Frommer's®

National Parks of the American West

7th Edition

by Don & Barbara Laine

with Shane Christensen, Jack Olson & Eric Peterson

Wiley Publishing, Inc.

Published by:

Wiley Publishing, Inc.

111 River St.
Hoboken, NJ 07030

ISBN 978-0-470-53767-1

Editor: Kathleen Warnock
Production Editor: Michael Brumitt
Cartographer: Guy Ruggiero
Photo Editor: Richard Fox
Production by Wiley Indianapolis Composition Services

Front cover photo: The Courthouse Towers, Arches National Park, Utah ©Markos Berndt / First Light / Alamy Images
Back cover photo: Adult mountain goat with summer coat, Glacier National Park, Montana ©Rolf Nussbaumer / Alamy Images

For information on our other products and services or to obtain technical support, please contact our Customer Care Department within the U.S. at 877/762-2974, outside the U.S. at 317/572-3993 or fax 317/572-4002.

Wiley also publishes its books in a variety of electronic formats. Some content that appears in print may not be available in electronic formats.

Manufactured in the United States of America

5 4 3 2 1

Contents

9 Capitol Reef National Park, UT 104

10 Carlsbad Caverns National Park, NM 115

11 Channel Islands National Park, CA 125

12 Crater Lake National Park, OR 138

13 Death Valley National Park & Mojave National Preserve, CA 147

19 Great Sand Dunes National Park & Preserve, CO 247

20 Guadalupe Mountains National Park, TX 253

21 Joshua Tree National Park, CA 261

22 Lassen Volcanic National Park, CA 273

23 Mesa Verde, Hovenweep, Chaco & Other Archaeological Sites of the Four Corners Region 281

30 Rocky Mountain National Park, CO 363

31 Saguaro National Park, AZ 379

32 Sequoia & Kings Canyon National Parks, CA 389

33 Theodore Roosevelt National Park, ND 409

34 Yellowstone National Park, WY & Little Bighorn Battlefield National Monument, MT 417

35 Yosemite National Park, CA 448

36 Zion National Park & Cedar Breaks National Monument, UT 475

37 Field Guide to Western Wildlife 493

38 Airline, Hotel & Car Rental Websites 499

Index 501

List of Maps

About the Authors

Residents of northern New Mexico for 40 years, **Don** and **Barbara Laine** have traveled extensively throughout the Rocky Mountains and the Southwest, exploring the mountains and deserts with their always-curious dogs. The Laines have authored or contributed to a number of Frommer's travel guides, including *Frommer's Zion & Bryce Canyon National Parks* and *Frommer's Utah.* They have also written *Little-Known Southwest, New Mexico & Arizona State Parks,* and *Best Short Hikes in Arizona* for The Mountaineers Books; and *The New Mexico Guide* for Fulcrum Publishing.

A Denver-based freelance writer, **Eric Peterson** has contributed to numerous Frommer's guides covering the American West, and has written *Frommer's Montana & Wyoming, Frommer's Colorado, Frommer's Yellowstone & Grand Teton National Parks,* and *Ramble: A Field Guide to the U.S.A.* Peterson also writes about travel and other topics for such publications as *ColoradoBiz, Delta Sky,* and the *New York Daily News.* In his free time, he's an avid camper and hiker, a lifelong Broncos fan, and a part-time rock star (at least in the eyes of his niece Olivia and nephews Mitch and Sam).

Jack Olson, a longtime resident of Denver, wanders the Rockies and the entire country as a freelance photographer and writer. He writes travel articles and supplies photographs for AAA magazines, and his photos have been seen in such publications as *Backpacker, Audubon, Sierra,* and *National Geographic Books.*

Shane Christensen has written extensively for Frommer's, including guides to Latin America, Europe, and the United States. Originally from California, he knows the American Southwest well and returns each year to the Grand Canyon to explore its wonders and ensure the accuracy of this guide. Shane has also held a variety of diplomatic assignments with the U.S. Department of State, and he is currently a research scholar and faculty advisor at Columbia University.

Acknowledgments

The authors offer sincere thanks to all the rangers and other employees of the National Park Service, U.S. Forest Service, Bureau of Land Management, state agencies, and various businesses who have reviewed chapters, provided information and tips, answered questions, and generally helped us assure the accuracy of this book.

How to Contact Us

In researching this book, we discovered many wonderful places—hotels, restaurants, shops, and more. We're sure you'll find others. Please tell us about them, so we can share the information with your fellow travelers in upcoming editions. If you were disappointed with a recommendation, we'd love to know that, too. Please write to:

Frommer's National Parks of the American West, 7th Edition
Wiley Publishing, Inc. • 111 River St. • Hoboken, NJ 07030-5774

An Additional Note

Please be advised that travel information is subject to change at any time—and this is especially true of prices. We therefore suggest that you write or call ahead for confirmation when making your travel plans. The authors, editors, and publisher cannot be held responsible for the experiences of readers while traveling. National parks are, by their very nature, potentially dangerous places. In visiting any of the places or doing any of the activities described herein, readers assume all risk of injury or loss that may accompany such activities. The publishers and the authors disavow all responsibility for injury, death, loss, or property damage that may arise from a reader's visit to any of the places or participation in any of the activities described herein, and the publisher and the authors make no warranties regarding the competence, safety, and reliability of outfitters, tour companies, or training centers described in this publication. Your safety is important to us, however, so we encourage you to stay alert and be aware of your surroundings. Keep a close eye on cameras, purses, and wallets, all favorite targets of thieves and pickpockets.

Frommer's Abbreviations

The following **abbreviations** are used for credit cards:

AE American Express
DC Diners Club
DISC Discover
MC MasterCard
V Visa

Travel Resources at Frommers.com

Frommer's travel resources don't end with this guide. Frommer's website, **www.frommers.com**, has travel information on more than 4,000 destinations. We update features regularly, giving you access to the most current trip-planning information and the best airfare, lodging, and car-rental bargains. You can also listen to podcasts, connect with other Frommers.com members through our active-reader forums, share your travel photos, read blogs from guidebook editors and fellow travelers, and much more.

1

Planning Your Trip to the National Parks of the American West

The National Park Service seems to be walking a tightrope. The service has two missions, and they sometimes seem to run in opposition to each other: Its first mission is to preserve some of America's most unique and important natural areas for future generations; the second is to make these places available for the enjoyment of all Americans. Because the number of visitors to our national parks has grown tremendously over the years, some of the busiest parks, including the Grand Canyon, Yosemite, Zion, and Yellowstone, are now searching for ways to make both of these goals a reality.

Park Service officials have often said that the real source of congestion in the most heavily visited parks is not the number of people, but rather the number of cars. (You don't go to a national park to get caught in a traffic jam, do you?) As a result, those parks with yearly attendance in the millions are now putting together plans to limit vehicle traffic within their boundaries.

If all this leads you to despair that you can't have a true "wilderness" experience at a national park in the American West, banish the thought! Even in a park as crowded as Yosemite, there are places where you can completely escape the crowds, where you'll be able to walk among the trees and hear nothing but the sound of your own footsteps. All it takes is a little effort and planning, and that's where this book can help.

Our authors have talked to the rangers, hiked the trails, and taken the tours, all the while asking, "How can our readers avoid the crowds?" In each of the following chapters, you'll find a section giving you straightforward, practical advice on just how to do this. Sure, if you're an outdoors iron man (or woman), you can avoid the crowds by taking off on the most strenuous backcountry hikes, but not everyone can manage that. So we've searched for secluded trails that can be hiked by the average person (not just the ones you'll see on the covers of *Outside* magazine), scenic drives where you won't get caught in bumper-to-bumper traffic, and points where, with only minimal effort, you'll be afforded spectacular views without feeling as if you're packed into Times Square on New Year's Eve.

We've also discovered that *when* you go is as important as *where* you go. Since most of the West's national parks and monuments are busiest in July and August, you can avoid many of the crowds by going in April or September, especially if you go just before students' summer vacation or just after classes resume. Most national parks are open year-round, though services are sometimes limited during the off season. In fact, many of the national parks are great places to go in winter for skiing and exploring, and you're less likely to feel mobbed. The hoodoos of Bryce Canyon, for example, are as strikingly beautiful when they're snow covered, and you won't be jostling with nearly as many people at the view points.

The last thing we've discovered (though it's not a big secret) is just how many hidden gems can be found among the national parks and monuments of the American West. Everyone knows about Mount Rainier and Carlsbad Caverns, but not always about the less-visited parks, such as Great Basin in Nevada, Great Sand Dunes in Colorado, the Channel Islands in California, Little Bighorn Battlefield in Montana, Jewel Cave in the Black Hills of South Dakota, and Guadalupe Mountains in Texas. These are places of great beauty or historical significance, but they're often overlooked because of their remoteness or simply because they're relatively new to the national park system.

As we all explore these parks and monuments, we should remember that they have been set aside not only for our enjoyment, but also for future generations. Let our gift to tomorrow's park visitors be that we have almost no impact on the beauty around us and, if anything, we leave it cleaner than we found it.

In this chapter, we've tried to give you the most useful general information you will need to help plan your trip to the national parks of the western United States. The individual park chapters that follow will answer your more specific questions.

1 The Parks Without the Crowds: Some General Tips

It's not easy to commune with nature when you're surrounded by hordes of fellow visitors. For each park, we've discussed the best times of year to go and listed certain areas, trails, and sites that are less visited than others. For specific information (such as a breakdown of the number of visitors to a particular park by the month), you can find park-use statistics at **www.nature.nps.gov/stats**. Beyond that, here are a few general guidelines.

- **Avoid the high season.** For most parks in the West, this means July and August, but anytime schools are not in session, parks are crowded with families. Spring and fall in many of these national parks offer mild weather, vibrant plant and animal life, and relatively empty trails and roads. The exception (at least, regarding crowds) is college spring break, which is usually in March or April. Some parks, such as Big Bend, get extremely crowded at that time.
- **Walk away if you find yourself in a crowd.** It sounds simple, but often when a scenic overlook is crowded, you'll find an equally good, completely empty view just a short stretch down the road or trail.
- **Visit popular attractions at off-peak hours,** especially early in the morning or late in the afternoon. You'll be surprised at how empty the park is before 9 or 10am. Dawn and dusk are also often the best times to see wildlife. Eat at off-peak hours—try lunch at 11am and dinner at 4pm. Campers using public showers will often find them jammed first thing in the morning and just before bedtime, but deserted the rest of the day.
- **Don't forget winter.** You may not see wildflowers, and some roads and areas may be closed, but many national parks are wonderful places to ski, snowshoe, snowmobile, or just admire the snowy landscape.
- **Remember that some parks are rarely crowded,** and we've made a special effort to include information about them in this book. Generally, the more difficult a park is to get to, the fewer people you'll encounter. And many of the smaller parks remain essentially undiscovered while offering scenery and recreation opportunities that rival or even surpass the big-names. Consider parks such as Great Basin, as well as one of America's newest national parks, Black Canyon of the Gunnison.

2 Visitor Information

Doing your homework can help you make the most of your trip; it can also help you avoid crowds. For park brochures and general planning information, contact each park directly, at the addresses included in each of the following chapters.

Another good source of information—and an important nonprofit advocate for America's national parks—is the **National Parks Conservation Association,** 1300 19th St., NW, Ste. 300, Washington, DC 20036 (© **800/628-7275** or 202/223-6722; www.npca.org).

Useful URLs for Planning Your Trip

In each of the following chapters we include pertinent websites, but here are a few for overall planning:

The National Park Service's website, **www.nps.gov**, has general information on national parks, monuments, and historic sites, as well as individual park maps that can be downloaded in a variety of formats. The site also contains a link to every individual park's website, and those often contain links to nearby attractions and other useful information. Unfortunately, the official national park websites are not as user-friendly as we would like, but you'll find most of the information you want if you're willing to do some searching. A good first step on the individual park websites is to look over the latest park newspaper, if it's available online.

Another useful website is **www.recreation.gov**, a partnership of federal agencies that can link you to information on national parks, national forests, Bureau of Land Management sites, Bureau of Reclamation sites, Army Corps of Engineers sites, and National Wildlife Refuges. You can make reservations at campsites, book tours, and either apply for or purchase various permits here.

Finally, those who like to travel with an animal companion should check out **www.petswelcome.com**, a site that provides tips on traveling with pets, as well as lists of lodgings that accept pets, kennels for temporary pet boarding, and veterinarians to call in an emergency.

Voices

Surely the great United States of America is not so poor we cannot afford to have these, nor so rich we can do without them.

—Newton Drury, National Parks Service Director, 1940–19[illegible]

A WORD ON NATURE ASSOCIATIONS

Throughout this book, you'll read that a certain nature association or organization operates a particular park's bookstore. Practically every national park has a **bookstore,** and some have several. Bookstores are excellent sources for maps, guidebooks, videos, postcards, posters, and the like. Most of the nature associations offer memberships (usually $25–$35 per year for individuals) that entitle the member to discounts of 15% to 20% on all purchases. You'll also usually get a regular newsletter. And for frequent travelers, here's the really good news: Membership in one nature association almost always entitles you to a 15% to 20% discount at other nature association bookstores and at national parks, monuments, historic sites, and recreation areas. For those of us who like to collect books, topographical maps, posters, and so on, the savings add up quickly. And we can also feel very smug about what a good deed we're doing in supporting these nonprofit groups.

3 Planning a National Park Itinerary

Even though distances seem vast in the western United States, it's possible to visit more than one of the region's national parks in a single trip. In fact, people often combine visits to Yellowstone with Grand Teton, Yosemite with Sequoia, and Zion with Bryce Canyon.

You can knit the parks of the California desert (Death Valley, Joshua Tree, and Mojave Preserve) into an itinerary that might even leave you time to stop off in Palm Springs. A popular trip for families is a drive through Badlands National Park and the Black Hills of South Dakota, through Devils Tower to Yellowstone. It's not a small stretch, but it's doable if you have more than a week.

Although it can be a lot of fun to combine several national parks in your vacation trip, try not to make the all too common mistake of attempting to see everything there is to see in too short a period of time. Be realistic about how much you want to see at each park, and create an itinerary that lets you thoroughly enjoy one or two aspects of a park rather than just glimpsing every corner as you speed by. And try to schedule a little relaxation time, especially for trips of more than a week—perhaps loafing in the campground one afternoon, or lounging by the motel swimming pool.

Following are two of our favorite park tours.

THE SOUTHWEST CIRCLE ITINERARY

This long circle drive hits five states and involves a lot of driving (or flying regional airlines and renting cars), but it takes you to a fantastic variety of parks—desert, cave, mountain, and deep canyon, plus one of the world's most fascinating archaeological preserves. We begin and end in Phoenix, Arizona, where almost all major airlines serve the airport, and car and RV rentals are available. We've laid it out for just under 2 weeks, but allowing more time would make it more satisfying.

Day 1: Phoenix, AZ

After arriving and picking up your rental car or RV, Phoenix is a good spot to stock up on supplies. The city is also famous for its golf resorts, so you may want to hit a few balls before heading south.

Day 2: Saguaro National Park, AZ

This is one of America's few national parks dedicated to protecting one plant—the saguaro cactus. You will see forests of them here. But you'll also see a variety of other plants and animals, such as javelinas—odd piglike animals with mouths so tough they can bite through prickly pear cactus pads. The park has two good **scenic drives,** as well as trails through the Sonoran Desert, including the **Valley View Overlook Trail,** which provides a close-up view of the desert, and the **Signal Hill Petroglyph Trail,** where you'll get a good look at some ancient petroglyphs. See chapter 31.

Days 3–5: Carlsbad Caverns, NM & Guadalupe Mountains, TX, National Parks

One of the largest and most spectacular cave systems in the world, **Carlsbad Caverns** in southern New Mexico has numerous cave formations, ranging from the fantastic to the grotesque. Take the **Big Room Self-Guided Tour** and the **King's Palace Guided Tour.** For a genuine caving experience, get

Voices

To preserve and protect . . . and to provide for the enjoyment of park visitors.

—National Park Service Organic Act, 1916

your clothes dirty on the **Slaughter Canyon guided tour.** Just over the state line in Texas, **Guadalupe Mountains** is a rugged wilderness of tall Douglas firs, offering panoramic vistas and the highest peak in Texas. Recommended for experienced hikers is the trek to the top of **Guadalupe Peak.** Everyone can enjoy the colors in **McKittrick Canyon**—either the trees in fall or the wildflowers in spring. See chapters 10 and 20.

Day ❻: Santa Fe, NM

It's a long drive from Carlsbad Caverns to Mesa Verde National Park, so we recommend breaking it up with an overnight stop in Santa Fe, famous for its art, history, and picturesque adobe buildings.

Days ❼–❾: Mesa Verde National Park, CO

The largest archaeological preserve in the United States, Mesa Verde contains intriguing, well-preserved cliff dwellings, plus mesa-top pueblos, pit houses, and kivas, built by the ancestral Puebloan (Anasazi) people hundreds of years ago. Recommended stops here are **Cliff Palace,** the largest cliff dwelling in the Southwest, and **Balcony House.** See chapter 23.

Day ❿: Petrified Forest National Park, AZ

Especially colorful after a rainstorm has washed away the dust, this park is a fascinating look at an unreal world of wood turned to stone. Take the 28-mile **scenic drive,** stopping at the pullouts and walking some of the short trails. We recommend the **Giant Logs Trail,** where you'll see some of the park's largest petrified logs, and **Blue Mesa Trail,** one of the prettiest and most otherworldly hikes in the park. At **Newspaper Rock,** early inhabitants pecked dozens of petroglyphs into the dark stone, including an image of the famous humpbacked flute player, Kokopelli. See chapter 27.

Days ⓫–⓬: Grand Canyon National Park's South Rim, AZ

The Grand Canyon truly is grand, and no matter how many photos you've seen, being there in person is an awe-inspiring experience. After stopping at the information center for a quick geology lesson, take the shuttle to some of the South Rim **view points,** and perhaps walk the **Rim Trail** a bit. Then, if you're physically able, walk down **Bright Angel Trail** at least a little way, watching the vegetation and rock layers change as you descend. Unless you are in very good condition, however, it is probably best to not go beyond the One-and-a-Half-Mile House, which has restrooms and drinking water, before heading back up to the rim. See chapter 16.

Day ⓭: Back to Phoenix, AZ

Back in Phoenix, you can practice your golf swing or visit some of the city's excellent museums before catching your plane for home.

THE GRAND CIRCLE ITINERARY

Southern Utah has five delightful national parks and several national monuments; the North Rim of the spectacular Grand Canyon is just over the border in Arizona, and perched along the state line is the awe-inspiring Monument Valley Navajo Tribal Park. Together they form a somewhat circuitous loop. This jaunt begins and ends in Las Vegas, Nevada, which is accessible by almost all major airlines and has car and RV rentals. You can complete this tour in 2 weeks, but it is much more satisfying in 3 weeks, as described here.

Day ❶: Las Vegas, NV

Fly in, pick up your rental car or RV, lay in some supplies, and maybe try the slot machines for a half-hour or so. Then hit the road and head northeast into the mountains of southern Utah.

Days ❷–❹: Zion National Park, UT

Famous for its mammoth natural stone sculptures and unbelievably narrow **slot canyon,** this park begs to be explored on foot. Hop on the shuttle bus that runs the length of the **Zion Canyon Scenic Drive,** getting off to take trails. We especially recommend the easy **Riverside Walk,** which follows the Virgin River through a narrow canyon past hanging gardens, as well as the **Emerald Pools Trail.** Especially pleasant on hot days, this walk through a forest of oak, maple, fir, and cottonwood trees leads to a waterfall, a hanging garden, and a shimmering pool. See chapter 36.

Days ❺–❻: Grand Canyon National Park's North Rim, AZ

The North Rim of the Grand Canyon receives far fewer visitors than the South Rim, but that doesn't mean it's any less spectacular. The North Rim (which is open in summer only) provides views of and access to the same overpowering canyon as the South Rim does, just from the other side. You'll want to stop at the **Grand Canyon Lodge,** listed on the National Register of Historic Places, and then hike a few of the **Rim Trails.** If you're in good enough physical shape, you might want to hike partway down into the canyon on the **North Kaibab Trail.** See chapter 16.

Days 7–8: Monument Valley Navajo Tribal Park, UT

Although not a national park, this Navajo Tribal Park is well worth a stop (and it's on your way). Monument Valley is, to many of us, the epitome of the Old West—we've seen it dozens of times in movies and on television. On the Utah/Arizona border, and part of the vast Navajo Nation, the park has a 17-mile self-guided **loop road** that lets you see most of the major scenic attractions, or you can get a personalized tour with a **Navajo guide.** Either way, you'll see classic Western scenery made famous in movies such as 1939's *Stagecoach*. ***Note:*** Federal passes, such as the America the Beautiful pass, are not valid here.

Days 9–12: Arches & Canyonlands National Parks, UT

Famed for its massive red and orange rock formations, this area is home to two national parks and the lively town of Moab. **Canyonlands National Park** (see chapter 8) is a great hikers' park. Make sure you stop at the **Grand Viewpoint Overlook,** in the **Island in the Sky District,** and hike the **Grand View Trail,** especially scenic in the late afternoon. **Arches National Park** (see chapter 2) is a bit more user-friendly. Take the scenic drive and walk a few trails—on the **Devils Garden Trail,** you can see more than a dozen arches, including picturesque **Landscape Arch.**

Days 13–14: Capitol Reef National Park, UT

Relatively unknown, this park offers brilliantly colored rock formations and a bit of history. The Fremont River created a lush oasis in this otherwise barren land, and 19th-century pioneers found the soil so fertile that they established the community of **Fruita,** named for the orchards they planted. Today you can explore the buildings and even pick fruit in season. Hikers can examine **Pioneer Register,** a rock wall where traveling pioneers "signed in," and explore canyons where famed outlaw Butch Cassidy is said to have hidden out between train and bank robberies. See chapter 9.

Days 15–18: Scenic Utah 12 & Bryce Canyon National Park, UT

From Capitol Reef, go south on Utah 12 over Boulder Mountain and through **Grand Staircase–Escalante National Monument,** possibly stopping for a short hike to Calf Creek Falls, before heading to **Bryce Canyon National Park.** Spend the night in the park or nearby so you can be on the rim of Bryce Amphitheater at **sunrise,** the best time to see the colorful and often whimsically shaped rock formations called hoodoos. Top hikes here include the colorful **Queen's Garden Trail,** named for a formation that resembles Britain's Queen Victoria. See chapter 7.

Days 19–20: Cedar Breaks National Monument, UT

This small, high-altitude park has an amphitheater reminiscent of Bryce Canyon's, as well as a 5-mile road that offers easy access to the monument's scenic overlooks and trail heads. Hike **Spectra Point Trail** along the rim for changing views of the colorful rock formations. The trail also takes you through fields of wildflowers, which are especially colorful in late July and August, and past bristlecone pines that are more than 1,500 years old. See chapter 36.

Day 21: Back to Las Vegas, NV

Back in Sin City, you can catch a show or feed the one-armed bandits befre flying home.

Carrying Firearms in National Parks

New National Park Service regulations, which went into effect in early 2010, make National Park Service properties subject to specific local, state, and federal firearms laws. Previously, the Park Service had a system-wide gun policy, which mostly prohibited the carrying of loaded weapons in parks. The Park Service has updated its website to provide links to state firearms laws and advises gun-carrying visitors to check those websites before visiting the parks. Visitors who would like to bring a firearm with them to a national park need to understand and comply with the applicable local laws. If a national park's boundaries extend from one state into another (and some 30 national parks do cross state lines), you'll need to be aware of the local laws in *both* jurisdictions. Federal law continues to prohibit the possession of firearms in designated "federal facilities" in national parks. For example, you can't bring a gun into visitor centers, offices, or maintenance buildings that are posted with "firearms prohibited" signs at public entrances. The new law also does not change prohibitions on the use of firearms in national parks and does not change hunting regulations.

The Federal Lands Name Game

Throughout this book, you'll read about America's most spectacular public lands, most designated as **national parks** and managed by the **National Park Service (NPS).** But you will also learn about national monuments, historical parks, and other public lands, also run by the NPS, as well as areas managed by other agencies. So what's in a name?

Although Yellowstone, America's first national park, was established by President Ulysses S. Grant in 1872, President Theodore Roosevelt is generally credited with spearheading the movement to preserve America's most beautiful scenic areas as public lands in the early 1900s. In 1916, President Woodrow Wilson signed an act creating the National Park Service as a division of the U.S. Department of the Interior. Today the NPS includes nearly 400 areas of public land covering more than 84 million acres in every state (except Delaware), as well as in Washington, D.C., and American Samoa, Guam, Puerto Rico, and the Virgin Islands.

These NPS properties go by a variety of names. Generally, a **national park** is the best of the NPS properties, covering a fairly large area and containing a variety of attributes. Traditionally, these parks have been set aside to be preserved and visited by the public, so mining, oil and gas drilling, hunting, cattle grazing, and other activities that would change the areas are not permitted. A **national monument,** which many consider "junior" national parks, are usually smaller and with fewer attractions than national parks; they still must include at least one feature considered nationally significant, and they are often managed with similar practices to national parks. **National preserves,** which are sometimes adjacent to national parks, are like national parks, except that they often allow mineral exploration, hunting, and other activities prohibited in national parks.

There are also **national historic sites,** which usually contain a single historical place of note; **national historical parks,** which include more than one historic site; **national memorials,** which are designated to commemorate a historic event or person; and **national battlefields,** which contain the sites of historic battlefields, usually from the Revolutionary or Civil wars. The NPS's 14 **national cemeteries** are significant historic cemeteries that mostly date to the Civil War era and are not the same as the national cemeteries managed by the U.S. Department of Veterans Affairs that contain the graves of more recent military veterans as well as veterans from earlier times.

National recreation areas are lands set aside primarily for recreation, such as boating or hiking; and **national seashores, lakeshores, rivers,** and **wild rivers** are usually scenic areas that include water sports and related activities. A **national trail** is a long-distance scenic or historic hiking trail, and a **national parkway** is a roadway through a scenic area.

Other departments and agencies also administer federal lands. The **U.S. Bureau of Land Management (BLM),** a separate division of the Department of the Interior, manages a lot of public land, almost always as multiple-use areas where recreation, cattle grazing, mining, and oil or gas drilling can go on side by side. While many national monuments are managed by the National Park Service, some are under the BLM. Another division of the Department of the Interior is the **U.S. Fish and Wildlife Service,** which manages America's **national wildlife refuges.** In addition, **national forests,** which abound throughout the American West, are under the jurisdiction of the **U.S. Department of Agriculture.** National Forests are also multiuse areas but often have a greater emphasis on recreation than BLM areas. Maybe that's because they usually have more trees!

4 Visitor Centers

Your first stop at any national park should be the **visitor center.** Some large parks have more than one, and we list the location of each. Not only will you learn the history of the park, but you'll also get timely information such as road and trail closures, updates on safety issues, and the schedule for ranger programs. Visitor center hours usually vary by season; most are open daily from 8am until 6 or 7pm in summer, closing earlier at other times. Many park visitor centers close for New Year's Day, Thanksgiving, and Christmas, even though the parks themselves usually remain open.

North to Alaska! The 49th State's Great National Parks

Although this book looks closely at the national parks in the American West of the continental United States, we must point out that some of the country's most beautiful and pristine national parks are in a destination a bit farther north: **Alaska.** In fact, more than two-thirds of America's national park acreage is in our northernmost state, encompassing huge areas of wilderness and near-wilderness, with few roads, buildings, or even airplane landing strips.

Most of the Alaska parks are challenging, both to get to and to explore. One exception is **Denali National Park** (✆ **907/683-2294;** www.nps.gov/dena), which provides visitors with easy access to genuine wilderness. Denali has sweeping tundra vistas, abundant wildlife, and North America's tallest mountain: 20,320-foot Mount McKinley. But what makes this park unique is that its accessibility hasn't spoiled the natural experience. That's because the only road through the park is closed to the public. To see Denali, you must ride a bus. The grizzly bears and other animals are still visible, and their behavior remains more normal than that of the animals seen in the more visited, vehicle-intensive parks such as Yellowstone and Yosemite.

Another recommended Alaska experience is **Glacier Bay National Park & Preserve** (✆ **907/697-2230;** www.nps.gov/glba), a rugged wilderness the size of Connecticut that can be seen only by boat or plane. Created by a receding glacier, this bay is a work in progress, where you'll see a vast variety of flora and fauna, including grizzly bears, mountain goats, seals, and especially whales, including humpback whales breaching (leaping all the way out of the water).

Other national parks in Alaska include **Katmai National Park & Preserve** (✆ **907/246-3305;** www.nps.gov/katm), the site of a phenomenal volcanic eruption in 1912 and now an excellent place to see relatively close up the huge Alaska brown bear as it devours a seemingly endless supply of red salmon. **Kenai Fjords National Park** (✆ **907/224-7500;** www.nps.gov/kefj/index.htm), a remote area of mountains, rocks, and ice, is the spot to see a vast array of sea lions, otters, seals, and birds. And **Wrangell–St. Elias National Park** (✆ **907/822-5234;** www.nps.gov/wrst), which, at over 8 million acres, is by far the largest unit in the National Park Service system, consists of numerous rugged mountains and glaciers, plus some fascinating history from its early copper mining days.

The above parks, plus a number of other national parks, monuments, and preserves, are explored fully in *Frommer's Alaska* (Wiley), by Charles P. Wohlforth, a lifelong resident of Alaska.

5 Fees & Permits

Though fees have increased in the past few years, visiting a national park is still a bargain—a steal compared to the prices you'd pay for a theme park or even a movie. Entry fees, ranging from free to $25, are usually charged per private vehicle (for up to 1 week), regardless of how many visitors you stuff inside. Those arriving on foot, motorcycle, or bicycle usually pay lower per-person fees. Some parks offer passes good for unlimited visits to the same park, or a few nearby parks, for 12 months.

NATIONAL PARKS/FEDERAL LAND PASSES

Those who enjoy vacationing at national parks, national forests and other federal lands have a new annual pass, but for most of us, it will cost more than the old passes that have now been phased out.

The **America the Beautiful–National Parks and Federal Recreational Lands Pass,** which is available for $80, provides free admission for the pass holder and those in his or her vehicle to recreation sites that charge vehicle entrance fees. These include lands administered by the National Park Service, U.S. Forest Service, U.S. Fish and Wildlife Service, Bureau of Land Management, and Bureau of Reclamation. At areas that charge per-person fees, the passes are good for the pass holder plus three additional adults. Children under 16 are admitted free.

The pass, which is valid for 1 year from the date of purchase, replaces the National Parks Pass, which was limited to only properties administered by the National Park Service, and the Golden Eagle Passport, which provided free entry to all the federal lands covered by the new pass. The **America the Beautiful Senior Pass** is available for U.S. citizens and permanent residents 62 and older for a lifetime fee of $10 (same as the former Golden Age passports), and the **America the Beautiful Access Pass** is free for U.S. residents and permanent residents

Tips on Renting an RV from the Experts

Shirley Slater and **Harry Basch** have been traveling the U.S. and Canada in their RV (and writing about it, authoring *Exploring America by RV* and *RV Vacations for Dummies* [Wiley]) for years; here, they offer some tips on what to look for, and where to look if you're thinking of renting an RV for a national parks trip. Harry and Shirley say:

A great many rental RVs are booked by European and Australian visitors to the United States who want to see our national parks, or drive along the coast of California. The most common unit available for rental is the motor home, either the larger type A or the type C mini–motor home which accounts for 90% of all rentals. Prices begin at around $975 a week.

Use of the **generator** is not usually included in the fee. You would need it only for operating the ceiling air-conditioning, microwave, and TV in a place without electrical hookups. The dealer will know how much time you've logged by reading the generator counter, usually located by the on/off switch.

If you're looking to rent a **travel trailer** (which you pull behind another vehicle), you'll find they usually require that you furnish your own tow vehicle, hitch, and electrical hookups on the tow vehicle.

Some companies offer a **furnishings package** with bedding, towels, dishes, cooking pots, and utensils for a flat price of around $100 for kitchen needs and $50 for bedding per trip. Other add-on kits are those containing power cords and hoses, plastic trash bags, toilet chemicals, and a troubleshooting guide. Remember to get a detailed list of what furnishings are included in your rental so you'll know what necessary items you have to supply. It may be easier to bring things from home than to spend vacation time searching for them on the road.

Be sure you're provided with a full set of **instruction booklets** and **emergency phone numbers** in case of a breakdown. The best thing to have is a 24-hour emergency toll-free number in case of a problem. When in doubt, ask fellow RVers what to do. They're always glad to help, but sometimes hesitant to offer for fear of offending. No matter how much you bustle around like you know what you're doing, the veterans in the campground can spot a goof-up a mile away.

Before setting out, be sure the dealer demonstrates how to operate all the **components and systems** of your unit. Take careful notes and, just as with rental cars, check for dents and damage from prior use before leaving the lot.

To find information about RV rental companies all over the United States and Canada, check out the website of **Recreation Vehicle Rental Association** (RVRA) (✆ **888/467-8464** or 703/591-7130; www.rvra.org). You'll find a directory with addresses, phone numbers, and prices for European, Canadian, and U.S. companies listed by city and state or province. There is also a companion

with permanent disabilities (also the same as the former Golden Access passports). The senior and access passes also provide 50% discounts on some other park fees, such as camping and guided tours. The passes are available at all national parks. For information, see www.nps.gov/fees_passes.htm or call ✆ **888/275-8747,** ext. 1.

BACKCOUNTRY PERMITS

At most national parks, it is necessary to obtain a **permit** to stay overnight in the park's undeveloped backcountry. Some parks have even more restrictions. To be safe, if you intend to do any backpacking, look in the individual park chapter or contact the park's backcountry office in advance. In some cases, it may be possible to obtain a permit by mail; in most cases, you must appear in person. Some parks charge for backcountry permits, while others do not; some restrict the number of permits issued and also the number of people in a group.

OTHER PERMITS

Hunting is generally not allowed in national parks, but **fishing** often is. You will usually need a state fishing license. Licenses are generally available at local sporting goods stores and state game and fish department offices. Fees vary for state residents and nonresidents, for various time periods, and sometimes by location within the state, but you can usually get a nonresident 1-day license for $5 to $15 and a 5- to 7-day nonresident license for $15 to $25.

page, **Rental Ventures,** with additional helpful information. Write to RVRA, 3930 University Dr., Fairfax, VA 22030-2525. Call for rental information (✆ 888/467-8464; www.rvra.org).

Your local Yellow Pages should also carry a listing for rentals under "Recreational Vehicle—Rentals." **Cruise America,** the largest rental company with more than 120 outlets, has added budget items such as camping vans, fully equipped travel trailers, and fold-out truck campers with compact pickups to tow them. It answers the requests from European campers in America, who are responsible for one-half to two-thirds of the company's rentals. Rentals will range from $800 to $6,350 a week. Contact them at 11 West Hampton Ave., Mesa, AZ 85250 (✆ **800/671-8042** or 480/464-7300; www.cruiseamerica.com).

Another important detail you need to take care of when you rent/before you leave: You also need to make sure your rental vehicle is insured. Normally, insurance on a rental RV is not covered on your personal automobile insurance, so ask your agent for a binder that extends your coverage to the RV for the full rental period. Many dealers require the binder before renting you a vehicle.

Along with Cruise America, some of the larger rental firms in the West include: **Adventure Rentals** in Ontario, California, which claims to have the largest trailer rental department in the United States, offering folding camping trailers from $520 a week and travel trailers from $750 a week. No rentals are made to anyone under 25. Renters supply a tow vehicle, hitch and electrical connections, bedding, and utensils. A cleaning deposit of $45 is required and forfeited if the vehicle is not returned clean; the company has its own dump stations for holding tanks. Contact them at 1200 W. Mission Blvd., Ontario, CA 91762 (✆ **909/983-2567;** www.adventurerentals.net). **Altman's Winnebago** in Carson, California, has type A and type C new motor homes for rent. A typical rental charge for a small type C motor home would be around $1,000 to $1,500 a week. Rental of a type A motor home would run around $1,988 a week. Additional charges would be $15 a day for insurance, with optional charges for a kitchen kit (pots, dishes, glasses; $99 per trip) and a bedroom kit (bedding and towels; $26 per person per trip; Contact them at ✆ **888/820-0800** or 310/518-6182; www.altmans.com.

Once you've made arrangements to rent an RV, if you're flying into the region to pick up your RV, many rental companies offer free airport pickup and return, if you notify them ahead of time.

Finally, if you fall in love with your rental vehicle (as we did our first one), you might be able to negotiate a purchase price that would subtract your rental fee from the total. If the vehicle is a couple of years old, the price should be even lower, since most dealers get rid of vehicles after 2 or 3 years.

In some parks (Yellowstone and Grand Teton, for example), you will need a special permit to go **boating.** In others, you may need a permit for **cross-country skiing.** Check individual park chapters for details on other required permits.

6 Getting a Campsite at a National Park

Although a growing number of national park campgrounds accept campsite reservations, many still do not. If you plan to camp and are heading to a first-come, first-served campground, the first thing to do upon arrival is to make sure a site is available. Campsites at major park campgrounds fill up early in summer, on weekends, and during other peak times, such as school holidays (try to avoid college spring breaks, often in Mar or Apr). A reservation or an early morning arrival (sometimes as early as 7 or 8am) is the best defense against disappointment. In each chapter, we've indicated whether a campground tends to fill up especially early and whether reservations are accepted.

Reservations for many National Park Service campgrounds, as well as national forest and other agency campgrounds, can be made through one central reservation center (✆ **887/444-6777** or 518/885-3639; TDD 877/833-6777; **www.recreation.gov**).

We also include information on nearby commercial campgrounds (both tent and RV) in individual chapters.

So You Like a Mystery? National Parks Set the Scene for Barr's Books

Author **Nevada Barr** (www.nevadabarr.com) spins a good yarn. A former National Park Service ranger, she writes what she knows—the settings for her mysteries are national parks, and her detective, Anna Pigeon, is a ranger. Anna's backstory is that she joined the Park Service after her actor husband was killed in New York City, and she finds safety in solitude. But occasionally someone breaks into her aloneness, such as the time she enjoyed a brief liaison with an FBI agent during a murder investigation at Lake Superior. Anna loves the wild country, and her work often takes her into strange situations. It's fascinating to see the parks through Anna's eyes, in the series' inaugural volume, *Track of the Cat* (Berkley, 1993), as she patrols the backcountry of Guadalupe Mountains on horseback—is the killer a mountain lion, as the tracks imply, or something more sinister?—or when she strives to uncover the cause of inexplicable deaths amid the ruins at Mesa Verde in *Ill Wind* (Berkley, 1995). The "accident" that befalls a spelunker in the depths of Carlsbad Caverns in *Blind Descent* (Berkley, 1998) takes the reader into subterranean territory, and the tense situation that develops among the small group of isolated firefighters during the aftermath of a forest fire at Lassen Volcanic National Park in *Firestorm* (Berkley, 1996) is riveting. In *High Country* (Berkley, 2004), set in Yosemite National Park, Anna goes undercover to find four missing seasonal workers. Ms. Barr makes Anna the new District Ranger at Rocky Mountain National Park in *Hard Truth* (Putnam, 2005), where a 6-week-old mystery seems to be winding down . . . until the disembodied voices start and small slayings turn into something bigger. In the latest (the 15th) installment of the series, *Borderline* (Putnam, 2009), Anna and her new husband, Paul, head down the Rio Grande on a raft in Big Bend, but the relaxing jaunt takes on nightmare proportions when their raft gets lost in rapids.

7 Maps

When you arrive at a national park, you'll receive a large, four-color brochure that has a good map of the park in it and in many cases, a park newspaper that also has maps; of course, you also have the maps in this book. If you plan to do some serious hiking, especially into backcountry and wilderness areas, you'll need detailed topographical maps.

Topographical maps can usually be ordered in advance from the individual park bookstores, which we list in the following chapters, and we suggest that you check with park personnel to see which maps they recommend. Maps can also often be purchased in electronic form and carried in a small PDA or laptop computer, or you can print out the sections of the areas you need to carry on the trail.

8 Tips for RVers

Many people prefer to explore the national parks in an RV—a motor home, truck camper, or camper trailer—especially in the warm months. One advantage to this type of travel is that early morning and early evening are among the best times to be in the parks if you want to avoid crowds and see wildlife. Needless to say, it's a lot more convenient to experience the parks at these times if you're already there, staying in one of the park campgrounds.

Carrying your house with you also lets you stop for meals anytime and anywhere you choose, and makes it easy to take care of individual dietary needs. RVing also means you don't have to worry about sleeping on a lumpy mattress, and you won't need to spend time searching for a restroom—almost all RVs have some sort of bathroom facilities, from a full bathroom with tub/shower combination to a Porta Potti hidden under a seat.

There are disadvantages, of course. If you already own an RV, you know what you had to pay for it. And even if you rent, you may not save a lot of money. Depending on the rate you get (and the cost of fuel at the time), renting a motor home could end up costing almost as much as renting a compact car, staying in moderately priced motels, and eating in family-style restaurants and cafes. That's because the motor home will go only one-quarter to one-third as far on a gallon of fuel as your compact car will, and they're expensive to rent. Some of the fancier private campgrounds now charge as much for an RV site with utility hookups as you'd expect to pay in a cheap motel.

Other disadvantages include the limited facilities in national park campgrounds (although they are being upgraded to the point where camping purists are starting to complain). Even in most commercial campgrounds, the facilities are less than you'd expect in moderately priced motels. And parking is often limited in national parks, especially for motor homes and other large vehicles. However, since most people are driving in the parks between 10am and 5pm, the solution is to head out on the scenic drives either early or late in the day, when there's less traffic. It's nicer then, anyway.

If you'll be traveling through the park in your RV and want to make it obvious that your campsite is occupied, carry something worthless to leave in it, such as a cardboard box with "Site Taken" clearly written on it.

Many national park campsites are not level. If your RV does not have built-in levelers, carry four or five short boards, or leveling blocks, that can be placed under the wheels. You'll discover that not only will you sleep better if your rig is level, but your food won't slide off the table and the refrigerator will run more efficiently.

You might consider purchasing as a companion to this book *Frommer's Exploring America by RV* (Wiley), by Shirley Slater and Harry Basch, which includes five road trips in the West (including one in Alaska) that pass through many national parks. There are also chapters on RV basics that people renting a vehicle for the first time will find useful.

You may also want to pick up *Frommer's Best RV and Tent Campgrounds in the U.S.A.* (Wiley), by David Hoekstra.

RENTING AN RV

If you're flying into the area and renting an RV when you arrive, choose your starting point carefully; not only do you want to keep your driving to a minimum—you'll be lucky to get 10 miles per gallon of gas—but rental rates vary depending on the city in which you pick up your RV. Do some research before you commit to a starting point. Rates are generally highest, between $1,000 and $1,500 per week, in midsummer. The country's largest RV rental company is **Cruise America** (© **800/671-8042;** www.cruiseamerica.com), with outlets in most major western cities. RV rentals are also available in many western states from **El Monte RV** (© **888/337-2214;** www.elmonte.com). Information on additional rental agencies, as well as tips on renting, can be obtained online from the **Recreation Vehicle Rental Association** (www.rvra.org). See "Tips on Renting an RV from the Experts," p. 8.

9 Tips for Traveling with Kids

Most parks offer **Junior Ranger Programs** that give kids the chance to earn certificates, badges, and patches for completing certain projects, such as tree or animal identification, or answering questions in a workbook. It's a good way to learn about the national parks and the resources that the Park Service protects. Also, many parks offer special discussions, walks, and other ranger-led activities for children.

For a complete list of national parks that offer Junior Ranger programs, visit **www.nps.gov/learn/juniorranger.htm**. WebRangers is an online component of the Junior Ranger program, and kids of all ages can play dozens of National Park–based games, look at and share photos in a web community, and even earn WebRanger patches at www.nps.gov/webrangers.

10 Tips for Travelers with Disabilities

The National Park Service has come a long way in the past 25 or 30 years in making the parks more accessible for visitors with disabilities. Most parks have accessible restrooms, and many have at least one trail that is wheelchair accessible—the Rim Trail at Bryce Canyon is a prime example. Several parks with sandy conditions, such as Great Sand Dunes, offer free use of specially designed wheelchairs with balloon tires for travel over sand.

Making Art in the Parks

The National Park Services offers opportunities for visual artists, photographers, sculptors, performers, writers, composers, and craft artists to live and work in the parks, in residencies that run from a week to a few months in length. The residencies are free of charge, and in some cases, the artists are asked to share their work by giving a reading, performance, or gallery show. There are currently 29 parks participating in the Artist-In-Residence program. The parks in this book that offer residencies are **Badlands** (ND), **Crater Lake** (OR), **Devils Tower** (WY), **Glacier** (MT), **Grand Canyon** (AZ), **Joshua Tree** (CA), **Mount Rushmore** (SD), **North Cascades** (WA), **Petrified Forest** (AZ), **Rocky Mountain** (CO), and **Yosemite** (CA). For more information on application requirements and deadlines, visit **www.nps.gov/archive/volunteer/air.htm**, or contact the individual park.

In addition, as campgrounds, boat docks, and other facilities are upgraded, improvements are being made to make them more accessible. Many parks now have campsites designed specifically for travelers in wheelchairs, most in-park lodging offers accessible rooms—some with roll-in showers—and park amphitheaters can usually accommodate wheelchair users.

But perhaps just as important as upgrades in facilities is the prevailing attitude of National Park Service personnel that these parks are for the public—the entire public—and they are going to do whatever it takes to help everyone enjoy his or her park experience. People with special needs are encouraged to talk with park workers, who can usually assist, opening locked gates to get vehicles closer to scenic attractions, or simply by pointing out trails with the lowest grades or with portable toilets that are accessible.

One note on service dogs: Seeing Eye and other service dogs are not considered pets and are legally permitted anywhere in the parks. However, because of potential problems with wildlife or terrain (sharp rocks on some trails can cut dogs' paws), it's best for people taking service dogs into the parks to discuss their plans with rangers beforehand.

Many of the major car-rental companies now offer hand-controlled cars for drivers with disabilities and can provide those vehicles with advance notice. **Wheelchair Getaways** (© **800/642-2042** or 859/873-4973; www.wheelchairgetaways.com) rents and sells specialized vans with wheelchair lifts and other features for visitors with disabilities. It has outlets in most western states.

And don't forget your **National Parks and Federal Recreational Lands Pass** (see "Fees & Permits," above). It is free and will grant you free admission to most national parks and a 50% discount on many park services and facilities.

11 Tips for Travelers with Pets

Most national parks, as well as other federal lands administered by the National Park Service, are not pet-friendly, and those planning to visit the parks should consider leaving their pets at home. Pets are almost always prohibited on hiking trails, in the backcountry, and in buildings, and must always be on a leash. Essentially, this means that if you take your dog or cat into the parks, they can be with you in the campgrounds and inside your vehicle, and you can walk them in parking areas, but that's about all. It's no fun for you or your pet.

Aside from regulations, you need to be concerned with your pet's well-being. Pets should never be left in closed vehicles, where temperatures can soar to over 120°F (49°C) in minutes, resulting in brain damage or death. No punishment is too severe for the human who subjects a dog or cat to that torture.

Those who do decide to take pets with them despite these warnings should take the pets' leashes, of course; carry plenty of water (pet shops sell clever little travel water bowls that won't spill in a moving vehicle); and bring proof that the dogs or cats have been vaccinated against rabies. Flea and tick spray or powder is also important, since fleas that may carry bubonic plague have been found on prairie dogs and other rodents in some parks, such as Mesa Verde and Bryce Canyon.

12 Health & Safety

Bears, rattlesnakes, and lightning can be dangerous, but that driver heading for you on a park road can be even more dangerous. In fact, **motor vehicle accidents** cause more deaths in the parks every year than anything else. Scenic drives are often winding and steep; take them slowly and carefully. And no matter how stunning the snowcapped peak you may glimpse is, keep your eyes on the road.

When out on the trails, even for a day hike, keep safety in mind. The wild, untouched nature of these parks is what makes them so exciting and breathtakingly beautiful—but along with wildness comes risk. The national parks are neither playgrounds nor zoos. The animals here are truly wild and sometimes dangerous. This doesn't mean that disaster could strike at any time, but visitors should exercise basic

Special Tip for Pet Owners

Although pets are not permitted on the trails or backcountry in most national parks, those traveling with their dogs can hike with them over trails administered by the U.S. Forest Service and Bureau of Land Management, as well as some of the state parks that are adjacent to many national parks.

Stay Hydrated: A Cautionary Tale!

Frommer's author Ethan Wolff lived in New Mexico, and loves to visit the Four Corners area whenever he can. However, he forgot an elementary safety rule on a recent visit (which he recounted in *Frommer's MTV USA Roadtrips*): "It can be a fine line between Paradise and Hell in the desert Southwest. Pretty landscapes can take on a sinister cast very quickly if you don't make basic preparations. In Natural Bridges National Monument in Southeast Utah, I found the scenery so gorgeous I couldn't bring myself to turn around, even though I had only planned on a quick ramble. I ended up hiking right through lunch, and right through my water supply. Somehow I managed to forget that the steep downhill that began the trail would be even steeper when it was time to climb back up. By then, it was the hottest part of the day, and with each step on rebelling legs, I was increasingly parched. Stupid? *Imbecilic.* And it's not like it would have taken some amazing effort to be properly outfitted: I had trail bars and Gatorade sitting in the car, and there was free water at the visitor center. When in doubt, make the minor effort it takes to be properly prepared. You'll feel freer to enjoy the scenery if you're not stressing about how much time you have, or whether you can afford to chance the next overlook. And the downside of not having it together out here is just too extreme."

caution and common sense at all times, respecting the wilderness around them and always following the rules of the park.

Never feed, bother, or approach animals. Even the smallest among them can carry harmful, sometimes deadly, diseases, and feeding them is dangerous not only to yourself, but also to the animals, who (like us) will eat what the animals' bodies can't handle. In addition, wild animals' dependence on handouts can lead to unpleasant confrontations, which often result in rangers' having to relocate or kill the animal. As the Park Service reminds us, "A fed bear is a dead bear."

In some parks where there are bears and mountain lions, it's often a good idea to make noise as you hike, to make sure you don't stumble upon and frighten an animal into aggression. Also, follow park rules on food storage when in bear country. Photographers should always keep a safe distance when taking pictures of wildlife—the best photos are shot with a telephoto lens.

It's equally important for your safety to know your limitations, to understand the environment, and to take the proper equipment when exploring the park. Always stop at the visitor center before you set out on a hike. Park staff there can offer advice on your hiking plans and supply you with pamphlets, maps, and information on weather conditions or any dangers, such as bear activity or flash flood possibilities on canyon hikes. Once out on the trail, hikers should always carry sufficient water and, just as important, remember to drink it. Wear sturdy shoes with good ankle support and rock-gripping soles. Keep a close eye on children in your group, and never let them run ahead.

Since many park visitors live at or near sea level, one of the most common health hazards is **altitude sickness,** caused by the high elevations of many of the parks in this book. Symptoms include headache, fatigue, nausea, loss of appetite, muscle pain, and lightheadedness. Doctors recommend that until you are acclimated—which can take several days—you should consume light meals and drink lots of liquids, avoiding those with caffeine or alcohol. It's a good idea to take frequent sips of water as well.

One proven method of minimizing the effects of high altitudes is to work up to them. For instance, on a visit to southern Utah, go to lower-elevation Zion National Park for a day or two before heading to the higher mountains of Bryce Canyon.

A waterborne hazard is *Giardia,* a **parasite** that wreaks havoc on the human digestive system. If you pick up this pesky hanger-on, it may accompany you on your trip home. The best solution is to carry all the water you'll need (usually a gal. a day). If you need additional water from the parks' lakes and streams, it should be boiled for 3 to 6 minutes before consumption.

13 Hiking Tips

Don't venture off on any extensive hike, even a day hike, without the following gear: a compass, a topographical map, bug repellent, a whistle, a watch, and sufficient water. In many western parks, sunglasses, sunscreen, and wide-brimmed hats are also considered essential. To be on the safe side, you should keep a **first-aid kit** in your car or luggage and have it handy when hiking. At a minimum, it should contain butterfly bandages, sterile gauze pads, adhesive tape, antibiotic ointment, pain relievers, alcohol pads, and a knife with scissors and tweezers (tweezers are especially useful for removing those nasty little cactus spines that seem to attack from the side of the trail). In many national parks, cellphone service is spotty or nonexistent, so don't depend on being able to call for help in an emergency unless you have a satphone (which is rather expensive to own but can be rented for your stay in a remote area).

14 Planning a Backcountry Trip

Here are some general things to keep in mind when planning a backcountry trip:

- **Permits.** In many parks, overnight hiking and backcountry camping require a permit.
- **Camping Etiquette & Special Regulations.** Follow the basic rules of camping etiquette: Pack out all your trash, including uneaten food and used toilet paper. Camp in obvious campsites. If pit toilets are not available, bury human waste in holes 6 inches deep, 6 inches across, and at least 200 feet from water and creek beds. When doing dishes, take water and dishes at least 200 feet from the water source, and scatter the wastewater. Hang food and trash out of reach of wildlife, use bear-proof containers, or follow other park rules to keep wildlife from human food.
- **Footwear.** Be sure to wear comfortable, sturdy hiking shoes or boots with good ankle support that will resist water, if you're planning an early season hike.
- **Sleeping Bags.** Your sleeping bag should be rated for the low temperatures found at high elevations. Most campers are happy to have a sleeping pad.
- **Water.** If you're not carrying enough water for the entire trip, you'll also need a good purifying system, because that seemingly clear stream is filled with a bacteria likely to cause intestinal disorders.
- **Your Pack.** The argument rages about the merits of old-fashioned external-frame packs and newer internal-frame models. Over the long run, the newer versions are more stable and allow you to carry greater loads more comfortably; however, they also cost more. The key issue is finding a pack that fits well and has plenty of padding, a wide hip belt, and a good lumbar support pad.

America's National Parks: We're Ready for Our Close-Up!

Ken Burns and Dayton Duncan's six-part, 12-hour 2009 documentary series *The National Parks: America's Best Idea* told the dramatic story of the origin of the National Park system. Starting with "The Scripture of Nature," it focused on the early appreciation (in the 1850s) of the areas that became Yosemite and Yellowstone national parks, followed by "The Last Refuge," depicting the ongoing battle between the preservation of the parks, starting in the 1890s, and industrialization and commercialization of the lands. "The Empire of Grandeur" profiled the formation of the National Park Service in 1916, spearheaded by wealthy, charismatic businessman Stephen Mather, who returned again and again to nature to restore his own health. "Going Home" featured people following in the footsteps of Mather in the 1920s and '30s to create more parks and protect the natural wonders all over the country, including John D. Rockefeller Jr.'s purchase of land to donate to the U.S. to expand Grand Teton National Park. "Great Nature" told the story of how the parks survived and changed in the Depression, with the creation of the WPA, and how President Franklin Roosevelt resisted pressure to use their natural resources during World War II. Set in the postwar years through about 1980, "The Morning of Creation" told how the parks have developed the balancing act between being cherished and visited by millions each year, and protecting the environments from being overrun and permanently altered. You can watch scenes from the series at **www.pbs.org/nationalparks** or purchase the DVDs, companion book, and soundtrack CD.

15 Protecting the Environment

Not long ago, the rule of thumb was to "leave only footprints"; these days, we're trying to do better and not leave even footprints. It's relatively easy to be a good outdoor citizen—just use common sense. Pack out all trash; stay on designated trails; be especially careful not to pollute water; don't disturb plants, wildlife, or archaeological resources; don't pick flowers or collect rocks; and, in general, do your best to have as little impact on the environment as possible. Some hikers go further, carrying a small trash bag to pick up what others may have left. As the Park Service likes to remind us, protecting our national parks is everyone's responsibility.

Be Gentle with Mother Nature, She's Fragile

Although you'll find westerners don't much stand on ceremony, there are a couple of things to be aware of out here. Much of America's historic and cultural heritage in the west runs on the honor system. Architectural sites can be damaged easily, so *please* keep off ruins with signs that warn people away. There are plenty of places where you can explore ruins up close without putting them at risk. When you think of it, it's a miracle any of this stuff survived—anything visitors can do to prolong its existence contributes to the miracle, and honors these unique, irreplaceable sites. Avoid touching petroglyphs, getting them wet, or walking on them. If you make it into the back country, you may see shards of pottery scattered around unexcavated sites. Taking things from archeological sites carries heavy penalties, but beyond the legal incentives, you can imagine the larger karmic reasons for not looting our national heritage. Most of the west is hearty enough that you can walk (or bike or drive) freely without worrying about damaging the land. There are some sensitive areas, however, especially around Canyonlands (chapter 8). The crust (sometimes called **cryptobiotic soil**) is alive with algae, lichens, and bacteria. You'll start recognizing it as a black, puffy growth. If you stay on trails and rock tops, and step carefully when you're around it, you'll help keep the desert alive. As the locals say: "Tiptoe through the crypto!"

2

Arches National Park, UT

by Don & Barbara Laine

Natural stone arches and fantastic rock formations, sculpted as if by an artist's hand, are the defining features of this park, and they exist in remarkable numbers and variety. Just as soon as you've seen the most beautiful, most colorful, most gigantic stone arch you can imagine, walk around the next bend, and there's another—bigger, better, and more brilliant than the last. It would take forever to see them all, with more than 2,000 officially listed and more being discovered, or "born," every day.

Just down the road from Canyonlands National Park (see chapter 8), Arches is more visitor-friendly, with relatively short, well-maintained trails leading to most of the park's major attractions. It's also a place to let your imagination run wild. Is Delicate Arch really so delicate? Or would its other monikers (Old Maid's Bloomers and Cowboy Chaps) be more appropriate? And what about those tall spires? You might imagine they're castles, giant stone sailing ships, or the petrified skyscrapers of some ancient city.

Exploring the park is a great family adventure. The arches seem more accessible and less forbidding than the spires and pinnacles at Canyonlands and most other western parks. Some think of arches as bridges, imagining the power of water that literally cuts a hole through solid rock. Actually, to geologists there's a big difference. Natural bridges are formed when a river cuts a channel; the often bizarre and beautiful contours of arches result from the erosive force of rain and snow, freezing and thawing, as it dissolves the "glue" that holds sand grains together and chips away at the stone.

Although arches usually grow slowly—*very* slowly—occasionally something dramatic happens, like that quiet day in 1940 when a sudden crash instantly doubled the size of the opening of Skyline Arch, leaving a huge boulder lying at its feet. Luckily, no one (that we know of) was standing underneath at the time. The same thing happened to the magnificently delicate Landscape Arch in 1991, when a slab of rock about 60 feet long, 11 feet wide, and 4½ feet thick fell from the underside of the arch. It's hard to believe that such a thin ribbon of stone can continue hanging on at all.

Spend a day or a week here, exploring the terrain, watching the rainbow of colors deepen and explode with the long rays of the setting sun, or glimpsing ribbons of moonlight on tall sandstone cliffs. Be on the lookout for mule deer, cottontail rabbits, and bright-green collared lizards as they go about the task of desert living. And let your imagination run wild among the Three Gossips, the Spectacles, the Eye of the Whale, the Penguins, the Tower of Babel, and the thousands of other statues, towers, arches, and bridges in this remarkable sandstone playground.

AVOIDING THE CROWDS

This is a very popular park, attracting more than 800,000 visitors annually. Expect to find crowded parking areas and full campgrounds daily from March through October, with the peak month being August. The quietest months are December, January, and February, but it can be cold then. Those wanting to avoid crowds might gamble on Mother Nature and visit in November or late February, when days can be delightfully sunny and just a bit cool, or bitterly cold, windy, and awful. As with most popular parks, avoid visiting during school vacations, if possible.

1 Essentials

GETTING THERE & GATEWAYS

The entrance to the park is 5 miles north of Moab, Utah, on U.S. 191. To get there from Salt Lake City, about 240 miles away, follow I-15 south to Spanish Fork, take U.S. 6 southeast to I-70, and follow that east to Crescent Junction, where you'll pick up U.S. 191 south. From Grand Junction, Colorado, take I-70 west until you reach Crescent Junction, and then go south on U.S. 191.

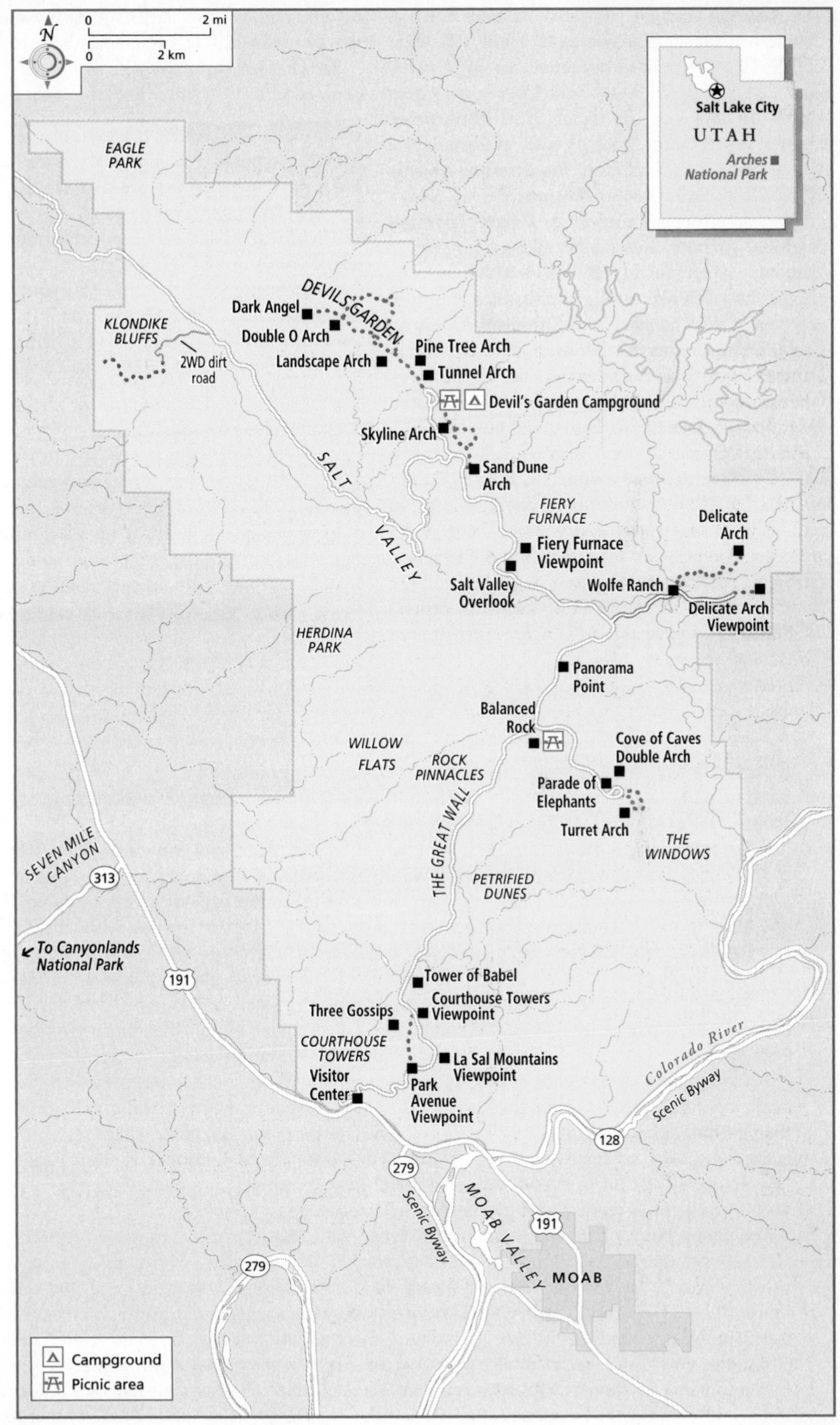

0
2 mi
0
2 km
Salt Lake City
UTAH
Arches National Park
EAGLE PARK
KLONDIKE BLUFFS
2WD dirt road
DEVILS GARDEN
Dark Angel
Double O Arch
Landscape Arch
Pine Tree Arch
Tunnel Arch
Devil's Garden Campground
Skyline Arch
Sand Dune Arch
SALT VALLEY
FIERY FURNACE
Fiery Furnace Viewpoint
Salt Valley Overlook
Delicate Arch
Wolfe Ranch
Delicate Arch Viewpoint
HERDINA PARK
Panorama Point
Balanced Rock
Cove of Caves
Double Arch
WILLOW FLATS
ROCK PINNACLES
Parade of Elephants
Turret Arch
THE WINDOWS
THE GREAT WALL
PETRIFIED DUNES
SEVEN MILE CANYON
313
To Canyonlands National Park
191
Tower of Babel
Courthouse Towers Viewpoint
Three Gossips
COURTHOUSE TOWERS
La Sal Mountains Viewpoint
Visitor Center
Park Avenue Viewpoint
Colorado River
Scenic Byway
128
279
Scenic Byway
MOAB VALLEY
191
279
MOAB
Campground
Picnic area

The Nearest Airport Located 16 miles north of downtown Moab, **Canyonlands Field** (✆ **435/259-7419;** www.moabairport.com) has daily scheduled flights between Moab and Denver on **Great Lakes Airlines** and car rentals from **Enterprise.** Shuttle service into Moab is also available from several companies, including **Roadrunner Shuttle** (✆ **435/259-9402;** www.roadrunnershuttle.com).

The closest major airport is **Grand Junction Regional Airport,** about 200 miles east in Grand Junction, Colorado (✆ **970/244-9100;** www.gjairport.com). It has direct flights or connections from most major cities on **Allegiant, American/American Eagle, Delta Connection/Skywest, Frontier, Great Lakes, United Express/Skywest,** and **US Airways.** Car rentals are available at the airport from **Alamo, Avis, Budget, Enterprise, Hertz,** and **National.**

Another option for air travelers is to fly into **Salt Lake City International Airport** (✆ **800/595-2442** or 801/575-2400; www.slcairport.com), about 240 miles from Moab, which has service from most major airlines and rental-car companies. From there, you can rent a car, take a US Airways Express flight (see above), or take a shuttle van with **Bighorn Express** (✆ **888/655-7433** or 801/417-5191; www.bighornexpress.com), which charges $69 each way and operates a varied schedule throughout the year.

See chapter 38 for website listings of major airlines, hotel/motel chains, and car-rental agencies.

GROUND TRANSPORTATION

Rentals (standard passenger cars, vans, and four-wheel-drive vehicles) are available from **Enterprise** (✆ **435/260-6081;** www.enterprise.com). Rugged four-wheel-drive vehicles are available from **Farabee's Jeep Rentals** (✆ **877/970-5337** or 435/259-7494; www.farabeejeeprentals.com), **Canyonlands Jeep Adventures** (✆ **866/892-5337** or 435/259-4413; www.canyonlandsjeep.com), and **Cliffhanger Jeep Rental** (✆ **435/259-0889;** www.cliffhangerjeeprental.com).

PARK INFORMATION

Contact **Arches National Park,** P.O. Box 907, Moab, UT 84532 (✆ **435/719-2299;** www.nps.gov/arch).

Books, maps, and videos on Arches, as well as Canyonlands National Park and other southern Utah attractions, are available from the nonprofit **Canyonlands Natural History Association,** 3015

Tips from a Park Ranger

A "good family park" is how Arches' former chief of interpretation Diane Allen describes this national park. "What makes Arches special is its variety of rock formations and the ease of accessibility," she says. "You can see quite a bit even if you have only a few hours."

Allen says that 2 hours is about the minimum time needed to tour the scenic drive, stopping at the view points and taking a few short walks, but 1 to 1½ days would give you a pretty good look at the park. She suggests that you start at the **visitor center** to find out about guided hikes and other ranger-led activities, and then get out on the trails early in the day, while it's still cool. The **Devils Garden Trail** provides a variety of experiences, Allen says, and is a fairly easy hike to scenic **Landscape Arch.** She says that hikers should carry and drink plenty of **water**—rangers recommend a gallon per person per day—because in this extremely arid climate, dehydration and heat problems can be fatal. If at the end of the day you have a slight headache and feel a bit lethargic and grouchy, it's likely because you didn't drink enough water.

Although park visitors will, of course, want to see the park's arches—**Delicate Arch** has practically become the symbol for the state of Utah—Allen says that Arches National Park is more than arches. "There are many other formations—spires, pinnacles, natural bridges, and great walls," she says, adding that the park is a prime example of Colorado Plateau vegetation. "We've got a little bit of everything: wildflowers, cactus, pinyon, juniper, a few riparian areas. And if you want to learn about geology, it's all exposed, easy to see."

The park is busiest between March and October, with August usually registering the most visitors. Summers are hot, and spring and fall are pleasant. One way to avoid crowds, Allen says, is to visit in winter: "You can get fantastic hiking days in February, but keep in mind that days are shorter then." The other proven way to avoid crowds, even at the height of the summer, is to get out onto the trails early in the day. "It's a much more pleasant time to be in the park," she says. "It's cooler, you have a better chance of seeing wildlife, and there are fewer people."

You can also ask rangers for suggestions on less used trails. Allen says she likes the **Tower Arch Trail,** which is more of a primitive experience where you are less likely to see a lot of other hikers.

If You Have Only 1 Day

Arches is one of the easiest national parks to see in a day if that's all you can spare. A **scenic drive** offers splendid views of natural rock arches and other formations, and several easy hikes open up additional scenery. The drive is 18 miles one-way, plus 5 miles for a side trip to The Windows and 4½ miles for a side trip to Delicate Arch.

Start at the **visitor center,** and ask rangers for their suggestions for a short hike so you can get a close-up view of some of the arches. Possibilities include the short, easy hike to **Double Arch** and the longer and sometimes hot hike to **Delicate Arch.** If you're up for a more strenuous excursion, and the timing's right, join one of the ranger-guided hikes to **Fiery Furnace.**

S. U.S. 191, Moab, UT 84532 (✆ **800/840-8978** or 435/259-6003; fax 435/259-8263; www.cnha.org). Some publications are available in foreign languages, and a variety of videos can be purchased in DVD and videotape formats. For more detailed descriptions of the park's hiking trails and backcountry roads, purchase *Hiking Canyonlands and Arches National Parks,* by Bill Schneider, at the visitor center or through the Canyonlands Natural History Association.

For area information, contact the **Moab Area Travel Council,** P.O. Box 550, Moab, UT 84532 (✆ **800/635-6622** or 435/259-8825; www.discovermoab.com). When you arrive, stop by the **Moab Information Center,** at the corner of Main and Center streets, open Monday through Saturday 8am to 8pm and Sunday from 9am to 7pm from July through September, with shorter hours the rest of the year.

VISITOR CENTER

The **Arches National Park Visitor Center** is just inside the entrance gate. It offers maps, brochures, and other information, and a museum explains arch formation and other features of the park. Be sure to take time to watch the orientation film, *Secrets of Red Rock,* shown in the auditorium. From April through October, the visitor center is open daily from 7:30am to 6:30pm; the rest of the year, it's open daily from 8am to 4:30pm. On Christmas Day, the park is open but the visitor center is closed.

FEES & PERMITS

Entry for up to 7 days costs $10 per private vehicle or $5 per person on foot, motorcycle, or bike. A $25 annual pass is also available; it's good for Arches and Canyonlands national parks, as well as Natural Bridges and Hovenweep national monuments. Campsites cost $20 per night. Required permits for overnight trips into the backcountry, available at the visitor center, are free.

SPECIAL REGULATIONS & WARNINGS

Ground fires are not permitted; the campground provides grills, but you must bring your own firewood. Be aware that although the desert terrain appears hardy, it is easily damaged. Rangers ask that hikers stay on trails and be careful around the bases of arches and other rock formations.

SEASONS & CLIMATE

Summer days are hot, often reaching 100°F (38°C), and winters can be cool or cold, dropping below freezing at night, with snow possible. The best time to visit, especially for hikers, is in the spring or fall, when daytime temperatures are usually between 60° and 80°F (16°–27°C) and nights are cool. Spring winds, although not usually dangerous, can be gusty, so hold on to your hat.

2 Exploring the Park by Car

You can see many of the park's most famous rock formations through your car windows, although we strongly urge you to get out and explore on foot. You have the option of walking short distances to a number of view points or stretching your legs on a variety of longer hikes (see "Day Hikes," below). The main road is easy to navigate, even for RVs, but parking at some view points is limited. Please be considerate and leave trailers at the visitor center parking lot or in a campground.

After leaving the visitor center, drive north past the Moab Fault to the overlook parking for **Park Avenue,** a solid rock "fin" that reminded early visitors of the New York skyline. From here, your next stop is **La Sal Mountain Viewpoint,** where you look southeast to the La Sal Mountains, named by early Spanish explorers who thought the snow-covered mountains looked like huge piles of salt. In the overlook area is a "desert scrub" ecosystem, composed mostly of blackbrush, with some sagebrush, saltbush, yucca, and prickly pear cactus, all plants that can survive in sandy soil with little moisture. The area's wildlife includes the black-tailed jackrabbit, rock squirrel, kangaroo rat, coyote, and several species of lizards.

Continuing on the scenic drive, you begin to see some of the park's major formations at **Courthouse Towers,** where monoliths such as Sheep Rock, the Organ, and the Three Gossips dominate the landscape. Leaving Courthouse Towers, watch for the **Tower of Babel** on the east (right) side of the road, and then proceed past the "petrified" sand dunes to **Balanced Rock,** a huge boulder weighing about 3,600 tons, perched on a slowly eroding pedestal.

You'll soon take a side road east (right) to **The Windows.** Created when erosion penetrated a sandstone fin, they are visible after a short walk from the parking area. Also in this area are **Turret Arch** and the **Cove of Caves.** As erosion continues in the back of the largest cave, it may eventually become an arch. A short walk from the parking lot takes you to **Double Arch,** which looks like exactly that. From the end of this trail, you can also see the delightful **Parade of Elephants.**

Return to the main park road, turn north (right), and drive to **Panorama Point.** You'll find an expansive view of Salt Valley and the Fiery Furnace, which can really live up to its name at sunset.

Next, turn east (right) off the main road onto the Wolfe Ranch Road and drive to the **Wolfe Ranch** parking area. A short walk leads to what's left of the century-old ranch. If you follow the trail a bit farther, you'll see some **Ute petroglyphs.** More ambitious hikers can continue for a moderately difficult 3-mile round-trip excursion to **Delicate Arch,** with a spectacular view at trail's end. You can also see this lovely arch, albeit from a distance, by getting back in your car, continuing down the road for 1 mile, and walking a short trail to the **Delicate Arch Viewpoint.**

Returning to the park's main road, turn north (right) and go to the next stop, the **Salt Valley Overlook.** Varying amounts of iron in the rock, as well as other factors, have caused the various shades and colors in this collapsed salt dome.

Continue now to the view point for **Fiery Furnace,** which offers a dramatic view of colorful sandstone fins. From here, drive to a pullout for **Sand Dune Arch,** down a short path from the road, where you'll find shade and sand along with the arch. It's a good place for kids to play. The trail also leads to **Broken Arch** (which isn't broken at all; it just looks that way from a distance).

Back on the road, continue to **Skyline Arch,** which doubled in size in 1940 when a huge boulder tumbled out of it. The next and final stop is the often crowded parking area for the **Devils Garden trail head.** From here you can hike to some of the most unusual arches in the park, including **Landscape Arch,** considered the longest natural rock arch in the world.

From the trail head parking lot, it's 18 miles back to the visitor center.

3 Organized Tours & Ranger Programs

From March through October, rangers lead 2-mile **guided hikes** into the Fiery Furnace area twice daily, by reservation. Cost is $10 per adult, $5 per child 6 to 12, and free for children under 6. The hikes, which take about 3 hours, are often booked a day or two in advance, and reservations can be made in person up to 7 days in advance and through the park's website. As you hike along, a ranger describes the desert plants, points out hard-to-find arches, and discusses the geology and natural history of the Fiery Furnace. Also see the section on the Fiery Furnace under "Day Hikes," below. From March through October, rangers lead daily nature walks from various park locations. **Evening campfire programs,** from April through October, cover topics such as rock art, geological processes, and wildlife. Check the schedule at the visitor center and on bulletin boards throughout the park.

4 Park Attractions

Although not many have left their mark in this rugged area, a few intrepid Ute Indians and pioneers have spent time here. Just off the Delicate Arch Trail is a **Ute petroglyph panel** that includes etchings of horses and possibly of bighorn sheep. Also, near the beginning of the trail is **Wolfe Ranch.** Disabled Civil War veteran John Wesley Wolfe and his son Fred moved here from Ohio in 1898; John's daughter Flora, her husband, and their two children arrived in 1907. They left in 1910, after which John's cabin was destroyed by a flash flood. The cabin used by Flora's family survived and has been preserved by the Park Service. You'll see the cabin, a root cellar, and a corral.

5 Day Hikes

Most trails are short and relatively easy, although because of the hot summer sun and lack of shade, it's wise to wear a hat and carry plenty of water on any jaunt expected to last more than 1 hour.

SHORTER TRAILS

Balanced Rock Trail This short, easy walk is perfect for visitors who want to stretch their legs and get a great close-up view of the precariously perched Balanced Rock. The loop takes you around the formation. The trail is wheelchair accessible. 0.3 mile RT. Easy. Access: Balanced Rock parking area, on east side of main park road.

Broken Arch This easy hike, with little elevation change, traverses sand dunes and slickrock to the arch. Watch for the rock cairns, in some places poorly defined, marking the path through the arch. A little farther along is a connecting trail to **Sand Dune Arch,** about .5 mile out and back. At the end of the loop is a .25-mile walk along the paved campground road back to your car. 1.2 mile RT. Easy. Access: End of Devils Garden Campground.

Double Arch This easy walk, with very little elevation change, leads you to the third-largest arch opening in the park—don't be fooled by how small it looks from the parking area. Along your way, look for the **Parade of Elephants,** off to the left. Once there, you can go a little farther and climb right up under the arch—just be very careful not to disturb the delicate desert vegetation or natural features. To the right of Double Arch are several alcoves that may one day become arches. If you're visiting in spring, look for the **sego lily,** Utah's state flower. It has three lovely cream-colored petals with a reddish-purple spot fading to yellow at the base. 0.25 mile one-way. Easy. Access: Double Arch parking area, in Windows section of park.

Park Avenue This downhill hike takes you into the canyon through scattered Utah juniper, singleleaf ash, blackbrush, and, in spring, wildflowers that sprinkle the sides of the trail with color. The park road allows views of **Courthouse Towers, Tower of Babel, Three Gossips,** and **Organ Rock,** but it's not nearly as awe-inspiring as actually walking among them. Have a friend provide a ride to the starting point so the trip is all downhill, or start at the **Courthouse Towers** end and make the 320-foot climb first, so the return to your vehicle is downhill. 1 mile one-way. Easy. Access: Park Avenue or Courthouse Towers parking area.

Sand Dune Arch This is an easy walk through low shrubs and grasses to the arch, which is hidden among and shaded by rock walls, with a naturally created giant sandbox below. Please resist the temptation to climb onto the arch and jump down into the sand—not only is it dangerous, but it can damage the arch. Just before **Sand Dune Arch,** a trail cuts off to the left that leads to **Broken Arch,** adding 1.2 miles to your hike. Those who try this should watch for mule deer and kit foxes, which inhabit the grassland along the way. 0.3 mile one-way. Easy. Access: Sand Dune Arch parking area.

Skyline Arch This is an easy walk along a flat, well-defined trail, with a view of Skyline Arch dominating the horizon. On a cold November night in 1940, a large boulder fell from the opening of this arch, doubling its size. 2 miles one-way. Easy. Access: Skyline Arch parking area.

The Windows This fairly flat hike leads to three massive arches, two of which appear to be almost perfectly round windows. It's a busy trail, but you'll find fewer people if you hike early or late in the day. On your way to **North Window,** take a short side trip to **Turret Arch.** Once you reach North and South Windows, take the loop around back and see for yourself why they are sometimes called Spectacles—the scene looks almost like a sea monster poking its large snout up into the air. 1-mile loop. Easy. Access: Windows parking area.

LONGER TRAILS

Delicate Arch Climbing about 480 feet, this hike is considered by many the park's best and most scenic; it's also complicated by slippery slickrock, no shade, and some steep drop-offs along a narrow cliff. The reward for your efforts is a dramatic, spectacular view of **Delicate Arch.** Along the way, you'll see the **John Wesley Wolfe Ranch** and have an opportunity to take a side trip to a **Ute petroglyph panel** that includes drawings of horses and what may represent a bighorn sheep hunt.

When you get back on the main trail, watch for **collared lizards,** bright-green foot-long creatures with stripes of yellow or rust and black collars. Feeding mostly in the daytime, they particularly enjoy insects and other lizards, and can stand and run on their large hind feet in pursuit of prey. Continuing along the trail, watch for **Frame Arch,** off to the right. Its main claim to fame is that numerous photographers have used it to "frame" a photo of Delicate Arch in the distance. Just past Frame Arch, the trail gets a little weird, having been blasted out from the cliff.

Should you choose not to take this hike, consider driving to the **Delicate Arch Viewpoint Trail,** which provides an ideal location for a photo, preferably with the arch highlighted by a clear blue sky. From the parking area, it is about a 5-minute walk to the viewpoint. 1.5 miles one-way. Moderate to strenuous. Access: Wolfe Ranch parking area.

Devils Garden Primitive Loop The whole Devils Garden loop is a fairly long, strenuous, and difficult hike, from which you can see 15 to 20 arches and some exciting scenery, as well as can't-miss **Landscape Arch.** Be sure to take plenty of water, and don't hurry.

You don't have to go the entire way to see some unusual formations. Just .25 mile from the trail head, a spur takes off to the right down a little hill. Here a left turn takes you to **Pine Tree Arch,** and turning right brings you to **Tunnel Arch.**

After returning to the main trail, stay to the left, and soon you'll reach the turnoff to **Landscape Arch,** a long (306-ft.), thin ribbon of stone that is one of the most beautiful arches in the park. This is about a 2-mile round-trip trail and is an absolute must-see during a visit to Arches National Park. Geologically speaking, Landscape Arch is quite mature and may collapse any day. Almost immediately after passing Landscape Arch, look to your right for **Wall Arch.** From here the trail is less well defined, but marked by cairns.

After another .25 mile, a side trip to the left has two spurs leading to **Partition Arch,** which you could see earlier behind Landscape Arch, and **Navajo Arch.** The spurs take you right up under the arches. Navajo Arch is shaded, providing a spot to stop and take a breather while absorbing the view.

Once back on the main trail, which gets rougher and slicker as you hike, it's .5 mile to the strange **Double O Arch,** where one arch stands atop another. Now you've reached another junction. The left spur leads to the **Dark Angel,** a dark sandstone spire reaching toward the heavens from the desert floor. The right spur takes you on to the **primitive loop,** a difficult trip through a dramatic desert environment with some drop-offs and narrow ledges. Along this part of the trail is just one major arch, **Private Arch,** on a short spur to the right. You'll have the primitive loop almost to yourself—most people turn back at Double O Arch rather than tackle this more difficult trail. 7.2 miles RT. Easy to strenuous. Access: Devils Garden parking area.

Fiery Furnace This is a difficult and strenuous hike to some of the most colorful formations in the park. The name comes from the rich reddish glow the rocks take on at sunset.

Guided hikes run twice daily from March through October (see "Organized Tours & Ranger Programs," above). You can also choose to head out on your own, although you must first obtain a **permit** (there's a fee) and watch a short video presentation. Trails aren't marked, so unless you are experienced in the Fiery Furnace, it's best to join a guided hike. 2 miles RT. Moderate to strenuous. Access: Fiery Furnace parking area.

Tower Arch This is a short but rugged hike on a primitive trail. It starts with a steep incline to the top of the bluff and proceeds up and down, with great views of the Klondike Bluffs to the right. Beware of the slickrock that makes up part of the trail, and watch for the cairns leading the way. The hardest part is near the end, where you struggle uphill through loose sand. Your reward is a grand sight: the immense **Tower Arch** standing among a maze of sandstone spires. Climb up under it for a soothing view while you take a much-deserved break. In spring, the majestic, snowcapped **La Sal Mountains** can be seen to the east through the arch opening. 1.7 miles one-way. Strenuous. Access: Follow Salt Valley Rd. for 7 miles, turn left toward Klondike Bluffs, and go 1.5 miles to the Tower Arch trail head. (Be careful not to take the left turn just before the Klondike Bluffs Rd., which is a difficult four-wheel-drive road.)

6 Exploring the Backcountry

There are no designated backcountry trails or campsites, and little of the park is open to overnight camping, but backcountry **hiking** is permitted. Ask park rangers to suggest routes. No fires are allowed, and hikers must carry their own water and practice low-impact hiking and camping techniques. Those planning to be out overnight need free **backcountry permits,** available at the visitor center.

7 Other Sports & Activities

Arches National Park and the surrounding public lands offer plenty for the do-it-yourselfer, and some 50 local outfitters offer excursions of all kinds just outside the park. They range from rugged mountain-bike treks to relatively comfortable four-wheel-drive adventures. You can also rent a canoe or take a guided boat trip on the Colorado River, which follows the park's southeast boundary.

The chart below lists some of the major companies that can help you fully enjoy this beautiful country. They are all in Moab. Advance reservations are often required, and it's best to check with several outfitters before deciding which best fits your needs. When making reservations, be sure to ask about the company's cancellation policy, just in case.

BIKING Bikes are prohibited on all trails and off-road in the backcountry. They are permitted on the scenic drive, although the 18-mile dead-end road is narrow and winding in spots, and can be crowded with motor vehicles during the summer.

Mountain bikers also have the option of tackling one of several four-wheel-drive roads (see the "Four-Wheeling" section, below). Cyclists can get information, as well as rent or repair bikes at **Poison Spider Bicycles,** 497 N. Main St. (✆ **800/635-1792** or 435/259-7882; www.poisonspiderbicycles.com). Bike rentals and repairs, plus shuttle services, will be found at **Chile Pepper Bike Shop,** 702 S. Main St. (✆ **888/677-4688** or 435/259-4688; www.chilebikes.com). Bike rentals range from $40 to $75 per day, with discounts for multiday rentals. Bike shuttle services are

Outfitter	4WD	Bike	Boat	Horse	Rent
Adrift Adventures 378 N. Main St., Box 577 ✆ 800/874-4483, 435/259-8594 www.adrift.net	Yes	No	Yes	Yes	No
Canyon Voyages Adventure Co. 211 N. Main St. ✆ 800/733-6007, 435/259-6007 www.canyonvoyages.com	Yes	Yes	Yes	Yes	Yes
Dan Mick's Guided Jeep Tours 600 Mill Creek Dr., Box 1234 ✆ 435/259-4567 www.danmick.com	Yes	No	No	No	No
Magpie Adventures Cycling Tours Box 1496 ✆ 800/546-4245, 435/259-4464 www.magpieadventures.com	No	Yes	No	No	No
Moab Adventure Center 225 S. Main St. ✆ 866/904-1163, 435/259-7019 www.moabadventurecenter.com	Yes	Yes	Yes	Yes	Yes
Moab Rafting Co. Box 801 ✆ 800/746-6622, 435/259-7238 www.moab-rafting.com	No	No	Yes	No	No
Navtec Expeditions 321 N. Main St., Box 1267 ✆ 800/833-1278, 435/259-7983 www.navtec.com	Yes	No	Yes	No	Yes
Sheri Griffith Expeditions 2231 S. U.S. 191, Box 1324 ✆ 800/332-2439, 435/259-8229 www.griffithexp.com	No	No	Yes	No	No
Tag-A-Long Expeditions 452 N. Main St. ✆ 800/453-3292, 435/259-8946 www.tagalong.com	Yes	No	Yes	No	Yes
Western Spirit Cycling 428 Mill Creek Dr. ✆ 800/845-2453, 435/259-8732 www.westernspirit.com	No	Yes	No	No	No

also available from several of the companies, including **Coyote Shuttle** (✆ **435/259-8656;** www.coyote shuttle.com) and **Roadrunner Shuttle** (✆ **435/259-9402;** www.roadrunnershuttle.com).

Several local companies (see the chart listing outfitters above) also offer guided mountain-bike tours, with rates starting at about $85 for a half-day and about $110 for a full day. Multiday biking/camping trips are also available.

BOATING, CANOEING & RAFTING Although there are no bodies of water inside Arches National Park, the Colorado River follows the park's boundary along its southeast edge, and river-running is a wonderful change of pace from hiking over the park's dry, rocky terrain. You can travel down the river in a canoe, kayak, large or small rubber raft (with or without a motor), or speedy, solid jet boat.

Do-it-yourselfers can rent kayaks or canoes for $35 to $55 for a full day, or rafts starting at $60 for a full day. Half-day guided river trips start at about $40 per person; full-day trips are usually $50 to $70 per person. Multiday rafting expeditions, which include meals and camping equipment, start at about $350 per person for 2 days. Jet-boat trips, which cover a lot more river in a given amount of time, start at about $80 for a half-day trip. Children's rates are usually about 20% lower. Some companies also offer sunset or dinner trips. See the chart above.

Public boat-launching ramps are opposite Lion's Park, near the intersection of U.S. 191 and Utah

128; at Take-Out Beach, along Utah 128 about 10 miles east of its intersection with U.S. 191; and at Hittle Bottom, also along Utah 128, about 24 miles east of its intersection with U.S. 191. The **Colorado Basin River Forecast Center** (✆ **801/539-1311** [recording]; www.cbrfc.noaa.gov) provides information on river flows and reservoir conditions.

FOUR-WHEELING There aren't as many four-wheel-drive opportunities here as in nearby Canyonlands National Park, but there are a few, including the **Salt Valley Road** and the **Willow Flats Road,** both of which can be extremely slick after a rain and are open to four-wheel-drive vehicles and mountain bikes. Check at the visitor center for directions and current conditions.

ROCK CLIMBING Technical climbing is permitted in some areas of the park, but only for experienced climbers. In addition, it is prohibited on many of the park's best-known arches, as well as Balanced Rock and a few other locations. Information is available from park rangers.

8 Camping

INSIDE THE PARK

At the north end of the park's scenic drive, **Devils Garden Campground** is Arches' only developed campground. The sites nestle among rocks, with plenty of pinyon and juniper trees. In the summer, the campground fills early, so it's a good idea to get **reservations** (✆ **877/444-6777;** www.recreation.gov; $9 booking fee) to make sure you'll have a site. Reservations are available March through October. Summer campers who haven't made reservations should arrive early; sites are available beginning at 7:30am.

NEAR THE PARK

More than a dozen commercial campgrounds are in and around Moab. Located at the junction of U.S. 191 and U.S. 313, **Arch View Resort RV Camp Park,** U.S. 191 (P.O. Box 938), Moab, UT 84532 (✆ **800/813-6622** or 435/259-7854; www.archviewresort.com), offers all the usual RV hookups, showers, and other amenities you'd expect in a first-class commercial RV park, plus great views into the park and trees throughout. Arch View has a grassy tent area, convenience store, pool, and playground, as well as propane, gasoline, and diesel sales. There are also log cabins and upscale cottages ($40 and up for two).

Canyonlands Campground & RV Park, 555 S. Main St., Moab, UT 84532 (✆ **800/522-6848** or 435/259-6848; www.canyonlandsrv.com), is surprisingly shady and quiet, given its in-town location. It's convenient to Moab's restaurants and shopping. On-site is a convenience store with food and some RV supplies. RV hookups include cable TV, and there is Wi-Fi throughout the campground. There are also six cabins ($52 double).

The **Moab KOA,** 3225 S. U.S. 191, Moab, UT 84532 (✆ **800/562-0372** for reservations, or 435/259-6682; www.moabkoa.com), about 3 miles south of Moab, has trees and great views of the La Sal Mountains. It has a miniature golf course, game room, playgrounds, cable TV hookups, Wi-Fi, and a convenience store with RV supplies and propane. About half of the sites are for tents only. There are also one- and two-room cabins ($51–$65 double).

On the north side of Moab, near the intersection of U.S. 191 and Utah 128, is **Moab Valley RV Resort,** 1773 N. U.S. 191, Moab, UT 84532 (✆ **435/259-4469;** www.moabvalleyrv.com). All sites offer great views of the surrounding rock formations. The park accommodates practically any size RV in its extra-large pull-through sites and provides cable television connections on full RV hookups. There are trees and patches of grass for both tenters and RVers, as well as Wi-Fi. You can refuel at the convenience store, which sells propane, groceries, and RV and camping supplies. Dogs are permitted in RV sites, but not in tent sites or cabins. There are 18 cabins and cottages ($50–$75 for two).

You'll find campgrounds at nearby Canyonlands National Park (see "Camping" in chapter 8) and in areas under the jurisdiction of the U.S. Forest Service, Bureau of Land Management, and Utah state parks. The **Mountain View RV Park** in Monticello (included in the campground chart here) is discussed in chapter 8. Also check at the **Moab Information Center** (see "Park Information," earlier).

9 Where to Stay

There are no lodging facilities inside the park.

NEAR THE PARK

Moab is the nearest town to Arches (5 miles south). Room rates are generally highest from mid-March through October, and sometimes drop by up to half in the winter.

Most visitors are here for the outdoors and don't plan to spend much time in their rooms; as a result, many book into one of the fully adequate chain and franchise motels, most of which are located on Main Street. Franchises here include our favorite, the very well-maintained **La Quinta Inn,** 815 S. Main St.

(✆ **435/259-8700;** www.laquintamoab.com), which is pet-friendly and has summer rates from $119 double, with off-season discounts. Other more than adequate franchises, with rates in the same general area, include **Super 8,** on the north edge of Moab, at 889 N. Main St. (✆ **435/259-8868**), which is the town's largest lodging, with almost 150 units; **Best Western Canyonlands Inn,** 16 S. Main St. (✆ **435/259-2300;** www.bestwesternutah.com); **Best Western Greenwell Inn,** 105 S. Main St. (✆ **435/259-6151;** www.bestwesternutah.com); **Comfort Suites,** 800 S. Main St. (✆ **435/259-5252**); **Days Inn,** 426 N. Main St. (✆ **435/259-4468**); **Motel 6,** 1089 N. Main St. (✆ **435/259-6686**); and **Sleep Inn,** 1051 S. Main St. (✆ **435/259-4655;** http://moabsleepinn.com). Website listings for the major hotel/motel chains are in chapter 38.

Also see the **cabins** at Arch View Resort RV Camp Park, Canyonlands Campground & RV Park, Moab KOA, and Moab Valley RV Resort, listed under "Camping," above.

Pets are not accepted unless otherwise noted.

Big Horn Lodge Spacious rooms with log furniture and knotty pine walls give the Big Horn a lodgelike atmosphere. All of the well-maintained units have two queen-size beds, refrigerators, microwaves, coffeemakers, dataports, hair dryers, and bathrooms with tub/showers. Bikes are permitted in the rooms. The property has an outdoor heated pool, a hot tub, a coin-op laundry, and a restaurant. All units are smoke-free.

550 S. Main St., Moab, UT 84532. ✆ **800/325-6171** or 435/259-6171. Fax 435/259-6144. www.moabbighorn.com. 58 units. A/C, TV, TEL. Apr–Oct $89–$109 double; check for Internet specials at other times. AE, DISC, MC, V. Pets accepted; $5 per night.

Bowen Motel This older family-owned and -operated motel offers fairly large, comfortable, clean, basic rooms with attractive wallpaper, a king-size or one or two queen-size beds, Wi-Fi, and combination tub/showers. Some units have a refrigerator and microwave; two family rooms sleep up to six each. Facilities include an outdoor heated swimming pool. All units are smoke-free.

169 N. Main St., Moab, UT 84532. ✆ **800/874-5439** or 435/259-7132. Fax 435/259-6641. www.bowenmotel.com. 40 units. A/C, TV, TEL. $74–$114 double; off-season discounts. Rates include continental breakfast. AE, DC, DISC, MC, V. Pets accepted.

Cali Cochitta Bed & Breakfast For a delightful escape from the hustle and bustle of Moab, head to the Cali Cochitta (Aztec for "House of Dreams"), a handsomely restored late-1800s Victorian home, with great views of the surrounding mountains and red rock formations. The spacious guest rooms have queen-size beds, handsome wood furnishings (including many antiques), and cotton robes. Our favorite room is the romantic "Cane," which has a high queen-size mahogany sleigh bed and French glass doors. The cottage has a refrigerator, and the suite can be rented as one or two rooms. The B&B has Wi-Fi, and all units have TVs with VCRs, hair dryers, and down comforters. Breakfasts include a hot entree (often prepared with herbs from the inn's garden), plus fresh muffins or other baked goods, fruit, and beverages. Bike storage is available. All units are smoke-free.

110 S. 200 E., Moab, UT 84532. ✆ **888/429-8112** or 435/259-4961. Fax 435/259-4964. www.moabdreaminn.com. 6 units. A/C, TV. Mar–Oct $125–$160 double; Nov–Feb $80–$120 double. Rates include full breakfast. AE, MC, V.

The Lazy Lizard International Hostel On the south side of town behind the A-l Self-Storage units, this hostel offers exceptionally clean, comfortable lodging at bargain rates for those willing to share. The main house, which is air-conditioned, has basic dorm rooms plus two private units. A separate building contains four additional private rooms, which look much like older motel units. The best facilities are the cabins, constructed of real logs and holding beds for up to six. There's also a camping area (no hookups). Everyone shares the bathhouses, and there's a phone in the main house. Guests also have use of a fully equipped kitchen; living room with TV, VCR, and movies; whirlpool; coin-op laundry; gas barbecue grill; and picnic tables. Groups should inquire about the nearby houses, which rent by the night ($120–$220 for 12–30 people).

1213 S. U.S. 191, Moab, UT 84532. ✆ **435/259-6057.** www.lazylizardhostel.com. 25 dorm beds, 10 private rooms, 8 cabins; total capacity 65 persons. A/C. $9 dorm bed; $26 private room double occupancy; from $31 cabin double occupancy; $7 per person camping space. Showers $3 for nonguests. Hostel membership not required. MC, V.

Red Stone Inn This centrally located motel is comfortable, quiet, and an especially good choice for mountain bikers. The exterior gives the impression that these are cabins, and the theme continues inside, with log furniture, knotty-pine walls, and colorful posters and maps of area attractions. Rooms are a bit on the small side, although perfectly adequate and spotlessly maintained. All rooms have kitchenettes with microwaves, 10-cup coffeemakers (with coffee supplied), refrigerators, and DSL dataports. Three units accessible for travelers with disabilities have tub/showers; the rest have showers only. There's an indoor hot tub, a 24-hour self-service coin-op laundry, a covered picnic area with tables and gas barbecue grills, and a bike work stand and bike wash station. Bikes are permitted in the rooms. There is no swimming pool on the premises, but guests have access to an outdoor heated pool at the motel across the street.

Campground	Total Elev.	RV Sites	Hookups	Dump Station	Toilets
Inside Arches					
Devils Garden	5,355	52	No	No	Yes
Inside Canyonlands					
Willow Flat	6,200	12	No	No	Yes
Squaw Flat	5,100	26	No	No	Yes
Near Canyonlands					
Dead Horse Point	5,900	21	21	Yes	Yes
Near Monticello					
Mountain View RV Park	7,050	35	29	Yes	Yes
Newspaper Rock	5,400	8	No	No	Yes
In and Near Moab					
Arch View Resort	5,000	71	54	No	Yes
Canyonlands Campground & RV Park	4,000	122	90	Yes	Yes
Moab KOA	5,000	154	73	Yes	Yes
Moab Valley RV Resort	4,000	108	69	Yes	Yes

535 S. Main St., Moab, UT 84532. ✆ **800/772-1972** or 435/259-3500. Fax 435/259-2717. www.moabredstone.com. 50 units. A/C, TV, TEL. $80–$90 double; check for Internet specials in winter. AE, DISC, MC, V. Pets accepted; $5 fee.

Sunflower Hill Luxury Inn This upscale country-style retreat, 3 blocks off Main Street, is our choice for a relaxing escape. The elegant rooms are individually decorated—for instance, the Summer House Suite boasts a colorful garden-themed mural—with handmade quilts on the queen-size beds. Deluxe rooms have jetted tubs and private balconies. The popular French Bedroom includes a hand-carved antique bedroom set, stained-glass window, vaulted ceiling, white lace curtains, and large whirlpool tub and separate tiled shower. The lush grounds are grassy and shady, with fruit trees and flowers, and a delightful swimming pool, all lending the air of an oasis. The substantial breakfast buffet includes fresh-baked breads and pastries, honey-almond granola, fresh fruits, and a hot entree such as a vegetable frittata, Belgian waffles, or a savory potato omelet. Guests have the use of an outdoor heated pool, hot tub, swing, picnic table, barbecue, locked bike storage, and coin-op laundry. The units are all smoke-free.

185 N. 300 East, Moab, UT 84532. ✆ **800/662-2786** or 435/259-2974. Fax 435/259-3065. www.sunflowerhill.com. 12 units. A/C TV. Mid-Mar through Oct and holidays $175–$245 double; Nov to mid-Mar $130–$190 double. Rates include full breakfast and evening refreshments. AE, DISC, MC, V. Children 9 and under are generally not allowed.

10 Where to Dine

There are no restaurants inside the park.

NEAR THE PARK

In addition to the restaurants discussed below, those looking for a foot-stompin' good time and a Western-style dinner will want to make their way to the climate-controlled dining room at the **Bar-M Chuckwagon Live Western Show and Cowboy Supper,** 7 miles north of Moab on U.S. 191 (✆ **800/214-2085** or 435/259-2276; www.barmchuckwagon.com). Diners go through a supper line to pick up sliced roast beef or barbecued chicken, baked potatoes, baked pinto beans, cinnamon applesauce, buttermilk biscuits, spice cake, and nonalcoholic beverages. Vegetarian meals can be prepared with advance notice, and beer and wine coolers are available.

After dinner, a stage show entertains with Western-style music, jokes, and down-home silliness from the Bar-M Wranglers. The grounds, which include a small Western village and gift shop, open at 6:30pm, with gunfights starting at 7pm, dinner at 7:30pm, and the show following supper. The Bar-M is usually open from April through mid-October but closed several evenings each week; call for the current schedule. Supper and show cost $27 for adults, $13 for children 4 to 12, and free for kids 3 and younger. Reservations are strongly recommended.

Another themed dining experience is offered by **Canyonlands by Night & Day** (✆ **800/394-9978** or 435/259-2628; www.canyonlandsbynight.com), which offers a variety of excursions in the area, including an evening river trip, operating spring through fall, that combines a sunset jet boat ride

Drinking Water	Showers	Fire Pits/ Grills	Laundry	Reserve	Fees	Open
Yes	No	Yes	No	Yes	$20	Year-round
No	No	Yes	No	No	$10	Year-round
Yes	No	Yes	No	No	$15	Year-round
Yes	No	Yes	No	Yes	$20	Year-round
Yes	Yes	No	Yes	Yes	$12–$22	May–Oct
No	No	Yes	No	No	Free	Year-round
Yes	Yes	Yes	Yes	Yes	$19–$36	Mid-Mar to mid-Nov
Yes	Yes	Yes	Yes	Yes	$22–$37	Year-round
Yes	Yes	Yes	Yes	Yes	$24–$35	Mar–Oct
Yes	Yes	Yes	Yes	Yes	$22–$42	Mar–Oct

with a Dutch-oven dinner. The office and dock are just north of Moab at the Colorado River Bridge. Cost for the boat trip and dinner is $65 for adults and $55 for children 4 to 12 (minimum age 4), with a family rate of $199 for two adults and two children. Reservations are recommended.

Buck's Grill House AMERICAN WESTERN This popular restaurant is Moab's best choice for steak. The dining room's subdued Western decor is accented by exposed wood beams and local artwork. The attractive patio, away from the road, has trees and a delightful rock waterfall. Especially good is the grilled 14-ounce rib-eye, or opt for the buffalo meat loaf with black onion gravy or the slow-cooked elk stew. Southwestern dishes include duck tamale with grilled pineapple salsa, and the grilled half-pound ground chuck burgers are an especially good deal, at $9. Pasta, pizza, ribs, and vegetarian items are also served. Buck's offers full liquor service and a good wine list, and serves a variety of Utah microbrews.

1393 N. U.S. 191, about 1½ miles north of town. ✆ **435/259-5201.** www.bucksgrillhouse.com. Main courses $9–$36. DISC, MC, V. Daily 5:30pm–closing.

Center Café CONTEMPORARY AMERICAN This excellent little restaurant—with white tablecloths, a stone fireplace, rich wood colors, and a bright, contemporary look—is the place to come for innovative seafood selections, plus a variety of seasonal beef, lamb, and vegetarian dishes. Dinner entrees, served from 5:30pm, include cedar-planked salmon with an applewood-smoked bacon-shallot crust; beef eaters will enjoy the grilled black Angus beef tenderloin with Pinot noir demi-glace. Another great choice is the grilled rack of lamb with mustard-currant sauce. The restaurant's small plates menu (available 4 –6pm) offers lighter fare, such as the pizza of the day, a cheese and fruit platter, or baby back ribs. Many ingredients are grown locally. There is also patio dining and full liquor service.

60 N. 100 West. ✆ **435/259-4295.** www.centercafemoab.com. Dinner reservations recommended. Small plates $3–$14; dinner main courses $18–$30. DISC, MC, V. Daily 4pm–closing. Closed mid-Dec to mid-Feb.

Eddie McStiff's AMERICAN This bustling, noisy brewpub is half family restaurant and half tavern, with a climate-controlled garden patio as well. The dining room has a Southwest decor, and the tavern looks just as a tavern should—long bar, low light, and lots of wood. The menu includes a good variety of charbroiled meats, excellent pizzas, and a selection of pasta dishes. Specialties include grilled Atlantic salmon and slow-smoked barbecued ribs. Prime rib is available after 4:30pm, and there are early bird dinner specials daily from 4:30 to 6:30pm. About a dozen fresh-brewed beers are on tap, and there is full liquor service.

In McStiff's Plaza, 57 S. Main St. (just south of the information center). ✆ **435/259-2337.** www.eddiemcstiffs.com. Main courses $7–$22. DISC, MC, V. Daily 11:30am–midnight.

Moab Brewery ECLECTIC An open, spacious microbrewery/restaurant on the south side of town, Moab Brewery serves fresh handcrafted ales brewed on-site, along with a wide variety of steaks, sandwiches, salads, soups, vegetarian dishes, and assorted house specialties. It's popular with families, who gobble down basic American fare such as half-pound burgers; fresh fish, including good tilapia

If You'd Like to Bend Your Elbow in Utah…

Since Utah is the home to many of the parks we cover in this book (Arches, Bryce Canyon, Canyonlands, Capitol Reef, Sequoia and Kings Canyon, and Zion national parks), you may want to keep the information below in mind if you're out socializing or staying in a gateway town. You can buy alcoholic beverages in Utah, but some fairly strict temperance laws can make the process a bit difficult. (Mormons, who make up a large portion of the population in the state, are supposed to abstain from tobacco, alcohol, or any beverage with caffeine). There were (until 2009) three kinds of liquor licenses for public houses: a tavern license, a restaurant license, and a private club license.

- **Tavern licenses** are granted to establishments that are for visitors 21 and over, and which serve only beer—and 3.2% beer at that. That's beer that has 3.2% alcohol by weight, and it's the only kind of beer that is sold at Utah establishments, unless you order an imported bottled beer. The 3.2% beer has less alcohol than most American beers: 3.2% alcohol by weight roughly translates to about 4% alcohol by volume, whereas the average American beer has 5% alcohol by volume. While you can buy 3.2% beer and malt liquor at convenience and grocery stores, anything containing more than 3.2% alcohol is sold only at state-run liquor stores.
- **Restaurant licenses** allow establishments to serve any type of alcoholic beverage, but there's one catch: To order a drink, you also have to order food. "Food" can be a snack or appetizer, or a full dinner, depending on the restaurant. Another thing to remember at a tavern: Bartenders are not allowed to free-pour. If you order a mixed drink or a shot, the bartender must use a state-approved and -mandated device that measures exactly one ounce of liquor, lest the establishment get slapped with some huge fines. Prior to the loosening of laws in 2009, a bartender had to walk around a glass partition (called by some "the Zion Curtain") separating the bartender from the patron to pour a drink.
- **Private club licenses** are now a thing of the past; prior to 2009, if you wanted to buy a drink in a bar or a lounge, you had to purchase a "membership." The 40-year-old system was finally abolished by government officials with their eye on increasing tourism, though it was accompanied by a tightening of DUI laws, and bars are required to scan the driver's license of patrons who appear to be younger than 35.

The state still strictly regulates the number of liquor licenses for bars and restaurants, linking the licenses available to the state's population.

tacos; and our top choice here, the St. Louis smoked pork ribs. The huge dining room is decorated with light woods, outdoor sports equipment—including a hang glider on the ceiling—and local artwork. Patio dining is available. You can sample the brews—from wheat ale to oatmeal stout—at the separate bar. Aside from the wares in the gift shop, you can also purchase beer-to-go in half-gallon jugs. Beer is sold in the bar; in the restaurant, diners can purchase beer, wine, or mixed drinks.

686 S. Main St. ✆ **435/259-6333.** www.themoabbrewery.com. Main courses $7–$20. AE, DISC, MC, V. Summer daily 11:30am–10pm; winter daily 11:30am–9pm.

Moab Diner & Ice Cream Shoppe AMERICAN/SOUTHWESTERN Late risers can get breakfast—among the best in town—all day here, featuring the usual egg dishes, biscuits and gravy, and a spicy breakfast burrito. Hamburgers, sandwiches, and salads are the offerings at lunch. For dinner, it's steak, shrimp, and chicken, plus liver and onions. The green chile is worth a try. In addition to ice cream, you can get malts and shakes, plus sundaes with seven different toppings. Decor is old-time diner, with comfy red vinyl booths, a bit of neon, photos of classic cars, and old Coca-Cola ads. No alcoholic beverages are served.

189 S. Main St. (2 blocks south of Center St.). ✆ **435/259-4006.** Main courses $5.50–$11 breakfast and lunch; $8–$15 dinner. MC, V. Daily 6am–10pm. Closed New Year's, Thanksgiving, and Christmas.

Sunset Grill AMERICAN Perched on a hill at the north edge of Moab, this fine restaurant offers the best sunset views in town. Once the home of miner Charles Steen, the Sunset Grill contains four tastefully decorated dining rooms and three patios. A favorite of locals celebrating special events, the restaurant serves excellent steaks, hand-cut in-house, plus such treats as roasted half duck with a raspberry sauce; and a grilled salmon filet with an

Asian glaze and served in a light soy-sherry cream sauce. Texas-style prime rib sells out often, so get here early if it's your first choice. The menu also includes a number of chicken dishes and several pasta selections. Utah microbrews, a good selection of wine, and full liquor service are available.

900 N. U.S. 191. ✆ **435/259-7146.** www.moab-utah.com/sunsetgrill. Main courses $14–$24. AE, DISC, MC, V. Mon–Sat 5pm–closing.

11 Picnic & Camping Supplies

The best grocery store in town is **City Market,** 425 S. Main St. (✆ **435/259-5181;** www.citymarket.com). You can pick up sandwiches from the deli, assemble your own salad at the salad bar, or choose fresh-baked items from the bakery. The store also sells fishing licenses, money orders, and stamps; offers photo finishing and Western Union services; and has a pharmacy.

For camping supplies and equipment for hiking, biking, and other outdoor activities, try **Moab Desert Adventures,** 415 N. Main St., Moab, UT 84532 (✆ **877/765-6622** or 435/260-2404; www.moabdesertadventures.com); **Red Canyon Outfitters,** 23 N. Main St. (✆ **435/259-3353**); or **Gearheads,** 471 S. Main St. (✆ **435/259-4327**), which also offers free filtered water (bring your own jugs).

12 Nearby Attractions

For a delightful escape from the desert heat, take a break at the **Scott M. Matheson Wetlands Preserve,** 934 W. Kane Creek Blvd. (✆ **435/259-4629;** www.nature.org/wherewework). Owned by the Nature Conservancy, this lush oasis attracts more than 200 species of birds and other wildlife, such as river otters, beavers, and muskrats. The preserve has a wheelchair-accessible 1-mile loop trail, boardwalks over the wet areas, and a two-story viewing blind. Guided bird walks are given (call for the current schedule), and bird and wildlife lists and self-guided tour brochures are available. In late spring and summer, visitors are advised to bring mosquito repellent.

The preserve is open daily year-round from dawn to dusk, and admission is free. From downtown Moab, go south on Main Street to Kane Creek Boulevard (btw. McDonald's and Burger King); go west about ¾ mile, passing the Moab Public Works Department, to a Y in the road. Take the left fork, and continue for about another ½ mile to the preserve entrance. From the parking area, a footpath and bridge lead over Mill Creek to an information kiosk and into the preserve.

Many visitors to Arches spend time at nearby **Canyonlands National Park.** See chapter 8.

Scouting Movie Locations Around Moab

Pick up a free "Moab Movie Locations" brochure in the **Moab Information Center,** Center and Main streets (or download it from the website, (**www.discovermoab.com/movie.htm**), and you can head to all your favorite movie locations in the area. See where scenes for *Indiana Jones and the Last Crusade* (1989) were shot in Arches National Park. At Canyonlands' Island in the Sky, Max von Sydow as Christ delivered the Sermon on the Mount in *The Greatest Story Ever Told* (1965); he stood facing the Green River at the Green River Overlook on a rock to the left of the fence. Just 2,000 years later in cinema time, the two heroines of *Thelma & Louise* (1991) drove off the cliff under Dead Horse Point 10 miles down the Shafer Trail (also called Potash Road), an unpaved road off Route 279, 19 miles south of Moab. Earlier in the film, at Arches' Courthouse Towers, they locked a pursuing police officer in his patrol car trunk, and several chase scenes were filmed in the La Sal Mountains outside the town of La Sal off Route 46.

For Western movie fans, in *Rio Grande* (1950), John Wayne rescued kidnapped cavalry children from a pueblo just off Utah Scenic Byway 128, a half-mile up a dirt road from Milepost 19, and located the hideout in *The Comancheros* (1961), 1 mile east of Milepost 21. In *Cheyenne Autumn* (1964), cavalryman Richard Widmark chased the Cheyenne across a fl at area south of the Arches' South Park Avenue. And Devils Garden in Arches served as the site where an Indian ambush trapped the U.S. Cavalry in the truly terrible *Taza, Son of Cochise* (1954), starring Rock Hudson and Barbara Rush. More recent movies that shot scenes in the area include *Geronimo, City Slickers II,* and *Mission Impossible II.*

3

Badlands National Park, SD

by Jack Olson

It's a strange and seemingly complicated place. From the ragged ridges and saw-toothed spires to the wind-ravaged desolation of Badlands Wilderness Area, Badlands National Park is an awe-inspiring sight and an unsettling experience. Few leave here unaffected by the vastness of this geologic anomaly, which spreads across 381 square miles of moonscape.

The Lakota Indians who once traversed this incredible land named it *mako sica,* or "land bad." Early French-Canadian trappers labeled it *les mauvaises terres à traverser,* or "bad lands to travel across."

Steep canyons, towering spires, and flat-topped tables all appear among Badlands buttes. Despite their apparent complexity, the unusual formations of the Badlands are essentially the result of two basic geologic processes: deposition and erosion.

The layered look of the Badlands comes from sedimentary rocks composed of fine grains that have been cemented into a solid form. Layers with similar characteristics are grouped into units called **formations.** The bottom formation is the **Pierre Shale,** deposited 68 to 77 million years ago during the Cretaceous period, when a shallow, inland sea stretched across the Great Plains. The mud of the sea floor hardened into shale, leaving fossil clamshells and ammonites that confirm a sea environment. The sea eventually drained away, and the upper layers of shale were weathered into soil, now seen as Yellow Mounds.

The **Chadron Formation,** deposited 32 to 37 million years ago during the Eocene epoch, sits above the Pierre Shale. By this time, a flood plain had replaced the sea, and each time the rivers flooded, they deposited a new layer of sediment on the plain. Alligator fossils indicate that a lush, subtropical forest covered the region. However, mammal fossils dominate. The Chadron is best known for large, elephant-size mammals called *titanotheres.*

Some of the sediment carried by rivers and wind was volcanic ash, the product of eruptions associated with the creation of the Rocky Mountains. This ash mixed with river and stream sediments to form clay stone, the main material from which Badlands buttes are constructed. After the Eocene epoch, the climate began to dry and cool, and tropical forests gave way to open savanna. Rivers deposited the **Brule** and **Sharps formations** during the Oligocene epoch from 26 to 32 million years ago, and today these formations contain the most rugged peaks and canyons of the Badlands.

Actually, the impressive serrated ridges and deep canyons of the Badlands did not exist until about 500,000 years ago, when water began to cut through the layers of rock, carving fantastic shapes into what had been a flat floodplain. Once again, the ancient fossil soils, buried for millions of years, became exposed. That erosion continues: Every time rain falls, or snow melts in spring, more sediment is washed from the buttes in this ongoing work of sculpting the earth. On average, the buttes erode an inch a year; scientists believe that the buttes will be gone in another 500,000 years.

In addition to its scenic wonders, the Badlands are one of the richest Oligocene fossil beds known to exist. Remains of three-toed horses, dog-size camels, saber-toothed cats, giant pigs, and other species have been found here; all date from 25 to 35 million years ago.

FLORA & FAUNA

Largely a mixed-grass prairie, the park contains 56 types of grasses, most of which are native species, including green needlegrass and buffalo grass. Wildflowers, including curlycup gumweed and pale purple coneflower, add color, with the best wildflower displays in June and July. You won't find many trees here.

Wildlife to watch for includes bison, Rocky Mountain bighorn sheep, pronghorns, and mule deer. Darting in and out of the grass are desert and eastern cottontail rabbits. Prairie dogs thrive here; a prairie dog town is just 5 miles down Sage Creek Rim Road. You might also see a prairie rattlesnake slithering through the grass, plus several nonpoisonous snake species.

AVOIDING THE CROWDS

The vastness of the park means that overcrowding is usually not a problem. Entrance stations, visitor centers, park concessions, and the Loop Road can become busy during the height of the summer season, especially in July and August, but most roads, trails, and services are not overtaxed at any time of the year.

As with most other national parks, those wishing to avoid crowds should visit during the shoulder seasons of April to May and September to October. If you must go in summer, visit early in the day, when the numbers of people are lowest and the sun hasn't begun to scorch the earth. Dawn and dusk are ideal times to photograph the unearthly beauty of the park and are the best times to see wildlife.

1 Essentials

GETTING THERE & GATEWAYS

Located in extreme southwestern South Dakota, Badlands National Park is easily accessible by car either on **S. Dak. 44** east of Rapid City, or off **I-90** at Wall or Cactus Flat. Westbound I-90 travelers take exit 131 south (Cactus Flat) onto S. Dak. 240, which leads to the park boundary and the **Ben Reifel Visitor Center** at Cedar Pass. This road becomes **Badlands Loop Road,** the park's primary scenic drive. After passing through the park, S. Dak. 240 rejoins I-90 at exit 110 at Wall. Eastbound travelers do the reverse, beginning in Wall and rejoining I-90 at exit 131.

THE NEAREST AIRPORT **Rapid City Regional Airport** (✆ **605/393-9924;** http://temp.rcgov.org/Airport/pages/index.html), 10 miles southeast of Rapid City on S. Dak. 44, provides direct access to the Badlands, Black Hills, and Mount Rushmore. **Frontier, Northwest, Delta/Skywest, United Express,** and **Allegiant** operate daily flights to Minneapolis, Salt Lake City, Chicago, Denver, Las Vegas, and Phoenix. Car-rental companies at the airport include **Alamo, Avis, Budget, Enterprise, Hertz,** and **National.** See chapter 38 for website listings of major airlines and car-rental companies.

INFORMATION

For Badlands National Park information, contact **Badlands National Park,** P.O. Box 6, Interior, SD 57750 (✆ **605/433-5361;** www.nps.gov/badl).

For information about the area, contact **South Dakota Tourism,** 711 E. Wells Ave., Pierre, SD 57501 (✆ **800/SDAKOTA** [732-5682] or 605/773-3301; fax 605/773-3256; www.travelsd.com), or the **Black Hills & Badlands Visitor Center,** north side of I-90 at exit 61, Rapid City, SD 57701 (✆ **605/355-3600;** www.blackhillsbadlands.com), open 8am to 5pm.

The National Park Service distributes a wide variety of brochures on topics including geology, prairie grasses, backpacking, biking, wildlife, plants, and use of horses in the park. You can pick up brochures at the park visitor centers and ranger stations or download them from the park's website.

The Badlands Visitor Guide, published by the nonprofit **Badlands Natural History Association,** P.O. Box 47, Interior, SD 57750 (✆ **605/433-5489;** www.nps.gov/archive/badl/exp/bnha.htm), provides up-to-date information on visitor center hours, park programs, camping, and hiking trails.

VISITOR CENTERS

Visitor centers are at Cedar Pass and White River. The **Ben Reifel Visitor Center** at Cedar Pass is open year-round and features exhibits on the park's natural and cultural history. The **White River Visitor Center,** on the Pine Ridge Indian Reservation, is open June through late August only. It includes exhibits about Oglala Sioux history.

Tips from the Chief of Interpretation

Badlands National Park's 244,000 acres of stark scenery deserve special attention on any visitor's itinerary, according to the park's chief of interpretation, Judy Olson. Just a short drive off I-90, the terrain changes dramatically.

"This park is larger than all of the other National Park Service units in the Midwest combined," Olson notes. "We have a great diversity of stories that converge here—the fossils, the prairie grasses and wildlife, Lakota history, pioneer history, and homesteading. It's all here waiting to be explored."

Olson suggests allowing no less than 2 days to fully experience the park. "Visitors to the Badlands should at least experience a night in the park. The air is so clear here that the stars shine."

She also advises visiting in the spring or fall. "The grasses are just greening in spring, the birds are migrating, and the prairie animals are giving birth to their young. In the fall, the canyons and the ravines are filled with beautiful golden colors, the birds are migrating . . . and you can enjoy an uncrowded hike, a bike ride, or just a solitary experience."

Badlands National Park

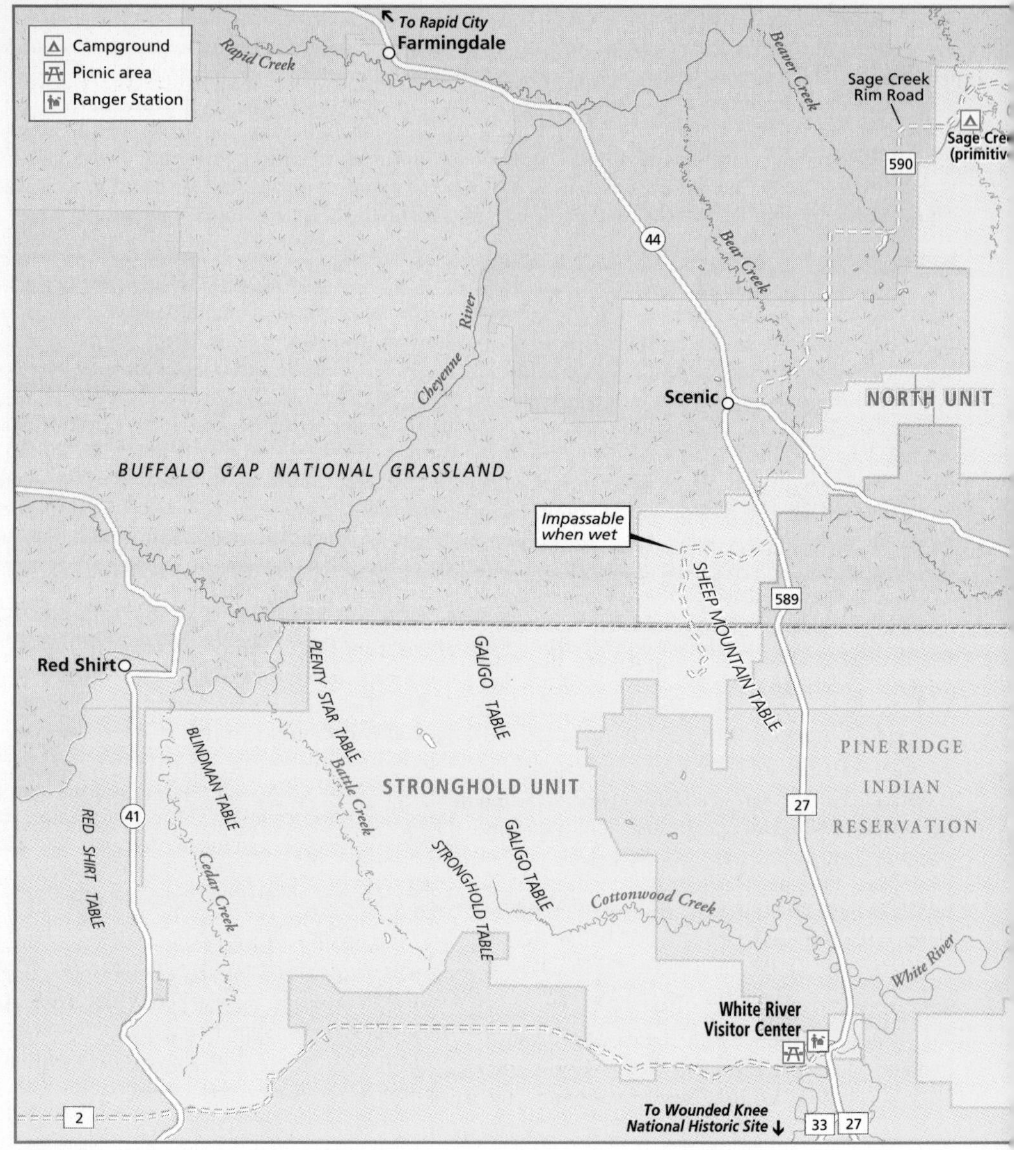

FEES

Park entry fees are $15 per passenger vehicle (up to 7 days), motorcycles $10, and each person on foot or bike pays $7. Members of the Oglala Sioux tribe pay half price. Camping costs $10 per site per night at the Cedar Pass Campground. Camping at Sage Creek Primitive Campground is free.

SPECIAL REGULATIONS & WARNINGS

Water in the Badlands is too full of silt for humans to drink and will quickly clog a water filter. When hiking or traveling in the park, always carry an adequate supply of water. Drinking water is available only at the Cedar Pass area, the White River Visitor Center, and the Pinnacles Ranger Station. No campfires are allowed. Climbing Badlands buttes and rock formations is allowed, but it can be extremely dangerous due to loose, crumbly rock. Unpaved roads in the park can be dangerous in winter and during thunderstorms, when surfaces may become extremely slippery.

SEASONS & CLIMATE

Badlands weather is often unpredictable. Heavy rain, hail, and high, often damaging winds are possible, particularly during spring and summer. Lightning strikes are common. Summer temperatures often exceed 100°F (38°C), so sunscreen, a broad-brimmed

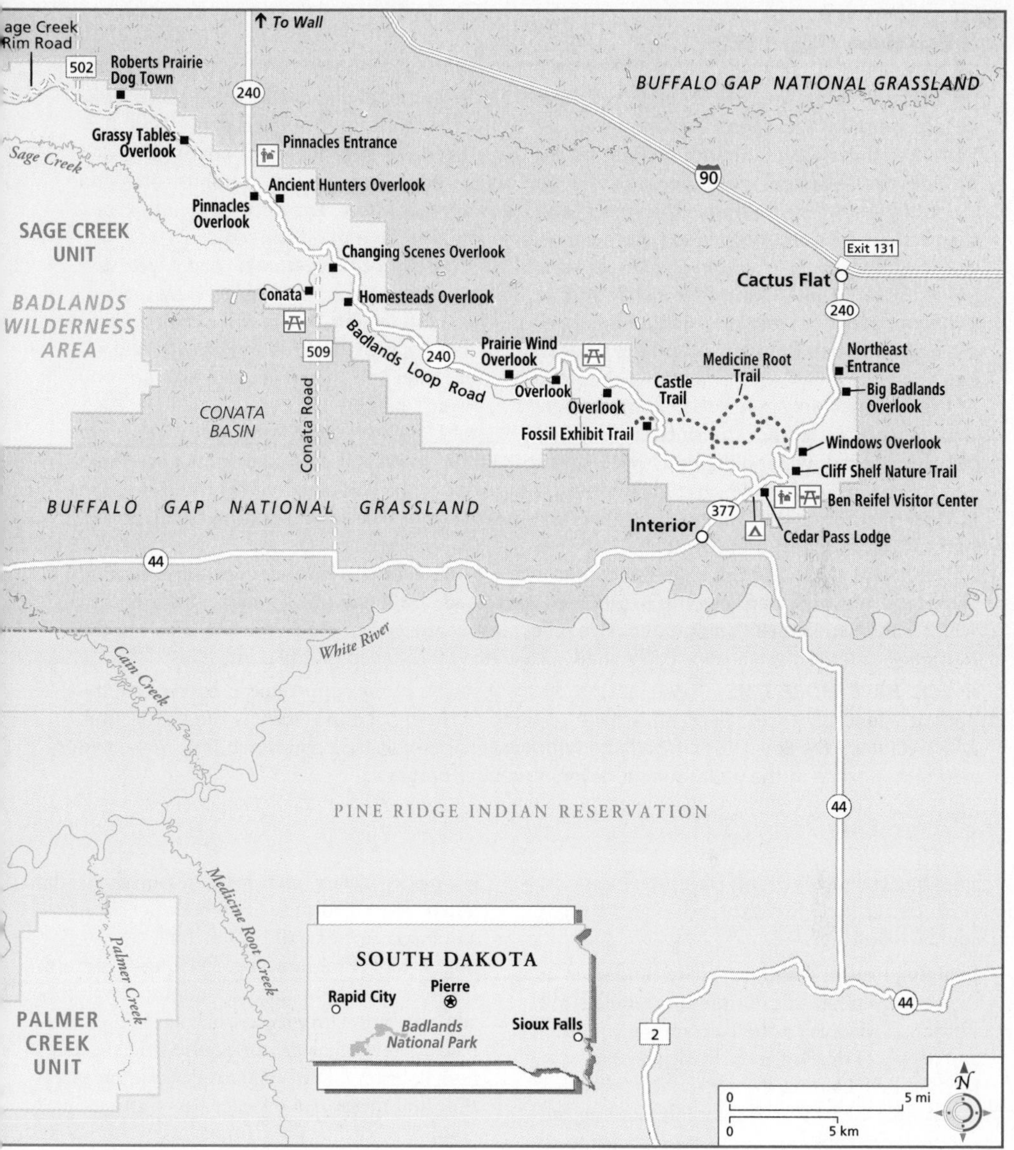

hat, and plenty of drinking water are essential to avoid severe sunburn, dehydration, and heat stroke. Winter travelers should be aware of approaching storms and be prepared for sleet, ice, heavy snow, and blizzard conditions.

2 Organized Tours & Ranger Programs

In addition to these suggestions, look at "Other Sports & Activities," below.

MOTOR COACH TOURS

Gray Line of the Black Hills, P.O. Box 1106, Rapid City, SD 57709 (✆ **800/456-4461** or 605/342-4461; www.blackhillsgrayline.com) does not schedule tours to Badlands National Park, but tours can be arranged by contacting Gray Line at the above number.

RANGER PROGRAMS

A limited schedule of **naturalist-led walks** and programs generally begins in mid-June, and offerings become more frequent as visitation increases. Check the activities board at the Ben Reifel Visitor Center

If You Have Only 1 Day

It's relatively easy to explore the highlights of the North Unit of Badlands National Park in a day or less. (Most visitors spend an average of 3–5 hr.) A few miles south of the park's northeast entrance, the closest entrance to I-90, is the **park headquarters.** It's open year-round and includes the Ben Reifel Visitor Center, Cedar Pass Lodge, and a campground, amphitheater, and dump station. After you stop at the visitor center exhibits, bookstore, and information desk, and then watch an orientation video (which we recommend), it's time to hit the trail.

The visitor center is within 5 miles of several trail heads, scenic overlooks, and three self-guided nature trails. Each of the seven trails in the area offers an opportunity to view some of the formations for which the Badlands is famous. The **Fossil Exhibit Trail** is wheelchair accessible. The **Cliff Shelf Nature Trail** and the **Door Trail** are moderately strenuous and provide impressive glimpses of Badlands formations. But none is longer than 1 mile, and you can hike any one of them comfortably in less than an hour. (See "Day Hikes," below.)

Leading directly from the visitor center is the 30-mile **Badlands Loop Road,** the park's most popular scenic drive. Angling northwest toward the town of Wall, it passes numerous overlooks and trail heads, each of which commands inspiring views of the Badlands and the prairies of the Buffalo Gap National Grassland. Binoculars will increase your chances of spotting bison, pronghorns, bighorn sheep, and coyote.

The paved portion of the Loop Road ends at the turnoff for the Pinnacles Entrance. Beyond this point, the road becomes the **Sage Creek Rim Road,** a 30-mile gravel road, at the end of which is the **Sage Creek Campground.** Five miles west of the end of the pavement, a visit to the **Roberts Prairie Dog Town** gives you a chance to watch black-tailed prairie dogs.

IF YOU HAVE MORE TIME Those staying overnight have more opportunities to explore the park at a leisurely pace, taking advantage of some of the other trails, such as the **Castle Trail,** which connects the Fossil Exhibit Trail and Window Fossil Exhibit Trail, and **Notch Trail.** You could also take in some of the park's summer evening ranger programs.

or campground bulletin boards for times, locations, and other details. Activities vary each year but often include the following:

- **Evolving Prairie Walk.** Generally conducted in the early evening, this 60-minute, 1-mile stroll introduces visitors to the paleontology, prairie, and people of the Badlands. Participants meet at the Ben Reifel Visitor Center.
- **Fossil Talk.** Generally slated for midmorning and late afternoon, this program allows participants to join a naturalist for a 20-minute discussion of the geological history and fossil resources of the White River Badlands. It's wheelchair accessible and meets at the Fossil Exhibit Trail.
- **Night Sky Program, or Evening Program.** Beginning at 9pm, these 45-minute amphitheater programs cover topics such as the night sky, paleontology, geology, the prairie, and the area's human history. The program is wheelchair accessible and meets at the Cedar Pass Campground amphitheater. The program begins when the sky is dark.

3 Day Hikes

Numerous hiking trails provide a closer look at the Badlands for those adventurous enough to leave the confines of their vehicles. All developed trails start from parking areas within 5 miles of the Ben Reifel Visitor Center at Cedar Pass.

Castle Trail Winding some 10 miles through the mixed-grass prairie and badlands, this is the longest developed trail in the park and runs parallel to some interesting formations. The fairly level trail connects the Fossil Exhibit Trail and the Door and Window parking area. Just walking this trail a short distance from the parking area brings the hiker close to outstanding formations. To make this a loop, follow the signs and turn off onto the well-marked Medicine Root Trail. The trail is not heavily used, making it an ideal spot to escape the crowds, but it can be treacherous during and just after a heavy rain. 10 miles RT. Moderate. Access: Trail heads at Fossil Exhibit Trail and at Door Trail parking area.

Cliff Shelf Nature Trail This popular trail takes you through a "slump" area where a good supply of water supports an oasis of green, which stands out in contrast to the stark badlands formations. You can pick up a brochure describing a self-guided excursion at the Visitor Center desk. The trail includes some steep sections and boardwalk stairs. Its parking lot cannot accommodate RVs towing other vehicles. .5 mile RT. Moderate. Access: .5 mile north of Ben Reifel Visitor Center.

Door Trail This trail winds through some of the "baddest" of the Badlands. The first 100 yards to a beautiful view at "The Door" are mostly downhill and accessible, with assistance, to those in wheelchairs. The more rugged section takes off to the right of the viewing area; striped posts mark the way, indicating the safest route. .6 mile RT. Moderate. Access: 2 miles northeast of Ben Reifel Visitor Center.

Fossil Exhibit Trail This easy boardwalk loop will give you an idea of what animal life was like 30 million years ago. Wheelchair accessible. .25 mile RT. Easy. Access: 5 miles northwest of Ben Reifel Visitor Center.

Notch Trail This trail takes you up a wash between the buttes, up a 45-degree angle wood-and-rope ladder, a climb that may rattle those afraid of heights. Follow the wash to the "Notch"; you'll find a striking view over the Cliff Shelf area and the White River Valley. 1.5 miles RT. Moderate. Access: North end of Door Trail parking area.

Saddle Pass Trail In less than .25 mile, this trail rises steeply 200 feet from the bottom of the Badlands Wall to the top, connecting with the Castle and Medicine Root trails. It's impassable after rains, so ask about trail conditions at the visitor center before you set out. .5 mile RT. Moderate to strenuous. Access: Branches off Castle Trail just west of intersection with Medicine Root Trail and leads to Badlands Loop Rd.

Window Trail A 100-yard boardwalk trail leads to a spectacular view through a "window," or opening, in the Badlands Wall. Wheelchair accessible. .25 mile RT. Easy to moderate. Access: Trail head at center of Door Trail parking area.

4 Exploring the Backcountry

The park encompasses the largest prairie wilderness in the United States, where expansive grasslands make cross-country travel unique. Vast ranges of classic badlands provide rugged, challenging terrain for even skilled hikers. Wildlife is close and abundant. Best of all, it's never crowded; hikers often have hundreds of acres to themselves.

The Badlands has no formal system of backcountry permits or reservations. Let friends and relatives know when you depart and when you expect to return. Rangers at the Ben Reifel Visitor Center can assist in planning a safe, enjoyable excursion by offering directions, safety tips, maps, and information sheets.

When planning your backcountry hike, examine past, present, and forecasted weather carefully. With even a small amount of precipitation, some trails can become slick and impassable. Carry water if you think you could be out for as little as a half-hour. Cross-country hikers are encouraged to carry a map, compass, and water, and to wear or carry appropriate clothing. No campfires are allowed. All overnight backcountry hikers should discuss their route with a park ranger before departure.

Spring and fall may be the best times to experience the Badlands backcountry. Days are often pleasant, and nights are cool. In summer, temperatures often exceed 100°F (38°C) and pose health hazards. Avoid heat sickness by drinking plenty of water and avoiding the midday sun. Only the hardiest hikers attempt winter backpacking trips. Severe winter temperatures coupled with strong winds and blizzards make backcountry survival difficult for the unprepared. Winter hikers should speak with a ranger at the Ben Reifel Visitor Center before setting out.

5 Other Sports & Activities

AERIAL TOURS If you want to see the Badlands from above, you have two options: helicopter and hot-air balloon. **Badger Helicopters** (✆ **605/433-5322**) takes off near the park's east entrance (take I-90, exit 131) between mid-May and mid-September. Call for current rates.

Those looking for a hot-air-balloon adventure can contact **Black Hills Balloons,** P.O. Box 210, Custer, SD 57730 (✆ **605/673-2520;** www.blackhillsballoons.com), which offers flights over the Badlands and Black Hills year-round.

BIKING Off-road biking is not allowed in the park, but the Loop Road is accessible to bikes. There are bike racks at the Ben Reifel Visitor Center. The 22-mile route from Pinnacles Overlook to the Ben Reifel Visitor Center is mostly downhill (though there are several steep passes to climb). Many bikers ride along Sage Creek Rim Road, past the prairie dog town, to spectacular views of the Badlands wilderness. During summer, though, car traffic is heavy and the temperatures hot. There are no bike rentals available in the park.

HORSEBACK RIDING Several companies offer guided trail rides through the backcountry of the Badlands (and the Black Hills). They include family-run **Dakota Badland Outfitters** (✆ **605/574-3412;** www.ridesouthdakota.com). Call for rates, activities, and reservations.

6 Camping

A chart summarizing facilities at campgrounds in the Badlands and Black Hills area is in chapter 6.

INSIDE THE PARK

Camping is available inside Badlands National Park at the Cedar Pass Campground and the Sage Creek Primitive Campground, on a first-come, first-served basis. Both are suitable for tents and small RVs, and offer scenic views but little shade. Campfires are not permitted. **Cedar Pass Campground,** with 96 sites, is just off the Loop Road and has an amphitheater and the Night Sky Interpretive Area. **Sage Creek Primitive Campground** is at the end of Sage Creek Rim Road, a gravel road that begins at the point where the park's Loop Road turns toward the Pinnacles Entrance. Impassable roads may limit access in winter. Up to 15 camping "units" can be accommodated.

Backcountry camping is also permitted (see "Exploring the Backcountry," above).

NEAR THE PARK

Badlands Ranch and Resort is much more than a campground. Here, in addition to the amenities noted in the campground chart in chapter 6, you'll find a barbecue area with gas grills, pool, whirlpool, playground, good fishing, rock hunting, and trail rides. For details, see "Where to Stay," below.

7 Where to Stay

INSIDE THE PARK

Cedar Pass Lodge Cabins The Cedar Pass Lodge, adjacent to the Ben Reifel Visitor Center, offers rustic but comfortable cabins in a great location. This is the spot to be to see the Badlands at dawn and dusk—an incredible experience.

Badlands National Park, P.O. Box 5, Interior, SD 57750. ✆ **605/433-5460.** Fax 605/433-5560. www.cedarpasslodge.com. 22 cabins. A/C, TEL. $85 double. AE, DISC, MC, V. May close mid-Oct to late Apr; check with lodge.

NEAR THE PARK

The closest lodging outside the park is in the tiny community of Interior. Wall, north of the park, and Rapid City, 55 miles west on I-90, offer hundreds of hotel and motel rooms, as well as quaint bed-and-breakfasts. Reliable chains in Wall include **Best Western Plains Motel,** 712 Glenn St., Wall, SD 57790 (✆ **800/637-5958** or 605/279-2145), which charges $71 to $172 double; **Days Inn,** 212 10th Ave., Wall, SD 57790 (✆ **800/329-7466** or 605/279-2000), $65 to $110 double; and **Super 8 Motel,** 711 Glenn St., Wall, SD 57790 (✆ **800/800-8000** or 605/279-2688), $60 to $95 double. A list of their websites is in chapter 38.

Chapter 6 lists accommodations in Rapid City and the Mount Rushmore area.

Rates vary by season, with the highest rates in summer. Some properties close for the winter.

IN INTERIOR

Badlands Ranch and Resort This friendly, year-round resort, which opened in 1997, is on 1,000 picturesque acres with views of the Badlands and plenty of wildlife to see. In addition to several accommodations options, there is a campground (see "Camping," above). The resort offers a pool and a hot tub, nightly bonfires and cookouts with entertainment, two fishing lakes, and horseback trails (moonlight trail rides can be arranged). If you wish, the owners can help arrange guided tours of

The Famous Wall Drug Store

You'll see the signs offering "free ice water" at the **Wall Drug Store,** 510 Main St., Wall, about 8 miles north of Badlands National Park on S. Dak. 240 and I-90. And you'll see them almost everywhere you go throughout the Black Hills region, all telling you how many miles it is to the small town of Wall and its eponymous drugstore. In fact, there are now more than 3,000 of these signs, all over the world. The advertising gimmick saved a small-town drugstore in an isolated community from bankruptcy during the Great Depression. Dorothy and Ted Hustead's marketing also turned their little establishment into a block-long Old West emporium that draws crowds from all over the United States and the world. You can buy pancakes or doughnuts (some of the best in the state, in fact), American Indian crafts, books, jewelry, and Western apparel, and watch the animated "cowboy band" perform every 15 minutes. Do you want a "genuine" jackalope? Yes, they've got those, too. Oh, and the ice water is still free. There's free entry to this 76,000-square-foot icon. Want to know more? Go to **www.walldrug.com**. Open 6:30am to 10pm.

the area's attractions and the adjoining American Indian reservation. Cabins and motel units are comfortable and well maintained. Rooms in the lodge are plusher—we suggest the top-floor honeymoon suite, which has a sunroom, a whirlpool, and great views of the Badlands.

S. Dak. 44 (HCR 53, P.O. Box 3), Interior, SD 57750. ✆ **877/433-5599** or 605/433-5599. Fax 605/433-5598. www.badlandsranchandresort.com. 8 cabins, 4 motel units, 35 RV hookups; large lodge space for up to 30. A/C TV. $83–$116 cabin; $61–$72 motel room; $25 RV hookup; $13–$15 tenting; $750 entire lodge. Winter rates negotiable. Lodge room rates include breakfast. AE, DISC, MC, V. From the park, head west on S. Dak. 44 approx. 6 miles toward Interior; when you pass the KOA Campground, look for the marked turnoff that leads to the resort.

8 Where to Dine

INSIDE THE PARK

Cedar Pass Lodge Restaurant Located near the Ben Reifel Visitor Center in the park's North Unit, the lodge's restaurant (the only dining choice inside the park) has a full menu ranging from buffalo burgers to steaks and trout, as well as ice-cold soft drinks, beer, and wine.

Cedar Pass Lodge. ✆ **605/433-5460.** www.cedarpasslodge.com. Main courses $13–$19. AE, DISC, MC, V. 3 meals daily; call for hours. May close mid-Sept to mid-May; check with lodge.

NEAR THE PARK

The towns around Badlands National Park, Interior, and Wall (see the sidebar "The Famous Wall Drug Store," above) offer several dining choices. Establishments in Rapid City and the communities surrounding Mount Rushmore are listed in chapter 6.

9 Picnic & Camping Supplies

Badlands National Park has two designated picnic areas, though you're likely to see people munching at nearly every overlook and trail head in the park. **Conata Picnic Area** is on Conata Road, just south of Dillon Pass and the Badlands Loop Road in the North Unit. It has tables, trash cans, and pit toilets. Camping and fires are not allowed, and there is no drinking water available. **Big Foot Picnic Area** is near Big Foot Pass on the Badlands Loop Road in the North Unit, about 7 miles northwest of the Ben Reifel Visitor Center. It also has tables and pit toilets, but no drinking water. Camping and fires are not allowed.

4

Big Bend National Park, TX

by Eric Peterson

Vast and wild, Big Bend National Park is a land of extremes, diversity, and a few contradictions. Its rugged terrain harbors thousands of species of plants and animals, some seen almost nowhere else on Earth. A visit to the park can be a hike into the sun-baked desert, a float down a majestic canyon-land river, or a trek in mountains where black bears and mountain lions rule.

Geologists tell us that an inland sea once covered this area. As it dried up, sediment of sand and mud turned to rock. Tectonic plates collided and mountains were created; later on, volcanic eruptions created further upheaval. It took millions of years of geologic activity and erosion to form the delightful canyons and rock formations we marvel at today. These rock formations, with their wonderful hues of red, orange, yellow, white, and brown, have created a unique and awe-inspiring world of immense and rugged beauty. This is not a fantasyland of delicate shapes and intricate carvings, such as Bryce Canyon in Utah, but a powerful and dominating landscape. Although the greatest natural sculptures are in the park's three major river canyons—the Santa Elena, Marsical, and Boquillas—throughout Big Bend you'll find spectacular and majestic examples of what nature can do with this mighty yet malleable building material we call rock.

Visitors to Big Bend National Park encounter not only a geologic wonder, but also a wild, rugged wilderness populated by myriad desert and mountain plants and animals, ranging from box turtles and black-tailed jackrabbits, to the piglike javelinas, to powerful black bears and mountain lions. The park is considered a birders' paradise, with more species than at any other national park. It's also a wonderful spot to see wildflowers and the colorful display of cactus blooms.

For hikers, the park offers a tremendous variety of options, from easy walks to rugged backcountry routes that barely qualify as trails. There are also opportunities to let the Rio Grande do the work, carrying watersports enthusiasts on rafts, canoes, and kayaks through canyons carved into 1,500 feet of solid rock. Adventurers with 4WDs enjoy exploring the backcountry roads, and history buffs enjoy a number of historical attractions and cultural experiences.

AVOIDING THE CROWDS

Average annual visitation is just over 350,000. Although the park is relatively uncrowded much of the year, lodging and campgrounds fill during several periods: college spring break (usually in Mar and early Apr), Easter weekend, Thanksgiving weekend, and the last week of December. Park visitation is generally highest in March and April, and lowest in August and September.

Although the park's visitor centers, campgrounds, and other developed facilities may be overburdened during busier times, visitors can still get some breathing room by seeking out lesser-used hiking trails. Discuss your hiking skills and expectations with rangers, who can offer advice on the best areas to get away from the crowds.

1 Essentials

GETTING THERE & GATEWAYS

Big Bend National Park is not really close to anything except the Rio Grande and Mexico. There is no public transportation to or through the park. The gateway towns of Marathon and Terlingua/Study Butte are quite small and remote.

Park headquarters is 108 miles southeast of the town of Alpine on **Tex. 118** and 69 miles south of Marathon on **U.S. 385.** There is train and bus service to Alpine, where you'll also find car rentals and the nearest hospital to the park. For information, contact the **Alpine Chamber of Commerce,** 106 N. 3rd St., Alpine, TX 79830 (✆ **800/561-3712** or 432/837-2326; www.alpinetexas.com).

From El Paso, 323 miles northwest of the park, take **I-10** east 121 miles to exit 140, follow U.S. 90 southeast 99 miles to Alpine, then turn south on Tex. 118 for 108 miles to park headquarters.

Big Bend National Park

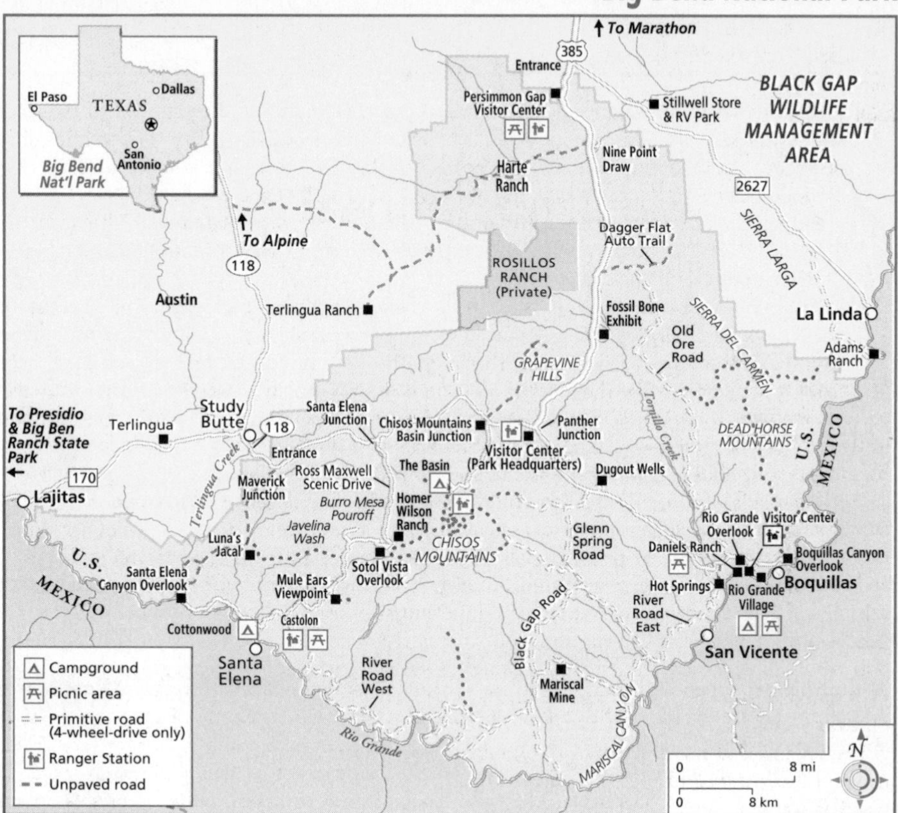

THE NEAREST AIRPORT The nearest commercial airport is **Midland International** (✆ **432/560-2200;** www.flymaf.com), 225 miles north and served by **American Eagle, Continental Express,** and **Southwest.** From the airport, located between Midland and Odessa, take I-20 west about 50 miles to exit 80 for Tex. 18, which you follow south about 50 miles to Fort Stockton. From there, take U.S. 385 south 125 miles through Marathon to park headquarters. Website listings for airlines and car-rental agencies are in chapter 38.

PARK INFORMATION

For information, contact **Big Bend National Park,** P.O. Box 129, Big Bend National Park, TX 79834 (✆ **432/477-2251;** www.nps.gov/bibe).

The free park newspaper, *The Big Bend Paisano,* published seasonally by the National Park Service, is a great source of information on seminars, new and special publications, suggested hikes, kids' activities, and local facilities.

Books, maps, and videos are available from **Big Bend Natural History Association,** P.O. Box 196, Big Bend National Park, TX 79834 (✆ **432/477-2236;** www.bigbendbookstore.org). *Big Bend: The Official National Park Handbook* (National Park Service, 2007) is a good introduction to the what and why of the park, describing in detail the terrain, flora, fauna, and human history of the area. Several Park Service booklets detail improved and unimproved roads and hiking trails. A particularly good hiking guide is *Hiking Big Bend National Park,* 2nd edition (Falcon Press, 2005), by Laurence Parent. Those planning backpacking trips will also want to get the appropriate topographical maps, which, along with the publications discussed above, are available at the park's visitor centers or by mail from the Big Bend Natural History Association.

For information on nearby attractions, as well as places to stay and eat, contact the **Big Bend Area Travel Association** (www.visitbigbend.com).

VISITOR CENTERS

The park has five visitor centers. **Panther Junction Visitor Center** (open daily year-round) is centrally located at park headquarters; **Persimmon Gap Visitor Center** (open year-round) is at the north entrance to the park on U.S. 385; **Rio Grande Village Visitor Center** (open Nov–Apr) is on the river in the eastern part of the park; **Castolon Visitor Contact Station** (open Nov–Apr) is near the river in the southwest end of the park; and **Chisos Basin**

Tips from a Park Ranger

"This park has something for everyone," says David Elkowitz, Big Bend's chief of interpretation and visitor services. High among the park's assets, he says, is its variety of activities, including both easy day hikes and extended backpacking trips, bird-watching, wildlife viewing, river running, and camping.

Big Bend is not a good choice for a quick visit, and Elkowitz recommends that people spend at least 3 days. "Be prepared for long distances, and don't expect all the amenities you might find in other places," he says.

Although Big Bend is one of America's less visited national parks, Elkowitz says that it does get busy occasionally, particularly during spring break, usually March and early April, when college students arrive en masse to hit the trails. The hottest months are May and June, according to Elkowitz, adding that the heat of July and August is usually tempered by afternoon thunderstorms. September is among the slowest times in the park, and it can be very nice, although still hot. "October is a great time, still quiet and a bit cooler," he says.

Elkowitz advises summer visitors to avoid hiking in the desert, but it's a "good time to visit the higher and cooler Chisos Mountains, which offer camping and miles of good trails." Here it can be 20° cooler than on the river. He also recommends hiking into the high country from October through December to see the beautiful fall colors. On the other hand, the desert is a "wonderful choice for fall and winter hiking into remote areas, with few, if any, other visitors."

Visitor Center (open year-round) is in the Chisos Mountains in the middle of the park, at 5,401 feet in elevation.

All visitor centers provide information, backcountry permits, books, and maps. They also have exhibits; a particularly impressive display on mountain lions is at Chisos Basin. Bulletin boards with schedules of ranger programs, notices of animal sightings, and other visitor information are at each of the visitor centers.

FEES & PERMITS

Entry into the park for up to a week costs $20 per passenger vehicle and $10 per person on foot or bicycle. Camping costs $14 per night in the three developed campgrounds. The concession-operated RV campground at Rio Grande Village has full hookups, costing $27. A $10 camping permit, available at any visitor center, is required for all backcountry camping; $10 permits are also required for all river-float trips (see "Camping" and "River Running," later in this chapter).

SPECIAL REGULATIONS & WARNINGS

Watch for wildlife along the roads, particularly javelinas, reptiles, deer, and rabbits. Be especially alert at night, when they may be blinded by your vehicle's headlights and freeze in the middle of the road. Feeding wildlife is prohibited, not only to minimize the risk of injuries to park visitors, but also because it's bad for the animals.

The **Basin Road Scenic Drive** into the Chisos Mountains has sharp curves and steep grades, and is not recommended for trailers longer than 20 feet or RVs longer than 24 feet. The **Ross Maxwell Scenic Drive** to Castolon is okay for most RVs and trailers but can present a problem for vehicles with insufficient power to handle the steep grade. These roads require extra caution by all users—drivers of motor vehicles, pedestrians, and bicyclists. Horses are not permitted on any paved roads in the park.

Desert heat can be dangerous. Hikers should carry at least 1 gallon of water per person per day; wear a hat, long pants, and long sleeves; and use a good sunscreen. Don't depend on springs as water sources, and avoid hiking in the middle of the day in summer. Early mornings and evenings are best for both comfort and sightseeing. Talk to rangers about your plans before heading out; they can help you plan a hike according to your ability and time frame. Check with rangers about weather forecasts—sudden summer thunderstorms are common and can cause flash flooding in dry washes and canyons.

Swimming is not recommended in the Rio Grande, even though it may look tantalizing on a summer day. Waste materials and waterborne microorganisms have been found in the river and can cause serious illness. Strong undercurrents, deep holes, and sharp rocks in shallow water are common. Should you decide to swim in spite of these conditions, be sure to wear a life jacket.

Wood or ground fires are prohibited, and caution is advised when using camp stoves, charcoal grills, and cigarettes. Smoking is prohibited on all trails in Chisos Basin. Check at the visitor centers for current drought conditions and for any special restrictions that may be in effect when you visit.

If You Have Only 1 Day (Consider Staying a Couple More . . .)

Big Bend National Park is huge, and you can't hope to see all of it in 1 day or even 2. It's best to allow at least 3 days, essentially devoting 1 day each to the desert, river, and mountains. If you have a limited amount of time in the park, however, the best choice is to start with the **Chisos Basin** and see the mountains in the middle of the park. Take the short, easy **Window View Trail,** a self-guided nature trail (see "Day Hikes," below) that highlights the flora and fauna of the Chisos Mountains. Then head back down and drive the **Ross Maxwell Scenic Drive** (see "Exploring the Park by Car," below) through the Chihuahuan Desert to the Rio Grande. If time allows, hike into **Santa Elena Canyon** (see "Day Hikes," below), one of the most beautiful canyons in the park. Finally, take in a ranger program at one of the park amphitheaters.

Crossing the Rio Grande for a visit to Mexico was once a staple of a visit to Big Bend, but the Department of Homeland Security now frowns on the practice. **DHS can slap violators with a $5,000 fine and a year of imprisonment.**

SEASONS & CLIMATE

Weather here is generally mild to hot, although because of the vast range of elevations—from about 1,800 feet at the eastern end of Boquillas Canyon to 7,825 feet on Emory Peak in the Chisos Mountains—conditions can vary greatly throughout the park at any given time. Essentially, the higher you go, the cooler you can expect it to be. Higher elevations are also wetter, although no section of the park gets a lot of precipitation.

Summers here are hot, often well over 100°F (38°C) in the desert in May and June, and afternoon thunderstorms are common from July through September. Winters are usually mild, although temperatures occasionally drop below freezing, and light snow is possible, especially in the Chisos Mountains. Fall and spring are usually warm and pleasant.

2 Exploring the Park by Car

The park has several paved roads—one goes through the park, and others take you to different sections. In addition, there are several roads that require high-clearance or four-wheel-drive vehicles (see "Backcountry Driving," below).

The park has two scenic drives, both with sharp curves and steep inclines, and not recommended for certain RVs and trailers (see "Special Regulations & Warnings," above).

The 7-mile **Chisos Basin Drive** climbs up Green Gulch to Panther Pass before dropping down into the basin. Near the pass are some sharp curves, and parts of the road are at a 10% grade. The views are wonderful any time of the year, particularly when the wildflowers dot the meadows, hills, and roadsides. The best month for wildflowers is usually October, after the summer rains.

When you've breathed your fill of clear mountain air, head back down and turn west toward the **Ross Maxwell Scenic Drive** through the Chihuahuan Desert and finally to the Rio Grande. This drive winds through the desert on the west side of the Chisos Mountains, providing a different perspective. Afterward, it passes through Castolon and then continues along and above the river to **Santa Elena Canyon.** Here you should park and hike the trail, which climbs above the river, offering great views into the steep, narrow canyon (see "Day Hikes," below).

Another worthwhile drive, recommended for all vehicles, begins at **Panther Junction Visitor Center** and goes to Rio Grande Village, a distance of 20 miles. From the visitor center, head southeast through the desert toward the high mountains that form the skyline in the distance. The first half of the drive passes through desert grasses, which are finally making a comeback after severe overgrazing in the decades before the establishment of the park in 1944. Recovery is slow in this harsh climate, but the land is beginning to revegetate.

As you progress farther into the desert, the elevation gradually decreases, and the grasses give way to lechuguilla and ocotillo stalks, cacti, and other arid-climate survivors. To the south is long, rather flat **Chilicotal Mountain,** named for the chilicote, or mescal-bean bushes, growing near its base. The chilicote's poisonous red bean is used in Mexico to kill rats. Several miles farther, the River Road turns off and heads southwest toward Castolon, more than 50 miles away. This primitive road is for high-clearance vehicles only.

If you feel adventurous, take the **Hot Springs** turnoff about a mile beyond the Tornillo Creek Bridge. It follows a rough wash to a point overlooking the confluence of Tornillo Creek and the Rio Grande. A trail along the riverbank leads to several springs. The foundation of a bathhouse is a remnant

Keeping the Wild in Wildlife, or How to Avoid an Unpleasant Encounter

The signs and warnings are everywhere: THIS IS BEAR AND MOUNTAIN LION COUNTRY, and although one of the thrills of visiting Big Bend National Park is the opportunity to see wildlife, for the safety of both humans and animals, always keep your distance. Rangers say that, since the 1950s, there have been more than 1,000 sightings of mountain lions in the park and numerous sightings of black bears. Although the vast majority of encounters have been uneventful—albeit definitely something to tell your friends about—four people have been attacked by mountain lions in the park. Fortunately, all recovered from their injuries; unfortunately, it was considered necessary to kill the mountain lions.

Hikers, especially in the Chisos Mountains, should be especially careful to minimize the danger of an encounter. First, discuss your hiking plans with park rangers to see if there have been any recent mountain lion sightings where you plan to hike. Don't hike alone, especially at dawn or dusk. Watch children carefully—never let them run ahead. If you do end up face-to-face with a mountain lion, rangers offer these tips: Don't run, but stand your ground, shout, wave your arms, and try to appear as large as possible. If you have children with you, pick them up. If the mountain lion acts aggressively, throw stones, and try to convince it that you are *not* prey, but actually dangerous. Then report the incident to a ranger as soon as possible.

The other animal you may see is one of the estimated 10 to 20 black bears that live in the Chisos Mountains. Bears are attracted to food, and the best way to avoid an unwanted encounter is to keep a clean camp. Park rangers recommend that you store all foodstuffs, cooking utensils, and toiletries in a hard-sided vehicle. Food storage lockers are available for hikers and campers in the Chisos Mountains. Always dispose of garbage properly in the receptacles provided. If you see a bear, keep a safe distance; do not approach or follow it, and, *never* attempt to feed a bear. If a bear approaches you, scare it away by shouting, waving your arms, or throwing rocks or sticks. Watch for cubs—you never want to be between a mother bear and her cubs. Report any bear sightings to a ranger.

Bears and mountain lions aren't the only wild animals in the park. Many visitors see javelinas (officially known as collared peccaries), which look a bit like their rather distant relatives, pigs, and are very nearsighted. A group of 10 to 20 is often seen in and near Rio Grande Village Campground. Some of them have learned to recognize the crinkling sound of potato chip bags and will run toward the sound in hopes of a snack. Although javelinas are not aggressive, they are easily frightened and could inflict some damage with the javelin-sharp tusks from which they get their name. Please help protect these wild animals: Never actively feed them, and always practice proper food storage.

Also deserving of mention are the park's poisonous snakes, scorpions, spiders, and centipedes, which are most active during the warmer months. Rangers advise that you watch carefully where you put your feet and hands, and use flashlights at night. Hikers may want to consider wearing high boots or protective leggings. It's also a good idea to check your shoes and bedding before use. Although few find these creatures cute or cuddly, they are an important part of the park's ecosystem, and they should be respected and protected—by avoiding them whenever possible.

of the town of Hot Springs, which thrived here about 20 years before the park was established and continued as a concession for another 10 years.

Back on the paved road, you'll soon pass through a tunnel in the limestone cliff, after which is a parking area for a short trail to a viewpoint overlooking Rio Grande Village. It's just a quick drive from here to **Rio Grande Village,** your destination, where you can take a .75-mile nature trail ending at a high point above the Rio Grande that offers terrific views up and down the river, as well as some great bird-watching opportunities.

3 Organized Tours & Ranger Programs

Park ranger naturalists offer a variety of programs year-round. Illustrated evening programs take place at the **Chisos Basin amphitheater** in summer. From November through April, evening programs are offered regularly in the amphitheater at **Rio Grande Village** and occasionally at Cottonwood

Campground. Subjects include the park's geology, plants, animals, and human history. Rangers also offer guided **nature walks** and occasionally lead **driving tours.** Workshops are also planned on subjects such as adobe construction or photography. Look for weekly schedules on the bulletin boards scattered about the park.

The **Big Bend Natural History Association** (see "Information," above) offers a variety of seminars. Cost is about $100 per day, and most seminars are for 1 or 2 days. Subjects could include black bears, archaeology, bats, birds, cacti, photography, and wildflowers.

4 Park Attractions

There is evidence that prehistoric American Indians and later Apaches, Kiowas, and Comanches occupied this area. Throughout the park you can find **petroglyphs, pictographs,** and other signs of early human presence, including ruins of **stone shelters.** Pictographs are along the Hot Springs Trail (see "Day Hikes," below) and along the river. Watch for **mortar holes** scattered throughout the park, sometimes a foot deep, where American Indians would grind seeds or mesquite beans.

Also within the park boundaries are the remains of several early-20th-century communities, a mercury mine, and projects by the Civilian Conservation Corps (see below).

The **Castolon Historic District,** in the southwest section of the park just off the Ross Maxwell Scenic Drive, includes the remains of homes and other buildings, many stabilized by the National Park Service, that were constructed in the early 1900s by Mexican-American farmers, Anglo settlers, and the U.S. Army. The first is the 1901 **Alvino House,** the oldest surviving adobe structure in the park. Nearby is **La Harmonia Store,** built in 1920 to house cavalry troops during the Mexican Revolution but never actually used by soldiers, because the war ended. Two civilians then purchased the building and converted it to a general store. The store continues to operate, selling snacks, groceries, and other necessities.

The village of **Glenn Springs,** in the southeast section of the park and accessible by dirt road off the main park highway, owes its creation to having a reliable water source in an otherwise arid area. It bears the name of a rancher called H. E. Glenn, who grazed horses in the area until he was killed by American Indians in the 1880s. By 1916 there were several ranches, a factory that produced wax from the candelilla plant, a store, a post office, and a residential village divided into two sections—one for Anglos and the other for Mexicans. But then Mexican bandit-revolutionaries crossed the border and attacked, killing and wounding a number of people, looting the store, and partially destroying the wax factory. Within 3 years, the community was all but deserted. Today the spring still flows, and you can see the remains of several adobe buildings and other structures.

Remains of a small health resort are visible at the **Hot Springs,** accessible by hiking trail or dirt road, along the Rio Grande west of Rio Grande Village in the park's southeast section. Construction of the resort was begun in 1909 by J. O. Langford, who was forced to leave during the Mexican Revolution. Langford returned and completed the project in the 1920s, advertising the Hot Springs as "The Fountain of Youth that Ponce de León failed to find." Today you'll see the ruins of a general store and post office, other buildings, and a foundation that fills with natural mineral water, at about 105°F (41°C), creating a great place to soak off those post-hike aches and pains.

To get to the **Marsical Mine,** you will likely need a four-wheel-drive or high-clearance vehicle. Located in the south-central part of the park, it is easiest to reach from River Road East, which begins 5 miles west of Rio Grande Village. The mine operated on and off between 1900 and 1943, producing 1,400 76-pound flasks of mercury (almost one-quarter of the total amount of mercury produced in the United States during that time). Mining buildings, homes, the company store, a kiln, foundations, and other structures remain in what is now a National Historic District.

Also in the park, you can see some excellent examples of work the **Civilian Conservation Corps** performed in the 1930s and early 1940s. These include stone culverts along the Basin Road, the Lost Mine Trail, and several buildings, including some stone-and-adobe cottages that are still in use at the Chisos Mountain Lodge.

5 Day Hikes

SHORTER TRAILS

Boquillas Canyon Trail This hike, a good choice for those who want to see some of the area's birds, begins by climbing a low hill and then drops down to the Rio Grande, ending near a shallow cave and huge sand dune. It affords good views of the scenic canyon and the Mexican village of **Boquillas,** across the Rio Grande. 1.4 miles RT. Moderate. Access: End of Boquillas Canyon Rd.

Burro Mesa Pour-Off This short hike takes you to the bottom of a desert pour-off. The beginning of the trail is a well-marked path, but as you turn into Javelina Wash, it becomes less obvious; watch for the lines of rocks pointing the way. The trail has an elevation gain of about 60 feet. The pour-off is a long, narrow chute that is usually dry, but the extensive cut gives testimony to the power of rushing water after a heavy summer rain. Don't attempt to climb to the top from here; it is quite hazardous. There is an easier way for those with good route-finding skills: See "Upper Burro Mesa Pour-Off," below. 1 mile RT. Easy. Access: Parking area at end of Burro Mesa spur road, about 12 miles down Ross Maxwell Scenic Dr. on the west (right).

Chihuahuan Desert Nature Trail A good introduction to the flora of the Chihuahuan Desert, this is an easy stroll along a relatively flat gravel path with signs describing the plants you see along the way. .5 mile RT. Easy. Access: Dugout Wells Picnic Area, 6 miles east of Panther Junction.

Chisos Basin Loop Trail This fairly easy walk climbs about 350 feet into a pretty meadow and leads to an overlook that offers good views of the park's mountains, including **Emory Peak,** highest point in the park, at 7,825 feet. 1.6-mile loop. Easy. Access: Chisos Basin trail head.

Hot Springs Trail An interpretive booklet available at the trail head describes the sights, including a historic health resort and homestead (see "Park Attractions," above), along this easy loop. Fairly substantial **ruins** remain, including a foundation that fills with natural mineral water, creating an inviting hot tub. Also along the trail are **pictographs** left by ancient American Indians and panoramic views of the Rio Grande and Mexico. 1 mile RT. Easy. Access: End of improved dirt road to Hot Springs, off road to Rio Grande Village.

Panther Path This is a short walk through a **garden of cacti** and other desert plants. A booklet discussing the park's plant life is available at the trail head. 50 yds. RT. Easy. Access: Panther Junction Visitor Center.

Rio Grande Village Nature Trail A good choice for sunrise and sunset views, this self-guided loop nature trail (booklet available at the trail head) climbs from the surprisingly lush river floodplain about 125 feet into desert terrain and up a hilltop that offers excellent panoramic views. .75 mile RT. Easy. Access: Southeast corner of Rio Grande Village Campground, across from site 18.

Santa Elena Canyon You may get your feet wet crossing a broad creek on this trail, which also takes you up a series of steep steps. But it's one of the most scenic short trails in the park, leading along the canyon wall (with good views of rafters on the Rio Grande) and continuing down among the boulders along the river. Interpretive signs describe the canyon environment. Beware of flash flooding as you cross the Terlingua Creek, and skip this trail altogether if the creek is running swiftly. 1.7 miles RT. Moderate. Access: End of Ross Maxwell Scenic Dr.

Upper Burro Mesa Pour-Off Trail This moderate hike takes you through some narrow, rocky gorges to the top of the Burro Mesa Pour-Off. The trail may not be well marked, so it's a good idea to carry a topographical map and compass. As you hike along the now-dry washes, you'll realize that the rock cairns marking the trail scatter quickly when water floods through them. There is a gradual decline of about 525 feet to the top of this desert waterfall, where the drainage drops suddenly and precipitously from the wash where you stand to the one below. Do not chance this hike in stormy weather, or you might get washed away with the rock cairns. 3.6 miles RT. Moderate. Access: Trail head parking about 7 miles down Ross Maxwell Scenic Dr. on the west (right).

Tuff Canyon This easy trail leads into a narrow canyon, carved from soft volcanic rock called tuff, with several canyon overlooks. .75 mile RT. Easy. Access: Ross Maxwell Scenic Dr., 5 miles south of Mule Ears Overlook access road.

Window View Trail Level, paved, and wheelchair accessible, this self-guided nature trail (a brochure is available at the trail head) runs along a low hill and has a variety of plant life. In addition, it offers magnificent sunset views through the **Window,** a V-shaped opening in the mountains to the west. .3 mile RT. Easy. Access: Chisos Basin trail head.

LONGER TRAILS

Chimneys Trail This flat trail through the desert follows an old dirt road to a series of chimney-shaped rock formations. American Indian **petroglyphs** can be seen on the southernmost chimney, and nearby are **ruins of rock shelters.** Those who want to extend this hike can continue to a **desert spring,** although the trail is difficult to follow after the Chimneys and a topographical map is highly recommended. 4.8 miles RT (to the chimneys). Moderate. Access: Ross Maxwell Scenic Dr., 1¼ miles south of Burro Mesa Pour-Off access road.

Emory Peak Trail A challenging hike to the high point in the park, the 7,832-foot Emory Peak, this trail begins in the Chisos Basin and gains over 2,400 feet on its way to the top. The final ascent is a scramble up a steep rock wall, but those who make it are rewarded with one of the best views in West Texas. 9 miles RT. Difficult. Access: Basin trail head.

Lost Mine Trail This self-guided nature trail (a booklet is available at the trail head) is a popular mountain hike that climbs about 1,100 feet. It was constructed in the 1940s by the Civilian Conservation Corps—evidence of the builders' rock work can still be seen. Along the way, the trail climbs through **forests of pinyon, juniper, and oak,** and offers splendid views. Those with limited time or ambition don't have to hike all the way—some of the trail's best views are about 1 mile from the trail head, from a saddle where you can look out over a canyon to the surrounding mountains and even deep into Mexico. 4.8 miles RT. Moderate. Access: Chisos Basin Rd. at Panther Pass.

Mule Ears Spring Trail This relatively flat desert trail crosses several arroyos and then follows a wash most of the way to Mule Ears Spring. It offers great views of unusual rock formations, such as the **Mule Ears,** and ends at a **historic ranch house and rock corral.** 3.8 miles RT. Moderate. Access: Mule Ears Overlook parking area, along Ross Maxwell Scenic Dr.

Pine Canyon Trail With a 1,000-foot elevation gain, this trail takes you from desert grasslands, dotted with sotols, into a pretty canyon with dense stands of pinyon, juniper, oak, and finally bigtooth maple and ponderosa pine. At the higher elevations, you'll also see **Texas madrones**—evergreen trees that shed their smooth reddish bark each summer. At the end of the trail is a **200-foot cliff,** which becomes a picturesque waterfall after heavy rains. At the cliff's base, you're likely to see the delicate yellow flowers of **columbine,** a member of the buttercup family. 4 miles RT. Moderate. Access: End of unpaved Pine Canyon Rd. (check on road conditions before setting out).

Slickrock Canyon This hike follows Oak Creek northwest to a small, scenic canyon, passing along the south edge of Slickrock Mountain. This is not a marked trail, but rather a route through sand and gravel washes; a topographical map is helpful. Hikers in this deep canyon will find desert plants such as mesquite and creosote bush, and possibly tracks of coyotes, javelinas, and mountain lions. 10 miles RT. Moderate. Access: Main Park Rd., about 12 miles west of Panther Junction, at Oak Creek Bridge.

Window Trail A scenic trail through Oak Creek Canyon, this hike involves descending about 800 feet to the base of the **Window,** a V-shaped opening in the mountains that frames panoramic desert scenes. Following the Oak Creek drainage, it provides a good chance to see deer, javelinas, rock squirrels, and a variety of birds. 4 miles RT. Moderate. Access: Chisos Basin trail head.

6 Exploring the Backcountry

The park offers numerous possibilities for backpacking, on established and marked hiking trails and on relatively unmarked hiking routes following washes, canyons, or abandoned rough dirt roads dating from the late 1800s. In all, the park has more than 150 miles of designated trails and routes. Cross-country hiking is also permitted. Because many trails and hiking routes are hard to follow, rangers advise that hikers carry detailed 7.5-minute topographical maps and compasses.

Campers can use numerous designated backcountry campsites and may camp in desert areas. The required $10 permits must be obtained in person, no more than 24 hours in advance. In the high Chisos Mountains, backcountry campers must stay at designated campsites and carry special permits, available on a first-come, first-served basis. These campsites are often difficult to obtain during the park's busiest times—Thanksgiving and Christmas holidays and college spring-break season (usually Mar and early Apr). Highly recommended is the South Rim, a 12-mile round-trip with a view that stretches far into Mexico.

Ground fires are prohibited throughout the park. Rangers warn that backcountry water availability is spotty and changeable, and advise backpackers to carry enough water for their entire trip.

7 Other Sports & Activities

Local companies that provide equipment rentals and a variety of guided adventures in both the park and the general area include **Desert Sports** (✆ **888/989-6900** or 432/371-2727; www.desertsportstx.com), located on FM 170, 5 miles west of the junction of FM 170 and Tex. 118, and **Far Flung Outdoor Center,** FM 170 (P.O. Box 377), Terlingua, TX (✆ **800/839-7238** or 432/371-2633; www.farflungoutdoorcenter.com).

BACKCOUNTRY DRIVING Big Bend has a number of unimproved roads requiring high-clearance and sometimes four-wheel-drive vehicles. Many have roadside campsites. Get details on current road conditions from rangers before setting out, and pick up the useful backcountry road guide, available at visitor centers. All overnight trips require backcountry permits. **Far Flung Outdoor Center** (see above) offers four-wheel-drive tours of the area, including trips into the national park. The most popular trip costs $64 per person for 3 hours. The nearest four-wheel-drive rentals are in Alpine, Texas, 108 miles northwest of the park.

HORSEBACK RIDING Horses are permitted on most dirt roads and many park trails (check with rangers for specifics), and may be kept overnight at many of the park's primitive road campsites, although not at the developed campgrounds. The **Government Springs Campsite,** 3½ miles from Panther Junction, is a primitive campsite with a corral that accommodates up to eight horses. It can be reserved up to 10 weeks in advance; call ✆ **432/477-1158.** Those riding horses in the park must get free stock use permits, which should be obtained in person up to 24 hours in advance at any of the park's visitor centers.

Although there are no commercial outfitters offering guided rides in the park as of this writing, there are opportunities for rides just outside the park on private land, such as nearby Big Bend Ranch State Park and across the river in Mexico. **Lajitas Stables** (✆ **800/887-4331** or 432/371-2212; www.lajitasstables.com) offers a variety of guided trail rides, lasting from 2 hours, to all day, to 5 days. Some trips follow canyon trails; others visit ancient Indian camps and ghost towns. Typical rates are $70 for 2 hours, $100 for 4 hours, and $150 for a full day; multiday trips are usually about $150 per day and include all meals and camping equipment, as well as the horse. There are also combination riding/rafting expeditions.

MOUNTAIN BIKING Bikes are not permitted on hiking trails but are allowed on the park's many established dirt roads. Mountain bikes are available for rent from **Desert Sports** (see above); prices start at $35 per day or $150 for a week. The company also offers 1-day and multiday guided trips, including a combination mountain-biking and float trip in the park (3 days, $550).

RIVER RUNNING The Rio Grande follows the southern edge of the park for 118 miles and extends another 127 miles downstream as a designated Wild and Scenic River. The river offers mostly fairly calm float trips, but it does have a few sections of rough white water during high-water times. It can usually be run in a raft, canoe, or kayak. Bring your own equipment, rent equipment near the park (none is available in the park), or take a trip with one of several local river guides under permit by the National Park Service. ***Note:*** The water can be quite low in summer, so call ahead if this is an important part of your visit.

Those planning trips on their own must obtain free permits at a park visitor center, in person only, no more than 24 hours before the trip. Permits for the lower canyons of the Rio Grande Wild and Scenic River are available at the **Persimmon Gap Visitor Center,** when it's open, and at a self-serve permit station at **Stillwell Store and RV Park,** 7 miles from the park's north entrance on FM 2627. Permits for the section of river through Santa Elena Canyon can also be obtained at the **Barton Warnock Environmental Education Center,** 1 mile east of Lajitas, Texas, about 20 miles from the park's west entrance. Park rangers *strongly* advise that everyone planning a river trip check with them to get the latest river conditions. A river-running booklet, with additional information, is available at park visitor centers and from the **Big Bend Natural History Association** (see "Park Information" under "Essentials," earlier in this chapter).

Several local companies rent rafts, inflatable kayaks, and canoes. Rafts typically cost about $25 per person per day (with a three-person minimum), inflatable kayaks cost about $40 per day, and canoes cost about $50 per day. There are discounts for multiday rentals. You can also take guided river trips; rates run about $125 for a full day. Multiday trips are also available.

Check with **Desert Sports** (see above) and **Far Flung Outdoor Center** (see above).

Big Bend River Tours (✆ **800/545-4240** or 432/371-3033; www.bigbendrivertours.com) offers several especially interesting river trips. Trips range from a delightful half-day float for about $72 per person to 10-day excursions for about $2,000 per person. Among the company's most popular trips is the 21-mile float through beautiful Santa Elena Canyon, which offers spectacular scenery and wonderful serenity, plus the excitement of a challenging section of rapids called the Rockslide. There are also often opportunities to see wildlife. The canyon can be explored on a day trip (about $140 per person), a 2-day trip (about $310 per person), or a 3-day trip (about $450 per person), with varying rates based on the number of people making the trip. The longer trips include a stop in a side canyon with waterfalls and peaceful swimming holes. Big Bend River Tours also offers guided canoe and inflatable kayak trips, provides a shuttle service, and rents equipment.

WILDLIFE VIEWING & BIRD-WATCHING Big Bend National Park has an absolutely phenomenal variety of wildlife. About 450 species of birds may be found here over the course of the year—that's more than at any other national park and nearly half of all those found in North America. At last count, there were also about 75 species of mammals, close to 70 species of reptiles and amphibians, and more than three dozen species of fish.

This is the only place in the United States where you'll find the **Mexican long-nosed bat,** listed by the federal government as an endangered species. Other endangered species that make their homes in the park include the **black-capped vireo** (a small bird) and the **Big Bend gambusia,** a tiny fish that we hope prospers and multiplies—its favorite food is mosquito larvae.

Birders consider Big Bend National Park a key bird-watching destination, especially for those looking for some of America's more unusual birds. Among the park's top bird-watching spots are Rio Grande Village and Cottonwood campgrounds, the Chisos Basin, and the Hot Springs. Species to watch for include the colorful **golden-fronted woodpecker,** which can often be seen year-round among the cottonwood trees along the Rio Grande; and the rare **Colima warbler,** whose range in the United States consists solely of the Chisos Mountains at Big Bend National Park. Among the hundreds of other birds that call the park home, at least part of the year, are scaled quail, spotted sandpipers, white-winged doves, greater roadrunners, lesser nighthawks, white-throated swifts, black-chinned hummingbirds, broad-tailed hummingbirds, acorn woodpeckers, northern flickers, western wood pewees, ash-throated flycatchers, tufted titmice, bushtits, cactus wrens, canyon wrens, loggerhead shrikes, Wilson's warblers, and Scott's orioles.

Mammals you may see in the park include desert cottontail rabbits, black-tailed jackrabbits, rock squirrels, Texas antelope squirrels, Merriam's kangaroo rats, coyotes, gray foxes, raccoons, striped skunks, mule deer, and white-tailed deer. There are occasional sightings of mountain lions (usually called panthers here), most commonly in the Green Gulch and Chisos Basin areas. Four attacks on humans are known to have occurred in the park (see "Keeping the Wild in Wildlife, or How to Avoid an Unpleasant Encounter," earlier in this chapter). Black bears, which were frequently seen in the area until about 1940, were mostly killed off by local ranchers, who saw them as a threat to their livestock. With the protection provided by national park status, however, they began to return in the mid-1980s and have now established a small population, and many have ignored regulations and crossed into the park from Mexico.

A number of reptiles inhabit the park, including some poisonous snakes, such as **diamondback, Mojave, rock,** and **black-tailed rattlesnakes,** plus the **trans-pecos copperhead.** Fortunately, you are unlikely to see a rattler or copperhead, since they avoid both the heat of the day and busy areas. You are more apt to encounter nonpoisonous **western coachwhips,** which are often seen speeding across trails and roadways. They're reddish, sometimes bright red, and among America's fastest snakes; sometimes they're called "red racers." Other nonpoisonous snakes that inhabit the park include Texas whipsnakes, spotted night snakes, southwestern black-headed snakes, and black-necked garter snakes.

Among the lizards you may see in the desert is the **southwestern earless lizard.** Adult males are green with black-and-white chevrons on their lower sides, and they often curl their black-striped tails over their backs. You'll also see **whiptail lizards** in the desert, but in the canyons and higher in the mountains, watch for the **crevice spiny lizard,** which is covered with scales and has a dark collar. Although rare, **western box turtles** inhabit the park, as do several types of more common **water turtles.**

8 Camping

A $10 camping permit, available at any visitor center, is required for use of the primitive backcountry roadside and backpacking campsites.

INSIDE THE PARK

The park runs three developed campgrounds, and a concessionaire operates an RV park. Reservations for Chisos Basin and Rio Grande Village campgrounds are available through the **National Recreation Reservation Service** (✆ **877/444-6777;** www.recreation.gov).

Rio Grande Village Campground is the largest. It has numerous trees, many with prickly pear cacti growing around them, and thorny bushes everywhere. Sites are either graveled or paved and are nicely spaced for privacy. They often fill up by 1pm in winter (the high season). One area is designated a "No Generator Zone." Separate but within walking distance is **Rio Grande Village RV Park,** a concessionaire-operated RV park with full hookups. It looks like a parking lot in the midst of grass and trees, fully paved with curbs and back-in sites (no pull-throughs). Tents are not permitted. A small store has limited camping supplies and groceries, a coin-operated laundry, showers for a fee, propane, and gasoline.

Chisos Basin Campground, although not heavily wooded, has small pinyon and juniper trees and well-spaced sites. The campground nestles around a circular road in a bowl below the visitor center. The access road to the campground is steep and curved, so take it slowly.

Cottonwood Campground is named for the huge old cottonwood trees that dominate the scene. Sites in this rustic area are gravel and spacious, within walking distance of the river. There are pit toilets.

NEAR THE PARK

About 7 miles east of the park's north entrance on FM 2627 is **Stillwell Store and RV Park,** HC 65, Box 430, Alpine, TX 79830 (✆/fax **432/376-2244;** www.stillwellstore.com), a casual RV park in desert terrain. There are two areas across the road from each other. The west side has full hookups. The east side has water and electric only, but it also features horse corrals and plenty of room for horse trailers. There is also almost unlimited space for tenters, who pay $5 per person. The park office is at the Stillwell Store, where you can get groceries, limited camping supplies, and gasoline. A small museum (donations accepted) features exhibits from the Stillwell family's pioneer days.

About 3 miles from the west entrance to the park is **Terlingua Oasis RV Park,** part of the Big Bend Motor Inn complex at the junction of Tex. 118 and FM 170 (✆ **877/386-4383** or 432/371-2218). This park offers pull-through and back-in sites, grassy tent areas, gasoline and diesel fuel, a restaurant, a convenience store, and a gift shop.

9 Where to Stay

INSIDE THE PARK

Chisos Mountains Lodge The lodge offers a variety of accommodations, from simple motel rooms to historic stone cottages. Motel rooms are small and simply decorated but well maintained. They have two double beds, air-conditioning, tub/showers, and terrific views of the Chisos Mountains, but no telephones or TVs. The **Casa Grande Motor Lodge,** part of the Chisos Mountains Lodge, offers somewhat larger motel rooms, air-conditioned and attractively furnished, with tiled bathrooms and tub/showers; most have two beds. Each room has a private balcony.

Built by the Civilian Conservation Corps in the 1930s, the six delightful stone cottages are our choice. Each has stone floors, a front patio, wooden furniture, three double beds, and shower only. Book as far in advance as possible. The lodge units are the least expensive accommodations and are a bit more rustic. They have one double and one single bed, a tiled bath, tub/shower, wood furnishings, painted brick walls with Western or Southwestern art (or both), and good views.

Chisos Basin, Big Bend National Park, TX 79834-9999. ✆ **877/386-4383** or 432/477-2292. Fax 432/477-2352. www.chisosmountainslodge.com. 72 units. A/C. $113–$144 double. AE, DISC, MC, V.

NEAR THE PARK

Just outside the national park's west entrance, this is the closest community to the park with lodging and other services. Here you'll find the **Big Bend Motor Inn,** at the junction of Tex. 118 and FM 170 (P.O. Box 336), Terlingua, TX 79852 (✆ **800/848-BEND** [2363] or 432/371-2218; www.foreverresorts.com), offering simple but comfortable and well-maintained modern motel rooms, with rates of $99 to $105 for doubles, and $149 to $199 for kitchenette 2-bedroom apartments. A restaurant and convenience store are on-site. In Terlingua Ghost Town, the formerly abandoned **Holiday Hotel,** behind the Terlingua Trading Company (✆ **432/371-2234**), has been nicely restored and features six rooms with double rates of $125 to $175. The proprietors also have numerous historic homes for rent in the area.

About 20 miles west of Terlingua, **Lajitas,** HC 70 (✆ **877/525-4827** or 432/424-5000; www.lajitas.com), offers double rooms and suites for $169 to over $700, including a pool and a wing of stylish rooms in a former cavalry post once under the command of "Black Jack" Pershing.

Gage Hotel Located 50 miles north of the park boundary, the historic Gage Hotel opened in 1927 as the social hub for area ranchers and miners, but fell into shambles under the desert sun in the ensuing decades. But that period is long over: The current owners restored the old redbrick's many charms in the early 1980s, melding history and an eye for Texas chic. The historic rooms have cow-skin rugs, hardwood floors, Navajo blankets, and oodles of personality; those with shared baths are a bit on the smallish side, but those with private baths are our personal favorites. With outdoor entrances closer to

Campground	Elev.	Total Sites	RV Hookups	Dump Station	Toilets
Inside the Park					
Chisos Basin	5,401	60	No	Yes	Yes
Cottonwood	2,169	31	No	No	Yes
Rio Grande Village	1,850	100	No	Yes	Yes
Rio Grande Village RV Park	1,850	25	25	No	No
Near the Park					
Terlingua Oasis	2,480	131	125	No	Yes
Stillwell Store and RV Park	2,600	65+	65	Yes	Yes

the magnificent pool and courtyards, the larger Los Portales rooms have adobe floors and coffeemakers, phones, hair dryers, and irons. The restaurant, **Café Cenizo,** serves steaks and gourmet Southwestern cuisine.

U.S. 90 (P.O. Box 46), Marathon, TX 79842. ✆ **800/884-4243** or 432/386-4205. www.gagehotel.com. 39 units (9 with shared bathroom), including 1 suite and 2 guesthouses. A/C. $76 double with shared bathroom; $98–$182 double with private bathroom; $208 suite; $303–$330 house. AE, DISC, MC, V.

La Posada Milagro ★ Built on the site of a former ruin that is now incorporated into the structure, La Posada Milagro overlooks Terlingua Ghost Town and is a terrific place to hang your hat. Featuring distinctive West Texas touches—thatched ceilings, corner hearths, and patio seating areas—three smaller rooms share a full bath and a half-bath, and a fourth room is the Chisos Honeymoon Suite, larger, with a private bath. Also available is a nearby guesthouse, **La Casita.**

100 Milagro Rd., Terlingua Ghost Town, Terlingua, TX 79852. ✆ **432/371-3044.** www.laposadamilagro.net. 5 units, 3 with shared bath, including 1 guesthouse. A/C. $145–$195 double with shared bathroom; $210 double with private bathroom; $350 guesthouse. AE, MC, V.

10 Where to Dine

INSIDE THE PARK

Chisos Mountains Lodge Restaurant AMERICAN Good food at reasonable prices, plus the best location in the area, is the draw here. The dining room is simply but attractively decorated, with good views from the large windows. The menu changes periodically but generally includes steak, burgers, and sandwiches, plus Southwestern and Tex-Mex dishes. At breakfast, there's a buffet as well as a menu.

Chisos Basin, Big Bend National Park. ✆ **432/477-2292.** Main courses $8–$20. AE, DISC, MC, V. Daily 7–10am, 11:30am–4pm, and 5–9pm.

NEAR THE PARK

For barbecue and steaks ($9–$18), **La Kiva,** FM 170 between Terlingua Ghost Town and then turnoff to Tex. 118 (✆ **432/371-2250;** www.lakiva.net), is a watering hole on Terlingua Creek that looks like a cave, complete with fossils in the walls and tree stumps for barstools. For breakfast, head into Terlingua Ghost Town for **Ms. Tracy's Café** (✆ **432/371-2888**).

Starlight Theatre NEW AMERICAN/MEXICAN A 1930s movie palace abandoned when the mines in Terlingua went bust in the following decade, the Starlight Theatre was reborn as an eatery and watering hole in 1991. The stage is still here, but the silver screen takes a backseat to the food (especially the game dishes, filet mignon, and chipotle pork medallions), drink (namely Texas beers and prickly pear margaritas), and desserts (such as cobbler for two). The funky West Texan decor, featuring numerous requisite longhorn skulls, is a contrast for the unexpectedly diverse menu, which highlights a number of vegetarian and seafood options. The theater still occasionally hosts movie nights and other entertainment. Mondays are known for two-for-one burgers and live music.

In Historic Terlingua Ghost Town, off U.S. 90. ✆ **432/371-2326.** www.starlighttheatre.com. Main courses $7–$33. AE, MC, V. Daily 5–10pm. Bar open later.

11 Picnic & Camping Supplies

Inside the park, limited groceries and camping supplies are available at Chisos Basin, Rio Grande Village, Castolon, and Panther Junction. There is also a gift shop in the lodge at the Basin. Gasoline is available at Rio Grande Village and Panther Junction only, so check your gas gauge before heading out—everything in this park is pretty far from everything else. Minor car repairs are available at Panther Junction.

Drinking Water	Showers	Fire Pits/ Grills	Laundry	Reserve	Fees	Open
Yes	No	Yes	No	Yes	$14	Year-round
Yes	No	Yes	No	No	$14	Year-round
Yes	No	Yes	No	Yes	$14	Year-round
No	No	No	Yes	No	$27	Year-round
Yes	Yes	Yes	Yes	Yes	$15–$29	Year-round
Yes	Yes	Yes	Yes	Yes	$16–$19	Year-round

Outside the north entrance to the park, southeast about 7 miles on FM 2627, is **Stillwell Store and RV Park** (✆ **432/376-2244;** http://stillwellstore.com), where you'll find groceries, limited camping supplies, and gasoline. Just outside the west entrance to the park, in Study Butte/Terlingua, you'll find several gas stations, car repair, a convenience store, and a liquor store. Also in the Study Butte/Terlingua area is **Desert Sports** (see above), with rental equipment, bike and boat parts and supplies, maps, and guidebooks.

12 Nearby Attractions

On the west side of Big Bend National Park, just beyond Study Butte and Terlingua, are three worthwhile side trips. Heading west, you'll encounter the **Barton Warnock Environmental Education Center,** 1 mile east of Lajitas on FM 170 (✆ **432/424-3327;** www.tpwd.state.tx.us/park/barton). Named for botanist and author Dr. Barton Warnock, the center is operated by Texas Parks & Wildlife. It features exhibits on the geology, archaeology, human history, and especially flora and fauna of the Big Bend area, with a museum plus 2½ acres of desert gardens with a self-guided walk among the various plants of the Chihuahuan Desert. There is also a gift shop and bookstore. Gates are open daily year-round from 8am to 4:30pm (closed Dec 25); admission costs $3 (free for children under 12) and is also good for the Fort Leaton State Historic Site (see below).

Continuing west, you enter **Big Bend Ranch State Park,** P.O. Box 2319, Presidio, TX 79845 (✆ **432/358-4444;** www.tpwd.state.tx.us), which covers some 300,000 acres of Chihuahuan Desert wilderness along the Rio Grande. Perhaps even more remote and rugged than Big Bend National Park, this mostly undeveloped state park (also called Big Bend Ranch Natural Area on some signs) contains two mountain ranges, extinct volcanoes, scenic canyons, a wide variety of desert plants, and wildlife including javelinas, mountain lions, deer, coyotes, a variety of lizards, several poisonous snakes, and numerous birds, including golden eagles and peregrine falcons. There is also a small herd of Texas longhorn cattle, a reminder of the property's ranching days. Hiking on and around the giant volcanic dome known as El Solitario is highly recommended. Day use is $3; camping is $8 per night. The bunkhouse at Sauceda charges $41 for a room and $25 for a bunk. Several outfitters offer river trips as well as mountain biking and hiking excursions in the state park. See "Other Sports & Activities," earlier in this chapter.

The 50-mile **Farm Road 170** between Lajitas and Presidio goes through the park, providing a wonderful scenic drive for 28 miles along the Rio Grande, and also offering access to several put-in and take-out points for rafts and canoes. The road is winding and hilly in places, with no shoulders and a maximum speed limit in most places of 45 mph. It meanders along the Rio Grande, passing among hillsides dotted with mesquite, yucca, ocotillo, prickly pear cactus, and a variety of desert shrubs. There are pullouts with picnic tables (protected from the weather by fake Indian tepees). Although paved, the road is subject to flash floods and rock slides, so we do not recommend driving it during or immediately after heavy rains. It washed out completely in 2008.

The park also has several miles of roads that require high-clearance four-wheel-drive vehicles, and about 30 miles of hiking and backpacking trails, with trail heads along FM 170. There are also a number of primitive camping areas. Those planning trips into the park can get permits and information (including a very good trail guide) at Barton Warnock Environmental Education Center (see above), Fort Leaton State Historic Site (see below), or the **ranch administrative offices.** Those driving through the park on FM 170 are not required to pay the entrance fee and can get out of their vehicles to look around, but should generally stay within sight of their vehicles.

Just west of Big Bend Ranch State Park is **Fort Leaton State Historic Site,** 4 miles east of Presidio on FM 170 (✆ **432/229-3613;** www.tpwd.state.tx.us/park/fortleat). Admission to the site costs $3 (free for children under 12; also good for the Warnock center). The site is a restored fort and trading post best known for the violence perpetrated both by and toward its residents. It was built by Benjamin Leaton in 1848, just after the end of the Mexican-American War, in which the United States acquired most of the Southwest from Mexico. Leaton had been working as a "scalp hunter"—killing American Indians for the governments of several Mexican states—and built the adobe fortress for his family and employees and to use as a base of operations for a trading business. It was said at the time that part of this business included encouraging area bands of Apaches and Comanches to steal livestock from Mexican settlements, which they would trade to Leaton for guns and ammunition. Leaton, considered a generally unsavory character, was known locally as *un mal hombre*—Spanish for "a bad man."

After his death in 1851, Leaton's widow married Edward Hall, who moved into the fort, from which he operated a freight business. Hall borrowed a large sum of money from a former associate of Leaton's,

John Burgess, and when in 1864 Hall could not repay the loan, Burgess foreclosed on the fort. Hall refused to leave and then was murdered, supposedly by Burgess, who then moved his family in. Burgess ran a successful freight business from there until 1875, when he was murdered by Bill Leaton, Ben Leaton's youngest son.

Despite this bloody chain of events, the remaining members of the Burgess family lived in the fort until 1926, when it was abandoned and began to fall into ruin. It was donated to the state in 1968 and has been partially restored so today's visitors can get a sense of what life was like at a trading-post fort in the untamed frontier of the 19th century. Twenty-five rooms are open to the public by guided (45–60 min.) or self-guided tour. The guided tours are especially good, giving visitors the guide's perspective on the building's violent past.

Fort Leaton State Historic Site includes a museum, with exhibits on the human history of the area—from the prehistoric American Indians who farmed here in the 15th century, to the Spanish and Mexican colonizers who followed, and, finally, the Anglo-Americans who arrived in the mid-1800s, including, of course, those who built and lived in Fort Leaton. The park holds periodic living-history demonstrations, such as how to make adobe bricks, blacksmithing, 19th-century cooking, and the like. The historic site is open daily from 8am to 4:30pm (closed Dec 25).

5

Black Canyon of the Gunnison National Park, CO

by Don & Barbara Laine

Early American Indians and, later, Utes and Anglos avoided the Black Canyon of the Gunnison, believing that no human could survive a trip through its depths. Now, the deepest and most spectacular 14 miles of this 48-mile canyon make up one of America's newest national parks.

The Black Canyon, which had been a national monument since 1933, became a national park on October 21, 1999. In a statement issued after the bill-signing ceremony, President Bill Clinton called it a "true natural treasure," adding, "Its nearly vertical walls, rising a half-mile high, harbor one of the most spectacular stretches of wild river in America."

The Black Canyon ranges in depth from 1,730 to 2,700 feet. Its width at its narrowest point (cleverly called "The Narrows") is only 40 feet at the river. This deep slash in the earth was created through 2 million years of erosion, a process that's still going on. At 30,300 acres, the Black Canyon is among the smallest of America's national parks.

Most visitors view the canyon from the **South Rim Road,** site of the visitor center, or the less used **North Rim Road.** Short paths branching off both roads lead to splendid view points with signs explaining the canyon's unique geology.

The park has hiking trails along both rims and backcountry hiking routes down into the canyon, and offers excellent trout fishing for anglers willing to make the trek to the canyon floor. It also provides an abundance of thrills for the experienced rock climbers who challenge its sheer canyon walls. In winter, much of the park is closed to motor vehicles, but it's a delight for cross-country skiers and snowshoers.

The Black Canyon shares its eastern boundary with **Curecanti National Recreation Area,** which offers boating and fishing on three reservoirs, as well as hiking and camping.

AVOIDING THE CROWDS

Although overcrowding has not been much of a problem in the past, with fewer than 200,000 people visiting each year, visitation is expected to increase now that the Black Canyon has gained national park status. Summer is the busiest time, with more than half the park visitors arriving between Memorial Day and Labor Day. December through February is the quietest time. Those seeking solitude should visit before Memorial Day and after Labor Day. Although winter can be beautiful, park access is limited.

1 Essentials

GETTING THERE & GATEWAYS

The park is on **Colo. 347,** 6 miles north of U.S. 50. To reach the south rim, travel east 8 miles from Montrose on U.S. 50 to the well-marked turnoff. To reach the north rim from Montrose, drive north 21 miles on U.S. 50 to Delta, east 31 miles on Colo. 92 to Crawford, then south on an 11-mile access road.

THE NEAREST AIRPORT The **Montrose Regional Airport,** 2100 Airport Rd. (✆ **970/249-3203;** www.montroseairport.com), is off U.S. 50, 2 miles northwest of town. Airlines serving the town include **American, Continental, Delta,** and **United.** Car-rental agencies with outlets at the airport include **Avis, Budget, Enterprise, Hertz,** and **National/Alamo.**

Voices

No other canyon in North America combines the depth, narrowness, sheerness, and somber countenance of the Black Canyon.

—Geologist Wallace Hansen, who mapped the canyon in the 1950s

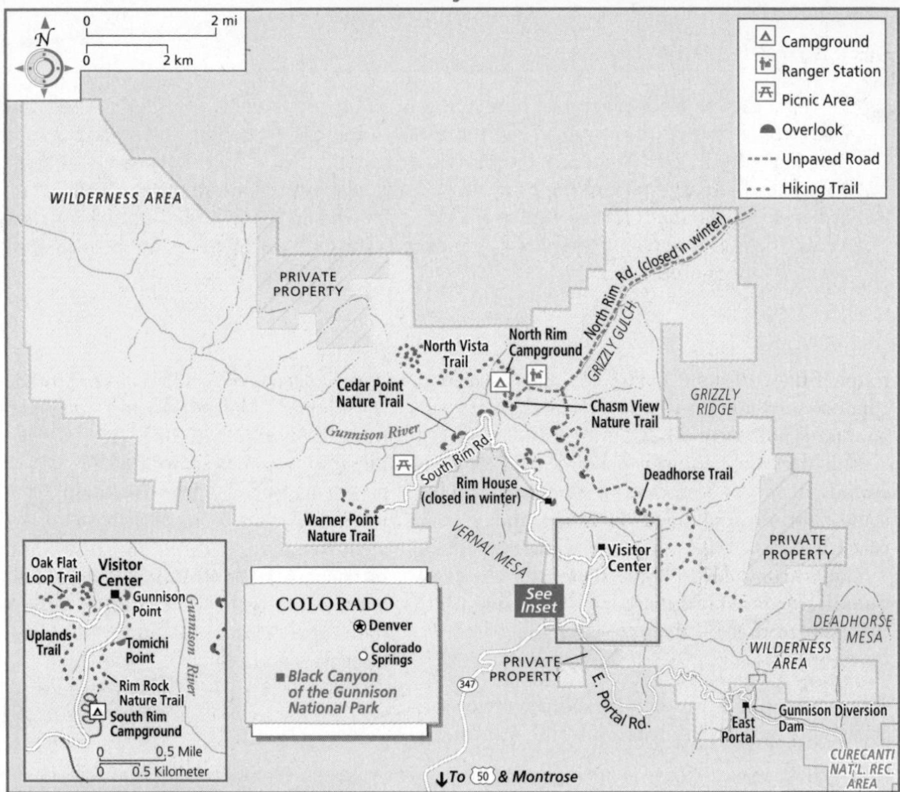

A bigger airport is **Grand Junction Regional Airport,** about 200 miles east in Grand Junction, Colorado (✆ **970/244-9100;** fax 970/241-9103; www.gjairport.com). It has direct flights or connections from most major cities on **Allegiant, American/American Eagle, Delta Connection/Skywest, United Express/Skywest,** and **US Airways.** Car rentals are available at the airport from **Alamo, Avis, Budget, Enterprise,** and **Hertz.**

Website listings for airlines, hotel chains, and car-rental companies appear in chapter 38.

INFORMATION

For information on both the national park and the adjacent Curecanti National Recreation Area, contact **Black Canyon of the Gunnison National Park,** 102 Elk Creek, Gunnison, CO 81230 (✆ **970/641-2337;** www.nps.gov/blca). A bookstore at the South Rim Visitor Center, operated by the Western National Parks Association, offers a variety of publications, including the very useful *South Rim Driving Tour Guide,* published by the association.

For information on other area attractions, lodging, and dining, contact the **Montrose Visitors & Convention Bureau,** 1519 E. Main St., Montrose, CO 81401 (✆ **800/873-0244;** www.visitmontrose.net), or stop at the **visitor center** in the **Ute Indian Museum,** 17253 Chipeta Dr. (✆ **970/249-3093**), on the south side of town off U.S. 550. Information on federal lands in the area, including those under the jurisdiction of the Bureau of Land Management, is available at the **Public Lands Center,** 2465 S. Townsend Ave. (✆ **970/240-5300**), open weekdays year-round.

VISITOR CENTERS

The park's **South Rim Visitor Center** is open daily year-round, except New Year's Day, Thanksgiving, and Christmas. Summer hours are 8am to 6pm, and hours the rest of the year are 8:30am to 4pm. The **North Rim Ranger Station** is open intermittently in summer but closed at other times; a self-registration board is available at the North Rim to pay entrance fees and obtain wilderness permits.

FEES & PERMITS

Admission for up to 7 days costs $15 per vehicle or $7 per person 17 or older on foot, bike, or motorcycle. Those under 17 are admitted free. Camping costs $12 per night for basic sites and $18 for sites with electric hookups. Required backcountry permits are free.

SPECIAL REGULATIONS & WARNINGS

Visitors are warned to not throw anything from the rim into the canyon, since even a single small stone thrown or kicked from the rim could be fatal to

If You Have Only 1 Day

It's fairly easy to see a great deal here in a short time, especially if you stick to the South Rim. First, stop at the **visitor center** to see the exhibits and get an understanding of how this phenomenal canyon was created. From the visitor center, drive 6 miles (one-way) to the end of South Rim Drive, stopping at the overlooks. Finally, take off on one of the rim hiking trails, such as the easy **Cedar Point Nature Trail** or the more challenging **Warner Point Nature Trail** (see "Day Hikes," below). If you'll be camping in the park or staying nearby, you might plan to attend the evening ranger program.

people below. Visitors are also advised to supervise children very carefully—many sections of the rim have no guardrails or fences.

Unlike at most national parks, leashed pets are permitted on two trails—Rim Rock and Chasm View—but are prohibited on others and are not permitted in the inner canyon or wilderness areas.

Those hiking down to the bottom of the Black Canyon are advised to watch out for poison ivy, which can grow to 5 feet tall along the Gunnison River.

SEASONS & CLIMATE

Temperatures and weather conditions often vary greatly between the canyon rim and the canyon floor; it gets progressively hotter as you descend into the canyon. Average summer temperatures range from highs of 60° to 90°F (16°–32°C), with summer lows dropping to 30° to 50°F (–1° to 10°C). In winter, highs range from 20° to 40°F (–7° to 4°C), with lows from 0° to 20°F (–18° to –7°C). Brief afternoon thunderstorms are fairly common in the summer. The South Rim Road usually remains open to the visitor center through the winter, but snow often closes the North Rim Road between December and March.

2 Exploring the Park by Car

The park's 7-mile (one-way) **South Rim Drive** provides an excellent and fairly easy way to see much of the park. There are a dozen overlooks along the drive, and in most cases you'll be walking from 140 feet to about 700 feet to reach the view points from your vehicle.

Among the not-to-be-missed overlooks are **Gunnison Point,** behind the visitor center, which offers stunning views of the seemingly endless walls of dark rock, capped by a pinkish rock layer; and the **Pulpit Rock Overlook,** which provides a splendid view of the rock walls and about 1½ miles of the Gunnison River, some 1,770 feet down. Farther along the drive is **Chasm View,** where you can see the incredible power of water, which here cut through more than 1,800 feet of solid rock. Near the end of the drive, stop at **Sunset View,** where there's a picnic area and a short (140-ft.) walk to a viewpoint, which offers distant views beyond the canyon as well as of the scenic canyon (but not the river). And if your timing is right, you might be treated to a classic Western sunset, in all its red-and-orange glory.

3 Organized Tours & Ranger Programs

A variety of free **ranger-conducted programs,** which might include nature walks, geology talks, and evening programs at the South Rim Visitor Center or campground, take place from Memorial Day through mid-September on the South Rim (check at the visitor center for the current schedule). During the winter, guided snowshoe walks and cross-country ski tours are usually offered on the South Rim when snow conditions are right (stop at the visitor center or call ahead for information and reservations).

4 Day Hikes

Trails on the monument's rims range from short, easy walks to moderate to strenuous hikes of several miles; hiking below the rim is difficult and not recommended for those with a fear of heights. Permits are not needed for rim trails, but free backcountry permits are required for treks below the rim.

SOUTH RIM TRAILS

Cedar Point Nature Trail With signs along the way describing the plants you'll see, this sunny trail not only offers a painless botany lesson, but at the end provides breathtaking views of the Gunnison River, 2,000 feet down, as well as the **Painted Wall,** at 2,250 feet, considered the tallest cliff in Colorado. .7 mile RT. Easy. Access: Cedar Point trail head, along South Rim Rd.

Oak Flat Loop Trail Dropping below the rim, this steep trail offers excellent views into the canyon while taking you through a grove of aspen, past Gambel oak, and finally through a forest of aspen, Gambel oak, and Douglas fir. Be aware that the trail is narrow in spots and a bit close to steep drop-offs. 2 miles RT. Moderate to strenuous. Access: Near visitor center.

Rim Rock Nature Trail Following the rim along a relatively flat path, this trail leads to an overlook providing good views of the Gunnison River and the canyon's sheer rock walls. A pamphlet available at the trail head describes plant life and other points of interest. 1 mile RT. Moderate. Access: Near entrance to South Rim Campground's Loop C.

Warner Point Nature Trail This trail offers a multitude of things to see, such as mountain mahogany, pinyon pine, Utah juniper, and other area flora; distant mountains and valleys; and the Black Canyon and its creator, the Gunnison River, 2,722 feet below. A trail guide is available at the trail head. 1.5 miles RT. Moderate. Access: High Point Overlook, at end of South Rim Rd.

NORTH RIM TRAILS

Chasm View Nature Trail Starting in a pinyon-juniper forest, this trail heads to the rim for good views of the canyon and the river; you'll also have a good chance of seeing swallows, swifts, and raptors. .3 mile RT. Moderate. Access: End of North Rim Campground loop.

Deadhorse Trail Actually an old service road, this trail offers a chance of seeing various birds, plus views of **Deadhorse Gulch** and the **East Portal area** at the southeast end of the park. 5 miles RT. Easy to moderate. Access: Kneeling Camel Overlook.

North Vista Trail Offering some of the best scenic views in the Black Canyon, this trail also provides hikers with a good chance of seeing red-tailed hawks, white-throated swifts, Clark's nutcrackers, and ravens. You might also be lucky enough to spot a peregrine falcon. The trail goes through a pinyon-juniper forest along the canyon's rim about 1.5 miles to **Exclamation Point,** which offers an excellent view into the canyon. Up to this point the trail is rated moderate, but it continues another 2 miles (rated strenuous) to **Green Mountain,** where you'll find broad, panoramic vistas. 7 miles RT. Moderate to strenuous. Access: North Rim Ranger Station.

5 Exploring the Backcountry

Experienced hikers in excellent physical condition may want to hike down into the canyon. Although the canyon has no maintained or marked trails, rangers can help you plot out several recommended routes. Free permits are required. A limited number of campsites are available for backpackers.

The most popular inner canyon hike is the strenuous **Gunnison Route,** which branches off the South Rim's Oak Flat Loop Trail (see above) and meanders down the side of the canyon to the river. Eighty feet of chain help keep you from falling on a stretch about a third of the way down. This hike has a vertical drop of 1,800 feet and usually takes a bit under 4 hours.

6 Other Sports & Activities

BIKING Although bikes are not permitted on any park trails, this is still a popular destination for bikers, who travel the **South Rim Road** to the various overlooks and trail heads. There are also plenty of mountain-biking opportunities outside the park. You can get maps, information, bike repairs, and accessories in Montrose at **Cascade Bicycles,** 21 N. Cascade Ave. (✆ **970/249-7375**), and **Jeans Westerner,** 147 N. Townsend Ave. (✆ **800/426-6756** or 970/249-3600; www.jeanswesterner.com), which rents mountain bikes starting at $29 per day.

CLIMBING The sheer vertical walls and scenic beauty of the Black Canyon make it an ideal and popular destination for rock climbers, but—we cannot emphasize this too strongly—this is no place for beginners. These cliffs require a great deal of experience and the best equipment. Free permits are required, and prospective climbers should discuss their plans first with park rangers.

FISHING Dedicated anglers can make their way to the Gunnison River at the bottom of the canyon in a quest for **brown** and **rainbow trout.** East Portal Road (open only in summer) provides access to the upstream section of the river from adjacent Curecanti National Recreation Area. The stretch of the Gunnison River within the park has been designated as Gold Medal Waters; only artificial lures are permitted, and other special rules apply (check with park rangers). A Colorado fishing license is required. For fly-fishing tips and equipment, stop at

Amazing Feat!

In September 1949, Ed Nelson accomplished what practically everyone considered impossible: He was the first man to boat through the Black Canyon of the Gunnison. Amazingly, he accomplished the feat in a 5-pound collapsible boat, using Ping-Pong paddles for oars!

Jeans Westerner (see "Biking," above) or **Cimarron Creek,** 317 E. Main St. (© **970/249-0408;** www.cimarroncreek.com).

WATERSPORTS Mostly, don't do it! Through the park, the Gunnison River is **extremely dangerous** for both swimmers and rafters (it's considered unraftable). Sections of river west of the park, however, are more suitable; information is available from the Public Lands Center office in Montrose (see "Information," above). The only exception is for experienced kayakers, who find the river an exhilarating challenge. Free permits are required.

WILDLIFE VIEWING The park is home to a variety of wildlife; you're likely to see chipmunks, ground squirrels, badgers, yellow-bellied marmots, and mule deer. Although not frequently spotted, there are also black bear, cougars, and bobcats, and you'll probably hear the lonesome high-pitched call of coyotes at night. The peregrine falcon can sometimes be spotted along the cliffs, especially in spring and early summer, and you may also see red-tailed hawks, turkey vultures, golden eagles, blue grouse, canyon wrens, and white-throated swifts.

WINTER SPORTS When the South Rim Road is closed by winter snow, the Park Service plows only to the South Rim Visitor Center, leaving the rest of the park the domain of cross-country skiers and snowshoers. The South Rim Road, running about 6 miles from the visitor center into the park, makes a great trail for **cross-country skiers,** providing fairly easy access to the scenic drive's overlooks. **Snowshoers** especially like the upper section of Oak Flat Loop Trail and the Rim Rock Nature Trail (see "Day Hikes," above). You can rent cross-country skis, at $9.50 per day, or snowshoes, at $15 per day, at **Jeans Westerner** (see "Biking," above).

7 Camping

There are campgrounds on both rims with toilets but no showers. There is drinking water available only from mid-May through mid-December, and because it must be trucked in, filling of RV water tanks is not permitted. The **South Rim Campground,** which rarely fills, has 88 sites (23 of which have electric hookups); some sites are open year-round. The **North Rim Campground,** which is open spring through fall only, has 13 basic sites and occasionally fills up. Sites at the North Rim Campground are available on a first-come, first-served basis, while some sites in the South Rim Campground can be reserved (© **877/444-6777;** www.recreation.gov), with a $3 reservation fee. Cost is $12 per night for basic sites and $18 for sites with electric hookups. RVs over 35 feet long are not recommended in either campground.

Campgrounds with hot showers and full RV hookups are available in Montrose. These include **Cedar Creek R.V. Park,** 126 Rose Lane, Montrose, CO 81401 (© **877/425-3884** or 970/249-3884; www.cedarcreekrv.com), which is open year-round, with spacious sites, lots of mature trees, and attractive landscaping. There are 43 RV sites (full hookup and water and electric only), including large pull-throughs for big rigs, a shady creekside tent area, free Wi-Fi and cable TV, a coin-op laundry, a well-maintained bathhouse, 18-hole minigolf, a playground, and a dump station. Tent sites are $20 per night, and RV sites run $26 to $34 per night. There are also several camping cabins, which share the campground's bathhouse, at $35 double without linens and $40 double with linens. Major credit cards are accepted.

8 Where to Stay

NEAR THE PARK

There is no lodging inside the park; the nearest facilities are in Montrose. National chain motels in Montrose include the **Best Western Red Arrow Motor Inn,** 1702 E. Main St. (© 970/249-9641), with rates for two from $86 to $120; **Econo Lodge,** 2100 E. Main St. (© 970/240-8000), with double rates from $70 to $100; **Holiday Inn Express Hotel & Suites,** 1391 S. Townsend Ave. (© 970/240-1800), with rates for two from $90 to $114; **Quality Inn & Suites,** 2751 Commercial Way (© 970/249-1011), with double rates from $85 to $120; and **Rodeway Inn,** 1705 E. Main St. (© 970/249-9294), charging $60 to $90 double.

Rates in Montrose are usually highest in July and August, and lowest November through April. Chapter 38 lists website info for the major national chains.

Looking for something more interesting than the standard chain motel? We like the **Uncompahgre Bed and Breakfast,** 21049 Uncompahgre Rd., Montrose, CO 81403 (✆ **800/318-8127** or 970/240-4000; www.uncbb.com). This quiet country retreat, housed in a renovated 1914 school building, offers seven spacious guest rooms, tastefully decorated in themes such as wild birds and Spanish flamenco or, our favorite, French country, which has an electric log fireplace and two-person whirlpool tub in addition to the subtle French countryside decor. Rates here are $110 to $150 double from mid-May through October and $90 to $125 double the rest of the year.

9 Where to Dine

NEAR THE PARK

In addition to the restaurant discussed below, we recommend the **Red Barn Restaurant,** 1413 E. Main St. (✆ **970/249-9202**), which specializes in beef. It's open Monday through Saturday from 11am to 10:30pm, Sunday from 9am to 2pm and 3 to 10:30pm. Another good choice is **Café 110,** 110 N. Townsend Ave. (✆ **970/249-0777;** www.cafe110montrose.com), serving innovative American breakfast and lunch items Monday through Saturday from 7am to 2pm.

Cazwellas INTERNATIONAL This upscale restaurant, in an historic downtown building, offers fine dining with excellent service and what we consider the best wine cellar in this part of the state. Serving what it describes as regional foods of the Americas, the menu includes fresh fish, wild game, steaks, and vegetarian items. The beef tenderloin, for example, is charbroiled and drizzled with truffle-infused smoked tomato butter sauce, and the duck breast is pan seared and oven roasted, and served with a wine and tart cherry demi-glace.

320 E. Main St. ✆ **970/252-9200.** Main courses $15–$39. AE, DISC, MC, V. Mon–Sat 5–9pm.

10 Picnic & Camping Supplies

A good bet for those seeking groceries, deli sandwiches, and baked goods is one of the two **City Market** grocery stores in Montrose. There's one at 128 S. Townsend Ave. (✆ **970/249-3405;** www.citymarket.com), which also has a pay-by-the-pound salad bar; and another at 16400 S. Townsend Ave. (✆ **970/249-3405;** www.citymarket.com). For general camping and other outdoor gear, stop at **Jeans Westerner** (see "Biking," above) or the 24-hour **Wal-Mart Supercenter,** at 16750 S. Townsend Ave. (✆ **970/249-7544;** www.walmart.com).

6

The Black Hills: Mount Rushmore National Memorial, Wind Cave National Park, Jewel Cave National Monument & Custer State Park, SD

by Jack Olson

Chiseled in granite high on a pine-clad cliff in South Dakota's fabled Black Hills are the portraits of four of America's greatest leaders. Since 1941, George Washington, Thomas Jefferson, Abraham Lincoln, and Theodore Roosevelt have gazed quietly across the Great Plains and a land they did so much to mold.

Most of the 2.7 million people who visit each year spend an hour or so at the memorial, maybe eating a sandwich, then moving on to Yellowstone National Park or some other "major" destination. But those with the time and inclination will discover much to enjoy at Mount Rushmore and the other attractions of the Black Hills. Within an hour's drive, you will find not only Wind Cave National Park and Jewel Cave National Monument, but also Custer State Park and the Crazy Horse Memorial—a work in progress that will be far larger than Mount Rushmore. And if you are willing to get off the beaten path—something that relatively few visitors do—you will find a backcountry dotted with trails through the region's pine forests, a nearly untrammeled wilderness where you can escape the crowds for days, or perhaps just an hour. As a bonus, you are almost certain to view a variety of wildlife matched in few places in the United States.

Geologists predict the presidents will continue their earthly vigil at **Mount Rushmore National Memorial** for many centuries, eroding less than 1 inch every 10,000 years.

As the "crown jewel" of South Dakota's state park system, **Custer State Park** offers 71,000 acres of prime Black Hills real estate, the largest and most diverse population of wildlife, the best accommodations and facilities, and the most memorable natural resources of any park in the state.

Located east of the town of Custer, the park is home to four lodges, four fishing lakes, wildlife loops, campgrounds, scenic drives, and granite spires so impressive that they make you want to get out of the car and walk the forest floor. With rolling meadows and foothills, pine forests, and the giant fingerlike granite spires of the Needles, Custer State Park is a must on any Black Hills itinerary.

Even after more than 100 years since the establishment of the park, there is still something to discover in the darkened depths of **Wind Cave National Park.** Although the cave formations here are generally not as ornate as those in some of the West's other caves, such as Carlsbad Cavern, Wind Cave has its share of fairyland-style decorations, including popcorn, shimmering needle-shaped crystals, and an abundance of formations called **"boxwork,"** which sometimes looks like fine lace. With more than 132 miles of mapped passageway, Wind Cave is one of the longest caves in the world. And with each succeeding expedition, the interconnecting network of known passages continues to grow, sometimes by a few paces, other times by several hundred feet. Barometric wind studies estimate that only 5% of the total cave has been discovered.

But there's a great deal more to Wind Cave than just its geological wonders. Aboveground, 28,295 acres of rolling prairie and ponderosa pine forests are ablaze with wildflowers and teeming with wildlife. Bison and pronghorn antelope graze on the park's lush grasslands, while prairie dogs watch from the relative safety of their "towns." In the fall, elk can be heard "bugling" throughout the confines of the park, and overhead, hawks, eagles, and vultures float on the thermal currents that rise from the rocky ridges of the Black Hills.

In the limestone labyrinth that rests below the Black Hills, **Jewel Cave National Monument** offers a mysterious, mazelike network of caverns and passageways, filled with rare specimens and beautiful jewel-like crystals that have yet to be fully explored.

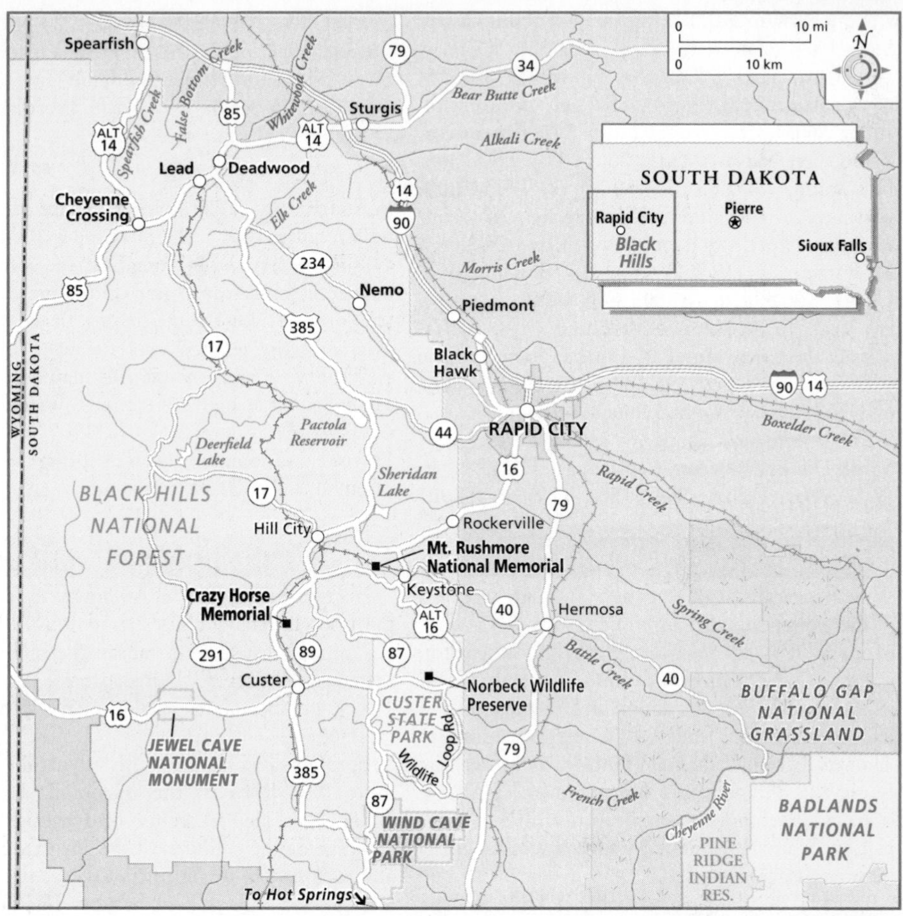

1 Essentials

GETTING THERE & GATEWAYS

Rapid City is the most popular gateway to the Black Hills and its bountiful selection of national and state parks, monuments, and memorials.

The most direct route to the Black Hills by car is I-90. To reach **Mount Rushmore,** take exit 57 to U.S. 16 (Mt. Rushmore Rd.) and continue approximately 23 miles southwest of Rapid City to the memorial entrance.

Custer State Park, between Mount Rushmore and Wind Cave National Park, is accessible via S. Dak. 79 and S. Dak. 36 from the east, U.S. 16A from the north and west, and S. Dak. 87 from the north and south.

Wind Cave National Park is best accessed via U.S. 385 north of Hot Springs, South Dakota, or S. Dak. 87 from Custer State Park, which shares its southern boundary with Wind Cave's northern perimeter. It's about an hour's drive south from Mount Rushmore.

The **Crazy Horse Memorial** is 5 miles north of Custer on U.S. 16/385.

Jewel Cave National Monument, the westernmost of the sites discussed in this chapter, is just off U.S. 16, 13 miles west of Custer.

THE NEAREST AIRPORT **Rapid City Regional Airport** (✆ **605/394-4195;** www.rcgov.org/Airport/pages), 10 miles southeast of Rapid City on U.S. 44, provides direct access to the Black Hills and Mount Rushmore. **Frontier, Northwest Airlines, Delta/Skywest, Allegiant,** and **United Express** serve the airport with daily flights to Minneapolis, Salt Lake City, Chicago, Denver, Las Vegas, and Phoenix. Car-rental agencies at the airport include **Alamo, Avis, Budget, Enterprise, Hertz, National,** and **Thrifty.** See chapter 38 for airline/car-rental website listings.

INFORMATION

For information on Mount Rushmore, contact the **Superintendent, Mount Rushmore National Memorial,** 13000 Hwy. 244, Building 31, Ste. 1, Keystone, SD 57751-0268 (✆ **605/574-2523;**

www.nps.gov/moru). For information about **Custer State Park,** contact the park at 13329 W. Hwy. 16A, Custer, SD 57730-9705 (✆ **605/255-4515;** www.custerstatepark.info). To get information about Wind Cave, contact the **Superintendent, Wind Cave National Park,** 26611 U.S. Hwy. 385, Hot Springs, SD 57747-9430 (✆ **605/745-4600;** www.nps.gov/wica). For details on Jewel Cave, contact the **Superintendent, Jewel Cave National Monument,** 11149 U.S. Hwy. 16, Building B12, Custer, SD 57730 (✆ **605/673-8300;** www.nps.gov/jeca). To get information about Crazy Horse, contact the **Crazy Horse Memorial,** Avenue of the Chiefs, Crazy Horse, SD 57730-9506 (✆ **605/673-4681;** www.crazyhorsememorial.org).

For information about the entire area, contact **South Dakota Tourism,** Capitol Lake Plaza, 711 E. Wells Ave., Pierre, SD 57501-3369 (✆ **800/SDAKOTA** [732-5682] or 605/773-3301; www.travelsd.com), or the **Black Hills Visitor Center,** north side of I-90 at exit 61, Rapid City, SD 57701 (✆ **605/355-3600;** www.blackhillsbadlands.com). Open 8am to 5pm.

SEASONS & CLIMATE

Summer days in the Black Hills are often sunny, with temperatures in the 80s (upper 20s–lower 30s Celsius), so a broad-brimmed hat and sunscreen are advised. Temperatures often drop rapidly after sunset, particularly in the mountains. In the fall, sunny skies and crisp temperatures can make for pleasant conditions, though snowstorms may occur as early as September at higher elevations. **Winter** daytime temperatures average 20° to 40°F (–7° to 4°C), and icy roads are common. Even in spring, weather can often be cold and wet.

2 Visiting Mount Rushmore National Memorial

Widely regarded as one of the man-made wonders of the world, Mount Rushmore is as much a work of art as it is an engineering marvel. Its creator, sculptor Gutzon Borglum, wanted to symbolize in stone the very spirit of a nation and, through four of its most revered leaders—George Washington, Thomas Jefferson, Abraham Lincoln, and Theodore Roosevelt—the country's birth, growth, preservation, and development. A half-century after its completion, Mount Rushmore remains one of America's most enduring icons.

In 1924, Borglum visited the Black Hills, looking for a place to carve a lasting legacy for himself and the nation. He hoped to locate a mountain with a suitable mass of stone, as well as a southeasterly exposure that would take advantage of the sun's rays for the greatest portion of the day. He decided on a rock outcropping named Mount Rushmore.

Inclement weather and lack of funds often stalled progress on the memorial. All told, the monument was completed at a cost of about $1 million during 6½ years of work over a 14-year period.

PLASTER PORTRAITS

Having studied under the master sculptor Auguste Rodin in Paris, Borglum understood art. When he arrived at Rushmore in 1925, Borglum was 58 years old and had already created a full roster of memorials to famous Americans, including Gen. Philip Sheridan, Gen. Robert E. Lee, and President Abraham Lincoln. Relying on his independent study of the four presidents, as well as life masks, paintings, photographs, and descriptions, Borglum created plaster sketches of the men. These sketches became the models for the memorial, and copies of each president's likeness were always on display on the mountain as a guide for the workmen.

Using a method of measurement called "pointing," Borglum taught his crews to measure the models, multiply by 12, and transfer the calibrations to the mountain carving. Using a simple ratio of 1:12, 1 inch on the model would equal 1 foot on the mountain.

Borglum and his crew used dynamite to carve more than 90% of the memorial. Powdermen became so skilled in the use of dynamite that they could grade the contours of the cheeks, chin, nose, and eyebrows to within inches of the finished surface. Skilled drillers used bumper bits and pneumatic drills to complete each portrait, leaving the surfaces of the presidents' faces as smooth as a concrete sidewalk. Up close, the pupils of each of the presidents' eyes are shallow recessions with projecting shafts of granite. From a distance, this shape makes the eyes sparkle. Several men were injured working on Mount Rushmore, but no one was killed during its construction.

As work neared completion in March 1941, Borglum died in a Chicago hospital at age 74. His son, Lincoln, carried on the work for another 6 months, but that work was interrupted by the winds of World War II. On October 31, as war clouds rumbled over Europe, the younger Borglum and his crew turned off the drills for good and removed the last scaffolding from the sculpture, returning the mountain to the eternal silence from which it had been awakened in 1927.

The efforts of the Borglums and their cadre of influential supporters resulted in a work of art for the ages. George Washington, the most prominent figure in the group, symbolizes the birth of a republic founded on the principle of individual liberty; Thomas Jefferson, who managed to fund the

Louisiana Purchase and balance the federal budget, signifies the growth of the United States; Abraham Lincoln, the Great Emancipator, imparts the strength of character responsible for preserving the union during the Civil War; and Theodore Roosevelt, the "Trust Buster" and friend of the common man, embodies the American spirit of independence, strength, and love of the wilderness.

AVOIDING THE CROWDS

Mount Rushmore is very popular, with peak visitation during June, July, and August. The best time to visit, though, is September and October, with April and May as alternatives. Although spring months can be wet and cold, the Hills' dry weather patterns make fall visits ideal. The varied mix of trees and plant life found in the high meadows and creek-carved canyons also makes the Black Hills a popular destination for avid "leaf-peepers."

If possible, view the sculpture at daybreak, when the golden orb of the sun crawls out of the morning mist of the badlands. Few vacationers are stirring at sunrise, making it among the best times to enjoy a more contemplative and less crowded experience. And there may be no finer setting for breakfast than the park's **Buffalo Dining Room,** which affords a commanding view of the presidents.

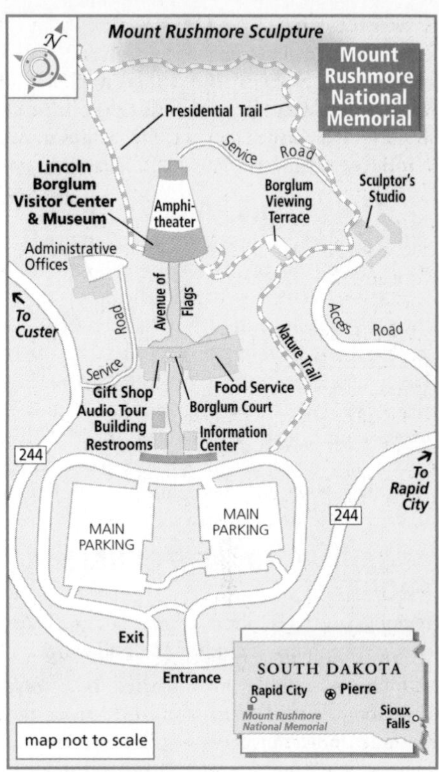

ESSENTIALS

VISITOR CENTER

Mount Rushmore is open 24 hours a day, year-round. The Information Center, just inside the entrance to the memorial, is open daily (except Christmas) from 8am to 5pm in winter, and 8am to 10pm in the summer. The Lincoln Borglum Museum maintains the same hours. This museum contains 5,200 square feet of exhibits, a bookstore operated by the Mount Rushmore History Association, and two 125-seat theaters. One interactive display features the dynamite blasting used to carve the mountain. This is an educational experience not to be missed. The museum also features some of the best views of the sculptures.

FEES

Mount Rushmore remains one of the few popular parks that have managed to avoid an entrance fee. However, you will have to pay a $10 fee for an annual **parking pass,** which funds the parking structure at the memorial. America the Beautiful Annual, Senior, and Access passes are not accepted for the parking fee, but because it's an annual ticket, you can come back later for no extra charge.

SPECIAL REGULATIONS & WARNINGS

Visitor access is prohibited within a restricted area around the Mount Rushmore sculpture. In other areas of the park, rock climbing and hiking are permitted.

Tips from the Park Superintendent

Mount Rushmore has undergone a great many changes recently, according to Superintendent Gerard Baker, who says, "The **Lincoln Borglum Museum** provides an interpretive experience unequaled in Western national park areas." Baker says that interactive displays depict sculptor Gutzon Borglum and his crew at work. There's also a large mural on the history of the United States that helps visitors understand why these four presidents were selected for the monument.

The **Presidential Trail** is a favorite of visitors, according to Baker, who adds, "This trail allows visitors to get close to the carving to better understand the scale of the sculpture." He adds that it also offers extraordinary views. "Our ranger program in the evening, with the lighting of the memorial, is a popular, patriotic experience," Baker says. "Cultural demonstrations at the Memorial depict the Native American way of life."

USEFUL PUBLICATIONS

The National Park Service has a number of informational pamphlets and other materials at the Information Center as you enter the memorial. A variety of books, maps, and videos are sold in the bookstore inside the Lincoln Borglum Museum.

EXPLORING THE PARK BY CAR

Although Mount Rushmore is best enjoyed on foot, many visitors overlook an impressive view of the sculpture that is best reached by car. After leaving the park's parking lot, turn right on S. Dak. 244 and proceed west then northwest around the memorial. Less than a mile from the parking lot, you'll discover the proud profile of George Washington in the upper-right corner of your windshield. While surveying the scene, keep an eye out for the Rocky Mountain goats that frequent the memorial and the Black Elk Wilderness Area to the west.

ORGANIZED TOURS & RANGER PROGRAMS

Mount Rushmore offers a variety of excellent interpretive programs, including the following:

- The 30-minute **Presidential Talk** leaves the Grand View Terrace six times a day in the summer. Join a ranger for a walk along the Presidential Trail to learn why Gutzon Borglum chose the four faces.
- The 15-minute **Studio Talk** (summer only) at the 1939 Sculptor's Studio examines techniques used by the artist to carve the memorial, as well as the original tools and plaster models employed in its construction.
- A 30-minute program at the **amphitheater** includes a talk and movie about the memorial, which coincides with its dramatic lighting ceremony. The program begins at 9pm from May through mid-August and at 8pm from mid-August through September. (The sculpture is illuminated nightly for 1–2 hr. year-round.)
- A 13-minute **film** narrated by noted reporter and South Dakotan Tom Brokaw is shown continuously at the visitor center and museum. Painting a broad overview of the memorial's history, construction, and subjects, the movie gives visitors a greater understanding of the colossal carving.

PARK ATTRACTIONS

The 1939 **Sculptor's Studio** played an important role in the final years of the construction of Mount Rushmore. Today the spacious studio and the artist's models it houses are integral to understanding how Borglum and his drill-dusty crew carved the sculpture from Black Hills granite.

Located on the walkway between the Concession Building and the Lincoln Borglum Museum, the Avenue of Flags features the flags of all U.S. states, territories, districts, and commonwealths, arranged in alphabetical order. The flags serve as a patriotic, colorful frame to Mount Rushmore.

DAY HIKES

The **Presidential Trail** begins near the main viewing terrace and proceeds west through the ponderosa pines to the talus slope at the base of the sculpture. The trail is .6 mile long, and a large portion of it is accessible to travelers with disabilities. The other portion consists of many steps, and depending on which direction a visitor walks, the trail can be a steep climb. The boardwalk circles the southeastern slope of the mountain before arriving at the Sculptor's Studio. In addition to decreasing crowding on the memorial's viewing terraces, this trail takes visitors into the woods and affords vantage points from which to view the four presidents.

A **Native American Heritage Village** is located on the first section of the Presidential Trail. The village illustrates the customs and traditions of local American Indian communities.

ROCK CLIMBING

Although climbing on the Mount Rushmore sculpture and within the restricted zone adjacent to the sculpture is prohibited, much of the park is open to climbing. The park is known as a world-class sports climbing area, with its massive spires and large rock faces nestled amid tall ponderosa pines.

3 Visiting Custer State Park

Custer State Park is one of the largest state parks in the Lower 48, and because of its unique historical, cultural, and natural resources, it attracts many visitors. If you want to avoid the crowds, the best times to visit are from May to mid-June and September through October. Spring offers a reawakening of the grasslands and the birth of cinnamon-colored bison calves, as well as elk, deer, antelope, and other wildlife. Fall beckons the change of colors in every canyon and ravine, as well as the bugling of bull elk as they search for mates. It's also the season for the annual buffalo roundup, held the last Monday in September, which draws nearly 11,000 spectators.

Creekside Lodge is open in the winter, and winter camping is available.

ESSENTIALS

VISITOR CENTERS

The Peter Norbeck Visitor Center, located between the State Game Lodge and the Coolidge General Store on U.S. 16A, offers brochures, interpretive exhibits, and a variety of educational items.

Crazy Horse Memorial: The "Fifth Face"

Known by locals as the "Fifth Face" in the Black Hills, the sculpture of the legendary Lakota Chief Crazy Horse began with the dedication of the work on June 3, 1948. More than a half-century later, work continues on what is expected to be the world's largest sculpture. The chief's nine-story-high face has been completed, and work has begun on carving the 22-story-high horse's head.

Begun by the late sculptor **Korczak Ziolkowski** (pronounced jewel-*cuff*-ski), and carried on by his widow, sons, and daughters, the mountain sculpture memorial is dedicated to all American Indians.

"My fellow chiefs and I would like the white man to know the red man has great heroes, too," Sioux Chief Henry Standing Bear wrote Ziolkowski in 1939, inviting him to create the mountain memorial. Seven years later, the sculptor agreed and began carving the colossal work.

When the sculpture is completed, Crazy Horse will sit astride his mount, pointing over his stallion's head to the sacred Black Hills. So large is the sculpture (563 ft. high) that all four presidents on Mount Rushmore would fit in Crazy Horse's head.

Visitors driving by the site on U.S. 16/385, 5 miles north of the town of Custer, might hear dynamite blasts, a surefire signal that work on the mountain carving is progressing. When night blasts are detonated, they tend to be among the most impressive events in the Black Hills.

In addition to viewing the carving in progress and watching an audiovisual display about the work, visitors may stop at the **Indian Museum of North America** at Crazy Horse, which is home to one of the most extensive collections of American Indian artifacts in the country. The museum's gift shop features authentic American Indian crafts.

For more information, go to the Crazy Horse Memorial website: **www.crazyhorsememorial.org**.

The Wildlife Station Visitor Center, located on the southeast part of the Wildlife Loop, has shade, information, exhibits, and educational items.

FEES

Entrance fees for 7 days are $6 per person or $15 per vehicle. Campsites with electricity are available for $22 per night in most of the park's eight campgrounds.

SPECIAL REGULATIONS & WARNINGS

The park's biggest attraction may be its 1,500 head of **bison.** Remember that all animals in the park are wild and can be dangerous. Bison are extremely fast and can be lethal if provoked, so give them plenty of space. Campers and hikers should never drink water from lakes, streams, or springs.

USEFUL PUBLICATIONS

The South Dakota Game, Fish and Parks Department provides a number of helpful brochures for the park, available at the Peter Norbeck Visitor Center. The park's newspaper, *Tatanka,* provides information on the park's resorts and activities. The newspaper is available at each park entrance station, the visitor center, and park headquarters.

EXPLORING THE PARK BY CAR

For a first-class excursion, pick any of the park's three scenic drives: the Needles Highway, the Wildlife Loop Road, or the Iron Mountain Road. When driving, it's important to keep an eye on the road and not your watch. Winding roads generally keep travel at 25 mph or less.

Be aware: Tunnels on Iron Mountain Road (U.S. 16A) are as low as 12 feet, 2 inches high and as narrow as 13 feet, 2 inches wide. Tunnels on the Needles Highway/Sylvan Lake Road (S. Dak. 87) are as low as 10 feet, 7 inches and as narrow as 8 feet, 4 inches.

NEEDLES HIGHWAY This is a mesmerizing 14-mile journey through pine and spruce forests, meadows surrounded by birch and quaking aspen, and giant granite spires that reach to the sky. Visitors pass the picturesque waters of Sylvan Lake, through tunnels, and near a unique rock formation called the Needle's Eye.

WILDLIFE LOOP ROAD This 18-mile drive takes you through open grasslands and pine-clad hills—an area that is home to most of the park's wildlife, including pronghorn, bison, white-tailed and mule deer, elk, coyote, begging wild burros, prairie dogs, eagles, hawks, and other birds. Stop by the Wildlife Station Visitor Center on the southeast part of the loop for information and exhibits. There are unpaved side roads off the Wildlife Loop Road that offer a quiet outdoor experience, in contrast to the main road in the summer. For example, one circle drive starts near the Wildlife Station Visitor Center. Take Park Road #3 (Oak Draw Rd.), then right on Park Road #4 (North Lame Johnny Rd.), right again on Park Road #5 (Swint Rd.), and one more right on Park Road #2 (Fisherman Flats Rd.), which will take you back to the Wildlife Loop Road and the Wildlife Station.

IRON MOUNTAIN ROAD Although only a portion of this scenic roadway rests in Custer State Park, it ranks as a must-see. The winding road runs between Mount Rushmore and the junction of U.S. 16A and S. Dak. 36. Along the route are wildfire exhibits, wooden "pig-tail" bridges, pullouts with wonderful views, and tunnels that frame the four presidents at Mount Rushmore.

DAY HIKES

Custer State Park is home to a wide variety of hiking experiences, ranging from short nature walks to backcountry treks. A 22-mile segment of the South Dakota Centennial Trail, the **Harney Peak Summit Trail,** extends through the park. The **Cathedral Spires Trail** is also a popular choice. Be aware that some trails are also open to mountain bikers and horseback riders.

4 Visiting Wind Cave National Park

For several centuries, American Indians have told stories of holes in the Black Hills through which the wind would blow and howl. But the first recorded discovery of Wind Cave came in 1881, when brothers Jesse and Tom Bingham were lured to the cave by a whistling noise. As the legend goes, the wind was rushing from the cave entrance with such force that it blew Tom's hat right off his head.

A few days later, when Jesse returned to the cave to show this phenomenon to friends, he was surprised to find that the wind had shifted directions and his hat was sucked into the cave. A hundred years later, we know that the direction of the wind is related to the difference in atmospheric pressure between the cave and the surface.

J. D. McDonald was the first person to attempt to establish a tourist attraction at Wind Cave, complete with stagecoach transportation, a hotel, and a gift shop. He did this primarily because there were no valuable mineral deposits in the cave to mine. But "ownership" of the cave came into question, and the matter entered a courtroom. The Department of the Interior decided in December 1899 that no party had a claim to Wind Cave. In 1901, the department withdrew all the land around the cave from homesteading.

On January 9, 1903, President Theodore Roosevelt signed the bill that established Wind Cave as what is now America's seventh national park, and the first created to protect the underground resources of a cave. In 1913 and 1914, the American Bison Society assisted in reestablishing a bison herd at Wind Cave, through the donation of 14 head from the New York Zoological Society. Also arriving in the park were 21 elk from Wyoming and 13 pronghorn antelope from Alberta, Canada. Today Wind Cave is home to 400 bison, as well as large herds of elk and pronghorn.

AVOIDING THE CROWDS

With more than 28,000 acres, two paved highways, two all-weather gravel roads, 30 miles of excellent trails, backcountry camping, and plenty of room to roam, avoiding the crowds in Wind Cave National Park is a cinch.

Tips from an Insider

Former Wind Cave National Park Superintendent Jimmy Taylor loves this park.

"This is truly an amazing park," says Taylor. "You can see and hear wildlife here. We have 800 to 900 head of elk, more than 300 bison, 50 antelope, two highways, and two all-weather gravel roads that make this park very accessible and suitable to the family sedan."

Wind Cave is "an intimate park" where road-weary travelers can put the brakes on and enjoy plant and animal life at its best, Taylor says. Visitors often settle back and just watch prairie dogs building their "towns" or bison grazing on the prairie grasses. In fall, Taylor says there's nothing quite like the sound of a lonely bull elk bugling from a rocky ridge in the park.

And beneath this remarkable place, says Taylor, is an underground wilderness whose depths have only been guessed at, and whose complexity we are only beginning to understand.

"Imagine," he says, "only a few hundred feet underground there are spaces people have never seen, and perhaps may never see. Think that every time someone crawls through a hole or peeks into the next opening, they may literally be the first person in the history of mankind who has ever seen it."

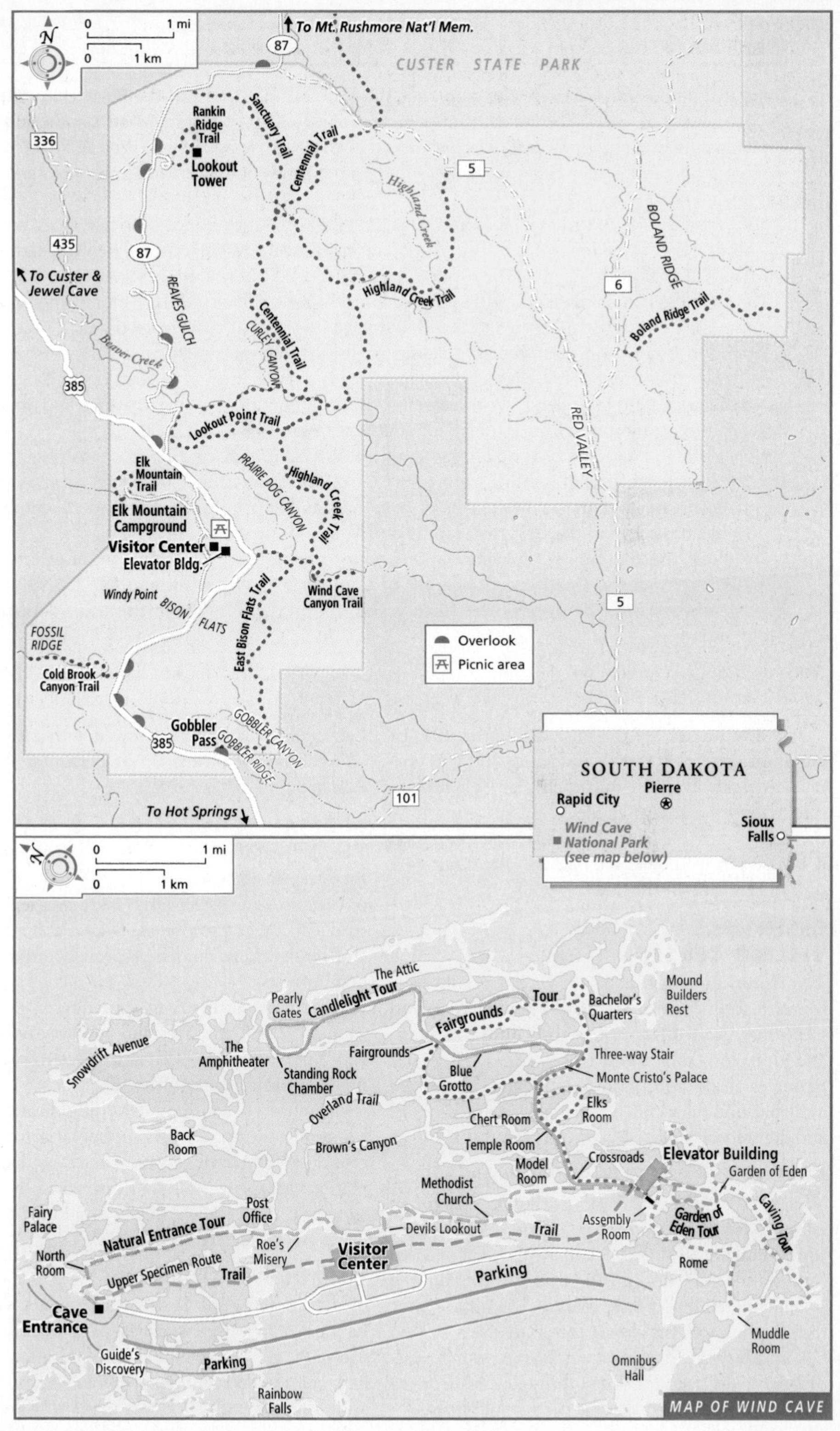
To Mt. Rushmore Nat'l Mem.
CUSTER STATE PARK
Rankin Ridge Trail
Lookout Tower
Sanctuary Trail
Centennial Trail
Highland Creek
Highland Creek Trail
BOLAND RIDGE
Boland Ridge Trail
To Custer & Jewel Cave
REAVES GULCH
Beaver Creek
Centennial Trail
CURLEY CANYON
Lookout Point Trail
RED VALLEY
PRAIRIE DOG CANYON
Highland Creek Trail
Elk Mountain Trail
Elk Mountain Campground
Visitor Center
Elevator Bldg.
Windy Point
BISON FLATS
East Bison Flats Trail
Wind Cave Canyon Trail
FOSSIL RIDGE
Cold Brook Canyon Trail
Overlook
Picnic area
Gobbler Pass
GOBBLER CANYON
GOBBLER RIDGE
To Hot Springs
SOUTH DAKOTA
Pierre
Rapid City
Wind Cave National Park (see map below)
Sioux Falls
0 1 mi
0 1 km
The Attic
Pearly Gates
Candlelight Tour
Tour
Bachelor's Quarters
Mound Builders Rest
Fairgrounds
Snowdrift Avenue
The Amphitheater
Fairgrounds
Three-way Stair
Standing Rock Chamber
Blue Grotto
Monte Cristo's Palace
Overland Trail
Elks Room
Chert Room
Back Room
Brown's Canyon
Temple Room
Crossroads
Elevator Building
Model Room
Garden of Eden
Methodist Church
Fairy Palace
Post Office
Natural Entrance Tour
Devils Lookout
Trail
Assembly Room
Garden of Eden Tour
Caving Tour
North Room
Roe's Misery
Upper Specimen Route
Trail
Visitor Center
Parking
Rome
Cave Entrance
Guide's Discovery
Parking
Muddle Room
Omnibus Hall
Rainbow Falls
MAP OF WIND CAVE

Deadwood: The Wildest & Woolliest Town in the West

There was a time when it wasn't safe to walk the cobblestone streets of the Black Hills' original Sin City. But that was a thousand gunfights and barroom brawls ago, when **Deadwood** was known as the wildest, wickedest, woolliest town in the West. It was where Wild Bill Hickok was gunned down and where Calamity Jane Canary claimed she could outdrink, outswear, and outspit any man.

Today the sounds of slot machines and streetside barkers have replaced the gunshots, crunching blows, and rowdiness of a century ago, when miners, gamblers, and painted ladies all searched for their pots of gold. They found gold, of course, but seldom retained it.

The city's merchants, bankers, and saloonkeepers, however, invested their money in beautiful Victorian buildings and residences that today stand as testament to a richer time.

Although Deadwood was labeled "a disaster" by historic preservation officials just over a decade ago, the town is still alive and kicking. This is due, to a great extent, to limited-stakes gambling, approved by South Dakota voters in 1989 to generate money to restore and preserve this mile-high community. The $5 maximum bet was raised to $100 in 2000.

Now state and national historic preservation officials call Deadwood's metamorphosis "a miracle." Brick streets, period lighting, and colorful trolleys greet visitors, who spend hours ducking in doorways and trying their luck in over 80 gambling halls. In addition to gambling, Deadwood has some of the best restaurants and hotels in the state.

For more information on accommodations, tours, museums, attractions, special events, and gambling, contact the **Deadwood Chamber of Commerce & Visitor Bureau (© 800/999-1876;** www.deadwood.org), or stop by the History and Information Center in the train depot at 3 Siever St.

July and August are the busiest months. Annual visitation averages 800,000, and about 100,000 people participate in a cave tour each year. When planning daily itineraries, include Wind Cave in either the early morning or late afternoon, when visitation is lowest and wildlife is most active. Buy your cave tour tickets early in the day.

ESSENTIALS

VISITOR CENTER

The visitor center (off U.S. 385) is open daily year-round (except New Year's Day, Thanksgiving, and Christmas) and offers books, brochures, exhibits, and video programs about the cave and other park resources. Cave tour information and tickets are available, and schedules of activities, including talks and nature walks, are posted.

FEES & PERMITS

Wind Cave National Park does not charge an entrance fee. It does, however, charge a fee for **cave tours,** ranging from $7 ($3.50 with a Senior Pass) for a simple guided tour ($3.50–$4.50 for children 6–16, children under 6 are free) to $23 for a 4-hour introduction to basic caving techniques.

Camping in Elk Mountain Campground costs $12 per night from mid-May through mid-September, and $6 per night during the rest of its season; all camping is on a first-come, first-served basis. Backcountry camping is allowed with a free **permit,** which must be picked up in person at the visitor center.

SPECIAL REGULATIONS & WARNINGS

The danger of wildfire is high year-round. Build fires only in the campground and only in fire grills or camp stoves. Never leave a fire unattended. Off-road driving is prohibited. Watch for rattlesnakes and black widow spiders, especially around prairie dog burrows.

Cave tour pathways may be uneven or wet and slippery. Watch your step and wear low-heeled, non-slip shoes. A jacket, sweater, or sweatshirt is recommended for protection from the cave's 53°F (12°C) temperature. If you have breathing, heart, or walking problems, or are claustrophobic, consult with a ranger before taking a tour. The cave's delicate formations are easily broken or discolored by skin oils, so please don't touch them. Smoking, food, and drink are prohibited in the cave.

USEFUL PUBLICATIONS

The National Park Service publishes a variety of handouts on topics such as park history, hiking, camping, geology, wildlife, bird life, prairie grasses and ecosystems, and environmental concerns. In addition, the park produces *Passages,* a free visitor newspaper that is available at the visitor center.

ORGANIZED CAVE TOURS

The park offers five different cave tours during the summer (a total of 30 tours per day) and one tour the remainder of the year. Adventurous cavers should consider the two tours limited to 10 people each; these will definitely take them away from the crowds.

THE GARDEN OF EDEN TOUR Entering and leaving Wind Cave by an elevator, this 1-hour tour takes participants past representative cave features. It's the park's least strenuous tour, climbing 150 stairs.

NATURAL ENTRANCE TOUR Beginning at the walk-in entrance to the cave and leaving by elevator, this moderately strenuous 75-minute tour has 300 stairs (though most of these are down) and leads visitors through the middle of the cave, with an abundance of "boxwork"—thin blades of calcite that project from the cave's walls and ceiling in a honeycomb pattern.

FAIRGROUNDS TOUR This includes some of the larger rooms found in the developed area of the cave. Participants view many cave formations, including boxwork. The tour enters and exits by elevator. This moderately strenuous excursion has 450 stairs and lasts 90 minutes.

CANDLELIGHT TOUR This is one of the most popular tours, especially for children 8 and over. Trekking through a less-developed, unlighted section of the cave, tour participants carry a candle bucket and experience the cave by candlelight. Shoes with nonslip soles are required; no sandals are allowed. This tour is limited to 10 people (minimum age is 8). This strenuous tour covers 1 mile of rugged trail and lasts 2 hours. Reservations, available no more than 1 month before the tour, are strongly advised (✆ **605/745-4600**).

WILD CAVE TOUR You can also explore Wind Cave away from the established trails. On this 4-hour adventure, visitors are introduced to basic, safe caving practices. You need to wear old clothes and gloves, since much of the tour is spent crawling. Long pants, long-sleeve shirts, and sturdy, lace-up boots or shoes with nonslip soles are a must. The park provides hard hats, lights, and kneepads. Do not bring jewelry, watches, or other valuables. This tour is limited to 10 people and the minimum age is 16. (Signed consent forms from a parent or guardian are required for 16- and 17-year-olds.) Reservations, which are available 1 month before the tour, are required (✆ **605/745-4600**).

TOURS FOR PEOPLE WITH DISABILITIES The visitor center and the cave are accessible to people with limited mobility. Call (✆ **605/745-4600**) to make arrangements or inquire about a special tour at the information desk. Some areas of the cave are accessible to wheelchairs. Fees are charged for special services.

EXPLORING THE PARK BY CAR

Wind Cave National Park is not just about a cave. The rolling prairies of western South Dakota run smack into the ponderosa pine forests of the Black Hills in the park, and its roadways provide access to some of the best **wildlife-viewing** opportunities in the region. Bison, pronghorn, elk, and other wildlife abound in this rugged preserve, and you'll be able to see many of them as you drive down through Custer State Park on S. Dak. 87 to Wind Cave. The combination of Wind Cave National Park and the adjoining Custer State Park presents a most attractive introduction to the Black Hills. Several scenic roadways lead through the Black Hills to Wind Cave. Roadside sightseers will find the Wildlife Loop Road, Iron Mountain Road, and Needles Highway particularly enjoyable. All of these are in Custer State Park, just north of Wind Cave National Park, and are described in the preceding section.

Warning: Tunnels on Iron Mountain Road (U.S. 16A) are 12 feet, 2 inches high and 13 feet, 2 inches wide. Tunnels on the Needles Highway/Sylvan Lake Road (S. Dak. 87) are as low as 10 feet, 7 inches and as narrow as 8 feet, 4 inches.

RANGER PROGRAMS

Park rangers provide a number of talks and programs at Wind Cave. Topics range from local wildlife, plants, and geology to area history and spelunking and cave surveying. Campfire programs are conducted most evenings during the summer. There is a 2-hour ranger-guided prairie hike daily in the morning during the summer. Check with the visitor center for times and locations.

DAY HIKES

More than 30 miles of trails crisscross the park's backcountry. Several can be combined to create round-trip hikes, or you may want to leave the trails and hike a ridgeline, explore a canyon, or trek across an open prairie bordered by ponderosa pine. Backcountry camping is permitted in the northwestern portion of the park with a free permit, available at the visitor center or either of the Centennial trail heads.

Park handouts also provide information on more than a half-dozen other trails, ranging from 1.4 miles to 8.6 miles.

Centennial Trail Wind Cave provides the southern terminus for the 110-mile-long Centennial Trail, built in honor of South Dakota's centennial in 1989. The trail leads through the heart of the Black Hills before ending at Bear Butte State Park near

Sturgis. A 6-mile section of the Centennial Trail is in the park, where it crosses the prairie, climbs the foothills and forested ridges, and also provides access to the wetter, riparian habitat of Beaver Creek. 6 miles one-way. Moderate. Access: Along S. Dak. 87, 3/4 mile north of its intersection with U.S. 385.

Elk Mountain Nature Trail This interpretive trail explores an ecotone, or meeting zone, where prairie and forest converge. Booklets are available at the trail head. .5 mile one-way. Easy. Access: Elk Mountain Campground.

Rankin Ridge Nature Trail This loop trail leads to the highest point in the park and is one of Wind Cave's most popular. You can stop at the lookout tower, about halfway around the loop. Booklets are available at the trail head. .75 mile RT. Moderate. Access: Rankin Ridge parking lot.

5 Visiting Jewel Cave National Monument

The exploration of Jewel Cave began in about 1900, when two South Dakota prospectors, Frank and Albert Michaud, and a companion, Charles Bush, happened to hear wind rushing through a hole in the rocks in Hell Canyon. After enlarging the hole, they discovered a cave full of sparkling crystals. The entrepreneurs filed a mining claim on the "Jewel Lode," but they found no valuable minerals, so they attempted to turn the cave into a tourist attraction. The business was never a success, but the cave did attract attention, and in 1908, President Theodore Roosevelt established Jewel Cave National Monument to protect this natural wonder.

A half-century later, exploration of the cave intensified. Led by the husband and wife team of Herb and Jan Conn, spelunkers explored and mapped miles of passageways.

When first asked to consider a trek below the surface, the Conns were reluctant. But after their first excursion into the underworld, the couple were hooked. In more than 2 decades of spelunking in Jewel Cave, the Conns logged 708 trips into the cave and 6,000 hours of exploration and mapping. Their efforts proved that Jewel Cave was among the most extensive and complex cave ecosystems in the world, filled with scenic and scientific wonders.

The explorers discovered chambers with exquisite calcite crystals and other rare specimens. One room mapped by the Conns, the Formation Room, is now a highlight of the Park Service tours. They also found rooms as large as 150 feet by 200 feet, passageways as long as 3,200 feet, and a place where the cave wind blows at speeds of 32 miles per hour. In 1980, after discovering more than 65 miles of passageways, the Conns retired, and a new generation of spelunkers have pushed the known boundaries of the cave to well over 145 miles.

When the Conns said, "We are still just standing on the threshold," they could not have known how accurate they were. Studies by the U.S. Geological Survey have since attempted to determine the number of passageways in the cave by measuring the volume of air leaving or entering the cave, depending on the barometric pressure outside. Results indicate that known passageways at Jewel Cave constitute less than 5% of what actually exists in the quiet darkness below the Black Hills.

Only Mammoth Cave in Kentucky is longer than Jewel Cave. More recent explorations of Jewel Cave have determined it is the second-longest cave system in the U.S.

Known for its calcite nailhead and dogtooth spar crystal, Jewel Cave is home to a variety of rare and unusual cave formations. The Cave's hydromagnesite "balloons," fragile silvery bubbles that look as if they might pop any minute, have been found in just a handful of other caves. Scintillites, reddish rocks coated with sparkling clear quartz crystals, were unknown until they were discovered in Jewel Cave. One particularly intriguing mineral, gypsum, combines with time and the ceaseless presence of seeping water to assume the shapes of flowers, needles, spiders, and cottony beards that sway from the heat of an explorer's lamp.

AVOIDING THE CROWDS

The highest visitation at Jewel Cave occurs June through August. With 1,274 acres above the surface and annual visitation of approximately 140,000, Jewel Cave is rarely overcrowded, even at the height of the season. However, because space on some tours is limited and more than 90,000 visitors participate in a cave tour annually, you should anticipate a wait to enter the cave. If you want to keep your wait to a minimum, reservations are recommended.

ESSENTIALS

VISITOR CENTER

The visitor center has books and brochures, and park rangers can assist travelers in planning their visit, pointing out interpretive programs, and answering questions about the park's cultural, historical, and geologic resources. Up-to-date cave information and tour tickets are available at the center, which is open daily year-round, except for Thanksgiving, December 25, and January 1.

FEES

There is no entry fee for the national monument, but there is a charge for **cave tours.** The Scenic and Lantern tours cost $8 ($4 for children ages 6–16);

the Discovery tour is $4 for adults and no charge for children under 16; the Wild Caving tour is $27. **Reservations** can be made by calling ✆ **605/673-8300.** Holders of the National Park Pass and their immediate families can take the Discovery tour free of charge, but not the other tours. Holders of the Senior Pass and Golden Access Pass and up to three family members can take the Discovery tour with no charge. If the holder wishes to take the Scenic, Lantern, or Wild Caving tour, only the cardholder may receive the benefit of a half-price tour.

SPECIAL REGULATIONS & WARNINGS

Low-heeled, rubber-soled shoes are highly recommended because trails can be slippery; some stair-climbing is required on each tour. A jacket, sweater, or sweatshirt will keep you comfortable in the 49°F (9°C) year-round temperature of the cave. Persons with respiratory or heart problems or who have been recently hospitalized, have lower joint problems, or have a fear of heights or confined spaces should talk with a park ranger before selecting a tour. Damaging or even touching cave formations is prohibited because of the fragile and irreplaceable nature of the formations. Pets and smoking are not allowed in the cave. Cameras are permitted on cave tours, but tripods are not.

USEFUL PUBLICATIONS

The National Park Service publishes brochures covering a variety of topics, such as bats, birds, surface trails, spelunking tours, and the history and exploration of the cave. Also refer to the park website at **www.nps.gov/jeca**.

ORGANIZED CAVE TOURS

Visitors can have an adventure in Jewel Cave by taking any of the park's ranger-guided tours. Tickets for the Scenic Tour, Lantern Tour, or Wild Caving Tour may be purchased by reservation or at the visitor center. Reservations for the Spelunking Tour are strongly encouraged. Call ✆ **605/673-8300,** ext. 0, for advance reservations. It's also a good idea to contact the monument before visiting to determine whether special hours, activities, or tour schedules are being observed.

SCENIC TOUR This ½-mile, 80-minute tour visits chambers decorated with calcite crystals and colorful stalactites, stalagmites, and draperies. The loop tour begins at the visitor center with an elevator ride into the cave. Participants take a paved, lighted path and climb up and down more than 700 stairs on this moderately strenuous journey into the underground. The tour, which is offered year-round, is conducted several times daily from May to September and is limited to 30 persons.

LANTERN TOUR This ½-mile, 105-minute tour follows in the footsteps of early Jewel Cave explorers. Tour participants see the cave's calcite-coated passageways lighted by old-style oil lanterns. This round-trip tour starts at the monument's historic cabin. The cave tour is moderately strenuous, with many steep stairs, and requires much bending and stooping. Long pants and sturdy, closed-toe shoes are highly recommended. The tour is offered several times daily from mid-June through Labor Day and is limited to 20 persons. (Definitely call ahead to find out if it will be offered when you are in the area.) Children under age 6 are not allowed.

WILD CAVING TOUR This physically and mentally challenging nearly ¾-mile, 3- to 4-hour tour gives participants a taste of modern-day cave crawling in a wild, undeveloped portion of Jewel Cave. The round-trip tour begins at the visitor center with an elevator ride into the cave. Old clothes and gloves are recommended; kneepads and ankle-high laced boots with lug soles are required. The park supplies hard hats and headlamps. To qualify for the tour, participants are required to crawl through an 8½-by-24-inch concrete block tunnel. This tour is offered

Tips from the Chief of Interpretation

"Jewel Cave is one of the most structurally complex caves in the world and it is still being explored," according to Chief of Interpretation Bradley Block. "This is not a cave that has been fully mapped, and it's probable that it will not be fully explored in any of our lifetimes." He adds, "To this point, we have been very successful in developing a visitor experience that allows people to enjoy the cave in a relatively pristine state."

For travelers with children over 6, Block recommends the "adventurous experience" of a **Lantern Tour** into the cave, the park's Junior Ranger Program, and the variety of surface programs that augment the cave tours.

Fall, winter, and spring are ideal times to visit the caves, Block says. Even with arctic blasts on the surface, temperatures within the cave are constant at 49°F (9°C), with humidity averaging 98%. "In the middle of winter, it can actually be quite pleasant in the cave," says Block.

Guided Tours of Jewel Cave

A number of charter bus park tours and guide services are available. **Gray Line of the Black Hills,** 1600 E. St. Patrick St., Rapid City, SD 57703 (© **800/456-4461** or 605/342-4461; www.blackhillsgrayline.com), offers daily bus tours of the area. **Golden Circle Tours Inc.,** P.O. Box 454, Custer, SD 57730 (© **605/673-4349;** www.goldencircletours.com), gives guided van tours of the area. Its office is located on U.S. 16A.

daily (12:30pm) from mid-June through mid-August; the limit is five persons (here's your chance to avoid the crowds). Children under 16 are not allowed; 16- and 17-year-olds must have a parent or guardian's written permission. You can (and should) reserve your place on a tour in advance by calling © **605/673-8300**.

JEWEL CAVE DISCOVERY For those with little time or limited physical abilities, this tour may be for you. You will visit one room of the cave in the 20-minute tour and learn Jewel Cave's natural and cultural histories. The cave is entered and exited by elevator and involves up to 15 steps. The entrance is wheelchair accessible.

RANGER PROGRAMS

In addition to the cave tours (see above), during the summer season, a number of special interpretive programs take place at the visitor center, including ranger talks, demonstrations, and guided walks. Check at the visitor center for specifics.

DAY HIKES

Travelers to Jewel Cave should also take time to experience life aboveground by taking a nature hike (there are two hiking trails), enjoying a picnic, or searching out the plants and animals that inhabit the rugged hills and canyon country of the Black Hills.

In the stillness of the ponderosa pine forest that blankets the park are mule deer, white-tailed deer, elk, porcupines, coyote, squirrels and chipmunks, and several species of birds, including golden eagles and hawks. Plants of both the prairie and the hills grow here, and in summer, wildflowers paint the landscape.

A huge wildfire burned about 90% of the monument's land area in August 2000, and visitors today will still see evidence of what is called the Jasper Fire, ranging from dead or damaged trees to plants that have come back since the blaze. Trail sections are occasionally closed on windy days if rangers think there is danger of burn-damaged trees falling. Check with the visitor center or a ranger for current conditions.

Canyons Trail This loop trail provides views of the limestone palisades of Hell Canyon and Lithograph Canyon, and offers a chance of seeing some of the deer, birds, and wildflowers that live in the ponderosa pine forest through which the trail winds. If you want to experience a part of the Canyon Trail without going the entire distance, you might try the 1.5-mile round-trip between the visitor center and the historic area of the cave. 3.5 miles RT. Easy to moderate. Access: Visitor center.

Walk on the Roof While visiting the "roof" of Jewel Cave on this self-guided interpretive walk, you'll learn how the monument's surface and subsurface resources interact. Interpretive trail guides for this walk are available at the information desk in the visitor center. .25 mile RT. Easy. Access: Visitor center.

6 Other Sports & Activities

AERIAL TOURS If you want to see the Black Hills from above, contact **Black Hills Balloons,** P.O. Box 210, Custer, SD 57730 (© **605/673-2520;** www.blackhillsballoons.com), which offers flights over the Black Hills, as well as Badlands National Park and Devils Tower National Monument, year-round.

BIKING The Black Hills region has more than 6,000 miles of fire trails, logging roads, and other undeveloped roads, and it is becoming a top spot for mountain biking. Custer State Park is a prime spot for mountain biking—most park trails and roads are open to bikers. (The Legion Lake Resort in Custer State Park rents mountain bikes; see the complete listing under "Where to Stay," below.)

FISHING Rainbow trout are stocked at Horsethief Lake, below Mount Rushmore, where there is a Forest Service campground (see "Camping," below). Center and Stockade lakes in Custer State Park are also good fishing spots. Many streams, including Grizzly Bear Creek, behind Mount Rushmore, have good fishing for brook trout. You'll need a **fishing license,** available at sporting-goods stores and many convenience stores.

HORSE-PACKING TRIPS Several companies offer guided trail rides through the backcountry of the Black Hills, including family-run **Dakota Badland Outfitters,** P.O. Box 85, Custer, SD 57730 (© **605/574-3412;** www.ridesouthdakota.com). Call for rates, activities, and reservations.

SNOWMOBILING The upper Black Hills have hundreds of miles of groomed snowmobile trails, and many guest ranches and resorts, such as Deadwood Gulch Resort (see "Where to Stay," below), rent snowmobiles to their guests. You can get more information on trails and companies that rent snowmobiles from South Dakota Tourism (see "Information," earlier in this chapter).

7 Camping

Although there are no campgrounds within the boundaries of Mount Rushmore National Memorial or Jewel Cave National Monument, there are several in Custer State Park and another in Wind Cave National Park, plus those in the Black Hills National Forest and privately operated campgrounds. Many commercial campgrounds offer free shuttle services, nightly entertainment, pools, convenience stores, and horseback riding. Reservations are recommended. Choice spots are often filled by midmorning, so arriving at popular campgrounds early in the day is advised.

For more information on camping opportunities, contact South Dakota Tourism (see "Information," earlier in this chapter). For information on National Forest Service campgrounds, contact the **Forest Supervisor,** Black Hills National Forest, 1019 N. 5th St., Custer, SD 57730 (✆ **605/673-9200;** www.fs.fed.us/r2/blackhills), or contact **Forest Recreation Management, Inc.,** 12620 Hwy. 244, Hill City, SD 57745 (✆ **605/574-2525**).

INSIDE WIND CAVE NATIONAL PARK

In the pine forests ½ mile north of the park visitor center, **Elk Mountain Campground** has shady sites suitable for tents and recreational vehicles. The campground fee is $12 per night per site mid-May through mid-September and $6 per night per site the remainder of its season, when water is turned off. Park rangers give campfire programs at the amphitheater in the summer. **Backcountry camping** is also permitted (contact the park office for details), and backcountry campers are encouraged to practice low-impact camping and hiking techniques.

INSIDE CUSTER STATE PARK

Campgrounds here require park entrance fees as well as camping fees.

Each campsite has a gravel or paved camping pad, drinking water and showers, fire grates, and a picnic table, and all campgrounds but Center Lake have flush toilets. About 270 campsites and 50 new camper cabins throughout the park may be reserved beginning in January, while other sites are available on a first-come, first-served basis. Campsites range from modern to primitive. There is electricity at campgrounds throughout the park.

For information and reservations, contact **Custer State Park,** 13329 W. Hwy. 16A, Custer, SD 57730 (✆ **800/710-2267** or 605/255-4515), or www.campsd.com.

Blue Bell Campground is in a mature stand of ponderosa pine near French Creek, not far from the site where Lt. Col. George Armstrong Custer and his 7th Cavalry discovered gold in 1874. It offers easy access to the Wildlife Loop Road, horseback riding, stream fishing, and fabulous hiking.

Game Lodge Campground was designed for larger RVs, but tent campers will find cool, shady sites and an occasional bison along the banks of Grace Coolidge Creek. It's near the park's Peter Norbeck Visitor Center and the State Game Lodge.

Legion Lake Campground is centrally located in Custer State Park, with fishing, boating, and hiking opportunities right at your doorstep. Historic sites are within walking distance, as is the Legion Lake Lodge across the highway.

You'd probably have to camp in Yosemite Valley to get a better view than the one at **Sylvan Lake Campground.** This mountain retreat is just off the incredible Needles Highway, near 7,242-foot **Harney Peak,** the highest point between the Rockies in the west and the Swiss Alps in the east, and offers the best Black Hills hiking and mountain climbing. Its campsites fill quickly, so make your reservations early; all sites are reservable.

The park's other three campgrounds are **Center Lake,** 5 miles northeast of the junction of U.S. 16A and S. Dak. 87; Grace Coolidge, 13 miles east of Custer on U.S. 16A; and **Stockade Lake,** just inside the park's western boundary on U.S. 16A.

Reservations are accepted at all campgrounds and camper cabins except Center Lake, which is all first come, first served.

INSIDE THE BLACK HILLS NATIONAL FOREST

You can make **National Forest camping reservations** by calling ✆ **877/444-6777** or online at www.reserveusa.com. Below are just two of 19 campgrounds in the Black Hills National Forest of South Dakota and Wyoming.

Horsethief Lake Campground, a mile west of Mount Rushmore, offers scenic sites adjacent to picturesque Horsethief Lake. At a 5,000-foot elevation, the campground has 28 sites for tents, travel trailers, and RVs; eight sites are for tents only. Sites not reserved (50% can be reserved) fill quickly, so you need to claim yours early in the day.

Roubaix Lake Campground, off U.S. 385 on FDR 255, is nestled in a ponderosa pine forest next

Campground	Total Sites	RV Hookups	Dump Station	Toilets	Drinking Water
Inside Badlands National Park (no open fires allowed)					
Cedar Pass	96	No	Yes	Yes	Yes
Sage Creek	15	No	No	Yes	No
Near Badlands National Park					
Badlands Ranch and Resort	35	Yes	No	Yes	Yes
Inside Wind Cave National Park					
Elk Mountain	75	No	No	Yes	Yes
Inside Custer State Park					
Blue Bell	30	No	No	Yes	Yes
Center Lake	71	No	No	Yes	Yes
Game Lodge	55	No	Yes	Yes	Yes
Grace Coolidge	26	No	No	Yes	Yes
Legion Lake	25	No	No	Yes	Yes
Stockade Lake	64	No	No	Yes	Yes
Sylvan Lake	38	No	No	Yes	Yes
Inside Black Hills National Forest					
Horsethief Lake	36	No	No	Yes	Yes
Roubaix	53	No	No	Yes	Yes
Private Campgrounds in the Black Hills					
American Presidents	70	Yes	No	Yes	Yes
Big Pine	90	Yes	Yes	Yes	Yes
Miners	28	Yes	No	Yes	Yes
Mount Rushmore KOA	500	Yes	Yes	Yes	Yes
Rapid City KOA	255	Yes	Yes	Yes	Yes
Whistler Gulch	127	Yes	Yes	Yes	Yes

*Campground opening and closing dates can vary from year to year.

to scenic Roubaix Lake, which offers great fishing and swimming at a 5,500-foot elevation. Spaces fill fast; some can be reserved.

COMMERCIAL CAMPGROUNDS

A variety of private campgrounds provide all the usual RV hookups and other services.

American Presidents Resort, 1 mile east of Custer on Hwy. 16A, P.O. Box 446, Custer, SD 57730 (✆ **605/673-3373;** www.presidentsresort.com), is a perfect base for touring the southern Black Hills. The campground's 40-by-60-foot heated pool and Jacuzzi are popular, as are its miniature golf and horseshoes. The campground, with 70 sites, has a store and fishing nearby. A 10% discount is offered on reservations made before May 15. Also available are 45 full-service cabins, some with kitchens, that sleep from two to eight people and a 15-unit motel (call for rates).

Big Pine Campground, R.R. 1, P.O. Box 52, Custer, SD 57730 (✆ **800/235-3981** for reservations, or 605/673-4054; www.bigpinecampground.com), secluded from traffic noises, offers level, naturally shaded sites plus fireplaces and wood, a store, game room, playground, hiking, and horseshoes.

Miners RV Park, P.O. Box 157, Keystone, SD 57751 (✆ **800/727-2421** or 605/666-4638; www.minersresort.com), in the heart of the former mining town of Keystone, is close to numerous attractions and only a stone's throw from Mount Rushmore National Memorial. The campground and its adjacent 43-unit motel offer cool shade and a gurgling brook, as well as a store, gas, ice, gifts, restaurant, heated pool, and hot tub. Take a fun walk down Keystone's Main Street while you're here.

Mount Rushmore KOA, P.O. Box 295, Hill City, SD 57745 (✆ **800/562-8503;** www.mtrushmorekoa.com), part of the Palmer Gulch Resort, is among the best campgrounds in the region. With 500 sites and 55 Kamping Kabins, two pools and spas, a water

Showers	Grills	Fire Pits/ Laundry	Reserve	Fees	Open*
No	No	No	No	$10	Year-round
No	No	No	No	Free	Year-round
Yes	Yes	Yes	Yes	$25	Year-round
No	Yes	No	No	$6–$12	Year-round
Yes	Yes	Yes	Yes	$18–$22	May 1–Oct 1
Yes	Yes	No	No	$16	May 1–Sept 15
Yes	Yes	Yes	Yes	$18–$22	May 1–Nov 1
Yes	Yes	No	No	$18–$22	May 1–Oct 1
Yes	Yes	No	Yes	$18	May 1–Sept 15
Yes	Yes	No	Yes	$18–$22	May 1–Sept 5
Yes	Yes	Yes	Yes	$18–$22	May 1–Sept 15
No	Yes	No	Yes	$23	May 24–Sept 13
No	Yes	No	Yes	$19	Year-round
Yes	Yes	Yes	Yes	$33–$44	Apr 1–Nov 30
Yes	Yes	Yes	Yes	$21–$31	May 1–Oct 1
Yes	Yes	Yes	Yes	$34–$39	Apr 15–Oct 15
Yes	Yes	Yes	Yes	$29–$70	May 1–Oct 1
Yes	Yes	Yes	Yes	$33–$73	Apr 15–Oct 15
Yes	Yes	Yes	Yes	$20–$50	May 1–Sept 30

slide, American Indian dancers, movies, miniature golf, fishing, hayrides, a restaurant, tours, and car rentals, this is what many commercial campgrounds want to be when they grow up.

Rapid City KOA, P.O. Box 2592, Rapid City, SD 57709 (✆ **800/KOA-8504** [562-8504] or 605/348-2111; www.rapidcitykoa.com), is on Rapid City's eastern flank. This large KOA offers a free pancake breakfast and a grand pool and spa. Bus tours and car rentals are available, and shopping, sightseeing, and Rushmore Plaza Civic Center are nearby.

Whistler Gulch Campground, 235 Cliff St., Hwy. 85 S., Deadwood, SD 57732 (✆ **800/704-7139** or 605/578-2092; www.whistlergulch.com), is in one of Deadwood's famous mining gulches. The campground offers 100 full-service RV sites and secluded tent sites. Facilities include a heated swimming pool, a sport court, and a small store. The town trolley takes visitors to Deadwood's casinos and historic sites.

8 Where to Stay

There are no accommodations at Mount Rushmore, Wind Cave, or Jewel Cave national parks, but inns, hotels, motels, lodges, and bed-and-breakfasts are plentiful in nearby Black Hills communities and parks. Custer State Park has four popular lodges; reservations are strongly recommended, especially in summer. For popular destinations such as Custer State Park, it's best to reserve 6 months to a year in advance of your visit. In addition to the properties listed below in Rapid City, Nemo, and Deadwood, you'll find accommodations in Keystone and Hill City (convenient to Mount Rushmore), as well as in Custer and Hot Springs (more convenient to Jewel Cave and Wind Cave, respectively). If you're continuing west, you might also consider lodging in Newcastle, Wyoming, 25 miles west of Jewel Cave National Monument.

For information on accommodations in the Black Hills, contact either the South Dakota Office of Tourism or the Black Hills & Badlands Association (see "Information," earlier in this chapter).

IN RAPID CITY

Abend Haus Cottages and Audrie's B&B Set on the banks of a rippling trout stream, Audrie's is a perfect choice for those couples seeking a romantic and luxurious escape during their visit to the Black Hills. The spacious cottages and suites ooze old-world charm, with European antiques, hot tubs, fireplaces, and patios. Among the cottages, an excellent choice is the Yuletide Haus, made of hand-peeled lodgepole pine logs, with a king-size bed, refrigerator, microwave, CD, and TV with DVD player. More upscale is Moonlight Lodge, a 1,100-square-foot log cabin that has a king bed, river rock gas fireplace, refrigerator and microwave, hot tub, and entertainment center complete with a 53-inch large-screen TV. Smoking is not permitted.

23029 Thunderhead Falls Rd., Rapid City, SD 57702-8524. ✆ **605/342-7788.** www.audriesbb.com. 9 units. TV. $145–$210 double. Rates include full breakfast. No credit cards. Couples only (no children). Located 7 miles west of town on U.S. 44.

Hotel Alex Johnson This finely restored hotel, listed on the National Historic Register, has a Germanic Tudor mixed with Lakota Sioux atmosphere on the inside, with a Germanic Tudor exterior. The furniture was handcrafted in Rapid City to replicate the hotel's original 1928 furnishings. It contains an Irish pub, gift shop, and highly recommended restaurant, **The Landmark,** that's open for breakfast, lunch, and dinner.

523 6th St., Rapid City, SD 57701. ✆ **800/888-2539** or 605/342-1210. Fax 605/342-7436. www.alexjohnson.com. 143 units. A/C, TV, TEL. $45–$115. AE, DC, DISC, MC, V.

Rushmore Plaza Holiday Inn This eight-story atrium hotel with a pool and waterfall offers all the spaciousness and amenities you would expect in a top-rated modern hotel. It also has a relaxing piano lounge and exercise facilities, and is close to downtown shopping, dining, and entertainment.

505 N. 5th St., Rapid City, SD 57701. ✆ **605/348-4000.** Fax 605/348-9777. 205 units. A/C, TV, TEL. Winter $129–$153 double; summer $145–$163 double. AE, DC, DISC, MC, V.

IN CUSTER

Bavarian Inn Motel The Bavarian Inn's location 1 mile north of downtown is convenient to many of the Black Hills' most popular attractions, including Mount Rushmore, Crazy Horse Memorial, and Custer State Park. There's a **restaurant** (German/American) and lounge on-site, plus heated indoor and outdoor pools, a tennis court, a sauna and hot tub, and a game room.

U.S. 16/385 N., Custer, SD 57730. ✆ **800/657-4312** or 605/673-2802. www.bavarianinnsd.com. 64 units, 1 condo. A/C, TV, TEL. $44–$115 double; $64–$189 suite. AE, DISC, MC, V.

IN DEADWOOD

The Bullock Hotel This is one of the finest hotels in South Dakota. You'll find turn-of-the-20th-century surroundings complemented by modern amenities. There's also 24-hour gambling, a full-service bar, and a quaint restaurant called **Bully's.** For a special treat, try one of the Jacuzzi suites. Keep an eye out for the hotel's namesake, legendary lawman Seth Bullock, whose ghost reportedly has a habit of reappearing here.

633 Historic Main St., Deadwood, SD 57732. ✆ **800/336-1876.** www.historicbullock.com. 28 units. A/C, TV, TEL. $65–$188 double, varied by seasons. AE, DISC, MC, V.

Deadwood Gulch Resort With a comfortable hotel, three casinos, a convention center, bars, a newly remodeled creekside restaurant, outdoor recreation, a 24-hour hot tub, and heated pools, this resort is a good home base for those exploring the area, as well as a destination to enjoy for its own merits. The attractive modern rooms have one or two queen-size beds; minisuites are also available. There's a convenience store and gas station, and trolley service to historic Main Street. In the summer, the resort has mountain-bike rentals; in the winter, you can rent snowmobiles, and special events are on offer year-round.

U.S. 85 S., 1 mile from Historic Main St. (P.O. Box 643, Deadwood, SD 57732). ✆ **800/695-1876** or 605/578-1294. Fax 605/578-2505. www.deadwoodgulch.com. 96 units. A/C, TV, TEL. Oct 4–May 21 $77 double; May 22–June 13 $189 double; June 14–Aug 31 $119; Sept 1–Oct 3 $89 double. AE, DC, DISC, MC, V. Rates include breakfast. No pets.

INSIDE CUSTER STATE PARK

Custer State Park is home to four distinct lodges, each with its own unique personality, that offer lodging, dining, and a wealth of recreational opportunities in the heart of the Black Hills.

The **State Game Lodge** (✆ **605/255-4541**), located on U.S. 16A near the park's main visitor center, served as the "Summer White House" for Presidents Calvin Coolidge and Dwight D. Eisenhower. The stone and wood lodge features stately lodge rooms, hotel rooms, and pine-shaded cabins, as well as meeting and banquet facilities. The dining room was rejuvenated in the 2009 season and continues to offer casual yet elegant breakfast and lunch dining, while creating a formal ambiance for dinner.

The lodge offers an excellent Buffalo Jeep Safari Ride into the backcountry and a Safari Ride cookout dinner tour.

Open year-round, **Creekside Lodge,** located on the grounds of the State Game Lodge, features 30 luxurious, oversized lodge rooms, a beautiful lobby, and two meeting rooms perfect for business or leisure gatherings.

The **Sylvan Lake Lodge** (✆ **605/574-2561**), on S. Dak. 87 in the northeast corner of Custer State Park, overlooking scenic Sylvan Lake and the Harney Range, features cozy lodge rooms and rustic family cabins. Sylvan's **dining room** was remodeled in 2009 and offers breakfast, lunch, and dinner with a view. Stop in at the lakeside general store to pick up your rental watercraft and snacks. The lodge is also close to a number of outdoor activities, including hiking, swimming, fishing, boating, and rock climbing.

The **Blue Bell Lodge** (✆ **605/255-4531**), located on S. Dak. 87 just before the turnoff for the Wildlife Loop Road (if you are traveling south), is among western South Dakota's best-kept secrets. The retreat has an Old West flavor, with handcrafted log cabins (our choice for the best place to stay in the park) scattered around a lodge with a newly remodeled dining room, lounge, and meeting room. A general store, gift shop, and gasoline station are located on-site, and fishing is available nearby. The Blue Bell also offers hayrides, chuckwagon cookouts, and trail rides.

The **Legion Lake Lodge** (✆ **605/255-4521**), located near the junction of the Needles Highway (S. Dak. 87 and U.S. 16A), dates from 1913 and features cottages in the pines near the lakeshore. The dining room and store provide guests with the best in deli, bakery, and burgers in a casual lakeside setting. Here you can pick up fishing licenses and all the supplies you need. The 110-mile Centennial Trail passes through the Legion Lake area.

Rates vary depending on the lodge and also by cabin and room type. Rates range from $130 per night (Legion Lake sleeping cabin) to $260 per night (10-person housekeeping cabin at Sylvan Lake Lodge). Several unique one-of-a-kind cabins are also available at a higher rate.

The more facilities and amenities, the more you pay. Most of the lodges open in late April or May and close down in late October. Creekside Lodge and a few cabins are kept open for winter visitors. Creekside Lodge is open year-round. These fill quickly, and some people call 6 months in advance for reservations. For more information or to make reservations at any of Custer State Park's lodges, contact Custer State Park Resort Co., 13389 W. Hwy. 16A, Custer, SD 57730 (✆ **888-875-0001;** www.CusterResorts.com).

9 Where to Dine

Dining in the Black Hills tends to be a casual affair, but the selection can be excellent, ranging from homemade pies and ranch-raised buffalo to hearty steaks and succulent pheasant. "Summer" means Memorial Day through Labor Day.

INSIDE THE PARKS

The only full-service dining for all meals within the National Park Service properties in the Black Hills is the Buffalo Dining Room at Mount Rushmore (see below). Wind Cave and Jewel Cave have vending machines. The four resorts at Custer State Park offer dining facilities that nonguests may enjoy as well; all offer what we might call upscale family dining, with mostly American fare at relatively moderate prices (see the individual resort descriptions under "Where to Stay," above).

In addition to the restaurants listed below, you might consider two places in Custer, east of Jewel Cave National Monument, west of Custer State Park, and northwest of Wind Cave National Park. **The Bavarian Inn,** at the junction of U.S. 385 and U.S. 16 (✆ **605/673-4412**), serves American and German dishes at reasonable prices, with live music most nights. **The Chief Restaurant,** 140 Mount Rushmore Rd. (✆ **605/673-4402**), offers family-style dining, with choices ranging from prime rib and steaks to pizza and buffalo burgers.

AT MOUNT RUSHMORE NATIONAL MEMORIAL

Buffalo Dining Room AMERICAN Every day, visitors to the Black Hills dine with presidents at Mount Rushmore's fabled Buffalo Dining Room. Operated by Xanterra Parks and Resorts, the Memorial's concessionaire, the dining room serves a wide array of food year-round in one of the world's most famous settings. Scrambled eggs, hash browns, homemade biscuits and sausage gravy, and country-fried steak, with coffee, tea, or milk, are a deal at $3.95. What's especially nice about the place is that most choices retain a homemade taste, not something you can say about all national park fare. The buffalo stew is excellent; you'll also find burgers, hot dogs, chicken, pot roast, spaghetti, baked fish, ham steaks, great pies and fudge, and monumental scoops of ice cream.

At Mount Rushmore N5.507; lunch and dinner entrees $6–$10. AE, DISC, MC, V. Summer daily 8am–9pm; other times of the year daily 8am–5pm (though hours may vary during the off season).

IN KEYSTONE

The Ruby House Restaurant and Red Garter Saloon STEAK/SEAFOOD/BUFFALO/ELK Steaks, seafood, game, and other specialties are served in a richly appointed Victorian dining room. If you've never tried buffalo, order one of the steaks or burgers here—they're similar to very lean beef, but pricier. This is a quiet stop in a tumultuous town.

126 Winter St., Keystone. ✆ **605/666-4404.** Main courses $6–$10 lunch, $9–$24 dinner. DISC, MC, V. Mid-Apr through Oct daily for lunch and dinner, 11am–9pm.

IN HILL CITY

The Alpine Inn STEAKS The Alpine Inn remains a favorite among most locals and all carnivores. This is a steak place, and steak is what the restaurant does well. The lack of a wide selection of entrees is mitigated by a choice of more than 30 desserts, most of which are homemade and all of which are delectable. An attractive porch overlooks the bustle of downtown.

225 Main St., Hill City. ✆ **605/574-2749.** Main courses $3–$9 lunch, $9–$11 dinner. No credit cards. Summer Mon–Sat 11am–2:30pm and 5–10pm; winter Mon–Sat 11am–2:30pm and 5–9pm. Closed Sun.

IN RAPID CITY

Botticelli Ristorante Italiano ITALIAN In business only since the late 1990s, Botticelli has quickly become a culinary hot spot. Featuring a wide selection of creamy pastas and delightful chicken and veal dishes, the fare smacks of northern Italy. Even though Botticelli is set in the heart of cattle country, the fresh seafood specials and other nonbeef items are generally the best choices. There's also a fine wine selection.

523 Main St., Rapid City. ✆ **605/348-0089.** Main courses $7–$10 lunch, $10–$25 dinner. AE, MC, V. Hours vary by day; separate hours for lunch and dinner.

Firehouse Brewing Co. CONTINENTAL/PUB FARE The brewing process is visible behind glass in this classic, renovated fire station. Burgers, buffalo, and chicken wings are favorites, but we also recommend the Reuben sandwich, the bean soup offered in fall, and the desserts, such as the Big Cookie—a freshly baked white and dark chocolate mix the size of a dinner plate that is topped with two large scoops of French vanilla ice cream and served with melba sauce on the side. Live entertainment is offered on a large, heated patio Wednesday through Saturday nights in the summer.

610 Main St., Rapid City. ✆ **605/348-1915.** Main courses $6–$12 lunch, $7–$18 dinner. AE, DC, DISC, MC, V. Summer Sun 11am–10pm Mon–Thurs 11am–11pm, Fri–Sat until midnight; other times of the year Sun 11am-9pm, Mon–Thurs 11am–10pm, Fri–Sat until 11pm.

Fireside Inn STEAKS/SEAFOOD/PASTA Bean soup is a great starter, but the Fireside Inn has made a name for itself with its prime rib and intimate fireside setting. Relax with refreshments on a spacious new patio before checking out the 20-ounce Cattlemen's Cut. Or you might want to sample the fresh salmon or the delicious chicken Wellington. The New York steak is among the best in the business.

On S. Dak. 44, 6 miles west of Rapid City. ✆ **605/342-3900.** Main courses $19–$27. AE, DISC, MC, V. Mon–Sat 5–9pm.

Golden Phoenix CHINESE A relaxed atmosphere with reasonable prices, quick service, and convenient parking make this a good choice in Rapid City. There is a wide selection of Chinese dishes, but it's hard to beat the Mongolian beef, sesame chicken, or Hunan shrimp.

2421 W. Main St., Rapid City. ✆ **605/348-4195.** Main courses $6 lunch, $6–$10 dinner. AE, DC, DISC, MC, V. Daily 11am–9:30pm.

IN PIEDMONT

Elk Creek Steakhouse & Lounge STEAKS/SEAFOOD/PASTA/CHICKEN Steak's the thing at Elk Creek, and the buffalo steaks are excellent. The Duchess potatoes are wonderful, and the Chef's Special—a rib-eye served on an English muffin, topped with broccoli, mock crab, and a hollandaise-cheese sauce—is wicked. The lounge features a live band on Saturday and Sunday nights.

I-90 at exit 46, Piedmont. ✆ **605/787-6349.** Main courses $8–$40. AE, DISC, MC, V. Mon–Thurs 5–9pm; Fri–Sat 5–10pm; Sun 4:30–9pm.

IN DEADWOOD

Deadwood Social Club STEAKS/PASTA A warm atmosphere is made even cozier with light jazz and blues in the background and one of South Dakota's largest wine selections in the cellar, which has received *Wine Spectator*'s Award of Excellence 5 years in a row. Pasta dishes, such as the smoked Tuaca pheasant, are exquisite. The South Dakota buffalo tenderloin and hand-cut rib-eye are served with fresh sautéed vegetables and garlic smashed potatoes, then topped with Florentine butter.

On the 2nd floor of Saloon No. 10, 657 Main St. ✆ **800/952-9398.** Reservations appreciated but not required. Main courses $5–$10 lunch, $11–$25 dinner. AE, MC, V. Summer 11am–10pm; winter Sun–Thurs 11am–9pm, Fri–Sat 11am–10pm.

Jakes NEW AMERICAN Before dining, browse handsomely displayed costumes worn by Kevin Costner in his feature films, including *The Postman, Dances with Wolves,* and *Tin Cup.* Kevin and partners Carla and Francis Caneva own Jakes, which features some of the most unique food in the region. Seasonal dishes include salmon, elk, chicken, duck, lamb, and buffalo, and a different chef's featured selection is part of the menu every night. Appetizers can range from escargot to buffalo carpaccio. There is also an excellent wine list.

Atop the Midnight Star, 677 Main St., Deadwood. ✆ **605/578-3656.** www.themidnightstar.com. Reservations highly recommended. Main courses $23–$38. AE, DC, DISC, MC, V. Daily 5–10pm.

7

Bryce Canyon National Park & Grand Staircase–Escalante National Monument, UT

by Don & Barbara Laine

Welcome to a magical land, a place of inspiration and spectacular beauty where thousands of intricately shaped hoodoos stir the imagination as they stand in silent watch.

Hoodoos, geologists tell us, are pinnacles of rock, often oddly shaped, left standing after millions of years of water and wind erosion have carved away softer or less protected rock. But perhaps the truth really lies in a Paiute legend. These American Indians, who lived in the area for several hundred years before being forced out by Anglo pioneers, told of a "Legend People" who lived here in the old days; for their evil ways, the powerful Coyote turned them to stone, and even today they remain frozen in time.

Bryce Canyon is unique. Its intricate and often whimsical formations are smaller and on a more human scale than the impressive rocks at Zion and Canyonlands national parks, and Bryce is easier to explore than the huge and sometimes intimidating Grand Canyon. The park is comfortable and inviting in its beauty; we feel we know it simply by gazing over the rim.

Although the hoodoos grab your attention first, before long you notice the deep amphitheaters that enfold them, with their cliffs, windows, and arches—all in shades of red, brown, orange, yellow, and white—that change and glow with the rising and setting sun. Beyond the rocks and light are the other faces of the park: three life zones, each with its own unique vegetation, changing with elevation; and a kingdom of animals, from the busy chipmunks and ground squirrels to stately mule deer and their archenemy, the mountain lion.

Human exploration of the Bryce area likely began with the Paiutes. Trappers, prospectors, and early Mormon scouts may have visited in the early to mid-1800s, before Maj. John Wesley Powell conducted the first thorough survey of the region in the early 1870s. Shortly after, Mormon pioneer Ebenezer Bryce and his wife, Mary, moved to the area and tried raising cattle. They stayed only a few years, but Bryce left behind his name and his oft-quoted description of the canyon as "a helluva place to lose a cow."

AVOIDING THE CROWDS

Although Bryce Canyon receives only two-thirds the number of annual visitors that pour into nearby Zion National Park, Bryce can still be crowded, especially during its peak season, from mid-June to mid-September. If you must visit then, try to hike some of the lesser-used trails (ask rangers for recommendations), and get out onto the trails as soon after sunrise as possible.

A better time to visit, if your schedule allows, is spring or fall. If you don't mind a bit of cold and snow, the park is practically deserted in the winter—a typical January sees some 22,000 to 25,000 visitors, less than a tenth of the number in August—and the sight of bright red hoodoos capped with fresh white snow is something you won't soon forget.

1 Essentials

GETTING THERE & GATEWAYS

Utah 12 crosses the park, which is in the mountains of southern Utah, from east to west. The bulk of the park, including the visitor center, is accessible from Utah 63, which turns south off Utah 12. West of the park, **U.S. 89** runs north to south. Utah 12 heads east to Tropic and eventually Escalante.

From Salt Lake City, it's about 250 miles to the park. Take **I-15** south about 200 miles to exit 95 and head east 13 miles on Utah 20, south on U.S. 89 for 17 miles to Utah 12, and east 17 miles to the park entrance road. The entrance station and visitor center are 3 miles south of Utah 12.

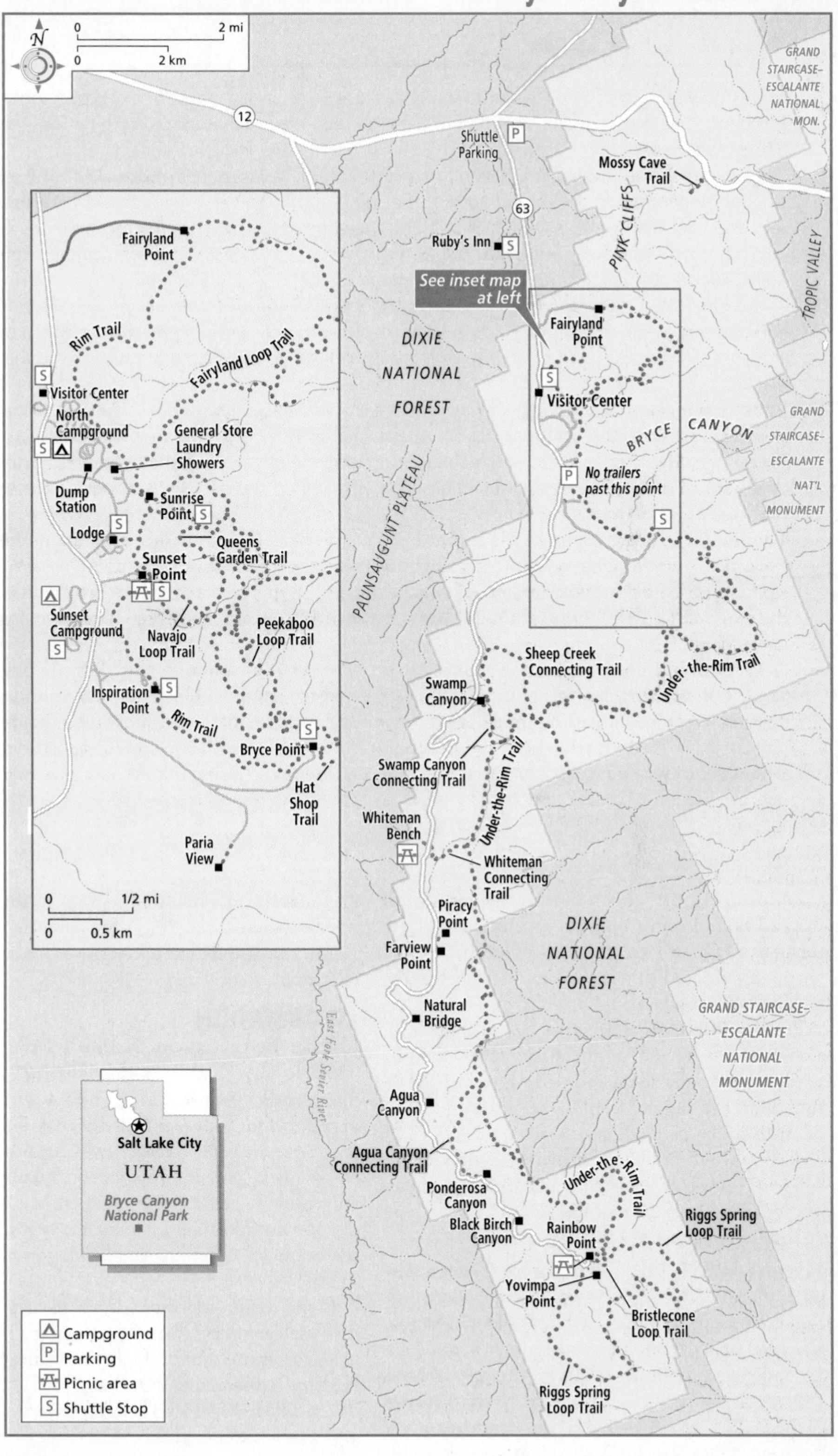

0 2 mi
0 2 km
N
12
63
Shuttle Parking
Mossy Cave Trail
GRAND STAIRCASE–ESCALANTE NATIONAL MON.
Ruby's Inn
PINK CLIFFS
TROPIC VALLEY
See inset map at left
Fairyland Point
Visitor Center
DIXIE NATIONAL FOREST
BRYCE CANYON
GRAND STAIRCASE–ESCALANTE NAT'L MONUMENT
No trailers past this point
PAUNSAUGUNT PLATEAU
Sheep Creek Connecting Trail
Under-the-Rim Trail
Swamp Canyon
Swamp Canyon Connecting Trail
Whiteman Bench
Whiteman Connecting Trail
Piracy Point
Farview Point
DIXIE NATIONAL FOREST
Natural Bridge
GRAND STAIRCASE–ESCALANTE NATIONAL MONUMENT
East Fork Sevier River
Agua Canyon
Agua Canyon Connecting Trail
Ponderosa Canyon
Black Birch Canyon
Rainbow Point
Yovimpa Point
Bristlecone Loop Trail
Riggs Spring Loop Trail
Riggs Spring Loop Trail
Fairyland Point
Rim Trail
Fairyland Loop Trail
Visitor Center
North Campground
General Store Laundry Showers
Dump Station
Sunrise Point
Lodge
Queens Garden Trail
Sunset Point
Sunset Campground
Navajo Loop Trail
Peekaboo Loop Trail
Inspiration Point
Rim Trail
Bryce Point
Hat Shop Trail
Paria View
0 1/2 mi
0 0.5 km
Salt Lake City
UTAH
Bryce Canyon National Park
Campground
Parking
Picnic area
Shuttle Stop

Tips from a Park Insider

"A lot of people think this is one of America's prettiest parks," says former park ranger Dave Mecham. "The hoodoos are what people come to see—that's what made Bryce famous—and it's the most popular thing."

Bryce Amphitheater has the best scenery in the park, in Mecham's opinion. "It's the place in the park where everything's coming together geologically to carve hoodoos at their best," he says. He particularly enjoys the **Rim Trail** along the edge of the canyon, and recommends the section between Inspiration and Bryce points, with perhaps the best view from **Upper Inspiration Point,** 300 to 400 yards south of Inspiration Point.

Mecham calls Bryce Canyon a "morning park" because the views are better illuminated in the early morning than at any other time of day. He recommends spending at least 1 night at or near the park. "If you're spending the night close by, I think it would be a big mistake to miss sunrise."

Getting up early is also the best way to avoid crowds, since most people don't get to the view points or out onto the trails until about 10am. The other way to avoid crowds is to walk away from them. Mecham says that you're not likely to see anyone at all on the two backcountry trails at the south end of the park, but avoiding crowds even in the park's most popular areas often takes only a short walk.

"Sunset Point is the busiest place in the park, especially in midsummer at midday," he says. "You finally get a parking spot, then walk out to a very crowded vantage point, where you're standing shoulder to shoulder and it's real hectic. But if you take a 5-minute walk south along the rim trail toward Inspiration Point, you'll leave the crowds immediately—they just cluster at those views."

Mecham says September and October are probably the best times to visit. "It's still busy," he says, "but less crowded on trails." If you *really* want to avoid people, you'll feel you have the park all to yourself if you visit midweek in the middle of the winter. "We plow the roads so people can drive to the view points and photograph the canyon with snow on it, and the people who ski or snowshoe will enjoy it the most," he says, adding, "Skiing is at its best in January and February, when it's really cold."

From St. George, about 135 miles southwest of the park, travel north on I-15 10 miles to exit 16, then head east on Utah 9 for 63 miles to U.S. 89, north 44 miles to Utah 12, and east 17 miles to the park entrance road.

From Cedar City (I-15 exits 57, 59, and 62), about 80 miles west of the park, take Utah 14 southeast 41 miles to its intersection with U.S. 89 and follow that north 21 miles to Utah 12, then east 17 miles to the park entrance road.

A couple of other handy driving distances: Bryce is 83 miles east of Zion National Park, 160 miles north of the North Rim of the Grand Canyon, and 245 miles northeast of Las Vegas, Nevada.

THE NEAREST AIRPORT **Bryce Canyon Airport** (✆ **435/834-5239;** www.brycecanyoncountry.com/county/airport.html), at a 7,586-foot elevation, is several miles from the park entrance on Utah 12 and has a 7,400-foot lighted runway. It hosts several charter services, including **Bryce Canyon Airlines** (✆ **435/834-5341;** www.rubysinn.com/bryce-canyon-airlines.html). Car rentals are available from **Hertz** (✆ **800/654-3131**), at the Chevron service station in the Ruby's Inn complex.

You can also fly to St. George or Cedar City and rent a car.

INFORMATION

Contact **Bryce Canyon National Park,** P.O. Box 640201, Bryce, UT 84764-0201 (✆ **435/834-5322;** www.nps.gov/brca). It's best to write at least a month before your planned visit. Ask for a copy of the park newspaper, *Hoodoo,* which contains a map of the park, plus information on hiking, weather, ranger-conducted activities, and current issues. You can also download information and maps, and make reservations for camping and lodging from the park's website.

If you desire even more details to help plan your trip, you can order books, maps, posters, DVDs, and videos from the nonprofit **Bryce Canyon Natural History Association,** P.O. Box 640051, Bryce, UT 84764-0051 (✆ **435/834-4601;** www.brycecanyon.org). Association members ($35 single or $50 family

If You Have Only 1 Day

There are several ways to see a good deal of Bryce in a short time. Start at the **visitor center** and watch the video program that explains some of the area's geology. Then drive the 18-mile (each way) dead-end **park road,** stopping at view points to gaze down into the canyon (see "Exploring the Park by Car," below), or visit the most popular view points on the **Bryce Canyon Shuttle.**

Whichever way you choose to get around, make sure you spend at least a little time at **Inspiration Point,** which offers a splendid (and, yes, inspirational) view into **Bryce Amphitheater** and its hundreds of statuesque pink, red, orange, and brown hoodoo stone sculptures. After seeing the canyon from the top down, walk at least partway down the **Queen's Garden Trail.** If you can spare 3 hours, hike down the **Navajo Loop Trail** and return to the rim on the Queen's Garden Trail (see "Day Hikes," below). Those who can't hike into the canyon can enjoy a leisurely walk along the **Rim Trail,** which provides spectacular views down into the canyon, especially just after sunrise and about an hour before sunset. In the evening, try to take in the **campground amphitheater program.**

annually) receive a 15% discount on purchases and discounts for programs presented by the High Plateaus Institute. Members also receive discounts at most other nonprofit bookstores at national parks, monuments, historic sites, and recreation areas.

For additional information on area lodging, dining, and activities, contact **Bryce Canyon Country,** operated by the Garfield County Office of Tourism (✆ **800/444-6689** or 435/676-1102; www.brycecanyoncountry.com).

VISITOR CENTER

At the north end as you enter the park, the visitor center has exhibits on the geology and history of the area and presents a short video program. Rangers answer questions, offer advice, and provide backcountry permits. You can also pick up free brochures and buy books, maps, videos, postcards, and posters. The visitor center is open daily year-round except Thanksgiving and Christmas. Summer hours are usually from 8am to 8pm, with shorter hours the rest of the year (in the dead of the winter, the visitor center closes at 4:30pm).

FEES & PERMITS

Entry into the park (for up to 7 days) costs $25 per private car, pickup truck, van, or RV, which includes unlimited use of the park shuttle (when it's operating). Individuals 16 and older entering on motorcycle, bike, or foot are charged $12 each; those under 16 are admitted free. Campsites cost $15 per night.

Backcountry permits are required for all overnight trips into the backcountry; for up to 7 days, the cost is $5 for one or two people, $10 for three to six people, and $15 for 7 to 15 people. Backcountry camping is permitted on only two trails (details are available at the visitor center).

SPECIAL REGULATIONS & WARNINGS

Although most visitors to Bryce Canyon enjoy an exciting vacation without serious mishap, accidents can occur. The most common injuries are sprained, twisted, and broken ankles. Park rangers strongly recommend that hikers, even those just out for short day hikes, wear sturdy hiking boots with good traction and ankle support.

Another concern in recent years has been **bubonic plague** (treatable with antibiotics if caught early). The bacteria that causes bubonic plague has been found on fleas in prairie dog colonies in the park, so you should avoid contact with wild animals, especially prairie dogs, squirrels, and other rodents. Those taking pets into the park should dust them with flea powder. Avoiding contact with infected animals will greatly minimize the chances of contracting this holdover from the Dark Ages, but caution is still necessary. Symptoms, which generally occur 2 to 6 days after exposure, may include high fever, headache, vomiting, diarrhea, and swollen glands. Anyone showing these symptoms after visiting the park should get medical attention immediately—the plague can be fatal if not treated promptly.

Backcountry hikers should carry water. Campfires are not permitted in the backcountry.

SEASONS & CLIMATE

With elevations ranging from 6,620 to 9,115 feet, Bryce Canyon is cooler than southern Utah's lower-elevation parks. From May through October, daytime temperatures are pleasant—usually from the low 60s to the upper 80s (high teens to low 30s Celsius)—but nights are quite cool, dropping into the 40s (single digits Celsius) even at the height of summer. Afternoon thunderstorms are common in July

The Best Time to Make the Scenic Drive

The scenic drive is practically deserted in early **mornings**—any time before 9am. This is the best time to see deer and the best time to see the hoodoos, when the light on them is at its richest.

and August. In winter, days are generally clear and crisp, with high temperatures often reaching the 40s (single digits Celsius), and nights are cold, usually in the single digits or teens, and sometimes dipping well below zero. Snow is common in winter, but the roads to the view points are plowed.

2 Exploring the Park by Car

The park's 18-mile (one-way) scenic drive follows the rim of Bryce Canyon, offering easy access to a variety of views into the fanciful fairyland of stone sculptures below. Trailers are not allowed on the road and must be left at one of several parking lots. Because all overlooks are on your left as you begin the drive, it's best to avoid crossing traffic on your way up, and instead drive all the way to the end of the road, turn around, and stop at the overlooks on your return. Allow 1 to 2 hours.

After leaving the visitor center, drive the 18-mile road to **Yovimpa and Rainbow Point overlooks,** which offer expansive views of southern Utah, Arizona, and sometimes even New Mexico. From these pink cliffs, you can look down on a platoon of stone soldiers, standing at eternal attention. A short loop trail from Rainbow Point leads to an **1,800-year-old bristlecone pine,** believed to be the oldest living thing at Bryce Canyon.

From here, drive north to **Ponderosa Canyon Overlook,** where you can gaze down from a dense forest of spruce and fir at multicolored hoodoos, and then continue to **Agua Canyon Overlook,** with some of the best color contrasts in the park. Looking almost straight down, watch for a hoodoo known as **The Hunter,** with its hat of green trees.

Continue on to **Natural Bridge,** actually an arch carved by rain and wind, spanning 85 feet. From here, continue to **Farview Point,** with a panoramic view to the distant horizon and the Kaibab Plateau at the Grand Canyon's North Rim. Next, pass through **Swamp Canyon** and continue until you hit a turnoff from the main road on the right.

This turnoff leads to three overlooks. The first is **Paria View,** looking off to the south of the White Cliffs, carved into light-colored sandstone by the Paria River. To the north of Paria View, you'll find **Bryce Point,** a splendid stop for seeing the **Bryce Amphitheater,** the largest natural amphitheater in the park, as well as distant views of the Black Mountains to the northeast and Navajo Mountain to the south. From here it's just a short drive to **Inspiration Point,** which offers views similar to those at Bryce Point, plus the best view in the park of the **Silent City,** a sleeping metropolis of stone.

Now return to the main road and head north to **Sunset Point,** where you can see practically all of Bryce Amphitheater, including **Thor's Hammer** and the 200-foot-tall cliffs of **Wall Street.**

Continue north to a turnoff for your final stop, **Sunrise Point,** where there's an inspiring view into Bryce Amphitheater. This is the beginning of the **Queen's Garden Trail,** an excellent choice for a walk (even a quick one) below the canyon rim.

3 Exploring the Park by Shuttle

In recent years, congestion has been increasing along the park's only road, making a drive through the park a less-than-pleasurable experience. To alleviate this, a **shuttle service** is now in effect from late May to mid-September, between 9am and 6pm. Visitors can park their cars at the parking and boarding area at the intersection of the entrance road and Utah 12, 3 miles from the park boundary, and ride the shuttle into the park. Those staying in the park at Bryce Canyon Lodge or one of the campgrounds can use the shuttle, at no additional charge (see "Fees & Permits," above). The shuttle has stops at various viewpoints, as well as at Ruby's Inn, Ruby's Campground, the visitor center, Sunset Campground, and Bryce Canyon Lodge. It runs every 12 to 15 minutes, it's free, and you can hop on and off. Note that using the shuttle is not required; you can use your own car if you wish.

4 Organized Tours & Ranger Programs

Park rangers present a variety of free programs and activities. One-hour **evening programs,** which may include a slide show, take place at Bryce Canyon Lodge, the visitor center, and occasionally at the North Campground amphitheater. Topics vary but could include such subjects as the animals and plants of the park, geology, and the role of humans in the park's early days. Rangers also give half-hour talks several times daily at various locations in the park and lead hikes and walks, including a **moonlight hike** (reservations required, so sign up at the visitor center) and a wheelchair-accessible, 1-hour **canyon rim walk.** Schedules are posted on bulletin boards at the visitor center, General Store, campgrounds, and Bryce Canyon Lodge.

Especially popular are the park's **Astronomy Programs,** which are usually offered 3 evenings a week through the summer. Telescopes are provided.

The **High Plateaus Institute,** which is affiliated with Bryce Canyon Natural History Association, occasionally presents educational programs for the public. For details, check with park offices or the Bryce Canyon Natural History Association's education specialist (✆ **435/834-4603;** www.brycecanyon.org).

For a bird's-eye view of the canyon and its numerous formations, contact **Bryce Canyon Airlines & Helicopters** (✆ **435/834-8060;** www.rubysinn.com) for scenic flights by helicopter or open cockpit biplane. Tours last from about 35 minutes to several hours, and the longer trips include surrounding attractions. Prices start at about $100 per person, and reservations are required.

Several **adventure tour operators** give guided biking, hiking, and backpacking trips in and near the park. Operators offering a variety of classic or multisport tours include **Austin-Lehman Adventures** (✆ **800/575-1540;** www.austinlehman.com), **Backroads** (✆ **800/462-2848;** www.backroads.com), **Bicycle Adventures** (✆ **800/443-6060** or 360/786-0989; www.bicycleadventures.com), **REI Adventures** (✆ **800/622-2236** or 253/437-1100; www.rei.com/adventures), and **The World Outdoors** (✆ **800/488-8483;** www.theworldoutdoors.com).

5 Park Attractions

Although American Indians and 19th-century pioneers spent some time in what is now Bryce Canyon National Park, they left little evidence. The park's main historic site is the sandstone and ponderosa pine **Bryce Canyon Lodge,** built by the Union Pacific Railroad in 1924. Much of it has been faithfully restored to its 1920s appearance.

6 Day Hikes

One of the wonderful things about Bryce Canyon is that you don't have to be an advanced backpacker to really get to know the park. But those looking for a challenge won't be disappointed, either.

All trails below the rim have at least some steep grades, so you should wear hiking boots with a traction tread and good ankle support to avoid ankle injuries, the most common accidents in the park. During the hot summer months, you'll want to hike either early or late in the day, always keeping in mind that it gets hotter the deeper you go into the canyon. Bryce's rangers do not rate hiking trails by difficulty, saying that what is easy for one person may be difficult for another. Ratings here are provided by the authors and other experienced hikers, and are entirely subjective.

SHORTER TRAILS

Bristlecone Loop An easy walk above the canyon rim, this trail traverses a subalpine fir forest. Here you'll find more bristlecone pines than along the other park trails. It takes just 45 to 60 minutes to complete the loop, which has an elevation change of 150 feet. 1 mile RT. Easy. Access: Rainbow Point parking area at end of scenic drive.

Hat Shop Trail This hike has a 1,336-foot elevation change. Leaving the rim, you'll drop quickly to the Hat Shop, so named because it consists of hard gray "hats" perched on reddish-brown pedestals. The trail offers close-up views of ponderosa pine and Douglas fir, as well as distant panoramas across the Aquarius Plateau toward the Grand Staircase–Escalante National Monument. This trail is also the beginning of the Under the Rim Trail (see

The Best of Two Great Trails

A great choice for getting down into the canyon and seeing the most with the least amount of sweat is to combine the **Navajo Loop Trail** with the **Queen's Garden Trail.** The total distance is just under 3 miles, and most hikers take 2 to 3 hours. It's best to start at the Navajo Loop Trailhead at Sunset Point and leave the canyon on the less steep Queen's Garden Trail, returning to the rim at Sunrise Point, .5 mile north of the Navajo Loop Trailhead.

"Exploring the Backcountry," below). 4 miles RT. Strenuous. Access: Bryce Point Overlook.

Mossy Cave Trail This often-overlooked trail outside the main part of the park offers an easy and picturesque 45-minute walk. The trail follows an old irrigation ditch up a short hill to a shallow cave, where seeping water nurtures the cave's moss. Just off the trail, you'll also see a small waterfall. Elevation gain is 200 feet. Hikers will usually get their feet wet; be careful when crossing the ditch. .8 mile RT. Easy. Access: Along Utah 12, about 3½ miles east of the intersection with Utah 63.

Navajo Loop Trail This trail descends from the canyon rim 550 feet to the canyon floor and back up again. Traversing graveled switchbacks, it affords terrific views of several impressive formations, including the towering skyscrapers of Wall Street, the awesome Twin Bridges, and the precariously balanced Thor's Hammer. The round-trip on this trail takes 1 to 2 hours. 1.3 miles RT. Moderate. Access: Trail head at central overlook point at Sunset Point.

Queen's Garden Trail This short trail, which drops 320 feet below the rim, takes you down into Bryce Amphitheater, with rest benches near the formation called Queen Victoria. At the beginning of the descent, keep an eye cocked to the distant views so you won't miss Boat Mesa, the Sinking Ship, the Aquarius Plateau, and Bristlecone Point. As you plunge deeper into the canyon, the trail passes some of the park's most fanciful formations, including "Queen Victoria" herself, for whom the trail and this grouping of hoodoos were named, plus the Queen's Castle and Gulliver's Castle. The round-trip takes 1 to 2 hours. 1.8 miles RT. Easy to moderate. Access: South side of Sunrise Point.

LONGER TRAILS

Fairyland Loop From Fairyland Point, this strenuous but little-traveled trail descends into Fairyland Canyon, and then meanders up, down, and around Boat Mesa. It crosses Campbell Canyon, passes Tower Bridge junction—a 200-yard side trail takes you to the base of Tower Bridge—and begins a steady climb to the Chinese Wall. About halfway along the wall, the trail begins the serious ascent back to the top of the canyon, reaching it near Sunrise Point. To complete the loop, follow the Rim Trail back through juniper, manzanita, and Douglas fir to Fairyland Point. The loop has an elevation change of 2,309 feet. 8 miles RT. Strenuous. Access: Fairyland Point Overlook, off park access road north of visitor center; also accessible from Sunrise Point.

Peekaboo Loop Open to hikers, mules, and horses, the Peekaboo Loop winds among hoodoos below Bryce and Inspiration points and has an elevation change of 1,555 feet. It has several steep inclines and descents, but the views make the effort worthwhile. You can see far to the east beyond Bryce Canyon—toward the Aquarius Plateau, Canaan Mountain, and the Kaiparowits Plateau—or enjoy the closer prospect of the Wall of Windows, the Three Wisemen, the Organ, and the Cathedral. Various connecting trails make Peekaboo easily adaptable. ***Note:*** Horse use is heavy from spring to fall, and hikers should step aside as horseback riders pass them on the trail. 5.5 miles RT. Strenuous. Access: Bryce Point Overlook parking area.

Rim Trail The Rim Trail, which does not drop into the canyon but offers splendid views from above, meanders along the rim with a total elevation change of up to 1,734 feet if you walk the entire length of the trail. This is more of a walk than a hike, and includes a half-mile section between two overlooks—Sunrise and Sunset—that is paved, fairly level, and suitable for wheelchairs. Overlooking Bryce Amphitheater, the trail offers almost continually excellent views. This is a good choice for an early morning or evening walk, when you can watch the changing light on the rosy rocks below. Another advantage is that you can access the trail from many locations, so you can have a short or long walk. You may also find this a convenient trail if you want to rush out to the rim for a quick look at sunrise over the hoodoos. Some people feel that the best view in the park is from the Rim Trail, south of Inspiration Point. 5.5 miles one-way. Easy to moderate. Access: North trail head at Fairyland Point; south trail head at Bryce Point. Also accessible from Sunrise, Sunset, and Inspiration points and numerous locations in between.

Sheep Creek Trail This trail takes you down into the canyon bottom and, if you follow the extension, out of the park into the Dixie National Forest. The first mile is on the rim. It then descends the Sheep Creek draw below pink limestone cliffs toward the canyon bottom, traversing part of the Under the Rim Trail along its way. Watch signs carefully; the route can be confusing. The trail has up to a 1,250-foot elevation change. 3–5 miles one-way. Easy to moderate. Access: Trail head and parking area 5 miles south of visitor center.

7 Exploring the Backcountry

For die-hard hikers who don't mind rough terrain, Bryce has two backcountry trails, usually open in the summer only. The truly ambitious can combine the trails for a weeklong excursion. Permits, which cost $5 and are available at the visitor center, are required for all overnight trips into the backcountry.

Riggs Spring Loop This hike can be done in 4 or 5 hours, or it can be more comfortably done as a relaxing overnight backpacking trip. The trail goes through a deep forest and also provides breathtaking views of the huge Pink Cliffs at the southern end of the plateau. It has an elevation change of 1,675 feet. 8.8-mile loop. Moderate to strenuous. Access: South side of parking area for Rainbow Point.

Under the Rim Trail This moderately strenuous trail runs between Bryce and Rainbow points; it offers the full spectrum of views of Bryce Canyon's scenery. Since the trail runs below the rim, it is full of steep inclines and descents, with an overall elevation change of 1,500 feet. Allow 2 to 3 days to hike the entire length. There are five camping areas along the trail, plus a group camp area. 23 miles one-way. Moderate. Access: East side of parking area for Bryce Point Overlook.

8 Other Sports & Activities

BIKING & MOUNTAIN BIKING Bikes are permitted only on the park's established roads, which are generally narrow, winding, and crowded with motor vehicles during the summer. However, you'll find plenty of mountain-biking opportunities just outside the park in the Dixie National Forest. For information, stop at the national forest's **Red Canyon Visitor Center** (✆ **435/676-2676**), along Utah 12 about 10½ miles west of the Bryce Canyon National Park entrance road. It's usually open daily from early May to early October and offers various interpretative programs on many Saturdays. Or contact the Powell District office of the **Dixie National Forest,** 225 E. Center St. (P.O. Box 80), Panguitch, UT 84759-0080 (✆ **435/676-9300;** www.fs.fed.us/dxnf).

Mountain bikes can be rented across the road from Ruby's Inn at the **American Car Care Center** (✆ **866/866-6616** or 435/834-5232; www.rubysinn.com) for $20 for up to 6 hours and $35 for a full day.

HORSEBACK RIDING To see Bryce Canyon the way early pioneers did, you need to look down from a horse or mule. **Canyon Trail Rides,** P.O. Box 128, Tropic, UT 84776 (✆ **435/679-8665;** www.canyonrides.com), offers a close-up view of Bryce's spectacular rock formations from the relative comfort of a saddle. The company has a desk inside Bryce Lodge. A 2-hour ride to the canyon floor and back costs $50 per person, and a half-day trip farther into the canyon costs $75 per person. Rides are offered April through November. Riders must be at least 7 years old for the 2-hour trip, at least 10 for the half-day ride, and weigh no more than 220 pounds.

Guided horseback rides in Red Canyon, just outside the national park, are provided by **Ruby's Inn Horserides** (✆ **866/782-0002** or 435/834-5341; www.horserides.net), at Ruby's Inn, for similar rates; in addition, Ruby's offers a full-day ride with lunch for $100. Ruby's will also board your horse (call for rates).

WILDLIFE WATCHING The park has a variety of wildlife, ranging from **mule deer,** which seem to be almost everywhere, to the often-seen **golden-mantled ground squirrel** and **Uinta chipmunk.** Occasionally, visitors catch a glimpse of a **mountain lion,** most likely on the prowl in search of a mule deer dinner; **elk** and **pronghorn** may be seen at higher elevations. Also in the park are **black-tailed jackrabbits, coyotes, striped skunks,** and **deer mice.**

The **Utah prairie dog,** which is listed as a threatened species, is actually a rodent. It inhabits park meadows in busy colonies and can be fascinating to watch. However, *keep your distance,* because its fleas may carry disease (see "Special Regulations & Warnings," above).

Many birds live in the park. You're bound to hear the rather obnoxious call of the **Steller's jay.** Other birds often seen include violet-green swallows, common ravens, Clark's nutcrackers, American robins, red-shafted flickers, dark-eyed juncos, and chipping sparrows. Watch for **white-throated swifts** as they perform their exotic acrobatics along cliff faces. The park is also home, at least part of the year, to peregrine falcons, red-tailed hawks, golden eagles, bald eagles, and great horned owls.

The **Great Basin rattlesnake,** although pretty, should be given a wide berth. Sometimes growing to more than 5 feet long, this rattler is the park's only poisonous reptile. Like most rattlesnakes, it is just as anxious as you are to avoid a confrontation. Other reptiles you may see are the mountain short-horned lizard, the tree lizard, the side-blotched lizard, and the northern sagebrush lizard.

WINTER SPORTS & ACTIVITIES The Bryce is beautiful in the winter, when snow settles over the red, pink, orange, and brown hoodoos.

Snowshoes may be used anywhere in the park except on cross-country ski tracks. **Cross-country skiers** will find several marked, ungroomed trails (all above the rim). They include the **Fairyland Loop Trail,** which leads 1 mile through a pine and juniper forest to the Fairyland Point Overlook. From here you can take the 1-mile **Forest Trail** back to the road, or continue along the rim for another 1.2 miles to the park boundary. There are also connections to trails in the adjacent national forest.

Although the entire park is open to cross-country skiers, rangers warn that it's impossible to safely ski the steep trails leading down into the canyon. Stop at the visitor center for additional trail information, and go to **Best Western Ruby's Inn,** just north of the park entrance (✆ **866/866-6616** or 435/834-5341;

www.rubysinn.com), for information on cross-country trails and snowmobiling opportunities outside the park. Ruby's grooms over 30 miles of ski trails and rents cross-country ski equipment.

9 Camping

INSIDE THE PARK

Typical of many of the West's national park campgrounds, the two facilities at Bryce offer plenty of trees with a genuine "forest camping" experience and easy access to trails, but limited facilities. **North Campground** is our top choice—it's closer to the Rim Trail, making it easier to rush over to catch those amazing sunrise and sunset colors. Reservations are available from early May through late September for North Campground (✆ **877/444-6777;** www.recreation.gov); an additional booking fee of $10 is required, regardless of the number of days. And we wouldn't turn down a site at **Sunset Campground.** Try to get to the park early (usually by 2pm in the summer) to claim a site. Showers ($2) are at a general store in the park, although it's a healthy walk from either campground. The Park Service also operates an RV dump station ($2 fee) in the summer.

The general store near the Sunrise Point parking area has a coin-operated laundry and a snack bar, plus bundles of firewood, food and camping supplies, and souvenirs. There are tables on a covered porch along one side of the building.

NEAR THE PARK

Just north of the entrance to the park is **Ruby's Inn RV Park & Campground,** 300 S. Main St., Bryce Canyon City, UT 84764 (✆ **866/866-6616** or 435/834-5301; www.rubysinn.com; credit cards accepted), which is on the park's shuttle bus route. The RV and tent sites are mostly shady and attractive. The campground contains a game room, horseshoes, a swimming pool, barbecue grills, two coin-op laundries, and a store with groceries and RV supplies. A lake and a horse pasture are nearby. Also on the grounds are several camping cabins ($55 double) and tipis ($33 double), which share the campground's bathhouse and other facilities.

Bryce Canyon Pines, milepost 10, Utah 12 (P.O. Box 640043, Bryce, UT 84764; ✆ **800/892-7923** or 435/834-5441; fax 435/834-5330; www.brycecanyonmotel.com; credit cards accepted), is part of a motel/restaurant/store/campground complex about 3½ miles west of the park entrance road. The campsites, set back from the highway behind a gas station and store, sit among ponderosa pines, junipers, wildflowers, and grasses. All RV sites have full hookups. Campers have access to the motel swimming pool across the street.

Bryce Pioneer Village, 80 S. Main St. (Utah 12; P.O. Box 119), Tropic, UT 84776 (✆ **866/657-8414** or 435/679-8546; fax 435/679-8607; www.bpvillage.com; credit cards accepted), is a small motel/cabins/campground combination in nearby Tropic, with some shade trees and easy access to several restaurants.

King Creek Campground, in the Powell District of the Dixie National Forest, 225 E. Canter St. (P.O. Box 80), Panguitch, UT 84759 (✆ **435/676-9300;** www.fs.fed.us/dxnf; no credit cards), is located above Tropic Reservoir, with graded gravel roads and sites nestled among tall ponderosa pines. The reservoir has two boat ramps and good trout fishing. From the intersection of Utah 63 and Utah 12, head west on Utah 12 about 2½ miles to the access road, turn south (left), and follow signs to Tropic Reservoir for about 7 miles to the campground.

About 9½ miles west of the park is another Dixie National Forest campground, **Red Canyon Campground** (same contact information as King Creek Campground, above). Set among the trees along the

Campground	Elev.	Total Sites	RV Hookups	Dump Station	Toilets
Inside the Park					
North	7,700	107	No	No	Yes
Sunset	8,000	101	No	No	Yes
Near the Park					
Bryce Canyon Pines	7,600	39	26	No	Yes
Bryce Pioneer Village	6,400	32	12	Yes	Yes
King Creek (USFS)	8,000	37	No	Yes	Yes
Kodachrome Basin SP	5,800	27	No	Yes	Yes
Red Canyon (USFS)	7,400	37	No	Yes	Yes
Ruby's Inn RV Park	7,600	227	127	Yes	Yes

south side of Utah 12, it offers terrific views of the red rock formations, although there is a bit of road noise. Reservations are available (✆ **877/444-6777;** www.recreation.gov). Showers cost $2 and use of the dump station costs $5, whether you're staying in the campground or not.

Kodachrome Basin State Park, P.O. Box 180069, Cannonville, UT 84718 (✆ **435/679-8562;** www.stateparks.utah.gov), about 22 miles southeast of Bryce Canyon National Park, has an attractive campground with sites among unusual rock "chimneys" and pinyon and juniper trees.

10 Where to Stay

INSIDE THE PARK

Bryce Canyon Lodge This is the perfect place to stay while you explore Bryce Canyon National Park. The location allows you to watch the play of changing light on the rock formations throughout the day. The handsome sandstone and ponderosa pine lodge opened in 1924. The luxurious lodge suites are wonderful, with white wicker furniture, ceiling fans, and separate sitting rooms. The motel units are simply pleasant, modern rooms, with two queen-size beds and either a balcony or a patio. The best choice is one of the historic cabins, restored to their 1920s appearance. They're not large, but they have two double beds, high ceilings, stone (gas-burning) fireplaces, and log beams—you might call the ambience "rustic luxury." At desks in the lobby, travelers can book horseback riding and other activities, and there is an excellent restaurant (see "Where to Dine," below). The gift shop sells everything from postcards and souvenirs to a fine selection of American Indian pawn jewelry. There is no swimming pool. All units are smoke-free.

Bryce Canyon National Park, UT. ✆ **435/834-5361.** Information and reservations: Xanterra Parks & Resorts, Central Reservations, 6312 S. Fiddlers Green Circle, Ste. 600N, Greenwood Village, CO 80111. ✆ **888/297-2757** or 303/297-2757. Fax 303/297-3175. www.brycecanyonlodge.com. 114 units. TEL. $130–$165 double; $175 cabin; $179 lodge suite. AE, DISC, MC, V. Closed Nov–Mar.

NEAR THE PARK

Best Western Bryce Canyon Grand Hotel This upscale hotel, which opened in 2009, offers excellent facilities a stone's throw from the entrance to Bryce Canyon National Park. The rooms and suites, in two four-story towers with interior corridors, are what we might call "Western luxury," with solid wood furnishings, good lighting, and top-quality beds—either one king or two queens. The deluxe suites, at 770 square feet, have a king bed, hide-a-bed couch, and jetted tub. All units have refrigerators and microwaves. The hotel caters to those who want to take care of business while on vacation, with large working desks, a well-equipped business center, and Wi-Fi. There is a heated outdoor pool, a whirlpool, a fitness center, a coin-op laundry, and a **restaurant** that serves American food. The hotel is under the same management as the nearby Best Western Ruby's Inn (see below). All units are smoke-free.

31 N. 100 E. (at the entrance to Bryce Canyon), Bryce Canyon City, UT 84764. ✆ **866/866-6634** or 435/834-5700. Fax 435/834-5701. www.brycecanyongrand.com. 162 units. A/C, TV, TEL. Summer $150 double, $200–$290 suite; rest of year $75 double, $140–$199 suite. Rates include a hot breakfast. AE, DC, DISC, MC, V.

Best Western Ruby's Inn This large Best Western provides most of the beds for tired hikers and canyon gazers visiting the park. The lobby is among the busiest places in the area, with an ATM, a small liquor store, car rentals, a beauty salon, a 1-hour film processor, and tour desks where you can arrange excursions, from horseback and all-terrain-vehicle rides to helicopter tours. Near the lobby are a restaurant; a Western art gallery; a huge general store that sells souvenirs, cowboy hats, camping supplies, and groceries; and a post office. Outside is a gas station with repair facilities.

Drinking Water	Showers	Fire Pits/ Grills	Laundry	Reserve	Fees	Open
Yes	No	Yes	No	Yes	$15	Year-round
Yes	No	Yes	No	No	$15	May to late Sept
Yes	Yes	Yes	Yes	Yes	$17–$25	Mar–Nov
Yes	Yes	No	No	Yes	$15–$25	Mar–Oct
Yes	No	Yes	No	No	$10	Mid-May to Sept
Yes	Yes	Yes	Yes	Yes	$16	Year-round
Yes	Yes	Yes	No	No	$12	Mid-May to Sept
Yes	Yes	Yes	Yes	Yes	$24–$39	Apr–Oct

Spread among nine buildings, the modern motel rooms are typical of this chain, and contain art depicting scenes of the area, wood furnishings, and tub/showers, as well as Wi-Fi access. Some units have whirlpools. Services include a concierge and courtesy transportation from the Bryce Airport; facilities include two indoor pools, one indoor and one outdoor whirlpool, a sun deck, nature and cross-country ski trails, a game room, a business center, conference rooms, two coin-operated laundries, and two restaurants (see "Where to Dine," below). All units are smoke-free.

26 S. Main St. (at the entrance to Bryce Canyon), Bryce Canyon City, UT 84764. ✆ **866/866-6616** or 435/834-5341. www.rubysinn.com. 368 units. A/C, TV, TEL. June–Sept $135–$169 double, $195 suite; Oct–May $70–$140 double, $145 suite. AE, DC, DISC, MC, V. Pets accepted.

Bryce Canyon Pines A modern motel with a Western flair, the Bryce Canyon Pines offers well-maintained rooms with light-wood furnishings, a table and two padded chairs, and two queen-size beds in most rooms. Some units have fireplaces (wood is supplied free in winter), some have fully stocked kitchenettes, and one has its own whirlpool tub. There's a covered, heated swimming pool and an adjacent restaurant (see "Where to Dine," below). All units are smoke-free.

Milepost 10, Utah 12 (3 miles west of intersection with park entry road; P.O. Box 640043), Bryce, UT 84764. ✆ **800/892-7923** or 435/834-5441. Fax 435/834-5330. www.brycecanyonmotel.com. 53 units. Mid-May to mid-Nov $85–$105 double, $105–$120 cottage, $120–$335 deluxe room and suite. Mid-Nov to mid-May $70–$95 double; $95–$250 cottage, deluxe room, and suite. AE, DC, DISC, MC, V.

Bryce Country Cabins There's something special about staying in a log cabin during a national park vacation, but there's also something appealing about hot showers and warm beds. Bryce Canyon Country Cabins offers both, with recently constructed log-style cabins and a historic two-room pioneer cabin, set on a 20-acre farm. The grounds surrounding the cabins are nicely landscaped, and you get views out over the park, although we wish the units were farther back from the highway. The intriguing part of the facility is the farm behind the buildings, where cattle graze in the fields and the chickens think they own the place.

The comfortable modern cabins have knotty pine walls and ceilings, exposed beams, and ceiling fans. Each has one or two queen-size beds, a table with two chairs, fridge, microwave, coffeemaker, hair dryer, and private porch. Some bathrooms have showers only; others have tub/showers. The pioneer log cabin, built in 1905, has two spacious rooms with country-style decor, each with its own entrance. Both of the rooms have two queen-size beds, fridges and microwaves, and full bathrooms with tub/showers combos. The pioneer cabin's two rooms can be rented together or individually. The property has Wi-Fi and outdoor barbecues for guests' use. All cabins are smoke-free.

320 N. Main St. (Utah 12; P.O. Box 141), Tropic, UT 84776. ✆ **888/679-8643** or 435/679-8643. Fax 435/679-8989. www.brycecountrycabins.com. 13 units. A/C, TV, TEL. Summer $95–$125 double; off-season discounts. Rates include a continental breakfast. AE, DC, MC, V.

Bryce Pioneer Village This is a good choice for those seeking a good night's rest at a reasonable rate. Decor is simple, with light-colored walls and rustic touches like rough log headboards in some units. The small, no-frills motel rooms are clean and comfortable, with one or two queen-size beds or two double beds, large walk-in closets, and showers only (no tubs). Cabins, relocated from inside the national park, are more interesting. Most are small but cute, with one queen-size bed plus a twin bed, one chair, and a small bathroom with shower. Several others are larger, with two queen-size beds and average-size bathrooms with tub/showers. There are also cabins with three queen-size beds. There is a campground on the property (see "Camping," above), two hot tubs, a picnic area, and a small curio shop. Just outside the motel office, you can see the cabin where Ebenezer and Mary Bryce, for whom the national park is named, lived in the late 1870s.

80 S. Main St. (Utah 12; P.O. Box 119), Tropic, UT 84776. ✆ **866/657-8414** or 435/679-8546. Fax 435/679-8607. www.bpvillage.com. 62 units. A/C, TV, TEL. Summer $70–$80 double, $75–$99 cabins and kitchenette units; winter rates lower. DISC, MC, V. Pets accepted in cabins.

Bryce Valley Inn A member of the America's Best Value Inn & Suites franchise, the Bryce Valley Inn offers simply decorated, basic motel rooms that are a clean, well-maintained, and relatively economical choice for park visitors. Units are furnished with either one king-size bed, one or two queen-size beds, or two double beds. There are also suites with either one queen or one king bed, plus a refrigerator and microwave. A **restaurant** serves American cuisine, and a gift shop offers a large selection of American Indian arts and crafts, handmade gifts, rocks, and fossils. There is also an on-site coin-op laundry. All units are smoke-free.

199 N. Main St., Tropic, UT 84776. ✆ **800/442-1890** or 435/679-8811. Fax 435/679-8846. www.brycevalleyinn.com. 65 units. A/C, TV, TEL. May to mid-Oct $95–$115 double and suite; rates from $59 double the rest of the year. AE, DISC, MC, V. 8 miles east of the park entrance road. Pets accepted ($20 fee).

Bryce View Lodge This basic modern American motel gets our vote for the best combination of economy and location. It consists of four two-story buildings, set back from the road and grouped around a large parking lot and attractively landscaped area. Rooms are simple but comfortable, recently refurbished, and quiet, and have Wi-Fi.

Guests have access to the amenities across the street at Best Western Ruby's Inn (see above).

991 S. Utah 63, Bryce Canyon City, UT 84764. ✆ **888/279-2304** or 435/834-5180. Fax 435/834-5181. www.bryceviewlodge.com. 160 units. A/C, TV, TEL. Summer $80–$110 double; rest of year $60–$85 double. AE, DC, DISC, MC, V. Pets accepted.

Foster's You'll find clean, quiet, economical lodging at Foster's. A modular unit contains small rooms, each with either one queen or two double beds, decorated with posters showing scenery of the area; bathrooms have showers only. Refrigerators and microwaves are available for a $10 fee. Also on the grounds is a **grocery store** with a nice **bakery** and a **restaurant** (see "Where to Dine," below). All units are smoke-free.

1150 Utah 12 (1½ miles west of the national park access road turnoff), Bryce, UT 84764. ✆ **435/834-5227.** Fax 435/834-5304. www.fostersmotel.com. 52 units. A/C, TV, TEL. Summer $50–$60 double; discounts available in winter. AE, DISC, MC, V.

Stone Canyon Inn This charming inn gets our vote as the best place to stay outside the park for those who seek upscale accommodations, an abundance of pampering, and fantastic views. Each of the six guest rooms is unique, with queen or king-size beds, colorful quilts, handsome wood furnishings, and a classic Western look. Three rooms have double whirlpool tubs and separate showers, two rooms have a whirlpool tub/shower, and a partially handicap-accessible room has a traditional tub/shower.

The four cottages—they're much too nice to be called cabins—each have two bedrooms and two bathrooms, a gas fireplace, full kitchen with stainless-steel appliances and granite countertops, living room with TVs with VCR/DVD players, tile floors, a private deck with a hot tub, and a barbecue grill. All units have Wi-Fi and phones with free long-distance calls in the continental United States. Room guests (not those in cottages) receive a home-cooked full breakfast. Smoking is not permitted.

1220 W. 50 South (P.O. Box 156), Tropic, UT 84776. ✆ **866/489-4680** or 435/679-8611. www.stonecanyoninn.com. From Utah 12 in Tropic, take Bryce Way Rd. west 1 mile to Fairyland Lane and follow the sign to the inn. 10 units. A/C, TV, TEL. Apr–Oct $125–$200 rooms, $300–$325 cottages; winter rates lower. Room rates include full breakfast; cottage rates do not. AE, DC, DISC, MC, V. No children 4 or under allowed in the inn; no age restrictions for cottages.

11 Where to Dine

INSIDE THE PARK

Bryce Canyon Lodge AMERICAN We would come here just for the mountain-lodge atmosphere, with two stone fireplaces and large windows looking out on the park. But the food's good, too, and reasonably priced, considering that this is the only real restaurant in the park. The service is good, although not always speedy, but this is not a fast-food restaurant. Breakfasts offer the usual American standards—we especially like the sourdough French toast—and an excellent buffet. At lunch, you'll find sandwiches, burgers, salads, and a do-it-yourself taco bar. The menu changes periodically but may include dinner specialties such as pan-seared Alaskan sockeye salmon topped with sun-dried tomato pesto, and cherry-glazed pork chops. The menu also offers steaks—including the tasty saloon steak (a grilled flatiron steak rubbed with fresh herbs and topped with marinated peppers) and a New York strip, topped with cilantro butter. Recent vegetarian selections have included Peekaboo Vegetable Strudel—seasoned vegetables sautéed in herb olive oil, rolled in phyllo dough and baked. The restaurant has full liquor service.

Bryce Canyon National Park. ✆ **435/834-8760.** www.brycecanyonlodge.com. Reservations required for dinner. Main courses $4–$11 breakfast and lunch, $13–$25 dinner. AE, DC, DISC, MC, V. Daily 6:30–10:30am, 11am–3pm, and 5–10pm. Closed Nov–Mar.

NEAR THE PARK

In addition to the restaurants below, **Ebenezer's Barn & Grill,** part of the Best Western Ruby's Inn complex at 26 South Main St. in Bryce Canyon City, offers a Western dinner and show nightly at 8pm during the summer. Similar to chuckwagon dinners elsewhere, diners go through a chow line and pick up their grub, and then head to large tables to eat and enjoy the show, a combination of Western-style music and humor. Dinner choices include steak, grilled salmon, baked chicken, and pulled pork, with prices from $26 to $30, and all meals include beans, potatoes, corn bread, dessert, and a nonalcoholic beverage. Tickets are available at the Best Western Ruby's Inn; for information, call ✆ **435/834-5341,** ext. 7099 (www.rubysinn.com/ebenezers).

Bryce Canyon Pines AMERICAN A country cottage–style dining room, with an old wood stove, is the perfect setting for the American food served here. Especially popular for its breakfasts, the restaurant is also known for its homemade soups and pies—all the usuals, plus some not-so-usual selections such as banana blueberry. Sandwiches and full meals are available at lunch and dinner. Recommended are the Utah trout; the 8-ounce tenderloin steak; and the hot sandwiches, such as the open-faced turkey with mashed potatoes and gravy. Beer and wine are available.

Utah 12, about 3 miles west of intersection with park entry road. ✆ **435/834-5441.** www.brycecanyonmotel.com. Sandwiches $4–$9; full dinners $10–$20. AE, DC, DISC, MC, V. Daily 6:30am–9:30pm (may close slightly earlier in spring and fall). Closed mid-Nov through mid-Mar.

Picnic & Camping Supplies

A small store inside the national park has groceries, camping supplies, and snacks, all at surprisingly low prices. Just outside the park, the huge general store in the Best Western Ruby's Inn (see "Where to Stay," above) offers camping supplies, groceries, Western clothing, and souvenirs.

Canyon Diner AMERICAN This fast-food restaurant is a great place to fill up the kids without going broke. Breakfasts, served until 11am, include bagels and egg croissants; for lunch and dinner you can get hoagies, burgers, hot dogs, nachos, good stuffed potatoes, fresh-made pizza, broiled chicken sandwiches, and salads. We especially recommend the English-style chips. Specialties include a fish-and-chips basket. No alcohol is served.

At the Best Western Ruby's Inn, 26 S. Main St., Bryce Canyon City. ✆ **435/834-5341.** www.rubysinn.com. Reservations not accepted. Individual items $4–$7; meals $6–$10. AE, DISC, MC, V. Daily 6:30am–9:30pm. Closed Nov–Mar.

Cowboy's Buffet and Steak Room STEAK/SEAFOOD The busiest restaurant in the Bryce Canyon area, this main restaurant at the Best Western Ruby's Inn moves 'em through with buffets at every meal, plus a well-rounded menu and friendly service. The breakfast buffet offers more choices than you'd expect, with scrambled eggs, fresh fruit, several breakfast meats, potatoes, pastries, and cereals. At the lunch buffet, you'll find country-style ribs, fresh fruit, salads, soups, vegetables, and breads; while the dinner buffet features charbroiled thin-sliced rib-eye steak and other meats, pastas, potatoes, and salads. Regular menu dinner entrees include prime rib, slow-roasted baby back ribs, breaded-and-grilled southern Utah rainbow trout, broiled chicken breast, burgers, and salads. In addition to the large, Western-style dining room, an outdoor patio is open in good weather. Full liquor service is available.

At the Best Western Ruby's Inn, 26 S. Main St., Bryce Canyon City. ✆ **435/834-5341.** www.rubysinn.com. Reservations not accepted. Breakfast and lunch $7–$16; dinner main courses and buffets $9–$26. AE, DC, DISC, MC, V. Summer daily 6:30am–10pm; winter daily 6:30am–9pm.

Foster's Family Steak House STEAK/SEAFOOD The simple Western decor here provides the right atmosphere for a down-to-earth steakhouse. Locally popular for its slow-roasted prime rib and steamed Utah trout, Foster's also offers several steaks (carnivores like us appreciate the 14-oz. T-bone), sandwiches, a soup of the day, and homemade chili with beans. All of the pastries, pies, and breads are baked on the premises. Bottled beer is available with meals.

At Foster's motel, 1150 Utah 12, about 1½ miles west of the park entrance road. ✆ **435/834-5227.** www.fostersmotel.com. Most breakfast and lunch items $4–$10; dinner main courses $10–$24. AE, DISC, MC, V. Mar–Nov daily 7am–10pm; call for winter hours.

12 Nearby Attractions

For excursions throughout the area, the Best Western Ruby's Inn, on Utah 63 just north of the Bryce Canyon National Park entrance (see "Where to Stay," above), is a one-stop entertainment center.

Directly across from the inn are the **Old Bryce Town Shops,** open daily 8am to 10pm from May through September. They include a rock shop and a variety of other stores where you can buy that genuine cowboy hat you've been wanting. There's a trail here especially for kids, where they can search for arrowheads, fossils, and petrified wood. You can also try your hand at panning for gold.

Nearby, **Bryce Canyon Country Rodeo** (✆ **866/782-0002;** www.rubysinn.com/rodeo.html) showcases broncos, bull riding, calf roping, and all sorts of rodeo fun in a 1-hour program from Memorial Day weekend through Labor Day weekend, Wednesday through Saturday evenings at 7pm. Admission is $10 for adults, $7 for children 3 to 12, and free for kids under 3.

13 Grand Staircase–Escalante National Monument

Covering almost 1.9 million acres, this vast area of canyons, mesas, plateaus, and river valleys became a national monument by presidential proclamation in 1996. Known for its rugged beauty, it contains a combination of geological, biological, paleontological, archaeological, and historical resources. In announcing the creation of the monument, President Bill Clinton proclaimed, "This high, rugged, and remote region was the last place in the continental United States to be mapped; even today, this unspoiled natural area remains a frontier, a quality that greatly enhances the monument's value for scientific study."

Unlike most other national monuments, almost all of this vast area is undeveloped—it has few all-weather roads, only one maintained hiking trail, and two small campgrounds. But the adventurous have access to miles upon miles of dirt roads and practically unlimited opportunities for hiking, horseback riding, mountain biking, and camping.

The national monument consists of three distinct sections: The **Grand Staircase** of sandstone cliffs—including five life zones, from Sonoran desert to coniferous forests—is the southwest section; the **Kaiparowits Plateau,** a vast, wild region of rugged mesas and steep canyons, is the center section; and the **Escalante River Canyons,** a delightfully scenic area containing miles of connecting river canyons, is the northern section.

ESSENTIALS

GETTING THERE

The monument covers an area almost as large as the states of Delaware and Rhode Island combined, with Bryce Canyon National Park to the west, Capitol Reef National Park along the northeast edge, and Glen Canyon National Recreation Area along the east and part of the south sides.

Access is on **Utah 12** along the monument's northwest edge, from Kodachrome Basin State Park and the communities of Escalante and Boulder; and by U.S. 89 to the southern section of the monument, east of the town of Kanab.

INFORMATION & VISITOR CENTERS

The national monument remains a rugged area, with limited facilities, poor roads, and changeable weather. We strongly suggest that before setting out, all visitors contact one of the monument's visitor centers to get maps and other information, and especially to check on current road and weather conditions. Also see the monument's website, **www.ut.blm.gov/monument**.

Visitor centers include the **Escalante Interagency Visitor Center,** on the west side of Escalante at 755 W. Main St. (Utah 12), Escalante, UT 84726 (✆ **435/826-5499**), open daily 7:30am to 5:30pm from mid-March through mid-November, and 8am to 4:30pm Monday through Friday the rest of the year. You can also get information at the Bureau of Land Management's **Kanab Visitor Center,** 745 E. U.S. 89, Kanab, UT 84741 (✆ **435/644-4680**), open daily 8am to 5pm.

The **Cannonville Visitor Center** is open daily from 8am to 4:30pm, mid-March through mid-November only, at 10 Center St. in Cannonville (✆ **435/826-5640**), east of Bryce Canyon National Park. The **Big Water Visitor Center** is along U.S. 89 near the southern edge of Glen Canyon National Recreation Area, at 100 Upper Revolution Way in Big Water (✆ **435/675-3200**). It is open daily from 9am to 6pm April through October, and daily 8am to 5pm the rest of the year.

FEES, REGULATIONS & SAFETY

There is no charge to enter most of the monument. **Calf Creek Recreation Area** charges $2 for day use and $7 for camping; camping at **Deer Creek** costs $4. Regulations are similar to those on other public lands and, in particular, forbid damaging or disturbing archaeological and historic sites.

The main safety concern is **water**—too little or too much. This is generally very dry country, so those going into the monument should carry plenty of drinking water. On the other hand, thunderstorms can turn the dirt roads into impassable mud bogs in minutes, stranding motorists. Potentially fatal **flash floods** through narrow canyons can catch hikers by surprise. ***The upshot:*** Everyone planning trips into the monument should check first with one of the offices listed above about current and anticipated weather and travel conditions.

SPORTS & ACTIVITIES

The monument offers numerous opportunities for outdoor adventures, including **canyoneering** through narrow slot canyons (with the aid of ropes). You can get information on the best areas for canyoneering at the monument's visitor centers, but we cannot emphasize too strongly that this is not a place for beginners. To put it bluntly, people die here, and you don't want to be one of them.

We recommend that, unless you are an expert at this specialized sport, you go with an expert. One of the best is Rick Green, owner of **Excursions of Escalante,** 125 E. Main St. (P.O. Box 605), Escalante, UT 84726 (✆ **800/839-7567;** www.excursionsofescalante.com). Trips, which are available year-round, usually include four people with one guide, and all equipment is provided. In addition to canyoneering trips, the company offers day hiking and backpacking excursions, specialized tours, and 3-day canyoneering courses ($450–$550). Day trips include lunch. Hiking trips cost $125 per person, canyoneering costs $145 to $160 per person, and a photo safari costs $170 per person. Overnight backpacking trips cost $225 per person per day, which includes practically everything you need, including food. Credit cards are not accepted; cash and checks are welcome. Excursions of Escalante also provides a flexible shuttle service; call for a quote.

HIKING, MOUNTAIN BIKING & HORSEBACK RIDING About 15 miles northeast of Escalante on Utah 12, the **Calf Creek Recreation Area** has a campground (see "Camping," below) and a picnic area with fire grates, tables, drinking water, and flush toilets. Well shaded, it lies along a creek at the bottom of a narrow, high-walled rock canyon.

The best part of the recreation area is the moderately strenuous 5.5-mile round-trip hike to **Lower Calf Creek Falls.** A sandy trail leads along Calf Creek, past beaver ponds and wetlands, to a beautiful waterfall cascading 126 feet down a rock wall into a tree-shaded pool. You can pick up an interpretive brochure at the trail head.

Even though the Calf Creek Trail is the monument's only officially marked and maintained trail, numerous unmarked cross-country routes are ideal for hiking, mountain biking, and horseback riding. We strongly recommend that hikers stop at the **Interagency Office** in Escalante or the **Bureau of Land Management office** in Kanab to get recommendations on hiking routes and to purchase topographical maps.

Among the popular and relatively easy-to-follow hiking routes is the footpath to **Escalante Natural Bridge.** It repeatedly crosses the river, so be prepared to get wet up to your knees. The easy 2-mile (one-way) hike begins at a parking area at the bridge that crosses the Escalante River near Calf Creek Recreation Area, 15 miles northeast of the town of Escalante. From the parking area, hike upstream to Escalante Natural Bridge, on the south side of the river. The bridge is 130 feet high and spans 100 feet. From here you can continue upstream, exploring side canyons, or turn around and head back to the parking lot.

Also starting at the Utah 12 bridge parking area is a hike downstream to **Phipps Wash.** Mostly moderate, this hike goes about 1.5 miles to the mouth of Phipps Wash, which enters the river from the west. On a north-side drainage of Phipps Wash, you'll find **Maverick Natural Bridge;** by climbing up the south side, you can get to **Phipps Arch.**

Hiking the **slot canyons** is very popular, but we can't stress too strongly that you must make sure to check on flood potential before starting out. One challenging and very strenuous slot canyon hike is through **Peek-a-boo** and **Spooky canyons,** which are accessible from the Hole-in-the-Rock Road (see "Sightseeing & Four-Wheeling," below). Stop at the Escalante Interagency Office for directions.

SIGHTSEEING & FOUR-WHEELING This is one of America's least-developed large sections of public land, offering a wonderful opportunity for exploration by the adventurous. Be aware, though, that roads inside the monument are dirt that becomes mud, and often impassable, when it rains.

One particularly popular road is the **Hole-in-the-Rock Scenic Backway,** which is partly in the national monument and partly in the adjacent Glen Canyon National Recreation Area. Like most roads in the monument, it is safe in dry weather only. Starting about 5 miles northeast of Escalante off Utah 12, this clearly marked dirt road travels 57 miles (one-way) to the Hole-in-the-Rock, where Mormon settlers in 1880 cut a passage through solid rock to get their wagons down a 1,200-foot cliff to the canyon floor and Colorado River below.

About 12 miles in, the road passes by the sign to **Devil's Rock Garden,** an area of classic red-rock formations and arches, where you'll find a picnic area (about 1 mile off the main road). The road continues across a plateau of desert terrain, ending at a spectacular scenic overlook of Lake Powell. The first 35 miles of the scenic byway are relatively easy (in dry weather) in a standard passenger car, but then it gets a bit steeper and sandier. The last 6 miles of the road require a high-clearance 4WD vehicle. Allow about 6 hours round-trip, and make sure you have plenty of fuel and water.

Another recommended drive is the **Cottonwood Canyon Road,** which runs from Kodachrome Basin State Park south to U.S. 89, along the monument's southern edge, a distance of about 46 miles. The road is sandy and narrow (and washboard in places) but usually passable for cars in dry weather. It mostly follows Cottonwood Wash, with good views of red-rock formations plus panoramas from hilltops. Unfortunately, two power lines mar views through the canyon and make photography a challenge—though in all fairness, we should acknowledge that the road would not exist at all if not for the power lines.

About 10 miles east of Kodachrome Basin State Park is a short turnoff from Cottonwood Canyon Road that leads to **Grosvenor Arch.** This magnificent stone arch, with an opening 99 feet wide, is well worth the trip. (It bears the name of National Geographic Society founder and editor Gilbert H. Grosvenor.)

WILDLIFE VIEWING & BIRD-WATCHING The isolated and rugged terrain offers a good habitat for a number of species, such as **desert bighorn sheep** and **mountain lions.** As for birds, more than 200 species have been spotted, including **bald eagles, golden eagles, Swainson's hawks,** and **peregrine falcons.** The best areas for seeing wildlife are along the Escalante and Paria rivers and Johnson Creek.

CAMPING

Backcountry camping is permitted in most areas of the monument with a free **permit,** available at the Interagency office in Escalante and the BLM office in Kanab. There are also two designated campgrounds. **Calf Creek Recreation Area,** about 15 miles northeast of the town of Escalante on Utah 12, has 13 sites and a picnic area. Open year-round, the tree-shaded campground often fills by 10am in summer. Located in a scenic, steep canyon along Calf Creek, surrounded by rock walls, the campground has a volleyball court and offers access to an interpretive hiking trail (see "Hiking, Mountain Biking & Horseback Riding," above). It has drinking water and restrooms with flush toilets, but no showers, RV hookups or dump station, or garbage removal. In addition, from November through

March, water is turned off and only vault toilets are available. To reach the campground, vehicles ford a shallow creek. The campground is not recommended for vehicles over 25 feet long. Campsites cost $7 per night; day use is $2 per vehicle.

The national monument's other designated campground is **Deer Creek,** 6 miles east of the town of Boulder along the scenic Burr Trail Road. It has four primitive sites and no drinking water or other facilities; camping costs $4 per night.

8

Canyonlands National Park, UT

by Don & Barbara Laine

Utah's largest national park, Canyonlands is a rugged high desert of rock, with spectacular formations and gorges carved over the centuries by the park's primary architects, the Colorado and Green rivers. This is a land of extremes, of vast panoramas, deep canyons, steep cliffs, broad mesas, and towering red spires.

The most accessible part of Canyonlands is the Island in the Sky District, in the northern section of the park between the Colorado and Green rivers. A paved road leads to sites such as Grand View Point, overlooking some 10,000 square miles of rugged wilderness. Island in the Sky also has several easy to moderate trails offering sweeping vistas of the park. A short walk provides views of Upheaval Dome, which resembles a large volcanic crater but may actually have been created by the crash of a meteorite. For the more adventurous, the 100-mile White Rim Road takes experienced mountain bikers and those with high-clearance four-wheel-drive vehicles on a winding loop tour through a vast array of scenery.

The Needles District, in the park's southeast corner, has only a few view points along the paved road, but it offers numerous possibilities for hikers, backpackers, and high-clearance 4WDs. Named for its tall, red-and-white-striped rock pinnacles, this district is home to impressive arches, including the 150-foot-tall Angel Arch, as well as meadows and the confluence of the Green and Colorado rivers. Backcountry visitors to the Needles District will also find ruins and rock art left by American Indians some 800 years ago.

Most park visitors don't get a close-up view of the Maze District, which lies on the west side of the Green and Colorado rivers, but instead see it off in the distance from Grand View Point at Island in the Sky, or Confluence Overlook in the Needles District. That's because it's inhospitable and practically inaccessible. You'll need a lot of endurance and at least several days to see even a few of its sites. In 1 day, hardy hikers can visit Horseshoe Canyon, where they can see the Great Gallery, an 80-foot-long rock art panel.

The park is also accessible by boat, which is how explorer Maj. John Wesley Powell first saw the canyons in 1869, when he made his first trip down the Green to its confluence with the Colorado, and then traveled farther downstream, eventually to the Grand Canyon. River access is from the towns of Moab and Green River; local companies offer boat trips of various durations.

You'll find a fascinating mixture of mountain and desert animals in Canyonlands; it varies depending on the time of year and your location. The best times to see most wildlife are early and late in the day, especially in the summer, when the midday sun drives all Canyonlands residents to search for shade. Throughout the park, you'll probably hear, if not see, coyotes, and you'll likely spot white-tailed antelope, squirrels, and other rodents scampering among the rocks. Watch for the elusive bighorn sheep along isolated cliffs, where you might also see a golden eagle or a turkey vulture soaring above the rocks in search of prey. In the pools of water that appear in the slickrock after rainstorms, you're likely to see tadpole shrimp—1-inch-long crustaceans. Among the cottonwoods and willows along the rivers, you'll find a variety of wildlife: deer, beaver, an occasional bobcat, and various migratory birds.

AVOIDING THE CROWDS

Although Canyonlands does not get as crowded as other major national parks—usually a bit under 400,000 visitors annually—the more popular trails can be busy. Spring and fall see the most visitors, but summer has recently become popular, despite scorching temperatures. Those who seriously want to avoid humanity should visit from November through mid-March, when the park is practically deserted, though some trails and 4WD roads may be inaccessible. College spring-break time (usually mid-Mar through Apr) can be especially busy, and any other school vacation usually brings more visitors as well. Hiking in the early morning—often the best time to hike anyway—is a good way to beat the crowds any time of year.

One thing that makes the backcountry experience here especially pleasant is that the number of permits for overnight trips is limited (and permits often sell out well in advance). If you're willing to hike, bike, or drive far enough, you're guaranteed that you won't be sharing the trail or road with a lot of other people.

Canyonlands National Park

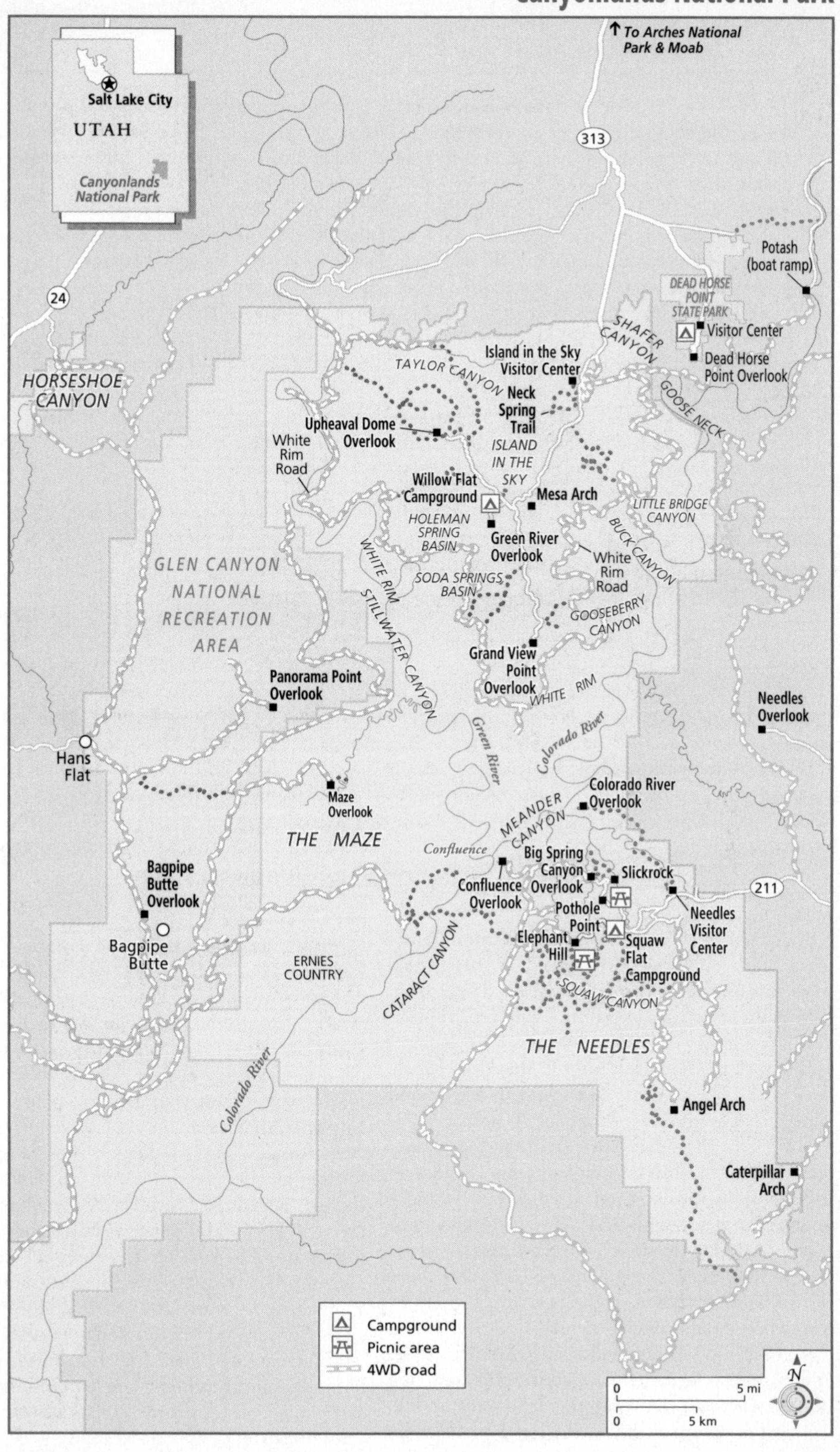

Tips from a Park Ranger

"A wilderness of rock" is how Paul Henderson, Canyonlands' chief of interpretation, describes the park, adding it contains some of the most remote country in the Lower 48. "There's some wonderful opportunities here to find solitude that don't exist in too many other places," Henderson adds.

"Island in the Sky District receives the highest visitation and has the most extensive frontcountry road system, so it's a place where folks that aren't equipped for a backcountry adventure can still get a good feeling for what this park is all about," he says. "There's a paved road system, and you can have a really good experience in half a day."

Henderson says that Island in the Sky is not only for the pavement-bound. "The premier opportunity at Island in the Sky is the White Rim Road," he says. "A network of old mining roads and cowboy trails that make about a 100-mile trip—it's one of the premier mountain-biking trips in the country."

The Needles District is not a good place to cycle, but has first-rate options for hiking, backpacking, and four-wheeling. "Needles is pretty rough country, with some classic four-wheel-drive roads that, for the most part, are not for novice four-wheel-drivers," he says. "I cringe when I see somebody in a brand-new $35,000 rig and it's probably the first time they've locked it into four-wheel-drive."

The park's third district, the Maze, is very rough backcountry, Henderson says, and not for everyone. It is a great destination if you don't want to see many people. In one recent year, there were about 40,000 people at Island in the Sky, about 20,000 at Needles, but only 546 at the Maze.

1 Essentials

There are campgrounds but no lodgings, restaurants, or stores inside the park. Most visitors stay in Moab.

GETTING THERE & GATEWAYS

For directions to Moab, see "Getting There & Gateways," in chapter 2.

To get to the Island in the Sky Visitor Center from Moab (about 34 miles), take **U.S. 191** (which runs north–south through eastern Utah from Wyoming to Arizona) north to Utah 313, and follow it south into the park.

To reach the Needles Visitor Center from Moab, leave U.S. 191 at **Utah 211** south of Moab, and head west into the park. It's about 75 miles.

To get to the Maze District, from Moab, take U.S. 191 north, then go west for about 11 miles on **I-70,** crossing Green River, and then take **Utah 24** south. Watch for signs and follow two- and four-wheel-drive dirt roads east into the park.

The Horseshoe Canyon area of the park is about 120 miles from Island in the Sky. To get there by two-wheel-drive vehicle, follow I-70 west from Green River to U.S. 24, and then go south about 24 miles to the Horseshoe Canyon turnoff (near the WATCH FOR SAND DRIFTS sign), where you turn left. Follow this maintained dirt road for about 30 miles to the canyon's west rim, where you can park. This is the trail head for the hike to the Great Gallery (see "Day Hikes," below).

THE NEAREST AIRPORT & RENTING A CAR See the sections "The Nearest Airport" and "Ground Transportation," in chapter 2.

INFORMATION

Contact **Canyonlands National Park,** 2282 SW Resource Blvd., Moab, UT 84532 (✆ **435/719-2313;** www.nps.gov/cany). Area information is available in advance from the **Moab Area Travel Council,** P.O. Box 550, Moab, UT 84532 (✆ **800/635-6622** or 435/259-8825; www.discovermoab.com). When you arrive, stop by the **Moab Information Center,** at the corner of Main and Center streets, open Monday through Saturday 8am to 8pm and Sunday from 9am to 7pm from July through September, with shorter hours the rest of the year. This multi-agency visitor center has information from the Park Service, Bureau of Land Management, U.S. Forest Service, Grand County Travel Council, and Canyonlands Natural History Association. You can get advice, watch videos on Southwest attractions, pick up brochures on local businesses and outfitters, and purchase books and other materials. A board displays current weather conditions and campsite availability.

If You Have Only 1 Day

If your schedule permits only a day, skip the Needles and Maze districts and drive to the **Island in the Sky Visitor Center.** After looking at the exhibits, drive to several of the overlooks, stopping for a short hike or two. Make sure you get to the **Grand View Point Overlook,** at the south end of the paved road. Among the best trails for a quick trip is the **Grand View Trail,** which starts at the overlook and is especially scenic in late afternoon. Allow about 1½ hours for this easy 2-mile walk. Also recommended is the **Upheaval Dome Overlook Trail,** which should take about a half-hour; it brings you to a mile-wide crater of mysterious origins.

Perhaps a better choice for a quick visit to the park, especially for those with a bit of extra cash, is to take a guided trip by four-wheel-drive vehicle or raft. See the "Organized Tours & Ranger Programs" and "Outfitters Based in Moab" sections, below.

Canyonlands Natural History Association offers a number of helpful books and maps for sale (see "Information," in chapter 2). A good guide for serious hikers is ***Hiking Canyonlands and Arches National Parks,*** by Bill Schneider.

VISITOR CENTERS

Canyonlands National Park operates **Island in the Sky Visitor Center,** in the northern part of the park, and **Needles Visitor Center,** in the southern section. At both, you can get advice from rangers, as well as maps and free brochures on hiking trails. Visitor center hours are 9am to 4:30pm, with extended summer hours, and both are closed Christmas and New Year's Day.

FEES & PERMITS

Entry into the park (for up to 7 days) costs $10 per private vehicle or $5 per person on foot, bike, or motorcycle. A $25 annual pass is also available; it's good for Canyonlands and Arches national parks, as well as Natural Bridges and Hovenweep national monuments. The camping fee at **Squaw Flat Campground** in the Needles District is $15; camping at **Willow Flat Campground** in the Island in the Sky District costs $10.

Backcountry permits, available at either visitor center, are required for all overnight stays in the park, except at the two established campgrounds. Permit reservations can be made in advance (© **435/259-4351;** www.nps.gov/cany/reserve.htm). Permits for overnight four-wheel-drive and mountain-bike trips are $30; for overnight backpacking trips, $15. The permit for white-water boating through Cataract Canyon is $30; flat-water boating costs $20. Permits are for groups, not individuals; see the park website for group size limitations.

Visitors bringing motor vehicles, horses, or mountain bikes on roads into Salt Creek/Horse Canyon and Lavender Canyon in the Needles District pay a $5 day-use fee.

SPECIAL REGULATIONS & WARNINGS

Backcountry hikers must pack out all trash, and wood fires are prohibited. Canyonlands National Park is not a good place to take pets. Dogs, which must be leashed at all times, are prohibited in public buildings, on all trails, and in the backcountry. This includes four-wheel-drive roads—dogs are not permitted even inside your vehicle.

The main safety problem at Canyonlands is that people underestimate the hazards. It's important that you know your limitations, as well as the limitations of your vehicle and other equipment. Rangers warn hikers to carry at least 1 gallon of water per person per day, to be careful near cliff edges, to avoid overexposure to the sun, and to carry maps in the backcountry. During lightning storms, avoid lone trees, high ridges, and cliff edges. Four-wheel-drive-vehicle operators should carry extra food and emergency equipment. Also, anyone going into the backcountry should let someone know where they're going and when they plan to return. Traveling alone in Canyonlands is not a good idea.

SEASONS & CLIMATE

Summers here are hot, with temperatures sometimes exceeding 100°F (38°C). Winters can be cool or cold, dropping below freezing at night. The best time to visit, especially for hikers, is in the spring or fall, when daytime temperatures are usually from 60° to 80°F (16°–27°C) and nights are cool. Late summer and early fall visitors should be prepared for afternoon thunderstorms.

2 Exploring the Park by Car

No driving tour has yet been designed to show off Canyonlands National Park. The Island in the Sky District has about 20 miles of paved highway, some gravel roads accessible to two-wheel-drive vehicles, and several view points. The Needles District has only 8 miles of paved roads. Many (but not all) of Needles' view points and trail heads are accessible only by high-clearance 4WD vehicles or on foot. The Maze District has only two main roads, neither of them paved. Both lead to trail heads.

If you happen to have a serious 4WD, and if you are equally serious about doing some hard-core four-wheeling, this is the park for you. See "Other Sports & Activities," below. Because of the constantly changing conditions of dirt roads, we strongly suggest that you discuss your plans with rangers before setting out.

3 Organized Tours & Ranger Programs

A variety of ranger programs run from March through October. In the **Island in the Sky** district, there are several programs daily, usually including geology presentations at Grand View Point at 10:30 and 11:30am, and talks at the Visitor Center at 10:30am and 1:30pm. In the **Needles** district, there are 1-hour evening programs at Squaw Flat Campground most nights, starting at 7:30pm.

Canyonlands by Night & Day (✆ **800/394-9978** or 435/259-2628; www.canyonlandsbynight.com) offers a variety of excursions, including an evening river trip, spring through fall, that combines a sunset jet boat ride with a Dutch-oven dinner. The office and dock are just north of Moab at the Colorado River Bridge. Cost for the boat trip and dinner is $65 for adults and $55 for children 4 to 12 (minimum age 4), with a family rate of $199 for two adults and two children. Reservations are recommended.

FLYING TOURS

Canyonlands is beautiful, but many of its most spectacular sections are difficult to get to. One solution is to take to the air. **Slickrock Air Guides, Inc.** (✆ **866/259-1626** or 435/259-6216; www.slickrockairguides.com) offers 1-hour scenic flights over Canyonlands National Park and nearby areas for $140 per person, 2½-hour flights that take in Canyonlands and Monument Valley for $260 per person, and 3-hour flights that add Lake Powell, the edge of the Grand Canyon, and Capitol Reef National Park for $385 per person.

4 Park Attractions

This land was once the domain of prehistoric American Indians, who constructed their buildings out of the region's rock, hunted deer and bighorn sheep, and left numerous drawings on rock walls. Most of the park's archaeological sites are in the Needles District. They include the well-preserved cliff dwelling called **Tower Ruin,** high on a cliff ledge in Horse Canyon, and an easy-to-reach **ancient granary,** near the Needles Visitor Center, that is accessible on the short self-guided Roadside Ruin Trail. Throughout the park you'll also find evidence of more modern peoples—the trappers, explorers, and cowboys of the 19th century.

In Horseshoe Canyon, a separate and remote section of the park on the west side of the Green River, you'll find the **Great Gallery,** one of the most fantastic rock art panels in the Southwest. More than 80 feet long, the panel contains many red-and-white paintings of what appear to be larger-than-life human figures. The paintings are believed to be at least 2,000 years old.

5 Day Hikes

Conditions along these trails can be tough in summer: little shade, no reliable water sources, and temperatures soaring to over 100°F (38°C). Because of this, rangers strongly advise that hikers carry at least 1 gallon of water per person per day, along with sunscreen, a hat, and all the usual hiking and emergency equipment. If you expect to do some serious hiking, try to plan your trip for the spring or fall, when conditions are much more hospitable.

All hikers should be careful on the trails that cross slickrock, a general term for any bare rock surface. As the name implies, it can be slippery, especially when wet. Also, because some of the trails may be confusing, hikers attempting the longer ones should take good topographical maps, available at visitor centers and at stores in Moab.

The following are some of the park's many hiking possibilities, arranged by district; check with rangers for other suggestions.

ISLAND IN THE SKY DISTRICT

SHORTER TRAILS

Aztec Butte Trail This short but steep trail, which climbs about 225 feet, leads up to a slickrock dome where you'll see some Ancestral Puebloan granaries, as well as fantastic panoramic views across a canyon. 1 mile one-way. Moderate. Access: Aztec Butte parking area.

Grand View Point Trail At the trail head, read the sign that points out all the prominent features you can see, such as the **Totem Pole** and the confluence of the **Colorado and Green rivers.** Although this is a fairly flat and easy trail, you should watch carefully for the cairns that mark the trail, because some are on the small side. And stay back from the cliff edge. This trail is especially beautiful at sunset, when the panorama seems to change constantly with the diminishing angle of sunlight. 1 mile one-way. Easy. Access: Grand View Point Overlook at south end of paved road.

Mesa Arch Trail This is a self-guided nature walk through an area of pinyon and juniper trees, mountain mahogany, cactus, and a plant called Mormon Tea, from which Mormon pioneers made hot drinks. The trail's main scenic attraction is the **Mesa Arch,** made of Navajo sandstone. It hangs precariously on the edge of a 500-foot cliff, framing a spectacular view of nearby mountains. .5 mile RT. Easy. Access: Trail head along paved road about 6 miles south of visitor center.

Upheaval Dome Overlook This hike to the overlook has a few steep inclines. Upheaval Dome doesn't fit with the rest of Canyonlands' terrain—it's the result not of gradual erosion (like the rest of the park), but of a dramatic deformity in which rocks have been pushed into a domelike structure. Experts say it may have been caused by a meteorite that struck Earth some 60 million years ago. Hiking another .5 mile takes you to a second overlook, closer to the Dome but with a less panoramic view. .5 mile one-way. Moderate. Access: Trail head at end of Upheaval Dome Rd.

Whale Rock Trail This trail provides breathtaking 360-degree views of the Island in the Sky District. It's a climb of 300 feet up a slickrock trail with handrails. Wander around on top a bit and study the varied formations; to those with some imagination, the outcrop you just climbed resembles a whale. .5 mile one-way. Moderate. Access: Trail head about 4 miles down Upheaval Dome Rd.

LONGER TRAILS

Gooseberry Trail Although the beginning of this trail is so steep it looks like a cliff, don't be deterred. True, it drops 1,400 feet over the course of the hike, and most of that (1,300 ft.) in the first 1.5 miles. But the trail is well made and, with a little care, is quite safe. As you gingerly hike down the switchbacks—be careful of the loose sand—you get superb views of this rugged red-rock country. Once down in Gooseberry Canyon, it's nearly a level walk out to the road. When you decide you're ready to face the climb back to the top, be sure to take lots of rest stops to admire the varying scenery. 2.7 miles one-way. Moderate. Access: Island in the Sky Picnic Area, about 11 miles south of visitor center.

Lathrop Canyon Trail The first 2.5 miles of this trail are on top of the mesa, but then it meanders down into the canyon, descending about 1,600 feet to the White Rim Road. This hike traverses steep terrain and loose rock—and remember, unless you have been able to arrange for someone to meet you at the road, you have to climb back up to your car. As you hike down the slope, you get grand views of **Lathrop Canyon** and glimpses of the **Colorado River.** It is possible to continue down to the river from the road (another 4 miles each way), but check with rangers about the feasibility of an overnight trip before attempting it. 5 miles one-way. Strenuous. Access: Trail head about 1½ miles south of visitor center along paved road.

Neck Spring Trail This hike follows the paths that animals and early ranchers created to reach water at two springs. You'll see water troughs, hitching posts, and the ruins of an old cabin. Because of the water source, you'll encounter types of vegetation not usually seen in the park, such as maidenhair ferns and Gambel oak. The water also draws wildlife, including mule deer, bighorn sheep, ground squirrels, and hummingbirds. Climbing to the top of the rim, you get a beautiful view of the canyons and even the **Henry Mountains,** some 60 miles away. 5.8 miles RT. Moderate to strenuous. Access: Trail head about ½ mile south of visitor center along paved road.

Syncline Loop Trail This is a long, hot day hike over one of only three loop trails in the Island in the Sky District. Be sure to start early and carry plenty of water. The trail drops 1,300 feet, and the best approach is clockwise, so you take the steepest part going down into **Upheaval Canyon.** Along the way, you'll follow dry washes, climb small hills and steep canyon sides, cross part of the Syncline Valley, pass **Upheaval Dome,** traverse some slickrock, and finally hit an area of lush vegetation. 8 miles RT. Strenuous. Access: Upheaval Dome Picnic Area, at end of Upheaval Dome Rd.

NEEDLES DISTRICT

Hiking trails here are generally not too tough, but keep in mind that slickrock can live up to its name and that there is generally little shade.

SHORTER TRAILS

Roadside Ruin Trail This self-guided nature walk leads to an ancient granary, probably used by the ancestral Puebloans (also known as the Anasazi) some 700 to 1,000 years ago to store corn, nuts, and other foods. For 25¢ you can get a brochure at the trail head that discusses the plants along the trail. Although it's flat, this trail can be muddy when wet. .3 mile RT. Easy. Access: Trail head just over ½ mile west of visitor center along paved road.

Slickrock Trail View points along this trail show off the stair-step topography of the area, from its colorful canyons and cliffs to its flat mesas and striped needles. Watch for bighorn sheep. 2.4 miles RT. Moderate. Access: Trail head about 6½ miles from visitor center, almost at end of road.

LONGER TRAILS

Big Spring Canyon to Squaw Canyon Trail This hike over steep slickrock winds through woodlands of pinyon and juniper, offering views along the way of the Needles rock formations for which the district is named, plus nearby cliffs and mesas as well as distant mountains. Watch for wildflowers from late spring through summer. You can complete this hike in about half a day, but several backcountry campsites make it available to overnighters. 7.5-mile loop. Strenuous. Access: Squaw Flat Campground.

Confluence Overlook Trail This hike has steep drop-offs and little shade, but the hard work is worthwhile—it shows off splendidly the many colors of the Needles District and offers excellent views into the Maze District of the park. The climax is a spectacular view overlooking the confluence of the **Green and Colorado rivers** in a 1,000-foot-deep gorge. This excursion can be done as a day hike (allow 4–6 hr.) or quite pleasantly as an overnight hike. 5.5 miles one-way. Moderate to strenuous. Access: Big Spring Canyon Overlook.

Druid Arch Trail A number of connecting trails lead into the backcountry from this trail head. The hike to Druid Arch, though not difficult, challenges hikers with steep drop-offs, quite a bit of slickrock, and a 1,000-foot increase in elevation. But the views make it well worth the effort. You hike through narrow rock canyons, past colorful spires and pinnacles, and up the steep climb to the bench just below the huge **Druid Arch,** its dark rock somewhat resembling the stone structures of Stonehenge. 5.5 miles one-way. Moderate. Access: Elephant Hill trail head at end of graded gravel road, manageable for most 2-wheel-drive passenger cars, but not for large vehicles such as RVs.

MAZE DISTRICT

Getting to the trail heads in the Maze District involves rugged four-wheel-drive roads; rangers can help you with directions.

The 3-mile **Maze Overlook Trail** is not for beginners or those with a fear of heights. It is quite steep in places, requiring the use of your hands. At the trail head, you get a fine view of the narrow canyons that inspired this district's name; the trail then descends 600 feet to the canyon bottom.

The 12-mile **Harvest Scene Loop** (difficult, 7–10 hr. or overnight) leads over slickrock and along canyon washes—watch for the cairns to be sure you don't wander off the trail—to a magnificent example of rock art.

Other trail heads lie in what is known as the **Doll House Area.** Check with a ranger for current trail conditions and difficulty.

HORSESHOE CANYON

This detached section of the park was added to Canyonlands in 1971 mainly because of its **Great Gallery,** an 80-foot-long rock art panel with larger-than-life human figures, which dates from 2000 B.C. to A.D. 500. The Horseshoe Canyon Unit is some 120 miles (one-way) from Island in the Sky, and only one road runs in (see "Getting There & Gateways," above). From the parking area, it's a 6.5-mile round-trip hike to see the rock art. The hike begins with a 1.5-mile section down an 800-foot slope to the canyon floor, where you turn right and go 1.75 miles to the Great Gallery. There is no camping in Horseshoe Canyon, but just outside the park boundary, primitive camping is available on Bureau of Land Management property on the rim.

6 Exploring the Backcountry

You'll find many opportunities for backpacking in Canyonlands National Park, although hikers will often be sharing trail/road combinations with four-wheel-drive vehicles and mountain bikes. Additional information is provided below.

7 Other Sports & Activities

If you've come to Utah for mountain biking, hiking, four-wheeling, or rafting, this is the place. The region holds surprises, too, from ancient American Indian dwellings and rock art to dinosaur bones.

Unlike most national parks, the backcountry at Canyonlands is not only the domain of backpackers. Here rugged four-wheel-drive and mountain-bike roads, as well as rivers navigable by boat, lead to some of the park's most scenic areas. Primitive campsites, strategically located throughout the backcountry, are available to all visitors, regardless of their mode of transport. Just be sure to make your backcountry campsite reservations well in advance—up to a year ahead for the more popular areas. You can get reservation forms and detailed information by mail, over the phone, or from the park's website (see "Information," above).

OUTFITTERS BASED IN MOAB

Some 50 local outfitters offer excursions of all kinds, from lazy canoe rides to hair-raising jet-boat and four-wheel-drive adventures. The chart below lists some of the major companies that want to help you fully enjoy this beautiful country. All are in Moab. Advance reservations are often required, and it's best to check with several outfitters before you decide on one. In addition to asking about what you'll see and do and what it will cost, it doesn't hurt to make sure the company is insured and has the proper permits with various federal agencies. Also ask about the cancellation policy, just in case.

BIKING Road bikes are of little use in Canyonlands, except for getting to and from trail heads, view points, visitor centers, and campgrounds in the Island in the Sky and Needles districts. Although bikes of any kind are prohibited on hiking trails and cross-country in the backcountry, they are permitted on designated two- and four-wheel-drive roads. Mountain bikers have many possibilities, although they will find themselves sharing dirt roads with motor vehicles and hikers. Some spots on the four-wheel-drive roads have deep sand that can turn into quicksand when wet—so you may find that mountain biking, while certainly a challenge, is not as much fun as you'd expect. It's wise to talk with rangers about conditions on specific roads before setting out.

Among popular rides are the **Elephant Hill** and **Colorado Overlook roads,** both in the Needles District. The 100-mile **White Rim Road,** in the Island in the Sky District, also makes a great mountain-bike trip (allow at least 4 days), especially for bikers who can arrange for an accompanying 4WD vehicle to carry water, food, and camping gear. See "Four-Wheeling," below.

Cyclists can get information and rent or repair bikes at **Poison Spider Bicycles,** 497 N. Main St. (✆ **800/635-1792** or 435/259-7882; www.poisonspiderbicycles.com). Bike rentals and repairs, plus shuttle services, will be found at **Chile Pepper Bike Shop,** 702 S. Main St. (✆ **888/677-4688** or 435/259-4688; www.chilebikes.com). Bike rentals range from $40 to $75 per day, with discounts for multiday rentals. Bike shuttle services are also available from several of the companies, including **Coyote Shuttle** (✆ **435/259-8656;** www.coyoteshuttle.com) and **Roadrunner Shuttle** (✆ **435/259-9402;** www.roadrunnershuttle.com).

Several local companies (see the "Outfitters" chart, at right) also offer guided mountain-bike tours, with rates starting at about $85 for a half-day and about $110 for a full day. Multiday biking/camping trips are also available.

BOATING, CANOEING & RAFTING After spending hours in the blazing sun looking at mile upon mile of huge red sandstone rock formations, it's easy to get the idea that Canyonlands National Park is a baking, dry, rock-hard desert. Well, it is. But both the Colorado and Green rivers run through the park, and one of the most exciting ways to see the park and surrounding country is from river level.

You can travel into the park in a canoe, kayak, large or small rubber raft (with or without motor), or speedy, solid jet boat. Do-it-yourselfers can rent kayaks or canoes for $35 to $55 for a full day, or rafts starting at $60 for a full day. Half-day guided river trips start at about $40 per person; full-day trips are usually $50 to $70 per person. Multiday rafting expeditions, which include meals and camping equipment, start at about $350 per person for 2 days. Jet-boat trips, which cover a lot more river in a given amount of time, start at about $80 for a half-day trip. Children's rates are usually about 20% lower. Some companies also offer sunset or dinner trips. See the "Outfitter" chart on next page.

The Colorado and Green rivers meet in the park and are calm before the confluence. But after they meet, the Colorado becomes serious white water; you will most likely want a guided raft trip here.

One fantastic canoe trip is along the Green River. Canoeists usually start in or near the town of Green River (put in at Green River State Park or at Mineral Bottom, just downstream) and spend about 2 days to get to the Green's confluence with the Colorado, where they can be picked up by a local outfitter.

Public boat-launching ramps in the Moab area are opposite Lion's Park, near the intersection of U.S. 191 and Utah 128; at Take-Out Beach, along Utah 128 about 10 miles east of its intersection with U.S. 191; and at Hittle Bottom, also along Utah 128, about 24 miles east of its intersection with U.S. 191. The **Colorado Basin River Forecast Center** (✆ **801/539-1311** [recording]; www.cbrfc.noaa.gov) provides information on river flows and reservoir conditions statewide.

FOUR-WHEELING Unlike most national parks, where motor vehicles and mountain bikes must stay on paved roads, Canyonlands has miles of rough four-wheel-drive roads where mechanized transport is king. We're talking serious four-wheeling here; most roads require high-clearance, short-wheelbase vehicles. Many of these roads also require the skill that comes only from experience, so it's usually a good idea to discuss your plans with rangers before putting your vehicle on the line. Four-wheelers must stay on designated 4WD roads, but here the term *road* can mean anything from a graded, well-marked two-lane gravel byway to a pile of loose rocks with a sign that says "that-a-way." Many of the park's jeep roads are impassable during heavy rains and for a day or two after.

Outfitter	4WD	Bike	Boat	Horse	Rent
Adrift Adventures 378 N. Main St., Box 577 ✆ 800/874-4483, 435/259-8594 www.adrift.net	Yes	No	Yes	Yes	No
Canyon Voyages Adventure Co. 211 N. Main St. ✆ 800/733-6007, 435/259-6007 www.canyonvoyages.com	Yes	Yes	Yes	Yes	Yes
Dan Mick's Guided Jeep Tours 600 Mill Creek Dr., Box 1234 ✆ 435/259-4567 www.danmick.com	Yes	No	No	No	No
Magpie Adventures Cycling Tours Box 1496 ✆ 800/546-4245, 435/259-4464 www.magpieadventures.com	No	Yes	No	No	No
Moab Adventure Center 225 S. Main St. ✆ 866/904-1163, 435/259-7019 www.moabadventurecenter.com	Yes	Yes	Yes	Yes	Yes
Moab Rafting Co. Box 801 ✆ 800/746-6622, 435/259-7238 www.moab-rafting.com	No	No	Yes	No	No
Navtec Expeditions 321 N. Main St., Box 1267 ✆ 800/833-1278, 435/259-7983 www.navtec.com	Yes	No	Yes	No	Yes
Sheri Griffith Expeditions 2231 S. U.S. 191, Box 1324 ✆ 800/332-2439, 435/259-8229 www.griffithexp.com	No	No	Yes	No	No
Tag-A-Long Expeditions 452 N. Main St. ✆ 800/453-3292, 435/259-8946 www.tagalong.com	Yes	No	Yes	No	Yes
Western Spirit Cycling 428 Mill Creek Dr. ✆ 800/845-2453, 435/259-8732 www.westernspirit.com	No	Yes	No	No	No

Several local companies offer four-wheel-drive vehicle rentals. They include **Farabee's Jeep Rentals** (✆ **877/970-5337** or 435/259-7494; www.farabeejeeprentals.com), **Canyonlands Jeep Adventures** (✆ **866/892-5337** or 435/259-4413; www.canyonlandsjeep.com), and **Cliffhanger Jeep Rental** (✆ **435/259-0889;** www.cliffhangerjeeprental.com).

The best four-wheel-drive adventure in Canyonlands' Island in the Sky District is the **White Rim Road,** which runs some 100 winding miles and affords spectacular and ever-changing views, from broad panoramas of rock and canyon to close-ups of red and orange towers and buttes. A high-clearance 4WD is essential. Expect the journey to be slow, lasting 2 to 3 days, although with the appropriate vehicle it isn't really difficult. There are primitive campgrounds along the way. Reservations on this route should be made well in advance.

Four-wheeling on one of many routes in the Needles District can be an end in itself or a means to get to some of the more interesting and remote hiking trails and camping spots. Four-wheelers will find one of their ultimate challenges on the **Elephant Hill Road,** which begins at a well-marked turnoff near Squaw Flat Campground. Although most of the 10-mile trail is only moderately difficult, the stretch over Elephant Hill near the beginning can be a nightmare, with steep and rough slickrock, drifting sand, loose rock, and treacherous ledges. Coming down the hill, one switchback requires you to back to the edge of a steep cliff before continuing. This is also a favorite of mountain bikers, although

Accommodations, Dining & Picnic & Camping Supplies

There are no facilities for lodging, dining, or buying supplies inside Canyonlands National Park. The nearest town is Moab. For information on restaurants, hotels, and supply stores in Moab, see the "Where to Stay," "Where to Dine," and "Picnic & Camping Supplies" sections in chapter 2.

riders will have to walk bikes on some stretches over an abundance of sand and rocks. The route offers views of numerous rock formations, from striped needles to balanced rocks, plus steep cliffs and rock "stairs." Side trips can add another 30 miles. Allow 8 hours to 3 days.

For a spectacular view of the Colorado River, the **Colorado Overlook Road** can't be beat. This 14-mile round-trip is popular with four-wheelers, backpackers, and mountain bikers. Considered among the park's easiest 4WD roads, the first part is very easy indeed, accessible by high-clearance two-wheel-drives, but the second half has a few rough and rocky sections that require four-wheel-drive. Starting at the Needles Visitor Center parking lot, the trail takes you past numerous panoramic vistas to a spectacular 360-degree view of the park and the Colorado River some 1,000 feet below.

Several local companies (see "Outfitters," above) provide guided trips, starting at about $70 per adult and $60 per child under 16 or 17, for a half-day.

8 Camping

For details on the following campgrounds, see the chart in chapter 2, Arches National Park.

INSIDE THE PARK

The park has two developed campgrounds, set among rugged rocks. **Willow Flat Campground** is in the Island in the Sky District, and **Squaw Flat Campground** is in the Needles District. Primitive campsites are available throughout the park for four-wheelers, boaters, bikers, and backpackers (see "Exploring the Backcountry," above).

NEAR THE PARK

Near Island in the Sky, the campground at scenic **Dead Horse Point State Park,** P.O. Box 609, Moab, UT 84532-0609 (✆ **435/259-2614;** www.stateparks.utah.gov), has electric hookups with 20-amp power. It accepts reservations from March through October with an $8 processing fee (✆ **800/322-3770;** www.reserveamerica.com). The **Newspaper Rock Campground** (contact the Bureau of Land Management, 365 N. Main St., Monticello, UT 84535; ✆ **435/587-1500;** www.blm.gov/ut/st/en/fo/monticello.html), along the road to the Needles District, has primitive campsites.

Additional camping facilities are available on nearby public lands administered by the Bureau of Land Management and U.S. Forest Service; check with the **Moab Area Travel Council,** P.O. Box 550, Moab, UT 84532 (✆ **800/635-6622** or 435/259-8825; www.discovermoab.com), or stop at the **Moab Information Center,** at the corner of Main and Center streets, open Monday through Saturday 8am to 8pm and Sunday from 9am to 7pm from July through September, with shorter hours the rest of the year. In and around Moab are over a dozen commercial campgrounds, some of which are discussed in chapter 2.

Near the Needles District are several commercial campgrounds in Monticello, along U.S. 191, about 15 miles south of the intersection of U.S. 191 and the park entry road. These include **Mountain View RV Park,** 632 N. Main St. (P.O. Box 910), Monticello, UT 84535 (✆ **435/587-2974**), a well-maintained campground with grassy sites, some trees, Wi-Fi, and cable TV hookups.

9

Capitol Reef National Park, UT

by Don & Barbara Laine

Capitol Reef National Park is one of those undiscovered gems, its rangers quietly going about the business of protecting and interpreting its natural wonders and historic sites while visitors flock to its more famous neighbors, Bryce Canyon and Zion.

But when people do stumble across this park, they are often amazed. Capitol Reef not only offers spectacular southern Utah scenery, but it also has a unique twist and a personality all its own.

The geologic formations here are incredible, if not downright peculiar. This is a place to let your imagination run wild, where you'll see the commanding Castle; the tall, rust-red Chimney Rock; the silent and eerie Temple of the Moon; and the appropriately named Hamburger Rocks, sitting atop a white sandstone table. A spectacular palette of colors paints Capitol Reef's canyon walls, which is why some Navajos called the area "The Land of the Sleeping Rainbow."

Capitol Reef is more than brilliant rocks and barren desert, however. Here the Fremont River has helped create a lush oasis in an otherwise unforgiving land. Cottonwood, willow, and other trees fill its banks. In fact, 19th-century pioneers found the land so inviting that they established the community that's now called Fruita, planting orchards that have been preserved by the National Park Service.

Because of differences in geologic strata, elevation, and water availability in different sections of the park, you'll find a variety of ecosystems and terrain, along with a selection of activities. There are trails for hiking; roads for mountain biking and four-wheel-drive touring; fruit orchards; green cottonwood groves and desert wildflowers; an abundance of songbirds; and a surprising amount of wildlife, from lizards and snakes to the bashful ring-tailed cat (which is really a member of the raccoon family). You'll also find thousand-year-old petroglyphs left behind by the ancient Fremont and ancestral Puebloan peoples, and other traces of the past left more recently by the Utes and Southern Paiutes. This was both a favorite hideout for Wild West outlaws and a home for industrious Mormon pioneers, who planted orchards while their children learned the three Rs and studied the Bible and the Book of Mormon in the one-room Fruita Schoolhouse.

The name Capitol Reef conjures up images of a shoreline—an odd choice for a park composed of cliffs and canyons in landlocked Utah. But many of the pioneers who settled the West were former seafaring men, and they extended the meaning of the word *reef* to include these rock barriers. They added *Capitol* to the name because the huge white, rounded domes of sandstone reminded them of the domes of capitol buildings.

The park should probably be called the Big Fold. When Earth's crust rose some 60 million years ago, creating the Rocky Mountains, most of the uplifting was relatively even. But here, through one of those fascinating quirks of nature, the crust wrinkled into a huge fold. Extending 100 miles, almost all within the national park, it's known as the Waterpocket Fold.

AVOIDING THE CROWDS

Although Capitol Reef receives fewer than 550,000 visitors annually, it can still be busy, especially during its peak season, which lasts from April through September. For this reason, the best time to visit is fall, particularly in October and November, when temperatures are usually warm enough for hiking and camping, but not so high as to send you constantly in search of shade. You also don't have to be as worried about flash floods through narrow canyons as you do during thunderstorm season, July through September.

1 Essentials

GETTING THERE & GATEWAYS

The park is about 121 miles northeast of Bryce Canyon National Park, 204 miles northeast of Zion National Park, 224 miles south of Salt Lake City, and 366 miles northeast of Las Vegas, Nevada.

It straddles **Utah 24,** which connects with I-70 to both the northeast and the northwest. Coming from the east along I-70, take exit 147 and follow Utah 24 southwest to the park. Traveling from the west along I-70, there are two options: Take exit 48

Capitol Reef National Park

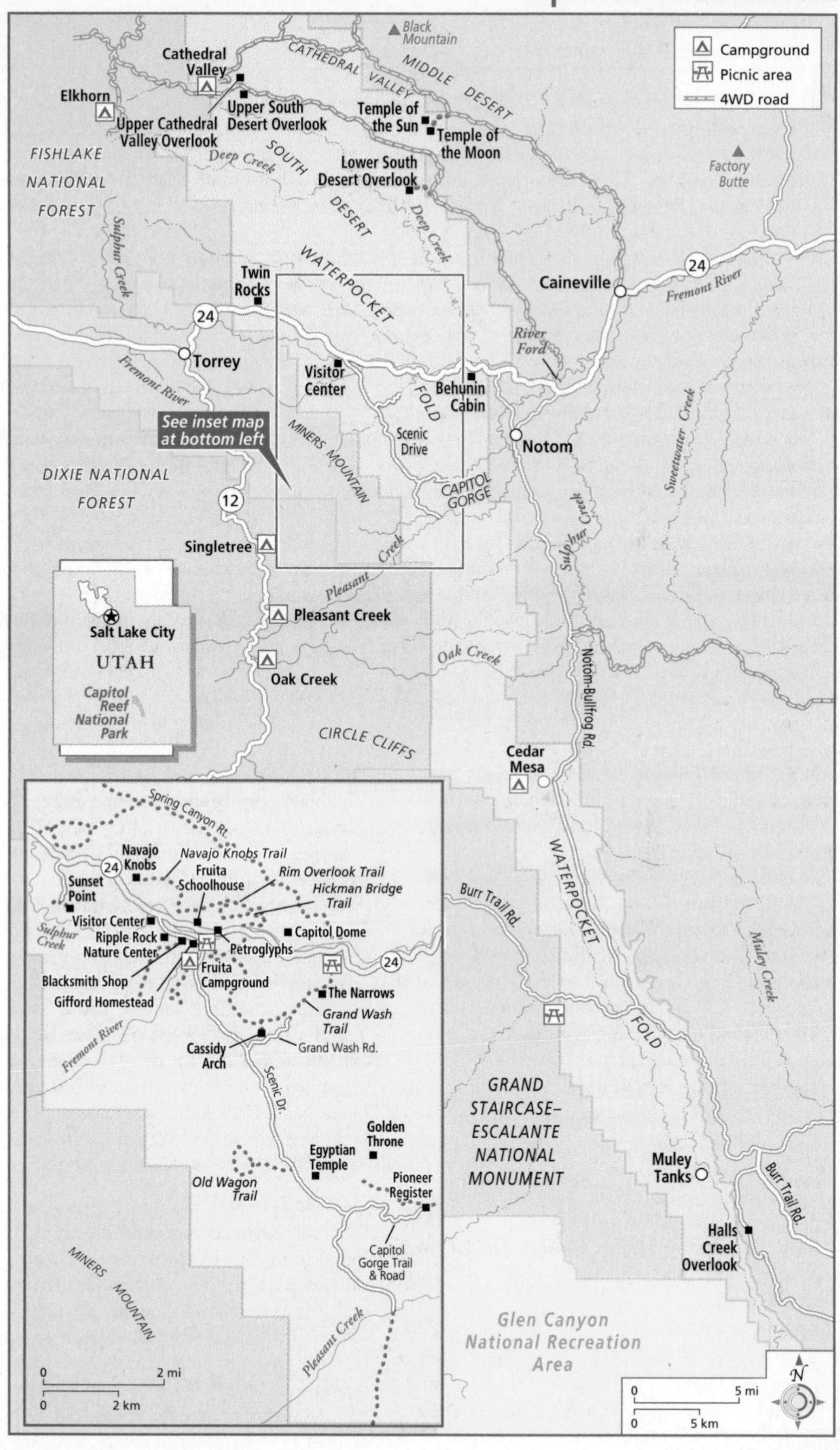

Tips from a Park Ranger

Thanks to the geology of the Waterpocket Fold, the park has a lot of variety in elevation, landscape, and terrain, according to Riley Mitchell, Capitol Reef's chief of interpretation.

"This tilted layer cake of geologic strata formed a variety of different microhabitats as it eroded," he says. "There's an immense desert wilderness, but within that you've got perennial streams that have created a very rich riparian habitat, where prehistoric and historic people settled."

Capitol Reef is still relatively unknown, he says, and hasn't changed much since *Outside* magazine sang its praises as one of America's eight most undervisited national parks—"parks as they were meant to be." Mitchell says, "When people stop here on their way to one of Utah's better-known national parks, they're usually pleasantly surprised."

The park is known for its wonderful colors, and Mitchell says you can see them practically everywhere. "At sunset along Utah 24 and along the Scenic Drive, you'll find a brilliant spectrum of colors—you can see them right from your car."

"The Frying Pan Trail is one of my favorite hikes," he says. "It's well marked, easy to get to, and you get wonderful views from the top as you hike along the crest of the Waterpocket Fold." Mitchell adds that another benefit to the trail is that it provides access to the spectacular spur trail to Cassidy Arch.

The dirt roads in the park can be a bit rugged, but most are accessible by two-wheel-drive, high-clearance vehicles, he says. However, Mitchell advises that a four-wheel-drive vehicle makes exploring the remote areas of the park easier and less worrisome in bad weather.

Given a choice, Mitchell would visit in the spring or fall, because it's a bit cooler. But, he adds, "summer's beautiful, too, because wildflowers are in bloom and the orchards are open for fruit picking."

for Sigurd and follow Utah 24 east to the park; or take exit 85 for Fremont Junction, then Utah 72 south to Loa, where you pick up Utah 24 east to the park.

Those coming from Bryce Canyon National Park can follow **Utah 12** northeast to its intersection with Utah 24 at the town of Torrey, and turn right (east) to Capitol Reef. If you're approaching the park from Glen Canyon National Recreation Area, take Utah 276 (from Bullfrog Basin Marina) or Utah 95 (from Hite Crossing) north to the intersection with Utah 24, and follow that west to the park.

THE NEAREST AIRPORT The closest major airport is **Grand Junction Regional Airport,** about 200 miles east in Grand Junction, Colorado (✆ **970/244-9100;** fax 970/241-9103; www.gjairport.com). It has direct flights or connections from most major cities on **Allegiant, American/American Eagle, Delta Connection/Skywest, Frontier, Great Lakes, United Express/Skywest,** and **US Airways.**

RENTING A CAR Car rentals are available at the Grand Junction airport from **Alamo, Avis, Budget, Enterprise, Hertz,** and **National.** See chapter 38 for websites for airlines and car rental companies.

INFORMATION

Contact **Capitol Reef National Park,** HC 70 Box 15, Torrey, UT 84775 (✆ **435/425-3791,** ext. 111; www.nps.gov/care). Books and maps are available from the nonprofit **Capitol Reef Natural History Association,** Capitol Reef National Park, HC 70, Box 15, Torrey, UT 84775 (✆ **435/425-3791,** ext. 113 or 115; www.capitolreefnha.org).

For additional information on area lodging, dining, and activities, contact the **Wayne County Travel Council,** P.O. Box 7, Teasdale, UT 84773 (✆ **800/858-7951** or 435/425-3365; www.capitolreef.travel), which operates a **visitor center** at the junction of Utah highways 12 and 24, from April through October Monday through Friday 9am to 5pm and Saturday and Sunday 8am to 7pm.

VISITOR CENTERS

The park **visitor center** is on the Scenic Drive at its intersection with Utah 24. A path connects it to the campground, passing the historic blacksmith shop, orchards, and a shaded picnic ground. The visitor center, open daily from 8am to 6pm in summer (shorter hours at other times), has exhibits on the geology and history of the area, and a video about the park. Rangers answer questions and provide backcountry permits. You can also pick up free brochures and buy books, maps, videos, postcards, and posters.

If You Have Only 1 Day

Because Capitol Reef is such a compact park, it's fairly easy to see a lot in a short time. Although 2 or 3 days in the park would be ideal, it is possible to have an enjoyable time with just half a day or so. Because there are no food services in the park (except fruit in season), pack a picnic lunch.

Start at the **visitor center,** and watch the short slide show explaining the park's geology and early history. Then head out on the paved 25-mile round-trip **Scenic Drive** (described below), stopping along the way for a short hike, perhaps the easy walk up the Grand Wash. In the historic pioneer community of **Fruita,** near the beginning of the Scenic Drive, you can wander among the orchards, where you're likely to see deer. Then visit the **Gifford Farmhouse,** where you can get a taste of the daily life of Fruita's Mormon settlers and purchase replicas of pioneer-era household items and crafts. Hike one of the shorter trails in the Fruita area before going to see the **Fruita Schoolhouse** and some of the park's **petroglyphs.** In the evening, try to take in a ranger program at the **amphitheater.**

The **Ripple Rock Nature Center,** located about ¾ mile south of the visitor center along the Scenic Drive, offers exhibits and activities especially for children. It's open from Memorial Day weekend through Labor Day weekend only. Check at the visitor center for its current hours.

FEES & PERMITS

Entry to the park is free, although it costs $5 per vehicle or $3 person on foot or bicycle to access the **scenic drive** (pass valid for up to 7 days). Camping in the main campground costs $10 per night; two primitive campgrounds are free. Free **backcountry permits** (available at the visitor center) are required for all overnight hikes.

SPECIAL REGULATIONS & WARNINGS

Although most visitors to the park enjoy a wonderful vacation without mishap, problems can occur. Hikers need to carry plenty of water, especially in summer. A major concern is weather: Afternoon thunderstorms in July, August, and September can bring flash floods, which fill narrow canyons suddenly and without warning. Steep-walled Grand Wash and Capitol Gorge can be particularly hazardous and should be avoided whenever storms are threatening.

Because wildlife refuses to follow park rules regarding wildlife diet, campers should be careful of where and how they store food, and dispose of garbage promptly.

SEASONS & CLIMATE

Because of its higher elevation, Capitol Reef doesn't get as hot as some other Southwestern parks, but summer temperatures can be uncomfortably warm on the trails without shade. Winters can be very pleasant—snow falls occasionally but doesn't usually last, and temperatures are often in the 50s (teens Celsius). Late winter and spring are frequently windy.

Depending on the weather, the Scenic Drive sometimes closes, most often in late summer during flash-flood season and occasionally in winter due to snow. When it's closed, you still have access to a network of trails from Utah 24 and can get to the picnic area and campground.

2 Exploring the Park by Car

Capitol Reef is relatively easy to see from the comfort of your automobile. From the visitor center, the **Scenic Drive** leads about 13 miles south into the park. Pick up a copy of the Scenic Drive brochure ($2 at the visitor center), then set out, stopping at view points to gaze at the array of colorful cliffs, monoliths, and commanding rock formations.

If the weather is dry, drive down the gravel **Capitol Gorge Road** at the end of the paved Scenic Drive for a look at what many consider to be the park's best scenery. It's a 5-mile round-trip drive. If you're up for a short walk, the relatively flat 2-mile (round-trip) **Capitol Gorge Trail,** which starts at the end of Capitol Gorge Road, takes you to the **Pioneer Register,** a rock wall where traveling pioneers "signed in" (see "Day Hikes," below).

Another dry-weather driving option is the **Grand Wash Road,** a maintained dirt road that is subject to flash floods but in good weather offers an easy route into a spectacular canyon. Along the 2-mile round-trip, you'll see **Cassidy Arch,** named for famed outlaw Butch Cassidy, who, at least by some accounts, hid out in this area.

Making the Scene as You Drive

The park's scenic drive runs mostly north–south, with most of the best rock formations on the east side of the road. In the morning you'll be looking into the sun, but drive the road in late afternoon or just before sunset, and the formations are richly illuminated.

Utah 24, which crosses Capitol Reef from east to west, also has several view points offering a look at some of the park's best features, such as the monumental **Capitol Dome, Chimney Rock,** the aptly named **Castle,** the **Fruita Schoolhouse,** and some **petroglyphs** left by the prehistoric Fremont people (see "Park Attractions," below).

3 Organized Tours & Ranger Programs

Park rangers present a variety of free programs and activities from spring through fall. **Campfire programs** take place most evenings at the outdoor amphitheater at Fruita Campground. Topics vary but may include the animals and plants, geology, and human history of the area. Rangers also lead **walks** and give **short talks** on a variety of subjects, such as the history of the Fruita Schoolhouse and the Gifford Farmhouse. Schedules are posted at the visitor center and campground.

Several local companies offer **guide services,** both in the national park and nearby. **Backcountry Outfitters,** 677 E. Utah 12 (P.O. Box 750298), Torrey, UT 84775 (✆ **866/747-3972** or 435/425-2010; www.ridethereef.com), offers a variety of guided trips, including hiking, canyoneering, biking, fishing, horseback riding, and four-wheel-drive excursions. **Hondoo Rivers and Trails,** 90 E. Main St. (P.O. Box 98), Torrey, UT 84775 (✆ **800/332-2696** or 435/425-3519; www.hondoo.com), offers multiday horseback trail rides plus half- and full-day hiking and four-wheel-drive tours, including special tours for photographers and to rock art sites.

4 Park Attractions

The Fremont people lived along the river as early as A.D. 700, staying until about 1300. Primarily hunters and gatherers, the Fremonts also grew corn, beans, and squash to supplement their diet. Their dwellings were pit houses, which were dug into the ground; the remains of one can be seen from the **Hickman Bridge Trail.** Many Fremont petroglyphs (images carved into rock) and pictographs (images painted on rock) are visible on the canyon walls. If we could understand them, they might tell us why these early Americans left the area, a puzzle that continues to baffle archaeologists. The most easily accessible site is 1½ miles east of the visitor center along Utah 24. There is a sign near the parking area, and a path leads to the petroglyph panels, which contain some of the most interesting images in the park.

Prospectors and other travelers passed through the **Capitol Gorge** section in the late 1800s, leaving their names on the **Pioneer Register,** reached on a 2-mile round-trip walk (see "Day Hikes," below).

Mormon pioneers established the community of Junction—later named **Fruita**—in 1880. Now a historic district listed on the National Register of Historic Places, the orchards those settlers planted continue to flourish, tended by park workers who invite you to sample the fruits of their labor. Nearby is a historic blacksmith shop. The tiny **Fruita Schoolhouse,** built in 1896, was a church, social hall, and meeting hall in addition to a one-room schoolhouse. The school closed in 1941 and was restored in 1984. It's furnished with old wood-and-wrought-iron desks, a wood stove, a chalkboard, and textbooks. A hand bell used to call students to class still rests on the corner of the teacher's desk.

Also in the Fruita district, the **Gifford Farmhouse,** built in 1908, is typical of rural Utah farmhouses of the early 1900s. Renovated and furnished by the Capitol Reef Natural History Association, it's off the Scenic Drive about 1 mile south of the visitor center, and is open from April through September. The former kitchen is a gift shop, selling reproductions of the household tools, toys, and utensils used by Mormon pioneers, crafts, jams and jellies, dried fruits, postcards, and books.

5 Day Hikes

Among the last areas in the continental United States to be explored, Capitol Reef has many parts that remain all but unknown, perfect for those who want to see this rugged country in its natural state.

Trails through the park offer panoramic views of colorful cliffs and domes; journeys through desolate, steep-walled canyons; and cool walks along the tree-shaded Fremont River. Watch for petroglyphs and other reminders of this area's first inhabitants. One of the best things about hiking here is the combination of scenic beauty, prehistoric American Indian rock art, and Western history you'll discover.

Guided hikes in the park and in other nearby locations are available from **Backcountry Outfitters** and **Hondoo Rivers and Trails** (see "Organized Tours & Ranger Programs," above). Prices vary, but as an example, half-day guided hiking trips cost about $90 and full-day guided hikes, including lunch, cost about $125.

SHORTER TRAILS

Capitol Gorge Trail This is a mostly level walk along the bottom of a narrow canyon. Looking up at the tall, smooth walls of rock conveys a strong sense of what the pioneers must have seen and felt 100 years ago when they moved rocks and debris to drive their wagons through this canyon. The trail leads past the **Pioneer Register,** where early travelers carved their names. 1.25 miles one-way. Easy. Access: End of Capitol Gorge dirt road.

Fremont River Trail This self-guided nature trail is quite easy—and wheelchair accessible—for the first .5 mile as it meanders past the orchards along the river. It becomes increasingly strenuous thereafter. The path climbs to an overlook of the lovely valley. Part of the trail is steep, with long drop-offs. 1.25 miles one-way. Easy to moderate. Access: Fruita Campground.

Goosenecks Trail This short walk affords great views of **Sulphur Creek Canyon.** It's a good trail for those with little time, because it offers both sweeping views of the geology of **Waterpocket Fold** and close-ups of interesting rock formations. .1 mile one-way. Easy. Access: Panorama Point Turnoff on Utah 24, 3 miles west of visitor center, then 1 mile on gravel access road.

Hickman Bridge Trail Starting at the Fremont River, this self-guided nature trail heads into the desert, ascending several short steep hills to **Hickman Natural Bridge,** which has an opening 133 feet wide and 125 feet high. The trail has a 400-foot elevation gain. 1 mile one-way. Moderate. Access: Hickman Bridge parking area on Utah 24, 2 miles east of visitor center.

Sunset Point Trail This hike affords panoramic views of cliffs and domes, most dramatic around sunset. .3 mile one-way. Easy. Access: Panorama Point Turnoff on Utah 24, 3 miles west of visitor center, then 1 mile on gravel access road.

LONGER TRAILS

Cassidy Arch Trail This trail offers spectacular views as it climbs steeply from the floor of Grand Wash to high cliffs overlooking the park. From the trail, you get several perspectives of Cassidy Arch, a natural stone arch named for outlaw Butch Cassidy, who is believed to have occasionally used the Grand Wash as a hideout. 1.75 miles one-way. Strenuous. Access: Scenic Dr. and Grand Wash Rd. to Grand Wash Trailhead.

Chimney Rock Trail This trail begins with a strenuous climb up switchbacks to the more moderate loop trail on top. It affords views of Chimney Rock from both below and above, plus panoramic views of the **Waterpocket Fold** and surrounding areas. 3.5 miles RT. Moderate to strenuous. Access: Chimney Rock parking area on Utah 24, 2 miles west of visitor center.

Cohab Canyon Trail After the first .25 mile, which is strenuous, this trail levels out a bit and has fewer steep grades. It climbs to a hidden canyon above the campground and has two short side trails leading to overlooks, from which you get good views of the **Fremont River, Fruita,** and the campground. 1.75 miles one-way. Moderate to strenuous. Access: Across from Fruita Campground.

Fremont Gorge Overlook Trail A strenuous climb to 1,000 feet above the Fremont River, this trail rewards you at the end with a great view into the Fremont Gorge. The middle of the hike, across Johnson Mesa, is fairly easy. The trail also affords good views of **Fruita** and the escarpment of the **Waterpocket Fold.** 2.25 miles one-way. Strenuous. Access: Blacksmith shop.

Frying Pan Trail This strenuous but scenic trail, which links Cohab and Cassidy Arch trails, follows the ridge of the **Waterpocket Fold escarpment,** with a number of climbs up and down canyons and over slickrock. You'll get good views of **Miners Mountain** to the southwest, rugged canyons to the side, and the **Grand Wash** below near the end of the trail. 3 miles one-way. Strenuous. Access: Across from Fruita Campground or Grand Wash parking area.

Golden Throne Trail A strenuous climb from the bottom of the gorge to the top of the cliffs at the base of the Golden Throne, this trail provides several panoramic vistas, which are good spots to catch your breath. The Golden Throne is a formation of Navajo sandstone that glows golden in the light of

---

Voices

The colors are such as no pigments can portray. They are deep, rich, and variegated; and so luminous are they, that light seems to flow or shine out of the rock.

—Geologist C. E. Dutton, 1880

the setting sun. 2 miles one-way. Strenuous. Access: Capitol Gorge parking area.

Grand Wash Trail This is a relatively easy hike along a narrow wash bottom with rock walls on both sides. The trail shows the phenomenal power of water as it winds between tall polished walls of stone, scoured smooth by flash floods. 2.25 miles one-way. Easy. Access: Grand Wash parking area, or on Utah 24 east of visitor center.

Old Wagon Trail This 1,100-foot climb up the east flank of **Miners Mountain** is certainly strenuous, but it affords spectacular and unusual views of the **Waterpocket Fold escarpment.** This hike is best done late in the day, when the cliffs are lit by the setting sun. 3.5 miles RT. Strenuous. Access: West side of Scenic Dr. near end.

Rim Overlook Trail After a strenuous 1,000-foot climb, hikers are rewarded with good views of **Fruita** and vistas to the south. 2.25 miles one-way. Strenuous. Access: Hickman Bridge parking area on Utah 24 east of visitor center.

6 Exploring the Backcountry

The park offers a variety of backpacking opportunities, including the 15-mile round-trip **Upper Muley Twist** route, which follows a canyon through the **Waterpocket Fold** and offers views of arches and narrows, and panoramic vistas from the top of the fold; and the 22-mile round-trip **Halls Creek Narrows,** which follows Halls Creek through a slot canyon (where you may have to wade or swim). **Free backcountry permits** (available at the visitor center) are required for overnight hikes, and groups cannot exceed 12 people. Backcountry hikers should discuss their plans with rangers before setting out, because many of these routes are prone to flash floods.

7 Other Sports & Activities

FOUR-WHEEL-DRIVE TOURING & MOUNTAIN BIKING As in most national parks, bikes and 4WD vehicles are restricted to established roads, but Capitol Reef has several such "established" roads—actually, little more than dirt trails—that provide exciting opportunities for those using 4WD or pedal power.

The only route appropriate for road bikes is the **Scenic Drive,** described above. Both the Grand Wash and Capitol Gorge roads (see "Exploring the Park by Car," above), plus three longer backcountry roads, are open to mountain bikes as well as four-wheel-drive vehicles. Be aware that rain can make the roads impassable, so it's best to check on current conditions before setting out.

One recommended trip is the **Cathedral Valley Loop.** It covers about 60 miles on a variety of road surfaces, including dirt, sand, and rock, and requires the fording of the Fremont River, where water is usually 1 to 1½ feet deep. The reward is unspoiled scenery, including sandstone monoliths and majestic cliffs, in one of the park's more remote areas. There's a primitive campground (see "Camping," below). Access is from Utah 24, outside the park, 12 miles east of the visitor center on the River Ford Road, or 19 miles east of the visitor center on the Caineville Wash Road.

Backcountry Outfitters and **Hondoo Rivers and Trails** (see "Organized Tours & Ranger Programs," above) offer full-day four-wheel-drive **tours,** including lunch, into the national park and surrounding areas, at rates of about $125. Early morning starting times are available for photographers who want to catch the light at sunrise, and specialized tours, including trips to rock art sites, are also available. Backcountry Outfitters, whose motto is "Get Out and Stay Out!" also rents mountain bikes, at $32 to $42 for a half-day and $38 to $48 for a full day. Those wanting to go four-wheel-drive touring on their own can rent a 4WD vehicle for about $95 per day, including 150 miles, at **Thousand Lakes RV Park & Campground** (see "Camping" below).

HORSEBACK RIDING Horses are prohibited in some areas of the park but permitted in others; check at the visitor center for details. One-, 3-, and 5-day guided horseback trips that include the national park or other areas are offered by **Hondoo Rivers and Trails** (see "Organized Tours & Ranger Programs," above), at rates from $125 per person, and Hondoo will also lead custom trips. **Backcountry Outfitters** (see "Organized Tours & Ranger Programs," above) also provides multiday trail rides and, in addition, offers 1-hour horseback rides for $40, 2-hour rides for $65, half-day rides for $120, and full-day rides, with lunch, for $160.

WILDLIFE VIEWING Summer in Capitol Reef is hot and sometimes stormy, but it's a good season for wildlife viewing. In particular, many species of **lizards** make their home in the park; you will probably catch a glimpse of one warming itself on a rock. The western whiptail, eastern fence, and side-blotched lizards are the most common; the most attractive is the collared lizard, which is usually turquoise with yellow speckles.

Especially for Kids

In addition to the **Junior Ranger Program** (see "Tips for Traveling with Kids," in chapter 1), children of all ages can become **Junior Geologists** by joining a ranger on a 30-minute field trip (usually held Tues–Sat in summer). Families can borrow a Family Fun Pack, containing park-related games and activities, at the visitor center and the Ripple Rock Nature Center, and the nature center also offers hands-on activities for kids (see "Visitor Centers," earlier in this chapter).

Watch for **deer** and **marmots** in Fruita, especially along the path between the visitor center and Fruita Campground. This area is also where you're likely to see **chipmunks** and **white-tail antelope squirrels.** Although they're somewhat shy and only emerge from their dens at night, **ring-tailed cats** (part of the raccoon family) also call the park home, as do **bighorn sheep, bobcats, cougar, fox,** and **coyote.**

If you keep your eyes to the sky, you may see a **golden eagle, Cooper's hawk, raven,** or any of the many other types of birds attracted by the park's variety of habitats. Year-round residents include chukars, common flickers, yellow-bellied sapsuckers, horned larks, canyon wrens, rock wrens, American robins, ruby-crowned kinglets, starlings, and American kestrels. In warmer months, you're also likely to see yellow warblers, red-winged blackbirds, western tanagers, northern orioles, violet-green swallows, white-throated swifts, and black-chinned hummingbirds. Bird-watching is particularly good along the Fremont River Trail in the spring and early summer.

8 Camping

INSIDE THE PARK

The pleasant **Fruita Campground,** located along the Scenic Drive, 1 mile south of the visitor center, has shade trees and modern restrooms, and is within walking distance of the Fruita Schoolhouse and other historic attractions. It also has an RV dump station that is open in summer only.

Capitol Reef also has two primitive campgrounds. To reach **Cedar Mesa Campground,** in the southern part of the park, go east on Utah 24 about 9 miles to Notom-Bullfrog Road, which you take about 23 miles south (the first 10 miles are paved) to the campground. The road may be impassable in wet weather. **Cathedral Valley Campground** is in the northern part of the park, about 35 miles from the visitor center (get directions at the center). *Note:* Access roads to Cathedral Valley Campground require a high-clearance or four-wheel-drive vehicle at all times and may be inaccessible in bad weather.

Backcountry camping is permitted in much of the park with a free permit, available at the visitor center.

NEAR THE PARK

Several commercial campgrounds are in the community of Torrey, about 5 miles west of the park entrance, and an attractive U.S. Forest Service campground is not too far away.

The closest full-service RV park and campground to the national park is **Wonderland RV Park,** at the junction of Utah 12 and 24 (P.O. Box 67), Torrey, UT 84775 (✆ **877/854-0184** or 435/425-3665; www.capitolreefrvpark.com). The grounds and bathhouses are immaculate, and there are shade trees, grass, big rig sites, and croquet, horseshoes, volleyball, and basketball. Wi-Fi, cable TV, and use of gas barbecue grills are included in the rates, and the bathhouses have hair dryers. Also on the grounds are two camping cabins ($24 double) and a cute sheep wagon ($40 double).

At **Sandcreek RV Park,** 540 Utah 24 (P.O. Box 750276), Torrey, UT 84775 (✆ **435/425-3577;** www.sandcreekrv.com), you'll find RV sites with full hookups, plus grassy tent sites, trees, and great views in all directions. There are horseshoe pits, an art gallery, and two attractive cabins that share the campground bathhouse ($28 double). There is also a horse corral with drinking water ($5 per horse).

About 1 mile west of Torrey on Utah 24 is **Thousand Lakes RV Park & Campground,** P.O. Box 750070, Torrey, UT 84775 (✆ **800/355-8995** for reservations, or 435/425-3500; www.thousandlakesrvpark.com). In addition to the usual amenities, this campground offers good views of surrounding rock formations, some shade trees, and Wi-Fi. RV sites are gravel; tent sites are grass. The campground also has a convenience store, a coin-op laundry, horseshoes, an outdoor heated pool, and barbecues. The campground has several cabins, some of which involve a walk to the bathhouse, and some deluxe cabins with private bathrooms, one of which sleeps five and has a kitchen. Cabin rates range from $35 to $95 double. In addition, from May through early October, Western dinners are offered Monday through Friday and some Saturdays

($15–$22 adults, $8–$10 children 12 and younger), and 4×4 rentals are available at $95 per day.

Those looking for a forest camping experience on the west side of the national park will like **Single Tree Campground,** on Utah 12 about 16 miles south of Torrey (Fremont River Ranger District of the Fishlake National Forest; office at 138 S. Main St. [P.O. Box 129], Loa, UT 84747; ✆ **435/836-2800;** www.fs.fed.us/r4; reservations 877/444-6777; www.recreation.gov). Located in a forest of tall pines, this campground has paved sites (some are especially large and will accommodate large RVs), and many offer distant panoramic views of the national park. The campground also has five multifamily sites ($20 per night), and there is a horseshoe pit and volleyball court.

9 Where to Stay

There are no lodging facilities in the park, but the town of Torrey, just west of the park entrance where Utah 12 meets Utah 24, can take care of most needs.

NEAR THE PARK

In addition to the properties discussed below, Torrey has a **Days Inn,** 675 E. Utah 24 (✆ **888/425-3113** or 435/425-3111), with rates of $70 to $95 double and $120 suite. Also see the information on cabins at **Sandcreek RV Park, Thousand Lakes RV Park & Campground,** and **Wonderland RV Park** under "Camping," above. Website listings for national hotel/motel chains can be found in chapter 38.

Austin's Chuck Wagon Motel This attractive family-owned and -operated motel offers a wide range of options. The well-maintained property includes modern motel rooms with Southwestern decor, phones, satellite TV, Wi-Fi, and two queen-size beds. Also available is a family suite, which has a living room with a queen sofa bed, a kitchen with microwave, and three bedrooms. Our choice is one of the plush Western-style cabins. Each cabin has two bedrooms (each with a queen-size bed), a living room with a queen-size sofa bed, a complete kitchen, a full bathroom with tub/shower, satellite TV, a covered porch, and a yard with a barbecue grill and a picnic table. The grounds are attractively landscaped, with a lawn and large trees, and facilities include an outdoor pool and whirlpool. On the property are a grocery store/bakery/deli, coin-op laundry, and salon.

12 W. Main St. (P.O. Box 750180), Torrey, UT 84775. ✆ **800/863-3288** or 435/425-3335. Fax 435/425-3434. www.austinschuckwagonmotel.com. 24 units. A/C, TV. Motel room $75 double (lower rates Mar and Nov); cabin from $135 for up to 4; family suite from $150 double. AE, DISC, MC, V. Closed Dec–Feb.

Best Western Capitol Reef Resort A mile west of the national park entrance, this attractive Best Western is one of the closest lodgings to the park. Try to get a room on the back side of the motel, where you'll be rewarded with fantastic views of the area's red-rock formations. Standard units have one king or two queen beds and hair dryers. Minisuites have a king bed and a queen sleeper sofa, plus a coffeemaker, refrigerator, microwave, iron, and wet bar; full suites add a sitting room for the sleeper sofa, a second TV and telephone, a jetted tub, and a patio. The heated pool, whirlpool, and sun deck are out back, away from road noise, with glass wind barriers and spectacular views. The hotel also has Wi-Fi, a tennis/basketball court, and a coin-op laundry. The **restaurant** serves breakfast and dinner daily.

2600 E. Utah 24 (P.O. Box 750160), Torrey, UT 84775. ✆ **888/610-9600** or 435/425-3761. Fax 435/425-3300. www.bestwestern.com. 100 units. A/C, TV, TEL. June–Sept $124–$134 double, $144–$154 minisuites and suites; Oct–May $51–$61 double, $70–$80 minisuites and suites. AE, DC, DISC, MC, V. Small pets accepted.

Boulder View Inn This attractive, well-maintained modern motel is a bargain for those who want a good night's sleep without a lot of frills. Guest rooms are large and comfortable, with combination tub/showers, queen or king beds, tables with chairs, and a Southwestern motif. The units all have Wi-Fi, but the inn has no swimming pool and smoking is not permitted.

Campground	Elev.	Total Sites	RV Hookups	Dump Station	Drinking Toilets
Cathedral Valley	7,000	6	0	No	Yes
Cedar Mesa	5,400	5	0	No	Yes
Fruita	5,500	71	0	Yes	Yes
Sandcreek	6,840	24	12	Yes	Yes
Single Tree	8,200	26	0	Yes	Yes
Thousand Lakes	6,840	67	58	Yes	Yes
Wonderland	6,980	47	33	Yes	Yes

385 W. Main St. (Utah 24; P.O. 750237), Torrey, UT 84775. ✆ **800/444-3980** or 435/425-3800. www.boulderviewinn.com. 11 units. A/C, TV, TEL. Apr–Nov $65 double; Nov–Mar $40 double. Rates include continental breakfast. AE, DISC, MC, V.

Capitol Reef Inn & Café This older, Western-style motel—small, nicely landscaped, and adequately maintained—offers guest rooms that are homey and comfortable. The furnishings are handmade of solid wood, and all rooms have refrigerators and coffeemakers. Only one unit has a combination tub/shower; the others have showers only. Facilities include a playground, 10-person whirlpool tub, and desert garden and kiva. Adjacent, under the same ownership, is a good **restaurant** (see "Where to Dine," below) and a gift shop that sells American Indian crafts, guidebooks, and maps.

360 W. Main St. (Utah 24), Torrey, UT 84775. ✆ **435/425-3271.** www.capitolreefinn.com. 10 units. A/C, TV, TEL. $53 double. AE, DISC, MC, V. Closed Nov–Mar.

Sandstone Inn If you want panoramic views in all directions and an attractive, comfortable room, this is the place. Perched high on a hill set back from the highway, the well-maintained property is peaceful and quiet. Standard motel rooms have two queen-size beds or one king, along with typical modern motel decor and some genuine wood touches. Deluxe rooms add refrigerators and microwaves, and suites have king-size beds, large whirlpool tubs, and private balconies. All units have hair dryers and Wi-Fi. Facilities include an indoor heated swimming pool, whirlpool, and **restaurant** (see "Where to Dine," below).

955 E. Utah 24, at the junction of Utah 24 and 12 (P.O. Box 750208), Torrey, UT 84775. ✆ **800/458-0216** or 435/425-3775. Fax 435/425-3212. www.sandstonecapitolreef.com. 50 units. A/C, TV, TEL. Apr–Oct $68–$88 double, $95 suite; Nov–Mar $58–$78 double, $80 suite. AE, DISC, MC, V. Pets accepted, for $10 nonrefundable fee.

Torrey Schoolhouse Bed and Breakfast This excellent inn offers a charming alternative to the standard motel. The imposing three-story red sandstone building served as the community's school from 1917 until 1954, and during its early days also hosted plays, boxing matches, and dances, which local residents claim were sometimes attended by famed outlaw Butch Cassidy and his "associates." Beautifully restored, the schoolhouse now houses a bed-and-breakfast which maintains the schoolhouse theme on the first and second floors, with furnishings such as an antique writing desk and musical instruments, while third-floor rooms have a pioneer theme. Units are spacious, with light-colored walls and high ceilings, which makes them feel even more spacious. The inn offers a good mix of historic ambiance and modern comforts and conveniences, including top-of-the line beds, massage recliners, hair dryers, and Wi-Fi. Organic breakfasts, often from locally grown ingredients, might include a breakfast quiche, Belgian waffles with fruit topping, or a breakfast burrito, with homemade muffins and breakfast meats. All units are smoke-free.

150 N. Center St. (P.O. Box 750337), Torrey, UT 84775. ✆ **435/633-4643.** www.torreyschoolhouse.com. 10 units. A/C. Apr–Oct $110–$150 double. Rates include full breakfast. Children 13 and older welcome. MC, V. Closed Nov–Mar.

10 Where to Dine

There are no dining facilities inside the park.

NEAR THE PARK

In addition to the restaurants discussed below, you'll find a good deli at **Austin's Chuck Wagon Motel,** 12 W. Main St., Torrey (✆ **800/863-3288** or 435/425-3335; www.austinschuckwagonmotel.com), open daily from mid-March through October (closed the rest of the year). It offers hot and cold sandwiches, wraps, and Mexican items such as burritos and enchiladas, at prices from $3 to $7. Although primarily for takeout, the deli does have several small tables.

Next to and under the same management as the Rim Rock Restaurant (see below), the **Rim Rock Patio** serves pizza, pasta, salads, and snacks in a publike atmosphere. Prices are in the $5-to-$10

Fire Pits/ Water	Showers	Grills	Laundry	Reserve	Fees	Open
No	No	Yes	No	No	Free	Year-round
No	No	Yes	No	No	Free	Year-round
Yes	No	Yes	No	No	$10	Year-round
Yes	Yes	Yes	Yes	Yes	$13–$21	Apr to mid-Oct
Yes	No	Yes	No	Yes	$10	Mid-May to Oct
Yes	Yes	Yes	Yes	Yes	$18–$29	Late Mar to late Oct
Yes	Yes	Yes	Yes	Yes	$20–$28	Apr–Oct

Picnic & Camping Supplies

In addition to groceries, the general store at **Austin's Chuck Wagon Motel,** 12 W. Main St., Torrey (✆ **800/863-3288** or 435/425-3335; www.austinschuckwagonmotel.com), has a bakery, a full-service deli, organic fruits and vegetables, a coin-operated laundry, and a salon. It is closed December through February.

range, and it's open 5 to 10pm year-round plus lunch in summer (call for hours). There is live music on summer weekends, and beer is served.

Cafe Diablo SOUTHWESTERN What appears to be a small-town cafe in a converted home is actually a fine restaurant—among southern Utah's best—offering innovative beef, pork, chicken, seafood, and vegetarian selections, many with a Southwestern flair. The menu varies but could include pumpkin seed–crusted local trout served with cilantro-lime sauce and wild rice pancakes; and Mayan tamales—eggplant, poblano peppers, roasted tomatoes, masa, and cesara cheese steamed in a banana leaf and served with chargrilled vegetables and brandied corn custard. Pastries and ice creams, all made on the premises, are spectacular, and beer, wine, and liquor are served.

599 W. Main St., Torrey. ✆ **435/425-3070.** www.cafediablo.net. Main courses $21–$29. AE, MC, V. Daily 5–10pm. Closed late Oct to early Apr.

Capitol Reef Inn & Café AMERICAN This popular restaurant offers a good selection of fresh, healthy cuisine, although service can be a bit slow, especially at dinner. Known for its locally raised trout, the cafe is equally famous for its 10-vegetable salad. Vegetables are grown locally, and several dishes—such as spaghetti and fettuccine primavera—can be ordered vegetarian or with various meats or fish. Steaks and chicken are also served. The atmosphere is casual, with comfortable seating, American Indian crafts, and large windows. The restaurant offers beer and wine.

360 W. Main St. ✆ **435/425-3271.** www.capitolreefinn.com. Main courses $5–$12 breakfast and lunch, $7–$19 dinner. AE, DISC, MC, V. Daily 7am–9pm. Closed Nov–Mar.

Chillzz Malt Shoppe PIZZA/BURGERS/ICE CREAM Want a pepperoni pizza and a chocolate malt? Head to Chillzz. This fast food restaurant with a 1950s atmosphere and a pool table serves great pizza, okay burgers, and excellent malts and shakes. Beer is available.

156 E. Main St., Torrey. ✆ **435/425-2600.** Shakes and malts $3–$5; burgers and sandwiches $5–$6; whole pizzas $8–$18. AE, DISC, MC, V. Summer daily 10am–9pm; call for off-season hours.

Sandstone Restaurant AMERICAN Perched on a hill back from the highway, the Sandstone offers tremendous views of the area's famed red-rock formations, plus good food at reasonable prices. The restaurant does an especially good job with barbecue—try the tender pork ribs—and beef, including a prime rib special most Tuesdays and Thursdays. There are also pasta and chicken dinners, a nightly salad bar, and excellent desserts, such as the four-layer chocolate cake and the huge brownie sundae. Breakfasts offer the usual American standards. Beer and wine are served.

Sandstone Inn, 955 E. Utah 24, at the junction of Utah 24 and 12. ✆ **435/425-3775.** www.sandstonecapitolreef.com. Main dinner courses $12–$20. AE, DISC, MC, V. Apr–Nov Daily 7–11am and 5–9pm. Call for hours at other times.

Slacker's Burger Joint BURGERS/SANDWICHES This fast-food restaurant serves good burgers—more than a half-dozen varieties, including one topped with pastrami!—plus sandwiches, fries, fish and chips, and, for those who insist on eating healthy, salads and a garden burger. There's a small dining room with '50s memorabilia and a lawn with picnic and patio tables. A wide variety of ice-cream cones and thick milkshakes is also available; no alcohol is served.

165 E. Main St., Torrey. ✆ **435/425-3710.** $2–$9. MC, V. Mon–Sat noon–8pm; Sun noon–5pm. Closed Nov–Mar.

Rim Rock Restaurant AMERICAN A local favorite for special occasions, this fine-dining restaurant is an excellent choice for beef, such as the grilled tenderloin with cranberry demi-sauce, or the blackened top sirloin with caramelized onions and button mushrooms. We also recommend the smoked pork barbecue ribs and, for an appetizer, the smoked trout. The menu also includes a pasta of the day, pan-seared Utah trout, several chicken dishes, a few vegetarian items, and homemade pies. The casual dining room has a Western look, with lots of windows providing stupendous views, and a raised outdoor dining area. Full liquor service is available.

2423 E. Utah 24. ✆ **435/425-3388.** www.therimrock.net. Main courses $15–$30. AE, DISC, MC, V. Daily 5–9pm. Closed Nov–Feb.

10

Carlsbad Caverns National Park, NM

by Don & Barbara Laine

One of the largest and most spectacular cave systems in the world, Carlsbad Caverns National Park comprises 116 known caves that snake through the porous limestone reef of the Guadalupe Mountains. Fantastic and grotesque formations fascinate visitors, who find every shape imaginable (and unimaginable) naturally sculpted in the underground—from frozen waterfalls to strands of pearls, soda straws to miniature castles, draperies to ice-cream cones.

Formation of the caverns began some 250 million years ago, when a huge inland sea covered this region. A reef formed, and then the sea disappeared, leaving the reef covered with deposits of salts and gypsum. Eventually, uplifting and erosion brought the reef back to the surface, and then the actual cave creation began. Rainwater seeped through cracks in the earth's surface, dissolving the limestone and leaving hollows behind. With the help of sulfuric acid, created by gases released from oil and gas deposits farther below ground, the cavern passageways grew, sometimes becoming huge rooms.

Once the caves were hollowed out, nature's artistry took over, decorating the rooms with a variety of fanciful formations. Water dripped down through the rock into the caves, dissolving more limestone and absorbing the mineral calcite and other materials on its journey. Each drop of water then deposited a tiny load of calcite, gradually creating the cave formations that lure visitors to Carlsbad Caverns each year.

Although American Indians had known of Carlsbad Cavern for centuries, settlers didn't discover it until sunset flights of bats emerging from the cave attracted ranchers in the 1880s. The first reported trip into the cave was in 1883, when a man supposedly lowered his 12-year-old son into the cave entrance. A cowboy named Jim White, who worked for mining companies that collected bat droppings for use as fertilizer, began to explore the main cave in the early 1900s. Fascinated by the formations, White shared his discovery with others, and word of the magical underground world soon spread.

Carlsbad Cave National Monument was created in October 1923. In 1926, the first electric lights were installed, and in 1930 Carlsbad Caverns gained national park status.

Underground development has been confined to the famous Big Room, one of the largest and most easily accessible of the caverns, with a ceiling 25 stories high and a floor large enough to hold more than six football fields. Visitors can tour parts of it on their own, aided by an excellent portable audio guide, and explore other sections and several other caves on guided tours. The cave is also a summer home to about 400,000 Brazilian (also called Mexican) free-tailed bats, which hang from the ceiling of Bat Cave during the day. They put on a spectacular show each evening as they leave the cave in search of food, and again in the morning when they return.

In addition to the fascinating underground world, the national park has a scenic drive, an interpretive nature trail, and backcountry hiking trails through the Chihuahuan Desert.

AVOIDING THE CROWDS

The park is open year-round and receives a bit over 400,000 visitors annually. Crowds are thickest in summer and on weekends and holidays year-round; visiting on weekdays between Labor Day and Memorial Day is the best way to avoid them. January is the quietest month.

Visiting during the park's off season is especially attractive because the climate in the caves stays the same regardless of the weather above. The only downside is that you won't be able to see the bat flights. The bats head to Mexico when the weather starts to get chilly, usually by late October, and don't return until May. There are also fewer guided cave tours off-season. The best time to see the park might be September, when you can still see the bat flights but there are fewer visitors than during the peak summer season.

Tips from an Insider

"If you can only see one thing here, see the **Big Room** in Carlsbad Cavern," advises Bridget Litten, the park's former public affairs specialist. "Allow an hour and a half, and if you have more time and are in good physical condition, take the Natural Entrance Route into the cave, which has a 750-foot descent and is a bit strenuous."

The potential for scientific discoveries from caves is tremendous, Litten says, adding that research is underway in Lechugilla Cave that may eventually provide a cure for certain types of cancer. "They're collecting microscopic life forms—bacteria that survive without sunlight and secrete an enzyme that appears to be able to kill breast cancer cells without harming healthy human cells."

Litten says that park visitors should not miss out on the aboveground attractions, such as the evening **bat flight,** and the 9½-mile **scenic drive,** which provides panoramic views of the surrounding desert. "A good time to take the drive is late afternoon or early evening after the visitor center has closed and before the bat flight program has begun," Litten says, adding that "it's usually cooler then, too." She also suggests a picnic at **Rattlesnake Springs,** a "birders' paradise," she calls it, and adds that those who want to experience the Chihuahuan Desert without any crowds should consider hiking the park's backcountry, which less than 1% of the park's visitors do.

1 Essentials

GETTING THERE & GATEWAYS

The main section of the park, with the visitor center and entrance to Carlsbad Cavern, is about 30 miles southwest of the city of Carlsbad by way of **U.S. 62/180** and **N. Mex. 7.** From Albuquerque, drive east on I-40 for 59 miles to Clines Corners, then turn south on U.S. 285 for 216 miles to the city of Carlsbad. For the caverns, continue southwest 23 miles on U.S. 62/180 to White's City, and go about 7 miles on N. Mex. 7, the park access road, to the visitor center. From El Paso, drive east 150 miles on U.S. 62/180 to White's City, then 7 miles on N. Mex. 7 to the visitor center.

THE NEAREST AIRPORT Air travelers can fly to **Cavern City Air Terminal** (✆ **575/887-1500**), at the south edge of the city of Carlsbad, which has commercial service from Albuquerque on **New Mexico Airlines** (✆ **888/564-6119;** www.flynma.com), plus **Enterprise** car rentals.

The nearest major airport is **El Paso International** (✆ **915/780-4749;** www.elpasointernationalairport.com), in central El Paso just north of I-10, with service from major airlines and car-rental companies. See chapter 38 for websites of the major airlines and car-rental companies.

INFORMATION

Contact **Carlsbad Caverns National Park,** 3225 National Parks Hwy., Carlsbad, NM 88220 (✆ **575/785-2232;** 575/785-3012 for bat flight information; www.nps.gov/cave).

Because the park's backcountry trails may be hard to follow, rangers strongly recommend that those planning any serious aboveground hiking obtain topographical maps. An excellent book for hikers is *Hiking Carlsbad Caverns and Guadalupe Mountains National Parks,* by Bill Schneider, which was published in partnership with the Carlsbad Caverns Guadalupe Mountains Association and is keyed to the Trails Illustrated topographical map of the park. Books and maps can be ordered from the **Carlsbad Caverns Guadalupe Mountains Association,** 727 Carlsbad Caverns Hwy. (P.O. Box 1417), Carlsbad, NM 88220 (✆ **575/785-2486,** or 575/785-2569 for orders; www.ccgma.org).

For additional information on area lodging, dining, and other attractions, contact or stop at the **Carlsbad Chamber of Commerce,** 302 S. Canal St., Carlsbad, NM 88220 (✆ **800/221-1224** or 575/887-6516; www.carlsbadchamber.com).

VISITOR CENTER

The park visitor center is open daily 8am to 7pm from Memorial Day to Labor Day; self-guided cave tours can begin from 8:30am to 5pm. The rest of the year, the visitor center is open daily from 8am to 5pm, with self-guided cave tours from 8:30am to 3:30pm. Tour times and schedules may vary during slower times in the winter. The park is closed December 25.

At the visitor center, displays depict the geology and history of the caverns, bats, and other wildlife; you can also see a 3D model of Carlsbad Caverns.

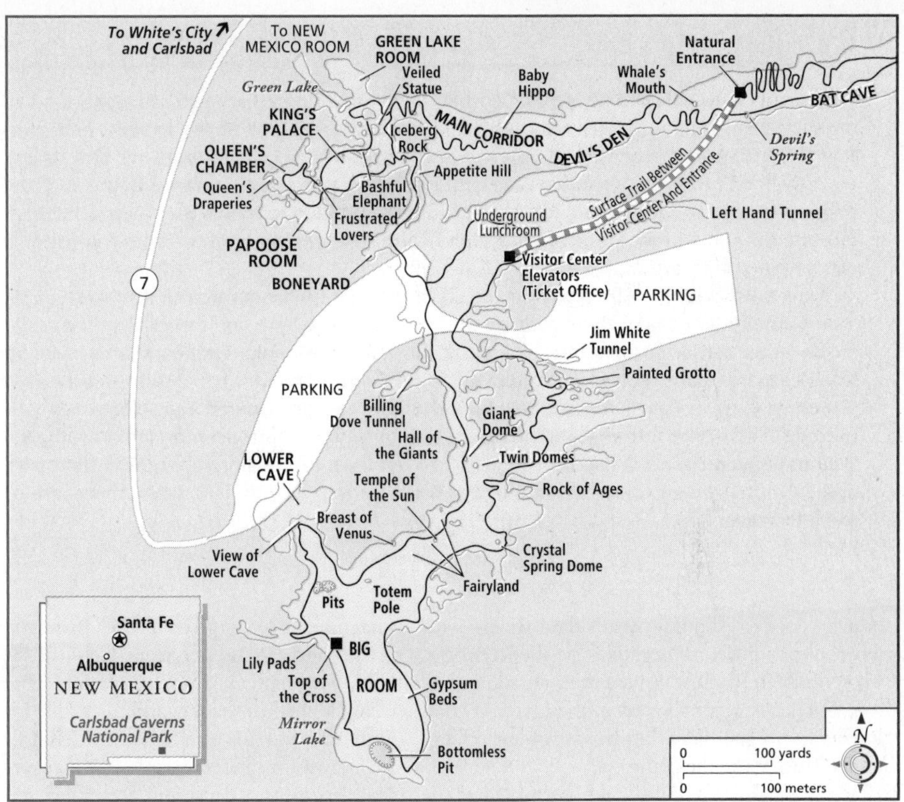

You can also get information about tours and other park activities, both below- and aboveground.

Attached to the visitor center is a family-style restaurant (see "Where to Dine," later in this chapter) and a gift shop that offers the usual souvenir items such as postcards and sweatshirts, plus a variety of gift items, including handmade American Indian crafts. Another gift shop is in the Underground Rest Area.

FEES & RESERVATIONS

Admission to the visitor center and aboveground sections of the park is free. The basic **cavern entry fee,** which is good for 3 days and includes self-guided tours of the Natural Entrance and Big Room, is $6 for adults 16 and older and free for children under 16. Holders of all America the Beautiful passes, plus their immediate families, are admitted free. An audio tour of the two self-guided routes is available for a $3 rental fee.

Reservations are required for all **guided tours.** In addition to tour fees, you will need a general cave admission ticket for guided cave tours, except those to Slaughter Canyon Cave and Spider Cave. Holders of the America the Beautiful Senior and Access passes receive a 50% discount on tours. Children under 16 must be accompanied by an adult 18 or older, and minimum age restrictions for tours also apply.

The King's Palace guided tour costs $8 for adults and $4 for children 4 to 15; younger children are not permitted. Guided tours of Left Hand Tunnel, limited to those 6 and older, cost $7 for adults and $3.50 for children 6 to 15. Guided tours of Spider Cave, Lower Cave, and Hall of the White Giant are limited to those 12 and older; they cost $20 for adults and $10 for youths 12 to 15. Slaughter Canyon Cave tours, for those 6 and older, cost $15 for adults, $7.50 for children 6 to 15.

You can make **reservations** for cave tours in advance by phone or on the Internet (✆ **877/444-6777;** www.recreation.gov).

SPECIAL REGULATIONS & WARNINGS

As you would expect, damaging the cave formations in any way is prohibited. Even touching the formations, walls, or ceilings of the caves can damage them. This is not only because many of the features are delicate and easily broken, but also because skin oils will discolor the rock and disturb the mineral deposits that are necessary for growth.

All tobacco use is prohibited underground. In addition, food, drinks, candy, and gum are not allowed on the underground trails. Do not throw coins or other objects into the underground pools.

If You Have Only 1 Day

Those with only 1 day to spend at Carlsbad Caverns National Park can see quite a bit if they organize their time well. First, stop at the **visitor center** to look at the exhibits and check out that day's tours and programs. If you would like to take any guided tours, it's best to buy tickets now. Then head into the main cave through the steep **Natural Entrance Route** and continue on a self-guided tour of the **Big Room.** For those not wishing to follow the steep switchback trail into the Natural Entrance, and anyone with health concerns, an elevator from the visitor center will deliver you to the Big Room.

You'll finish your Big Room tour at the elevators near the **Underground Rest Area,** so pick up a sandwich there or take the elevator up to the surface, where you can dine in the restaurant at the visitor center or drive out for a picnic lunch at **Rattlesnake Springs.** (Rattlesnake Springs is a picnic area with tables, grills, drinking water, and restrooms. It's along the access road to Slaughter Canyon Cave.) After lunch, take the **King's Palace Guided Tour** (for which you purchased tickets earlier). Then walk the nature trail outside the visitor center and drive the 9½-mile **Walnut Canyon Desert Drive.** If possible, try to get back to the amphitheater at the cave's Natural Entrance by dusk to see the nightly **bat flight** (spring through fall), when thousands of bats leave the cave.

Cave visitors should wear flat shoes with rubber soles and heels to negotiate the slippery paths. Children under 16 must remain with an adult at all times. Strollers are not allowed in the caves, so child backpacks are a good idea, but beware of low ceilings and doorways along the pathways.

Photography of any kind is not permitted at the evening bat flight programs.

Pets are not permitted in the caverns, on park trails, or in the backcountry. Because of the hot summer temperatures, pets should not be left unattended in vehicles. A **kennel** is available at the visitor center. It has cages in an air-conditioned room but no runs, and is primarily used by pet owners for a few hours while they are on cave tours. Pets are given water but not food, and there are no overnight facilities. Reservations are not necessary.

SEASONS & CLIMATE

The climate aboveground is warm in the summer, with highs often in the 90s (30s Celsius) and sometimes exceeding 100°F (38°C); evening lows are in the mid-60s (upper teens Celsius). Winters are mild, with highs in the 50s and 60s (10s and mid-teens Celsius) in the day and nighttime lows usually in the 20s and 30s (low negatives Celsius). Summers are known for sudden intense afternoon and evening thunderstorms; August and September see the most rain. Underground it's another story entirely, with a year-round temperature that varies little from its average of 56°F (13°C), making a jacket or sweater a welcome companion.

SEASONAL EVENTS

A "bat flight breakfast," planned from 5 to 7am on a summer Saturday, encourages visitors to watch the bats return to the cavern after their night of insect hunting. Park rangers prepare breakfast for early morning visitors for a small fee and then join them to watch the early morning return flight. Call the park for the date, cost, and other details.

2 Exploring the Park by Car

No, you can't take your car into the caves, but it won't be totally useless, either. For a close-up as well as panoramic view of the Chihuahuan Desert, head out on the **Walnut Canyon Desert Drive,** a 9½-mile loop. You'll want to drive slowly on the one-way gravel road, both for safety and to appreciate thoroughly the dramatic scenery. Passenger cars can easily handle the tight turns and narrow passage, but the road is not recommended for motor homes or cars pulling trailers. Pick up an interpretive brochure for the drive at the visitor center bookstore. Allow about 1 hour.

3 Organized Tours & Ranger Programs

In addition to cave tours (discussed below), rangers give a talk on bats at sunset each evening from mid-May through mid-October at the cavern's Natural Entrance (check at the visitor center or call ✆ **575/785-3012** for the schedule). They also offer a variety of demonstrations, talks, guided nature walks, and other programs daily. Especially popular are climbing programs, during which rangers demonstrate caving techniques. A schedule of ranger-led activities is posted at the visitor center.

4 Park Attractions

Although this park is devoted primarily to the work of nature, observing human activities in the caves is part of the Carlsbad Caverns experience. Throughout the main cavern, you'll see evidence of human use (and misuse) of the caves. Those taking the guided Lower Cave tour will see artifacts left by early cave explorers, including members of a 1924 National Geographic Society expedition.

5 Cave Exploration

Carlsbad Cavern (the park's main cave), Slaughter Canyon Cave, and Spider Cave are open to the public. Experienced cavers with professional-level equipment can request permission to explore some of the park's other caves.

Most visitors head first to Carlsbad Cavern, which has elevators, a paved walkway, and the Underground Rest Area. A 1-mile section of the Big Room self-guided tour is accessible to those in wheelchairs (no wheelchairs are available at the park), though it's best to have someone along to assist. Pick up an accessibility guide at the visitor center.

MAIN CARLSBAD CAVERN ROUTES

Most visitors see Carlsbad Cavern by taking the following three trails, all of which are lighted and paved and have handrails. However, the Big Room is the only one of the three that's considered easy.

The formations along these trails are strategically lit to display them at their most dramatic. The odd tints of green and yellow that may appear in your photos are caused by the lighting.

Big Room Self-Guided Tour Considered the one essential of a visit to Carlsbad Caverns National Park, this trail meanders through a massive chamber—it isn't called the Big Room for nothing—where you'll see some of the park's most spectacular formations and likely be overwhelmed by the enormity of it all. Allow about 1½ hours. 1-mile loop. Easy. Access: Visitor center elevator to Underground Rest Area, or Natural Entrance Route (see below).

King's Palace Guided Tour This ranger-led 1½-hour walk wanders through some of the cave's most scenic chambers, where you'll see fanciful formations in the King's Palace, Queen's Chamber, and Green Lake Room. Watch for the Bashful Elephant formation between the King's Palace and Green Lake Room. Along the way, rangers discuss the geology of the cave and early explorers' experiences. Although the path is paved, the 80-foot elevation change makes this more difficult than the Big Room trail. Children under 4 are not permitted. 1-mile loop. Moderate. Access: Visitor center elevator to Underground Rest Area.

Natural Entrance Route This moderately strenuous hike takes you into Carlsbad Cavern on the same basic route used by its early explorers. You leave daylight to enter a big hole, then descend more than 750 feet into the cavern on a steep and narrow switchback trail, moving from the "twilight zone" of semidarkness to the depths of the cave, which would be totally black without the electric lights conveniently provided by the Park Service. The self-guided tour takes about 1 hour and ends near the elevators, which can take you back to the visitor center. However, it is strongly recommended that from here you proceed on the Big Room Self-Guided Tour, which is described above, if you have not already been there. 1.25 miles. Moderate to strenuous. Access: Outside visitor center.

CAVING TOUR PROGRAMS IN CARLSBAD CAVERN

Ranger-led tours to these less developed sections of Carlsbad Cavern provide more of the experience of exploration and genuine caving than the above routes, which follow well-trodden trails. Caving tours vary in difficulty, but all include a period of absolute darkness or "blackout," which can make some people uncomfortable. Because some tours involve walking or crawling through tight spaces, people who suffer from claustrophobia or who have other health concerns should discuss specifics with rangers before purchasing tickets.

See below for age restrictions and required equipment. Rangers provide headlamps and helmets on some tours. All tours must be reserved; the cost is separate from the general entrance fee. Tours can book up weeks in advance, so reserve early.

Hall of the White Giant If you want a strenuous 4-hour trip during which you crawl through narrow, dirty passageways and climb slippery rocks, this tour is for you. The highlight is the huge formation called the White Giant. Only those in excellent condition should consider this tour; children must be at least 12. Four AA batteries for the provided headlamp, sturdy hiking boots, kneepads, gloves, and long pants are required. .5 mile one-way. Strenuous. Access: Visitor center.

Left Hand Tunnel The easiest of the caving tours, this one allows you to actually walk—rather than crawl—the entire time! Hand-carried lanterns (provided by the Park Service) light the way, and the trail is dirt but relatively level. You'll see a variety of formations, fossils from Permian times, and pools of water. Children must be at least 6. The tour takes about 2 hours. .5 mile one-way. Easy. Access: Visitor center, near the elevator.

Lower Cave This 3-hour trek involves descending or climbing over 50 feet of ladders, and an optional crawl. It takes you through an area that was explored by a National Geographic Society expedition in the 1920s, and you'll see artifacts from that and other excursions. In addition, you'll encounter a variety of formations, including cave pearls, which look a lot like the pearls created by oysters and can be as big as golf balls. Participants must be at least 12. Four AA batteries are required for the provided headlamp. Hiking boots or good sneakers and gloves are also required. 1 mile RT. Moderate. Access: Visitor center, near the elevator.

OTHER CAVING TOURS

It takes some hiking to reach the other caves in the park, so carry drinking water, especially on hot summer days. Children under 16 must be accompanied by an adult; other age restrictions apply as well. Each tour includes a period of total darkness or "blackout." Fees apply for both, but a general cave admission ticket is not required. Tours are popular and are frequently fully booked; call a few months ahead for reservations.

Slaughter Canyon Cave Discovered in 1937, this cave was commercially mined for bat guano (used as fertilizer) until the 1950s. It consists of a corridor 1,140 feet long with many side passageways. The excellent guided tour lasts about 2 hours, plus at least another half-hour to hike up the steep trail to the cave entrance. No crawling is involved, although the smooth flowstone and old bat guano on the floor can be slippery. You'll see a number of wonderful cave formations, including the crystal-decorated Christmas Tree, the 89-foot-high Monarch, and the menacing Klansman. Children must be at least 6. Participants must take strong flashlights with fresh batteries, drinking water, and good hiking boots. 1.25 miles RT (plus .5-mile hike to and from cave entrance). Moderate. Access: Take U.S. 62/180 from Carlsbad, going south 5 miles from White's City, to marked turnoff that leads 11 miles to parking lot. Driving time is 45 min. Tours meet at and depart from cave entrance.

Spider Cave Very strenuous, this tour is ideal for those who want the experience of a rugged caving adventure, as well as some great underground scenery. Highlights include climbing down a 15-foot ladder, squeezing through tight passageways, and climbing on slippery surfaces—all this after a fairly tough half-mile hike to the cave entrance. But it's worth it. The cave has numerous beautiful formations—most much smaller than those in the Big Room—and picturesque pools of water. Allow 4 hours. Participants must be at least 12, need four AA batteries for the provided headlamps, and should have good hiking boots, kneepads, gloves, long pants, and drinking water. 1-mile loop (plus .5-mile hike to and from cave). Strenuous. Access: Visitor center; follow ranger to cave.

WILD CAVING

Experienced cavers with the proper gear can request permits from the park's **Cave Resources Office** (✆ **575/785-2232,** ext. 3104, 3105, 3106, or 3107) to enter one of several undeveloped caves in the park on their own. In addition, Ogle Cave is open to experienced vertical cavers on ranger-led trips. Applications should be submitted at least 1 month ahead of time. There is a $15 fee for entry to Ogle Cave; permits for other caves are free. Further information is available from the Cave Resources Office.

6 Other Sports & Activities

HIKING & BACKPACKING Most of the hiking here is done underground, but there are opportunities on the earth's surface as well. The park's busiest trail is the **Nature Trail,** a fairly easy, 1-mile paved loop that begins just outside the visitor center and has interpretive signs describing the various plants of the Chihuahuan Desert.

About a half-dozen other trails wander through the park's 30,000 acres of designated wilderness. These **backcountry trails** are usually poorly marked—rangers strongly recommend that hikers carry topographical maps, which are for sale at the visitor center. Watch for rattlesnakes, especially in warmer months. Lighting fires and entering backcountry caves without permits are prohibited. For overnight hikes, you'll need to pick up a free permit at the visitor center.

Backcountry trails include the 3.7-mile (one-way) **Old Guano Road Trail,** with an elevation change of 710 feet; the 2.2-mile (one-way) **Rattlesnake Canyon Trail,** with an elevation change of 670 feet; the 5.3-mile (one-way) **Slaughter Canyon Trail,** which has an elevation change of 1,850 feet; the 7.7-mile (one-way) **Yucca Canyon Trail,** with a 1,520-foot elevation change; the 12-mile (one-way) **Guadalupe Ridge Trail,** with an elevation change of 2,050 feet; and the 2.8-mile (one-way) **Juniper Ridge Trail,** with an 800-foot elevation change.

Especially for Kids

Children usually love the self-guided walk through the main cavern's **Big Room,** with its many bizarre and beautiful shapes, especially when they're encouraged to let their imaginations run wild. Younger children are often bored on the **King's Palace Guided Tour** because it has several stops and everyone must remain with the group. (Children under 4 are not permitted on the King's Palace tour.) Families with children at least 6 years old (and preferably a bit older) enjoy the **Slaughter Canyon Cave** tour, which has some spectacular formations and gives the feeling of exploring a wild cave.

Backcountry camping is allowed (with a free permit) on all of the above trails except Old Guano Road. Additional trail information is available from park rangers.

HORSEBACK RIDING Most of the backcountry trails are open to those on horseback. A small corral is available, with advance arrangements. Contact the park **Resource Management Office** (✆ **575/785-3091**).

WILDLIFE VIEWING & BIRD-WATCHING At sunset, roughly from April or May until late October or early November, a crowd gathers at the Carlsbad Cavern Natural Entrance to watch hundreds of thousands of bats take off for the night. All day long, the **free-tailed bats,** which spend the winter in Mexico, sleep in the cavern; they strike out on an insect hunt each night. An amphitheater in front of the Natural Entrance provides seating, and ranger programs are held each evening from mid-May through mid-October (check the schedule at the visitor center or call ✆ **575/785-3012**). The most bats are seen in August and September, when baby bats born earlier in the summer join their parents, along with migrating bats from the north, on the nightly forays. Early risers can see the bats return just before dawn. Cameras, including video cameras, are not permitted.

Bats aren't the only wildlife at Carlsbad Caverns. The park has a surprising number of **birds**—more than 300 species—many of which are seen in the Rattlesnake Springs area. Among species you're likely to see are turkey vultures, red-tailed hawks, scaled quail, killdeer, mourning doves, lesser nighthawks, black-chinned hummingbirds, vermilion flycatchers, canyon wrens, northern mockingbirds, black-throated sparrows, and western meadowlarks. In addition, several thousand cave swallows build their mud nests each summer on the ceiling just inside the Carlsbad Cavern Natural Entrance. (The bats make their home farther back in the cave.)

Among the park's **larger animals** are mule deer and raccoons, which are sometimes spotted near the Natural Entrance at the time of the evening bat flights. The park is also home to porcupines, hog-nosed skunks, desert cottontails, black-tailed jackrabbits, rock squirrels, and the more elusive ringtails, coyotes, and gray fox. These are sometimes seen in the late evenings along the park entrance road and the Walnut Canyon Desert Drive. In recent years there have also been a few sightings of mountain lions and bobcats.

7 Camping

There are no developed campgrounds or vehicle camping of any kind inside the national park. Backcountry camping, however, is permitted in some areas. (See the description of backcountry trails under "Hiking & Backpacking," above.) Pick up free permits at the visitor center.

NEAR THE PARK

The closest camping to the national park that we recommend is in the city of Carlsbad at **Carlsbad RV Park & Campground,** 4301 National Parks Hwy., Carlsbad, NM 88220 (✆ **888/878-7275** or 575/885-6333). This tree-filled campground offers pull-through sites large enough to accommodate big rigs with slideouts, as well as tent sites and sites for everything in between. Some sites have cable TV hookups, and all sites have Wi-Fi. There's an indoor heated pool, a game room, a playground, a free petting zoo, and a meeting room with kitchen. Breakfast is available on weekends. A convenience store sells groceries, gifts, and RV supplies.

The most luxurious camping in the area for both RVers and tenters is at **Carlsbad KOA,** 2 Manthei Rd., Carlsbad, NM 88220 (✆ **800/562-9109** or 575-457-2000; www.carlsbadkoa.com). Near Brantley Lake State Park (see below), the KOA is 13 miles north of the city of Carlsbad, just off U.S. 285. The top-rated RV park in the entire state by several respected RV park publications, the facility is nicely landscaped with grass and trees and boasts large (40-by-70-ft.) sites that can accommodate the

Campground	Elev.	Total Sites	RV Hookups	Dump Station	Toilets
Brantley Lake State Park	3,300	51+	51	Yes	Yes
Carlsbad KOA	3,420	132	102	No	Yes
Carlsbad RV Park & Campground	3,110	136	95	Yes	Yes

largest rigs with slideouts. All RV sites have full hookups, including cable TV and Wi-Fi, and there is an outdoor heated pool, hot tub, playground, coin-op laundry, and fenced pet park where dogs can be off-leash. Some tent sites have water and electric available, and there are two meticulously maintained bathhouses. Barbecue dinners and sandwiches are prepared each evening and can be ordered for campsite delivery, and hot breakfasts are available weekends. An on-site wind turbine provides a portion of the campground's electricity. There are also 12 cabins, ranging from basic to luxurious, at rates from $55 to $140 per night.

Another good choice for those who will be exploring the area is **Brantley Lake State Park,** P.O. Box 2288, Carlsbad, NM 88221 (✆ **575/457-2384;** www.nmparks.com). Located 12 miles north of the city of Carlsbad (take U.S. 285, then go 4½ miles northeast on Eddy C.R. 30), this quiet and relaxing park is just under 40 miles from the Carlsbad Caverns Visitor Center. Activities include boating, swimming, and fishing on the 3,000-acre lake, as well as bird-watching. The park also has boat ramps, picnic tables, two playgrounds, and exhibits on the 19th-century community of Seven Rivers, considered one of the West's wildest towns, which now lies at the bottom of the lake. The day-use fee is $5 per vehicle. There are 51 developed RV campsites (48 with water and electric hookups, 3 with water, electric, and sewer), plus primitive camping along the lakeshore for 20 to 50 RVs or tents, depending on the lake level. Rangers present programs in the campground Saturday evenings during the summer. Reservations, for a $11 processing fee (in addition to the campsite fee), are available from spring through early fall by calling ✆ **877/664-7787,** or on the Web at www.newmexico.reserveworld.com.

8 Where to Stay

There are no accommodations within the park. We recommend staying in the city of Carlsbad, where the lodging choices are not exciting, but you will find several clean, well-maintained chain motels, including our favorite, the **Best Western Stevens Inn** (see below). Other options include the **Comfort Inn,** 2429 W. Pierce St., Carlsbad, NM 88220-3515 (✆ **575/887-1994**), with rates of about $110 double; **Days Inn,** 3910 National Parks Hwy., Carlsbad, NM 88220 (✆ **575/887-7800**), $70 to $120 double; and **Super 8 Motel,** 3817 National Parks Hwy., Carlsbad, NM 88220 (✆ **575/887-8888**), $49 to $59 double. See chapter 38 for website listings of the national chains.

Best Western Stevens Inn Well-landscaped gardens surround this handsome property, composed of several buildings spread across spacious grounds. Rooms have Southwestern decor, coffeemakers, hair dryers, and high-speed Internet. They have one king- or two queen-size beds, and some units have refrigerators and microwaves. Some units, with peaked ceilings that make them feel even larger, also have back-door patios. There are also wheelchair-accessible rooms with roll-in showers. The motel has a good restaurant, **The Flume** (see "Where to Dine," below), room service, courtesy airport transportation, coin-op laundry, 24-hour front desk, large outdoor swimming pool, whirlpool, exercise room, and playground.

1829 S. Canal St., Carlsbad, NM 88220. ✆ **800/730-2851** direct, or 575/887-2851. www.stevensinn.com. 220 units. A/C, TV, TEL. $104–$114 double. Rates include full breakfast buffet. AE, DC, DISC, MC, V. Pets accepted, $10 per night.

9 Where to Dine

INSIDE THE PARK

There are two concessionaire-operated restaurants at the park (✆ **575/785-2281**). A family-style, full-service restaurant at the **visitor center** serves three meals daily. It offers standard breakfasts and a variety of sandwiches, burgers, and salads for lunch and dinner. Prices are in the $5-to-$12 range. The restaurant is open daily 8am to 7pm in summer, with shorter hours the rest of the year. The **Underground Rest Area,** inside the cavern 750 feet belowground, has a cafeteria-style eatery that offers a limited menu of fast food items, including sandwiches, and has summer hours of 8:30am to 5pm, with shorter hours at other times. Prices are in the $4-to-$8 range. There is also a gift shop.

Drinking Water	Showers	Fire Pits/ Grills	Laundry	Reserve	Fees	Open
Yes	Yes	Yes	No	Yes	$8–$18	Year-round
Yes	Yes	Yes	Yes	Yes	$28–$55	Year-round
Yes	Yes	Yes	Yes	Yes	$19–$34	Year-round

NEAR THE PARK

The Flume AMERICAN This relatively elegant restaurant, with comfortable seating and attractive wall sconces and chandeliers, is our top dining choice in Carlsbad. For breakfast and lunch, you can choose from a good selection of American favorites. The dinner menu includes the house specialty prime rib, a variety of steaks, seafood such as the broiled halibut, chicken, pasta, and Mexican items. Lighter dinners for those 55 and older are also available.

At the Best Western Stevens Inn, 1829 S. Canal St., Carlsbad. ✆ **575/887-2851.** Main courses $5–$9.95 lunch, $9.95–$22 dinner. AE, DC, DISC, MC, V. Mon–Sat 6am–10pm; Sun 6am–9pm.

A Quick Guide to New Mexican Cuisine

For me, half the fun of a trip to the Southwest is getting to eat New Mexican food. I don't even care about the high-end places: A burrito or bowl of green chile from a takeout stand is good enough for me. Even if you're familiar with Mexican and Tex-Mex, you'll find New Mexico cooking is its own thing. Like the state itself, Anglo, Spanish, and Indian influences blend together. The chile pepper (they use the Spanish spelling out here) is the key, served red or green, often as a sauce to top enchiladas and burritos. The following glossary refers to New Mexican food, which overlaps with its Four Corner neighbors.

- **Carne adovada** Tender pork marinated in red chile sauce and then baked. Tends to be spicy. Insanely good.
- **Chorizo** Mexican sausage, often found in breakfast burritos, along with eggs, potatoes, Jack cheese, and red or green chile.
- **Christmas** Tortured over which sauce to try, the red or the green chile? Get 'em both; just ask for it "Christmas."
- **Green chile stew** Chile soup with meat, potatoes, and sometimes beans. Tends to be hot. The best.
- **Huevos rancheros** Fried eggs on tortillas, topped with cheese and chile and/or salsa. Often served with pinto beans.
- **Masa** The corn dough used in tortillas and tamales. New Mexican corn comes in six colors, with yellow, white, and blue the most common.
- **Navajo frybread** Fried dough. When topped with honey or powdered sugar, similar to fairground faves like funnel cakes, dough boys, and elephant ears.
- **Navajo tacos** Frybread topped with beans, beef, and cheese.
- **Piñon nuts** Pine nuts, more or less. Available at roadside stands, great smoky flavor.
- **Posole** Hominy corn in a soup or stew, sometimes with pork and chile. Very hearty, good cold weather food.
- **Ristra** Those strings of chiles you see dangling from porches.
- **Sopaipilla** Airy fried dough pocket served with honey, or stuffed with meat and vegetables.

New Mexican food seems like it should travel easily, but like French bread or New York bagels, you just can't find it done right once you get away from the source. I say, eat as much of it as you can while you have the chance.

—Ethan Wolff

10 Nearby Attractions

Many visitors to Carlsbad Caverns also spend time at nearby **Guadalupe Mountains National Park,** which is discussed in chapter 20.

We also highly recommend spending a few hours at **Living Desert Zoo & Gardens State Park,** located on the northwest edge of the city of Carlsbad off U.S. 285 (✆ **575/887-5516;** www.emnrd.state.nm.us/PRD/livingDesert.htm), where you'll get a close-up look at the plants and animals of the Chihuahuan Desert. A 1.3-mile trail meanders through the various habitats that make up the desert, from sand hills, to gypsum rock formations, to the mountainous pinyon-juniper zone. Animals here include elk, mule deer, pronghorn, black bear, bison, mountain lion, badger, and porcupine. There's also a small herd of javelina, named for their short, javelin-sharp tusks, that enjoy a meal of tasty prickly pear cactus, spines and all. There's a Reptile House, an aviary, and a pond that attracts migrating ducks and geese.

There are numerous plants of the Chihuahuan Desert and an amazing collection of cacti and succulents from around the world—those hardy species that can endure extreme heat and cold, sandy soil, and very little water.

From Memorial Day weekend through Labor Day weekend, the park is open daily from 8am to 5pm, with the last entry to the zoo at 3:30pm. Hours the rest of the year are shorter, and it is closed Christmas Day. Especially in summer, it's best to get to the park during the cooler morning hours, when the animals are more active. Admission costs $5 for those 13 and older, $3 for children 7 to 12, and is free for kids under 7.

Picnic & Camping Supplies

You'll find a good variety of stores in the city of Carlsbad, including an **Albertson's** grocery store, 808 N. Canal St., at West Church Street (✆ **575/885-2161;** www.albertsonsmarket.com), that has a well-stocked deli and bakery.

Channel Islands National Park, CA

by Eric Peterson

A rusted windmill watches over Scorpion Ranch on Santa Cruz Island, a reminder of man's impact on even our wildest places. It is but one of an array of archaeological and historic sites in this national park.

But the Channel Islands are still defined more by the sea and the wind than anything else. On land, the dry grasses and shrubs remain in motion, mimicking the white-capped water of the Santa Barbara Channel that separates the islands from the mainland. These waters contain a diversity of life matched by few places.

Although they make up one of America's less visited national parks, the Channel Islands offer plenty of reasons to keep visitors coming back. Opportunities for sea kayaking and hiking are numerous, you'll find plants and animals that live nowhere else, and archaeological remains serve as reminders of long-vanished cultures. It's also a draw for underwater explorers from all over—twice as many people come here to explore the waters around the islands as ever set foot on the shore.

Channel Islands National Park encompasses the five northernmost islands of an eight-island chain: Santa Barbara, Anacapa, Santa Cruz, Santa Rosa, and San Miguel. (The park does not include Santa Catalina, San Clemente, and San Nicolas.) Not limited to the islands themselves, the park also encompasses 1 nautical mile of ocean around each island, and the 6 nautical miles around each island have been designated a national marine sanctuary. The smallest of the park's islands, tiny Santa Barbara, lives a solitary existence off by itself. The four northern islands cluster in a 40-mile-long chain. During the last ice age, before the continental ice sheets melted, driving up the level of the sea, these islands were connected in one huge island that geologists now call Santarosae.

Although it was once theorized that the Channel Islands broke off the California coast some 600,000 years ago, geologists now believe that the islands were never connected to the mainland, ultimately owing their origins to underwater volcanic activity.

FLORA & FAUNA

The isolation of the Channel Islands has allowed a diverse array of life to develop and evolve, prompting some biologists to dub the islands the "North American Galápagos." Most of the differences from mainland species are in size, shape, or color variation. Perhaps the most curious of the islands' former inhabitants was the pygmy mammoth, only 4 to 6 feet tall, which roamed over Santarosae during the Pleistocene era—fossilized remains have been found on San Miguel, Santa Cruz, and Santa Rosa.

Other island species have survived. Like the mammoth, the **Santa Cruz gopher snake, island spotted skunk,** and endangered **island fox** (two of the islands' three endemic mammal species—the other is the deer mouse) have all evolved to be smaller than their mainland relatives. At just 4 pounds, the island fox is the smallest fox species in North America. Like Darwin's finches in the Galápagos, the islands' native birds also show marked adaptation: The **Santa Cruz Island scrub jay,** for instance, displays "gigantism"—it is one-third larger than mainland jays.

But the diversity of animal life is outdone by the array of native plant life. One of the most spectacular of the islands' plants is the **yellow coreopsis,** or tree sunflower, which grows on all five islands (as well as the mainland). Other species of plants live nowhere else on Earth—the islands support a number of endemic varieties of plants. Santa Rosa's endemic **Torrey pine** population dates from the Pleistocene era, though a remnant mainland subspecies survives at Torrey Pines State Reserve, north of La Jolla, California.

Marine life around the islands easily wins the diversity award. The islands are the meeting point of two distinct marine ecosystems: the cold, nutrient-rich waters of Northern California and the warmer, clearer currents of Baja California. Everything from microscopic plankton to the largest creature ever to live on Earth, the blue whale, calls these waters home. Orcas and great white sharks, anemone and abalone, lobsters and starfish, plus dozens of varieties of fish, live in the tide pools, kelp forests, and waters surrounding the islands. Six varieties of seal and sea lions beach themselves on San Miguel, four of which breed here, making it one of the largest seal and sea lion breeding colonies in the United States. The islands are also the most important seabird nesting area in Southern California.

AVOIDING THE CROWDS

Unlike many of the more popular (and more easily accessible) national parks, the Channel Islands rarely have a crowding problem. In a given year, about 300,000 people stop in at the park visitor center and 600,000 go into the park waters, but only about 100,000 set foot on the islands. Although visitors to any given island rarely number more than a few hundred a day, the open section of Anacapa (the closest and most popular day-trip destination) is so small that it may be difficult to completely separate yourself from the flock. As for the other four islands in the park, you should have no trouble finding a secluded picnic spot or overlook. Santa Barbara Island is the least crowded, Santa Rosa allows for backcountry beach camping, and San Miguel is the most remote (the boat trip takes 3–4 hr.) and the wildest.

1 Essentials

GETTING THERE & GATEWAYS

Most people travel to the islands by boat from **Ventura.** Although there are no park fees, getting there is expensive—anywhere from $26 to $130 per person, the higher price being for a trip by air to Santa Rosa. If you fly, you may leave from the **Camarillo** airport. Anacapa, 14 miles out, is closest to the mainland, about a 1-hour boat ride.

THE NEAREST AIRPORT The closest major airport to the Channel Islands is **Los Angeles International Airport,** or LAX (✆ **310/646-5252;** www.lawa.org/welcomeLAX.aspx). It's served frequently by all major airlines, with connections to almost anywhere you want to go. Los Angeles is 66 miles southeast of Ventura and 96 miles southeast of Santa Barbara. All major **car-rental** companies have vehicles at LAX. Websites for airlines and car rental companies appear in chapter 38.

GETTING TO THE ISLANDS BY BOAT **Island Packers,** at Ventura Harbor at 1691 Spinnaker Dr. (✆ **805/642-1393;** www.islandpackers.com), is one of the park's two concessionaires for boat transportation to and from the islands. They will take you on a range of scheduled excursions, from 3½-hour nonlanding tours of the islands to full-day excursions, and will transport you to and from the islands for overnight trips. Prices start at $30 per person for nonlanding tours and run $45 to $75 for full-day excursions or $60 to $108 for campers. Island Packers also arranges specialty trips, primarily sea kayaking and snorkeling. Private yachts and commercial dive and tour boats also visit the park on a regular basis. Specializing in dive trips, the second boat concessionaire is **Truth Aquatics** (✆ **805/962-1127;** www.truthaquatics.com). It leaves from Santa Barbara Harbor and charges about $100 for a nonlanding round-trip to Santa Cruz; overnight live-aboard trips are also available. The trips take about 3 hours each way.

IF YOU HAVE YOUR OWN BOAT If you want to take your own boat, check with the mainland visitor center. Access to the islands is prohibited in some places and difficult in others—going ashore often requires a skiff, raft, or small boat. More details:

- You may land without a permit on East Anacapa, Santa Barbara, and east Santa Cruz, between Prisoner's Harbor and Valley Anchorage.
- West Anacapa, except the beach at Frenchy's Cove, is closed to the public to protect nesting brown pelicans.
- Access to middle Anacapa requires a ranger escort.
- At San Miguel, landings at Cuyler Harbor are allowed, and hiking access is limited without a permit and ranger escort.
- Landings and beach use on Santa Rosa do not require a permit; inland hiking excursions are also allowed. Special closures may exist; contact the park for up-to-date information.
- To land on the private western portion of Santa Cruz, boaters must obtain a permit from the **Nature Conservancy,** Attn.: Santa Cruz Landing Permit Program, 3639 Harbor Blvd., Ste. 201, Ventura, CA 93001 (✆ **805/642-0345;** www.nature.org/cruzpermit). A fee is charged, no overnight stays are permitted, and processing the request may take 2 weeks. Applications are available from the mainland visitor center or by contacting the Nature Conservancy directly.

GETTING TO THE ISLANDS BY AIR If you want to get to Santa Rosa in a hurry, **Channel Islands Aviation,** 305 Durley Ave., Camarillo, CA 93010 (✆ **805/987-1301,** ext. 0; www.flycia.com), will fly you there from Camarillo or Santa Barbara in one of its small, fixed-wing aircraft (around $160 per adult round-trip, $250 if you're camping).

INFORMATION

Contact **Channel Islands National Park,** 1901 Spinnaker Dr., Ventura, CA 93001 (✆ **805/658-5730;** www.nps.gov/chis).

For information on Ventura, try the **Ventura Visitors & Convention Bureau,** 101 S. California St., Ventura, CA 93001 (✆ **800/483-6214** or 805/648-2075; www.ventura-usa.com).

VISITOR CENTERS

The main visitor center for the islands is on the mainland, in Ventura Harbor, where you'll also find the park headquarters. Visit the **Channel Islands National Park Headquarters and Visitor Center,** 1901 Spinnaker Dr., Ventura, CA 93001 (✆ **805/658-5730**), to get acquainted with the various programs and individual personalities of the islands through maps and displays. A wide variety of publications are available; among the most helpful are the free handouts focusing on the individual islands. The center is open daily from 8:30am to 5pm (closed Thanksgiving and Dec 25). The visitor center on the mainland in **Santa Barbara,** 113 Harbor Way, 4th floor, Santa Barbara, CA 93109 (✆ **805/884-1475**), is open daily; call for hours.

Anacapa, Santa Cruz, and **Santa Barbara islands** also have smaller visitor centers with exhibits and other information. Rangers and volunteers run interpretive programs on the islands and the mainland year-round.

FEES

The park does not charge entrance fees, but you should consider the cost of getting to the islands when planning your budget. There is a nightly $15-per-site charge for camping on all five islands; you must make reservations (see the "Camping" sections for each island, below).

SPECIAL REGULATIONS & WARNINGS

The islands' relative inaccessibility makes preplanning a must. The boat concessionaires are often booked a month or so in advance, so be sure to make reservations. Also remember to bring anything you might need (including water, food, and equipment if you're camping). If you're camping, bring a good tent. If you don't know the difference between a good and a bad tent, the island wind will gladly demonstrate.

SEASONS & CLIMATE

Although the climate is mild, upper 40s to high 60s (about 8–20°C), with little variation in temperature year-round, the weather on the islands is always unpredictable. Winds of 30 mph can blow for days, or sometimes a fog bank will settle in and smother the islands for weeks at a time. Winter rains can turn island trails into mud baths. In general, plan on wind, lots of sun (bring sunscreen), cool nights, and the possibility of hot days. Water temperatures are in the 50s and 60s (teens Celsius) year-round. Also be aware that inclement weather or sea conditions can cause concessionaires to cancel trips on the day of the excursion, so it's a good idea to have a plan B just in case.

SEASONAL EVENTS

January through March, **gray whales** can be viewed from the islands as they pass by on their annual 10,000-mile migration from their warmer breeding grounds off the coast of Baja California to their cold-water feeding grounds in the Arctic Ocean. **Blue and humpback whales** can be seen in the waters off the islands between June and October.

Which Island Should You Visit?

ANACAPA Families with children might want to start here, and they will want to be especially cautious near the island's unfenced cliff edges. There are more **organized activities** here than on the other islands, and the crossing to Anacapa is the shortest. If you're interested in **sea kayaking,** Anacapa's scores of sea caves make it your best bet. Though much smaller than its huge neighbor Santa Cruz, Anacapa has several times more caves, many of which are accessible by kayak.

SANTA CRUZ It has fewer caves than Anacapa, but Santa Cruz, the largest of the islands, is still a good choice for sea kayakers—on Nature Conservancy land, the island's **Valdez Cave** (or Painted Cave) is the largest and deepest sea cave in the world. The Nature Conservancy owns much of Santa Cruz, and you must apply for permission to visit the portions of the island it manages (see "Getting There & Gateways," above). **Backcountry enthusiasts,** take note: Landing at Prisoner's Harbor here allows for the most challenging hikes in the park. It's also a good pick for families with younger kids.

SANTA ROSA This is a good bet if you want to visit one of the islands for more than a day. (It's relatively big, so there's more to explore.) Those interested in **ranching history** and ***vaqueros*** (Mexican cowboys) will find Santa Rosa appealing. Santa Rosa's hundreds of undisturbed **archaeological sites** (please leave them undisturbed) also may attract anthropology buffs and others interested in Chumash culture. (The Chumash were the American Indians who inhabited all four of the islands.) Those interested in **endemic plant life** will probably also enjoy a visit. Though a century of ranching has wreaked havoc on the island's traditional landscape, the prehistoric **stand of Torrey pines** is spectacular—the species grows in only one other spot on Earth (near San Diego).

SAN MIGUEL If adventure is what you're after, the choice is pretty simple: The ranger-led 16-mile trek to Point Bennett and back offers the greatest diversity of scenery among the park's hikes. San Miguel is also your best choice if you want to **observe wildlife**—over 30,000 seals and sea lions gather at Point Bennett, and seabirds nest on Prince Island at the mouth of Cuyler Harbor.

SANTA BARBARA This is the smallest of the island chain, not to mention one of the most **distant and solitary.** After a 3-hour boat trip, you'll be free to hike this tiny island as alone as you care to be.

If you have only a day, Anacapa and east Santa Cruz are the closest to the mainland and the easiest to get to. The bad side: They're the most crowded (though *crowded* is a relative term here).

2 Exploring the Islands

EXPLORING ANACAPA

Sitting only 15 nautical miles off the Ventura coast, tiny Anacapa has historically been the most visited of the park's islands. (Santa Cruz recently overtook it in terms of visitation.) Referring to Anacapa as an island is somewhat misleading, because it is a chain of three small islets—East, Middle, and West Anacapa—inaccessible to each other except by boat. From the shore, the flat landscapes of East and Middle Anacapa stand out in sharp contrast to West Anacapa's twin peaks.

Anacapa is the only island in the chain to keep anything resembling its original name—Anacapa is from the Chumash word ***Eneepah,*** meaning "island of deception or mirage," and on a foggy or hot day, it is easy to see why: Tricks of light make the island's cliff walls seem enormous or almost nonexistent, and 40-foot-high **Arch Rock,** a natural offshore bridge, can seem to dominate the eastern end of the island or barely emerge from the water.

At 1 square mile (700 acres), Anacapa is not the best choice for people who need room to roam. To cramp things even more, only East Anacapa is completely open to the public. Visitors to Middle Anacapa must be accompanied by a park ranger.

Visitors interested in seeing the island's marine life may want to head for **Frenchys Cove** on West Anacapa instead of East Anacapa. Unlike most of the mainland tide pools, the island's tide pools are pristine, housing thriving marine communities. Only the beach at Frenchys Cove is open to visitors, though. The rest of West Anacapa is closed to protect the nesting areas of the endangered brown pelican—the islet houses the largest breeding rookery for the bird on the West Coast.

Seabirds are easily the island's most abundant wildlife. Because of the island's relative lack of predators, thousands of birds nest on the island, including the endangered brown pelican, rare xantus murrelets, and western gulls. Cormorants, scoter ducks, and black oystercatchers can be seen plying the air and waters above and around the island. To protect seabirds, the park removed non-native rats from Anacapa in the largest-scale rodent-eradication program on any island in the world.

The island also harbors a community of California sea lions and harbor seals. The animals rest and breed on Anacapa's rocky shores and feed in the kelp forests surrounding the island. Overlooks at **Cathedral Cove, Pinniped Point,** and **Inspiration Point** offer visitors views of them.

Although scrubby brownish vegetation covers the island for most of the year, winter rains bring the island's flora to vibrant life—the bright blossoms of the yellow coreopsis, or tree sunflower, are often so numerous that they're visible from the mainland.

ORGANIZED TOURS & RANGER PROGRAMS

Rangers, volunteers, and concessionaire-employed naturalists lead guided nature walks daily during the summer, and self-guided trail booklets are available at the visitor center on the island.

At 2pm Tuesday through Thursday from Memorial Day through Labor Day, rangers plunge into the kelp forest off the island with a camera. The rangers allow visitors to view the undersea world on the monitor on the island's landing dock (or on a large screen in the mainland visitor center).

PARK ATTRACTIONS

In 1853, the steamer *Winfield Scott* grounded and sank off the coast of Middle Anacapa (remains of the wreck can still be seen off the north coast of the islet), prompting the government to build a 50-foot tower supporting an acetylene beacon.

In 1932, the U.S. Lighthouse Service replaced the tower with the present **lighthouse** and facilities on East Anacapa. The fully automated lighthouse used the original handmade Fresnel lens until 1990, when a more modern lighting system was installed. The original lead crystal lens is on display in the island's visitor center. The U.S. Coast Guard operates the lighthouse. ***Do not approach the building***—the foghorn can cause permanent hearing damage.

Today the other lighthouse service buildings house the visitor center and ranger residences. A churchlike building holds two 55,000-gallon water tanks that supply fresh water for the residences and fire fighting, intriguingly designed to resemble a Spanish mission.

DAY HIKES

The 2-mile, figure-eight **Loop Trail** on East Anacapa serves up great views and is a good introduction to the island's natural history. Follow signs from the boat-landing area to the trail head. A pamphlet describing the island's most significant features is available in the visitor center. Naturalists also lead guided nature walks daily year-round.

CAMPING

Camping is allowed on East Anacapa year-round, but don't bring more than you're able to carry up the 154-stair, half-mile trail from the landing cove. The campground has seven sites and a capacity of 30 people. The campsites are primitive; there is no shade, and food and water are not available. Pit toilets are provided. No fires are allowed, but cooking is permitted on enclosed, backpack-type stoves. Bring earplugs and steer clear of the foghorn. There is a nightly $15-per-campsite charge, and a reservation is required (© **877/444-6777;** www.recreation.gov). Campground reservations fill quickly, so be sure to call well in advance.

EXPLORING SANTA CRUZ

By far the biggest of the islands—nearly 100 square miles—Santa Cruz is also the most diverse. It has huge canyons, year-round streams, beaches, cliffs, the highest mountain in the Channel Islands (2,400 ft.), abandoned cattle and sheep ranches, and Chumash village sites.

The pastoral **central valley** that separates the island's two mountains is still being created by a major tectonic fault. The island is home to an amazing display of flora and fauna, including 650 species of plants, 9 of which are endemic; 140 land-bird species; and a small group of other land animals, including the endangered island fox. Lying directly between cold northern and warm southern waters, the waters off the island contain a marine community representing 1,000 miles of coastline.

Originally called ***Limuw*** by the Chumash (who believed the island was the site of their creation, before they took to the mainland over the mythological Rainbow Bridge), Santa Cruz gained its present moniker after a priest's staff was accidentally left on the island during the Portola expedition of 1769. A resident Chumash found the cross-tipped staff and returned it to the priest, inspiring the Spaniards to dub the island *La Isla de Santa Cruz* (The Island of the Holy Cross).

Much of the island is still privately owned; the Nature Conservancy holds the western three-quarters. In 1997 the Park Service acquired the eastern end from the Gherini family, which had operated a sheep ranch here. Most visitors come to **Scorpion**

Anacapa Island

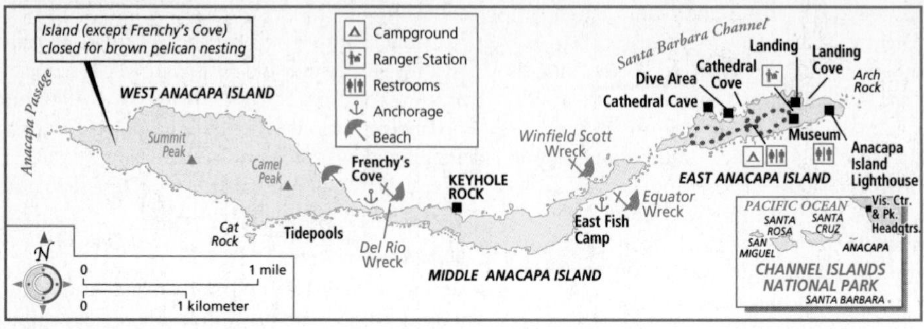

Ranch and **Smuggler's Ranch** on the Park Service's land. Much of the most beautiful land is on Nature Conservancy property, which includes Santa Cruz's lush Central Valley and the islands' highest peaks.

Unfortunately, the island's ranching heritage has left its mark on the land and created a serious domino effect. In 2003, the last of the island's feral sheep population (which had badly overgrazed the land) was shipped off; focus was then on eradicating feral pigs, a project completed in 2007. The pigs provided food for golden eagles, which moved in after DDT decimated the native bald eagle population in the 1970s. Bald eagles don't hunt island foxes, but golden eagles do; the population boom ultimately resulted in a 93% decline in the island fox population. The multiyear restoration plan involves removing golden eagles, reintroducing island foxes and bald eagles, and controlling the growth of fennel. The island fox has recovered nicely, with the park's population roughly tripling since the program began.

It's difficult, but not impossible, to get access to the more pristine Conservancy land; Island Packers (see "Getting There & Gateways," above) runs occasional trips to **Prisoner's Harbor.** At one point, it was possible to arrange stays at Christy Ranch on the windswept west end of the island and visits to the main ranch in the Central Valley, but at press time the ranches were under restoration, and access was limited. Contact the **Nature Conservancy** (✆ **805/642-0345**) for up-to-date information.

Valdez Cave (also known as Painted Cave for its colorful rock types, lichens, and algae) is the largest and deepest known sea cave in the world. The huge cave stretches nearly a quarter of a mile into the island and is nearly 100 feet wide. The entrance ceiling rises 160 feet, and in the spring, a waterfall tumbles over the opening. Located on the northwest end of the island, the cave can be entered in a dinghy or kayak, and many concessionaire-operated boat tours also have boats that can fit inside. See "The Extra Mile: Exploring the Coastline & Waters off the Channel Islands," later in this chapter.

PARK ATTRACTIONS

After more than a century of ranching, Santa Cruz has acquired its fair share of historic buildings, including adobe houses, barns, blacksmith and saddle shops, wineries, and a chapel. The ranch house at **Scorpion Ranch** is a private residence today, just as it was in the early 20th century; the old adobe bunkhouse is now a ranger station and visitor center. All around Scorpion Ranch, ranch and farm implements, some dating back decades, speckle the landscape. A **visitor center** opened in an 1886 ranch outbuilding, featuring interactive exhibits focusing on Santa Cruz's Island Chumash and ranching eras.

DAY HIKES

Most hikes in the national parkland of Santa Cruz begin at Scorpion Ranch. The easiest and shortest is the **Historic Ranch Walk.** The ranch area is visible from the beach. This hike is basically the beginning leg of all the hikes described below, so if you are planning to take one of those, you don't really need to allocate much additional time for this hike.

The hike up to **Cavern Point** leads you to the bluffs northwest of Scorpion Harbor, providing spectacular views of the north coast of the island. Between January and March, this is an excellent vantage from which to spot **migrating gray whales.** Follow the main trail from the beach through the ranch area. Beyond the ranch, look for the second side canyon on your right (west). Follow the signed trail through the eucalyptus grove and up the side of the canyon to Cavern Point. Avoid the unstable cliff ledges at the top and return to Scorpion Beach by following the trail to the east. At 2 miles round-trip, the hike is rated moderate to difficult due to a 200-yard uphill climb, uneven terrain, and loose rock.

A little longer than the Cavern Point hike, the hike up to the **Potato Harbor Overlook** also provides magnificent coastal views. Head past the ranch about .75 mile until you come to a big break in the eucalyptus trees. A trail sign marks the spot. Follow the old road on the right (west) until you reach the bluff trail to Potato Harbor Overlook. Avoid cliff edges, and return the way you came (or make a loop

Santa Cruz Island

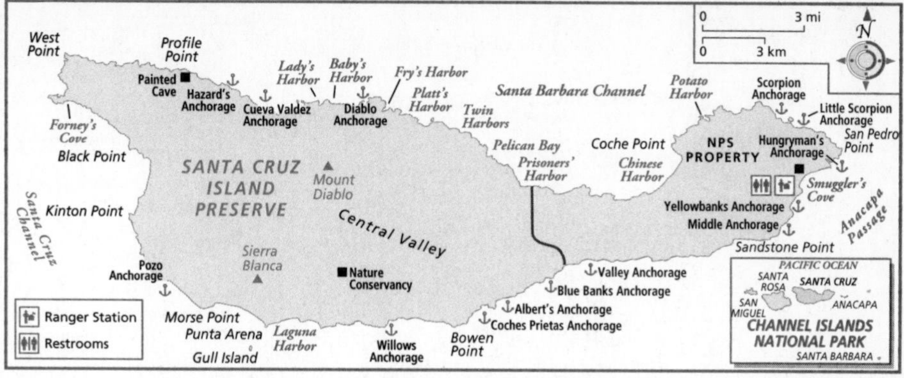

of it on the scenic Northwest Bluff Trail). The round-trip is 4 miles and is rated moderate due to a 1-mile uphill climb.

For another coastal view, you can head up to **Scorpion Bluffs.** Approximately 100 feet past the ranch area, before the eucalyptus grove, turn left (east) on the road/trail across the streambed to the base of Smugglers Road. At the top of the road, follow the trail that goes along the bluffs. Avoid cliff ledges, and return the way you came. The round-trip is 2 miles and is rated moderate for its 300-foot elevation gain.

Your best chance to see the island jay is to head up **Scorpion Canyon.** Follow the main road/trail through the ranch area and into the eucalyptus grove. The trail will eventually wind in and out of an old streambed before reaching the first oak tree after approximately 1.5 miles. You may continue up the streambed, but the terrain is rocky and uneven.

For those with a little more time, the hike to **Smugglers Cove** is a nice way to spend a day. At 7 miles round-trip, it is not recommended for visitors with time constraints. Easy to follow, the hike follows Smugglers Road all the way from Scorpion Ranch to the white-sand and cobblestone beaches of Smugglers Cove. Because of the 600-foot elevation gain over many uphill sections, the hike is rated strenuous. Another longer option is the strenuous hike up to **Montañon Ridge,** an 8-mile round-trip.

CAMPING

Camping is allowed at the Scorpion Ranch Campground on the east end of Santa Cruz year-round. All gear must be carried about a half-mile to the numerous sites. The campsites are primitive, but there is plenty of shade. Potable water is available; food is not. Pit toilets are provided. Cooking is permitted on enclosed backpack-type stoves, and open fires are allowed only on the beach from December to May. There are four backcountry campsites at Del Norte Campground. There is a nightly $15 per campsite charge. A **reservation** is required and can be obtained at the park visitor center or by calling ✆ **877/444-6777** or visiting www.recreation.gov. Camping is not allowed on Nature Conservancy land (the western 76% of the island).

EXPLORING SANTA ROSA

Windy Santa Rosa was California's only singly owned, entirely private island until the 1980s, when the National Park Service bought it from the Vail and Vickers ranching company for $30 million. In 1998, the company ceased all cattle operations, ending nearly 2 centuries of ranching on the islands that now form the national park.

The second-largest island in the park, Santa Rosa consists of widely different landscapes. Because of its ranching past, rolling non-native grasslands cover about 85% of the island. Elsewhere are high mountains with deep canyons. A unique **coastal marsh** on the east end of the island is among the most extensive freshwater habitats found on any of the Channel Islands.

As with Santa Cruz, the island's size allows for a fantastic variety of life. Although the impact of ranching has been severe, native plant species survive, primarily in the rocky canyons and on the upper slopes. Santa Rosa is home to a large concentration of endangered plant species, 34 of which occur only on the islands. **Torrey pines** grow only in two places. One is on Santa Rosa, where two ancient groves lie near Bechers Bay. (The trees also grow on the mainland near San Diego.) The island's vast grasslands provide prime habitat for over 100 **bird species;** shore birds and waterfowl prefer the marshy terrain on the island's eastern tip.

Santa Rosa is also home to the **island fox,** a tiny cousin of the gray fox that has become nearly fearless, as it has evolved in the predator-free environment. Golden eagles nearly wiped out the fox population, leading to a captive breeding program. As of 2009, the program was successful, to the tune of bolstering the population from a low of 15 to over 50 animals.

Santa Rosa Island

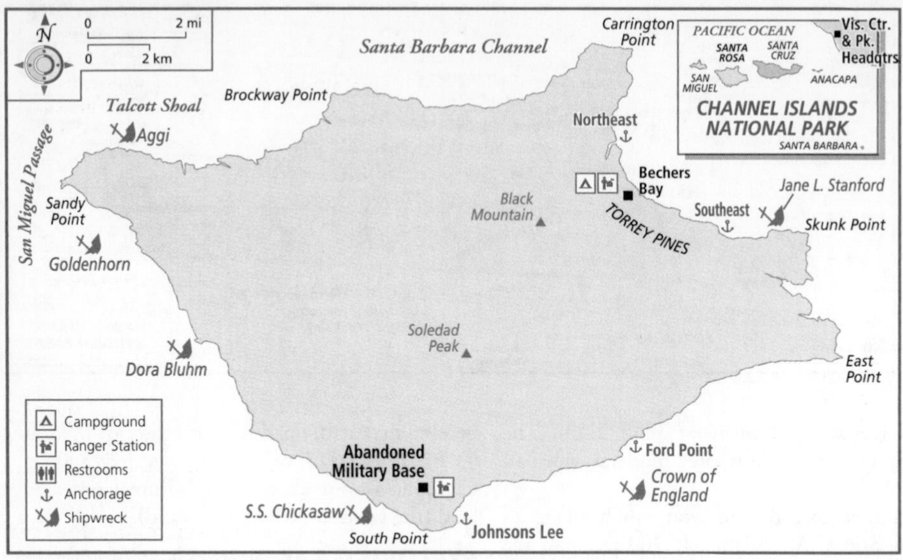

The **kelp beds** that surround the island function as an invaluable nursery for the sea life that feeds the Channel Islands' marine mammals and seabirds.

PARK ATTRACTIONS

The Chumash lived on ***Wima*** (their name for the island) until they were moved to mainland missions around 1820. Through radiocarbon dating, scientists have been able to date human use of the island back 13,000 years, making Santa Rosa an invaluable archaeological resource. Thousands of largely undisturbed **archaeological sites** have been recorded, and visitors are asked to be especially careful not to disturb any sites that they encounter. In 1959 archaeologist Philip Orr discovered an individual we now refer to as Arlington Springs Man (though the remains are actually those of a woman). Lacking evidence of a traditional burial site, scientists believe she was killed accidentally some 13,000 years ago, possibly while gathering food. Her bones may be the oldest human remains found in the United States.

The island provides an important fossil record. A fossilized pygmy mammoth skeleton, carbon-dated at 12,000 years old, was found on the island in 1994, the most complete specimen ever discovered.

The island also provides insights into a more modern culture, with the buildings and other remains of a **cattle ranch.** Owned by the Vail and Vickers Company, it operated here from 1902 until 1998, with few changes except the addition of modern vehicles.

DAY HIKES

Because of its large size, Santa Rosa offers a diverse array of possible hikes. To get to all the trail heads, follow signs from the boat-landing area. Volunteers and concessionaire employees lead guided hikes.

The white sands of **Water Canyon Beach** are a popular destination for hikers and day-trippers. The trail is 2 miles round-trip and is rated easy.

The **Lobo Canyon Trail** descends through Lobo Canyon to a Chumash village site and on to an excellent tide-pooling area. Unlike most mainland tide pools, the Channel Islands' intertidal zones have not been destroyed by human impact on the fragile habitats. The hike is 13 miles round-trip and is rated moderate.

The hike to the island's endemic stand of **Torrey pines** is 5 miles round-trip and affords unbelievable views. **East Point Trail** is a strenuous 12-mile round-trip that also allows for more views of these rare trees, as well as the brackish marsh at the island's eastern tip.

CAMPING

Camping is allowed in Water Canyon on Santa Rosa's northeast end year-round. All gear must be carried 1½ miles from the pier on Bechers Bay. The campground has water and toilets, and each of the 15 sites has its own picnic table and windbreak. There is a nightly $15 charge per campsite for the campground; the required reservations can be obtained by calling ✆ **877/444-6777** or visiting www.recreation.gov.

Camping is permitted on a limited number of beaches that are at least a 10-mile hike from the landing site around the island from June to December. Although the winds will definitely test your tent, this is a good option for those who want to sleep in relative solitude near the water. A free permit (✆ **805/658-5711**) is necessary.

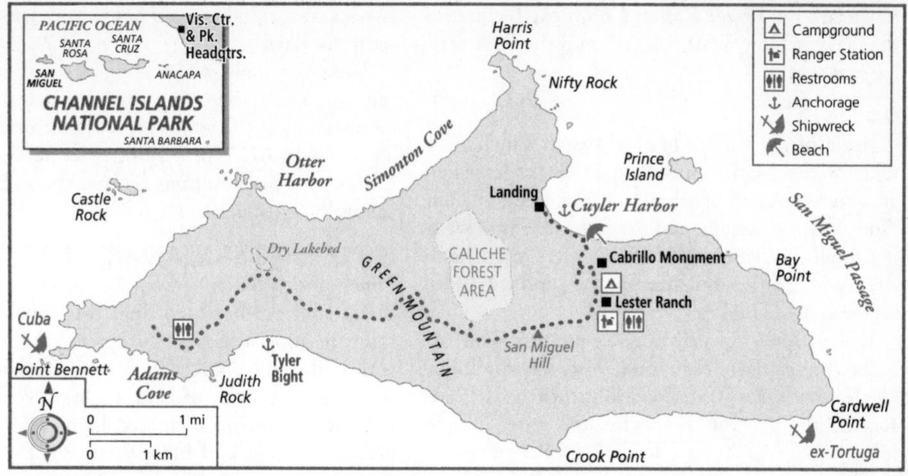

EXPLORING SAN MIGUEL

People often argue about the location of the wildest place left in the Lower 48. They bat around places such as Montana, Colorado, and Idaho. Curiously, no one ever thinks to consider San Miguel, the farthest west of the Channel Islands. They should, for this 9,500-acre island is a wild, wild place. The wind blows constantly here, and fog can shroud the island for days at a time. Human presence is definitely not the status quo.

Visitors land at **Cuyler Harbor,** a half-moon-shaped cove on the island's east end. Arriving here is like arriving on Earth the day it was made: perfect sand, outrageously blue water, seals basking on the offshore rocks. The island's **caliche forest** appears otherworldly. Created by caliche (calcium carbonate) sand castings, these natural stone sculptures are the remains of a once-living forest.

As it did on most of the other islands in this chain, a long history of ranching nearly destroyed native vegetation. The removal of the imported grazing animals has given the island's recovery a major boost. Today many native species are reclaiming their ancestral lands.

Though widely hunted during the 19th century, the island's seal and sea lion populations have clearly recovered and can be seen on ranger-guided hikes. At certain times of the year—June is often the best—over 30,000 animals, including California sea lions, northern elephant seals, and northern fur seals, occupy the beach at **Point Bennett,** making it one of the largest concentrations of wildlife in the world. The Guadalupe fur seal and Stellar sea lion, former island residents, also appear occasionally. Harbor seals haul out on other island beaches.

Prince Island, just outside the mouth of Cuyler Harbor, is an important nesting area for western gulls, brown pelicans, cormorants, and Cassin's auklets. And San Miguel's inland bird species can once again count the peregrine falcon among their number. After years of decimation by the pesticide DDT, the falcon has been reintroduced to the island and is now nesting successfully.

The waters around San Miguel are the richest but most dangerous surrounding the Channel Islands—this island is exposed to wave action from all sides. Harsh sea conditions have resulted in a fair number of shipwrecks, including the luxury liner *Cuba,* which went under on September 8, 1923. Fortunately, everyone on board was rescued, along with $2.5 million in gold and silver bullion.

Swimming among the wrecks are a wide variety of sea mammals. In addition to the pinnipeds (seals and sea lions), dolphins, porpoises, gray whales, orcas, and even blue whales can sometimes be seen off the island's shore.

The boat concessionaires' schedule to San Miguel is sporadic in summer and almost nonexistent in winter, so call ahead.

PARK ATTRACTIONS

Like Santa Rosa, San Miguel has more than 500 Chumash archaeological sites.

The island also holds the remains of the earliest modern structure on any of the islands. In the 1850s, Capt. George Nidever established a sheep, cattle, and horse ranch on the island. The **adobe** he built is barely visible today.

In the 1930s, Herbert and Elizabeth Lester became the island's caretakers. During his time on the island, Herbert became known as "the King of San Miguel." After being asked to leave San Miguel during World War II by the Navy, which owned the island, Herbert committed suicide in 1942. Both he and Elizabeth are buried on San Miguel. Today only a few fence posts and small piles of rubble near the trail mark the **Lester Ranch Complex.** Technically the Navy still owns San Miguel, and the Park Service manages it.

DAY HIKES

Outside of the Cuyler Harbor/Lester Ranch Area, hikes on San Miguel must be led by a ranger. There are three trails, all of which meet at Lester Ranch. Due to terrain, length, and the tiring effects of walking in all that wind, all three are rated moderately strenuous. Concessionaire employees and volunteers also lead guided hikes.

If you don't feel up to a serious trek, you can make the relatively easy walk from the landing at Cuyler Harbor to Cabrillo Monument and Lester Ranch, the starting point for the three official hikes.

The first trail heads north to **Harris Point,** allowing marvelous views of Prince Island to the east and Simonton Cove to the west. Taking the trail southeast from Lester Ranch will lead you to **Cardwell Point.**

San Miguel's most popular hike is the 5-mile round-trip trek along the **Point Bennett Trail** to the aforementioned caliche forest.

For those with more time and stamina, consider following the trail all the way to Point Bennett, a 16-mile round-trip. Camping along the trail is forbidden. The diversity of scenery and wildlife on view is seemingly endless for those hikers hardy enough to endure the wind and weather. After crossing San Miguel Hill, the trail passes the caliche forest. The trail then heads west to Point Bennett, passing south of the island's other peak, Green Mountain. At the end of the trek, the barking of sea lions will signal your arrival at Point Bennett, where 30,000 pinnipeds sometimes congregate.

Note: San Miguel Island was used as a bombing range for the U.S. Navy between 1948 and 1970. Live ordnance is still occasionally uncovered in the shifting sand, so it is extremely important to ***stay on established trails.***

CAMPING

Camping is allowed on San Miguel year-round, though camping dates are subject to Island Packers' schedule. Located 1 mile south of Cuyler Harbor, between Cabrillo Monument and the old Lester Ranch complex, the **campground** has nine primitive sites and a capacity of 30 people. The hike to the campground includes a steep climb up Nidever Canyon—keep this in mind before packing your accordion. There is a pit toilet and basic wind shelter at each site, but food and water are not available. No fires are allowed, but cooking is permitted on enclosed backpack-type stoves. Be sure to bring a strong tent, a sleeping bag, and waterproof clothes—the wind is often fierce, and damp fog can set in for days.

There is a nightly $15 charge per site for camping, and a reservation is required. Reservations can be obtained at the park visitor center or by calling ✆ **877/444-6777** or visiting www.recreation.gov. Campground reservations fill quickly, so be sure to call well in advance.

EXPLORING SANTA BARBARA

Lonely, lonely Santa Barbara. As you come upon the island after a 3-hour crossing, you may think that someone took a medium-size grassy hill, ringed it with cliffs, and plunked it down in the middle of the ocean. In terms of land, there's not a lot here. Even the Chumash eschewed living on the island because of its lack of fresh water. But the upside is that, of all the islands, Santa Barbara gives you the best sense of what it's like to be stranded on a desert isle, surrounded by the immense Pacific Ocean.

The island's deserted appearance is somewhat misleading. During the 1920s, farming, overgrazing, intentional burning by island residents, and the introduction of rabbits all but destroyed the island's native vegetation. To survive the island conditions, plants must be tolerant of salt water and wind—and, unfortunately, the Santa Barbara ice plant is perfectly suited to this type of environment.

Originally imported from South Africa in the early 1900s, the non-native ice plant survives by capturing moisture from sea breezes and subsequently leaches salt into the soil, raising the soil's salt concentration. It has wreaked havoc on the natural ecosystem, virtually taking over much of the island. Through its resource-management program, the Park Service is taking steps to eradicate non-native species from the islands.

Other than the **landing cove,** there's no access to the water's edge. (The snorkeling in the chilly cove is great.) You can hike the entire 640-acre island in a few hours, then spend some time staring out to sea. You won't be let down. The cliffs and rocks are home to elephant seals (weighing up to 6,000 lb.) and sea lions that feed in the kelp forests surrounding the island. Because of the island's small size, the barking of sea lions is audible almost everywhere. The **Sea Lion Rookery, Webster Point,** and **Elephant Seal Cove** all provide excellent overlooks from which to observe the animals. Be sure to stay at least 100 yards away, particularly from January through July during pupping time—young animals may become separated from their mothers if disturbed.

Santa Barbara's cliffs and rocks are home to swarms of seabirds such as you'll never see on the mainland, including western gulls, endangered brown pelicans, and the world's largest colony of xantus murrelets. Inland species include the horned lark, orange-crowned warbler, and house finch, all found only on Santa Barbara Island.

There's also a tiny **museum** chronicling island history. ***Note:*** Island Packers schedules boats to Santa Barbara only during the summer. (See "Getting to the Islands by Boat," earlier in this chapter, for more information.)

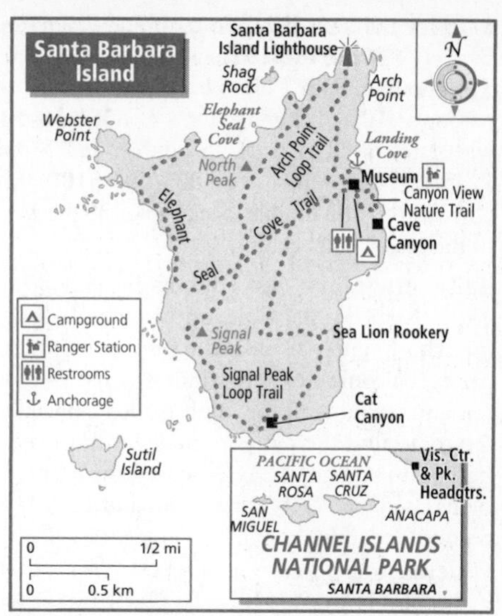

DAY HIKES

Hiking the short **Canyon View Nature Trail** is a good introduction to Santa Barbara, but since it's such a small island, it's not that difficult to hike all three of the island's main trails. All trails begin and end at the campground and visitor center; guided hikes are available.

At 5 miles round-trip, the **Elephant Seal Cove Trail** heads southwest from the visitor center to the west coast of the island, then heads up by Webster Point, a favorite beach for sea lions and elephant seals, and continues to Elephant Seal Cove.

The **Arch Point Trail** heads north from the visitor center to Arch Point, the northernmost tip of the island. You can then turn south and follow the island's northwestern bluffs, before turning inland and crossing the Elephant Seal Cove Trail. Once across the Elephant Seal Cove Trail, the trail becomes the **Signal Peak Loop Trail** and continues southwest and up Signal Peak. It then follows the bluffs around the southern portion of the island, cutting inland briefly to bypass Cat Canyon. Once on the southeastern side of the island, the trail heads up to Sea Lion Rookery, where it runs inland and then north back to the visitor center.

CAMPING

Camping is allowed on Santa Barbara year-round. Note that all gear must be carried up the 131 steps to the campground, located approximately ¼ mile inland. The 10 campsites are primitive; there are pit toilets, but food, water, and shade are not available. No fires are allowed, but cooking is permitted on enclosed backpack-type stoves. There is a nightly $15-per-site charge for camping, and a reservation is required. **Permits** can be obtained at the park visitor center or by calling © **877/444-6777** or visiting www.recreation.gov; campground reservations fill up quickly, so be sure to call in advance.

3 The Extra Mile: Exploring the Coastline & Waters off the Channel Islands

SEA KAYAKING One of the best ways to explore the fascinating coastline of the islands is by kayak. **Aquasports** (© **800/773-2309** or 805/968-7231; www.islandkayaking.com) and **Paddle Sports** (© **805/899-4925;** www.kayaksb.com), both offer guided trips out of Santa Barbara starting around $175 per day per person. Trips can also be arranged through Island Packers or Truth Aquatics (see "Diving," below) and other concessionaires (see the park website for the entire list).

DIVING Half of Channel Islands National Park is underwater. In fact, twice as many visitors visit the waters annually than the number of people who set foot on the islands. Scuba divers come here from all over the globe for the chance to explore stunning kelp forests, shipwrecks, and underwater caves, all with the best visibility in California. Everything from sea snails and urchins to orcas and great white sharks call these waters home.

Truth Aquatics in Santa Barbara (© **805/962-1127;** www.truthaquatics.com) is the best provider of single- and multiday dive trips to the islands; 1-day trips begin at $130. **Ventura Dive & Sport** (© **805/650-6500;** www.venturadive.com) also offers guided trips, instruction, and rentals, as does **Pacific Scuba** in Oxnard (© **805/984-2566;** www.pacificscuba.com).

4 Where to Stay in Ventura

Although no accommodations other than camping are available on any of the islands, the town of Ventura has lots of options.

In addition to the lodgings below, chain motels include the **Ventura Beach Marriott,** 2055 Harbor Blvd. (© **805/643-6000**), which charges $159 to

$229 for a double; **Best Western,** 708 E. Thompson Blvd. (✆ **805/648-3101**), which charges $109 to $149 double; **Four Points by Sheraton,** also at the harbor at 1050 Schooner Dr. (✆ **805/658-1212**), with rates of $125 to $245 double; and **Motel 6,** 2145 E. Harbor Blvd. (✆ **805/643-5100**), which costs $60 to $82 double. See chapter 38 for websites of the major hotel chains.

Bella Maggiore Inn European elegance pervades the Bella Maggiore, an intimate Italian-style inn whose simply furnished rooms (some with fireplaces, balconies, or bay window seats) overlook a romantic courtyard or roof garden. Breakfast is served around the patio fountain, an intimate spot known to nonguests as **Nona's Courtyard Cafe.** Nona's also serves breakfast and lunch daily (and dinner Wed–Sun).

67 S. California St. (½ block south of Main St.), Ventura, CA 93001. ✆ **800/523-8479** or 805/652-0277. Fax 805/648-5670. 28 units. TV, TEL. $75–$175 double; $150 suite. Rates include full breakfast and afternoon refreshments. AE, DISC, MC, V.

Crowne Plaza Ventura The beachfront Crowne Plaza recently underwent a multimillion-dollar renovation that made it the most luxurious place to hang your hat in downtown Ventura. Featuring plush guest rooms with the full assortment of in-room perks, as well as a restaurant and bar with tremendous ocean views, a heated outdoor pool, and attractive modern furnishings throughout, the Crowne Plaza balances the best location in town, with plenty of style and service.

450 E. Harbor Blvd. (adjacent to the Ventura pier), Ventura, CA 93001. ✆ **800/842-0800** or 805/648-2100. www.cpventura.com. 258 units. A/C, TV, TEL. $99–$239 double. AE, DC, DISC, MC, V.

Pierpont Inn Established in 1910, the Pierpont Inn has seen the adjacent coastline change dramatically, but the property's top-notch service and unassuming elegance have endured. Nestled in exquisitely maintained gardens, the Pierpont offers an array of lodging, from hotel-style rooms with exterior entry to lavish cottages furnished with period antiques from several different periods: The '50s Flat exudes midcentury modern, while the Vickers Estate reflects the Spanish Colonial Revival style that was the rage in the 1930s. There's a restaurant, a private racquet club, and great views of the beach. My only complaint is that the property is fairly close to U.S. 101, and traffic noise is omnipresent outdoors.

550 San Jon Rd., Ventura, CA 93001. ✆ **800/285-4467** or 805/643-6144. www.pierpontinn.com. 77 units. A/C, TV, TEL. $145–$195 double; $195–$395 cottage or suite. Rates include continental breakfast. AE, DC, DISC, MC, V.

5 Where to Dine in Ventura

There is no food available on any of the islands in the park. Ventura has several good places to eat. For breakfast or lunch, hit the excellent **Savory Cafe & Bakery,** 419 E. Main St. (✆ **805/652-7092**). If you want a box lunch to go, try the **Sandwich Factory,** 4531 Market St. (✆ **805/650-0465**). Both conveniently open before the boats leave at 7am.

Anacapa Brewing Company MICROBREWERY An attractive eatery with brick walls, copper fermenting vats, and local art, this microbrewery makes excellent beers and offers respectable steaks and pasta dishes, as well as burgers, pizzas, and salads. Of the beers, I'm partial to Pierpont Pale Ale and Santa Rosa Red.

472 E. Main St. ✆ **805/643-2337.** www.anacapabrewing.com. Main courses $9–$20. AE, DISC, MC, V. Mon 5:30–9pm; Tues–Thurs and Sun 11:30am–9pm; Fri–Sat 11:30am–10pm. Bar open later.

Andria's Seafood Restaurant and Market SEAFOOD Set aside your reservations at seeing the fast-food decor here and proceed to the counter to place your order. Andria's, which doubles as a fresh seafood market, has been voted Ventura County's best seafood restaurant for over a decade. The fish go directly from the ocean into the deep-fat fryer (charbroiled selections are also available) and onto your plate, with only a short stint on the boat in between. The food isn't fancy, but it's fresh, and the harborside seating is pleasant.

In Ventura Harbor Village, 1449 Spinnaker Dr. ✆ **805/654-0546.** Main courses $9–$16. MC, V. Sun–Thurs 11am–9pm; Fri–Sat 11am–10pm.

Jonathan's at Peirano's MEDITERRANEAN Inhabiting the first commercial building in Ventura County (1877), Jonathan's is the sleek anchor of the west end of downtown Ventura. The attractive room, with a Douglas fir floor, is an ideal setting for a selection of fresh fish, pastas, stews, and entrees from Italy, Spain, Portugal, Morocco, and other Mediterranean locales. Among the specialties are a spicy cioppino (with a pinch of saffron). Attached (and under the same ownership) is **J's,** a casual tapas bar with live entertainment.

204 E. Main St. ✆ **805/648-4853.** www.jonathansatpeiranos.com. Main courses $9–$20 lunch, $17–$35 dinner. AE, MC, V. Tues–Thurs 11:30am–2:30pm and 5:30–9pm; Fri–Sat 11:30am–4pm and 5–10pm; Sun 11:30am–4pm and 5:30–9pm.

71 Palm FRENCH/ECLECTIC Housed in a restored 1910 Craftsman home, 71 Palm is a nice pick for a romantic dinner in Ventura, in a quiet location just off the main drag with several intimate seating areas, indoors and out. Chef-owner Didier Poirier's fare is quite good—try terrific horseradish-crusted Chilean sea bass, tender and with just the

Picnic & Camping Supplies

Food is not available on any of the islands, so you'll need to bring a picnic lunch and water for day trips, and enough food and water (1 gal. a day per person) if you are camping. You can buy supplies in Ventura at **Von's** grocery store, 2433 Harbor Blvd. (© **805/642-6761**), or the **Village Market** (© **805/644-2970**) in Ventura Harbor Village. There is a **Big 5 Sporting Goods** in Ventura at 3860 E. Main St. (© **805/644-0668**).

right amount of bite. The menu also includes a nice range of seafood, pasta, and meat.

71 Palm St. © **805/653-7222.** www.71palm.com. Main courses $7–$16 lunch, $11–$33 dinner. AE, DC, DISC, MC, V. Mon–Sat 11:30am–2pm; Mon–Sat 5–9pm.

The SideCar NEW AMERICAN Originally opening as a diner in the 1930s in an authentic 1910 Pullman railcar, this restaurant was reinvented in 2004 by chef-owner Tim Kilcoyne. The Pullman opens onto an intimate dining room and bar featuring live jazz, decorated with rich red hues and a classic-meets-contemporary vibe. The food is as good as anything you'll find in L.A., let alone Ventura, and nearly all of the ingredients, from beets to beef, are sourced within 25 miles. Depending on your taste, try a Niman Ranch pork chop or a roasted tofu steak; the horseradish mashed potatoes are terrific. Lunch includes a gourmet egg salad sandwich, penne pasta, and a fresh fish of the day.

3029 E. Main St. © **805/653-7433.** www.thesidecarrestaurant.com. Main courses $7–$18 lunch, $16–$27 dinner. AE, DISC, MC, V. Mon–Fri 11:30am–2pm and Wed–Sun 5–9pm.

The Sportsman AMERICAN You might walk right by the inconspicuous facade of Ventura's oldest restaurant. Like the intriguingly retro lettering on its awning, the interior hasn't changed a lick since it opened in 1950: plush leather booths, brass lamps, wood-paneled bar, giant trophy swordfish on the wall, and light at levels normally reserved for planetariums. The Sportsman serves hearty omelets at breakfast, and burgers, steaks, and other grilled items for lunch and dinner. Or you can just wet your whistle with the stiff drinks from the bar.

53 California St. (½ block south of Main St.). © **805/643-2851.** Main courses $6–$16 breakfast, $8–$25 lunch, $11–$39 dinner. AE, DISC, MC, V. Mon–Thurs 11am–9:30pm; Fri 11am–10pm; Sat 9am–2pm and 5–10pm; Sun 9am–2pm and 4–10pm. Bar open later.

12

Crater Lake National Park, OR

by Eric Peterson

To many people, southern Oregon means one thing: Crater Lake. It's the deepest lake in the country, and it's arguably the most beautiful. Visitors to the area can't imagine the sudden impact of the awesome grandeur that lies ahead as they approach the rim of the caldera, and that makes the lake's appearance 1,000 feet below all the more stunning.

With Mount Shasta, Mount Lassen, the Trinity Alps, and the Marble Mountains just south of the Oregon–California border, it's hard to get excited about the low peaks of southern Oregon. Evidence of past volcanic activity is less vertical here, but more dramatic. Mount Mazama, in which Crater Lake is located, once stood as tall as its neighbors to the south. Then, 7,700 years ago, it erupted with almost unimaginable violence, a blast estimated at about 100 times greater than that of Mount St. Helens. When it had finished erupting, the volcano collapsed in on itself, forming a vast caldera 6 miles wide and almost 4,000 feet deep. Within 500 years, the caldera filled with water to become today's Crater Lake. The sapphire-blue lake's surface is at the base of 1,000- to 2,000-foot cliffs that rise to a total elevation of more than 8,000 feet.

The lake has no inlet or outlet streams and is fed solely by springs, snowmelt, and rainfall. Evaporation and ground seepage keep the lake at a nearly constant level. Because it is so deep, it rarely freezes over entirely, despite long, cold winters. The high elevation of the caldera rim and heavy winter snowfalls mean that the summer season here is short.

Gold prospectors stumbled upon the lake's rim in 1853. The American Indian tribes of the region, who considered the lake sacred, had never mentioned its existence to explorers and settlers. By 1886, explorers had made soundings and established its depth at 1,996 feet, making it the deepest lake in the United States. Sonar soundings later set the depth at 1,943 feet. In 1902, the lake was designated a national park.

"I came, I saw, I left," could be the motto of many of the almost 500,000 annual visitors. From mid-July to mid-September, they ride dutifully around the Rim Road and then move on. If you're looking to interact with the landscape on a more personal level, you have some options, such as road biking around the Rim Road or day hiking to the summits of several peaks, including that of 760-foot Wizard Island in the middle of the lake. The area also offers superb cross-country skiing and snowshoeing opportunities in winter.

The Pacific Crest Trail passes through the park, with a 6-mile stretch on the west side of the lake. Wildlife is mostly limited to the lowlands surrounding the caldera, although at the summit you can see hawks, eagles, and many types of birds and small mammals. In addition, the spotted owl has been found nesting within the park boundaries. The forested slopes provide refuge for deer, elk, porcupine, coyote, and fox, and trout and salmon live in the lake.

AVOIDING THE CROWDS

It's hard to avoid crowds here when the snow is melted. Given the area's harsh winters, most visitors come during the relatively short "summer" season between late June and the end of September. Many day visitors drive some distance to the park, so the Rim Road is not crowded early in the morning. Circle the lake before 10am, and you can easily pick your overlook. The best advice is to stay longer than the single day that 90% of the visitors allot to the park. Once you've seen and appreciated the lake (take a cruise early, before the crowds form), go off and hike some of the less trampled paths. Several of the longer trails will lead you to fabulous, relatively uninhabited view points. Especially recommended are the Watchman Peak, Garfield Peak, and Mount Scott trails (see "Day Hikes," below).

1 Essentials

GETTING THERE & GATEWAYS

There are three ways into Crater Lake National Park, the most convenient being from the west and south on **Ore. 62,** which runs through the southwest corner of the park.

To get to the park's west entrance, drive northeast from Medford 75 miles on Ore. 62.

If You Have Only 1 Day

Most people enter the park's west and south entrances on Ore. 62. Bypass the Mazama Village area unless you need to load up on snacks, and stop at the **Steel Information Center** for a preview.

At this point, provided you have the stamina to hike down to the lakeshore, it might be a good idea to head for the requisite **boat trip** to Wizard Island before it gets too late in the day and, consequently, too crowded at the boat dock. The first boat leaves at 10am.

Drive north, clockwise around the rim from the Rim Village entrance, to the **Cleetwood Cove Trailhead** (the only trail in the park that leads to the lakeshore), approximately 5 miles past the junction of the northern route to the Pumice Desert.

The trip down Cleetwood Cove Trail is for the muscles in the front of your thighs, and the trip back is for your calves. It's a steep, strenuous trail, equal to a climb of 65 flights of stairs, or an elevation change of about 700 feet over 1 mile in distance. Consider carefully whether you are in good enough shape to make the 1-mile climb back up before you head down to the boat dock. There are benches along the way, if you have to rest (you will). At the trail head is a concessionaire who sells tickets for the guided boat ride. The tour takes approximately 2 hours to return you to the shore, provided that you don't lay over on Wizard Island when the boat stops there during the tour.

It's perfectly fine to explore **Wizard Island** for a while, climbing 760 feet to its summit on the Wizard Island Trail and catching the next boat back. You might want to eat lunch on the beach at Cleetwood Cove before you head back up the trail. After all, this is the only area of the park where you can get next to the water, so why not take advantage?

After the boat trip, it's time for the **Rim Drive.** Go clockwise toward the **Cloudcap Overlook** turnoff, for a brief drive that gives you 2,000-foot views of the lake and, farther off on the horizon to the south, Mount Scott and Mount Shasta. Then keep heading clockwise. You'll eventually approach a turnoff to view **The Pinnacles,** an area of unique rock formations. These spires are the remnants of fumaroles that formed in hot volcanic debris from the great eruption of Mount Mazama. The road back to the rim terminates at a junction with another great view, the **Phantom Ship Overlook.** The "ship" is an ornate piece of eroded basalt jutting up from the lake; it sometimes seems to be sailing when the wind whips up the water just right. You might want to skip this if you took the boat ride and got an up-close look.

Next, make a short stop to admire pretty **Vidae Falls;** there may be lovely wildflowers blooming along the cascade. Return to the Rim Village for the last stop of the day, a little walk to the **Rim Village Visitor Center** (which closes at 5pm) and down the path to the **Sinnott Overlook,** which has exhibits that tell you about the lake and the geology of the volcano.

You can get a cup of coffee at the Rim Village Cafeteria, or sit back and watch the sun go down with a meal at the Crater Lake Lodge (see "Where to Stay & Dine," below), just east of the visitor center. Be sure to call ahead for reservations. Way ahead.

If you skipped the boat ride, you'll have time for a short hike. Two of the easy, short trails in the park are the Annie Creek Canyon and Godfrey Glen trails, which begin around Mazama Village. A third is the Castle Crest Wildflower Trail, which begins at the Steel Information Center. None of these trails is over 2 miles (see "Day Hikes," below).

IF YOU HAVE MORE TIME Even though most summer visitors come into the park's west or south entrances, you can reach Crater Lake from the north. And it would be a shame to miss the northern perimeter lands; the sands of the Pumice Desert are otherworldly when wildflowers are scattered across its flat canvas. If you have the time, detour north when driving in from the south—it's worthwhile just to see this area. From the south entrance, it adds only an extra 15 miles or so, depending on how far toward the north entrance station you want to drive.

If you'd rather spend any extra time you have outside your car, try hiking a section of the moderate to strenuous Pacific Crest Trail (listed under "Longer Trails," below).

Crater Lake National Park

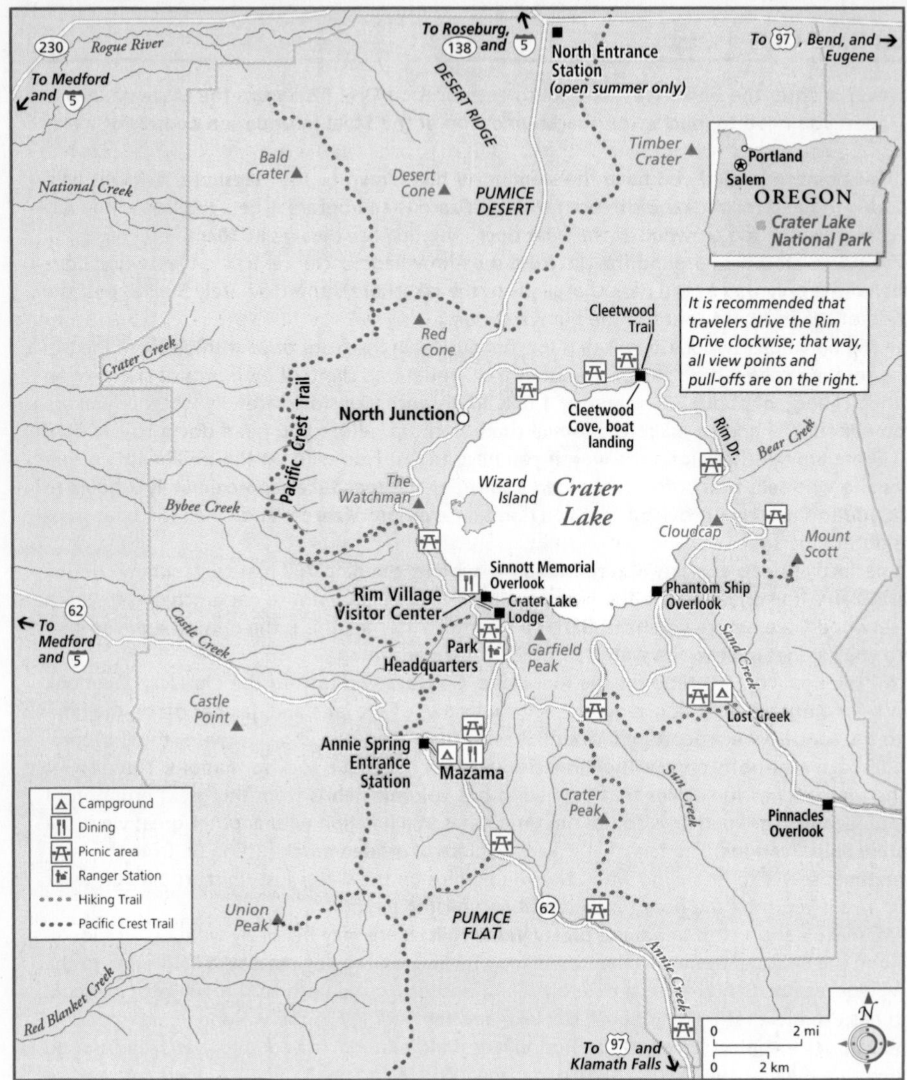

To get to the park's south entrance from Klamath Falls, travel north on U.S. 97, then northwest on Ore. 62; the total distance is 60 miles.

To get to the park's summer-only north entrance from Roseburg, take **Ore. 138** east; the total distance to Rim Drive is approximately 92 miles.

If you're arriving in winter, call park headquarters for road information (✆ **541/594-3000**).

THE NEAREST AIRPORTS Area airports include **Rogue Valley International–Medford Airport** (✆ **541/776-7222;** www.co.jackson.or.us), in Medford, which is served by **Allegiant Air, Delta Connection, Horizon,** and **United/United Express,** with car rentals from **Avis, Budget, Hertz,** and **National.** The **Klamath Falls Airport** (✆ **541/883-5372;** www.flykfalls.com) is served by **United Airlines,** and **Budget, Enterprise,** and **Hertz** offer car rentals. See chapter 38 for listings for airlines and car-rental agencies.

INFORMATION

Contact **Crater Lake National Park,** P.O. Box 7, Crater Lake, OR 97604 (✆ **541/594-3000;** www.nps.gov/crla), for the free park guide, *Crater Lake Reflections,* which has a good summary of most of the park's trails, accommodations, and seasons. You can obtain a catalog of books and maps about the park from the **Crater Lake Natural History Association,** P.O. Box 157, Crater Lake, OR 97604 (✆ **541/594-3110;** www.craterlakeoregon.org).

The Crater Lake Rim Drive

Exploring the park by car is *de rigueur* for most people. There are 33 miles of the famous Rim Drive, with more than 30 overlooks lining the summer-only, two-lane road, and a couple of spur roads that lead to spectacular spots in the southeastern section of the park. Allow 2 hours to complete the drive, adding time if you plan to enjoy any of the many trails and overlooks that are accessible from it. Gasoline is available only at Mazama, and then only from late May to mid-October. Otherwise, gas up in Medford, Roseburg, or any of the other outlying communities.

It's best to travel clockwise on Rim Drive because all the lake view points are on the inside (right side) of the road as you drive that way, so entering and exiting the view points is easier. There are also some view points on the outside of the ring that offer views of mountain scenery.

VISITOR CENTERS

The park has two visitor centers. **Steel Information Center,** south of the lake off Ore. 62, is open daily year-round and contains the park headquarters. You can talk to a ranger, find out about local weather forecasts, pick up general park information, purchase books and maps, and watch an 18-minute film. The **Rim Village Visitor Center** is along the southern edge of the caldera rim. It's open daily from June through September. Here you can obtain general park information, books, videos, and maps. In addition, a short paved trail leads from the visitor center to the Sinnott Overlook, which offers a fine view of the lake and several interpretive exhibits.

FEES & PERMITS

Entrance to the park costs $10 per vehicle. Camping in Mazama Campground is $21 per tent site and $25 to $27 per RV site. Camping in the Lost Creek Campground is $10 per site. Backcountry camping requires registration but no fee.

SPECIAL REGULATIONS & WARNINGS

You may not climb into the caldera. After getting a view of some of the steep and sharp-looking volcanic boulders lining the trip down, you won't want to try. The only access to the lake is through the Cleetwood Cove Trail. Fire prevention is also a big concern in this park.

SEASONS & CLIMATE

Crater Lake basically has two seasons. The main tourist season lasts from mid-June, when most of the park's facilities open, through September. The busiest months are July and August. Summer temperatures in southern Oregon can be scorching, sometimes hovering near the 100°F (38°C) mark in the lower elevations. The upper elevations remain cooler; the lake's rim can get up to 80°F (27°C) in summer.

In the winter, snowfall averaging 44 feet a year buries the park, making it virtually impassable to everyone save skiers and snowshoers. Roads along the lake rim are left unplowed and are open to non-car travelers exclusively. The winter season generally includes fall and spring, stretching from late October to mid-June or even early July.

2 Organized Tours & Ranger Programs

Numerous ranger-led programs and tours take place in the summer. At Rim Village, 20-minute talks run several times daily. Check the park newspaper, bulletins boards, or the visitor center for the current program schedule.

At Mazama Campground, evening programs at an outdoor amphitheater focus on a variety of topics; details are posted daily at the visitor centers. The talks generally start at 9pm in July, and earlier from August to Labor Day.

The most famous Crater Lake tour is the guided **boat tour** that leaves Cleetwood Cove every hour, daily from early July to early September, from 10am to the last shove-off at 4pm. Remember, the trail down to the boat landing is steep. Some boats stop at Wizard Island and then glide past the Phantom Ship before heading back to the Cleetwood Dock; others are purely scenic cruises. Take a jacket, because weather here can change rapidly. Tickets are available at the trail head beginning at 8am. Tickets cost $27 for adults, $17 for children 2 to 11, free for children under 2; the prices are, respectively, $37 and $22 if you want to be dropped off on Wizard Island. For information, contact park concessionaire **Xanterra** (© **888/774-2728;** www.craterlakelodges.com).

3 Park Attractions

In addition to the Crater Lake Lodge, which you might want to take a look at even if you don't spend the night, the **Sinnott Memorial Overlook** has evidence of past travels through and visits to this area by numerous people over the last 150 years. If you're lucky, you might find some wagon tracks; the faint impressions can be found here and there throughout the outer perimeter of the park. Ask the rangers at the visitor center to suggest trails where you might be able to see them.

4 Day Hikes

Over 90 miles of trails lead into the park's backcountry. They're usually snow-free from mid-July to early October. There's no smoking on all trails.

SHORTER TRAILS

Annie Creek This is a scenic walk through old-growth forest and wildflower meadows. It's a nice little break from all the ancient volcanic starkness going on up at the rim. There is an elevation gain of about 200 feet. 1.7 miles RT. Easy. Access: Mazama Campground Trailhead, btw. the D and E loops of the campground.

Castle Crest Wildflower Garden Summer is short on the rim of Crater Lake, so when the snow finally melts, wildflowers burst forth with nearly unrivaled abandon. This trail meanders through one of the best displays of wildflowers in the park. Late July and early August are the best wildflower periods. Although this trail is rated "easy," be careful of slick rocks. Hiking boots, or shoes with good tread, are helpful. The trail has an elevation gain of about 100 feet. .5 mile RT. Easy. Access: Park headquarters, Mazama Village.

Cleetwood Cove Trail This is the only trail down to the shore of Crater Lake, and it stays busy with those trying to get to the water or to Cleetwood Cove to take the boat tour. Because the trail leads downhill, many visitors are lured into thinking that this is an easy trail. It's not! Volcanic boulders line the trail, and the climb 700 feet back up from the water to the rim is strenuous and steep. 2.2 miles RT. Strenuous. Access: North side of the lake, 4½ miles east of the North Junction.

Discovery Point This trail, like most trails around the rim, provides brilliant views of the vast lake and Wizard Island below, ending after a short climb at an overlook where John Hillman, one of the first European explorers of the area, first witnessed the beauty of Crater Lake in 1853. 2.2 miles RT. Easy to moderate. Access: West end of Rim Village parking area.

Godfrey Glen This trail is a very easy walk through an old-growth forest overlooking the Annie Creek Valley (also accessible by trail). You'll cross Munson Creek at Duwee Falls before you head back to the car. It's a good walk for kids, with lots of possibilities to see deer, elk, rabbits, and grouse. 1 mile RT. Easy. Access: 1½ miles past Mazama Village Entrance, on right side of the road.

Sun Notch This trail, with an elevation gain of 115 feet, takes hikers through a meadow to a terrific overlook of Crater Lake and Phantom Ship. There are steep drop-offs, so be careful. .5 mile RT. Moderate. Access: 4 miles east of park headquarters on East Rim Dr.

Watchman Peak With a historic fire lookout perched on its summit, the Watchman is one of the high points on the rim of the caldera. A short but steep (420-ft. elevation gain) hike leads to the top for an outstanding view of the lake, with conical Wizard Island rising from the deep blue of the foreground. This is the shortest climb you can make along the rim of the caldera. 1.6 miles RT. Moderate. Access: 3¾ miles northwest of Rim Village on West Rim Dr.

Wizard Island Though it is small, Wizard Island is a great place to visit. The island, with its steep volcanic cone rising from the deep, is fun to explore for a few hours. This trail climbs 760 feet up to the island's summit. To spend some time here, take an early boat tour, get off on the island, and return on a later boat. Because most of the hiking is on jagged lava rock, be sure to wear sturdy boots. 2 miles RT. Moderate. Access: Cleetwood Cove Trail (see above), then boat tour; disembark on the island.

LONGER TRAILS

Bald Crater/Boundary Springs The ashy, flat, and rolling Pumice Desert stretches north along the trail as you travel approximately 3 miles toward the 8,763-foot summit of the Red Cone, a miniature Mount Mazama before it collapsed and created the caldera that holds the lake. The plains give way to ancient forests interspersed with fields of wildflowers. At the junction of the Pacific Crest Trail and the Bald Crater Trail, turn right to head for Bald Crater Peak. The peak is about 2 miles south of some fine campsites at the end of the Bald Crater Trail, along Boundary Springs, near the headwaters of the beautiful Rogue River. 20 miles RT. Easy to moderate. Access: Rim Dr. to northwest of Rim Village area; continue to the Northern Park Junction of the Rim Dr. and the northern access road; from here, it's 3 miles down the northern access road to the trail head, on the left.

Crater Peak This beautiful hike takes you to a peak that is also a crater. How? The summit of the hike is the rim of yet another little volcanic cone, south of once-huge Mount Mazama.

The trail begins with an uphill climb through 2 miles of alpine forest and meadow. The steep final .5 mile leads to the summit of Crater Peak, with its panoramic vistas of the Klamath Basin to the south and the rim of Crater Lake to the north. To the west lies Arant Point, near Mazama, and to the east the Grayback Ridge. All of them combine to form an incredible view. Early in the morning or late in the evening, you may see deer or elk. 6.4 miles RT. Moderate to strenuous. Access: From park headquarters, head east around the Rim Dr.; trail head is at the Vidae Falls Picnic Area.

Dutton Creek If you think the whole volcano experience is about ash and pumice, check out the old-growth forest of hemlocks, fir, and pine on the sometimes-vertiginous Dutton Creek Trail. This is also the section of the Pacific Crest Trail that leads the long-distance hiker up to the rim. For short-timers heading south, it provides an opportunity to get away from the crowds and see something besides a volcano's mouth: perhaps a deer or an elk that appears as you hike down this narrow, forested valley along Dutton Creek. The route meets the Pacific Crest Trail, where you climb back the way you came. 4.8 miles RT. Easy to moderate. Access: West end of Rim Village parking area.

Garfield Peak Sure, the view from the Rim Village borders on sublime, but this is even better. You'll leave most of the crowds behind, get in a good hike, and treat yourself to a breathtaking (literally—the hike starts above 7,000 ft.) view of the lake. This hike leads to the summit of 8,054-foot Garfield Peak, which lies just east of the Rim Village. The route gains all of its 1,010 feet of elevation in 1.7 miles of nearly constant switchbacks. From the summit, the entire lake is visible below, including the island called Phantom Ship, which is hard to see from the Rim Village. To the south, Mount Shasta is visible. 3.4 miles RT. Moderate to strenuous. Access: East end of Rim Village parking area.

Mount Scott If the trail to Garfield Peak had a few too many other hikers on it for your tastes, try this trail to the top of 8,929-foot Mount Scott. This is the highest point within Crater Lake National Park, and the trail is longer and entails more elevation gain (1,250 ft.) than the trail up Garfield Peak. The views from the summit are the most far-reaching in the park, encompassing not only the entire lake, but also such surrounding peaks as Mount Thielsen, Mount Shasta, and Mount McLoughlin, as well as the vast expanse of Klamath Lake to the south. 5 miles RT. Strenuous. Access: 14 miles east of park headquarters on East Rim Dr., across the road from Cloudcap Junction.

Pacific Crest Trail Section For those who want to chalk up this particular section of the Pacific Crest Trail, which stretches along the West Coast from the Mexican to the Canadian border, there's a lot to chalk up. The trail essentially bisects the park, with only one section that follows the rim and allows views of the lake. Otherwise, you're pretty much out there in the flatlands.

From the trail head, the path follows the base of the mountain's curve to the west, with views of the mountain's slow climb to its rim to your right, and the rolling high desert plains to your left. At the northern end of the walk, before crossing into the vast Pumice Desert, there is an opportunity to circle back to the rim at North Junction. 33 miles one-way. Moderate to strenuous. Access: Approx. ¼ mile west of Mazama Village, trail head is on the left.

Pumice Flat This is the southern equivalent of the park's northern Pumice Desert area. The dusty trail takes you through gently rolling, forested pumice and ash plains littered with sharp volcanic rocks, before intersecting the Pacific Crest Trail for the loop to Mazama. You can also return on the shorter route back to the trail head where you started. 6 miles RT. Easy to moderate. Access: 3 miles south of Mazama Village on Ore. 62.

Stuart Falls Stuart Falls is outside the park's boundaries, but the trail head isn't. You'll experience a nice contrast as you climb down to the dusty, volcanically beautiful Pumice Flat before heading into the Red Blanket Valley after the junction with the Pacific Crest Trail. You'll begin to notice a bare trickle of water turning into a creek, turning into a much bigger creek that ends up as a fine crashing mist of spray known as Stuart Falls. Folks have been known to take a rest in Stuart Falls' fine white spray before heading back up the steep and often parched trail. 11 miles RT. Easy to moderate. Access: 3 miles south of Mazama Village park entrance on Ore. 62.

5 Other Summer Sports & Activities

BIKING The 33-mile circuit of Crater Lake is one of the most popular road–bike trips in the state, despite the heavy car traffic. Although it seems like an easy trip at first, numerous ups and downs (especially on the east side of the lake) turn the circuit into a demanding ride. Keep in mind that there are more hills on the east side, but also more views. An alternative is to do the 21-mile out-and-back ride from the Rim Village to the Cleetwood Cove Trailhead (and maybe add a boat tour of the lake).

Diamond Lake Resort (see "Where to Stay & Dine," below) rents bikes in the summer for $30 a day; no rentals are available in the park.

FISHING Anglers occasionally try for rainbow trout and kokanee salmon near the boat dock or from Wizard Island. License aren't required and only artificial lures and flies are allowed, but because fishing in the lake generally isn't very good, I suggest you stick to sightseeing and hiking in the park. However, fly-fishing in streams outside the park is pretty good—stop at the fly-fishing shop at Steamboat Inn (see "Where to Stay & Dine," below) for information.

SWIMMING/SCUBA DIVING Although Crater Lake is too deep to ever reach a truly comfortable temperature (even in the summer), plenty of people do a few quick strokes to cool down after hiking the Cleetwood Cove Trail or after exploring Wizard Island. But this is an informal activity, and there are no facilities for swimmers. The lake has also emerged as a diving destination for hardcore types. The only diving access is at Cleetwood Cove and Wizard Island. There are no refills or rentals available in the immediate vicinity.

6 Winter Sports & Activities

CROSS-COUNTRY SKIING The **Diamond Lake Nordic Center,** 4 miles north of the park on Ore. 138 (✆ **800/733-7593**), offers Crater Lake ski tours that include a Sno-Cat ride. The Nordic Center has 8 miles of groomed trails and more than 50 miles of marked backcountry trails. It also rents cross-country skis and boots. Maps of ski areas are available at the Steel Information Center at park headquarters.

Without a doubt, the **rim** of Crater Lake National Park offers some of the best cross-country skiing in the country. Not only are there numerous views of sapphire-blue Crater Lake 1,000 feet below you, but the views to the west and south take in Mount McLoughlin, Mount Shasta, and countless ridges and seemingly endless forest vistas as well.

The **ultimate ski tour** is the 30- to 33-mile circuit of the lake. Although racers have completed this route in a single day, most skiers take 3 days and enjoy the views along the way. Because the weather is better and there's still plenty of snow, March and April are the most popular months. The route is straightforward, although you may have to do some route finding on the northeast side of the lake. Be sure to get a backcountry permit for overnight trips, and check weather forecasts and avalanche danger.

The **West Rim Trail,** which follows Rim Drive, is the most popular day skiing area. By late November, the road is unplowed and the snow cover turns it into an excellent trail that requires a little climbing. It's best done in good weather and good snow conditions. Consult a park ranger for snow conditions before heading out.

The **East Rim Trail** is not as popular as the West Rim Trail, for the simple reason that the first view of the lake (depending on where you start) is between 4.25 and 5.4 miles along. This trail also has a lot more ups and downs. So, why would you want to start on this section at all? To stay out of the wind, that's why. If, after driving all the way up here, a gale-force wind is blowing up the west slopes, you don't have much choice. Never set out without checking with the rangers at park headquarters to find out about avalanche conditions and other dangers.

SNOWMOBILING During the winter, snowmobiling is allowed, but only on the north entrance road up to its junction with Rim Drive. Snowmobiles are not allowed on Rim Drive. You cannot drive snowmobiles on any park trails, either. Snowmobile rentals are available from **Diamond Lake Resort** (see "Where to Stay & Dine," below) at $100 for 2 hours, $200 for a half-day, and $300 for a full day, plus gas and oil. Guided snowmobile tours start at $85 for one rider.

SNOWSHOEING With its jewel of a lake for a centerpiece and views that extend all the way to Mount Shasta in California, Crater Lake National Park is a natural magnet for snowshoers. The **West Rim Trail** is the most popular route with both snowshoers and cross-country skiers, but snowshoers have the advantage of being able to go where few skiers can. Before you head out, discuss possible routes with the rangers and ask about avalanches and other potential dangers.

If you've never snowshoed before, you can give it a try at Rim Village, where 90-minute guided snowshoe hikes begin at 1pm on weekends from late November through April. Call the visitor center for reservations; snowshoes are provided free.

7 Camping

Within Crater Lake National Park, there are only two campgrounds, one large and one small. No reservations are taken.

Mazama Village Campground ($21 per tent, $25 to $27 per RV per night) has 213 sites, some of which are available by reservation (✆ **888/774-2728**). A few sites have electric hookups, but most have no hookups. There is drinking water, a dump station, restrooms with showers, a coin-op laundry, a public phone, and fire pits. It's at Mazama Village off Ore. 62. There is also a general store and an adjacent post office. It's usually open from mid-June to early October.

First-come, first-served **Lost Creek Campground** ($10 per night) has 16 sites for tents only. There is running water and flush toilets; each site has a fire ring, picnic table, and bear-proof food locker. It is in the southeastern section of the park, on the spur road to The Pinnacles. It's usually open from early July to early October.

8 Where to Stay & Dine

INSIDE THE PARK

Aside from the Crater Lake Lodge Dining Room (see below), places to eat include the Rim Village Café (at Rim Village) and Annie Creek in the Mazama Village area.

The Cabins at Mazama Village The Cabins at Mazama Village are a short drive away from the rim of the caldera. The modern motel-style guest rooms are in 10 steep-roofed buildings that look like traditional mountain cabins. Rooms have one or two queen-size beds, and bathrooms have showers only. A coin-op laundry, gas station, and general store make Mazama Village a busy spot in the summer.

1211 Ave. C, White City, OR 97503. ✆ **888/774-2728** or 541/830-8700. Fax 541/830-8514. www.craterlakelodges.com. 40 units. $126 double. AE, DISC, MC, V. Closed Nov–May.

Crater Lake Lodge Perched on the edge of the rim overlooking Crater Lake, this is the finest national park lodge in the Northwest. Not only are the views breathtaking, but the amenities are modern without sacrificing the rustic atmosphere that visitors expect in a mountain lodge. Among the lodge's original features are the stone fireplace and ponderosa pine bark walls in the Great Hall. Slightly more than half the guest rooms overlook the lake. Most rooms have modern bathrooms, and eight units have claw-foot bathtubs. The very best rooms are the corner ones on the lake side of the lodge. As at other national park lodges, reservations should be made as far in advance as possible.

The lodge's **dining room** features creative Northwest cuisine and provides views of Crater Lake and the Klamath River basin. The only full-service restaurant in the park, it serves three meals daily when the lodge is open, from mid-May to mid-October. Lunches ($10–$15) feature salads, burgers, sandwiches, fish and chips, and specialties such as fettuccine alfredo with Alaskan salmon. Dinner main courses ($21–$35) include steak, chicken, venison, vegetarian items, and seafood, like Pacific halibut filet with a roasted hazelnut crust, seared in brandy. Reservations (✆ **541/594-2255,** ext. 3217) are highly recommended for dinner.

1211 Ave. C, White City, OR 97503. ✆ **888/774-2728** or 541/830-8700. Fax 541/830-8514. www.craterlakelodges.com. 71 units. $151–$282 double. AE, DISC, MC, V. Closed mid-Oct to mid-May.

NEAR THE PARK

Because the park is so isolated, the range of accommodations and dining options in the small surrounding communities is limited.

Diamond Lake Resort On the shores of Diamond Lake just outside the park's north entrance, this resort has long been a popular family vacation spot. With Mounts Thielsen and Bailey flanking the lake, it's also one of the prettiest settings in the Oregon Cascades. There is a variety of accommodations. My favorites are the lakefront cabins, which are large enough for a family or two couples, with great views. If you want to do your own cooking, you'll find kitchenettes in both the cabins and the studios, or you can dine at the resort's three restaurants—all family-friendly, with standard American menus and moderate prices. Boat, mountain-bike, and horse rentals are available, and there's a small sandy beach and a bumper-boat area. In winter, the resort is most popular with snowmobilers but also attracts a few cross-country skiers; it also offers snow cat backcountry skiing. The **Diamond Lake RV Park** (✆ **541/793-3318**), nearby, is open in summer only. It has full hookups; prices begin at $33.

350 Resort Dr., Diamond Lake, OR 97731-9710. ✆ **800/733-7593** or 541-793-3333. www.diamondlake.net. 91 units. TV. $89 motel double; $99 studio for 2; $165–$285 cabin. Winter discounts available. AE, DISC, MC, V.

Prospect Historic Hotel-Motel On peaceful, gardened grounds near three waterfalls, this hotel, 34 miles from Crater Lake's Rim Village in the tiny town of Prospect, combines vintage and modern style. The beautiful historic (1889) hotel has a wraparound veranda on which sit several bent-willow couches and a comfy swing. The cozy rooms are period-furnished with quilts and considerable country flair. The modern motel rooms have cable TVs, telephones, refrigerators, microwaves, and coffeemakers; some also have kitchenettes. There is also free Wi-Fi. The elegant **dining room,** open seasonally, serves a fixed-price dinner, with prices in the $23 to $33 range.

391 Mill Creek Dr. (P.O. Box 50), Prospect, OR 97536. ✆ **800/944-6490** or 541/560-3664. Fax 541/560-3825. www.prospecthotel.com. 24 units. May–Sept hotel $135 double, $195 suite; motel $90–$120 double. Oct–Apr hotel $100 double, $175 suite; motel $70–$95

double. Hotel rates include full breakfast. DC, DISC, MC, V. Pets accepted in motel rooms but not in hotel.

Steamboat Inn Midway between Roseburg and Crater Lake, this inn is the finest lodging on the North Umpqua River. The beautiful gardens, luxurious guest rooms, and gourmet meals attract people looking for a quiet getaway in the forest and a base for hiking and biking. The suites have their own soaking tubs overlooking the river; the next best are the stream-side rooms (the units the inn calls "cabins"). All are nicely maintained, with gas fireplaces, and open onto a long deck that overlooks the river. The hideaway cottages are more spacious, but they don't have river views and are half a mile from the lodge (and the dining room). **Dinners** ($50) are elaborate multicourse affairs served in a cozy dining room. The innovative American menu changes nightly, utilizing local, seasonally available ingredients. There's also a fly-fishing shop on the premises, where anglers congregate in the fall.

42705 N. Umpqua Hwy., Steamboat, OR 97447-9703. ✆ **800/840-8825** or 541/498-2230. Fax 541/498-2411. www.thesteamboatinn.com. 20 units. Cabin $175 double; cottage or house $215–$245; suite $300. MC, V. Closed Jan–Feb.

Union Creek Resort Practically across the road from the Rogue River Gorge, this rustic resort has been catering to Crater Lake visitors since the early 1900s; it's on the National Register of Historic Places. In my opinion, it's the best (as well as the closest) lodging option outside the west entrance to Crater Lake National Park. Tall trees shade the grounds of the resort, which is on Ore. 62 about 23 miles from Rim Village. Accommodations include lodge rooms, with a bit of historic charm, and very basic cabins (many of which have kitchenettes). Lodge units accommodate two to four people and share bathrooms; cabins sleep 2 to 10. ATV and snowmobile rentals are available, as are Wi-Fi access, DVDs, and TVs. Across the road is an ice-cream shop and **Beckie's Cafe,** which serves three home-style meals a day in summer for $5 to $18.

56484 Ore. 62, Prospect, OR 97536. ✆ **866/560-3565** or 541/560-3565. Fax 541/560-3339. www.unioncreekoregon.com. 32 units. May–Sept $59–$69 lodge unit, $90–$130 cabin for 2–4, $145–$255 cabin for 6–12; Oct–Apr $54–$60 lodge unit, $75–$220 cabin. AE, DISC, MC, V.

13

Death Valley National Park & Mojave National Preserve, CA

by Eric Peterson

In 1994, Death Valley National Monument became Death Valley National Park. The '49ers, whose suffering gave the valley its name, would've howled at the notion. To them, several four-letter words other than *park* would have come to mind, including—but not limited to—*gold, mine, lost,* and *dead.*

Americans looking for gold in California's mountains in the winter of 1849–50 got lost in the parched desert here trying to avoid the severe snowstorms in the nearby Sierra Nevada. One person perished along the way, and the land became known as Death Valley. Little about the valley's essence has changed since. Its mountains stand naked, unadorned. The bitter waters of saline lakes evaporate into odd, thornlike crystal formations. Jagged canyons jab deep into the earth. The ovenlike heat, the frigid cold, and the driest air imaginable combine to make this one of the world's most inhospitable locations.

Death Valley is raw, bare earth, the way things must've looked before life began. Here, Earth's forces are exposed with dramatic clarity; just looking out on the landscape, you'll find it impossible to know what year, or century, it is. It's no coincidence that many of Death Valley's topographical features are associated with hellish images: Funeral Mountains, Furnace Creek, Dante's View, Coffin Peak, and Devil's Golf Course. But the valley can be a place of serenity as well.

Human nature being what it is, it's not surprising that people have long been drawn here to challenge the power of Mother Nature. The area's first foray into tourism was in 1926, a scant 77 years after the '49ers' harrowing experiences. It probably would have begun sooner, but the valley had been consumed by lucrative borax mining since the late 1880s, when teamsters drove 20-mule-team wagons filled with the mineral through the dusty landscape. This white compound is used as a cleaning agent, preservative, and flux; in fireproofing; and as a water softener.

In one of his last official acts, President Herbert Hoover designated Death Valley a national monument in February 1933. With the stroke of a pen, he not only authorized the protection of a vast and wondrous land, but helped to transform one of the earth's least habitable spots into a tourist destination.

The naming of Death Valley National Monument came at a time when Americans were discovering the romance of the desert. Land that had previously been considered devoid of life was being celebrated for its spare beauty; places that had once been feared for their harshness were being admired for their uniqueness.

In 1994, when President Bill Clinton signed the California Desert Protection Act, Death Valley National Park became the largest national park outside Alaska, with more than 3.3 million acres. Though remote, it attracts nearly a million visitors a year, from all over the world.

FLORA & FAUNA

Most of Death Valley's climate zones are harshly limiting to plants and animals, but they are diverse nevertheless. Within the park, elevations range from 282 feet below sea level (Badwater, the lowest point in the Western Hemisphere) to 11,049 feet above sea level (Telescope Peak, blanketed by snow during winter and early spring). Little sign of life is found at the lowest elevations; any groundwater is highly saline and supports predominantly algae and bacteria. One notable exception is the unique **desert pupfish,** an ancient species that has slowly adapted to Death Valley's increasingly harsh conditions. In the spring, you can see the tiny fish in the marshes of Salt Creek, halfway between Furnace Creek and Stovepipe Wells, where a boardwalk lined with interpretive plaques allows an up-close look.

Hardy desert shrubs such as **mesquite, creosote,** and **arrowweed** flourish wherever there's groundwater below or snowmelt trickling from above. You have to look closely to see the surprising number of small mammals and birds that live at the lower elevations (from below sea level to 4,000 ft.); **rabbits, rodents, bats, snakes, roadrunners,** and even **coyotes** all get by on very little water. At the higher elevations, where **pinyon** and **juniper** woodlands blanket the slopes, animals are more plentiful and can include **bobcats** and

mule deer. Elusive **bighorn sheep** are found on rocky slopes and in desert canyons. Above 10,000 feet, look for small stands of **bristlecone pine,** the planet's longest-lived tree; some specimens on Telescope Peak are more than 3,000 years old.

AVOIDING THE CROWDS

You may think that no one would plan a vacation in a 120°F-plus (49°C-plus) remote desert, but Death Valley is a year-round destination. Visitors tend to avoid the summer and crowd Death Valley on weekends and school holidays the rest of the year, especially in the spring. December and January are the quietest months (with the exception of Christmas week and Martin Luther King Jr. Day weekend). The following advice will help ease the crush during your visit.

- **Make accommodations reservations** as far in advance as you can, at least 2 or 3 months ahead. Facilities are limited inside the park, and Death Valley's isolation makes it time-consuming to base yourself elsewhere. Those planning to set up in one of the first-come, first-served camping areas should try to claim a site between 9am and noon.
- **Avoid visiting on weekends** and during school vacation periods. Plan to enjoy the most popular activities early in the day, before crowds start building up (around 10am). An alternative, particularly on summer days, is to wait until crowds dissipate, around 4pm. Remember, the sun doesn't set until after 7pm between June and September, and it stays hot well past midnight.
- With the help of a **high-clearance, four-wheel-drive vehicle** with upgraded tires, you'll find a whole world of hidden valleys, ghost towns, sand dunes, and remote canyons that are inaccessible to most of Death Valley's visitors. Check the Park Service's official map, where roads are clearly marked according to how passable they are, and ask at the visitor center about current road conditions.

1 Essentials

GETTING THERE & GATEWAYS

All of the routes into the park involve crossing one of the steep mountain ranges that isolate Death Valley. The most common access route from Los Angeles and points south is **Calif. 127** from I-15 at the town of Baker; from Death Valley Junction, Calif. 190 leads to the park's center. From Las Vegas, **Nev. 160** leads to Pahrump, 2 miles past which the route heads west to Death Valley Junction on Belle Vista Road. Perhaps the most scenic entry is on **Calif. 190** from the west, reached from Calif. 14 and U.S. 395 by taking Calif. 178 from Ridgecrest. To reach the same route from the north, pick up Calif. 190 directly from U.S. 395 at Olancha, or via Calif. 136 at Lone Pine. You can also approach the park from Nevada by taking **Nev. 374** from Beatty, which is on U.S. 95.

THE NEAREST AIRPORT The nearest airport is Las Vegas's **McCarran International Airport,** 5757 Wayne Newton Blvd. (✆ **702/261-5211;** www.mccarran.com), with scheduled flights on most major airlines, and offices of all major car-rental agencies. See chapter 38 for website listings.

It's a 2½-hour drive from Las Vegas to Death Valley. A four-wheel-drive vehicle is necessary for backcountry travel, and you'll need one to reach 2 of the 10 campgrounds (see "Camping," later). If you rent a car, be sure to read the fine print about driving off-road.

INFORMATION

Contact **Death Valley National Park,** P.O. Box 579, Death Valley, CA 92328 (✆ **760/786-3200;** www.nps.gov/deva). Be sure to pick up the official *Visitor Guide,* a newspaper-style free handout listing most of the park basics. It's available at ranger stations and the Furnace Creek Visitor Center (see below). Also, it's not a bad idea to ask a ranger for tips on avoiding heat exhaustion and on high-temperature auto care (although the latter is usually a problem only with older vehicles).

The **Death Valley Natural History Association,** P.O. Box 188, Death Valley, CA 92328 (✆ **800/478-8564;** www.dvnha.org), operates the park bookstores and organizes a number of events.

VISITOR CENTERS

Park headquarters are at the **Furnace Creek Visitor Center** (✆ **760/786-3200**), open daily from 8am to 5pm year-round in Furnace Creek, 15 miles inside the eastern park boundary on Calif. 190. You'll find well-done interpretive exhibits and an hourly slide program, as well as an extensive bookstore. There's also a museum, a bookshop, and an information center at **Scotty's Castle** (✆ **760/786-2392**), also open daily year-round (see "Park Attractions," below).

Ranger stations that collect fees and can provide you with information are at **Stovepipe Wells** (no phone) and **Grapevine** (no phone).

FEES

Entry to the park for up to 7 days costs $20 per car (or $10 per person on foot, motorcycle, or bike). Be sure to keep the receipt handy; you'll be required to show it when passing the entry checkpoint near Scotty's Castle (Grapevine).

Death Valley National Park

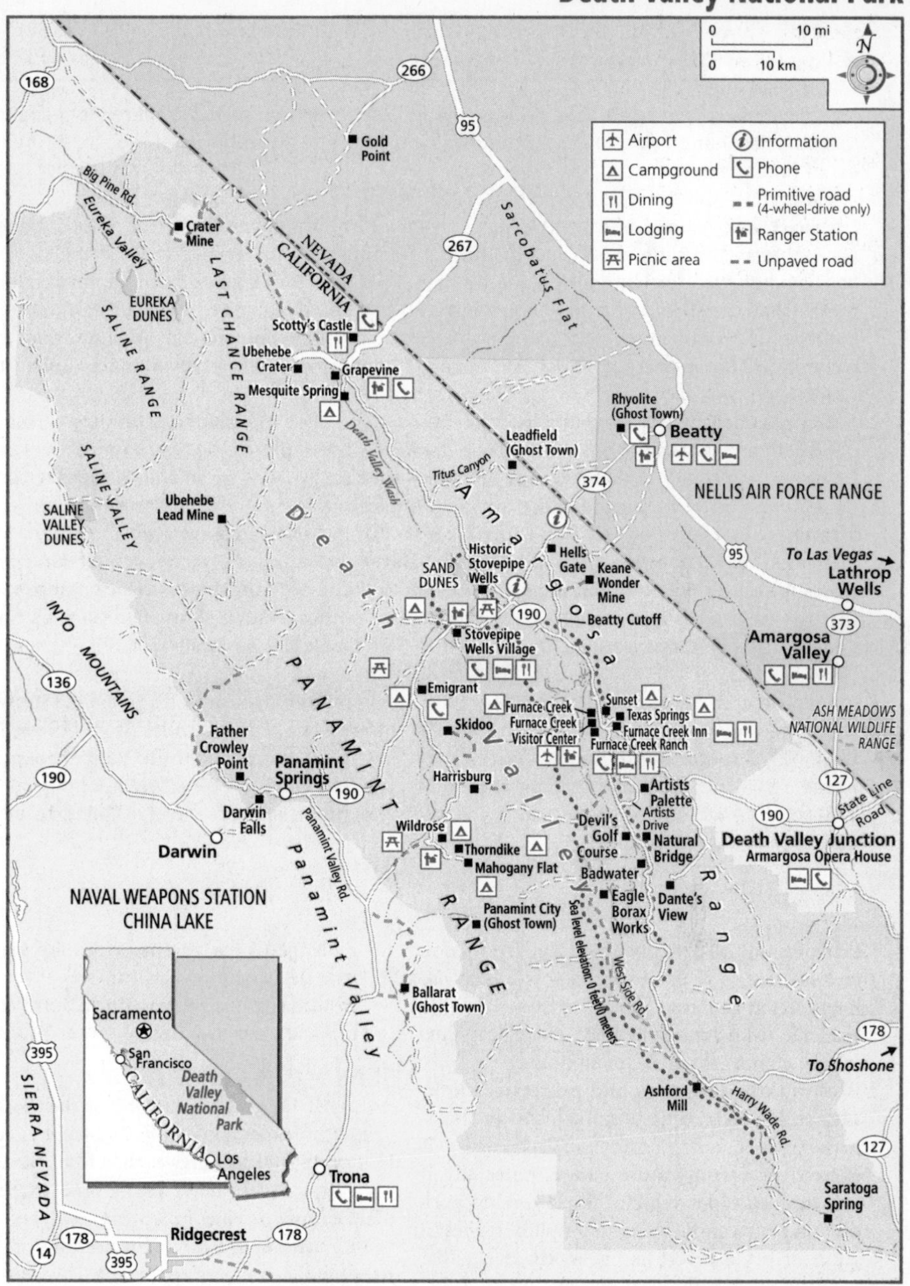

There are nine campgrounds within park boundaries. Four are free; overnight fees elsewhere range from $12 to $18.

SPECIAL REGULATIONS & WARNINGS

It isn't called Death Valley for nothing, but there's little chance you'll encounter any life-threatening situations, especially if you follow common-sense safety tips. You'll find these and many more in brochures available at the park's visitor centers.

- **Always carry a supply of water for everyone,** including your car. Dehydration is your most urgent concern, particularly in summer, when temperatures routinely reach at least 120°F (49°C) at the arid lower elevations. Recommended minimum amounts are 1 gallon per person per day, twice that if you're planning strenuous activity. Drink often, whether you feel thirsty or not, and be alert for the signs of

If You Have Only 1 Day

The distances inside Death Valley National Park are enormous, so this is merely a guideline. If there's a destination you don't want to miss, you'll have to pass up something else in the interest of time.

If you have only 1 day and want to get a sampling of the park's best-loved spots, start at the **Furnace Creek Visitor Center,** at the center of the action in Furnace Creek (see "Visitor Centers," above). View the **slide show** (shown throughout the day) for an overview of the park. This advice holds even for visitors with several days. Step over to the center's museum for a look at the 10×20-foot **relief map** of the park, which will give you a feel for where your destinations are in the context of the region, including the all-important elevation factor. If you have time, check out the tiny **Borax Museum,** in an old miners' boardinghouse at nearby Furnace Creek Ranch. Admission is free.

Scotty's Castle is a must-see for most people, but you need to plan ahead because of the popularity of ranger-guided house tours. Even if you want to explore only the grounds, the castle is 53 miles north of Furnace Creek, over an hour's drive each way. A good plan is to make the castle your first activity after breakfast, avoiding the crowds and freeing up the afternoon for seeing other sites or squeezing in a short hike. If it's hot, reverse course and hit Scotty's in the afternoon. Easily reached spots are **Artists Palette** (we especially recommend taking Artists Drive), **Harmony Borax Works, Badwater, Devil's Golf Course, Zabriskie Point,** and **Dante's View.**

If the weather is agreeable, replace one or two of these with a short hike (such as **Golden Canyon, Mosaic Canyon, Sand Dunes,** or the **Salt Creek Nature Trail**)—for details, see "Day Hikes," below.

Because each gateway to Death Valley has its own features, visitors with time limitations can maximize their experience by choosing a different entrance and exit route. If you drove in on Calif. 127 through Death Valley Junction, try leaving on the scenic route west through the Panamint Valley. If you entered from the Panamint side, try following Badwater Road (aka Calif. 178) south from Furnace Creek, across the Black Mountains and Greenwater Valley, to pick up Calif. 127 at Shoshone.

dehydration: dizziness, headache, and cool, clammy skin. It's a good idea to stow several gallons for the car, even though radiator water is available from tanks placed at strategic points (uphill climbs) along the main roads.

- **Always carry sunscreen and protective clothing,** including a wide-brimmed hat and sunglasses.
- **Watch your temperature gauge, especially if you have an older vehicle.** When driving, turn off your air-conditioning on uphill grades if your car begins overheating. In the event that your car overheats, keep the engine running, turn the heat on full blast, and turn the car into the breeze. Remove the cap only if the engine has cooled significantly.
- **Be alert for wildlife on the road,** and don't let yourself be distracted by the scenery. Single-car accidents are the number-one cause of death in Death Valley, and they can occur summer or winter, daylight or nighttime. Many long miles of roads run through the park; though well paved, they often have sharp curves, dips, and steep downhill grades. If your tires wander off the edge of the pavement at high speed, don't jerk the wheel, which can cause you to skid. Instead, gradually slow down until it's safe to bring all four tires back onto the road.

SEASONS & CLIMATE

Although Death Valley is one of the world's driest deserts, altitudes range from 282 feet below sea level to over 11,000 feet above; therefore, "desert" doesn't always equal "hot." From June to September, temperatures in the valley can soar above 120°F (49°C), making the mountain sections of the park a relief, with temperatures in the 70s and 80s (20s Celsius). From November to February, when valley temperatures are comfortable—in the 60s and 70s (upper teens to mid-20s Celsius)—many higher areas are frigid and snowy.

SEASONAL EVENTS

The weeklong **Death Valley '49ers Encampment** (www.deathvalley49ers.org) is held in early November. It features a fiddlers' contest, square dancing, tours, a Western art show, and a golf tournament. Contact the visitor center for information.

2 Exploring the Park by Car

A network of roads, ranging from washboard remnants of old mining days to well-maintained highways built during the 1930s, crisscrosses Death Valley National Park. You'll find that most of the popular destinations, as well as the five major entry routes, have superior-quality roads suitable for all passenger vehicles, as well as trailers and RVs. One exception is the Emigrant/Wildrose Canyon pass between Calif. 190 and Calif. 178, sections of which are rough, narrow, and winding; vehicles over 25 feet are prohibited, and other drivers may want to consult a ranger about road conditions before attempting the unpaved section south of Wildrose.

Because of its vast area and unforgiving climate, the park is ideal for viewing by car. Some of the most beautiful sites have handy access roads, vista turnouts, or loop drives to facilitate viewing. These include **Artists Palette,** where the 9-mile (one-way) Artists Drive takes you through a colorful display hidden from the main road. Over millions of years, mineral deposits have created brilliant swaths of color across the low, rocky hills. There's a scenic overlook at the beginning of the drive, as well as a parking area farther along, in case you want to stop and scramble amid the pink, blue, red, orange, and green patches. (Sci-fi buffs, take note: This area served as a location in the original *Star Wars.*)

South of Artists Drive, Badwater Road takes you past several of Death Valley's highlights, which best illustrate this environment of low-elevation extremes. **Devil's Golf Course,** accessible by a short spur of graded dirt road, sets your car right in the middle of a forbidding landscape created by salt and erosion on a lake bed that dried up about 2,000 years ago. The results are spikes, pits, craters, and jagged ridges stained brown and smoothed by human feet near the parking area; walk just 2 minutes in any direction and you'll see the salty white surface in its natural state.

About 5 miles south of this is **Badwater,** whose name indicates the lowest, hottest, and (curiously) wettest spots on the valley floor. At 279 feet below sea level, Badwater is the lowest spot in the park accessible by auto and is marked by permanent spring-fed pools. The basin drops 3 feet from the road to the continental superlative of 282 feet below sea level. The water at first seemed like relief to early travelers—until they tasted the chloride, sodium, and sulfate. It isn't poisonous, and it is home to beetles, soldier fly larvae, and a snail that slowly adapted to these harsh conditions.

A similar site is 25 miles north on Calif. 190: **Salt Creek,** home to the **Salt Creek pupfish,** found nowhere else on Earth. In the spring, you can glimpse this little fish, which has made some amazing adaptations to survive in this arid land, from a wooden boardwalk nature trail. In spring, a million pupfish might be wriggling in the creek; they're not visible at any other time of year.

Your car will also take you all the way to two of the best lookout points around, both along Calif. 190 southeast of Furnace Creek. Before sunrise, photographers set up their tripods at **Zabriskie Point,** 5 miles southeast of Furnace Creek off Calif. 190, and aim their cameras down at the pale mudstone hills of Golden Canyon and the great valley beyond. The panoramic view is magnificent.

Another grand park vista is at **Dante's View,** 25 miles south of Furnace Creek by way of Calif. 190 and Dante's View Road. This 5,475-foot point looks out over the shimmering Death Valley floor backed by the high Panamint Mountains.

Nearly everyone takes the scenic drive up Scotty's Castle Road to visit the park's major man-made attraction, **Scotty's Castle** (see below). While you're there, it's worth taking the 15-minute drive to **Ubehebe Crater,** 9 miles west of the castle. The otherworldly pockmark resulted from a volcanic explosion that occurred as recently as 300 years ago. You'll know that you're close when the landscape begins to darken from layers of cinders that were spewed from the half-mile crater. A convenient loop road takes you up to the most scenic lip. An explanatory sign graces the parking area, and there's a hiking path (for those willing to brave the often-gusting winds) to an even more dramatic overlook and a field of smaller craters.

3 Organized Tours & Ranger Programs

In addition to providing hourly **Scotty's Castle** "Living History" tours (see below), Death Valley rangers keep busy giving lectures, group discussions, and film presentations on varied topics. For those eager to get their shoes dusty, several hikes and guided walks are available on a seasonal basis. Contact park headquarters for a seasonal schedule of day and evening events; nearly all programs (except for year-round Scotty's Castle tours) cease between mid-April and late October.

Pink Jeep Tours out of Las Vegas offers day trips to various park destinations for $119 per day and up. Among the tours is an expedition into the remote Racetrack area, where rocks mysteriously skate around on an ancient dry lakebed. Call **888/900-4480** or visit **www.pinkjeep.com** for reservations or additional information.

4 Park Attractions

Scotty's Castle, the Mediterranean-style hacienda in the northern part of the park, is Death Valley's premier attraction. Visitors are wowed by the Spanish tiles, well-crafted furnishings, and innovative construction with ahead-of-its-time solar water heating. Even more compelling is the colorful history of this villa in remote Grapevine Canyon, brought to life by park rangers dressed in 1930s clothing. Construction of the "castle"—officially, Death Valley Ranch—began in 1922. It was to be a winter retreat for Chicago millionaire Albert Johnson. The insurance tycoon's unlikely friendship with prospector/cowboy/spinner-of-tall-tales Walter Scott put the $2.3-million structure on the map and captured the public's imagination. Scotty greeted visitors and told them fanciful stories from the early mining days of Death Valley.

The 50-minute guided tour of Scotty's Castle is excellent, both for its inside look at the mansion and for what it reveals about the eccentricities of Johnson and Scotty. Tours depart about every 20 minutes from 9am to 5pm in the winter and 9:30 to 4pm in the summer; they fill up quickly, so arrive early for the first available spots. The tour costs $11 for adults, $9 seniors, $6 children 6 to 15, and is free for kids under 6. During busy periods, you may have to wait an hour or more, perusing the gift shop, relaxing in the snack bar, or hiking to Scotty's grave on the hill behind the castle. There's also a self-guided walking tour (excluding the interiors); the pamphlet *A Walking Tour of Scotty's Castle* leads you on an exploration from stable to pool, from bunkhouse to powerhouse. Organized groups (only) can reserve tour times by calling ✆ **760/786-2392.**

There are also **seasonal tours** of Scotty's true domicile, Lower Vine Ranch, and the amazing "Underground Mysteries Tour" below the castle. Call ✆ **760/786-2392** for current information; fees are the same as the castle tour for the latter and $15 per person for the former.

In 2000, Congress passed a bill that returned 7,000 acres (including about 300 in the Furnace Creek area) in and around the park to the Timbisha Shoshone, an American Indian tribe that inhabited the area for thousands of years before it became a national monument. This represents the first time that an Indian reservation has been established within the boundaries of a national park, and nearly 50 tribal members now live in the valley year-round in a private community. For more information, contact the **Timbisha Shoshone Tribe** (✆ **760/786-2374;** www.timbisha.org).

For yet another side of the human experience here, visit the **Harmony Borax Works,** 1 mile north of Furnace Creek off Calif. 190 (take a short spur road and a very short trail). This is a rocky landscape as tortured as you'll ever find. Death Valley prospectors called borax "white gold," and though it wasn't a glamorous substance, it was a profitable one. From 1883 to 1888, more than 20 million pounds of it were transported from the Harmony Borax Works; some borax mining continues in Death Valley to this day. A short trail with interpretive signs leads past the ruins of the old borax refinery and some outlying buildings.

Transport of borax was the stuff of legends, too. The famous 20-mule teams hauled the huge loaded wagons 165 miles to the rail station at Mojave. (To learn more about this colorful era, visit the Borax Museum at Furnace Creek Ranch, near the park visitor center.) Other remnants of human industry are the **Eagle Borax Works** ruins, 20 miles south of Furnace Creek on Badwater Road and the unpaved dirt West Side Road, and the **Wildrose Charcoal Kilns,** 39 miles south of Stovepipe Wells off Emigrant Canyon Road, where vast amounts of charcoal were manufactured for use in the lucrative silver mine near neighboring Panamint Valley. Located near the Wildrose campground, the road to the kilns is partially paved and twists precariously; vehicles over 25 feet are prohibited.

5 Day Hikes

The park has routes to suit all levels of expertise and at varying elevations. Wherever you hike, never forget to carry enough water; even in seemingly mild weather conditions, hikers can become dehydrated quickly. Park rangers can provide topographical maps, current weather conditions, and detailed directions to each trail head.

SHORTER TRAILS

Eureka Dunes This area is approachable only from the remote north end of the park and by rutted dirt and gravel roads that are subject to washout, so travel to the area requires a sturdy vehicle. The magnificent dunes are the tallest in California. The whole family will enjoy hiking here, spotting dune grass and wildflowers or the tracks of lizards and rodents. (Tread lightly, because this area is home to myriad endangered and threatened plant species.) The view from atop the highest dune (680 ft.) takes in the contrast of creamy sand against the layer-cake band of nearby rock, and small avalanches of sand create the trademark "singing" peculiar to such dunes. 1 mile RT. Moderate. Access: Eureka Valley, at the end of South Eureka Rd.

Golden Canyon Interpretive Trail A good choice for a quick hike in just about any weather, Golden Canyon is convenient to Furnace Creek accommodations and offers an opportunity to get up close with an interesting rock formation. The fairly level trail twists and turns a mile up Golden Canyon, to the foot of the aptly named Red Cathedral. An interpretive trail guide is available for a small fee at the trail head, with signposts marking the trail side; the Red Cathedral is a quarter-mile past the last signpost. 2 miles RT. Easy. Access: 2 miles south of Calif. 190 on Badwater Rd.

Little Hebe Crater Trail You get to the bleakly beautiful crater on a steep but plain trail that leads from the parking area, up to the crater's lip, around some of the contours, and past several lesser craters. Black cinders and volcanic fragments cover the countryside surrounding the apocalyptic-looking Ubehebe Crater, which erupted as recently as 300 years ago. Fierce winds can hamper your progress, but you'll get an exhilarating feeling, as though you're visiting another planet. High-top boots or shoes are recommended for the pebbly path. Adventurous types can also descend a short, steep trail to the crater floor, about 500 feet below the rim. 1.5 miles RT. Moderate. Access: Trail head leads up from parking area for Ubehebe Crater, 7 miles northwest of the Grapevine Ranger Station.

Mesquite Flats Sand Dunes Although not as majestic as the remote Eureka Dunes in northern Death Valley, these golden mounds off U.S. 190 are easy to reach and fun to romp on. There's no formal trail—simply explore to your heart's content. Kids especially will enjoy a barefoot romp on the fine sand dotted with stands of mesquite. Don't forget an adequate supply of water; in the midday sun, the dunes get very hot. 2 miles RT. Easy. Access: 2 miles east of Stovepipe Wells Village on Calif. 190.

Mosaic Canyon This short stroll requires a bit of rock scrambling into a canyon where water has polished the marble into white, gray, and black mosaics. The first mile is easy, suitable for every skill level; children will love running their hands over the water-smoothed rock walls. More adventurous climbers can continue up a series of chutes and dry waterfalls in the latter half of the hike. 1 to 4 miles RT. Moderate. Access: End of a short, graded dirt road just east of Stovepipe Wells on Calif. 190.

Natural Bridge Canyon This short walk takes you into a colorful narrow canyon. The loose gravel underfoot makes for a tiring walk, but it's less than .5 mile to the distinctive formation that gives the canyon its name: a rock bridge overhead, formed when rushing waters cut through softer lower layers. If you wish to hike past the bridge, it's another half-mile to the end of the canyon, making for a 2-mile hike. 1 mile RT. Moderate. Access: Take Badwater Rd. 15 miles south of Furnace Creek and continue 2 miles on unpaved spur road suitable for passenger vehicles.

Salt Creek Nature Trail A leisurely hike on a wooden boardwalk leads you along the unique salt marshes, passing a few plants (including the unusual pickleweed) along the way. In the spring, watch for the amazingly adaptive Salt Creek pupfish flashing about in the shallow water. .5 mile RT. Easy. Access: Take Calif. 190 14 miles north of Furnace Creek or 13 miles east of Stovepipe Wells, then follow 1-mile graded dirt spur road.

Titus Canyon Narrows As you hike, watch for vehicle traffic coming one-way from the other direction. The canyon's rock walls are an amateur geologist's dream—layers of orange, black, and blue-gray volcanic sediment streaked with threads of gleaming white calcite. Though you can augment this easy hike by continuing through the canyon, there's a broad pullout from the road at 1.5 miles; it's a good place to enjoy the view, and perhaps a picnic, before returning the way you came. More adventurous types can hike 5 more miles to walls bedecked with petroglyphs near Klare Springs. 3 miles RT. Easy. Access: Up a signed dirt road off Scotty's Castle Rd. (about 15 miles north of Calif. 190) that leads to the mouth of Titus Canyon, where it meets a one-way road for 4WD vehicles from Nev. 374; trail begins where the road becomes one-way coming toward you (from Nevada).

LONGER TRAILS

Gower Gulch Loop This trail's proximity to Furnace Creek, plus its varying degrees of difficulty, makes it quite popular. Start by hiking along the once-paved route that allowed cars to drive into the canyon but which was destroyed by flash flooding. Soon you'll be scrambling around the "badlands," hills of mud and silt deposited by ancient lakes. Those with more stamina can continue past Manly Beacon (a sandstone formation), across gullies and washes, and then up to Zabriskie Point for panoramic views of the forbidding badlands. ***Note:*** If you hike beyond Manly Beacon, be sure to pick up a map at one of the park's visitor centers—it is easy to lose your bearings in this area. 4 miles RT. Easy to moderate. Access: Golden Canyon parking lot along Calif. 178, about 2 miles south of Furnace Creek Inn.

Grotto Canyon This route is marked by deep "grottos" (smooth hollows formed by erosive floodwaters) in the rocks. The first mile follows a rugged gravel road up the canyon's alluvial fan; if you have an off-highway vehicle, drive this portion as far as the wash. Continue on foot from there, as the canyon narrows and you begin to encounter the grottos, beyond which waterfalls occasionally trickle. The cool hidden grottos are a nice place to stop for a snack, sheltered from the sun. 4 miles RT.

Campground	Elev.	Total Sites	RV Hookups	Dump Station	Toilets
Emigrant****	2,100	10	No	No	Yes
Furnace Creek**	–196	136	No	Yes	Yes
Mahogany Flat*	8,200	10	No	No	Yes
Mesquite Spring	1,800	30	No	Yes	Yes
Panamint Springs Resort	N/A	62	12	No	Yes
Stovepipe Wells	Sea level	204	14	Yes	Yes
Sunset	–196	270	No	Yes	Yes
Texas Spring	Sea level	92	No	Yes	Yes
Thorndike*	7,400	6	No	No	Yes
Wildrose***	4,100	23	No	No	Yes

* Road not passable for trailers, campers, or RVs. Passenger cars not advised; four-wheel-drive vehicle may be necessary.

** Reservations can be made Oct 15–Apr 15 only.

*** Water not available at Wildrose in winter.

**** Tents only.

Moderate to strenuous. Access: 2½ miles east of Stovepipe Wells on Calif. 190.

Jayhawker Canyon This out-of-the-way route follows the path of a desperate group of pioneers who attempted to find a way out of Death Valley in 1849–50. The footing in the debris-filled canyon is treacherous, and several forks and tributaries can distract you from staying in the main wash. At the end of the route lies a spring marking the Jayhawkers' camp, also a popular stopping place for the native Shoshone. Boulders in the area are marked with petroglyphs depicting bighorn sheep, along with the initials of several pioneers scratched into the rocks. 4.2 miles RT. Moderate. Access: Off Calif. 190, just west of Emigrant Ranger Station.

Telescope Peak Trail A grueling 3,000-foot climb ultimately leads to the 11,049-foot summit, where you'll be rewarded with the view described thusly by one pioneer: "You can see so far, it's just like looking through a telescope." Snow-covered in winter, the peak is best climbed from May to November; the trail is snowed in the rest of the year and recommended only for experienced winter climbers. Consult park rangers for current conditions and detailed advice—and ***never attempt this climb alone.*** 14 miles R. Strenuous. Access: Mahogany Flat Campground, past Wildrose Charcoal Kilns (4WD vehicles only).

Wildrose Peak Trail Consisting mostly of steady and unrelenting ascents, this steep hike has several level portions for rest stops. And you'll need them, because you'll be climbing over 2,000 feet on the way to the 9,060-foot summit. Marvelous views along the way present the stark Panamint Range, a bird's-eye view of Death Valley, and panoramas of the Sierras on the western horizon. It's unwise to attempt this hike in winter or without obtaining a topographical map from the ranger station. 8.4 miles RT. Strenuous. Access: Wildrose Charcoal Kilns, usually accessible by passenger vehicles (check with park rangers for road conditions).

6 Other Sports & Activities

BIKING Cycling is allowed on the 1,000 miles of dirt and paved roads used by motor vehicles in the park, but not on hiking trails or anywhere else. Weather conditions between May and October make bicycling at the lower elevations dangerous at times other than early morning.

There are no bike rentals available in the park, and given the park's isolation, the only practical option is to bring your own. You'll need a pretty rugged mountain bike to do most of these routes.

Good choices are **Racetrack** (28 miles one-way), **Greenwater Valley** (30 miles one-way, mainly level), **Cottonwood Canyon** (20 miles one-way), and **West Side Road** (40 miles one-way, fairly level with some washboard sections). **Artists Drive** is 9 miles long and paved, with some steep uphill stretches. Other favorites include **Titus Canyon** (28 miles on a one-way hilly road—it has some very difficult uphill and downhill stretches) and **Twenty-Mule Team Canyon Road** (a one-way 2¾-mile graded gravel road through colorful badlands).

Drinking Water	Showers	Fire Pits/ Grills	Laundry	Reserve	Fees	Open
Yes	No	No	No	Yes	No	Year-round
Yes	Nearby (fee)	Yes	Nearby	Yes	$12–$18	Year-round
No	No	Yes	No	No	No	Mar–Nov
Yes	No	Yes	No	No	$12	Year-round
Yes	Yes	Yes	No	Yes	$15–$30	Year-round
Yes	Nearby (fee)	Yes	No	No	$12–$30	Oct–Apr (full hookups year-round)
Yes	Nearby (fee)	No	No	No	$12	Oct–Apr
Yes	Nearby (fee)	Yes	No	No	$14	Oct–Apr
No	No	Yes	No	No	No	Mar–Nov
Yes	No	Yes	No	No	No	Year-round

7 Camping

Death Valley offers little variety to those seeking conventional accommodations, but campers (tent, trailer, and RV) can expect to find comforts similar to those at most other desert parks. You should take care, however, when selecting a campground. Although most locations are closed seasonally to protect visitors from the harshest elements (only five campgrounds are open year-round), there's always a risk of unseasonably hot temperatures at the none-too-shady campgrounds on the valley floor, as well as early or late snow at remote mountain sites. Always inquire with the park ranger about current conditions before setting up camp.

Furnace Creek Campground, just north of the Furnace Creek Visitor Center, has showers nearby (for a fee) from a strained water supply. (During peak times, there are quotas.) The campground also has group sites, which can be reserved. The huge **Sunset Campground,** just a quarter-mile east of the Furnace Creek Ranch, has individual sites and nearby showers (fee). **Texas Spring,** near Sunset Campground, has 92 sites and two group sites. The fee for an individual site at these campgrounds ranges from $12 to $18 a night.

Stovepipe Wells Campground has 204 spaces, with 14 RV hookups in two areas, and pay showers; the fee is $12 for a campsite, or $30 if you want an RV utility hookup. The basic, tents-only **Emigrant Campground** is 9 miles southwest of Stovepipe Wells on Calif. 190.

Thorndike Campground, 37 miles south of Stovepipe Wells and 1 mile from Mahogany Flats Campground, off the Trona-Wildrose Road, is accessible only by four-wheel-drive vehicle. It has eight primitive campsites with pit toilets but no other facilities. **Wildrose Campground,** 30 miles south of Stovepipe Wells off the Trona-Wildrose Road, has pit toilets and drinking water. **Mahogany Flats Campground,** 38 miles south of Stovepipe Wells, off Trona-Wildrose Road, can be reached only by four-wheel-drive vehicle. It has pit toilets but no other facilities. **Mesquite Spring Campground** is 5 miles south of Scotty's Castle on Grapevine Road.

The **Panamint Springs Resort** (✆ **775/482-7680**), 30 miles west of Stovepipe Wells on Calif. 190, operates a commercial campground with 40 spaces (12 with RV utility hookups). It charges $30 per night for full RV hookups, $20 for a water-only RV site, and $15 for a tent campsite.

Reservations for Furnace Creek are available from the **National Park Reservation Service** (✆ **877/444-6777;** www.recreation.gov).

8 Where to Stay

INSIDE THE PARK

Furnace Creek Inn The Furnace Creek Inn is exceptional, a 1920s resort whose charm has been preserved. Like an oasis in the middle of stark Death Valley, the inn's red-tiled roofs and hot spring–fed pool hint at the elegance within. The deluxe rooms and suites have every modern amenity. Stroll the lush, palm-shaded gardens before sitting down to a meal in the elegant **dining room,** where the food is excellent. Tennis courts and nearby golf and horseback riding are available; there's even a shuttle from the Furnace Creek private airstrip.

Calif. 190, 1 mile south of Furnace Creek Visitor Center (P.O. Box 1), Death Valley, CA 92328. ✆ **760/786-2345**; 800/297-2757 or 303/297-2757 for reservations. www.furnacecreekresort.com. 66 units. A/C, TV, TEL. $305–$455 double. AE, DC, DISC, MC, V. Closed mid-May to mid-Oct.

Furnace Creek Ranch Run by the same folks who maintain the elegant Furnace Creek Inn, the year-round Furnace Creek Ranch is more down-to-earth, with rustic cabin units and motel rooms that are great for families. Amenities include a naturally heated, spring-fed pool, the world's lowest 18-hole golf course (at 214 ft. below sea level), tennis and basketball courts, a playground, and a selection of dining options (see below).

Calif. 190, adjacent to the Furnace Creek Visitor Center (P.O. Box 1), Death Valley, CA 92328. ✆ **760/786-2345**; 800/297-2757 or 303/297-2757 for reservations. Fax 760/686-2514. www.furnacecreekresort.com. 224 units. A/C, TEL. $124–$213 double. AE, DC, DISC, MC, V.

Panamint Springs Resort The privately owned Panamint Springs Resort, across the Panamint Range and about a 45- to 60-minute drive west of Furnace Creek, is a bit off the beaten path—not just geographically, but also philosophically. A welcome change from the touristy overtones of Death Valley, this charming rustic motel has plain rooms, as well as a full-service **restaurant** that serves traditional American fare at breakfast, lunch, and dinner—and has 100 different brands of beer.

Calif. 190, 30 miles west of Stovepipe Wells (P.O. Box 395), Ridgecrest, CA 93555. ✆ **775/482-7680**. Fax 760/482-7682. www.deathvalley.com/psr. 14 units, 1 cottage. A/C. $79–$94 double; $149 cottage. AE, DISC, MC, V.

Stovepipe Wells Village The truly budget-conscious opt for Stovepipe Wells Village, where the modest air-conditioned motel rooms (sans phones and TVs) surround a small pool. About 23 miles northwest of Furnace Creek, Stovepipe Wells has a general store, Internet kiosk, saloon, and dining room (see below). Rooms have two twin beds, two double beds, or one king.

Calif. 190 at Stovepipe Wells, Death Valley, CA 92328. ✆ **760/786-2387**; 800/297-2757 or 303/297-2757 for reservations. Fax 760/786-2389. www.stovepipewells.com. 83 units. A/C. $76–$116 double. AE, DC, DISC, MC, V.

NEAR THE PARK

Because accommodations in Death Valley are limited, you might consider the money-saving (but inconvenient) option of spending a night in one of the gateway towns. **Lone Pine,** on the west side of the park, is a good choice, with a wide selection of lodgings and great Western views and charm. **Beatty, Nevada,** and **Shoshone** have inexpensive lodgings. Each is about an hour's drive from the park's center, but accommodations are limited to unremarkable motels. In Death Valley Junction, the one-of-a-kind **Amargosa Opera House and Hotel** (✆ **760/852-4441;** www.amargosa-opera-house.com) offers 15 air-conditioned rooms in a historic out-of-the-way place, 30 miles from Furnace Creek. Room rates are $67 to $84, and credit cards (AE, MC, V) are accepted. See the box, "Death Valley's Unique Opera House and Its Creator," for more on the story of the Amargosa Opera House.

9 Where to Dine

INSIDE THE PARK

There aren't many restaurants inside the park, or much variety (most of them serve basic American fare), but here's a rundown.

There are three dining options at the **Furnace Creek Ranch,** all relatively informal. The best and most economical is the **Forty Niner Cafe,** a diner with better-than-average food and a widely varied menu. It's open daily from 7am to 9pm October to May and from 10am to 9pm the rest of the year. The adjacent **Wrangler Steakhouse** offers an all-you-can-eat buffet for breakfast (6–9am) and lunch (11am–2pm). The prices are higher than average, but the buffet is a good choice for families with hearty eaters. From 5:30 to 9:30pm, the Wrangler offers table service, grilling steaks, ribs, and other satisfying specialties; the servings are generous, but the dinners are pricey. At the golf course, the **19th Hole Bar & Grill** serves sandwiches and pub fare from October to May. All of these places accept major credit cards (AE, DC, DISC, MC, V).

At the elegant dining room at the **Furnace Creek Inn** (✆ **760/786-2345**), the menu highlights several Continental and regional cuisines. The peaceful setting and attentive service can be a welcome (though pricey) treat during exhausting travels through the park. Breakfast, lunch, and dinner are served. The Sunday buffet brunch is truly decadent; reservations are necessary. The dining room closes from 2:30 to 5:30pm daily and closes with the hotel from mid-May to mid-October. Major credit cards (AE, DC, DISC, MC, V) are accepted. T-shirts and tank tops are not allowed.

The restaurant at **Stovepipe Wells** (✆ **760/786-2604**) is kind of a cross between a camp dining room and a casual cafe. It's open daily 7am to 2pm and 6:30 to 10pm (with shorter hours in the hot season), and accepts major credit cards (AE, DC, DISC, MC, V). Other choices are a snack bar at **Scotty's Castle** and a rustic (and affordable) burgers-and-beer cafe at **Panamint Springs.**

Death Valley's Unique Opera House and Its Creator

The town of Death Valley Junction has as many opera houses as it does residents: exactly one. And though the closest town to the **Amargosa Opera House** (✆ **760/852-4441**; www.amargosa-opera-house.com) is 30 miles away, it manages to pack the house every weekend it's open. For many years, the sole performer was Marta Becket, who is now in her mid-80s, and has retired from performance (or so she says; reports have her making guest appearances in the new show). You can still visit and stay at the hotel, and see a show inspired by Becket's remarkable life and art.

Located on the edge of Death Valley, the opera house is the culmination of a dream of the bizarre Becket, who arrived by accident in 1967. A dancer, Becket had been touring in California. She and her husband were driving back east when their car had a flat tire. The closest garage was in Amargosa, which at the time was a company town run by the Pacific Borax Company. While the tire was being fixed, Beckett poked around the old adobe structures and instantly fell in love with the opera house. "As I looked into that hole, into this empty building, I had this distinct feeling I was looking into the other half of my life," Beckett recalls.

Though the floors and ceilings were falling apart and there were rats living in the space, to Becket, it symbolized freedom and independence. So she did it. She and her husband abandoned their lives in New York City to move out here, at the intersection of nowhere and nothing.

The opera house itself is a work of art—and so is the hotel it's attached to. Before she began performing, Becket wanted to guarantee herself an audience. She spent 4 years painting its walls to resemble the inside of a theater, with level upon level of character-filled balconies. There are whimsical nuns, prostitutes, court jesters, and royalty. Two years were spent on the blue ceiling, illustrated with cherubs flying amid clouds. The people she painted were a silent guarantee, to her anyway, that she'd never be performing to an empty house. Since the beginning, she's performed whether there was an actual audience or not.

Often, there wasn't, and her painted characters sufficed. An unexpected stroke of luck befell the opera house 6 years into its run when a writer from National Geographic stumbled upon the show. He loved it, wrote about it, and the place has been packed ever since.

The Opera House is more than just a roadside attraction. It's a labor of love and showcases the true (though slowing) talent of Becket, whose husband left a few years after they moved there. For 23 years she took on a partner, a maintenance man with a flair for comedy. He passed away in 2005.

Becket stopped performing in her Amargosa Opera House at the end of the 2008–2009 season, but it still hosts performances: In November 2009, "If These Walls Could Talk," a show Inspired by Marta Becket, created and performed by Sandy Scheller, opened at the facility, which runs Saturday nights and Sunday afternoons from November through April. Tickets are $15 for adults, $12 for children. Reservations are required.

—Kate Silver

Helpful hint: Meals and groceries are costly inside the park because of its remote location. If possible, consider bringing a cooler with some snacks, sandwiches, and beverages. Ice is easy to find, and you'll also be able to keep water chilled.

NEAR THE PARK

Too far away for a round-trip excursion once you're in Death Valley, **The Mad Greek** (✆ **760/733-4354**) in Baker is a restaurant you must stop at on the way in or out. At the junction of I-15 and Calif. 127, this roadside treasure is an ethnic surprise beloved by many. White tiles, Aegean-blue accents, and plenty of Athenian kitsch complement a menu of Greek specialties such as souvlaki, spinach-and-feta spanakopita, stuffed grape leaves, green salad with tangy feta, exquisite pastries, and even Greek beer. The mile-long menu also includes traditional road fare, such as hamburgers and hot sandwiches, and killer strawberry shakes. In Beatty, Nevada, the **Ensenada Grill,** 600 U.S. 95 S. (✆ **775/553-2600**), is another good pick, serving good Mexican standards for breakfast, lunch, and dinner daily.

10 Picnic & Camping Supplies

Within park boundaries, **Furnace Creek Ranch** has a market carrying a fairly wide selection of groceries and ice; propane is available at the adjacent service station. **Stovepipe Wells** offers ice, limited groceries, propane, and white gas.

Outside the park, if you want to stock up before entering, groceries and supplies are available in the towns of **Baker, Beatty, Shoshone, Pahrump,** and **Ridgecrest.** For visitors approaching on U.S. 395 from the south, Ridgecrest is the best choice—it's a sizable city with chain grocery stores, fast-food restaurants, and a selection of gas stations. If you're coming from Las Vegas, booming **Pahrump** is the place to stop; it has a pair of good-size grocery stores to fill most travelers' needs.

11 A Nearby Desert Wonderland: Mojave National Preserve

To most Americans, the eastern Mojave is a bleak, interminable stretch of desert to be crossed as quickly as possible. But many consider the national preserve, just southeast of Death Valley National Park along California's I-15 and I-40, the crown jewel of the California desert.

This is a hard land to get to know—it has no accommodations or restaurants, few campgrounds, and only a handful of roads suitable for the average passenger vehicle. But hidden within this natural fortress are some true gems—its 1.6 million acres include the world's largest Joshua tree forest; abundant wildlife; spectacular canyons, caverns, sand dunes, and volcanic formations; tabletop mesas; and a dozen mountain ranges.

Paradoxically, the eastern Mojave owes much of its appearance to water—canyons carved by streams, mineral-encrusted dry lake beds, and mountains whose colorful layers represent limestone deposited in ancient oceans. Today the landscape is distinguished primarily by its extreme dryness. The climate changed dramatically following the end of the last ice age, about 10,000 years ago; around this time, the first humans are believed to have migrated into the area. Lakes fed by glacial runoff supported fish, mammoths, camels, and diverse vegetation. When traditional food such as antelope diminished, the inhabitants adapted a lifestyle better suited to the arid climate, ultimately relying on small game and plants.

The European invasion started in the 18th century, when Spanish missionaries and explorers ventured north from Mexico. In the 19th century, American pioneers arrived, crossing the Mojave on their way west to the coast. Then in 1883, the railroad arrived, boosting existing mining and ranching operations.

By the 1970s, environmentalists had become gravely concerned with the region's protection. Destructive off-road use, the theft of rare desert plants, the plunder of archaeological sites, and the killing of threatened desert tortoises all endangered the delicate ecological balance. Then in 1994, President Bill Clinton signed the California Desert Protection Act, creating Mojave National Preserve.

The Mojave's elevated status hasn't attracted hordes of sightseers, and devoted visitors are happy to keep it that way. Unlike a national park, the national preserve allows hunting and continued grazing and mining within its boundaries, practices that are sore spots for ardent preservationists.

FLORA & FAUNA

There's much more life in the Mojave Desert than the human eye can immediately discern. Many animals are well camouflaged or nocturnal (or both), but if you tread lightly and keep your eyes open, the experience is rewarding. Wildlife includes the hopping kangaroo rat, ground squirrels, cottontails and jackrabbits, bobcats, coyotes, lizards, snakes, and the threatened desert tortoise. Consider yourself lucky to spot elusive bighorn sheep or shy mule deer. Migrating birds that stop off in the Mojave are met by permanent residents such as quail, pinyon jays, sparrows, noisy cactus wrens, and the distinctive roadrunner.

You'll see familiar desert plants such as the fragrant creosote bush, several varieties of cacti (including the deceptively fluffy-looking cholla, or "teddy bear"), and several strains of yucca. On and around Cima Dome grows the world's largest and densest **Joshua tree forest.** Botanists say that Cima's Joshuas are more symmetrical than their cousins elsewhere in the Mojave. The dramatic colors of the sky at sunset provide a breathtaking backdrop for Cima's Joshua trees, some more than 25 feet tall and over 100 years old.

Other desert flora include Mormon tea, cliff rose, desert sage, desert primrose, and cat's-claw; these flowering plants are among many that make the spring wildflower season a popular time to visit. Junipers, nut-bearing pinyon pines, and scrub oaks are found in the preserve's higher elevations.

ESSENTIALS

GETTING THERE

I-15, the major route between Los Angeles and Las Vegas, extends along the northern boundary of the preserve. **I-40,** the major route between southern California and Arizona, is the southern access route.

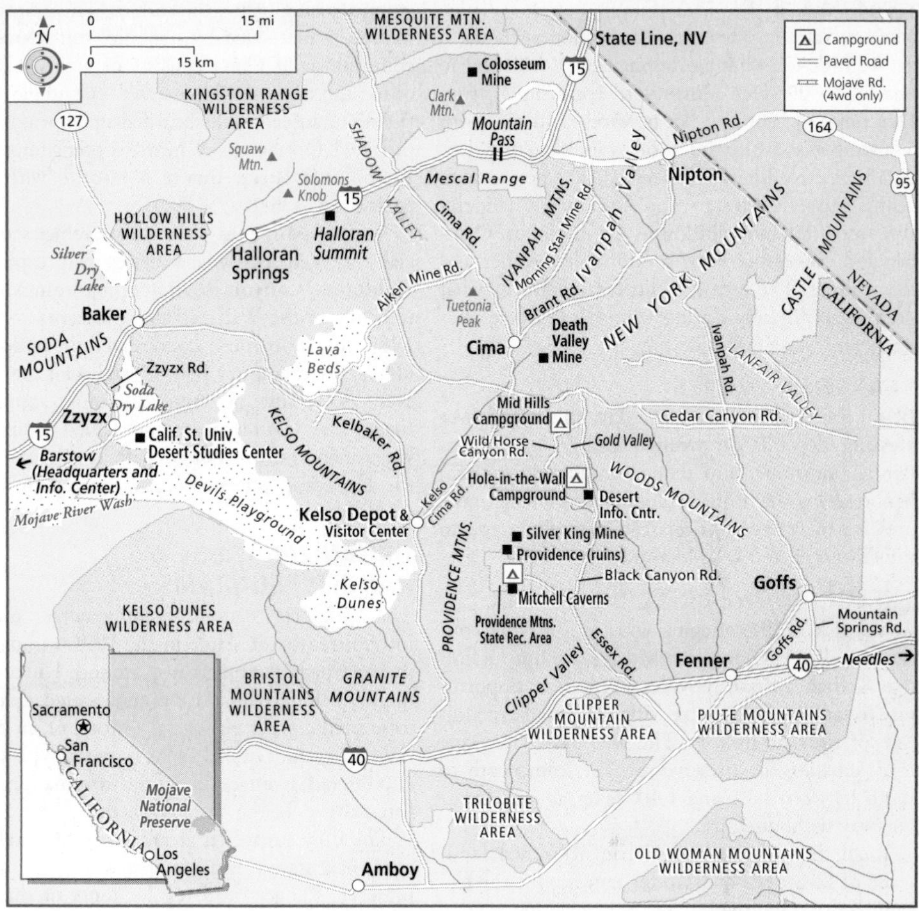

Common entry points include **Kelbaker Road,** which crosses the preserve from Baker to Kelso. There are Kelbaker Road exits from both I-15 and I-40. The **Essex Road** exit from I-40, 25 miles east of Kelbaker Road, is the access point for **Providence Mountains State Recreation Area** (Mitchell Caverns) and two other campgrounds. The **Cima Road** exit from I-15 near Mountain Pass leads into the center of the preserve.

The town of **Nipton,** technically outside preserve boundaries, is a common destination for Mojave travelers. Take Nipton Road from I-15, within sight of the Nevada border.

The nearest airport is Las Vegas's **McCarran International,** discussed earlier in this chapter.

INFORMATION & VISITOR CENTERS

Contact the Superintendent, **Mojave National Preserve,** 2701 Barstow Rd., Barstow, CA 92311 (✆ **760/252-6100;** www.nps.gov/moja).

The best source for up-to-date weather conditions and a free map is the **Mojave National Preserve–Kelso Depot Visitor Center,** 90942 Kelso-Cima Rd., Kelso, CA 92309 (✆ **760/252-6108**), which offers a superior selection of books. The historic depot in the heart of the preserve is open daily from 9am to 5pm year-round. Additional information and maps are available inside the preserve at the **Hole-in-the-Wall Ranger Station** (✆ **760/928-2572** or 760/252-6104), open on weekends in summer from 9am to 4pm and Wednesday through Sunday in winter from 9am to 4pm.

FEES & WARNINGS

Entry to the preserve is free. Campsites at two developed campgrounds cost $12, but dispersed camping is free. A constant threat in the desert is **dehydration.** Rangers recommended drinking 1 gallon of water per person per day, twice that if you're planning strenuous activity.

SEASONS & CLIMATE

Mojave National Preserve's 1.6 million acres lie in the high desert, with elevations from 1,000 feet to nearly 8,000 feet. Although conditions from December to February can be windy and cold with a dusting of snow, summers often see blistering temperatures exceeding 100°F (38°C). The best time to visit is between February and April, when temperatures are mild and wildflowers are in bloom. October and November have comfortable weather and few visitors. The area gets little rainfall, but what does occur (usually during winter) can begin suddenly and cause flash flooding.

SEASONAL EVENTS

Best between February and May, the **wildflower viewing** depends on weather conditions such as rainfall, sunshine, and temperatures, but you can bet on seeing the brilliant blooms somewhere in the preserve each year. Rangers can help direct you to the flowers currently in bloom.

EXPLORING THE PRESERVE BY CAR

At the risk of discouraging you from leaving your car to really experience the Mojave, we must admit that **Kelbaker Road** provides an excellent opportunity to sample the preserve with a minimal expenditure of time or trouble. The well-paved two-lane road, crossing the preserve roughly from north to south between I-15 and I-40, takes about 1 hour one-way without stops.

You'll drive through the eerie blackened landscape of **lava beds** and **cinder cones,** visit the elegant **Kelso Depot,** and see the towering golden mounds of **Kelso Dunes.** This 45-square-mile formation of sculpted sand dunes is famous for its "booming," a low rumble emitted when small avalanches or blowing sands pass over the underlying layer. Geologists speculate that the extreme dryness of the East Mojave Desert, combined with the wind-polished, rounded nature of the sand grains, has something to do with the musicality. Sometimes the low rumbling resembles a Tibetan gong; other times it sounds like a 1950s doo-wop musical group. After Kelso Dunes, you'll end your trip with views of the **Granite Mountains,** where erosion has removed all but the most resilient chunks of extraordinarily hard rock, leaving piles of rosy-hued boulders that are alternately smooth and jagged.

Leading northeast from Kelso Depot, the **Kelso-Cima Road** provides another scenic diversion, running alongside railroad tracks to the tiny community of **Cima** (Spanish for "summit"), at the foot of a geological oddity called **Cima Dome,** an almost perfectly rounded landform rising 1,500 feet above the desert. The dome is a batholith, created by molten rock that, unlike its volcano cousin, stopped rising below the surface. This unusual formation is blanketed by majestic Joshua trees. The community of Cima consists of a tiny U.S. post office and a ramshackle market, but no gas station. (Don't be fooled by its boarded-up appearance.) Be prepared for the many heart-stopping dips in the Kelso-Cima Road; they're a favorite with young backseat passengers.

Visitors with four-wheel-drive vehicles or especially rugged two-wheel drives can explore the **Wildhorse Canyon Road,** looping from Mid Hills to Hole-in-the-Wall, at the preserve's heart. In 1989, this short route was declared the nation's first official "Backcountry Byway," an honor that federal agencies bestow on America's most scenic back roads. The 11-mile horseshoe-shaped route crosses wide-open country dotted with cholla cactus, but the landscape was irrevocably altered by a 2005 wildfire.

ORGANIZED TOURS & RANGER PROGRAMS

The Park Service holds evening ranger programs intermittently at Hole-in-the-Wall campground; they're worth planning a stop around. The programs might include talks on the endangered desert tortoise or the area's geological history, or an evening slide program. Guided walks to petroglyph sites are also offered. Contact one of the information centers listed above for the current schedule.

The only organized attraction is **Mitchell Caverns,** in a state recreation area within the national preserve. Rangers lead regular tours of these rock rooms, where you'll see stalactites, stalagmites, and other limestone formations, plus archaeological artifacts from the area's early human inhabitants. The caves, where the temperature is an almost constant 65°F (18°C), provide a welcome respite during hot weather. Tours run daily between Labor Day and Memorial Day, weekdays at 1:30pm and weekends at 10am, 1:30pm, and 3pm. In summer, tours are daily at 1:30pm. Cost is $5 for adults, $2 for kids 6 to 16, and free for children under 6 (but the tour is not recommended for younger kids). Tours are limited to 25 people and fill quickly, so arrive early to ensure a spot. For information, call ✆ **661/942-0662.** ***Note:*** Tours are often added without notice during periods of high demand. To check last-minute schedules or find out whether a particular tour is sold out, call the visitor center (✆ **760/928-2586**).

PARK ATTRACTIONS

In the days of steam trains, the town of Kelso was a critical watering spot for locomotives. Built in 1924, the elegant **Kelso Depot** is Spanish Mission style, with the requisite red-tile roof and graceful arches.

At its peak, during World War II, the town supported 2,000 residents, and the depot's diner, the **Beanery,** served customers 24 hours a day. Once slated for demolition, the depot has been restored by the National Park Service for use as the preserve's visitor center.

Skirting the preserve's northern boundary is the whistle-stop town of **Nipton.** Founded in 1885, Nipton was a true ghost town, until nearly a century later, Los Angeles transplants Jerry and Roxanne Freeman began restoring its dilapidated buildings. At its height, Nipton was at the center of Mojave industry, providing railroad access for miners and ranchers; silent film star Clara Bow was a visitor. Call ✆ **760/856-2335** or visit **www.nipton.com** for additional information on Nipton.

At the preserve's western boundary, on the shores of the stark white Soda Dry Lake, is **Zzyzx** (a cryptic name, pronounced *Zeye*-zix, that's puzzled generations of motorists). Reached by taking the Zzyzx Road exit from I-15 and carefully negotiating a 4-mile rocky dirt road, the springs have a colorful history. In addition to being an important watering hole for those crossing the desert, the site was an American Indian camp, a military outpost, a wagon station, the headquarters of a Hollywood radio evangelist, and a trendy health resort (with the fanciful name of Zzyzx Mineral Springs). The springs are still active, feeding the elegant pools left over from the resort's heyday and supporting an entire ecosystem of wildlife at the lake bed's edge. You can stroll among the buildings, now used by **California State University's Desert Studies Center** (http://biology.fullerton.edu/dsc), and learn more about the area's history from interpretive signs on a trail around Lake Tuendae.

Throughout the preserve are remnants of the historic **Mojave Road,** a 19th-century wagon route to the West Coast. Check with preserve rangers for tips on where to find sections of the old road.

DAY HIKES

In addition to the preserve's marked and maintained hiking trails, many hikers create their own routes using the dirt roads that crisscross the area. Some are so poor that they're passable only by off-road vehicles, so there's little or no traffic.

There are several good hiking areas along **New York Mountains Road,** west of Ivanpah Road (itself unpaved and rough), an area of mine ruins, ranch structures, and cool, pine-studded canyons. Several sections of the historic **Mojave Road** are also great for hiking but accessible only by four-wheel-drive vehicles; remains of a wagon route stretch from Piute Wash beyond the eastern boundary of the preserve, through Cedar Canyon and past the lava beds, all the way to Zzyzx Springs on Soda Dry Lake at the western edge. When you're hiking in the backcountry, please respect private lands, which are not always well marked.

SHORTER TRAILS

Kelso Dunes Trail These are the second-highest dunes in California, covering 45 square miles and reaching almost 700 feet in height. The dunes are visible from Kelbaker Road. Three miles of graded dirt road lead to a parking area, where several interpretive signs give information on dunes ecology. Follow the trail out past the vegetation, then ramble to your heart's content, trying to spot examples of the many plants and animals that live in the seemingly barren dunes. Among them are rodents, kit foxes, lizards, sand verbena, and desert primrose, which color the dunes with brilliant blooms of yellow, white, and pink in springtime. ***Note:*** Climbing the soft dunes requires time and exertion, but tumbling back down is the fun reward. 3 miles RT (to the dunes). Moderate. Access: Parking area 10 miles south of Kelso Depot.

Mary Beal Nature Trail Suitable for all ages, the path winds past examples of the diverse plant and animal life found in the Mojave. Named for a prominent naturalist who spent 50 years exploring this desert, the trail has numbered posts keyed to a brochure that's for sale at the visitor center. .5 mile RT. Easy. Access: Providence Mountains State Recreation Area Visitor Center, Essex Rd., 16 miles northwest of I-40.

LONGER TRAILS

Mid Hills/Hole-in-the-Wall Trail Stretching between the two campgrounds, this maintained trail can be hiked in part or full. The entire hike is a grand tour of canyons and tabletop mesas, large pinyon trees, and colorful cacti; it's an all-day, one-way undertaking if you can arrange a car shuttle, and is much more enjoyable in the downhill direction, from Mid Hills to Hole-in-the-Wall. If you're not up for a long day hike, the 2-mile hike from Hole-in-the-Wall Campground to Banshee Canyon offers an easier alternative. From Hole-in-the-Wall, the initial segment of the trail offers the most adventure; climbers descend through a vertical chute in the rock using a series of metal rings. Even with handholds, the climb requires agility and concentration—don't try it if you have any doubts. ***Note:*** Much of the area between Mid Hills and Hole-in-the-Wall was charred by a 2005 wildfire. 1 mile RT to 8 miles one-way. Easy to strenuous. Access: Hole-in-the-Wall Picnic Area.

Teutonia Peak Trail This trail leads up about 600 feet to Teutonia Peak, atop Cima Dome, an unusual volcanic formation. The top affords panoramic views of the dome and desert. You'll walk among Joshua trees, Mojave yucca, and cholla

Especially for Kids

There's a lot for kids to enjoy in Mojave, from scrambling on sandy **Kelso Dunes** to exploring **Mitchell Caverns,** which resemble an *Indiana Jones* movie set. You can show them **lava beds** so similar to the moon's surface that U.S. astronauts once trained here, or you can make a contest of finding familiar shapes and profiles in the jagged Granite Mountains.

("teddy bear") cactus. Near the summit, the trail is faint but marked with cairns (small piles of stones). 4 miles RT. Moderate. Access: On Cima Rd. btw. I-15 and the town of Cima.

BIKING

Opportunities are as extensive as the preserve's hundreds of miles of lonesome dirt roads. The 140-mile-long historic **Mojave Road,** a rough four-wheel-drive route, crosses the preserve east to west and visits many of the most scenic areas in the East Mojave; sections of this road make excellent bike tours, but you'll definitely need a mountain bike. Prepare well—the Mojave's dirt roads are rugged routes surrounded by miles of desert wilderness. There are no bike rentals in the park.

CAMPING

The preserve has three established campgrounds, all open year-round on a first-come, first-served basis. None have showers, laundry facilities, or RV hookups, though the Hole-in-the-Wall Campground has a dump station.

The **Mid Hills Campground** was damaged in the 2005 wildfire but restored for use; about half of its 26 sites were back in commission at press time. It is 36 miles northwest of Essex, off Black Canyon Road. The mile-high camp is the coolest in the East Mojave. Pit toilets, fire grates, and drinking water are provided, but there are no public telephones. Cost is $12 per night.

Nearby **Hole-in-the-Wall Campground** perches above two dramatic canyons, 26 miles northwest of Essex, on Black Canyon Road near the Mid Hills Campground. There are 37 sites; the fee is $12. You'll find pit toilets, drinking water, public phones, fire grates, and a dump station.

The sites at **Providence Mountain State Recreation Area** (✆ **760/928-2586**) are adjacent to the Mitchell Caverns Visitor Center. There are only six first-come, first-served sites, for $25 per night. You'll find flush toilets, drinking water, public telephones, and fire grates.

A highlight of the East Mojave is camping in the open desert all by your lonesome; **backcountry camping** requires no registration. Backcountry campers need to pack out all trash and take care to set up in only previously impacted campsites 200 yards from any water source. It's advisable to contact an information center before establishing camp. And please respect private lands.

In addition to the campgrounds in the preserve, 30 acres of camping space are available in a privately owned campground in Nipton, in the open desert beyond the town's historic B&B inn (double rates are about $80, continental breakfast included). Other facilities include hot tubs, showers, drinking water, a Wi-Fi network ($3.50/stay), a restaurant, five "eco-cabins" ($65–$85 per night, breakfast included), and four RV hookups ($35 per night). For information, call ✆ **760/856-2335** or visit **www.nipton.com**.

14

Devils Tower National Monument, WY

by Eric Peterson

Rising 1,267 feet above the Belle Fourche River, the stone stump of Devils Tower greets visitors miles before they arrive. Established in 1906 by President Theodore Roosevelt as the country's first national monument, Devils Tower is well off the beaten path in northeast Wyoming, but it's well worth the trip.

Col. Richard I. Dodge, who commanded a military escort for a U.S. Geological Survey party that visited the Black Hills in 1875, is credited with giving the formation its name. In his book *The Black Hills* (1876), Dodge described Devils Tower as "one of the most remarkable peaks in this or any other country."

The steep-sided mass of igneous rock rises abruptly from the grasslands and pine forests, and it remains one of the Black Hills' most conspicuous geologic features. Movie buffs will recognize the tower as the landing site of an alien spaceship in Steven Spielberg's 1977 Oscar-winning film *Close Encounters of the Third Kind,* starring Richard Dreyfuss, François Truffaut, and Teri Garr.

GEOLOGY

Although the 50-million-year-old tower is composed of hard igneous rock, much of the other exposed rock within the 1,347-acre monument is made of soft sediments from the warm, shallow seas of the Mesozoic era. These colorful bands of rock encircling the igneous core include layers of sandstone, shale, mudstone, siltstone, gypsum, and limestone.

The story of Devils Tower's geology is but one chapter in the history of the Black Hills. Even now, after extensive study and detailed geologic mapping, modern scientists are still debating the origins of Devils Tower. While scientists agree it is an igneous (or volcanic) intrusion, their theories diverge on the tower's original size and shape. The most popular suggests that it is the result of volcanic activity in the early Tertiary period, some 50 million years ago. Scientists believe that a mass of molten rock forced its way up from below the surface of the earth, forming an inverted, cone-shaped structure beneath layers of sedimentary rock in what is now northeastern Wyoming. As the molten rock slowly cooled, it cracked and fractured, creating one of the most striking features of the monument, its polygonal columns. Most of the columns are five-sided, and others are four- or six-sided. The largest columns measure 15 to 20 feet in diameter at their base and gradually taper upward to about 10 feet in diameter at the summit.

Over centuries, the gentle waters of ancient streams and rivers carried away sedimentary layers, leaving the more erosion-resistant igneous rock behind. Today the tower appears to sit quietly on the crest of a wooded hill, but its base is actually the top of the unexposed magma, covered with fallen columns and soil.

AMERICAN INDIAN LEGEND

American Indians have their own names for Devils Tower, which earned its current moniker from a translation of "bad god's tower." Since long before 1875, the Lakota have called it *Mato Tipila,* or Grizzly Bear Lodge, and descendants of several American Indian nations of the Great Plains share similar legends of how the prominent butte was formed.

Day's End at Devil's Tower

Visitors to Devils Tower should take the time to stay a night, if only to watch the drama that unfolds at dusk. Head to Joyner Ridge via Joyner Ridge Rd., about 2½ miles up the main road from the park entrance, with a picnic dinner on a nice night, and just gaze at the tower and watch the moon rise. It also offers a tremendous vantage point to photograph the tower. There are also occasional guided full-moon hikes here in the summer; contact the park for details.

According to the Kiowa version of the tale, seven sisters watched with horror as their brother was turned into a bear. The sisters ran from him to the stump of a large tree, which beckoned them to climb on. (In other versions, they ran to a large, flat stone.) When they did, the stump rose up into the sky, and the bear, unable to climb up the stump to reach the sisters, scored it with its claws. The sisters were then raised into the sky, becoming the seven stars of the Big Dipper.

Devil's Tower is a sacred place to many native peoples. In deference to the religious significance of the tower, the National Park Service has requested that climbing of the tower be voluntarily suspended during the month of June so that ceremonies may be conducted without interference.

FIRST ASCENT

As a battle to preserve the monument from commercial encroachment was being waged in 1893, two local ranchers decided it was time someone made the first recorded climb to its summit.

William Rogers and Willard Ripley planned for months before making their first attempt on the southeast face on July 4, 1893. As the date approached, the pair began distributing handbills offering such amenities as ample food and drink, daily and nightly dancing, and plenty of grain for horses. The flyers also touted the feat as the "rarest sight of a lifetime."

Rogers and Ripley used a wooden stake ladder for the first 350 feet of the climb. As more than 1,000 spectators watched, the pair made the harrowing climb in about an hour, raised Old Glory, and then sold pieces of it as mementos of the occasion. Thereafter, the tower became a popular place for Independence Day family gatherings. At the annual affair in 1895, Mrs. Rogers used her husband's ladder to become the first woman to reach the summit.

ON TOP OF THE TOWER

From its base, most visitors would surmise that the top of Devils Tower is a flat, barren pinnacle. As the approximately 4,000 climbers who make it to the peak each year will attest, the top of the tower isn't much different from the countryside that surrounds it—except that it's said you can see five states.

The summit is actually slightly domed, with a few small outcroppings, and is covered with prairie grasses, prickly pear cactus, currant and gooseberry bushes, and native big sage, thanks to prairie falcons and turkey vultures that nest in the tower's columns and deposit seeds on top. A number of animals also have been spotted on the crown of Devils Tower, including rattlesnakes, pack rats, and cute red squirrels that have slithered and scampered up the cracks and fissures.

At the top, climbers may sign a register and record any unusual aspect or oddity of their adventure. More than 60,000 signatures have been gathered since records of tower climbs were established in 1937. In that time, climbers have used more than 220 routes to the top; in 1941 parachutist George Hopkins jumped from an airplane to the cap of the tower, then lost his escape rope and was stranded on top for 6 days.

AVOIDING THE CROWDS

Traffic patterns at the monument are similar to those of national park areas throughout the West. Expect the highest visitation from June through August, with lower visitation in the shoulder months of April, May, September, and October; the lowest visitation is during winter. Parking is limited in summer.

If you visit during the summer, stop at the tower early in the day or take in a fireside ranger talk when crowds have thinned in the evening. Each year during the second week in August, a huge motorcycle rally takes place in nearby Sturgis, South Dakota. Attendance may significantly increase during that period.

1 Essentials

GETTING THERE & GATEWAYS

Because of Devils Tower's remote location, the best access is by private vehicle. The monument entrance is 33 miles northeast of Moorcroft, Wyoming, and 27 miles northwest of Sundance, Wyoming, on **U.S. 14** (travel to the immediate area on **I-90**). Scheduled

Voices

A dark mist lay over the Black Hills, and the land was like iron. At the top of the ridge I caught sight of Devils Tower upthrust against the gray sky as if in the birth of time the core of the earth had broken through its crust and the motion of the world was begun. There are things in nature that engender an awful quiet in the heart of man; Devils Tower is one of them.

—N. Scott Momaday, Pulitzer Prize–winning author of *House Made of Dawn*

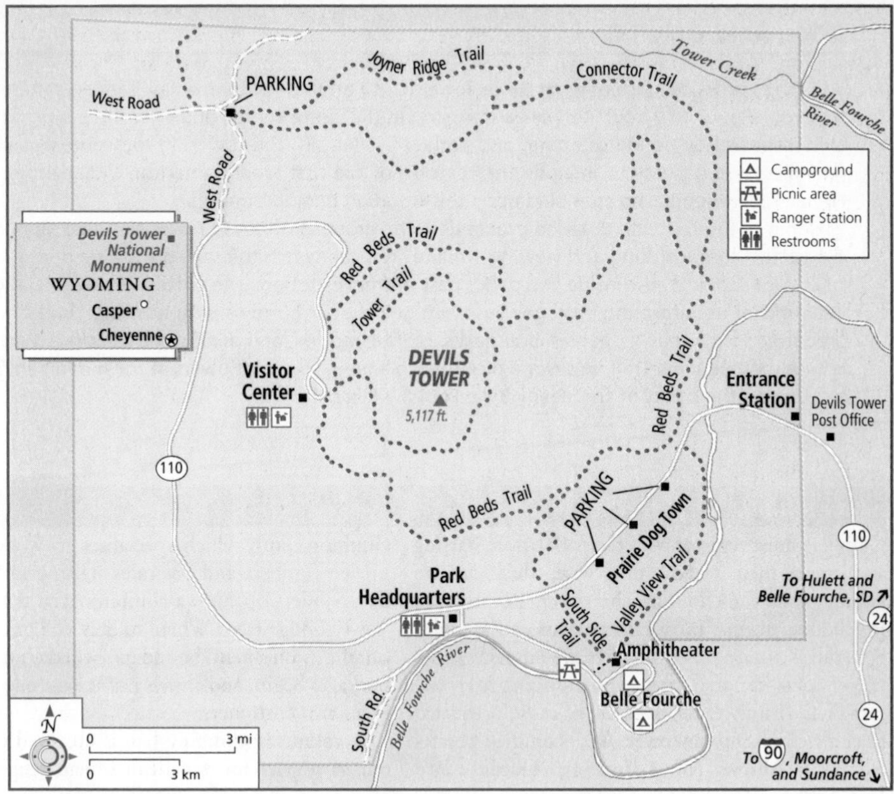

airlines serve **Gillette-Campbell County Airport** (www.iflygillette.com), in Wyoming, with regional commuter flights via Delta, Frontier, and United, and their partners; and Rapid City, South Dakota. For information on the Rapid City airport and car-rental options, see chapter 3, "Badlands National Park."

INFORMATION

Contact **Devils Tower National Monument,** P.O. Box 10, Devils Tower, WY 82714-0010 (✆ **307/467-5283;** www.nps.gov/deto). The **Devils Tower Natural History Association,** P.O. Box 37, Devils Tower, WY 87214-0037 (✆ **307/467-5283**), operates a bookstore at the monument's visitor center and offers a variety of publications.

VISITOR CENTER

Open from early April through November, the visitor center is 3 miles from the monument's entrance. It has exhibits about the tower's history and geology.

FEES

There is an entrance fee of $10 per car or motorcycle, and $5 per person on foot or bike. Camping costs $12 per night.

SPECIAL REGULATIONS & WARNINGS

Do not feed, chase, or disturb prairie dogs; they bite and may carry diseases. Abandoned prairie dog holes are often homes to black widow spiders and rattlesnakes. Disturbing any wildlife or gathering items such as rocks or flowers is prohibited. Also see "Climbing the Tower," below.

SEASONS & CLIMATE

The monument is open year-round. The climate and seasons at Devils Tower echo those in the Black Hills region. Summer days can be hot and dry, although thunderstorms are not uncommon; evenings and early mornings are usually damp and cool. Spring weather is often chilly and rainy, and fall weather is often pleasant but can be cool and often cold at night. Winters are usually cold, but snow and sunlight can combine to create incredible pictures of the landmark.

If You Have Only 1 Day

You can experience much of what Devils Tower has to offer in less than a day. Rangers recommend that you allow 2 to 4 hours to walk a trail, stop at the visitor center, and view the prairie dogs.

Surrounded by ponderosa pines and bathed in blue sky, the towering rock obelisk is visible for miles, and it's easy to imagine the reaction of the first lonely American Indian scouts and French fur trappers who stumbled upon this stunning geologic anomaly.

Home to the feisty black-tailed **prairie dog,** the grounds of Devils Tower National Monument are perfect for picnicking and viewing wildlife. You can watch the sociable prairie dogs in their colony, or "town," just inside the park's east entrance station. The critters excavate elaborate networks of underground passageways, then guard their burrows with warning "barks" when predators such as hawks, eagles, bullsnakes, coyote, red fox, and mink come too close. Walk the leisurely **Valley View Trail,** or savor a picnic lunch among the wildflowers at the monument's picnic area on the banks of the sleepy Belle Fourche River.

2 Climbing the Tower

Climbers must **register** with the park before starting and upon their return; otherwise, there are no requirements for climbing the tower. Be prepared for sudden storms; carry rain gear and a flashlight. Rockfall is common, so helmets are advised. Ask a ranger for additional safety and climbing information. The visitor center has a list of those permitted to guide climbs up the tower. We recommend Frank Sanders's **Above All Climbing Guides and Instruction** (© **888/314-5267;** www.devilstowerclimbing.com), which specializes in working with novice climbers and has rates starting at $300 per day. Sanders operates a climbing gym at his Devils Tower Lodge (see "Where to Stay & Dine," below) on the monument boundary, where introductory packages begin, and always has at least one guide for every two customers.

A voluntary climbing ban is observed each June out of respect for American Indian religious ceremonies on Devils Tower at that time.

3 Organized Tours & Ranger Programs

A variety of talks, walks, and other activities are scheduled, mostly in summer. Check at the visitor center for locations and times.

Interpretive Talks. Meet a park ranger in front of the visitor center for bear tales and interpretive talks about climbing, geology, and tower trivia. Programs last about 20 minutes and are wheelchair accessible.

Tower Walk. Meet a park ranger in front of the visitor center and enjoy a lively walk as the sun rises above the tower. Good walking shoes and water are recommended. These guided walks last about 1½ hours and end on the Tower Trail (see "Day Hikes," below).

Evening Programs. Learn more about America's first national monument by the glow of a campfire. On many nights, you can join a park ranger in the monument's amphitheater from Memorial Day through Labor Day. During inclement weather, programs may move to the picnic shelter.

Cultural Program Series. During the summer, Devils Tower plays host to scholars, artists, and performers who bring their expertise to the monument. They include American Indian storytellers, musicians, historians, costumed interpreters, photographers, poets, and astronomers.

If you're a writer who'd like to be considered for a residency at Devil's Tower (one of the many national parks that offers space to artists), contact Christine Czazasty at © **307/467-5283,** ext. 224, MST or christine_czazasty@nps.gov. For additional information, write to **Writers-In-Residence Program,** Devils Tower National Monument, WY 82714 or Bearlodge Writers, PO Box 10, Devils Tower, WY 82714.

4 Day Hikes

Devils Tower will announce itself (through your windshield) miles before you arrive. In fact, you may drive to within a few hundred yards of the tower, but the real highlight of any nonclimbing visit to Devils Tower is the park's trails; get out and enjoy them. Pets are not allowed on trails.

The paved 1.3-mile **Tower Trail,** rated easy, goes all the way around the tower, offering close-up views of the tower on fairly level ground. Wayside exhibits tell the Devils Tower story.

There are several other trails: the scenic **Red Beds Trail,** 3 miles; **Southside Trail,** .6 mile; **Joyner Ridge Trail,** 1.5 miles; **Valley View Trail,** .6 mile (or you can combine Southside and Valley View for 1.2 miles). None of the trails gets very crowded, so these are a good way to examine the terrain around the monument, including the pine forest and the prairie dog town, and avoid some of the summer crowds.

5 Camping

Located a mile from the monument's headquarters, **Belle Fourche Campground** is open from April through October and rarely fills up except around the Sturgis Motorcycle Rally in August. The campground's 50 sites accommodate RVs (up to 35 ft. long) and tents on a first-come, first-served basis. Each campsite has a cooking grill, table, and nearby drinking water. There are no showers, RV hookups, or dump station. Sites costs $12 per night; there are three group sites, which cost $2 per person per night, with a six-person minimum. The adjacent Valley View Trail skirts a giant prairie dog town. The campground's amphitheater offers excellent interpretive ranger programs.

Those looking for a commercial campground with RV hookups and hot showers will find the **Devils Tower KOA,** P.O. Box 100, Devils Tower, WY 82714 (✆ **800/562-5785** or 307/467-5395; www.devilstowerkoa.com), just outside the monument entrance. Open from May through September, it offers 56 RV sites, 100 tent sites, 11 camping cabins (which share two bathhouses and other campground facilities), and a camping lodge. Rates for two adults are $25 to $80 in hookup sites, $20 to $60 for tents, $75 to $300 for the camping lodge, and $45 to $80 for cabins (DISC, MC, V). Amenities include a heated outdoor pool, self-service laundry, free Wi-Fi, game room, cafe, two gift shops (featuring homemade fudge), horseback rides, hayrides, propane sales, and a nightly showing of *Close Encounters of the Third Kind* Memorial Day to Labor Day, which was filmed in part at Devils Tower.

6 Where to Stay & Dine

There are no lodging facilities or restaurants within the monument boundaries.

NEAR THE PARK

Recommended in Sundance is the **Bear Lodge,** 218 Cleveland St., on Wyo. 14 at Business Loop I-90 (P.O. Box 912), Sundance, WY 82729 (✆ **307/283-1611;** fax 307/283-2537; www.bearlodgemotel.com). It offers 32 well-maintained basic motel rooms, all air-conditioned and with TVs, free Wi-Fi, and phones. The double rate is about $64 to $68 during the summer and fall, and a bit less in winter and spring. Major credit cards (AE, DISC, MC, V) are accepted. Another good choice is the **Best Western Inn at Sundance,** 2719 E. Cleveland, at I-90 exit 189 (P.O. Box 927), Sundance, WY 82729 (✆ **800/238-0965** or 307/283-2800; fax 307/283-2727). It offers everything you would expect from a top-notch Best Western, at rates of $120 to $130 double in summer, and lower prices from fall through spring.

There are two moderately priced restaurants, open year-round, across the street from the Best Value Inn Bear Lodge: **Aro Restaurant,** 203 Cleveland St. (✆ **307/283-2000**), is open daily from 7am to 9pm in summer, with slightly shorter hours in winter. It serves a home-style American menu of sandwiches, burgers, and steak, plus a few Mexican dishes, with lunch prices from $4 to $8 and dinner prices from $8 to $20. **Higbee's Café,** 101 N. 3rd St. (✆ **307/283-2165**), generally serves breakfast and lunch Monday through Friday, plus dinner on Wednesday. It offers homemade soups and a variety of sandwiches, with most prices from $4 to $6, and serves breakfast anytime.

Immediately outside of the monument's boundaries, climbing guru Frank Sanders runs the **Devils Tower Lodge,** P.O. Box 66, Devils Tower, WY 82714 (✆ **888/314-5267** or 307/467-5267; www.devilstowerlodge.com), an eclectic yet nicely appointed four-room B&B in the former superintendent's residence. The rooms all have private bathrooms; the facilities are geared toward climbers, and the communal mood makes guests feel as if they're staying in a home instead of an inn. Room rates ($150–$225) include full breakfast; dinners (about $12) are available upon request. Checks and credit cards (MC, V) are accepted.

In Hulett, try the **Hulett Motel,** 202 Main St., Hulett, WY 82720 (✆ **307/467-5220;** www.hulettmotel.com). Double rates are $65 to $85; major credit cards (MC, V) are accepted. Rooms are well maintained, and there's also a row of trim and tidy cabins on the Belle Fourche River.

15

Glacier National Park, MT & Waterton Lakes National Park, AB

by Eric Peterson

Majestic and wild, this vast preserve beckons visitors with stunning mountain peaks (many covered year-round with glaciers), verdant mountain trails, and a huge diversity of plant and animal life. Every spring, Glacier is a postcard come to life: Wildflowers carpet its meadows; bears emerge from months of hibernation; and moose, elk, and deer play out the drama of birth, life, and death. The unofficial mascot in these parts is the grizzly, a refugee from the high plains.

Here you'll see nature at work: The glaciers are receding (the result of global warming, many say), and avalanches have periodically ravaged Going-to-the-Sun Road, the curving, scenic 50-mile road across the park. For the time being, the park is intact and very much alive, a treasure in a vault that opens to visitors.

Named in honor of the slow-moving glaciers that carved awe-inspiring valleys throughout this expanse of over 1 million acres, Glacier National Park exists because of the efforts of George Bird Grinnell, a 19th-century magazine publisher and cofounder of the Audubon Society. Following a pattern established with Yellowstone and Grand Teton, Grinnell lobbied for a national park to be set aside in the St. Mary region of Montana, and in May 1910 his efforts were rewarded. Just over 20 years later, it became, with its northern neighbor Waterton Lakes National Park in Canada, **Glacier-Waterton International Peace Park**—a gesture of goodwill and friendship between the governments of two countries.

If your time is limited, motor along Going-to-the-Sun Road, viewing the dramatic mountain scenery. Visitors with more time will find diversions for both families and hard-core adventurers; while some hiking trails are suitable for tykes, many more will challenge those determined to conquer and scale the park's tallest peaks. The park's lakes, streams, ponds, and waterfalls are equally engaging. Travelers board cruise boats to explore the history of the area; recreational types can fish, row, and kayak.

To truly experience the park requires more effort, interest, and spunk than a simple drive through—abandon the pavement for even a short, easy hiking trail, and you'll discover a window into Glacier's soul.

AVOIDING THE CROWDS

The simplest way to leave the crowds behind is to avoid visiting the park in its peak season, from mid-June to Labor Day. July is the busiest month. Late September and October, when fall colors light up the park, are excellent months to visit. A highlight is the display the larch trees put on throughout the western portions of the park. Entire hillsides turn bright yellow, fading to a dull orange glow as October wanes.

If visiting in the off season isn't possible, consider the following: Find a trail head that is equidistant from two major points, and head for the woods. Because most people congregate in proximity to the major hotels, this strategy should gain you a measure of solitude. If you must drive, to make the trip more enjoyable (and traffic-free), journey across the Going-to-the-Sun Road before 8:30am; you'll be astounded at the masterful job Mother Nature does of painting her mountains. You can always see more wildlife in the early morning (or just before dark) than at other times.

1 Essentials

GETTING THERE & GATEWAYS

Glacier National Park is in the northwest corner of Montana, on the Canadian border. The closest cities with airline service are **Kalispell,** 29 miles southwest of the park; **Great Falls,** 200 miles southeast; and **Missoula,** 150 miles south. If you're driving, the easiest ways to reach the park are from **U.S. 2** and **U.S. 89.**

Among the park's entrances are those at West Glacier, Camas Road, St. Mary, Many Glacier, Two Medicine, and Polebridge. Access is primarily at either end of Going-to-the-Sun Road: at West Glacier on the southwest side and St. Mary on the east.

From the park's western boundary, you may enter at Polebridge to reach Bowman and Kintla lakes or take Camas Road to Going-to-the-Sun Road.

Glacier National Park

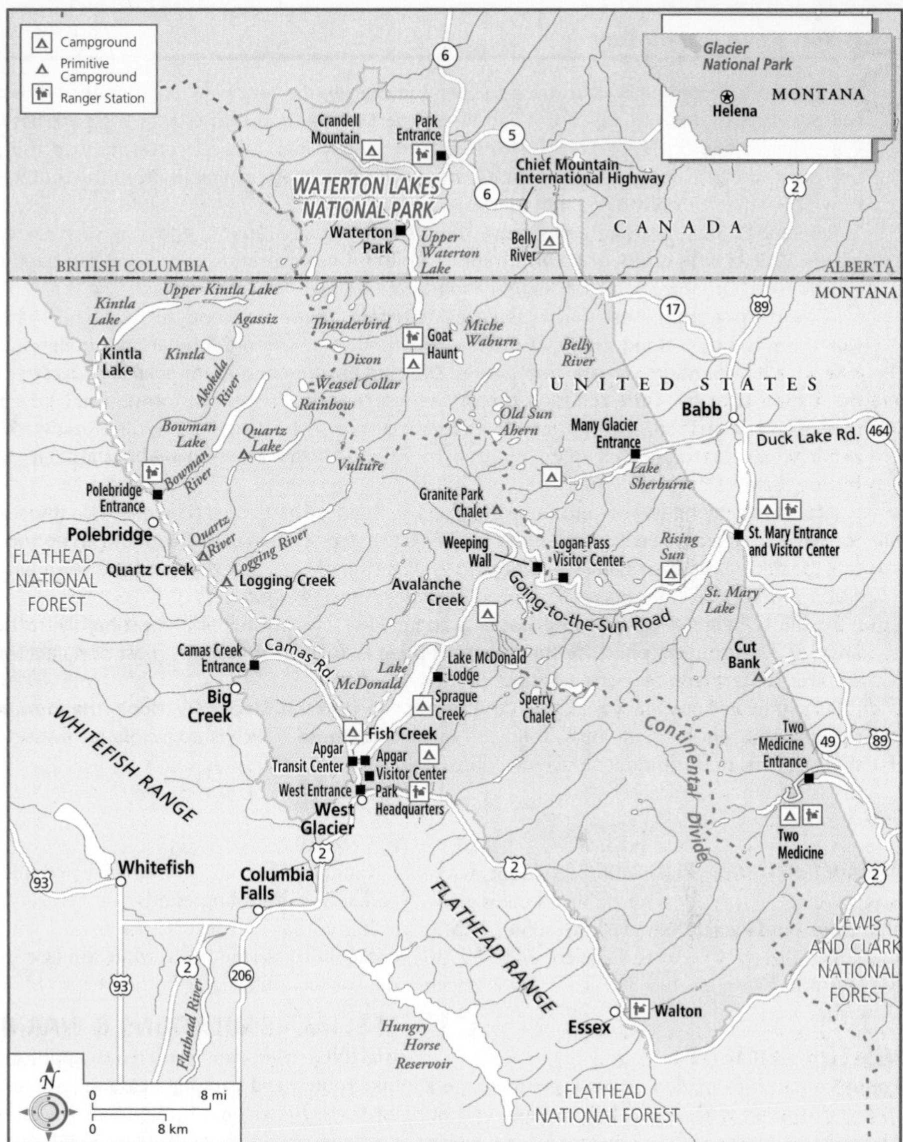

The following east-side entrances are primarily hiking trails designed to access specific places and do not necessarily take you into the heart of the park: Essex, East Glacier, Two Medicine, Cut Bank, and Many Glacier.

Visitor entrance passes are sold at the West Glacier, Two Medicine, Many Glacier, Polebridge, and St. Mary Park entrances. Entrance is restricted during the winter, when most of Going-to-the-Sun Road is closed. (See "Seasons & Climate," below.)

THE NEAREST AIRPORTS **Glacier Park International Airport,** north of Kalispell at 4170 U.S. 2 (✆ **406/257-5994;** www.glacierairport.com), is serviced by United, Allegiant, Delta, and Horizon. Avis, Budget, Hertz, and National have counters at the airport. The airports in Missoula and Great Falls are within a relatively easy drive of Glacier as well. See chapter 38 for websites of the major airlines, car-rental companies, and hotel/motel chains.

BY RAIL **Amtrak's *Empire Builder*** (✆ **800/872-7245;** www.amtrak.com), a Chicago-Seattle round-trip train, stops between May 1 and October 1 at East Glacier and year-round at West Glacier and Essex.

INFORMATION

Contact the Superintendent, **Glacier National Park,** P.O. Box 128 West Glacier, MT 59936

If You Have Only 1 Day

If you have a limited amount of time to spend in Glacier, the best way to experience the park's full beauty is to drive **Going-to-the-Sun Road,** the 50-mile road that crosses the park between West Glacier and St. Mary. Points of interest are clearly marked and correspond to the park brochure *Points of Interest Along the Going to the Sun Road,* available at visitor centers and downloadable from **www.nps.gov/glac** as a podcast.

Remember that the road gains more than 3,400 feet in 32 miles, and it is very narrow in places. Visitors with a fear of heights might consider a guided van tour or using the park's free shuttle (see "Organized Tours & Ranger Programs," below).

A short drive from West Glacier is **Lake McDonald,** the largest body of water in the park. Numerous turnouts along the way present opportunities to photograph panoramic views of the lake with its mountainous backdrop. **Sacred Dancing Cascade** and **Johns Lake** are visible by taking a short hike from the roadside through a red cedar and hemlock forest. You'll often see moose and waterfowl. The **Trail of the Cedars** is a short, wheelchair-accessible boardwalk trail rich in vibrant, verdant hues. All hiking trails mentioned below are described in the "Day Hikes" section, below.

Almost exactly halfway along Going-to-the-Sun Road is **The Loop,** an excellent vantage point for views of **Heaven's Peak.** Just 2 miles farther is the **Bird Woman Falls Overlook,** an outlook for falls located across the valley. The **Weeping Wall,** a wall of rock that does, in fact, weep groundwater profusely in the summer, is a popular subject for photographers.

At the 32-mile mark from West Glacier is **Logan Pass,** one of the park's most highly trafficked areas and the starting point for the hike to **Hidden Lake,** one of Glacier's most popular. There's a visitor center here, atop the Continental Divide.

As you head downhill, you'll reach the turnout for **Jackson Glacier Overlook,** the most easily recognizable glacier in the park, followed by **Sunrift Gorge,** which is accessible via a short trail that presents opportunities to view wildlife.

(✆ **406/888-7800;** TDD 406/888-7806; www.nps.gov/glac). A vast array of publications is available from the **Glacier Association,** 12544 U.S. 2 E., (P.O. Box 310), West Glacier, MT 59936 (✆ **406/888-5756;** fax 406/888-5271; www.glacierassociation.org).

VISITOR CENTERS

For up-to-date information on park activities, check in at visitor centers at **Apgar, Logan Pass,** and **St. Mary;** Travel Alberta staffs a center at **West Glacier.** St. Mary is open from mid-June through mid-October; Logan Pass, from mid-June through late September; and Apgar, from May through October (and weekends during the winter). Park information is also available from the **Two Medicine, Polebridge,** and **Many Glacier** ranger stations or from park headquarters.

FEES & PERMITS

A vehicle pass good for 7 days costs $25; an individual pass for walk-ins, bicycle riders, and motorcyclists, also good for 7 days, is $12. In winter, the fees drop to $15 and free, respectively. An annual park pass costs $35. Visitors to Waterton Lakes National Park (which is located in Canada) pay a separate entrance fee.

Camping fees are $10 to $23 per night at the park's drive-in campgrounds.

If you plan to backpack overnight, you'll need a backcountry permit before your trip (see "Exploring the Backcountry," later in this chapter).

SPECIAL REGULATIONS & WARNINGS

BIKING Bikes are restricted to established roads, bike routes, and parking areas, and are not allowed on trails. Restrictions apply to the most hazardous portions of Going-to-the-Sun Road during peak travel times, from around mid-June to Labor Day; call ahead to find out when the road will be closed to bikers. During low-visibility periods of fog or darkness, a white front light and a red back reflector are required.

BOATING Although boating is permitted on some of Glacier's lakes, motor size is restricted to 10 horsepower on Bowman and Two Medicine lakes. A detailed list of other regulations is available at park headquarters and staffed ranger stations. Park rangers may inspect or board any boat to determine regulation compliance.

FISHING A fishing license is not required within the park's boundaries; however, there are guidelines, so check with rangers at visitor centers or ranger stations for regulations. Also keep in mind that the eastern boundary of the park abuts the Blackfeet Indian Reservation, so you may find yourself fishing in their territorial waters. To avoid a problem, purchase a $20 use permit from businesses in the gateway towns; the permit covers fishing, hiking, and biking in the reservation. Fishing outside the park in Montana waters requires a state license; check in at a local fishing shop to make certain you're within the law.

HORSES Although visitors may bring their own horses and pack animals into the park, restrictions apply to private stock. A free brochure detailing regulations regarding horseback riding is available from the Park Service.

VEHICLES RVs and vehicles longer than 21 feet or wider than 8 feet are prohibited on the 24-mile stretch of Going-to-the-Sun Road between Avalanche Campground and Sun Point on St. Mary Lake; vehicles over 10 feet are discouraged. Snowmobiling is prohibited in the park.

SEASONS & CLIMATE

Glacier is magnificent at any time of the year, but some roads are closed and park access is limited in the winter. By far the most popular time to visit is during the summer, when Going-to-the-Sun Road is fully open; in summer, sunrise is around 5am and sunset is nearly 10pm, so you have plenty of time for exploring. Spring and fall are equally magnificent, with budding wildflowers and variegated leaves and trees, but these sights can be viewed only from the park's outer boundaries and a limited stretch of the scenic highway.

In winter, Glacier shuts itself off from much of the motorized world. Going-to-the-Sun Road, which is generally fully open only from mid-June to mid-September, is usually plowed from West Glacier to the head of Lake McDonald. U.S. 89 provides access to the St. Mary area. The North Fork Road from Columbia Falls is open for winter travel to North Fork and the Polebridge Ranger Station. Temperatures sometimes drop to –30°F (–34°C), so appropriate dress is essential.

2 Exploring the Park by Car

Because of the massive mountains that surround Glacier National Park, visitors inevitably compare it to Grand Teton. Perhaps the most significant difference is that here one drives among the mountain peaks; at Teton, you view the mountains from a distance, unless you're willing to head for the hiking trails.

Going-to-the-Sun Road is by far the most driver-friendly avenue on which to enjoy the park and see some of the more spectacular views. See the previous section, "If You Have Only 1 Day," for an idea of what you'll see along this road.

You can easily circumnavigate the lower half of the park in 1 long day, without traveling at warp speed. Along the way, you'll get a bird's-eye view of Big Sky country. After a leisurely breakfast in West Glacier, you'll be in East Glacier in plenty of time for lunch at the Glacier Park Lodge (see "Where to Stay," later in this chapter) and at St. Mary or Many Glacier for dinner. (***Note:*** Going-to-the-Sun Road's multiyear rehabilitation will cause 30-min. to 4-hr. delays for several years.)

U.S. 2 between West Glacier and East Glacier, which is approximately 57 miles, is a well-paved, two-lane affair that winds circuitously around the western and southern edges of the park and follows the Middle Fork of the Flathead River. In the summertime, you'll see inner tubes and white-water rafts galore. As you descend to the valley floor, you'll drive through beautiful Montana ranchland and farmland. Shortly after entering the valley, look to the north and admire the park's massive peaks—spires as beautiful as any on the planet. The Goat Lick parking lot, on U.S. 2 just east of Essex, gets you off the beaten path and provides a view into a canyon carved by the Flathead River; if you have time, take the short hike down to the stream and look on the hillside for mountain goats.

Beyond East Glacier, as you head northwest on Mont. 49 and west toward Two Medicine, you'll notice that the earth appears to fall off. The contrast is inescapable—mountains tower in the west, but to the east the Hi-Line begins, with a horizon that extends far and flat. But round a corner on the Two

Picnicking Tips

The best picnicking spot on the Going-to-the-Sun Road is at **Sun Point,** which is also the trail head for the 1.6-mile round-trip to Baring Falls, a trail that follows the shoreline of the lake. From the picnic area, the views across the lake to the mountains are unrivaled. Even better: Be there at sunrise.

Medicine Road, and suddenly you'll find yourself faced with three mountains (Appistocki Peak, Mount Henry, and Bison Mountain), bare of vegetation, but as red as their Southwest counterparts. The difference here is that snow fills the crevasses, even in mid-August. Ten miles later, continuing the route north on U.S. 89, you'll come across a wide panorama of mountain peaks, valleys, ridges, and forested mountains that truly characterize Glacier's personality. Conclude the bottom half of your long loop by winding downward from these high elevations to the village of St. Mary. Not a bad day's drive!

There are two ways to see the park's western boundary and to reach the Polebridge area, in the north; one is slow and uncomfortable, the other slightly faster and less uncomfortable. The **North Fork Road** (Mont. 486) from Columbia Falls takes about an hour to negotiate. It's a sometimes-paved (mostly gravel and pothole-filled) stretch that follows the North Fork of the Flathead River; spectacular views ameliorate the condition of the drive. Not much is there besides water and scenery, but the area around Polebridge is a popular spot for the outdoor crowd—an excellent location to experience Montana's natural beauty.

The **Inside North Fork Road,** just north of Apgar, also runs to Polebridge. However, it's totally unpaved, takes an hour longer, and is much harder on driver, passenger, and equipment. Unless you are a glutton for punishment, take the faster route and spend that extra hour relaxing on a riverbank.

3 Organized Tours & Ranger Programs

Ranger-guided activities and evening campfire and slide-show programs run daily throughout the park. The park's *Glacier Visitor Guide* publication—free upon entering the park and also available at visitor centers—is a thorough source for days, times, and locations of various educational programs. Local tribal members provide programs highlighting **American Indian culture and history.** Most programs are free; there may be a minimal charge for some of the American Indian programs and those including boat trips.

For kids, there is a **Junior Ranger** program with an activity book; backpacks with kid-oriented naturalist activities can also be checked out at the St. Mary and Apgar visitor centers.

The park offers a **free shuttle bus service.** Visitors simply park their cars at the Apgar Transit Center on the west side or the St. Mary Visitor Center and take the shuttle to about 20 stops throughout the park, most of them on Going-to-the-Sun Road. The shuttles connecting the two lots run from about 7am to 7pm. For detailed information on the schedule and routes, visit the park's website or check the insert in the *Glacier Visitor Guide.*

Glacier Park Boat Co., P.O. Box 5262, Kalispell, MT 59903 (✆ **406/257-2426;** www.glacierparkboats.com), offers narrated boat tours from Lake McDonald, St. Mary, Two Medicine, and Many Glacier from mid-June to mid-September. These "scenicruises" combine the comfort of an hour-long lake cruise with a short hike or picnic. Spectacular views of Lake McDonald sunsets, the awe-inspiring Grinnell Glacier, and the panoramic rugged cliffs ringing St. Mary Lake are just a few of the possible photo opportunities you may have while aboard. The boats typically depart every hour, usually seven times each day (although schedules are subject to change in late season or if the weather is inclement). Ticket prices top out at $22. Check ahead for a complete listing of prices and departure times. The concessionaire also offers charter service for larger groups and guided hikes in the park.

"Jammer" coach tours run along Going-to-the-Sun Road and north to Waterton. Thirty-three classic bright-red coaches from the 1930s, long identified with Glacier, are in service after a restoration project that began in 1999. Drivers provide insightful commentary about the park and its history, and you don't have to worry about how close you may be to the edge of the often-precipitous road! Full-day rates are about $80 for adults and about $40 for children, with tours departing from both sides of the park. Half-day tours (for about half the price) are also available. For schedules, contact **Glacier Park Inc.** (✆ **406/892-2525;** www.glacierparkinc.com).

Historical-cultural 25-passenger **motor coach tours** of Going-to-the-Sun Road conducted by knowledgeable guides from the Blackfeet Nation originate from West Glacier, East Glacier, Browning, and St. Mary. Rates start at $40 for a 4-hour trip and $75 for a full day. Contact **Suntours** (✆ **800/786-9220;** www.glaciersuntours.com).

Scenic **helicopter tours** are offered by **Glacier Heli Tours** (✆ **800/879-9310** or 406/387-4141; www.glacierhelitours.net) and **Kruger Helicop-Tours** (✆ **800/220-6565** or 406/387-4565; www.krugerhelicopters.com). Prices start at $110 per person for four people for a half-hour trip.

The **Glacier Institute,** 137 Main St. (P.O. Box 1887), Kalispell, MT 59903 (✆ **406/755-1211;** www.glacierinstitute.org), conducts summer field classes that examine the park's cultural and natural resources. These 1- to 4-day courses include instruction, transportation, park fees, and college credit.

Picture This: Glacier Park Photo Tips

The adventurous shutterbug will find that the best photo ops occur early in the morning. Near bodies of water, the sunrise provides a multitude of oranges, blues, and yellows. Then, as the earth warms, lakes are transformed to fog-covered valleys, creating a mystical photographic opportunity.

One of the most picturesque spots is the west end of St. Mary Lake; not only does sunrise paint the lake orange and yellow, but it paints the mountains red and orange. A close runner-up is the view west from an overlook across St. Mary Lake to Wild Goose Island in the foreground and the peaks and glaciers at the west end of the lake. Logan Pass, when it's carpeted with wildflowers, is breathtaking.

Late-day photos of the Garden Wall from west of Logan Pass are also very dramatic.

Highly skilled instructors bring an intimate knowledge of the region and subject matter to each course. The classroom is Glacier National Park and other areas in northwest Montana; courses cover wildflowers, grizzlies, weather systems, and nature photography. Prices range from $65 to $850 per course. (The pricier classes include lodging.) Contact the institute or visit the website for a listing of the current catalog.

Finally, **Glacier Guides,** P.O. Box 330, West Glacier, MT 59936 (✆ **800/521-7238** or 406/387-5555; www.glacierguides.com), organizes backpacking trips into the Glacier National Park backcountry. The company has been the exclusive backpacking guide service in the park since 1983. See "Exploring the Backcountry," below.

4 Day Hikes

With more than 700 miles of maintained trails, the park is best explored by hiking. Because most of these trails are rather short, you might also wish to check out "Exploring the Backcountry," below. Many of the longer trails described there can be done fully (or at least partially) in a day, and are likely to take you farther off the beaten path than the shorter routes, and away from the crowds.

Trail maps are available at outdoor stores in Whitefish and Kalispell, as well as at visitor centers and the major ranger stations at each entry point. The park's new free shuttle can take you to numerous trail heads; there is a comprehensive guide in the *Glacier Visitor Guide* newspaper. **Glacier Park Inc.** (✆ **406/892-2525**) also operates a **hiker's shuttle** on the east side to get people from St. Mary to Many Glacier, Waterton, and East Glacier.

Before setting off, check with the nearest visitor center or ranger station to determine the accessibility of your destination, trail conditions, and recent bear sightings. It can be a bummer when, 10 miles into a trip, a ranger turns you back.

The Park Service asks you to stay on trails to keep from eroding the park's fragile components. Also, do not traverse snowbanks, especially the steeper ones. Before approaching any trail head, you should have proper footwear and rain gear, enough food, and, most importantly, enough water. A can of **pepper spray** can also come in handy when you're in grizzly habitat. If you plan on hiking in Canada, be sure the spray is USEPA-approved. Contact **Canadian Customs** (✆ **204/983-3500** or 506/636-5064) for regulations. See "Exploring the Backcountry," below, for more information.

LAKE MCDONALD AREA

Trail of the Cedars Nature Trail This level trail, consisting of a wheelchair-accessible boardwalk, offers a respite from the crowds in a forested area. There are interpretive signs along the way. .75 mile RT. Easy. Access: Across from Avalanche Campground Ranger Station.

Trout Lake This is a good workout if you're around Lake McDonald Lodge, sipping coffee and skipping rocks off the lake. The hike is straight up and straight down, 2,100 feet each way. The trail takes you from the north end of Lake McDonald to the foot of Trout Lake and back. 8.4 miles RT. Moderate. Access: North end of Lake McDonald, 1½ miles west on Lake McDonald Rd.

LOGAN PASS AREA

Hidden Lake Overlook Nature Trail This trail climbs 460 feet and requires more spunk than others in the area, yet it's not too hard. It's a popular trail, but if you go past the overlook up to the lake, you'll get past most of the crowds. This is an interpretive nature trail, with signs along the way that

Voices

Give a month to this precious reserve. The time will not be taken from the sum of your life. Instead of shortening, it will indefinitely lengthen it and make you truly immortal.

—John Muir, naturalist and conservationist

point out what you are seeing. 3 miles RT. Easy to moderate. Access: Logan Pass Visitor Center.

The Loop Not considered easy mainly because of its altitude gain of 2,200 feet, The Loop is a popular hiking trail that winds up to Granite Park Chalet and back. Many people use it as a continuation of the Highline Trail (see below), but this is the section to do if you're short on time. The Highline Trail is 7.6 miles one-way to the chalets, but not nearly as steep as the Loop; see the descriptions of the chalets under "Camping," below. If you want to spend the night in a chalet, contact **Granite Park Chalet** for reservations (✆ **888/345-2649;** www.graniteparkchalet.com). 8 miles RT. Moderate. Access: Along Going-to-the-Sun Rd., about halfway btw. Avalanche Campground and Logan Pass Visitor Center.

Sunrift Gorge Trail Most hikers approach Siyeh Pass from the Piegan Pass trail head, but we prefer ascending to this gorgeous glacial valley from Sunrift Gorge. The creekside trail climbs through a forest and switches back to reveal a hanging glacier and several waterfalls, before ascending the pass up a wall that is prime bighorn habitat. 11.2 miles RT. Difficult. Access: Sunrift Gorge parking area, 10 miles west of St. Mary.

MANY GLACIER AREA

Iceberg Lake This beautiful hike traverses flower-filled meadows to a high lake backed against a mountain wall. Even in summer, there may be snow on the ground and ice floating in the lake. Look for mountain goats or bighorn sheep on the cliffs above. As in many of the backcountry areas, keep an eye out for the grizzlies. 9.6 miles RT. Moderate. Access: Trail head in a cabin area east of the Swiftcurrent Coffee Shop and Campstore.

Swiftcurrent Nature Trail This is a fun hike along the shore, through the woods, and near a marsh. You may see deer and birds—keep an eye out for blue grouse. If you have time, continue on the trail as it circles Lake Josephine, another easy hike that adds 2.8 miles to the trip. Dramatic Mount Gould towers above the far end of the lake. Midsummer wildflowers can be spectacular. Access to a longer, 10-mile round-trip trail to Grinnell Glacier, the park's largest, is also from this area. 2.5 miles RT. Easy. Access: Picnic area ½ mile west of the hotel turnoff.

TWO MEDICINE AREA

Appistoki Falls This trail, with an elevation gain of only 260 feet, climbs through a forest of fir and spruce, then runs along Appistoki Creek before ending at an overlook that provides views of a 65-foot waterfall. 1.2 miles RT. Easy. Access: ¼ mile east of Two Medicine Ranger Station.

Running Eagle Falls Hardly even a hike, the easiest trail in the area leads to Running Eagle Falls along a path that winds through a heavily forested area to a large, noisy waterfall. The path is wheelchair accessible. .6 miles RT. Easy. Access: 1 mile west of the Two Medicine entrance.

Twin Falls Trail The most popular hiking path in this area is the one to Twin Falls, which originates at the campground. Hikers may walk the entire distance to Twin Falls on a clearly identified trail, or boat across Two Medicine Lake to the foot of the trail head and hike the last mile. 7.6 miles RT. Easy. Access: Two Medicine Campground.

5 Exploring the Backcountry

Depending upon your point of view, negotiating the backcountry may translate to a leisurely stroll or a strenuous experience in the high country. Choices range from 4-mile day hikes to multiday treks, so consider your experience and fitness level before heading out. Study a park map that illustrates trails and campsites in the area you want to explore.

Backcountry campgrounds have maps at the entrance to show you the location of each campground, the pit toilet, food-preparation areas, and, perhaps most important, food-storage areas. In addition, you can obtain a free loan of bear-resistant food containers at most backcountry permit-issuing stations. If you fish while camping, it's recommended you exercise catch-and-release to avoid attracting wildlife in search of food. If you eat the catch, be certain to puncture the air bladder and throw the entrails into deep water at least 200 feet from the nearest campsite or trail. When backpacking in Glacier, especially in the high country, it's important to remember to pack as lightly as possible and make sure you're aware of the trail's degree of ascent. And remember the cardinal rule: Pack it in, pack it out. No exceptions.

Wherever you decide to go, remember that you must secure a **backcountry permit** before your overnight trip. Advance reservations can be made June 15 to October 31 for $30; a fee of $5 per night per camper is also charged. Call ✆ **406/888-7857** for additional information.

A Guided Backcountry Trip. Many folks like to let someone else make the arrangements, leaving themselves free to concentrate on the hiking experience. The exclusive backpacking guide service in Glacier National Park is **Glacier Guides,** P.O. Box 330, West Glacier, MT 59936 (✆ **800/521-7238** for reservations, or 406/387-5555; www.glacierguides.com). For a price, the company will put together any kind of trip; it has several regularly scheduled throughout the season, from the end of June through the beginning of September. These include a 3-day "taste" of the park for about $450 per person, and an entire week in the wilderness for about $850 per person. Custom trips run $150 a day per person, with a four-person minimum. Glacier Guides will even organize a trip that lets you spend the day hiking and the night cuddled in a comfy inn inside the park or in the Granite Park Chalet (see "Camping," below). Gear rentals are also available.

The main office is 1½ miles west of West Glacier on U.S. 2. For information and reservations, contact the company.

KINTLA LAKE AREA

Kintla Lake to Upper Kintla Lake Skirting the north shore of Kintla Lake above Polebridge for about 7 miles, before climbing a couple of hundred feet, this stretch of the Boulder Pass hike is a breeze. However, once you hit Kintla Creek, you may want to reconsider going farther. With 12 miles under your belt at this point, climbing 3,000 feet may not seem like a great idea. The trail, once it breaks into the clear, offers views of several peaks, including Kinnerly Peak to the south of Upper Kintla Lake. 12 miles one-way. Moderate. Access: Kintla Lake Campground.

POLEBRIDGE AREA

Bowman Lake This trail (14 miles to Brown Pass) is similar to the Kintla Lake hike in difficulty and, like the Kintla Lake Trail, passes the lake on the north. After a hike through rolling hills sheathed in foliage, the trail climbs out of reach for anyone not in top shape, ascending 2,000 feet in less than 3 miles to join the Kintla Lake Trail at Brown Pass. A left turn takes you back to Kintla Lake (23 miles), and a right takes you to Goat Haunt at the foot of Waterton Lake (9 miles). 7.1 miles one-way. Moderate. Access: Bowman Lake Campground; follow Glacier Rte. 7 to Bowman Lake Rd., just north of Polebridge, then follow signs to Bowman Lake Campground.

Quartz Lake The loop runs up and over an 1,800-foot ridge and down to the south end of Lower Quartz Lake. From there it's a level 3-mile hike to the west end of Quartz Lake, then 6 miles back over the ridge farther north (and higher up) before dropping back to Bowman Lake. An interesting aspect of this trail is evidence of the Red Bench Fire of 1988, which took a chunk out of the North Fork area. 12 miles RT. Moderate. Access: Bowman Lake Picnic Area; cross the bridge over Bowman Creek and you're on your way.

LOGAN PASS AREA

Highline Trail This relatively easy hike gains a mere 200 feet in elevation over 7.6 miles. It begins at the Logan Pass Visitor Center and skirts the Garden Wall at heights of over 6,000 feet to Granite Park Chalet. Give yourself plenty of time for the return hike to Logan Pass. Or, rather than retracing your steps, continue from the chalet to The Loop, the aptly named section of Going-to-the-Sun Road. The trail terminates here (an additional 3.5 miles), although you'll need to plan for a shuttle back to your car. (It's also possible to continue all the way to Upper Waterton Lake, but if you do, you should allow 3 days for the trip.) 12 miles one-way (including The Loop). Moderate. Access: Granite Park Chalet.

TWO MEDICINE AREA

Pitamakan Pass Trail This trail presents several options: You can take one or two long day hikes, or you can use it as the jumping-off point for an extended trip. From the trail head, the path winds to Old Man Lake and a campground, and then up 2,400 feet to Pitamakan Pass. At this point, your options are to return on the same trail or to continue to Dawson Pass, through Twin Falls, and then back to the campground, which adds about 10 miles to the trip and completes the loop. Or you could head north on the Cut Bank or Nyack Creek trails, which will add days to your trip. 6.9 miles one-way. Moderate. Access: Two Medicine Campground.

6 Other Summer Sports & Activities

BOATING At Apgar and Lake McDonald, you will find kayaks, canoes, rowboats, and motorboats for rent; gas-powered outboard motors of 10 horsepower or less are permitted at Two Medicine Lake and Bowman Lake. You can also rent kayaks, canoes, rowboats, and electric motorboats at Two Medicine. At Many Glacier, you can rent kayaks, canoes, and rowboats. For details, contact **Glacier Park Boat Co.** (✆ **406/257-2426;** www.glacierparkboats.com).

FISHING The crystal-clear mountain streams and lakes of Glacier are home to many native species of trout. Anglers looking to hook a big one should try the North Fork of the Flathead for cutthroat, and any of the three larger lakes in the park (Bowman Lake, St. Mary Lake, and Lake McDonald) for lake trout and cutthroat. For equipment or sage advice, or to schedule a guided foray ($325 for one or two people for a half-day), contact **Glacier Anglers** (✆ **800/235-6781;** www.glacierraftco.com), at the Glacier Outdoor Center in West Glacier.

HORSEBACK RIDING If you want to saddle up Old Paint and take an Old West approach to transportation, **Swan Mountain Outfitters** (✆ **406/888-5121** or 406/732-4203; www.swanmountainoutfitters.com) offers horseback riding at Lake McDonald, Apgar Village, and Many Glacier. The company offers hourly ($40) to half-day rides ($105) into the nearby wilderness.

KAYAKING Most kayaking in the park involves passages across lakes; the most popular are Bowman Lake and Lake McDonald. Inquire at any ranger station for details and conditions (for rentals, see "Boating," above).

MOUNTAIN CLIMBING The peaks of Glacier Park rarely exceed elevations of 10,000 feet, but these are incredibly difficult climbs; you must inquire at a visitor center or ranger station regarding climbing conditions and closures. In general, the peaks are unsuitable except for experienced climbers or those traveling with experienced guides. The park administration does not recommend climbing because of the unstable nature of the rock.

RAFTING & FLOAT TRIPS Though the waters in the park don't lend themselves to white-water rafting, the boundary forks of the Flathead River are some of the best in the northwest corner of the state. For just taking it easy and floating along in the summer sun, the North Fork of the Flathead River stretching from Polebridge to Columbia Falls and into Flathead Lake is ideal. The same may be said for the Middle Fork of the Flathead, which forms the southern border of the park.

For white-water voyagers, the North Fork of the Flathead River (classes II and III) and the Middle Fork (class III) are the best bets. Flow rates change dramatically as snow melts or storms move through the area; inquire at any ranger station for details and conditions.

The Middle Fork is a little more severe and isn't the sort of river you enjoy with an umbrella drink in hand. The names of certain stretches of the Middle Fork are instructive (the Narrows, Jaws, Bonecrusher), but you can book a trip with several outfitters that offer expert, sanctioned guides.

Established in 1975, **Glacier Raft Company,** P.O. Box 210, West Glacier, MT 59936 (✆ **800/235-6781** or 406/888-5454; www.glacierraftco.com), is Montana's oldest raft company. Offerings include half-day trips ($48 adult, $36 child), full-day excursions ($82 adult, $59 child), 2-day trips ($335 adult, $275 child), and 3-day outings ($455 adult, $370 child). Prices include all necessary equipment and food. The company also offers scenic trips, inflatable-kayak rentals, and other services. Other local raft guides include **Great Northern Whitewater,** 12127 U.S. 2 East (P.O. Box 270), West Glacier, MT 59936 (✆ **800/735-7897;** www.gnwhitewater.com); **Montana Raft Company,** P.O. Box 330, West Glacier, MT 59936 (✆ **800/521-7238** or 406/387-5555; www.glacierguides.com); and **Wild River Adventures,** P.O. Box 272, West Glacier, MT 59936 (✆ **800/700-7056** or 406/387-9453; www.riverwild.com).

7 Winter Sports & Activities

All unplowed roads become trails for snowshoers and cross-country skiers, who rave about the vast powdered wonderland here. Guided trips into the backcountry are a great way to experience the park in winter, or you can strap on a pair of snowshoes and explore on your own. ***Note:*** Snowmobiles are prohibited in the park.

SNOWSHOEING & CROSS-COUNTRY SKIING Glacier has many cross-country trails, the most popular of which is the **Upper Lake McDonald Trail** to the Avalanche picnic area. This 8-mile trail offers a relatively flat route up Going-to-the-Sun Road with views of McDonald Creek and the mountains looming above the McDonald Valley. For the advanced skier, the same area presents a more intense trip that heads northwest in a roundabout fashion to the Apgar Lookout.

The most popular trail on the east side is the **Autumn Creek Trail** near Marias Pass. Avalanche paths cross this area, so inquire about weather conditions before setting out. Yet another popular spot is in Essex along the southern boundary of the park at the **Izaak Walton Inn.**

In West Glacier, **Glacier Outdoor Center** (✆ **800/235-6781**) rents snowshoes and cross-country ski packages for $15 and $18 per day, respectively.

8 Camping

INSIDE THE PARK

You can spend your evenings at the park in the hotel lounge looking over your cocktail at the folks in the campground, and vice versa. For those who prefer the latter, Glacier offers 13 campgrounds, 8 of which are accessible by paved road.

Most campgrounds are available on a first-come, first-served basis. Fish Creek and St. Mary campgrounds may be reserved through the **National Park Service Reservation System** (✆ **877/444-6777;** www.recreation.gov). Most campgrounds have restrooms with flush toilets and cold running water. Despite its proximity to the center of the hotel and motel activity, the **Many Glacier Campground** is a well-forested, almost secluded campground that provides as much privacy in a public area as you'll see anywhere. The campground has adequate space for recreational vehicles and truck-camper combinations, but space for vehicles pulling trailers is limited. It is a veritable mecca for tent campers.

Apgar Campground is at the bottom of Lake McDonald, near the West Glacier entrance and the Apgar Visitor Center. The **Avalanche Campground** may be the nicest of all, because it is 4 miles north of Lake McDonald on Going-to-the-Sun Road in a heavily treed area adjacent to the creek. Of its 87 sites, 50 are suitable for RVs.

Bowman Lake Campground is at the end of a primitive dirt road in the northwest section of the park (accessible through the Polebridge entrance). It's not recommended for RVs. The bad news about the **Cut Bank Campground** road is that it's not paved. The good news is that it's only 5 miles from the pavement of U.S. 89 to the ranger station and campground, which are in the southeast portion of the park between St. Mary and Two Medicine. And the unpaved road deters many from heading into the outback to this primitive campground, which sits in the shadow of Bad Marriage and Medicine Wolf mountains. The campground only recently reopened after being rebuilt, so is relatively undiscovered; the road and campground are best suited to recreational vehicles 21 feet or shorter.

Fish Creek Campground is 2 miles from Apgar, on the western shore of Lake McDonald. **Kintla Lake Campground** is in the northwest section of the park, reached by primitive dirt roads through the Polebridge entrance station, so it is not recommended for RVs. **Logging Creek** is a primitive campground just beyond Quartz Creek and reached by dirt roads. **Quartz Creek** is another primitive campground, accessible by dirt roads through the Polebridge entrance.

Sprague Creek Campground is on the eastern shore of Lake McDonald. No towed trailers or vehicles longer than 21 feet are allowed. **St. Mary Campground** is outside the town of St. Mary. **Rising Sun Campground,** 6 miles west of St. Mary, is near the public showers at Rising Sun Motor Inn.

The **Two Medicine Campground** is in the shadows of major mountains near three lakes and a stream. It is a forested area that has beautiful sites, plenty of shade, and opportunities to wet a fishing line or dangle your feet in cool mountain water.

Some campgrounds are open early in the season as primitive campgrounds, with limited facilities and lower fees than the bulk of the summer.

BACKCOUNTRY CAMPING

Glacier has 65 backcountry campgrounds. Fortunately, many are at lower elevation, so inexperienced backpackers have an opportunity to take advantage of them. For an accurate estimation of your itinerary's difficulty and advice on what you may need, check with rangers in the area you contemplate visiting. One of the main dangers is running into a bear.

Visitors planning to camp overnight in Glacier's backcountry must stop at a visitor center, ranger station, or the Apgar Backcountry Permit Office and obtain a **backcountry use permit.** Backcountry permits may be reserved in advance (see "Exploring the Backcountry," above). Permits are good only for the prearranged dates and locations, with no more than 3 nights allowed at each campground. Certain campgrounds have a 1-night limit. There are separate fees for advance reservations ($30 per permit) and backcountry camping ($5 per person per night or $3 for kids under 16).

You can obtain backcountry camping permits in person from the backcountry office at Apgar, Waterton Townsite, and St. Mary, or the ranger stations at Many Glacier, Two Medicine, and Polebridge. During summer months, permits may be obtained no earlier than 24 hours before your trip.

WINTER BACKCOUNTRY CAMPING

Though snow camping isn't for everyone, it's a great way to see the park in winter and to complement a winter excursion. Permits are required for all overnight trips, but there is no fee to reserve one up to 7 days in advance. There are a few rules that take effect beginning each November 20, so double-check at visitor centers for details.

CHALETS

Two of the park's most popular destinations, Granite Park and Sperry Chalets, are National Historic

Campground	Total Sites	RV Hookups	Dump Station	Toilets
Inside the Park				
Apgar	194	No	Yes	Yes
Avalanche	87	No	No	Yes
Bowman Lake*	48	No	No	Yes
Cut Bank*	14	No	No	Yes
Fish Creek	178	No	Yes	Yes
Kintla Lake*	14	No	No	Yes
Logging Creek*	7	No	No	Yes
Many Glacier	110	No	Yes	Yes
Quartz Creek*	7	No	No	Yes
Rising Sun	83	No	Yes	Yes
Sprague Creek	25	No	No	Yes
St. Mary	148	No	Yes	Yes
Two Medicine	99	No	Yes	Yes
Near the Park				
Glacier Campground	160	Yes	Yes	Yes
Johnson's of St. Mary	157	Yes	Yes	Yes
Lake Five Resort	45	Yes	Yes	Yes
Y Lazy R	30	Yes	Yes	Yes

* Campground accessible only by narrow dirt roads. RVs not recommended.

** Public showers nearby, for a fee.

Landmarks built by the Great Northern Railway between 1912 and 1914. Granite Park is a basic hikers' shelter, and Sperry is a full-service chalet.

Granite Park Chalet has 12 rooms (all with single bunk beds) and sleeps two to six per room. The chalet runs $148 double, and the kitchen facilities are shared.

Sperry Chalet, a rustic backcountry chalet, is accessible by trail only. It operates from mid-July through mid-September. Services include overnight accommodations and full meal service for a double rate of $285. Reservations are required. For information and reservations for either chalet, contact **Belton Chalets,** P.O. Box 189, West Glacier, MT 59936 (✆ **888/345-2649;** www.graniteparkchalet.com and www.sperrychalet.com).

NEAR THE PARK

IN EAST GLACIER

Y Lazy R Just off U.S. 2, this campground is within walking distance of East Glacier and is the closest to town with laundry facilities. Arrive early if you want to snag one of the few sites with trees. This place is a great value and an ideal place to base yourself while exploring the region.

Washington St. and U.S. 2 (P.O. Box 13), East Glacier, MT 59434. ✆ **406/226-5505.** 10 tent sites, 20 RV sites. $16 tent; $18 water and electric only; $20 full hookup.

IN ST. MARY

Johnson's of St. Mary From April through September (depending on the weather), this is where you want to camp if you can get a spot. The campground has showers, an 18-hole miniature golf course, and a laundromat. Campers both inside the park and out come to St. Mary for a good meal at **Johnson's Cafe,** which serves homemade American grub family style (with serving dishes placed on each table) at breakfast, lunch, and dinner daily. Lunches include burgers, sandwiches, and homemade soup (most items $3–$8), and dinners usually include your choice of entrees such as fried chicken, trout, sirloin or T-bone steak, or pork chops, with prices from $10 to $18.

St. Mary, MT 59417. ✆ **406/732-4207.** www.johnsonsofstmary.com. 75 tent sites, 82 RV sites. $23 tent; $32–$35 RV with electricity and water only; $40 full hookup; $26 RV, no hookup.

IN WEST GLACIER

Glacier Campground One mile west of West Glacier on U.S. 2 is the closest campground outside the park. Set in a forested area overgrown with evergreens, it's a quiet, comfortable place to retreat under the shade of the trees, especially on hot days. Most sites have water and electric hookups; the rest are perfect for tent camping. Five rather primitive cabins are also available, with modest furnishings, electricity, beds with mattresses, and use of the

Drinking Water	Showers	Fire Pits/ Grills	Laundry	Reserve	Fees	Open
Yes	No	Yes	No	No	$10–$20	Year-round
Yes	No	Yes	No	No	$20	Mid-June to Labor Day
Yes	No	Yes	No	No	$10–$15	Mid-May to mid-Sept
No	No	Yes	No	No	$10	Late May to mid-Sept
Yes	No	Yes	No	Yes	$23	June to Labor Day
Yes	No	Yes	No	No	$10–$15	Late May to mid-Sept
No	No	Yes	No	No	$10	July to mid-Sept
Yes	Yes**	Yes	No	No	$10–$20	Late May to late Sept
No	No	Yes	No	No	$10	July to early Dec
Yes	Yes**	Yes	No	No	$20	Late May to mid-Sept
Yes	No	Yes	No	No	$20	Mid-May to mid-Sept
Yes	No	Yes	No	Yes	$10–$23	Year-round
Yes	No	Yes	No	No	$10–$20	Late May to late Sept
Yes	Yes	Yes	Yes	Yes	$19/$22–$29	Mid-May to Sept
Yes	Yes	Yes	Yes	Yes	$23/$26/$32–$40	Apr–Oct
Yes	Yes	Yes	Yes	Yes	$40–$45	Early May to mid-Oct
Yes	Yes	Yes	Yes	Yes	$16/$18–$20	June to mid-Sept

campground's bathhouse. Recreational facilities include volleyball, horseshoes, and a basketball court; also on the premises are an excellent cafe, a laundromat, and a small general store.

P.O. Box 477, 12070 U.S. 2, West Glacier, MT 59936. ✆ **888/387-5689** or 406/387-5689. www.glaciercampground.com. 80 tent sites, 80 RV sites, 5 cabins. $19 tent; $22–$29 RV; $40–$50 cabin.

Lake Five Resort Located 3 miles west of West Glacier and less than a mile from U.S. 2, this cabin and campground arrangement is an alternative to potentially crowded park campgrounds but is still close to the park. The resort is on a 235-acre lake. Seven of the nine cabins are on the lakefront; all are equipped with bathrooms and showers.

540 Belton Stage Rd. (P.O. Box 338), West Glacier, MT 59936. ✆ **406/387-5601.** www.lakefiveresort.com. 9 cabins, 6 tepee lodges; 31 sites with electricity and water, 14 sites with electricity, water, and sewer hookup. $115–$175 cabin; $50–$60 tepee; $40–$45 site.

9 Where to Stay

INSIDE THE PARK

With only one exception, **Glacier Park, Inc.** (GPI) operates all of the hostelries in Glacier National Park, which fall into two categories. Lake McDonald Lodge, Glacier Park Lodge, and Many Glacier Hotel are first-tier properties that have been popular destinations since early in the 20th century; Swiftcurrent Motor Inn is typical of the casual motel-style properties at the other end of the spectrum that provide good accommodations for less money.

Although the lodges have a certain stately charm, don't expect in-room hot tubs or even air-conditioning. The structures may have been constructed to withstand natural disasters, but little thought was given to interior soundproofing. If you're an eavesdropper, you'll be in heaven; if you're a light sleeper, bring earplugs. Although all of the lodges are comfortable, their greatest attribute, aside from the architecture, may be their stunning setting.

Reserve well in advance; July and August dates may fill before the spring thaw. For more information on the GPI-operated properties and to make reservations, contact **Glacier Park Inc.,** P.O. Box 2025 Columbia Falls, MT 59912 (✆ **406/892-2525;** fax 406/892-1375; www.glacierparkinc.com).

Apgar Village Lodge The Apgar Village Lodge, on the south end of Lake McDonald, is one of two lodgings in Apgar Village. A less expensive alternative to the park's GPI-managed properties, the log-and-frame cabins have a rustic charm but lack in-room amenities.

Apgar Village, Box 410, West Glacier, MT 59936. ✆ **406/888-5484.** www.westglacier.com. 28 cabins, 20 motel rooms. TV. $95–$125 double; $105–$275 cabin. AE, DISC, MC, V. Closed Oct to mid-May.

Glacier Park Lodge Just outside the southeast entrance at East Glacier, this is the park's flagship inn, an imposing timbered lodge that stands as a stately tribute to the Great Northern Railroad and its early attempts to lure tourists to Glacier. The immaculate lawn and ever-blooming wildflowers frame the grounds in colors that rival the mountain backdrop. The interior features massive Douglas fir pillars, some 40 inches in diameter and 40 feet tall. In fact, stand in the middle of the lobby and look up—beams carved from massive trees are the structural supports for the entire building. Skylights, wrought-iron chandeliers, and a desk hewn from a 36-inch-diameter log add to the Old West flavor. Rooms are nicely furnished, but showers are elbow-banging small, and sinks are significantly smaller than those found in today's modern hotels and motels. There's an immaculately groomed executive-style 9-hole golf course, and some evenings, members of the Blackfeet tribe recount their history and culture around the fireplace.

East Glacier, MT 59434. ✆ **406/892-2525.** Fax 406/892-1375. www.glacierparkinc.com. 154 units. TEL. $140–$199 double; $299–$449 suite. AE, DISC, MC, V. Closed Oct to late May.

Lake McDonald Lodge, Cabins & Inn This place feels like a genuine mountain lodge. Although the two-story building doesn't have the same towering ceilings and open spaces as other park hotels, its wood construction lends it a warm, cozy feel. Lodge rooms, located on the second and third floor (there's no elevator), are pleasantly decorated and have a historic feel. Motel units are simply well-maintained motel rooms. The well-preserved cottages are in multiunit buildings in a wooded area. Situated on the shore of the park's largest lake, the lodge provides a marvelous central base for exploring the western part of the park. The lodge is a center for boating activity; scenic cruises depart daily, and canoe rentals are popular. Common lounging areas are furnished with heavy couches, sofas, and chairs that surround a stone fireplace. The lodge houses a dining room, gift shop, and lounge; a coffee shop, post office, and sundries store are also on the grounds. The entire lodge is smoke-free.

Glacier National Park, MT 59936. ✆ **406/892-2525.** Fax 406/892-1375. www.glacierparkinc.com. 62 lodge and motel units, 38 cottage units. TEL. $177 lodge room; $137 motel unit; $124–$177 cottage. AE, DISC, MC, V. Closed late Sept to late May.

Many Glacier Hotel Built in 1915 by the Great Northern Railway, this is the largest hotel in the park and our top choice for a place to stay. The alpine-style hotel may be the most-photographed building in the park. When you arrive at Many Glacier after driving along the park's interior road from Babb, it comes slowly into view, as picturesque as a Swiss chalet and almost as inviting as the turquoise blue waters of Swiftcurrent Lake. In August, after the huckleberries ripen, you can almost count on seeing grizzly bears on the nearby mountains. Rooms, decorated in keeping with the hotel's historic roots, are in the main lodge overlooking the lobby or in the adjoining annex. We like the lakeside rooms, for their views of Swiftcurrent Lake; the smaller units without a view are less expensive. A dining room, coffee shop, gift shop, and lounge are in the hotel. In the evenings (Mon–Sat) starting in midsummer, David Walburn, a Montana singer/songwriter, entertains with his guitar, harmonica, and stories.

Glacier National Park, MT 59936. ✆ **406/892-2525.** Fax 406/892-1375. www.glacierparkinc.com. 216 units. TEL. $150–$232 double; $289 suite. AE, DISC, MC, V. Closed mid-Sept to early June.

Rising Sun Motor Inn & Cabins Located 6½ miles from St. Mary, just off Going-to-the-Sun Road, the Rising Sun is a complex made up of a restaurant, a motor inn, cottages, stores, and a service station. The basic rooms are just that—uninspiring motel rooms that are completely adequate for a good night's rest in an excellent location for those who want to explore the eastern side of the park. The cottage rooms (half of a duplex) are more interesting but a bit on the rustic side. All units here are smoke-free.

Glacier National Park, MT 59936. ✆ **406/892-2525.** Fax 406/892-1375. www.glacierparkinc.com. 63 units. TEL. $121–$137 double; $124 cottage. AE, DISC, MC, V. Closed mid-Sept to mid-June.

Swiftcurrent Motor Inn & Cabins The appeal here is for those satisfied with modest prices and decor—primarily active types interested in spending lots of time exploring the backcountry trails. Like Many Glacier, which is just up the street, the inn sits against a mountain backdrop in what is considered a hiker's paradise. Motel rooms have standard decor—functional, but nothing special. Cabins are a bit more interesting, with one or two bedrooms and perhaps a bathroom (communal facilities are nearby). There's also a coffee shop and restaurant on the premises. All units are smoke-free.

Glacier National Park, MT 59936. ✆ **406/892-2525.** Fax 406/892-1375. www.glacierparkinc.com. 88 units and cabins, some cabins without private bathroom. $121–$137 double in motor inn; $65–$89 double in cabin. AE, DISC, MC, V. Closed mid-Sept to mid-June.

Village Inn at Apgar Not to be confused with Apgar Village Lodge (see above), the Village Inn at Apgar is the smallest of the properties GPI operates in Glacier. Located lakeside in Apgar Village, the inn is near the general store, cafes, and boat docks.

The Village Inn is comfortably outfitted with modest furnishings, making it a cozy and convenient place. Rooms spread over two floors of the inn; 12 of them have kitchenettes. Second-level rooms have the same lake views as those downstairs, but they have less people traffic. Though there's no in-house dining, the restaurants of Lake McDonald and Apgar are all nearby. Close to the Apgar corral and the docks of Lake McDonald, not to mention a plethora of hiking trails, Apgar Village bustles with activity during the summer. The entire property is smoke-free.

Glacier National Park, MT 59936. ✆ **406/892-2525.** Fax 406/892-1375. www.glacierparkinc.com. 36 units. $137–$205 double. AE, DISC, MC, V. Closed mid-Sept to early June.

NEAR THE PARK

If the convenience of staying on Glacier's back porch is important to you, these are the towns to stay in. For greater variety in lodging, dining, and nightlife, head for Whitefish.

IN EAST GLACIER

Backpacker's Inn Low-cost, low-end sleeping accommodations for those willing to share bathroom facilities are what you get at this dorm-style hostel.

29 Dawson Ave. (P.O. Box 94), East Glacier, MT 59434. ✆ **406/226-9392.** 8 beds in 1 cabin, 2 private cabins. $12 per person in single-sex dorms; $30 for 1 person, $40 for 2 people in private cabin. AE, DISC, MC, V. Closed mid-Oct to Apr.

Brownies Grocery and HI Hostel Reservations are recommended at this popular grocery store/hostel, which offers comfortable rooms at affordable prices. Dorm and family rooms are on the second floor of a rustic, older log building with several common rooms for guests to share, including a porch, kitchen, bathrooms, and laundry. Family rooms sleep two to six. A bakery and deli (with Internet access) are in the grocery, there's a restaurant next door, and tent sites ($10) are available out back.

1020 Mont. 49 (P.O. Box 229), East Glacier, MT 59434. ✆ **406/226-4426.** www.brownieshostel.com. 10 units, all with shared bathroom, 1 family room, 2 bunk rooms. HI members $13 bunk, $28–$33 double private room, $40 family room; nonmembers $16 bunk, $31–$34 double private room, $43 family room. DISC, MC, V. Closed Oct to mid-May, depending on the weather.

Jacobson's Cottages In a nicely wooded area, these quaint cottages are small but comfortable. All have cable TV, and one has a kitchen. Entertainment and good food are nearby, and it's a 12-mile drive to the Two Medicine trail.

1204 Mont. 49 (P.O. Box 454), East Glacier, MT 59434. ✆ **406/226-4422.** Fax 406/226-4425. jacobcot@sofast.net. 12 cottages. TV. $70–$90 double. AE, DISC, MC, V. Closed Oct–Apr.

Mountain Pine Motel This property is a one-story, 1950s-type remodeled motel that provides well-furnished rooms in a shaded, timbered area just off the main highway. Most standard rooms have two queen-size beds, reading chairs and table, and bathrooms with tub/shower. Considering that rooms here are about a third as expensive as those at the park hotels, this is an excellent alternative.

909 Mont. 49 (P.O. Box 260), East Glacier, MT 59434. ✆ **406/226-4403.** www.mtnpine.com. 25 units. TV, TEL. $60–$80 double; lower rates off season. AE, DC, DISC, MC, V.

IN ESSEX

Izaak Walton Inn Built in 1939 by the Great Northern Railway, this historic Tudor lodge once served as living quarters for rail crews who serviced the railroad. Located just off U.S. 2 on the southern boundary of Glacier Park, the Izaak Walton is extremely popular with tourists from near and far, many of whom choose to travel by Amtrak train, which stops a mere 100 yards from the front door of the lodge. Both lodge rooms and the converted cabooses offer comfortable and attractive lodging, with wood-paneled walls and various Western touches. And who can pass up the opportunity to sleep in a caboose or the new-in-2009 deluxe locomotive? During the winter, this inn is a popular jumping-off spot for cross-country skiers.

290 Izaak Walton Inn Rd., Essex, MT 59916. ✆ **406/888-5700.** Fax 406/888-5200. www.izaakwaltoninn.com. 33 units, 4 caboose cottages, 1 locomotive lodging. $117–$168 double; $235–$255 suite; $230 cabins and caboose cabins; $299 locomotive lodging. 2-night minimum stay in cabins; 3-night minimum stay in cabooses and locomotive. MC, V.

IN POLEBRIDGE

North Fork Hostel and Square Peg Ranch Formerly part of the Quarter Circle MC Ranch inside the park, this lodge was moved to its present location near Polebridge in the late 1960s, and it is ideal for the back-to-nature traveler. It sits within a stone's throw of the North Fork of the Flathead River, right across the river from the park. Accommodations are ultrarustic, with a mountain-cabin feel—heat is from an old-fashioned woodstove. There are separate facilities for men and women, as well as couples' accommodations, washrooms with hot showers, and clean outhouses. There are also several small cabins suitable for families. Hostel guests should bring linens or sleeping bags (sheets are available for rent) and flashlights. The Ranch offers two rustic log homes, with decor similar to the hostel's, and a few bare-bones, summer-only tepees and campsites for $10 a night. The log homes have solar-heated showers, or guests can use the hostel showers. The hostel and cabins have kitchen facilities, and the former has a relaxing 6-foot-long claw-foot bathtub. Equipment rentals and free Wi-Fi access are also available.

80 Beaver Dr., Polebridge, MT 59928. ✆ **406/888-5241** or 406/253-4321. www.nfhostel.com. 7 bunks, 2 private rooms, 2 cabins, 2 log

homes. $20 bunk; $45 cabin; $80 log home. 2-night minimum stay in log home. MC, V. Reservations required in winter.

Polebridge Mercantile and Cabins If you can make the trek up the gravelly North Fork Road, then give these bare-bones cabins a try. They don't have running water, let alone bedding—it's BYO sleeping bag at the Merc, which is also home to a fantastic bakery. Each cabin has a propane cooking stove and lights, and the views out over the west side of Glacier National Park make the price a steal, especially if you bring the kids. Polebridge is a happening spot in the summer, when all the river rats and seasonal residents converge for whopping good times and tall tales about running rapids and climbing peaks.

265 Polebridge Loop, Polebridge, MT 59928. ✆ **406/888-5105.** 4 cabins. $35–$45 cabin. MC, V.

IN ST. MARY

St. Mary Lodge and Resort At the St. Mary end of Going-to-the-Sun Road, this lodge is one of the few area properties that isn't managed by GPI. The main lodge and rooms are standard Montana fare, with tasteful ironwood furnishings. Lodging is in three different areas near the center of the complex; lodge and motel rooms are nicely done motel-style units that may have two single beds or a queen. The nicest units are the cabins, many of which were built in 2009; they boast living areas with dining tables and queen beds in a separate sleeping area, and some have kitchenettes. Most rooms have TVs and air-conditioning. The surrounding complex includes a market, several restaurants, and a lounge.

U.S. 89 and Going-to-the-Sun Rd., St. Mary, MT 59417. ✆ **800/778-6279** or 406/732-4431. Fax 406/732-9265. www.stmarylodgeandresort.com. 136 units, including 28 cabins. A/C, TV, TEL. $159–$199 double; $229–$269 cabin; $229–$329 suite. AE, DISC, MC, V.

IN WEST GLACIER

Belton Chalets and Lodge A National Historic Landmark, this facility across from the railroad station has been completely restored to the elegance of an early-20th-century hotel. The rooms are small, simple, and old-fashioned. The bathrooms are also small. But the feel of the place is comfortable, and the staff is very friendly. Many of the rooms have private balconies looking out over the rounded timber foothills of Glacier National Park.

12575 U.S. 2, West Glacier, MT 59936. ✆ **888/235-8665** or 406/888-5000. Fax 406/888-5005. www.beltonchalet.com. 25 rooms, 2 cottages. Early June to early Sept $145–$299; early Sept to early June $120–$225. MC, V.

Glacier Outdoor Center Built in three stages since 1996, the cabins at the Glacier Raft Company's HQ are delightful, functional, and tasteful, sporting trout, moose, and bears on everything from dishes to lampshades. Backing up to the Flathead National Forest just west of the park entrance on U.S. 2, the cabins are well off the road, nestled around a grassy glen with a picnic area, volleyball court, and trout pond where casting clinics are held in the summer. Each cabin has a fully equipped kitchen, one to three bedrooms, and a private deck with a barbecue; the two-bedroom units can sleep up to 14 people. There is free Wi-Fi and a full rental/retail/guide operation in the main center, and in the winter, 15km of cross-country ski trails are groomed daily.

12400 U.S. 2, P.O. Box 210, West Glacier, MT 59936. ✆ **800/235-6781** or 406/888-5454. www.glacierraftco.com. 10 cabins. A/C TV. $275–$449 cabin; lower rates in winter. AE, DISC, MC, V.

Great Northern Chalets This small, rafting-oriented resort near West Glacier offers log chalets that have balconies facing flower gardens and a pond, with mountain views in the distance. The largest chalet is a beautifully furnished two-story, two-bedroom unit with a full bathroom upstairs and a half-bath downstairs. Smaller chalets have one large bedroom upstairs, and a downstairs level with a full-size sleeper sofa and a kitchen with service for six. The lobby offers free Wi-Fi, and there's a pond used for fly-fishing instruction.

12127 U.S. 2, West Glacier, MT 59936. ✆ **800/735-7897** or 406/387-5340. Fax 406/387-9007. www.gnwhitewater.com. 5 units. TEL. $200–$300 double; lower rates in winter. DISC, MC, V.

Vista Motel Perched atop a hill at the west entrance to Glacier National Park, the Vista boasts tremendous views of the mountains. There's a small heated pool, free Wi-Fi in the lobby, and family-sized rooms. Accommodations are not luxurious, but the modern motel rooms are clean and comfortable, the customer service is among the best in town, and it's cheaper than the competition.

12340 U.S. 2 E. (P.O. Box 90), West Glacier, MT 59936. ✆ **877/888-5311** or 406/888-5311. www.glaciervistamotel.com. 25 units, including 5 cabins. $80–$140 double. AE, DISC, MC, V.

West Glacier Motel Formerly the River Bend Motel, this property has two locations. Half of the units are in West Glacier on Going-to-the-Sun Road, about 1 mile from the park entrance, and a second set of units is a quarter-mile away on forested grounds on a bluff above the river. This 1950s-style motel has small rooms and smaller bathrooms, but the prices are considerably lower than what you'll find in the park. The Western-style cabins are better suited for families; they come with two queen beds and fully equipped kitchens.

200 Going-to-the-Sun Rd., West Glacier, MT 59936. ✆ **406/888-5662.** www.westglacier.com. 32 units. Motel $85–$105 double; cabin $145–$225. AE, DISC, MC, V. Closed late Sept to mid-May.

IN WHITEFISH

Duck Inn Featuring magnificent views, this recently remodeled inn has style to spare and is a good value, to boot. The building is 2 blocks off the U.S. 93 strip, yet in a tranquil spot overlooking the Whitefish River. The rooms are large, each with a fireplace and a bathroom with a deep soaking tub. The lobby area is lovely, and the hot tub is in a broad-windowed room with a view of the river.

1305 Columbia Ave., Whitefish, MT 59937. ✆ **800/344-2377** or 406/862-3825. www.duckinn.com. 15 units. A/C, TV, TEL. $94–$199 double. Rates include continental breakfast. AE, DISC, MC, V.

Garden Wall Inn The Garden Wall Inn is right on the main Whitefish drag but in a world of its own. Owners Rhonda Fitzgerald and Chris Schustrom clearly take pride in providing all of the little luxurious extras. The inn is full of country charm—it was built in 1923, and all of the furnishings are period antiques, including claw-foot tubs and Art Deco dressers, depending on your room. Every detail is just about perfect, right down to the towels, which are large and fluffy enough to dry two adults. Rhonda and Chris are both trained chefs, so breakfast is a gourmet event.

504 Spokane Ave., Whitefish, MT 59937. ✆ **888/530-1700** or 406/862-3440. www.gardenwallinn.com. 4 units. $145–$195 double; $255 suite. Rates include full breakfast and afternoon refreshments. AE, MC, V.

10 Where to Dine

INSIDE THE PARK

Food options inside the park are primarily dining rooms operated by GPI. They're convenient, and you're almost always assured of friendly service from a staff of 20-something students from around the country. Credit cards accepted at all GPI properties include American Express, Discover, MasterCard, and Visa. Breakfasts range from about $5 to $10, lunch entrees are $6 to $13, and most dinner entrees cost $10 to $30.

You'll find above-average food served at above-average prices in the dining rooms at the major properties. Glacier Park Lodge has the **Great Northern Dining Room,** which has Western decor and a menu of beef, barbecued ribs, fish, and chicken, plus a full breakfast buffet; and the **Empire Bar & Grill,** which offers a bar menu of sandwiches and appetizers.

At Lake McDonald Lodge you'll find **Russell's Fireside Dining Room,** which has a hunting-lodge atmosphere with rough-hewn beams and hunting trophies; it specializes in American standards, including beef tenderloin, roast duckling, seared mountain trout, roast turkey, Alaskan salmon, and steaks. There's also a full breakfast buffet. Also at Lake McDonald Lodge is **Lucke's Lounge,** which serves a bar menu, and the family-oriented **Jammer Joe's Grill & Pizzeria.**

Many Glacier Hotel has the **Ptarmigan Dining Room,** which has Swiss decor in keeping with the lodge, enjoys spectacular mountain views, and serves Continental and Swiss cuisine plus a breakfast buffet. Many Glacier also has the **Swiss Room and Interlaken Lounge,** with a bar menu, and **Heidi's,** a fast-food counter known for its huckleberry frozen yogurt. The dining rooms open with the park and close sometime in September, depending on the facility. At each dining room, breakfast is served from 6:30 to 9:30am, lunch from 11:30am to 1:30pm, and dinner from 5:30 to 9:30pm. Coffee and snack shops open at 7 or 8am and close at 9pm. All are smoke-free.

The alternatives include second-tier restaurants in proximity to the hotels, most of which are comparable to chain restaurants in both quality and price. The **Two Dog Flats Grill** at the Rising Sun Motor Inn serves "hearty American fare." The Swiftcurrent Motor Inn restaurant is the **Italian Gardens Ristorante,** where lunch and dinner feature combinations of salads, sandwiches, pasta dishes, and create-your-own pizzas. At Apgar you'll find a deli and a family dining arrangement.

NEAR THE PARK

The gateway cities have a number of restaurants, and there are even more choices in Whitefish.

EAST GLACIER & VICINITY

Serrano's MEXICAN Perhaps the area's best restaurant (although that's not saying too much), Serrano's is just off the highway at the center of town. Serrano's is one of the only eateries in town, so don't be surprised if you encounter masses of people in the dining room and on the outdoor deck at the height of summer. You can expect hearty portions of Mexican food, an ample selection of imported beers and microbrews, and a full bar featuring margaritas.

29 Dawson Ave., East Glacier. ✆ **406/226-9392.** Main courses $9–$18. AE, DISC, MC, V. Daily 5–10pm (until 9pm in early May and late Sept). Closed Oct–Apr.

Two Sisters Cafe AMERICAN This longstanding favorite serves perhaps the best pie in the area, with a fun atmosphere and a huge license plate collection to boot. Susan and Beth Higgins, the eponymous sisters who run the place, specialize in hearty American fare, with a menu that includes dishes like chili cheeseburgers, hand-battered chicken-fried steak, and big brownie sundaes. As for libations, there are margaritas, microbrews, and a nonalcoholic "lemonade of the day."

4 miles north of St. Mary on U.S. 89, Babb. ✆ **406/732-5535.** MC, V. Daily June–Sept 11am–10pm. Closed Oct–May.

IN WEST GLACIER

Belton Tap Room AMERICAN This restaurant, located in restored buildings that were once the Great Northern Railway Chalet, serves respectable food geared toward American tastes—steaks, buffalo, chicken, ribs, trout, and salmon, as well as some vegetarian selections. A large stone fireplace dominates the tap room, which serves several brands of locally brewed beer.

12575 U.S. 2, West Glacier. ✆ **406/888-5000.** Main courses $9–$30. MC, V. Daily 5–10pm. Bar open at 3pm, with a limited menu.

Glacier Highland Restaurant AMERICAN This may be the spot to satisfy your sweet tooth; a baker is on hand, so the pies are worth the stop, and the cinnamon rolls are immense. The Highland Burger is, by any standard, a great hunk of beef, and fresh trout is a dinner specialty.

U.S. 2, West Glacier. ✆ **406/888-5427.** Breakfast items $4–$9; main courses $5–$10 lunch, $6–$20 dinner. AE, DISC, MC, V. Daily 7am–10pm, with some seasonal variations. Closed mid-Nov to Mar.

IN WHITEFISH

Red Caboose Diner AMERICAN This new eatery caters to rail travelers with its always-open hours and railroad-themed decor. The menu offers a creative spin on traditional diner fare, with such appetizers as crab cakes and deep-fried artichoke hearts, hearty egg dishes for breakfast, po-boys and burgers for lunch, and steaks, catfish, meatloaf, and other American standards for dinner. Kids will love the paper chef's hats for coloring. There is a full bar.

101 Central Ave. ✆ **406/863-4563.** Breakfast items $5–$10; lunch and dinner main courses $6–$19. AE, DISC, MC, V. Sun–Thurs 7am–11pm (until 10pm in winter); Fri–Sat 7am–2:30am.

Tupelo Grille CAJUN/NEW AMERICAN The Tupelo is the best restaurant in downtown Whitefish, especially if you like New Orleans–style food. Creole chicken and dumplings in mustard-sage cream sauce and a Cajun Creole combo (a platter of shrimp Creole, crawfish étouffée, and chicken and sausage jambalaya) are specialties. The rack of lamb is tough to beat.

17 Central Ave. ✆ **406/862-6136.** Reservations recommended for large parties. Main courses $17–$32. AE, MC, V. Summer daily 5:30–10pm; winter Mon–Sat 5:30–9:30pm.

11 Picnic & Camping Supplies

In **East Glacier,** there's a gas station, a post office, several gift shops, and a small market with a limited supply of fresh meats and produce, as well as beer, wine, and a modest supply of fishing and camping accessories. **West Glacier** offers a gas station, general store, laundromat, photo shop, rafting companies, post office, and gift shop, as well as a bar and restaurant. In **St. Mary,** the **grocery store** (✆ **406/732-4431**) at St. Mary Lodge and Resort will never be confused with a metropolitan-area supermarket, but it's the closest thing you will find in any of the gateway towns. There's fresh produce, canned goods, and beverages, including beer and wine, but at tourist-town prices. There's also a post office.

12 A Side Trip to Waterton Lakes National Park in Canada

It's worth finding the time to explore the upper regions of this area. From St. Mary, head north to visit Waterton Lakes National Park, Glacier's Canadian counterpart. You'll be rewarded with different yet equally beautiful scenery and a touch of European culture.

Located in Alberta, Canada, Waterton is the place where the Canadian mountains meet the rolling prairie, which means it has an incredible variety of flowers and animals. As you travel along the high ridge, you'll see meadows and boggy areas that are ideal habitat for moose; later you'll find lakes all around and the Canadian Rockies filling the horizon. The area is also a haven for elk, mule deer, and bighorn sheep, and both grizzly and black bears are found in the park.

ESSENTIALS

GETTING THERE

From the eastern entrance of Glacier National Park at St. Mary, drive north through Babb, which is barely a whistle-stop, until you reach the intersection of Mont. 17—it's very well marked. Head northwest to the Canadian border, where Mont. 17 becomes Alberta Hwy. 6. ***Remember:*** **You'll need a passport** to cross the border. Head down into the valley until you reach the park entrance on your left.

VISITOR INFORMATION

The park's **Visitor Reception Centre** (✆ **403/859-2224;** www.parkscanada.gc.ca/waterton) is just inside the park.

FEES & PERMITS

Park entrance costs about C$8 (about US$7) per person, with a maximum of about C$20 (US$19) per vehicle. Day hiking does not require a permit, but backcountry overnight trips do; permits cost about C$10 (US$9) per person per day.

A BRIEF HISTORY

Compared with its counterparts in the Lower 48, Waterton is a tiny park; the total size is only 203 square miles. However, the park has great historical significance: Based on more than 200 identified archaeological sites, historians think that Aboriginal people first populated the area 11,000 years ago.

In modern times, Waterton Lakes became a national park about 6 years before oil was discovered here. (Oil and mineral exploration was allowed in Canada's national parks during the system's infancy.) It was set aside as a national park in 1895, thanks to the efforts of a local rancher.

In 1932, following an initiative by the Rotary Clubs of Alberta and Montana, Waterton Lakes and Glacier national parks were designated the world's first **International Peace Park.** They have since come to represent the need for cooperation between nations where sharing resources and ecosystems is possible. The areas were designated **Bio-Sphere Reserves** by the UNESCO Man and Bio-Sphere Program, in order to provide information about the relationships between people and the environment. The two parks were jointly designated a UNESCO **World Heritage Site** in 1995.

EXPLORING THE PARK

Unlike most "park centers"—essentially a smattering of restaurants, souvenir shops, and gas stations clustered around the primary lodging—Waterton Village actually is a village. As you cruise the perimeter of the lake heading for Waterton Village, you'll pass three large lakes, the habitat of bald eagles that often perch atop the snags of dead trees. The park bears a striking resemblance to Grand Teton, in that its attractions spread out across a narrow valley floor; however, the valley is narrower and peaks surround three-fourths of it, so the overall effect is cozier but equally dramatic.

By most standards, it's also windier here, though locals say that they don't acknowledge the wind unless there are whitecaps in the toilets at the Prince of Wales Hotel (see "Where to Stay," below).

Hiking, cruising the lake, and just doing nothing are all great pastimes around here. Most of the 120 miles of trails are easily accessible from town. They range in difficulty from short strolls to steep treks for overnight backcountry enthusiasts.

DAY HIKES

The park is a popular destination for European, Canadian, and American hiking fanatics. For nearly 20 years, the 11-mile **Crypt Lake Trail** has been rated as one of Canada's best hikes—except for those prone to seasickness: To reach the trail head, hikers take a 2-mile boat ride across Upper Waterton Lake. Contact the **Waterton Shoreline Cruise Company** (✆ **403/859-2362;** www.watertoncruise.com) for details about the boat shuttle. After that, the trail leads past Hellroaring Falls, Twin Falls, and Burnt Rock Falls before reaching Crypt Falls and a passage through a 60-foot rock tunnel. The elevation gain is 2,300 feet, but veterans say the hike is doable in 3 hours, one-way.

A second, extended tour starts at the marina and heads south across the international boundary to **Goat Haunt,** Montana, an especially popular trip because of the sightings of bald eagles, bears, bighorn sheep, deer, and moose, as well as numerous unusual geologic formations.

The **International Peace Park Hike,** a free guided trip that follows Upper Waterton Lake, takes place on Wednesday and Saturday from the end of June through the end of August. Participants meet at the Bertha Trailhead in the morning and spend the day on an 8.5-mile trail with U.S. and Canadian rangers. At the end of the trail, hikers return by boat to the main dock.

CAMPING

At the west end of the village is **Townsite Campground,** a Parks Canada–operated facility with 235 sites that's a popular jumping-off spot for campers headed into the park's backcountry. Prices range from roughly C$16 (US$15) to C$38 (US$35); half of the sites have electricity and sewage disposal. Also available on the premises are kitchen shelters, washrooms, and shower facilities. The site perches right on the lake, so views are excellent and trails await evening strollers.

There are also a number of designated **wilderness campgrounds** with dry toilets and surface water, some of which have shelters.

WHERE TO STAY

Although the Prince of Wales Hotel (see below) is clearly the flagship in these woods, a worthwhile alternative is the **Waterton Lakes Lodge Resort** (✆ **888/985-6343** or 403/859-2150; www.watertonlakeslodge.com), with a great location in the heart of Waterton Village. The lodge offers lake and mountain views, and some rooms have fireplaces, whirlpool tubs, and kitchenettes. Other facilities include a health-center spa and indoor pool. Basic lodge doubles start at C$185 (US$170) in summer.

The Prince of Wales Hotel The Prince of Wales compares with the finest park hostelries in Montana and Wyoming. Built in 1927 by the Great Northern Railway, the hotel boasts soaring roofs, gables, and balconies that convey the appearance of a giant alpine chalet. Rooms, though small, have aged well, with dark-stained, high-paneled wainscoting and heavily upholstered chairs. Bathrooms have European-style tubs with wraparound curtains; one look at the washbasins, and you'd surmise that guests were Lilliputian size when the hotel was first constructed.

The lobby, like those in many of the old railroad hotels, is wood, wood, and more wood—in this case, accented by tufted furniture and carpeting. Two-story-high windows overlook the lake and village, minutes away by footpath. If you don't spend the night at the Prince of Wales, stop in for a traditional **British high tea,** served daily from 2 to 5pm. Waterton Lakes National Park, AB T0K 2M0. ✆ **403/859-2231** or 406/892-2525 in winter. Fax 403/859-2630. www.glacierparkinc.com. 87 units. TEL. C$235–C$278 (US$219–US$259) double; C$857 (US$799) suite. AE, DISC, MC, V. Closed mid-Sept to mid-June.

WHERE TO DINE

All of the village's restaurants and retail outlets are within a 4-block area around Waterton Avenue (which the locals call Main St.). So despite the fact that many buildings aren't numbered, you'll have no problem finding places to eat or shop.

The **Royal Stewart Dining Room** in the lobby of the Prince of Wales Hotel (✆ **403/859-2231**) serves Continental and English fare at breakfast, lunch, and dinner. At Waterton Lakes Lodge Resort, the casual **Vimy's Ridge Lounge and Grill** (✆ **403/859-2150**) serves three meals a day in a room with spectacular views.

16

Grand Canyon National Park, AZ

by Shane Christensen

The first thing you notice about the Grand Canyon is its size. At 277 river miles long, roughly 4,000 feet deep, and an average of 10 miles across, it's so big that even the breezes seem to draw a deep breath at the rims. But it's so much more than an enormous gulch. In the past 6 million years, while the river or rivers that eventually became the Colorado River were carving the main canyon, runoff from the rims cut hundreds of side canyons that funnel like capillaries into the larger one. As the side canyons deepened and spread, they gradually isolated buttes and mesas that tower thousands of feet above the canyon floor. Early cartographers and geologists noticed similarities between these rock pinnacles and some of the greatest works of human hands. They called them temples and shrines, and named them after deities such as Brahma, Vishnu, and Shiva.

The canyon not only inspires reverence, but tells the grandest of stories. Half the earth's history is represented in its rocks. The oldest and deepest rock layer, the Vishnu Formation, began forming 2 billion years ago, before aerobic life forms even existed. The layers of sedimentary rock that piled atop the Vishnu Formation tell of landscapes that changed like dreams. They speak of mountains that really did move, eroding into nothingness; of oceans that poured forth across the land before receding; of deserts, swamps, and rivers the size of the Mississippi—all where the canyon now lies. The fossils in these layers illustrate the very evolution of life.

Many of the latest products of evolution—more than 1,500 plant and 400 animal species—survive at the canyon today. If you include the upper reaches of the Kaibab Plateau (on the canyon's North Rim), this small area of northern Arizona includes zones of biological life comparable to ones found as far south as Mexico and as far north as Alaska. The species come in every shape, size, and temperament, ranging from tiny ant lions dwelling in the canyon floor to 1,000-pound elk roaming the rims. And for every species, there is a story within a story. Take the Douglas fir, for example. Once part of a forest that covered both rims and much of the canyon, the tree has endured since the last ice age on shady, north-facing slopes beneath the South Rim—long after the sun-baked rim itself became too hot and inhospitable.

A number of Native American tribes have lived in or around the canyon, and the Navajo, Havasupai, Kaibab Paiute, Hopi, Zuni, and Hualapai tribes still dwell in this area. The Hopi still regard the canyon as their place of emergence and the place to which their dead return. Their predecessors left behind more than 3,000 archaeological sites and artifacts up to 10,000 years old.

In the 1500s, Spanish missionaries and gold-greedy explorers passed through the area, but it wasn't until the 1800s that Europeans began settling here. Prospectors clambered through the canyon in search of precious minerals, and some of them stayed after their mines, plagued by high overhead costs, shut down. The first tourists followed, and vacationers began flooding the area after the railroad linked Grand Canyon Village to Williams, Arizona, in 1901.

When President Theodore Roosevelt visited in 1903, he was moved to use the Antiquities Act to declare Grand Canyon a national monument in 1908. Congress established Grand Canyon National Park in 1919.

Although designated a "park," Grand Canyon has a daunting, even ominous side. Visitors, no matter how many times they enter it, must negotiate with it for survival. One look at the clenched jaw of a river

Voices

Leave it as it is. You cannot improve on it. The ages have been at work on it, and man can only mar it. What you can do is to keep it for your children, your children's children . . . as the one great sight which every American . . . should see.

—Theodore Roosevelt

Grand Canyon National Park

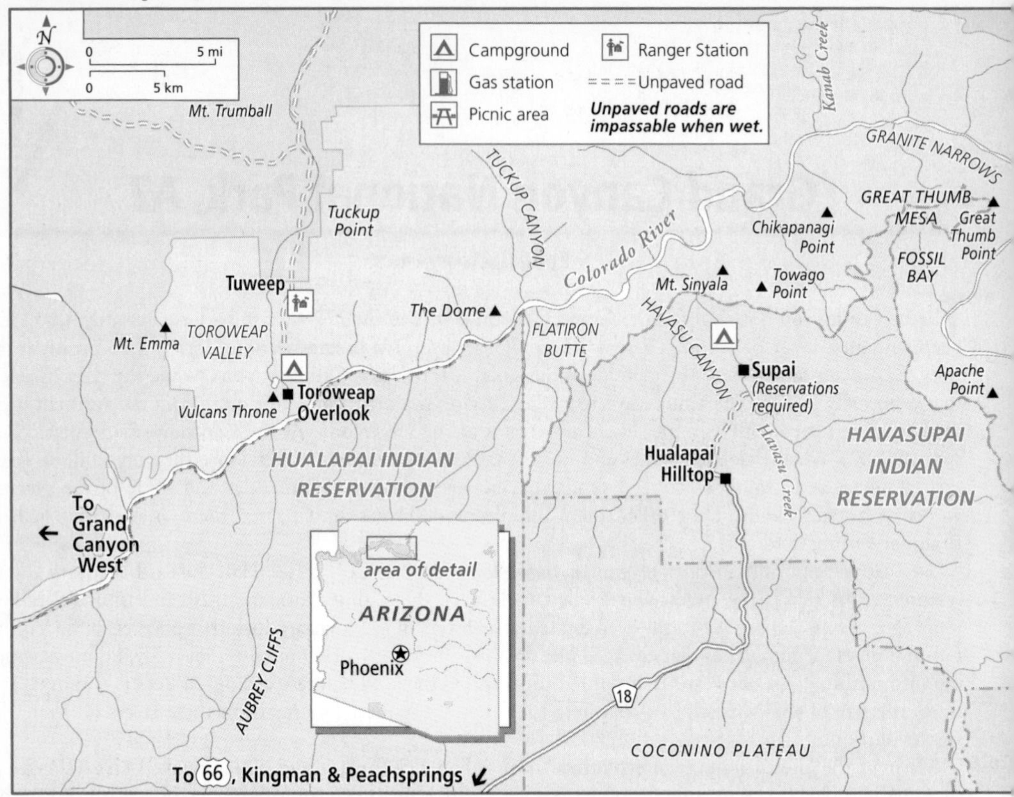

guide as he or she rows into Lava Rapids will remind you that the canyon exacts a heavy price for mistakes. The most common mistake is to underestimate it. Try to escape, and it becomes a prison, with walls 4,000 feet high. The canyon's menace reminds us that we still haven't completely conquered nature. It even has its own symbols: the rattlesnake's warning; the elegant symmetry of the black widow; the seductive, lilylike flower of the deadly sacred datura.

Clearly, you can suffer here, but reward is everywhere. It's in the spectrum of colors: The Colorado River, filled with runoff from a recent rain in the Painted Desert, runs blood red beneath slopes of orange Hakatai shale; cactus flowers explode in pink, yellow, and red; and lichens paint rocks orange, green, and gray, creating art more striking than the works in any gallery. It's in the shapes, too—the spires, amphitheaters, temples, ramps, and cliffs—and in the shadows that bend across them before lifting like mist. It's in the myriad organisms and their struggles for survival. Most of all, it's in the constancy of the river, which reminds us that, in time, all things move forward, wash away, and return to the earth.

AVOIDING THE CROWDS

High season runs from April through October, with visitation peaking in midsummer. Maureen Oltrogge, the public affairs officer for Grand Canyon National Park, offers this straightforward advice for people wanting to avoid the crowds at the park: "Prime season is July and August. Try to visit at another time. If you can't come during the off season, we recommend that you come before 10am or after 2pm, so that you can avoid both the lines at the entrance gates and the parking problems inside the park."

Oltrogge's advice applies to both rims. She points out that because the North Rim lacks facilities for large numbers of people, it sometimes feels as crowded as the South Rim, despite having roughly one-eighth the visitation. Outside of spring break and midsummer, however, crowds should not be a big issue on either rim.

1 Essentials

GETTING THERE & GATEWAYS

The nearest cities to the South Rim of the Grand Canyon are Flagstaff, Arizona, 78 miles south of Grand Canyon Village on U.S. 180; and Williams, Arizona, 59 miles south on Ariz. 64.

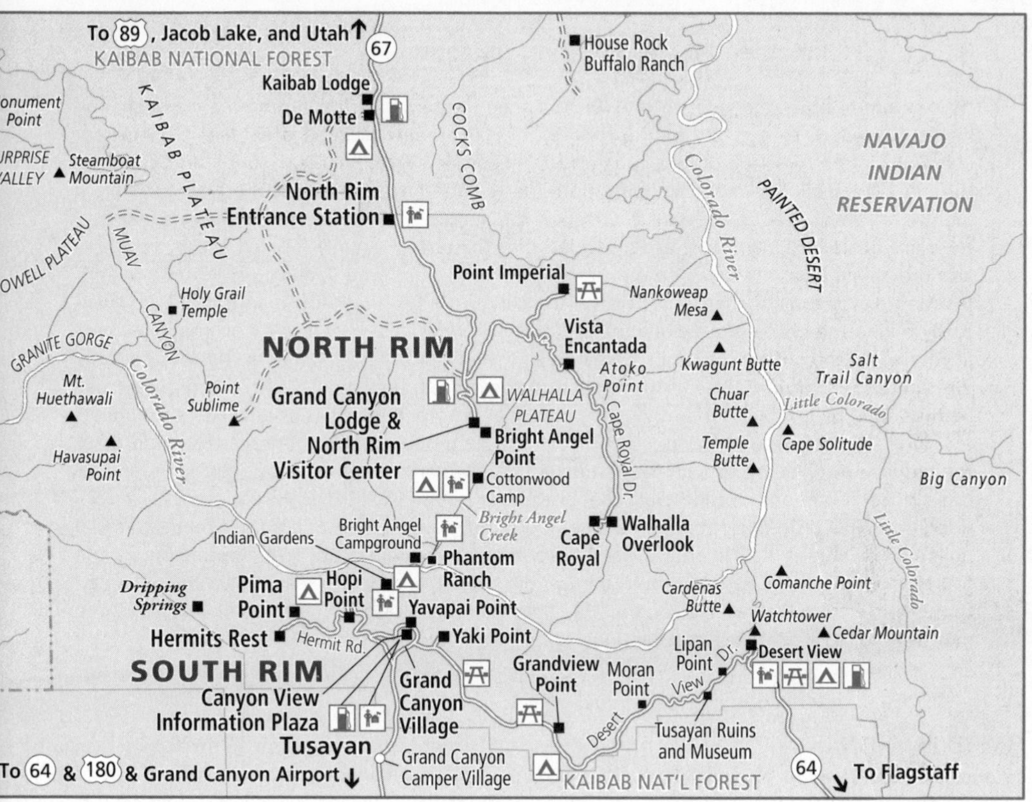

The closest small town to the park is Tusayan, Arizona, 1 mile south of the south entrance gates on Ariz. 64. The closest substantial town to the North Rim is Kanab, Utah, 78 miles northwest of Grand Canyon National Park on U.S. 89A.

THE NEAREST AIRPORTS Many travelers fly to **Phoenix Sky Harbor International Airport** (✆ **602/273-3300;** http://skyharbor.com), 220 miles from the South Rim, or to **McCarran International Airport** (✆ **702/261-5211;** www.mccarran.com), in Las Vegas, 263 miles from the North Rim. The major airlines and car-rental companies serve both airports. See chapter 38 for website listings of the major airlines, hotels, and car-rental companies.

Grand Canyon Scenic Airlines (✆ **800/634-6801;** www.scenic.com) and **Grand Canyon Airlines** (✆ **866/235-9422;** www.grandcanyonairlines.com) offer daily service between Grand Canyon National Park Airport and Boulder City (BLD), Nevada (30 min. south of Las Vegas). The cost for these flights, which often include air tours of the canyon, is about $200 one-way. **Vision Air** (✆ **800/256-8767;** www.visionholidays.com) serves Canyon National Park Airport from **North Las Vegas Airport** (✆ **702/261-3806**).

BY RAIL **Amtrak** (✆ **800/872-7245** or 928/774-8679; www.amtrak.com) regularly stops in downtown Flagstaff, where lodging, rental cars, and connecting bus service are available, and in Williams, where lodging and connecting rail service (on the historic Grand Canyon Railway) are available.

The **Historic Grand Canyon Railway** (✆ **800/843-8724;** www.thetrain.com) offers daily service linking Williams and Grand Canyon Village. Pulled by historic steam engines during the summer, the train leaves Williams in the morning and returns in late afternoon.

BY BUS **Open Road Shuttle** (✆ **877/226-8060;** www.openroadshuttle.com) provides bus service between Flagstaff and Grand Canyon National Park for $33 one-way, $60 round-trip (prices include entry fee).

Daily shuttle service between the North and South rims is available from mid-May to mid-October on the **Trans-Canyon Shuttle** (✆ **928/638-2820;** www.trans-canyonshuttle.com).

RENTING A CAR Most major car-rental companies have offices in Flagstaff. See chapter 38 for their websites.

Heads Up: Change in Overnight Permit Procedure

As we went to press, managers of the Grand Canyon National Park announced a major change in the procedure to get one of the roughly 11,500 permits granted each year to backpack overnight in the park; the change took effect in February 2010. Previously, applicants could try their luck via mail, by fax, or by lining up in person the day that permits became available 4 months before the requested date. Nearly half the people who applied for permits via mail and fax were denied. NPS administrators decided that the system unduly favored nearby residents and those who have the time and resources to travel to the Grand Canyon just to get a permit. In order to even out the chances for visitors traveling from far away (and in anticipation of eventually taking the entire process online), the park will now issue backcountry overnight permits as follows (in this stiffly worded press release): "Grand Canyon National Park will consider **only written requests during the fourth-month-out** starting February 1, 2010. Written requests may be submitted by fax, by letter or by hand delivery as before. Regardless of how they are submitted, written requests are considered based on the date on which they are received, and all of the requests received by 5pm on the first day of the fourth-month-out will be placed in random order by computer and considered in that new order before the next day's requests receive consideration. This procedural change will mean that advance backcountry permit requestors will no longer be able to walk in and have their requests receive immediate consideration during the fourth-month-out (the earliest month permits are available.) Instead, the request will be added to the written requests received on that day. Permit requests made in person one, two and three months prior to start-of-trip will continue to be considered immediately."

INFORMATION

Contact **Grand Canyon National Park,** P.O. Box 129, Grand Canyon, AZ 86023 (✆ **800/638-7888;** www.nps.gov/grca), for a free copy of the *Grand Canyon Trip Planner.* Those who want more in-depth information can buy books, maps, and videos from the **Grand Canyon Association,** P.O. Box 399, Grand Canyon, AZ 86023 (✆ **800/858-2808;** www.grandcanyon.org). Among the hundreds of books written on the Grand Canyon, several stand out. For a general overview, leaf through *Grand Canyon: A Natural History Guide* (Houghton Mifflin Co., 1993), by Jeremy Schmidt. For a discussion of the human history of the Grand Canyon, try *Living at the Edge: Explorers, Exploiters and Settlers of the Grand Canyon Region* (Grand Canyon Association, 1998), by Michael F. Anderson. In *An Introduction to Grand Canyon Geology* (Grand Canyon Association, 1999), author L. Greer Price explains the geology of the Grand Canyon in terms anyone can understand. ***Frommer's Grand Canyon National Park*** is a comprehensive guide to the park written by the author of this chapter, Shane Christenson. If you're planning a longer trip to the area, you might also pick up a copy of *Frommer's Arizona* or *Frommer's American Southwest.*

FEES & PERMITS

Admission to Grand Canyon National Park costs $25 per private vehicle and $16 for those on foot, bicycle, or motorcycle. The receipt is good for a week and includes both rims.

Permits are required for all overnight camping in the backcountry that falls within the park's boundaries. This includes all overnight stays below the rims (except in Phantom Ranch's cabins and dorms) and on park land outside of designated campgrounds. Good for up to 11 people, each permit costs $10, plus an additional $5 per person per night (so the cost for four people, for example, would be $30).

Permits for the month desired go on sale on the first of the month, 4 months earlier called the "four-month-out." For example, permits for all of May go on sale on January 1; permits for June go on sale February 1, and so on. If you're not purchasing a permit in person (at the **Backcountry Information Center;** ✆ **928/638-7875;** www.nps.gov/grca), you'll need to complete a Backcountry Permit Request Form, included in the free *Backcountry Trip Planner,* which also suggests itineraries for first-time Grand Canyon hikers and offers advice about safe, low-impact hiking. To get one, call the park's main line at ✆ **928/638-7888** and choose the "backcountry information" option. Or write to Grand Canyon National Park, P.O. Box 129, Grand Canyon, AZ 86023, and request a Backcountry Trip Planner (not to be confused with the park's regular trip planners).

You can also download a Permit Request Form and instructions by going to the backcountry section of the park's website: **www.nps.gov/grca.** To increase your odds of receiving a permit, be as flexible as possible. It helps to request three alternative hikes, in order of preference, and more than one starting date. Keeping your group small also helps.

The **Backcountry Information Center** takes calls weekdays between 1 and 5pm MST at © **928/638-7875.** You can also visit the office from 8am to noon and 1 to 5pm daily. Representatives can help if you have questions about a trail or about applying for a permit.

VISITOR CENTERS

Completed in the fall of 2000, Canyon View Information Plaza, near Mather Point, has become the first stop for visitors to the South Rim. The **Grand Canyon Visitor Center** is here, and the whole complex has the streamlined appearance of a modern mass-transit hub. Various kiosks provide basic information about tours, trails, overlooks, cycling, weather, ranger-guided programs, and other topics. A parking lot accommodating up to 600 vehicles was opened in the fall of 2009. Free shuttles connect the Information Plaza with Grand Canyon Village and the Kaibab Trail.

Grand Canyon Visitor Center sits inside a long, glass-fronted building. Here you'll find displays about the canyon and the Colorado Plateau, an area for ranger presentations, a large bookstore run by the Grand Canyon Association, an information desk, and restrooms. To get here, you can take a free shuttle, walk, bicycle, or park. The Visitor Center is open daily 8am to 6pm in summer, 8am to 5pm during the rest of the year.

The **Yavapai Observation Station,** a half-mile west of the Canyon View Information Plaza on Yavapai Point, has an observation room where you can identify many of the monuments in the central canyon. Rangers here frequently lead interpretive programs.

The **Desert View Bookstore & Park Information,** 26 miles east of Grand Canyon Village, is small and staffed by volunteers. It sells books and provides information on the canyon.

Located 3 miles west of Desert View, **Tusayan Museum** has an information desk staffed by rangers, in addition to displays on the area's indigenous peoples.

Historic Kolb Studio, on the rim at the west end of Grand Canyon Village, houses a small bookstore and an art gallery with free exhibits.

The **North Rim Visitor Center** has a small bookstore and information desk staffed by rangers, volunteers, and employees of the Grand Canyon Association.

Verkamps Visitor Center is the park's newest visitor center within the century-old Vercamp's Curios building; it features displays depicting the canyon's history, as well as a bookstore.

SPECIAL REGULATIONS & WARNINGS

It's illegal to remove any resources from the park. These can be anything from flowers to pottery fragments. Even seemingly useless articles like bits of metal from the canyon's old mining operations have historical value and are protected by law.

Fires are strictly prohibited except at North Rim, Desert View, and Mather campgrounds. In the backcountry, use a small camp stove for cooking.

Bicycles are allowed on all paved and unpaved park roads and the new greenway trail. However, they are not permitted on other trails, including the Rim Trail. Bicyclists must obey all traffic regulations and should ride single file with the flow of traffic. On the narrow Hermit Road, they should pull to the right shoulder and dismount when large vehicles are passing.

Leashed pets are permitted on trails throughout the developed areas of the South Rim, but not below the rim. The only exceptions are certified service animals.

If, by chance, you have a hang glider and are considering jumping into the canyon, forget it. It's illegal, and you'll be fined.

SEASONS & CLIMATE

The climate at Grand Canyon varies greatly not only from season to season, but from point to point. At over 8,000 feet in elevation, the North Rim is by far the coldest, dampest part of the park. Its temperatures run about 30° cooler than Phantom Ranch at the canyon bottom, more than 5,000 feet below, and 7° cooler than the South Rim, roughly 1,000 feet below. It averages 25 inches of precipitation per year, compared to just 8 inches at Phantom Ranch and 16 inches on the South Rim.

The North Rim doesn't open until mid-May, so your only choice in early spring is the South Rim, where daily highs average 60°F and 70°F (16°C and 21°C) in April and May, respectively. Travelers should be prepared for late-winter storms, which occasionally bring snow to the rim. Spring is an ideal time to hike the inner canyon, with highs in April averaging 82°F (28°C).

In summer, the rims seldom become unbearably hot. Summer highs are usually in the 80s (upper 20s Celsius) on the South Rim and in the 70s (low 20s Celsius) on the North Rim. The canyon bottom, on the other hand, can be torrid, with highs in July averaging 106°F (41°C). Localized thunderstorms frequently drench the park in late July and August, the wettest month of the year, when nearly 2¼ inches of rain fall on the South Rim. On the North Rim, nights can be nippy even during July, when low temperatures average a chilly 46°F (8°C).

After the thunderstorms taper off in mid-September, fall is a great time to be anywhere in the park.

If You Have Only 1 Day

After stopping at one of the information centers to get your bearings, hike a short distance down the **Bright Angel** or **North Kaibab** trail in the morning. (If the weather is hot or if your condition is not top-notch, a rim trail may be preferable.) At midday, attend a ranger presentation; *The Guide* lists times and locations. Later in the day, go on a scenic drive. On the South Rim, your best choice on the first day is **Desert View Drive,** which remains open to cars year-round and offers expansive views of the central and eastern canyon. On the North Rim, travel the **Cape Royal Road.** To complete your scenic drive, watch sunset from **Lipan Point** on the South Rim or from **Cape Royal** on the North Rim. The scenic drives and corridor trails are detailed later in this chapter.

Highs on the South Rim average 76°F (24°C) in September, 65°F (18°C) in October, and 52°F (11°C) in November. The North Rim has highs of 69°F (21°C) in September and 59°F (15°C) in October. (It closes in mid-Oct.) The Inner Gorge remains hot in September but cools off considerably, to an average high of 84°F (29°C), in October. The first winter storms can hit the North Rim as early as mid-October.

In winter, the North Rim is closed, and drivers to the South Rim should be prepared for icy roads and occasional closures. When the snow isn't falling, the South Rim warms up nicely, with average highs of 41°F (5°C) in January. Hiking trails remain open but are often snow-packed and icy.

SEASONAL EVENTS

For 3 weeks every September, world-renowned musicians gather for the **Grand Canyon Music Festival,** P.O. Box 1332, Grand Canyon, AZ 86023 (✆ **800/997-8285** or 928/638-9215; www.grandcanyonmusicfest.org). Most of the offerings are chamber-music concerts, and are at the acoustically superb Shrine of the Ages Auditorium on the canyon's South Rim. Tickets for the 7:30pm concerts cost $25 for adults and $8 for children (park admission not included) and are available in advance through the festival office. To ensure that you receive the tickets you want, order by early July.

For up-to-date information on other special events, consult the park's newspaper, *The Guide.*

2 Exploring the Park by Car

HERMIT ROAD

This 8-mile road from Grand Canyon Village to Hermits Rest is open to private cars December to February only, when shuttles aren't running.

Your first stops are at **Trailviews 1 and 2.** Looking north from these view points, you can see straight down the side canyons that formed on either side of the Colorado River along the Bright Angel fault. Below, you may spot lush vegetation growing around a spring. This area is Indian Garden, where Havasupai Indians once farmed.

The next stop, **Maricopa Point,** overlooks the old Orphan Mine, which produced some of the richest uranium ore in the Southwest during the 1950s and 1960s. Below and to the west, you can see the metal framework from the tramway used to move ore to the rim from 1956 to 1969.

Continue to the **Powell Memorial,** which honors John Wesley Powell, the one-armed Civil War veteran thought to be the first non-native person to float through the canyon. From atop the memorial, you can get an especially fine view 60 miles southeast to the San Francisco peaks, including Humphreys Peak, which, at 12,633 feet, is the highest point in Arizona.

Because the next stop, **Hopi Point,** projects far into the canyon, its tip is the best place on Hermit Road to watch the sunset. As the sun drops, its light plays across four of the canyon's loveliest temples. The flat mesa almost due north of the point is Shiva Temple. The temple southwest of it is Osiris; the one southeast is Isis. East of Isis is Buddha Temple.

The next stop, **Mohave Point,** is a great place to observe some of the Colorado River's most furious rapids. Farthest downstream (to your left) is Hermit Rapids. Above it, you can make out the top of the dangerous Granite Rapids. Just above Granite Rapids, you can discern the bottom of Salt Creek Rapids. As you look at Hermit Creek Canyon and the rapids below it, you can visualize how floods washed rocks into the Colorado River, forming the natural dam that creates the rapids.

Next you'll come to **The Abyss,** where the steep canyon walls drop 2,600 feet to the base of the Redwall Limestone.

Monument Creek Vista is a new shuttle stop on the way to Hermits Rest that lets you access the new greenway trail. Cyclists can bring their bikes on the shuttle to this point and then ride 2.8 miles along the greenway to Hermits Rest.

Three thousand feet below the next stop, **Pima Point,** you'll see some of the foundations and walls from the old Hermit Camp, a tourist destination built in 1912 by the Santa Fe Railroad. Before descending to Hermit Camp, tourists took a break at the next stop, **Hermits Rest.** In this 1914 building, Mary Colter celebrated the "hermit" theme by building what resembled a crude rock shelter, with stones heaped highest around the chimney. Inside, Colter covered the ceiling above the fireplace with soot, so it has the look of a cave warmed by fire. Nearby are restrooms and a snack bar.

Highlights: Closed to cars during high season, the overlooks are quieter than those on the Desert View Drive and afford excellent river views.

Drawbacks: Occasional long waits for buses.

DESERT VIEW DRIVE

The first stop, Yavapai Point, features some of the most expansive views up and down the canyon. A historic observation station here has huge plate-glass windows overlooking the canyon, along with interpretive panels identifying the major landmarks.

People entering the park from the south generally catch their first glimpse of the canyon from the next stop, Mather Point. It's a clamorous place with one redeeming feature: a canyon view. (There's no such thing as a bad canyon view.) You can park here and walk to the South Rim's **Visitor Center at Canyon View Information Plaza.**

Grand Canyon Village

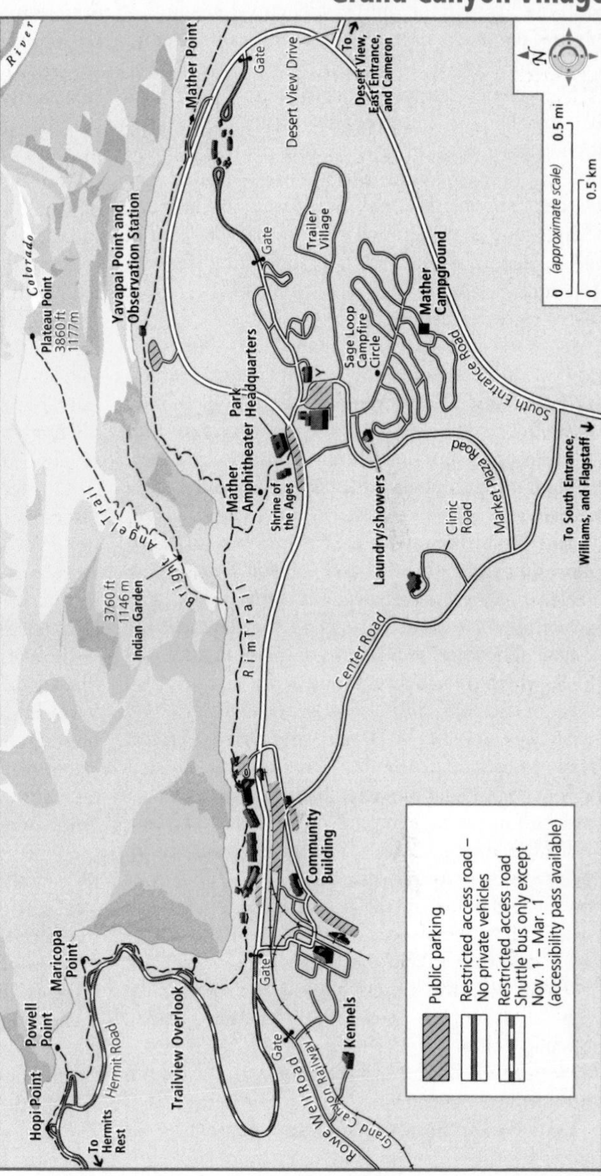

Yaki Point, the first stop off Ariz. 64, is accessible by car only when the shuttles aren't running. It's a great place to see the monuments of the central canyon, including Wotan's Throne, Vishnu Temple, and Zoroaster Temple. Two trails are also easy to spot from here. To the north, the South Kaibab Trail descends in switchbacks below Skeleton Point. Meanwhile, the Tonto Trail meanders across the broad blue-green terrace known as the Tonto Platform.

The next stop, 7,406-foot-high **Grandview Point,** is one of the highest spots on the South Rim. In the 1890s, one of the canyon's early prospectors, Pete Barry, built a trail from Grandview Point to nearby Horseshoe Mesa, where he mined copper. He then built cabins and a dining hall on the mesa, and a hotel a short distance from Grandview Point. Today only a trace of the hotel's foundation remains, but the trail is still in use, and Horseshoe Mesa bears the remnants of Barry's mines.

Next you'll come to **Moran Point,** named for landscape painter Thomas Moran. This is the best place from which to view the tilting block of rock known as the **Sinking Ship.** Stand at the end of the point and look southwest at the rocks level with the rim. The "ship" appears to be "submerged" in the horizontal layers of Coronado Butte (in the foreground). It's part of the Grandview Monocline, a place where rocks have bent in a single fold around a fault line.

Next comes **Tusayan Pueblo,** built in the 12th century by the ancestral Puebloan (sometimes known as Anasazi) people. Among the 3,500 documented archaeological sites in and around the Grand Canyon, this may have been the last one abandoned. A self-guided tour takes you around the pueblo. Built in 1932, the adjoining Tusayan Museum celebrates the traditions of the area's Native American tribes.

Don't miss the next stop, **Lipan Point.** With views far down the canyon to the west, it's a great place to catch the sunset. It also overlooks the Colorado River where the river makes two sweeping curves to form an enormous S. Just downstream from the S, the river begins cutting through the 2-billion-year-old Vishnu Formation, and the steep-walled Inner Gorge begins.

Like Lipan Point, the next stop, **Navajo Point,** offers fine views of the Grand Canyon Supergroup, a formation of igneous and sedimentary rocks that have eroded altogether in many other parts of the canyon. The long, thin streaks of maroon, gray, and black, which tilt at an angle of about 20 degrees, are layers of this formation.

The last stop on the Desert View Drive is **Desert View,** where you'll find the Watchtower, a 70-foot-high historic stone building that was modeled after towers found at ancient pueblos such as Mesa Verde and Hovenweep. Atop the Watchtower is an enclosed observation deck, which, at 7,522 feet, is the highest point on the South Rim. The rim at Desert View offers spectacular views of the northeast end of the canyon.

If you take the Desert View Drive shuttle, be aware that the buses stop only at Mather, Yavapai, and Yaki points.

Highlights: Spectacular views of both the central and northeastern canyon.

Drawbacks: Sometimes closes temporarily in winter because of snow. Allow a half-day for this 25-mile scenic drive on Ariz. 64, which connects South Entrance Rd. with Desert View.

NORTH RIM: CAPE ROYAL DRIVE

Start your driving tour at Cape Royal, where a gentle, paved .3-mile (each way) trail passes a natural bridge, Angel's Window, carved into a rock peninsula along the rim. The trail ends at the tip of Cape Royal, with views of the looming butte known as Wotan's Throne.

Your next stop may be at the **Cliff Springs Trail,** a .5-mile walk that ends at a small spring (see "Day Hikes," below).

From the next stop, **Walhalla Overlook,** you can follow with your eyes the tan line of Unkar Creek as it snakes down toward Unkar Delta. The soil and abundant water at the delta made for excellent farming for the ancestral Puebloan people, who occupied the canyon through about A.D. 1175. Many of these people migrated seasonally to dwellings such as the two small pueblos across the street from this overlook.

The next stop, **Roosevelt Point,** is one of the best places to see the confluence of the gorge of the Little Colorado River with the Grand Canyon. They meet at nearly a right angle, unusual in that most tributaries enter at close to the same direction as the larger rivers.

By starting your driving tour of the Walhalla Plateau early in the day, you can reach the next stop, **Vista Encantada,** in time for a late picnic on one of several tables with canyon views.

From there you can finish your driving tour by taking the 3-mile spur from the Cape Royal Road to Point Imperial, at 8,803 feet, the highest point on the North Rim. It's also the best place on either rim to view the northeastern end of the park.

Highlights: Sparse crowds and lovely views of the eastern canyon.

Drawbacks: The Colorado River is not visible as often on this drive as on the South Rim drives. Also, there's no shuttle on the north rim, so you must do all the driving yourself. From the Grand Canyon Lodge on the North Rim, it's best to go the length of the scenic drive 23 miles directly to Cape Royal, on the Walhalla Plateau, then make your stops on the way back. That way, you can do the short hikes near Cape Royal while your legs are fresh, and stop at the picnic areas, closer to the lodge, on your way back. Allow a half-day to a day for this drive.

3 Exploring the Park by Shuttle

Once at the South Rim, you can ride the park's free shuttles from March 1 through November 30 (year-round on the loop serving Grand Canyon Village). Three shuttle routes serve all of Grand Canyon Village, Canyon View Information Plaza, Mather Point, Yavapai Point, Yaki Point, and Hermit Road. When the shuttles run, Hermit Road and Yaki Point (including the South Kaibab trail head) are closed to private vehicles.

When the shuttles aren't running, take advantage of the park's **24-hour taxi service** (**© 928/638-2822**). These taxis do not have meters, as their fares vary according to distance and the number of passengers. The trip from Grand Canyon Village to Tusayan costs $10 for one or two adult passengers, plus $5 for each additional adult.

Protecting the Environment: What You Can Do

Here are a few things you can do during your stay to protect Grand Canyon National Park:

- **Respect the animals.** When accustomed to handouts, wild animals are nuisances, at best, and dangerous, at worst. Deer will sometimes butt, kick, or gore people who have food; squirrels, which may carry rabies and even bubonic plague, won't hesitate to bite the hand that feeds them. And human food isn't good for wildlife. In recent years, park management has been forced to shoot deer that have become sick from eating human food. So don't feed the critters.
- **Report sightings of California condors, and stay at least 300 feet away from the birds.** The endangered California condor, the largest land bird in North America, was reintroduced to the wild just north of Grand Canyon in 1996. Unafraid of people, many of the condors eventually began venturing to crowded areas on the South Rim. If the condors become accustomed to people, their survival will be jeopardized. Already, people have killed a few. The park asks that visitors stay at least 300 feet from the birds and report any sightings to a ranger.
- **Stay on designated trails.** Short-cutting is riskier on the steep trails at Grand Canyon than at other parks. In addition to risking a fall, people who cut trails often kick off rock fall, which is dangerous to those below. Short-cutting also digs paths that channel water during storms, causing unnecessary erosion of desert soils. Throughout the canyon, off-trail hikers frequently trample cryptogamic soils—delicate plants that take as long as 100 years to form.
- **Pack it out.** Even when day-hiking, remember to carry out anything that you bring in.
- **Pick up litter and recycle.** Even small bits of litter such as cigarette butts can add up to a big mess in the crowded areas on the rim. Pieces of paper that blow into the canyon can take decades to decay in the dry desert air. So can organic material such as fruit rinds and apple cores.
- **Leave plants, rocks, and artifacts in place.** Removing any of these things not only detracts from the beauty of the park, but is against the law. While it may seem innocuous to pick a flower, imagine what would happen if each of the park's five million visitors did so.
- **Use the shuttles.** From March 1 to November 30, free shuttles serve Grand Canyon Village, Hermits Rest Route, the Canyon View Information Plaza, and Yaki and Yavapai points. By using the shuttles, all of which pass through the Maswik Transportation Center, you can ease congestion, noise, and air pollution.

If you'd like to do something extra to help the park and make some new friends, sign up for the canyon's **Habitat Restoration Program,** which works to restore the park's natural environment. Activities include seed gathering, the removal of exotic species, and revegetating areas where the soils have been disturbed. During high season on the South Rim, a group usually meets in the morning and works for an hour or two. To find out more, ask at the Canyon View Center.

4 Organized Tours & Ranger Programs

The park offers a host of free ranger programs; the schedule changes seasonally. A typical schedule includes guided hikes and walks, kids' programs, and discussions of geology, native species, and natural and cultural history. Evening programs are scheduled nightly and run year-round on the South Rim (in winter, the North Rim is closed). For an up-to-date schedule, consult the park newspaper, *The Guide.*

GUIDED HIKES & TRIPS The nonprofit **Grand Canyon Field Institute,** P.O. Box 399, Grand Canyon, AZ 86023 (www.grandcanyon.org/fieldinstitute), schedules dozens of backpacking trips and outings lasting 1 to 9 days. Some explore broad subjects such as ecology; others hone narrow skills such as orienteering or drawing. An expert on the topics covered guides each excursion. Because the courses vary greatly, the Field Institute assigns a difficulty level to each and tries to help participants find ones suited to their skill levels and interests.

BUS TOURS Of the many private companies that offer bus tours, **Fred Harvey** (operated by Xanterra) presents the largest number of options. Among the tour choices are Desert View Drive (East Rim) and Hermits Rest Tour ($42 and $24, respectively, for adults; free for those under 16), sunset tours ($19), sunrise tours ($19) to one of several rim stops, and all-day outings that combine Desert View Drive with any other tour ($52). Unlike those on the free shuttles, Xanterra's drivers narrate the tours.

Though they mean well and offer some valuable information, these guides were not hired for their command of natural science and history. For advance reservations, call ✆ **888/297-2757** or visit www.grandcanyonlodges.com. Once at the canyon, visit the transportation desks at Yavapai, Maswik, or Bright Angel lodges, or call ✆ **928/638-2631,** ext. 6015, to make reservations.

Open Road Tours (✆ **800/766-7117;** www.openroadtours.com) offers 1-day guided canyon tours that depart from Flagstaff at 9:30am and return by 5:30pm. The cost is $95 for adults, $48 for children 11 and under.

5 Park Attractions

Most of the historic buildings on the South Rim cluster in **Grand Canyon Village,** a National Historic District. Hermits Rest, on Hermit Road, and the Watchtower, on the Desert View Drive, are also of historical significance (see "Exploring the Park by Car," above).

More than a half-dozen of these historic buildings were designed by Mary Colter, a Minneapolis schoolteacher who in 1902 began decorating the shops that sold American Indian art along the Santa Fe Railroad line. Both a decorator and a self-trained architect, Colter designed these Grand Canyon landmarks: **Hopi House** (1905), **The Lookout** (1914), **Hermits Rest** (1914), **Phantom Ranch** (1922), **Watchtower** (1932), and **Bright Angel Lodge** (1935). Colter's work drew heavily on the architectural styles of Native Americans and Spanish settlers in the Southwest. Another historic building, the **El Tovar Hotel** (1905), was designed by Charles Whittlesey in a style reminiscent of a northern European hunting lodge.

Grand Canyon Lodge (1928), on the North Rim, is on the National Register of Historic Places.

6 Day Hikes

There's no better way to enjoy the canyon than by walking down into it, watching the vegetation and rock layers change as you descend. The experience is far more rewarding than merely looking down from the rims.

Unfortunately, hiking below the rims can be dangerous, especially at midday during summer. Changes in temperature and elevation can make hiking difficult even in ideal conditions. The jarring descent can strain your knees; the climb back out will test your lungs and heart. If it's hot out or you aren't up to climbing, consider walking on one of the rim trails or on the new greenway being constructed on the South Rim. If nothing else, this will help you move away from the crowds at the overlooks. The rim trails are especially peaceful in the forests on the North Rim.

First-time hikers in the canyon should consider one of the corridor trails: North Kaibab, South Kaibab, and Bright Angel. Park rangers regularly patrol the trails, which are well maintained and easy to follow. Each has at least one emergency phone and pit toilet. Drinking water is available at several sources along both the Bright Angel and North Kaibab trails, but not on South Kaibab.

Wherever you hike, carry plenty of water and food, and check with the rangers about the availability of additional water along the trail. Eat and drink regularly. Wear sunscreen, sunglasses, and protective clothing. If you hike into the canyon, allow yourself twice as much time for the trip out as for the descent, and remember that the mileage indicated represents, in large part, vertical distance.

RIM TRAILS: SOUTH RIM

South Rim Trail This walk starts in Grand Canyon Village and goes both east and west along the rim, with the westbound section of the trail spanning 8 miles to Hermits Rest and the eastbound part extending 3.7 miles past Mather Point to Pipe Creek Vista. Both sections can be very busy, especially near Grand Canyon Village, and both offer stunning canyon views while passing through less-than-pristine rim-top scenery. The eastbound section is paved, wide, and easy to traverse; the westbound part is longer and more rugged, and has lonesome stretches. Unfortunately, much of it is close to Hermit Road.

West on the South Rim Trail Walking instead of driving along the rim is a great way to see the canyon while putting some room between yourself and the crowds at the overlooks. The trail travels parallel to Hermit Road and passes through the same scenic overlooks described in the driving tour (see above). The 1.4-mile stretch from the Village to Maricopa Point is paved, with one 200-vertical-foot climb. Past Maricopa Point, the trail planes off somewhat, and the pavement ends. For the next 4 miles, there's a well-defined dirt trail that meanders through pinyon-juniper woodland along the rim (when not passing overlooks). The scenery is lovely, and the crowd thins as you move farther west.

Because 16 miles might be too much for 1 day, I recommend hiking out on this trail from Grand Canyon Village and taking the shuttle back (Mar–Nov). By hiking out, you can avoid revisiting the same overlooks on the shuttle ride back—the shuttles stop at every turnout en route to Hermits Rest, but only at Mohave Point, Pima Point, and Hopi Point on their way back to Grand Canyon Village.

East on the South Rim Trail This smooth, paved trail connects Grand Canyon Village and **Mather Point.** Around the lodges, the path is a flat sidewalk teeming with people. The crowds dissipate somewhat between the village's east edge and **Yavapai Point.** Near Yavapai Point, there are many smooth, flat rocks along the rim—great places from which to contemplate the canyon. Located 1.75 miles northeast of the village's historic district, Yavapai Point has a historic observation station (it was built in 1928), with large windows overlooking the canyon and geology-related exhibitions. From here, you can walk another .7 miles to Mather Point on a portion of the park's greenway trail, then on to **Pipe Creek Vista.** This 10-foot-wide, paved walkway is usually within a few feet of the rim, away from crowds and providing ever-changing canyon views. If you grow fatigued, you can catch shuttles at Mather Point, Yavapai Point, or Pipe Creek Vista.

RIM TRAILS: NORTH RIM

Cape Final Trail This relatively flat, boulder-free trail is a good choice for a first hike in the backcountry. It meanders through ponderosa pine forest on an old jeep trail, ending at Cape Final, where you'll have partial views of the northern canyon and Juno Temple. 2 miles one-way. Easy. Access: Unmarked dirt parking area off Cape Royal Rd., 4.9 miles south of Roosevelt Point.

Cliff Springs Trail Both scenic and fairly short, this hike is perfect for active families. The dirt trail seems to head into forest away from the canyon, but it soon descends into a narrow, rocky side canyon that drains into the larger one—a reminder that the Walhalla Plateau is a peninsula in the Grand Canyon. It hugs the north wall of the side canyon, passing under limestone overhangs, in light-colored green by the canopies of box elder trees. The springs drip from one of these overhangs, where mosses carpet fissures in the rock. The spring water is not potable and must be purified before drinking. A waist-high boulder marks the end of the trail. .5 mile one-way. Moderate. Access: Small pullout a little more than ¼ mile north of Cape Royal on Cape Royal Rd.

Ken Patrick Trail This steeply rolling trail travels through ponderosa pine and spruce-fir forest between the head of Roaring Springs Canyon and Point Imperial. Starting at the North Kaibab end, the first mile of the trail has been pounded into dust by mules. The path becomes very faint about 4 miles in, after passing the trail head for the old Bright Angel Trail. Past the Cape Royal Road, the trail descends into, then climbs out of, a very steep drainage overgrown with thorn-covered New Mexican locust. Although challenging, the 3-mile section between the Cape Royal Road and Point Imperial is also the prettiest stretch, skirting the rim of the canyon above upper drainages of Nankoweap Creek. You'll see plenty of scarlet bugler, identifiable by its tubular red flowers with flared lower petals, as well as a number of Douglas firs interspersed among the ponderosa pines. 10 miles one-way. Strenuous. Access: From south side of parking area for Point Imperial, or from parking area for North Kaibab Trail (on North Rim entrance road, 2 miles north of Grand Canyon Lodge).

The Transept Trail & Bright Angel Point Trail To familiarize yourself with the North Rim, start with these trails, which are different sections of the same pathway. At the bottom of the stairs behind Grand Canyon Lodge, the Bright Angel Point Trail goes to the left and the Transept Trail goes right.

The paved **Bright Angel Point Trail** travels a quarter-mile to the tip of a narrow peninsula dividing Roaring Springs and Transept canyons. It passes a number of craggy outcroppings of Kaibab limestone, around which the roots of wind-whipped juniper trees cling like arthritic hands. The trail ends at 8,148-foot-high Bright Angel Point.

The **Transept Trail** ventures northeast along the rim of Transept Canyon, connecting the lodge and the North Rim Campground. Passing through old-growth ponderosa pine and quaking aspen, it descends into, then climbs out of, three shallow side drainages, with ascents steep enough to take the breath away from people unaccustomed to the altitude. Approximate round-trip hiking time for this trail is 1½ hours. Bright Angel Point Trail .25 mile each way. Transept Trail 1.5 miles RT. Easy. Access: Behind Grand Canyon Lodge.

Widforss Trail Named for landscape painter Gunnar Widforss, this trail skirts the head of Transept Canyon before venturing south to Widforss Point. For the first 2 miles, the trail undulates through ponderosa pine and spruce-fir forest, with spruce fir on the shady side of each drainage. Past the head of Transept Canyon, the trail heads south through a stand of old-growth ponderosa, part of which has been singed by forest fires. The trail reaches the rim again at Widforss Point, where you'll have a view of five temples. Near the rim are a picnic table and several good campsites. This is a self-guided hike; obtain brochures at the trail head.

5 miles one-way. Moderate. Hiking time approximately 6 hr. round-trip. Access: Dirt road a little more than ¼ mile south of Cape Royal Rd. Follow this road about ¾ mile to well-marked parking area.

CANYON TRAILS

Because of the huge elevation changes on the canyon trails, none should be called easy. (More people are rescued off the Bright Angel Trail, generally considered the "easiest" trail into the canyon, than off any other trail.) In general, please note that rating a trail easy, moderate, or difficult oversimplifies the situation; for this reason, we've avoided doing so below. For example, among the wilderness trails, the Hermit Trail is fine for many day-hikers going to Santa Maria Spring, but it becomes more rugged and harder to follow beyond that point; the trail offers day hikes that vary in distance up to 12 miles. The Tonto Trail is often easy to walk on, but it has little water or shade. It's always a good idea to discuss your plans and your experience with a ranger before setting out.

SOUTH RIM CORRIDOR TRAILS

Bright Angel Trail Both Native Americans and early settlers recognized this as a choice location for a trail. First, there's an enormous fault line that creates a natural break in the cliffs. Then there's the water—more of it than anywhere else on the South Rim.

On a day hike, follow the switchbacks below Grand Canyon Village to **One-and-a-Half-mile House** or **Three-mile House,** each of which has shade, an emergency phone, and drinking water (seasonally). The Park Service, which responds to hundreds of emergency calls on this trail every year, discourages many day-hikers from going past One-and-a-Half-mile House.

If you continue on the trail past Three-mile House, you begin a long descent to the picnic area near the spring at **Indian Garden,** where lush vegetation surrounds you and large cottonwood trees provide shade. At 4.6 miles and more than 3,000 vertical feet from the rim, Indian Garden is dangerously deep for many people. However, a few well-prepared day-hikers may wish to hike an additional 1.5 miles past Indian Garden on the relatively flat (in this area) Tonto and Plateau Point trails. The Plateau Point Trail eventually dead-ends at an overlook of the Colorado River 1,300 feet below. 4.6 miles to Indian Garden, 7.8 miles to Colorado River, 9.3 miles to Bright Angel Campground. Access: Just west of Kolb Studio, near Grand Canyon Village. 6,860 ft. at trail head,; 3,800 ft. at Indian Garden; 2,450 ft. at Colorado River. Water sources at One-and-a-Half-mile House (seasonal), Three-mile House (seasonal), Indian Garden, Colorado River, Bright Angel Campground.

South Kaibab Trail Unlike the Bright Angel Trail, which follows natural routes into the canyon, the South Kaibab was built using dynamite and hard labor. And unlike the Bright Angel Trail, which stays near creek beds for much of the distance to the Colorado River, the South Kaibab Trail travels on ridgelines with expansive views. Because the South Kaibab has no water and little shade, it is best for descending. The Bright Angel Trail is a safer trail for most hikers. Work is planned on the trail during the next couple years in order to minimize erosion and improve tread. During this period, mules won't be allowed on the trail.

For a good day hike, follow the trail as it makes a series of switchbacks through the upper rock layers, down the west side of Yaki Point. Below the Coconino Sandstone, the trail heads north to Cedar Ridge, a platform that has pit toilets and a hitching post for mules. Shaded by pinyon and juniper trees, it affords expansive views down side canyons to the east and west. This is an excellent place for day-hikers to picnic and rest before hiking the 1.5 miles and 1,500 vertical feet back out. 6.7 miles to Colorado River, 6.8 miles to Bright Angel Campground. Access: Yaki Point (Ariz. 64, East Rim Dr., 5 miles east of Grand Canyon Village). 7,260 ft. at trail head; 2,450 ft. at Colorado River. Water sources at trail head, Colorado River, and Bright Angel Campground.

North Kaibab Trail Less crowded than the South Rim corridor trails, this one begins at a parking area off the North Rim entrance road. It starts with a long series of switchbacks through thickly forested terrain at the head of Roaring Springs Canyon. The first major landmark is **Supai Tunnel.** At 2.7 miles from the trail head, with seasonal water, shade, and restrooms available, this is an excellent turnaround point for day-hikers. Beyond the tunnel, the trail descends in relatively gradual switchbacks through the bright red Supai Formation rocks, then crosses a bridge over a creek bed. Past the bridge, the trail travels along the south wall of Roaring Springs Canyon, on ledges atop cliffs of Redwall limestone.

A spire known as **The Needle** marks the point where the trail begins its descent of the Redwall cliffs. Roaring Springs, the water source for both rims, becomes audible just above the confluence of Bright Angel and **Roaring Springs** canyons. A .2-mile spur trail descends to the springs. In the lush vegetation around it, you'll find drinking water (seasonally), shade, and picnic tables. Roughly 5 miles and 3,000 vertical feet below the rim, this is the farthest a day-hiker should go. 2.7 miles to Supai Tunnel, 4.7 miles to Roaring Springs, 6.8 miles to Cottonwood Campground, 14 miles to the Colorado. Access: North Rim entrance road, 2 miles north of Grand Canyon Lodge. 8,250 ft. at North Kaibab Trailhead; 5,200 ft. at Roaring Springs; 4,080 ft. at

Cottonwood Campground; 2,400 ft. at Colorado River. Water sources at Roaring Springs (seasonal), Bright Angel Creek, Cottonwood Campground (seasonal), Phantom Ranch, Bright Angel Campground.

WILDERNESS TRAILS

Rangers are seldom encountered on the wilderness trails, which are not maintained by the park. The boulder-strewn trails have all but washed away in some places; in others, they descend steeply through cliffs.

Two South Rim wilderness trails, the Grandview and Hermit trails, work well for day hikes. Day-hikers often descend 2,600 vertical feet on the **Grandview Trail** to Horseshoe Mesa (avoid when wet or icy). This trail does not provide direct access to the Colorado River. Another option is to follow the **Hermit Trail** to Santa Maria or Dripping Springs (on a spur on the Dripping Springs Trail). Other South Rim wilderness trails include the Tanner, New Hance, Boucher, and South Bass. North Rim wilderness trails include the Bill Hall, Thunder River, Deer Creek, North Bass, and Nankoweap.

You can ask questions about wilderness trails and obtain free trail descriptions at the **Backcountry Information Center** (✆ **928/638-7875**), in the Maswik Transportation Center on the South Rim, and in the Backcountry Reservations trailer on the North Rim (no phone), approximately 11 miles south of the North Rim entrance gate, and marked by a sign. More detailed descriptions can be found in guidebooks and individual trail guides sold through the **Grand Canyon Association** (✆ **800/858-2808;** www.grandcanyon.org).

7 Other Sports & Activities

BIKING Inside the park on the South Rim, cyclists are allowed on all paved and unpaved roads, as well as on the **Greenway Trail** (there are plans to extend this trail through forest land and btw. canyon overlooks, connecting Grand Canyon Village to Tusayan, Hermits Rest, and Desert View). Cyclists are not permitted on hiking trials or pedestrian paths, including the South Rim Trail. Hermit Road is open to cyclists year-round and makes for a terrific ride, but you'll need to yield to tour buses, shuttles, private vehicles, and pedestrians.

You can mountain-bike on trails in the Kaibab National Forest, which borders the park on both rims.

For the South Rim, higher-end bicycles can be rented in Flagstaff at **Absolute Bikes** (✆ **928/779-5969**), 202 E. Rte 66. Prices vary from $15 to $70 for a full day, $15 to $50 for a half-day.

On the North Rim, **Forever Resorts** (✆ **928/638-2611,** ext. 758) rents mountain bikes at the Sinclair Gas and Outfitter Station located at the entrance to the North Rim Campground. Adult mountain bikes cost $40 per day or $7.50 per hour; kid-size mountain bikes cost $25 per day or $4 per hour. Helmets are required and provided.

For visitors to the North Rim, **Escape Adventures,** in Moab, Utah (✆ **800/596-2953** or 435/259-7423; www.kaibabtours.com), rents bikes for a half-day ($35) or full day ($55).

CONDOR VIEWING In recent years, many Grand Canyon visitors have spotted the largest land bird in North America. Of the 180 California condors in the wild, 75 now live in the canyon country of northern Arizona and southern Utah. Members of the vulture family, California condors will cruise well over 100 miles a day, at speeds approaching 50 mph. When mature, condors are grayish-black except on their heads, which are orange and featherless. Under each wing, a triangular white patch is visible.

Because condors have poor olfactory senses, they sometimes follow turkey vultures and other raptors to carrion. Other than size, the easiest way to tell the species apart is the way they soar: Vultures hold their wings in a V; condors keep theirs in a plane. Unless the condors change their habits, they will probably reappear above the South Rim in the years to come.

North of the canyon, you might spot a condor by driving 14 miles east of Jacob Lake on Hwy. 89A to House Rock Valley Road (the first road to your left after you leave the National Forest). Turn left (north) and go 2 miles to a small ramada. Scientists leave food for the youngest birds on cliffs above the ramada. If the condors are in the area, you'll probably meet workers who are tracking them. They carry a spotting scope and binoculars and will help you sight the birds.

Wherever you spot them, please don't approach, feed, or otherwise disturb the condors. If you see one who appears to be hurt or sick, notify the **Peregrine Fund Condor Project** (✆ **928/355-2270;** www.peregrinefund.org). Be prepared to identify the time and location of the sighting and, if possible, the bird's wing-tag number.

CROSS-COUNTRY SKIING Cross-country skiing is unreliable on the South Rim. When there is sufficient snow, the Kaibab National Forest grooms trails near the Grandview Lookout Tower. For information about which trails are open in winter, call the **Kaibab National Forest Tusayan Ranger District Office** at ✆ **928/638-2443.**

FISHING There's great trout fishing in the Colorado River just upstream of the national park, between Glen Canyon Dam and Lees Ferry. For advice on fishing this area, contact **Lees Ferry Anglers Guides and Fly Shop** (✆ **800/962-9755** or 928/355-2261), at Cliff Dwellers Lodge, about 2½ hours north of Flagstaff on U.S. 89A. Before you can fish in or near the park, you'll need an Arizona Fishing Permit and trout stamp, available at Lees Ferry Anglers or at the **Canyon Village Marketplace** (✆ **928/638-2262**) in Grand Canyon Village.

The best trout fishing inside the park is at the eastern end of the canyon, upstream of Phantom Ranch. The river is clear and cold (48°F/9°C) year-round directly below the dam, making this a great trout hatchery—and a chilling place for the native species, which evolved to live in muddy water and extreme variations in temperature. Downstream the river gradually warms and gathers sediment from its tributaries, causing the trout population to dwindle and enabling the bottom-feeders to survive. The five most abundant fish species in the park are carp, speckled dace, flannel-mouth sucker, rainbow trout, and blue-head sucker.

HORSEBACK RIDING For horseback riding near the South Rim, go to **Apache Stables** (✆ **928/638-2891;** www.apachestables.com), which operates from April through October behind the now-closed Moqui Lodge, just outside the park's south entrance. This is a great, albeit expensive, family activity. Children as young as 8 are allowed on the 1-hour trail rides, which, like the 2-hour ones, loop through the Kaibab National Forest near the stables. Apache Stables also offers a 4-hour ride east through the forest to a viewpoint at the East Rim. You must be 10 or over to go on the 2-hour ride, 14 to go on the 4-hour ride. Weight limits are 230 pounds, 220 pounds, and 200 pounds for the 1-, 2-, and 4-hour rides, respectively. Prices are $86 for the 2-hour ride, $46 for the 1-hour ride, $56 for the campfire trail ride, and $26 for the campfire wagon ride.

MULE RIDES The prospect of descending narrow trails above steep cliffs on animals hardly famous for their intelligence might make you nervous. Once on the trail, however, you'll soon discover that the mules are no more enthralled by the idea of falling than you are. Although the mules walk close to the edges, there has never been a fatal accident on a Fred Harvey mule ride.

From the South Rim, you can take a 12-mile round-trip day ride to Plateau Point, or purchase a package that includes the ride into and out of the canyon, and lodging and meals at Phantom Ranch. Because the rides are strenuous for both riders and mules, the wranglers strictly adhere to the following requirements: You must weigh less than 200 pounds fully dressed; be at least 4 feet, 7 inches tall; speak English; and not be pregnant.

The least expensive ride—the 1-day trip to **Plateau Point**—may also be the most grueling, since it involves a whopping 6 hours in the saddle. It travels down Bright Angel Trail to Indian Garden, then follows Plateau Point Trail across the Tonto Platform to Plateau Point, which overlooks the Colorado River. Having descended 3,200 feet, riders then return up the same trails. This 12-mile round-trip, which breaks for lunch at Indian Garden, doesn't reach the rim until mid- to late afternoon. Cost: $162, including tax.

The other rides are part of 1- or 2-night packages that include lodging and meals at **Phantom Ranch.** Going down, they follow Bright Angel Trail to the river, then travel east on the River Trail before finally crossing the river via the Kaibab Suspension Bridge. Coming back, they use the South Kaibab Trail. The 10.5-mile descent takes 5½ hours; the 8-mile-long climb out is an hour shorter. The Phantom Ranch overnight costs $477 for one person, $842 for two, and $378 for each additional person (prices include tax). The Phantom Ranch 2-night trip, offered only from November to March, costs $667 for one person, $1,011 for two people, and $469 for each additional person. A livery service is also available, costing $64 per duffle bag.

Mule rides on the North Rim are through a small, family-run outfit called **Canyon Trail Rides**. Four types of rides, open to ages 7 and up, are offered; the easiest goes 1 mile along the rim on the Ken Patrick Trail before turning back. This 1-hour ride costs $40 per person, while the two half-day rides each cost $75 per person. One stays on the rim, following the Ken Patrick and Uncle Jim trails to a canyon view point; the other descends 2 miles into the canyon on the North Kaibab Trail, turning back at Supai Tunnel. The all-day ride ($165, including lunch) travels 5 miles on the North Kaibab Trail to Roaring Springs before turning back. Riders must be at least 12 years old to go on the all-day ride. No one over 200 pounds is allowed on the canyon rides; for the rim rides, the limit is 220. All riders must speak English. Long pants are recommended, and you shouldn't carry anything more than a camera. Water is provided.

AIR TOURS A handful of companies, based at Grand Canyon National Park Airport in Tusayan, offer scenic airplane or helicopter rides over the canyon. With hundreds of thousands of people taking air tours over the canyon every year, the flights, which generate a great deal of noise in parts of the park and have raised safety concerns following a few crashes over the years, have become a politically charged issue.

The following companies offer air tours originating from Tusayan:

Papillon Grand Canyon Helicopters (✆ **800/528-2418;** www.papillon.com), **Air Grand Canyon** (✆ **800/247-4726** or 928/638-2686; www.airgrandcanyon.com), **Maverick Helicopters** (✆ **800/962-3869;** www.maverickhelicopter.com), **Grand Canyon Airlines** (✆ **866/235-9422;** www.grandcanyonairlines.com), and **Scenic Airlines** (✆ **800/634-6801;** www.scenic.com). Some of these companies also offer longer, more expensive tours that combine flights with short river cruises and lunch.

Most airplane tours remain airborne for 40 to 50 minutes and cost about $125 per person; most helicopter tours fly for 25 to 50 minutes and range from $150 to $235. The planes also cover more ground, crossing the canyon near Hermits Rest and returning along the East Rim, near Desert View. The helicopter tours, meanwhile, usually fly out and back in the same corridor near Hermits Rest (though some do go for the full loop.) The helicopters cruise lower—just above the rim.

RAFTING DAY TRIPS **Colorado River Discovery** (✆ **888/522-6644;** www.raftthecanyon.com) offers half-day guided smooth-water float trips from the base of Glen Canyon Dam to Lees Ferry (where most companies *begin* their trips). The excursions last about 6 hours and cost $64 for adults, $54 for children 12 and under. This trip is offered March 1 through November 30.

Grand Canyon Airlines (✆ **866/235-9422;** www.grandcanyonairlines.com) has teamed up with Colorado River Discovery to offer full-day guided smooth-water float trips from the base of Glen Canyon Dam to Lees Ferry. Round-trip bus transportation is provided to and from the Glen Canyon National Recreation Area, transferring through Grand Canyon National Park and the Navajo Indian Reservation. Cost for this tour is $179 ($159 for ages 11 and under), including lunch. Tours are offered year-round and include a flight over the canyon for an additional charge.

One-day guided motorized raft trips through the Grand Canyon's westernmost section are available through **Hualapai River Runners** (✆ **888/255-9550;** www.destinationgrandcanyon.com). Riders begin at Diamond Creek's rapids and finish at Lake Mead's banks. Time spent on the river is about 5 ½ hours and includes seven to nine cluster rapids. At the end of the day (weather permitting), participants are helicoptered off the river. Meeting time is 7:30am at Hualapai Lodge, on the Hualapai Indian Reservation in Peach Springs, and return time is between 6 and 7pm that same day. Lunch is included, and participants should bring a change of clothes, since they will get wet. These guided trips cost $353 per person and run from mid-March through October. The Hualapai Indian Reservation is about a 2-hour drive from Grand Canyon Village.

RAFTING OVERNIGHT TRIPS Guided motorized trips are fastest, often covering the 277 miles from Lees Ferry (above the canyon) to South Cove (in Lake Mead) in 6 to 8 days, compared to as many as 19 days for nonmotorized trips. The motorized trips use wide pontoon boats (known colloquially as "bologna boats") that almost never capsize, making them slightly safer. Also, it's easier to move about on these solid-framed boats than on oar or paddleboats, a plus for people who lack mobility. Because of the speed, however, there's less time for hiking or resting in camp. If motorized trips are for you, consider using **Moki Mac River Expeditions** (✆ **800/284-7280;** www.mokimac.com) or **Wilderness River Adventures** (✆ **800/992-8022;** www.riveradventures.com).

For mobile people who want to bask in the canyon's beauty, I strongly recommend guided nonmotorized trips, even if it means seeing half the canyon instead of it all. There are two types of nonmotorized boats: paddleboats and oar boats. Sixteen companies are authorized to provide rafting trips in the Grand Canyon. For a comprehensive list, visit **www.nps.gov/grca** under "River Trips."

8 Camping

INSIDE THE PARK

You can make reservations for campsites in the Mather and North Rim campgrounds by calling ✆ **877/444-6777** (928/638-7851 from outside the U.S.) or visiting **www.recreation.gov**.

Inside the park on the South Rim, 26 miles east of Grand Canyon Village on Ariz. 64, you'll find **Desert View Campground** (no phone). At dusk, the yips of coyotes drift over this campground in pinyon-juniper woodland at the eastern edge of the park. Elevated, cool, and breezy, the peaceful surroundings offer no clue that the bustling Desert View Overlook is within walking distance. The floor of the woodland makes for smooth tent sites, the most secluded being on the outside of the loop drive. The only drawback: The nearest showers are 28 miles away at Camper Services. During high season, this first-come, first-served campground usually fills up by noon.

Near Grand Canyon Village on the South Rim is **Mather Campground** (✆ **877/444-6777** or 928/638-7851). Despite having 319 sites in a relatively small area, this is a pleasant place. Pinyon and juniper trees shade the sites, spaced just far enough

Campgrounds in the Grand Canyon Area

Campground	Rim	Total Sites	RV Hookups	Dump Station	Toilets
Cameron Trading Post RV Park	South	48	48	Yes	No
Desert View Campground	South	50	No	No	Yes
Diamond Creek Campground	South	Open tent camping	No	No	Yes
Flintstone Bedrock City	South	Unlimited tent sites	27	Yes	Yes
Grand Canyon Camper Village	South	300	250	Yes	Yes
Jacob Lake Campground	North	53	No	No	Yes
Kaibab Camper Village	North	130	70	Yes	Yes
Kaibab Lake Campground	South	72	No	No	Yes
Mather Campground	South	323	No	Yes	Yes
North Rim Campground	North	87	No	Yes	Yes
Ten X Campground	South	70	No	No	Yes
Trailer Village	South	84	84	Nearby	Yes

apart to afford some privacy. The Aspen and Maple loops are the roomiest. Also, don't stay too near the showers, in the Camper Services building next to the campground—you'll have hundreds of campers tramping past your site.

For RV drivers on the South Rim, **Trailer Village** in Grand Canyon Village (P.O. Box 699), Grand Canyon, AZ 86023 (✆ **888/297-2757** for advance reservations, or 928/638-2631 for same-day reservations and campground questions), offers full hookups. The neighbors are close, the showers far (half a mile) away, and the vegetation sparse. However, a few sites at the end of the numbered drives have grass, shade trees, and one neighbor-free side. You can catch a shuttle bus at a stop near the campground.

Inside the park on the North Rim, the **North Rim Campground** (✆ **877/444-6777** for advance reservations) is 44 miles south of Jacob Lake on Ariz. 67. Shaded by old-growth ponderosa pines and situated alongside Transept Canyon (part of Grand Canyon), this is a delightful place to spend a few days. The 1.5-mile Transept Trail links the campground to Grand Canyon Lodge, and the North Rim General Store is within walking distance. The most spectacular sites are the rim sites, which open onto the canyon. These cost an extra $7 but are worth it. Showers ($1.50/5 min.) are within walking distance.

With only 87 sites, the North Rim Campground fills up for much of the summer. If you show up without a reservation only to find the SORRY, CAMPGROUND FULL sign on the entry booth, don't be afraid to ask if there have been any cancellations—you might just end up with a campsite. The best time to ask about openings is 8am, when sites made available by the previous night's cancellations go up for sale. The campground is open May 15 to October 15, with a limited number of sites remaining open until the first snowfall.

NEAR THE PARK: SOUTH RIM

Just outside the park is **Grand Canyon Camper Village** in Tusayan, 1 mile south of the park entrance on Ariz. 64 (✆ **877/638-2887**). This campground's advantage is its location, within easy walking distance of Tusayan's stores and restaurants on one side, and of Kaibab National Forest on the other. Its disadvantages are its relatively narrow (average width: 27 ft.) campsites and the noise from the nearby Grand Canyon National Park Airport. At least the restrooms are clean, the showers hot, and the laundry facility up and running. There's also a playground and a gravel basketball court.

Ten X Campground (✆ **928/638-2443**) lies 2 miles south of Tusayan on Ariz. 64. Large, wooded campsites make this the most peaceful campground within 20 miles of the South Rim. With plenty of

Drinking Water	Showers	Fire Pits/Grills	Laundry	Advance Reservations	Fees	Dates Open
Yes	No	No	No	Yes	$15 per site	Year-round
Yes	No	Yes	Nearby	No	$12 per site	Mid-May to mid-Oct
No	No	Yes	No	No	$25 per person	Year-round (weather permitting)
Yes	Yes	No	Yes	Yes	$14 two-person tent, $16 electric hookup, $18 water/electric, $2 each additional person	Year-round
Yes	Yes	Yes	Yes	Yes	$43 water/electric, $37 electric, $20 tent sites	Year-round
Yes	No	Yes	No	No	$17 per site	Year-round
Yes	Yes	Yes	No		$34 hookups, $17 dry sites, $17 tent sites, $85 cabin-style room	May 15–Oct 15
Yes	No	Yes	No	No	$18 per site	May 1–Sept 30
Yes	Yes	Yes	Yes	Mar–Nov	$18 Apr–Nov, $15 rest of year	Year-round
Yes	Nearby	Yes	Yes	Yes	$18–$25 per site, $6 tent only (no car)	May 15–Oct 15
Yes	No	Yes	No	No	$10 per site	May–Sept
Yes	Nearby	Yes	Nearby	Yes	$32, plus $2 each additional person	Year-round

distance between you and your neighbors, you'll find it a great place to linger over a fire. All sites have fire pits and grills, and the campground host sells wood. Later you'll find the soft, needle-covered floor perfect for sleeping. This campground, which is first-come, first-served, does sell out. If you're driving from Flagstaff or Williams, consider snagging a site before going to the canyon for the day. Open May to September.

NEAR THE PARK: NORTH RIM

Kaibab Camper Village is a half-mile west of Ariz. 67, just south of Jacob Lake (© **928/643-7804;** Mon–Fri 8am–5pm, or 928/526-0924 when closed; www.kaibabcampervillage.com). Compared to most South Rim RV parks, where sagebrush is often the largest plant in sight, this is like a fairy tale. Ponderosa pines tower above the campsites, making this easily the prettiest RV park in the Grand Canyon area. The use of generators is forbidden so everyone can enjoy the quiet. The campground has two showers ($2.25 for 5 min.).

Just north of Jacob Lake on U.S. 89A, nestled into rolling hills covered with ponderosa pine forest, **Jacob Lake Campground** (© **877/444-6777**) is a beauty of a Forest Service campground. Towering pines shade sites only a short drive from Jacob Lake Inn (where you'll find a gas station, store, restaurant, and motel). Sites are available on a first-come, first-served basis, but it seldom fills up.

Bundle up for the night at **DeMotte Park Campground** (© **928/643-8100**), a Forest Service campground 5 miles north of the park boundary on Ariz. 67. At 8,760 feet high, it's usually cold. The road through the campground curves sharply and some of the spaces are small, so this place may not work for large RVs. Because this campground is relatively small and located just outside the park entrance, it tends to fill up early. Try to get a site on your way into the park instead of on your way out. The campsite host will come around to collect your fee. Drinking water, toilets, and cooking grills are available on the campground.

9 Where to Stay

When planning a visit to Grand Canyon, try to reserve a place inside the park for at least 1 night. This lets you savor the twilight hours at the canyon without driving far in the dark.

If you're hoping to spend the night at or near the rim, be sure to reserve well in advance. During busy years, accommodations inside the park and in

Tusayan frequently fill up, forcing would-be lodgers to backtrack away from the park.

INSIDE THE PARK

Lodging inside the park on the South Rim is handled by **Xanterra** (✆ **888/297-2757** or 303/297-2757; www.xanterra.com), and on the North Rim by **Forever Resorts** (✆ **877/386-4383** or 480/998-1981; www.grandcanyonforever.com). Book well ahead: The most desirable rooms, like those at the Grand Canyon Lodge, El Tovar, or Bright Angel's rim cabins, can fill up a year in advance. All lodges usually sell out from mid-March to mid-October (in summer you can often find a room more easily for late Aug or early Sept). It is possible to reserve a room up to 13 months in advance (which you would need to do for Phantom Ranch), and the rate is guaranteed for the first night, even if the price increases later. If you're flexible with dates and travel in fall or winter, you can usually find rooms 1 or 2 months in advance. Because Xanterra and Forever Resorts both allow cancellations without penalty up to 48 hours in advance, you can sometimes grab a room at the last minute, even at the busiest times. A few rooms become available each day, so try walking into the lodge of your choice to ask about vacancies. Checkout is 11am, so the staff will know by that time whether a room will be available.

Rates listed are for double occupancy during high season, which lasts March through October and includes holidays. Prices may fall substantially in the off season at off-rim lodges (they remain the same year-round at El Tovar, Bright Angel, Kachina, and Thunderbird Lodges). A 6.74% tax will be added. Xanterra and Forever Resorts accept American Express, Diner's Club, Discover, MasterCard, and Visa. Kids under 16 stay free with their parents. Pets are not allowed in accommodations inside the park (service dogs are permitted), and there is no smoking at any of the lodges.

Most of the rooms in the park have relatively new furnishings, though only a few have telephones and televisions. Only El Tovar, Yavapai East (at Yavapai Lodge) and Maswik North have air-conditioning; Thunderbird and Kachina lodges have evaporative cooling systems. The only conspicuous difference in decor is at upscale El Tovar.

SOUTH RIM

Bright Angel Lodge & Cabins Guests of Bright Angel Lodge, which was renovated in 2007, stay in tightly clustered buildings along the rim west of the main lodge. In the 1930s, the Fred Harvey Co. sought to develop new, affordable lodging for the many visitors who had begun driving to the canyon. The company contracted Mary Colter to design the lodge and cabins. She built the cabins around several historic buildings, including the park's old post office and the Bucky O'Neill Cabin, the rim's oldest continually standing structure. Since those days, Bright Angel Lodge has become the South Rim's hub—and most crowded area. Visit the Bright Angel History Room for highlights of the legacies of Fred Harvey, Mary Jane Colter, and the Santa Fe Railway at the Grand Canyon.

Low-end accommodations start with clean, spare rooms in two long buildings adjacent to the main lodge. The lodge rooms are the park's least expensive, and each has a double bed and desk but no television; some also share bathrooms. Rooms in the historic cabins are slightly more expensive but still an excellent value. Most of these popular cabins house two guest rooms; the majority of them have open-frame ceilings and windows with bright-colored frames. The units nearer the rim are quieter than the ones along Village Loop Road, where traffic can get heavy. At the high end of the price range are the 12 rim-side cabins, which offer views of the canyon and probably the neatest overnight experience available at the canyon. Four include fireplaces; the historic **Bucky O'Neill Cabin,** one of the park's oldest structures, boasts a fireplace, a wet bar, and canyon views. The rim-side cabins tend to fill up far in advance, so plan ahead.

✆ **928/638-2631** (main switchboard) or 888/297-2757 (reservations only). Fax 303/297-3175. 34 units, 14 with bathroom, 10 with sink only, 10 with sink and toilet; 55 cabin units. $69 double with sink only; $79 double with sink and toilet only; $90 double with bathroom; $111 historic cabin; $142–$174 historic rim-side cabin; $333 rim-side Bucky O'Neill Suite. AE, DC, DISC, MC, V. **Amenities:** Restaurant; snack bar; lounge; Internet kiosk. *In room:* TV in most rooms; fridge in rim cabins; ceiling fan in rim-side and historic cabins.

El Tovar Hotel The grande dame of the South Rim hotels serves as a dark, cool counterpoint to Mary E. Jane Colter's warm, pueblo-style buildings. Completed in 1905 to accommodate the influx of tourists from the Santa Fe Railroad, the hunting-style lodge stands just steps from the rim and casts a long shadow over Grand Canyon Village. A pointed cupola sits like a witch's cap atop its three stories of Oregon pine and native stone, and spires rise above an upstairs deck. Inside, tourists wander through historic corridors that lead past the dimly lit lobby to the elegant dining room. El Tovar looks much as it did at its inception, when it offered all manner of luxury, including a music room, art classes, and a rooftop garden.

While these amenities have gone the way of the Flagstaff-to-Grand Canyon stagecoach, the hotel remains the canyon's most upscale, and the only one to offer room service and nightly turndown. During the renovation, rooms were given a significant facelift; CD radios were added, as were photos of the Grand Canyon. Bathrooms got pedestal sinks, beveled mirrors, and hair dryers. The deluxe rooms now offer more space, and some have balconies. Twelve individually themed suites, including the **Zane Grey Suite** (which has a porch) and the **Charles Whittlesey Suite** (named after the hotel's architect, this one has blueprints of the building's original design), start at $321. The most stunning accommodations are the three **view-suites,** each of which boasts a sitting room and a private deck overlooking the canyon. These suites, which cost $426, often fill up a year or more in advance. Stay at El Tovar if you can, but remember that you don't have to be a guest to enjoy spending time here.

✆ **928/638-2631** (main switchboard) or 888/297-2757 (reservations only). Fax 303/297-3175. 78 units. Standard rooms $174–$205; deluxe rooms $268; suites $321–$426. AE, DC, DISC, MC, V. **Amenities:** Restaurant (international) in a stunning dining room; lounge w/veranda overlooking the rim; concierge; room service. *In room:* A/C, cable TV, fridge, hair dryer.

Maswik Lodge Built in the 1960s, Maswik Lodge sits in a wooded area that's a 5-minute walk from the rim. If you're not up to walking, catch a free shuttle in front of the lodge, which also offers a transportation desk, cafeteria, gift shop, and sports bar with billiards and air hockey. The guest rooms fill 16 two-story wood-and-stone buildings known as Maswik North and South. Most **Maswik North** rooms feature vaulted ceilings, large bathrooms with vanities, private balconies, and forest views, making them among the park's loveliest accommodations. Because of their spaciousness and price, they're an excellent family value—and it's easy to get a roll-away bed, if needed. Rooms in **Maswik South** are older and a bit smaller, and have less pristine views. With only one window each, they can be hot during summer. However, they were renovated in 2007, and their low cost—less than Maswik North, which was renovated in early 2006—makes them a good value, despite their shortcomings.

Maswik is an especially smart choice for those traveling with children (lodgings here can easily fit a roll-away bed), and all rooms include two queen-size beds or one king. During summer, Maswik also rents out 40 guest rooms in 10 rustic, thin-walled cabins. If you're staying anywhere at Maswik, bring a flashlight, as the area is dark at night.

✆ **928/638-2631** (main switchboard) or 888/297-2757 (reservations only). Fax 303/297-3175. 278 units. Maswik South $90; Maswik North $170; cabin rooms $90. AE, DC, DISC, MC, V. **Amenities:** Cafeteria; sports lounge; ATM machine; Internet kiosk. *In room:* TV. In Maswik North only: A/C, fridge, hair dryer.

Thunderbird and Kachina Lodges The '60s-era dormitory architecture is impossible to miss in these lodges' flat roofs, decorative concrete panels, and metal staircases. The exteriors notwithstanding, the hotel has since been renovated and has both a friendlier look and an excellent location next to the rim. Inside, rooms are basic but comfortable, with wide windows and upgraded bathrooms. Most upstairs units on the more expensive canyon side offer at least a partial canyon view. Check-in for Thunderbird takes place at Bright Angel Lodge; for Kachina, it's at El Tovar.

✆ **928/638-2631** (main switchboard) or 888/297-2757 (reservations only). Fax 303/297-3175. 55 units at Thunderbird, 49 at Kachina. Street-side $170; canyon-side $180. AE, DC, DISC, MC, V. *In room:* TV, fridge, hair dryer.

Yavapai Lodge The largest lodge at the canyon, Yavapai lies a mile from the historic district but is close to Canyon Village Marketplace, the post office, and Chase bank. Built between 1970 and 1972, the lodge houses a large cafeteria and gift shop. Its 358 rooms are spread among 10 single-story buildings known as **Yavapai West** and six two-story wood buildings collectively called **Yavapai East.** Most Yavapai West rooms are compact with cinder-block walls but afford guests the benefit of parking right in front of their room's door. Yavapai East's units are larger, with king-size beds and air-conditioning. As many of them offer forest views, they're worth the extra money. The gravel paths connecting the buildings are very dark at night, so bring a flashlight.

✆ **928/638-2631** (main switchboard) or 888/297-2757 (reservations only). Fax 303/297-3175. 358 units. $107 Yavapai West; $153 Yavapai East. Winter $85–$105. AE, DC, DISC, MC, V. **Amenities:** Cafeteria; Internet kiosk. *In room:* TV, hair dryer. In Yavapai East only: A/C, fridge.

CANYON BOTTOM

Phantom Ranch This has got to be one of the world's most remote accommodations. Accessible only by floating down the Colorado River or by hiking (or riding a mule) to the bottom of the Grand Canyon, Phantom Ranch is the only park lodging below the rims, and it often sells out on the first day of availability—13 months in advance. To reserve a spot, call as early as possible. If you arrive at the canyon without a reservation, contact the **Bright Angel Transportation Desk** (✆ **928/638-2631,** ext. 6015) for information about next-day openings. Hikers will have an easier time getting lodging here in winter, when fewer mule rides head down.

The reason for the booked slate? Clean sheets never felt better than at the bottom of the Grand Canyon, cold beer never tasted as good (not even close), and a hot shower never felt so, well, miraculous. The ranch's nine air-conditioned cabins are a simple pleasure. Mary Colter designed four of them—the ones with the most stone in the walls—using rocks from nearby Bright Angel Creek. Connected by dirt footpaths, these cabins sit, natural and elegant, alongside picnic tables, under cottonwood trees' shade. Inside each cabin, there's concrete flooring, a desk, and 4 to 10 bunk beds, as well as a toilet and a sink. A shower house for guests sits nearby.

While most of Phantom Ranch was completed in the 1920s and '30s, four 10-person male and female dorms, each with its own bathing facilities, were added in the early 1980s. Used exclusively by hikers, these are ideal for individuals and small groups looking for a place to bed down; larger groups are better served by reserving cabins, which provide privacy and a lower per-person price than the dorms.

During the day, some guests hike to Ribbon Falls or along the River Trail, while others relax, read, or write postcards that, if sent from here, will bear a unique postmark: "Mailed by mule from the bottom of the Grand Canyon." In the late afternoon, guests and hikers from Bright Angel Campground gravitate to the canteen, which sells snacks and serves meals. Note that guests must book meals in advance. (For more about dining here, see "Inside the Canyon" under "Where to Dine," later this chapter.)

At the bottom of the canyon, ½ mile north of the Colorado River on the North Kaibab Trail. ✆ **928/638-2631** (main switchboard) or 888/297-2757 (reservations only). 7 4-person cabins, 2 cabins for up to 10 people, 4 10-person dorms. $42 dorm bed; $90 cabin (for 2); $11 each additional person. Most cabins are reserved as part of mule-trip overnight packages. Duffel service (baggage service via mule): $65 (each way). AE, DISC, MC, V. **Amenities:** Restaurant. *In room:* A/C, no TV, no phone.

NORTH RIM

Grand Canyon Lodge I love this lodge, a timeless stone and log structure that stands majestically at the edge of the North Rim over one of Earth's most breathtaking panoramas. A new park concessionaire took over management of the lodge in 2008 and has retained and enhanced its historic character.

The lodge's architect, Gilbert Stanley Underwood, was best known for designing edifices such as train stations and post offices. After opening in 1928 and burning in 1932, the lodge reopened in 1937 and seems to have grown into the landscape. Its green-shingled roof merges with the needles on nearby trees, its log posts match their trunks, and its Kaibab limestone walls blend with the rim rock. Beyond the grand lobby, with its 50-foot-ceiling and exquisite native American rugs, the octagonal **Sun Room** features leather sofas and chairs pointed toward three enormous picture windows overlooking the canyon. Two long decks with faux-wood chairs flank this room, providing a platform from which to view the canyon from outside. Just below lies another romantic lookout, the **Moon Room,** which is a favorite for marriage proposals. The lodge also houses a deli, saloon, and breathtaking dining room offering panoramic views of the world wonder before it (see "North Rim," under "Where to Dine," later in this chapter).

One hundred and forty cabins made of the same materials as the lodge have sprouted like saplings around it (unlike El Tovar, none of the units connect to the main lodge). There are four types of cabins, all of which received new mattresses and other updates when Forever Resorts took over management of the lodge in 2008. With rustic wood furnishings, gas fireplaces, fridges, bathtubs, and small vanity rooms, **Western Cabins** and **Rim Cabins** are the most luxurious. Western Cabins cost $12 less than the four Rim Cabins, but for paying the extra cash, you'll get magnificent views of Bright Angel Canyon. Rim Cabins generally fill up on their first day of availability, which is 13 months in advance.

The two other types of accommodations here—**Pioneer Cabins** and **Frontier Cabins**—are more rustic inside. Tightly clustered along Transept Canyon's rim, they feature exposed-log walls and ceilings, electric heaters, and showers instead of bathtubs. Pioneer Cabins were all renovated in 2009 with new handmade furnishings, and each cabin has two guest rooms—one with a queen bed, the other with twin bunks and a futon. For $136 to $146, a family of five can stay in comfort in a Pioneer Cabin. More primitive Frontier Cabins each have one guest room with a double bed and a twin bed. Getting the right shower temperature requires delicate balancing.

Tip: A few inexpensive motel rooms are also available here. Though comfortable and quiet, their ambience doesn't compare with the cabins' historic feel. Unlike the cabins, they offer ceiling fans. If you're concerned about it being too hot but want to stay in a cabin, request one that remains shaded during the peak afternoon sun. There's limited cellphone coverage here; Wi-Fi access, however, is available at the General Store, a short drive away.

At North Rim, 214 miles north of South Rim on Hwy. 67. ✆ **928/638-2611** (main switchboard) or 877/386-4383 (reservations only). Fax 928/638-2554. www.grandcanyonforever.com. 218 units. $116 Frontier Cabin; $112 motel unit; $136–$146 Pioneer Cabin; $158 Western Cabin; $170 Rim Cabin. AE, DC, DISC, MC, V. **Amenities:** Restaurant; deli; coffee shop and bar; post office; porter service. *In room:* No TV; fridge, hair dryer (in all rooms except Frontier Cabins).

OUTSIDE THE PARK

NEAR THE NORTH ENTRANCE

Jacob Lake Inn In 1922, Harold and Nina Bowman bought a barrel of gas and opened a gas "stand" near the present-day site of this inn. Seven years later, they built the inn at the junction of highways 67 and 89A, about an hour drive from the closest viewpoint on the North Rim. Today Jacob Lake Inn is the main hub of activity between the North Rim and Kanab, Utah. To serve the growing summer crowds, the Bowmans' descendants and their friends travel south from their homes in Utah. Together they run the inn's various businesses: the bakery, which churns out excellent fresh-baked cookies and pies; the soda fountain, which serves milkshakes made from soft-serve ice cream; and the gift shop, which features museum-quality pieces by Native American artists. There's also a restaurant, a motel, and a full-service gas station.

Lodgers can choose between inn rooms, motel units, and cabins. In 2006, a two-story stone and wood "hotel" building was added; it has country-style rooms with a king or two queen beds and small balconies with views of the surrounding ponderosa pines. Though pleasant inside, the motel rooms in the front building are not nearly as peaceful as the rooms and cabins behind the lodge. Built in 1958, the motel rooms in back are solid and clean. The bathrooms have showers but no tubs, and many of them drain onto the same tile floor as the bathroom itself—a curious design. Most people prefer the rustic cabins, which cost less than the motel rooms. The cabin floors creak and the guest rooms (from one to four per cabin) are small—in other words, they're exactly how cabins should be. Another advantage to the cabins is that each has its own private porch.

The **Jacob Lake restaurant,** with a U-shaped counter and dining room, serves burgers, sandwiches, and steaks, but the most appetizing entree may be the fresh trout cooked in the Dutch-style oven. A potent lunch item is the Grand Bull, a thick ground beef sandwich with grilled onions, chiles, cheese, mushrooms, tomatoes, and bacon. Even if you don't need a meal, it's worth stopping at Jacob Lake Inn to buy a few home-baked cookies, a piece of pie, or a milkshake.

Junction of Hwy. 67 and 89A, Jacob Lake, AZ 86022. ✆ **928/643-7232.** Fax 928/643-7235. www.jacoblake.com. 24 hotel units; 12 motel units; 27 cabins (shower only). May 14–Nov 30 $84–$143 double; Dec 1–May 13 $65–$75 double. Pets accepted for $10 extra. **Amenities:** Restaurant; playground. *In room:* No phone (motels and cabins only).

Kaibab Lodge Open from mid-May (the opening date is weather dependent) to November 2, Kaibab Lodge feels as warm and comfortable as a beloved summer camp. It has an open-framed ceiling and enormous pine beams that date from its construction in the 1920s. Guests tend to congregate in front of the 5-foot-wide fireplace (where there are Adirondack-style chairs), in the small television room, or at the tables across from the counter that doubles as the front desk and the beer bar.

Each cabinlike building houses two to four of the guest rooms, each of which sleeps from two to five people. The rooms are sparse but clean, with paneling of rough-hewn pine. Most have showers but not tubs, and there are no in-room phones or TVs. Because the older units' walls are very thin, it's best just to share a cabin with friends. Just a short distance from the highway, the rooms open onto the soothing, broad expanse of DeMotte Park, one of the large, naturally occurring meadows on the Kaibab Plateau.

HC 64, Box 30 (26 miles south of Jacob Lake on Hwy. 67, and 5 miles north of North Rim park entrance), Fredonia, AZ 86022. ✆ **928/638-2389.** Fax 928/638-9864. www.kaibablodge.com. 35 units. $90–$170 double. DISC, MC, V. Pets allowed. **Amenities:** Restaurant; bar. *In room:* No phone.

NORTHEAST OF THE PARK

The Marble Canyon area, at the northeast tip of the park (closer to the north entrance than to the east entrance), is a great place to stop if you're driving from rim to rim. In addition to Lees Ferry Lodge, you can find pleasant accommodations in the Marble Canyon area at **Cliff Dwellers Lodge** (✆ **800/962-9755;** www.cliffdwellerslodge.com), 9 miles west of Navajo Bridge on North Hwy. 89A (HC 67-30), Marble Canyon, AZ 86036. Another reliable option is **Marble Canyon Lodge** (✆ **800/726-1789** or 928/355-2225; www.marblecanyoncompany.com), a quarter-mile west of Navajo Bridge on Hwy. 89A, Marble Canyon, AZ 86036. Rates at both lodges are about $60 to $70 double.

Lees Ferry Lodge Some of the world's best porch-sitting can be enjoyed on the patios outside of this 1929 lodge's low sandstone buildings (a popular stopping place for trout fishers trying their luck above Lees Ferry). The patios, like those at nearby Cliff Dwellers, afford stunning views south across the highway toward the greenish-pink Marble Platform or north to the Vermilion Cliffs. Though the motel sits close to the road, traffic is slow at night.

The older rooms, which are small and rustic, have been redecorated in themes ranging from cowboy to, yes, fish. Double rooms in newer, prefab-style buildings are available for groups of up to five people.

HC 67-Box 1 (4 miles west of Navajo Bridge on N. Hwy. 89A), Marble Canyon, AZ 86036. ✆ **800/451-2231** or 928/355-223. www.leesferrylodge.com. 10 units. $65–$105 double. AE, MC, V. Pets accepted. **Amenities:** Restaurant; bar. *In room:* A/C, no phone.

EAST OF THE PARK

Cameron Trading Post Motel Each room features baby-blue bedding and Southwestern-style furnishings, many of them handmade by the motel's staff. The motel's **Hopi building** borders a terraced garden with stone picnic tables, a fountain, and a large grill. Ask for a room on the second floor of the Hopi or **Apache building** to get the best view. Next to the motel, **Cameron Trading Post RV Park** offers full hookups for $15 per night, but there are no restrooms or showers.

P.O. Box 339 (54 miles north of Flagstaff on Hwy. 89, and 1 mile north of the east Grand Canon Desert View access road), Cameron, AZ 86020. ✆ **877/221-0690** or 928/679-2231. Fax 928/679-2350. www.camerontradingpost.com. 66 units. June 1–Oct 19 $99–$109 double, $149–$179 suite; Oct 20–Dec 31 $69–$79 double; Jan 1–Mar 1 $59–$69 double; Mar 2–May 30 $79–$89 double. AE, DC, DISC, MC, V. Pets accepted for $15 extra. **Amenities:** Restaurant. *In room:* A/C, TV, hair dryer.

TUSAYAN

Tusayan is about 1 mile south of the park. The town is neither cheap nor particularly charming, with gas, lodging, and food priced about 20% higher than the same items in other gateway towns. However, Tusayan's location makes it the best option for folks who don't have a room inside the park and wish to stay closer than Flagstaff or Williams. A midpriced chain hotel in Tusayan is **Red Feather Lodge** (✆ **800/538-2345** or 928/638-2414; www.redfeatherlodge.com), on Hwy. 64, 1 mile south of the park. Next door is a **Holiday Inn Express** (✆ **888/473-2269** or 928/638-3000). Rates typically range from $100 to $150 for double occupancy.

Best Western Grand Canyon Squire Inn There's a lot to do at this hotel, which prides itself on being the Grand Canyon's only full-service resort. You can exercise, get a haircut, or pause to consider the lobby's three-story-high waterfall and Grand Canyon–themed mural by Southwestern artist Kenton Pies. Kids will love the recreation center, which includes a six-lane bowling alley, billiards, and video games. Adults tend to gravitate to the fine-dining **Coronado Room** restaurant and **Saguaro Lounge,** Tusayan's most popular bar.

All rooms were renovated in 2008 and 2009 with rustic wood furnishings and Southwestern accents. Standard rooms, in two older buildings, are no larger than the rooms at the other area motels. Costing about $20 more than standard rooms, deluxe rooms are more spacious and have better bathrooms (with Roman tubs).

P.O. Box 130 (1½ miles south of the park on Hwy. 64), Grand Canyon, AZ 86023. ✆ **800/622-6966** or 928/638-2681. Fax 928/638-2782. www.grandcanyonsquire.com. 250 units. High season $185–$205 double; low season $120–$145 double. AE, DC, DISC, MC, V. **Amenities:** 2 restaurants; 2 bars (lounge and sports bar); bowling; exercise room; Jacuzzi; outdoor pool (seasonal). *In room:* A/C, TV, fridge upon request, hair dryer, free Wi-Fi.

Canyon Plaza Resort Previously the Quality Inn, this hotel changed management in March 2009, upgrading all rooms and injecting new life into the service. In summer, guests here sun themselves around the large outdoor swimming pool and hot tub. In winter, they head for the hotel's stunning atrium, where tropical plants and palm trees shade an 18-foot-long Jacuzzi spa with a waterfall. As the area's hot tubs go, this one is the grandest, with jets to massage every aching joint. When guests finally finish soaking, they find themselves occupying some of the town's nicest accommodations, including a handful of rooms with private decks and refrigerators. A few rooms bordering the atrium have only tiny windows to the outside (and larger ones facing the atrium). Ask for a room with a large exterior window if darkness bothers you.

P.O. Box 520 (on Hwy. 64, 1 mile south of the park entrance, next to the IMAX theater), Grand Canyon, AZ 86023. ✆ **800/995-2521** (reservations only) or 928/638-2673. Fax 928/638-9537. www.grandcanyonqualityinn.com. 176 units, 56 suites. Apr 1–Oct 20 $145–$190 double; Oct 21–Mar 31 $100 double. AE, DC, DISC, MC, V. **Amenities:** Restaurant; lounge; 2 Jacuzzis; outdoor pool (seasonal); sauna. *In room:* A/C, TV, fridge (suites only), hair dryer, minibar (60 rooms), free Wi-Fi.

Grand Hotel Modeled after an Old West lodge, the Grand's lobby features an enormous fireplace, hand-woven carpets, and hand-oiled, hand-painted goatskin lanterns. Imitation ponderosa pine logs rise from the stone-tile floors to the high ceiling. The rooms are inviting, decorated with prints of the canyon and simple Southwest furnishings. The choicest ones are the third-story rooms that have balconies facing away from the highway.

P.O. Box 3319 (on Hwy. 64, 1½ miles south of the park entrance), Grand Canyon, AZ 86023. ✆ **888/634-7263** or 928/638-3333. Fax 928/638-3131. www.grandcanyongrandhotel.com. 121 units. High season $189 standard, $209 balcony; low season $99 standard, $119 balcony. AE, DISC, MC, V. **Amenities:** Restaurant; bar; exercise room; Jacuzzi; indoor pool. *In room:* A/C, TV, hair dryer.

7-Mile Lodge This is the cheapest motel in town. Instead of taking reservations, the owners of this lodge start selling spaces at around 9am and usually sell out by early afternoon. If you need a reasonably priced place to stay, think about stopping here on your way into the park. Don't be put off by the motel's cramped office—surprisingly, the rooms are decent and large enough to hold two queen-size beds. Thick walls and doors muffle the noise of planes from the nearby airport.

P.O. Box 56 (1½ miles south of Hwy. 64 park entrance), Grand Canyon, AZ 86023. ✆ **928/638-2291.** Reservations not accepted. 20 units. High season (spring to early fall, holidays) $80 double; low season (rest of year) $68 double. AE, DISC, MC, V. *In room:* A/C, TV, no phone, Wi-Fi.

WILLIAMS

Williams is 59 miles south of the park. It has one moderate to expensive chain hotel we recommend: **Best Western Inn of Williams,** 2600 Rte. 66 (✆ **928/635-4400**). Rates run about $149 double.

Recommended midpriced chain hotels in Williams include **Fairfield Inn by Marriott** (✆ **928/635-9888**), 1029 N. Grand Canyon Blvd. (off I-40 exit 163); **Quality Inn Mountain Ranch Resort** (✆ **928/635-2693**), 6701 E. Mountain Ranch Rd. (6 miles E. of Williams on I-40, exit 171); and **Holiday Inn Williams** (✆ **928/635-4114**), 950 N. Grand Canyon Blvd. (off I-40 exit 163). Rates range from $89 to $129 for double occupancy.

Inexpensive chain hotels include **Travelodge,** 430 E. Rte. 66 (✆ **928/635-2651**); **Motel 6 East,** 720 W. Rte. 66 (✆ **928/635-4464**); and **Motel 6 West,** 831 W. Rte. 66 (✆ **928/635-9000**). Rates range from $66 to $79 for double occupancy.

Canyon Motel & RV Park Kevin and Shirley Young have lovingly restored their 18 historic flagstone cottages, as well as the eye-catching guest rooms in two **Santa Fe cabooses** and one former **Grand Canyon Railway coach car.** From the outside, the cabooses resemble, well, cabooses, only with private decks. They even sit on segments of train track. They are wonderful for families of up to six, with a bed for the parents in the larger section, a compact bathroom and shower, and additional beds for the kids in the caboose's copula. The two largest guest rooms are in the Grand Canyon Railway car. Unlike the cabooses, these rooms have windows that open and enough space to accommodate a queen-size bed and a sleeper sofa. The cottage rooms are a good choice for travelers on a budget. The Youngs have also opened an adjacent **RV park** with full hookups.

1900 E. Rodeo Rd., Williams, AZ 86046-9527. ✆ **800/482-3955** or 928/635-9371. Fax 928/635-4138. www.thecanyonmotel.com. 18 cottage units (10 with shower only), 5 train-car units, 47 RV spaces, 6 tent sites. Cottage unit $36–$74 double; train-car unit $99–$106 double; caboose $128–$132 double; RV space with full hookup $29–$36 for up to 4 people; tent site $20–$25. DISC, MC, V. **Amenities:** Indoor pool (may close seasonally). *In room:* A/C (11 units), TV, fridge (18 units), microwave (18 units), no phone, free Wi-Fi (free).

El Rancho Motel It's sure not much from the outside, but this two-story 1966 motel between the eastbound and westbound lanes of Route 66 is one of the best lodging values in Williams. Guests can swim in the outdoor pool, cook on barbecue grills, or recline in the spotless rooms, which come with a host of amenities. The only drawback is the proximity of certain rooms to the noisy traffic. As for decor, one owner aptly describes it as "blue."

617 E. Rte. 66, Williams, AZ 86046. ✆ **928/635-2552.** Fax 928/635-4173. 25 units. Winter $38–$50 double; summer $58–$88 double. AE, DISC, MC, V. One small pet allowed per room for $5 extra. **Amenities:** Outdoor pool (seasonal); barbecue grills. *In room:* A/C, Direct TV, fridge, microwave.

Grand Canyon Railway Hotel This sprawling train-lovers' lodge beside the depot replaced the original Fray Marcos Hotel. Today an array of fun amenities, like an indoor pool and outdoor sports courts, make this a great spot for families. Bellmen carry luggage to the spacious (but somewhat spartan) Southwestern-style rooms, all of which come with two queen beds. Suites feature a separate bedroom and living room with a sleeper sofa and kitchenette. **Spenser's Lounge,** which features a beautiful 100-year-old bar imported from Scotland, offers simple dining and top-shelf liquor. The all-paved **Grand Canyon Railway RV Park** has opened next door.

235 N. Grand Canyon Blvd., Williams, AZ 86046. ✆ **800/843-8724** or 928/635-4010. Fax 928/635-2180. www.thetrain.com. 298 units. May 15–Oct 14 $169 and up double, $229 suites; Oct 15–May 14 $109 and up double, $159 suites. AE, DISC, MC, V. **Amenities:** 2 restaurants; lounge; exercise room; Jacuzzi; playground; indoor pool; free Wi-Fi in lobby. *In room:* A/C, TV.

Legacies Bed and Breakfast This two-story home on a quiet residential street offers only four rooms, but each is different, inviting, and reasonably priced. The **Hawaiian room** represents a tropical escape from the dry Southwest; the **Route 66** room, a walk down memory lane; the **Virginia Room,** a throwback to colonial times; and the 600-square-foot **Legacies Suite,** a romantic retreat with a raised canopy king-size bed, fireplace, and lighted two-person whirlpool. A wood-burning stove warms the lobby, and there's an inviting sitting area in the upstairs alcove. The highlight of the gourmet breakfast (included) is the orange-pecan toast served with warm maple syrup.

450 S. 11th St., Williams, AZ 86046. ✆ **866/370-2288** or 928/635-4880. www.legaciesbb.com. 4 units. $140–$210 double. Rates include full breakfast. MC, V. No children 15 and under. *In room:* Satellite TV w/DVD player, free Wi-Fi (free), fireplace and whirlpool in 2 rooms.

The Red Garter Bed & Bakery In the early 1900s, this Victorian Romanesque building had a brothel upstairs, a saloon downstairs, and an opium den in the back. The innkeeper, John Holst, has worked hard to preserve the building, built in 1897, and its colorful history. A general contractor specializing in restoration work, he fully refurbished the structure, which served as a tire storage facility in the early 1970s. Using early family and city records, he fleshed out the building's bawdy history, which he gladly shares with visitors. Each of the four guest rooms has custom moldings (made by Holst), a 12-foot-high ceiling, a ceiling fan, and antique furnishings.

137 W. Railroad Ave. (P.O. Box 95), Williams, AZ 86046. ✆ **800/328-1484** or 928/635-1484. www.redgarter.com. 4 units, all with private bathroom, 3 with shower only. $120–$155. Rates include Continental breakfast. DISC, MC, V. Closed Dec–Jan. *In room:* TV, no phone.

Sheridan House Inn Few B&Bs offer an inclusive package that rivals the one at this inn. Guests enjoy a social hour with complimentary snacks and nonalcoholic beverages, and a gourmet breakfast that includes fresh fruits, juice, yogurt, and a hot plate. There's also a video library, a game room, billiards, a stocked refrigerator, and hot drinks. Most of the guest rooms have brass beds (with tempting chocolates on the nightstands), glass-topped coffee tables, TVs, stereos, and VCRs. The **Rosewood Room** has been decorated with a lighthouse theme and includes a fireplace, DVD player, and large marble bathroom with separate shower and tub. Two **family suites** offer separate bedrooms for parents and kids, each with its own TV and VCR.

460 E. Sheridan Ave., Williams, AZ 86046. ✆ **888/635-9345** or 928/635-9441. Fax 928/635-1005. www.grandcanyonbedandbreakfast.com. 6 units. $145–$195 double. Rates include full breakfast and nonalcoholic drinks. AE, DISC, MC, V. **Amenities:** Jacuzzi during summer season; free Wi-Fi. *In room:* TV/VCR, fridge (in some rooms), phone, stereo.

FLAGSTAFF

Flagstaff is 78 miles south of Grand Canyon Village. A recommended chain hotel in Flagstaff is **Radisson Woodlands Hotel Flagstaff** (© **928/773-8888**), 1175 W. Rte. 66. A comfortable, midpriced chain hotel in Flagstaff is the **Holiday Inn Flagstaff** (© **928/714-1000**), 2320 E. Lucky Lane (off I-40 exit 198). A recommended B&B in Flagstaff is **England House** (© **877/214-7350** or 928/214-7350; www.englandhousebandb.com), 614 W. Santa Fe Ave. Rates range from $75 to $195 for double occupancy.

Comfi Cottages In the 1970s, Pat Wiebe, a nurse at the local hospital, began purchasing and renovating small homes in Flagstaff. Today she rents out seven of these quaint cottages, all but one of which were built in the 1920s and 1930s. Wiebe has modernized the cottages somewhat, adding thermostat-controlled fireplaces, televisions, DVD/VCRs, and washer/dryers. She goes out of her way to make accommodations comfortable and treats her guests like they're part of the family.

1612 N. Aztec St., Flagstaff, AZ 86001. © **888/774-0731** or 928/774-0731. Fax 928/773-7286. www.comficottages.com. 7 units in different locations in Flagstaff. $130–$280 double. Rates include breakfast. DISC, MC, V. Inquire about pets. **Amenities:** Free bicycle use. *In room:* A/C, TV, DVD/VCR, gas barbecue, fridge stocked w/breakfast foods, kitchen, picnic baskets, sleds.

Hotel Weatherford Constructed in 1898, this historic three-story hotel in downtown Flagstaff transports you back to the turn of the 20th century. An upstairs sitting room features quirky antiques such as a cider press and an antique sewing machine, as well as panoramic period photos of Flagstaff. The **Zane Grey Room,** which serves drinks on the hotel's third floor at night, boasts a hand-carved Brunswick bar next to a fireplace and across from an original painting by the legendary 19th-century landscape artist Thomas Moran. The guest rooms, only some of which have private bathrooms, are varied and eccentric.

23 N. Leroux, Flagstaff, AZ 86001. © **928/779-1919.** Fax 928/773-8951. www.weatherfordhotel.com. 11 units, 3 with shared bathrooms. $49–$75 double with shared bath; $85 double with private bath; $130 suite. AE, DC, DISC, MC, V. Parking behind the hotel. **Amenities:** Restaurant (Southwestern/American); 3 excellent bars.

The Inn At 410 Bed & Breakfast Gordon Watkins still runs the most charming, friendly B&B in the vicinity of the Grand Canyon. Peering into each of his nine guest rooms here is like flipping through pages in an issue of *House & Garden.* Each expertly decorated room is daringly different, yet tasteful. The romantic **Tea Room,** adjacent to the first-floor living area, is elegantly furnished with a king bed, fireplace, mahogany woodwork, porcelain tea sets, and Jacuzzi bathroom. Another room, called **Monet's Garden,** is reminiscent of a French country garden, with a private sitting area that opens to the garden. All the guest rooms here have gas fireplaces; three have jetted tubs.

410 N. Leroux St., Flagstaff, AZ 86001. © **800/774-2008** or 928/774-0088. Fax 928/774-6354. www.inn410.com. 9 units. $170–$235 double. MC, V. **Amenities:** Small gym; movie library; free Wi-Fi. *In room:* A/C, Direct TV with DVD/VCR, fridge, hair dryer, no phone.

Little America Hotel Strangely enough, one of the most highly regarded chain hotels in Flagstaff adjoins a truck stop. Little America's rooms are enormous—they have sitting areas, dressing areas, dining tables, and oversized tubs. They're lavishly decorated in French Colonial style (think Versailles), and were renovated in 2006 with plasma TVs and new carpeting and color schemes. Guest rooms facing the forest cost $20 more and are quieter because there's less train noise. An even better surprise: Five hundred mostly wooded acres, owned by the hotel, provide access to Flagstaff's urban trail system and, farther out, the Arizona Trail.

2515 E. Butler (off I-40 exit 198), Flagstaff, AZ 86001. © **800/352-4386** or 928/779-7900. Fax 928/779-7983. www.flagstaff.littleamerica.com. 247 units, 8 specialty suites. High season $149–$189 double; low season $89–$149 double. AE, DC, DISC, MC, V. **Amenities:** Restaurant; lounge; exercise room; outdoor Jacuzzi; playground; outdoor pool (seasonal); room service; complimentary shuttle. *In room:* A/C, TV w/pay movies and video games, fridge, hair dryer, free Wi-Fi.

A Shooting Star Innkeeper Tom Taylor's mesmerizing solar-paneled house serves as a B&B, observatory, and photography and music recording studio. Most guests come to this remote location under Arizona's clear dark skies to witness an amazing astronomy program (presented by Tom and included in the rate) that lets you view the moon, stars, and other planets through the lens of a powerful telescope. Three guest rooms—aptly named Galileo, Einstein, and Cassini—sit just off the great room, where guests come together under 25-foot ceilings to discuss the wonder of the stars. The house fronts the San Francisco peaks and sits next to a national forest, offering a breathtaking panorama in all directions.

27948 N. Shooting Star Lane (21 miles north of Flagstaff at milepost 236 on Hwy. 180), Flagstaff, AZ 86001. © **928/606-8070.** www.shootingstarinn.com. 3 units. $195 double. No credit cards. **Amenities:** Observatory; photo gallery; free Wi-Fi. *In room:* No phone.

KANAB, UTAH

Kanab, about 78 miles northwest of the park, has one chain hotel that's very good and slightly more expensive than the others: **Holiday Inn Express and Suites,** 217 S. 100 E. (© **877/320-8454** or 435/644-3100). It also has a number of more inexpensive hotels. Consider **Shilo Inn Suites Kanab,** 296 W. 100 N. (© **800/222-2244** or 435/644-2562; www.shiloinns.com); or **Comfort Inn,** 815 E. Hwy. 89 (© **435/644-8888**). For a comfortable, inexpensive campground smack in downtown with tent and RV spaces, as well as a few log cabins, try **Hitch N' Post,** 196 E. 300 S. (✆ **800/458-3516** or 435/644-2142; www.hitchnpostrvpark.com).

Parry Lodge Many of the older rooms (known as "movie units") in this 1929 Colonial-style lodge display plaques bearing the names of stars (Dean Martin, Gregory Peck, and Sammy Davis, Jr., among others) who stayed in them while filming Westerns here. One unit (no. 134) was built specially to house Frank Sinatra's mother-in-law while the crooner starred in *Sergeants Three.* (Sinatra stayed in an adjoining room.) The movie units are smaller and closer to Center Street than the newer rooms, but they're far more charming.

89 E. Center St., Kanab, UT 84741. ✆ **800/748-4104** or 435/644-2601. Fax 435/644-2605. www.parrylodge.com. 89 units. May 1–Oct 31 $62–$102 double; Nov 1–Apr 30 $49–$69 double. AE, DISC, MC, V. Pets accepted ($10 extra). **Amenities:** Restaurant (seasonal); heated outdoor pool (seasonal); free Wi-Fi. *In room:* A/C, TV.

10 Where to Dine

SOUTH RIM

Arizona Room STEAKHOUSE This is the locals' first choice for dinner and a less time-consuming option than El Tovar. The informal restaurant dishes up the South Rim's most consistently tasty meals. Entrees include hand-cut New York strip steaks, blackened prime rib, barbecue beef brisket, honey-lime grilled chicken, and pan-seared salmon with melon salsa. My favorite is the baby back ribs with prickly-pear or spicy *chipotle* barbecue sauce. To accompany your meal, choose from a variety of midpriced California wines or flavored margaritas. Arriving before the 4:30pm dinner opening isn't a bad idea, since the wait can be an hour long at sunset (the large windows facing the canyon are a huge draw). The restaurant is now open for lunch, too, offering a barbecue-centric menu. Consider the Serrano chicken salad if you've had your fill of beef.

At Bright Angel Lodge. ✆ **928/638-2631.** Reservations not accepted. Lunch $10–$13; dinner $17–$28. AE, DC, DISC, MC, V. 11:30am–3pm and 4:30–10pm daily. Closed for lunch Nov–Feb, and for lunch and dinner Jan–Feb.

Bright Angel Restaurant AMERICAN This busy restaurant serves average coffee-shop food. Basic breakfast and lunch fare such as omelets, French toast, burgers, and large salads usually pass muster. At dinnertime, the restaurant supplements the lunch menu by adding no-fuss entrees such as grilled tri-tip steak, sour cream chicken, roast pork loin, and three-cheese lasagna. A kids' menu and activity book are also available. This is a good place for families, who can dine without worrying much about the children's behavior.

Also in Bright Angel Lodge is **Canyon Coffee House,** which opens at 5:30am and serves coffee drinks, as well as light breakfast items. At night, the coffeehouse becomes a cocktail lounge.

At Bright Angel Lodge. ✆ **928/638-2631.** Reservations not accepted. Breakfast $5–$13; lunch $8–$11; dinner $11–$27. AE, DC, DISC, MC, V. 6am–10pm daily.

El Tovar Restaurant INTERNATIONAL One hundred years after opening its doors, this restaurant remains a memorable dining experience. Best of all is the stunning dining room, which features banks of windows at the north and south ends, and Oregon pine walls graced with murals depicting Native American dances.

At dinner, a Southwestern influence spices the Continental cuisine. Consider starting with the mozzarella roulades with prosciutto, tomatoes, olives, and a basil pesto. Delicious main courses include the salmon tostada served with organic greens and a tequila vinaigrette, the enormous New York strip steak accompanied by buttermilk-cornmeal onion rings, and grilled chicken with a fresh tomato ragout and feta dumplings. The French onion soup is an excellent lunch choice. At breakfast, sample the coffee—it's the park's best—and order the eggs Benedict with smoked salmon. All entrees are served in large portions, and children can order half-portions at discounted prices. Service is friendly and refined.

In El Tovar Hotel. ✆ **928/638-2631,** ext. 6432. Reservations accepted for dinner only. Breakfast $5–$13; lunch $7–$17; dinner $22–$36. AE, DC, DISC, MC, V. 6:30–11am, 11:30am–2pm, and 5–10pm daily.

Maswik and Yavapai Cafeterias CAFETERIAS For the price of a burger, fries, and a soft drink at the Tusayan McDonald's, you get a full meal at either Maswik or Yavapai cafeteria. Though the food costs about the same at both places, there are some key differences: Maswik more closely resembles a food court, where meals come complete with side dishes. One Maswik station serves Mexican fare; another provides home-style entrees like roast turkey, meatloaf, chicken, or fish; a third offers spaghetti and other pastas; and a fourth serves burgers, hot dogs, and chicken sandwiches.

At Yavapai, you can mix and match from different stations, picking up fried chicken from one, pizza from another, potatoes from another—and, when you put it all together, a case of indigestion. The salad bar is priced by weight.

Given a choice between Maswik and Yavapai, I'd choose Yavapai. The fried chicken is particularly tasty, as is the chicken potpie. If you're craving a burger, however, go to Maswik, where the meat is grilled instead of fried. Both cafeterias offer Dreyer's soft-serve ice cream and box lunches to go.

At Maswik and Yavapai lodges, respectively. ✆ **928/638-2631.** Reservations not accepted. Breakfast $3–$8; lunch and dinner $4–$12. AE, DC, DISC, MC, V. Maswik 6am–10pm daily; Yavapai 6am–9pm daily (closed early Nov to mid-Feb, except on holidays).

INSIDE THE CANYON

Phantom Ranch AMERICAN At the bottom of the Grand Canyon, whether you travel in by foot or by mule, pretty much anything tastes good. Would the food at Phantom Ranch taste as great on the rim as alongside Bright Angel Creek? That's hard to say.

Every evening, just three options are offered: a steak (drench it in steak sauce and you're in heaven) or vegetarian dinner at 5pm, and a hearty beef stew at 6:30pm. The vegetarian plate comes with a lentil loaf (better put steak sauce on this, too) and the same side dishes as the steak dinner: vegetables, cornbread, baked potato, and salad. With either dinner, dessert is chocolate cake.

The family-style, all-you-can-eat breakfasts are excellent, with heaping platters of eggs, bacon, and pancakes laid out on long tables in the canteen. The box lunch ($13) includes a bagel, cream cheese, summer sausage, juice, an apple, peanuts, raisins, pretzels, and cookies. Alternatively, you could pack your own lunch and, if necessary, supplement it with snacks from the canteen.

Because the cooks here produce only a certain amount of food, hikers and mule riders must reserve meals ahead of time through **Xanterra** (p. 204) or at the Bright Angel Transportation Desk. As a last resort, inquire upon arrival at Phantom Ranch to find out whether any meal reservations remain. Up until 4pm, you can do this at the canteen. After 4pm, ask at the side window behind the canteen. Between 8am (8:30am in winter) to 4pm and from 8 to 10pm, anyone is allowed in the canteen, which sells snacks, soda, beer, wine, first-aid items, souvenirs, and film. The lemonade is fantastic.

Inside the canyon ½ mile north of the Colorado River on the North Kaibab Trail. To reserve meals more than 1 day in advance, call ✆ **888/297-2757;** to reserve next-day meals, contact the Bright Angel Transportation Desk at ✆ 928/638-2631, ext. 6015. Steak dinner $42; vegetarian meal $26; stew $26; sack lunch $13; breakfast $20. AE, DC, DISC, MC, V (DC not accepted for advance reservations).

NORTH RIM

Deli in the Pines AMERICAN This snack bar serves simple breakfast, lunch, and dinner options, including cereals, sandwiches, pizza whole or by the slice, pasta dishes, and hot dogs. Grab one of the tables or booths, or take it to go. If all you desire is good coffee, stop by the **Roughrider Saloon** (straight across from the deli), which doubles as a cafe in the morning, open from 5:30 to 10:30am.

In Grand Canyon Lodge (west wing). ✆ **928/638-2611.** Reservations not accepted. Breakfast $3–$7; lunch and dinner $4–$22; AE, DISC, MC, V. 7am–9pm daily.

Grand Canyon Lodge Dining Room CONTINENTAL This is, without question, one of the world's most scenic restaurants. Long banks of west- and south-facing windows look out on Transept Canyon and help warm this dining room, gently lit by table candles by night. The high, open-framed ceiling absorbs guests' clamor.

For a park restaurant operated by a concessionaire, this unforgettable dining room offers a remarkably creative menu, which incorporates sustainable agricultural products. At dinner, consider starting with the blue crab and artichoke dip served with house-fried tortilla chips, or with the assortment of chargrilled vegetables accompanied by a sunflower dipping sauce. Fresh Utah ruby trout is served nightly as a main course with a different sauce (mine came with a deliciously light pear, apple, and raisin butter sauce), the 10-oz. prime rib is a favorite, and the thinly sliced bison will make your mouth water. There are a variety of pasta dishes and options for lighter appetites.

A sampling of the lunch menu includes beef stew, Angus hamburgers, veggie burgers, chicken or turkey sandwiches, and Navajo tacos; a lunch buffet with pasta and salad is also offered. Both the breakfast and lunch buffets cost less than $13.

Note there are only nine window-adjacent tables, which cannot be reserved. Though you can opt to wait (likely for an hour or more), you will still not be guaranteed a window seat. However, you can see through the windows from any part of the dining room, and you are always welcome to walk up to them for a closer view. Service is generally good.

At Grand Canyon Lodge. ✆ **928/638-2611.** Reservations recommended for dinner, not accepted for breakfast or lunch. Breakfast $6–$12; lunch $6–$12; sack lunch $11; dinner $12–$34. AE, DC, DISC, MC, V. Daily 6:30–10am, 11:30am–2:30pm, and 4:45–9:45pm.

NORTHEAST OF THE PARK

Vermilion Cliffs Bar & Grill AMERICAN After rigging boats for trips down the Colorado, many river guides come to this remote restaurant, and not just for the 85 types of bottled beer. The baby back ribs with homemade barbecue sauce taste fabulous, and the chef also prepares excellent hand-cut steaks, including New York strip. The staff provides low-key service in a dining room whose wood walls, tables, chairs, and bar all seem to have been hewn from the same tree. The restaurant can be very crowded at dinnertime during peak fishing periods (generally fall and spring). Hearty breakfasts are also served.

In Lees Ferry Lodge, Hwy. 89A, 4 miles west of Navajo Bridge, Marble Canyon, AZ. ✆ **928/355-2231.** Breakfast $5–$10; lunch $6–$14; dinner $10–$25. Daily 6am–9pm.

TUSAYAN

Cafe Tusayan AMERICAN/SOUTHWESTERN Since opening Cafe Tusayan in a space formerly occupied by a Denny's, the restaurant's owners have kept the menu small. They serve a few varieties of salads, appetizers such as jalapeño poppers and sautéed mushrooms, and a half-dozen entrees, including salmon with herb butter, baked chicken, and stroganoff. For breakfast, you can choose from Continental, Southwestern, and standard American options, including some vegetarian choices. Perhaps because the chefs are able to focus on just a few dishes, the food is some of Tusayan's best. However, servers tend to lose their focus when busy, and the table and booth decor still screams "chain restaurant."

Next to Red Feather Lodge (1½ miles south of the park on Hwy. 64 at U.S. 180), Tusayan. ✆ **928/638-2151.** Reservations not accepted. Breakfast $6–$13; lunch $7–$11; dinner $12–$23. MC, V. Daily 7am–9pm during summer; hours vary rest of year.

Canyon Star Restaurant REGIONAL The entertainment at this festive restaurant seems designed to give tourists exactly what they hope to find in the American West. Most nights, a lonesome cowboy balladeer performs for diners. Specialty items include the barbecue buffalo brisket, smoked baby back ribs, and the "ultimate T-bone" which is part New York strip, part filet mignon. Salmon and trout are usually served, and there's a commendable kids' menu ($8). The adjacent **Canyon Star Saloon** is Tusayan's leading hangout.

In Grand Hotel on Hwy. 64 (1½ miles from the park's south entrance), Tusayan. ✆ **888/634-7263** or 928/638-3333. Breakfast $7–$12; lunch $6–$16; dinner $15–$28. AE, DISC, MC, V. Daily 7–10am, 11am–2pm, and 5–9:30pm.

Coronado Dining Room CONTINENTAL Tasty food and attentive service make this Tusayan's most upscale restaurant. The nattily attired waiters, lavender-colored tables and chairs, and dim lighting create a more formal atmosphere than that at other Tusayan eateries (even though the dining room looks like the destination point for a time machine to the 1970s). The restaurant puts a heavy emphasis on steaks, including filet mignon, New York strip, rib-eye, and prime rib; a few chicken and seafood dishes are thrown in for good measure. The most delicious entree may be the elk tournedos served with sweet red wine demi-glacé. Fresh, dark bread accompanies the meal. The adjoining, family-oriented **Canyon Room** offers breakfast and a buffet lunch seasonally.

In Best Western Grand Canyon Squire Inn (1½ miles south of the park on Hwy. 64), Tusayan. ✆ **928/638-2681,** ext. 4419. Reservations recommended. Entrees $23–$30. AE, DC, DISC, MC, V. Daily 5–10pm.

FLAGSTAFF

Brix AMERICAN/WINE BAR Adjacent to the Inn at 410, this casually elegant restaurant and wine bar competes with Cottage Place as Flagstaff's finest dining room. Closely spaced candlelit tables fill the inside, and there's a charming outdoor patio with heat lamps for those who prefer fresh air. The seasonal contemporary American menu draws inspiration from local farmers; its selections are mostly organic.

413 N. San Francisco St., Flagstaff. ✆ **928/213-1021.** www.brixflagstaff.com. Reservations recommended. Lunch $11–$14; dinner $24–$32. AE, DISC, MC, V. Mon–Sat 11am–2pm and 5–9pm. Closed Sun.

Charly's SOUTHWESTERN/AMERICAN Charly's is spacious and cool, both inside, where the 12-foot-high ceilings of the Hotel Weatherford (built in 1897) provide breathing room, and on the sidewalk, a favorite place for summertime dining. Try the *posole*—New Mexican hominy with pork, chili, and spices served in a flour tortilla bowl—or the Navajo tacos served with frybread. Besides steaks, fish, and burgers, the restaurant also offers a number of vegetarian dishes. The hotel's **bars** are among the town's hottest nightspots and are open well after Charly's kitchen closes.

In historic Hotel Weatherford, 23 N. Leroux St., Flagstaff. ✆ **928/779-1919.** Reservations accepted. Breakfast $6–$10; lunch $10–$12; dinner $18–$24. AE, DC, DISC, MC, V. Sun–Thurs 8am–9pm; Fri–Sat 8am–10pm.

Cuvée 928 AMERICAN/WINE BAR Combination restaurants/wine bars have grown increasingly popular in Flagstaff, and this is the most spirited. Though Brix (see above) is primarily for fine dining, Cuvée 928 is first and foremost a wine bar, a place where spirited locals (and singles) enjoy sports on TV, festive music, and delightful California and international wines. Patrons can choose their selections right out of the impressive cellar, and wine tastings are offered every Wednesday evening.

This is also a place where the food is very, very good. The menu is written on a board; to give you a sense of it, the outstanding chef cures the salmon himself, and Flagstaff's only original hot sauce is served here. There's also a wonderful selection of sandwiches, *panini,* salads, and other light teasers. Cuvée 928 opens up on to Heritage Square, which is home to concerts, art walks, and movies on weekend nights.

6 E. Aspen Ave., Flagstaff. ✆ **928/214-9463.** www.cuvee928winebar.com. $6–$12. AE, DISC, MC, V. Mon–Tues 11:30am–9pm; Wed–Sat 11:30am–10pm.

Cottage Place COUNTRY FRENCH The quiet serenity of Flagstaff's most elegant restaurant is ideal for special occasions, a wonderful spot to peacefully celebrate your vacation to the Southwest. Original artwork decorates three rose-colored rooms, where soft conversations are heard from candlelit tables. Chateaubriand (for two) is chef-owner Frank Branham's signature dish. It comes with fresh vegetables, whipped potatoes, and tomato Provençal. As for other entrees, I find it hard to choose between the rack of lamb, which is seared on an open-flame broiler and accompanied by a port wine demi-glacé and English mint sauce, and the Gorgonzola tournedos: choice medallions of beef tenderloin pan-seared and flavored with Gorgonzola and blue cheese. All entrees are served with soup du jour, green salad, and fresh breads. A six-course tasting menu is offered nightly, with or without matching wines, plus you can order the "Twilight Menu" from 5 to 6pm, which comes with soup or salad and an entree for $19.

126 W. Cottage Ave., Flagstaff. ✆ **928/774-8431.** Reservations recommended. Dinner $19–$37; chateaubriand for 2 $74. AE, MC, V. Wed–Sun 5–9:30pm.

Fratelli Pizza PIZZERIA This is not a place to come for a relaxing, romantic, or even sit-down dinner. There are only a few tables, so most people order takeout. There's not much more to say about Fratelli, except that its pizza is Northern Arizona's best. The hand-tossed pies come with a selection of traditional, vegetarian, and specialty toppings. Antipasto, salads, and giant calzones also enliven the menu, as do a handful of beer and wine selections.

119 W. Phoenix Ave., Flagstaff. ✆ **928/774-9200.** Reservations not accepted. Pizza $11–$20. AE, DISC, MC, V. Sun–Thurs 11am–9pm; Fri 11am–10pm.

Tinderbox Kitchen AMERICAN Opened in May 2009, Tinderbox Kitchen quickly established itself as Flagstaff's hottest new table. Co-owners Kevin Heinonen and chef Scott Heinonen have created an inspirational menu centered on American comfort food, although it's been kicked up several notches above "comfort." The menu varies daily and is packed with creative entrees such as succulent seared scallops served with homemade bacon creamed corn and wild rice hushpuppies, jalapeno mac-'n'-cheese topped with a duck leg confit, homemade sausage links, and a fresh fish selection prepared any number of ways. The decor matches the contemporary simplicity of the cuisine, with a dozen interior tables complemented by a handful of tables on the back patio.

34 S. San Francisco St., Flagstaff. ✆ **928/226-8400.** www.tinderbox.com. Reservations recommended. Lunch $8–$15; dinner $16–$28. AE, DISC, MC, V. Mon 5–9pm; Tues–Sat 11am–2pm and 5–9pm. Closed Sun.

WILLIAMS

Cruisers Cafe 66 AMERICAN Built in an old Route 66 gas station, this restaurant is jammed with gas-station memorabilia, including stamped glass, filling-station signs, vintage gas pumps, and photos of classic service stations. It's exactly what you would expect from a family-run cafe along Route 66. The burgers are tasty, but the best choice, if you really want to fill up, is the pork-back ribs. Healthier options are available, too.

233 W. Rte. 66, Williams. ✆ **928/635-2445.** www.cruisers66.com. Reservations not accepted. Lunch and dinner $9–$21. AE, DISC, MC, V. Daily 11am–10pm (may vary seasonally).

Pine Country Restaurant AMERICAN Many locals who dine at this recently expanded restaurant in downtown Williams eat their pie first, *then* order dinner. One taste of any of the 25-plus varieties of fresh-baked pie (if it's summer, you'll be able to choose from more than *50*)—including unusual flavors such as banana peanut butter and strawberry cream cheese—will convince you that the pie-eaters have their priorities straight. But pie ($4 a piece) is just a slice of the offerings here. Dinner entrees, like country-fried steak, grilled shrimp skewers, and rotisserie chicken, are moderately priced and taste home cooked. The lunch menu mostly consists of burgers, hot sandwiches, and salads.

107 N. Grand Canyon Blvd., Williams. ✆ **928/635-9718.** Reservations accepted. Breakfast $5–$8; lunch $6–$8; dinner $10–$22. AE, DISC, MC, V. Daily 5:30am–9pm.

Rod's Steak House STEAKHOUSE If you're a steak lover, brake for the cow-shaped sign on Route 66 as if it were real livestock. This landmark Route 66 restaurant, which sprawls across a city block between the highway's east- and westbound lanes, has hardly changed since Rodney Graves, an early member of the U.S. Geological Survey, opened it in 1946. It's almost always crowded. Printed on a paper cutout of a cow, the fold-out menu is still only about 6 inches across—more than enough space for its laconic descriptions of the restaurant's offerings. The best choices are the corn-fed, mesquite-broiled steaks, which have kept this place humming for a half-century. For dessert, try the mud pie.

301 E. Rte. 66, Williams. ✆ **928/635-2671.** Reservations accepted. $13–$42. AE, DISC, MC, V. Mon–Sat 11am–9:30pm. Closed Sun and first 2 weeks of Jan.

KANAB, UTAH

Escobar's Mexican Restaurant MEXICAN There's not much to make you feel like you're in Mexico here, save for a few shiny sombreros and toy chile peppers dangling from the ceiling. But this ultracasual Kanab favorite (indeed, there are sometimes as many kids as adults in the small dining room) serves Mexican food far more authentic than what you might expect to find here.

373 E. 300 S. ✆ **435/644-3739.** Reservations not accepted. Breakfast $6–$7; lunch $3–$7; dinner $8–$16. No credit cards. Sun–Fri 11am–9:30pm. Closed mid-Dec to mid-Jan.

Houston's Trails' End Restaurant AMERICAN Generations of ranchers have eaten in this restaurant, as evidenced by the many rifles, branding irons, and spurs hanging on the walls. While country music plays over the stereo, waitresses wearing toy weapons serve up meaty dishes, including the house specialty, chicken-fried steak topped with country gravy. For something a bit more exotic, try the honey-jalapeno pork tenderloin. The soup is made fresh daily, as are the enormous yeast rolls that come with dinner.

32 E. Center St. ✆ **435/644-2488.** Reservations accepted. Breakfast $4–$12; lunch $6–$13; dinner $10–$23. AE, DISC, MC, V. Daily 7am–10pm. Closed mid-Nov to mid-Mar.

Rocking V Café ECLECTIC In 2000, Vicky Cooper left her stressful job as a TV news reporter to open this eclectic cafe, easily Kanab's best restaurant. The fresh, all-organic menu might include chicken and mushroom Alfredo, cornmeal-crusted trout, Asian stir-fry, and Thai curry with fresh veggies. My favorite dish is the grilled buffalo tenderloin—free-range buffalo with a burgundy-balsamic reduction served with soup or salad. Finish with the chocolate silk or Key lime pie. The restaurant occupies a glass-fronted 1892 building that has seen duty as a general store, a mortuary, a grocery, and a bank. The wine cellar occupies the old safe, and there's a gallery with local and regional art upstairs. Service is excellent.

97 W. Center St. ✆ **435/644-8001.** Reservations accepted. Dinner $12–$38. MC, V. Wed–Sun 5–9pm (daily in high season). Closed Nov–Feb.

11 Picnic & Camping Supplies

If possible, stock up on camping items at a grocery store in a large city, such as Flagstaff. In general, prices rise steadily as you near the canyon, peaking at the **Canyon Village Marketplace** inside the park on the South Rim, in Market Plaza at Grand Canyon Village (✆ **928/638-2262**). Also on the South Rim is the **Desert View Store** at Desert View off Ariz. 64 (✆ **928/638-2393**). On the North Rim is the **North Rim General Store** (✆ **928/638-2611**), adjacent to North Rim Campground.

Outside the park, in Tusayan, is **Tusayan General Store,** 1 mile south of the park entrance on Ariz. 64 (✆ **928/638-2854**). Williams has a **Safeway,** 637 W. Rte. 66 (✆ **928/635-0500**).

In Kanab you'll find **Glazier's Market,** 264 S. 100 E. (✆ **435/644-5029**), and **Honey's Jubilee Foods,** 260 E. 300 S. (✆ **435/644-5877**).

Flagstaff has four large supermarkets: **Albertson's,** 1416 E. Rte. 66 (✆ **928/773-7955**); **Basha's,** 2700 Woodlands Village Blvd. (✆ **928/774-3882**); and another location at 1000 N. Humphreys St. (✆ **928/774-2101**); and **Fry's,** 201 N. Switzer Canyon Dr. (✆ **928/774-2719**).

17

Grand Teton National Park, WY

by Eric Peterson

Every time you focus your camera in Grand Teton, the frame will likely center on one of its many stately peaks. As a whole, the towering mountains of the Teton Range define this park, unlike neighboring Yellowstone, distinguished by its pastiche of thermal features and subtle beauty. You'll still see wildlife—eagles and osprey along the Snake River; moose and, if you're lucky, a black bear in the vicinity of the Jackson Lake Junction; and pronghorn on the valley floor—but it is the landscape that makes Grand Teton.

Compared with the undulations of Yellowstone, Grand Teton presents two vistas: a long, wide valley bordered on all sides by vertical peaks. If possible, once you enter the park, head for the summit of Signal Mountain, near Jackson Lake. There you will have a 360-degree view that will put the park and surrounding areas in perspective. It's also the view point from which some of the most famous early photos of the park were taken.

From the Jackson Point Overlook on Signal Mountain, you'll see a valley floor that was once covered with a freshwater sea and, later, thousands of tons of ice; to the west are views of a mountain formation towering more than a mile overhead.

Consider that the tops of the Tetons, which sit on a 40-mile-long fault, were displaced by geological upheaval that caused 30,000 feet of movement of the earth's crust over the last 13 million years—the valley floor dropped by 24,000 feet as the mountains shot up 6,000 feet. Ice-age glaciers, which also gouged out hundreds of lakes in the park, carved the canyons that punctuate the mountains.

One advantage of Grand Teton over Yellowstone is that it's significantly easier to navigate, in part because the park is smaller and activity centers are closer to each other. Jackson Lake and the Snake River, prime recreational areas for anglers and boaters, are near the hiking trails and campsites. Though not as stately as Old Faithful Inn, Jackson Lake Lodge is quite appealing and comfortable in its own right.

The first homesteaders began arriving in the area in the 1880s. Many discovered, though, that the frigid winters and short growing season made it difficult—indeed, virtually impossible—to eke out a living, so they abandoned the area. By 1907, cattle ranchers discovered that wealthy Eastern hunters were attracted to the area as a vacation site, and the dude-ranching industry secured its first foothold in Jackson Hole, the great valley that runs the length of the Tetons on the east side.

When cattle interests learned of a movement to convert privately owned grazing land on the valley floor into a national park, a rancorous tug-of-war began. Congress had designated the area south of Yellowstone National Park the Teton Forest Reserve in 1897 and attempted to create a larger sanctuary in 1918; however, local opposition defeated the measure. In 1923, a better-reasoned and successful attempt was made to preserve the area for future generations. Maud Noble, a conservation-minded entrepreneur, and a group of other concerned locals, aided by Yellowstone Superintendent Horace Albright, prepared a plan for setting aside a portion of the Jackson Hole as a national recreation area. Congress first set aside 96,000 acres of mountains and forests (excluding Jackson Lake) as a national park in 1929.

John D. Rockefeller, Jr., got into the act by establishing the Snake River Land Company, which became the vehicle through which he anonymously accumulated more than 35,000 acres of land between 1927 and 1943. His goal was to donate the property for an enlarged park, but opponents in Congress prevented the government from accepting his gift.

Finally, in 1950, the feds and the locals reached a compromise: The government agreed to reimburse Teton County for revenue that would have been generated by property taxes and to honor existing leaseholds, and present-day Grand Teton National Park was born.

AVOIDING THE CROWDS

Most of the travelers who visit Grand Teton are visiting Yellowstone on the same trip—and this means that when winter closes in on Yellowstone, the crowds abandon both parks. Grand Teton usually holds out against winter a bit longer than the higher plateau to the north, so you may enjoy a wonderful, traffic-free visit in early June and late October at Grand Teton. But I emphasize the word *may:* Snow can fall as early as September and as late as June.

Another off-season risk, in addition to unpredictable snowfall, is that it's sometimes harder to get around. In the spring, higher trails are still blocked by snow or the mud that follows it. This soggy season can last well into June. In the fall, temperatures can drop at night, and icy winds sometimes blow.

In spring, however, wildflowers are particularly dynamic, filling the meadows and hillsides with vast arrays of color. In the fall, golden aspens rustle amid the evergreens, and the thinning crowds provide a respite for both visiting humans and resident wildlife. In some streams, this is the best time for angling. It's cheaper, too: Motels drop their rates during the off season.

If crowds make you claustrophobic, the key months to avoid are July and August. But most of the people who come through the gates in midsummer go only to the developed campgrounds and lodges at Colter Bay, Jenny Lake, Jackson Lake, and Signal Mountain; to the lakes and views accessible by car; and to the short paths that stay within view of the visitor center. If you have the energy to hike up into Cascade Canyon and beyond, you'll see an entirely different landscape. And, of course, summer is a beautiful time of year, with wildflowers blooming well into July and wildlife always in evidence.

1 Essentials

GETTING THERE & GATEWAYS

The park is essentially the east slope of the Tetons and the valley below; if you drive to it, you enter from the south, east, or north. From the north, you can enter Grand Teton from Yellowstone National Park via the **John D. Rockefeller, Jr., Memorial Parkway** (U.S. 89/191/287). You will already have paid your fee for entrance to both parks, so there is no entrance station, but you can stop at **Flagg Ranch,** approximately 5 miles north of the park boundary, and get park information. From December to March, Yellowstone's south entrance is open only to snowmobiles and snow coaches.

You can also approach the park from the east, on **U.S. 26/287.** This route comes from Dubois, 55 miles east on the other side of the Absaroka and Wind River mountains, and crosses Togwotee Pass, where you'll get your first and one of the best views of the Tetons from above the valley. Travelers who come this way can continue south on U.S. 26/89/191 to Jackson without paying an entrance fee, though they are within the park boundaries.

You can also enter Grand Teton from Jackson in the south, driving 12 miles north on U.S. **26/89/191** to the Moose turnoff and the park's south entrance. You'll find the park headquarters and visitor center, and a community with dining and shops.

THE NEAREST AIRPORT Inside the southern boundary of Grand Teton National Park, **Jackson Hole Airport** (© **307/733-7682;** www.jacksonholeairport.com) is the most convenient airport. It's served by **American, Delta, Northwest,** and **United.** Most major car-rental companies have outlets here. See chapter 38 for websites of the major airlines and car-rental firms.

INFORMATION

To receive park maps and information before your arrival, contact **Grand Teton National Park,** P.O. Drawer 170, Moose, WY 83012 (© **307/739-3300;** www.nps.gov/grte).

The **Grand Teton Association,** P.O. Drawer 170, Moose, WY 83012 (© **307/739-3403;** www.grandtetonpark.org), provides information about the park and books of interest to visitors at the park visitor centers. You can also order books online or by mail. The following titles are recommended: *Teton Trails,* by Katy Duffy and Darwin Wile, available from the Grand Teton Association; *A Guide to Exploring Grand Teton National Park,* by Linda Olson and Tim Bywater (RNM Press); and *An Outdoor Family Guide to Yellowstone and Grand Teton National Parks,* by Lisa Gollin Evans (The Mountaineers).

The **Jackson Hole Chamber of Commerce,** 990 W. Broadway, P.O. Box 550, Jackson, WY 83001 (© **307/733-3316;** www.jacksonholechamber.com), provides information on just about everything in and around Jackson. Along with the U.S. Forest Service and National Park Service, representatives of the chamber staff the informative **Greater Yellowstone Visitor Center,** 532 N. Cache, about 3 blocks north of the town square, with a view of the National Elk Refuge. For information on lodging, events, and activities, contact the chamber.

VISITOR CENTERS

Grand Teton National Park has three visitor centers. New in 2007, the dazzling **Craig Thomas Discovery and Visitor Center,** a half-mile west of Moose Junction at the southern end of the park, features exhibits on alpinism, geology, and wildlife; an art gallery; a "video river" and other multimedia installations; and a theater. You can pick up maps and permits for boating and backcountry trips.

The **Jenny Lake Visitor Center,** at South Jenny Lake, has maps, publications, and a geology exhibit.

Grand Teton National Park

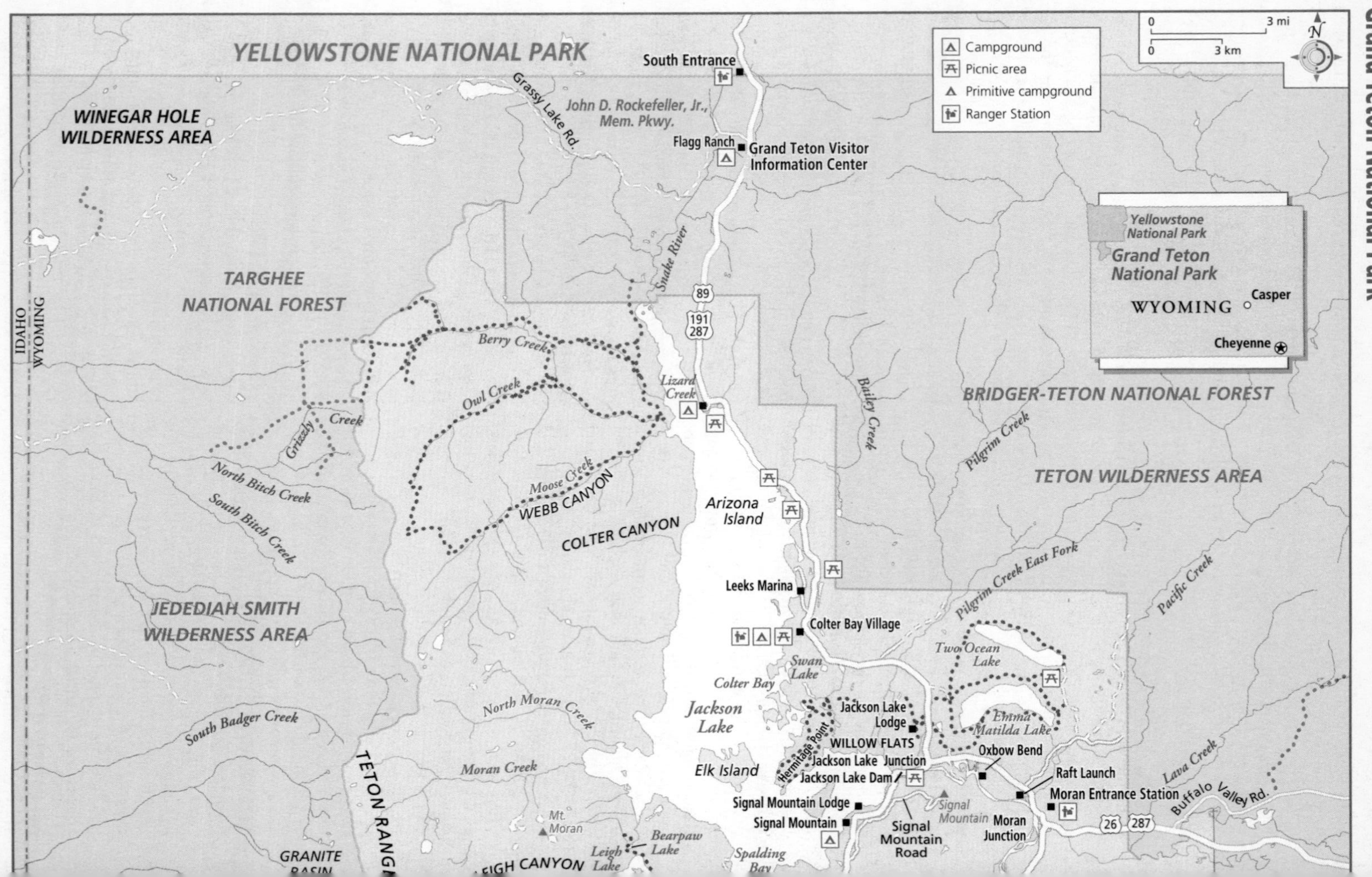

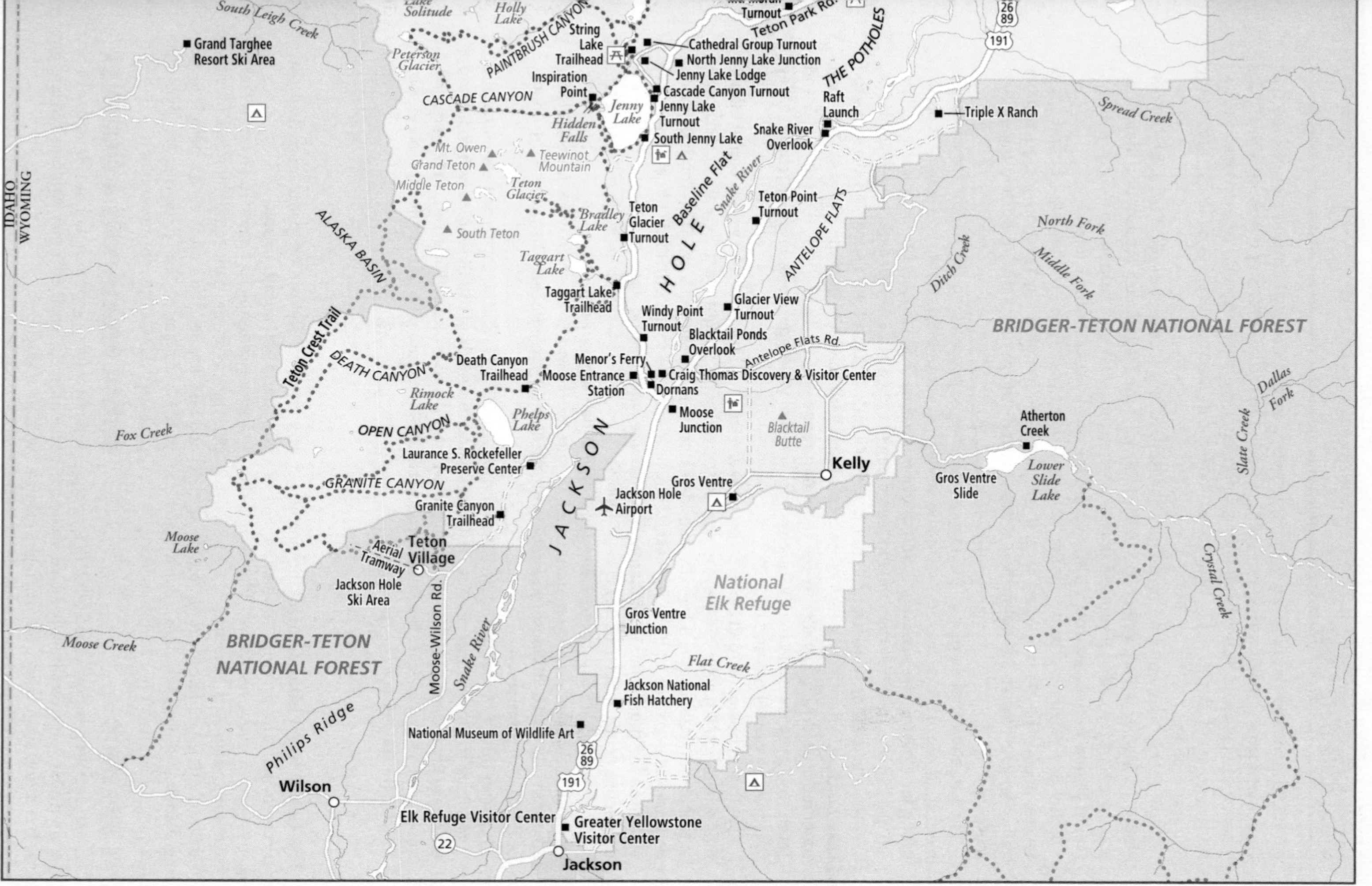
BRIDGER-TETON NATIONAL FOREST
Dallas Fork
Slate Creek
Crystal Creek
Spread Creek
North Fork
Middle Fork
Ditch Creek
Triple X Ranch
Atherton Creek
Lower Slide Lake
Gros Ventre Slide
THE POTHOLES
Teton Park Rd.
Cathedral Group Turnout
North Jenny Lake Junction
Jenny Lake Lodge
Cascade Canyon Turnout
Jenny Lake Turnout
South Jenny Lake
Raft Launch
Snake River Overlook
Teton Point Turnout
ANTELOPE FLATS
Antelope Flats Rd.
Glacier View Turnout
Blacktail Ponds Overlook
Craig Thomas Discovery & Visitor Center
Blacktail Butte
Kelly
Snake River
Baseline Flat
HOLE
Windy Point Turnout
Dornans
Moose Junction
Gros Ventre
National Elk Refuge
Flat Creek
String Lake
Trailhead
Jenny Lake
Inspiration Point
Hidden Falls
Teewinot Mountain
Teton Glacier Turnout
Bradley Lake
Taggart Lake
Taggart Lake Trailhead
Menor's Ferry
Moose Entrance Station
JACKSON
Jackson Hole Airport
Gros Ventre Junction
Jackson National Fish Hatchery
National Museum of Wildlife Art
Greater Yellowstone Visitor Center
Jackson
Elk Refuge Visitor Center
PAINTBRUSH CANYON
Holly Lake
CASCADE CANYON
Mt. Owen
Grand Teton
Teton Glacier
South Teton
Middle Teton
Lake Solitude
Peterson Glacier
Death Canyon Trailhead
Phelps Lake
Laurance S. Rockefeller Preserve Center
Granite Canyon Trailhead
Rimock Lake
OPEN CANYON
DEATH CANYON
GRANITE CANYON
ALASKA BASIN
Teton Crest Trail
Teton Village
Moose-Wilson Rd.
Aerial Tramway
Jackson Hole Ski Area
BRIDGER-TETON NATIONAL FOREST
Phillips Ridge
Wilson
South Leigh Creek
Grand Targhee Resort Ski Area
Moose Lake
Fox Creek
Moose Creek
IDAHO
WYOMING
26
89
191
22

If You Have Only 1 Day

A 1-day trip around this park is not unreasonable, given its size. You can complete a loop that encompasses many major attractions without having to retrace your steps. Although this 1-day itinerary assumes you are entering Grand Teton from the north, possibly after visiting Yellowstone, you could just as easily begin your itinerary in Jackson, 13 miles south of the Moose Entrance Station.

Begin at the south entrance of Yellowstone National Park, driving through the **John D. Rockefeller, Jr., Memorial Parkway** on U.S. 89/181/287 past the **Flagg Ranch Information Station.** As you drive south, you'll find yourself skirting the northern shore of Jackson Lake, with a view of **Mount Moran** to the west and, farther south, the towering **Cathedral Group.**

Colter Bay Village on the northeast shore of Jackson Lake is one of the park's busiest spots. Several popular hiking trails start here. If you turn right at Colter Bay Junction and go another half-mile, you'll be at the **Colter Bay Visitor Center;** stop here for the interesting **Indian Arts Museum.**

The **Lakeshore Trail** begins at the marina entrance and runs along the harbor for an easy 2-mile round-trip. It's level, paved, shady, and wheelchair accessible, offering you your best opportunity for a hike in this area if you don't have much time. The Douglas firs and pine trees here are greener and healthier than the lodgepole pines you see at higher elevations in Yellowstone.

A few minutes' drive south of Colter Bay, you'll pass **Jackson Lake Lodge** and then **Jackson Lake Junction,** where a right turn puts you on **Teton Park Road,** the beginning of a 43-mile loop tour. You'll be driving parallel to the mountain range and its 13,770-foot centerpiece, Grand Teton. You'll see lakes, created by glaciers thousands of years ago, bordering a sagebrush valley inhabited by pronghorn and elk.

Just 5 miles down the road along Jackson Lake, a left (east) turn will take you up **Signal Mountain,** where you'll have a 360-degree view of the valley. You might want to grab a quick lunch at Signal Mountain Lodge, a friendly lakeside eatery with a beautiful view. Then continue south on Teton Park Road to **South Jenny Lake.** If you have time, go to the other side (it's a 2-mile hike) and make the short climb to **Hidden Falls.** Otherwise, your best bet for a day hike in this area is the **Moose Ponds Trail** (see "Day Hikes," below).

When you leave South Jenny Lake, you'll drive a flat, sagebrush stretch to Moose, the southernmost of the park's service centers. One half-mile before Moose Junction is the **Moose Visitor Center.** While you're in Moose, you might visit the **Menor/Noble Historic District** and the **Chapel of the Transfiguration.**

Coming out of Moose, turn left (north) on U.S. 26/89/191, which crosses the flats above the Snake River to Moran Junction. The best views along this road are the **Glacier View Turnout** and the **Snake River Overlook,** both of which are right off the road and well marked. At Moran Junction, turn left for a 5-mile drive back to Jackson Lake Junction, past **Oxbow Bend,** a great spot for wildlife watching.

The **Colter Bay Visitor Center,** the northernmost centers, provides permits, information audiovisual programs, and a bookstore. This is also the home of the **Indian Arts Museum.**

Finally, there is an information station at the **Flagg Ranch** complex, which is approximately 5 miles north of the park's northern boundary.

FEES & PERMITS

There are no park gates on U.S. 26/89/191, so the views are free as you pass through the park on that route, but if you want to get off the highway and explore, you'll pay $25 per automobile for a 7-day pass (good for both Yellowstone and Grand Teton). If you expect to visit the parks more than once a year, buy a $50 annual permit.

Fees for **camping** in Grand Teton are $18 to $20 per night at all the park campgrounds($7 for hike- and bike-in sites). You must have a **permit** to sleep in the backcountry. See "Exploring the Backcountry," later this chapter, for information.

SPECIAL REGULATIONS & WARNINGS

It is unlawful to approach within 100 yards of a bear or within 25 yards of other wildlife. Feeding any wildlife is illegal.

SEASONS & CLIMATE

A popular song once romanticized "Springtime in the Rockies," but what the rest of the world calls **spring** is likely to be chilly and spitting snow or rain here. Snow and mud still clog trails. Cold and snow may linger into April and May, though temperatures are generally warming. The average daytime readings are in the 40s and 50s (single digits and 10s Celsius), gradually increasing into the 60s and 70s (upper teens and 20s Celsius) by early June. A warm jacket, rain gear, and water-resistant walking shoes are advised.

Summer is finally under way in mid-June; wildflowers start to bloom in May in the lower valleys and plains, and in July in the higher elevations. Temperatures are typically 75° to 90°F (24°–32°C) in the lower elevations and are especially comfortable because of the lack of humidity. Nights, however, will be cool, even during the warmest months, with temperatures dropping into the low 40s (single digits Celsius), so you'll want to pack a light jacket. Summer thunderstorms are common.

As **fall** approaches and temperatures remain mild but begin to cool, you'll want an additional layer of clothing. The first heavy snows typically fall by November 1 and continue through March or April.

Winter is a glorious season here, though it's not for everyone—it can get very cold. But the air is crystalline, the snow is powdery, and the skiing is fantastic. You'll need long johns, heavy shirts, vests and coats, warm gloves, and thick socks to combat daytime temperatures hovering in single digits and subzero overnights. If you drive in the park's vicinity in the winter, always carry sleeping bags, extra food, flashlights, and other safety gear.

If you're planning on visiting Yellowstone as well as Grand Teton and are considering making your trip to the parks before the middle of June, think about beginning your exploration in Grand Teton before working north to Yellowstone. Elevations here are slightly lower and snow melts earlier, so less water accumulates on trails, and temperatures are more moderate.

ROAD OPENINGS

Teton Park Road opens to conventional vehicles and RVs around May 1. The **Moose-Wilson Road** opens to vehicles at about the same time. Roads close to vehicles on November 1 and open for snowmobiles in mid-December, though they never close for nonmotorized use.

2 Exploring the Park

A 1-day whirlwind tour of Grand Teton is far from ideal. Like Yellowstone, this park demands a visit of 2 days or more. An extended stay allows for some relaxed hiking, picnicking, and sightseeing—you'll gain a greater appreciation for the park and the area's culture and history.

We begin at the northern end of the park. But you could also start exploring from the southern end, near Jackson. From Jackson, it's 13 miles to the Moose Entrance Station, another 7 miles to the Jenny Lake Visitor Center, another 12 miles to the Jackson Lake Junction, and 5 miles to Colter Bay.

JACKSON LAKE & THE NORTH END OF THE PARK

Many people enter Grand Teton National Park from the north end, emerging from Yellowstone's south entrance with a 7-day park pass that is good for admission to Grand Teton as well. Yellowstone connects to Grand Teton by a wilderness corridor called the **John D. Rockefeller, Jr., Memorial Parkway,** through which the highway runs for 8 miles, over the Snake River, past meadows sometimes dotted with elk, along the shores of Jackson Lake, and through forests.

On the parkway, not far from Yellowstone, you'll pass **Flagg Ranch Resort** (see "Where to Stay," later in this chapter), with gas, restaurants, lodging, and other services.

Giant **Jackson Lake,** a huge expanse of water that fills a deep gouge left 10,000 years ago by retreating glaciers, dominates the north end of the park. Though it empties east into the Snake River, curving around in the languid **Oxbow Bend**—a favorite wildlife-viewing float for canoeists—the water from Jackson Lake eventually turns south and then west through Snake River Canyon and into Idaho. Stream flow from the dam is regulated both for potato farmers downstream in Idaho and for rafters in the canyon, so, for better or ill, we have an irrigation dam in a national park. Elsewhere on the lake, things look quite natural, except when water gets low in the fall.

As the road follows the east shore of the lake from the north, the first development that travelers encounter is **Leeks Marina,** where boats can launch, gas up, and moor from mid-May to mid-September. There are numerous scenic pullouts along the lake, some good for picnics.

Just south of Leeks is **Colter Bay,** a busy outpost of park services—a visitor center, a general store, a laundry, two restaurants, a boat launch, boat rentals, and tours. Colter Bay has lots of overnight options, from cabins to old-fashioned tent camps to a trailer park. You can take pleasant short hikes in this area, including a walk around the bay or out to **Hermitage Point** (see "Day Hikes," below).

The **Indian Arts Museum** at the Colter Bay Visitor Center is worth a visit, though it is not strictly about the Native American cultures of this area. The artifacts are mostly from Plains Indian tribes, but there are also some Navajo items from the Southwest. The collection includes moccasins, pipes, shields, dolls, and war clubs sometimes called "skull crackers." Visiting American Indian artists work in the museum all summer long and sell their wares on-site. Admission is free.

From Colter Bay, the road swerves east and then south again past Jackson Lake Lodge. Numerous trails emanate from here, both to the lakeshore and east to **Emma Matilda Lake.** The road then comes to **Jackson Lake Junction,** where you can either continue west along the lakeshore or go east to the park's Moran Entrance Station. If you go out through the Moran entrance, you are still in the park and may turn south on U.S. 26/89/191 and drive along the Snake River to Jackson, making the most of your journey within the park's borders.

If you're here to enjoy the park, you should turn right (west) on **Teton Park Road** at Jackson Lake Junction. After 5 miles, you will arrive at **Signal Mountain.** Like its counterpart at Colter Bay, this developed recreation area, on Jackson Lake's southeast shore, offers camping sites, accommodations in cabins and multiplex units, two restaurants, and a lounge with one of the few televisions in the park. If you need gas or food, stock up at the convenience store here. Boat rentals and scenic cruises of the lake are also available.

If you turn east instead of west off Teton Park Road at Signal Mountain, you can drive up a narrow, twisty road to the **top of the mountain,** 700 feet above the valley, where you'll have a fine view of the ring of mountains—Absarokas, Gros Ventres, Tetons, and Yellowstone Plateau—that create the Jackson "Hole." Note also the potholes created in the valley's hilly moraines left by retreating glaciers. Below the summit, about 3 miles from the base of the hill, is **Jackson Point Overlook,** a paved path 100 yards long leading to the spot where the Hayden Expedition's photographer William Henry Jackson shot his famous wet-plate photographs of Jackson Lake and the Tetons more than a century ago—proof to the world that such spectacular places really existed.

Looking for a hideaway? On the right (west) side of the road between Signal Mountain and North Jenny Lake Junction, approximately 2 miles south of the Mount Moran Turnout, is an unmarked, unpaved road leading to **Spalding Bay.** It's a sheltered little campsite and boat launch area with a primitive restroom. There isn't much space if others have beaten you there, but it's a great place to be alone, with fantastic views of the lake and mountains. An automobile or SUV driving slowly will have no problem with this road. You'll pass through brush and forest and might spot a moose.

JENNY LAKE & THE SOUTH END OF THE PARK

Continuing south along Teton Park Road, you move into the park's southern half, where the tallest peaks rise abruptly above a string of smaller lakes strung together in the foothills—**Leigh Lake,** the appropriately named **String Lake,** and **Jenny Lake,** many visitors' favorite. At North Jenny Lake Junction, you can take a turnoff west to Jenny Lake Lodge. The road then continues as a one-way scenic loop along the lakeshore before rejoining Teton Park Road about 4 miles later.

Jenny Lake gets a lot of traffic throughout the summer, both from hikers who circumnavigate the lake on a 6-mile trail and from more sedentary folks who pay for a boat ride across the lake to Hidden Falls and the short, steep climb to **Inspiration Point** (see "Day Hikes," below). The parking lot at **South Jenny Lake** is often jammed, and there can be a long wait for the boat ride, so you might want to get there early. Or you can save your money by taking the 2-mile hike around the lake—it's level and easy. Also here are a tents-only campground, a visitor center, and a general store. You'll have to buy a ticket and wait in line for the trip across the lake in a powerboat that holds about 30 people. Hours and prices change from year to year, but generally in peak season, boats leave every 15 minutes from 8am to 6pm. The trip costs $10 round-trip for adults, $5 for children 5 to 12, and free for children under 5. One-way trips cost $7 for adults, $5 for children, free for children under 5. Contact **Jenny Lake Boating Company** (✆ **307/734-9227;** www.jennylakeboating.com) for more information.

South of the lake, Teton Park Road crosses open sagebrush plains with views of the mountains. You'll pass the Climbers' Ranch and some trail heads for **hikes to Taggart Lake** and elsewhere. Look in the sagebrush for the shy pronghorn, an antelope-like creature. This handsome animal, with tan cheeks and black accent stripes, can spring along at up to 60 mph. If you wander in the sagebrush here, you may encounter a badger, a shy but mean-spirited creature that sometimes comes out of its hole in the morning or at twilight.

The **Teton Glacier Turnout** presents a view of a glacier that grew for several hundred years until, pressured by hotter summer temperatures in the past century, it reversed direction and began retreating.

The road arrives at the park's south entrance—again, actually well within the park boundaries—and the **Craig Thomas Discovery and Visitor Center** in Moose, also home to park headquarters and a village with shops, restaurants, and lodgings.

Visiting the LSR Preserve

In 2007, the Rockefeller family donated to the National Park Service their former private retreat, the 1,106-acre **JY Ranch,** on the shore of Phelps Lake in the southern reaches of the park. Buildings came down and a 3-mile trail system went in, along with a staffed "reflection center" to allow visitors to make a personal connection with nature. The facility and trail system opened in 2008.

Behind the visitor center is **Menor's Ferry.** Bill Menor had a store and operated a ferry across the Snake River at Moose in the late 1800s. The ferry and store have been reconstructed, and you can buy items like those once sold here. Also in the area is the **Chapel of the Transfiguration.** In 1925, this chapel was built in Moose so that settlers wouldn't have to make the long ride into Jackson. It's still in use for Episcopal services from spring to fall, and it's a popular place for weddings, with a view of the Tetons through a window behind the altar.

Dornan's is a small village area just south of the visitor center on a chunk of private land owned by one of the area's earliest homesteading families. There are a few shops and a semi-gourmet grocery store, a collection of nice **rental cabins** (**© 307/733-2522;** www.dornans.com) that sleep four to six ($175–$250 in the summer), a post office, restaurants, a bar with occasional live music, and even a first-rate wine shop.

THE EAST SIDE OF THE PARK

At Moose Junction, just east of the visitor center, drivers can rejoin the highway and turn south to Jackson and the Gros Ventre turn, or cruise north up U.S. 89/26/191 to Moran Junction. This 18-mile trip is the fastest route through the park and, because of its distance from the mountains, offers views of a broader mountain tableau.

The junction of U.S. 89 with **Antelope Flats Road** is 1¼ miles north of the Moose Junction. The 20-mile route beginning here is an acceptable biking route. It's all on level terrain, passing by the town of Kelly and the Gros Ventre campground before looping back to U.S. 26/89/191 at the Gros Ventre Junction to the south. If you continue straight on Antelope Flats Road, you'll reach the **Teton Science School** (see "Organized Tours & Ranger Programs," below) at the road's end, about a 5-mile trip.

Less than a mile farther along U.S. 26/89/191, on the left, **Blacktail Ponds Overlook** offers an opportunity to see how beavers build dams and how they affect the flow of the streams. The area is marshy early in summer, but it's worth the quarter-mile hike down to the streams, where you can view the beaver activity more closely.

Traveling 2 miles farther along U.S. 89 brings you to the **Glacier View Turnout,** which offers views of an area that 140,000 to 160,000 years ago was filled with a 4,000-foot-thick glacier. The view of the gulch between the peaks offers testimony of the power of the glaciers that carved this landscape. Lower **Schwabacher Landing** is at the end of a 1-mile, fairly well-maintained dirt road that leads down to the Snake River; you'll see the turnoff 4½ miles north of Moose Junction. The road winds through an area filled with glacial *moraine* (the rocks, sand, gravel, and so forth left behind as glaciers passed through the area) remaining from several different ice ages. At the end of the road is a popular launch site for float trips and fly-fishing. It's also an ideal place to retreat from the crowds. Don't be surprised to see bald eagles, osprey, moose, river otter, and beaver, which regularly patrol the area.

The **Snake River Overlook,** 4 miles down the road beyond the Glacier View Turnout, is the most famous view of the Teton Range and the Snake River, immortalized by Ansel Adams. From this overlook, you'll also see at least three 200-foot-high plateaus that roll from the riverbed to the valley floor, a vivid example of the power of the glaciers and ice floes as they sculpted this area.

A half-mile north of the Snake River Overlook is the recently repaved road to **Deadman's Bar,** a peaceful clearing on the riverbank. Many float trips launch here, and there is limited fishing access.

Cunningham Cabin, 1¾ miles north of Deadman's Bar, is a historic site at which homesteaders Pierce and Margaret Cunningham built their ranch in 1890. By 1928, they had been defeated by the elements and sold out to Rockefeller's Snake River Land Co. You can visit it at any time.

If you head down the highway in the other direction (south) from Moose Junction on U.S. 26/89/191, you can turn east on the **Gros Ventre River Road** 5 miles before you reach Jackson and follow the river east into its steep canyon—a few miles past the little town of Kelly, you leave the park and enter **Bridger-Teton National Forest.**

In 1925, a huge slab of mountain broke off the north end of the Gros Ventre Range on the east side of Jackson Hole, a reminder of nature's violent and unpredictable side. The slide left a gaping open gash in the side of Sheep Mountain, sloughing off nearly 50 million cubic yards of rock and forming a natural dam across the Gros Ventre River half a mile wide. Two years later, the dam broke, and a cascade of water rushed down the canyon and through the little town of Kelly, taking several lives. The town of **Kelly** is a quaint, eccentric community with a large number of yurts. Up in the canyon formed by the Gros Ventre River is a roadside display with photographs of the slide area and a nature walk from the road down to the residue of the slide and **Lower Slide Lake.** Signs identify the trees and plants that survived or grew in the slide's aftermath.

3 Organized Tours & Ranger Programs

The **Grand Teton Lodge Company** (© **800/628-9988** or 307/543-2811 for information; www.gtlc.com) runs half- and full-day bus tours of Grand Teton ($36 adults, $18 children 3–11) and Yellowstone ($66 adults, $41 children 3–11) from late May to early October, weather permitting.

The **Teton Science Schools,** 700 Coyote Canyon Rd., Jackson, WY 83001 (© **307/733-1313;** www.tetonscience.org), offer an excellent curriculum for students of all ages, from integrated science programs for junior-high kids to adult seminars covering everything from botany to astronomy. Classes take place at campuses in Jackson and Kelly, and other locations in Jackson Hole. The school's **Wildlife Expeditions** (© **888/945-3567**) offers tours that bring visitors closer to the park's wildlife. These trips range from a half-day to a week, covering everything from bighorn sheep to the wolves of Yellowstone.

Within the park, there are several interesting ranger programs. These include a ranger-led 3-mile hike from the Colter Bay Visitor Center to Swan Lake, as well as a relaxed evening chatting with a ranger on the deck of the Jackson Lake Lodge while you watch for moose and birds through a spotting scope. There are numerous events during the summer at Colter Bay, South Jenny Lake, and the Craig Thomas Discovery and Visitor Center at Moose. Check the daily schedules in the park's newspaper, *The Teewinot,* which is available at any visitor center.

From Moose, rangers lead visitors out to the "lek"—the mating ground of the strutting grouse, whose males' displays are dramatic during the springtime mating season. In winter, **guided snowshoe hikes** begin at the visitor center in Moose.

There are guided morning hikes to Phelps Lake at the Laurance S. Rockefeller Preserve and Hidden Falls from Jenny Lake (you take the boat across the lake), among other activities.

Youngsters 8 to 12 can join **Young Naturalist programs** at Colter Bay or Jenny Lake and learn about the natural world for 2 hours while hiking with a ranger. Signups are at the visitor centers (the fee is a mere $1); kids will need basic hiking gear.

There are also evening campfire gatherings at most of the campground amphitheaters on a variety of park-related topics.

4 Day Hikes

COLTER BAY AREA

Lakeshore Trail Originating in the Colter Bay area, this short jaunt starts at the marina and leads out to pebble beaches on the west side of Jackson Lake. The trail is wide and shady, and views of the entire Teton Range leap out at you from across the lake when you arrive at the end of the trail. 2 miles RT. Easy. Access: Marina entrance.

TRAILS FROM THE HERMITAGE POINT TRAIL HEAD

The **Hermitage Point trail head** near the marina is the starting point for a variety of trips ranging from 1 to 9 miles. With careful planning, it's possible to start the day with a hike beginning at Colter Bay that leads past **Cygnet Lake** across **Willow Flats** to Jackson Lake Lodge (where you can stop for lunch). Then, after a break, take the same path and return to Colter Bay in time for the evening barbecue. All told, that's 10 miles round-trip.

When choosing your route, keep in mind that the three trails running through this same forested part of the Colter Bay area—Heron Pond Trail, Swan Lake Trail, and Hermitage Point Loop—have virtually identical foliage and terrain. The numerous options can be confusing, so carry a map.

Hermitage Point Loop This trail goes through a thickly forested area to the isolated Hermitage Point, a peninsula jutting into Jackson Lake, from which you can look across the bay to the Signal Mountain Lodge. If you're seeking solitude, this is an excellent place to find it, though you should check with rangers before leaving—this is bear country. 9.4 miles RT. Moderate. Access: Swan Lake/Heron Pond trail intersection.

Heron Pond Trail If you take this trail in the early morning, you will improve your chance of seeing the beavers that live in the pond. This is bear territory as well as a home for Canada geese, trumpeter swans, and moose. Wildflowers are part of the show in the early summer—look for lupine, gilia, heartleaf arnicas, and Indian paintbrush. The first 200 yards of the trail are steep, but after reaching the top of a rise, it levels out and has only moderate elevation gains from that point on. 3 miles RT. Easy. Access: Hermitage Point trail head.

Swan Lake Trail Finding swans at Swan Lake requires a trip to the south end, where a small island offers them isolation and shelter for nests. From Swan Lake, it's only .3 mile through a densely forested area to the intersection with the trail to Heron Pond. Hermitage Point is 3 miles from this junction along a gentle path that winds through a wooded area that is a popular bear hangout. 3 miles RT. Easy. Access: Hermitage Point trail head.

Willow Flats An alternative to mountainous, forested trails, this trip from Colter Bay to Jackson Lake Lodge takes you across marshy flats where you'll have an excellent view of the Tetons and a chance of seeing moose and other wildlife. You begin by skirting the sewage ponds at Colter Bay (sorry), then pick up a trail east to Cygnet Lake. Instead of looping back to Colter Bay, you take a spur that crosses Pilgrim Creek going east across the flats. You can hike in either direction, but drop a car at each end if you don't want to double back on foot. 10 miles RT. Easy. Access: Horse corrals at Colter Bay.

JACKSON LAKE LODGE AREA

Christian Pond Trail This trail begins with a half-mile walk through a grassy, wet area to a pond with nesting trumpeter swans and other waterfowl. You can circle the pond, adding another 3 miles to the trip. In May and June, this is a great wildflower walk, but it's also prime habitat for bears, so check with rangers first. The south end of the pond is covered with little grassy knolls upon which the birds build their nests and roost, and beavers have constructed a lodge here, too. It's a restful sanctuary but often infested with gnats and mosquitoes. 1 mile RT. Easy. Access: 200 yards south of Jackson Lake Lodge entrance (it's unmarked, so look carefully).

Signal Mountain Summit Trail This up-and-down trail gives you a few fine hours of solitude with views of the mountains, wildflowers, and, at the end, a grand panorama of the glacially carved valley. After negotiating a steep climb at the beginning of the trail, you'll come upon a broad plateau covered with lodgepole pines, grassy areas, and seasonal wildflowers. Cross a paved road to a lily-covered pond, and just beyond you'll choose one of two trails—take the right one up (ponds, wildlife, maybe moose and bear) or the left one down (open ridges with views). 8 miles RT. Moderate. Access: Near Signal Mountain Lodge entrance, or 1 mile (by car) up Signal Mountain Rd. to a pond on the right.

TWO OCEAN & EMMA MATILDA LAKE TRAILS

You can come to these lakes from the east or west: From the west, you'd begin at the Grand View Point trail head, 1 mile north of Jackson Lake Lodge, or at the Christian Pond trail head, just east of Jackson Lake Lodge. From the east, you'd go up Pacific Creek Road, 4 miles east of Jackson Lake Junction on the road to the Moran entrance. There is a pull-out for Emma Matilda Lake 2 miles up this road, or you can go a half-mile farther, take a left on Two Ocean Lake Road, and go to the Two Ocean Lake trail head parking lot, with trails leading to both lakes.

Emma Matilda Lake Trail Circumnavigating this lake is a pleasant, up-and-down journey with great views of the mountains and a good chance of seeing wildlife. The hike winds uphill for .5 mile from the parking area to a large meadow favored by mule deer. The trail follows the north side of the lake through a pine forest 400 feet above the lake, then descends to an overlook where you'll have panoramic views of the Tetons, Christian Pond, and Jackson Lake. The trail on the south side of the lake goes through a densely forested area populated by Englemann spruce and subalpine fir. Be watchful and noisy, because this is grizzly bear country. It's possible to branch off onto the Two Ocean Lake Trail along the north shore of the lake. 11.8 miles RT. Easy to moderate. Access: Emma Matilda Lake trail head on Pacific Creek Rd., or trail head off Two Ocean Lake Rd. north of Jackson Lake–Moran Rd.

Two Ocean Lake Trail Take your time and take a picnic on this delightful, underused trail around Two Ocean Lake. You can start at either end, the walk around the lake is fairly level, and ducks, swans, grebes, and loons are commonly seen on the water. The variety of habitat—marshes, lakes, woodlands, and meadows—means that you'll see these birds, as well as wildflowers, butterflies, and possibly bear, beaver, elk, deer, and moose. As usual, awesome views of the Tetons abound; for the best perspective, take the 1.3-mile trip up 600 feet to Grand View Point, a somewhat difficult climb through lodgepole and fir en route to a hilltop covered with orange arrowleaf balsamroot. You'll look down on lakes, meadows, and volcanic outcrops, and in the distance, you'll gaze at the Tetons, the Mount Leidy Highlands, and Jackson Lake. It's possible to branch off onto the Emma Matilda Lake Trail at the east end of Two Ocean Lake. 5.8 miles RT. Easy to moderate. Access: Two Ocean Lake trail head on Two Ocean Lake Rd., or Grand View Point trail head.

JENNY LAKE AREA

Amphitheater Lake Trail Here's a trail that can get you up into the high mountains and out in a day, if you're in good shape and acclimated to the altitude (you'll climb 3,000 ft.). You'll cross glacial moraines and meadows quilted with flowers, and enter forests of fir and lodgepole and whitebark pine (a bear food—be alert!). Finally, you clear the trees and come into an amphitheater of monstrous rock walls topped by Disappointment Peak, with the Grand and Teewinot in view. Surprise Lake and Amphitheater Lake sit in this dramatic setting, with a few gnarled trees struggling to survive on the slopes. 9.6 miles RT. Strenuous. Access: Lupine Meadows trail head. From Moose Entrance Station on Teton Park Rd., drive a little over 6¾ miles to Lupine Meadows Junction and follow signs to trail head; from Jenny Lake, trail head is at the end of a road less than 1 mile south of South Jenny Lake.

Cascade Canyon Trail For those who have time to go a little farther, Cascade Canyon Trail is the most popular in the park. You can begin the hike from South Jenny Lake, but you can shave 2 miles off each way by riding the boat across the lake and beginning your hike at the dock (see "Jenny Lake & the South End of the Park," earlier in this chapter). At this point, you're only a steep 1-mile hike from Inspiration Point (see "Hidden Falls & Inspiration Point Trail," below), which is as far as many visitors go. From here, you make a brief steep climb to the glacially rounded canyon, where the trail levels out and you're in a wonderland of wildflowers, waterfowl, and busy pikas. On a nice day, the warblers will be singing and you may see moose and bear. If you want to go farther once you reach forks of North and South Cascade Canyon, follow either the South Fork to Hurricane Pass or the North Fork to Lake Solitude. These are overnight trips.

A less taxing alternative to the Cascade Canyon trip mentioned above is a detour to **Moose Ponds,** which begins on the Inspiration Point trail. The ponds, 2 miles from either the west or east boat dock, are near the south end of the lake and are alive with birds. The area near the base of Teewinot Mountain, which towers over the area, is populated with elk, mule deer, black bears, and moose. The trail is flat (at lake level), short, and easy to negotiate in 1 to 1½ hours. The best times to venture forth are in early morning and evening. 9.1 miles RT. Moderate to strenuous. Access: Inspiration Point.

Hidden Falls & Inspiration Point Trail Many people cross Jenny Lake, either by boat or on foot around the south end, and then make the short, forest-shaded uphill slog to Hidden Falls (less than 1 mile of hiking if you take the boat, 5 miles roundtrip if you walk around), which tumbles down a broad cascade. Some think that's enough and don't go another steep half-mile to Inspiration Point. Up there you get a great view of Jenny Lake below, and you can see the glacial moraine that formed it. If you're going only to these two overlooks, we recommend a relaxed and easy hike around the south end of the lake. 1.8–5.8 miles RT. Moderate. Access: East or west shore boat dock.

Jenny Lake Loop Trail Another lake to circumnavigate, following the shore. You can cut the trip in half by taking the Jenny Lake boat shuttle from the east shore boat dock to the west shore boat dock. The lake occupies a pastoral setting at the foot of the mountain range, providing excellent views throughout the summer. ***Warning:*** This is one of the most popular spots in the park; to avoid crowds, travel early or late in the day. The trails to Hidden Falls, Inspiration Point, and the Moose Ponds branch off this trail on the southwest shore of the lake. The trails to String and Leigh lakes branch off this trail on the northern shore of Jenny Lake. 6.5 miles RT. Easy to moderate. Access: Trail head at east shore boat dock.

5 Exploring the Backcountry

Grand Teton may seem small compared with Yellowstone, but it has more than 250 miles of backcountry trails that provide good opportunities for solitude and adventure. You must have a **permit** from the Park Service to sleep in the backcountry—the permits are free, but reservations are not. The permit is valid only on the dates for which it is issued. There are two methods of securing permits: They may be picked up at park visitor centers the day before you start your trip, or you can make a reservation for a permit in advance of your arrival, for a $25 fee. To avoid the fee, you may pick up a permit the day before you commence your trip. Reservations are accepted only from January 1 to May 15; it's wise to reserve a camp area if you're going in July or August. Reservations may be made by writing the **Permits Office,** Grand Teton National Park, P.O. Drawer 170, Moose, WY 83012, or faxing 307/739-3438. Reservations can also be made online at **www.nps.gov/grte**.

Remember that this region has a short summer and virtually no spring. Although the lower-elevation areas of the park are open in May, some of the high-country trails may not be clear of snow or high water before late June or early July. Look in the "Backcountry Camping" brochure available at the visitor center for approximate dates when specific campsites will be habitable.

Perhaps the most popular backcountry trail in Grand Teton is the 19.3-mile **Cascade Canyon Loop,** which starts on the west side of Jenny Lake, winds northwest 7.2 miles on the **Cascade Canyon Trail** to Lake Solitude and the Paintbrush Divide, then returns on the 10-mile-long **Paintbrush Trail** past Holly Lake. It is one of the most rigorous hikes in either Grand Teton or Yellowstone because of gains in elevation—more than 2,600 feet—rocky trails, and switchbacks through loose rock and gravel that can become slippery, especially in years when snow remains until the middle of summer on the north-facing side of Paintbrush Divide.

Rangers recommend the hike for several reasons, the most noteworthy of which is unsurpassed scenery. Moose and black bears inhabit this part of the park, so hikers are cautioned to be diligent about making noise. There's also the possibility of sighting harlequin ducks, which nest near the trail in Cascade Creek. You'll see many types of wildflowers, large stands of whitebark pine trees, and an almost unimaginable array of bird life.

Though it adds 5.1 miles to the trip (one-way), a detour west from the Cascade Canyon Trail to **Hurricane Pass** will reward you with a view from the foot of **Schoolroom Glacier.** If you're after an extended trip, head west into the Jedediah Smith Wilderness on a trail that eventually crosses into Idaho. This trail doesn't stop anytime soon—you can continue trekking all the way to Alaska.

If you're unable to complete the hike in 1 day, you can trek 7.2 miles on the Cascade Canyon Trail to **Solitude Lake** and return on the same trail. If you can afford a 2-day trip, camping zones are 6 miles west of the trail head on the Cascade Canyon Trail and 8.7 miles northwest on the Paintbrush Canyon Trail at Holly Lake. Be sure to get a reservation.

Perhaps the quickest way to get up high in these mountains for a backcountry foray is to hitch a ride up **Rendezvous Mountain** on the Jackson Hole Ski Resort Tram. This puts you at 10,450 feet in **Bridger-Teton National Forest,** just south of the park, and ready to embark north toward the park's Middle Fork Cutoff. From here you can head down into Granite Canyon to Phelps Lake, or go north along the **Teton Crest Trail** to Fox Creek Pass (over 8 difficult miles from the tram) and **Death Canyon** and beyond. If you are hardy enough to make it to **Death Canyon Shelf,** a wildflower-strewn limestone ledge that runs above Death Canyon toward **Alaska Basin,** you'll have an extraordinary high-altitude view of the west side of the Tetons' biggest peaks. If you are on an extended backcountry trip, you can continue north to Hurricane Pass, where you can come back down to the valley floor by way of Cascade Canyon.

This kind of backcountry trip is really an expedition, and it requires skill and experience. Go over your plans with park rangers, who can help you evaluate your ability to take on the challenge.

6 Other Summer Sports & Activities

BIKING Bikes are banned from hiking trails in the park. On the paved roads, the problem is safety—huge RVs career about, and some roads have only narrow shoulders. Teton Park Road has been widened somewhat, but traffic is heavy here. Debuting in 2009, a popular new 8-mile multiuse trail was opened between Jenny and Moose lakes. Road bikers should also try **Antelope Flats,** beginning at a trail head 1 mile north of Moose Junction and going east. Sometimes called **Mormon Row,** this paved route crosses the flats below the Gros Ventre Mountains, past old ranch homesteads and the small town of Kelly. It connects to the unpaved **Shadow Mountain Road,** which actually goes outside the park into national forest, climbing through the trees to the summit. Total distance is 7 miles, and the elevation gain is 1,370 feet; you'll be looking at Mount Moran and the Tetons across the valley.

Mountain bikers have a few more options: Try **Two Ocean Lake Road** (reached from the Pacific Creek Rd. just north of Moran Junction) or the **River Road,** a 15-mile dirt path along the Snake River's western bank. (Bison use it, too, and you'd be smart to yield.) Ambitious mountain bikers may want to load their overnight gear and take the **Grassy Lake Road,** once used by American Indians, west from Flagg Ranch on a 50-mile journey to Ashton, Idaho.

A map that shows bicycle routes is available from the Park Service at visitor centers, or from **Adventure Sports** at Dornan's in the town of Moose (✆ **307/733-3307**), which is inside the boundaries of Grand Teton National Park. You can also rent various bikes here.

BOATING If you bring your own boat, you must register it: For human-powered craft, it's $10 for 7 days, or $20 for a 1-year permit; motorized skippers pay $20 for 7 days and $40 for an annual permit, which you can buy at the Colter Bay and Moose visitor centers. Boat and canoe rentals, tackle, and fishing licenses are available at **Colter Bay** and **Signal Mountain** (rental fees of $30 to $40 per hour for motorboats include permits; kayaks, canoes, and deck cruisers are also available). Sailboat tours are also available at Signal Mountain. The **Jenny Lake Boating Company** (✆ **307/733-9227**) runs shuttles to the west side of Jenny Lake and offers scenic cruises.

Motorized boats are allowed on Phelps, Jackson, and Jenny lakes, but on Jenny Lake the motor can't be over 8 horsepower. Only human-powered vessels are permitted on Emma Matilda, Two Ocean, Taggart, Bradley, Bearpaw, Leigh, and String lakes. Rafts, canoes, dories, and kayaks are allowed on the Snake River within the park. No boats are allowed on Pacific Creek or the Gros Ventre River.

Scenic cruises of Jackson Lake are conducted daily by the **Grand Teton Lodge Company** (✆ **307/543-2811;** www.gtlc.com). Breakfast cruises run Saturday through Thursday, and dinner cruises run Monday, Wednesday, and Friday. Both depart from the **Colter Bay Marina** from May through September. You'll travel to Elk Island, where they cook up a good meal: trout and steak for dinner, and pancakes and eggs for breakfast. The scenic trips are 1½ hours long and cost $24 for adults and $12 for kids 3 to 11; the meal cruises are twice that length and run $36 (breakfast) or $57 (dinner) for adults, and $22 or $37, respectively, for kids 3 to 11.

Additionally, you can rent kayaks and canoes at **Adventure Sports** at Dornan's in the town of Moose (✆ **307/733-3307**), which is within the boundaries of Grand Teton National Park.

CLIMBING The Tetons have a strong allure for climbers, even inexperienced ones, perhaps because you can reach the tops of even the highest peaks in a single day. The terrain is mixed, with snow and ice year-round—knowing how to self-arrest with an ice axe is a must—and the weather can change suddenly. The key is to get good advice, know your limitations, and, if you're not already skilled, take some lessons and hire a guide at a local climbing school. Two long-standing operations offer classes and guided climbs of Grand Teton: **Jackson Hole Mountain Guides** in Jackson (✆ **800/239-7642** or 307/733-4979; www.jhmg.com) and **Exum Mountain Guides** in Moose (✆ **307/733-2297;** www.exumguides.com). Expect to pay around $700 to $1,000 for a guided 2-day climb of Grand Teton, or $150 to $200 for a class. The **Jenny Lake Ranger Station** (✆ **307/739-3392;** open only in summer) is the center for climbing information; climbers are encouraged to stop in and obtain information on routes, conditions, and regulations.

FISHING The lakes and streams of Grand Teton are popular fishing destinations. Jackson, Jenny, and Phelps lakes are loaded with lively cutthroat trout, whitefish, and mackinaw (lake) trout. Jackson has produced monsters weighing as much as 50 pounds, but you're more likely to catch fish under 20 inches, fishing deep with trolling gear from a boat during hot summer months.

The Snake River runs for about 27 miles in the park, and it has cutthroat and whitefish up to about 18 inches. It's a popular drift-boat river for fly-fishers. If you'd like a guide who knows the holes, try **Jack Dennis Sports** (✆ **800/570-3270** or 307/733-3270; www.jackdennisfishingtrips.com), **Triangle X Float Trips** (✆ **307/733-5500;** www.trianglex.com), or **Westbank Anglers** (✆ **800/922-3474** or 307/733-6483; www.westbank.com). The going rate is $425 to $475 for a full day for two people. **Signal Mountain Lodge** (✆ **307/543-2831**) offers guided half-day trips on motorized craft in **Jackson Lake** for one or two people for $280. As an alternative, stake out a position on the banks below the dam at **Jackson Lake,** where you'll have plenty of company and just might snag something. You need a Wyoming state **fishing license** and must check creel limits, which vary from year to year and place to place.

FLOAT TRIPS One of the most effective and environmentally sound (not to mention relaxing) methods of viewing wildlife in Grand Teton is aboard a floating watercraft that silently moves downstream without disturbing the animals. The park's 27-mile stretch of river is wonderful for viewing wildlife, with moose, eagles, and other animals coming, like you, to the water's edge. Most of the commercial float operators in the park operate from mid-May to mid-September (depending on weather and river flow conditions). These companies offer 5- to 10-mile scenic floats, some with early morning and evening wildlife trips. Try **Solitude Float Trips** (✆ **888/704-2800** or 307/733-2871; www.grand-teton-scenic-floats.com), **Barker-Ewing Float Trips** (✆ **800/365-1800** or 307/733-1800; www.barkerewing.com), **Grand Teton Lodge Company** (✆ **307/543-2811;** www.gtlc.com), or **Signal Mountain Lodge** (✆ **307/543-2831;** www.signalmtnlodge.com). Scenic float trips cost about $50 to $60 for adults, with discounts for children under 12.

HORSEBACK RIDING The **Grand Teton Lodge Company** offers tours from stables next to popular visitor centers at Colter Bay and Jackson Lake Lodge. Choices are 1- and 2-hour guided trail rides daily aboard well-broken, tame animals. An experienced rider may find these tours too tame; wranglers refer to them as "nose-and-tail" tours. In Jackson, try **Jackson Hole Outfitters** (✆ **307/654-7008**), **Spring Creek Ranch Riding Stables** (✆ **800/443-6139**), or the **Mill Iron Ranch** (✆ **307/733-6390**). Rates usually run about $50 for 2 hours.

7 Winter Sports & Activities

Park facilities pretty much shut down during the winter, except for a skeleton staff at the Moose Visitor Center, and the park shows no signs of becoming the winter magnet for snowmobilers or backcountry skiers that Yellowstone is. That may be just as well—you can enjoy some quiet, fun times in the park without the crowds.

SKIING You can ski flat or you can ski steep in Grand Teton. The two things to watch out for are hypothermia and avalanches. As with climbing, know your limitations, and make sure you're properly equipped. Check with local rangers and guides for trails that match your ability. Among your options is the relatively easy **Jenny Lake Trail,** starting at the Taggart Lake Parking Area, about 8 round-trip miles of flat and scenic trail that follows Cottonwood Creek. A more difficult ski is the **Taggart Lake–Beaver Creek Loop,** about a 3-mile route that has some steep and icy pitches coming back. About 4 miles of the **Moose-Wilson Road**—the back way to Teton Village from Moose—is unplowed in the winter, and it is an easy trip through the woods. You can climb the windy, unplowed road to the top of **Signal Mountain** and have some fun skiing down. An easy ski trail runs from the Colter Bay Ranger Station area to **Heron Pond;** it's about 2.6 miles, with a great view of the Tetons and Jackson Lake. Get a ski trail map from a visitor center.

Skiers who come to Jackson Hole are usually after the hard, steep stuff at the Jackson Hole Mountain Resort, but a growing contingent of backcountry telemark skiers ski off Teton Pass and out of the ski resort boundaries.

SNOWMOBILING The subject of controversy for over a decade, snowmobiling is a popular winter option, and it looks like it's here to stay. The **Continental Divide Snowmobile Trail** in Grand Teton is groomed, providing access to trails in the nearby **Bridger-Teton National Forest,** the area to the immediate east of Grand Teton National Park, and into Yellowstone. **High Country Snowmobile Tours, Wyoming Adventures,** and **Rocky Mountain Snowmobile Tours** share a website and reservation service (✆ **800/647-2561;** www.snowmobiletours.net), offering guided trips in Jackson Hole and the adjacent wildlands. For snowmobile rentals in Jackson, contact **Leisure Sports** (✆ **307/733-3040**).

8 Camping

INSIDE THE PARK

The campground chart below lists amenities for each campground in the park. All the campgrounds except Jenny Lake can accommodate tents, RVs, and trailers, but none has utility hookups. **Jenny Lake Campground,** a tents-only area with 51 sites, is in a quiet, wooded area near the lake. You have to be here first thing in the morning to get a site.

The largest campground, **Gros Ventre,** is the last to fill, if it fills up at all—probably because it's on the east side of the park, a few miles from Kelly on the Gros Ventre River Road. It has 350 sites, a trailer dump station, a tents-only section, and no showers. If you arrive late in the day and you have no place to stay, go here first.

Signal Mountain Campground, with views of the lake and access to the beach, is another popular spot that fills first thing in the morning. It has 81 sites overlooking Jackson Lake and Mount Moran, as well as a pleasant picnic area and boat launch. There are no showers or laundry, but a store and service station are nearby.

Colter Bay Campground and Trailer Village has 350 sites, some with RV hookups, showers, and a launderette. The area has access to the lake but is far enough from the village to offer a modicum of solitude; spaces are usually gone by noon.

Lizard Creek Campground, at the north end of Grand Teton National Park near Jackson Lake, occupies an aesthetically pleasing wooded area near the lake with views of the Tetons, bird-watching, and fishing (and mosquitoes; bring your repellent). It's only 8 miles from facilities at Colter Bay and has 60 sites that fill by 2pm.

NEAR THE PARK

There are several places to park the RV or pitch a tent around Jackson Hole, and a few of them are reasonably priced and not too far from the park. Some of your best bets are either out of Jackson or way out of Jackson. Most campgrounds are open from late spring to early fall.

A concessionaire-operated campground is at the **Flagg Ranch Resort** on the John D. Rockefeller, Jr., Memorial Parkway. The campground, in a wooded area next to the parkway, has 171 sites for RVs and campers, showers, and a launderette.

Away from the crowds, the **Snake River Park KOA Campground** is on U.S. 89, 10 miles south of Jackson (✆ **307/733-7078**), and has 83 sites.

9 Where to Stay

INSIDE THE PARK

Grand Teton's lodging options are few but varied. You can get information about or make reservations for Jackson Lake Lodge, Jenny Lake Lodge, and Colter Bay Village through the **Grand Teton Lodge Company,** P.O. Box 250, Moran, WY 83013 (✆ **800/628-9988** or 307/543-2811; www.gtlc.com). For Signal Mountain Lodge, contact **Signal Mountain Lodge,** P.O. Box 50, Moran, WY 83013 (✆ **307/543-2831;** www.signalmountainlodge.com).

In Moose, **Dornan's Spur Ranch Cabins** (✆ **307/733-2522;** www.dornans.com) sleep four to six for $175 to $250 in the summer. Nearby, **Moulton Ranch Cabins** (✆ **307/733-3749;** www.moultonranchcabins.com) charges $80 to $220 for a cabin.

Grand Teton National Park properties have in-room telephones, but none have in-room televisions or air-conditioning. You'll find televisions in the lounge areas at the Jackson Lodge, Signal Mountain Resort, and Flagg Ranch.

COLTER BAY VILLAGE AREA

Colter Bay Village You might call this the people's resort of Grand Teton, with simpler lodgings, lower prices, and a lively, friendlier atmosphere that is well suited to families. On the eastern shore of Jackson Lake, Colter Bay Village is a full-fledged recreation center. Guest accommodations are in rough log cabins on a wooded hillside; they are clean and simply furnished with area rugs on tile floors and reproductions of pioneer furnishings—chests, oval mirrors, and extra-long bedsteads with painted headboards. If you want to take a trip back to the early days of American auto travel, when car camping involved unwieldy canvas tents on slabs by the roadside, you can spend an inexpensive night in tent cabins. The shower and bathroom are communal. Overall, the village provides an excellent base of operations for visitors because it has the most facilities of any area in the park. Free Wi-Fi is available in certain areas.

P.O. Box 240, Moran, WY 83013. ✆ **800/628-9988** or 307/543-2811. www.gtlc.com. 166 units. $41–$165 log cabin; $48 tent cabin. MC, V. Closed late Sept to late May.

Jackson Lake Lodge Much the way that Old Faithful Inn or the Lake Yellowstone Hotel captures historic eras of Yellowstone tourism, Jackson Lake Lodge epitomizes the architectural milieu of the period when Grand Teton became a park. That era was the 1950s, an age of right angles, flat roofs, and big windows. While not as distinctive as Yellowstone's standouts, the lodge is more functional and comfortable than its northern counterparts. The setting is sublime, overlooking Willow Flats with the lake in the distance, and, towering over it without so much as a stick in the way, the Tetons and Mount Moran. You don't even have to go outside to see this impressive view—the lobby has 60-foot-wide windows showcasing the panorama. A few guest rooms are in the three-story main lodge, but most are in cottages scattered about the property, some of which have large balconies and mountain views. Newly remodeled in 2009, rooms are spacious and cheery, and most offer double beds, electric heat, and newly tiled bathrooms. For a premium, the view rooms provide guests with a private picture window facing the Tetons. Free Wi-Fi is available in certain areas.

P.O. Box 240, Moran, WY 83013. ✆ **800/628-9988** or 307/543-2811. www.gtlc.com. 385 units. $219–$319 double; $550–$750 suite. MC, V. Closed mid-Oct to mid-May.

SIGNAL MOUNTAIN AREA

Signal Mountain Lodge Signal Mountain has a different feel—and different owners—from the other lodgings in Grand Teton, adding to the sense

Campground	Total Sites	RV Hookups	Dump Station	Toilets	Drinking Water
Inside the Park					
Colter Bay	350	No	Yes	Yes	Yes
Colter Bay Trailer Village	112	Yes	Yes	Yes	Yes
Gros Ventre	350	No	Yes	Yes	Yes
Jenny Lake*	51	No	No	Yes	Yes
Lizard Creek	60	No	No	Yes	Yes
Signal Mountain	81	No	Yes	Yes	Yes
Near the Park					
Flagg Ranch	171	Yes	Yes	Yes	Yes
Snake River Park KOA	83	Yes	Yes	Yes	Yes

*Tents only.

that any place you choose to stay in this park is going to give you a fairly unique atmosphere. What they all have in common is the Teton view, and this lodge, on the banks of Jackson Lake, might have the best. To top it off, it's got lakefront retreats, which you can really inhabit, with stoves and refrigerators and foldout sofa beds for the kids. Other accommodations, mostly rustic log cabins, come in a variety of flavors, from motel-style rooms in four-unit buildings set amid the trees to beachfront family bungalows. These carpeted units feature handmade pine furniture, electric heat, covered porches, and tiled bathrooms; some have fireplaces, and all are nonsmoking. Recreational options include rafting and fishing, and sailboat tours on the lake. A convenience store and gas station are on the property; free Wi-Fi is available in the lodge lobby.

P.O. Box 50, Moran, WY 83013. ✆ **307/543-2831.** www.signalmountainlodge.com. 80 units. $151 double; $120–$240 cabin units. AE, DISC, MC, V. Closed late Oct to early May.

JENNY LAKE AREA

Jenny Lake Lodge My favorite property in any national park, this lodge justifiably prides itself on seclusion, award-winning food, and the individual attention that comes with a cabin resort kept intentionally small. Catering to an older, affluent, and loyal clientele, the style here is a throwback: a blend of peaceful rusticity and occasional reminders of class and formality. The property is a hybrid of mountain-lake resort and dude ranch, with various extras included in its prices, such as horseback rides, meals, walking sticks, umbrellas, and cool cruiser bicycles. The cabins, each named for a resident flower, are rustic on the outside and luxurious within—decorated with bright braided rugs, dark wood floors, beamed ceilings, cushy plaid armchairs, and tiled bathrooms. Rooms have one queen-size, one king-size, or two queen beds. Some were old dude-ranch cabins from the 1920s, and some were built in the 1990s; the latter have larger baths and more modernity, but less character. Free Wi-Fi is available in the main lodge.

Box 240, Moran, WY 83013. ✆ **800/628-9988** or 307/543-2811. www.gtlc.com. 37 units. $585 double; $760–$825 suite. Extra person $150 a night. Rates include breakfast, dinner, and activities. AE, MC, V. Closed mid-Oct to May.

NEAR THE PARK

FLAGG RANCH VILLAGE AREA

Like Grant Village in Yellowstone, Flagg Ranch offers travelers the full gamut of services: cabins, tent and RV sites, an above-average restaurant (at the Flagg Ranch Resort), and a gas station. Until a ban on snowmobiling was recently reinstated, it was a popular jumping-off spot for snowmobilers during winter months. However, it's in a stand of pines in the middle of nowhere, and there's not much to do in the immediate vicinity except watch the Snake River pass by.

Flagg Ranch Resort At this resort on the Snake River with log-and-luxury ambience, accommodations are duplex and fourplex log cabins that were constructed in the 1990s. The rooms feature patios with rocking chairs, king- and queen-size beds, spacious sitting areas with writing desks and chests of drawers, and bathrooms with a tub/shower and separate vanities. There are float trips, horseback rides, and excellent fishing in Polecat Creek or the Snake River. The lodge is a locus of activity, with its double-sided fireplace, fancy **dining room,** gift shop, espresso bar and pub with large-screen television, convenience store, and gas station. A campground is situated on the grounds amid a stand of pine trees.

P.O. Box 187, Moran, WY 83013. ✆ **800/443-2311** or 307/543-2861. www.flaggranch.com. 92 cabins, 171 RV sites. $179–$189 cabin double; $50 RV site; $25 tent site. AE, DISC, MC, V. Closed mid-Oct to mid-May.

Showers	Fire Pits/ Grills	Laundry	Public Phone	Reserve	Fees	Open
Yes	Yes	Yes	Yes	No	$19	Late May to late Sept
No	Yes	Yes	Yes	Yes	$48–$54	Late May to late Sept
No	Yes	No	Yes	No	$19	Early May to mid-Oct
No	Yes	No	Yes	No	$19	Mid-May to late Sept
No	Yes	No	Yes	No	$18	Early June to early Sept
No	Yes	No	Yes	No	$20	Mid-May to Oct
Yes	Yes	Yes	Yes	Yes	$25–$50	Mid-May to late Sept
Yes	Yes	Yes	Yes	Yes	$39–$62	Mid-Apr to early Oct

IN JACKSON

Clustered together near the junction west of downtown where Wyo. 22 leaves U.S. Hwy. 26/89 and heads north to Teton Village is a colony of chain franchises: a surprisingly chic **Motel 6,** 600 S. U.S. Hwy. 89 (✆ **307/733-1620**); **Super 8,** 750 S. U.S. Hwy. 89 (✆ **307/733-6833;** www.super8.com); and the more upscale and expensive **Days Inn,** 350 S. U.S. Hwy. 89 (✆ **307/733-0033;** www.daysinn.com), with private hot tubs and fireplaces in suites. High-season prices for the motels range from about $100 to $200.

On the inexpensive end of the scale, the **Anvil Motel,** 215 N. Cache St. (✆ **800/234-4507** or 307/733-3668; www.anvilmotel.com), offers hostel beds in the well-kept "Bunkhouse" for $25 a night, with ski lockers, a communal kitchen, and a hot tub. Motel rooms run $128 to $148 in summer. I also like the summer-only **Buckrail Lodge,** at the base of Snow King Mountain at 110 E. Karns Ave. (✆ **307/733-2079;** www.buckraillodge.com), a comfortable independent that's been nicely maintained by the two families that have owned it since it opened in the 1960s. Doubles are $85 to $135. Find website listings for the major chains in chapter 38.

Alpine House Stylish, environmentally conscious, and melding the best of the B&B and hotel worlds, Alpine House began as a six-room operation in 1996 and expanded nearly fourfold in 2000 when it also opened a **spa.** Modeled after Scandinavian lodging, the rooms are woodsy and Western but modern and functional, with one king, one queen, or two queens and nice views. Some have lofts with additional beds; all have a shared or private balcony, a fireplace, and a soaking tub. The public areas are quiet and serene. New in 2009 were five spacious creekside cottages a block away from the main building. Owners Hans and Nancy Johnstone are former Olympians and great resources for planning outdoor adventures in Jackson Hole.

285 N. Glenwood St. (P.O. Box 1126), Jackson, WY 83001. ✆ **800/753-1421** or 307/739-1570. Fax 307/734-2850. www.alpinehouse.com. 27 units. $175–$260 double; $195–$295 suite; $195–$400 cottage. Rates include full breakfast. AE, MC, V.

Rusty Parrot Lodge and Spa The name sounds like an out-of-tune jungle bird, but the Rusty Parrot demonstrates excellent pitch, cultivating a country lodge and spa right in the heart of busy Jackson. Across from Miller Park, the Parrot is decorated in the nouveau Western style of peeled log, with an interior appointed with elegant furnishings and river-rock fireplaces. One very attractive lure is the **Body Sage Spa,** where you can get yourself treated to all sorts of scrubs, wraps, massages, and facials. Another is the excellent restaurant, **Wild Sage.** The breakfast that comes with your room includes omelets, fresh pastries, fruits, cereals, and freshly ground coffee; food also appears later in the day, but the lodge likes to make that a surprise (sorry). Featuring free Wi-Fi and other perks, rooms are gigantic, and several have private balconies.

175 N. Jackson (P.O. Box 1657), Jackson, WY 83001. ✆ **800/458-2004** or 307/733-2000. www.rustyparrot.com. 31 units. A/C, TV, TEL. $290–$425 double; $625–$750 suite; lower rates spring and fall. Rates include full breakfast. AE, DC, DISC, MC, V.

Trapper Inn Just 2 blocks from Town Square, the Trapper Inn was reborn as a slick hotel when it opened 36 new rooms in a pair of attractive "mountain contemporary" buildings in 2006. The rooms are stylish and spacious—the newest are all suites that adjoin, with a kitchen in every other unit—and the employees here are some of the most helpful you'll find in Jackson.

235 N. Cache, Jackson, WY 83001. ✆ **800/341-8000,** or 307/733-2648 for reservations. www.trapperinn.com. 90 units. A/C, TV, TEL. $119–$219 double; $159–$289 suite. AE, MC, V.

Virginian Lodge It's not brand new, it's not a resort, and it doesn't have a golf course, but the Virginian is one of the better motels in Jackson. On the busy Broadway strip, its courtyard seems a world away, and the prices remain reasonable. All in all, it's a busy, cheerful place to stay. A large outdoor pool is open seasonally, and you can get a room with a Jacuzzi. Kids can romp in the arcade, and parents can relax in the **Virginian Saloon.**

750 W. Broadway, Jackson, WY 83001. ✆ **800/262-4999** or 307/733-2792. Fax 307/733-4063. www.virginianlodge.com. 170 units. A/C, TV, TEL. $119 double; $159–$220 suite. AE, DC, DISC, MC, V.

Woods Hotel Originally opened in 1950, the Woods Hotel was collecting cobwebs from 1998 to 2006 until new ownership reinvented the place as a boutique lodge in 2007. The brick exterior (and vintage sign) belies the innlike rooms, with their spare Western-chic style—leather headboards, warm earth tones, and a few rugged touches. The standard rooms are small and lack air-conditioning, but the brick structure stays surprisingly cool, and the suites and one family room (with bunk beds) give guests more space to stretch out, plus free Wi-Fi, microwaves, and minifridges.

120 N. Glenwood St., Jackson, WY 83001. ✆ **307/733-2200.** www.thewoodshotel.com. 11 units. TV. $149 double; $179–$189 suite. AE, MC, V.

Wort Hotel On Broadway just off the Town Square, the Wort stands like an old tree. Opened in the early 1940s by the sons of Charles Wort, an early-20th-century homesteader, the Tudor-style two-story building was largely rebuilt after a 1980 fire. Nowadays it has an old-fashioned style, both in the relaxed **Silver Dollar Bar** (distinctively graced with 2,032 silver dollars) and in the quiet, formal

dining room. In the manner of an old cattle-baron hotel, the lobby holds a warm, romantic fireplace; another fireplace and a huge, hand-carved mural accent a mezzanine sitting area, providing a second hideaway. The rooms aren't Tudor at all—the Wort labels them "New West." Brass number plates and doorknobs welcome you into guest rooms, which have modern decor, thick carpeting, and armoires. The Silver Dollar Suite features a wet bar inlaid with the same silver dollars found in the bar below.

50 N. Glenwood, Jackson, WY 83001. ✆ **307/733-2190.** www.worthotel.com. 59 units. A/C. $165–$339 double; $399–$699 suite. AE, DISC, MC, V.

NEAR JACKSON

A Teton Tree House This B&B is an architectural marvel "and a quiet port in the storm" of bustling Jackson Hole, says innkeeper, builder, and longtime Jackson adventurer Denny Becker. Built on a forested hillside above Wilson where flying squirrels glide amidst the sunset canopy, the labyrinthine inn is 95 steps up from the parking lot and full of books, staircases, and all sorts of funky nooks and crannies. Most every room has a private deck with a splendid view of the valley; the Downy Woodpecker room has a queen bed and an outdoor swing, and adjoins with the Clark's Nuthatch room with two queens for larger parties. Denny and his wife, Sally, eat heart-healthy breakfasts (meaning no eggs or meat) with their guests; Denny is known for his breakfast banana splits (with light yogurt), Sally for her baking, and both have plenty of good advice.

6175 Heck of a Hill Rd. (P.O. Box 550), Wilson, WY 83014. ✆ **307/733-3233.** www.atetontreehouse-jacksonhole.com. 6 units. $205–$250 double; 3-night minimum. Rates include full breakfast. No children 4 or under. DISC, MC, V. Closed mid-May to Mid-Oct. Located 8 miles west of Jackson.

Amangani Chopped into the side of East Gros Ventre Butte, Amangani's rough rock exterior blends in so well that the lights from its windows and pool appear to glow from within the mountain. The style is understated and rustic, but every detail is expensively done. Owner Adrian Zecha has resorts like this around the world, from Bali to Bhutan; although the designs are tailored to the landscape, the approach is the same: personal service, luxury, and all the little touches. To name a few of the latter, there are iPod cradles in every bedroom, cashmere throws on the daybeds, and stunning slate and redwood interiors.

1535 NE Butte Rd., Jackson, WY 83002 (on top of East Gros Ventre Butte). ✆ **877/734-7333** or 307/734-7333. www.amanresorts.com. 40 units. A/C, TV, TEL. $565–$1,400 double. AE, DC, DISC, MC, V.

Spring Creek Ranch Perched atop East Gros Ventre Butte, 1,000 feet above the Snake River and minutes from both the airport and downtown Jackson, this resort commands a panoramic view of the Grand Tetons and 1,000 acres of land populated by deer, moose, and the horses at its riding facility in the valley below. It seems a little less exclusive now that Amangani has opened next door. But Spring Creek still has much going for it: The rooms, divided among nine buildings with cabinlike exteriors, all have wood-burning fireplaces, Native American floor and wall coverings, and balconies with views of the Tetons. Most rooms have a king- or two queen-size beds, and the studio units boast kitchenettes. In addition to its own rooms, the resort arranges accommodations in the privately owned condominiums and vacation homes that dot the butte—large, lavishly furnished, and featuring completely equipped kitchens. The resort also has free Wi-Fi, an **"Adventure Spa,"** offering a combination of guide service and post-outing treatments, and in-house naturalists who lead guests on "Wildlife Safaris" into the parks.

1800 Spirit Dance Rd. (on top of East Gros Ventre Butte), P.O. Box 4780, Jackson, WY 83001. ✆ **800/443-6139** or 307/733-8833. 125 units. A/C, TV, TEL. $340–$500 double; $375–$2,200 condo or home. AE, MC, V.

Wildflower Inn A terrific B&B on 3 lush and secluded acres near Teton Village, the Wildflower Inn is the brainchild of jack-of-all-trades Ken Hern, a log-home builder and climbing guide, and his wife, Sherrie, a former ski instructor who now runs the inn full-time. Besides being founts of local information, the Herns are remarkable hosts who pride themselves on both the big picture and the little details. Rooms, named after local wildflowers, are comfortable and luxurious, with private decks, exposed logs, and a remarkable sense of privacy for an inn. Guests also get access to house bikes, rain gear, and trekking poles—not to mention hammocks. Breakfasts are excellent, including veggie frittatas, sour cream coffee cake, and yeast-raised waffles.

3725 Teton Village Rd. (P.O. Box 11000), Jackson, WY 83002. ✆ **307/733-4710.** Fax 307/739-0914. www.jacksonholewildflower.com. 5 units. TV. $320–$350 double; $400 suite. MC, V.

IN TETON VILLAGE

Although lodging in the town of Jackson tends to be a little cheaper in the winter than in the summer, at Teton Village the pattern is reversed—rooms by the ski hill get more expensive after the snow falls.

The Alpenhof No other spot in the village has quite the Swiss-chalet flavor of this long-standing hostelry, which has a prize location only 50 yards from the ski-resort tram. Four stories tall, with a pitched roof and flower boxes on the balconies, it offers a little old-world atmosphere, as well as excellent comforts and service. The rooms feature brightly colored alpine fabrics, handcrafted Bavarian furnishings, and tiled bathrooms with big, soft towels. You can choose from two junior suites with wet bars and five rooms with fireplaces, and many rooms have balconies or decks. Economy rooms offer two doubles or one queen-size bed, while deluxe units are larger. The resident **Alpenrose** restaurant specializes in fondue.

3255 W. Village Dr., Teton Village, WY 83025. ✆ **800/732-3244** or 307/733-3242. Fax 307/739-1516. www.alpenhoflodge.com. 42 units. A/C, TV, TEL. $189–$379 double; $539 suite. Lower rates in spring and fall. AE, DC, DISC, MC, V. Closed Nov.

Four Seasons Resort Jackson Hole The most deluxe lodging option in Teton Village, the ultrastylish Four Seasons sets a high bar for ski-in, ski-out luxury. From a year-round pool landscaped to resemble a mountain creek to the cowboy-hatted doorman to the rooms—stately, luxurious, and definitively Western—this is one of the top slopeside properties in the country. The range of rooms starts at the high end and goes up from there, but even the standard kings are large and plush, and most units have a balcony or a fireplace. One especially notable perk: the hotel's "Base Camp," a full-service outdoor-activity concierge who can arrange mountain biking, hiking, fishing, and ballooning excursions, and who will outfit you in style. In winter, the service transforms into a first-rate ski concierge, and s'mores and hot chocolate are served poolside. The eating and drinking facilities are also a cut above and range from casually hip to extravagant.

7680 Granite Loop (P.O. Box 544), Teton Village, WY 83025. ✆ **307/732-5000.** www.fourseasons.com. 156 units. A/C, TV, TEL. $400–$750 double; $700–$4,000 condo or suite. AE, DC, DISC, MC, V.

The Hostel If you came to Wyoming to ski, not to lie in the lap of luxury, get yourself a room at the Hostel and hit the slopes. Open since 1967 and fortuitously spared the wrecking ball—and known as Hostel X until 2008—it's a great bargain for those who don't need the trimmings. And it's not just dormitory bunks, either—the comfortable but simple private rooms (about the caliber of a roadside motel) hold up to four people; they have either one king bed or four twins. There's also a good place to prep your skis, a library, and a common room with chessboards, a ping-pong table, a fireplace, Internet access, and a TV. You can walk to the Mangy Moose and other fun spots, and nobody will be able to tell you apart from the skiers staying at the Four Seasons.

3315 W. Village Dr., Box 543, Teton Village, WY 83025. ✆ **307/733-3415.** www.thehostel.us. 52 rooms, 36 dormitory-style bunks. $79–$89 double; $18–$32 bunk. MC, V.

Hotel Terra The newest—and greenest—property in Teton Village, Hotel Terra combines sustainable design and contemporary Western style, with satisfying results. The LEED-certified hotel incorporates granite stonework and understated decor into inviting and sleek spaces. The rooms, which range from studios to three-bedroom suites with full kitchens, demonstrate superior attention to detail; there are organic cotton sheets and towels, rain-shower heads, fair trade coffee, and touch-screen telephones. The hotel's facilities are uniformly excellent, including the terrific **CHILL Spa** and an excellent restaurant, **Il Villagio Osteria** (see "Where to Dine," below).

3315 W. Village Dr. (P.O. Box 543), Teton Village, WY 83025. ✆ **800/631-6281** or 307/739-4000. www.hotelterrajacksonhole.com. 132 units. A/C, TV, TEL. $359–$499 double; $499–$1,700 suite; lower rates spring and fall. AE, DISC, MC, V.

Snake River Lodge & Spa This perpetually changing establishment has gained some stability under the management of RockResorts. Lodgepole beams, wooden floors, and stone fireplaces accent the main reception area. The main lodge provides accommodations where classy overshadows rustic, with exposed wooden-beam ceilings, down comforters, and luxurious furnishings. There are three levels of suites, from oversize versions of the standard rooms to three-bedroom versions with top-of-the-line kitchens, good sound systems, and Jacuzzi tubs. The 17,000-square-foot **spa** is the state's largest, featuring everything from microdermabrasion to hydrotherapy to free weights. Winter visitors can ski directly to a ski valet and drop their skis off for an overnight tune-up.

7710 Granite Loop Rd. (Box 348), Teton Village, WY 83025. ✆ **866/975-7625** or 307/732-6000. www.snakeriverlodge.com. 130 units. TV, TEL. $299–$499 double; $699–$2,000 suite. Lower rates spring and fall. Lower rates in spring and fall. AE, MC, V.

10 Where to Dine

INSIDE THE PARK

COLTER BAY

John Colter Cafe Court DELI/FAST FOOD These are the two sit-down restaurants in the village (although there's also a snack shop in the grocery store). Three meals are served daily during the summer months. The **cafe** serves sandwiches, burgers, and pretty good Mexican fare. Breakfasts at the **Ranch House** are hearty; lunch is a soup-and-salad bar and hot sandwiches; dinner is more of an event but nonetheless family-friendly. Among the dinner entrees are trout, lasagna, pork chops, beef stew, and New York strip steaks. The bar is worth a look, emblazoned with the brands of a number of Jackson Hole–area ranches.

Across from the visitor center and marina in Colter Bay Village. ✆ **307/543-2811.** Reservations not accepted. Breakfast and lunch $6–$13; dinner $6–$22. MC, V. Daily 6:30am–10pm. Closed Oct–Apr.

JACKSON LAKE JUNCTION

The casual dining choice at the Jackson Lake Lodge is the **Pioneer Grill;** entrees are light and less expensive than those at the Mural Room (see below). The **Blue Heron** lounge at Jackson Lake Lodge is one of the nicest spots in either park to enjoy a cocktail.

The Mural Room STEAKS/WILD GAME Jackson Lake's main dining room is quiet and fairly formal, catering to a more sedate crowd as well as corporate groups; it's also more expensive than other park restaurants. The floor-to-ceiling windows provide stellar views across a meadow that is moose habitat and to the lake and the Cathedral Group. (The staff applauds sunset every night.) Walls inside are adorned with hand-painted Western murals created by Carl Roters. The food is the perfect complement to the view and markedly superior to most of what you'll find in Yellowstone. Three meals are served daily in summer. Breakfast items include a "healthy start" breakfast, organic granola, and fruit smoothie. Dinner might be a grand five-course event that includes pan-seared ostrich, butternut bisque, and house salad, followed by an entree of blue corn and plantain–crusted trout, slow-roasted prime rib, vegetable tart, or peppered elk loin. Dessert includes delicious homemade ice cream and a rich fudge cake. Aside from the dining room at Jenny Lake Lodge and Lake Yellowstone Hotel, this is the most romantic and upscale eatery in either park.

At Jackson Lake Lodge. ✆ **800/628-9988** or 307/543-2811. Reservations not accepted. Breakfast $6–$15; lunch $9–$17; dinner $18–$38. MC, V. Daily 7–9:30am, 11:30am–1:30pm, and 5:30–9pm.

Signal Mountain Lodge AMERICAN/MEXICAN There are actually two restaurants here, serving delicious food in the friendliest style in the park. The fine dining room and lounge are called **Peaks** and **Deadman's Bar,** respectively, and the **Trapper Grill** supplements the continental fare with Mexican entrees, pizzas, and plump sandwiches. You eat up the scenery, too, with a view of Jackson Lake and Mount Moran. Bargain hunters flock to the bar for the decadent Nachos Supreme: a foot-tall mountain of chips, cheese, chicken, beef, beans, and peppers that runs a mere $15. You'll easily fill four people for that price, leaving you plenty of change for the bar's signature blackberry margaritas. Because the bar has one of three televisions in the park and is equipped with cable for sports nuts, the crowd tends to be young and noisy. Full meals are served in the proper dining room, with an emphasis on sustainable cuisine. Entrees include free-range chicken, vegetarian lasagna, and filet mignon.

At Signal Mountain Resort. ✆ **307/543-2831.** Reservations required for breakfast and dinner. Breakfast $7–$10; lunch $8–$16; dinner $19–$35. AE, DISC, MC, V. Daily 7–10am and 11:30am–10pm.

JENNY LAKE

Jenny Lake Lodge Dining Room CONTINENTAL The finest meals in either park (or, for that matter, in *any* park) are served here, where a talented chef creates culinary delights for guests and, occasionally, a president of the United States. Breakfast, lunch, and dinner are served here, and all are spectacular. (Nonguests should have lunch here, if they can.) The five-course dinner is the bell-ringer, though. Guests choose from appetizers that might include elk carpaccio; salads with organic greens, pecans, and dried cherries; and entrees such as pan-roasted squab, herb-rubbed rabbit leg, or a venison strip loin. Desserts are equally creative and tantalizing. Price is no object, at least for guests, because meals are included in the room charge; nonguests should expect a hefty bill. Casual dress is discouraged, with jackets requested for dinner.

At Jenny Lake Lodge. ✆ **307/733-4647.** Reservations required. Prix-fixe breakfast $22; lunch main courses $9–$14; prix-fixe dinner $72, not including alcoholic beverages. AE, MC, V. Daily 7:30–9am, noon–1:30pm, and 6–8:45pm.

NEAR THE PARK

The Bear's Den AMERICAN Served at the main lodge at Flagg Ranch, the food at this oasis is better than what's typically found in a "family restaurant," and servings are generous. The dinner menu includes fish, chicken, and beef dishes, as well as home-style entrees such as ranch beef stew and chicken potpie; lunch and dinner are unadventurous but hearty. The ambience is also pleasant during both winter and summer months; wooden chairs and tables with colorful upholstery liven up this newly constructed log building.

At Flagg Ranch, John D. Rockefeller Jr. Pkwy. ✆ **800/443-2311.** Reservations accepted. Breakfast $5–$12; lunch $8–$13; dinner $12–$26. AE, DISC, MC, V. Daily 7–10:30am, 11:30am–1pm, and 5–9:30pm.

Il Villaggio Osteria ITALIAN The swankest restaurant in Teton Village, Il Villaggio Osteria features tables as well as a 12-seat wine bar and 8-seat salami bar where imported meats and cheeses are sliced to order. The menu includes gourmet wood-fired pizzas with such exotic toppings as figs, arugula, and hummus, as well as creative dishes with Mediterranean influences: wild mushroom risotto, braised pork with polenta, and house-made wild boar ragu. The tantalizing dessert list includes a delectable tiramisu. The lunch menu focuses on salads, pizzas, paninis, and lighter versions of the dinner entrees; from 2:30 to 5:30pm, a limited "cafe menu" is served.

In the Hotel Terra, 3335 W. Village Dr., Teton Village. ✆ **307/739-4100.** Reservations recommended. Lunch $10–$19; dinner $15–$27. AE, DISC, MC, V. Daily 11am–10pm.

Mangy Moose AMERICAN Coming off the slopes at the end of a hard day of skiing or snowboarding, you can slide right to the porch of this Teton Village institution. Good luck getting a seat, but if you like a lot of noise and laughter, a beer or a glass of wine, and tasty food, you'll be patient—it beats getting into your car and driving into town. The decor matches the pandemonium: It looks like an upscale junk shop, with bicycles, old signs, and, naturally, a moose head or two hanging from the walls and rafters. The food is customary Wyoming fare (steak, seafood, and pasta)—I'm a big fan of the buffalo meatloaf and the fresh Idaho trout. There is often live music in the saloon, which serves both lunch and dinner. An affiliated cafe, the **RMO Cafe,** serves breakfast, lunch, and pizza in a separate room from 7am to 8pm.

1 W. Village Dr., Teton Village. ✆ **307/733-4913.** www.mangymoose.net. Reservations recommended for larger parties. Main courses $12–$30 in the dining room; $4–$10 in the bar and cafe. AE, MC, V. Daily 5–10pm (dining room), 7am–5pm (cafe), and 11:30am–10pm (bar).

Nora's Fish Creek Inn AMERICAN If you like to eat among locals, and if you like to eat a lot, Nora's is the place to hang out in Wilson, 6 miles northwest of Jackson—just look for the 15-foot trout on the roof. At once rough and cozy, it's an institution, and if you come here often, you'll start to recognize the regulars, who grumble over their coffee and gossip about doings in the valley. Breakfast is especially good, when there are pancakes and huevos rancheros that barely fit on the huge plates. Trout and eggs is another specialty. Prices are inexpensive compared to those at any of the other restaurants in town. Dinner is burgers, barbecue, and smoked trout.

5600 W. Wyo. 22, Wilson. ✆ **307/733-8288.** Reservations accepted for dinner. Breakfast and lunch $5–$10; dinner $10–$15. AE, DISC, MC, V. Mon–Fri 6:30am–2pm; Sat–Sun 6:30am–1:30pm; daily 5–9pm. Call for winter hours.

North Grille NEW AMERICAN The resident eatery at the Jackson Hole Golf and Tennis Club, the North Grille is located at the LEED-certified clubhouse, a slick and stylish new building with incredible views of the Tetons. For sunset watching, I recommend the outdoor patio, but the dining room, clad in dark wood and bookcases, is a cozy setting for the winter months. The menu is neatly organized into categories by price point: $14 nets you a garlic roaster chicken breast or steamed clams, $20 brings halibut medallions on biscuits with lobster gravy or a spicy pork filet, and $28 allows for rack of lamb or chargrilled king salmon. Lunch brings similar but lighter fare.

5000 Spring Gulch Rd. ✆ **307/733-7788.** www.jhgtc.com. Reservations recommended. Lunch $8–$12; dinner $14–$28. AE, DISC, MC, V. Daily 11:30am–2:30pm and 5:30–9pm.

Stiegler's AUSTRIAN Austrian cuisine isn't exactly lurking on every street corner, waiting to be summoned with a Julie Andrews yodel, but the discerning Austrian will certainly appreciate Stiegler's. Since 1983, Stiegler's has been confusing, astonishing, and delighting customers with such favorites as elk *Försterin,* bratwurst, and schnitzel, as well as less recognizable (and not as heavy as Austrian food's reputation might suggest) delicacies. Each plate is served with at least three veggies for a terrific presentation and variety of tastes. The desserts are more familiar: apple strudel and crepes. Peter Stiegler, the Austrian chef, invites you to "find a little *Gemütlichkeit*"—the feeling you get when you're surrounded by good friends, good food, and, of course, good beer. The inviting copper bar has its own menu ($10–$19, with great burgers) and there are intimate tables and booths inside and a poolside patio outside.

Teton Village Rd. at the Aspens. ✆ **307/733-1071.** Reservations recommended. Main courses $16–$37. AE, MC, V. Tues–Sun 5:30–9:30pm. Closed Mon.

IN JACKSON

The Blue Lion CONTINENTAL In the fast-moving, high-rent world of Jackson dining, the Blue Lion stays in the forefront by staying the same. Owned and operated by Ned Brown since 1978, the restaurant is in a two-story blue clapboard building across from a park that looks like a comfy family home. Inside, in intimate rooms accented with soft lighting, or outside on a picture-perfect patio, diners enjoy slow-paced and elegant meals. The menu features rack of lamb and wild-game specialties, such as grilled elk loin in a peppercorn sauce. Fresh fish is flown in daily for dishes such as the nori-crusted ahi.

160 N. Millward St. ✆ **307/733-3912.** www.bluelionrestaurant.com. Reservations recommended. Main courses $15–$33. AE, DC, DISC, MC, V. Summer daily 5:30–10pm; winter daily 6–10pm.

Burke's Chop House STEAKS/GAME/SEAFOOD Longtime Jackson chef Michael Burke's ambitious eatery in downtown Jackson features a sleek dining room—punctuated by plenty of dark wood, a sweeping bar, and a few antique car parts and scenic photographs. The understated setting is a perfect backdrop for the unpretentious but excellent fare. The menu includes smoked baby back pork ribs with homemade bourbon barbecue sauce and a nice selection of steaks and chops. The buffalo tenderloin and filets are particularly satisfying.

72 S. Glenwood St. ✆ **307/733-8575.** Reservations recommended. Main courses $20–$40. AE, DC, DISC, MC, V. Daily 6pm–close (usually 9–10pm).

The Cadillac Grille CALIFORNIA ECLECTIC Neon and a hip menu give this restaurant a trendy air that attracts see-and-be-seen visitors more than locals. The chefs work hard on presentation, but they also know how to cook a wide-ranging variety of dishes, from fire-roasted elk tenderloin to pancetta-crusted Alaskan halibut. The wine list is equally long and varied. The upscale dining room is one of three options at this address; you can also eat at the posh bar or in the '50s-themed confines of **Billy's Giant Hamburgers,** where a great burger runs about $6. For the best of both worlds, order a burger at the bar.

55 N. Cache St. ✆ **307/733-3279.** Reservations recommended. Lunch $5–$18; dinner $12–$35. AE, MC, V. Daily 11:30am–3pm and 5:30–9:30pm.

Jedediah's House of Sourdough AMERICAN You feel as if you've walked into the kitchen of some sodbuster's log cabin home when you enter Jedediah's, and with good reason—the structure dates from 1910. Bring a big appetite for breakfast, and a little patience—you may have to wait for a table; then you may have time to study the interesting old photos on the wall as you wait for your food. But it's worth it, especially for the rich flavor of the sourjacks (a stack of sourdough pancakes), served with blueberries. Lunches include soups, salads, and burgers and sandwiches—on sourdough, of course. The sourdough starter here is also historic: It dates to the 1870s.

135 E. Broadway. ✆ **307/733-5671.** Reservations not accepted. Breakfast $5–$12; lunch $7–$11. AE, DC, DISC, MC, V. Daily 7am–2pm.

Koshu Wine Bar ASIAN FUSION In the back half of the Jackson Hole Wine Company, this small, sleek dining room serves ingenious, addictive, Asian-inspired creations. The Far East is just a starting point, with offerings that meld dozens of influences into dishes such as buttermilk-battered soft-shell crab and pork ribs; the menu changes on a near-daily basis. Thanks to its location in a wine store, patrons can choose from 800 varieties of wine at retail price (plus a nominal corking fee).

200 W. Broadway, in the back of the Jackson Hole Wine Company. ✆ **307/733-5283.** Reservations recommended. Main courses $15–$30. AE, MC, V. Daily 6–10:30pm. Bar open until 2am, depending on crowd.

Nani's Genuine Pasta House ITALIAN In a warmly appointed dining room with red-and-white checkered tablecloths and a slick wine bar, the food is extraordinary at Nani's. You are handed two menus when you are seated: a "Carta Classico" featuring pasta favorites such as *amitriciana* (tomato, onion, guanciale, and freshly ground black pepper) and fresh mussels in wine broth, and a list of specialties from a different featured region of Italy. Depending on when you visit, it might be Sicily, where head chef Camille Parker's family has its roots, or Emilia-Romagna, where prosciutto, Parmesan, and balsamic vinegar are culinary staples. Parker ventures to Italy annually for research, and you can literally taste her passion. Your only problem with her restaurant might be finding it—it's tucked away behind a little relic of a motel, but it is definitely worth seeking out.

242 N. Glenwood St. ✆ **307/733-3888.** Reservations recommended. Main courses $14–$33. MC, V. Daily 5–10pm. Bar open later.

Rendezvous Bistro AMERICAN/SEAFOOD The Rendezvous opened in 2001 and garnered a fast local following. It's easy to see why: The place is contemporary yet casual, the food is affordable but very good, and the service is excellent. Climb into one of the intimate booths and order a dozen oysters on the half-shell and slurp away, but save some room for a main course, ranging from steak frites to spicy chipotle trout to grilled chile-rubbed pork chops. It might sound formal, but it's really not—the beauty is that the food is the best upscale value in town, while the atmosphere is very laid-back.

380 S. Broadway. ✆ **307/739-1100.** Reservations recommended. Main courses $15–$25. AE, DISC, MC, V. Summer daily 5:30–11pm; fall to spring Sun–Thurs 5:30–10pm; Fri–Sat 5:30–11pm. Closed Sun fall to spring.

Snake River Brewery MICROBREWERY One of the West's best (and busiest) microbreweries, the industrial-meets-contemporary-looking establishment offers a menu of pasta, applewood-fired pizzas and panini, and salads, plus a few entrees like "Slash and Burn Trout," served with fennel relish. The real standouts are the beers, especially Custer's Last Ale and Zonker Stout, winners at the Great American Beer Fest. This place is a local favorite and a great lunch spot, with daily $7 specials like turkey-and-brie wraps and chipotle BBQ sandwiches.

265 S. Millward St. ✆ **307/739-2337.** www.snakeriverbrewing.com. Most dishes $8–$14. AE, DISC, MC, V. Daily 11:30am–11pm. Bar until midnight.

Snake River Grill NEW AMERICAN This is a popular drop-in spot for locals, including some of the glitterati who spend time in the valley. The front-room dining area overlooks the busy Town Square, and there's also a more private, romantic room in the back. It's an award-winning restaurant for both its wine list and its menu, which features regular fresh-fish dishes (ahi tuna is a favorite), crispy pork shank, and some game-meat entrees such as venison chops and Idaho trout. The pizzas—cooked in a wood-burning oven—are topped with exotic ingredients such as venison pepperoni or steak tartare.

84 E. Broadway, on the Town Square. ✆ **307/733-0557.** www.snakerivergrill.com. Reservations recommended. Main courses $20–$40. AE, MC, V. Summer daily 5:30–10pm; winter daily 6–10pm. Closed Nov and Apr.

Nearby Attractions: National Elk Refuge

The U.S. Fish & Wildlife Service makes sure that the elk at the **National Elk Refuge,** just north of Jackson on U.S. Hwy. 26/89 (✆ **307/733-9212;** http://nationalelkrefuge.fws.gov), eat well during the winter by feeding them alfalfa pellets. It keeps them out of the haystacks of area ranchers and creates a beautiful tableau on the flats along the Gros Ventre River: Thousands of elk, some with huge antler racks, dot the snow for miles. Though the elk are absent in the summer, there is still plenty of life on the refuge, including, most recently, a quite visible mountain lion and cubs.

Each winter (mid-Dec to Mar), the Fish and Wildlife Service offers horse-drawn sleigh rides that weave among the elk. Rides early in the winter will find young bulls playing and banging heads, while later visits wander through a more placid scene. Riders embark at the **Greater Yellowstone Visitor Center,** 532 N. Cache St., between 10am and 4pm on a first-come, first-served basis. Tickets for the 45-minute rides cost $18 for adults, $14 for children 5 to 12.

Sweetwater Restaurant AMERICAN Though this little log restaurant serves American fare, it does so in a decidedly offbeat way. The eclectic menu includes, for example, a Greek salad, a Baja chicken salad, and a cowboy-grilled roast beef sandwich. The dinner menu is just as quirky; try the unique chile-lime crab cakes before diving into the giant salmon filet or buffalo pot roast. Vegetarians will want to sample the spinach and feta casserole.

85 King St. ✆ **307/733-3553.** Reservations recommended. Lunch $5–$8; dinner $13–$22. AE, DISC, MC, V. Summer daily 11:30am–3pm and 5:30–10pm; winter daily 11:30am–2:30pm and 5:30–9:30pm.

Trio NEW AMERICAN Opened in 2005 by a trio (thus the name) of owner/chefs who formerly worked at the Snake River Grill, this instant local favorite offers a winning combination of inviting atmosphere and remarkable food. Served in a dimly lit, social room with a fossil-rock bar and semi-open kitchen, the seasonal menu might include appetizers such as sautéed shrimp with Szechuan peppercorns and wonton crisps, and entrees like elk medallions and a killer Idaho rainbow trout on a bed of blackened corn and avocado. Everything is uniformly mouthwatering, and the portions are perfectly sized and impeccably presented and served. The restaurant is perhaps best known for its killer fries—served with scallions, black pepper, and an addictive blue cheese fondue.

45 S. Glenwood Dr. ✆ **307/734-8038.** www.bistrotrio.com. Reservations recommended. Main courses $12–$32 dinner. AE, MC, V. Mon–Fri 11am–2pm; daily 5:30–close, usually 9–10pm.

18

Great Basin National Park, NV

by Don & Barbara Laine

Great Basin National Park, along the Utah–Nevada border, provides an intimate glimpse of a vast, rugged section of America, with opportunities for outdoor (and underground) adventures. A region of desert, valleys, mountains, lakes, and streams, North America's Great Basin includes Nevada, Utah, and parts of California, Oregon, and Idaho. It got its name because the rainwater that falls here has no outlet to the sea.

Founded in 1986, this park not only looks out at the Great Basin's expanse of desert and mountains from the summit of 13,063-foot Wheeler Peak, but descends beneath the earth's surface for a subterranean tour of the intricate and delicate stalactites, stalagmites, and other formations in the unreal world of Lehman Caves.

Hiking trails abound, through pine and aspen forests, or above the tree line to a world of barren, windswept rocks. Camping in the park is a delight, with quiet campgrounds, plenty of trees, and splendid scenery. The park contains forests of bristlecone pine—a species scientists believe is the oldest living tree on Earth—as well as pinyon, juniper, spruce, fir, pine, and aspen. You'll see wildflowers like yellow aster and Parry's primrose during the summer; also watch for mule deer, bighorn sheep, squirrels, and golden eagles.

Like most of the American West's national parks, Great Basin offers ample activities to keep you busy for at least a week, and we strongly suggest you plan to spend at least 1 full day in the park. For the best experience, try to allow at least 3 full days, to provide enough time to tour Lehman Cave and explore the scenic drive, and to hike to the bristlecone pine forest and perhaps to one of the park's high-mountain lakes.

Because of its remoteness—Great Basin isn't near any other popular tourist destinations or even along a route to one—you'll find it relatively quiet and uncrowded, similar to what you would have found 30 or 40 years ago in America's loved-to-death parks such as Yosemite and Grand Canyon. Although Great Basin National Park is in Nevada, many visitors are Utah residents on long-weekend excursions from Salt Lake City. Visitors to the national parks of Arizona and Utah who start their trips in Las Vegas, Nevada, can easily add Great Basin to the beginning or end of their driving loops.

AVOIDING THE CROWDS

Because Great Basin National Park is seemingly in the middle of nowhere, it receives far fewer visitors than most other national parks. However, it isn't deserted. During the relatively busy summer season, you'll need

Tips from a Park Insider

Anne Hopkins Pfaff, who worked as a park ranger at Great Basin National Park for a number of years, says that during her time at Great Basin she enjoyed both the park and the surrounding desert. "It's a gorgeous area," she says. "I like the remoteness."

Asked what she especially likes about the 77,100-acre park, Pfaff replies, "The variety of vegetation and habitats, and the views—especially the views that include both Wheeler Peak and out across the Great Basin, such as you get from Mather Overlook." This park, she says, "is one of America's real treasures, where you can get out on the trails and not see another human being." Pfaff says that as far as national parks go, Great Basin's campgrounds offer minimal services, and although many visitors enjoy this aspect, others miss their creature comforts, such as hot showers and RV hookups.

Pfaff says she's impressed by the age and beauty of the bristlecone pines and considers a hike to the bristlecone pine forest among the park's top experiences. Also on her list of things all visitors should do are touring Lehman Caves and taking the Wheeler Peak Scenic Drive. She recommends visiting the park in September, "when the crowds are gone and the weather is usually beautiful—not too hot at the lower elevations, but not yet snow-covered in the upper elevations."

to arrive at the visitor center early for your cave tour tickets (or purchase them in advance), and don't count on finding a campsite if you arrive late in the day, especially on weekends. The busiest times are on Memorial Day weekend and from July through Labor Day. Although the park is quieter in spring, weather can be a problem, with snow in the higher elevations. The park has its lowest visitation in January and February, but that is also when it is coldest and snowiest. The best time to visit is from just after Labor Day through the end of September, when there are fewer people and the weather is beautiful—warm days and crisp, cool nights. Early October is also *usually* nice, but you may also find yourself in an early snowstorm.

1 Essentials

GETTING THERE & GATEWAYS

Great Basin National Park is 5 miles west of Baker, Nevada; 70 miles southeast of Ely, Nevada; 385 miles east of Reno, Nevada; 286 miles north of Las Vegas, Nevada; 200 miles north of St. George, Utah; and 234 miles southwest of Salt Lake City, Utah.

From west-central Utah, take **U.S. 50** west across the state line into Nevada, go south on Nev. 487 to Baker, and then west on **Nev. 488** into the park. From St. George, take **I-15** north to Cedar City; continue north on Utah 130 to Minersville; take Utah 21 west through Milford to the Nevada state line, where it becomes Nev. 487, which you follow to Baker; and then take Nev. 488 west to the park.

From Las Vegas, follow **U.S. 93 north** to U.S. 50, go east to Nev. 487, where you turn south to Baker, and then follow Nev. 488 into the park.

From Ely and Reno, Nevada, follow U.S. 50 east to Nev. 487, and follow directions above.

THE NEAREST AIRPORTS The closest major airports are **McCarran International Airport** in Las Vegas, Nevada (✆ **702/261-5211;** www.mccarran.com), and **Salt Lake City International Airport** (✆ **800/595-2442** or 801/575-2400; www.slcairport.com) in Salt Lake City, Utah. Both are served by most major airlines and national car-rental agencies, whose website listings can be found in chapter 38.

INFORMATION

Contact **Great Basin National Park,** 100 Great Basin National Park, NV 89311 (✆ **775/234-7331;** www.nps.gov/grba). Be sure to ask for a copy of the park's excellent newspaper-style guide, *Bristlecone,* which includes a map, current activities and costs, and nearby services. Those who want to buy maps and books can contact the nonprofit **Western National Parks Association,** which operates two bookstores in the park, through a link on the park's website. For information on businesses outside the park in the nearby community of Baker, see the **Great Basin Business & Tourism Council**'s website, **www.greatbasinpark.com**.

VISITOR CENTER

The visitor center, on Nev. 488 at the northeast corner of the park, sells tickets for cave tours. It contains the Great Basin Association's bookstore, distributes brochures and other free information, and shows exhibits on the park's geology, history, flora, and fauna. In addition, a short film provides an introduction to the park.

The park is open daily, but the visitor center and cave are closed January 1, Thanksgiving, and December 25.

FEES

Park entry is free. The 90-minute cave tour costs $10 for adults, $5 for children 5 to 15 (kids under 5 not permitted); the 60-minute tour costs $8 for adults, $4 for children 5 to 15, and free for kids under 5. **Cave tour tickets** can be purchased by phone (✆ **775/234-7331,** ext. 242) from 24 hours to 30 days in advance. Camping costs $12 per night in the developed campgrounds, free at backcountry campsites.

If You Have Only 1 Day

In some ways, Great Basin is actually two parks: the caverns and the mountains. Because of the frequency of afternoon thunderstorms in the summer, it is usually best to do outdoor activities early in the day. Those with only 1 day at the park should spend the morning on the **Wheeler Peak Scenic Drive,** possibly allowing time to hike at least part of one of the trails. Then, after a picnic lunch or sandwich from the cafe, take a **cave tour** (it's best to purchase tickets in advance; see "Fees," above), see the exhibits and programs in the **visitor center,** and walk along the **Mountain View Nature Trail.**

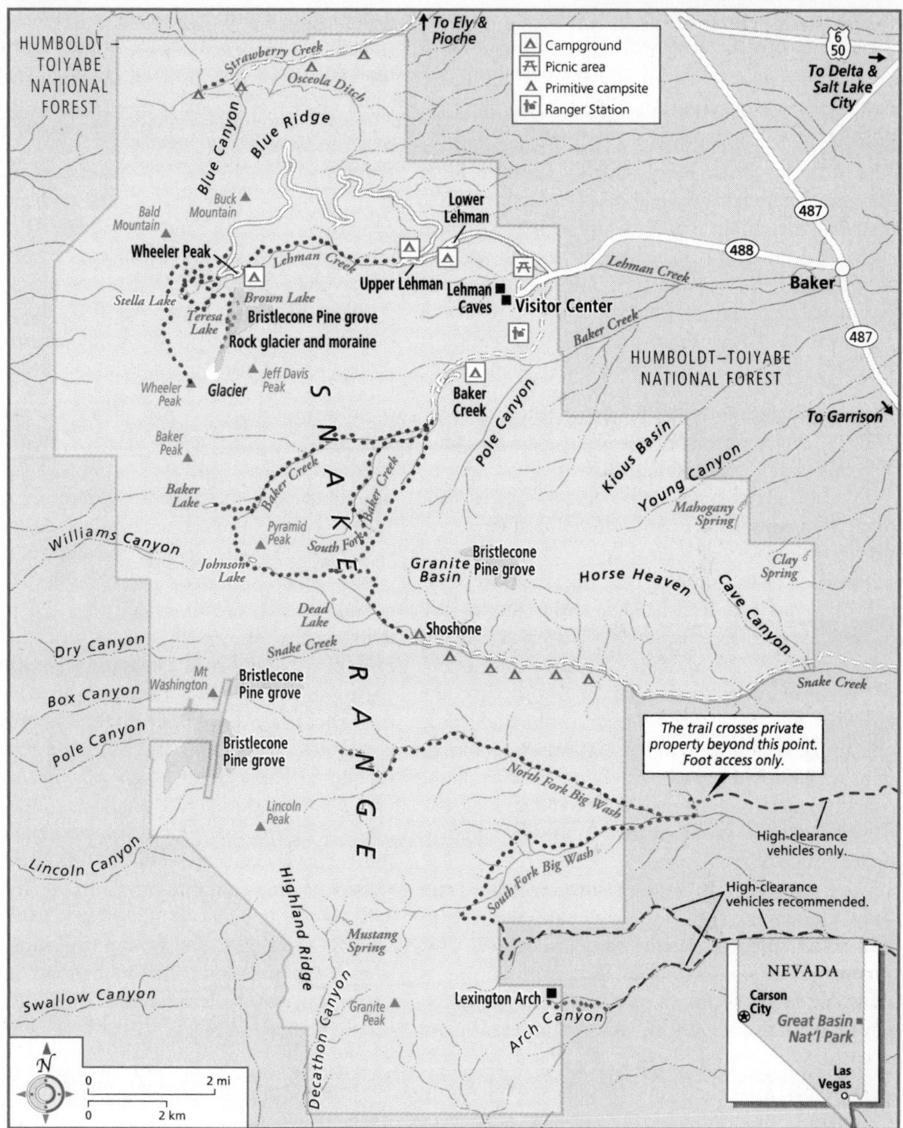

SPECIAL REGULATIONS & WARNINGS

Although backcountry permits are not required, those planning to go into the backcountry are encouraged to **register** at the visitor center, where they will also receive information on the latest backcountry conditions and regulations. Hikers going to the top of 13,063-foot Wheeler Peak may develop symptoms of **altitude sickness** (headache, nausea), in which case they should turn back immediately. Vehicles are also sometimes affected by the elevation and steep roads. The 12-mile Wheeler Peak Scenic Drive, which leads to several trail heads, is steep and winding, and trailers and motor homes over 24 feet long are prohibited after the first 3 miles (to Upper Lehman Creek Campground).

At this writing, cellphone service in the park was not reliable. For regulations and advice concerning Lehman Caves, see "Organized Tours & Ranger Programs," below.

SEASONS & CLIMATE

Although the park is open year-round, deep snow and bitter cold limit aboveground activities during the winter. The cave, which has a year-round temperature of 50°F (10°C) and humidity of 90%, can be visited at any time. Outdoors, conditions are tied to elevation, which ranges from 6,825 feet at the visitor center to 13,063 feet at Wheeler Peak. Hiking trails at lower elevations are usually free of snow from late spring through early fall, but above 10,000 feet, snow is possible at any time. Summer thunderstorms are common during the afternoon but can occur at any time.

2 Exploring the Park by Car

The **Wheeler Peak Scenic Drive** runs 12 miles one-way. The road is paved but steep (about an 8% grade) and winding. It ascends over 3,000 feet from the visitor center, at 6,825 feet elevation, to the base of Wheeler Peak, at almost 10,000 feet. Along the way, there are pullouts where you can stop to take in views of the Great Basin and Wheeler Peak. At the first pullout, a short walk brings you to the remnants of an 18-mile aqueduct built in 1890 to carry water from Lehman Creek to a gold-mining operation. The road ends at Wheeler Peak Campground, where several hiking trails begin. Motor homes and trailers over 24 feet long may go the first 3 miles to Upper Lehman Creek Campground, but not beyond. The road is usually closed by snow (except for the first 3 miles) from fall through spring.

3 Organized Tours & Ranger Programs

The only way to see **Lehman Caves** is on a guided tour led by a park ranger, who points out the intricately formed stalactites, stalagmites, draperies, and shields that have been created by the oozing and dripping of water. Although Lehman lacks the vastness of the caves at Carlsbad Caverns National Park in New Mexico (see chapter 10, "Carlsbad Caverns National Park"), it makes up for that in the number of beautiful formations in this small space, and the fact that Lehman can be seen easily and fairly quickly. In addition, Lehman Caves possess formations called **shields,** rarely seen in other caves. These consist of two roughly circular halves that look like flattened clamshells. Scientists have yet to agree on how the shields are formed.

Cave tours begin near the visitor center and run daily year-round (call for schedules; see "Fees," above for prices), except on New Year's Day, Thanksgiving, and Christmas. A part of the tour is accessible to those in wheelchairs, with assistance. Adults must accompany all children under 16, and children under 5 are not permitted on the 90-minute cave tour. The temperature in Lehman Caves is 50°F (10°C) year-round, so a jacket or sweater is advised. Because the path is often wet, good traction shoes with rubber soles are strongly recommended. Some passageways are narrow, so items such as fanny packs, purses, and backpacks are prohibited. Hand-held cameras are permitted.

Although the park's main ranger-led activity is the Lehman Caves tour, during the summer rangers also guide nature walks and hikes and present other programs. These change each year, but recent programs have included a 1.4-mile hike (one-way) to the bristlecone pine grove. Rangers usually present short talks several times daily at the visitor center, as well as evening campfire programs at Wheeler Peak and Upper Lehman campgrounds, with subjects such as the night sky, gold prospecting, and the area's bat population. One-hour programs for children, who must be accompanied by adults, have also been scheduled in recent years.

4 Park Attractions

Throughout the park are reminders of the region's mining days, and along several trails you will see the ruins of miners' cabins, mining equipment, and mine shafts and tunnels (which are dangerous and should not be entered). Just outside the visitor center is the historic **Rhodes Cabin,** which dates from between 1920 and 1932, when Clarence Rhodes and his wife, Beatrice, were custodians of the property for the U.S. Forest Service. The cabin, constructed of Englemann spruce and white fir, was one of nine tourist cabins built in the 1920s, along with a log lodge, a dining room, a dance hall, and a swimming tank. This particular cabin was rented to tourists until 1933, and from then until 1936, it was the home of the national monument custodian and his family. It was then used for storage before the Park Service restored it.

5 Day Hikes

There are a wide variety of trails, ranging from easy walks to challenging, high-altitude hikes. Higher-elevation areas may be closed by snow from late October until mid-June, and afternoon thunderstorms are common in July and August. Avoid exposed ridges during lightning storms. Hikers should be aware that they may be sharing trails with rattlesnakes, which have the right of way.

Because of loose rock and steep grades on some trails, sturdy hiking boots with good ankle support are recommended. Hikers also need to carry plenty of water—usually 1 gallon per person per day. Park rangers emphasize that although the rocky alpine sections of the park at its highest elevations may appear rugged, they are quite fragile. Plants grow slowly, and even under the best of conditions, their survival rate is low. Therefore, hikers should be diligent about staying on trails and having the least possible impact on the land.

SHORTER TRAILS

Alpine Lakes Loop With an elevation gain of only about 600 feet, this is a relatively easy and accessible trail, popular with families. However, keep in mind that those not accustomed to the 10,000-foot elevation may find any activity tiring. The loop can be hiked in either direction, passing through forests of spruce and pine trees, as well as meadows dotted with wildflowers. Teresa and Stella lakes are shallow and clear, and the reflections of snowcapped peaks often appear in their smooth surfaces. 2.7 miles RT. Easy to moderate. Access: Just north of Wheeler Peak Campground.

Bristlecone and Glacier Trail Those who want a relatively easy hike through a unique forest will enjoy this trail. It goes through a grove of bristlecone pines and then on to a view of an ice field and a rock glacier—a rock-covered permanent mass of ice moving very slowly downhill—which rangers say is the only glacier in Nevada. Distance to the bristlecone pine grove is 1.4 miles one-way, and the ice field is another .9 mile. During summer, rangers sometimes lead hikes to the bristlecone grove. Elevation is about 10,000 feet. 4.6 miles RT. Easy to moderate. Access: Near Wheeler Peak parking area.

Lexington Arch This six-story arch is a bit out of the way, but the splendidly framed views through its 75-by-120-foot opening prove an ample reward. After driving into Utah and then following a dirt road, you will find yourself hiking a sunny path that takes you past wildflowers, mountain mahogany, fir, and pinyon. The easy-to-follow trail ends at the arch, which is unique because it has been carved from limestone, not sandstone, as is usually the case in the American West. Some geologists believe it is not really an arch, but a natural bridge (arches are formed by wind, rain, and ice, while bridges are created by the eroding force of streams and rivers). Leashed dogs are permitted on the trail. 3.4 miles round trip. Moderate. Access: About 18 miles south of the visitor center off a dirt road; ask park rangers for specific directions and current road conditions.

Mountain View Nature Trail This is a self-guided loop through a pleasant forest, with a brochure available at the visitor center that provides information on plants, animals, and geology. The short trail is popular among those with 20 to 30 minutes to wait before their guided cave tour. .3 mile RT. Easy. Access: Outside the visitor center.

LONGER TRAILS

Baker Lake Trail Following Baker Creek, this trail leads to Baker Lake, climbing from about 2,600 feet in elevation to over 10,500 feet. It passes through meadows and forests, past pinyon, juniper, aspen, and pine, changing with the elevation. It's a good choice for wildlife viewing; you are likely to see mule deer, rock squirrels, and a variety of birds. Anglers often stop to catch a trout in the creek (see "Fishing," below), and the trail provides excellent views of the surrounding peaks. Along the way, you pass the remains of a miner's log cabin before reaching Baker Lake. 12 miles round-trip. Moderate to strenuous. Access: End of Baker Creek Rd.

Johnson Lake Trail This rugged trail follows an old mining road, with an elevation gain of about 2,400 feet, before arriving at Johnson Lake. The lake bears the name of Alfred Johnson, who mined and processed tungsten here in the early part of the 20th century. Rangers warn hikes to stay out of mine structures, which are dangerous. The Johnson Lake Trail can be combined with the Baker Creek Trail to produce a loop, starting with the Baker Creek Trail and descending along Snake Creek. Parts of this loop are difficult to follow, and topographical maps and good mountaineering skills are needed. 7.4 miles round-trip. Moderate to strenuous. Access: End of Snake Creek Rd.

Lehman Creek Trail Although there is a 2,050-foot elevation change along this trail, it's an easy downhill walk for those who start at Wheeler Peak Campground and have a vehicle waiting at Lehman Creek Campground. The trail mostly follows a bluff above Lehman Creek, crossing through several separate life zones and offering views of a wide variety of plant life, from sagebrush and cactus to forests of aspen, spruce, pinyon, and tall Douglas fir. Along the way, you will also see mountain mahogany and, if your timing's right, an abundance of wildflowers. 3.4 miles one-way. Easy. Access: Connects Upper Lehman Creek Campground with Wheeler Peak Campground.

Wheeler Peak Summit Trail Those looking for stupendous panoramic vistas should consider this strenuous trail, which begins as a relatively gentle walk through a forest of pine and becomes considerably steeper as it reaches the tree line. Eventually, you find yourself on the summit, at an elevation of 13,063 feet, the second-highest point in Nevada. During its 2,900-foot ascent, the trail passes through several plant communities, including forests of Englemann spruce and pine, before climbing above the tree line. This is generally an all-day

Especially for Kids

The park's **Junior Ranger Program** offers a book at the visitor center for kids under 12. After they complete several activities, attend a ranger program, and do a service project such as picking up trash at a campsite, they receive a certificate and a Junior Ranger badge.

hike, and rangers advise starting early so you're off the summit by the time afternoon thunderstorms appear. Hikers are also advised to carry plenty of drinking water, extra clothing, and rain gear. 8.2 miles RT (from campground). Strenuous. Access: Summit Trailhead, about .5 mile from Wheeler Peak Campground, or from the campground on Alpine Lakes Loop Trail, which intersects with Summit Trail.

6 Exploring the Backcountry

The park has numerous opportunities for backcountry hiking, but few maintained trails. The most commonly used routes follow river valleys or ridgelines. Topographical maps, available at the visitor center, are essential; although backcountry permits are not required, rangers strongly recommend that those planning to go into the backcountry register and discuss their plans with park staff before setting out.

Backcountry camping is permitted in most areas, but not within a quarter-mile of most trails, in bristlecone pine forests, in Wheeler Peak and Lexington day-use areas, or within 100 feet of a water source. Backcountry campers must camp in groups of 15 or less and are encouraged to use backpacking stoves; campfires are permitted below 10,000 feet elevation only, and you are not allowed to burn any wood from the bristlecone pine tree. Trash, including toilet paper, should be packed out, and human waste should be buried at least a half-foot deep and no less than 100 feet from water sources.

7 Other Sports & Activities

BIKING Although biking is permitted only on designated motor vehicle roads, the park has miles of dirt roads, many of which handle little traffic. Bikers should check with rangers about which roads are open and their current conditions.

FISHING The park's small, clear mountain streams provide good but somewhat challenging fishing for rainbow, brook, and brown trout. Anglers over 11 will need a Nevada fishing license, available at **T&D's Country Store, Restaurant & Lounge** in Baker (see "Where to Dine," below).

HORSEBACK RIDING Some of the backcountry trails are open to horseback riding; check with park rangers.

WILDLIFE VIEWING Almost every visitor will see wildlife, whether some of the mule deer that frequent the campgrounds, meadows, and creek sides; or birds such as pinyon jays, western tanagers, and Clark's nutcrackers. Park visitors should also watch for golden eagles, bighorn sheep, bobcats, and small mammals, including rock squirrels, wood rats, and marmots.

WINTER SPORTS Although there are no designated cross-country ski trails, once snow falls—sometimes as early as October—the park becomes a winter playground, especially at higher elevations. You can use cross-country skis or snowshoes on many of the trails and several roads, although it's best to talk with rangers about your plans before setting out so you can avoid trails that might be too steep for your ability. In lean snow years, you may have to hike a bit from parking areas to snow that's right for skiing, but there's almost always plenty of snow at the higher elevations.

One favorite cross-country ski trip is up **Baker Creek Road,** which leads to Baker Creek Campground, and then on up the Baker Creek Trail for a while before heading back. Those particularly skilled and in good physical condition might ski the 4-mile trail from **Upper Lehman Creek Campground** up

Campground	Elev.	Total Sites	RV Hookups	Dump Station	Toilets
Baker Creek	7,530	34	No	No	Yes
Border Inn RV Park	5,300	22	Yes	Yes	Yes
Lower Lehman Creek	7,300	11	No	No	Yes
Upper Lehman Creek	7,752	22	No	No	Yes
Wheeler Peak	9,886	37	No	No	Yes

to **Wheeler Peak Campground.** The trail climbs about 2,500 feet. Although Wheeler Peak Campground is technically closed from about mid-October through mid-June, skiers are welcome to spend the night.

Trails and roads in the park that are suitable for cross-country skiing and snowmobiling are not groomed, although the most popular ones are flagged with tape. For equipment rentals, check with Silver Jack Inn (see "Where to Stay," below).

8 Camping

INSIDE THE PARK

The park has four developed campgrounds—Lower Lehman Creek, Upper Lehman Creek, Baker Creek, and Wheeler Peak—with just over 100 sites. They have lots of trees, pit toilets, and picnic tables. Those with large RVs will want to arrive as early in the day as possible, because only a limited number of sites can easily accommodate rigs over 25 feet.

One campground is open year-round; the others are open from spring through fall, weather permitting. There are also some primitive campsites along **Strawberry Creek,** in the far northern reaches of the park, and along **Snake Creek,** in the southern half of the park. These sites have tables and fire grates but no drinking water. There are a few pit toilets along Snake Creek, but no toilets along Strawberry Creek.

Backcountry camping is also permitted; see the section "Exploring the Backcountry," above. The park has an RV dump station near the visitor center ($5), usually open from late May through October, but no hookups or showers. All campsites are assigned on a first-come, first-served basis.

NEAR THE PARK

The **Border Inn RV Park,** on U.S. 50/6 at the Nevada–Utah border (P.O. Box 30), Baker, NV 89311 (✆ **775/234-7300;** www.greatbasinpark.com/borderinn.htm), is about 13 miles northeast of the national park. It has 22 gravel pull-through RV sites with full hookups, plus shower and coin-op laundry facilities. Showers are free for registered campers, $5 for others. There are also a motel, restaurant, casino and bar, and 24-hour store (see below). Also see the listing for the **Silver Jack Inn,** below.

9 Where to Stay

There are no lodging facilities in the park, but the tiny community of Baker, 5 miles east of the park entrance, has several places to stay. You can get additional information on the Baker businesses, as well as other facilities, from the **Great Basin Business & Tourism Council**'s website (www.greatbasinpark.com). Otherwise, park visitors will find services in Ely, Nevada, 70 miles west, and Delta, Utah, about 100 miles east. Both Ely and Delta also have a variety of restaurants, plus fuel, groceries, and camping supplies.

NEAR THE PARK

The Border Inn This comfortable motel has basic rooms and 12 kitchenette units in Utah, and a restaurant and casino with a bar a few feet away in Nevada. The wood-paneled rooms are simply but attractively furnished, and satellite TV offers a good choice of channels. The inn offers a coin-operated laundry as well as VCR and videotape rentals. Gasoline and diesel fuel are available, and there is a 24-hour convenience store. Also see "Where to Dine," below.

U.S. 50/6, at the Nevada–Utah border, 13 miles northeast of the national park (P.O. Box 30), Baker, NV 89311. ✆ **775/234-7300.** www.greatbasinpark.com/borderinn.htm. 29 units. A/C, TV, TEL. $42–$49 double. AE, DISC, MC, V. Pets accepted ($5 one-time fee).

Silver Jack Inn This well-maintained motel is the closest lodging to the national park. Basic motel rooms have either one or two double beds, and one unit has two double beds plus a twin bed in a separate room. Some units have a tub/shower, while others have showers only. There is an attractive patio with a fountain where guests sit, chat, and watch the hummingbirds. The separate efficiency units are several blocks away; each has a queen-size bed, refrigerator, microwave, and coffeemaker. Pets are

Drinking Water	Showers	Fire Pits/ Grills	Laundry	Reserve	Fees	Open
Yes	No	Yes	No	No	$12	May–Oct
Yes	Yes	No	Yes	No	$20	Year-round
Yes	No	Yes	No	No	$12	Year-round
Yes	No	Yes	No	No	$12	May–Oct
Yes	No	Yes	No	No	$12	June–Sept

Picnic & Camping Supplies

In addition to the snacks available at the cafe and gift shop in the park, you can find takeout food, ice, packaged liquor, and other supplies at **T&D's Country Store, Restaurant & Lounge,** in Baker (see "Where to Dine," above). The **Border Inn,** along U.S. 50/6 at the Nevada–Utah border (see "Where to Stay," above), has a 24-hour convenience store plus gasoline and diesel fuel.

permitted at the inn but not in the efficiencies. All units are nonsmoking. An onsite **restaurant** and bakery, open from May through November, serves breakfast and dinner daily and prepares lunches to go. There are also five RV spaces, offering water and electric hookups plus showers, at $22 per night.

Downtown Baker, 5 miles east of the national park (P.O. Box 69), Baker, NV 89311. ✆ **775/234-7323.** www.silverjackinn.com. 7 motel units, 3 efficiency units. A/C, TV. $49–$69 double. DISC, MC, V. Closed Dec–Mar.

10 Where to Dine

INSIDE THE PARK

The only food services in the park are the visitor center's **cafe** and gift shop (✆ **775/234-7221**), open daily from April through October (8am–5pm in summer, slightly shorter hours at other times). Your choices here include light breakfasts, soup and sandwich lunches, and snack items, including excellent homemade ice-cream sandwiches.

NEAR THE PARK

In addition to the restaurants discussed below, you'll find good food at the **Lextrolux Café,** open May through October at Silver Jack Inn (see "Where to Stay," above).

The Border Inn AMERICAN Especially good burgers and chicken-fried steak are on the menu at this roadside restaurant, which also specializes in homemade soups and baked items, and has a daily special. The dining room is large and open, and there is a casino with a bar in a separate room. There is also a convenience store (open daily 24 hr.), an ATM, and a gas station with diesel fuel.

U.S. 50/6 at the Nevada–Utah border, 13 miles northeast of the national park. ✆ **775/234-7300.** www.greatbasinpark.com/borderinn.htm. Lunch $6–$9, dinner $8–$20, with most items about $10. AE, DISC, MC, V. Daily 6am–10pm; bar open later. Closed Christmas.

T&D's Country Store, Restaurant & Lounge AMERICAN/MEXICAN The restaurant is in a bright and cheery sunroom attached to a small grocery store. It's known for its pizzas, deli sandwiches, homemade salsa and chips, and big burritos and other Mexican specialties. The restaurant also serves burgers, steak sandwiches, pita sandwiches, a good selection of vegetarian items, and several more elaborate meals, including barbecued ribs and Asian chicken salad. You can also get your food to go. There is a full bar, with several beers on tap, and a surprisingly good stock of wines available by the glass. There is patio dining plus a separate lounge, and the complex has a full liquor store and sells camping and fishing gear.

1 Main St. (corner of Elko and Main, downtown Baker). ✆ **775/234-7264.** www.greatbasinpark.com/td.htm. Sandwiches $4–$8; meals $6–$11; large pizzas $12–$23. DISC, MC, V. Summer restaurant daily 11am–8pm; store daily 8am–7pm. Call for winter hours.

19

Great Sand Dunes National Park & Preserve, CO

by Don & Barbara Laine

Here in southern Colorado, far from any sea or even a major desert, is a startling sight—a huge expanse of sand, piled nearly 750 feet high. The towering dunes, the tallest on the continent, seem incongruous, out of place in a land best known for the Rocky Mountains. But here they are, some 30 square miles of light brown sand dunes, restlessly grasping at the western edge of the Sangre de Cristo Mountains. (*Sangre de Cristo* is Spanish for "Blood of Christ"; the name comes from the deep red reflected onto the snow-capped mountains by the setting sun.)

The dunes were created over thousands of years by southwesterly winds blowing across the San Luis Valley. They were formed when streams of water from melting glaciers carried rocks, gravel, and silt down from the mountains. Accumulating on the valley floor, the sand was picked up by the wind and carried toward the mountains.

Even today the winds are changing the face of the dunes. So-called "reversing winds" from the mountains pile the dunes back upon themselves, building them higher and higher. Though it's physically impossible for sand to be piled steeper than 34 degrees, the dunes often appear more sheer because of deceptive shadows and colors that change with the light: gold, pink, tan, sometimes even bluish.

Great Sand Dunes became a national monument in 1932, but in recent years concerns over the possible effects on the dunes and their ecosystem from water usage in the surrounding area have increased. In 2000, Congress passed a law approving park status pending the acquisition of "sufficient land having a sufficient diversity of resources." The necessary property was acquired with the help of the nonprofit Nature Conservancy, and on September 13, 2004, the U.S. Secretary of the Interior arrived at Great Sand Dunes to publicly announce the designation of Great Sand Dunes National Park.

AVOIDING THE CROWDS

Overcrowding has not been a major problem at Great Sand Dunes. In recent years, the park has received fewer than 250,000 visitors annually, compared to almost three million at Rocky Mountain National Park, just a half-day's drive north. But national park status and the additional acreage and attractions have been producing an increase in visitation. Therefore, we suggest that you try to visit at times other than school vacations and holiday weekends. Early fall can be especially pleasant here. Memorial Day weekend is particularly busy, with limited parking and traffic congestion. If you do happen to visit on a busy day, a hike along Sand Ramp Trail (see "Day Hikes," below) usually gets you away from the crowds.

1 Essentials

GETTING THERE & GATEWAYS

From Alamosa, two main routes lead to Great Sand Dunes. Go east 14 miles on U.S. 160, then north on Colo. 150; or drive north 14 miles on Colo. 17 to Mosca, then east on Six Mile Lane to the junction of Colo. 150.

If You Have Only 1 Day

Great Sand Dunes is fairly easy to see in a day or less. First stop at the **visitor center** for a look at the exhibits (and an explanation of how these dunes were and are being formed), then drive to a parking area and walk into the **dunes.** If time permits, also walk one of the shorter **trails,** such as the Montville Nature Trail or Visitor Center Trail.

Exploring the Park by Car

Although you will use your vehicle to get to the visitor center, the dunes, and a few spots where you'll get good views, the Great Sand Dunes environment is best explored on foot or in a special wheelchair (see "Day Hikes," below).

THE NEAREST AIRPORTS The **San Luis Valley Regional Airport,** 2490 State St. (✆ **719/589-4848**), 3 miles off U.S. 285 South, has service to and from Denver on **Great Lakes Airlines.** Car rentals are available at the airport from **Budget** and **Hertz,** and a local company, **L&M Automobile Rental** (✆ **719/589-4651**). See chapter 38 for website listings of major airlines and car-rental companies.

INFORMATION

Contact **Great Sand Dunes National Park & Preserve,** 11500 Colo. 150, Mosca, CO 81146-9798 (✆ **719/378-6300;** www.nps.gov/grsa).

For information on other area attractions, lodging, and dining, contact the **Alamosa Convention & Visitors Bureau,** 601 State Ave., Alamosa, CO 81101, at the corner of State Avenue and U.S. 160 (✆ **800/258-7597** or 719/589-4840; www.alamosa.org). This building, a restored historic train depot, also houses a **Colorado Welcome Center,** open daily 8am to 6pm except New Year's Day, Easter, Thanksgiving, and Christmas. Also in the depot is the ticket booth for the **Rio Grande Scenic Railroad** (see "Nearby Attractions," at the end of this chapter).

VISITOR CENTER

The visitor center (✆ **719/378-6399**) has exhibits on dune formation and life in the dunes, a bookstore, and a short video that shows throughout the day. It's open daily year-round, except for federal holidays. From Memorial Day weekend through Labor Day weekend, hours are 9am to 6pm, and hours are shorter the rest of the year.

FEES & PERMITS

Admission to the park for up to 7 days costs $3 per person, free for children under 16. Camping costs $14 per night.

If you are planning to explore the backcountry, you'll need a free backcountry permit, which is available at the visitor center.

SPECIAL REGULATIONS & WARNINGS

Although summer air temperatures are pleasant, sand temperatures can soar to 140°F (60°C), so park officials strongly advise that shoes be worn when hiking in the dunes. Also, summer thunderstorms are fairly common. Hikers are advised to leave the dunes quickly when lightning threatens, to avoid the chance of being struck.

Elevations range from 7,515 feet to 13,604 feet, so those from low elevations are warned that they should take it easy until they have adapted and drink plenty of water to avoid altitude sickness, which causes shortness of breath, headaches, and nausea.

Pets are permitted throughout the park and preserve but must be leashed, and officials ask that owners clean up after their pets. They also warn that the sand in the dunes can be hot and will burn the pads on dogs' feet, so they suggest dune hiking with pets early or late in the day, when the sand is cooler.

SEASONS & CLIMATE

Pleasant summers and cool to cold winters are the rule here. Daytime summer temperatures average 70° to 80°F (21°–27°C), with nighttime lows often dropping into the 40s and low 50s (single digits and 10s Celsius). Thunderstorms are common in July and August. High winds can be expected at any time and are often especially ferocious from April through early June, when northeast winds have been clocked at over 90 mph. From fall through spring, expect moderate daytime temperatures; winter days can see daytime temperatures in the 40s (single digits Celsius), but winter nights are usually below freezing and often below zero. Snowfall averages a bit over 3 feet annually, with March being the snowiest month.

2 Organized Tours & Ranger Programs

In the summer, rangers offer guided nature walks, short talks at the visitor center patio, and evening amphitheater programs. Great Sand Dunes also offers a Junior Ranger program, in which children complete various activities to earn badges.

3 Day Hikes

You can hike anywhere you want in the sand dunes, although there are no designated trails. If you make it all the way to the top, you'll be rewarded with spectacular views of the dunes and the nearby mountains. It usually takes about 1½ hours to get to the crest of a 750-foot dune and back to the base.

Great Sand Dunes National Park & Preserve

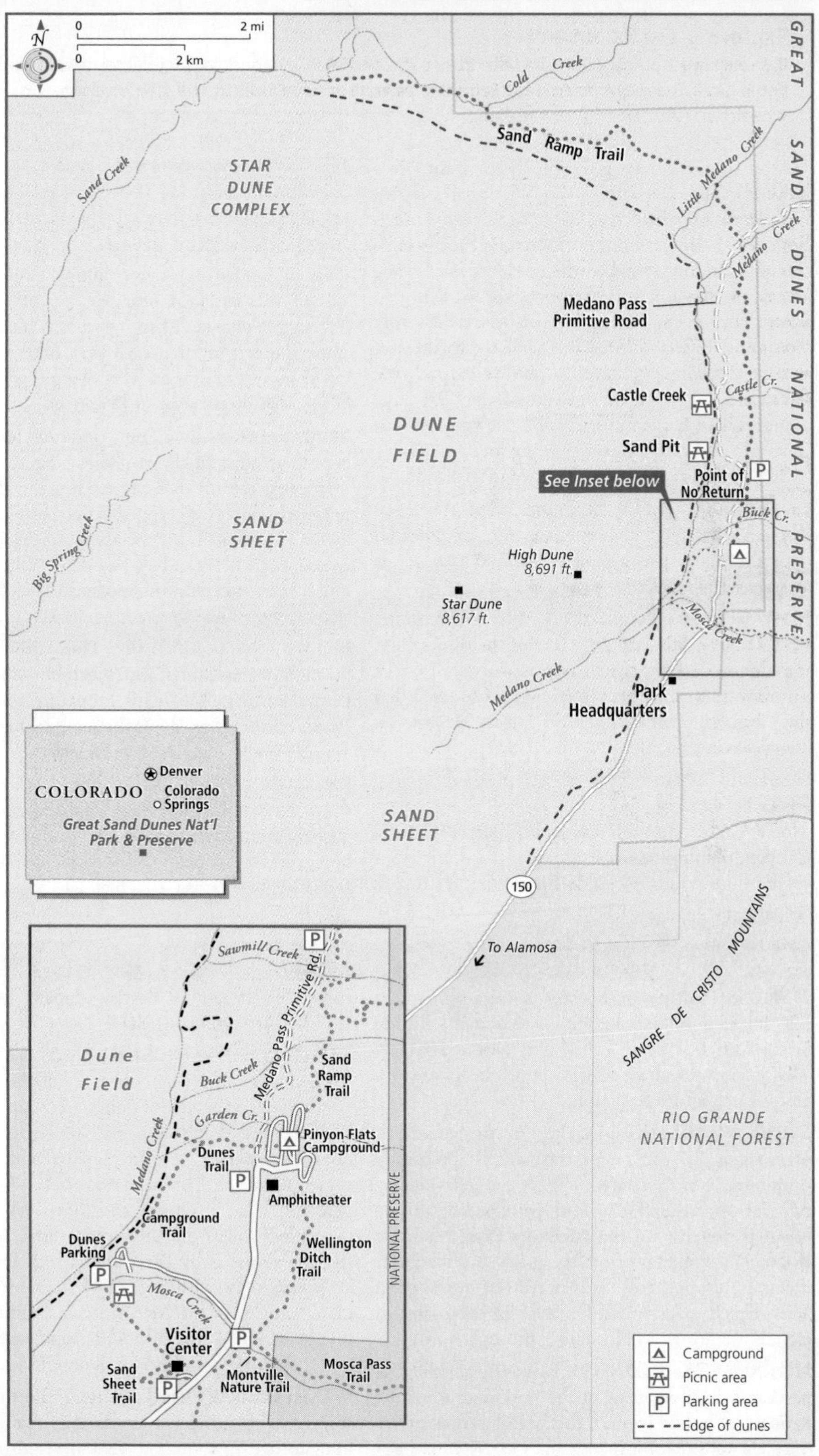

Exploring the Backcountry

Backpacking is permitted throughout the park, and there are backcountry campsites along the Sand Ramp Trail. The required free **backcountry permits** are available at the visitor center.

Hiking in the dunes is especially pleasant on a moonlit night.

In the past, wheelchair users were pretty much limited to seeing the dunes from their motor vehicles and parking areas, because the loose sand made access to the dunes nearly impossible. But two wheelchairs specially designed for over-sand travel, with large, inflatable tires, are available for loan at the visitor center. A helper is needed to push the chair, and the chairs are not suitable for very large adults. There is also an accessible viewing deck at the north end of the dunes parking lot.

The park also has miles of conventional trails.

Campground Trail This convenient trail runs through a grassy area, connecting the campground with the dunes parking area. 1 mile RT. Easy. Access: Campground (near site 32) or dunes parking area.

Medano Creek to Castle Creek This route, which leads north along the face of the dunes from the dunes parking area, follows Medano Creek upstream to a spot where the dunes are so steep that they avalanche into the creek. 5 miles RT. Moderate. Access: Dunes parking area.

Montville Nature Trail This pleasant loop—especially nice on hot days—runs along shady Mosca Creek, through the lower part of Mosca Canyon, offering dramatic views of the dunes from several high points. A guide for the nature trail is available at the visitor center. .5 mile RT. Easy. Access: Parking area on east side of main park road, just north of the visitor center.

Mosca Pass Trail This challenging hike, which climbs 1,463 feet into the mountains, passes through forests of pinyon, juniper, aspen, spruce, and fir to grasslands near the top of the pass. It offers good chances of seeing quite a bit of wildlife. ***Note:*** Rangers say that each year, hikers report seeing bears and mountain lions along this trail. 7 miles RT. Strenuous. Access: Montville Parking Lot.

Sand Ramp Trail Those looking for a longer hike than most of those at Great Sand Dunes can escape any crowds that happen to be in the park by following this trail along the northern edge of the dunes, crossing Little Medano Creek and Cold Creek. For a pleasant half-day jaunt, hike the first 3 miles, then turn around and head back. 22 miles RT. Moderate. Access: Campground, near site 62.

Sand Sheet Loop Trail This fairly level loop through a grassland features exhibits on the area's natural history. Watch for miniature short-horned lizards in the grass along the trail during the summer. .25 mile RT. Easy. Access: Visitor center.

Wellington Ditch Trail This level trail offers good views of the dune field. Part of the trail follows an irrigation ditch that was hand-dug by a 1920s homesteader named Wellington. 2 miles RT. Easy. Access: Montville Parking Lot or Loop 3 in Campground.

4 Other Sports & Activities

FISHING Although this area is not a prime fishing destination, anglers with a Colorado fishing license can fish Sand Creek and Medano Creek. Medano is stocked with Rio Grande cutthroat trout and is catch-and-release only.

FOUR-WHEELING Driving in the dunes or off-road in any section of the park is specifically prohibited, but those with 4WDs can get wonderful views of the dunes and gain access to the national preserve on the **Medano Pass Primitive Road,** which takes off from the main park road near the amphitheater and heads north out of the park. This rugged road, which has a lot of deep sand, is closed by snow from November through April.

HORSEBACK RIDING Horseback riding is permitted in most areas of the park and all of the national preserve; contact the visitor center or see the park website for information. Guided horseback trips are offered at nearby Zapata Ranch (see "Nearby Attractions," below).

SANDBOARDING, SKIING & SLEDDING Who needs snow when there is all this sand? All unvegetated areas of the dunes are open to sliding, sledding, and skiing. Rangers advise that cardboard doesn't work at all, so come prepared with a flat-bottomed plastic sled, snowboard, or skis. Also be prepared to hike. Even the medium-sized slopes are over a half-mile from the parking area. Among the steepest slopes is by the Castle Creek Picnic Area, accessible only with a high-clearance four-wheel-drive vehicle via the Medano Pass Primitive Road, but be careful—this 300-foot slope ends abruptly and may dump you into Medano Creek.

WILDLIFE VIEWING Among the animals that survive in this unusual environment are the **Ord's kangaroo rat,** a creature that never drinks water, plus several insects found nowhere else on Earth, including the **Great Sand Dunes tiger beetle.** Among more common wildlife you're apt to see are Rocky Mountain elk, mule deer, coyotes, black-tailed and white-tailed jackrabbits, desert cottontail rabbits, golden-mantled ground squirrels, and Colorado chipmunks. Just outside the park, look for bison. More than 150 species of **birds** have been sighted in the park, including both golden and bald eagles, ravens, white-throated swifts, broad-tailed hummingbirds, Lewis's woodpeckers, Say's phoebes, violet-green swallows, yellow-rumped warblers, black-headed grosbeaks, and chipping sparrows. Prime bird-watching areas include the Montville and Wellington Ditch trails. You're also likely to see all kinds of wildlife along Medano Creek, which runs along the base of the dunes and usually flows in spring and early summer.

Also see the sections on **Zapata Ranch** and the **Alamosa/Monte Vista/Baca National Wildlife Refuge Complex** under "Nearby Attractions," below.

5 Camping

The shady **Pinyon Flats Campground,** with an abundance of pinyon and juniper trees, offers great views of the dunes and nearby mountains. It has 88 sites and is open year-round. There are picnic tables, fire grates, flush toilets, and drinking water, but no showers or RV hookups. Campsites are assigned on a first-come, first-served basis, and cost $14 per night. There are also **commercial campgrounds** with showers and RV hookups in Alamosa; get details from the Alamosa Convention & Visitors Bureau (see "Information," above).

6 Where to Stay & Dine

There are no lodging or dining facilities in the park, so, except for Great Sand Dunes Lodge (discussed below), your base for exploring Great Sand Dunes will likely be Alamosa, which has motels and a variety of restaurants. Reliable chains in Alamosa include the **Best Western Alamosa Inn,** 2005 Main St. (✆ **719/589-2567**), with double rates of $76 to $97; **Comfort Inn,** 6301 U.S. 160 (✆ **719/587-9000**), charging $75 to $110 double; **Days Inn,** 224 O'Keefe Pkwy., at the junction of U.S. highways 160 and 285 (✆ **719/589-9037**), with rates for two of $51 to $86; and **Super 8,** 2505 W. Main St. (✆ **719/589-6447**), charging $63 to $100 double. See chapter 38 for website listings of the national hotel/motel chains.

You'll find a number of restaurants in downtown Alamosa. We like the Mexican food at **Oscar's Restaurant,** 520 Main St. (✆ **719/589-9230**), open Tuesday through Sunday for lunch and dinner; and **Mrs. Rivera's Kitchen,** 1019 Sixth St. (✆ **719/589-0277**), open Monday through Saturday for lunch and dinner. Most items at both restaurants are under $10. For American food—especially beef—try **True Grits Steakhouse,** 100 Santa Fe Ave. (✆ **719/589-9954**), which is open for dinner nightly and for lunch Saturday and Sunday. The decor pays homage to John Wayne, and most prices are in the $7 to $16 range. Fans of real beer will want to make sure they get to the **San Luis Valley Brewing Company,** 631 Main St. (✆ **719/587-2337;** www.slvbrewco.com), which produces an excellent, well-hopped IPA. Its restaurant is open for lunch and dinner daily in summer and Monday through Saturday the rest of the year. The menu is a step above the usual brew pub offering, with items such as Mongolian barbecue ribs, smoked salmon pasta, and smoked bacon burgers, and most prices are in the $8 to $22 range.

Great Sand Dunes Lodge At the edge of the national park, this small motel offers clean, well-maintained basic lodging at reasonable rates, and it's the best location for those who want to explore the park early or late in the day, when the lighting is perfect. The average-sized standard rooms have two queen beds, the usual amenities, and private patios with views out over Great Sand Dunes. The more spacious deluxe rooms have one king-size bed plus a refrigerator, microwave, and outdoor private gas barbecue. There is Wi-Fi, an indoor heated pool, and a restaurant nearby (May–Sept only). All rooms are nonsmoking.

7900 Colo. 150 N, Mosca, CO 81146. ✆ **719/378-2900.** www.gsdlodge.com. 10 units. A/C, TV, TEL. $89–$105 double standard room; $110–$135 double deluxe room. AE, DISC, MC, V. Closed mid-Oct to mid-Mar.

Picnic & Camping Supplies

For groceries and other necessities, head to Alamosa and stop at **City Market,** 131 Market St. (✆ **719/589-2492;** www.citymarket.com). You'll find a variety of camping supplies, plus groceries and just about everything else you might want, at the **Walmart SuperCenter,** 3333 Clark Ave., Alamosa (✆ **719/589-9071;** www.walmart.com).

7 Nearby Attractions

Bordering great Sand Dunes National Park and Preserve is **Zapata Ranch,** 5305 Colo. 150, Mosca, CO 81146 (✆ **888/592-7282** or 719/378-2356; www.zranch.org), owned by The Nature Conservancy. It is a working cattle, bison, and guest ranch where visitors can take **ranch vacations,** *City Slicker* style, and enjoy other activities. All-inclusive rates for 7 nights (lodging, food, and all activities) costs about $1,700 per adult. The ranch also rents rooms by the night for $200 to $300 double, which includes all meals. All rooms have private bathrooms and Wi-Fi, and there is a hot tub. Day visitors are invited to take **Bison Tours** to see the ranch's herd of some 2,000 head of bison, as well as other wildlife such as elk, deer, pronghorn, porcupines, and large numbers of birds, the historic ranch headquarters. Bison tours are by reservation only and cost $50 for adults (13 and older), $25 for children 6 to 12, and free for kids under 6 with four paying customers.

The **Alamosa/Monte Vista/Baca National Wildlife Refuge Complex** (✆ **719/589-4021;** www.fws.gov/alamosa) together have preserved nearly 118,000 acres of vital land for a variety of marsh birds and waterfowl, including many migrating and wintering species. Sandhill cranes visit in early to mid-October and early March; at other times of the year, there may be egrets, herons, avocets, bitterns, and other avian species. A wide variety of ducks are year-round residents, and waterfowl numbers are at their peak March through May. There is also a herd of several hundred elk that often winter in the Monte Vista refuge.

The Baca National Wildlife Refuge is currently closed to the public, but the Alamosa and Monte Vista refuges have self-guided driving tours with a number of view points, and also several hiking trails. Bring binoculars, since they'll be useful. To get to the Alamosa refuge, which contains the visitor center (✆ **719/589-4021)** and refuge headquarters, go 4 miles east of Alamosa on U.S. 160 and then south 2 miles on El Rancho Lane. Monte Vista refuge is located 6 miles south of the community of Monte Vista on Colo. 15. Admission to the refuges is free, and they are open daily from sunrise to sunset. The visitor center is open sporadically (based on volunteer availability) from March through November, and closed the rest of the year.

Visitors staying in Alamosa might want to check out the **Rio Grande Scenic Railroad,** with its depot at 601 State Ave. (✆ **877/726-7245;** www.riograndescenicrailroad.com). Steam or diesel locomotives haul classic Pullman passenger railroad through the mountains and valleys of southern Colorado, with several trips available, over routes more than a hundred years old. Typical is the half-day round-trip excursion between Alamosa and Antonito, but you can also go one-way, perhaps catching a train back in a day or two, or go round-trip between Alamosa and the mountain community of La Veta. The passenger cars are climate controlled with comfortable seating, and the trains have snack bars and open-air observation cars. Allow at least a half-day. Round-trip fares are from $12 adult (13–59), $11 senior (60 and older), $10 child (12 and under), and infants under 2 that do not occupy a seat ride free. The season generally runs from spring through fall, and there may also be a special train at Christmastime.

20

Guadalupe Mountains National Park, TX

by Eric Peterson

Once it was a long reef just below the ocean's surface, then it inched skyward and ultimately became a forested area surrounded by wooded canyons and desert lowlands. Today Guadalupe Mountains National Park is a rugged wilderness of tall Douglas firs and sometimes lush vegetation rising out of a vast desert. Here you will find numerous hiking trails, panoramic vistas, the highest peak in the state, plant and animal life unique in the Southwest, and a canyon that many believe is the prettiest spot in all of Texas.

As you approach from the northeast, the mountains seem to rise from the landscape, but seen from the south they stand tall and dignified. El Capitan, the southern tip of the escarpment, watches over the landscape like a sentinel. In the south-central section of the 86,416-acre park, Guadalupe Peak, at 8,749 feet the highest mountain in Texas, provides hikers with views of the surrounding mountains and desert.

Park headquarters and the visitor center are at Pine Springs, along the park's southeast edge. There you'll also find a campground and several trail heads, including one with access to the Guadalupe Peak Trail, the park's premier mountain hike. Nearby, a short dirt road leads to historic Frijole Ranch, with a museum and more trail heads. A horse corral is nearby for those with their own mounts. The McKittrick Canyon area of the park, near its northeast corner, may be the most beautiful spot in Texas, especially in fall, when its oaks, maples, and other trees produce a spectacular show of color. A day-use area only, McKittrick Canyon has a delightful (though intermittent) stream, a variety of plant and animal life, several trail heads, and historic buildings. Along the park's northern boundary, almost in New Mexico, is secluded, forested Dog Canyon.

Particularly impressive is Guadalupe Mountains National Park's vast variety of flora and fauna. You'll find species here that don't seem to belong in west Texas, such as the maple, ash, and walnut trees that produce the fall colors in McKittrick Canyon, and even black bears, which are usually found only farther north. Scientists say these seemingly out-of-place plants and animals are leftovers from a time when this region was cooler and wetter. As the climate changed and the desert spread, some species were able to survive in these mountains, where conditions remained somewhat cooler and moister. At the base of the mountains, at lower elevations, you'll find desert plants such as sotol, agave, and prickly pear cactus; as you start to climb, especially in stream-nurtured canyons, expect to encounter ponderosa pine, ash, walnut, oak, and ferns. Wildlife abounds, including mule deer, elk, and all sorts of birds and snakes.

AVOIDING THE CROWDS

Guadalupe Mountains National Park is one of America's less visited national parks, with attendance of only about 225,000 each year. This is partly because it is primarily a wilderness park, where you'll have to tackle rugged hiking trails to get to the best vistas. But it's also out of the way and somewhat inconvenient—the closest lodging is 35 miles away from the park's main section. In fact, about the only time the park might be considered even slightly crowded is during spring break at Texas and New Mexico colleges, usually in March, when students bring their backpacks and hit the trails. Quite a few families visit during summer, although the park is not usually crowded even then. Visitation drops a lot once schools open in late August.

An exception is McKittrick Canyon, renowned throughout the Southwest for its beautiful fall colors, which are at their best in late October and early November. The one road into McKittrick Canyon will be busy then, but once you get out on the trails, you can distance yourself from others.

Checking Out Carlsbad

Many visitors to Guadalupe Mountains also spend time at nearby **Carlsbad Caverns National Park** in New Mexico. See chapter 10.

1 Essentials

GETTING THERE & GATEWAYS

Located on the border of New Mexico and Texas, the park is 55 miles southwest of Carlsbad, New Mexico, along **U.S. 62/180.** From Albuquerque, drive east on I-40 for 59 miles to Clines Corners, turn south and take U.S. 285 for 216 miles to the city of Carlsbad, then head southwest 55 miles on U.S. 62/180 to the park entrance at Pine Springs. From El Paso, drive northeast 110 miles on U.S. 62/180 to Pine Springs.

THE NEAREST AIRPORT Air travelers can fly to **Cavern City Air Terminal** (✆ **575/887-1500**), at the south edge of the city of Carlsbad, which has commercial service from Albuquerque on **New Mexico Airlines** (✆ **888/564-6119;** www.flynma.com), plus **Enterprise** car rentals.

The nearest major airport is **El Paso International** (✆ **915/780-4749;** www.elpasointernationalairport.com), in El Paso, just north of I-10, with service from most major airlines and car-rental companies. See chapter 38 for websites for the airlines and major car-rental firms.

INFORMATION

Contact **Guadalupe Mountains National Park,** 400 Pine Canyon Rd., Salt Flat, TX 79847-9400 (✆ **915/828-3251;** www.nps.gov/gumo). Books and maps can be ordered from the **Carlsbad Caverns Guadalupe Mountains Association,** 727 Carlsbad Caverns Hwy. (P.O. Box 1417), Carlsbad, NM 88220 (✆ **575/785-2486;** www.ccgma.org).

Because the park's backcountry trails often crisscross each other and can be confusing, rangers strongly recommend that those planning any serious hiking carry topographical maps. An excellent book for hikers is *Hiking Carlsbad Caverns and Guadalupe Mountains National Parks,* 2nd edition (Falcon Press, 2005), by Bill Schneider, which was published in partnership with the Carlsbad Caverns Guadalupe Mountains Association and is keyed to the Trails Illustrated topographical map of the park. Also very useful is a shorter and less expensive guide, *Trails of the Guadalupes* (Environmental Associates, 1992), by Don Kurtz and William D. Goran. These are often available at the visitor center bookstore or from the Carlsbad Caverns Guadalupe Mountains Association.

A small seasonal park newspaper contains pertinent up-to-the-minute information for visitors. It is available free at the visitor center.

VISITOR CENTERS

Park headquarters and the main visitor center are at Pine Springs just off U.S. 62/180. There are three other access points on this side of the park: Frijole Ranch, about 1½ miles east of Pine Springs and a mile north of the highway; McKittrick Canyon (day use only), about 7 miles east and 4 miles north of the highway; and Williams Ranch, about 8 miles south of Pine Springs and 8 miles north of the highway on a four-wheel-drive road.

The **Pine Springs Visitor Center,** open daily year-round (closed Dec 25), has natural history exhibits, a bookstore, and an introductory slide program. **McKittrick Canyon** has a visitor contact station with outdoor exhibits and a slide program on the history, geology, and natural history of the canyon.

On the north side of the park is **Dog Canyon Ranger Station,** at the end of N. Mex. 137, about

Tips from a Park Ranger

"This is a hiking park," says Michael Haynie, an interpretive ranger at the park. He says the park's two main attractions, which he recommends to all visitors, are the hike to the top of Guadalupe Peak and the colors in McKittrick Canyon, either the trees in fall or the wildflowers in spring.

Haynie says his two favorite hikes in the park are the Bowl Trail and the hike to the Notch in McKittrick Canyon, noting that you can visit any time of year. "Both offer nice variety and great views," he says. "The Bowl offers panoramic, 100-mile views of the desert."

There are five species of rattlesnakes in the park, but visitors probably won't see any, says Haynie. In the history of the park, there have been no reported rattlesnake bites. The biggest threat here is the sun, he says. "The biggest thing to stress is the water. Hikers unfamiliar with desert environments tend to underestimate how much water they need." Haynie says hikers should carry a gallon of water per day, and drink it.

He also warns that because many trails have a lot of loose rock, good hiking boots are essential. The other thing he wants park visitors to keep in mind is that there is no gasoline or other services close to the park, so you should have plenty of fuel and anything else you might need.

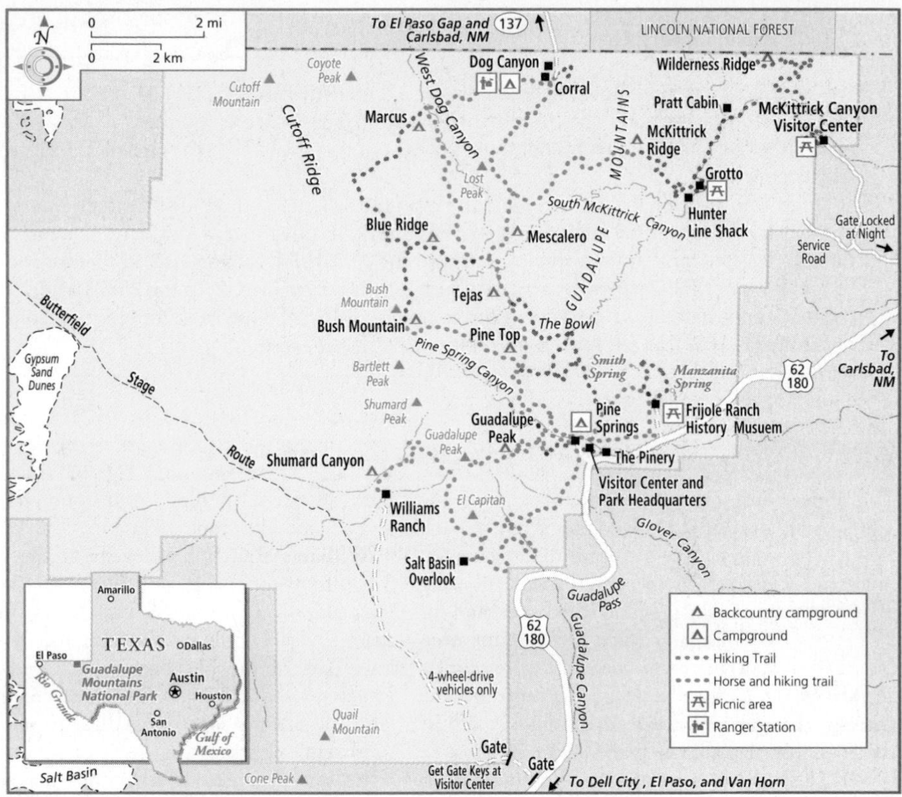

70 miles from Carlsbad and 110 miles from park headquarters. Information, restrooms, and drinking water are available.

FEES & PERMITS

The entrance fee (collected at trail heads) is $5 per person, free for children under 16, and good for 7 days. Camping at developed campgrounds costs $8 per night. Backcountry camping is free, but a **permit** is required. Corrals are available for those who bring their horses to ride in the park (call the park for reservations); permits are required for horseback riding. All permits are available at the Pine Springs Visitor Center and Dog Canyon Ranger Station, and must be requested in person, either the day before or the day of use.

SPECIAL REGULATIONS & WARNINGS

Visitors to McKittrick Canyon, a day-use area, must stay on the trail; entering the stream is not permitted. The McKittrick Canyon **entrance gate** opens at 8am daily and closes at 4:30pm during standard time and at 6pm when daylight saving time is in effect.

Neither wood nor charcoal fires are allowed anywhere in the park. Horses are prohibited in the backcountry overnight.

SEASONS & CLIMATE

In general, summers in the Guadalupe Mountains are hot, with highs in the 80s and 90s (mid-20s and lower 30s Celsius) and lows in the 60s (teens Celsius). Winters are mild, with highs in the 50s and 60s (lower teens Celsius) and lows in the upper 20s and 30s (just below zero Celsius). October tends to have the best weather, but sudden and extreme changes in the weather can occur at any time. In winter and spring, high winds can whip down the mountain slopes in gusts reading 100 mph, and on hot summer days, thunderstorms can blow up quickly. The sun is warm even in winter, and summer nights are generally cool, no matter how hot the afternoon. Clothing that can be layered is best, comfortable and sturdy walking and hiking shoes are a must, a hat and sunscreen are highly recommended, and plenty of drinking water is essential for hikers.

SEASONAL EVENTS

McKittrick Canyon's beautiful display of **fall colors** usually takes place between late October and early November. It varies, however, so call before going. On weekend evenings in the summer, rangers offer programs at the campground amphitheater.

If You Have Only 1 Day

This park is best explored over a period of 2 or 3 days, with at least 1 day devoted to the visitor center, historic attractions, and trails in the Pine Springs section, and another full day allotted to McKittrick Canyon. Those with additional time could then head over to the park's third section, Dog Canyon.

Those who have only 1 day can see quite a bit but will need to decide on either Pine Springs or McKittrick Canyon. If it's fall and the colors are right, drive to the **McKittrick Canyon Visitor Contact Station,** look at the exhibits, and hike the **McKittrick Canyon Trail** to the historic **Pratt Lodge.** If it's not fall or if you don't care about fall colors, go directly to the **Pine Springs Visitor Center,** see the exhibits, and hike one of the trails—the **Guadalupe Peak Trail** for the ambitious, or the **Devil's Hall Trail** for those who prefer less physical exertion.

2 Park Attractions

The **Pinery** was one of 200 stations along the 2,800-mile Butterfield Overland Mail Coach Route. The stations provided fresh mules every 20 miles and a new coach every 300 miles, allowing drivers to maintain the grueling speed of 5 mph for 24 hours a day. John Butterfield had seen the need for overland mail delivery between the eastern states and the West Coast, so he designed a route and the coaches, then secured a federal contract to deliver the St. Louis mail to San Francisco in 25 days. In March 1857, this was a real feat. The Pinery commemorates his achievement.

Named for nearby stands of pine, the Pinery had abundant water and good grazing. It was a high-walled rock enclosure with a wagon repair shop, a blacksmith shop, and three mud-roofed rooms where passengers could get a warm meal, if they had time. The first mail coach came through on September 28, 1858. It continued until August 1859, when the route was abandoned for a new road that better served the West's military forts.

Located in McKittrick Canyon, **Pratt Lodge** was built by Wallace E. Pratt in 1931–32 from stone quarried at the base of the Guadalupe Mountains, using heart of pine from east Texas for rafters, collar beams, and roof supports. Pratt, a geologist for the Humble Oil Co. (now ExxonMobil), and his family came for summer vacations when the heat in Houston became unbearable. He retired here in 1945. Soon after, he and his family built a second house, **Ship on the Desert,** outside the canyon. In 1957, the Pratts donated 5,632 acres of their 16,000-acre ranch to the federal government to begin the national park. In addition to the grand stone lodge, there are several outbuildings, stone picnic tables, and a wonderful stone wall.

Williams Ranch house rests at the base of a 3,000-foot rock cliff on the west face of the Guadalupe Mountains. The just over 7¼-mile access road, navigable only by high-clearance 4WDs, follows part of the old Butterfield Overland Mail Route for about 2 miles. The road crosses private land and has two locked metal gates for which you must sign out keys at the visitor center.

It's not clear exactly who built the house and when, but it's believed to have been constructed around 1908. The first inhabitants for any significant period of time were almost certainly Henry and Rena Belcher. For almost 10 years, they maintained a substantial ranch here, running up to 3,000 head of longhorn cattle. Water was piped from Bone Spring down the canyon to holding tanks in the lowlands. James Adolphus Williams acquired the property around 1917 and, with the help of an American Indian friend, ranched and farmed the land until he moved to New Mexico in 1941. After Williams's death in 1942, Judge J. C. Hunter bought the property, adding it to his already large holdings in the Guadalupes.

Another historic site is **Frijole Ranch,** which was a working ranch from the 1870s until 1972. Inside the ranch house is a museum with exhibits on the cultural history of the Guadalupe Mountains, including information on the prehistoric American Indians, the Mescalero Apaches who came later, the Spanish conquistadors, and ranchers of the 19th and 20th centuries. On the grounds are several historic buildings, including a schoolhouse.

3 Day Hikes

This is a prime hiking park, with more than 80 miles of trails that range from easy walks to steep, strenuous, and sometimes precarious adventures.

SHORTER TRAILS

Indian Meadow Nature Trail This exceptionally easy stroll follows a series of numbered stops keyed to a free brochure, available at the trail head. You'll learn about the native vegetation and cultural history of the area as you ramble along a virtually level dirt path in a lovely meadow. .6 mile RT. Easy. Access: Dog Canyon Campground; walk south from the water fountain.

McKittrick Canyon Nature Trail An ideal way to discover the variety of plants and animals that inhabit the canyon, this trail has some steep climbs. Read the numerous interpretive signs along the path, telling you all you wanted to know about, for example, why rattlesnakes are underappreciated and how cacti supply food and water for wildlife. .9 mile RT. Easy to moderate. Access: McKittrick Canyon Visitor Center.

Pinery Trail Paved and accessible by wheelchair, the Pinery Trail gives visitors an introduction to the low-elevation environment here. The interpretive signs discuss both the plants along the trail and the history of the area. About a quarter of a mile from the visitor center, the trail leads to the ruins of an old station left over from the Butterfield Stage Route (see "Park Attractions," above). .75 mile RT. Easy. Access: Trail head by the Pine Springs Visitor Center, or from parking area on U.S. 62/180, ½ mile north of visitor center entrance road.

Smith Spring Loop The Smith Spring Loop begins in the dry desert and climbs 440 feet to the lush oasis of Smith Spring. The first part of the trail, which takes you to Manzanita Spring, is easy and navigable by people with mobility impairments. If you take this walk in the evening, you might catch a glimpse of an elk, deer, or other animal coming to the spring for water. After Manzanita Spring, the trail begins the climb to Smith Spring, following a good example of a desert riparian zone along Smith Canyon. Look for the damage caused by a lightning fire in 1990, and note how the desert environment has recovered and even improved. Smith Spring itself is a magnificent oasis, with enough water seeping out to form a small waterfall and stream. Here you'll find maidenhair fern, bigtooth maple, chinquapin oak, and Texas madrone—all in the middle of the Chihuahuan Desert. Although lush, the area is fragile, so please remain in the designated area to preserve the ecosystem. 2.3 miles RT. Easy to moderate. Access: North edge of Frijole Ranch and Museum.

LONGER TRAILS

El Capitan Trail This trail climbs over 1,500 feet and takes a long day to complete, including the drive to Williams Ranch (see "Park Attractions," above), which requires a four-wheel-drive vehicle. This is the only trail into the remote western part of the Guadalupe Mountains, and it offers little shade. The incredible scenery along the first 2 miles more than makes up for the long, slow, and usually hot climb up Shumard Canyon, an elevation gain of over 1,300 feet. Stop occasionally to look back down the canyon to the west, and ahead toward Shumard Peak and the impressive escarpment of the Guadalupes. After Shumard Canyon, the hike takes you 3 miles around El Capitan, keeping in the shadow of the escarpment and climbing another 200 feet. After about 5 miles, the Salt Basin Overlook loop takes off to the right and you stay to the left, gradually dropping down into Guadalupe Canyon, where you meet the other end of the lower Salt Basin Overlook loop. From here the last 3.4 miles of the trail are fairly easy, level walking to Pine Springs. The trail can also be hiked out and back from Pine Springs, an arduous 19-mile overnight hike, which is why many hikers get lifts from friends to the ranch and hike back to Pine Springs. An alternative you may consider is to hike from Pine Springs to the Salt Basin Overlook Trail, hike around it, and then head back to Pine Springs, a trip of 11.3 miles. 9.4 miles one-way. Moderate to strenuous. Access: Williams Ranch.

Guadalupe Peak Trail This trail is strenuous, climbing almost 3,000 feet, but the views from the 8,749-foot-high Guadalupe Peak are magnificent. The peak is the highest in Texas. If you are an average or better hiker and have only 1 day to explore the park, this is the hike you should choose. Start early, take plenty of water, and be prepared to work. When you've gone about halfway, you'll see what seems to be the top not too far ahead, but beware: This is a false summit. Study the changing life zones as you climb from the desert into the higher-elevation pine forests—this will take your mind off your straining muscles and aching lungs. A mile short of the summit, a campground lies in one of the rare level spots on the mountain. If you plan to spend the night, anchor your tent strongly—the winds can be ferocious, especially in spring.

From the summit, the views are stupendous. To the north are Bush Mountain and Shumard Peak, the next two highest points in Texas, with respective elevations of 8,631 and 8,615 feet. The Chihuahuan Desert stretches to the south, interrupted only by the Delaware and Sierra Diablo mountains. This is one of those "on a clear day you can see forever" spots—

(Not) Exploring the Park by Car

The Guadalupe Mountains are not the place for the vehicle bound. No paved scenic drives traverse the park; roads here are simply a means of getting to historical sites and trail heads.

Campground	Elev.	Total Sites	RV Hookups	Dump Station	Toilets
Brantley Lake State Park	3,300	51+	51	Yes	Yes
Carlsbad KOA	3,420	132	102	No	Yes
Carlsbad RV Park & Campground	3,110	136	95	Yes	Yes
Dog Canyon	6,320	13	0	No	Yes
Pine Springs	5,840	39	0	No	Yes

sometimes all the way to 12,003-foot-high Sierra Blanca, near Ruidoso, New Mexico, 100 miles north. 8.5 miles RT Strenuous. Access: Pine Springs Campground.

Lost Peak A moderate hike you can probably complete in a half-day, Lost Peak is especially good near dawn or dusk, when you may see wild turkey, deer, and other wildlife. A fire caused by lightning fire scorched the area in 1994, and although many plants have been recovering, the loss of the tall trees will be felt for a long time. After leaving the trail head, follow the Tejas Trail up Dog Canyon on a gradual climb for about 1.5 miles. Just before reaching Dog Canyon Springs, the trail starts to switchback up the west side of the canyon to a ridgeline, offering great views back to the campground. If you continue all the way to the peak, the next 1.5 miles climb about 1,100 feet, the steepest section of the trail. There's no sign for the peak, and it's easy to hike on by, so watch your topographical map carefully—the peak is just a bit to the right of the trail. After scrambling up to the summit for a panoramic view, head back down the trail. The elevation change is 1,420 feet. 6.4 miles RT. Moderate. Access: Dog Canyon Trailhead.

McKittrick Canyon McKittrick Canyon is one of the most famous scenic areas in Texas, and this trail explores the length of it. The first 2.4 miles to the Pratt Lodge are relatively easy, the following mile to the Grotto gains 340 feet in elevation and is considered moderate, and the strenuous climb to the Notch rises 1,300 feet in 1.6 miles. This is one of the most popular hikes in the park, though not everyone makes it to the Notch.

The canyon is forested with conifers and deciduous trees. In fall the maples, oaks, and other hardwoods burst into color, painting the world in bright hues set off by the variety of the evergreens. The stream in the canyon, which appears and disappears several times in the first 3 miles of the trail, is a unique, permanent desert stream, with reproducing trout. Hikers may not drink from, wade in, fish, or disturb the stream in any way.

The first part of the trail is wide and seems flat, crossing the stream twice on its way to Pratt Lodge, which is wonderfully situated at the convergence of North and South McKittrick canyons. About a mile from the lodge, a short spur veers off to the left to the Grotto, a recess with odd formations that look as if they belong in a cave. This is a great spot for lunch at one of the stone picnic tables. Continuing down the spur trail to its end, you reach the Hunter Line Cabin, which served as temporary quarters for ranch hands of the Hunter family. Beyond the cabin, South McKittrick Canyon has been preserved as a Research Natural Area with no entry. To return, continue on the main trail, or head back down the canyon to your vehicle. In another half-mile, the trail begins to switchback up the side of South McKittrick Canyon for the steepest ascent in the park, until it slips through the Notch, a distinctive narrow spot in the cliff. Sit down and rest while you absorb the incredible scenery. The view down the canyon is magnificent, and dazzling in autumn. You can see both Hunter Line Cabin and Pratt Lodge in the distance. Remember to start down in time to reach your vehicle well before the gate is locked. 10 miles RT. Moderate to strenuous. Access: McKittrick Canyon Trailhead.

4 Exploring the Backcountry

A variety of backpacking possibilities exist. It's always best to discuss your plans with rangers before heading out, to find out about current trail conditions and to decide on the trail or trails you want to take. The required free **backcountry campsite permit** can be obtained no more than 24 hours in advance at the Pine Springs Visitor Center or Dog Canyon Ranger Station. Also, see "Camping," below.

The Bowl This hike climbs 2,546 feet in elevation if you go to the top of Hunter Peak. It is primarily an overnight hike; you'll camp either at Pine Top, about 3.9 miles down the trail and a bit off to the left, or at Tejas Campsite, about 5.5 miles along. The trail crosses a dry wash, follows the Tejas Trail up a hill, has a fairly level stretch, and then starts the climb up to Pine Top, rising 2,000 feet over 3 miles of switchbacks. The view from the top of the escarpment is breathtaking. The trail then continues through a magnificent pine forest—watch for elk along the way. There are some old

Drinking Water	Showers	Fire Pits/ Grills	Laundry	Reserve	Fees	Open
Yes	Yes	Yes	No	Yes	$8–$18	Year-round
Yes	Yes	Yes	Yes	Yes	$28–$55	Year-round
Yes	Yes	Yes	Yes	Yes	$19–$34	Year-round
Yes	No	No	No	No	$8	Year-round
Yes	No	No	No	No	$8	Year-round

water tanks and a pipe running along the trail in spots, left over from a water system used by ranchers years ago. You can take a side trip to the top of Hunter Peak for another incredible view before heading back down. 13-mile loop. Strenuous. Access: Pine Springs Campground.

5 Other Sports & Activities

HORSEBACK RIDING About 60% of the park's trails are open to horses for day trips, although horses are not permitted in the backcountry overnight. There are **corrals** at Frijole Ranch (near Pine Springs) and Dog Canyon (see "Fees & Permits," above). Each set of corrals contains four pens that can accommodate up to 10 horses. No horses or other pack animals are available for hire in or near the park. Park rangers warn that horses brought into the park should be accustomed to steep, rocky trails.

WILDLIFE VIEWING & BIRD-WATCHING Because of the variety of habitats, and because these canyons offer some of the few water sources in western Texas, Guadalupe Mountains National Park offers excellent wildlife viewing and bird-watching. **McKittrick Canyon** and **Frijole Ranch** are among the best wildlife viewing spots, but a variety of species can be seen throughout the park. Those spending more than a few hours will likely see mule deer; the park is also home to a herd of some 50 to 70 elk, which are sometimes observed in the higher elevations or along the highway in winter. Other **mammals** include raccoons, striped and hog-nosed skunks, gray foxes, coyotes, gray-footed chipmunks, Texas antelope squirrels, black-tailed jackrabbits, and desert cottontails. Black bears and mountain lions also live in the park but are seldom seen.

About two dozen varieties of **snakes** make their home in the park, including five species of rattlesnakes. There are also numerous **lizards,** usually seen in the mornings and early evenings. These include the collared, crevice spiny, tree, side-blotched, Texas horned, mountain short-horned, and Chihuahuan spotted whiptail. The most commonly seen is the southwestern fence lizard, which is identified by two light-colored stripes down its back.

More than 200 species of **birds** spend time in the park, including peregrine falcons, golden eagles, turkey vultures, and wild turkeys. You are also likely to encounter rock wrens, canyon wrens, black-throated sparrows, common nighthawks, mourning doves, rufous-crowned sparrows, mountain chickadees, ladder-backed woodpeckers, solitary vireos, and western scrub jays.

6 Camping

INSIDE THE PARK

Two developed vehicle-accessible campgrounds are in the park. **Pine Springs Campground** is near the visitor center and park headquarters just off U.S. 62/180. There are 19 spaces for RVs, 20 very attractive tent sites, and 2 group campsites. There is usually a campground host on duty. About half a mile

Lodging, Dining, and Picnic Supplies

There are no accommodations within the park. The nearest recommended lodgings are 65 miles south in **Van Horn, Texas,** and 55 miles northeast in **Carlsbad, New Mexico.** For information, see "Where to Stay" in chapter 10. There are also no restaurants within the park. Aside from the **Salt Flat Cafe,** 23 miles west of the park visitor center on U.S. 62/180 (✆ **915/964-2838**), the closest dining possibilities we recommend are in Carlsbad. See "Where to Dine" in chapter 10.

For picnics, you'll find a variety of stores in the city of Carlsbad, including an **Albertson's** grocery store, 808 N. Canal St., at West Church Street (✆ **575/885-2161**), which has a well-stocked deli and bakery.

inside the north boundary of the park is **Dog Canyon Campground,** accessible from N. Mex. 137. Here there are nine tent sites and four RV sites. Although reservations are not accepted, you can call ahead to check on availability of sites (✆ **915/828-3251**). Camp stoves are allowed, but wood and charcoal fires are prohibited.

The park also has 10 designated backcountry campgrounds, with five to eight sites each. Be sure to pick up free permits at the Pine Springs Visitor Center or Dog Canyon Ranger Station the day of or the day before your backpacking trip. No drinking water is available in the backcountry, and all trash, including toilet paper, must be packed out. Fires are strictly prohibited; use cookstoves only. You may camp only in designated campgrounds.

NEAR THE PARK

The closest commercial campgrounds are across the state line in New Mexico. We recommend the facilities in the Carlsbad area, at **Carlsbad RV Park & Campground, Carlsbad KOA,** or **Brantley Lake State Park** in Carlsbad. For information on these campgrounds, see "Camping" in chapter 10, "Carlsbad Caverns National Park."

Joshua Tree National Park, CA

by Eric Peterson

At Joshua Tree National Park, the trees are merely the starting point for exploring the seemingly barren desert. Viewed from the roadside, the dry land only hints at hidden vitality, but closer examination reveals a giant mosaic of an ecosystem, intensely beautiful and complex. From lush oases teeming with life to rusted-out relics of man's attempts to tame this wilderness, from low plains of tufted cacti to mountains of exposed, gnarled rock, the park is much more than a tableau of the curious tree for which it's named.

The Joshua tree is said to have been given its name by early Mormon settlers (ca. 1850). Its upraised limbs and bearded appearance reminded them of the prophet Joshua leading them to the promised land. It's actually a treelike variety of yucca, a member of the agave family.

At Joshua Tree National Park, the peculiar tree reaches the southernmost boundary of its range. The park straddles two desert environments: The mountainous, Joshua tree–studded Mojave Desert forms the northwestern part of the park, while the hotter, drier, and lower Colorado Desert, characterized by a wide variety of desert flora such as cacti, ocotillo, and native California fan palms, comprises the park's southern and eastern sections. Between them runs the "transition zone," displaying characteristics of each.

The area's geological timeline stretches back almost 2 billion years. Eight million years ago, the Mojave landscape was one of rolling hills and flourishing grasslands; horses, camels, and mastodons abounded, with saber-toothed tigers and wild dogs filling the role of predator. Displays at the Oasis Visitor Center show how climactic, volcanic, and tectonic activity created the park's signature cliffs and boulders and turned Joshua Tree into the arid desert you see today. Human presence has been traced back nearly 10,000 years with the discovery of the Pinto culture, and you can see evidence of more recent habitation throughout the park in the form of American Indian rock art. Miners and ranchers began coming in the 1860s, but the boom went bust by the turn of the 20th century. Then Pasadena doctor James Luckie, treating World War I veterans suffering from respiratory and heart ailments caused by mustard gas, prescribed the desert's clean, dry air—and modern interest in the area was born.

During the 1920s, a worldwide fascination with the desert emerged, and cactus gardens were much in vogue. Entrepreneurs hauled truckloads of desert plants into Los Angeles for quick sale or export, and souvenir hunters removed archaeological treasures. Incensed that the beautiful Mojave was in danger of being picked clean, Pasadena socialite Minerva Hoyt organized the desert conservation movement and successfully lobbied for the establishment of Joshua Tree National Monument in 1936.

In 1994, under provisions of the federal California Desert Protection Act, Joshua Tree was "upgraded" to national park status and expanded to nearly 800,000 acres.

FLORA

The eastern half of the park is typical of the lower Colorado Desert, dominated by the abundant and fragrant **creosote** bush, a drought-resistant survivor that releases secretions into the surrounding soil to inhibit competing seedlings. Adding interest to the arid land are small stands of spidery, tenacious **ocotillo,** a split personality that drops its leaves in times of drought, making it appear dry and spindly. When the rains come, the ocotillo can sprout bushy leaves in a few days, and its flaming blooms atop leafy green branches bear little resemblance to its dormant alter ego.

Most people associate desert plants with cacti, which are indeed here in abundance. One of the more unusual members of the cactus family is the **Bigelow cholla cactus** ("teddy bear" or "jumping" cactus). Cholla's fine spines appear soft and fluffy from afar, but the folks who have accidentally gotten a clump stuck to their skin or clothing know the truth about these deceptively barbed spines. Most of the park's points of interest lie in the higher, slightly cooler and wetter Mojave Desert, the special habitat of the burly **Joshua tree,** which displays huge white flowers following a good rainy season. Early pioneers tried to chop down the trees for firewood, only to discover that they were actually full of water and fireproof. Five **fan palm** oases (in both climate zones) flourish in areas where water is forced to the surface along fault lines.

Joshua Tree National Park

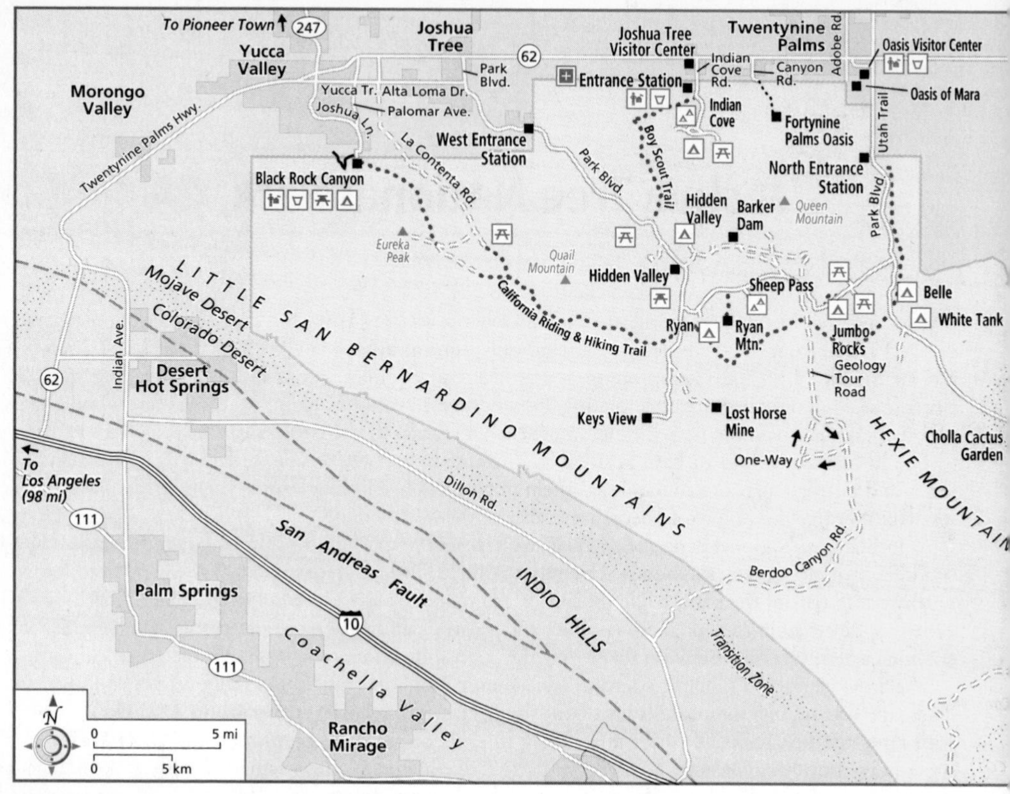

Wildflower lovers, take note: The Joshua Tree area has traditionally been an excellent place to view nature's springtime bonanza, and the lower elevations of the park are hot spots. In addition to the flowering plants discussed above, the desert is home to sand verbena, desert dandelion, evening primrose, and dozens more varieties, some so tiny that you must crouch down to make out their brightly colored petals—veteran viewers call these "belly flowers."

FAUNA

One of the more wonderful aspects of the Joshua Tree desert is the way this seemingly harsh and barren landscape slowly reveals itself to be richly inhabited. From the black-tailed **jackrabbits** abundant at the Oasis of Mara and throughout the park to **bobcats** and the occasional **cougar** prowling around less-traveled areas, the desert teems with life.

Some other frequently spotted residents: the **roadrunner,** a member of the cuckoo family with long, spindly legs and that telltale gait; the **coyote,** a fearless scavenger who'll openly trot along the road in search of food (***Beware:*** They'll eat tennis shoes or picnic trash as eagerly as they eat rabbits, but it is illegal to feed them anything); and **bighorn sheep,** most often seen atop the rocky hills they ascend with sharp cloven hooves. Perhaps the most unusual animal is the **desert tortoise,** a slow-moving burrow dweller not often seen by casual visitors. The tortoises, which can live more than 50 years, are a protected threatened species, and you're prohibited from touching or interfering with them in any way. A poignant exception to this is if you encounter a tortoise on the road in danger of being hit—you're permitted to pick it up gently with two hands and carry it off the road, placing it facing in the same direction in which it was traveling.

AVOIDING THE CROWDS

Joshua Tree chief of interpretation Joe Zarki knows all about the park's natural flora and fauna. He offers the following tips for maximizing your enjoyment even during the most crowded months:

- Joshua Tree's greatest visitation occurs in spring, when temperatures are moderate and wildflowers are blooming. From March to May, the number of monthly visitors is 150,000 and up. Compared to summer, which sees about 60,000 to 70,000 people each month, these figures are staggering. The fall months are also popular, with numbers around 100,000. If you can, time your visit outside of these crowded periods, and stay away during spring break. If you can't, try to visit during the week to avoid the crush of weekenders from nearby Los Angeles.

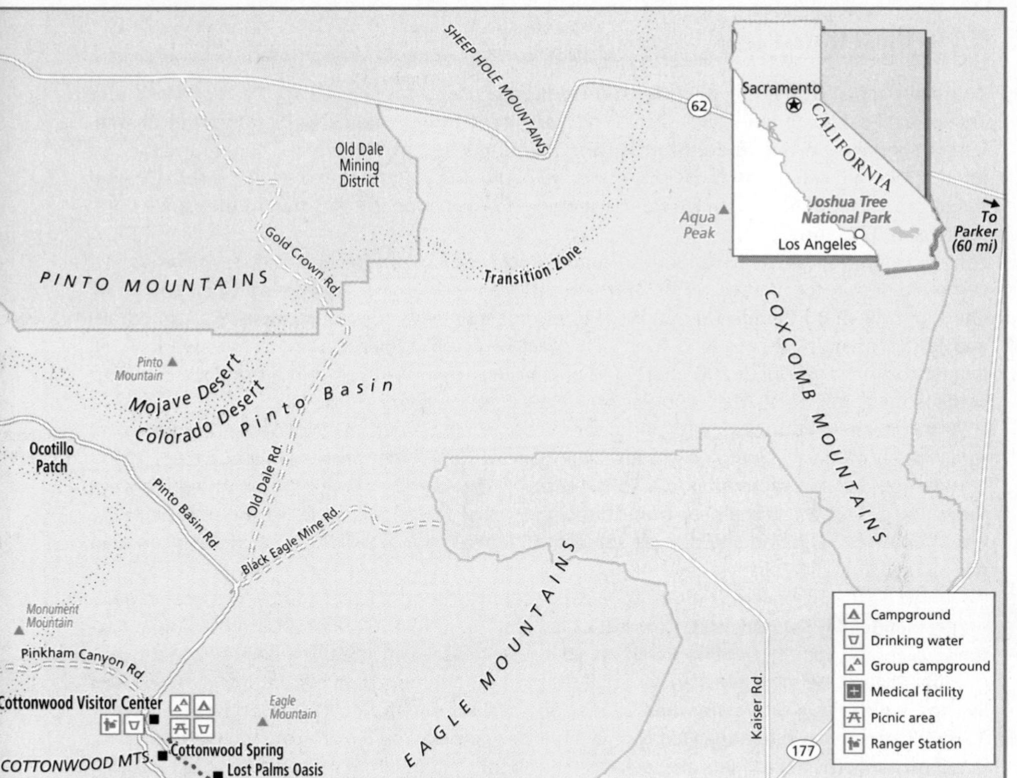

- Choose to enjoy the more popular activities (such as designated nature trails and easy hiking routes) before 9 or 10am. Most people see the park between 10am and 4pm, so the evening hours can also offer some respite from crowds. Remember that the sun sets after 7pm from May to September. In addition, you'll enjoy cooler temperatures during the morning and evening hours.
- Campers eager to stake their claim in the campground of their choice need to be diligent in the spring, because all but two of the park's campgrounds are first come, first served. (Black Rock Canyon and Indian Cove take reservations.) Generally, it's best to arrive between 9am and noon to snatch an available space. The campsites near popular rock-climbing areas (Hidden Valley, Jumbo Rocks, Indian Cove) fill first. If you're staying over a weekend in peak season, try to claim your site Friday morning, before weekenders arrive.

1 Essentials

GETTING THERE & GATEWAYS

There are three roads into the park. The most commonly used is the **West Entrance Station,** on Park Boulevard in the town of Joshua Tree along Calif. 62. The **North Entrance Station,** at the end of Utah Trail in the town of Twentynine Palms, on Calif. 62, 40 miles north of its junction with I-10, is also a popular gateway to the park. On the southern side of the park is the **Cottonwood Visitor Center,** about 40 miles east of Palm Springs along I-10.

THE NEAREST AIRPORT The closest airport is the **Palm Springs International Airport,** 3400 E. Tahquitz Canyon Way (✆ **760/318-3800;** www.palmspringsca.gov). **Alaska, Allegiant, American, Delta, Northwest, Sun Country, United,** and **US Airways** fly here, and **Alamo, Avis, Budget, Dollar, Enterprise, Hertz, National,** and **Thrifty** rent cars. See chapter 38 for website listings for airlines and car-rental firms.

INFORMATION

Contact **Joshua Tree National Park,** 74485 National Park Dr., Twentynine Palms, CA 92277 (✆ **760/367-5500;** www.nps.gov/jotr). A terrific website with abundant info on the park and surrounding communities is www.desertgold.com.

If You Have Only 1 Day

An excellent first stop is the main **Oasis Visitor Center,** located alongside the Oasis of Mara, also known as the Twentynine Palms Oasis. For many generations, the native Serrano and Chemehuevi tribes lived at this "place of little springs and much grass." Get maps, books, and the latest in road, trail, and weather conditions before beginning your tour, and stroll the short, paved nature trail through the oasis behind the center—it provides an introduction to the park's flora, wildlife, and geology.

From the Oasis Center, drive south to **Jumbo Rocks,** which captures the essence of the park: a vast array of rock formations, a Joshua tree forest, and the yucca-dotted desert, open and wide. Check out the many boulders that appear to resemble humans, dinosaurs, monsters, cathedrals, and castles; if you're visiting with kids, it's a great way to put their imaginations to work. Stroll among the giant rock piles and observe the rock climbers who travel from around the world to practice their craft here—they're one of the park's most distinctive features.

At Cap Rock Junction, the main park road swings north toward the **Wonderland of Rocks,** 12 square miles of massive jumbled granite. This maze of stone hides groves of Joshua trees, trackless washes, and several small pools. To the south is the road that dead-ends at mile-high **Keys View.** You get a view of the park from this wind-whipped overlook; several plaques explain the topography you're seeing and provide some insight into the delicate desert ecosystems found in the park.

Don't miss the contrasting Colorado Desert terrain along Pinto Basin Road—to conserve time, simply plan to exit the park on this route, which ends up at I-10. You'll pass both the **Cholla Cactus Garden** and spindly **Ocotillo Patch** on your way to vast Pinto Basin, a barren lowland surrounded by austere mountains and a small ridge of sand dunes. Then continue to **Cottonwood Springs,** which has a cool, palm-shaded oasis and groves of mature cottonwood trees.

Try to participate in a ranger-led tour or hike (see below). You'll learn to appreciate the park in a short time, for the rangers are as exuberant about their patch of wilderness as they are well informed.

In addition to the free newspaper offered by the park, the following publications might prove helpful: Robert Cates's *Joshua Tree National Park: A Visitors Guide* (Chatsworth, California: Live Oak Press, 1984), and Patty Knapp's *Joshua Tree Trails* (M.I. Adventure Press, 2001). Order them from the **Joshua Tree National Park Association,** 74485 National Park Dr., Twentynine Palms, CA 92277 (**© 760/367-5525;** www.joshuatree.org).

VISITOR CENTERS

Your best sources of information in the park are the Park Service's three visitor centers. The park headquarters and **Oasis Visitor Center,** 74485 National Park Dr. in Twentynine Palms, is on the road to the North Entrance Station. The **Cottonwood Visitor Center,** at the south end of the park, houses a gift shop and bookstore, as well as an interpretive exhibit on the area's wildlife. The **Joshua Tree Visitor Center,** 6554 Park Blvd. in Joshua Tree, is on the road to the West Entrance Station. In addition to providing visitor materials and information, this center has a bookstore and gift shop, a cafe, and an exhibit gallery. Oasis and Joshua Tree are open daily from 8am to 5pm, and Cottonwood 9am to 3pm.

FEES

Admission to the park is $15 per car (valid for 7 days). The nine developed campgrounds charge fees of $10 to $15 for individual sites, more for group sites. Backcountry camping is free, but self-registration is required.

SPECIAL REGULATIONS & WARNINGS

In addition to the standard national park regulations designed to protect fragile ecosystems, keep these in mind while enjoying Joshua Tree:

- **Dehydration** is a constant threat in the desert; even in winter, carry plenty of drinking water and drink regularly even if you don't feel thirsty. Recommended minimum supplies are 1 gallon per person per day, or twice that if planning strenuous activity. Water is available at five park locations: Cottonwood Springs, the Black Rock Canyon Campground, the Indian Cove Ranger Station, West Entrance, and the Oasis Visitor Center. The water for RVs at the Oasis Visitor Center comes from a coin-operated fountain—bring plenty of quarters.

- Sections of the park (identified on the official map) contain **abandoned mines** and associated structures. Use extreme caution in the vicinity, watching for open shafts and prospect holes. Supervise children closely, and never enter abandoned mines.
- **Flash flooding** is a potential hazard following even brief rain showers, so avoid drainage areas and be especially observant of road conditions at those times.

SEASONS & CLIMATE

Joshua Tree National Park's 794,000 acres—585,000 of them designated as wilderness— straddle two distinct desert climates. The eastern half of the park is hot, dry, Colorado Desert, and most points of interest lie in the higher, slightly cooler and wetter Mojave Desert. The Mojave will occasionally get a dusting of snow in winter, but neither section sees more than 3 to 6 inches of annual rainfall. Winter temperatures are in the comfortable 50s or 60s (lower teens Celsius) during the day and often approach freezing overnight; summer days can blaze past 100°F (38°C) at noon, and even nighttime offers little relief in August and September, when lows are still in the 80s (upper 20s Celsius). At the park's higher elevations, however, the summer climate is much more bearable. Overall, the fall tends to be the best season for hiking.

SEASONAL EVENTS

Best between February and May, the springtime **wildflower viewing** is dependent on rainfall, sunshine, and temperatures, but you can see brilliant blooms somewhere in the park most years. Rangers lead interpretive walks to the best displays, and 24-hour recorded information on prime viewing sites (updated at least weekly during the Mar–May wildflower season) is available from the park at ✆ **760/367-5500.** Information is also available online at www.nps/gov/jotr.

2 Exploring the Park by Car

There are two main roads through the park, and by driving them both you'll be able to see virtually every feature that distinguishes Joshua Tree; there are even a couple of easy opportunities to stop and stretch your legs.

Park Boulevard loops through the high northern section between the North Entrance Station in Twentynine Palms and the West Entrance Station in Joshua Tree. Along the drive, which takes about 1 hour one-way, you'll get an eyeful of the rock formations and oddly shaped Joshua trees. Stop at one of the well-marked interpretive trails along the way (see "Day Hikes," below), but don't miss the detour to **Keys View,** one of the most popular spots in the park. A paved road leads to this mile-high mountain crest, where a series of plaques describe the land below and a panoramic view that encompasses both the highest (Mt. San Gorgonio) and the lowest (Salton Sea) points in Southern California.

Pinto Basin Road crosses the park from top to bottom, forking away from Park Boulevard near the North Entrance Station and winding down to the Cottonwood Entrance off I-10. Driving it, you'll pass from the higher Mojave Desert into the lower Colorado Desert, across the "transition zone" snaking through the middle of the park, a fascinating melting pot where the two climates are both represented. Stop to marvel at the Cholla Cactus Garden (see "Day Hikes," below) or the Ocotillo Patch, where the spidery, tenacious desert shrub sports flaming red blooms following spring rains. At the park's southern end, you can explore the lush Cottonwood Spring or see relics of World War II training maneuvers (see "Park Attractions," below). Driving from end to end takes about an hour.

3 Organized Tours & Ranger Programs

A multitude of ranger-led seminars and guided hikes are available. They change annually but might include topics such as "Meet the Joshua Tree," "Clever Desert Plants," "Rock of Ages," and "Oasis Walk," as well as guided hikes on many of the park's popular trails and evening campfire talks on weekends. Throughout the wildflower blooming season, and especially during Easter week, special walks visit the most abundantly flowering areas.

The Park Service also conducts guided tours of the historic **Keys Ranch** (see below). From approximately October to May, tours run twice daily ($5 adults, $2.50 kids 6–11 and seniors). Contact the Oasis Visitor Center for a schedule; tours operate by appointment only during the hot summer. Arrive early—these events are popular, and groups are limited to 25. You can make advance reservations by calling ✆ **760/367-5555.**

Visitors can go more in-depth by enrolling in a workshop offered by the **Desert Institute,** 74485 National Park Dr., Twentynine Palms, CA 92277

(✆ **760/367-5535;** http://desertinstitute.homestead.com). The Institute's course catalog covers subjects ranging from desert survival and orienteering to poetry and basket weaving; workshops typically run one to three daily sessions and cost $50 to $150.

4 Park Attractions

Miners and ranchers began coming in the 1860s, including the McHaney brothers, who established the Desert Queen Ranch. Later on, Bill Keys acquired it, and he lived with his family on the property, now known as the **Keys Ranch,** until his death in 1969. Many of the ranch structures have been restored to their Keys-era condition, painting a compelling picture of how one hardy family made a home in the unforgiving desert. Admittance is limited to official Park Service tours (see above).

You can find petroglyphs near **Barker Dam,** where an easy 1.1-mile loop hiking trail leads to a small artificial lake framed by the Wonderland of Rocks. After scrambling a bit to get to the dam, you'll find a sandy path leading to the "Disney Petroglyph" site. Its wry name stems from the fact that a 1950s movie crew retraced the ancient rock carvings to make them more visible to the camera, defacing them forever. If you investigate the cliffs along the remainder of the trail, you're likely to find some untouched drawings depicting animals, humans, and other aspects of desert life as interpreted by long-ago dwellers. You'll see more petroglyphs along the 18-mile **Geology Tour Road,** a sandy, lumpy dirt road accessible only by four-wheel-drive vehicles or hardy mountain bikers.

During World War II, George S. Patton trained over a million soldiers in desert combat at several sites throughout the Mojave and Colorado deserts. Tank tracks are still visible in the desert around the former Camp Young, near Cottonwood Springs. The **Camp Young Memorial** marker is 1 mile east of Cottonwood Springs Road, just before the park entrance; an informational kiosk there gives details of the training maneuvers and daily camp life. To learn more, you can visit the **General Patton Memorial Museum** (✆ **760/227-3483;** www.generalpattonmuseum.com) in Chiriaco Summit, on I-10 about 4 miles east of the Cottonwood Entrance. The museum contains an assortment of memorabilia from World War II and other military glory days, as well as displays of tanks and artillery; it's open daily from 9:30am to 4:30pm (except Thanksgiving and Dec 25). Admission is $4 for adults, $3.50 for seniors 62 and older, and free for children under 12.

5 Day Hikes

Joshua Tree's natural wonders are accessible to everyone, not just the extreme outdoor adventurer. Nowhere is this more apparent than in the diversity of hiking and nature trails, which range from a half-mile paved nature trail (ideal for even strollers and wheelchairs) to trails of 15-plus miles requiring strenuous hiking and backcountry camping.

SHORTER TRAILS

Barker Dam Nature Trail This sandy path leads to a small lake formed in a natural rock basin by an artificial dam. It's a relic of the ranchers who used such "tanks" to water their stock. Signs along the way describe some of the plant and animal life found here, including migratory wildfowl that use the lake as a watering hole on their journeys. After scrambling up the dam, you'll come to some petroglyph sites (see "Park Attractions," above). 1.3 miles RT. Easy. Access: Barker Dam parking area.

Cap Rock Nature Trail Climbers gather here, and they're as interesting as the short, informative trail leading from the parking lot. In between identifying different desert plants along the paved path, test your footing on some of the rocks to get a feel for the climbing experience. .4 mile RT. Easy. Access: Cap Rock parking area.

Cholla Cactus Garden Nature Trail This trail winds through an unusually dense concentration of Bigelow cholla, one of the desert's more fascinating residents. Often called "teddy bear cactus" for its deceptively fluffy appearance, cholla is also nicknamed "jumping cactus" for the ease with which its barbed spines stick to the clothing and skin of anyone who passes too close. Any ranger can tell you horror stories of people who've tripped into a cholla bush and emerged porcupine-like and suffering—but please don't let that stop you from enjoying this pretty roadside diversion. .25 mile RT. Easy. Access: Middle of the park, about halfway btw. the north and south entrances.

Cottonwood Springs Nature Trail The trail leads through rolling desert hills long inhabited by Cahuilla Indians. Signs along the way relate how they used native plants in their everyday lives; the trail culminates at lush Cottonwood Springs. The prolific underground water source supports thick groves of cottonwood and palm trees, plus the birds and animals that make them home. 1 mile RT. Easy. Access: Cottonwood Campground.

Desert Queen Mine The "trail" meanders and forks through the ruins of a gold mine that yielded several million dollars' worth of ore between 1895 and 1961. Building ruins, steel machinery parts, and sealed mine shafts dot the hillsides and ravine; there's a signboard at the overlook with information about mine operations. 1.5 miles RT. Easy to moderate. Access: Dirt road leading north from Park Blvd., opposite the Geology Tour Rd.

Fortynine Palms Oasis This hike begins with a steep, harsh ascent 300 feet up to a ridge fringed with red-spined barrel cacti. Down the other side, a rocky canyon contains the spectacular oasis whose fan palm and cottonwood tree canopy shades clear pools of green water. Plants (especially spring wildflowers), birds, lizards, and other wildlife are abundant in this miniature ecosystem, and the scorched trunks of trees bear witness to past fires that have nourished rather than destroyed the life here. Beware of rattlesnakes in the shaded brush around the oasis. 3 miles RT. Strenuous. Access: End of Canyon Rd. in Twentynine Palms (outside the park, down Canyon Rd.).

Hidden Valley Nature Trail This trail is fun for kids and adults who like rock climbing and intrigue. You can see sport climbers surrounding the small valley, which is reputed to have been a hideout for 19th-century cattle rustlers. Signs posted along the trail talk about the area's geology and history. The trail is relatively level, though there's some scrambling through rocky areas along the route. 1-mile loop RT. Easy. Access: Paved spur near Hidden Valley picnic area.

Hi-View Nature Trail This well-maintained and popular trail involves a steady, moderately steep climb to one of Joshua Tree's many spectacular vistas. Alternately rocky and sandy, the trail matches up with numbered signposts keyed to a leaflet that is available at the Black Rock Ranger Station from October through May. Benches dot the trail at intervals and at the summit. 1.3 miles RT. Moderate. Access: Dirt-road turnoff immediately before entrance to Black Rock Campground at park's northwest edge.

Mastodon Peak Trail Well-worn and scenic, this is the longest loop trail in the park, offering great views of the Eagle Mountains and the nearby Salton Sea. For history buffs, it also passes a long-abandoned gold mine. There is a small amount of elevation gain, about 400 feet on the way to the 3,371-foot summit of Mastodon Peak. 3 miles RT. Moderate. Access: Cottonwood Spring or Cottonwood Campground.

Oasis of Mara Nature Trail Leading into a miniature ecosystem of palm trees, small ponds, and abundant animal life (especially birds), this incredibly easy paved path is lined with interpretive signs. It's a great place to start your first visit to Joshua Tree and an excellent introduction to the centuries of human inhabitants who used the oasis to sustain life. .5 mile RT. Easy. Access: Behind the Oasis Visitor Center.

Pine City This path takes you to a cluster of boulder formations and sandy washes. Pinyon trees thrive in the moisture provided by these natural drainage courses; their pine nuts were a food source for early inhabitants. Birds now gather in the trees, and bighorn sheep occasionally appear among the rocks. 3 miles RT. Easy. Access: Dirt road leading from Park Blvd., opposite the Geology Tour Rd.

Ryan Mountain A steep climb (almost 1,000 ft.) leads to the best panoramic views in the park, encompassing snowcapped mountain peaks, tree-dotted valleys, and volcanic mounds. Ascending through a juniper and pinyon pine woodland, the trail is mostly rocky, well maintained, and easy to follow—you'll likely spot rock climbers to the west of the mountain. 3 miles RT. Strenuous. Access: Marked parking area along Park Blvd.

Skull Rock Nature Trail Leading to an unusually anthropomorphic rock formation, the trail meanders through boulders, desert washes, and a rocky alleyway. Watch for the "ducks" (small stacks of rocks) that mark the pathway. The official trail ends at the main road, but a primitive trail continues on a mile-long loop across the street. 1.5 miles RT. Easy. Access: Jumbo Rocks Campground (Loop E).

LONGER TRAILS

Boy Scout Trail From the trail head, you progress downhill, through picturesque, sandy washes lined with oak and pine trees. Traveling through a variety of terrain, this trail can also be taken one-way in either direction. The latter portion skirts a rocky mountainside, then finishes through open desert, ending up at the Indian Cove Ranger Station and backcountry board. 16 miles RT. Moderate. Access: Keys West backcountry board, 6½ miles east of the West Entrance Station.

California Riding and Hiking Trail Marked by distinctive brown posts stenciled with "CRH," the many miles of this trail pass through distinct areas of the park, from pinyon and juniper forests to flat, lower desert terrain. In general, traveling from west to east is easier than the reverse, because the western sections are at higher elevations. Hiking the entire trail takes 2 to 4 days, but you can break it into sections ranging from 4.4 to 11 miles. In deciding which of the six access points to use, your best bet is to consult with park rangers and obtain a topographical map to help you stay on track. 35 miles RT. Easy to strenuous. Access: 6 points along the trail.

Lost Horse Mine This trail leads to the ruins of the area's most successful mining operation. Well-preserved remnants include the steam engine that powered the machinery, a winch for lowering equipment into the mine, settling tanks, and stone building foundations. The trail, actually an old wagon road, winds gradually up through rolling hills; once there, you can take an additional short, steep hike to the hilltop behind the ruins for a fine view into the heart of the park. Hikers with children should keep a watchful eye around the mine ruins. Hikers can head back the way they came or continue on a loop trail that is 6.2 miles. 4 miles RT. Moderate. Access: End of a dirt road leading from Keys View Rd., 2½ miles south of its junction with Park Blvd.

Lost Palms Oasis This long trail leads through sandy washes and rolling hills to the oasis overlook. A steep, rugged, and strenuous trail then continues to the canyon bottom. Whether or not you're up to the entire challenge, the beauty of birdsong and rustling palms echoing through the canyon makes this a special hike. Lost Palms is the park's largest oasis; look closely for elusive bighorn sheep in the remote canyon bottom. 7.2 miles RT. Moderate. Access: Park at Cottonwood Spring, accessible by paved road just beyond the Cottonwood Campground.

6 Other Sports & Activities

BIKING Because most of Joshua Tree National Park is designated wilderness, visitors must take care not to damage the fragile ecosystem. That means bicycles are restricted from hiking trails and allowed only on roads, none of which have bike lanes. This effectively puts biking out of reach for most casual pedalers. If you're into mountain biking and up to a challenge, however, miles of unpaved roads are open to bikers. Distraction from cars is rare, particularly on four-wheel-drive roads such as the 18-mile dirt **Geology Tour Road,** which begins 2 miles west of Jumbo Rocks. Dry lake beds contrast with boulders along this sandy, lumpy downhill road; you can stop to see a Joshua tree woodland, abandoned mines, and petroglyphs. ***Note:*** The park has devised a plan to open 29 miles of trails to bikes, but at press time was still awaiting the congressional stamp of approval.

A short but rewarding ride starts at Covington Flats, accessible only by unpaved (two-wheel-drive okay) La Contentata Road in the town of Joshua Tree. From the picnic area, ride west to **Eureka Peak,** about 4 miles away through lush high desert vegetation such as mammoth Joshua trees, junipers, and pinyons. The road is steep near the end, but your reward is a panoramic view of Palm Springs to the south, the Morongo Basin to the north, and the jagged mountain ranges of the park in between. For other bike-accessible unpaved and four-wheel-drive roads, consult the park map available at all visitor centers. There are no bike rentals available in the park, so you'll have to bring your own.

Especially for Kids

Joshua Tree National Park is a great place for the kids. They'll see unusual plants and animals, learning just enough to stimulate their imaginations but not so much that they zone out. From identifying familiar shapes in rock formations to investigating the mysterious "teddy bear" cactus, the possibilities are endless. Parents must exercise caution with regard to the weather and other dangers. Bring plenty of water, sunscreen, and protective clothing for children, and keep a close eye (if not a grip) on them at all times to prevent their straying into perilous desert terrain with prickly cacti, steep rocks, and abandoned mine shafts.

Start by taking the kids on a designated nature trail (listed in the free *Joshua Tree Guide* and indicated by roadside signs). The park's 11 nature trails have numerous plaques along the way to help your family interpret the rocks, plants, and other characteristics you'll see in the context of their geological history and significance to animal and human desert dwellers. They're all short (.25- to 1.3-mile loops) and relatively flat, making them ideal for most visitors. Three of these (**Oasis of Mara, Bajada Trail,** and **Cap Rock**) are paved and wheelchair accessible.

The Park Service is eager for younger visitors to learn nature appreciation and conservation. Available at the park's visitor centers, the ***Junior Ranger*** publication offers several educational activities for kids, ranging from sketching rock formations and plants to taking quizzes on the park's facilities. If your youngster is interested enough to complete five of the activities, rangers at the Oasis and Cottonwood visitor centers will reward him or her with an official Junior Ranger badge.

ROCK CLIMBING During most of the year, visitors to the park can observe rock climbers scurrying up, down, and across the many geological formations in the northwestern quadrant. Joshua Tree is one of the sport's premier destinations, with more than 4,000 individually rated climbs.

Spectacular geological formations have irresistible names such as **Wonderland of Rocks** and **Jumbo Rocks.** Lovers of Stonehenge and Easter Island will delight in bizarre stacks with names such as **Cap Rock** (for the single flat rock perched atop a haphazard pile) and **Skull Rock** (where the elements have worn an almost-human countenance into a boulder arrangement). But human hands had nothing to do with nature's sculptural artistry here; these fantastic formations are made of **monzogranite,** once a molten liquid forced upward that cooled before reaching the surface. Tectonic stresses fractured the rocks, and as floods eventually washed away the ground cover and exposed the monzonite, natural erosion wore away the weakened sections, creating the bizarre shapes and piles you see today. Climbers of every skill level travel here from around the world, drawn by the otherworldly splendor of rock piles worn smooth by the elements.

Hidden Valley is another good place to watch enthusiasts from as far away as Europe and Japan scaling sheer rock faces with impossible grace. Climbers sometimes practice bouldering—working on strength and agility on smaller boulders within jumping distance of the ground. You can try some bouldering to sample the high-friction quartz monzogranite; even tennis shoes seem to grip the rock surface.

If you'd like to learn the sport of rock climbing, it's easier than you think—there are 30 climbing guides with permits for the park. The folks at (aptly named) **Uprising** (✆ **888/254-6266** or 760/366-3799; www.uprising.com) in Joshua Tree have accredited, experienced guides who'll orchestrate your excursion, starting with detailed instruction on rock-climbing basics. Later the guide will lead each climb, setting up ropes for belay and rappelling, then guiding students every step of the way. All-day excursions are about $150 per person in groups of three or more, $175 each for two people, or $315 for one person. The company operates year-round, and prices include all necessary gear.

7 Camping

The park has nine developed drive-in campgrounds. At this writing, you can make reservations for individual sites only at Black Rock Canyon and Indian Cove (✆ **877/444-6777;** www.recreation.gov). You can make group camping reservations (sites accommodate 10–70 people) at the same number and website. **Belle Campground** is on Pinto Basin Road 9 miles south of Twentynine Palms. **Black Rock Campground** is in the northwest corner, at the head of the 35-mile California Riding and Hiking Trail (to reach it, you have to leave the park boundaries), and is the most developed campground. There is also a visitor center here. **Cottonwood Campground** is in the southern portion of the park, near the Cottonwood Visitor Center. **Hidden Valley Campground,** 14 miles south of Joshua Tree, California, is on the main park road. **Indian Cove** is just inside park boundaries west of Twentynine Palms; as at Black Rock, there are hiking trails leading farther into Joshua Tree, but no roads. **Jumbo Rocks Campground,** named for its—surprise!—jumbo rocks, is 11 miles south of Twentynine Palms. Take Park Boulevard to reach **Ryan Campground,** 16 miles southeast of Joshua Tree, California. **Sheep Pass group camp,** a few miles east of Ryan Campground, has group sites only. **White Tank Campground** is 2 miles beyond the Belle Campground. There are no showers or laundry facilities at any of the campgrounds, and you can make fires only in the fire pits provided at each campsite (bring your own wood).

The park also allows **backcountry camping** in the wilderness areas; regulations include mandatory registration on boards at the trail heads (see the Park Service map for locations). Park staffers recommend backcountry enthusiasts buy the Trails Illustrated topographic map of the park (available through the park association) before embarking on a backpacking trip.

Outside of the park boundaries, there are a few commercial campgrounds. One of the best is the **Joshua Tree Lake RV & Campground,** 5 miles north of Calif. 62 on Sunfair Road near the town of Joshua Tree (✆ **760/366-1213;** www.jtlake.com). It has a fishing lake (with bass, bluegill, and catfish), a dump station, a small convenience store, laundry machines, and 44 RV hookups ($28 per night). Tent sites are $16 for two people. Showers cost $5 for walk-ins but are free for guests.

Campground	Total Sites	RV Hookups	Dump Station	Toilets	Drinking Water
Belle	18	No	No	Yes	No
Black Rock	100	No	Yes	Yes	Yes
Cottonwood	62 individual, 3 group	No	Yes	Yes	Yes
Hidden Valley	39	No	No	Yes	No
Indian Cove	101 individual, 13 group	No	No	Yes	Yes
Joshua Tree Lake	200	Yes	Yes	Yes	Yes
RV & Campground (private)					
Jumbo Rocks	125	No	No	Yes	No
Ryan	31	No	No	Yes	No
Sheep Pass	6 group	No	No	Yes	No
White Tank	15	No	No	Yes	No

* Reservations can be made (by mail) for group sites.

** Schedule based on demand; call for current information.

8 Where to Stay

Aside from camping, there are no overnight accommodations available within the park.

NEAR THE PARK

America's Best Value Inn & Suites: Oasis of Eden It may look like a plain roadside motel, but the Oasis of Eden has surprises behind its doors. If you think the name makes it sound like a good place for illicit liaisons, wait till you see one of the 14 "theme rooms," each with a whirlpool and VCR. The Oasis of Eden is a less grand cousin to San Luis Obispo's famous Madonna Inn; here you can go back to the heyday of Elvis and sleep in a bed shaped like a '59 Cadillac in the '50s Room, revisit Caesar's Palace in the marble-pillared Roman Suite, or return to your vine-swinging roots in the popular Jungle Room. The 24 standard rooms, some of which have kitchenettes, are less expensive than the theme units. As motels go, this one's a cut above, offering a heated outdoor pool and spa, as well as free Wi-Fi; rates include continental breakfast.

56377 Twentynine Palms Hwy., Yucca Valley, CA 92284. ✆ **800/606-6686** or 760/365-6321. Fax 760/365-9592. www.oasisofeden.com. 38 units. A/C, TV, TEL. $55–$145 double; $99–$375 theme room. Rates include continental breakfast. AE, DC, DISC, MC, V.

Joshua Tree Inn Not all local lore has to do with pioneering miners and ranchers. If fact, one vintage motel boasts of a more recent rock-'n'-roll history. Built in the 1950s, the Joshua Tree Inn has been the choice of the Rolling Stones, the Flying Burrito Brothers, and the cast of *Saturday Night Live.* The lobby is decorated with posters of folk singer–songwriter Gram Parsons, who died of an overdose here in 1973, and Room 8 is dedicated to his memory, decorated with rock posters and psychedelic art. Legends aside, the low-slung adobe-style rooms are basic but charming, surrounding a large pool near the west entrance of Joshua Tree National Park, set back far enough from the highway to escape most traffic noise.

61259 Twentynine Palms Hwy., Joshua Tree, CA 92252. ✆ **760/366-1188.** www.joshuatreeinn.com. 10 units, including 2 suites. A/C, TV. $85–$105 double; $175 suite. AE, DISC, MC, V.

Pioneertown Motel Built as a "living movie set" in 1946, Pioneertown saw numerous movie shoots in its day, including vehicles for such stars as Roy Rogers, Gene Autry, and the Sons of the Pioneers—for whom the town was named. When the scenes were shot, this well-kept motel is where the cast and crew hung their hats and played poker. The small, rustic, but comfortable rooms have kitchenettes, unique furnishings, and vintage movie posters; perks include satellite TV and free Wi-Fi, and proximity to walk to Pappy & Harriet's (see "Where to Dine," below) for dinner.

5040 Curtis Rd., Pioneertown, CA 92277. ✆ **760/365-4879.** www.pioneertownmotel.com. 18 units. A/C, TV. $78–$92 double. MC, V.

Spin and Margie's Desert Hide-a-Way Words like *funky* and *eclectic* come to mind when describing Spin and Margie's, but they don't really do the place justice. Proprietors Mindy Kaufman and Drew Reese have seamlessly blended kitsch and high-desert style into one of the best properties in the area. Featuring inflatable taxidermy, Our Lady of Guadalupe iconography, Navajo blankets, and Reese's photography, the rooms are both artful and functional. They have sleeper sofas, foldout futons, flatscreen TVs, free Wi-Fi, CD and DVD players with excellent in-room libraries, and—except for the standalone cabin—full kitchens. (The cabin, however, has a

Showers	Fire Pits/ Grills	Laundry	Reserve	Fees	Open
No	Yes	No	No	$10	Oct–May**
No	Yes	No	Yes	$10	Year-round
No	Yes	No	No*	$15–$30	Year-round
No	Yes	No	No	$10	Year-round
No	Yes	No	Yes*	$15–$40	Year-round
Yes	Yes	Yes	Yes	$15–$27	Year-round
No	Yes	No	No	$10	Year-round
No	Yes	No	No	$10	Oct–May**
No	Yes	No	Yes*	$25–$40	Year-round
No	Yes	No	No	$10	Oct–May**

private yard populated with ceramic deer.) Outside there's a great courtyard, a barbecue area, and plenty of shady nooks, off-kilter sculptures, and found art. Just 3 miles from the park boundary and the center of the town of Joshua Tree, the Hide-a-Way is well removed from the bustle, but not ridiculously so.

Sunkist Rd. and Twentynine Palms Hwy. (P.O. Box 1092), Joshua Tree, CA 92252. ✆ **760/366-9124** or 760/774-0850. www.deserthideaway.com. 5 units, including 1 cabin. A/C, TV. $125–$160 double; $135 cabin. AE, DISC, MC, V.

29 Palms Inn In town, but a world apart, this rustic, family-run inn dates from the 1920s. It consists of adobe cottages and cabins scattered among 70 acres of the Oasis of Mara, the other side of which holds the main visitor center for the park. It has been discovered by Hollywood celebrities in need of a low-key resort dedicated to the art of relaxation. The breathtaking grounds feature an artesian pond shaded by the namesake 29 original palms, and sublime views of the desert mountains. The cozy cottages have distinct personalities; most have a fireplace or wood stove and patio or deck, but all have evaporative coolers or air-conditioning for the sweltering summer. Our favorite: Irene's Historic Adobe, a one-bedroom, one-bunkroom house with a top-notch kitchen and an enclosed courtyard that's been used in music videos. Next to the outdoor pool—a perfect antidote to the desert heat—is a poolside bar. Other perks: weekend naturalist walks, art classes, and a 2-acre garden that provides veggies for the inn's **restaurant,** one of the best in town (see "Where to Dine," below).

73950 Inn Ave., Twentynine Palms, CA 92277. ✆ **760/367-3505.** Fax 760/367-4425. www.29palmsinn.com. 24 units, including 4 guesthouses. A/C, TV. Mid-Sept to June $132–$190 double, $230–$340 guesthouse; July to mid-Sept $85–$150 double, $155–$280 guesthouse. Lower midweek rates. Rates include morning coffee and sweet breads. AE, DC, DISC, MC, V.

9 Where to Dine

There are no restaurants in the park.

NEAR THE PARK

Beyond the choices listed below, in Joshua Tree is **Royal Siam Thai,** 61599 Twentynine Palms Hwy. (✆ **760/366-2923**), a very good Thai restaurant. For tasty muffins, scones, and other baked goods, head across the street to **Teacakes Bakery,** 61740B Twentynine Palms Hwy. (✆ **760/974-6209;** www.teacakes.biz). And for coffee, gourmet takeout fare, including calzones, wraps, and a number of vegan dishes, and an eclectic store with everything from newspapers, to wine, to fashion, stop at **Ricochet,** 61705 Twentynine Palms Hwy. (✆ **760/366-1898;** www.ricochetjoshuatree.com).

Crossroads Café and Tavern AMERICAN A favorite post-hiking or -climbing destination, this bustling eatery serves fresh coffee flown in from Washington State, fresh fruit smoothies, and fresh fish, plus some tasty hot and cold gourmet sandwiches—try the Grilled Coyote (chicken and portobello mushrooms with balsamic mayo). The bar pours several draught microbrews. Besides the local color, there is plenty to distract yourself on the walls: original art, bumper stickers, and bric-a-brac.

61715 Twentynine Palms Hwy., Joshua Tree. ✆ **760/366-5414.** www.crossroadscafeandtavern.com. Main courses $4–$11. AE, DISC, MC, V. Sun–Tues and Thurs 6:30am–8pm; Fri–Sat 6:30am–9pm.

Desert Bizarro

The Joshua Tree area has long attracted outcasts, misfits, and eccentrics looking for a place where they can let it all hang out. And they've definitely left a mark. Check out the landmarks left by two late desert notables, George Van Tassel and Noah Purifoy, in the respective forms of the **Integratron** near Landers (✆ **760/364-3126;** www.integratron.com), and the **Noah Purifoy Sculpture Park Museum** in the town of Joshua Tree (✆ **213/382-756** for an appointment to visit). The former is an amazing wooden dome with unbelievable acoustics and public sound baths on Sundays at noon and on other days by appointment, and the latter is an outdoor museum of contemporary art made mostly from media that other artists would have thrown away.

Pappy and Harriet's Pioneertown Palace BARBECUE The Pappy and Harriet's motto, "Retire now, work later," is fitting for this low-key outpost, a culinary and musical mecca in the California desert. You can definitely make a case for the succulent, mesquite-grilled chicken and steaks as the best in the Joshua Tree area. There are also some seafood and vegetarian options. Drinks are served in mason jars, paper towels serve as napkins, and the atmosphere of the grand, old-fashioned Western bar would best be described as rough around the edges. But truth be told, the joint has long been a favorite of Southern California musicians, including the late, great Gram Parsons and Led Zeppelin frontman Robert Plant. More recently, rockers have used the stage as a recording studio. There's live music every night Pappy and Harriet's is open, from 7pm until "y'all stop drinking"—usually well after midnight.

Pioneertown Rd., Pioneertown. ✆ **760/365-5956.** www.pappyandharriets.com. Reservations recommended on weekends. Main courses $7–$27. AE, DISC, MC, V. Mon 5–9:30pm; Thurs–Sun 11am–9:30pm. Bar open later. Take Pioneertown Rd. 4 miles north of Yucca Valley.

29 Palms Inn NEW AMERICAN A favorite spot for local artists to display their work, this restaurant is tucked away behind its namesake hotel's postage stamp–size pool. It consists of a paneled dining room whose large, hospitable bar sports a vaguely nautical Polynesian theme. The reasonably priced meals enjoy their own fame, separate from the hotel's, and deservedly so. Starting with fresh vegetables from the inn's garden (which flourishes in this fertile oasis) and quality meat, poultry, and fresh fish, the kitchen sends out simple meals accented with zesty condiment inventions (such as citrus-tinged mustard-herb salad dressing). Lunch choices include fluffy quiche du jour, creamy soups, crunchy salads, and tostadas, plus a variety of hot and cold sandwiches—call ahead if you'd like a sack lunch prepared. Dinner is more robust, featuring grilled meats and fish, seafood sautéed in butter and garlic, and specials such as prime rib on Friday and Saturday.

73950 Inn Ave., Twentynine Palms. ✆ **760/367-3505.** www.29palmsinn.com. Reservations recommended for dinner. Brunch and lunch entrees $6–$14; full dinners $12–$27. AE, DC, DISC, MC, V. Daily 11am–2pm (from 9am Sun); Sun–Thurs 5–9pm; Fri–Sat 5–9:30pm.

10 Picnic & Camping Supplies

SERIOUS GEAR

Experienced climbers in need of backpacking or climbing equipment should step into **Nomad Ventures,** 61795 Twentynine Palms Hwy. (✆ **760/366-4684**), an outfitter located next to the Joshua Tree Visitor Center. Open daily, it rents and sells climbing shoes and sells packs, harnesses, and other necessities. **Joshua Tree Outfitters,** 61707 Twentynine Palms Hwy. (✆ **888/366-1848** or 760/366-1848; www.joshuatreeoutfitters.com), rents camping gear and bouldering pads.

PICNIC SUPPLIES

You can stock up for picnicking or camping on the way into Yucca Valley, where **Walmart, Von's,** and **Stater Brothers** loom large on Hwy. 62, along with every fast-food joint you can imagine. Once you're in Twentynine Palms, try the **Twentynine Palms Market,** 73544 Twentynine Palms Hwy. (✆ **760/367-7216**), across from the chamber of commerce in the Historic Plaza at the northwest corner of Adobe and Two Mile roads. This friendly local market is convenient to the park's north entrance. Both **Crossroads Café and Tavern** and **Ricochet** (see "Where to Dine," above) are good places to pick up sandwiches, salads, and other takeout dishes.

22

Lassen Volcanic National Park, CA

by Eric Peterson

Stashed in the northeastern corner of California, Lassen Volcanic National Park is a remarkable reminder that North America is still evolving and that the ground below is alive with the forces of creation—and sometimes destruction. Lassen Peak is the southernmost volcano in the Cascade Mountain Range, a chain that also includes Mount St. Helens and stretches all the way north to British Columbia.

Though the 10,457-foot Lassen Peak is quiet, the surrounding landscape is very much alive. The peak last awakened in May 1914, beginning a cycle of eruptions that spit lava, steam, and ash until 1921. The eruption climaxed in 1915 when Lassen blasted forth a 6-mile-high mushroom cloud of ash that was seen from hundreds of miles away. Though the peak has not erupted for more than three-quarters of a century, the park's hydrothermal features continue to boil with ferocious intensity; boiling springs, *fumaroles* (vents for volcanic steam and gases), and mud pots are all very active. Volcanologists cannot predict when any of the volcanoes in the area will erupt again, but they are fairly sure such an event will eventually take place.

Until then, the park gives you an interesting chance to watch a landscape recover from the destruction brought on by an eruption. To the north of Lassen Peak is the aptly named Devastated Area, a swath of volcanic scars steadily repopulating with conifers. Forest botanists have revised their earlier theories that forests must be preceded by herbaceous growth after watching the Devastated Area immediately revegetate with a diverse mix of eight conifer species, four more than were present before the blast.

The 106,000-acre park is a place of great beauty. The flora and fauna are an interesting mix of species from the Cascade Range, which stretches north from Lassen; species from the Sierra Nevada, extending south; and species from the Basin Range, to the east. The resulting blend accounts for an enormous diversity of plants, with 745 distinct species identified in the park. Though it's snowbound in winter, Lassen is an important summer feeding ground for black bears and transient herds of mule deer.

In addition to the dozens of volcanoes and geothermal features, Lassen Volcanic National Park includes 150 miles of hiking trails, more than 50 beautiful lakes, large meadows, cinder cones, lush forests, cross-country skiing, and great backcountry camping. In fact, three-quarters of the park is designated wilderness.

Four groups of American Indians inhabited the Lassen area before the arrival of Europeans. The Atsugewi, Maidu, Yana, and Yahi all used portions of the park as their summer hunting grounds. The white man's diseases and encroachment into their territory quickly decimated their population. By the turn of the 20th century, they were thought to be gone from the wilds of the Lassen area. In 1911, however, butchers discovered a nearly naked American Indian man at a slaughterhouse in Oroville. When they couldn't communicate with him, the sheriff locked the man in a cell.

News of the "Wild Man" found a receptive audience among anthropologists at the University of California at Berkeley, who quickly rescued the man. Ishi, as he came to be known, turned out to be the last of the Yahi tribe. He lived at the university's Museum of Anthropology for 5 years before succumbing to tuberculosis. Ishi, who shared his knowledge with anthropologist Alfred Kroeber and others, is responsible for much of what's known about Yahi culture in California.

AVOIDING THE CROWDS

Crowds? Forget it. Lassen is one of the least visited national parks in the Lower 48. Unless you're here on July 4 or Labor Day weekend, you won't encounter anything that could rightly be called a crowd. Even then, you can escape simply by skipping the popular sites, such as Bumpass Hell, Lassen Peak, and the Sulphur Works, and heading a few miles down any of the backcountry trails.

1 Essentials

GETTING THERE & GATEWAYS

Part of the reason Lassen Volcanic National Park is one of the least visited national parks is its remoteness, which is partly perception. The most foolproof route is to take **Calif. 44** east from Redding (on I-5), which leads to the park's northwest entrance. If you're

If You Have Only 1 Day

The highlights of Lassen are the **volcanoes** and their offshoots: boiling springs, fumaroles, mud pots, and so on. You can see many of the most interesting sites in a day, making it possible to visit Lassen as a short detour from I-5 or U.S. 395 on the way to or from Oregon.

Bumpass Hell, a 1.5-mile walk off the main road in the southern part of the park, is the largest hydrothermal site in the park—16 acres of bubbling mud pots cloaked in a stench of rotten egg–smelling sulfur. The colorful name comes from an early Lassen area homesteader guide, K. V. Bumpass, who suffered a severe burn on his leg after falling though thin earth into boiling mud during one of his tours. Don't make the same error.

Sulphur Works is another stinky, steamy example of Lassen's residual heat. Two miles from the southwest park entrance, the ground hisses with seething gases escaping from the ground.

Boiling Springs Lake and **Devils Kitchen** are two of the more remote hydrothermal sites; they're in the Warner Valley section of the park, usually reached from the Feather River Drive/Warner Valley Road near the small town of Chester.

coming from the south along I-5, take Calif. 36 east from Red Bluff, which leads to the park's southwest entrance.

If you're arriving from the east on I-80, take the U.S. 395 turnoff at Reno and head to Susanville. Depending on which end of the park you're shooting for, take either Calif. 44 (to the northwest entrance) or **Calif. 36** (to the southwest entrance) from Susanville.

Calif. 89 leads to the main park road, which crosses the park in a 30-mile half-circle, with entrances and visitor contact stations at either end.

Most visitors enter the park at the **Southwest Entrance Station,** drive through the park, and leave through the **north entrance,** or vice versa. Three other entrances lead to remote portions of the park. **Warner Valley** and **Juniper Lake** are accessible from the south on the road from Chester. The **Butte Lake** entrance is on a dirt road from Calif. 44 between Old Station and Susanville.

THE NEAREST AIRPORT The closest airport is **Redding Municipal Airport,** 6751 Woodrum Circle (✆ **530/224-4320**). It's served by **Horizon Air** and **United Express,** with car rentals from **Avis, Budget,** and **Enterprise.** See chapter 38 for airline/car-rental websites. The closest major airports are in Sacramento and Reno.

INFORMATION

Contact **Lassen Volcanic National Park,** P.O. Box 100, Mineral, CA 96063 (✆ **530/595-4480;** www.nps.gov/lavo). *Peak Experiences* is a free, handy little newspaper listing activities, hikes, and points of interest. Also useful is Larry Eifert's *Lassen Volcanic National Park: Auto Tours, Trips & Trails* (Estuary Press, 2007), which gives a tour of the park from a motorist's viewpoint. These and other books, plus maps and videos, are available from the **Lassen Association** (✆ **530/595-3399;** www.lassenassociation.org).

VISITOR CENTERS

There is a visitor center just inside the northwest entrance at the **Loomis Museum.** The Loomis Museum (daily late June to late Sept) has interpretive exhibits, videos, and leaflets. Ranger-led walks are offered late June to early September.

Just inside the southwest entrance, the terrific new **Kohm Yah-mah-nee Visitor Center** features interpretive exhibits, a bookstore, and a cafe. Named for the Mountain Maidu people's moniker for "Snow Mountain," Kohm Yah-mah-nee is open daily year-round.

The **park headquarters,** on Calif. 36 in Mineral, southwest of the park, offers information and publications Monday to Friday (except holidays) year-round. There are ranger stations at Summit Lake and in the more isolated reaches of the park at Warner Valley, Juniper Lake, and Butte Lake.

FEES & PERMITS

Entry to the park for up to a week costs $10 per vehicle or $5 per person on foot, horse, or bicycle. Camping fees range from $10 to $18. Anyone spending the night in the backcountry must obtain a free **wilderness permit.**

SPECIAL REGULATIONS & WARNINGS

Because of the dangers posed by the park's **thermal features** (specifically the boiling, acidic water), always remain on trails in active areas and heed warning signs. Fires are allowed in campgrounds only. Warm clothing is needed year-round.

SEASONS & CLIMATE

The park is in one of the colder areas of California, and temperatures at night can drop below freezing

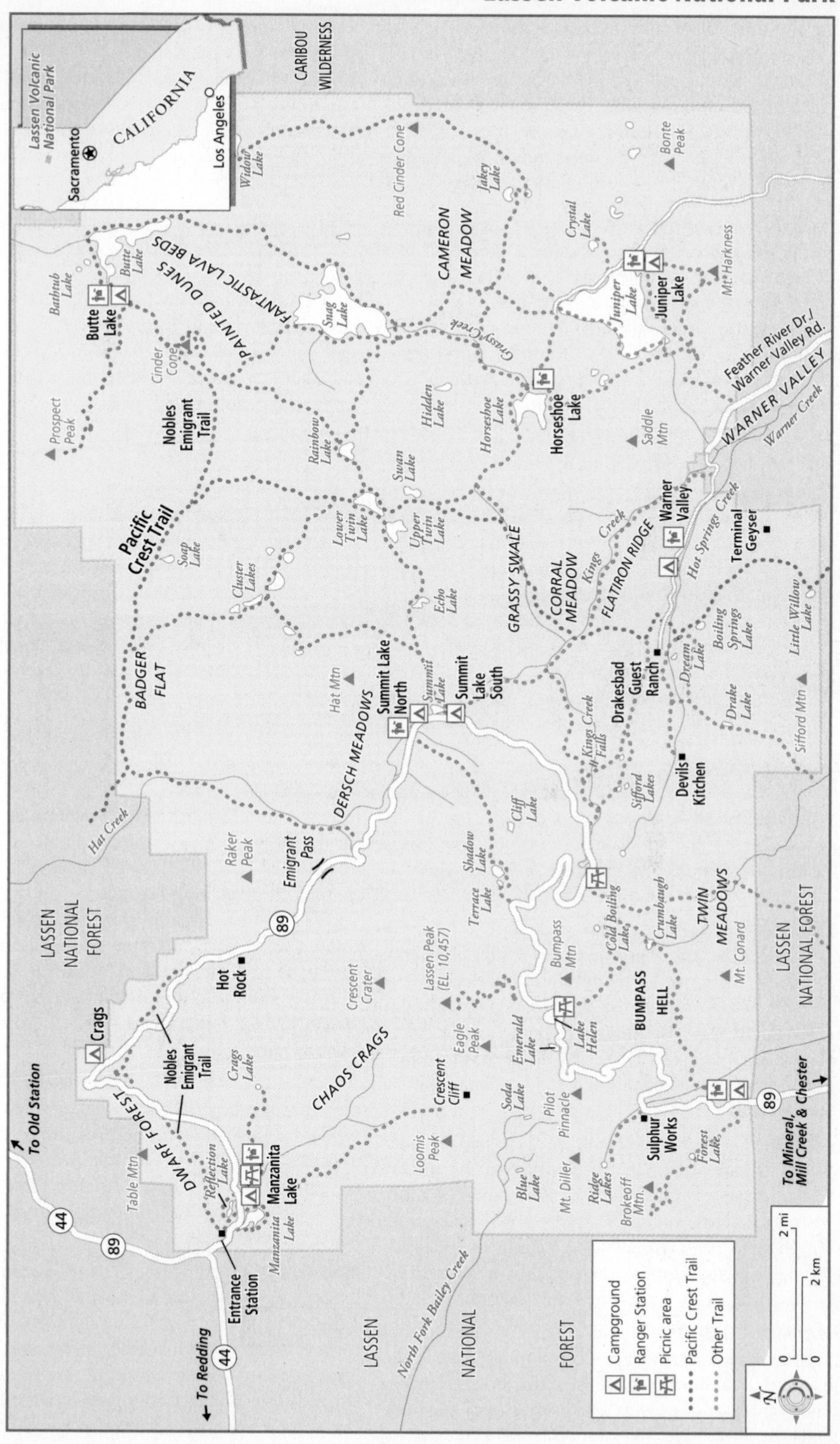

Lassen Volcanic National Park
CALIFORNIA
Sacramento
Los Angeles
CARIBOU WILDERNESS
LASSEN NATIONAL FOREST
LASSEN NATIONAL FOREST
LASSEN NATIONAL FOREST
To Old Station
To Redding
To Mineral, Mill Creek & Chester
Entrance Station
Manzanita Lake
Reflection Lake
Table Mtn
DWARF FOREST
Nobles Emigrant Trail
Crags
Crags Lake
CHAOS CRAGS
Crescent Cliff
Loomis Peak
Hot Rock
Crescent Crater
Lassen Peak (EL. 10,457)
Eagle Peak
Emerald Lake
Lake Helen
Soda Lake
Pilot Pinnacle
Blue Lake
Mt. Diller
Ridge Lakes
Brokeoff Mtn.
Sulphur Works
Forest Lake
BUMPASS HELL
Bumpass Mtn
Cold Boiling Lake
Crumbaugh Lake
TWIN MEADOWS
Mt. Conard
Terrace Lake
Shadow Lake
Cliff Lake
Raker Peak
Emigrant Pass
DERSCH MEADOWS
Hat Creek
BADGER FLAT
Hat Mtn
Summit Lake North
Summit Lake
Summit Lake South
Echo Lake
Cluster Lakes
Soap Lake
Pacific Crest Trail
Nobles Emigrant Trail
Prospect Peak
Cinder Cone
Butte Lake
Bathtub Lake
PAINTED DUNES
FANTASTIC LAVA BEDS
Rainbow Lake
Lower Twin Lake
Upper Twin Lake
Swan Lake
Snag Lake
Widow Lake
Red Cinder Cone
CAMERON MEADOW
Jakey Lake
Hidden Lake
Horseshoe Lake
Grassy Creek
GRASSY SWALE
CORRAL MEADOW
Kings Creek
Kings Creek Falls
FLATIRON RIDGE
Sifford Lakes
Drakesbad Guest Ranch
Devils Kitchen
Warner Valley
Hot Springs Creek
Terminal Geyser
Dream Lake
Drake Lake
Boiling Springs Lake
Little Willow Lake
Sifford Mtn
Saddle Mtn
Crystal Lake
Juniper Lake
Mt. Harkness
Bonte Peak
WARNER VALLEY
Warner Creek
Feather River Dr./ Warner Valley Rd.
North Fork Bailey Creek
Manzanita Lake
44
89
Campground
Ranger Station
Picnic area
Pacific Crest Trail
Other Trail
0
2 mi
0
2 km
N

at any time. Blanketing the area with an average of 500 inches of snow a year, winter can begin in late October, and the main park road can be closed until mid-June. Even in summer, you should be prepared for the possibility of rain and snow. In some years, you might see snowbanks lining the main park road into July. Winter, however, shows a different and beautiful side of Lassen that people are starting to appreciate. Since most of the park is over a mile high and the highest point is 10,457 feet, snow accumulates in incredible quantities. Altitude is also a consideration if you intend to stay in the area—the high elevation can affect some medical conditions.

2 Exploring the Park by Car

The **main park road** crosses the park in a half-circle with entrance stations at either end. It is usually open from mid-June through late November. Most visitors enter the park at the Southwest Entrance Station, drive through, and leave through the northwest entrance, or vice versa.

The 30-mile tour through this rugged yet captivating region should take no more than a couple of hours, though it's a good idea to factor in a few more hours to hike up Lassen Peak or explore the Devastated Area and Bumpass Hell. If there's time, make an effort to stop at Sulphur Works near Mineral (about 2 miles from the southwest entrance), an acrid, noisy cauldron of steam vents that let off a mighty pungent odor.

3 Organized Tours & Ranger Programs

Free interpretive programs take place daily in summer, highlighting everything from flora and fauna to cultural history and volcanic processes. Junior Ranger programs are offered to kids aged 7 to 12; check park bulletin boards or the park's website or newspaper for a current schedule.

From January to early April, a park ranger leads free 1½- to 2-hour snowshoe hikes across Lassen's snow-packed hills. The tours begin on Saturday at 1:30pm at the park's southwest entrance. You must be at least 8 years old, warmly dressed, and wearing boots. Snowshoes are provided free of charge on a first-come, first-served basis, though a small donation ($1) is requested for upkeep. For details, call park headquarters (✆ **530/595-4480**).

4 Day Hikes

Most visitors drive through in a day or two, see the hydrothermal hot spots, and move on. That leaves 150 miles of trails and expanses of backcountry to the few who take the time to get off-road.

Bumpass Hell Trail This walk leads you to the middle of the largest geothermal site west of Yellowstone—16 acres of bubbling mud pots cloaked in a stench of sulfur. Stay on the wooden boardwalks that guide you past the pyrite pools, steam vents, and noisy fumaroles. 3 miles RT. Moderate. Access: Well-marked trail head just off the main park road in the southern part of the park.

Cinder Cone Trail Black and charred, Cinder Cone is almost barren, but surrounded by picturesque dunes of multihued volcanic ash. If 4 miles seems too short, you can extend the hike by heading in about 8 miles from Summit Lake on the Park Road or by diverting to the east side of Butte Lake. 4 miles RT. Moderate. Access: Butte Lake Campground.

Lassen Peak Trail This climb to the top of Lassen Peak is among the most popular hikes in the park. The distance may seem short, but the trail is steep and partially covered with snow until late summer. At 10,457 feet in elevation, you'll get a view of the surrounding wilderness that's worth every step. On clear days you can see the Sacramento Valley to the south and Mount Shasta and the Trinity Alps to the north. Every 5 to 7 years, millions of California tortoiseshell butterflies ascend Lassen to escape the summer heat, making for quite a spectacle. With a steep 2,000-foot elevation gain, the round-trip takes about 4 to 5 hours, and often longer for those unaccustomed to high elevation. Keep an eye out for lightning storms on and near the summit. 5 miles RT. Strenuous. Access: 7 miles from the southwest entrance on the main park road.

Manzanita Lake Trail This trek runs along the shoreline of pretty Manzanita Lake, which is 2 miles inside the northwest entrance to the park. It's easy to get to by car, and an easy hike for almost anyone. (If you want a bit more distance, you can hike around Reflection Lake as well.) 1.5 miles RT. Easy. Access: Loomis Museum.

Nobles Emigrant Trail One of the park's easiest longer hikes is this scenic trail that passes though an old-growth forest, past Chaos Jumbles (pink-hued rocks shaken from volcanoes 300 years ago), and into Lassen's Dwarf Forest, a bizarre region of stunted trees. The trail continues into the northeastern edge of the park for overnight trips. Trail length varies. Easy. Access: Northwest entrance.

Pacific Crest Trail This is a small section of the Pacific Crest Trail, which runs some 2,650 miles from Mexico to Canada. The most scenic section of the trail in the park is the 5-mile segment south of Drakesbad that leads toward the park's boundary past Boiling Springs Lake. For information on the Pacific Crest Trail, contact the **Pacific Crest Trail Association,** 5325 Elkhorn Blvd., PMB #256, Sacramento, CA 95842 (✆ **916/349-2109;** www.pcta.org). 17.8 miles one-way. Moderate. Access: Warner Valley Rd., or long hike from Hat Lake.

Paradise Meadow This hike rises at a steady grade along a creek, eventually coming to a series of small waterfalls and a picture-perfect meadow with outstanding wildflower displays during midsummer. 2.8 miles RT. Moderate. Access: Hat Lake parking area, off Calif. 89 btw. Emigrant Pass and Summit Lake campgrounds.

Summit Lake Trail This is a walk around a pristine alpine lake that's often frequented by deer in the evening. 1.5 miles RT. Easy. Access: Either Summit Lake campground.

Summit Lake to Echo and Twin Lakes A popular day or overnight hike, this trek passes several lakes and wildflower-filled meadows on the way to Lower Twin Lake. After you pass the first moderately steep crest, the rest of the hike is less strenuous. Backcountry camping is allowed at Twin Lakes but not at Echo Lake; a wilderness permit is required. 8 miles RT. Moderate. Access: From midpoint of the Summit Lake Trail (see above).

5 Other Sports & Activities

CANOEING & KAYAKING Paddlers can take canoes, rowboats, and kayaks on any of the park lakes except Reflection, Emerald, Helen, and Boiling Springs. Motors, including electric motors, are prohibited on all park waters. Lakes accessible from the main park road include Manzanita and Summit. You can get to Butte Lake, in the northeast section of the park, on a gravel road from Calif. 44. Juniper Lake is accessible from a gravel road in the southeast section of the park.

WINTER SPORTS & ACTIVITIES

The main park road usually closes to cars in late October due to snow, and most years it doesn't open until June, so winter recreationists have their run of the area. Snowmobiles are forbidden.

CROSS-COUNTRY SKIING & SNOWSHOEING Trails of all skill levels leave from the northwest and southwest entrances. Heated bathrooms and running water are available at Loomis Plaza at Manzanita Lake and in the new Kohm Yah-mahnee Visitor Center, which opened at the end of 2008. Popular trips are the trails to Sulphur Works. More advanced skiers and snowshoers can make the trek to Lake Helen.

You can also ski the popular 30-mile course of the main park road, but doing this overnight trek involves a long car shuttle. For safety reasons, the park requires all skiers to register at the southwest entrance or Loomis Ranger Station before heading into the backcountry, even for a day trip. A free wilderness permit is required for overnight camping.

SLEDDING During winter, heavy snows close the main road through the park, but roads going into both the southwest and northwest entrances are kept open for a mile or two. On weekends, you can bring the family, snow toys, and picnic baskets to enjoy the slopes.

6 Camping

Car campers have their choice of eight park campgrounds with over 400 sites. Reservations for Manzanita Lake, Summit Lake, and Butte Lake campgrounds are available through the **National Recreation Reservation Service** (✆ **877/444-6777;** www.recreation.gov). Sites do fill up on weekends, so if you don't have a reservation, your best bet is to get to the park early Friday to secure a spot. There are no RV hookups at the park, but you'll find them at nearby private campgrounds, as well as **Lassen Mineral Lodge** (see "Where to Stay," below).

By far the most "civilized" campground in the park is at **Manzanita Lake,** where you'll find flush toilets and a camper store. There is also the **Crags Campground,** about 5 miles away, which is much more basic, with vault toilets. Farther into the park along the main park road is the **Summit Lake Campgrounds,** on the north and south ends of Summit Lake, where you'll find flush toilets in the north campground and vault toilets in the south campground. It's a pretty spot, often frequented by deer, and is a launching point for some excellent day hikes. In the southern end of the park is **Southwest Campground,** a walk-in camp directly adjacent to the southwest entrance parking lot and the park's only year-round campground.

The remote entrances to Lassen have their own campgrounds: **Warner Valley, Butte Lake,** and **Juniper Lake** campgrounds. All are reached on dirt roads, and Warner Valley and Juniper Lake are not

Campground	Elev.	Total Sites	RV Hookups	Dump Station	Toilets
Butte Lake	6,100	101	No	No	Yes
Crags	5,700	45	No	No	Yes
Juniper Lake	6,792	18	No	No	Yes
Manzanita Lake	5,890	179	No	Yes	Yes
Southwest	6,700	21	No	No	Yes
Summit Lake (North)	6,695	46	No	No	Yes
Summit Lake (South)	6,695	48	No	No	Yes
Warner Valley	5,650	18	No	No	Yes

Note: Campgrounds usually open in May or June and close in Sept or Oct, but weather can affect dates; call the park for current information.

recommended for trailers. All campgrounds except Juniper Lake have potable water in the summer.

Backcountry camping is allowed in much of the park, and traffic is light. Ask about closed areas when you get your free wilderness permit, which is issued at the visitor stations and required for anyone spending the night in the backcountry. Fires and dogs are prohibited in the backcountry.

If park campgrounds are full, myriad campgrounds are available in surrounding **Lassen National Forest,** so you'll find a site somewhere. For information, contact the Forest Supervisor's Office, 2550 Riverside Dr., Susanville, CA 96130 (✆ **530/257-2151;** www.fs.fed.us/r5/lassen).

7 Where to Stay

INSIDE THE PARK

Drakesbad Guest Ranch The only lodge operating in Lassen Volcanic National Park is Drakesbad, hidden in a high mountain valley and surrounded by meadows, lakes, and streams. The 100-year-old Drakesbad is famous for its rustic cabins, lodge, and steaming thermal swimming pool, fed by a natural hot spring. Horseback riding is also a big draw. The ranch is as deluxe as a facility with very little electricity and no phones can be, with quilts on every bed, propane heaters for warmth, and kerosene lamps for light. Food is hearty American fare, with an emphasis on fresh fruits and vegetables, and often creative variations on standard dishes. Breakfast and lunch are buffets (sack lunches are also available), and dinners are served at the table. The lodge is very popular, so reservations are booked as far as 2 years in advance.

Warner Valley Rd. (Mailing address: California Guest Services, 2150 Main St., Ste. 5, Red Bluff, CA 96080.) ✆ **530/529-1512.** www.drakesbad.com. 19 units. $155–$176 per person double. Rates include all meals and activities. Discounts available in fall. MC, V. Closed mid-Oct to early June. From Chester, enter southern part of the park on Warner Valley Rd., which ends at the ranch.

NEAR THE PARK

The Bidwell House In 1901, Gen. John Bidwell, a California senator who made three unsuccessful bids for the presidency, built a country retreat and summer home for his beloved young wife, Annie. After her death, when Chester had developed into a prosperous logging hamlet, the building, with its farmhouse-style design and spacious veranda, was converted into the headquarters for a local ranch.

The house sits at the eastern end of Chester, adjacent to a rolling meadow. The lake is visible across the road, and inside, Eva and Filip Laboda maintain one of the most charming B&B inns in the region. Seven of the rooms have whirlpool tubs, and three offer wood-burning stoves. The cottage (which sleeps up to six) has a full kitchen. The gourmet omelets are a breakfast favorite.

1 Main St. (P.O. Box 1790), Chester, CA 96020. ✆ **530/258-3338.** www.bidwellhouse.com. 14 units, 12 with private bathroom; 1 cottage. TEL. $85–$175 double. Rates include full breakfast. MC, V.

Lassen Mineral Lodge A mere 9 miles south of the park's southern entrance, this family-owned and -operated lodge (established in 1896) offers a homey atmosphere in a delightful forest setting. The motel-style rooms, constructed in the 1940s, are comfortable. Most have king or queen beds; several larger rooms also have two twin beds and kitchenettes, making them a good choice for families. In summer, the lodge is almost always bustling with guests and customers who venture into the gift shop, general store, and full-service **restaurant and bar** (see "Where to Dine," below). There's good fishing within walking distance. Also on the property is a full-service RV park and campground ($18–$22).

38348 Calif. 36 East (P.O. Box 160), Mineral, CA 96063. ✆ **530/595-4422.** Fax 530/595-4452. www.minerallodge.com. 20 units. $72–$100 double. AE, DISC, MC, V.

Drinking Water	Showers	Fire Pits/ Grills	Laundry	Reserve	Fees	Open
Yes	No	Yes	No	Yes	$16	June–Oct
Yes	No	Yes	No	No	$12	May–Sept
No	No	Yes	No	No	$10	June–Sept
Yes	Yes	Yes	Yes	Yes	$18	May–Oct
Yes	No	Yes	No	No	$14	Year-round
Yes	No	Yes	No	Yes	$18	July–Sept
Yes	No	Yes	No	Yes	$16	July–Oct
Yes	No	Yes	No	No	$14	Year-round

Mill Creek Resort Set deep in the forest, the Mill Creek is a rustic mountain retreat that is well off the beaten path. A homey country general store and diner serve as the resort's center, a good place to stock up on food while exploring Lassen Volcanic National Park. The housekeeping cabins, available on a daily or weekly basis, are basic but cute, furnished with rustic wooden lodgepole beds. All of the cabins have kitchens. The campground here is open May through October; RV sites are $25 nightly, tent sites $16.

Calif. 172 (3 miles south of Calif. 36), Mill Creek, CA 96061. ✆ **888/595-4449** or 530/595-4449. www.millcreekresort.net. 9 cabins. $80–$110 cabin. No credit cards. Pets accepted.

The Weston House Located 19 miles west of Lassen's northwest entrance, the Weston House is a modern, Big Sur–style B&B in a spectacular forested location above a wild horse sanctuary. Sumptuous views of the upper Sacramento Valley abound, from each room and from the massive redwood deck, which has a lap pool and whirlpool tub. The rooms are uniquely decorated with antiques and art. I like Jennifer's Room, spacious with a full private bathroom, queen-size and twin beds, sofa, love seat, TV/DVD player, and woodstove. Vanessa's Room has a private deck, and Helen's features a kitchenette. The gourmet breakfast might include frittatas or croissant French toast, accompanied by fresh fruit and beverages. The inn is nonsmoking and family-friendly.

6741 Red Rock Rd. (P.O. Box 276), Shingletown, CA 96088. ✆ **530/474-3738.** www.westonhouse.com. 4 units. $155–$195 double. Rates include full breakfast. MC, V. Pets accepted ($25 one-time fee). Located 1½ miles south of Calif. 44 via Shingletown Ridge Rd.

8 Where to Dine

INSIDE THE PARK

There is a **cafe** at the new **Kohm Yah-mah-nee Visitor Center.** Hours are 9am to 5pm fall to spring and 9am to 6pm in the summer. There's also a **snack bar,** with sandwiches, hot dogs, and the like, at the **Manzanita Lake Camper Store** (✆ **530/335-7557**), at the park's north entrance. It's open late May to early October, daily from 8am to 8pm in midsummer, 9am to 5pm at the beginning and end of the season.

NEAR THE PARK

Restaurant choices in the area are limited. The best approach may be to stay at a B&B or lodge that offers meals or to book a room (or stay at a campsite) where you can prepare your own. See "Where to Stay" and "Camping," above.

A few eateries are fairly close to the park, primarily in Chester and on the shores of Lake Almanor. From the south entrance, the closest restaurant is the **Lassen Mineral Lodge** (see "Where to Stay," above), which serves three meals of basic American fare a day, plus a few Italian, Mexican, and vegetarian items. You can also head southeast on Calif. 36 to Chester and dine at the **Kopper Kettle Café,** 243 Main St. (✆ **530/258-2698**), for a hearty breakfast, or the **Knotbumper,** 274 Main St. (✆ **530/258-2301**), for lunch or dinner. Another solid option in Chester is the **Red Onion Grill,** 384 Main St. (✆ **530/258-1800**), which has an eclectic menu that includes Cajun salmon, steaks, and Italian fare.

On the Lake Almanor Peninsula, **Tantardino's,** 401 Ponderosa Dr. (✆ **530/596-3902**), is a time-tested pizzeria and Italian restaurant. For a fancy dinner, locals head to **Gamboni's Peninsula Grill,** 401 Peninsula Dr. (✆ **530/596-3538**), for steaks, seafood, and pasta dishes.

9 Picnic & Camping Supplies

The **Manzanita Lake Camper Store** (✆ **530/335-7557**), at the park's north entrance, is a good place to stock up on groceries, ice, firewood, and basic outdoor gear. It also sells gasoline.

At the southern end of the park, you'll find just about everything you need for your outdoor adventure in the old-fashioned general store at **Lassen Mineral Lodge,** on Calif. 36 in Mineral (see "Where to Stay," above).

North of the park, just south of Old Station, try the store at **Hat Creek Resort,** on Calif. 89 (© **530/335-7121;** www.hatcreekresortrv.com), where you'll also find a restaurant, an RV park, and an assortment of cabins and motel rooms.

23

Mesa Verde, Hovenweep, Chaco & Other Archaeological Sites of the Four Corners Region

by Don & Barbara Laine

With about 4,700 archaeological sites, Mesa Verde National Park is the largest archaeological preserve in the United States. Among the sites are some of the largest cliff dwellings in the world, as well as mesa-top pueblos, pit houses, and *kivas* (subterranean rooms used for meetings and religious ceremonies)—all of which were built by the ancestral Puebloans (also called the Anasazi). The sites here tell the story of a 750-year period (A.D. 550–1300) during which these people shifted from a seminomadic hunter-gatherer lifestyle to a largely agrarian way of life centered on large communities in cliff dwellings.

Mesa Verde must have looked inviting to the ancestral Puebloans, whose descendants are such modern Pueblo tribes as the Hopi, Zuni, and Acoma. On the mesa's north side, 2,000-foot-high cliffs form a natural barrier to invaders. The mesa slopes gently to the south, and erosion has carved numerous canyons, most of which receive abundant sunlight and have natural overhangs for shelter.

The ancestral Puebloans became adept at surviving here. The mesa tops were covered with *loess,* a red, wind-blown soil good for farming. And although water was scarce, it could seep into the sandstone overhangs where they eventually made their homes. For food, they farmed beans, corn, and squash; raised turkeys; foraged in the pinyon-juniper woodland; and hunted for game such as cottontail rabbits and deer. They wove sandals and clothing from yucca fibers and traded for precious stones and shells, which they used to make jewelry.

To the visitor today, their most impressive accomplishments are the multistory cliff dwellings, which were largely ignored until ranchers Charlie Mason and Richard Wetherill chanced upon them in 1888. Looting of artifacts followed their discovery until a Denver newspaper reporter's stories aroused national interest in protecting them. In 1906, the 52,000-acre site was declared a national park, the only U.S. national park devoted entirely to the works of humans.

The **Cliff Palace,** the park's largest and best-known site, is a four-story apartment complex with stepped-back roofs forming courtyards for the dwellings above. Accessible by guided tour only, it is accessible by a quarter-mile downhill path. Its towers, walls, and kivas are all set back beneath the rim of a cliff. Another ranger-led tour takes visitors up a 32-foot ladder to explore the interior of **Balcony House.** Each of these tours runs only in summer and fall.

Two other important sites—**Step House** and **Long House,** both on Wetherill Mesa—are open to visitors in summer only. Rangers lead tours to **Spruce Tree House,** a major cliff-dwelling complex, only in winter, when other park facilities are closed; during the summer, you can see Spruce Tree House on your own.

What's in a Name?

The prehistoric inhabitants of the ancient villages of the Four Corners region have long been known as the **Anasazi.** That word is being phased out, however, in favor of the term **"ancestral Puebloans,"** because modern American Indians who trace their roots to the ancestral Puebloans consider the word *Anasazi* demeaning. *Anasazi* is a Navajo word that means, at least according to some sources, "enemy of my people" (the Navajos considered the ancestral Puebloans their enemies). Some are also using the term "ancient Pueblo people."

Desert Safety Advice from an Expert

Frommer's author Ethan Wolff did a Four Corners roadtrip for *Frommer's MTV USA Roadtrips*, and his experience living and traveling in the area gave him the knowledge on how to stay comfortable and safe in the Southwest desert. He says: A few of my friends scoffed when I told them I was off to the southwest in July. Desert summers are indeed extreme, but the Four Corners can be a lot easier to enjoy than, say, Phoenix. My biggest issue turned out to be the cold—while the rest of the west was wilting under 117 degrees, I was underdressed and shivering through 55° Santa Fe nights. Elevation is the big factor. Flagstaff, Santa Fe, and the South Rim of the Grand Canyon are all around 7,000 feet, so you can expect reasonable temperatures there. Lower stretches, like Moab, can get hellishly hot, but that doesn't mean they can't be enjoyed. The west has low humidity, so shade is a lot more useful than it is back east, and temperatures often drop significantly overnight. Mornings can also be quite cool, with the hottest part of the day coming in late afternoon and early evening, after the earth has baked all day. If you plan on heavy hiking, try to get as early a start as possible. In the afternoons, lie low in the shadows, hit the pool, or rack up some miles with the car's A.C. cranking. Evenings are also great times to explore. As an added bonus for avoiding midday, you'll catch "magic hour," when the sun's angles shade the rocks and canyons in extraordinary ways. No matter what the temperature, there are a few precautions you must take in the desert:

- During lightning storms, avoid being the tallest object around (stay away from lone trees, high ridges, and cliff edges).
- Sunscreen and sunglasses are essential, as are wide-brimmed hats (not baseball caps).
- Hikers should carry at least a gallon of water per person per day.
- Water alone isn't enough: Backpacks should also be filled with energy bars, fruit, and trail mix.
- If you drink too much water too fast, you risk water intoxication, which can be fatal.
- Salty snacks and sports drinks such as Gatorade can help keep electrolytes balanced.

For reasons not yet understood, these cliff homes were fully occupied for only about a century; their residents left around 1300.

Although Mesa Verde is the largest and probably the most impressive archaeological site in the Four Corners region, it is not the only one. In fact, archaeologists say that from about 700 to 1,000 years ago, this area teemed with busy communities. Following the discussion of Mesa Verde is a quick look at a few of the other important archaeological attractions in the region.

AVOIDING THE CROWDS

With close to 500,000 visitors annually, Mesa Verde seems packed at times. But park officials point out that the numbers are much lower just before and after the summer rush. June 15 to August 15 is the high summer visitation period. Visitors during the first 2 weeks of June or the last 2 weeks of August encounter fewer crowds.

Another way to beat the crowds is to make the 12-mile drive to Wetherill Mesa. In one recent year, only 5% of the park's visitors—just over 30,000 people—ventured to the mesa, which has some of the park's most interesting archaeological sites. The third and perhaps best way to beat the crowds is to hike one of the backcountry trails. As one former park ranger told us, "With our backcountry closed to camping, our hiking trails aren't used very much, and these are great ways for people to get away."

1 Essentials

GETTING THERE & GATEWAYS

Mesa Verde National Park is in southwestern Colorado, just under 400 miles southwest of Denver and 252 miles northwest of Albuquerque. The park entrance is on U.S. 160, 10 miles east of the town of Cortez and 6 miles west of Mancos.

From Cortez, **U.S. 491** (formerly U.S. 666) runs north to Monticello, Utah (and on to Salt Lake City), and south to Gallup, New Mexico (on I-40). **U.S. 160** runs east through Durango to Walsenburg and I-25, and west through the Four Corners area into Arizona. At the east end of town, **Colo. 145,** which runs north to Telluride and Grand Junction, intersects U.S. 160.

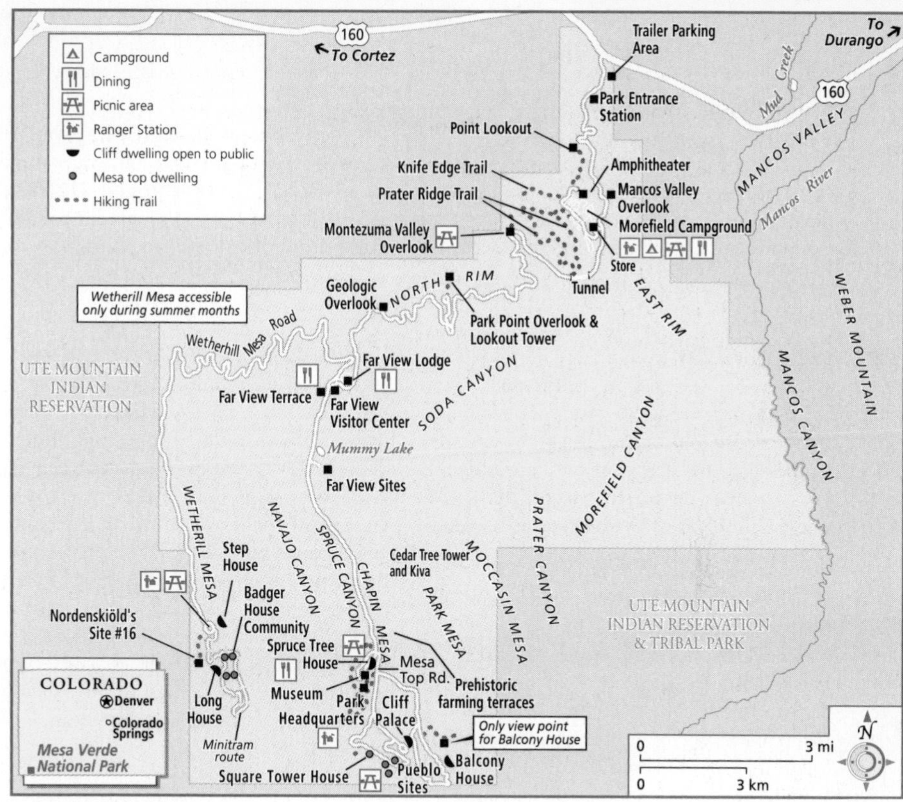

THE NEAREST AIRPORT **Cortez Municipal Airport** (✆ **970/565-7458;** www.cityofcortez.com), about 3 miles southwest of town off U.S. 491 and U.S. 160, is served by **Great Lakes Airlines,** which offers daily service between Cortez and Denver and has rental cars from **Hertz** and **Budget.** See chapter 38 for websites of the major airlines and rental-car firms.

INFORMATION

Contact **Mesa Verde National Park,** P.O. Box 8, Mesa Verde N.P., CO 81330-0008 (✆ **970/529-4465;** www.nps.gov/meve). Books on the park are available from the **Mesa Verde Museum Association,** P.O. Box 38, Mesa Verde, CO 81330 (✆ **800/305-6053** or 970/529-4445; www.mesaverde.org).

For area information, stop at the **Colorado Welcome Center at Cortez,** Cortez City Park, 928 E. Main St. (✆ **970/565-3414**), open daily from 8am to 6pm in summer and from 8am to 5pm the rest of the year; or contact the **Mesa Verde Country Visitor Information Bureau,** P.O. Box HH, Cortez, CO 81321 (✆ **800/253-1616;** www.mesaverdecountry.com), or the **Cortez Area Chamber of Commerce,** P.O. Box 968, Cortez, CO 81321 (✆ **970/565-3414;** www.cortezchamber.org).

VISITOR CENTERS

The **Far View Visitor Center,** 14 miles southwest of the park entrance, is the only place that sells tickets for ranger-guided hikes. It has an information desk, a display of American Indian art, and a small bookstore. It's open from early April to mid-October only, from 8am to 7pm daily at the height of summer, and closes at 5pm at the beginning and end of the season.

The staff at the small **Morefield Ranger Station** in Morefield Village also provides park information. It's open in summer only, usually during the afternoon and early evening.

The **Chapin Mesa Archaeological Museum,** open daily year-round (8am–6:30pm from early Apr to mid-Oct, until 5pm the rest of the year), has dioramas and interpretive displays on Pueblo culture, a ranger-staffed information desk, and a bookstore.

FEES

Admission to the park for up to 1 week for private vehicles costs $15 from Memorial Day weekend through Labor Day weekend and $10 the rest of the year; rates for motorcyclists are $8 and $5, respectively. There are also fees for guided tours (see "Organized Tours & Ranger Programs," below).

Keeping Fido Safe & Happy

Human visitors to Mesa Verde National Park have plenty to do, but the U.S. Park Service is not very welcoming to our canine friends and prohibits them on all trails (the only exceptions are for service dogs). If you want to explore the park, you'll need to leave your dogs behind. Fortunately, the area has several kennels, including the **Dog Hotel,** 33350 Colo. 184, Mancos (✆ **970/882-5416;** tomoverington@gmail.com), which is a well-run facility that also offers accommodations for cats. Appointments are necessary, and pet owners must have proof of current vaccinations.

GETTING AROUND

The Park Service operates a **minitram** in the Wetherill Mesa area during the summer season. It runs from the Kiosk to the main archaeological sites and is a time-saver, because your only other choice is to hike; cars aren't permitted beyond the Kiosk. Check at the visitor center for the current schedule.

SPECIAL REGULATIONS & WARNINGS

To protect the many park's archaeological sites, the Park Service has outlawed backcountry camping and off-trail hiking. It's also illegal to enter cliff dwellings without a ranger present. All artifacts and archaeological sites are protected by federal law.

The Wetherill Mesa Road cannot accommodate vehicles over 25 feet. Cyclists must have lights to pedal through the tunnel on the entrance road.

In 2005, park officials announced that a rock squirrel in the park had tested positive for **plague,** the first occurrence of the potentially deadly disease since 1993. Plague is transmitted by fleas, so visitors are advised to use insect repellent on their shoes and socks and the lower sections of their pants, and to treat pets with flea repellent. Diagnosed early, plague can be treated successfully.

SEASONS & CLIMATE

With an average annual precipitation of just 18 inches, Mesa Verde remains dry despite being between 6,000 and 8,572 feet high. June is the driest month, with just over ½ inch of rain, and August is the wettest, with 2 inches. The park typically receives 80 inches of snow in a season. Summer temperatures tend to be about 10° cooler than in the nearby Montezuma Valley. Even during July, the hottest month, highs average an easily bearable 87°F (30°C), and nighttime lows dip into the mid-50s (lower teens Celsius). In winter, temperatures on the mesa can sometimes be 10° warmer than in the valley. This happens during calm, clear periods when cold air is trapped in the lowlands. Daytime highs on the mesa average in the low 40s (single digits Celsius) in December, January, and February.

Because winter storms often continue well into March, spring tends to come late. Warm autumns, however, are not uncommon. In April, average temperatures are 5° cooler than in October, with 60s (teens Celsius) for highs and 30s (single digits Celsius) for lows.

2 Exploring the Park by Car

The main scenic drive in the park is the **Mesa Top Loop Road.** Each of the 10 stops along this 6-mile loop either overlooks cliff dwellings or is a short walk from mesa-top dwellings. The sites date from A.D. 675 to 1275 and include structures from the three Pueblo periods. By reading the panels at each site, you can learn about the developments in architecture and the changes in Pueblo culture during those periods. Highlights include the **Square Tower House Viewpoint,** where binoculars are handy for spotting the myriad cliff dwellings in the canyon; **Sun Point Pueblo,** where a tunnel links a *kiva*—a subterranean room used in ceremonies—to a lookout tower; and the mysterious **Sun Temple,** a D-shaped structure that may have been a shrine or community gathering area.

On your way back to the Far View Visitor Center, consider stopping at the **Far View Sites Complex,** 1 mile south of the visitor center; six sites are within walking distance, including what seem to be the remains of an ancient reservoir.

3 Organized Tours & Ranger Programs

Three of the park's spectacular cliff dwellings—Cliff Palace, Balcony House, and Long House—can be visited only during ranger-guided tours. Tickets ($3) go on sale daily at 8am at the Far View Visitor Center. Visitors may tour Long House and either Cliff Palace or Balcony House on the same day, but may not tour both Cliff Palace and Balcony House in a day. We suggest that first-time visitors with only

1 day to spend here tour Cliff Palace, the largest site in the park.

Departing every half-hour between 9am and 6pm in summer (shorter hours in spring and fall, and hourly until early May and after mid-October), the ¼-mile **Cliff Palace** tour involves a 100-vertical-foot descent to the dwelling and a climb to the same height to exit. In between, you'll have to scale four 10-foot-high ladders. The effort is well worth it. With 151 rooms and 23 kivas, Cliff Palace is the largest cliff dwelling in the Southwest and one of the largest in the world. Especially striking is the original red-and-white wall painting that remains inside a four-story tower.

Merely reaching the 45-room **Balcony House,** the most fortresslike of the Mesa Verde dwellings, will make you appreciate the agility of the ancestral Puebloans, who used hand- and footholds and log ladders to scale the cliffs. During the tour, you'll descend 90 vertical feet of stairs, climb 32- and 20-foot-long ladders, and slip through a narrow 12-foot-long crawl space. When you do reach the dwelling, you'll be standing on a level stone floor 700 feet above the floor of Soda Canyon. The Puebloans dumped tons of fill inside 15-foot-high stone retaining walls below this floor, creating a level surface on which to build. Tours run every half-hour between 9am and 5pm in summer, less frequently at the beginning and end of the season.

Some people remember the **Long House** tour for its ¾-mile walk, the flight of 52 stairs, and the two 15-foot-high ladders they have to negotiate. Others will recall the dwelling itself, with its 21 kivas and 150 rooms stretching across a long alcove in Rock Canyon. At its center is a large plaza where the community gathered and danced. Granaries are tucked like mud dauber nests into two smaller alcoves (one above the other) to the rear of the large one. The 90-minute tours meet at the Wetherill Mesa Kiosk and run regularly from 10am to 4pm.

Cliff Palace tours run from early April to early November, a few weeks longer than the season for Balcony House. Wetherill Mesa, site of Long House, is open only from Memorial Day weekend through Labor Day. To replace these attractions during the off season, the park offers free ranger-guided tours of Spruce Tree House, a self-guided area in summer. Call the park to find out the exact dates of the tour season.

In summer, rangers also lead 90-minute **evening tours** of Cliff Palace. The 7pm tours are limited to 20 people and cost $10 per person. Tickets are available at the Far View Visitor Center. Four-hour **bus tours** include short hikes to sites along the Mesa Top Loop and a walking tour of Cliff Palace. Cost is $49 adults, $38 children 5 to 12, and free for children under 5 with a paying adult.

Also in summer, rangers lead **free walks** daily and present **evening programs** at Morefield Campground and Far View lodge. Schedules are available at the Far View Visitor Center and Chapin Mesa Museum.

4 Day Hikes

Although none of the trails to the Mesa Verde sites is strenuous, the 7,000-foot elevation can be tiring for visitors who aren't used to the altitude.

SHORTER TRAILS ON CHAPIN MESA

Spruce Tree House Open from 8:30am to 6:30pm daily during summer, this paved trail descends from behind the Chapin Mesa Museum to Spruce Tree House, a dwelling with 130 rooms and 8 kivas. Because Spruce Tree House sits in an 89-foot-deep alcove, this is the best-preserved dwelling at Mesa Verde. Rangers are here to answer questions during high season. Off season, they guide tours here. The trail is accessible to the mobility impaired, although they may require assistance on some of its grades. .25 mile one-way. Easy. Access: Chapin Mesa Museum.

ON WETHERILL MESA

Badger House Community Trail This trail visits mesa-top sites on Wetherill Mesa. Usually uncrowded, the gravel and paved trail is accessible from one of three minitram stops or by making a

If You Have Only 1 Day

If you have only a day to spend at the park, stop first at the Far View Visitor Center to buy tickets for a late-afternoon tour of either **Cliff Palace** or **Balcony House**—visitors are not allowed to tour both on the same day. Then travel to the **Chapin Mesa Museum** for a look at the history behind the sites you're about to see. From there, walk down the trail behind the museum to **Spruce Tree House.** Lunch at Spruce Tree Terrace, and then take the **Mesa Top Loop Road.** Cap your day with the guided tour. If time permits, you may wish to stop at **Far View Sites** on your way out of the park.

longer walk from the parking area. The 12-stop self-guided tour details 600 years of history. 2.5 miles RT. Easy. Access: Wetherill Mesa Kiosk.

Nordenskiold's Site No. 16 Trail Begin this quiet hike by taking the minitram to its trail head or walking from the parking area. Mostly flat, the dirt trail descends over rocks for the last few yards before it reaches an overlook of Site No. 16, a 50-room cliff dwelling that was occupied for most of the 13th century. On the way, the self-guided tour identifies many of the plants in the area. 1 mile RT. Easy. Access: Wetherill Mesa Kiosk.

Step House This loop descends roughly 75 feet of stairs and switchbacks to Step House, a cliff dwelling that dates from A.D. 1226. Three modified pit houses dating from 626 sit to the left of Step House (as you look toward it). A set of prehistoric stone stairs climbs from these dwellings toward a break in the cliffs. .5 mile RT. Moderate. Access: Wetherill Mesa Kiosk.

NEAR MOREFIELD CAMPGROUND

Knife Edge Trail This trail follows the old Knife Edge Road, the only automobile route into the park until a tunnel was blasted between Prater and Morefield canyons in 1957. Now, during wet years, wildflowers brighten the old roadbed, which hugs the side of Prater Ridge on one side and drops off all the way to the Montezuma Valley on the other. A self-guided tour identifies many of the plant species along the trail. From the end of this trail, you can watch the sun set behind Sleeping Ute Mountain. 2 miles RT. Easy. Access: Near Morefield Village.

Point Lookout Trail This trail rises in tight switchbacks from the northeast corner of the campground to the top of Point Lookout, a monument conspicuous from near the park's entrance. It then traverses the top of this butte to a stunning overlook of the Montezuma Valley. Sheer drops in several places make the trail unsuitable for small children. 2.2 miles RT. Moderate. Access: Near Morefield Village.

Prater Ridge Trail This loop rises 700 feet from the campground's west side to the top of Prater Ridge. Once atop the ridge, the trail forks, looping around the top of the mesa and opening onto views of the Montezuma and Mancos valleys and the La Plata Mountains. A cutoff trail halves the mesa-top loop, which zigzags around a number of side canyons. Because the trail is faint in places where it crosses the sandstone, some route-finding skills may be necessary. Fire in the summer of 2000 damaged the area, leaving almost no shade along the trail. 7.8 miles RT. Moderate. Access: Near Morefield Village.

LONGER TRAILS ON CHAPIN MESA

Three backcountry trails on Chapin Mesa are open to day hikers. Before hiking the Petroglyph Point and Spruce Canyon trails, register at the trail head or museum where you can borrow or buy a booklet for the self-guided tour on the Petroglyph Point Trail. No registration is required for the Soda Canyon Overlook Trail.

Petroglyph Point Trail This loop trail travels just below the rim of a side canyon of Spruce Canyon. It eventually reaches Petroglyph Point, one of the park's most impressive panels of rock art. Just past the petroglyphs, the trail climbs to the rim. It stays on the relatively flat rimrock for its return to the Chapin Mesa Museum. 2.4 miles RT. Moderate. Access: Short paved trail to Spruce Tree House site, just below Chapin Mesa Museum and Chief Ranger Station.

Soda Canyon Overlook Trail This trail crosses the rim from a kiosk on the Cliff Palace Loop Road to overlooks of Soda Canyon and Balcony House. To view Balcony House, go right when the trail forks. 1.2 miles RT. Easy. Access: Pullout on Cliff Palace Loop Rd.

Spruce Canyon Trail This loop descends 500 feet into a tributary of Spruce Canyon. Turning to the north, it travels up the bed of Spruce Canyon before climbing in steep switchbacks to the rim. It reaches the rim near the park's picnic area, a short walk from the Chapin Mesa Museum. The vegetation along the bottom of the canyon includes Douglas firs and ponderosa pines, which flourish in the moist canyon bottom soil. Damaged by fire in 2002, the exit area of the trail has little shade in the afternoon. 2.4 miles RT. Moderate. Access: Short paved trail to Spruce Tree House site, just below Chapin Mesa Museum and Chief Ranger Station.

5 Camping

The **Morefield Campground,** c/o Aramark, P.O. Box 277, Mancos, CO 81328 (© **800/449-2288** or 970/533-1944; www.visitmesaverde.com), 4 miles past the entrance station on the park's entrance road, is among the largest in the national park system with 435 sites, including 15 with full RV hookups. Open from mid-May to mid-October, the campground sits on rolling hills in a grassy area with scrub oak and brush. The attractive sites line four loop roads on the gently sloping floor of Morefield Canyon. For tent campers, the sites on Navajo Loop afford extra privacy. Though lower than the others, this loop is free of RVs and cuts into dense clusters of Gambel oak. If you prefer panoramic vistas, head for Hopi Loop, where the campsites are higher and less wooded than the others, affording views down the canyon. At dusk on most nights, mule deer browse in the bushes around many campsites.

Showers are available just outside the campground entrance at Morefield Village, which also has a coin-operated laundry. The campground has toilets, drinking water, public phones, picnic tables, grills, and an RV dump station. Programs on the area's human and natural history and other subjects take place at the campground amphitheater nightly from Memorial Day weekend through Labor Day weekend. Campsites cost $23, $31 with hookups. Reservations are accepted.

6 Where to Stay

INSIDE THE PARK

Far View Lodge In the heart of Mesa Verde National Park, Far View Lodge offers not only the most convenient location for visiting the park, but the best views of any accommodations in the area. The facility lodges guests in 17 buildings spread across a hilltop. Rooms aren't fancy and some are a bit on the small side, but they are well maintained and more than adequate, with Southwestern decor, refrigerators, coffeemakers, hair dryers, and irons. The upscale "Kiva" rooms have air-conditioning (standard rooms do not), handcrafted furniture, one king- or two queen-size beds, bathrobes, CD players, and other amenities. Most standard rooms have one queen-size bed or two doubles, although a variety of bed combinations are available. We prefer the rooms with one bed—they seem less cramped than rooms with two beds. There are no TVs, but each unit has a private balcony, and the views are magnificent. The lodge **restaurants** serve three meals daily, and Wi-Fi is available in the lobby only. All units are nonsmoking.

Mesa Verde National Park (P.O. Box 277), Mancos, CO 81328. © **866-292-8295.** Fax 970/564-4311. www.visitmesaverde.com. 150 units. TEL. $122–$158 double. AE, DC, DISC, MC, V. Closed mid-Oct through mid-Apr. Pets accepted in standard rooms only, with $50 deposit and $10 nonrefundable fee per pet per night.

NEAR THE PARK

Lodging in Cortez is adequate but not very exciting, although since you probably are just using Cortez as a base for exploring the area, this may not matter. Therefore, we recommend that you stay in your favorite chain. Summer is the busy season here, and that's when you'll usually pay the highest rates. Among those offering clean, comfortable, and relatively reasonably priced rooms in Cortez are **Best Western Turquoise Inn & Suites,** 535 E. Main St. (© 800/547-3376 or 970/565-3778; www.bestwesternmesaverde.com), charging $90 to $150 double; **Budget Host Bel Rau Lodge,** 2040 E. Main St. (© 970/565-3738; www.budgethostmesaverde.com), charging $55 to $89 double; **Econo Lodge,** 2020 E. Main St. (© 970/565-3474), with double rates of $80 to $110; **Holiday Inn Express,** 2121 E. Main St. (© 970/565-6000; www.coloradoholiday.com), charging $128 to $136 for two; **Rodeway Inn,** 1120 E. Main St. (© 970/565-3761), charging $60 to $98 double; and **Super 8,** 505 E. Main St. (© 970/565-8888). Websites for the national chains are listed in chapter 38.

7 Where to Dine

INSIDE THE PARK

Reservations are not accepted at restaurants in the park, which are all operated by **Aramark** (© **866/292-8295;** www.visitmesaverde.com). In addition to the restaurants below, a cafe at the Morefield Campground serves an all-you-can-eat pancake breakfast when the campground is open.

Far View Terrace AMERICAN/REGIONAL This food court offers a variety of foods, buffet style, such as salads, sandwiches, burgers, pizzas, and Southwestern dishes—the Navajo taco is a specialty—and also has an espresso bar. While dining, you can see as far as New Mexico through a long bank of windows.

Across from the Far View Visitor Center. Buffets $10–$12. AE, DISC, MC, V. Daily 7am–7pm. Closed late Oct to mid-Apr.

Metate Room SOUTHWESTERN The best restaurant in the park, the Metate Room specializes in Southwestern and American Indian–inspired dishes. We recommend the Rocky Mountain elk tenderloin, spiced and pan roasted with a chokecherry demiglace; blue corn and pine nut–crusted boneless trout; or the slow-cooked lamb shank. Several lighter

Picnic & Camping Supplies

Inside the park, a **general store** in Morefield Village sells camping supplies and groceries from late April through late October. In Cortez, **City Market,** 508 E. Main (© **970/565-6505;** www.citymarket.com), which has a deli, bakery, and excellent salad bar, sells everything you might want for a picnic or family outing, including fishing licenses.

Kokopelli: Casanova or Traveling Salesman?

Of the many subjects of rock art found in the West, one claims both a name and a gender: He's **Kokopelli,** and he's been found in ruins dating as early as A.D. 200 and as late as the 16th century. The consistency of the depictions over a wide geographic area indicates that Kokopelli was a well-traveled and universally recognized deity. The figure is generally seen as hunchbacked and playing a flute. His image is still used by potters, weavers, and painters, as well as for decoration on jewelry and clothing. Kokopelli has never been an evil character, although he's frequently been a comic one.

Until quite recent times, legends of Kokopelli were still current among the Pueblo peoples of the Four Corners area. Although the many stories differ in detail, almost all connect Kokopelli to a fertility theme. Sometimes he's a wandering minstrel with a sack of songs on his back; other times he is greeted as a god of the harvest.

The Hopi of First Mesa seem to identify him with an unethical guide of Spanish friars searching for the Seven Cities of Cibola in 1539. This guide was more interested in making passes at Hopi maidens than in searching for the fabled cities, according to legend, and Hopi men consequently shot him with arrows and buried him under a pile of rocks. Another Hopi village holds Kokopelli to be a sort of traveling salesman who traded deerskin shirts and moccasins for brides. Yet another Hopi legend has him seducing the daughters of a household and sewing shirts while his wife chased the men.

The Hopi also make kachina dolls of Kokopelli and of his wife, Kokopelli-mana, both of which are sold to tourists. As with most kachina dolls, there was also a real-life kachina dancer, who used to make explicit gestures to female tourists and missionaries—until the visitors found out what the gestures meant. Many early peoples welcomed Kokopelli around corn-planting time, and married women who hoped to conceive sought his blessing. Single maidens, however, fled in panic.

dishes are also offered, including buffalo bratwurst and a burger. A must-try from the dessert menu is Napoleon Looking West, locally grown grilled fruit, layered with sweet mascarpone cream and crispy wontons, with a java-caramel sauce. The restaurant displays high-quality American Indian rugs and pottery, which you might not notice, given the breathtaking views from the windows.

Far View Lodge, across from Far View Visitor Center, 17 miles down the park entrance road. ✆ **970/529-4736.** Main courses $8.50–$31. AE, DISC, MC, V. Daily 5–9:30pm. Closed late Oct to mid-Apr.

Spruce Tree Terrace AMERICAN Hamburgers, cheeseburgers, and hot dogs dominate the menu at this fast-food cafeteria, which also serves sandwiches, salads, yogurt, and ice cream. Sit in the Southwestern-style dining area, or take your food out onto the deck.

Across from Chapin Mesa Museum. Most items $4.95–$8.95. AE, DISC, MC, V. Mid-Apr to Oct daily 10am–7pm; shorter hours Nov to mid-Apr.

NEAR THE PARK

Main St. Brewery AMERICAN Fans slice the air under a stamped-tin ceiling, and fanciful murals splash color above subdued wood paneling. The pleasant contrasts found in the decor carry over to the menu. In addition to brewpub staples such as fish and chips, pizza, and bratwurst, this restaurant serves steaks and prime rib—dry aged Angus beef from its own herd of Angus cattle, raised with no artificial growth stimulants or antibiotics—plus a vegetarian stir-fry plate and Rocky Mountain trout. The beers brewed here go well with everything. We especially recommend the hoppy, slightly bitter Pale Export and the Munich-style Pale Bock.

21 E. Main St., Cortez. ✆ **970/564-9112.** Main courses $6.95–$24. AE, MC, V. Daily 3:30pm–close.

Nero's ITALIAN/AMERICAN Our top choice in this area when we're craving something a bit different. The innovative entrees, prepared by Culinary Institute of America chef Richard Gurd, include house specialties such as the Cowboy Steak (a charbroiled 12-oz. sirloin seasoned with a spicy rub and served with pasta or fries); our favorite, the mushroom ravioli served with an Alfredo sauce, sautéed spinach, sun-dried tomatoes, and pecans; and shrimp Alfredo—sautéed shrimp with spinach served over fettuccine with Alfredo sauce and Romano cheese. There's an excellent selection of beef, plus seafood, fowl, pork, veal, and lots of homemade pasta. A small, homey restaurant with a Southwestern art-gallery decor, Nero's also offers pleasant outdoor seating in warm weather.

Archaeological Sites of the Four Corners Area

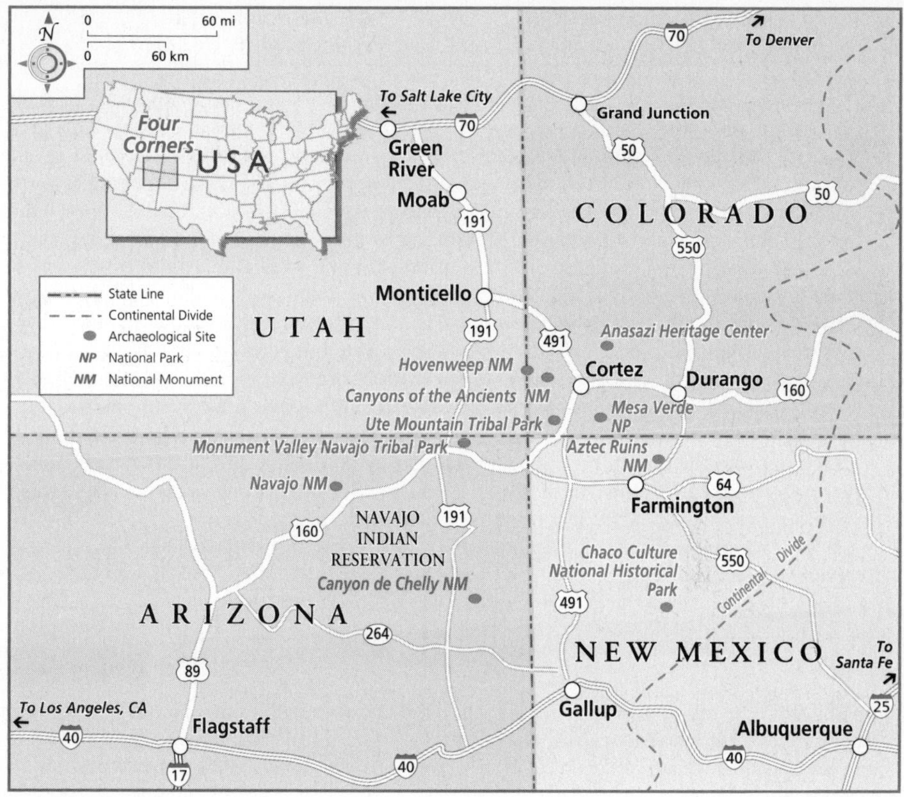

303 W. Main St. ✆ **970/565-7366.** http://subee.com/neros/home.html. Reservations recommended in summer. Entrees $8.95–$21. AE, MC, V. Daily 5–9:30pm. Closed Sun in winter.

Pippo's Café AMERICAN This friendly, down-home cafe is an easy place to like, especially if you appreciate a casual atmosphere, good basic American cooking, speedy service, and reasonable prices. On busy Main Street, Pippo's serves breakfast and lunch, and the specialty is breakfast, served during all open hours. We especially like the Pippo's Omelet—three eggs, green chilies, tomatoes, olives, mushrooms, and cheese—and the homemade hash browns. The lunch menu (served from 11am) includes half-pound burgers, hot and cold sandwiches, homemade soups, and hot plates including chicken fried steak with gravy.

100 W. Main St. ✆ **970/565-6039.** Main courses $3.80–$8.90. DISC, MC, V. Mon–Sat 6:30am–3pm; Sun 6:30am–2pm.

8 Nearby National Monuments & Archaeological Sites

The major archaeological center of the United States, the **Four Corners** area—where the states of Colorado, New Mexico, Arizona, and Utah meet—is surrounded by a vast complex of ancient villages that dominated this region a thousand years ago. Here among the reddish-brown rocks, abandoned canyons, and flat mesas, you'll discover another world, once ruled by the ancestral Puebloans and today largely the domain of the Navajo.

In addition to the archeological sites discussed below, the **Crow Canyon Archeological Center,** 23390 Rd. K, Cortez, CO 81321 (✆ **800/422-8975** or 970/565-8975; www.crowcanyon.org), offers tours of its current excavation sites. The full-day tours are offered Wednesday and Thursday from May through September, and cost $50 for adults and $25 for youths from 10 to 17 (children under 10 are not permitted). Lunch is included. Call ahead for reservations.

HOVENWEEP NATIONAL MONUMENT, CO

Preserving some of the most striking and isolated archaeological sites in the Four Corners area, this national monument straddles the Colorado–Utah border, 40 miles west of Cortez.

Hovenweep is the Ute word for "deserted valley," appropriate because its inhabitants apparently left

Safety Tips for Driving in the Four Corners (Learned the Hard Way)

The wild, wild West is mostly relegated to our national imagination. Those used to their well-serviced urban area or suburb, however, may find the infrastructure in the Four Corners a little lacking. This is a sparsely populated region with searing heat and little water, so it's not entirely a surprise that paved roads can seem more luxury than necessity. There are many opportunities to get off solid ground, and unless you're rocking your 4WD vehicle, take it easy on the back roads. Flash floods are a particular hazard. There may not be a cloud in the sky, but desert drainage carries water immense distances at breakneck speeds. Don't try to cross washes when they're flowing, as you may get swept away, or you may soak your brakes and find yourself unable to stop. Steep ledges with deadly drop-offs offer further incentive to keep your speed down. Another thing you'll want to avoid is bottoming out your rental car on a patch of rough road, like the last little hill on the approach to Chaco Canyon, because you don't want to deal with the car stalling in the middle of the road, coolant pouring out of your engine, and a couple of park employees graciously trying to pour water into your dinged-up radiator, which just drains out into the desert, before the employees laugh politely and shrug when you ask about the nearest taxi or Dodge dealer or tow truck, all of which are many, many miles away. You'll wind up being stuck in the canyon for 6 hours without food while waiting for the car rental place in Albuquerque to send a flatbed with a new rental car to replace the one you just ruined, resulting in a bill of $3,275.16, all for hitting one lousy little bump. Trust me on this one.

—Ethan Wolff

around 1300. The monument contains six separate sites and is noted for mysterious, 20-foot-high sandstone towers, some square, others oval, circular, or D-shaped. Archaeologists have suggested their possible function as everything from guard or signal towers, celestial observatories, and ceremonial structures to water towers or granaries.

A ranger station, with exhibits, restrooms, and drinking water, is at the **Square Tower Site,** in the Utah section of the monument, the most impressive and best preserved of the sites. The **Hovenweep Campground,** with 30 sites, is open year-round. Sites are fairly small—most appropriate for tents or small pickup-truck campers—but a few sites can accommodate RVs up to 36 feet long. The campground has flush toilets, drinking water, picnic tables, and fire pits, but no showers or RV hookups. Cost is $10 per night; reservations are not accepted, but the campground rarely fills.

From Cortez, take **U.S. 160** south to County Road G (McElmo Canyon Rd.), and follow signs into Utah and the monument. The other five sites are difficult to find, and you'll need to obtain detailed directions and check on current road conditions before setting out. Summer temperatures can reach over 100°F (38°C), and water supplies are limited, so take your own and carry a canteen, even on short walks. Bug repellent is advised; gnats can be a nuisance in late spring.

The visitor center/ranger station is open daily from 8am to 6pm from April through September and 8am to 5pm the rest of the year; it's closed New Year's Day, Thanksgiving, and Christmas. Admission for up to a week costs $6 per vehicle or $3 per person on bike, motorcycle, or foot. For advance information, contact **Hovenweep National Monument,** McElmo Route, Cortez, CO 81321 (© **970/562-4282;** www.nps.gov/hove). Allow a half-day for the Square Tower Site and at least 1 full day to visit Square Tower plus a few other sites.

UTE MOUNTAIN TRIBAL PARK, CO

If you liked Mesa Verde but would have enjoyed it more without the company of so many fellow tourists, you'll *love* the Ute Mountain Tribal Park, P.O. Box 109, Towaoc, CO 81334 (© **800/847-5485** or 970/565-3751 ext. 330; www.utemountainute.com/tribalpark.htm).

Set aside by the Ute Mountain tribe to preserve its heritage, the 125,000-acre park—which abuts Mesa Verde National Park—includes wall paintings and ancient petroglyphs, as well as hundreds of surface sites and cliff dwellings that are similar in size and complexity to those in Mesa Verde.

Access to the park is limited to guided tours. Full- and half-day tours begin at the **Ute Mountain Visitor Center/Museum** (© **970/749-1452**) at the junction of U.S. 491 and U.S. 160, 20 miles south of Cortez. Mountain-biking and backpacking trips are also offered. No food, water, lodging, gasoline, or other services are available within the park. Some climbing of ladders is necessary on the full-day tour.

There's one primitive **campground** ($12 per vehicle; reservations required).

Charges for tours in your vehicle start at $27 per person for a half-day, $45 for a full day; it's $10 per person extra to go in the tour guide's vehicle, and reservations are required. Special private tours to remote sections of the park are also offered, with a minimum of four persons, from $60 per person per day. Credit cards are not accepted (cash or checks only), dogs are not permitted on the property, and professional photography is not allowed.

CORTEZ CULTURAL CENTER, CO

The center, 25 N. Market St., Cortez (✆ **970/565-1151;** www.cortezculturalcenter.org), includes a museum with exhibits on both prehistoric and modern American Indians, an art gallery with displays of regional art, and a good gift shop offering crafts by local tribal members. A variety of programs are offered year-round, ranging from guided kids' hikes to photo exhibits, and from late May through early September there are American Indian dances and cultural programs most evenings starting at 7:30pm. The center is open daily from 10am to 10pm from June through August, with shorter hours the rest of the year. Admission is free, and you should plan to spend at least an hour in the museum (more if there are dances or other programs). Nearby, the **Hawkins Preserve** covers 122 acres, offers hiking trails and rock-climbing opportunities, and includes several prehistoric archaeological sites. Check with the Cortez Cultural Center about current tours and other activities.

ANASAZI HERITAGE CENTER, CO

When the Dolores River was dammed and McPhee Reservoir created in 1985, some 1,600 ancient archaeological sites were threatened. Four percent of the project costs was set aside for archaeological work, and several million artifacts and other prehistoric items were rescued. Many are on display here. Located 10 miles north of Cortez, it is set into a hillside near the remains of 12th-century sites.

Operated by the Bureau of Land Management, the center emphasizes visitor involvement. Children and adults are invited to examine corn-grinding implements, a loom and other weaving materials, and a re-created pit house. You can touch artifacts 1,000 to 2,000 years old, examine samples through microscopes, use computer programs, and engage in video lessons in archaeological techniques.

A half-mile wheelchair-accessible trail leads from the museum to the small **Dominguez Pueblo Ruins,** atop a low hill, with a beautiful view across the Montezuma Valley. It was probably home to a family of four to six people and has low walls marking four rooms. Nearby are ruins of the much larger **Escalante Pueblo,** with about 28 rooms surrounding a kiva. Archaeologists say that Escalante Pueblo was one of the northernmost settlements influenced by the Chaco culture.

The center also serves as the visitor center for Canyons of the Ancients National Monument (see below). It is located at 27501 Colo. 184, Dolores (✆ **970/882-5600;** www.co.blm.gov/ahc). It's open March through October daily from 9am to 5pm, November through February daily from 10am to 4pm, and closed New Year's Day, Thanksgiving, and Christmas. An admission fee of $3 for adults is charged March through October only; admission is free for those 17 and under. Allow 2 hours.

CANYONS OF THE ANCIENTS NATIONAL MONUMENT, CO

The 164,000-acre Canyons of the Ancients contains over 6,000 archaeological sites—what some claim is the highest density of archaeological sites in the United States—including the remains of villages, cliff dwellings, sweat lodges, and petroglyphs at from 700 to perhaps as much as 10,000 years old.

Its primary excavated site is **Lowry Pueblo,** a prehistoric village that is located about 27 miles west of Cortez via U.S. 491, on C.R. CC, 9 miles west of Pleasant View. This pueblo, which was built about 1060 and likely abandoned by 1200, is believed to have housed about 100 people. It has standing walls from 40 rooms plus 9 kivas (circular underground ceremonial chambers). A short, self-guided interpretive trail leads past a kiva and continues to the remains of a great kiva, which, at 54 feet in diameter, is among the largest ever found. Hiking is permitted throughout the monument, but hikers are asked to stay on developed trails. The area offers a picnic area, drinking water, and toilets. There is primitive, dispersed camping but no developed campsites.

Canyons of the Ancients is overseen by the Bureau of Land Management and as yet has no on-site visitor center or even a contact station. Those wishing to explore the monument are strongly advised to contact or, preferably, stop first at the visitor center located at **Anasazi Heritage Center** (see above) for information, especially current road conditions and directions. Information is also available online at **www.co.blm.gov/canm** and from the welcome center in Cortez (see the Information section in "Essentials," at the beginning of this chapter). Allow at least 2 hours.

CHACO CULTURE NATIONAL HISTORICAL PARK, NM

A stunning setting and well-preserved ruins makes the long drive to Chaco Canyon extremely worthwhile. The stark desert seems strange as a center of culture, but the ancient ancestral Puebloan people (the group here are also called Chacoans) successfully farmed and built elaborate public buildings, which connected with other Chacoan sites over a wide-ranging network of roads.

From about A.D. 850 to 1250, Chaco was the religious and economic center of the San Juan Basin, with some 2,000 to 5,000 residents living in about 400 settlements in the immediate area. Stone walls rose more than four stories high, and some are still in place today.

Chaco's decline after centuries of success coincided with a drought in the San Juan Basin between 1130 and 1180, but anthropologists still argue over why the site was abandoned. Many believe that an influx of outsiders may have brought new and troubling influences. One controversial theory maintains that cannibalism existed at Chaco, practiced by the ancestral Puebloans themselves or by invaders, such as the Toltecs of Mexico. Most, however, contend that, for some reason, the Chacoan people left gradually, and today their descendants live among the region's Pueblo people.

Walking and hiking among the ruins are the most popular activities here. The key ruin is **Pueblo Bonito,** one of the largest prehistoric dwellings ever excavated in the American Southwest. It has some 800 rooms covering more than 3 acres, and you'll get good views from above along the **Pueblo Alto Trail.** Other easily accessible ruins are Chetro Ketl, Pueblo del Arroyo, Kin Kletso, Casa Rinconada, Hungo Pavi, and Una Vida.

The park is open daily year-round. A visitor center, with a bookstore and a museum that shows films on ancestral Puebloan culture, is open daily year-round 8am to 5pm, except for Thanksgiving, Christmas, and New Year's Day. **Gallo Campground** ($10 per night) has 49 sites with toilets, nonpotable water, and no shade. Drinking water is available only at the visitor center.

The primary entrance is off **U.S. 550** and San Juan County roads 7900 and 7950. To get to Chaco from Santa Fe, take I-25 south to Bernalillo (exit 242), then U.S. 550 northwest through Cuba to mile marker 112. Turn left onto San Juan County Road 7900 for 5 miles, and turn right. Go 16 miles on San Juan County Road 7950 to the park entrance. Farmington is the nearest population center, and it's a 75-mile, 1½-hour drive to the park. From Farmington, head east on **U.S. 64** to Bloomfield and turn right onto U.S. 550. Three miles south of the Nageezi Trading Post (the last stop for food, gas, or lodging), turn onto San Juan County Road 7900 and proceed as above.

For information, contact **Chaco Culture National Historical Park,** P.O. Box 220, Nageezi, NM 87037 (✆ **505/786-7014;** www.nps.gov/chcu). Admission for up to 7 days costs $8 per vehicle or $4 per person on foot, bike, or motorcycle.

AZTEC RUINS NATIONAL MONUMENT, NM

Misnamed by Anglo settlers who thought these ruins were built by the Aztec people of Mexico, this 500-room pueblo with a huge central kiva was actually the home of the ancestral Puebloans about 7 centuries ago, long before the time of the Aztecs.

You'll see the Chaco culture here, plus signs of Mesa Verde influence from a later occupation. Aztec's **Great Kiva** is the only completely reconstructed great kiva in existence. The circular ceremonial chamber is 50 feet in diameter, with a main floor sunken 8 feet below the surface of the surrounding ground.

Allow at least an hour to see the ruins on the half-mile self-guided trail, and also stop in the visitor center to see the exhibits and watch the 25-minute film on the history of the prehistoric people of the area. There is no camping at the monument.

Aztec Ruins is approximately a half-mile north of N.M. 516 (off U.S. 550) on Ruins Road (C.R. 2900), on the north edge of the city of Aztec, about 14 miles northeast of Farmington, New Mexico. The monument is open daily year-round except Thanksgiving, Christmas, and New Year's Day. Hours from Memorial Day weekend through Labor Day weekend are 8am to 6pm; the rest of the year, it's open daily 8am to 5pm.

For information, contact **Aztec Ruins National Monument,** 84 C.R. 2900, Aztec, NM 87410 (✆ **505/334-6174;** www.nps.gov/azru). Admission for up to 7 days is $5 per person, free for children under 16.

NAVAJO NATIONAL MONUMENT, AZ

This national monument, deep inside the Navajo Nation, contains three of the best-preserved ancestral Puebloan cliff dwellings in the region—Betatakin, Keet Seel, and Inscription House. You can visit both Betatakin and Keet Seel, but fragile Inscription House is closed to the public. There are also exhibits on the Navajo culture.

Stop first at the **visitor center** (daily year-round 8am–6pm from Memorial Day weekend through Labor Day weekend and 9am–5pm the rest of the year) to see the displays on the ancestral Puebloan and Navajo cultures, including artifacts from Tsegi Canyon. Several short films are shown, and a shop sells Navajo and Pueblo arts and crafts.

Betatakin, which means "ledge house" in Navajo, is the only one of the three ruins that can be seen easily, and that is from a distance on the easy 1-mile round-trip Sandal Trail. Built in a huge amphitheater-like alcove in the canyon wall, Betatakin was occupied only from 1250 to 1300, and at its peak may have housed 125 people. A strenuous 5-mile round-trip **hike to the ruin** is led by a ranger and involves descending more than 700 feet to the floor of Tsegi Canyon and later hiking back up to the rim.

Keet Seel, which means "broken pieces of pottery" in Navajo, was occupied from as early as A.D. 950 until 1300, and at its peak may have housed 150 people. Twenty people a day receive permits to make the strenuous 17-mile round-trip hike to Keet Seel. The trail is open only in summer.

Other trails in the park, open year-round, are the .8-mile round-trip Aspen Trail, which branches off the Sandal Trail to drop some 300 feet into an aspen forest; and the Canyon View Trail, a .6-mile round-trip walk that offers views of Betatakin Canyon.

The free, shady **Sunset View Campground** has 31 small sites (RVs 28 ft. long or less), paved roads, toilets, and drinking water, and is open year-round. Another free campground, **Canyon View,** is open April through September and has 16 sites, dirt roads, pit toilets, but no water.

From Cortez, follow **U.S. 160** south and west 137 miles into New Mexico and Arizona, to Ariz. 564, which leads north 9 miles to the monument. For information, contact **Navajo National Monument,** HC 71 Box 3, Tonalea, AZ 86044 (© **928/672-2700;** www.nps.gov/nava). The park is open daily year-round. Admission is free.

CANYON DE CHELLY NATIONAL MONUMENT, AZ

People have lived in these deep canyons for more than 2,000 years, and there are more than 100 prehistoric dwelling sites in the area. The monument includes two major canyons—**Canyon de Chelly** (which comes from the Navajo word *tségi,* meaning "rock canyon") and **Canyon del Muerto** (Spanish for "Canyon of the Dead"). The smooth sandstone walls of rich reds and yellows contrast sharply with the deep greens of corn, pasture, and cottonwood on the canyon floor.

Stop first at the **visitor center** (daily 8am–5pm year-round except Christmas) to see exhibits on both the present-day Navajo residents and the ancient peoples who inhabited the canyons. There's often a silversmith at the visitor center demonstrating Navajo jewelry making.

The two rim drives cover about 20 miles each and, with stops, can easily take 2 hours apiece.

The **North Rim Drive** overlooks Canyon del Muerto. From view points, you'll see **Ledge Ruin,** occupied between A.D. 1050 and 1275, and, nearby, a *kiva* (circular ceremonial building). Farther along, **Mummy Cave**—named for two mummies found in burial urns—is a large amphitheater with two caves, believed to have been occupied from 300 to 1300. There's a three-story structure similar to dwellings at Mesa Verde; altogether there are 80 rooms.

The **South Rim Drive** climbs the South Rim of Canyon de Chelly, providing views of canyons, the junction of Canyon del Muerto and Canyon de Chelly, and several ruins, including **First Ruin,** with 22 rooms and 2 kivas. Farther along is the **White House Overlook.** The final stop offers a spectacular view of **Spider Rock,** twin towers that rise 800 feet from the canyon floor.

The **White House Ruins Trail,** the only trail into the canyon you can take without a guide, descends 600 feet to the canyon floor, crosses Chinle Wash, and approaches the White House Ruins. Among the largest ruins in the canyon, it contains 80 rooms and was inhabited between 1040 and 1275. You're not allowed to wander off this trail, and please respect the privacy of those Navajo living here. It's a 2.5-mile round-trip hike and takes about 2 hours.

Access to the floor of Canyon de Chelly is restricted. To enter the canyon, **you must be accompanied by a park ranger or an authorized guide** (unless you're on the White House Ruins Trail). **Navajo guides** will lead you into the canyon on foot or in your own or their four-wheel-drive vehicle, and there are also guided horseback tours. Check at the visitor center for fees and other details.

The shady (and free) **Cottonwood Campground** has 96 sites, a dump station, and toilets. There is water in summer only.

To get to Canyon de Chelly from Cortez, follow **U.S. 160** south and west 76 miles into Arizona to U.S. 191, which you take south 62 miles to Chinle, where you turn east to enter the park, which is open daily year-round. Admission is free.

For information, contact **Canyon de Chelly National Monument,** P.O. Box 588, Chinle, AZ 86503 (© **928/674-5500;** www.nps.gov/cach).

24

Mount Rainier National Park, WA

by Eric Peterson

On summer weekends, when "the mountain is out," as the locals say, busloads of noisy tourists descend on Mount Rainier, cameras at hand. But for anyone willing to expend a little bit of energy to get away from the crowds, this mountain, which dominates the Puget Sound and western Washington skyline for miles, has many secrets to share: mountain goats and marmots, streaming waterfalls, ominous walls of ice deep in the rainforest, and thousand-year-old trees set against subalpine meadows teeming with summer wildflowers.

Should you visit on a wet, dreary October day, you may theorize that Mount Rainier was named for the weather. In fact, Capt. George Vancouver named it in 1792 for his friend Rear Adm. Peter Rainier (who never saw it). The region's native people had been calling it Tahoma, or other variations, for centuries, however, and the name remained contentious until the early 19th century (and it still remains a touchy issue for some). Nevertheless, the mountain is known as Rainier to most people, and a sprawling city to the northwest, Tacoma, wound up with the American Indian name. Rainier was finalized as the name when the park was established in 1899.

Native peoples hunted deer, elk, and mountain goat and gathered huckleberries on its lower slopes for thousands of years. Today Mount Rainier is a symbol of the wild Northwest, providing constant reassurance of the beauty that lies beyond the sprawl of suburbia.

Although the early pioneers saw most of the mountains in the West as obstacles, 14,411-foot Mount Rainier so captivated the settlers that, as early as the 1850s, less than a decade after Seattle was founded, mountaineers were heading for its snowcapped slopes. In 1857, an army lieutenant, August Valentine Kautz, climbed to within 400 feet of the summit. In 1870, Gen. Hazard Stevens and Philemon Van Trump made the first recorded complete ascent. (Trapped near the summit at dark, they survived the night huddled in ice caves formed by sulfurous steam vents, with the steam providing enough heat to keep them from freezing.) In 1884, James and Virinda Longmire opened the mountain's first hotel, at a spot that now bears their name. In 1899, Mount Rainier became the nation's fifth national park, and by 1916, the system now known as the Wonderland Trail was completed, forming a loop nearly 100 miles long around the mountain.

Because of its massive network of glaciers and unpredictable weather, Mount Rainier is an unforgiving peak. Dozens of climbers have died on its slopes, yet each year about 10,000 people set out for the summit of the dozing volcano. Only about half reach the top, however. The rest are turned back by bad weather, altitude sickness, exhaustion, and hazardous glacial crossings. This is not a mountain to be treated lightly.

Although the mountain is a magnet for climbers, the adventurers make up only a fraction of the two million visitors who arrive each year. This mountain is really all about hiking through subalpine meadows, the main activity pursued by the vast majority of park visitors, most of whom visit during the short summer season (July–Sept in the higher elevations).

Scenic idylls through flower-strewn meadows aside, the Cascades are not dead—they're just sleeping. The eruption of Mount St. Helens in 1980 drove that fact home. But what of Mount Rainier? Snow and glaciers notwithstanding, Rainier has a heart of fire. Steam vents at the mountain's summit are evidence of that. Though the volcanic peak has not erupted for more than 150 years, it could erupt again at any time. Some scientists believe that Rainier's volcanic activity occurs in 3,000-year cycles; if this holds true, it'll be another 500 years (give or take) before another big eruption. So go ahead and plan that trip. In all likelihood, only the scenery will blow you away.

TERRAIN

According to local legend, Martha Longmire, who helped found the first hotel in the area, was supposed to have exclaimed, "This must be what paradise is like," upon her first visit to the subalpine meadows that now bear that name. These meadows, now the site of the Paradise Inn and the Jackson Visitor Center, are

Mount Rainier National Park

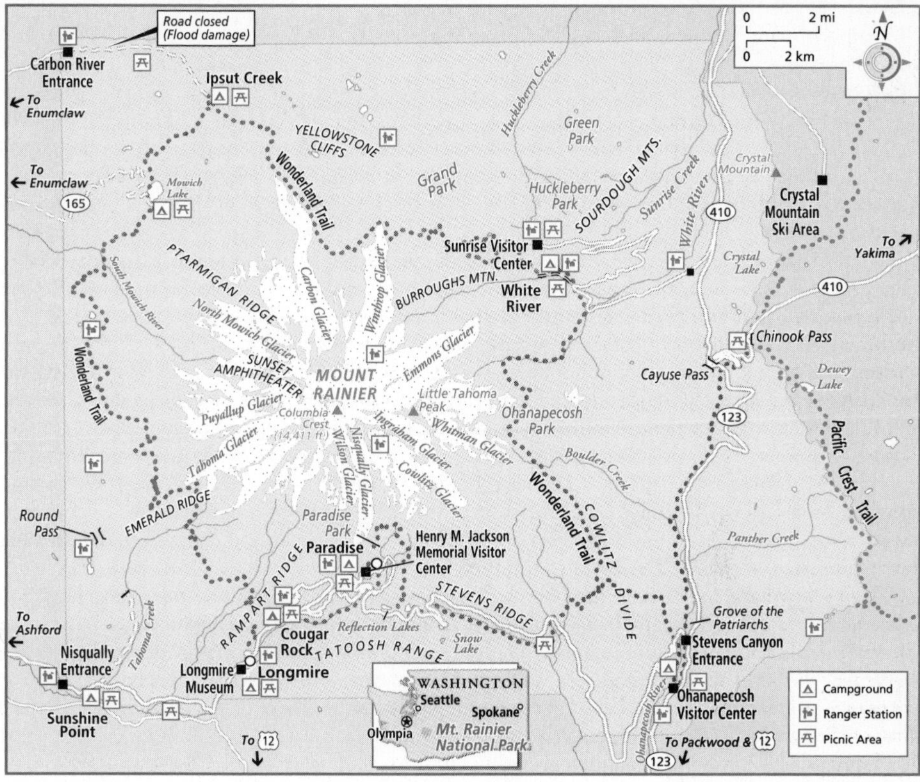

the most popular spots in the park. Wildflowers cover the slopes, and the vast bulk of the mountain rises so steeply overhead that it is necessary to strain one's neck to gaze up at the summit.

Mount Rainier lies toward the southern end of the Washington Cascades. Here the crags of the North Cascades give way to a volcanic landscape of rolling hills punctuated by Mount Rainier, Mount St. Helens, and, to the east, Mount Adams and Goat Rocks: the latter but a remnant of an ancient volcano, the former, a snow cone as impressive as Mount Rainier.

It is said that Rainier makes its own weather, and more often than not, it isn't what people consider good weather. Rising more than 2 miles above the surrounding landscape, Mount Rainier interrupts the eastward flow of moisture-laden air that comes in off the Pacific Ocean. Forced upward into the colder altitudes, this moist air drops its load of water on the mountain. At lower elevations on the west side, the moisture falls as rain, which creates a **rainforest** in the Carbon River Valley. However, at higher elevations, the precipitation falls as snow. On average, about 680 inches of snow falls each winter at Paradise on Mount Rainier, but in the winter of 1971–72, 1,122 inches (94 ft.) of snow were recorded at Paradise, setting a world annual snowfall record. And in November 2006, 17 inches of rain drenched the mountain in 48 hours, causing significant damage to the trails and roads (see "The 2006 and 2009 Floods" sidebar, below).

Mount Rainier is the single most glaciated mountain in the Lower 48. So much snow falls here each winter that it can't melt over the short summer. Each year the snow accumulates, eventually compressing into ice that adds to the mountain's **glaciers.** There are 26 named glaciers on Mount Rainier and another 50 unnamed ones. Among these are the largest (Emmons) and the lowest (Carbon) in the Lower 48.

These glaciers, in turn, feed a half-dozen rivers. The Muddy Fork of the **Cowlitz River** and the **White River** take their names from the color that the glacial flour (silt) imparts to them. Fortunately, the **Carbon River** is not as black as its name implies. The river instead takes its name from the coal deposits found in the area. The **Nisqually,** the **Puyallup,** and the Cowlitz all retain names given to them centuries ago by the region's American Indian tribes. All of these rivers eventually flow westward to the Puget Sound, with the exception of the Cowlitz, which flows into the Columbia River.

Surrounding the park are four **national forests:** Mount Baker, Snoqualmie, Wenatchee, and Gifford Pinchot. Within these forests are seven wilderness areas and thousands of miles of logging roads and trails.

FLORA & FAUNA

In a national park, where animals need not fear hunters, you often get unexpected chances to encounter wildlife up close and personal, sometimes whether you want to or not. Yes, **cougars** live in this park, as do **black bears,** but neither is seen very often. Much more common large mammals are the park's deer, elk, and mountain goats. **Deer,** mostly black-tailed, are the most frequently spotted. **Elk,** much larger and more majestic in stature, are less in evidence but sometimes appear in the Sunrise area in the summer and throughout the eastern regions of the park during the autumn. **Mountain goats,** which are actually not goats but rather longhaired relatives of the antelope, keep to the rocky cliffs above alpine and subalpine meadows during the summer.

Perhaps the most entertaining and enviable of the park's wild residents are its **marmots.** These largest members of the squirrel family spend their days nibbling wildflowers in subalpine meadows and stretching out on rocks to bask in the sun. In meadows throughout the park, these chubby creatures seem oblivious to the presence of humans, contentedly grazing only steps away from hikers.

Marmots share these subalpine zones with **pikas,** tiny relatives of rabbits that are more often heard than seen. Living among the jumbled rocks of talus slopes, pikas skitter about their rocky domains calling out warnings with a high-pitched beep that is surprisingly electronic in tone.

Monkeyflowers, elephant's heads, parrot's beaks, bear grass: They represent just a small fraction of the variety of **wildflowers** on the slopes of Mount Rainier. This mountain's subalpine meadows are among the most celebrated in the Northwest and the world. Although not as colorfully named as the flowers mentioned above, lupines, asters, gentians, avalanche lilies, phlox, heather, and Indian paintbrush all add distinctive splashes of color to the slopes in summer.

The meadows at Paradise are much wetter than those at Sunrise, which lie in a rain-shadow zone and, consequently, are relatively dry. In the northwest corner of the park, the **Carbon River Valley** opens out to the Puget Sound and channels moisture-laden air into its valleys. As a result, this valley is a rainforest where tree limbs are draped with moss and lichen, and where Douglas fir and western red cedar grow to enormous proportions. In the southeast corner of the park, in the **Grove of the Patriarchs** near the Stevens Canyon Entrance, stand some of the oldest trees—Douglas firs more than 1,000 years old and western red cedars more than 25 feet in circumference.

AVOIDING THE CROWDS

On a sunny summer weekend, it is sometimes necessary to park more than a mile from Paradise and walk on forest trails and the road to the meadows. You can avoid the crowds by **visiting in the spring or fall.** Keep in mind that, in May, Paradise and Sunrise will still be snow-covered and most park roads will be closed; weather may still be unsettled. Even in June, Paradise may remain snow-covered and some park roads may be closed. Also, the rainy season starts in mid- to late October and continues until early summer.

Perhaps the best tip, if you're traveling in busy months, is to **visit on weekdays** rather than weekends. You might also consider avoiding the Sunrise and Paradise areas altogether, heading instead to the **more remote sections** of the park, such as the Carbon River area in the northwest section, or the Denman Falls/Gobblers Knob area in the southwest. Both are accessible, at least part of the way, by car, and they provide the same sorts of stunning vistas you get at Sunrise and Paradise. The Carbon River Road is subject to flood closures; check with park staff. The Westside Road, which leads to the Denman Falls area (open summer only), is closed due to flood damage 3 miles up, so you will have to do some hiking. Be sure to check at the ranger station for the latest info.

Otherwise, a good plan is to arrive at either Sunrise or Paradise early in the day—before 10am—spend an hour checking out the visitor center, and then high-tail it out to a trail. Likewise, people generally leave the park between 4 and 6pm, so if you can arrange to arrive at a visitor center around 5pm (with the idea of staying put for an hour or so), you can avoid a lot of the traffic.

Finally, you might try reversing this advice, hitting Sunrise at sundown. Most park visitors are leaving through the Nisqually Entrance in the park's southwest corner late in the day; you'll be heading in the opposite direction.

1 Essentials

GETTING THERE & GATEWAYS

Unlike its cousin across the Puget Sound, Olympic National Park, Rainier does not lie within a circle of roads; the northwest corner of the park, for example, is accessible only through one entrance.

The **Nisqually Entrance** (also known as the Nisqually-Longmire Rd.), in the southwest corner of the park, is the park's main access point. Just to the west on Wash. 706 is **Ashford,** where most of the area's accommodations and services are. A few miles farther west is **Elbe,** with a few more choices.

At the park's northeast corner, the **White River Entrance,** off Wash. 410, provides easier access from Seattle and points north if your goal is the Sunrise area. The town closest to this entrance is **Greenwater,** which has some overnight options.

In the northwest corner, the **Carbon River Entrance** is off Wash. 165 but is closed to vehicular traffic inside the park because of flooding in 2006. **Enumclaw** offers motels, restaurants, and fuel.

At the southeast corner, the **Stevens Canyon Entrance,** off Wash. 123 from U.S. 12, provides access from Yakima. **Packwood** and **Randle,** both south of the park on U.S. 12, are two of the larger towns in the nearby area. You'll find some accommodations in Packwood.

During the summer, it is also possible to enter the park from the east on **Wash. 410,** which also leads to Yakima by way of Chinook Pass. Entering this way gives you the option of heading north to the White River Entrance and Sunrise, or south to Stevens Canyon.

In winter, only the Nisqually Entrance is open. Severe winter road damage often closes roads during summer; contact the park for current information.

THE NEAREST AIRPORT The **Seattle–Tacoma International Airport** (✆ **206/787-5388;** www.portseattle.org/seatac), is 70 miles northwest of the park. Allow about 2 hours for the drive on I-5, Wash. 7, and Wash. 706 to the Nisqually Entrance. The airport is served by practically all major airlines and car-rental companies; see chapter 38 for website listings.

INFORMATION

Contact **Mount Rainier National Park,** 55210 238th Ave. E., Ashford, WA 98304 (✆ **360/569-2211;** www.nps.gov/mora). The park publishes a free newspaper, the *Tahoma,* available at visitor centers with information about park activities.

VISITOR CENTERS

When you arrive, stop at one of the park's four visitor centers. The **Longmire Museum** (✆ **360/569-2211,** ext. 3314) is inside the park beyond the Nisqually Entrance and is the welcoming center for the park. The **Henry M. Jackson Visitor Center** (✆ **360/569-2211,** ext. 6036), near Paradise Meadows, is the park's main visitor center. The **Ohanapecosh Visitor Center** (✆ **360/569-2211,** ext. 6046), off Wash. 123 in the southeast corner of the park, is near the Stevens Canyon Entrance. It's open in summer only. The **Sunrise Visitor Center,** off Wash. 410, past the White River Entrance (✆ **360/663-2425**), is in the northeast section of the park. It's open in summer only.

FEES

Entry to the park for up to 7 days costs $15 per vehicle, $5 for individuals on foot, bike, or motorcycle. Camping costs $12 to $15 per night, depending on the campground and season.

SPECIAL REGULATIONS & WARNINGS

The main thing to remember in the heavily visited spots in the subalpine portions of the park is to stay on the trails and stay off the wildflowers. Off-trail trampling erodes the thin loam topsoil that supports the fragile vegetation.

Be sure to boil any water taken from the park's rivers, as it has been known to carry ***Giardia,*** the little bug that causes mighty intestinal disorder.

Don't even think about heading for a day climb anywhere near the upper altitudes of Rainier without checking in at a ranger station or employing a guide. Steep snowfields can become slippery in the sun or contain unstable ice bridges. Remember, people die in the high altitudes every year.

Additionally, the National Park Service wants visitors to be aware of some other risks: Mud flows, glacial outburst floods, and falling rocks are hazards that may be encountered here.

SEASONS & CLIMATE

Summer is the warmest and driest time of the year, with frequent fog banks rolling in late and early in

The 2006 and 2009 Floods

A massive rainstorm on November 2006 dumped nearly 18 inches of rain in 36 hours on Mount Rainier National Park, turning every river into a raging torrent and burying trails and roads under landslides all over the park. Afterwards, a violent windstorm uprooted trees, causing further damage. Much of Wash. 123 on the east side of the park and Carbon River Road in the northwest corner were damaged, as were numerous trails and backcountry bridges. Another flood in January 2009 destroyed sections of Stevens Canyon and Nisqually roads. Contact the park for current information.

the day, and temperatures ranging from the upper 40s to the low 80s (10s to mid-20s Celsius). The spring and fall are cool and drizzly, with occasional days of warm weather late in the spring and early in the fall. The greatest rainfall comes in January and December, with daytime temperatures in the 40s (10s Celsius). Weather generally gets colder and nastier the higher up you go, and there is lots of snow in the higher elevations. This snow can linger well into the summer, even at popular Paradise.

It's important that you dress in layers for a day visit, when you may encounter any type of weather. It can go from warm to cool very quickly as you climb in altitude. Rain can come in suddenly, so rain gear is a good precaution.

2 Exploring the Park

Longmire, just inside the Nisqually Entrance, is the park's oldest developed area and the site of the historic hotel, which opened in 1899. Here you'll find the old Mount Rainier National Park Headquarters, now the National Park Inn, a year-round lodge and restaurant. There's also a museum, a general store, a wilderness information center, and a post office. Although it sounds as if this must be a small city, it is actually quite compact and rarely very crowded. Other important features of the area are the Trail of the Shadows, Historic District Walking Trail, and a Transportation Exhibit.

Paradise, in the south-central portion of the park, is a subalpine meadow and one of the most popular areas for visitors. Nearby you'll find the Jackson Visitor Center, the park's main visitor center, a gracefully curving stone and concrete structure that houses a snack bar and the only public showers in the park. Interesting exhibits on geology, glaciers, and the local flora and fauna are here. Paradise is also the site of the Paradise Inn, a historic mountain lodge that's undergoing extensive renovations.

Ohanapecosh, off Wash. 123 in the park's southeast corner, offers scenic views of the Ohanapecosh River near a visitor center. Inside, look for exhibits focused primarily on the old-growth forest ecosystem that surrounds this area. The 188-site Ohanapecosh Campground is here, as are several good, short hikes.

At 6,400 feet, **Sunrise,** in the northeast part, is the highest point to which you can drive in the park. This is the second most popular spot in the park. You'll find displays and naturalist-led walks, a snack bar and restaurant, and interpretive programs on the subalpine and alpine ecosystems. You can look at the glaciers up close with free telescopes. The visitor center is open daily from July through mid-September, when the roadway is open.

The **Carbon River area,** in the northwest corner, provides access to the most heavily forested area in the park. The jury is still out as to whether the terrain is actually lowland forest or temperate rainforest. The road here is indefinitely closed to vehicle traffic, but trails lead into the backcountry and connect with the **Wonderland Trail.** A separate road (Wash. 165) reaches the Mowich Lake area, open to the lake in summer only.

3 Organized Tours & Ranger Programs

Gray Line of Seattle (✆ **800/426-7532** or 206/626-5200; www.graylineofseattle.com) offers bus tours into the park from May through September. Cost for a 1-day tour is $62 for adults, $31 for children. Three- and seven-day tours that include accommodations and explore both Mount Rainier and Seattle are also available for about $300 and $750 per person, respectively, based on double occupancy.

Ranger-led tours, discussions, and seminars take place or begin at Longmire, Ohanapecosh, Paradise, and Sunrise visitor centers.

At **Longmire,** short history talks take place daily in summer. There are evening programs at Cougar Rock Campground.

At **Ohanapecosh,** there are ranger-led hikes and walks along popular trails almost daily, as well as evening programs during July and August devoted to natural and cultural history and resources.

From **Paradise,** there are daily walks to view wildflowers and glaciers. Park naturalists also roam the area answering questions.

From the **Sunrise** area, there are daily ranger-led walks. During July and August, evening campfire programs take place at White River Campground.

Programs change each year and season. Check at a visitor center for specific programs and times during your visit.

4 Day Hikes

Some trails, especially those near Sunrise and Paradise, are packed throughout the summer. However, many forest trails offer solitude. Trails in the northwest corner, near the Carbon River Entrance, are relatively quiet but now require a 4-mile hike along the destroyed roadway to get to the former trail head. Mowich Lake sees more weekend foot traffic, since the road is open in the summer.

For current information on trail availability or closures, call the **Longmire Wilderness Information Center** (✆ **360/569-4453**) in summer, or the Longmire Museum (✆ **360/569-2211,** ext. 3314) year-round.

In addition to the trails discussed below, a section of the famed **Pacific Crest Trail** skirts the park's eastern edge. This trail runs some 2,600 miles from Mexico to Canada. For information on the entire route, contact the **Pacific Crest Trail Association,** 5325 Elkhorn Blvd., PMB #256, Sacramento, CA 95842-2526 (✆ **916/349-2109;** www.pcta.org).

ALL THE WAY AROUND MOUNT RAINIER

Wonderland Trail With varying degrees of difficulty, this 93-mile loop is the mother of all trails in the park. It circles Mount Rainier, with numerous connecting trail heads. To some, making this loop through some of the most stunning vistas in the continental United States is a Northwest rite of passage. Think hard and plan ahead before you try to take it all at once. You'll want to leave yourself about 2 weeks' time to make the whole loop.

There are more things to see on this trail than you can name. But expect to find yourself traveling through subalpine meadows, glacial streams, mountain passes, valley forests, and an ultimate summit point of 6,500 feet at Panhandle Gap. Many backcountry camping spots along the way provide water in the summer, but be sure to purify every drop. In the interest of planning shorter trips, keep in mind that you can connect with this trail from any of the spokelike trails that crisscross and touch the trail throughout the park, allowing you to set up a hiking mileage and time schedule all your own. It's possible for 1 day's elevation gain to be as much as 7,000 feet. 93 miles RT. Allow 10–14 days. Strenuous. Access: Start from Longmire, Paradise, Sunrise, Mowich Lake, or Carbon River.

LONGMIRE AREA

Although flood damage has closed Westside Road 3 miles up, the **Lake George and Gobblers Knob Lookout Trail** is open.

Carter Falls Trail This trail passes a wooden pipeline that once carried water, which generated electricity for Longmire. Go past Carter Falls about 50 yards for a look at the second waterfall, the zany Madcap Falls. This trail is part of the Wonderland Trail, between Paradise to the east and Indian Henry's to the west. 2.2 miles RT. Easy. Access: 100 yards downhill from Cougar Park Campground, on the road to Paradise.

Rampart Ridge Trail This is a somewhat steep trail at first (the elevation gain is 1,339 ft.), before you arrive at the top of an ancient lava flow called the Ramparts, which offers panoramic views of the Nisqually Valley to the south, Mount Rainier to the north, and, to the west, the site of the massive Kautz Creek Mudflow of 1947. It's also your connection with many of the other trails in the area, including the Van Trump, Comet, and Christine Falls trails. 4.6 miles RT. Moderate. Access: Across road from Longmire Museum.

Trail of Shadows Nature Trail This short, level loop trail is an enjoyable walk through the forest around Longmire Meadow. It takes you past the former site of the Longmire Springs Hotel, as well as a log cabin that's the oldest man-made structure in the park. Don't drink from the springs. .7 miles RT. Easy. Access: Across road from Longmire Museum.

Van Trump Park & Comet Falls Trail This steep trail (total elevation gain of 2,200 ft.) leads 1.9 miles through old-growth forest to Comet Falls, the second-highest falls in the park at 320 feet. Hiking another mile uphill takes you to beautiful views of the Nisqually, Van Trump, and Kautz glaciers. This is a popular trail in the summer, but it can be dangerous in early summer due to trail damage and steep, icy slopes; stop at the ranger station and ask for information on trail conditions before going. Up to 5.8 miles RT. Moderate. Access: Below Christine Falls Bridge on road to Paradise.

PARADISE AREA

Alta Vista This popular day hike meanders through subalpine meadows along a trail that leads to the top of an overlook with views of Paradise Meadows, Mount Adams, and Mount St. Helens to the south. There's a 600-foot elevation gain. 1.75 miles RT. Easy. Access: Jackson Visitor Center parking lot.

Bench & Snow Lakes Trail You can catch both lakes on this trail of gradual ups and downs over low ridges before reaching Bench Lake after .75 mile, then continuing another .5 mile to Snow Lake, with beautiful views of beargrass and meadow flowers. The round-trip takes about an hour, with a 700-foot elevation gain. 2.5 miles RT. Easy to moderate. Access: Stevens Canyon Rd., 1 ½ miles east of Reflection Lakes.

Dead Horse Creek Trail The Dead Horse Trail serves as a conduit to the Moraine and Glacier Vista trails, as well as providing views of the Nisqually Glacier to your left as you head up the ridge. You will be rewarded with dramatic views if you take the Moraine Trail spur to the left, .75 mile up the path. 2.5 miles RT. Easy to moderate. Access: Northern end of Jackson Visitor Center parking lot.

Nisqually Vista Trail This interpretive trail leads across rolling terrain, with a 200-foot elevation gain, to explore the high-country flowers, with views of

If You Have Only 1 Day

Most folks who make Mount Rainier a day trip are coming from the Seattle area, and they work their way around from the southwest corner of the park, driving first through **Longmire** to **Paradise,** then **Ohanapecosh,** and on to **Sunrise.** But, Sunrise being named what it is, you might want to go the other way around to get the best daylight, in which case you'll want to enter on Wash. 410 at the park's northeast corner. If you're coming from the south or from Yakima, adjust your entry point and itinerary accordingly. The day-tripper will probably not be able to visit the Carbon River area in the northwest and fit in Paradise and Sunrise. But Carbon River also makes a great 1-day visit, but the flood-caused road closure makes it a hike or a bike instead of a drive.

It might be a bit pedestrian, but if you want to get the whole flavor of what Mount Rainier is about, you will probably want to do the normal route and head into the park through the Longmire Entrance in late summer. You get old-growth forests, subalpine meadows blooming with flowers, and a look at the rocky scree underneath the Emmons and Winthrop glaciers. If you'd rather avoid lines of cars later in the day, start early in the morning. By noon, Rainier is packed, especially on weekends.

For an 80-mile trip, start out at the **Nisqually Entrance** on Wash. 706, and check out the **Longmire Museum** and its exhibits on American Indian culture, European exploration, and the area's natural history, as well as the local flora and fauna. If you've already been driving a bit, take a walk on the excellent .7-mile **Trail of the Shadows** across from the National Park Inn. The trail passes by the mineral springs that once were home to the early hotel, as well as a cabin (reconstructed) built by one of the Longmires in 1888. Don't drink the mineral water; it will make you very sick.

Next is an up-close-and-personal look at the fantastic burst of colors in **Paradise**'s fields of brilliant paintbrush, anemones, and gentians. But first visit the **Jackson Visitor Center** and figure out what you're looking at. It might be the Nisqually or Wilson glacier hanging over your head. For a more up-close view of the Nisqually Glacier, take the 1.2-mile (1 hr. round-trip) **Nisqually Vista Trail** from the visitor center. Otherwise, numerous trails leading from the parking lot will allow you to create your own wildflower stroll. Please stay on the trails to protect the wildflowers.

the Nisqually Glacier. 1.2 miles RT. Easy. Access: Jackson Visitor Center.

Skyline Trail This trail is a good choice for high-elevation hiking, without going all the way to the top of Mount Rainier. They're sort of extended versions of all the trails that surround Paradise, offering lots of beautiful subalpine meadows and close-up views of the Nisqually Glacier, one of the most visible and beautiful glaciers in the park. At Panorama Point, there is a pit toilet for a quick stop before the trail begins to loop back around to the southeast. At the top of this loop, you may have to traverse some snow. There's a 1,700-foot elevation gain. On the way back, check out the views of Mount Adams and Mount St. Helens. 5 miles RT. Moderate. Access: Left of Paradise Ranger Station, next to restrooms.

SUNRISE & NORTHEASTERN AREAS

Berkeley Park/Grand Park Trail Head for the high tableland meadows and the wildflower and green field bonanza at Grand Park. Stay on the trails to protect fragile vegetation. Bring plenty of water—there's none up here. Head out of the Sunrise parking lot to the Sourdough Ridge Trail, where the view is the most scenic and the road the easiest. At 6,700-foot Frozen Lake, descend toward Berkeley Park, keeping right with the trail to Mystic Lake. Berkeley Camp is 4 miles from Sunrise, and it's another 2.5 miles, mostly uphill, to the Plateau of Grand Park. 13 miles RT. Strenuous. Access: Branches off Sourdough Ridge/Dege PeakTrail (described below).

Burroughs Mountain Trail If you can't handle the snow, you might not want to take this trail. This is ice-ax territory, sometimes until early August, so come prepared. Follow the Sunrise Rim Trail, which begins on the south side of the Sunrise Visitor Center parking lot, to Shadow Lake and Sunrise Campground, and to a sharp upturn toward the First Burroughs Peak at 7,000 feet. Beyond this point, you're in a delicate tundra climate, one of the few in the Lower 48. It's possible to take the Frozen Lake Trail at First Burroughs and make a loop back to Sunrise if you don't feel like climbing anymore. However, should you decide to head up the remaining 400 vertical feet, you'll be treated to fantastic views of Mount Rainier and the Emmons and Winthrop glaciers. Total elevation gain is 1,200 feet.

From Paradise, head east toward the **Stevens Canyon Entrance.** Your next goal is a short hike along the **Grove of the Patriarchs** at Ohanapecosh. This 1.3-mile walk, one of the most popular in the park, is famous for its absolutely huge Douglas fir and western red cedar, located on a small island accessible by a bridge across the beautiful Ohanapecosh River. If you have time, take the **Hot Springs Nature Trail,** which begins at the visitor center, a quick .4-mile jaunt where you will see a shallow hot spring alongside the trail as you gaze down at a meadow of lush grass. Other worthy stops are at Reflection Lakes and Box Canyon along Stevens Canyon Road.

Finally, wind your way through forests of fir, cedar, and hemlock on the way to **Sunrise.** The big snowcapped mountain in your rearview mirror to the south is Mount Adams, equal in beauty to Mount Rainier but more remote. This side of the mountain is glacier-packed. Check out **Emmons Vista** for views of Little Tahoma and the Emmons Glacier, or take the 1.5-mile **Sunrise Rim Trail,** which also leads away from the day lodge. For a close-up view, use the telescopes at the visitor center.

IF YOU HAVE MORE TIME The best way to explore the park is on foot, and if you have more than 1 day, you'll be able to get out on the trails. The mother of all park trails is the Wonderland Trail, which, as it winds its labyrinthine route around the entire mountain, takes you through any section of the park you might be interested in. Although most folks plan 10 days to 2 weeks to do this one, there's no law that says you can't do a small portion of the Wonderland Trail. Since it's accessible from all the major park centers, you can do a piece as a day hike (see "Day Hikes," below).

The least visited sections of the park, including the beautiful **Carbon River** area northwest of the mountain, are really some of the best. If you have the time, go there. The Carbon River basin contains a temperate rainforest. The only other temperate rainforest in the United States is on the Olympic Peninsula, making the Carbon River area a unique jewel of an ecosystem. You'll need to allow time to hike around, though, as the road was closed to cars by flooding; bikes and pedestrians are welcome.

7 miles RT. Moderate to strenuous. Access: Branches off Sunrise Rim Trail (described below).

Glacier Basin Trail Watch for rusting machinery on this journey through a part of the park that wasn't always so protected. You'll see remnants of a mining operation from the late 1800s in this glacial valley. Follow an old road up past the headwaters of the White River. After 1 mile, veer to the left for beautiful views of the Emmons Glacier. Beyond the junction of the trail with the Burroughs Mountain Trail, you'll arrive at Glacier Basin Camp. Look for climbers making the ascent to the summit here, along a secondary route. Elevation gain is about 1,300 feet. 7 miles RT. Moderate to strenuous. Access: Past White River Entrance, in upper area of White River Campground.

Mt. Fremont Lookout Trail From the trail head, you climb for about .3 mile along this popular trail through the surrounding meadows, then follow Sourdough Ridge to the left toward Frozen Lake. At the end of the lake, take the fork to the right for the easy 1.3-mile hike to the Mt. Fremont Lookout, where you can get excellent glimpses of the surrounding Cascades. On a clear day, you might even be able to see Seattle. Elevation gain is about 1,200 feet. 5.5 miles RT. Moderate. Access: North end of Sunrise Visitor Center parking lot.

Naches Peak Loop Trail This is a popular hike, with stunning views from the top of Naches Peak of the meadows and lakes stretching toward Rainier's icy summit. From the Pacific Crest trail head (see the intro to the "Day Hikes" section, above), head south, traversing the east side of the Naches Peak. There's the junction with the loop that can be taken back to Tipsoo Lake, or continue ahead .5 mile to Dewey Lake, where there are campsites. Elevation gain is 500 feet. A wheelchair-accessible path is at Tipsoo Lake, near the Pacific Crest trail head junction. 3.5 miles RT. Easy. Access: Pacific Crest trail head, near Tipsoo Lake. Follow trail to junction with Naches Peak Loop Trail.

Palisades Lake Trail This is a popular trail, so don't expect to get away from other hikers. However, if you're out for a fairly invigorating stroll through forest and meadowlands, this is a good one. It includes small rises and falls in elevation as you wander past small alpine lakes toward a rock outcropping called, appropriately enough, the Palisades. There are also good wilderness campsites a little farther on, at Dick's Lake and Upper Palisades Lake, though they tend to be crowded in the summertime. 7 miles RT. Easy to moderate. Access: Sunrise Visitor Center.

Sourdough Ridge Nature Trail This loop provides you with a brief glimpse of what's on the longer Sourdough Ridge/Dege Peak Trail (described below). This self-guided tour of the summer wildflowers and subalpine meadows is quite popular, and it's good for kids. 1 mile RT. Easy. Access: Sunrise Visitor Center parking lot.

Sourdough Ridge/Dege Peak Trail From the trail head, climb to a ridge top and turn east beneath the gaze of Antler Peak, after which you'll cruise along the ridge for wonderful views of Rainier to the south and the brilliant greens of the Yakima parklands below. At the top of Dege Peak, look south for close-up views of the Cowlitz Chimneys and farther-off views of snowcapped Mount Adams. 4.2 miles RT. Easy to moderate. Access: Sunrise Visitor Center.

Summerland Trail If you want to see some mountain goats, take this trail to Panhandle Gap, about 1.5 miles past the end of the 4-mile, one-way entrance to the Frying Pan Glacier area. Hundreds of hikers can flock to this trail on a peak summer day, so beware. And please stay *on* the trails to avoid trampling the wildflowers. It's a 3.5-mile graded walk through mature forests before entering the Frying Pan Creek area, where the scenery opens up into the brushy upper Frying Pan Valley. From there it's a steep .5-mile climb to the spectacular Summerland Meadows. The total elevation gain is 1,500 feet. 8.5 miles RT. Easy to moderate. Access: Past White River Entrance, on the way to Sunrise or White River area.

Sunrise Rim Trail This is a nature trail with many interpretive signs to tell you what to look for as you gaze up at Mount Rainier, to the north. About 1.5 miles into the trail, you'll arrive at Shadow Lake and, just beyond, the walk-in Sunrise Campground. With a little more effort, you can hike south to the glacier overlook and be awed by the blue-white overhangs of Emmons Glacier and on to the first Burroughs Mountain. Total elevation gain is 900 feet. 4.8 miles RT. Easy to moderate. Access: Sunrise Visitor Center.

OHANAPECOSH AREA

Grove of the Patriarchs Trail This short, level, and popular trail follows the Ohanapecosh River before crossing over a bridge to an island of incredibly huge, thousand-year-old Douglas firs and western red cedars. Even though it's well traveled, it's still a pretty awe-inspiring place—if you can manage to find a little silence in which to meditate on the grandeur of the trees. 1.3 miles RT. Easy. Access: Just west of Stevens Canyon Entrance on Stevens Canyon Rd.

Silver Falls Trail This trail, a fairly level one, is popular with families. It winds its way through old-growth forests and over a bridge above the pristine waters of the Ohanapecosh River facing the falls that give the area its name. The misty falls themselves drop 75 feet. Across the bridge below the falls is the return trail to the Ohanapecosh Campground. 3 miles RT. Easy. Access: Ohanapecosh Visitor Center; start at far end of "B" Loop of Ohanapecosh Campground.

NORTHWESTERN RAINIER

In 1999, the Carbon River Road reopened after years of storm damage. This is a very flood-prone area, and the road closed again after floods washed it out again in 2006. There are no plans to reopen it to cars, but bicyclists and hikers are welcome. For all trails listed below, visitors bike or walk a rough trail 4.5 miles from the ranger station at the park entrance to the Ipsut Creek Campground and the trail heads. Be sure to call the **Park Information Line** (✆ **360/569-2211**) for information before taking any of the northwest Rainier trips.

Storm damage notwithstanding, the best way to reach trails from the Carbon River Road is connecting with the Wonderland Trail or driving in on the Mowich River Road (Wash. 165). Access to the Wonderland Trail along this corner of the park by car, unlike those on the southern and northeastern sides, is limited. The Carbon Glacier, Rainforest, Mystic Lake, Moraine Park, Mowich Lake, and Tolmie Peak trails are accessible from the Carbon River Entrance by foot and the Mowich Lake Road by car, or from the Wonderland Trail on an extended hike.

Carbon Glacier & Moraine Park Trails After hiking in the first 4.5 miles on the Carbon River Road, you begin this hike toward Moraine Park on the Wonderland Trail, the first 3 miles of which are a gentle uphill grade as they parallel the beautiful glacial waters of the Carbon River. Subsequently, the trail crosses the river on a suspension bridge just below the lower edge of the Carbon Glacier. Take a right turn on the Wonderland Trail at its junction with the Northern Loop, and the trail will lead you to the edge of this, the lowest and seemingly most monstrous glacier in the Lower 48. The trail then becomes a series of steep switchbacks that lead you through the neighboring forest to Moraine Park. Along the way, you'll pass several campsites (Carbon River, Dick Creek, and, farther along, Mystic Lake). The elevation gain is 1,200 to 3,300 feet, depending on the route you take. 12–16 miles RT. Moderate to strenuous. Access: Carbon River Entrance Station.

Mystic Lake Trail To reach Mystic Lake, you must first hike to the narrow, subalpine valley of Moraine Park, a moderate to strenuous trip. When the hike includes Mystic Lake, the round-trip distance becomes 20.8 miles, with elevation gains of 3,900 feet. Beyond the park, the trail goes over two small, wooded ridges, then descends a short distance to Mystic Lake. The trail was named by two early naturalists who claimed to have seen a mysterious whirlpool near the lake's outlet. Many people use the campsites around Mystic Lake as base camps for exploring the Curtis Ridge area; they have spectacular views of the Winthrop and Carbon glaciers. 20.8 miles RT. Moderate to strenuous. Access: Carbon River Entrance Station.

Spray Park Trail Go to Spray Falls at sunset if you want to see the light hit the spray action. Set amid subalpine meadows, Spray Falls is a spectacular sight in the summer when the flowers are blooming, although most of the hike proceeds through forested terrain. The trail head intersects the Wonderland Trail after a .25-mile descent. Follow the Spray Park Trail east for 2 miles, through the woods, across Lee Creek, and eventually to a junction with a spur trail to overlook the falls. The next .5 mile to the Spray Park Meadows is a steep climb up a series of switchbacks. Even more extensive meadows come into view in another .5 mile. The whole trip has an elevation gain of 1,300 feet. 6 miles RT. Moderate. Access: Southeast side of Mowich Lake Walk-in Campground, at the end of Mowich Lake Rd.

Tolmie Peak This is a hugely popular day hike, with lots of traffic from weekenders and kids, but you can't really go that wrong anywhere around here. The trail proceeds gently through 1.25 miles of forested woodland to the junction at Ipsut Pass (elevation 5,100 ft.). Stay left and proceed uphill another 1.75 miles to the subalpine meadows at Eunice Lake for a look at how far you're going to have to climb to Tolmie Peak. ***Note:*** Tolmie Peak is closed to overnight backpackers. The entire hike has a 1,010-foot elevation gain. 6.5 miles RT. Moderate. Access: End of Mowich Lake Rd. on left side of lake.

5 Other Summer Sports & Activities

BIKING No trails are open to mountain bikes in Mount Rainier National Park. However, there are plenty of trails to ride at nearby Crystal Mountain and White Pass ski areas during the summer. Crystal Mountain is by far the most popular and is known for its grueling climbs and brake-turning downhills. Luckily, you can avoid much of the climbing by riding the lifts up. The lifts generally operate only on weekends. A good gravel road for great biking is Westside Road, which you can reach through the Nisqually Entrance of Mount Rainier National Park. It is completely closed to motorized vehicles after 3 miles. One of the best reasons to ride this road is the chance to get on some of the little-used west-side hiking trails (closed to bikes). Try strapping some hiking boots on your bike; this is a great way to get away from the crowds and see some of the rare, less crowded areas of the park. However, you might want to call ahead for information on the usage of Westside Road. Another option is Carbon River Road, closed to vehicles since the 2006, with 4.5 miles open to only bikes and pedestrians en route to the Ipsut Creek Campground and myriad trail heads.

BOATING & CANOEING Located in the northwest corner of the park, Mowich Lake is a pristine little lake with a peekaboo view of the mountain from its west side. The water is incredibly clear, and it's fun to paddle around gazing down into the deep at the large logs and boulders lying on the bottom. Early morning and late afternoon are particularly good times. You might catch a glimpse of an otter, and in the evening, deer often feed in the meadows by the lake's edge. A walk-in campground beside the lake makes this a great spot for a weekend camping and paddling trip. Yes, there are even a few fish in the lake, if you want to try your luck (see "Fishing," below).

FISHING The good news about fishing in Mount Rainier National Park is that no fishing license is required. The bad news is that the fishing isn't very good. However, there are some fish out there, and you're welcome to try to catch a few. Lots of people do. Remember that only artificial lures and flies can be used in the park, and some posted waters are closed to fishing. Ask for details.

For the most part, glacial silt keeps Mount Rainier's rivers too cloudy for fishing in the summer. The Ohanapecosh River is one exception. This river, in the southeast corner of the park, flows clear throughout the summer and is designated for fly-fishing only. Anglers are encouraged to release the trout they catch. Most of the park's many lakes are home to one or another species of trout. In most cases, you have to hike in to fish. Some shorter hikes include Sunrise Lake (below Sunrise Point) and Louise, Bench, and Snow lakes, east of Paradise off the road to the Stevens Canyon Entrance.

HORSEBACK RIDING If you'd like to do some horseback riding, you have a few options in the area. In Elbe, you'll find **EZ Times Outfitters,** 18703 Wash. 706 (✆ **866/675-7700** or 253/350-1141; www.eztimeshorserides.com), which leads rides into the Elbe Hills State Forest. On the east side of the park, 19 miles east of Chinook Pass on Wash. 410, you'll find **Chinook Pass Outfitter & Guides** (✆ **800/726-3631** or 509/653-2633; www.chinookpass.com). East of White Pass on U.S. 12, you'll find **Indian Creek Corral** (✆ **509/672-2400;** www.indiancreekcorral.com), near the shore of Rimrock Lake. Horse rides cost $25 to $45 an hour.

MOUNTAINEERING Each year, more than 10,000 people set out to climb the 14,411-foot summit of Mount Rainier. That only slightly more than half make it to the top is a testament to how difficult the climb is. Although the ascent does not require rock-climbing skills, the glacier crossings require basic mountaineering knowledge, and the 9,000-foot climb from Paradise is physically demanding. Also, the elevation often causes altitude sickness. This is not a mountain to be attempted by the unprepared or the untrained; over the years, dozens of people have died attempting the summit. Because of the many difficulties presented by summit ascents at Mount Rainier, this mountain often serves as a training ground for expeditions headed to peaks all over the world.

The easiest and most popular route starts at Paradise, at 5,400 feet, and climbs to the stone climbers' shelter at 10,188-foot Camp Muir. From here, climbers, roped together for safety, set out in the middle of the night to reach Columbia Crest, the mountain's highest point at 14,411 feet. From the summit on a clear day, seemingly all of Washington and much of Oregon stretches below.

The best way for most of us to climb Mount Rainier is with somebody who knows what he or she is doing, and that means **RMI Expeditions,** P.O. Box Q, Ashford, WA 98304 (✆ **888/892-5462** or 360/569-2227; www.rmiguides.com); **International Mountain Guides,** P.O. Box 246, Ashford, WA 98304 (✆ **360/569-2609;** www.mountainguides.com); and **Alpine Ascents,** 121 Mercer St., Seattle, WA 98109 (✆ **206/378-1927;** www.alpineascents.com). Each offers a variety of mountaineering classes, as well as guided summer climbs. A class combined with the 2- or 3-day summit climb runs about $900 to $1,300.

WILDLIFE VIEWING Hunting is prohibited in Mount Rainier National Park; consequently, deer, elk, and mountain goats within the park have lost their fear of humans. Anyone hiking the park's trails in the summer can expect to encounter some of these large mammals. Deer are the most common, although the park's mountain goats seem to command the greatest interest. Look for goats on Goat Island Mountain across the White River valley from Sunrise (use binoculars) on the Summerland Trail, on Mount Fremont (5.5-mile round-trip hike from Sunrise), and at Skyscraper Pass (7-mile round-trip hike from Sunrise).

Undoubtedly, the most seen mammals in the park are marmots, which resemble beavers but have round tails and live in the subalpine meadows. These big, shaggy members of the squirrel family are frequently seen lying on rocks soaking up the sun. They often allow people to get fairly close, but when alarmed, they let loose with a shrill whistle.

Wild animals are fun to see, but they *are* wild. For both their safety and yours, keep your distance.

6 Winter Sports & Activities

CROSS-COUNTRY SKIING There are several ungroomed cross-country trails around the Paradise and Longmire areas. Perhaps equally satisfying in winter is the absence of crowds and cars that haunt these regions during the summer months. Peace and quiet abound when snow covers the landscape, although there is often a threat of avalanches (check at the Jackson Visitor Center or Paradise Ranger Station). The slopes above the Paradise Inn usually stay covered with snow well into June. You can rent cross-country skis at **Longmire** at the National Park Inn (✆ **360/569-2411;** www.guestservices.com). Skis, poles, and shoes will cost you about $20 per day.

West of the park, the Mount Tahoma Trails Association trail system maintains 50 miles of easy to difficult trails, which are accessible from Ashford (follow signs to the snow parks). For information, maps, or hut reservations, contact the **Mount Tahoma Trails Association,** P.O. Box 206, Ashford, WA 98304 (✆ **360/569-2451;** www.skimtta.com), or stop by headquarters in Ashford, which is usually open on winter weekends. There are about 10 miles of trails at **White Pass** (✆ **509/672-3101;** www.skiwhitepass.com), about 20 miles southeast of the park. There are also 32 downhill runs served by 5 lifts here.

Outside the northeast entrance of the park, downhill resort **Crystal Mountain ski area** (✆ **360/663-2265;** www.skicrystal.com) offers good backcountry skiing, though there are no maintained trails. Only experienced skiers should attempt backcountry skiing here due to the difficult conditions and danger of avalanches.

SNOWMOBILING Snowmobiles are permitted on designated roadways, and only when snow closes the roadways to normal traffic. Do not attempt to travel cross-country on trails or on undesignated roads. Obtain a copy of the park's snowmobile regulations.

SNOWSHOEING If you've never tried snowshoeing and want to, visit Mount Rainier National Park when free, ranger-led **snowshoe walks** lasting about 90 minutes are offered, on winter weekends and holidays from late December to early April. Snowshoes are available for rent for $1. For more information, call the **Longmire Museum** (✆ **360/569-2211,** ext. 3314).

One of the better snowshoeing options in the park is the marked route from the Paradise parking lot behind the Jackson Visitor Center to the Nisqually Glacier Overlook. The Nisqually Vista Trail is only 1.25 miles long and twists and turns as it meanders up and down hills. At the turnaround, you have a great view of the glacier and the rest of the mountain, but don't get too close to the edge!

Lower down on the mountain, at Longmire, snowshoers can make a 4.6-mile loop up Rampart Ridge. This steep trail requires some route finding and the snow level is not always reliable, but if conditions are right, it makes for an enjoyable and rigorous hike. Another good snowshoeing trail in this same area is the trail to Carter Falls, which starts above Longmire just before the Cougar Rock Campground. This 2.2-mile round-trip trail follows a section of the Wonderland Trail. It's all uphill to Carter Falls, and it crosses several avalanche chutes.

7 Camping

Mount Rainier has more than 400 campsites in three drive-in campgrounds. None of the campgrounds in the park has RV utility hookups, nor are there laundry or shower facilities.

You should definitely make reservations at Cougar Rock and Ohanapecosh campgrounds between the last Friday in June and Labor Day; call ✆ **877/444-6777** or visit www.recreation.gov. Other campgrounds are on a first-come, first-served basis.

Cougar Rock Campground, a little more than 2¼ miles northwest of Longmire, has an amphitheater for ranger programs. **Ohanapecosh Campground,** 11 miles north of Packwood, Washington, on Wash. 123, also has an amphitheater. **White River Campground** is 5 miles west of the White River Entrance. **Sunshine Point Campground** was closed in 2006 due to flood damage.

There are two walk-in campgrounds that often have spaces available, even on weekends. **Mowich Lake Campground** is in the northwest corner of the park, at the end of unpaved S.R. 165, and the sites are only 100 yards from a parking lot. A walk-in campground since the 2006 flooding, **Ipsut Creek Camp Campground** is about 5 miles east of the park's Carbon River Entrance. A backcountry permit is required. If you're prepared for a longer walk, consider the **Sunrise Campground,** about a mile from the Sunrise parking lot. A backcountry permit is required.

A **permit** is required for all overnight stays in the wilderness. **Backcountry camping** is free with a permit obtained at any of the ranger stations, although the first-come, first-served permits are grabbed up quickly. Reservations ($20 per permit) can be made by mail or fax beginning in mid-March for the period from May through September. For information, call ✆ **360/569-4453.**

Other camping options are in the nearby Gifford Pinchot National Forest. **La Wis Wis Campground,** in the national forest's Cowlitz Valley Ranger District, 10024 U.S. 12 (P.O. Box 670), Randle, WA (✆ **360/497-1100;** www.fs.fed.us/r6), is along U.S. 12 and the Cowlitz River, near the southeast entrance to the park. The campground has numerous tall trees and offers some sites that can accommodate RVs up to 24 feet long. Reservations (✆ **877/444-6777;** www.recreation.gov) are available.

Numerous other National Forest Service campgrounds lie along U.S. 12 east of White Pass and along Wash. 310 east of the park. These campgrounds represent your best chance of finding a campsite on a Friday or Saturday night in summer. The campgrounds along Wash. 410 tend to be less crowded, since they are harder to reach and are not near any fishing lakes. National Forest campgrounds are also within a few miles of the southwest and northeast entrances, and dispersed camping is permitted in some areas. Check the forest service website (**www.fs.fed.us/r6**) for more information.

8 Where to Stay

For information about or reservations at the lodgings inside the park, contact **Mount Rainier Guest Services,** 55106 Kernahan Rd. E., Ashford, WA 98304 (✆ **360/569-2275;** fax 360/569-2770; http://rainier.guestservices.com).

There are a number of places to stay in the surrounding communities in addition to those reviewed here. For a list, contact **Seattle's Convention and Visitors Bureau** (✆ **206/461-5840;** www.seeseattle.org) or the **Enumclaw Chamber of Commerce** (✆ **360/825-7666;** www.enumclawchamber.com).

INSIDE THE PARK

National Park Inn In Longmire in the southwest corner of the park, this rustic lodge opened in 1920 and was fully renovated in 1990. Relatively small and open year-round, the National Park Inn makes a great little getaway or base for exploring the mountain. The inn's front veranda has a view of Mount Rainier, and inside there's a guest lounge with a river-rock fireplace that's perfect for relaxing on a winter night. The guest rooms vary in size but come with rustic furniture, new carpeting, and coffeemakers. In winter this lodge is popular with cross-country skiers; skis and snowshoes can be rented here. The inn has a **restaurant,** plus full bar service, and all rooms are nonsmoking. You'll need to book reservations well in advance for the summer months. If at first you don't succeed, keep trying, because there are often cancellations.

At the Longmire Entrance, off Wash. 706 (mailing address: P.O. Box 108, Ashford, WA 98304). ✆ **360/569-2275.** http://rainier.guestservices.com. 25 units, 18 with bathroom. $114 double without bathroom; $150–$210 double with bathroom. B&B package Nov–Apr from $106. AE, DC, DISC, MC, V.

Paradise Inn First opening in 1917, the grand Paradise Inn recently had a multimillion-dollar overhaul, reopening in May 2008. The renovation included replacing the foundation and installing blizzard- and earthquake-resistant technologies, but it retained its historic look, with stone fireplaces and massive wood timbers. Rooms—which were not renovated—are similar to the rustic appointed rooms in the National Park Inn. There is a **restaurant** and snack bar on-site.

At Paradise, off Wash. 706 (mailing address: P.O. Box 108, Ashford, WA 98304). ✆ **360/569-2275.** http://rainier.guestservices.com. 121 units, 92 with bathroom. $107 double without bathroom; $158–$225 double with bathroom. AE, DC, DISC, MC, V.

OUTSIDE THE SOUTHWEST (NISQUALLY) ENTRANCE

Budget travelers might want to look into the hostel-style accommodations at **Whittaker's Bunkhouse,** 30205 Wash. 706 E., Ashford, WA 98304 (✆ **360/569-2439;** www.whittakersbunkhouse.com), with bunks for $35 and private rooms for $85 to $115 double, as well as an espresso bar. The rates are lower in winter, but bunks are not available.

Alexander's Country Inn Just outside the park's Nisqually Entrance, this appealing bed-and-breakfast opened as an inn in 1912. Today, as then, it is one of the preferred places to stay in the area, offering not only comfortable rooms but also some of the best food around (see "Where to Dine," below). Much care went into the restoration, with antique European stained-glass windows and antique furnishings. The dining room takes up the first floor; on the second floor, you'll find a big lounge where you can sit by the fire on a cold night. By far the best room is the tower suite, which is in a turret and has plenty of windows looking out on the woods. After a hard day of playing on the mountain, there's no better place to relax than in the hot tub overlooking the inn's trout pond—or in the **day spa** enjoying a massage. The inn also rents two guesthouses (call for details).

37515 Wash. 706 E., Ashford, WA 98304. ✆ **800/654-7615** or 360/569-2300. www.alexanderscountryinn.com. 12 units, 2 houses. May–Oct $125–$155 double, $165–$179 suite, $225–$235 house; Nov–Apr $99–$110 double, $135 suite, $185 house. Rates include full breakfast. MC, V.

Deep Forest Cabins Tucked into two forested fairyland locations off the road to the park, Deep Forest Cabins dates back to the 1930s, but each has been renovated since the turn of the millennium. Featuring blonde woods and attractive hardwoods, the cabins are romantic retreats with two-person jetted tubs inside and hot tubs on the decks outside, as well as full kitchens, TVs with VCRs and DVD players (but no reception), and gas fireplaces.

33823 Wash. 706, Ashford, WA 98330. ✆ **866/553-9373** or 360/569-2954. www.deepforestcabins.com. 5 cabins. TV. July–Aug $165–$215 double; Sept–May $135–$195 double. MC, V.

The Hobo Inn If you're a railroad buff, you won't want to pass up the opportunity to spend the night in a remodeled boxcar. Each of the railroad cars is a little different (one even has a kitchenette), but all

Campground	Total Sites	RV Hookups	Dump Station	Toilets	Drinking Water
Cougar Rock	173	No	Yes	Yes	Yes
Ipsut Creek*	22	No	No	Yes	No
La Wis Wis**	100	No	No	Yes	Yes
Mowich Lake	30	No	No	Yes	Yes
Ohanapecosh	188	No	Yes	Yes	Yes
Sunrise*	8	No	No	No	No
White River	112	No	No	Yes	Yes

*Camping requires a Mount Rainier National Park backcountry permit.

** National Forest site on reservation program.

have comfortable beds and bathrooms. Some have bay windows, while others have cupolas. For the total railroad experience, dine in the adjacent **Mount Rainier Railroad Dining Co.** restaurant and go for a ride on the **Mount Rainier Scenic Railroad** (✆ **888/STEAM-11** [783-2611] or 360/569-2351; www.mrsr.com).

54106 Wash. 7 (P.O. Box 20), Elbe, WA 98330. ✆ **360/569-2500.** 6 units. $115 double. Rates include full breakfast. AE, DC, DISC, MC, V.

Mountain Meadows Inn Bed & Breakfast Set beneath tall trees beside a small creek, this B&B was built in 1910 as the home of the superintendent for the lumber mill in the town of National, which was the site of the largest sawmill west of the Mississippi. Today this old home is filled with unique collections, including an outstanding display of memorabilia of John Muir and the national parks, Northwest coast American Indian basketry, and a 1,000-volume nature library. There are three rooms in the main house, a bit dated but attractively decorated with antiques and American Indian art, plus three rooms in a separate guesthouse, which are more modern. Some have shower only, some have tub only, and some have both. We especially like the Mountain Berry Room in the main house because of its claw-foot tub and handsome early American furnishings. The main house's big front porch overlooks the creek, and there is room to roam on the nature trail that meanders a mile through the inn's 11 acres of woodland. An outdoor whirlpool tub and free Wi-Fi are also on the property.

28912 Wash. 706 E. (P.O. Box 291), Ashford, WA 98304. ✆ **360/569-2788.** www.mountainmeadowsinn.com. 6 units. $139–$165 double. Rates include full breakfast. MC, V.

Nisqually Lodge This modern lodge is well located near the Nisqually Entrance to Mount Rainier National Park, and it is next door to a popular restaurant, the Rainier Overland. Rooms are of the modern motel style, average size, with wood-toned furnishings, upholstered chairs, and a few homey touches, such as flowers. The Nisqually offers a coin-op laundry, an outdoor hot tub, wireless Internet access, and satellite TV. You can read or relax by the fireplace in the Great Room. All units are nonsmoking; pets are not allowed.

31609 Wash. 706, Ashford, WA 98304. ✆ **888/674-3554** or 360/569-8804. Fax 360/569-2435. www.escapetothemountains.com. 24 units. A/C, TV, TEL. $105–$125 double; lower rates in winter. Rates include continental breakfast. AE, MC, V.

Stone Creek Lodge Located only 200 yards from the park's Nisqually Entrance, these cabins sit on green lawns that attract deer throughout the year. These are not the most elaborate of the cabins right outside the park entrance, but they're clean, functional, and recently renovated. Big picture windows let in plenty of light. Larger cabins have kitchens and fireplaces and sleep up to four people (these are good for families), some smaller ones have microwaves and refrigerators, and all have gas-log fireplaces and hot tubs. Some cabins have one queen bed, and some have one queen plus two singles. All cabins are nonsmoking.

38624 Wash. 706, Ashford, WA 98304. ✆ **800/819-3942** or 360/569-2355. www.stonecreeklodge.net. 10 cabins. $105–$150 double. AE, DISC, MC, V.

Stormking Cabins and Day Spa Especially appealing for active, outdoorsy adult couples, Stormking started out as a popular hot tub and massage facility. But people enjoyed the setting and experience so much that they kept telling co-owner Deborah Sample that she should build secluded, romantic cabins and take overnight guests. That's just what she and co-owner Steven Brown did. All of the gorgeous cabins have private hot tubs, two-person showers, and gas fireplaces. Spa treatments are offered, and Stormking is nonsmoking.

37311 Wash. 706 E. (P.O. Box 126), Ashford, WA 98304. ✆ **360/569-2964.** www.stormkingspa.com. 4 cabins. Cabin $160–$205 double (2-night minimum). MC, V.

OUTSIDE THE NORTHEAST (WHITE RIVER) ENTRANCE

Alta Crystal Resort at Mount Rainier This is the closest lodging to the northeast (White River) park entrance and the Sunrise area. The resort has

Showers	Fire Pits/ Grills	Laundry	Reserve	Fees	Open
No	Yes	No	Yes	$12–$15	Mid-May to mid-Oct
Yes	No	No	No	Free	Year-round
No	Yes	No	Yes	$18–$36	Mid-May to late Sept
No	Yes	No	No	Free	Mid-May to mid-Oct
No	Yes	No	Yes	$12–$15	Late May to mid-Oct
No	Yes	No	No	Free	Year-round
No	Yes	No	No	$12	Late June to early Oct

wooded grounds and makes a good base in winter, when skiers flock to the slopes of Crystal Mountain, just minutes away, but it is just as good for a summertime visit. The resort features suites in chalets and a log honeymoon cabin, all with a mountain-lodge atmosphere and lots of homey touches, such as dried flowers. Chalets can sleep up to four adults and two children under 12. No matter what size suite you choose, you'll find a full kitchen, fireplace or wood stove, phone with dataport, and TV with DVD player and VCR. The honeymoon cabin, set apart from the other buildings, is for two adults only; no children. Also available are a rustic recreation lodge, an outdoor pool and hot tub, and horseback riding, hiking, and mountain-bike trails from your door.

68317 Wash. 410 E., Greenwater, WA 98022. ✆ **800/277-6475** or 360/663-2500. Fax 360/663-2556. www.altacrystalresort.com. 24 units. TV, TEL. $160–$280 unit for 1–6 people. AE, MC, V.

OUTSIDE THE SOUTHEAST (STEVENS CANYON) ENTRANCE

Cowlitz River Lodge With easy access to Mount Rainier, Mount St. Helens, and White Pass skiing, this lodge offers comfortable accommodations with many amenities. Owned by the same company as the Nisqually Lodge (see above), rooms here are typical of modern American motel style—average size, with wood-toned furnishings, upholstered chairs, and a few homey touches. There's an outdoor hot tub, coin-op laundry, and waxing room for cross-country skiers. You may see deer or elk on the lawn, and you can laze by the lobby fireplace. There is free Wi-Fi and satellite TV.

13069 U.S. 12 (P.O. Box 488), Packwood, WA 98361. ✆ **888/305-2185** or 360/494-4444. www.escapetothemountains.com. 31 units. A/C, TV, TEL. $75–$95 double; lower rates in winter. Rates include complimentary continental breakfast. AE, DC, MC, V.

Hotel Packwood Two stories tall, with a wraparound porch and weathered siding, this funky, cozy 1912 hotel looks like a classic mountain lodge even though it's right in the middle of a small town. The tiny rooms aren't for the finicky, but they are comfortable and most welcome after a day spent traipsing around on park trails. There are iron bed frames in some rooms and a fireplace in the lobby. Packwood is about 10 miles from the southeast entrance to the park. All units are nonsmoking.

104 Main St., Packwood, WA 98361. ✆ **360/494-5431.** www.packwoodwa.com. 9 units, 2 with bathroom, 7 with shared bathroom. TV. $39–$49 double. DISC, MC, V.

9 Where to Dine

INSIDE THE PARK

The dining rooms at the **Paradise Inn** and the **National Park Inn** (see "Where to Stay," above) serve American and regional dishes, including salmon, chicken, steak, and pasta at dinner, with interesting sandwiches and burgers at lunch. Lunch prices are mostly in the $9 to $14 range; dinners run $14 to $23. Specialties include a slow-roasted pot roast sandwich for lunch and bourbon buffalo meatloaf at dinner. The restaurants do not accept reservations, and because they are the only formal dining option within the park, you may have to wait a bit for a table. But we think the wait is worth it. For quick meals, there is fast food at the **Jackson Visitor Center, Paradise Inn,** and **Sunrise Lodge.**

In Ashford you'll find a place that bakes great blackberry pie, the **Copper Creek Inn,** 35707 Wash. 706 E. (✆ **360/569-2326;** www.coppercreekinn.com), which is one of the closest restaurants to the park's southwest (Nisqually) entrance. It's open daily year-round, serving three meals in summer, and lunch and dinner the rest of the year. Cuisine is American Northwest, with burgers, sandwiches, and lots of salads on the lunch menu ($5–$10). The dinner menu ($13–$23) includes steak, chicken, pasta, and fish—such as grilled salmon filet with blackberry vinaigrette.

In Elbe, the **Mount Rainier Railroad Dining Company** (✆ **360/569-2505**), in an old dining car at the Hobo Inn (see "Where to Stay," above), is your best bet, serving steaks, seafood, and alder-smoked chicken and ribs; prices range from $5 to $15 at breakfast and lunch, and $5 to $21 at dinner.

Alexander's AMERICAN Alexander's, which is also a popular B&B (see "Where to Stay," above), is the best place to dine outside the Nisqually Entrance to the park. Dining outside beside the pond and waterfall is an option in the summer. Fresh pan-fried trout from the inn's pond is the dinner of choice, but you'll also find chicken, steaks, fresh salmon, stuffed pork chops, and homemade lasagna. Whatever you order, just be sure to save room for wild blackberry pie.

37515 Wash. 706 E., Ashford. ✆ **360/569-2300.** www.alexanderscountryinn.com. Dinner reservations recommended. Main courses $6–$12 breakfast and lunch, $10–$25 dinner. MC, V. Daily 8:30–10:30am and 11:30am–8pm.

25

North Cascades National Park, WA

by Eric Peterson

The Cascade Range, in many stretches of its span, receives significant visitation, but here in the northern reaches lies the largest wilderness in the state of Washington. Here gray wolves and grizzly bears still roam, and human encroachment is limited.

The North Cascades National Park Service Complex is at the heart of this region. Note the name; this is not just a park, but a complex, which includes the national park as well as Ross Lake and Lake Chelan national recreation areas. A 1988 act of Congress designated about 93% of the acreage of the entire complex the Stephen Mather Wilderness. Unlike many national recreation areas, both Ross Lake and Lake Chelan are wild and remote, with minimal development.

A trip beyond the highway corridor is a true wilderness experience. Hiking here takes time and preparation. Although there are several shorter trails, many attract the rugged few to take a few days or weeks to get reacquainted with the natural state of things. If you're prepared, there's nothing else like it in the continental United States.

Geologically speaking, the North Cascades are some of the most complex and least understood mountains in North America. These peaks were formed over millions of years as a tectonic plate drifting northward from the South Pacific slammed into the North American coast, causing the area's sedimentary rocks to buckle, fold, and transform. In some areas, the rock in the North Cascades is obviously the result of this collision and subsequent metamorphosis. In other areas, there is rock that predates the tectonic collision—one upthrust mountain is believed to be 10 million years old.

Glaciation both past and present has further augmented geologic complexity in the North Cascades. In past ice ages, both alpine glaciers and the continental ice sheet covered this region. The visual legacy of this activity endures today in the wide U-shaped valleys carved out by the ice sheet. The single most fascinating legacy of this glaciation is Lake Chelan, which lies in the heart of the North Cascades southern section.

AVOIDING THE CROWDS

It's not hard to avoid the crowds in the North Cascades. The lack of roads, the weather, and the ruggedness of the terrain all work in concert to keep this one of the best-kept secrets in the national park system.

If it's true isolation you seek, hike in the northern unit of the national park. Nonetheless, Stehekin (the developed unit of the southern park section) also offers plenty of solitude, especially in the fall and winter. Lake Chelan, Ross Lake, and Diablo Lake are relatively tourist-heavy spots.

In high season, this park can be like many others. You're more likely to run into folks on the Big Beaver Trail or on your way to Hozomeen in the summer than in the fall, which is about the last part of the year during which you can easily get anywhere in the park. Ross Lake is thicker with boaters on summer holiday weekends, and the heaviest load of visitors all year is in Stehekin and the Cascade Pass area during July and August. The deeper into the backcountry you go, the fewer people you are likely to encounter. Winter is not to be underestimated in this park, and Wash. State Route 20 will almost certainly be closed.

1 Essentials

GETTING THERE & GATEWAYS

Only one paved road, **Wash. State Route 20,** goes through the park complex. There are a few unpaved side trips, though. The **Cascade River Road,** which leaves Wash. 20 at Marblemount, enters the national park proper as an unpaved road. The gravel **Stehekin Valley Road** above High Bridge also enters the national park. This road does not connect with the outside world, however; rather, the park concessionaire provides a shuttle service along this road from mid-May to mid-October.

From **Seattle** on the west side, take the Wash. State Route 20 exit 230 off I-5 and head east, toward Rockport and Marblemount, into the park. From **Spokane,** the major metropolitan area on the east side, it's U.S. 2 West, linking up with U.S. 97 North, to Wash. State Route 153 and, finally, Wash. State Route 20. And remember, in the winter, these

North Cascades National Park

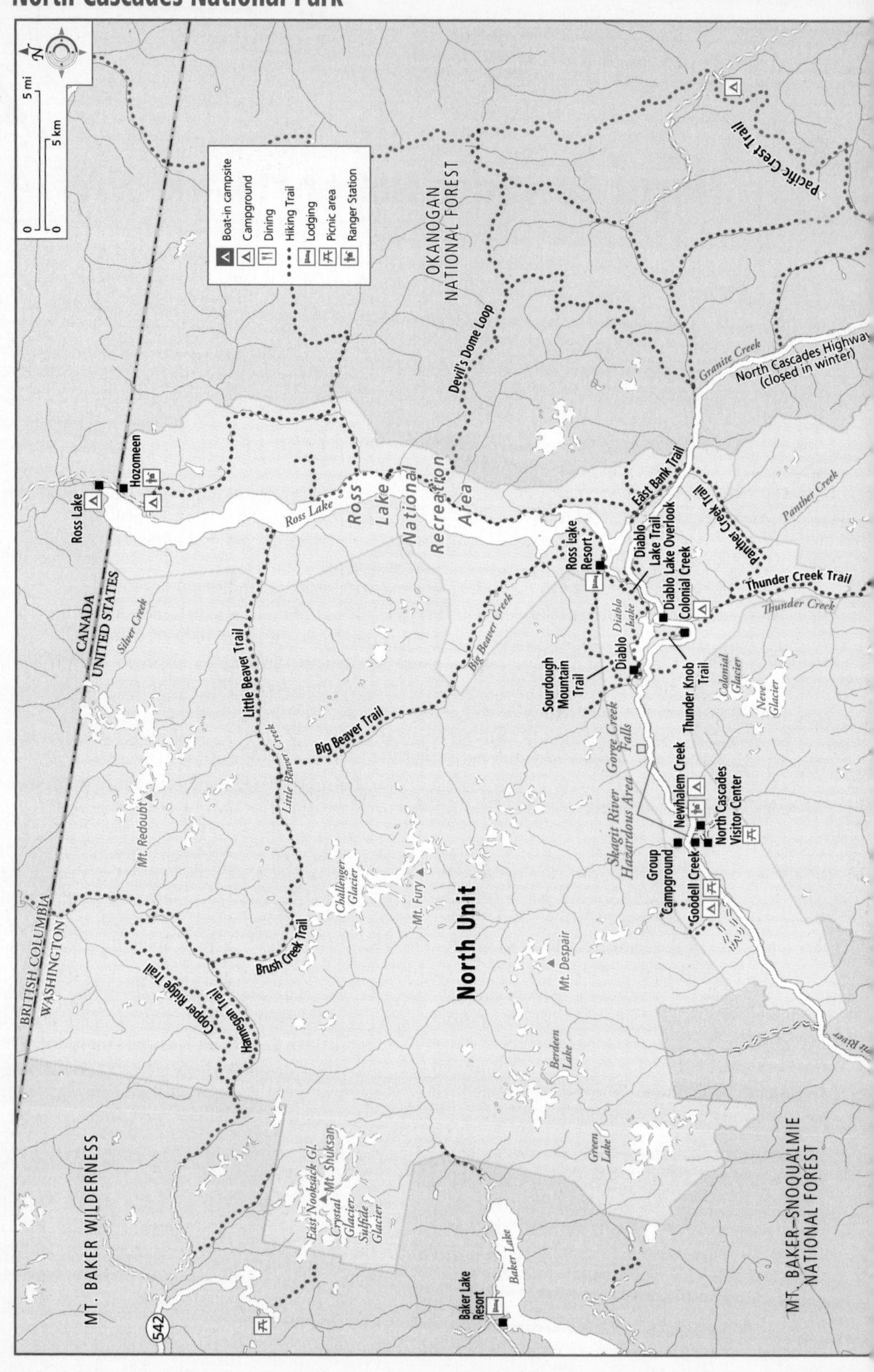

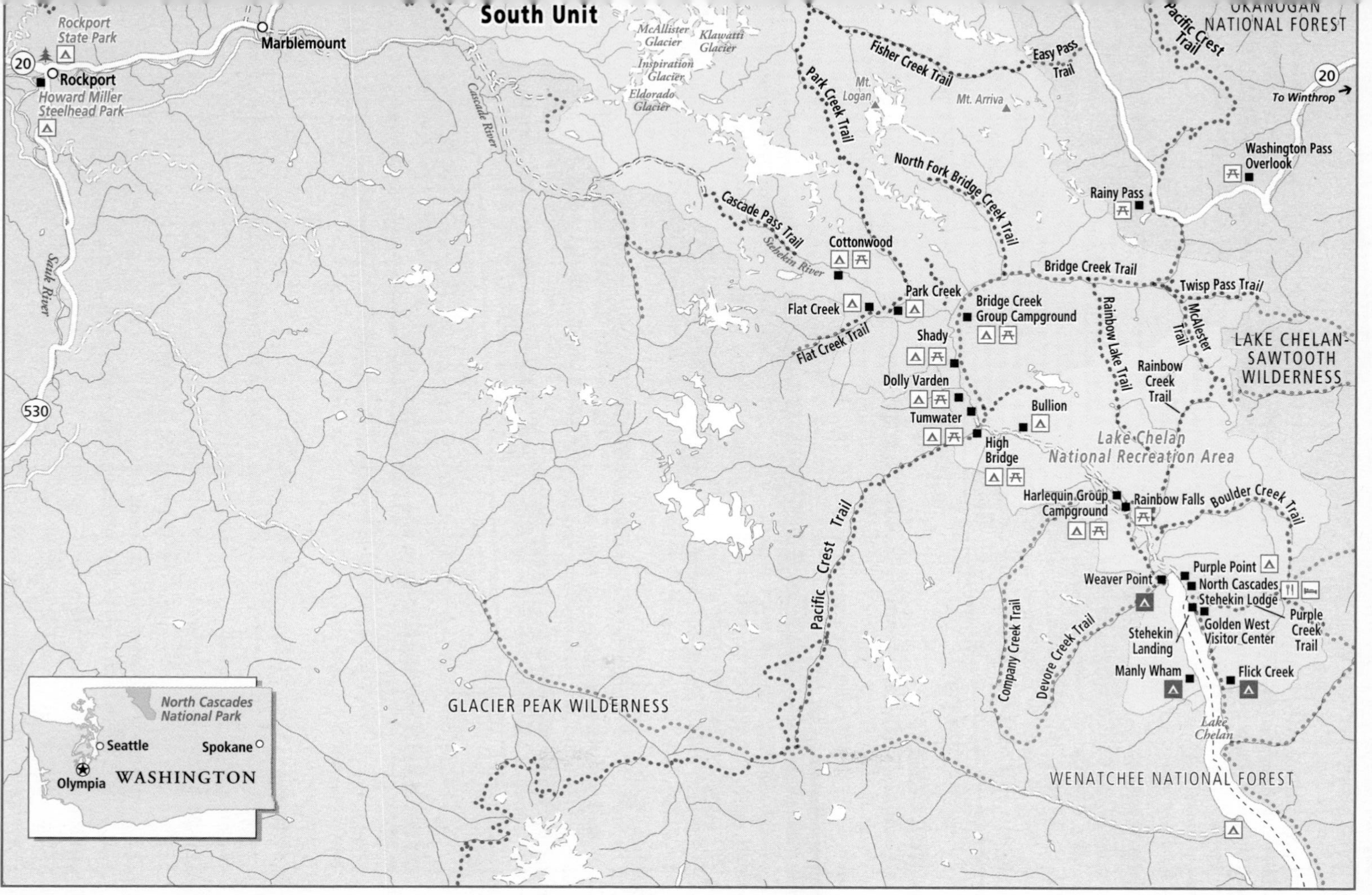

South Unit
OKANOGAN NATIONAL FOREST
Pacific Crest Trail
Rockport State Park
20
Rockport
Marblemount
Howard Miller Steelhead Park
McAllister Glacier
Klawatti Glacier
Inspiration Glacier
Eldorado Glacier
Cascade River
Fisher Creek Trail
Easy Pass Trail
Mt. Logan
Mt. Arriva
To Winthrop
Park Creek Trail
North Fork Bridge Creek Trail
Washington Pass Overlook
Rainy Pass
Cascade Pass Trail
Stehekin River
Cottonwood
Bridge Creek Trail
Twisp Pass Trail
Sauk River
Park Creek
Flat Creek
Bridge Creek Group Campground
Rainbow Lake Trail
McAlester Trail
LAKE CHELAN-SAWTOOTH WILDERNESS
Shady
Flat Creek Trail
Rainbow Creek Trail
Dolly Varden
530
Bullion
Tumwater
Lake Chelan National Recreation Area
High Bridge
Harlequin Group Campground
Rainbow Falls
Boulder Creek Trail
Pacific Crest Trail
Purple Point
Weaver Point
North Cascades Stehekin Lodge
Purple Creek Trail
Golden West Visitor Center
Stehekin Landing
Company Creek Trail
Devore Creek Trail
Manly Wham
Flick Creek
Lake Chelan
North Cascades National Park
GLACIER PEAK WILDERNESS
Seattle
Spokane
Olympia
WASHINGTON
WENATCHEE NATIONAL FOREST

roads may close at any time from late October to early May. Be sure to call ahead.

THE NEAREST AIRPORT **Seattle–Tacoma International Airport** (✆ **206/787-5388;** www.portseattle.org/seatac) is 15 miles south of Seattle on I-5. The airport is served by practically all major airlines and car-rental companies. See chapter 38 for their website listings.

INFORMATION

Contact **North Cascades National Park Service Complex,** 810 Wash. State Rte. 20, Sedro-Woolley, WA 98284 (✆ **360/854-7200;** www.nps.gov/noca). The park publishes an annual newspaper, the *North Cascades Challenger,* full of useful information. For current information, such as road closures, call or check the park's website.

VISITOR CENTERS

The **North Cascades Visitor Center,** mile marker 120, Wash. State Rte. 20, Newhalem (✆ **206/386-4495,** ext. 11), open daily in the summer, offers exhibits, audiovisual programs, a bookstore, and assistance from rangers. A wheelchair-accessible trail (Sterling Munro Viewpoint) leads from the back of the building and affords excellent views of the surrounding mountains. Several other universally accessible trails, including the Rock Shelter Trail, are nearby.

The **Golden West Visitor Center,** P.O. Box 7, Stehekin, WA 98852 (✆ **360/854-7365,** ext. 14), is on the banks of the northern tip of Lake Chelan. It provides information on camping, hiking, backcountry permits, and the local environs, and has interpretive exhibits and a bookstore. It's open daily in the summer and keeps shorter hours in winter. You can also rent bicycles from a concessionaire.

GETTING AROUND INSIDE THE PARK

BY AIR If you want to get to Stehekin in a hurry, you can make the trip by floatplane on **Chelan Seaplanes** (✆ **509/682-5555;** www.chelanseaplanes.com), which leaves from the dock next to the ferries at Chelan. The fare is $160 round-trip adults, $100 for kids under 12.

BY BOAT On Lake Chelan in the spring and summer, the ***Lady Express*** and the ***Lady of the Lake II*** run between the Lake Chelan boat landing and Stehekin, at the north end of the lake. In the fall and winter, only the *Lady Express* operates. Rides cost $39 to $59 round-trip, depending on the boat. Contact **Lady of the Lake** (✆ **509/682-4584;** www.ladyofthelake.com). The **Ross Lake Resort** (✆ **206/386-4437**) operates water taxis to trail heads and campgrounds on Ross Lake and offers portage service.

BY SHUTTLE BUS A shuttle bus provides transportation up the Stehekin Valley Road.

No reservations are required, and the cost is $5 one-way. If you want to ride as far as the Stehekin Pastry Company, the fare is only $2 each way.

Taxi service is also available from the North Cascades Stehekin Lodge at the boat landing.

FEES & PERMITS

There are currently no entrance fees for the park complex, though there are fees for **camping** (see the campground chart, later). The Northwest Forest Pass ($5 per day, $30 per year) is required for Forest Service trail heads. A **dock fee pass** ($5 per day, $40 per year) is required on Lake Chelan from May 1 until October 31. **Backcountry permits** are required but free.

10 Essential Items for Hikers in the North Cascades

The Park Service considers the following 10 items absolute essentials for hikers—even day hikers—in the North Cascades National Park Service Complex. Hikers should carry them and know how to use them.

- **Navigation** (a topographical map and compass)
- **Food and water** (boiling water can kill *Giardia,* but some treatment pills can't)
- **Clothing** (including rain gear, wool socks, sweater, gloves, and hat)
- **Light** (a flashlight with spare bulb and batteries)
- **Fire** (waterproof matches and a fire starter, such as a candle)
- **Sun protection** (sunglasses and sunscreen)
- **First aid** (a kit, including any special medications you might need)
- **Knife** (a folding pocket knife is best)
- **Signals** (both audible and visual: whistle and metal mirror)
- **Emergency shelter** (a plastic tube shelter or waterproof bivouac sack)

If You Have Only 1 Day

Since this is one of the most rugged wilderness areas in the United States, any attempt to see the park in a day must be made with the understanding that you're not going to see it all. For most folks with limited time, the choice is a **summer drive** across the park on Wash. State Route 20 (North Cascades Hwy., described below), and perhaps a hike to Pyramid Lake or on another of the more accessible trail heads.

SPECIAL REGULATIONS & WARNINGS

Wash. State Route 20 is usually closed from mid-November through mid-April. Call the park complex headquarters in Sedro-Woolley (✆ **360/854-7200**), or check the park's website, www.nps.gov/noca, for current information.

Check in at a visitor center for full details on trails before you head into the backcountry. This is bear and mountain lion (cougar) country; pick up the free handout on hiking and camping safety.

Other than the general precautions that anyone would take when camping in a wilderness area, keep in mind that the North Cascades National Park Service Complex can be extremely remote for both the backcountry hiker and the park driver. Even when day hiking, remember to carry enough water (and all of the 10 essential items; see box, earlier). Don't forget bug spray—the area has a lot of water (not necessarily to drink) and, consequently, lots of insects during some seasons at some locations.

SEASONS & CLIMATE

As can usually be expected in the Northwest, rains arrive westerly from the Pacific in the spring and fall, with summer being the most pleasant all around. At any time, though, expect rain and bring rain gear. The eastern side of the mountains is less wet than the western. Few visit the North Cascades area in the winter, which begins creeping up in October in the upper elevations and mid-November in the lower elevations. It lasts until mid- to late April and necessitates the regular closure of Wash. State Route 20. Closure depends on snow and avalanche conditions.

From April to September, daytime temperatures range from 50° to 80°F (10°–27°C), depending on the elevation. However, this is a land of extremes: Trails at higher elevations are usually snow-covered into early July (though this varies considerably from year to year), and summer temperatures of 100°F (38°C) are not unusual at Ross Lake and Lake Chelan. With the extremes in altitude here, it's always good to bring some warm clothing, even in the summer months.

SEASONAL EVENTS

The Golden West Visitor Center mounts several **art exhibits** in the summer. Contact the park for dates.

North Cascades is also one of the national parks that offers an artist-in-residence program, which gives artists a chance to "discover and interpret this landscape through their own projects." The residencies are for 4 to 6 weeks and take place in the spring and fall. For information and an application, visit **www.nps.gov/noca/supportyourpark/artist-in-residence.htm**.

2 Exploring the Park

The road into the park is a beautiful drive along the banks of the Skagit River, past the Mount Baker–Snoqualmie National Forest. Your last connection with civilization, and the last chance to stock up on groceries, is Marblemount, the oldest town in the region. From here, you can head south or east. South is the Cascade River Road, and east is Wash. State Route 20.

The **Cascade River Road** is a 23-mile stretch of mostly gravel road that leads to Cascade Pass. The road, at the very beginning, crosses the Skagit River and then passes near a fish hatchery before terminating at the **Cascade Pass trail head,** where you can see a majestic tableaux of glaciers and waterfalls Many folks hike the 3.7-mile one-way trip to the top of Cascade Pass, which leads the hiker up a relatively modest set of switchbacks to beautiful views of glaciers and subalpine meadows.

If you're not up to the unpaved twisting of the Cascade River Road, continue on Wash. State Route 20 to **Newhalem,** where the North Cascades Visitor Center has exhibits and regularly scheduled ranger-led walks and talks. This is a good place to get information about the many short walks and hikes in the immediate vicinity. A short boardwalk trail (Sterling Munro Viewpoint) begins behind the visitor center and affords beautiful views of the surrounding mountains. In addition, if you're there late enough in the day, check out the trail to **Ladder Creek Falls** (which is not on National Park Service property but is owned by Seattle City Light), which is fun in a most decidedly touristy manner.

The National Park Service recommends the short, accessible **Newhalem Rockshelter Trail** to an archaeological site near the visitor center, as well as the **River Loop Trail** from the visitor center.

Next up is the little town of **Diablo,** at the foot of 389-foot-high Diablo Dam, which holds back the blue-green waters of Diablo Lake. A tour operated by Seattle City Light's **Skagit Tours** (✆ **206/684-3030;** www.seattle.gov/light/tours/skagit) takes you out on Diablo Lake. Tours last 2½ hours and cost $25 for adults, $20 for seniors over 62, $12 for youths 6 to 12, free for children under 6. Reservations are recommended. A 4-hour dinner tour is also available.

As the road loops south from Diablo, look for fantastic views of **Neve Glacier.** In fact, beautiful views spread out from a plethora of turnouts along the road. Between Newhalem and Diablo is the new, universally accessible **Gorge Overlook Trail,** with great views and interpretive signs.

At the **Ross Lake Dam,** the lake begins its 24-mile dogleg up the eastern side of the park complex to the Canadian border. For views of the lake from the dam, stop the car and take the steep, 1-mile walk down the **Ross Dam Trail.** This trail leads over the top of the dam, eventually winding its way to the Ross Lake Resort and the North Cascades backcountry. Several longer hikes lead along Ross Lake, including the West Bank and the Happy-Panther trails. Another good choice is the accessible **Happy Creek Forest Walk,** a quarter-mile past the Ross Dam trail head, a .3-mile boardwalk stroll through old-growth forest, with interpretive signs. Farther along Wash. State Route 20, take the turnout at the **Ross Lake Overlook,** where you can see the Ruby Arm (leading to Ruby Creek), as well as Ross Lake proper, heading north toward Canada (with Hozomeen Mountain in the distance).

The **Stehekin Area,** at the head of Lake Chelan, is not accessible by car. To get there, you have to hike in and take a passenger ferry or floatplane from the southern resort town of Chelan. A ferry ride up the lake from Chelan is the only quick and relatively affordable way to the Stehekin Area. (A floatplane is the quickest, most expensive option.)

Once you make it to Stehekin, you can rent a bike to ride the roads in the area, but bikes are not permitted on trails. Give yourself enough time and strength for the hike out.

If you wish to visit the **northern sections of the park,** you have a couple of options. From the Ross Dam area, park the car and hike the trail into the **Ross Lake Resort.** You can hike around the general area or, better yet, catch a water taxi up the shores of the lake. Call the Ross Lake Resort to arrange for **water taxi service** (✆ **206/386-4437**). The taxis will drop you off at any of the trail heads that intersect both sides of the shores of this lake all the way to Hozomeen, the northernmost part of the lake in U.S. territory. Ross Lake Resort also rents small outboards, canoes, and kayaks for those who want to fish or explore the lake on their own.

The only practical way to get near the **northwest section of the park** by vehicle is to head east from the Mount Baker Wilderness Area, which is popular and easily accessible because of the Mount Baker Ski Area. Beyond the Mount Baker area, take **Hannegan Road** (Forest Service Rd. 32), which is accessible by two-wheel drive. As usual, it's a good idea to call ahead for road conditions. Beyond the end of the road lie the **Hannegan Pass, Copper Ridge,** and **Chilliwack trails.** These are popular trails in the summer, but they are multiday hikes and require a permit for camping overnight. Backcountry permits are available at the Glacier Public Service Center in Glacier. Permits are issued in person only, on the day of your trip or up to a day in advance. Permits are issued on a first-come, first-served basis. The trails offer views of glaciers spreading southward through the park, especially the Nooksack Glacier along the ridges overhanging the Nooksack River. The Northwest Forest Pass is required for all trail head parking on U.S. Forest Service lands in Washington and Oregon.

3 Organized Tours & Ranger Programs

For tours of Diablo Lake and Ross Dam, call Seattle City Light's **Skagit Tours** (✆ **206/684-3030**).

Want to track radio-collared mountain caribou? Stalk newts, frogs, and salamanders in Heather Meadows? Learn about Lummi Indian basketry? Delve into the mysteries of mycology? Hang with some bats? You can do any of these things if you sign up for the right class through the North Cascades Institute. Offering more than 60 field seminars each year, **North Cascades Institute,** 810 Wash. State Rte. 20, Sedro-Woolley, WA 98284-1239 (✆ **360/856-5700;** www.ncascades.org), is a nonprofit educational organization that offers a wide range of courses each year. Many of the seminars are now held at the North Cascades National Park.

A variety of day trips operate in conjunction with the three passenger ferries of **Lady of the Lake** (✆ **509/682-4584**). Tours include a popular bus ride to 312-foot Rainbow Falls ($7 adults, $4 children 6–11, free for children under 6).

4 Day Hikes

Day hikes do not require a hiking permit; however, a Northwest Forest Pass for vehicle parking may be required. Those going into the backcountry overnight must obtain a free permit at one of the visitor centers, the National Park Service Complex headquarters in Sedro-Woolley, or the Wilderness Information Center in Marblemount. In addition to the hikes discussed below, a small section of the famed Pacific Crest Trail, which runs some 2,650 miles from Mexico to Canada, goes through the park (see "Bridge Creek Trail," below). For information on the entire Pacific Crest Trail, contact the **Pacific Crest Trail Association,** 5325 Elkhorn Blvd., PMB #256, Sacramento, CA 95842-2526 (✆ **916/349-2109;** www.pcta.org).

ROSS LAKE NATIONAL RECREATION AREA

Desolation Peak This is the peak that inspired Jack Kerouac's *Desolation Angels,* and it's no wonder that people (and in the middle of summer, there are often quite a few) would be inspired to meditate on desolation after hiking up this steep hillside through alpine meadows. On the way to the top—4,400 feet up—there are spectacular views of Hozomeen Mountain, Jack Mountain, and below, beautiful Ross Lake. This can be a very hot and dry hike in the summer, and the full round-trip takes several days. Carry plenty of water. Desolation Lookout is closed to the public. 13.6 miles RT. Strenuous. Access: Desolation Landing on Ross Lake (take the Ross Lake Resort water taxi), or hike north along East Bank Ross Lake Trail. Northwest Forest Pass required for parking.

Diablo Lake Trail This is the "Grand Central" of the Diablo Lake area. You get views of Ross Dam and of the power lines, which the trail intersects, but you'll also see some old-growth trees and varied forests. The trail starts at Seattle City Light's power project dock, where you can pick up the summer boat for a ride to the base of upstream Ross Dam (call for schedules). Better to follow the trail as it winds along what was once the Skagit River but is now Diablo Lake. In front of Ross Dam, you get a good idea of how well the dams work. Check out the view as you cross the suspension bridge, which once traversed the Skagit River Gorge which now is part of the system of dams that makes the Ross and Diablo lake areas. 7.6 miles RT. Moderate. Access: At end of road, across Diablo Dam.

East Bank Trail During the summer, this is one of the most popular trails in the park because of its plentiful and well-maintained campsites, the easy grade of its path, and its proximity to Wash. State Route 20. To avoid crowds, you might want to wait until late in the season or hike midweek. The path, near the eastern perimeter of the park, borders the Pasayten Wilderness and the Okanogan National Forest, from which several trails intersect the East Bank Trail. The highest point along the trail is the Desolation Peak Trail, to the north. Along the way, be prepared for black bears, fall foliage, and, on the northern section of the trail, the remote possibility of sighting a member of one of the few remaining wolf packs in the Lower 48. 5–31 miles one-way. Easy to moderate. Access: Several points along the shore of Ross Lake (take the Ross Lake Resort water taxi), or from trail head on Wash. State Rte. 20 to terminus of trail at Hozomeen Campground. Northwest Forest Pass required for parking.

Fourth of July Pass/Panther Creek For a day hike through some of the most astonishing country in the Lower 48, this section of trail isn't too shabby. It's a popular summer hike to the top of Fourth of July Pass, which offers views of the majestic Neve Glacier and Colonial Peak to the west. It isn't easy, though—this is a switchback-cursed climb from Thunder Creek up to the 3,500-foot top of the pass. But that's the hardest part. You return downhill through the beautiful Panther Creek Valley for 5 miles to the junction with Wash. State Route 20 at the Panther Creek Bridge and the East Bank trail head. 10 miles RT. Moderate to strenuous. Access: Hike 1.8 miles up Thunder Creek Trail to junction with trail head. Northwest Forest Pass required for parking at Panther Creek Trailhead on Wash. State Rte. 20.

Pyramid Lake This trail is like many in the park—steep. The hike is a beautiful but relatively sharp climb—it gains 1,500 feet in just over 2 miles—passing through pine and fir forests. It ends at a pond, fed by the Colonial Glaciers looming above along the southeast side of Pyramid Peak. You're liable to see climbers descending from the peaks at the end of the day, looking tired but happy after having ascended the 7,000 feet to the top of Pyramid. 4.2 miles RT. Moderate. Access: 1 mile east of Diablo, on south side of highway near creek, close to mile marker 127. Northwest Forest Pass required for parking.

Sourdough Mountain From the west, the trail is easily accessible by car. But rest assured, either way, you're going to be doing some serious climbing: Try a 3,000-foot climb from the Diablo direction, and in just 2 miles, too. And then there's the remaining 2,000 feet or so along the next 4 miles. It's a densely forested walk over the first couple of miles. Be sure to take the right fork at the 3-mile mark to get to the summit for spectacular views of the lake and the glaciers that dot the horizon to the north. This area is hot and dry in the summer, so take extra water. Sourdough Lookout is closed to the public. Up to 20 miles RT. Strenuous. Access: In Diablo, or water taxi on the West Bank Trail to the Pierce Mountain Trailhead.

Stetattle Creek This is a pleasant summer hike down a gentle, scenic path along a creek. The trail meanders north for some 2.5 miles before hitting a stretch of giant, moss-hung trees and finally petering out in the middle of the forest. The waters of Stetattle Creek often flow milky blue-white from the glacial silt that comes down from McMillan Spire and Mount Terror. The total elevation gain is 1,100 feet. 6 miles RT. Moderate. Access: Exit before the green bridge on Wash. State Rte. 20, just before Diablo, along Gorge Lake.

Thornton Lake Trail Although the first part of the trail is basically an old logging road that might remind you of resource-stripping, this trip is not to be missed. It's a moderately steep walk to the lakes, with a scramble route to Trapper Peak, for sublime views of the Picket Range. Even if you don't take the side route, the sight of Mount Triumph's glaciers to the north, from the nestled valleys in which the lakes sit, is worth the hike. The trail gains 2,400 feet in elevation in just over 5 miles. 10.4 miles RT. Moderate to strenuous. Access: Wash. State Rte. 20 to Thornton Lakes Rd., 3 miles west of Newhalem. Gravel road climbs steeply to trail head. Northwest Forest Pass required for parking.

Thunder Creek Trail There are plenty of options if you decide to take the Thunder Creek Trail. You can amble past the Thunder Creek Arm of Diablo Lake to the intersection with the Fourth of July Pass Trail (also called the Panther Creek Trail), then head to the left and make a loop around the hub of everlooming (and, it goes without saying, snowcapped and gorgeous) Ruby Peak. Or you can make an overnight trek through the rugged wilderness that lines the trail north to south on its way to its terminus in the Park Creek Area along the Stehekin River. Along the way, you can intersect with the Fisher Creek Trail, sloping left along the creek toward an intersection with a possible terminus over Easy Pass at Wash. State Route 20.

From Diablo Lake, the trail is a broad and easy path for the first couple of miles. It then begins to slope upward for the next several miles, through the Panther Creek junction on the way to McAlester Creek Camp. This is the 6-mile mark, and a lot of day hikers head back the way they came at this point. Otherwise, it's off for several days in some of the most gorgeous country in the continental United States, through the rugged and lush valleys in the southern part of the park. Distance and difficulty vary; up to 39.2 miles RT. Access: Trail head south of Diablo Lake, at Colonial Creek Campground parking lot.

LAKE CHELAN NATIONAL RECREATION AREA

Agnes Gorge Trail This is an easy hike along the west-side cliffs of Agnes Gorge, with beautiful views of looming Agnes Mountain above you. This is a good walk for a day visitor to the Stehekin area. 5 miles RT. Easy. Access: High Bridge (accessible by shuttle bus).

Coon Lake Trail This hike, the beginning of the McGregor Mountain Trail, leads to a pretty lake created by beavers. Wildlife, especially waterfowl, is plentiful on and around the 15-acre lake. On the far side is a waterfall on Coon Creek. Though forests surround the lake, there are views to the southwest toward Agnes Mountain. 2.5 miles RT. Moderate. Access: High Bridge (accessible by shuttle bus).

Rainbow Falls At 312 feet high, Rainbow Falls is among the most impressive falls in Washington and a popular destination for day-trippers who visit Stehekin by boat (see "Getting Around Inside the Park," above). The falls were created when a glacier scraped out the walls of the Stehekin Valley, leaving Rainbow Creek hanging high above the valley floor. The falls are 3.5 miles from Stehekin Landing by road and make a good day-hike destination if you are staying at the North Cascades Stehekin Lodge; you get there by walking along the road. The lodge also offers a bus tour of the falls (it's open to anyone and timed for the convenience of the day-tripper). Or, if the shuttle bus is running, you can take it to and from the falls or just one-way. 7 miles RT. Easy. Access: Stehekin Landing.

Rainbow Loop Trail Trails in the Stehekin area tend to be flat valley-bottom hikes or grueling climbs straight up steep walls. This hike makes a good in-between choice. Views of the Stehekin Valley and Lake Chelan are the payoff. Start the hike from the Rainbow Creek trail head, which is accessible from the shuttle bus. From here, climb 1,000 feet in 2.5 miles—along the way passing a bluff with a view of the valley—to a bridge over Rainbow Creek. Just before the creek is a trail junction. If you turn left here and hike up this trail .5 mile, you'll have views even more stunning than the ones along the main trail. The creek marks the midpoint of the trail. The lower trail head is 2.5 miles down a steep trail with more great views. 9.2 miles RT. Moderate. Access: Rainbow Creek Upper Trailhead, 5 miles from Stehekin.

NORTH CASCADES NATIONAL PARK—SOUTHERN UNIT

The interior of the southern unit of the North Cascades National Park is remote. Most of the trails concentrate on the northern or southern end. The northern trails are accessible from Wash. State Route 20. The access route to the southern trails is the Cascade River Road, a winding, sometimes rugged stretch of mostly gravel road, which will get you to the Cascade Pass Trail. Call ahead to the **Wilderness Information Center** in Marblemount (✆ **360/854-7245**) for road conditions; sometimes the route is not easily accessible to the average vehicle. Backpackers can take Thunder Creek Trail, an artery through the interior, for access to the Chelan/Stehekin area, but it's not a day hike.

Bridge Creek Trail This backcountry hike ascends steadily (though never too steeply) to Wash. State Route 20 through some beautiful valleys, after a short hike along a section of the Pacific Crest Trail (see the introduction to this section, above). The trail affords beautiful views of Goode Mountain and Mount Logan, as well as the massive ice-hangs below Memaloose Ridge. 29 miles RT. Moderate. Access: Trail head at Bridge Creek Bridge on Stehekin Valley Rd.; other end of trail is at Bridge Creek trail head, east of Rainy Pass on Wash. State Rte. 20. Northwest Forest Pass is required for parking at the Wash. State Rte. 20 end.

Cascade Pass/Sahale Arm Trail This is one of the most popular hikes in the park. Starting high above the valley of the North Fork Cascade River, the trail follows an ancient American Indian trading route over the Cascades to Lake Chelan. Today the trail is popular as a day trip, an overnight trip, a climber's route to some challenging North Cascades rock, and a through trail to Stehekin. For a spectacular day hike, climb to the top of Cascade Pass (3.7 miles), then continue to ascend on a trail to the left until you cross a ridge. Soon you will be traversing Sahale Arm, far above jewel-like Doubtful Lake. From here, there are sweeping views of the North Cascades. The elevation gain is 1,700 feet to the top of the pass and 2,200 feet up to Sahale Arm. 12 miles RT. Moderate. Access: From Marblemount on Wash. State Rte. 20, cross bridge and drive east 23 miles on Cascade River Rd. to trail head. Northwest Forest Pass is required for parking along Cascade River Rd. and at Cascade Pass trail head.

Park Creek Pass Though this hike is often crowded in the summer with people passing through Stehekin, it's still worth it. Make your way up the steep, forested slopes toward the alpine meadows beyond Five Mile Camp. From here on up, it's glacier lilies and the cracking of calving glacier ice on the slopes of Goode Mountain. Huge chunks of ice have been known to crash into the valley below the slopes. Look for slabs as big as your average house. Beyond the 6,000-foot Park Creek Pass, you can connect with the Thunder Creek Trail (see above) for a much longer hike to the Ross Lake Area and State Route 20. 8 miles one-way. Moderate to strenuous. Access: Park Creek Campground, Stehekin Valley Rd.

NORTH CASCADES NATIONAL PARK—NORTHERN UNIT

The backcountry trails in this region, such as **Hannegan Trail** and **Big Beaver Trail,** aren't easy to get to, but they're worth the effort. Here you'll find some of the most stupendous mountain views in the park complex. This is the most remote wilderness area in the state, home to abundant wildlife. From virgin forests in glacial valleys to high meadows with head-on views of the park's jagged Picket Range, these hikes have everything.

Start at the Mount Baker Wilderness trail head in the Mount Baker–Snoqualmie National Forest, near the north section of the North Cascades National Park Northern Unit. From the town of Glacier, drive 13 miles to F.S. 32 (Hannegan Rd.), and continue to the trail head at Hannegan Camp at the road's end. You can also take a water taxi, which must be arranged in advance, up Ross Lake and start your hike from the Big Beaver Landing. Check with the **Ross Lake Resort** (✆ **206/386-4437**) for information and fares.

5 Other Sports & Activities

BIKING Riding off the road is not allowed in the park, but there are several good biking routes. Keep in mind that biking is usually best in late July and August, but even then, bad weather can descend suddenly, ruining views and soaking riders.

The trip along Wash. State Route 20 through the park and west of the park between Rockport and Marblemount is strenuous but beautiful. The road has a wide shoulder in many (though not all) places, and developed campgrounds. There are some extremely steep stretches.

Mountain bikers will want to try the Stehekin Valley Road route, a 21-mile stretch from the community of Stehekin to Flat Creek, on Lake Chelan. The road parallels the glacier-fed Stehekin River and provides plenty of great views of the North Cascades peaks. The 312-foot-high Rainbow Falls is a wonderful stop along the way.

CROSS-COUNTRY AND DOWNHILL SKIING West of the park complex, the **Mount Baker Ski Area** (✆ **360/671-0211;** www.mtbaker.us) is where most downhill skiers end up. Another good source of information is **www.nooksacknordicskiclub.org** for cross-country skiing in the North Cascades area. If you want to do some cross-country skiing away from the crowds, consider **Stehekin.** The chance to ski past 312-foot-tall Rainbow Falls should not be missed.

FISHING Anglers must have Washington State **fishing licenses,** which are available at sporting goods stores. The **Washington Department of Fish and Wildlife** (✆ **360/902-2200;** www.wdfw.wa.gov) publishes a pamphlet that lists regulations and seasons.

Ross Lake contains populations of both native rainbow and cutthroat trout, as well as eastern

Campground	Total Elev.	RV Sites	Dump Hookups	Station	Toilets
Colonial Creek	1,200	162	0	Yes	Yes
Goodell Creek	500	21	0	No	Yes
Howard Miller Steelhead Park	400	64	51	Yes	Yes
Hozomeen	1,600	75	0	No	Yes
Marble Creek	1,000	23	0	No	Yes
Newhalem Creek	500	111	0	Yes	Yes

brook trout and a few bull trout (which must be released). The **Ross Lake Resort** (✆ **206/386-4437**) rents fishing boats. Fishing season on Ross Lake is July 1 to October 31.

Lake Chelan, although it looks like an awesome fishing hole, is so large, so deep, and so cold that it doesn't support a large fish population. However, it does have quite a variety, including kokanee; land-locked chinook salmon; cutthroat, rainbow, and Mackinaw trout; and freshwater ling cod (burbot). The **Stehekin River** and its tributary streams offer excellent fly-fishing. Check fishing regulations for seasons.

HANG GLIDING & PARAGLIDING In recent years, Lake Chelan has become one of the nation's hang gliding and paragliding meccas. However, neither activity is allowed in the national park or the adjacent national recreation area. Strong winds and thermals allow flyers to sail for a hundred miles or more from the Chelan Sky Park atop Chelan Butte, on the outskirts of town. Paragliding lessons are available here through **Aerial Paragliding School** (✆ **509/782-5543;** www.paragliding.us). The website for the local Chelan Flyers club, **www.chelanflyers.com**, is another good resource.

KAYAKING & CANOEING Diablo Lake and Ross Lake both offer excellent flat-water paddling. They are among the few inland waters in the Northwest with extensive boat-in campsites. However, there is no road access to **Ross Lake** in the U.S. (the unpaved Silver Skagit Rd. enters the park from Hope, British Columbia, and leads 40 miles to the north end of the lake). **Ross Lake Resort** (✆ **206/386-4437**) offers a canoe and kayak shuttle service from Diablo Lake (which is accessible by car) around Ross Dam to Ross Lake. Check with the resort for charges per canoe or kayak. You can also rent outboard motorboats, kayaks, and canoes at the resort.

You'll need a backcountry permit, available at the Wilderness Information Center in Marblemount, to overnight on Ross Lake. A permit allows you to stay at the many campsites along the shores of Ross Lake. Backcountry permits are also available at the Hozomeen Ranger Station. Here you can explore the Narrow Ruby Arm using Green Point Campground (1 mile above the dam) as a base camp. Farther north are the Cougar Island (2 miles above the dam), Roland Point (4 miles above the dam), McMillan (5½ miles above the dam), and Spencer's (6 miles above the dam) campgrounds.

Because of the 24-mile length of the lake and the strong winds that often blow in the afternoon, many paddlers stick to the lower end (unless they enter at Hozomeen at the lake's north end).

If you aren't inclined to spend the money for the shuttle, you can have a similar experience paddling on **Diablo Lake,** which is an amazing turquoise color due to the amounts of glacial flour suspended in the water. Diablo also has three boat-in campsites (Thunder Point, Hidden Cove, and Buster Brown), as well as a couple of small islands. Backcountry permits are needed for boat-in campgrounds on Diablo Lake. Alternatively, you can explore the lake from the drive-in Colonial Creek Campground on the Thunder Arm of the lake.

SNOWSHOEING The **Stehekin Valley** makes an ideal snowshoeing destination, with trails that offer opportunities for exploring the mountain slopes surrounding the valley. The road is plowed to a point 9 miles north of Stehekin Landing.

6 Camping

Reservations for Newhalem Creek Campground and several group campgrounds are available through the **National Recreation Reservation Service** (✆ **877/444-6777;** www.recreation.gov); other campgrounds are first come, first served. Camping in the backcountry requires a free **backcountry permit,** available at visitor centers or the Wilderness Information Center in Marblemount. The only drive-in campsites are along Wash. State Route 20 through the Ross Lake area, except Hozomeen, which is accessible by car only through the Silver Skagit Road, 40 miles south of Hope, in British Columbia, Canada.

Backcountry permits are issued on a first-come, first-served basis, in person only, on the day of your

Drinking Water	Showers	Fire Pits/ Grills	Laundry	Reserve	Fees	Open
Yes	No	Yes	No	No	$12	Mid-May to mid-Oct
Yes	No	Yes	No	No	$10	Year-round
Yes	Yes	No	No	Yes	$22	Year-round
Yes	No	Yes	No	No	Free	Late May to late Oct
No	No	Yes	No	No	$12–$24	Late May to mid-Sept
Yes	No	Yes	No	Yes	$12–$21	Mid-May to mid-Oct

trip into the backcountry or up to a day in advance. There are no advance reservations by phone.

IN ROSS LAKE NATIONAL RECREATION AREA

For information, contact the national park offices (✆ **360/854-7200**). The following campgrounds assign sites on a first-come, first-served basis.

Goodell Creek Campground, just west of Newhalem, is popular with paddlers and anglers. It has a good view of the Picket Range from just across the highway. Drinking water is not available from late fall through winter. A raft and kayak launch adjacent to the campground is available for whitewater runs down the Skagit River. This campground is open year-round.

Newhalem Creek Campground, one of the area's busiest, is at the center of the action near the North Cascades Visitor Center. It's wheelchair accessible and has many short hiking trails nearby. Park rangers present weekend campfire programs in the summer.

Colonial Creek Campground, on the banks of the Thunder Arm part of Diablo Lake, is the largest campground on the highway, and the busiest. It has pleasant sites on the water and access to boat ramps. Park rangers present nightly interpretive programs during the summer.

Hozomeen Campground is a more primitive campground, with no garbage facilities, at the northern tip of Ross Lake. Drinking water is provided.

IN LAKE CHELAN NATIONAL RECREATION AREA

At the north end of the lake, near Stehekin, are 11 campgrounds, most of which are served by the shuttle bus from Stehekin. Purple Point Campground is right in Stehekin and is the most convenient to the boat landing.

For information on campgrounds in the Stehekin Valley, contact the **Golden West Visitor Center,** P.O. Box 7, Stehekin, WA 98852 (✆ **360/854-7365**). A free backcountry permit is needed for these campgrounds. Permits are available in person only at the Golden West Visitor Center, on a first-come, first-served basis.

ALONG THE NORTH CASCADES HIGHWAY

Right in Rockport, there are campsites in a large open field at the Skagit County–run **Howard Miller Steelhead Park** (✆ **360/853-8808**). If you make a reservation, there is a $6 fee for the first night. Camping in Rockport State Park has been closed for an indefinite time. Call ✆ **360/853-8461** for the latest information.

East of Marblemount are a couple of small National Forest Service campgrounds on the Cascade River Road, which leads to the trail head for the popular hike to Cascade Pass. Among them, **Marble Creek** is 8 miles east of Marblemount, and **Mineral Park** is 18 miles east.

For U.S. Forest Service campground reservations, call ✆ **800/444-6777** or visit www.recreation.gov.

7 Where to Stay

There aren't a lot of choices for lodging in the park. To the west, along Wash. 20, you can find places in and near Marblemount and Rockport; to the east there's Mazama and Winthrop, also on Wash. 20.

INSIDE THE PARK

Ross Lake Resort There may not be another lodging of this type in the United States. All 15 of the resort's cabins are built on logs that float on Ross Lake. If you're looking to get away from it all, this place comes pretty close. No roads run to the resort. To reach it, you drive to the Diablo Dam on Wash. 20, then take a tugboat to the end of Diablo Lake, where a truck carries you around the Ross Dam to the lodge. Or you can hike in on a 2-mile trail from mile marker 134 on Wash. 20. There is no restaurant or grocery store, so bring enough supplies for your stay. All cabins have some cooking facilities, ranging from stovetops to full kitchens. Most cabins have private bathrooms; some share with one other cabin. What do you do once you get here? Rent a boat and go fishing, rent a kayak or canoe, do some hiking, or simply sit and relax.

Rockport, WA 98283. ✆ **206/386-4437.** www.rosslakeresort.com. 15 cabins. $128–$279 double. Most cabins 20% discount Sept–Oct weekdays. Closed Nov to mid-June. MC, V.

Stehekin Landing Resort Located at Stehekin Landing, the Stehekin Landing Resort sits in the shade of tall trees and overlooks the lake. It has a variety of rooms, ranging from basic units with no lake view to spacious apartments. The studio apartments, which have kitchens and lake views, are the best deal. Fishing boat and bike rentals are available.

P.O. Box 3, Stehekin, WA 98852. ✆ **509/682-4494.** Fax 360/856-2579. www.stehekinlanding.com. 28 units, including 1 guesthouse. $112–$185 double; $398 guesthouse. Closed Oct–May. MC, V.

Stehekin Valley Ranch If you're a camper at heart, then the tent cabins at the Stehekin Valley Ranch should be just fine. With canvas roofs, screen windows, and no electricity or plumbing, these "cabins" are little more than permanent tents. Bathroom facilities are in the nearby main building. For slightly more comfortable accommodations, opt for one of the permanent cabins. Activities (available at additional cost) include horseback riding, river rafting, mountain biking, and kayak tours and instruction.

P.O. Box 36, Stehekin, WA 98852. ✆ **800/536-0745** or 509/682-4677. www.stehekinvalleyranch.com. 7 cabins, 7 tent cabins. Cabins $105–$115 per adult, $75–$85 per child 4–12, $30–$40 per child 3 and under; tent cabins $85–$95 per adult, $55–$65 per child 4–12, $15–$25 per child 3 and under. Rates include all meals and transportation in lower valley. 2 kitchenettes $170. MC, V for advance phone payment only. No credit cards or checks accepted at ranch.

IN ROCKPORT AND MARBLEMOUNT

Buffalo Run Inn This old 1889 roadhouse has been slowly renovated into a solid lodging option across the street from the dirt road to Cascade Pass. With decor alternately inspired by Europe and local wildlife, the ground-level rooms have private bathrooms, air-conditioning, and TV. Upstairs, five "hostel rooms" share two baths and a TV room.

60084 Wash. 20 (P.O. Box 133), Marblemount, WA 98267. ✆ **360/873-2461** or 360/873-2103. Fax 360/873-4078. www.buffalorunrestaurant.com. 15 units. $79–$109 double with private bath; $49–$59 double with shared bath. AE, DISC, MC, V.

Clark's Skagit River Resort Of a number of different lodging options, the theme cabins keep people coming back to this riverside resort: Western, nautical, Victorian, American Indian, Adirondack, hacienda, and mill are the current decor choices. There are also five new chalets named for local wildlife. Other cabins on the property are equally comfortable, but the theme cabins are what make Clark's just a bit different. The cabins are popular in winter, when folks flock to the area to watch bald eagles congregate on the Skagit River. The resort also has a B&B lodge with a conference room and patio for groups. Also on the property are two **RV parks** ($30–$35) and **tent camping** ($20–$25), as well as a restaurant, **The Eatery.** The Brookhaven Lodge has guest accommodations and hosts music performances.

58468 Clark Cabin Rd., Rockport, WA 98283. ✆ **800/273-2606** or 360/873-2250. Fax 360/873-4077. www.northcascades.com. 40 units. TV. Cabins $79–$169; Brookhaven Lodge $99–$109; call for seasonal rates. AE, DISC, MC, V.

IN MAZAMA

Freestone Inn At the upper end of the Methow Valley outside the community of Mazama, the Freestone Inn is one of the most luxurious lodgings in the North Cascades. The inn's main building is a huge new log structure with a massive stone fireplace in a cathedral-ceilinged great room that serves as lobby and dining room. The lodge sits on the shore of Freestone Lake and has a superb view of the mountains rising beyond the far shore. Guest rooms are thoughtfully designed, with gas fireplaces and sunken tubs that open to the bedroom. All in all, these are some of the most memorable rooms in the state. For more privacy, you can opt to stay in a cabin. Families may want to go all the way and rent one of the large lakeside lodges. **Meals** here are every bit as nice as the rooms. Northwest cuisine is the focus, with prices in the $18-to-$30 range.

The inn also offers tour arrangements, a heli-ski operation, cross-country ski lessons, ski and mountain-bike rentals, an extensive equestrian program, and sleigh rides. Nearby, there are ski trails and a lake for swimming or ice skating.

31 Early Winters Dr., Mazama, WA 98833. ✆ **800/639-3809** or 509/996-3906. Fax 509/996-3907. www.freestoneinn.com. 43 units. TEL. Summer $155–$205 double, $205–$305 cabin, $480–$730 lodge; winter $140–$190 double, $190–$290 cabin, $365–$715 lodge. Lower rates in spring and fall. AE, MC, V.

The Mazama Country Inn Set on the flat valley floor but surrounded by rugged towering peaks and tall pine trees, this modern mountain lodge is secluded and peaceful, offering an escape from the crowds in Winthrop. If you're out here to hike, mountain bike, cross-country ski, or horseback ride, the Mazama Country Inn makes an excellent base of operations. It also has a private outdoor tennis court, a swimming pool, and an athletic facility with a squash court and workout room. After a hard day of outdoor fun, you can soak in the hot tub and eat in the rustic **dining room,** with its massive freestanding fireplace and high ceiling. The medium-size guest rooms are simply furnished and modern. Four deluxe rooms have king beds, gas fireplaces, and jetted tubs. The 13 cabins range in size from one to five bedrooms. This is a nonsmoking facility. No pets are allowed in the inn, but some cabins permit pets.

15 Country Rd., Mazama, WA 98833. ✆ **800/843-7951** or 509/996-2681. Fax 509/996-2646. www.mazamacountryinn.com. 22 units. Summer $90–$140 double; winter $190–$240 double. Off-season discounts available. Winter rates include all meals. DISC, MC, V.

IN WINTHROP

Hotel Rio Vista The Hotel Rio Vista, ravaged by a 2002 fire, arose from the ashes with all brand-new units that include more king suites, minisuites, and rooms with single and doubles. The suites offer kitchenettes, DVDs, and VCRs. Step onto your private balcony for a view of the confluence of the Chewuch and Methow rivers; guests often see deer, bald eagles, and many other species of birds. A hot tub overlooks the river, and there's a riverside picnic area. The hotel is in downtown Winthrop, so it's an easy walk to shops and restaurants. The **Aspen Loft Cabin** is 10 miles from Winthrop and sleeps six.

285 Riverside Ave. (P.O. Box 815), Winthrop, WA 98862. ✆ **800/398-0911** or 509/996-3535. www.hotelriovista.com. 29 units. A/C, TV, TEL. $75–$155 double; $116–$160 Aspen Loft Cabin. MC, V.

River Run Inn & Cabins Secluded from the bustle of downtown Winthrop but only a short stroll away, the River Run Inn is right on the banks of the Methow River and a great spot for families and couples alike. There are lodge rooms, cabins, a suite, and a guesthouse that sleeps up to 13. The rooms are fittingly rustic but quite comfortable, and hammocks and porch swings abound. Guests can tube the river and get a ride back for $25, and bikes are provided free of charge. There is an indoor pool and hot tub and free Wi-Fi.

27 Rader Ave., Winthrop, WA 98862. ✆ **800/757-2709** or 509/996-2173. www.riverrun-inn.com. 15 units, including 1 house, 4 cabins, and 1 suite. A/C, TV, TEL. $105–$140 double; $145–$180 suite; $165–$195 cabin; $350–$500 house. MC, V.

Sun Mountain Lodge If you're looking for luxury and proximity to the trails, the Sun Mountain Lodge should be your first choice in the region. Perched on a mountaintop with grand views of the Methow Valley and the North Cascades, this luxurious lodge captures the spirit of the West in both its breathtaking setting and its rustic design. Most guest rooms feature rustic Western furnishings and views of the surrounding mountains. The newest (and priciest) rooms are in the Mount Robinson wing. If seclusion is what you're after, opt for one of the cabins on Patterson Lake. The **dining room** is excellent, as are the views. Prices for Northwest-inspired main courses range from about $20 to $40. The lodge offers a full slate of summer and winter recreational activities and rentals. Guests can also use the outdoor heated pools, two whirlpools, tennis courts, exercise room, children's playground, spa, and ice-skating pond.

P.O. Box 1000, Winthrop, WA 98862. ✆ **800/572-0493** or 509/996-2211. Fax 509/996-3133. www.sunmountainlodge.com. 98 units, 16 cabins. Summer $220–$435 double, $350–$895 cabin; fall–spring $160–$360 double, $255–$695 cabin. AE, DC, MC, V.

The Virginian Just south of downtown Winthrop, the Virginian is a collection of small cabins and motel rooms on the banks of the Methow River. The deluxe rooms overlooking the river are our favorites. They have high ceilings, balconies, and lots of space. The quaint cabins don't have river views. The rooms and cabins are all lined with cedar, which gives them a rustic feel. There's a horseshoe pit and volleyball court. A cross-country ski and mountain-bike trail is out the front door.

808 Hwy. 20, Winthrop, WA 98862. ✆ **800/854-2834** or 509/996-2535. www.virginian-resort.com. 37 units, 7 cabins. A/C, TV. $69–$89 double; $74–$169 cabin. DISC, MC, V. Pets accepted.

8 Where to Dine

Stock up on chow in Marblemount or Winthrop before you head into the park. In most places, including Ross Lake Resort, there's no food to be had.

IN STEHEKIN

There are several dining options in Stehekin, but if you plan to stay in a cabin or camp out, be sure to bring all the food you'll need. Otherwise, simple meals are available at **Stehekin Landing Resort** (✆ **509/682-4494**), at the boat dock in Stehekin. If you just have to have something sweet, you're in luck—the **Stehekin Pastry Company** (✆ **509/682-7742**), 2 miles up valley from the boat landing, serves pastries and ice cream, as well as pizza and espresso.

IN MARBLEMOUNT

Buffalo Run Restaurant AMERICAN From the outside, this looks like any other roadside diner, but once you see the menu, it's obvious this place is something more. The owners have a buffalo ranch, and the menu includes buffalo burgers, buffalo chili, and buffalo T-bones. They also serve venison, elk, and ostrich, as well as salmon and mussels, plus a full menu page of vegetarian items. After a day of hiking, the garden patio is a pleasant setting for a meal. The restaurant offers beer, wine, and cocktails. Of course there's a buffalo head (and hide) on the wall. Rooms are also available (see "Where to Stay").

60084 Wash. 20 (mile marker 106), Marblemount. ✆ **360/873-2461.** www.buffalorunrestaurant.com. Main courses $5–$40. AE, DISC, MC, V. Daily 11am–9pm.

IN THE WINTHROP AREA

The best meals in the Winthrop area are at the dining room at **Sun Mountain Lodge,** where you'll also enjoy one of the most spectacular views in the state. See "Where to Stay," above.

The Duck Brand MEXICAN/AMERICAN Named for Winthrop's original watering hole, the Duck Brand is a casual restaurant with a big, multi-level deck that's a great spot for a meal on a warm summer day. In cold or rainy weather, you can grab a table in the small dining room, its walls clad in historic photos, antlers, and pinecones, and order a plate of enchiladas or a burger and a microbrew to wash it all down. The Duck Brand's muffins and cinnamon rolls make great trail-side snacks. There are also five basic rooms for rent here for $59 to $69 a night.

Wash. 20 (Riverside Ave.). ✆ **509/996-2192.** www.methownet.com/duck. Main courses $6–$21. AE, DC, DISC, MC, V. Daily 7am–9pm.

Old Schoolhouse Brewery AMERICAN In a tiny, wedge-shaped former schoolhouse, this local brewpub is the liveliest joint in town. There's a deck out back overlooking the river with a beer garden in summer, and on weekends the place usually books some kind of live music. The menu is typical pub fare—burgers, fish and chips, wraps, steaks, sandwiches, chicken, and ribs. The house specialties are the homemade sweet potato fries and the Double D Blonde Ale.

155 Riverside Ave. ✆ **509/996-3183.** www.oldschoolhousebrewery.com. Main courses $7–$16. MC, V. Sun–Mon and Wed–Thurs 11am–10pm; Fri–Sat 11am–midnight; shorter hours in winter.

26

Olympic National Park, WA

by Eric Peterson

Get ready for sensory overload. Olympic National Park is an area of such variety in climate and terrain that it's hard to believe it's just one park. Here you can view white, chilled alpine glaciers; wander through a green, sopping-wet rainforest; or soothe your muscles with a soak in a hot springs pool. Or perhaps you'd prefer to ponder the setting sun from the sandy Pacific coastline, or disappear from the outside world altogether in the deep green forests of largely untouched mountains.

In the Olympic Mountains, remnants survive of 20,000-year-old glaciers that continue to grind and sculpt the mountains now as they did then, albeit on a smaller scale—the glaciers have been shrinking rapidly in the past half-century. Farther down in some of the peninsula's west-facing valleys are some of the best remaining examples of temperate rainforests in the contiguous United States. In addition, Olympic National Park contains one of the longest stretches of uninterrupted coastal wilderness in the country, 73 miles in all.

Water is serious business here. Precipitation in the peninsula's rainforests is measured in feet, not inches, with some areas receiving over 12 feet each year. Contrast this with some parts of the drier northeastern section of the peninsula, which receive a comparatively paltry 15 to 20 inches on average. Again, variety is the rule. If the crystalline, jade waters of the glacier-fed lakes feel a little too cold for comfort, you have the opportunity to warm your bones in hot springs in the northern section of the park.

Despite its inherent ruggedness, rainy, and mysterious nature, the interior of the park has long been known to native peoples, as well as white settlers since the mid- to late 1800s. Unbridled curiosity and the inevitable desire for timber, mineral, and tourism dollars played a part in its recent exploration. Homesteads had been established by westward-moving pioneers on the periphery of the peninsula as early as the mid-1800s. However, the first documented exploration of the interior by white settlers didn't occur until 1885, and it was no easy feat. One group of explorers spent a grueling month hacking through dense brush to get from Port Angeles to Hurricane Ridge. (Today the trip takes approx. 45 min. by car.)

On the advice of some of these adventuresome explorers, Congress declared most of the peninsula a national forest. Then, in 1909, just before leaving office, President Theodore Roosevelt, an avid hunter, established Mount Olympus National Monument. It was set aside to preserve the summer range and breeding grounds of dwindling herds of Roosevelt elk (flatteringly named for the president himself in a brilliant piece of prelegislative public relations). In 1938, President Franklin Roosevelt signed the bill that turned the national monument into a national park, and in 1953 the coastal strip was added. In 1981, the park was declared a World Heritage Park, and in 1988, 95% of the park was designated a wilderness area.

Today Olympic National Park encompasses more than 900,000 acres of mountains and rainforests, crystalline lakes, and Pacific shoreline. By a fortunate stroke of planning or a fortunate lack of money, no roads divide the interior of the park. Consequently, large sanctuaries exist here for elk, deer, eagles, bear, cougars, and other inhabitants and visitors to its interior.

AVOIDING THE CROWDS

Avoiding the crowds in Olympic National Park is not as simple as you may think. With easy access from both Seattle and Victoria, BC, the park is a magnet for visitors from around the world. However, a few options are within your control.

The easiest solution is to go in the off-season, especially in the fall. September is a great time to visit for the fall colors and visible wildlife. However, starting in mid-October, the west side of Olympic is often deluged with rain.

You might also try driving to the park from the southwest via Aberdeen. If you choose this route, you can see everything the peninsula offers in a nutshell. Instead of going to the Hoh, try the Queets. Although less traveled, this area affords the same rainforest views as the more popular Hoh.

Finally, if you absolutely have to come in the summer and don't want to miss the most popular views, such as those on **Hurricane Ridge,** try heading up in the late afternoon when everyone else is on their way

Olympic National Park

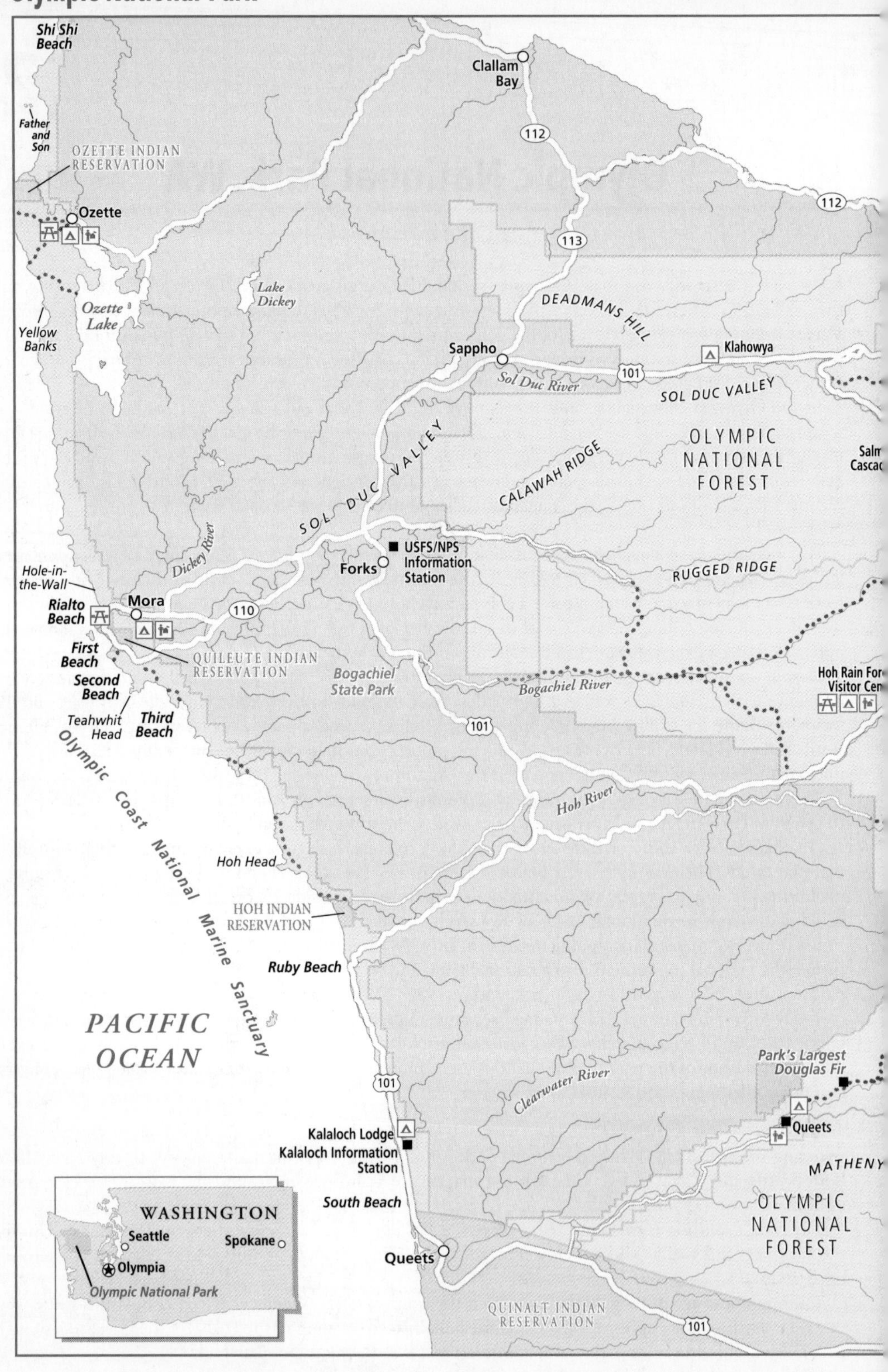

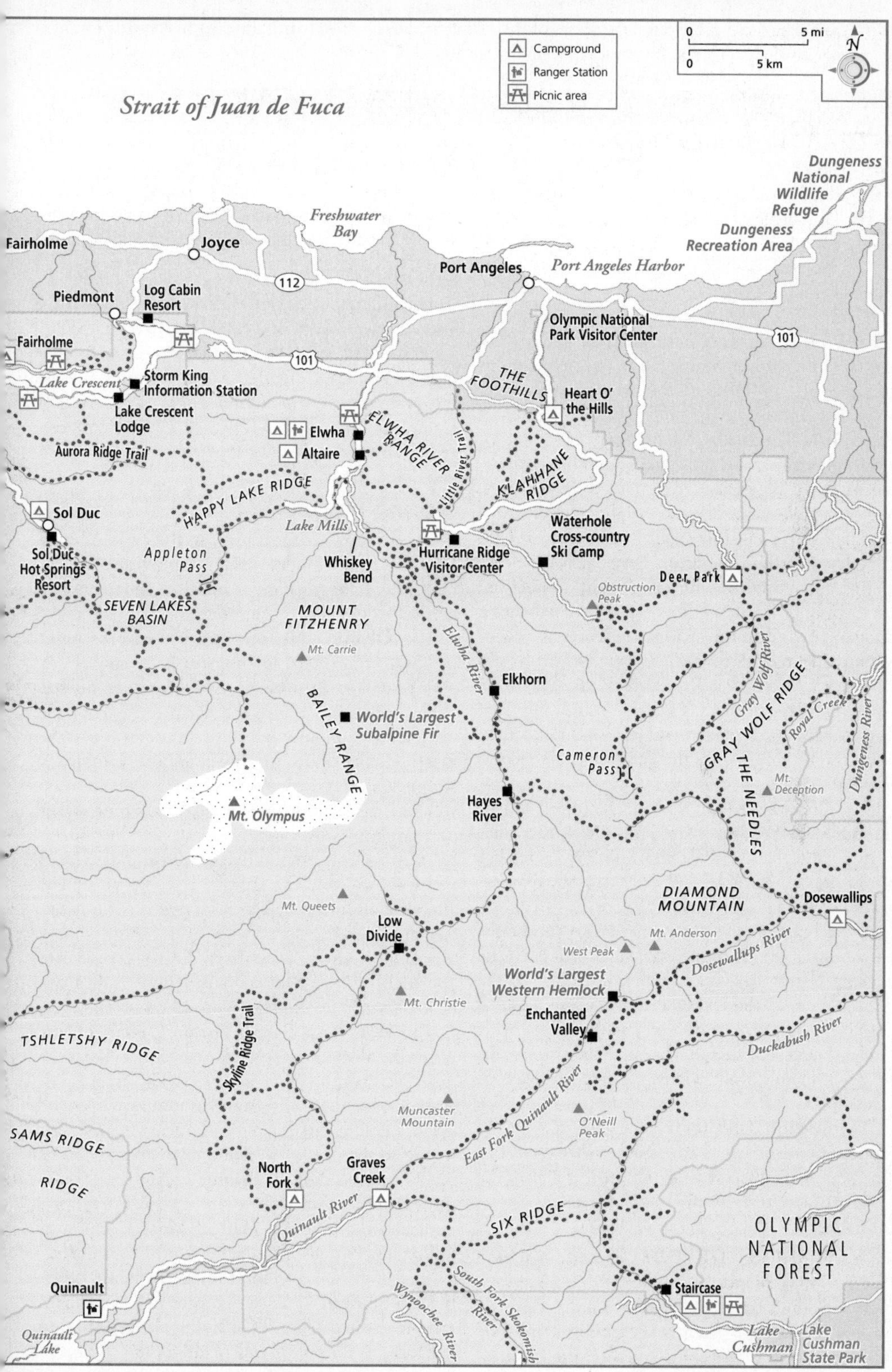
Campground
Ranger Station
Picnic area
0
5 mi
0
5 km
N
Strait of Juan de Fuca
Freshwater Bay
Fairholme
Joyce
112
Port Angeles
Port Angeles Harbor
Dungeness National Wildlife Refuge
Dungeness Recreation Area
Piedmont
Log Cabin Resort
Olympic National Park Visitor Center
101
Fairholme
Lake Crescent
Storm King Information Station
Lake Crescent Lodge
THE FOOTHILLS
Heart O' the Hills
Elwha
Altaire
ELWHA RIVER RANGE
Little River Trail
KLAHHANE RIDGE
Aurora Ridge Trail
HAPPY LAKE RIDGE
Sol Duc
Sol Duc Hot Springs Resort
Appleton Pass
Lake Mills
Whiskey Bend
Hurricane Ridge Visitor Center
Waterhole Cross-country Ski Camp
Obstruction Peak
Deer Park
SEVEN LAKES BASIN
MOUNT FITZHENRY
Mt. Carrie
Elwha River
Elkhorn
Gray Wolf River
GRAY WOLF RIDGE
Royal Creek
Dungeness River
BAILEY RANGE
World's Largest Subalpine Fir
Cameron Pass
THE NEEDLES
Mt. Deception
Hayes River
Mt. Olympus
DIAMOND MOUNTAIN
Dosewallips
Mt. Queets
Low Divide
Mt. Anderson
West Peak
Dosewallups River
World's Largest Western Hemlock
Mt. Christie
Enchanted Valley
Skyline Ridge Trail
TSHLETSHY RIDGE
Duckabush River
Muncaster Mountain
O'Neill Peak
East Fork Quinault River
SAMS RIDGE
RIDGE
North Fork
Graves Creek
Quinault River
SIX RIDGE
OLYMPIC NATIONAL FOREST
South Fork Skokomish River
Wynoochee River
Quinault
Staircase
Quinault Lake
Lake Cushman
Lake Cushman State Park

down. You're liable to get spectacular views of the sunset as the fog rolls in and the deer make their evening pilgrimage to the parking lot at the Hurricane Ridge Visitor Center.

1 Essentials

GETTING THERE & GATEWAYS

The main travel artery for all visitors to Olympic National Park is **U.S. 101.** This northernmost point of the famous coastal highway encircles and only briefly enters the park. Most of the traffic into and out of the park is on the northeastern side, from Vancouver and Seattle.

If you're departing from **Seattle,** you can take either of the ferries that run regularly every day from the same downtown Seattle dock. No reservations are available for most of the ferries, which cost about $15 one-way for a standard passenger vehicle. The **Seattle–Bainbridge Island Ferry** takes you for a half-hour ride across the Puget Sound before arriving in Bainbridge Island. From there, take Wash. 305 north through Poulsbo to the Hood Canal floating bridge, and then Wash. 104 across to U.S. 101. The **Seattle–Bremerton Ferry** arrives in Bremerton after a 60-minute ride. From Bremerton, take Wash. 3 north to the Hood Canal floating bridge. The **Edmonds–Kingston Ferry** is a 30-minute ride to Kingston, where you take Wash. 104 24 miles to U.S. 101. In addition, the **Keystone Ferry** shuttles between Whidbey Island and Port Townsend, but it's smaller and runs less frequently; reservations, available for this ferry only, are recommended

For all ferry **schedules and rates,** contact **Washington State Ferries,** 2901 Third Ave., Ste. 500, Seattle, WA 98121 (✆ **888/808-7977** or 511 statewide, or 206/464-6400 local and out of state; www.wsdot.wa.gov/ferries).

If you'd rather drive your car over dry land only, head west from **Tacoma** on Wash. 16 over the Tacoma Narrows Bridge, which connects with the eastern shore of the Kitsap Peninsula just south of Gig Harbor. Drive north on Wash. 16 to Port Orchard and Bremerton. From Bremerton, take Wash. 3 to the Hood Canal floating bridge and across to U.S. 101.

To reach the park from the south, take I-5 to **Olympia,** where you can connect with U.S. 101 North, or with Wash. 8 West to the other side of the U.S. 101 loop, to enter the Pacific Ocean section of the park.

THE NEAREST AIRPORT Seattle–Tacoma International Airport (✆ **206/787-5388;** www.portseattle.org/seatac) is 15 miles south of Seattle on I-5. It's served by most major airlines and car-rental companies. **William R. Fairchild International Airport** (✆ **360/457-1138;** www.portofpa.com/airports) is in Port Angeles, site of the park's main visitor center, and is served by **Kenmore Air** (✆ **866/435-9524;** www.kenmoreair.com), which offers service between Port Angeles and Seattle. **Budget** provides car rentals. See chapter 38 for websites of the airlines and car-rental companies.

INFORMATION

Contact **Olympic National Park,** 600 E. Park Ave., Port Angeles, WA 98362-6798 (✆ **360/565-3130,** TTY 800/833-6388, or 360/565-3131 for a recording; www.nps.gov/olym). Several free publications, including the *North Olympic Peninsula Visitor's Guide,* published by the *Peninsula Daily News* twice yearly, and the park's *The Bugler* newspaper, offer a good look at the area.

VISITOR CENTERS

There are three visitor centers in the park, offering exhibits, maps, guides, and information. Smaller ranger and information stations at popular trail heads are open only in summer.

The **Olympic National Park Visitor Center** (✆ **360/565-3130**), on the northern end of the park near Port Angeles, is a good jumping-off station before heading into the northwest part of the park. It's a 45-minute drive from there to one of the most popular spots in the park, the **Hurricane Ridge Visitor Center,** where you'll find beautiful views of the Olympic Mountains and alpine meadows blooming with wildflowers each summer. It also has a snack bar, interpretive exhibits, and trails. If you want to avoid the crowds, drive up in the late afternoon, as everyone else is leaving. Wait for sunset, and you might get a view of the mists coming in, and perhaps a visit from deer—but do not approach or feed any animals. Those who arrive before 10am will also find more elbow room.

The **Hoh Rain Forest Visitor Center,** on the west side of the main part of the park, is some 15 miles off a turnoff from U.S. 101. This is an excellent spot for those who want to experience a temperate rainforest without spending a couple of days hiking in the elements. The information center is, like Hurricane Ridge, a favorite spot for tourists in the summer season. There are several interpretive trails and the beautiful **Hall of Mosses** nearby, as well as longer trails into the heart of the rainforest.

Smaller centers include the **Storm King Information Station,** on Lake Crescent in the northern section of the park, and the **Kalaloch Information Station,** on the south end of the beach section of the park. You can get food and some supplies near

If You Have Only 1 Day

Decide in advance what you would like to see. This is a big park, and no roads go completely through it. The roads that do venture inside (and they're major tourist attractions) are generally short and pleasant. It's 19 miles from U.S. 101 to the Hoh Visitor Center, and 17 miles to Hurricane Ridge.

If you want to see the **rainforests** and **the coastal strip,** drive north from Aberdeen on U.S. 101 (which circumnavigates the peninsula) through the coastal region, perhaps stopping at the Kalaloch Information Station and Ruby Beach, and then head to the Hoh Rain Forest Visitor Center, from where you can explore further. To see the **glaciers and the alpine meadows** of the east side of the park, start by driving to the Olympic National Park Visitor Center in Port Angeles, and from there head up to Hurricane Ridge, where you set out on a hike or drive even farther into the park. From Seattle, the eastern option is closer.

the **Sol Duc Ranger Station** at the Sol Duc Hot Springs Resort.

FEES & PERMITS

Entrance to the park for up to a week costs $15 per vehicle, or $5 per individual hiking, biking, or on a motorcycle. Camping in the wilderness (for groups up to 12 people) costs $5 for a backcountry permit, plus $2 per person per night. Camping in the park campgrounds costs $10 to $18 a night. Dump station use costs $5.

SPECIAL REGULATIONS & WARNINGS

Wilderness use permits, available at the Wilderness Information Center (just behind the main visitor center in Port Angeles) and at all ranger stations, are required for overnight stays in the backcountry. During the summer, you may also need reservations for certain areas. Call the **Wilderness Information Center** (✆ **360/565-3100**) for details.

When hiking, be prepared for sudden and extreme weather changes.

SEASONS & CLIMATE

The climate of the entire peninsula is best described as varied, of the marine type. In the winter, the temperatures stay in the 30s and 40s (single digits Celsius) during the day, and 20s and 30s (negative single digits Celsius) at night. The lower elevations, near the water, rarely receive more than 6 inches of accumulated snow per season, and it melts quickly. However, on the upper slopes, the snowfall can become quite heavy.

Spring is the late half of the rainy season, mostly wet, mild, and windy. Temperatures range from 35° to 60°F (2°–16°C), with lingering snow flurries in the mountains.

Summer temperatures range from a low of 45°F (7°C) in the evening to 75°F (24°C) and up to 80°F (27°C) or higher during the afternoons. In the latter half of the summer and early fall, fog and cloud banks often drift into the valleys and remain until midday, burn off, and sometimes return in the evening. Thunderstorms may occur in the evening in the upper elevations.

The fall is moderately cold and blustery; it ushers in the rainy season, which usually begins in mid- to late October. Snow begins to fall in the mountains as soon as early autumn. Temperatures range from 30° to 65°F (–1° to 18°C).

Rainfall varies throughout the Olympic Peninsula, but about three-quarters of the precipitation falls during the 6-month period from October through March, primarily on the Pacific side of the peninsula.

SEASONAL EVENTS

Seasonal events take place across the Olympic Peninsula, if not within the park itself. They include salmon cook-offs; classical, jazz, and bluegrass festivals; boat races; light opera; and arts and crafts festivals. For a full list, as well as other information about the area, contact the **Port Angeles Chamber of Commerce Visitor Center** (which operates a visitor center at 121 E. Railroad Ave. in Port Angeles; ✆ **360/452-2363;** www.portangeles.org), or the **Olympic Peninsula Tourism Commission** (✆ **800/942-4042** or 360/452-8552; www.olympicpeninsula.org).

2 Exploring the Park by Car

THE RAINFORESTS & THE COAST

If the rainforests are your destination, your best bet is to drive west and north from Olympia (or, if you're coming from Seattle on a ferry, west and south from Port Angeles or Port Townsend) along the western side of the peninsula. The first opportunity to see a bit of the rainforest is near the north shore of **Lake Quinault,** at the southern end of the

Organized Tours & Ranger Programs

Olympic National Park offers a variety of programs, including **campfire talks** and **beach walks**. You'll find **rainforest tours** originating from the Hoh and Quinault ranger stations, **alpine wildflower walks** from the Hurricane Ridge area, and **lakeside and waterfall walks** from the Storm King Ranger Station. Check the park newspaper, *The Bugler,* for a current schedule.

main part of the park. If you plan to stay the night, this area has a number of lodges, motels, and campgrounds. From the ranger station on the south shore, there are several interpretive hikes along the lake; those who want to delve into the rainforest should start on the north side of the lake. The view of the mountains from Lake Quinault is quite spectacular on a sunny day, but the area serves as a good hors d'oeuvre more than anything else.

Drive north on U.S. 101. You should be able to get to **Queets Ranger Station** if the road is open (it washes out frequently); the Queets River Valley is home to some of the most beautiful (and remote) rainforests on the peninsula. Or you can keep driving northwest on U.S. 101 to the **Kalaloch Information Station,** where you can enjoy views of the Pacific from Kalaloch to Ruby Beach. Of the two options, it's a tough call. You might get to see elk in some of the former homestead meadows in the early morning or late afternoon on the 3-mile **Sams River Loop Trail** in the Queets, but understand that it's the least accessible of the rainforests. Watch for seasonal closures during the winter and late fall.

After leaving the coastal area at Ruby Beach, continue your northward drive on U.S. 101 to the turnoff for the **Hoh Rain Forest Visitor Center.** It's a 19-mile drive from U.S. 101 to the center, with excellent views of the Hoh River along the way. You could also spend a long day hiking the 9 miles (one-way) from the Hoh Visitor Center parking lot up to the **Olympus Guard Station.** In just a few hours, this hike goes from temperate rainforest to alpine meadows with stunning views of Mount Olympus. If you're not feeling so ambitious, take the short **Hall of Mosses** or **Spruce Nature trail,** and get ready to head north again, to Sol Duc.

The last leg of our excursion takes you to one of the most commercially developed areas in the park, **Sol Duc** and the **Sol Duc Hot Springs Resort.** It might be a nice idea, before you head back down the coast to Olympia, or to sleep in your campsite or hotel room, to have a dip in these famous hot springs (open from late spring to early fall). The hot springs experience costs $12 to enter ($8.50 for kids); packages, including a sauna and a massage, are available. You also have your choice of comfort levels, anywhere from 70° to 158°F (21°–70°C). But be forewarned: There's a resort here, and the springs can be crowded. Still, if you're into luxuriating after a long day of hiking, it may be just the thing.

The area has more than hot springs. Try taking the 1.5-mile round-trip hike from the springs through some wonderfully dense forest to **Sol Duc Falls.** Or take the **Mink Lake Trail** through 2.5 miles of uphill grade and forest to get a look at one of the many higher-altitude lakes that dot the Sol Duc region.

THE EAST SIDE OF THE PARK

Seen the rainforests? You could do a lot worse than spending a day seeing the glaciers and the alpine meadows of the east side of the park. This time, the jumping-off point is probably **Port Angeles.** First, visit the **Olympic National Park Visitor Center,** to get acquainted with what you're about to see.

As in the rainforest tour, this trip starts with a choice: Head back through Port Angeles for the **Elwha/Altair area,** or from the visitor center to **Hurricane Ridge.** Either way, you're in for a variety of Olympic experiences.

The Elwha area has a small ranger station and, farther up the road, a nice observation point for viewing **Lake Mills** (a reservoir slated to be drained as part of an ecosystem restoration project) and the surrounding hills. In addition, if you don't want to deal with the crowds at Sol Duc, you can hike 2.5 miles from Elwha to the only other hot springs inside the park. On the banks of Boulder Creek, the **Olympic Hot Springs** is not accessible by car, and don't expect amenities or guarantees of sanitation, either. In other words, use at your own risk.

Along the way to Hurricane Ridge from Port Angeles, pass the **Heart O' the Hills Ranger Station.** At Hurricane Ridge, one of the most popular spots in the park, there are a number of short interpretive trails, very good for seeing wildflowers during times of big blooms. Many larger trails intersect here as well. The visitor center has numerous interpretive exhibits and a snack bar.

Leaving Hurricane Ridge, Port Angeles, or the Elwha area, drive a little farther southeast. Off a turnoff from U.S. 101 is the less crowded **Deer Park Ranger Station,** where you get the same sort of views as at Hurricane Ridge without jostling for position. The road to Deer Park is steep and graveled. It's not suitable for RVs and trailers, and prepare to deal with steep inclines, turns, and potholes. The road is closed in winter.

Outside Olympic National Park, consider visiting other locations along U.S. 101, such as the

Attractions Within the Park

There aren't many man-made attractions within the park, although it's dotted with **old homestead sites,** such as those found along the **Geyser Loop Trail** in the Elwha Valley. Also, there's an old cabin behind the Olympic National Park Visitor Center that will leave you wondering how early settlers managed in such a claustrophobic environment.

community of **Dungeness** and **Sequim Bay State Park** on the northeastern tip of the peninsula, with their beautiful shorelines and views of the strait. As you travel farther south, the **Hood Canal** will appear on your left. There are numerous places here to see seals on the rocks, especially at **Seal Point.**

3 Day Hikes

The park has a vast number of trails, and they all seem to connect somewhere. Consequently, it's possible to tie several trails together to create your own route. It's also easy to get lost—make sure to carry a map (and tide tables for coastal hikes), a compass, and water at all times. For a complete listing, visit the park's website or write ahead for a free **Olympic National Park map** from the Wilderness Information Center, Olympic National Park, 600 East Park Ave., Port Angeles, WA 98362.

The following is a partial, though representative, list of some of the many wonderful trails in the park. **Backcountry permits** are required for overnight trips. They're available at the **Wilderness Information Center,** behind the main visitor center in Port Angeles (✆ **360/565-3100**), and at all ranger stations. During the summer, you may also need reservations for certain areas. You'll pay a $5 fee for wilderness camping for groups of up to 12 people, plus $2 per person per night. Call the Wilderness Information Center for information.

COASTAL AREA

Cape Alava/Sand Point Loop This loop begins with a stroll over a cedar-plank boardwalk through teeming coastal marsh and grasslands. (Careful! Boards are slippery when wet, which is most of the time.) The trail connects to its second leg on a wilderness beach strip of the Pacific shoreline, the westernmost point in the Lower 48. Camping is permitted on the beach, but it's a popular spot in the summer and reservations are required. Continue south 1 mile past the petroglyphs that can be seen from the rocks along the shore next to the high-tide line. Two miles south of this area, the trail connects to the Sand Point leg, which is an easy stroll back to the Ozette Ranger Station. A permit and reservation are required here. Call the Wilderness Information Center. 9 miles RT. Easy. Access: Ozette Ranger Station.

Hoh River to Queets River The beaches here are wide and flat, and the surf fishing is good. With this trail's proximity to U.S. 101, you can expect to see a lot of people here in the summer, but camping is not allowed. This section, compared to the more northern trails, is fairly tame. Destruction Island Overlook is famous for its whale-watching from March to April and November to December.

Warning: Coastal hiking can be treacherous. Tides can trap you. Never round headlands without knowledge of the tide heights and times. Carry a tide chart. Obtain additional information from the Wilderness Information Center. Up to 15 miles one-way. Easy to moderate. Access: Ruby Beach parking lot.

Sand Point to Rialto Beach This is a coastline famous for its shipwrecks, the memorials of which dot the beach at many points, along with an abandoned mine. Other than that, there are few signs of human activity. Enjoy the sand and the mist, take in the forests that come down to land's end, and get ready for the storms that visit here regularly. Up to 20 miles one-way. Easy to strenuous. Access: Ozette Ranger Station from the north or Rialto Beach from the south.

Second Beach Trail Wander through a lovely forest to a sandy beach, with tide pools and sea stacks. A long set of stair steps awaits at the end. For a short walk, this is hard to beat. .7 mile one-way. Easy. Access: Second Beach parking area on La Push Rd., 14 miles west of U.S. 101.

Third Beach to Hoh River This trail is not a leisurely stroll. You'll do a bit of inland skirting along old oil company roads to avoid some of the more wicked headlands, and there are some sand ladders (contraptions constructed of cables and wooden slats) just beyond Taylor Point. In addition, a slightly treacherous crossing is farther south at Goodman Creek. So what's the reward for the intrepid hiker? Toleak Point is 5 miles down the beach, where there is a sheltered campsite that's famous for its wildlife. The entire area is well known for its shipwrecks, wildlife, coastal headlands, and sea stacks. The trail ends at Oil City, north of the Hoh Indian Reservation. 17 miles one-way. Moderate to strenuous. Access: Third Beach parking area, 3 miles beyond La Push Rd. left fork.

WESTERN PARKLANDS & RAINFORESTS

Bogachiel River This hike, an equally beautiful cousin to the often-crowded Hoh River Trail, is as long or short as you want to make it. The beginning, outside of the national park boundary, has been harvested, but once you enter Olympic proper, you'll enter a rainforest extravaganza—huge Douglas firs, spruce, cedar, and big-leaf maples, including the world's largest silver fir, some 8 miles from the trail head. Approximately 6 miles into the trail is the Bogachiel Shelter, and 8 miles in is Flapjack Camp, both good backcountry campsites. This is pretty much the end of the flatland; farther up, the trail begins to get steep. Length varies. Easy to moderate in the lowlands, more strenuous farther inland. Access: 5 miles south of Forks, turn left across from Bogachiel State Park onto Undie Rd., and continue 5 miles to the trail head.

Hoh River Valley This is one of the most heavily traveled trails in the park, at least in the lower elevations, and it won't take you long to figure out why. Huge Sitka spruces hung with moss shelter the Roosevelt elk that wander among its lowlands. The first 13 miles, through the massive rainforests and tall grass meadows along the Hoh River Valley bottomlands, are relatively flat. The number of fellow walkers drops off after the first few miles. Happy Four Camp (6 miles in) and Olympus Guard Station (9 miles in) provide excellent camp or turnaround sites. The trail continues climbing east for the remaining 4 or 5 miles. You can eventually find yourself at the edge of the famous Blue Glacier on Mount Olympus, elevation 7,965 feet. Be careful. After July, hiking near the park's glaciers can be dangerous because of snowmelt. Up to 17 miles one-way. Easy to moderate in the lowlands, more strenuous farther inland. Access: Hoh Rain Forest Visitor Center.

Lake Quinault Loop Inside the Olympic National Forest, not the park, this trail is easily accessible, is well maintained, and offers beautiful views. Consequently, it's quite crowded in the summer. Elevation changes are gentle, making this an excellent walk for kids.

The trail wanders about the shore of Lake Quinault, past historic Lake Quinault Lodge as well as the adjacent campgrounds and other lakeside attractions, before heading into its most popular section, the Big Tree Grove. Here you can wander among the huge trunks of 500-year-old Douglas firs. Watch for the interpretive signs. In addition, the Big Tree Grove is accessible on a 1-mile loop trail that originates from the Rain Forest Nature Trail parking lot. 4 miles RT. Easy. Access: Trail heads at various spots along the loop, including South Shore Rd., Quinault Lodge, Willaby Campground, Quinault Ranger Station, and Falls Creek Campground. All access originates from south shore of Lake Quinault.

Maple Glade Rain Forest Trail This is a beautiful, peaceful trail with lots of exhibits. Take the kids, or enjoy it yourself. As you meander, you'll pass through trees, open meadows, and an abandoned beaver pond. Keep your eyes peeled for the ever-possible elk sighting. .5 mile RT. Easy. Access: Quinault Rain Forest Ranger Station.

North Fork of the Quinault The North Fork Trail could conceivably take you 47 miles, all the way through the park to the Elwha Valley on the north side—if you make the right connections and are maniacal enough. The trail is relatively benign for the first dozen miles as it winds inward along the river toward its source near Mount Seattle. Wilderness camping areas are available at Wolf Bar (2.5 miles in), at Halfway House (5.3 miles in), and in a gorge in Elip Creek (6.5 miles in). Next, the trail climbs steeply toward Low Divide, Lake Mary, and Lake Margaret, where you can get beautiful views of Mount Seattle, at an elevation of 6,246 feet. Snow can remain at this elevation until midsummer, so be ready. There's a summer ranger station at Low Divide, and many high-elevation campsites here as well. Up to 15 miles one-way. Moderate. Access: End of North Fork Rd.

Queets River Trail This is the trail for the serious rainforest and wilderness lover. Part of its appeal is that the average hiker must exert a bit of an effort to reach the trail's solitude and quietly majestic scenery. Within 50 yards of your car, you'll be crossing the Queets River—without a bridge. Even on this first of several trips across the river, the water can be treacherous. It's best to visit during the dry season in late summer. An option is to cross the Sams River to the right of the Queets, connecting and crossing the Queets River farther up. At 2.5 miles, gape at one of the largest Douglas firs in the park. After 5 miles of hiking through elk and giant fern territory, you'll arrive at Spruce Bottom, which is a common haunt for steelhead anglers and has several good campsites. The trail ends at Pelton Creek, where more campsites are available. Up to 16 miles one-way. Moderate to strenuous. Access: Queets River Campground.

Sam's River Loop Trail This short loop parallels both the Sams River and the Queets River, providing a view of some old homestead meadows, beautiful spruce trees, and perhaps an elk or two in the meadows in the evening. 2.8 miles RT. Easy to moderate. Access: Queets River Ranger Station.

NORTHERN PARK REGIONS

Deer Lake This trail is a steady climb through beautiful woods to a tree-lined lake. Canada jays wait to eat your food, but don't feed them. There are some switchbacks on this trail, and it can get pretty bumpy in spots. 8 miles RT. Moderate. Access: Junction of Sol Duc Falls.

Elwha River Trails The serious backpacker arranges a pickup car at the Dosewallips or North Fork trail heads and heads for a week or so along the trail that was blazed by the famed 1889 Press Expedition, the first Anglo excursion across the Olympic Mountains. For a good distance, the trail follows the blue-green of the Elwha River to its source on the sometimes snow-slushy peak at Low Divide (elevation 3,600 ft.), which is also the head of the Quinault River. You can follow the trail downhill to the North Fork of the Quinault.

What can you expect on such a monumental trip? Old-growth forests, moist valley flatlands, and gently sloping hills appear around you as you explore the Elwha Valley before you begin your ascent toward the sometimes calf-busting Low Divide. Roosevelt elk, black bears, mountain lions, marmots, or a grouse or two might show up. At Low Divide, you're treated to spectacular views of Mount Seattle to the north and Mount Christie to the south. From here, you begin your descent from alpine heights to the rainforests along the Quinault.

As with any overnight wilderness trip, be sure to check in at the park's **Wilderness Information Center** (© **360/565-3100**) beforehand. Up to 50 miles one-way. Difficulty varies. Access: Drive just beyond Elwha Ranger Station to Whiskey Bend Rd. Go past Glines Canyon Dam, 1½ miles up the road. At road's end is Whiskey Bend trail head, just beyond Upper Lake Mills trail head.

Geyser Valley Loop From the Whiskey Bend trail head, hike down the trail to the Eagles Nest Overlook for a view of the meadows that stretch from valley to valley. You may see an elk or black bear if you're lucky. Head back to the trail and proceed a half-mile to the Rica Canyon Trail for a view of Goblin's Gate, a rock formation in the Canyon Gorge that might look like a bunch of goblins' heads staring at you, if you stare back hard enough. The trail to Goblin's Gate drops 325 feet on the half-mile walk to the viewing area. At this point, you can follow a riverside trail for another half-mile to some prime fishing spots, or continue to the Krause Bottom and Humes Ranch area; you can get a glimpse into the park's homesteading history. At any one of these points, you can return to the Whiskey Bend Trail or continue northeast past Michael's Cabin, another old homestead. 6 miles RT. Moderate. Access: Whiskey Bend Rd.

High Divide Loop Like many trails in the park, this one gives you a chance to design your own hike—be sure to bring a map. From the Sol Duc trail head, climb a relatively easy wooded route of less than a mile to Sol Duc Falls and keep going. You can take a leg out to the Seven Lakes Basin Area. On clear summer days, you can enjoy the wildflowers along the slopes of Bogachiel, the view to the south of the glaciers of Mount Olympus, or the brilliant sunsets on the western Pacific horizon. As with any park trails, permits are required for all overnight stays. Up to 20 miles RT. Moderate. Access: Sol Duc Ranger Station.

Lover's Lane Loop This trail creates a loop that links the campground, resort, and Sol Duc Falls. Cross the bridge at the falls and continue around on the trail, which will return you to the resort and campground area after taking you through beautiful Douglas-fir groves and fern glades. Portions of the trail are narrow and rocky and can get muddy until things dry out in midsummer. You may spot grouse along the trail. 5.8 miles RT. Easy to moderate. Access: Sol Duc trail head or Sol Duc Hot Springs Resort.

Marymere Falls This is one of the most popular hikes in the park. It's well maintained, sits close to U.S. 101, and has a definite goal: beautiful Marymere Falls. It's a popular trail for kids, but the littlest ones will have trouble with the steep ascent to the viewing platform. Start out on the Barnes Creek Trail, which leads .7 mile through beautiful maples and conifers to the Marymere Trail turnoff. Continue up to the falls, where silvery water drops from a moss-covered outcropping some 100 feet to the basin below. 1.8 miles RT. Easy. Access: Storm King Ranger Station.

Mink Lake Trail This is a long climb up to Mink Lake, where herons are known to pursue an elusive trout or two. In late summer, brilliant buckbean flowers fill the marshy edges of the lake, and huckleberries are abundant. 5.2 miles RT. Moderate. Access: Opposite end of Sol Duc Resort parking lot from the pools.

North Fork of the Sol Duc On this trail, you climb the ridge between the main and north forks of the river before descending into the North Fork Valley. The trail passes through old-growth forests before arriving at the deep-green pools of the river. The curious can venture upriver for several more miles. 2.4 miles RT. Moderate. Access: North Fork trail head, 3¾ miles down Sol Duc Rd. away from the resort.

Sol Duc Falls One of the more popular spots on the peninsula, Sol Duc Falls is viewed from a bridge that spans the canyon just below the falls. On the way, check out the huge hemlocks and Douglas firs, some of which are 300 years old. This trail is wide, graveled, and level, making it great for kids. 1.7 miles RT. Easy. Access: Sol Duc Ranger Station.

Spruce Railroad This is the trail you want to take for a leisurely stroll on a hot summer afternoon. The flat, wide trail wanders around the unbelievably blue-green waters of Lake Crescent, along an old stretch of abandoned railroad, with excellent views of Mount Storm King. There are two abandoned railroad tunnels (don't go in!) and a much-photographed arch bridge at Devil's Punchbowl. 8 miles RT. Easy. Access: End of North Shore Rd. along Lake Crescent, or from east end near Log Cabin Resort.

HURRICANE RIDGE AREA

Cirque Rim Trail & Big Meadow Loops These trails provide a wonderful little taste of subalpine meadows, deer, and the summer displays of wildflowers, along with excellent views of Port Angeles, the Strait of Juan de Fuca, and the Olympic Mountains. .5 mile and .25 mile RT. Easy. Access: Hurricane Ridge Visitor Center parking lot.

Grand Ridge (Obstruction Point to Green Mountain) This is the highest section of trail in the park, a fact you might notice as you gaze out to Victoria, BC, and the Strait of Juan de Fuca to the north, or to the south, toward the Grand Valley with its string of lakes and the numerous snow-clad peaks of the Olympic interior. There is a shortage of both trees and water on this hike.

From the parking lot, follow the trail to the left. (The right goes to Grand Valley.) In 2 miles you'll find yourself at the breathtaking top of Elk Mountain. Over the next 5.5 miles, you will pass through Roaring Winds Camp (not misnamed) on your way up to Maiden Peak. This is a good turnaround point, unless you want to descend to Deer Park. 11 miles RT. Moderate. Access: From Hurricane Ridge, turn right onto dirt road to Obstruction Point, and continue 8½ miles to end of road.

High Ridge, Alpine Hill to Klahhane Ridge You can take the short, paved 1-mile High Ridge Route (which is chock-full of interpretive exhibits) and then return to the parking lot. Or you can proceed along the unpaved portion to Sunrise Ridge, a rocky little backbone of a view point off the High Ridge Trail, providing excellent panoramas of the Olympic Mountains, the Strait of Juan de Fuca, Port Angeles, and numerous beautiful alpine glaciers and wildflowers. The rest of the 3.3-mile, somewhat strenuous walk climbs to the top of Klahhane Ridge. As numerous signs warn, do not feed or approach the deer and marmots here. 1–8 miles RT. Easy to moderate. Access: Hurricane Ridge Visitor Center.

Hurricane Hill This is a popular trail in the summertime. The broad, paved trail climbs along an abandoned work road up to brilliant alpine meadows, with fantastic views of the Strait of Juan de Fuca and Port Angeles to the north and glacier-crowned Mount Olympus to the south. 3.2 miles RT. Moderate. Access: 1½ miles from Hurricane Ridge Visitor Center.

EASTERN & SOUTHEASTERN SECTION

Note: At press time, Dosewallips Road was washed out and no timeline was set for repair (the U.S. Forest Service has prepared a Draft Environmental Impact Statement to address the future of this road, but it doesn't look like the road will be rebuilt or reopened anytime soon). Hikers and stock can still explore the area, but the new trek to the trail head adds about 5.5 miles (one-way) to the hikes below.

Main Fork Dosewallips/Constance Pass Take the Main Fork Dosewallips to the north, and you'll find yourself on a moderate climb through old-growth forest for 7.5 miles before the trail flattens out at Constance Pass. Fields of wildflowers skirt the edge of Mount Constance. The trail ends in another 3.4 miles at Boulder Shelter in Olympic National Forest. You can also catch the Upper Big Quilcene Trail or the Upper Dungeness Trail here. 11 miles one-way. Moderate. Access: Dosewallips trail head.

Main Fork of the Dosewallips This is a versatile trail. You can catch a lot more of the inland trails from here, including Constance Pass Trail, the Gray Wolf Trail, and the Elwha River Trail. The Dosewallips side of the park sometimes seems like the neglected side—it's not as flashy as a glacial meadow or a rainforest. But the Dosewallips is one of the most beautiful rivers in the country, its jade-green water crashing down among narrow cliffs. And you might skirt some of the crowds. 31 miles RT. Moderate. Access: Dosewallips trail head.

4 Other Sports & Activities

BIKING Almost all trails in the park are closed to mountain bikes. The only exception is the **Spruce Railroad Trail,** which was once a railroad grade that ran along the shore of the lake. It is quite flat and easy for its 4-mile length; an additional 1½-mile stretch of road extends past the North Shore Picnic Area. The highlight of the trail is a much-photographed arched bridge across a rocky cove. A few **dirt roads** for mountain bikers extend from paved roads; they include the section from Hurricane Ridge to Obstruction Peak.

For road bikers, U.S. 101 can be treacherous, with eager motorists rubbernecking and all. But if you get through that, you can find some pleasant rides on any of the roads that poke into the park.

KAYAKING & CANOEING Although large and often windy, glacier-carved **Lake Crescent** is a beautiful place to do a little paddling. Lush, green forests rise straight up from the shores of the 624-foot deep lake, giving the waters a fjordlike quality unmatched on the peninsula. Boat ramps are on U.S. 101 at Storm King (near the middle of the lake) and at Fairholme (at the west end of the lake). On East Beach Road, on the lake's northeast shore, there is a private boat ramp at the Log Cabin Resort.

If you launch at Storm King, you can explore around Barnes Point, away from U.S. 101 traffic noise (but in view of the Lake Crescent Lodge). From Fairholme, you can paddle along the north shore. From the Log Cabin Resort, you can explore the bay that feeds the Lyre River, the lake's outlet stream. When winds blow down this lake, as they often do, the waters can be dangerous for small boats.

Fairholm Store & Marina, at the west end of the lake (✆ **360/928-3020;** www.fairholmstore.com), rents canoes, kayaks, and rowboats for about $10 per hour. Boats are for rent at the **Log Cabin Resort,** 3183 E. Beach Rd., Port Angeles (✆ **360/928-3325;** www.logcabinresort.net), on the lake's northeast shore, at similar rates.

Lake Ozette, surprisingly deep and nearly 10 miles long, is the third-largest natural lake in Washington and a fascinating place to explore by sea kayak or canoe. Only a mile from the Pacific Ocean, the lake is indented by numerous coves and bays, and surrounds three small islands. Campsites along the shore include the boat-in sites at Erickson's Bay.

The **Swan Bay boat launch,** one of two on the large lake, is probably the best choice for paddlers. For a leisurely half-day paddle, just explore the shores of the convoluted bay, in the middle of which is Garden Island. For a daylong trip, try paddling down the lake to Tivoli Island. For an overnighter, head to the lake's western shore and the campsites at Erickson's Bay. From here, you can explore up and down the west shore.

Both Lake Crescent and Lake Ozette are big lakes subject to quick changes of weather and wind. Whitecaps can come up suddenly, and cold waters can cause hypothermia. Check the weather forecast before leaving, and keep an eye on the sky. Also see "White-Water Kayaking & Rafting," below.

LLAMA TRIPS The park and surrounding areas have become a favorite for llama pack trips. **Kit's Llamas** (✆ **253/857-5274;** www.northolympic.com/llamas) offers day trips and overnights starting at $75 per person.

SNOWSHOEING & CROSS-COUNTRY SKIING Any of the roads leading into the mountains will offer a satisfying winter trek; check with park rangers about avalanche hazards before you go. If you seek views, head to **Hurricane Ridge** with the rest of the winter crowd and set out on any of the area's trails. One place to rent snowshoes is **Olympic Outdoor Center,** 18971 Front St. in Poulsbo (✆ **800/592-5983** or 360/697-6095; www.olympicoutdoorcenter.com), which charges $15 a day.

WHITE-WATER KAYAKING & RAFTING White-water rafting, scenic floats, and sea kayaking are options in and around Olympic National Park. Guided trips last approximately half a day. Canoe and kayak rentals are available from **Olympic Raft & Kayak,** 123 Lake Aldwell Rd., Port Angeles (✆ **888/452-1443** or 360/452-1443; www.raftandkayak.com); prices start at $50 per day. Rates for guided trips start at $54 for adults and $44 for kids 5 to 11. The company also offers classes (call for details).

Another respected company that provides guided white-water trips outside the park, classes, and rentals is **Olympic Outdoor Center** (see "Snowshoeing & Cross-Country Skiing," above).

5 Camping

Many campgrounds here are open seasonally, and their exact schedules are subject to change. Campgrounds at higher elevations may be snow-covered (and closed) from early November to late June; seasonal campgrounds at lower elevations may open earlier.

There are no showers or laundry facilities inside the park; the Log Cabin Resort, on the north shore of Lake Crescent at the northern edge of the park, has both.

The park has no RV hookups, and many sites can accommodate RVs of only 21 feet or less. Use of the park's RV dump stations costs $5. The Log Cabin Resort offers RV sites with hookups (see below).

NORTH- & EAST-SIDE CAMPGROUNDS

The six campgrounds on the northern edge of the park are some of the busiest in the park, due to their proximity to U.S. 101.

Deer Park is the easternmost of these campgrounds (to get there, take Deer Park Rd. from U.S. 101 east of Port Angeles); at 5,400 feet, it's also the only high-elevation campground in the park. The winding one-way gravel road to the campground will have you wondering how you're ever going to get back down the mountain. (RVs and trailers are prohibited.) Deer frequent the campground, and hiking trails head out across the ridges and valleys.

Because of its proximity to Hurricane Ridge, **Heart O' the Hills** is especially popular. It's on Hurricane Ridge Road, 5 miles south of the Olympic National Park Visitor Center. Several trails start at or near the campground.

Two campgrounds are on Olympic Hot Springs Road, up the Elwha River, which is popular with kayakers and anglers. **Elwha** is the trail head for a trail leading up to Hurricane Ridge. **Altair** has a boat ramp often used by rafters and kayakers. And,

Campground	Total Elev.	RV Sites	Dump Hookups	Drinking Station	Toilets
Altair	450	30	No	No	Yes
Deer Park*	5,400	14	No	No	Yes
Dosewallips**	1,540	30	No	No	Yes
Elwha	390	40	No	No	Yes
Fairholme	580	88	No	Yes	Yes
Graves Creek	540	30	No	No	Yes
Heart O' the Hills	1,807	105	No	No	Yes
Hoh	578	88	No	Yes	Yes
Kalaloch	50	170	No	Yes	Yes
Log Cabin Resort	580	40	Yes	Yes	Yes
Mora**	32	94	No	Yes	Yes
North Fork	9	520	No	No	Yes
Ozette	40	15	No	No	Yes
Queets	290	40	No	No	Yes
Sol Duc	1,680	82	No	No	Yes
South Beach	50	50	No	No	No
Staircase	765	47	No	No	Yes

* Trailers/RVs prohibited.

** Walk-in sites.

yes, there are undeveloped hot springs pools, just a 2.5-mile hike away.

The only national park campground on Lake Crescent is **Fairholme,** at the west end of the lake. This campground is popular with power boaters and can be rather noisy. South of this area, nearby **Sol Duc** sits amid impressive stands of old-growth trees near the Sol Duc Hot Springs (and the resort there). Not surprisingly, it is often crowded.

You'll find RV sites with full hookups at the **Log Cabin Resort,** 3183 E. Beach Rd., on the north shore of Lake Crescent (✆ **360/928-3325;** www.logcabinresort.net). Because there are no hookups at any of the national park campgrounds, this is a good choice for RVers. The resort accepts credit cards (DISC, MC, V) and is open year-round.

SOUTHEAST-SIDE CAMPGROUNDS

Along the Dosewallips River, you'll find the walk-in-only **Dosewallips Campground** in a forested setting. The campground is a 5.5-mile hike from the road; a landslide closed the road for cars.

The remote **Staircase Campground** is inland from the Hood Canal and is a good base for day hikes or as a starting point for a longer backpacking trip. It's up the Skokomish River from Lake Cushman on F.S. 24 and is the trail head for the Six Ridge, Flapjack Lakes, and Anderson Pass trails.

SOUTH- & SOUTHWEST-SIDE CAMPGROUNDS

If you want to say you've camped in the wettest rainforest in the Lower 48, head for **Hoh,** a busy campground near the Hoh Rain Forest Visitor Center.

East of Lake Quinault, **North Fork** and **Graves Creek,** reached only by unpaved roads that are prone to washouts and not recommended for RVs, provide access to several long-distance hiking trails.

Queets was closed due to flooding in 2005, but the park rerouted the road and reopened it in 2008. The road often washes out; call for the latest information.

COASTAL CAMPGROUNDS

Along the peninsula's west side are several beach campgrounds. Busy **Kalaloch,** at the southernmost portion of the park's coastal strip, is the only Olympic National Park campground that accepts reservations, and only for the period from mid-June through early September (✆ **877/444-6777;** www.recreation.gov).

Up the coast is **Mora,** along the Quillayute River about 2 miles from beautiful Rialto Beach. About 3 miles in from the coast is the remote **Ozette,** on the north shore of Lake Ozette. It's a good choice for kayakers and canoeists, as well as people wanting to day-hike to the beaches on either side of Cape Alava. This campground may be closed during periods of heavy rain because of flooding.

Fire Pits/ Water	Showers	Grills	Laundry	Reserve	Fees	Open
Yes	No	Yes	No	No	$12	Seasonal
No	No	Yes	No	No	$10	Seasonal
No	No	Yes	No	No	Free	Seasonal
Yes	No	Yes	No	No	$12	Year-round
Yes	No	Yes	No	No	$12	Seasonal
Yes	No	Yes	No	No	$12	Seasonal
Yes	No	No	No	No	$12	Year-round
Yes	No	Yes	No	No	$12	Year-round
Yes	No	Yes	No	Yes	$14–$18	Year-round
Yes	Yes	Yes	Yes	Yes	$40	Seasonal
Yes	No	Yes	No	No	$12	Year-round
No	No	No	No	No	$10	Seasonal
Yes	No	Yes	No	No	$12	Seasonal
Yes	No	Yes	No	No	$12	Seasonal
No	No	No	No	No	$10	Year-round
No	No	Yes	No	No	$10	Seasonal
Yes	No	Yes	No	No	$12	Seasonal

6 Where to Stay

INSIDE THE PARK

Kalaloch Lodge This rustic, cedar-shingled lodge and its cluster of cabins perch on a grassy bluff. Below, the Pacific Ocean thunders against a sandy beach where huge driftwood logs are scattered like so many twigs. The breathtaking setting makes this one of the most popular lodges on the coast, and it's advisable to book rooms at least 4 months in advance (11 months in advance for July, Aug, and major holidays). The rooms in the old lodge are the least expensive, but the ocean-view bluff cabins are the most popular. The log cabins across the road from the bluff cabins don't have the knockout views. Amenities in the cabins vary—some have cooktops, refrigerators, microwaves, and Franklin stoves. For comfort, you can't beat the motel-like rooms in the Sea Crest House. All units have coffeemakers, two walking sticks, and tide tables! The **dining room** serves breakfast, lunch, and dinner, and there is a casual **coffee shop.** The lodge also has a general store and gas station.

157151 U.S. 101, Forks, WA 98331. ✆ **866/525-2562.** Fax 360/962-3391. www.visitkalaloch.com. 64 units. Late May to mid-Oct $171–$193 lodge or motel room double; $308 suite; $188–$311 cabin. Lower rates rest of year. AE, MC, V. Pets accepted in cabins ($15 per night).

Lake Crescent Lodge This historic lodge, built in 1916, lies 20 miles west of Port Angeles on the south shore of Lake Crescent. It is the lodging of choice for those wishing to stay on the north side of the park. The five guest rooms in the main building are the oldest and have shared bathrooms. If you'd like more modern accommodations, there are also standard motel-style rooms. If you have family or friends along, we recommend reserving a cottage. Those with fireplaces are the most comfortable and the most popular. All rooms have views of the lake or the mountains. Wood paneling, hardwood floors, a stone fireplace, and a sunroom make the lobby a popular spot for just sitting and relaxing. The **Lodge Dining Room** serves three meals daily. A lobby **lounge** provides a quiet place for an evening drink. Rowboat rentals are available. All units are nonsmoking.

416 Lake Crescent Rd., Port Angeles, WA 98363. ✆ **360/928-3211.** www.lakecrescentlodge.com. 52 units. $107 double with shared bathroom; $156–$171 double with private bathroom; $188–$241 cottage. $15 per additional person. AE, DC, DISC, MC, V. Children 17 or under not accepted in main building. Pets accepted in cottages ($25 per pet).

Log Cabin Resort This resort on the north shore of Lake Crescent first opened in 1895 and still has buildings that date from the 1920s. The least expensive accommodations are rustic one-room log cabins in which you provide the bedding and share a bathroom a short walk away. More comfortable are the 1928 cabins with private bathrooms (shower or tub), some of which also have kitchenettes. (You provide the cooking and eating utensils.) The lodge rooms (with showers, microwaves, and coffeemakers) and a chalet (with a shower, kitchen sink, and refrigerator) offer the greatest comfort and best views. The lodge **dining room,** which offers organic and natural foods, overlooks the lake. The resort also has a general store and RV sites (see "Camping," above).

3183 E. Beach Rd., Port Angeles, WA 98363. ✆ **360/928-3325.** www.logcabinresort.net. 24 cabins, 8 with bathroom; 4 motel units; 2 chalet units. $65 cabin for 2 without bathroom; $93–$115 cabin for 2 with bathroom; $120 double lodge unit; $160 chalet. DISC, MC, V. Closed Nov–Mar. Pets accepted in cabins ($12 per pet).

Sol Duc Hot Springs Resort At the end of Sol Duc Road, the Sol Duc Hot Springs area has been a popular family vacation spot for years. Campers, day-trippers, and resort guests all spend the day soaking and playing in the hot spring–fed sitting pools. The grounds of the resort are grassy and open, but the forest is within arm's reach. The cabins, done in modern motel style, are comfortable, if not spacious. Cabins are available with or without kitchenettes. The excellent **restaurant** serves breakfast and dinner, and the poolside deli serves lunch. The resort also has a gift shop and a convenience store. The focal point is the three **soaking pools,** which are open to the public ($12 adults, $8.50 children 4–12, free for kids under 4; room rates include pool access for guests). Massages are available.

Sol Duc Rd., U.S. 101 (P.O. Box 2169), Port Angeles, WA 98362. ✆ **866/476-5382.** Fax 360/327-3593. www.visitsolduc.com. 32 cabins. $151–$184 double; $320 suite. Rates include full breakfast and pool access. AE, DISC, MC, V. Closed late Oct to early Mar. Pets accepted ($15 per night).

NEAR THE PARK IN PORT ANGELES

Domaine Madeleine Looking for a romantic getaway? You won't find a better spot than Domaine Madeleine. Set on beautifully gardened grounds overlooking the water, this B&B has a secluded and relaxing atmosphere. The guest rooms are in several different buildings surrounded by colorful gardens. All have views of the Strait of Juan de Fuca and the mountains beyond, fireplaces, and hair dryers, plus romantic touches such as French perfumes and his-and-hers designer robes. Four units have whirlpool tubs for two, and three have kitchenettes. The breakfasts, offering items such as Dungeness crab cakes, smoked salmon, and apple crepes, are superb. There is a DVD library and Wi-Fi. All rooms are nonsmoking.

146 Wildflower Lane, Port Angeles, WA 98362. ✆ **888/811-8376** or 360/457-4174. www.domainemadeleine.com. 5 units. TV, TEL. Summer $195–$310 double; winter $160–$225 double. Rates include full breakfast. AE, MC, V. Children 12 and under not accepted.

Red Lion Hotel Port Angeles If you're on your way to or from Victoria, there's no more convenient hotel than the Red Lion. Located on the waterfront, it's steps from the ferry terminal. Most rooms have balconies and large bathrooms, and the more expensive rooms overlook the Strait of Juan de Fuca. A seafood restaurant is adjacent to the hotel. Laundry and valet service is available, and there's a heated outdoor pool and hot tub.

221 N. Lincoln St., Port Angeles, WA 98362. ✆ **360/452-9215.** Fax 360/452-4734. www.redlion.com/portangeles. 186 units, including 2 suites. A/C, TV, TEL. $149–$209 double; $179–$229 suite. Lower rates off season. AE, DC, DISC, MC, V.

The Tudor Inn In a quiet residential neighborhood, this 1910 Tudor home is surrounded by a large yard and pretty gardens. Upstairs are nicely restored guest rooms furnished with European antiques. Several rooms have good views of the Olympic Mountains; one unit has a balcony, fireplace, and claw-foot tub. On the ground floor are a lounge and library, both with fireplaces that get a lot of use. The delicious breakfast of fresh-baked pastries, egg dishes, and specialty items is served by candlelight in the formal dining room. The inn is nonsmoking.

1108 S. Oak St., Port Angeles, WA 98362. ✆ **866/286-2224** or 360/452-3138. www.tudorinn.com. 5 units. $125–$160 double. AE, DISC, MC, V. Children 11 and under not accepted.

IN THE FORKS AREA

Manitou Lodge Bed & Breakfast This terrific B&B is secluded on 10 forested acres only minutes from some of the most beautiful and remote beaches in the Northwest. The rooms are decorated in an eclectic style and a touch of class that combines handmade furniture, quilts, and other crafts with antiques. All units have microwaves and Wi-Fi. The largest guest room, Sacagawea, has a wood-burning fireplace, king bed, handmade tables, and an old oak freezer chest as a dresser. There are five rooms in the main lodge, two more in a separate cottage, and two primitive, summer-only cabins with access to a bathroom in the main lodge. There is also a "luxury campsite" with everything set up; guests need bring only cooking gear. Guests tend to gravitate to the comfortable **great room,** where a stone fireplace is the center of attention.

813 Kilmer Rd. (P.O. Box 600), Forks, WA 98331. ✆ **360/374-6295.** Fax 360/374-7495. www.manitoulodge.com. 9 units. $99–$179 double; primitive cabins (May–Oct only) $69–$99 double; luxury campsite $45 double. Rates include full breakfast. AE, MC, V. Take Wash. 110 west from 1 mile north of Forks; after 8 miles, turn right on Mora Rd. and then right on Kilmer Rd. Pets accepted in several units ($10 fee).

Miller Tree Inn This charming and comfortable old farmhouse, a few blocks east of downtown Forks, is surrounded by large trees and pastures. There's nothing fussy or pretentious—it's just a friendly inn that caters primarily to outdoors enthusiasts and fans of the *Twilight* books and movies (set right here in Forks). Two rooms have two-person whirlpool tubs, two more have one-person tubs, and three have gas fireplaces. A hot tub is on the back deck. The breakfasts are worth getting up for—specialties include gingerbread pancakes with lemon sauce, and caramel-peach French toast. All rooms are nonsmoking.

654 E. Division St. (P.O. Box 1565), Forks, WA 98331. ✆ **800/943-6563** or 360/374-6806. Fax 360/374-6807. www.millertreeinn.com. 8 units. June to mid-Sept $125–$205 double; mid-Sept to May $100–$185 double. Rates include full breakfast. AE, DISC, MC, V. Pets accepted in 1 unit ($10 fee).

SOUTH OF THE PARK

Lake Quinault Lodge On the shore of Lake Quinault at the southwest corner of the park, this imposing grande dame of the Olympic Peninsula exudes ageless tranquillity. Huge old firs and cedars shade the rustic lodge, and Adirondack chairs on the deck command a view of the lawn. In the main lodge are small rooms, modern rooms with TVs and little balconies, and rooms with fireplaces. Many rooms have been recently renovated. The Boathouse or annex rooms are more rustic, but they allow pets. There's an indoor heated pool and a sauna. Canoe, rowboat, and kayak rentals are available, as are rainforest tours, led by the Forest Service in the summer. Hiking trails abound. The **dining room** is a large, dark place befitting such a lodge, with beautiful lake views. The menu reflects the bounties of the Olympic Peninsula, especially seafood.

P.O. Box 7, Quinault, WA 98575. ✆ **800/562-6672** or 360/288-2900. Fax 360/288-2901. www.visitlakequinault.com. 91 units. Mid-June to late Sept and winter holidays $130–$228 double, $256 suite; late Sept to mid-June $90–$175 double, $200 suite. AE, MC, V. Pets accepted ($15 per night).

7 Where to Dine

INSIDE THE PARK

Restaurant choices inside the park are slim. On the north side, on the shore of Lake Crescent, the dining room at **Lake Crescent Lodge** (open early May to mid-Oct) serves Continental and Northwestern cuisine with an emphasis on local seafood. Also along the lakeshore, the **Log Cabin Resort** (open Memorial Day to Labor Day), offers a Northwestern menu, specializing in organic and natural fare. On Lake Quinault, try the dining room at **Lake Quinault Lodge** (see "Where to Stay," above). The restaurant at **Sol Duc Hot Springs Resort** is open from early May through mid-October. It offers traditional American breakfasts and Northwest cuisine at dinner. On the premises is a deli that serves lunch.

To pick up packaged sandwiches, beverages, and snacks at Lake Crescent, stop at the **Fairholm Store & Marina,** 221121 U.S. 101 (✆ **360/928-3020;** www.fairholmstore.com), at the west end of the lake. It's open from May through September.

IN PORT ANGELES

Bella Italia ITALIAN This lively, colorfully decorated restaurant in Port Angeles offers a fun atmosphere. Meals begin with a basket of fresh-baked bread accompanied by a dipping sauce of olive oil, balsamic vinegar, garlic, and herbs. The menu includes all the favorite Italian dishes. Daily specials include fresh local seafood. Also on the menu are local mussels, steamed clams, and smoked salmon fettuccine. If you've had your fill of seafood, try vegetarian lasagna, manicotti, one of the specialty pizzas, or Tuscan steak—sliced marinated flank steak grilled with garlic whipped potatoes. The Italian desserts are excellent. This is a good choice for families, as well as fans of *Twilight*—this is the site of Edward and Bella's first date.

118 E. 1st St. ✆ **360/457-5442.** www.bellaitaliapa.com. Main courses $10–$32. AE, DC, DISC, MC, V. Daily 4–10pm (until 9pm fall to spring). Closed major holidays.

C'est Si Bon FRENCH Open since the early 1980s on the east side of Port Angeles, C'est Si Bon is an attractive restaurant with reproductions of European works of art, crystal chandeliers, and old musical instruments used as wall decorations. Most tables have a view of the restaurant's pretty garden, and there is a large sunroom on the garden side. The menu is primarily French with some Northwestern influences; sauces are mostly lighter than those at many other French restaurants. Selections include Cornish game hen with mushroom stuffing, scampi in whiskey sauce, beef tenderloin in red currant sauce, roast duck, and rack of lamb. Desserts are limited but rich and creamy, and the wine selection is very good. The cozy bar is decorated with signed photos of stars; chef-owner Michelle Juhasz formerly worked as a Hollywood caterer.

23 Cedar Park Rd. (north side of U.S. 101, just off Buchanan Rd.). ✆ **360/452-8888.** www.cestsibon-frenchcuisine.com. Reservations recommended. Main courses $28–$32. AE, DISC, MC, V. Tues–Sun 5–11pm. Closed Jan 1.

Downriggers SEAFOOD/STEAK At the back of a mall, convenient to the ferry landing, you'll find this large, casual restaurant. Walls of glass provide great views of the harbor and take in some stunning sunsets. A long menu nearly guarantees that you'll find something you like. We especially recommend the king salmon and top sirloin combo, but the salmon crab cakes are also very popular, and everyone raves about the clam chowder. The bar features two dozen beers on tap.

At the Landing Mall, 115 E. Railroad Ave., 2nd level. ✆ **360/452-2700.** Reservations recommended for dinner. Main courses $10–$25. AE, DISC, MC, V. Daily noon–10pm.

Drake's Pizza & Subs SANDWICHES/PIZZERIA This basic restaurant is not much to look at—four tables and somewhat random decor—but it serves good food at a good price. The menu is split between subs, wraps, salads, and pizza, with something for everybody, from vegetarians to carnivores. I liked the Caesar chicken wrap. This is a great place to pick up a to-go lunch before heading into the park.

819 S. Lincoln St. © **360/452-4955.** Menu items $4–$7; pizzas $7–$15. MC, V. Mon–Fri 10am–8pm; Sat 10am–7pm; Sun 11am–4pm.

IN FORKS

Forks Coffee Shop AMERICAN An extensive menu of well-prepared American food and a casual atmosphere make the Forks Coffee Shop a good bet. It features all the usual breakfast items, including gigantic hotcakes and create-your-own omelets. A limited number of breakfast basics are available all day. Lunch consists of a variety of sandwiches, burgers, and baskets such as fish and chips and fried chicken. Dinners are primarily steak and seafood, with local fresh fish whenever possible, and include the soup and salad bar. There is a good selection of homemade pies for dessert.

241 S. Forks Ave. (U.S. 101). © **360/374-6769.** www.forkscoffeeshop.com. Main courses $4–$13 breakfast and lunch, $11–$19 dinner. DISC, MC, V. Daily 5am–8pm.

The Smoke House Restaurant AMERICAN The name says it all. This place smokes fish, and the salmon is just about the best we've ever had. It has a good smoky flavor yet is tender and moist. If you don't feel like sitting down for the smoked salmon dinner, smoked salmon salad, or smoked salmon and cheddar cheese tray appetizer, then consider getting some to go. A few other items are served, including beef and chicken, but the smoked salmon is so good, it's hard to recommend ordering anything else. The pie is also some of the best in the state.

193161 U.S. 101 (at La Push Rd.). © **360/374-6258.** Main courses $6–$18 lunch, $8–$23 dinner. DISC, MC, V. Summer Mon–Fri 11am–10pm, Sat–Sun noon–10pm; winter Mon–Fri 11am–9pm, Sat–Sun noon–9pm. Closed Thanksgiving and Dec 24–25.

27

Petrified Forest National Park, AZ

by Eric Peterson and Don & Barbara Laine

The first things you'll notice at Petrified Forest National Park are the dozens of logs lying atop hills as if on display, many of them pointing in the same direction. Closer up, you can see the colors in the wood—reds, greens, yellows, blues, and purples, all of them rich and moist looking, like wet paint. The colors might tempt you to touch the wood, and if you do, you'll find that it isn't wood at all, but cold, hard stone.

More than 200 million years ago, these petrified trees were enormous conifers growing in a tropical forest. Floods swept them into large rivers, tearing off their branches in the process. Eventually, the trees bottomed out in the shallow waters of the floodplain, where silt, mud, and volcanic ash buried them. Because almost no oxygen could reach the entombed trunks, they were slow to decay. Silica from the ash permeated the trunks, replacing or filling the wood's cells before leaving quartz in its place. Minerals such as iron and manganese streaked the quartz with colors. The end result: The wood became beautiful rock.

Recognizing the value of this rock, early settlers began shipping it out on East Coast–bound trains. When the residents of the Territory of Arizona realized that the "wood" might soon be gone, they petitioned Congress to protect the "forests." Using the Antiquities Act, President Theodore Roosevelt created Petrified Forest National Monument in 1906. Congress designated it a national park in 1962.

The same sediments that entombed the trees buried other plants and animals, preserving them as fossils as well. Erosion has exposed these clays and sandstones, collectively known as the **Chinle Formation.** With little or no vegetation to hold them in place, the sediments erode quickly and unevenly, forming mesas, buttes, and furrowed, conical badlands, unearthing thousands of fossils, including bones from some of the most remarkable creatures ever to inhabit the earth. In addition to the 200-million-year-old fossils, there is evidence that the ancestral Puebloans (also known as Anasazi), ancestors of the modern Pueblo people, once occupied this area. Evidence of other human occupation dates from 10,000 years ago.

Even without these wonders, it would be worth coming here to see the rich reds, grays, and maroons of the Painted Desert. Shaped like a tusk (with the wider end near Cameron, Arizona), the desert spreads from near Holbrook in the south to the Hopi mesas in the northeast, to near the Grand Canyon in the west—far beyond the boundaries of the park. Its seemingly barren landscape is home to a rich diversity of plant and animal life: desert grasses; wildflowers, including Indian paintbrush and globemallow; juniper and other trees; mammals, including pronghorns, cottontails, and porcupines; reptiles, including collared lizards and western rattlesnakes; and birds, the most prominent being the raven.

AVOIDING THE CROWDS

About 600,000 people visit the park each year, in part because it is so convenient for cross-country travelers, just a few hundred yards off I-40. Nearly everyone heads down the same 28-mile scenic drive, and the drive's 20 pullouts can get crowded.

We offer three suggestions for avoiding the crowds: Arrive early in the day, because there aren't many visitors in the first few hours, it's also before the heat peaks, and the lighting on the rocks is great. Second, stroll away from the parking areas. The pullouts attract far more people than the trails. But the most effective place to get away from it all here is a day hike into the Painted Desert Wilderness.

1 Essentials

GETTING THERE & GATEWAYS

Petrified Forest National Park is 117 miles east of Flagstaff and 180 miles north of Phoenix. The north entrance is 25 miles east of Holbrook on **I-40;** the south entrance is 20 miles east of Holbrook on **U.S. 180.** From Flagstaff, simply take I-40 east.

THE NEAREST AIRPORT Flagstaff's **Pulliam Airport** (✆ **928/556-1234**) is served by **Horizon Air** and **US Airways Express,** and has rental cars from **Avis, Budget, Hertz,** and **National.** See chapter 38 for airline/car-rental websites.

INFORMATION

Contact **Petrified Forest National Park,** P.O. Box 2217, Petrified Forest National Park, AZ 86028 (✆ **928/524-6228;** www.nps.gov/pefo). The **Petrified Forest Museum Association,** P.O. Box 2277, Petrified Forest, AZ 86028 (✆ **928/524-6228,** ext. 239), has several excellent books on the park. Written by retired geology professor Sidney Ash, *Petrified Forest: The Story Behind the Scenery* provides a good overview of the human and natural history of the park. Stephen Trimble's book *Earth Journey: A Road Guide to Petrified Forest* is almost as good as a guided tour of the park's scenic drive.

For information about area lodging and dining, contact the **Holbrook Chamber of Commerce,** 100 E. Arizona St., Holbrook, AZ 86025 (✆ **800/524-2459** or 928/524-6558; www.gotourholbrook.com).

VISITOR CENTERS

The park has a visitor center at each end. Both sell books, videos, and area maps, and offer free brochures on the park's geology, flora, and fauna. Both centers are open daily year-round, from 7am to 7pm in summer, with shorter hours at other times, and both are closed Christmas.

The **Painted Desert Visitor Center,** outside the park's north entrance gate, has general information on the park and shows a 20-minute film about the park on the hour and the half-hour. Two miles north of the park's south entrance station, the **Rainbow Forest Museum** shows the same film on the same schedule as the Painted Desert Visitor Center, plus it has displays on the formation of petrified wood, fossilized bones and teeth of ancient animals, and a display of letters from people who stole wood from the park and later regretted it. The latter is particularly compelling and often quite funny.

Also see the section on the **Painted Desert Inn National Historic Landmark** under "Park Attractions," below.

FEES & PERMITS

Entrance to the park costs $10 per vehicle, $5 per visitor on foot, bicycle, or motorcycle. The required but free **backcountry camping permits** are issued at visitor centers.

SPECIAL REGULATIONS & WARNINGS

Because an estimated 25,000 pounds of petrified wood are stolen from the park every year, the National Park Service has adopted a **zero-tolerance policy** for visitors who remove even the smallest pieces. Violators are subject to fines starting at $325. If rangers suspect you of removing any wood or other resources, they may detain you and search your car.

There are long stretches between water sources at the park, so fill containers at either visitor center before starting on the scenic drive.

While pets must be leashed, dogs are permitted on most trails in the park.

SEASONS & CLIMATE

With an average of just over 9½ inches of precipitation annually, the park couldn't get much drier. Because it averages a lofty 5,800 feet in elevation, however, it's not as hot as many other areas in Arizona. Even in July, daily highs average in the mid-80s (30s Celsius), with nightly lows in the low 50s (10s Celsius). Of course, the park occasionally heats up—temperatures sometimes top 100°F (38°C) in midsummer. The hottest months, July and August, are also the wettest, with afternoon storms cutting the morning heat and depositing nearly a third of the yearly precipitation. Storms continue into early fall, but the weather dries out as it cools. By winter it can get very cold, and snowstorms occasionally close the park. In January, daily highs average 42°F (6°C) and lows 19°F (–7°C). Spring tends to be blustery and dry, with daily highs increasing from the mid-50s (lower teens Celsius) in March to about 80°F (27°C) in June—the driest month of all, with just over ¼ inch of rainfall.

SEASONAL EVENTS

During March, special events mark **Arizona Archaeology Month.** Call the park office for details.

For about a week both before and after the June 21 **summer solstice,** rangers meet with visitors from 8 to 10am daily at Puerco Pueblo. The sun shines through a natural crack, directing a beam of light onto a smaller boulder beside it. The beam gradually moves down the edge of the rock to a small, circular petroglyph; it touches the center of the petroglyph on the summer solstice. Archaeologists believe the ancestral Puebloans used this petroglyph to monitor the summer solstice.

If You Have Only 1 Day

The most obvious and easiest way to see the park is to first stop at one of the visitor centers and then take the 28-mile **scenic drive,** stopping at the pullouts and taking some of the short trails to get close-up views of the petrified wood. With a bit of extra time, you might consider a hike into the **Painted Desert Wilderness.** Combine this with a pre- or post-hike picnic at the **Chinde Point Picnic Area.**

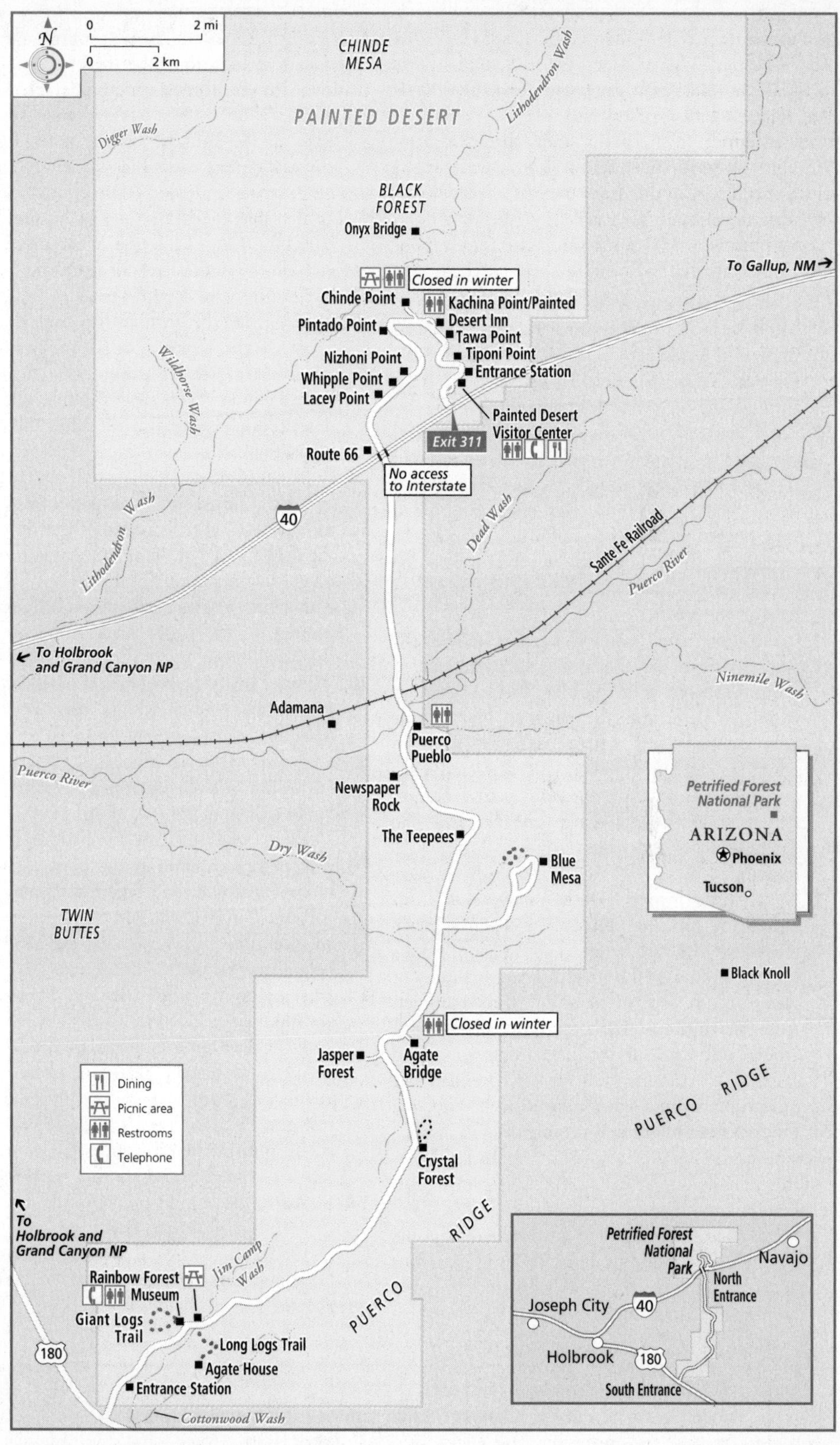
0
2 mi
0
2 km
N
CHINDE MESA
PAINTED DESERT
Digger Wash
Lithodendron Wash
BLACK FOREST
Onyx Bridge
Closed in winter
To Gallup, NM
Chinde Point
Kachina Point/Painted
Desert Inn
Pintado Point
Tawa Point
Tiponi Point
Nizhoni Point
Entrance Station
Whipple Point
Lacey Point
Wildhorse Wash
Painted Desert Visitor Center
Exit 311
Route 66
No access to Interstate
40
Lithodendron Wash
Dead Wash
Sante Fe Railroad
Puerco River
To Holbrook and Grand Canyon NP
Ninemile Wash
Adamana
Puerco Pueblo
Puerco River
Newspaper Rock
The Teepees
Dry Wash
Blue Mesa
Petrified Forest National Park
ARIZONA
Phoenix
Tucson
TWIN BUTTES
Black Knoll
Closed in winter
Jasper Forest
Agate Bridge
Dining
Picnic area
Restrooms
Telephone
PUERCO RIDGE
Crystal Forest
To Holbrook and Grand Canyon NP
RIDGE
Jim Camp Wash
Rainbow Forest Museum
Giant Logs Trail
Long Logs Trail
Agate House
180
PUERCO
Entrance Station
Cottonwood Wash
Petrified Forest National Park
Navajo
North Entrance
Joseph City
40
Holbrook
180
South Entrance

2 Exploring the Park by Car

The direction you choose for the scenic drive depends on which way you're traveling on I-40. If you're coming from the west, take U.S. 180 east from Holbrook to the park's south entrance, drive through the park, then rejoin I-40 at the park's north entrance. Coming from the east, do the opposite, driving through the park from the north and exiting onto U.S. 180 at the south end. Trails mentioned here are discussed in "Day Hikes," below.

1. If you enter the park from the south entrance, you'll start at the **Rainbow Forest Museum.** Behind the museum is the **Giant Logs Self-Guided Trail,** the first of several easy trails through the forests of petrified wood.
2. Leave your vehicle at the museum parking area. Just past the museum, you'll see an access trail to the **Long Logs** and the **Agate House** trail heads. The Agate House Trail ends at a prehistoric pueblo made of petrified wood. Forking to the left, the Long Logs Trail winds among some of the longest and most spectacular petrified trees in the area.
3. Continuing, you'll come to the **Crystal Forest,** where visitors in the late 1800s discovered ground covered with sparkling bits of petrified wood. At that time, the petrified logs in this area were flecked with quartz and purple amethyst crystals. The crystals attracted gem hunters, some of who went so far as to dynamite the trees. Although many crystals and the smaller pieces are gone, some colorful logs remain.
4. Next comes **Jasper Forest,** an overlook from atop a 150-foot-high bluff. This is a great place to observe the various effects of erosion. Looking downhill, you'll notice that large chunks of sandstone and petrified wood have tumbled from the bluff to the desert floor. Soft clay eroded out from under the harder wood and sandstone, undermining it and sending it downhill. Because erosion continues, someday the rocks underfoot will tumble down as well.
5. The first thing you'll notice at **Agate Bridge** is the remarkable bridge itself. With each end firmly embedded in sandstone, a petrified log forms a natural bridge across an arroyo that cuts through the ground underneath its midsection. The next thing you'll probably notice is the concrete span that "supports" it. In 1917, workers who wanted to preserve the bridge as a tourist attraction buttressed it with concrete.
6. Next, a short loop trail takes you to **Blue Mesa.** Like all the badlands in the park, Blue Mesa consists of soft rocks that can erode at the rate of 3 inches a decade—fast enough to change appreciably in the span of a human lifetime. The Blue Mesa Trail, one of the prettiest walkways in the park, descends from the fourth and last overlook on the spur road.
7. Next comes the turnoff for conical badlands known as the **Tepees.** The flat rocky surface you see is called **desert pavement,** created when strong winds sweep away the fine sands of the desert floor, exposing small stones and petrified-wood fragments.
8. From an overlook 2 miles past the Tepees, you can look down on **Newspaper Rock.** Early inhabitants pecked dozens of petroglyphs into the dark surface of the stone. Among them is an image of the famous humpbacked flute player, Kokopelli. The petroglyphs in this area aren't limited to Newspaper Rock, so be sure to scan the surrounding rocks with your binoculars.
9. With so many petroglyphs around Newspaper Rock, it seems inevitable that a prehistoric dwelling is nearby. Sure enough, a mile down the road is **Puerco Pueblo,** the remains of a 100-room pueblo occupied by the ancestral Puebloans from 1250 to about 1400. To see this dwelling, walk the easy .3-mile loop trail.
10. The newest pullout in the park focuses on a more recent era: the heyday of **Route 66.** Here you can pose with an old Studebaker and read an interpretive plaque about the Mother Road before moving on.
11. The remaining stops between Puerco Pueblo and the Painted Desert Visitor Center are overlooks of the Painted Desert. Each one affords a unique view, but the panorama from the hilltop at **Pintado Point** may be the most spectacular. Just past Pintado Point is **Chinde Point,** where you'll find sheltered picnic tables, restrooms (open seasonally), and another overlook.
12. A quarter of a mile past Chinde Point is the turnoff for **Kachina Point** and the **Painted Desert Inn National Historic Landmark.** Here you can descend into the desert on the Painted Desert Wilderness Trail or, if the drop

Organized Tours & Ranger Programs

A changing program of **guided hikes** and **talks** runs at locations throughout the park, with the greatest number during the summer. Check at either visitor center to see what's on tap each day.

seems a bit imposing, hike to Tawa Point on the Painted Desert Rim Trail. After hiking, be sure to visit the landmark itself (see "Park Attractions," below).

3 Park Attractions

The **Painted Desert Inn National Historic Landmark** (http://home.nps.gov/pefo/historyculture/pdi.htm), which overlooks the desert from Kachina Point, once served as a lunch counter and trading post for early travelers on Route 66. After the Park Service purchased the inn from private owners in 1936, Civilian Conservation Corps workers rebuilt it in the Southwestern style, not so cleverly covering some of the building's original petrified-wood walls with stucco. Upon completion in 1940, the 28-room inn became an immediate hit with travelers. It closed, however, during the last years of World War II. After the war, the Fred Harvey Company managed the building, using it as a visitor center and restaurant until 1963, when the new Painted Desert Visitor Center opened.

In 1947, Fred Kabotie, the renowned Hopi artist whose work also graces the Desert Watchtower at the Grand Canyon, painted several murals inside, including one that depicted the coming-of-age journey of the Hopi to the sacred Zuni salt lake. Kabotie's murals may have helped save the building, which had structural problems caused by expansion and contraction of the clay underneath it. When it was threatened with demolition in the 1960s, preservationists cited the value of Kabotie's art as they called for protecting the building. The Painted Desert Inn was declared a National Historic Landmark in 1987 and a year-long restoration project was completed in the spring of 2006. The landmark, which contains a museum and bookstore, is open daily from 9am to 5pm year-round.

4 Day Hikes

Agate House An enjoyable walk takes you to Agate House, a pueblo that archaeologists believe was briefly occupied around A.D. 1100. (Archaeologists suspect a brief occupation because little trash was found in the area.) Colorful bits of petrified wood dot the ground on the way to the eight-room pueblo, which sits atop a knoll overlooking a vast expanse of arid badlands. Made from petrified wood and mortar, Agate House must have been one of the prettiest dwellings anywhere in its time—a house of jewels, on a hill. Workers reconstructed the pueblo's largest room in the 1930s. ***Note:*** Combine this loop with the Long Logs Trail (below) for a 2.6-mile hike. 1 mile RT. Easy to moderate. Access: .5-mile one-way walk down access trail from Rainbow Forest Museum.

Blue Mesa Trail This paved loop trail descends steeply to the floor beneath the blue-, gray-, and white-striped badlands at Blue Mesa—some of the prettiest land in the park. You may notice that it's hard to determine the size of the hills: Because they lack vegetation, there is little to provide a sense of scale. At the bottom, you can observe how the different colors of these hillsides streak and blend where the clay has washed into drainages. Look for small fossils, abundant in the area (and please leave them where you find them!). The trail has numerous interpretive panels, spaced to give you a chance to catch your breath as you walk. 1 mile RT. Moderate. Access: Blue Mesa sun shelter.

Crystal Forest Trail This paved trail, which includes a few steep grades, reminds us of why it's important to leave petrified wood in place. As in other parts of the park, there is evidence of where visitors have broken off, and continue to break off, pieces of petrified wood. What's left is still lovely. Still, it's hard not to wonder what this area looked like before the scavengers arrived. .75 mile RT. Moderate. Access: Crystal Forest parking lot.

Giant Logs Trail This paved trail loops past some of the park's largest petrified logs, including "Old Faithful," which spans nearly 10 feet at its base. The trail has 11 stops, each corresponding to a page in a guide (free to borrow, small fee to keep) available in the museum. At each stop, you'll find out about the trees or the area's geology. Constructed in the 1930s by the Civilian Conservation Corps, the trail has some steps, making access difficult for people in wheelchairs. .4 mile RT. Easy. Access: Behind Rainbow Forest Museum.

Long Logs Trail This relatively flat, paved loop will give you an idea of the immensity of the Araucarioxylon trees that grew in this area during the Triassic period. Many of the longest, including one that measures 116 feet, lie alongside the trail on the north end of the loop. You'll see places where petrified logs protected the softer clay underneath them and prevented it from eroding. The trail also takes you within a few feet of the rugged badlands. The different-colored layers are caused by mineral deposits in the clay. .6 mile RT. Easy. Access: .5-mile one-way walk down access trail from Rainbow Forest Museum.

Painted Desert Rim Trail As this cinder trail meanders along the Painted Desert rim between Kachina and Tawa points, it affords stunning views of the gray, pink, and red badlands that stand out against the green grasses at their bases. The trail is atop the basalt of the Bidahochi formation, which, at 8 million years old, is much younger than most other rocks in the park. This layer has disappeared in many areas of the park but is widespread in other parts of northern Arizona. Here it provides fertile soil for a diversity of vegetation, including juniper, Mormon tea, sagebrush, and cliffrose. The trail also features wayside exhibits and plant identification signs. 1 mile RT. Easy. Access: Kachina Point stop on scenic drive.

Painted Desert Wilderness Route This cross-country hike—we can't really say there is a trail here—descends in switchbacks down the face of the badlands below Kachina Point, then follows a wash for a short distance before heading out into the grasslands on the floor of the Painted Desert. You won't find water or shade, but you will have a chance to experience the desert's colors and landforms. Before wandering far, be sure to identify landmarks to retrace your steps. (The Painted Desert Inn makes an especially good landmark.) If you carry a topographical map and plenty of water and sunscreen, you should have few problems in this desert, which has excellent sight lines and few insurmountable obstacles. Walk on the dry streambeds when possible. Besides being easier, this minimizes the damage to the fragile plant life.

It's worth spending the night just to watch the sun dip below the red sands of the desert. Before bedding down, you must obtain a **backcountry permit** at one of the visitor centers, then walk at least a mile into the 43,000-acre Painted Desert Wilderness, which starts on the other side of Lithodendron Wash. The direction you take from the bottom of the wash will depend on which "use area" you sign up for. You'll find spots smooth enough for camping near many of the mesas and badlands. (Keep in mind, however, that runoff can create problems during storms.) Don't forget to pack insect repellent; in spite of its dry climate, the park has been known to host a large population of no-see-ums. About .5 mile minimum one-way. Moderate to strenuous. Access: Kachina Point.

Puerco Pueblo Trail This relatively flat loop travels through the 100-room Puerco Pueblo. The 30 excavated rooms hint at the floor plan of the buildings—a trapezoid around an outdoor plaza where most of the activity in the community took place. As you walk, you'll observe places where the rooms were one, two, or three deep around the plaza. Where they were two deep, the rooms on the outside may have been used to store crops harvested from the floodplains below. The inside rooms, which opened onto the plaza, were probably used for sleeping or shelter from inclement weather. Three *kivas*—ceremonial rooms dug into the ground—were inside the plaza, and one is obvious alongside the trail. Partway around the loop, a short trail leads down to an overlook from which you can see numerous petroglyphs. .3 mile RT. Easy. Access: Puerco Pueblo parking lot.

5 Camping

There are no campgrounds in the park. Backpackers with backcountry permits can stay in the park after it closes for the evening, but they must hike at least 1 mile into the wilderness before setting up camp. For drive-in camping, head to Holbrook, 25 miles west of the park on I-40, where several commercial campgrounds offer all the usual amenities.

The **Holbrook/Petrified Forest KOA,** 102 Hermosa Dr., Holbrook, AZ 86025 (✆ **800/562-3389** for reservations, or 928/524-6689; www.koa.com), has a large, inviting outdoor pool that shimmers like a mirage on sunny days (open in summer). There are 22 grassy tent sites and 100 RV sites. The cost is $22 to $28 for tents and $29 to $36 for RV hookups. Major credit cards are accepted. The campground has a playground, game room, snack bar, public phones, coin-op laundry, propane, dump station, and Wi-Fi (for a fee). It's open year-round. During the high season, campers feast at relatively inexpensive evening cookouts. Several camping cabins (from $45 double) share the bathhouse and other facilities.

The **OK RV Park,** 1576 Roadrunner Rd., Holbrook, AZ 86025-2143 (✆ **866/403-1392** or 928/524-3226; www.okrvpark-llc.com), is an exceptionally well-maintained campground with everything you might want except a pool. There are about 150 gravel sites, with some trees, a coin-op laundry, and a convenience store. RV sites, at $29 to $34 for two people, include electric, water, sewer, Wi-Fi, and cable TV. Tent sites are $14 for two people. Major credit cards are accepted. The campground is open year-round.

6 Where to Stay

There is no lodging inside the park.

NEAR THE PARK

The place to get a bed for the night is Holbrook, 25 miles west of the park. In addition to the

Picnic & Camping Supplies

Just inside the north entrance to the park, you'll find a gas station with a convenience store. In Holbrook, picnic supplies and general foodstuffs are available at **Safeway,** 702 W. Hopi Dr. (✆ **928/524-3313;** www.safeway.com).

fascinating Wigwam Motel, discussed below, Holbrook offers the **Best Western Adobe Inn,** 615 W. Hopi Dr. (✆ **928/524-3948**), with rates for two of $89 to $104; **Best Western Arizonian,** 2508 Navajo Blvd. (✆ **928/524-2611**), with double rates of $93 to $128; **Comfort Inn,** 2602 E. Navajo Blvd. (✆ **928/524-6131**), $80 to $85 double; **Days Inn,** 2601 E. Navajo Blvd. (✆ **928/524-6949**), $51 to $77 double; **Econo Lodge,** 2596 E. Navajo Blvd. (✆ **928/524-1448**), $45 to $55 double; **Holiday Inn Express,** 1308 E. Navajo Blvd. (✆ **928/524-1466**), $104 to $120 double; and **Super 8,** 1989 Navajo Blvd. (✆ **928/524-2871**), $50 to $60 double. See chapter 38 for the national chains' websites.

Wigwam Motel Tired of the same boring chain motel rooms? Then it's time for a night at the Wigwam! And even if you don't stay here, the Wigwam Motel makes a wonderful photo op. Each of the motel's 15 rooms is inside its own 32-foot-high wood-and-concrete wigwam, built during Route 66's glory days in the 1940s by the same family that's running it today. The wigwams are clean and well maintained, and each is furnished with the motel's original hand-carved hickory furniture. The only drawbacks—which we consider a small price to pay for the experience of this unique motel—are that both the bathrooms and windows are somewhat small by today's standards. The motel's owners have done a good job of preserving this bit of Americana. A small museum on the property contains family items, including giant petrified-wood slabs, Civil War artifacts, Route 66 artifacts, and American Indian items. Also on the property are close to a dozen classic cars. All rooms are nonsmoking.

811 W. Hopi Dr. (P.O. Box 788), Holbrook, AZ 86025. ✆ **928/524-3048.** Fax 928/524-3668. www.wigwamgazette.info. 15 units. A/C, TV. $52–$58 double. MC, V. Office opens at 3pm in summer, 4pm in winter. Pets accepted.

7 Where to Dine

INSIDE THE PARK

Harvey's Diner AMERICAN/REGIONAL This is a convenient and quick family-oriented cafeteria. It serves hot breakfasts, including eggs and pancakes, and fast food such as home-style chili, burgers, Navajo tacos, and sandwiches for lunch.

Next to the Painted Desert Visitor Center, off I-40 exit 311. ✆ **928/524-3756.** Most items $3–$9. AE, DISC, MC, V. Summer daily from about 8am until the lunch crowd moves out in midafternoon; shorter hours the rest of the year.

NEAR THE PARK

In addition to the choices discussed below, you can choose from a pair of highly rated Mexican restaurants in Holbrook: **Romo's Café,** 121 W. Hopi Dr. (✆ **928/524-2153**), and **El Rancho,** 867 Navajo Blvd. (✆ **928/524-3332**).

Joe and Aggie's AMERICAN/MEXICAN In 1943, Joe and Aggie Montaño opened this restaurant, and today a third generation of the family continues to operate their popular eatery at the same Route 66 location. It's a friendly, down-home place, with plenty of historic Route 66 charm. Recommended at breakfast are the chili-cheese omelet and the egg burro (scrambled eggs with hash browns and cheese rolled in a flour tortilla). At lunch and dinner you can select from Mexican platters, traditional American dishes, and combinations of both, such as a Mexican hamburger steak with red or green chile. For a sort of Mexican pizza, try the cheese crisp—a deep-fried flour tortilla with melted cheese and toppings such as green chile and taco meat.

120 W. Hopi Dr., Holbrook. ✆ **928/524-6540.** Most main courses $6–$14. AE, DISC, MC, V. Mon–Sat 6am–8pm.

Mesa Italiana Restaurant ITALIAN/STEAKS Generally regarded as the best restaurant in Holbrook, Mesa Italiana serves steaks and traditional Italian dishes, including baked ziti, stuffed shells, lasagna, linguine, and pizza, at reasonable prices. Italiana mushrooms (stuffed with chicken, spinach, and fresh herbs, all topped with garlic white-wine sauce) are great. Also recommended is chicken Jerusalem—a chicken breast sautéed with butter, garlic, artichoke hearts, mushrooms, and shrimp, all swimming in white-wine and lemon sauce.

2318 E. Navajo Blvd., Holbrook. ✆ **928/524-6696.** Main courses $9–$18. AE, DISC, MC, V. Daily 4–9pm. Closed Thanksgiving and Christmas.

28

Point Reyes National Seashore, CA

by Eric Peterson

Point Reyes is a 100-square-mile peninsula of dark forests, wind-sculpted dunes, endless beaches, and plunging sea cliffs. Aside from its beautiful scenery, it boasts man-made historical treasures that offer a window into California's coastal past, including lighthouses, turn-of-the-20th-century dairies and ranches, and the site of Sir Francis Drake's 1579 landing, plus a complete replica of a Coast Miwok Indian village.

The national seashore system was created to protect rural and undeveloped stretches of America's coast from the pressures of soaring real estate values and increasing population; nowhere is the success of the system more evident than at Point Reyes. Layers of human history coexist here with one of the world's most dramatic natural settings. Residents of the surrounding communities—Inverness, Point Reyes Station, and Olema—have resisted runaway development. You won't find any strip malls or fast-food joints here, just laid-back coastal towns with cafes and country inns where gentle living prevails. The park, a 71,000-acre hammer-shaped peninsula jutting 10 miles into the Pacific and backed by Tomales Bay, abounds with wildlife, ranging from tule elk, birds, and bobcats to gray whales, sea lions, and great white sharks.

The often idyllic scene on the surface is a sharp contrast to the seismic turmoil below. The infamous San Andreas Fault separates Point Reyes, the northernmost landmass on the Pacific Plate, from the rest of California, which rests on the North American Plate. Point Reyes is making its way toward Alaska at a rate of about 2 inches per year, but at times it has moved much faster. In 1906, Point Reyes jumped north almost 20 feet in an instant, leveling San Francisco and jolting the rest of the state. The .5-mile Earthquake Trail, near the Bear Valley Visitor Center, illustrates this geological drama with a loop through an area torn by the fault. Shattered fences, rifts in the ground, and a barn knocked off its foundation by the quake illustrate that the earth is alive here. If that doesn't convince you, a look at a seismograph in the visitor center will.

AVOIDING THE CROWDS

Though the park is heavily visited, crowds are a problem only at a few places and during certain times. If you visit the lighthouse on a weekend or holiday during whale season (Dec–Mar), be prepared for crowds and a wait for the shuttle that operates from Drakes Beach to the lighthouse area. Trails leaving from Bear Valley tend to be more crowded on weekends. Try the **Five Brooks** or **Palomarin trail heads** to avoid hordes of hikers. As a rule, a weekday visitor will encounter far fewer people than the weekender.

1 Essentials

GETTING THERE & GATEWAYS

Point Reyes is 30 miles northwest of San Francisco, but it takes at least 90 minutes to reach by car. (It's all the small towns, not the topography, that slow you down.) The easiest route is **Sir Francis Drake Boulevard** from U.S. 101 south of San Rafael; it takes its time getting to Point Reyes but does so without any detours. For a much longer but more scenic route, take the Stinson Beach/Hwy. 1 exit off U.S. 101 just south of Sausalito and follow **Hwy. 1 north.**

THE NEAREST AIRPORT San Francisco International Airport (✆ **650/821-8211;** www.sfoairport.com), 14 miles south of downtown San Francisco on U.S. 101, is served by all major airlines and car-rental companies. See chapter 38 for information on airline and car-rental websites.

INFORMATION

Contact **Point Reyes National Seashore,** Point Reyes Station, CA 94956-9799 (✆ **415/464-5100,** ext. 2; www.nps.gov/pore). Kathleen Goodwin and Richard Blair's *Point Reyes Visions Guidebook* (Color & Light Editions, 2004) is a handsome, photographically enhanced tome covering Point Reyes and vicinity.

VISITOR CENTERS

As soon as you arrive at Point Reyes, stop at the **Bear Valley Visitor Center** on Bear Valley Road (look for the small sign posted just north of Olema

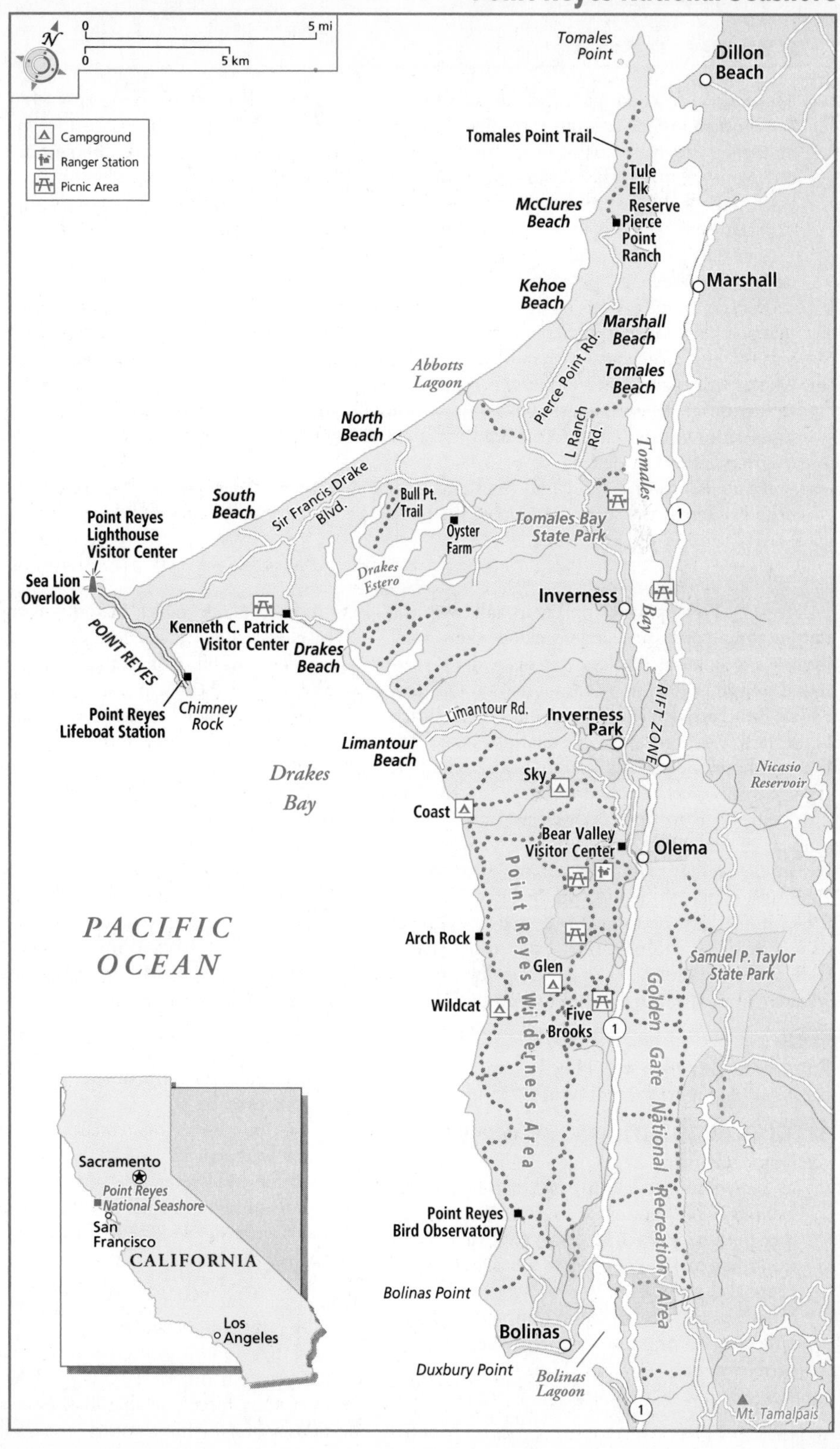

0
5 mi
0
5 km
N
Campground
Ranger Station
Picnic Area
Tomales Point
Dillon Beach
Tomales Point Trail
Tule Elk Reserve
McClures Beach
Pierce Point Ranch
Marshall
Kehoe Beach
Marshall Beach
Pierce Point Rd.
Abbotts Lagoon
Tomales Beach
North Beach
L Ranch Rd.
Tomales
South Beach
Sir Francis Drake Blvd.
Bull Pt. Trail
Oyster Farm
Tomales Bay State Park
1
Point Reyes Lighthouse Visitor Center
Sea Lion Overlook
Drakes Estero
Inverness
Bay
Kenneth C. Patrick Visitor Center
Drakes Beach
POINT REYES
RIFT ZONE
Point Reyes Lifeboat Station
Chimney Rock
Limantour Rd.
Inverness Park
Limantour Beach
Drakes Bay
Sky
Nicasio Reservoir
Coast
Bear Valley Visitor Center
Olema
Point Reyes Wilderness Area
PACIFIC OCEAN
Arch Rock
Samuel P. Taylor State Park
Glen
Wildcat
Five Brooks
Golden Gate National Recreation Area
Sacramento
Point Reyes National Seashore
San Francisco
CALIFORNIA
Los Angeles
Point Reyes Bird Observatory
Bolinas Point
Bolinas
Duxbury Point
Bolinas Lagoon
Mt. Tamalpais

If You Have Only 1 Day

First, stop at the **Bear Valley Visitor Center** and pick up the free Point Reyes map, which lists all the trails and roads open to cars, bikes, horses, and hikers. While you're here, spend some time at the nearby **Kule Loklo,** an authentic reconstruction of a village of the indigenous Coast Miwok Indian tribe, and at **Morgan Horse Ranch,** a good place to see park patrol horses. Afterward, take a short stroll on the **Earthquake Trail,** an informative .5-mile walk along the San Andreas Fault, and, time permitting, the .7-mile self-guided **Woodpecker Nature Trail.**

The most popular (and crowded) attraction at Point Reyes National Seashore is the **Point Reyes Lighthouse,** at the westernmost tip of Point Reyes. The drive alone is worth the trip—a 45-minute, 20-mile scenic excursion on the **Sir Francis Drake Highway** through windswept meadows and dairy ranches (watch out for cows on the road). When the fog burns off, the lighthouse and the headlands provide a fantastic lookout for common murres, basking sea lions, and gray whales as they migrate along the coast from December through March. The road closes at Drakes Beach on weekends from January through mid-April, when buses take visitors from the Ken Patrick Visitor Center to the lighthouse and back from 9am to 5:15 pm. Adult tickets are $5; children under 17 ride free.

If you still have some time, the **Point Reyes Bird Observatory**—an ornithological research organization at the southeast end of the park—is a must for bird-watchers.

on Hwy. 1). Pick up a free trail map, talk with the rangers about your plans, and check out the natural history and cultural displays. It's open daily year-round from 8 or 9am to 5 or 6pm (closed Dec 25).

The **Ken Patrick Visitor Center** at Drakes Beach houses a 250-gallon saltwater aquarium and a 16-foot minke whale skeleton, among other exhibits. It's open only weekends and holidays (except Dec 25) from 10am to 5pm, as well as Monday and Tuesday in summer. The **Lighthouse Visitor Center,** at the westernmost point of the Point Reyes Peninsula, offers information on the lighthouse and life-saving services performed over the 125 years of its use, as well as natural history exhibits on whales, seals, and wildflowers. It's open Thursday through Monday from 10am to 4:30pm (closed Dec 25).

FEES

Entrance to the park is free. Hike-in camping is $15 per night (and more for groups of 7–25).

SPECIAL REGULATIONS & WARNINGS

- Dogs and other pets are not permitted on trails, in campgrounds, or on beaches that are seal habitats or bird nesting areas. On other beaches they must be leashed. Check at park visitor centers before taking your dog to a beach, to avoid seasonal closures.
- Wood fires are prohibited in campgrounds. Use only charcoal or gas stoves. Driftwood fires are permitted only on sandy beaches below the high-tide line; you must obtain a free **permit** at a visitor center.
- Check the tide tables before walking on the beaches. Rising water can trap you against a cliff with no possibility of escape.
- Sleeping on the beach is prohibited; it can be dangerous. High tide frequently comes to the base of the cliffs and can trap the unwary.
- Do not climb cliffs—they can crumble easily. Walking or sitting below cliffs is also dangerous due to falling rock.
- In wooded areas, keep an eye out for poison oak's waxy three-leaf clusters. Also be sure to check for ticks—the Lyme disease–carrying black-legged tick is common here.
- The pounding surf and rip currents are treacherous, especially at McClures Beach and Point Reyes beaches, north and south. Stay away from the water.
- Don't disturb any baby seals or sea lions you may encounter on the beach. The mother may be preoccupied with finding lunch, and she won't come back until you leave. In fact, you could be fined up to $10,000 for your good intentions. However, if a pup looks injured or appears to be in danger, call the **Marine Mammal Center** (✆ **415/289-7325**).

SEASONS & CLIMATE

Weather at Point Reyes is fickle. The seasons here generally reverse expectations: Summer tends to be cold and foggy until the afternoon (the point is the foggiest place on the West Coast), while winter is clear and often more tolerable. But these are generalizations at best—winter storms can rage for weeks, and sometimes the summer fog holds off for days. Spring and fall usually see the best weather (that is, little fog, warm temperatures).

To make matters more frustrating, the clearing of fog often signals the onset of strong winds. So if you plan to explore the park on foot, prepare yourself for cool weather, dampness, and wind (*lots* of wind—gusts have reached up to 133 mph, the highest wind speed recorded on the Pacific Coast). The best plan is to take advantage of variations in local weather by being flexible with your itinerary: Save indoor sightseeing for rainy or foggy days, and hit the beach or go hiking when the sun comes out.

SEASONAL EVENTS

Point Reyes National Seashore plays host to an annual **Native American celebration** (aka the Big Time Festival) on the third Saturday of July. American Indian basket-makers, flint-knappers, singers, and dancers convene at Point Reyes for an annual public celebration at Kule Loklo, a reconstruction of a village of the indigenous Coast Miwok Indian tribe. The **Miwok Archaeological Preserve of Marin** (✆ **415/479-3281;** www.mapom.org) offers classes in traditional California Indian skills in the spring and fall.

2 Exploring the Park by Car

The main scenic road in the park is the **Sir Francis Drake Highway.** An excellent turnoff on this road is **Mount Vision Road,** which winds its way up to the Mount Vision Overlook for a panoramic view of the entire peninsula.

There are two other major roads within the park. **Pierce Point Road** forks north from the Sir Francis Drake Highway toward Tomales Point, passing Tomales Bay State Park (a popular picnicking area that offers relatively warm and safe waters) and Abbotts Lagoon (a bird-watchers' paradise) before ending at McClures Beach. The other major road is **Limantour Road,** which crosses the park before ending at Limantour Beach, a popular spot for beachcombing, picnicking, and bird-watching at nearby Estero de Limantour. Both roads are primarily used to reach trail heads and beaches, but they can double as scenic alternatives to touring the Sir Francis Drake Highway.

The Sir Francis Drake Highway closes at South Beach on weekends from January through mid-April, when buses take visitors to the lighthouse and back from 9am to 5:15 pm. Tickets ($5 adults, free for children under 17) are available at the Ken Patrick Visitor Center.

3 Organized Tours & Ranger Programs

Rangers lead free programs within Point Reyes National Seashore year-round. Offerings include wildlife hikes, local history lessons, and habitat-restoration demonstrations. Call the **Bear Valley Visitor Center** (✆ **415/464-5100,** ext. 2) for up-to-date schedules.

Point Reyes Field Seminars (✆ **415/663-1200;** www.ptreyes.org) offers half-day to 3-day classes year-round, on topics ranging from fitness walking, to birding, to visual arts. Half-day seminars usually cost about $50, 3-day courses about $200.

4 Park Attractions

Kule Loklo is a re-creation of a Coast Miwok Indian village that often schedules displays of dancing, basket-making, cooking, and indigenous art. Until recently, **Morgan Horse Ranch** was the only working horse-breeding farm in the National Park System. Although breeding is defunct, the ranch remains a good place to see park patrol horses. Also, exhibits here offer an interpretive glimpse into the area's horse ranching past. Both are near the **Bear Valley Visitor Center** on Bear Valley Road and are open year-round.

If you want a behind-the-scenes look at shellfish aquaculture, head to **Drakes Bay Oyster Company,** 17171 Sir Francis Drake Blvd., about 6 miles west of Inverness (✆ **415/669-1149;** www.drakesbayoyster.com). Located in the park, on the edge of Drakes Estero (a large saltwater estuary on the Point Reyes Peninsula that produces about 10% of California's commercial oyster yield), the farm may not be much to look at, with its cluster of trailer homes, shacks, and oyster tanks surrounded by piles of oyster shells, but these tasty bivalves are raised in an organic and sustainable manner, and they don't come any fresher. The Park Service has threatened to shut the farm down come 2012, so this may be a limited-time opportunity.

The typical modus operandi is: 1) buy a couple of dozen (reserve them in advance if you can—they go quickly), 2) head for a picnic area along nearby Drakes Beach, 3) fire up the barbecue pit (don't forget the charcoal), 4) split and barbecue the little guys, 5) slather them in sauce, and 6) slurp 'em down. The farm is open daily 8am to 4:30pm.

5 Day Hikes

There's a little of everything for hikers here—32,000 acres, crisscrossed by 70 miles of trails, set aside as wilderness where no motor vehicles or bicycles are allowed. The principal trail heads are Bear Valley, Palomarin, Five Brooks, and Estero. Pick up a free trail map at a visitor center.

Abbotts Lagoon Trail If you're looking for a short, easy trail well away from the masses, this is the one. After climbing a small ridge, you continue down to Abbotts Lagoon, a popular watering hole for migratory birds. You can add 1 mile to the round-trip if you continue on to Great Beach. 3 miles RT. Easy. Access: Abbotts Lagoon trail head parking area on Pierce Point Rd.

Bear Valley Trail This is your best bet for a beautiful walk through the woods to the rocky coast. The well-worn trail leads through wooded hillsides until it reaches the shore at Arch Rock, where Coast Creek splashes into the sea through a "sea tunnel" (actually the arch of Arch Rock). 8.2 miles RT. Easy. Access: Bear Valley trail head, south of visitor center parking area.

Coast Trail Recommended by locals, this trek is one of Point Reyes's prettiest. This section of the trail skirts a cliff offering stunning views and then passes several small lakes and meadows before it reaches Alamere Falls, a freshwater stream that cascades down a 40-foot bluff onto Wildcat Beach.

The longest trail at the national seashore, the Coast Trail continues for a 15-mile one-way hike along the coast that is usually done in 2 days, camping a third of the way through at Wildcat Beach. (There's another campground at Santa Maria Beach.) The trail ends at the Point Reyes Hostel. You'll need a second car to shuttle you back to the trail head where you began, or else make a 5-mile loop with the Coast, Fire Lane, and Laguna trails. 7 miles RT. Easy to moderate. Access: Palomarin Trailhead, just off Mesa Rd. at southern tip of park.

Estero Trail A favorite with birders, this mellow trail meanders along the edge of Drakes Estero and Limantour Estero. (*Estero* is the Spanish word for "estuary.") The brackish waters draw flocks of waterfowl and shorebirds, as well as many raptors and smaller species. Along the way, you cross a dam and a bridge over Home Bay. 5 miles one-way. Easy to moderate. Access: Estero Parking Area.

Mount Wittenberg Trail For the Rambo in your group, this huffer-puffer weeds out the weenies with its elevation, peaking at 1,407 feet rather abruptly. From the Bear Valley trail head, turn right onto the Mount Wittenberg Trail after .2 mile. The trail up the ridge is steep but rewards hikers with great views back east across the Olema Valley. Instead of turning around directly, if you still have the energy, you can loop back along Baldy Trail and take a path such as the Meadow Trail back to Bear Valley Trail, the main route home. 5 miles RT. Strenuous. Access: Bear Valley trail head, south of visitor center parking area.

Stewart Trail This trek to Wildcat Beach, one of the few trails in the park open to mountain bikes, is also popular with horseback riders. It's quite steep and not as scenic as most other trails. 13.4 miles RT. Moderate. Access: Five Brooks parking area.

Tomales Point Trail This trail gives hikers a tour of the park's rugged shoreline and passes through an elk reserve, home to the park's 400-strong herd of tule elk. Watch for their V-shaped tracks on the trail. About halfway through, you come to the highest spot on Pierce Point, where on a clear day you can see over the bay to the Sonoma coast and to Mount St. Helena to the northeast. 9.5 miles RT. Easy to moderate. Access: Parking lot at end of Pierce Point Rd.

6 Beaches

The **Great Beach** is one of California's longest. It is also one of the windiest, and home to large and dangerous waves. You can't swim here, but the beachcombing is some of the best in the world. Tide-poolers should go to **McClures Beach** at the end of Pierce Point Road during low tide or hike out to **Chimney Rock,** east of the lighthouse. Swimmers and dog owners will want to stick to **Limantour Beach,** in the protected lee of Point Reyes. **Kehoe Beach,** in the northwest part of the park, is known for its spring wildflower blooms. **Hearts Desire Beach,** at Tomales Bay State Park (© **415/669-1140;** www.parks.ca.gov), has the warmest, safest swimming, as well as a $6-per-vehicle fee.

Sir Francis Drake reputedly landed the *Pelican* (later rechristened the *Golden Hind*) on the sandy shore of Drakes Bay in June 1579, to replenish supplies and make repairs before sailing home to England. **Drakes Beach** is now home to the Kenneth C. Patrick Visitor Center and **Drakes Beach Cafe** (© **415/669-1297;** Thurs–Fri and Mon 11am–3pm; Sat–Sun 11am–5pm), the only food concession in the park and famous for its Sunday oyster cookouts. Prix-fixe dinners are also seasonally available on Friday and Saturday nights; reservations are required. This beach is good for swimming, and beach fires are permitted.

7 Other Sports & Activities

BIKING As most ardent Bay Area mountain bikers know, Point Reyes National Seashore has some of the finest mountain-bike trails in the region—narrow dirt paths winding through densely forested knolls and ending with spectacular ocean views. A trail map (available free at the Bear Valley Visitor Center) is a must, because many of the park trails are off-limits to bikes.

BIRD-WATCHING Point Reyes National Seashore boasts one of the most diverse bird populations in the country, with over 490 different species sighted. Popular bird-watching spots are Abbotts Lagoon and Estero de Limantour. You can hang out with the pros at the **Point Reyes Bird Observatory–Palomarin Field Station** (✆ **415/868-0655;** www.prbo.org), one of the few full-time ornithological research stations in the United States, at the southeast end of the park on Mesa Road. This is where ornithologists keep an eye on the myriad feathered species that call the seashore home. Admission to the visitor center and nature trail is free, and visitors are welcome to observe the tricky process of catching and banding the birds. The observatory is open Tuesday to Sunday sunrise to sunset spring to fall, with more limited hours in the winter (banding hours vary; call for exact times).

HORSEBACK RIDING Equestrian activities are very popular at Point Reyes, where all of the trails (save Bear Valley Trail on weekends and holidays) are horse-friendly. A good resource is **Five Brooks Ranch** (✆ **415/663-1570;** www.fivebrooks.com), located at the Five Brooks Trailhead, 3½ miles south of Olema on Highway 1. The ranch offers guided trail rides (horses provided) at prices ranging from $40 for an hour-long ride to about $200 for a 6-hour beach ride. Horse boarding is available.

KAYAKING **Blue Waters Kayaking** (✆ **415/669-2600;** www.bwkayak.com) offers kayak trips, including 3-hour sunset outings, 3½-hour full-moon paddles, yoga tours, day trips, and longer excursions. Instruction and clinics are available, and all ages and skill levels are welcome. Prices start at $68 for tours. Four-hour rentals begin at $45 for one person, $65 for two. Basic skill classes last a full day and run $110. There are no waves to contend with in placid Tomales Bay, a haven for migrating birds and marine mammals. The launching point is on Calif. 1 at the Marshall Boatworks in Marshall, 8 miles north of Point Reyes Station.

WHALE-WATCHING Each year, gray whales (the barnacles make them appear gray) migrate from their winter breeding grounds in the warm waters off Baja California to their summer feeding grounds in Alaska. You can observe them as they undertake their 10,000-mile journey from just about anywhere in Point Reyes National Seashore. The most popular vantage point is the Point Reyes Lighthouse.

During peak season (Dec–Mar), you might see dozens of whales from the lighthouse, and the **Lighthouse Visitor Center** offers great displays on whale migration and maritime history. During this period, the Park Service runs a shuttle from Drakes Beach to the **Point Reyes Lighthouse** ($5 adults, free for children under 17), where watchers have been known to see as many as 100 whales in a single afternoon. Even if the whales don't materialize, the lighthouse itself, a fabulous old structure teetering high above the sea at the tip of a promontory, is worth a visit. Two other spots, **Chimney Rock,** east of the lighthouse, and **Tomales Point,** at the northern end of the park, offer just as many whales without the crowds.

8 Camping

Camping within the park is limited to four hike-in camps. **Wildcat Camp,** near Alamere Falls, is a 6.7-mile hike from Bear Valley trail head. **Coast Camp** is on an open bluff, 2.3 beach miles west of the Limantour Beach parking lot. These camps near the sea are often foggy and damp, so bring a good tent and sleeping bag. **Sky Camp** (1.2 miles from Sky trail head on Limantour Rd.) and **Glen Camp** (4.6 miles from the Bear Valley trail head) are in the woods away from the sea, more protected from the coastal elements.

In all camps, individual sites hold up to eight people and have picnic tables and food lockers. Pit toilets are available. Stays are limited to 4 nights. Sites can be reserved up to 3 months in advance by calling ✆ **415/663-8054** Monday to Friday 9am to 2pm.

Just outside the park is the **Olema RV Resort & Campground** (✆ **415/663-8106;** www.olemarvresort.com), which accommodates tents and RVs and is close to restaurants and a grocery store. It's about a half-mile north of downtown Olema on Highway 1. Reservations are recommended. Credit cards are not accepted in person, but they are on the website.

Campground	Total Sites	RV Hookups	Dump Station	Toilets	Drinking Water
Coast Camp	12	No	No	Yes	Yes
Glen Camp	12	No	No	Yes	Yes
Olema Ranch Campground (private)	184	Yes	Yes	Yes	Yes
Sky Camp	12	No	No	Yes	Yes
Wildcat Camp	12	No	No	Yes	Yes

9 Where to Stay

INSIDE THE PARK

Point Reyes Hostel Deep inside Point Reyes National Seashore, this beautiful old ranch-style complex can accommodate 40 guests in dormitory-style bunk rooms. The hostel has a pair of common areas, each warmed by stoves during chilly nights, as well as a fully equipped kitchen, a computer with Web access ($1 for 10 min.), a barbecue, and patio. If you don't mind sharing your sleeping quarters with strangers, this is a deal that can't be beat. Reservations (and earplugs) are strongly recommended. The maximum stay is 5 nights.

Off Limantour Rd. (P.O. Box 247), Point Reyes Station, CA 94956. ✆ **415/663-8811.** www.norcalhostels.org. 40 bunks, 1 private room. $22 bunk; $64 private room double. AE, DISC, MC, V. Reception daily 7:30–10am and 4:30–9:30pm.

NEAR THE PARK

The four towns in and around the Point Reyes National Seashore boundary—Olema, Point Reyes Station, Inverness Park, and Inverness—are so close together that it really doesn't matter where you stay, because you'll be within a stone's throw of the park. Although the accommodations in Point Reyes are excellent, they're also expensive, with most rooms averaging $200 per night. Make reservations far in advance during the summer and holidays, and dress warmly: Point Reyes gets darn chilly at night.

Note: If you're having trouble finding a vacancy in Point Reyes, call the **Point Reyes Lodging Association** (✆ **800/539-1872;** www.ptreyes.com) or the **West Marin Network** (✆ **415/663-9543;** www.westmarinnetwork.com) for information on available lodgings.

Manka's Inverness Lodge Nestled in the forest with a certain aura of mystery, this lovable, elegantly funky lodging is one of the top places to stay on the West Coast, but suffered a devastating blow when the main lodge and revered restaurant burned down in 2006. With the lodge being rebuilt with an eye toward reopening sometime in 2012, the surviving cabins (with hot tubs and outdoor showers) and quartet of annex rooms that survived the fire balance rural charm and refined sophistication. Supper is available in-room for $50 a person on Friday and Sunday nights.

Argyle St., off Sir Francis Drake Blvd., 2 blocks north of downtown (P.O. Box 1110), Inverness, CA 94937. ✆ **415/669-1034.** www.mankas.com. 6 units. $285–$715 double. AE, MC, V.

Motel Inverness Inside, this motel has the feel of a country inn, with a lobby that overlooks Tomales Bay and features a pool table. There are comfortable small rooms and suites with kitchens; the motel rooms are a good deal, with rates on the low end of the spectrum for the Point Reyes area, and the two-bedroom suite is a good bet for families. Ask about the unique Dacha, a bayfront cottage built in Russian Orthodox style a mile away—it's often booked up to a year in advance.

12718 Sir Francis Drake Blvd. (P.O. Box 958), Inverness, CA 94937. ✆ **866/453-3839** or 415/236-1967. www.motelinverness.com. 7 units. $99–$190 double; $190–$290 suite. MC, V.

Nick's Cove This historic cottage resort that's over the water on the east side of Tomales Bay was given a 21st-century revamp in recent years. A fishing and boating hot spot since the 1930s, Nick's is now a foodie destination, thanks to its standout **seafood restaurant,** and has plenty of contemporary style blended with funky nautical charm. Five cottages are built over the bay, and the rest have a water view or are across the road on a creek. Plasma screens and Wi-Fi access in most rooms balance with wood-burning stoves and wood-paneled walls for a satisfying, if pricey, whole.

2340 Hwy. 1, Marshall, CA 94940. ✆ **866/636-4257** or 415/663-1033. www.nickscove.com. 11 cottages. $335–$695 cottage. AE, DISC, MC, V.

Olema Druids Hall Formerly the lodge for a chapter of the United Ancient Order of Druids, an Elks-like organization of men in funny hats holding secret meetings, this 1885 structure has been transformed into a terrific inn. Inside the lodge are two deluxe rooms with a European feel. The suite and the cottage are quite lavish: The suite, once the Druids' secret throne room, has a stainless-steel kitchen that is sometimes used for culinary classes, a private deck, and an antique mantle above the wood-burning fireplace; the cottage (which once served as a woodshed) features Asian-meets-Arts-and-Crafts decor.

Showers	Fire Pits/ Grills	Laundry	Reserve	Fees	Open
No	Yes	No	Yes	$15	Year-round
No	Yes	No	Yes	$15	Year-round
Yes	Yes	Yes	Yes	$34–$53	Year-round
No	Yes	No	Yes	$15	Year-round
No	Yes	No	Yes	$15	Year-round

9870 Hwy. 1 (P.O. Box 96), Olema, CA 94950. ✆ **866/554-4255** or 415/663-8727. Fax 415/663-1830. www.olemadruidshall.com. 4 units, including 1 cottage. $165–$285 double; $295–$465 suite or cottage. Rates include expanded continental breakfast. MC, V.

Point Reyes Country Inn & Stables This five-bedroom, ranch-style home on 4 acres offers pastoral accommodations for two- and four-legged guests (humans and horses, that is) and easy access to plenty of hiking and riding trails. Each room has a private bathroom and either a balcony or a garden. Above the stables are two studios with kitchens, and two cottages on Tomales Bay in Inverness are equipped with decks, kitchens stocked with breakfast supplies, fireplaces, and a shared dock.

12050 Hwy. 1, Point Reyes Station, CA 94956. ✆ **415/663-9696.** Fax 415/663-8888. www.ptreyescountryinn.com. 10 units, including 2 studios and 2 cottages. $115–$185 double; $95–$345 studio; $185–$225 cottage. $10–$15 per horse. Rates include breakfast (studios excepted). MC, V.

10 Where to Dine

Cafe Reyes PIZZA This bustling and casual eatery is a local favorite, operating as a coffeehouse, beer (and wine) joint, and grill. With counter service and a colorful and social atmosphere, Cafe Reyes is the best deal in the area. The menu focuses on tasty Neapolitan-style pizzas made with dough cultures from Italy in an imported Italian oven (with toppings like local blue cheese and fennel sausage), as well as local oysters.

11101 Hwy. 1, Point Reyes Station. ✆ **415/663-9493.** www.cafereyes.net. Menu items $6–$15. MC, V. Daily noon–9pm.

Station House Café AMERICAN A local favorite, the Station House Cafe is known for its good food and animated atmosphere, particularly when live music plays on weekends. The menu changes every week but always features vegetarian selections (with veggies from the cafe's garden), locally raised beef, and a good selection of fresh fish. For breakfast, try the famous Hangtown Fry: Drakes Bay oysters, bacon, and three eggs, which always seems to taste better at a table outside on the shaded garden patio. A lunch specialty is double-cheese polenta served with portobello mushrooms and blue cheese. For dinner, start with a platter of local oysters and mussels, followed by a soft-shell crab sandwich, *osso buco,* or one of the old standbys such as meatloaf with garlic mashed potatoes. Rounding out the menu are homemade turkey chili, calamari, steamed clams, fresh soup, and mouthwatering desserts made daily. The cafe has an extensive list of fine California wines, plus local and imported beers.

11180 Main St., Point Reyes Station. ✆ **415/663-1515.** www.stationhousecafe.com. Reservations recommended. Breakfast $6–$10; lunch items $7–$17; dinner main courses $9–$19. AE, DISC, MC, V. Thurs–Tues 8am–9pm. Closed Wed.

Vladimir's Czechoslovakian Restaurant CZECHOSLOVAKIAN An Inverness institution, Vladimir's has been dishing out fantastic dishes since 1960 and is still going strong. The menu is dynamic, changing depending on the availability of ingredients; one night, goose or pheasant might be featured; on others, cabbage rolls, kielbasa, or Wiener schnitzel could be among your choices. You can sit inside in the quaint but elegant dining room or outside on the patio. There is a full bar with its own menu (about $7–$12). ***Note:*** Call ahead—the restaurant's hours are subject to the unpredictable Point Reyes weather and owner-chef's annual ski trips.

12785 Sir Francis Drake Blvd., Inverness. ✆ **415/669-1021.** Main courses $15 lunch, $28 dinner. No credit cards. Tues 3–9pm; Wed–Thurs 1–9pm; Fri–Sun noon–9:30pm.

29

Redwood National & State Parks, CA

by Eric Peterson

It's impossible to explain the feeling you get in the old-growth forests of Redwood National and State Parks without resorting to *Alice in Wonderland* comparisons. Like a tropical rainforest, the redwood forest is a multistoried affair, the tall trees being only the top layer. Everything is big, misty, and primeval; flowering bushes cover the ground, 10-foot-tall ferns line the creeks, and the smells are rich and musty. Out on the parks' crowd-free trails, it's impossible not to feel as if you've shrunk, or the rest of the world has grown, or else that you've gone back in time to the Jurassic epoch—dinosaurs would fit in here nicely.

When Archibald Menzies noted the existence of the coast redwood in 1794, more than 2 million acres of redwood forest carpeted California and Oregon. By 1965, logging had reduced that to 300,000 acres, and it was obvious something had to be done. The state created several parks around individual groves in the 1920s, and in 1968 the federal government created Redwood National Park. In 1994, the National Park Service and the California Department of Parks and Recreation signed an agreement to manage the four contiguous redwood parks cooperatively—hence the name Redwood National *and* State Parks.

The modern 131,983-acre park complex offers a lesson in ecology. When the park was created to protect the biggest coast redwoods, logging companies continued to cut much of the surrounding area, sometimes right up to the park boundary. Redwoods in the park began to suffer as the quality of the Redwood Creek drainage declined from upstream logging, so in 1978 the government purchased a major section of the watershed, having learned that you can't preserve individual trees without preserving the ecosystem.

Although the logging of old-growth redwoods is still a major bone of contention for the government, private landowners, and environmentalists, the trees thrive. They are living links to the age of dinosaurs and reminders that the era of mankind is but a hiccup in time to the venerable *Sequoia sempervirens.*

AVOIDING THE CROWDS

The parks include three major features—the ocean setting, the old-growth forests, and the prairies. Not many people discover the bald hills (called "prairies" here) that offer excellent views over the tops of the redwoods and down to the ocean. And while the coastal environment and the shade of the redwoods can chill a hiker's bones year-round, these treeless spots are warm and sunny sanctuaries in the summertime. The prairie region also offers many opportunities to explore the park by hiking to the historic barns used during the ranching days before the park's establishment, visiting the School House Peak Firelook to check out the view, or hiking to the valley bottom along the Dolason Prairie Trail.

1 Essentials

GETTING THERE & GATEWAYS

The parks lie on a narrow strip near the coast in northern California, about 350 miles north of San Francisco. There are three major routes to the Redwood Coast. **U.S. 101** links San Francisco and Brookings, Oregon, traversing much of the length of the parks. **U.S. 199** takes off from U.S. 101 just north of the parks and heads northeast to Grants Pass, Oregon. The main route to the east is **Calif. 299,** which goes from Redding, California, to meet up with U.S. 101 south of the park.

If you're heading from the south, you'll want to stop just before you get to Orick. If you're heading from the north (Oregon), you'll want to stop in Crescent City. Both have excellent information centers crammed with useful (and important) information about the parks, including free maps.

THE NEAREST AIRPORTS **Arcata-Eureka Airport** (© **707/839-5401**) is in McKinleyville, 28 miles south of the Redwood Information Center near Orick. **McNamara Field** (© **707/465-3804**) is in Crescent City, at the north end of the park. Both are served by **United;** Arcata-Eureka is also served by **Horizon** and **Delta.** Much farther south, **San Francisco International Airport** (© **650/821-8211;** www.sfoairport.com) is 14 miles south of downtown San Francisco on U.S. 101. All major **car-rental chains** have offices at San Francisco International Airport; some rentals are available at the Arcata-Eureka and Crescent City airports. Airline and car-rental websites are listed in chapter 38.

INFORMATION

Contact **Redwood National and State Parks,** 1111 2nd St., Crescent City, CA 95531 (✆ **707/464-6101;** www.nps.gov/redw). The park's *Visitor Guide* newspaper describes activities in the parks, plus the wildlife you're likely to see. Books and other resources are available from the **Redwood Park Association** (✆ **707/465-7325;** www.redwoodparkassociation.org) and the **North Coast Redwood Interpretive Association** (✆ **707/465-7354** or 707/488-2169; www.ncria.org).

VISITOR CENTERS

The southern gateway to the Redwood National and State Parks is the town of Orick, on U.S. 101. You can't miss it: Just look for the dozens of burl stands alongside the road. Just south of town you'll find the sleek **Thomas H. Kuchel Visitor Center,** P.O. Box 7, Orick, CA 95555 (✆ **707/465-7765**), where you can get a free map and see a variety of exhibits. It's open daily from 9am to 5pm year-round, with extended summer hours. If you missed the Kuchel Visitor Center, don't worry: About 7 miles farther north on U.S. 101 is the **Prairie Creek Visitor Center** (✆ **707/465-7354**), which carries the same maps and information. It's open daily from 9am to 5pm year-round.

The northern gateway to the National and State Parks is Crescent City. The town has its charms, but the face it presents along U.S. 101 isn't exactly alluring. (To combat this, a beautification project is ongoing.) Still, it's your best bet for a motel, gas, fast food, and outdoor supplies. Before touring the park, pick up a free guidebook at the **Crescent City Information Center,** 1111 2nd St. (at K St.), Crescent City, CA 95531 (✆ **707/465-7335**). It's open daily 9am to 6pm (until 4pm in winter).

If you happen to be arriving on U.S. 199 from Oregon, the rangers at the **Hiouchi Information Center** (no phone) and **Jedediah Smith Visitor Center** (✆ **707/458-3496**) can supply maps and advice. Both are open daily in the summer 9am to 6pm; Hiouchi is closed spring to fall and Jedediah Smith is open winter weekend as staffing allows.

FEES & PERMITS

Admission to the national park is free, but to enter any of the three state parks (which contain some of the best redwood groves), you'll have to pay a $6 **day-use fee,** good at all three.

The **camping fee** is $35 for drive-in sites. Walk-in sites are free or $5. Most do not require permits, but free permits, available in person at visitor centers, are required for **backcountry camping** along the Redwood Creek Trail.

To travel the Tall Trees Trail (see "If You Have Only 1 Day," below), you'll have to get a free **permit** from the Kuchel Visitor Center near Orick (see "Visitor Centers," above).

SPECIAL REGULATIONS & WARNINGS

Many of the best scenic drives in these parks are on roads not suitable for motor homes or trailers. If possible, those with RVs should consider towing a car, traveling with a friend who is driving a car, or maybe even renting a car near the parks.

- **Don't disturb abandoned baby seals or sea lions** you may encounter on the beach. The mother may be nearby, but she will not return until you leave. In fact, you may be fined up to $10,000 for your good intentions. If a pup looks injured or appears to be in danger, call the **North Coast Marine Mammal Center** (✆ **707/465-6265**).
- On the beach, **be aware of tidal fluctuations.** Swimming is hazardous because of cold water, strong rip currents, and sneaker waves.
- **Watch for poison oak,** particularly in coastal areas.
- **Follow park regulations regarding bears** and food storage; all food and scented personal-care items should be secured and hidden from view in vehicles, placed in bear-proof lockers (located at each drive-in campsite), or hung from trees. Roosevelt elk are wild and unpredictable; do not approach them on foot.
- **Treat water** from natural sources before drinking.
- **Tree limbs can fall** during high winds, especially in old-growth forests.

SEASONS & CLIMATE

All those huge trees and ferns wouldn't have survived for 1,000 years if it didn't rain a lot here. Count on rain or at least a heavy drizzle during your visit, then get ecstatic when the sun comes out—it can happen anytime. Spring is the best season for wildflowers. Summer is generally foggy along the coast. (It's called "the June gloom," but it can continue into July and Aug.) Fall is the warmest and (relatively) sunniest time of all, and winter isn't bad, though it can be cold and wet, and some park facilities are closed. A storm can provide the most introspective time to see the park, since you'll probably be alone. And after a storm passes through, sunny days often follow. On an even brighter note, chances are, you won't freeze to death in winter or wither and melt in summer, because the average annual temperature along the Redwood Coast varies only 16°, ranging from an average low of 45°F to an average high of 61°F (7°–16°C).

Redwood National Park

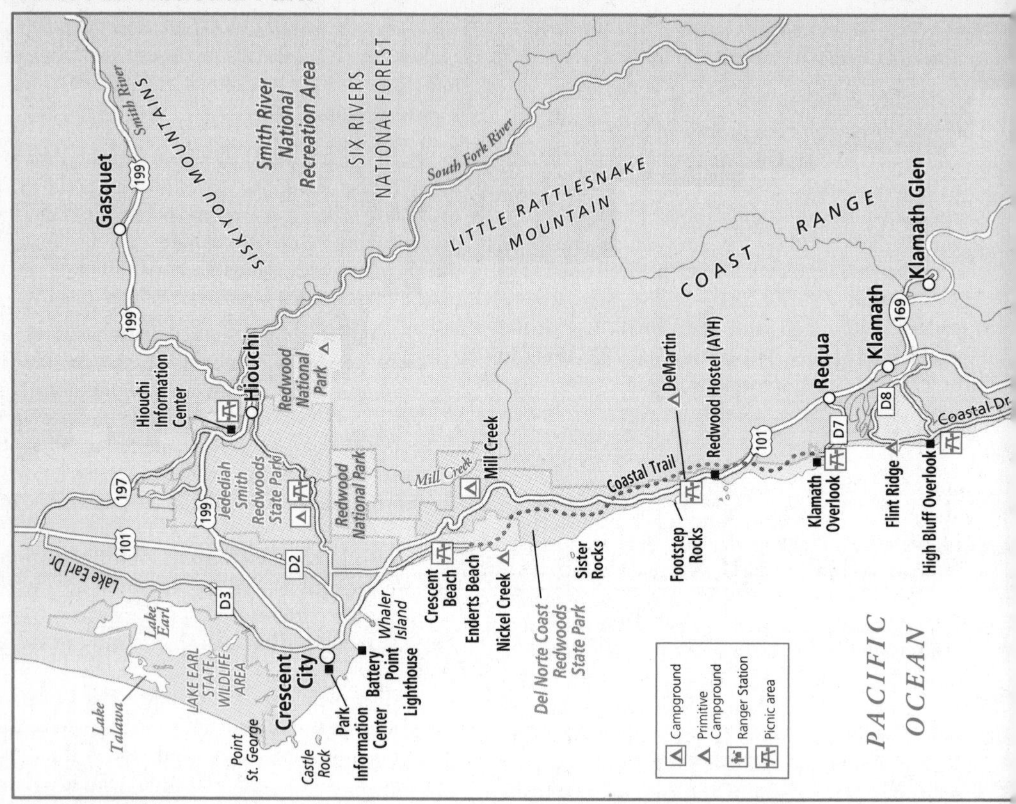

SEASONAL EVENTS

Annual events include an **Earth Month beach cleanup** in April, the **Eco Fun Fest** in August, and the **Discovery Ride through the Ancient Forest** in October. Contact the park for exact dates and times. Also, Crescent City holds a **surf contest** in October, and the park holds a **candlelight celebration** through the old growth in December.

2 Exploring the Park by Car

A number of scenic drives cut through the park. Steep, windy **Bald Hills Road** (a few miles north of Orick on U.S. 101) will take you back into the Redwood Creek watershed and up to the shoulder of 3,097-foot Schoolhouse Peak. Don't even think of driving a motor home up here or pulling a trailer. A few miles farther north is the **Lost Man Creek Trail,** a short, unpaved scenic drive through the redwood forest. The 1½-mile trip leads past the World Heritage Site dedication area and on to a cascade on Lost Man Creek. Again, anyone with a motor home or pulling a trailer can forget this one.

A don't-miss detour along U.S. 101 is the **Newton B. Drury Scenic Parkway,** which passes through redwood groves and elk-filled meadows before returning to the highway 8 miles later. While you're cruising along, take the **Cal-Barrel Road** turnoff, a narrow, packed-gravel road (no trailers or motor homes) just north of the Prairie Creek Visitor Center off the Newton B. Drury Scenic Parkway. It offers a spectacular 3-mile tour through an old-growth redwood forest.

One of the premier coastal drives on the Redwood Coast starts at the mouth of the Klamath River and runs 8 miles south toward Prairie Creek Redwoods State Park. The narrow, partially paved **Coastal Drive** winds through stands of redwoods, with spectacular views of the Pacific and numerous pullouts for picture taking (sea lions and pelicans abound) and short hikes. Keep an eye out for the World War II radar station, disguised as a farmhouse and barn. If you're heading south on U.S. 101, take the Alder Camp Road exit just south of the Klamath River Bridge and follow the signs to the Mouth of Klamath. Northbound travelers should take the Redwood National and State Parks Coastal Drive exit off the Newton B. Drury Scenic Parkway. Motor homes and vehicles with trailers should not take this road.

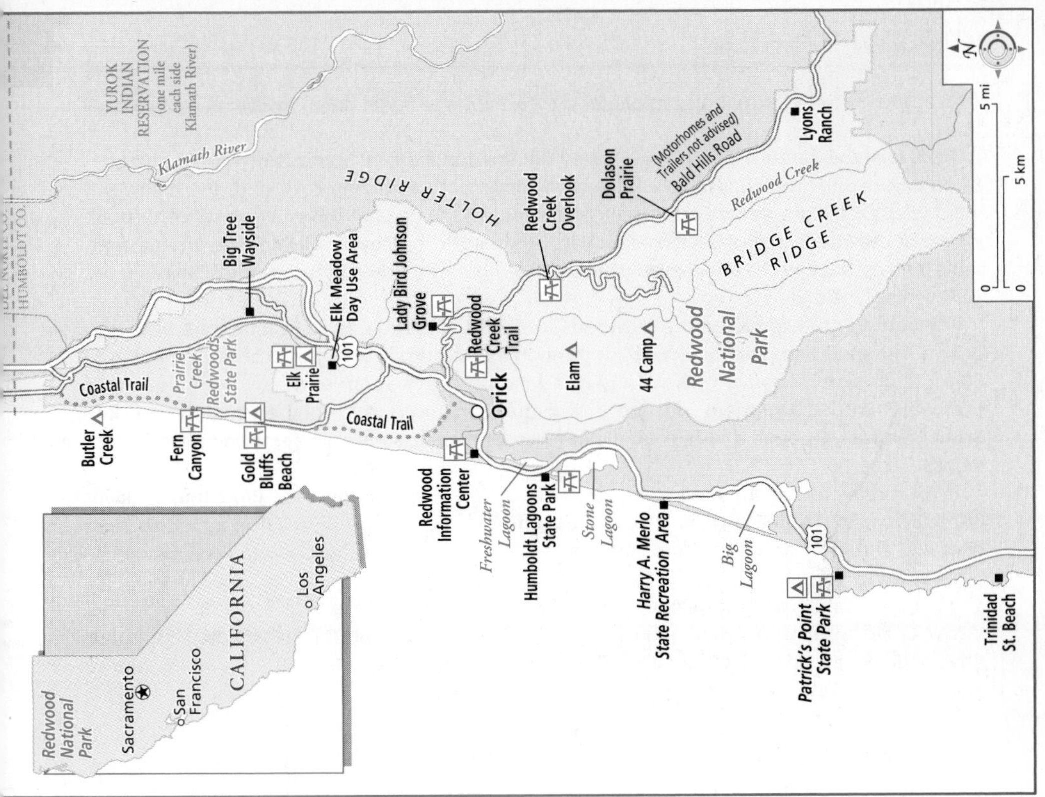

The most amazing car-friendly trail in all of the Redwood National and State Parks is the hidden, well-maintained gravel **Howland Hill Road.** It winds for about 12 miles through Jedediah Smith Redwoods State Park, an unforgettable journey through a spectacular old-growth redwood forest. To get there from the northbound lanes of U.S. 101, keep an eye out for the southernmost traffic light coming into Crescent City, at Elk Valley Road, and turn right. Follow Elk Valley to Howland Hill Road, which will be on your right. After driving through the park, you'll end up at U.S. 199 near Hiouchi, and from there it's a short jaunt west to get back to U.S. 101. Plan at least 2 to 3 hours for the 45-mile round-trip, or all day if you want to do some hiking or mountain biking in the park. Driving a motor home or towing a trailer is not recommended.

3 Day Hikes

Regardless of the length of your hike, dress warmly and bring plenty of water and sunscreen. The website of Redwood Hikes Press, **www.redwoodhikes.com**, is a great resource, and they also sell printed maps. **Redwood Adventures,** north of Orick (✆ **866/733-9637;** www.redwoodadventures.com), offers guided hikes; a half-day runs $85 per person.

Big Tree Trail For the nonhikers in your group (including those in wheelchairs), this is a short paved trail leading to an impressively large tree. You can return the way you came or make a 2- or 3-mile loop if you continue on the Foothill, Cathedral Tree, and Prairie Creek trails. .25 mile RT. Easy. Access: Big Tree turnoff along Newton B. Drury Scenic Pkwy.

Boy Scout Tree Trail After taking this trail through Jedediah Smith Redwoods State Park, you might understand why an activist such as Woody Harrelson would chain himself to the Golden Gate Bridge to protest logging old-growth forests. This is nature primeval, a lush, cool, damp forest brimming with giant ferns and redwoods. Just being here is truly an emotional experience. 5.3 miles RT. Easy. Access: Off Howland Hill Rd.; ask for directions and map at Jedediah Smith Information Center.

Enderts Beach Trail This short trail leads down to Enderts Beach. In the summer, free 2½-hour ranger-guided tide pool and seashore walks are offered when the tides are right. You start at the

If You Have Only 1 Day

Stop at one of the information centers for a free map, which will detail the parks' main attractions.

Next, take the detour along U.S. 101 called the **Newton B. Drury Scenic Parkway,** which passes through groves of redwoods and elk-filled meadows before leading back onto the highway 8 miles later. Or try one of two other spectacular routes: the **Coastal Drive,** which winds through stands of redwoods and offers grand views of the Pacific, or **Howland Hill Road,** an unforgettable journey through an unbelievably beautiful old-growth redwood forest (see "Exploring the Park by Car," below).

The best way to experience the redwoods is on foot, so be sure to fit in time for a brief hike or two. The short **Fern Canyon Trail** leads through a fantastically lush grotto of ferns clinging to 50-foot-high vertical canyon walls. **Lady Bird Johnson Grove Loop** is an easy self-guided tour that winds around a glorious lush grove of mature redwoods. And the best trail of all is **Boy Scout Tree Trail,** through a lush, cool, damp forest brimming with giant ferns and majestic redwoods.

If you prefer to see the area from the water, take a **Klamath River Jet Boat Tour** (**© 800/887-5387** or 707/482-5822; www.jetboattours.com) up the Klamath River Estuary to view bear, deer, elk, and more along the riverbanks, or a **kayak tour** around the Klamath River Estuary or other waters.

If you're determined to see some of the world's tallest trees, make your first stop the Kuchel Visitor Center near Orick. Here you can get a permit to travel the **Tall Trees Trail.** This 4-hour drive-and-hike expedition is limited to 50 permits each day, so get yours early. It's an experience you'll never forget.

beach parking lot, descend to the beach, and explore rocky tide pools at its southern end. 1.2 miles RT. Easy. Access: End of Enderts Rd. at south end of Crescent City (about 3 miles south on U.S. 101 from downtown).

Fern Canyon Trail This short, heavily traveled trail leads to an unbelievably lush grotto of lady, deer, chain, sword, five-finger, and maidenhair ferns clinging to 50-foot-high vertical walls divided by a babbling brook. It's only about a 1.5-mile walk from Gold Bluffs Beach, but be prepared to scramble across the creek several times on small footbridges. This short loop connects with a number of trails, allowing the adventurous hiker to get in a 10-mile hike if he or she desires. 1.5 miles RT. Easy. Access: From U.S. 101, take Davison Rd. exit, which follows Gold Bluffs Beach to Fern Canyon parking lot. Day-use fee $6. No trailers or motor homes over 24 ft. long.

Friendship Ridge, Coastal Loop Trail This is possibly the most varied and beautiful hike in Redwood National Park. Beginning at the Fern Canyon Trailhead, you'll follow the Coastal Loop Trail north, then veer right and follow the Friendship Ridge Trail. For the next 3 miles, you'll walk through a fern and redwood forest, then join the West Ridge Trail through old-growth forest to Ossagon Creek Camp and back south along the Coastal Loop Trail. 8 miles RT. Moderate. Access: Fern Canyon Trailhead on Davison Rd.

Lady Bird Johnson Grove Loop Here's a self-guided tour that loops around a lush grove of mature redwoods. It's the site at which Lady Bird Johnson dedicated the national park in 1968. The following year, it was named for her. 1.4 mile RT. Easy. Access: Lady Bird Johnson Grove. Take Bald Hills Rd. exit off U.S. 101, ½ mile north of Orick.

Tall Trees Trail To see the some of the world's tallest trees—about 360 feet tall and more than 600 years old—you'll have to go to the Kuchel Visitor Center near Orick (see "Visitor Centers," earlier in this chapter) to obtain a free **map** and **vehicle permit** to drive to the Tall Trees Grove Trailhead. Once thought to be the world's tallest, these trees lost their title when 378-foot Hyperion was discovered elsewhere in the park in 2006. Hyperion's location is kept secret to protect the surrounding soil. Only 50 permits are issued per day, on a first-come, first-served basis. After driving to the trail head—a slow, 15-mile one-way drive on a rough gravel road (trailers and motor homes not permitted)—you have to walk a steep trail down into the grove, but it's a small price to pay to see some of the tallest trees in the world. Once you figure in the drive and hike to get to the tree, the whole expedition takes at least 4 hours. 3.9 miles RT. Moderate. Access: End of Tall Trees Access Rd., off Bald Hills Rd. Permit required.

Organized Tours & Ranger Programs

The parks run interpretive programs on subjects ranging from trees to tide pools, legends to landforms, at the Hiouchi and Kuchel information centers and in the Crescent Beach area during summer months, and year-round at the park headquarters in Crescent City. Park rangers lead campfire programs and numerous other activities throughout the year. Check the free park newspaper or call the **Kuchel Visitor Center** (✆ **707/465-7765**) for current schedules.

4 Exploring the Backcountry

The long, beautiful **Coastal Trail,** which runs the entire 37-mile length of the parks' coastal section and as near the ocean as possible, can be hiked by the day in small segments. It also makes a great 3- or 4-day trip using backcountry camps on the route. One of the nicest runs is from Crescent Beach south into the Del Norte Coast Redwoods State Park. A free permit is required if you stay overnight at Ossagon Creek or along Redwood Creek.

Redwood Creek Trail This hike is a beauty, passing through Tall Trees Grove (where some of the tallest trees in the world grow on the banks of Redwood Creek), periodic meadows, new-growth forests, and awesome vantage points overlooking the grove. You'll camp along the sandbars of Redwood Creek. The bridges on Redwood Creek are installed from May 15 to September 15 only, and from the end of October to the beginning of April, heavy rains make creek crossings dangerous. 15.4 miles RT. Moderate to strenuous. Access: End of Redwood Creek access road, off Bald Hills Rd.

5 Other Sports & Activities

BEACHES The park's beaches vary from long white-sand strands to cobblestone pocket coves. The water temperature is in the high 40s to low 50s (single digits to 10s Celsius) year-round, and it's often rough out there. Swimmers and surfers should be prepared for adverse conditions.

Crescent Beach is a long, sandy beach just 2 miles south of Crescent City that's a popular destination for beachcombing, surf fishing, and surfing. Just south of Crescent Beach is **Enderts Beach,** a protected spot with a hike-in campground and tide pools at its southern end.

The Crescent Beach Overlook, along Enderts Road (off U.S. 101 about 4 miles south of Crescent City), is one of the prettiest picnic sites on the coast. Pack a picnic lunch from Good Harvest Cafe (see "Where to Dine," below), park at the overlook, lay your blanket on the grass, and admire the ocean view from atop your personal 500-foot bluff.

BICYCLING Most of the hiking trails throughout the National and State Parks are off limits to mountain bikers. However, **Prairie Creek Redwoods State Park** has a 19-mile mountain-bike trail through dense forest, elk-filled meadows, and glorious mud holes. Parts of it are difficult, though, so beginners should sit this one out. Pick up a $3 trail map at the Prairie Creek Visitor Center. Bike Rentals are available from **Redwood Adventures** north of Orick (✆ **866/733-9637;** www.redwoodadventures.com) for $50 a day.

A few other mountain-bike loops are about 20 miles long, but they are serious thigh burners and make the one above look easy. These loops are the **Holter Ridge Trail** and **Little Bald Hills.** Also, mountain biking is permitted on the old U.S. 101, now the **Coastal Trail** within Del Norte Coast Redwoods State Park.

The park recently completed the **Davison Trail,** which connects the Prairie Creek bike trails and the Newton B. Drury Scenic Parkway with U.S. 101 and the Holter Ridge Trail.

FISHING The Redwood Coast's streams are some of the best steelhead trout– and salmon-breeding habitat in California. Park beaches are good for surfcasting, but you should be prepared for heavy wave action. A California **fishing license** (available at local sporting goods stores) is required. Be sure to check with rangers about closures or other restrictions, which seem to change frequently. **Rivers West Outfitters** (✆ **707/482-5822** or 707/465-5501; www.riverswestoutfitters.com) offers guide service for $150 per person per day.

HORSEBACK TRAIL RIDES Equestrians can go on a variety of guided trail rides, including lunch and dinner trips, with **Redwood Trails Horseback Riding** (✆ **707/498-4837;** www.redwoodhorserides.com) and **Redwood Adventures** (✆ **866/733-9637;** www.redwoodadventures.com). Rates range from about $50 for a 1-hour ride to $250 for a full day.

JET-BOAT TOURS Tours aboard a jet boat take visitors 22 miles upriver from the Klamath River Estuary to view bear, deer, elk, osprey hawks, otters,

Campground	Total Sites	RV Hookups	Dump Station	Toilets	Drinking Water
Crescent City Redwoods KOA	94	42	Yes	Yes	Yes
Elk Prairie	75	0	Yes	Yes	Yes
Gold Bluffs Beach	25	0	No	Yes	Yes
Jedediah Smith	106	0	Yes	Yes	Yes
Mill Creek	145	0	Yes	Yes	Yes

and more along the riverbanks. It's about $40 for a 45-mile scenic trip. Kids pay half-price, and children under 4 ride free. Tours run May through September. Contact **Klamath River Jet Boat Tours,** Klamath (✆ **800/887-JETS** [887-5387] or 707/482-5822; www.jetboattours.com).

WHALE-WATCHING & BIRD-WATCHING High coastal overlooks such as **Klamath Overlook** and **Crescent Beach Overlook** make great whale-watching outposts during the December–January southern migration and the March–April return migration. The northern sea cliffs also provide valuable nesting sites for marine birds such as auklets, puffins, murres, and cormorants. Birders will also love the park's coastal freshwater lagoons, which are some of the most pristine shorebird and waterfowl habitats left and are chock-full of hundreds of different species.

WILDLIFE VIEWING One of the most striking aspects of Prairie Creek Redwoods State Park is its herd of **Roosevelt elk,** usually found in the appropriately named Elk Prairie in the southern end of the park and other spots in the Orick area. These gigantic beasts can weigh up to 1,000 pounds and are most definitely not tame. The bulls carry huge antlers from spring to fall. Elk are also sometimes found at Gold Bluffs Beach—it's an incredible rush to suddenly come upon them out of the fog or after a turn in the trail. Nearly 100 **black bears** also call the park home but are seldom seen. Unlike those in Yosemite, these bears avoid people.

6 Camping

Most drive-in camping is in the state parks. In the southern part of the complex, Prairie Creek Redwoods State Park (✆ **707/465-7354**), known for its old-growth redwoods and herds of elk, has two drive-in campgrounds. **Elk Prairie Campground,** 5 miles north of Orick on U.S. 101, is near hiking trails, has a nature center, and offers evening campfire talks. Make reservations through **ReserveAmerica** (✆ **800/444-7275;** www.reserveamerica.com). **Gold Bluffs Beach Campground** is 3 miles north of Orick on U.S. 101, then 5 miles west on Davison Road. It's somewhat more primitive and offers trail access.

In the northern part of the complex, the campground at **Jedediah Smith Redwoods State Park** (✆ **707/458-3018**), along U.S. 199 at Hiouchi, provides easy access to some of the area's biggest and most spectacular redwoods, as well as campsites along the scenic Smith River. Also in the northern section is **Mill Creek Campground,** in Del Norte Coast Redwoods State Park (✆ **707/465-2146**), 7 miles south of Crescent City on U.S. 101. It has sites for both RVs and tents, and the walk-in tent sites nestle among the redwoods. Both Jedediah Smith and Mill Creek take reservations through ReserveAmerica (see above).

Those seeking RV hookups and the usual commercial campground amenities will find several choices in Crescent City, including the quiet, well-maintained **Crescent City Redwoods KOA,** 4241 U.S. 101 N., Crescent City, CA 95531 (✆ **707/464-5744**). Tent sites are among the redwoods, and some RV sites are also shaded. The KOA has farm animals, a recreation room, a laundromat, a convenience store with RV supplies, propane, free wireless Internet, and cable TV hookups. Also here are several cabins ($40–$70 double) and one modernized cottage that sleeps six ($100–$150), situated among the redwoods.

In addition to the developed drive-in campgrounds discussed above, eight small, primitive hike-in campgrounds are in the national park; they require a walk of .25 to .5 mile. Some are free, others are $5 per person per night, and all have fire rings and toilets. Contact the park office (✆ **707/464-6101**) for information.

Four campgrounds are in the mountains above the park, along U.S. 199, in the **Smith River National Recreation Area** (✆ **707/457-3131**). We like the Panther Flat campground, with coin-op showers, where sites run $15 per night. The other, more primitive campgrounds charge $8 to $14 per night. To reserve any of the four sites, contact **www.recreation.gov** or call ✆ **800/444-6777.**

Showers	Fire Pits/ Grills	Laundry	Reserve	Fees	Open
Yes	Yes	Yes	Yes	$30–$50	Year-round
Yes	Yes	No	Yes	$35	Year-round
Yes	Yes	No	No	$35	Year-round
Yes	Yes	No	Yes	$35	Year-round
Yes	Yes	No	Yes	$35	Summer only

7 Where to Stay

There are a number of bed-and-breakfasts and roadside motels in Crescent City, Orick, and Klamath. The **Crescent City/Del Norte Chamber of Commerce** (© **800/343-8300;** www.northerncalifornia.net) is a good resource.

INSIDE THE PARK

Elk Meadow Cabins Built in the 1950s and 1960s as employee housing for a lumber company, these three-bedroom units completely surrounded by park land have been converted to stylish guesthouses. Featuring full kitchens, Wi-Fi, and king beds in two of the three bedrooms, the cabins are perfect for families, with a lawn perfect for kids with lots of energy (not to mention grazing elk). This is also the base camp for **Redwood Adventures,** offering bike rentals, horseback rides, guided hikes, and other recreation.

U.S. 101 (P.O. Box 66), Orick, CA 95555. © **866/733-9637.** www.redwoodadventures.com. 6 units. A/C, TV, TEL. $199–$310 double. AE, MC, V. Located just north of Orick.

Hostelling International–Redwood Hostel The only lodging in the park, this 1908 settler's ranch was remodeled in 1987 to accommodate 30 guests dormitory style (bunks and shared bathrooms). The location—100 yards from the beach, surrounded by hiking trails along the Redwood Coast—more than makes up for the lack of privacy. Two private rooms that accommodate two (one has a loft bunk for a child as well) are available with advance reservations. The nightly rate includes showers and use of a common room, two redwood decks, a kitchen, a dining room, and a stove. Reservations are strongly recommended. ***Note:*** The hostel will be closed all of 2010 for foundation work; construction will potentially finish by summer 2011. Call for current information.

14480 U.S. 101 (at Wilson Creek Rd., about 7 miles north of town), Klamath, CA 95548. © **800/295-1905** or 707/482-8265. www.redwoodhostel.org. 26 bunks, 2 couple's rooms. Bunk $21 per adult, half-price for children 12 or under; $59 couple's room. AE, DISC, MC, V. Closed Jan; limited availability Nov, Dec, and Feb.

NEAR THE PARK

Curly Redwood Lodge This is a blast from the past, the kind of place where you might have stayed as a kid during one of those cross-country vacations in the family station wagon. It was built in 1957 on grasslands across from the town's harbor, and completely trimmed with rare curly-grained lumber from a single ancient redwood. Although they're not full of the latest high-tech gadgets, the guest rooms are among the largest and most soundproof in town, and certainly the most evocative of a bygone, more innocent age. Overall, the retro aura is more akin to Oregon than anything you might imagine in 21st-century California.

701 U.S. 101 S., Crescent City, CA 95531. © **707/464-2137.** Fax 707/464-1655. www.curlyredwoodlodge.com. 36 units. TV, TEL. Summer $65–$70 double; winter $54–$58 double. AE, DC, MC, V.

Hampton Inn & Suites Built in 2003, this property immediately became the top place to stay in Crescent City, thanks to a jaw-dropping oceanfront location near the historic Battery Point Lighthouse out of earshot of noisy U.S. 101. (In fact, it's California's newest hotel within 35 ft. of the ocean in more than 20 years.) Rooms are typical of a Hampton Inn, featuring free Wi-Fi, fridges, microwaves, coffeemakers, and comfortable beds; some have balconies and jetted tubs. The views make the place: The rocky coastline is on full display from the picture windows in the lobby.

100 A St., Crescent City, CA 95531. © **707/464-465-5400.** Fax 707/465-0962. 53 units. A/C, TV, TEL. Summer $239–$299 double; lower in winter. AE, DISC, MC, V.

Historic Requa Inn Established in 1914 as a fishing lodge, this two-story charmer on the banks of the lower Klamath River offers guest rooms modestly decorated with antique furnishings. Bathrooms have showers, a tub/showers, or claw-foot tubs. Six units offer views of the lower Klamath River. The inn's main attraction is the cozy parlor downstairs, where guests bury themselves in the plump armchairs to read beside the fireplace or just relax and watch the river run. There are plenty of enticements just outside, including a hot tub, river access, numerous hiking trails in nearby Redwood National Park, and, of course, fishing.

451 Requa Rd., Klamath, CA 95548. © **707/482-1425.** www.requainn.com. 10 units. $99–$169 double; lower rates in off season. Rates include full breakfast. AE, DISC, MC, V. Closed Dec–Jan. From U.S. 101, take Requa Rd. 2½ miles north of Klamath River Bridge.

Picnic & Camping Supplies

Groceries are available in Crescent City at **Safeway,** 475 M St. (✆ **707/465-3353**), and **Ray's Food Place,** 625 M St. (✆ **707/465-4045**). **Walmart,** 900 Washington St., Crescent City (✆ **707/464-1198**), sells camping supplies and sporting goods.

8 Where to Dine

Beachcomber SEAFOOD The decor is as nautical as its name implies: rough-cut planking and a scattering of driftwood, fishnets, and buoys, dangling above a dimly lit space. The restaurant lies beside the beach, 2 miles south of Crescent City's center. Proprietor-chef Monty Roberts grills many dishes over madrone-wood barbecue pits, a technique perfected here since the restaurant opened in 1975. The house specialty is a sumptuous Parmesan halibut, but Roberts' family recipe for a marinated New York strip is a close second. Nightly specials include such tantalizing options as vanilla-champagne-hazelnut halibut and ginger mahi-mahi.

1400 U.S. 101 S., Crescent City. ✆ **707/464-2205.** Reservations recommended. Main courses $10–$20. AE, DISC, MC, V. Daily 5–9pm.

Cazadores Family Mexican Restaurant MEXICAN Nondescript from the parking lot, and fairly typical from the Formica-topped tables, Cazadores nonetheless plates up excellent Mexican dishes, including the standards like tacos, burritos, and enchiladas, plus a solid column of Mexican seafood dishes. We favor the *rellenos,* spicy chile wrapped in thin layers of egg and cheese. Service is remarkably efficient: It will probably take you longer to eat your order than you wait for it.

1461 Northcrest Dr., Crescent City. ✆ **707/464-2388.** Main courses $7–$14. AE, DISC, MC, V. Mon–Sat 11am–9pm; Sun 11am–8:30pm. Shorter hours in winter.

Good Harvest Café AMERICAN A Crescent City stalwart established in 1993 and moving to swank new quarters in 2009, Good Harvest is a comfortable woodsy eatery with a social atmosphere and local loyalty. Breakfast includes fluffy frittatas, spinach-and-artichoke-heart omelets, and baked goods, while lunch tends toward sandwiches, burgers, and salads. Dinner tends toward fresh seafood and grain-fed beef, but there are also plenty of vegetarian options here. This is a great place to pick up a sack lunch to eat on the trail.

575 U.S. 101 S., Crescent City. ✆ **707/465-6028.** Main courses $5–$10 breakfast and lunch; $8–$24 dinner. DISC, MC, V. Daily 6:30am–10pm.

Steelhead Lodge AMERICAN At the end of the road next to the river levee in Klamath Glen, Steelhead Lodge is a woodsy landmark known for its hearty dinners. Dishes are named for riffles—or frothy spots—in the Klamath River: A Terwer Riffle is a 16-ounce rib-eye, a Bear Creek Riffle is a half-chicken and pork spareribs, and a Van Pelt Riffle is local red snapper. Salad is served family style, and dinners come with your choice of baked potato, chili beans, or rice pilaf. A map of the river is tiled into the vintage bar's floor, and the dining room is bedecked with old bottles and logging implements.

330 Terwer Riffle Rd., Klamath Glen. ✆ **707/465-6028.** Main courses $5–$10 breakfast and lunch; $8–$24 dinner. MC, V. Sun–Thurs 5–8:30pm; Fri–Sat 5–9:30pm. Shorter hours in winter. Located 3 miles east of U.S. 101.

30

Rocky Mountain National Park, CO

by Eric Peterson

Snow-covered peaks stand watch over lush valleys and alpine lakes, creating the perfect image of America's most dramatic and beautiful landscape: the majestic Rocky Mountains. Here the pine- and fir-scented forests are deep, the air is crisp and pure, and the mountain peaks reach up to grasp the deep-blue sky.

What makes Rocky Mountain National Park unique is not only its breathtaking scenery, but also its variety. In relatively low areas, up to 9,000 feet, ponderosa pine and juniper cloak the sunny southern slopes, with Douglas fir on the cooler northern slopes. The thirstier blue spruce and lodgepole pine cling to the banks of streams, along with occasional groves of aspen. Elk and mule deer thrive. On higher slopes, forests of Engelmann spruce and subalpine fir dominate, interspersed with wide meadows vibrant with wildflowers in spring and summer. This is also home to bighorn sheep, which have become a symbol of the park. Above 11,500 feet, the trees become increasingly gnarled and stunted, until they disappear altogether and alpine tundra takes over. Fully one-third of the park is in this bleak, rocky world, where many of the plants are identical to those found in the Arctic.

Within the park's 415 square miles are 17 mountains above 13,000 feet. Longs Peak, at 14,259 feet, is the highest.

Trail Ridge Road, which cuts west through the middle of the park from Estes Park, then south down its western boundary to Grand Lake, is one of America's most scenic highways. Climbing to 12,183 feet, it's the highest continuously paved highway in the United States. The road is usually open from Memorial Day into October, depending on snowfall. The 48-mile drive from Estes Park to Grand Lake takes about 3 hours, allowing for stops at numerous view points. Exhibits at the Alpine Visitor Center at Fall River Pass, 11,796 feet above sea level, explain life on the alpine tundra.

Fall River Road, the original park road, leads from Estes Park to Fall River Pass via Horseshoe Park. As you negotiate its graveled switchbacks, you get a clear idea of what early auto travel was like in the West. This road, too, is closed in winter. Among the few paved roads in the Rockies that lead into a high mountain basin is Bear Lake Road, which stays open year-round, with occasional half-day closings to clear snow.

AVOIDING THE CROWDS

The park is fully accessible for only half the year, so few of the park's almost three million visitors come in the off season. The busiest time is from mid-June through mid-August—essentially during school vacation—so just before or just after that period is best. But winter is gaining in popularity, too, because it is the quietest time. You won't be able to drive the entire Trail Ridge Road, and the park can be bitterly cold, but it is also beautiful. Regardless of when you visit, the best way to avoid crowds is to head out on a trail.

1 Essentials

GETTING THERE & GATEWAYS

Entry to the park is from either the east (through the town of **Estes Park**) or the west (through the town of **Grand Lake**). Connecting the east and west sides of the park is **Trail Ridge Road,** open during summer and early fall, but closed to all motor vehicle traffic by snow the rest of the year. Most visitors enter the park from the Estes Park side. The Beaver Meadows Entrance, west of Estes Park on U.S. 36, leads to the Beaver Meadows Visitor Center and park headquarters; it is the most direct route to Trail Ridge Road. U.S. 34 west from Estes Park takes you to the Fall River Visitor Center, just outside the park, and into the park through the Fall River Entrance, which is north of the Beaver Meadows Entrance. From there you have access to Old Fall River Road or Trail Ridge Road.

Estes Park is about 71 miles northwest of Denver, 44 miles northwest of Boulder, and 42 miles southwest of Fort Collins.

The most direct route from Denver is **U.S. 36** through Boulder. At Estes Park, that highway joins **U.S. 34,** which runs up the Big Thompson Canyon from I-25 and Loveland, and continues through

Tips from a Park Insider

The ease with which visitors can experience the many faces of Rocky Mountain National Park helps make it a special place, according to former park spokesman Dick Putney.

There are other alpine tundra areas in the United States, but you usually have to do a lot of hard hiking, Putney says. "What makes Rocky Mountain National Park unique is that Trail Ridge Road takes you up to the tundra—above tree line—in the comfort of your car; you can see plant and animal communities that, if not for this park, you would have to go to the Arctic Circle to see."

Those willing and able to hike can see plenty of tundra country. Putney suggests having a friend drop you off at the **Ute Trail** turnout on Trail Ridge Road, where you can hike the 6 miles down through Forest Canyon to Upper Beaver Meadows. He says this canyon is among the wildest in the park, adding that the hike along its steep side provides spectacular views of the canyon and Longs Peak, the park's tallest mountain.

Another hike that Putney recommends is the 2-mile (one-way) **Gem Lake Trail,** on the park's east side. "When you're going up that trail, there are several places to look across the Estes Valley to Longs Peak, and the lake is a wonderful spot for a picnic," he says. Those who want to work a bit harder will be well rewarded on another of Putney's favorites, the East Inlet Trail on the west side of the park. "Once you get up there a couple of miles and gain some elevation, you look back toward Grand Lake and think you're in Switzerland."

Longs Peak, at 14,259 feet elevation, is the northernmost of Colorado's famed "fourteeners" (mountains that exceed 14,000 ft. elevation), and it's a popular hike. "You don't need technical climbing gear once the ice is gone, usually by mid-July," Putney says, adding that hikers may have some physical problems with the altitude at first. "It's wise to give yourself at least a couple of days to acclimate before tackling Longs Peak." He also recommends that high-elevation hikers drink plenty of nonalcoholic fluids, eat regularly, carry energy bars, take it slow, and listen to their bodies. Another tip for hikers is to spend time discussing their plans with rangers in the park's Backcountry Office before setting out. "We'd much rather spend time with them beforehand to try to get to know their abilities and expectations, and advise them where to go, than be called out on a search-and-rescue mission."

One activity that many visitors miss out on is viewing the night sky, says Putney. He suggests taking a picnic supper and stopping at one of the Trail Ridge Road **view points** after dark, when most park visitors are in their motel rooms or campsites. "We don't have any light pollution here," he says. "You think you can just reach up and touch the Milky Way. You can see satellites, and the Perseid meteor shower in August is something you won't soon forget."

Putney says the easiest method to avoid crowds, even during the park's busiest season, is to take off down a hiking trail, since most visitors remain close to the roads. "The farther you go up the trail, the fewer people you'll encounter," he says. He adds that another sure way to escape humanity is to visit in winter and explore the park on snowshoes or cross-country skis.

And when would he visit? "Fall—from September through mid-October—is the best time," he says. "Days are warm and comfortable, nights are cool and crisp, there are fewer people than in summer, and the aspens are changing. You can see hundreds of elk and watch the bulls bugle as they protect their harems from the other bulls. But it might snow!"

Rocky Mountain National Park to Grand Lake. An alternative scenic route to Estes Park is **Colo. 7,** the "Peak-to-Peak Scenic Byway" that transits Central City (Colo. 119), Nederland (Colo. 72), and Allenspark (Colo. 7).

Heading south from Estes Park on Colo. 7, you can reach two trail heads in the southeast corner of the national park, but there are no connecting roads to the main part of the park from those points. These are **Longs Peak Trailhead** (the turnoff is 9 miles south of Estes Park and the trail head about another mile) and **Wild Basin Trailhead** (another 3½ miles south to the turnoff and then 2¼ miles to the trail head).

Every day from late spring to early fall, free national park **shuttle buses** take hikers to some of the more popular spots and trail heads on the park's east side. There is a Park and Ride parking area west of Glacier Basin Campground; one route goes to Bear Lake, and the other goes to Moraine Park and

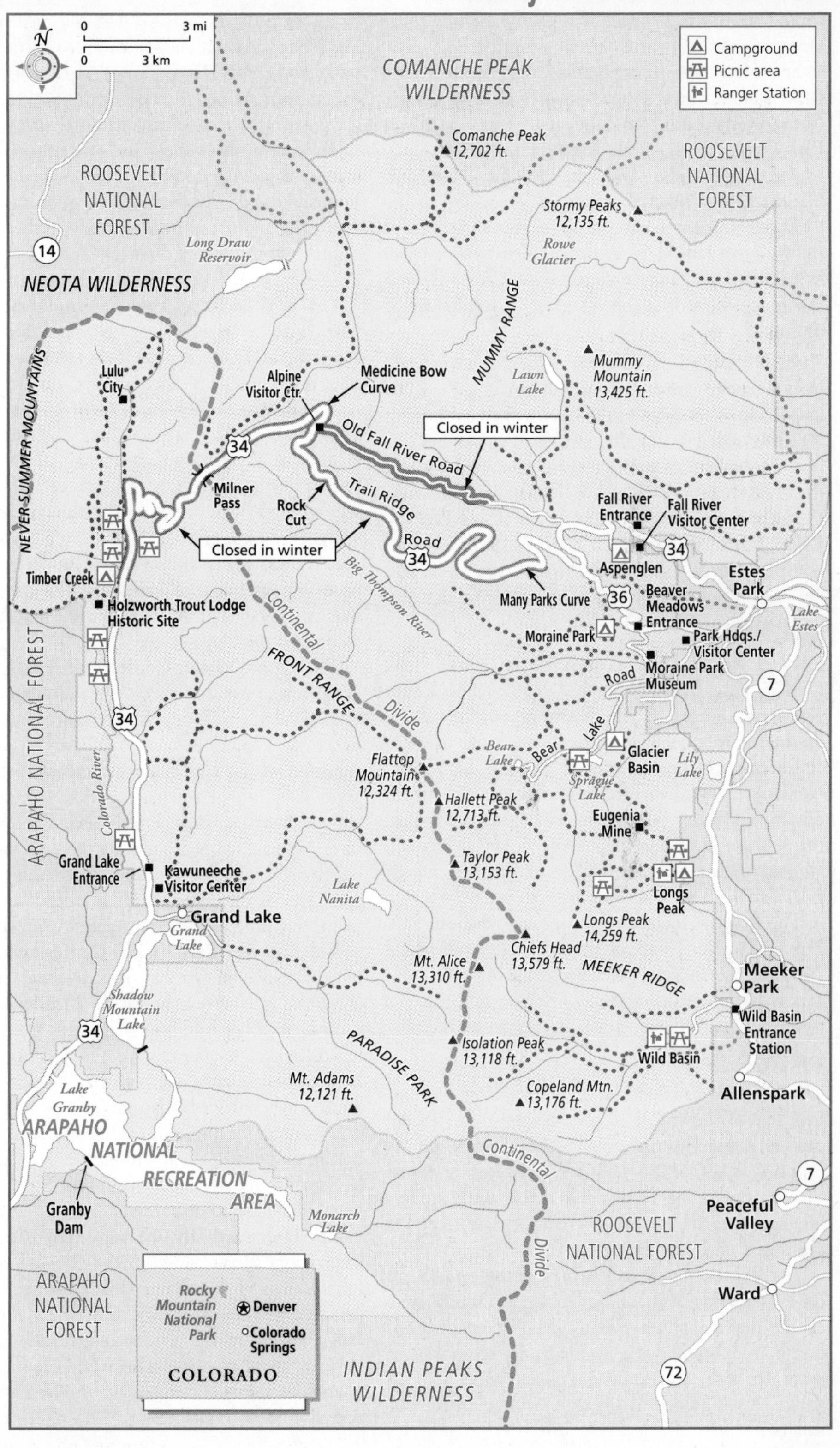
0 3 mi
0 3 km
Campground
Picnic area
Ranger Station
COMANCHE PEAK WILDERNESS
Comanche Peak 12,702 ft.
ROOSEVELT NATIONAL FOREST
ROOSEVELT NATIONAL FOREST
Stormy Peaks 12,135 ft.
Rowe Glacier
Long Draw Reservoir
14
NEOTA WILDERNESS
MUMMY RANGE
Mummy Mountain 13,425 ft.
Lawn Lake
NEVER SUMMER MOUNTAINS
Lulu City
Alpine Visitor Ctr.
Medicine Bow Curve
Closed in winter
Old Fall River Road
34
Milner Pass
Rock Cut
Trail Ridge Road
Closed in winter
Fall River Entrance
Fall River Visitor Center
Aspenglen
Estes Park
Timber Creek
Holzworth Trout Lodge Historic Site
Big Thompson River
Continental Divide
Many Parks Curve
36
Beaver Meadows Entrance
Lake Estes
Moraine Park
Park Hdqs./ Visitor Center
Moraine Park Museum
7
FRONT RANGE
ARAPAHO NATIONAL FOREST
Bear Lake Road
Bear Lake
Glacier Basin
Lily Lake
Sprague Lake
Flattop Mountain 12,324 ft.
Hallett Peak 12,713 ft.
Colorado River
Eugenia Mine
Taylor Peak 13,153 ft.
Grand Lake Entrance
Kawuneeche Visitor Center
Longs Peak
Lake Nanita
Grand Lake
Grand Lake
Longs Peak 14,259 ft.
Chiefs Head 13,579 ft.
Mt. Alice 13,310 ft.
MEEKER RIDGE
Meeker Park
Wild Basin Entrance Station
Shadow Mountain Lake
Isolation Peak 13,118 ft.
Wild Basin
PARADISE PARK
Mt. Adams 12,121 ft.
Copeland Mtn. 13,176 ft.
Allenspark
Lake Granby
ARAPAHO NATIONAL RECREATION AREA
Granby Dam
Monarch Lake
Peaceful Valley
ROOSEVELT NATIONAL FOREST
ARAPAHO NATIONAL FOREST
Rocky Mountain National Park
Denver
Colorado Springs
COLORADO
Ward
72
INDIAN PEAKS WILDERNESS

several nearby trail heads. Contact park offices or visit the website for the current schedule.

From late June to Labor Day, the town of Estes Park also operates a free summer **shuttle** service (www.estesparkcvb.com) that connects the Estes Park Visitor Center with downtown, the surrounding campgrounds, and the Rocky Mountain National Park's hiker shuttles.

Those who want to enter the national park from the west can take **U.S. 40** north from I-70 through Winter Park and Tabernash to Granby, and then follow U.S. 34 north to the village of Grand Lake and on into the park.

THE NEAREST AIRPORT Visitors usually fly into **Denver International Airport** (✆ **800/247-2336** or 303/342-2000; www.flydenver.com), 90 miles southeast of the park's east entrances. It's served by most major airlines and car-rental companies. See chapter 38 for their website listings. From the airport, travelers can also get to Estes Park on **Estes Park Shuttle** (✆ **970/586-5151;** www.estesparkshuttle.com). The 2-hour trip costs $45 per person one-way or $85 per person round-trip.

INFORMATION

Contact **Rocky Mountain National Park,** 1000 U.S. 36, Estes Park, CO 80517 (✆ **970/586-1206;** www.nps.gov/romo). There's also great information on the Internet. Start at the park's main website, but check out the Environmental Education Department's site, **www.heartoftherockies.net**. Park visitor centers sell U.S. Geological Survey topographical maps. Also available is *Hiking Rocky Mountain National Park,* by Kent and Donna Dannen, which gives detailed trail descriptions.

The **Rocky Mountain Nature Association,** P.O. Box 3100, Estes Park, CO 80517 (✆ **800/816-7662** or 970/586-0108; www.rmna.org), offers a variety of trip-planning tools. The association sells a number of park maps, guides, books, and videos.

VISITOR CENTERS

When entering the park, it's wise to make your first stop one of the visitor centers. Except as noted, all can be contacted through the main park phone number (✆ **970/586-1206**). Visitor center hours vary seasonally and based on available staff; the following hours are subject to change. Visitor centers are closed on December 25.

The **Beaver Meadows Visitor Center,** on U.S. 36 on the east side of the park, has a good interpretive exhibit that includes a relief model of the park, a 23-minute film on the park, a wide choice of books and maps for sale, and knowledgeable people to give advice. A self-guided nature trail just outside the visitor center identifies many of the park's plants. It's open daily year-round with varying hours, longest in summer.

Just outside the park on U.S. 34, just east of the Fall River entrance on the east side of the national park, is the **Fall River Visitor Center.** In a beautiful mountain lodge–style building, it contains exhibits on park wildlife, including some spectacular full-size bronzes of elk and other animals, plus an activity/discovery room for children, an information desk, and a bookstore. It is open daily 9am to 5pm from late spring through early fall, with slightly shorter hours on weekends only the rest of the year. Next door is **Rocky Mountain Gateway** (✆ **970/577-0043;** www.rockymountaingateway.net), with a large, pricey souvenir and clothing shop, a grocery store, a laundromat, and a cafeteria-style restaurant that serves snacks and sandwiches.

The **Kawuneeche Visitor Center** is at the Grand Lake end of Trail Ridge Road. In addition to exhibits on the geology, plants, animals, and human history of the park's west side, there is a small theater where a film on the park is shown, and a short self-guided nature trail. The center is open daily year-round, with varying hours; hours are 8am to 6pm in the heart of summer. *Kawuneeche* (kah-wuh-*nee*-chee) is an Arapaho word that translates as "Valley of the Coyote."

The **Alpine Visitor Center,** at Fall River Pass, has exhibits that explain life on the alpine tundra and a viewing platform from which you are almost certain to see elk. Next door is the Fall River Store, open in summer, with a snack bar and gift shop that has a good selection of souvenirs, gifts, arts and crafts, and clothing, at surprisingly reasonable prices. The center is usually open late May through early October, weather permitting, and closed the rest of the year. Hours vary; the center is open 9am to 5pm from mid-June to early September.

The **Moraine Park Visitor Center and Museum** is a great spot for families. It is on Bear Lake Road, about 1½ miles from the Beaver Meadows entrance station, in a log building that dates from 1923. It has full visitor-center facilities, in addition to excellent natural-history exhibits that describe the creation of the park's landscape, as well as the plants and animals of the park. There's also a half-mile nature trail outside. The museum is open daily from late spring to early fall, with hours of 9am to 5pm from mid-June to early September.

The **Holzwarth Trout Lodge Historic Site** is off Trail Ridge Road—it's a half-mile walk—about 7 miles north of the Grand Lake entrance station. It consists of several historic buildings, including a lodge, with displays of furnishings, tools, and other items from when it was a busy dude ranch. The site is open in summer only, daily 10:30am to 4:30pm. A trail guide is available.

If You Have Only 1 Day

This park simply begs for an extended visit—4 to 7 days would be ideal—but it offers wonderful experiences for visitors who have only a short amount of time or who are not able or willing to hike.

Those arriving in summer or early fall with only 1 day to see the park will want to stop at one of the visitor centers and then drive the fantastically scenic **Trail Ridge Road,** described below. Stop at the view points and take the half-hour walk along the **Tundra World Nature Trail** to get a close-up view of the plants, animals, and terrain of the tundra. Those returning to the east or west side will have time for little else—the 48-mile drive takes about 3 hours each way—but those passing through the park on their way to somewhere else might want to take another short hike.

FEES & PERMITS

Park admission costs $20 per vehicle for up to 1 week and $10 for solo bicyclists, motorcyclists, and pedestrians. Camping in developed campgrounds costs $20 per night during the summer and $14 in the off season when the water is turned off, usually from late September to May. Required **overnight backcountry permits** cost $20 from May through October and are free the rest of the year (see "Exploring the Backcountry," below).

SPECIAL REGULATIONS & WARNINGS

Rocky Mountain National Park's high elevation and extremes of climate and terrain are among its most appealing features, but also its greatest hazards. Hikers should try to give themselves several days to acclimate to the altitude before hitting the trails that climb above timberline, and hikers with respiratory or heart problems would do well to discuss their plans with their physicians before leaving home. Hikers need to be prepared for rapidly changing conditions, including sudden afternoon thunderstorms in July and August. If lightning threatens, stay clear of ridges and other high points.

SEASONS & CLIMATE

Even though the park is open year-round, **Trail Ridge Road,** the main east–west thoroughfare, is always closed in winter. Assume that you will not be able to drive clear across the park from mid-October until Memorial Day—even into June and again in September, snow can close the road for hours or even a day or more. That's not to say that travelers can't enjoy the park in winter. All park entrances are open, trails accommodate snowshoers and cross-country skiers, and roads to a number of good view points and trail heads are plowed. Those with the proper skills and equipment can cross-country ski into the high country, although they need to be aware of storm and avalanche dangers. Always check with rangers before setting out.

Weather is a key factor that will affect your trip to the park in any season. In summer, temperatures typically climb into the 70s (20s Celsius) during the day and drop into the 40s (single digits Celsius) at night, but because of the park's high elevation and range of elevations, temperatures vary greatly. The higher into the mountains you go, the cooler it gets. Rangers say that for every 1,000 feet in elevation gain, the climate changes the equivalent of traveling 600 miles north. The tree line in the park—the elevation at which trees can no longer grow—varies but is at about 11,500 feet.

Winters usually see high temperatures in the 20s and 30s (below 0 Celsius) and lows from –10°F (–23°C) to 20°F (–7°C). Spring and fall temperatures can vary greatly, from pleasantly warm to bitterly cold and snowy. For this reason, spring and fall are when you need to be flexible and ready to adjust your itinerary to suit current conditions. Particularly at higher elevations, wind-chill factors can be extreme. Hypothermia can be a problem at any time, even in summer, when afternoon thunderstorms sometimes cause temperatures to drop dramatically and suddenly.

SEASONAL EVENTS

The **elk rutting season** in September and October brings hundreds of elk to the lower elevations, where you can often hear the bulls bugle and watch them trying to keep other bulls away from their females.

2 Exploring the Park by Car

Although Rocky Mountain National Park is generally considered the domain of hikers and climbers, it's easy to enjoy this park without working up a sweat. For that we can thank **Trail Ridge Road,** built in 1932 and undoubtedly one of America's most scenic highways. This remarkable 48-mile

Organized Tours & Ranger Programs

Campfire talks and other programs occur between June and September. Activities vary from talks on the park's wildlife and geology to photo walks, fly-fishing, and orienteering programs. At night, rangers lead night-sky programs using the park's computerized telescopes. They also give nightly talks during the elk rutting season. Winter visitors will find a variety of activities, including moonlight hikes and snowshoe and cross-country ski trips. Check at visitor centers for current schedules.

road rises to over 12,000 feet in elevation and crosses the Continental Divide. Along the way it offers spectacular vistas of snowcapped peaks, deep forests, and meadows of wildflowers full of browsing bighorn sheep, elk, and deer. Allow at least 3 hours for the drive, and consider a short walk or hike from one of the many vista points.

To get a close-up look at the tundra, pull off Trail Ridge Road into the **Rock Cut Parking Area** (elevation 12,110 ft.), about halfway along the scenic drive. You'll have splendid views of glacially carved peaks along the Continental Divide, and on the .5-mile **Tundra Nature Trail** you'll find signs identifying and discussing the hardy plants and animals that inhabit this region.

Trail Ridge Road is left unplowed and closed by winter snows. In recent years, it has usually been clear by late May and closed sometime in October, depending how fast winter comes. But even well into June and again in September and through early October, the road can be closed for snow for hours or even days at a time.

There are two other roads within the park. **Old Fall River Road,** 9 miles long and unpaved, is one-way uphill only (you'll return on Trail Ridge Rd.). It's usually open from July 4 through mid-October. **Bear Lake Road,** the access road to Bear Lake, is open year-round.

3 Park Attractions

Remnants from the area's mining and ranching days of the late 1800s and early 1900s persist in the park. Hikers will encounter the ruins of several historic cabins on the Lulu City and Eugenia Mine trails (see "Day Hikes," below). Exhibits in the **Moraine Park Visitor Center and Museum** on Bear Lake Road are mainly on natural history, but the building itself—a log structure built as a social center in 1923—is listed on the National Register of Historic Places. The **Holzwarth Trout Lodge Historic Site,** a dude ranch dating back to the 1920s, is an easy half-mile walk from Trail Ridge Road on the west side of the park. Denver saloon owner John Holzwarth started it as a cattle ranch after Prohibition forced him to find a new line of work. But Holzwarth discovered that it was easier, and more profitable, to take in paying guests (at $2 per day or $11 per week, including room, meals, and a horse) than to do the hard work of actual ranching. The ranch buildings contain many of their original furnishings, and visitors can see the bunkhouses, kitchens, a taxidermy shop, wagons, and sleds.

4 Day Hikes

The park contains over 350 miles of hiking trails, ranging from short, easy walks to extremely strenuous hikes that require climbing skills. Trail difficulty can also vary by time of year—the higher elevations usually have snow until at least mid-July. Many of the park's trails, such as Longs Peak, can be either day hikes or overnight backpacking trips. Hikers are strongly advised to discuss their plans with park rangers before setting out. The following are some favorites; there are many more.

SHORTER TRAILS

Alberta Falls Trail With an elevation change of only 210 feet, this is an easy, scenic walk along Glacier Creek to Alberta Falls. Along the sunny trail, you'll see beaver dams and an abundance of golden-mantled ground squirrels. 1.2 miles RT. Easy. Access: Glacier Gorge parking area.

Bear Lake Nature Trail Head out early in the day if you want some quiet time on this very popular walk. From the beginning of the trail, on the eastern side, 12,713-foot Hallett Peak dominates the view; along the lake's north side, you'll be looking at the national park's highest mountain, 14,259-foot Longs Peak. Expect to see ground squirrels, chipmunks, and snowshoe hares; in the clear waters of the lake, you may catch a glimpse of a greenback cutthroat trout. (No fishing is allowed.) The Rocky Mountain Nature Association's booklet *Bear Lake Nature Trail* ($2), available at park visitor centers, makes a handy companion. This is an easy stroll, most of which is wheelchair accessible—one section has stairs. .6-mile loop. Easy. Access: Bear Lake trail head, at the end of Bear Lake Rd.

Bierstadt Lake Trail This trail climbs 566 feet through an open forest of aspen to Bierstadt Lake. From the northwest side of the lake, you'll have good views of Longs Peak. This trail connects with several other trails, including one that leads to Bear Lake. 2.8 miles RT. Moderate. Access: North side of Bear Lake Rd., 6½ miles from Beaver Meadows.

Emerald Lake Trail This trail offers spectacular scenery on its route past Nymph and Dream lakes to its destination, Emerald Lake. The .5-mile hike to Nymph Lake is easy, climbing 225 feet. The trail is then rated moderate to Dream Lake (another .6 mile) and Emerald Lake (another .7 mile), which is 605 feet higher than the starting point at Bear Lake. In addition to the mountain lakes, you'll see the surrounding mountains, which are especially pretty reflected in the surface of Nymph Lake or towering over Dream Lake. In summer, an abundance of wildflowers borders the path between Nymph and Dream lakes. 3.6 miles RT. Easy to moderate. Access: Bear Lake.

Eugenia Mine Trail This walk to an abandoned mine follows the Longs Peak Trail for about .5 mile and then forks off to the right, heading through groves of aspens and then evergreens before arriving at the site of the mine. There you'll see hillside tailings, the remnants of a cabin, and abandoned mine equipment. The trail has an elevation gain of 508 feet. 2.8 miles RT. Moderate. Access: Longs Peak Ranger Station.

Gem Lake Trail A relatively low-elevation trail, starting at only 7,740 feet, this route has an elevation change of 1,090 feet. It offers good views of Estes Park and Longs Peak; the destination is a pretty lake. 3.2 miles RT. Moderate. Access: Lumpy Ridge trail head on Devil's Gulch Rd., north of Estes Park.

Mills Lake Trail This trail leads to a mountain lake nestled in a valley among towering mountain peaks. Among the best spots in the park for photographing Longs Peak (the best lighting is usually in late afternoon or early evening), this is also the perfect place for a picnic. The trail has an elevation change of about 750 feet. 5.6 miles RT. Moderate. Access: Glacier Gorge Junction.

Ouzel Falls Trail This hike climbs about 950 feet and crosses Cony Creek on two bridges before delivering you to a picture-perfect waterfall, among the park's prettiest. The trail passes through areas that were burned in 1978—good spots to see wildlife—and also offers fine views of Longs Peak and Mount Meeker. 5.4 miles RT. Moderate. Access: Wild Basin Ranger Station.

Roger Toll Memorial Trail Named for one of the park's first superintendents, this wheelchair-accessible nature trail has exhibits identifying various tundra plants and animals, and describing how they have adapted to the harsh tundra environment. .5-mile loop. Easy. Access: Near Rock Cut parking area on Trail Ridge Rd.

LONGER TRAILS

East Inlet Trail This trail is an easy walk for the first .3 mile, to scenic Adams Falls. It then wanders along some marshy areas, crosses several streams, and, becoming more strenuous, climbs sharply in elevation to Lone Pine Lake, about 5.5 miles from the trail head. It is another 1.5 miles, partly through a subalpine forest, to Lake Verna. The trail continues, unmaintained, after the lake. Total elevation gain to Lake Verna is 1,809 feet. 13.8 miles RT. Moderate to strenuous. Access: West portal of Adam's Tunnel, southeast of the town of Grand Lake.

East Longs Peak Trail Recommended only for experienced mountain hikers and climbers in top physical condition, this trail climbs 4,855 feet along steep ledges and through a narrows to the top of 14,259-foot Longs Peak, the highest point in the park. The trek takes most hikers about 15 hours to complete and can be done in 1 or 2 days. Those planning a 1-day hike should consider starting extremely early, so they will be well off the peak before the summer afternoon thunderstorms arrive. For a 2-day hike, go 5 or 6 miles the first day, stay at a designated backcountry campsite (a permit is required), and complete the trip the following day. Those making the hike in early summer (usually until mid-July) should be prepared for icy conditions. 16 miles RT. Strenuous. Access: Longs Peak Ranger Station.

Lawn Lake Trail This hike, with an elevation gain of 2,249 feet, follows the Roaring River through terrain dotted with ponderosa pine. Along the way you can see all too plainly the damage done by a massive flood that occurred when the Lawn Lake Dam broke in 1982, killing three campers. At higher elevations, there are scenic views of Mummy Mountain. 12.4 miles RT. Strenuous. Access: Trail head on Fall River Rd.

Lulu City Trail This trail gains just 300 feet in elevation as it winds along the river floodplain, through lush vegetation, past an 1880s mine and several mining cabins, and then along an old stage route into a subalpine forest before arriving at Lulu City. Founded in 1879 by prospectors hoping to strike gold and silver, it was abandoned within 10 years. Little remains except the ruins of a few cabins. An interpretative brochure ($1) is available. 6.2 miles RT. Moderate. Access: Colorado River trail head, near the western park boundary.

Timber Lake Trail You'll work hard on this hike but be amply rewarded with views of timberline lakes and alpine tundra. With an elevation change of 2,060 feet, this hike takes you through a forest of lodgepole pines, follows a creek lined with subalpine wildflowers, and then arrives at the lake, surrounded by rocks, tundra, snow, and a few trees. 9.6 miles RT.

Strenuous. Access: East side of Trail Ridge Rd., a little more than 9½ miles north of the Grand Lake Entrance.

Ute Trail An excellent way to see the tundra, this moderate hike can become fairly easy if you can get a ride to the top and walk down the 3,300-foot descent to Beaver Meadows. The hike down the side of a canyon provides great views. 6 miles one-way. Moderate. Access: Ute Trail turnout on Trail Ridge Rd.

5 Exploring the Backcountry

The park allows numerous opportunities for backpacking and technical climbing, and hikers and climbers will generally find that the farther they go into the backcountry, the fewer humans they see. Some of the day hikes discussed above can also be done as overnight hikes; for example, the East Longs Peak Trail, which takes most people about 15 hours round-trip, is often completed over 2 days. Hikers can also combine various shorter trails to produce loops that can keep them in the park's backcountry for up to a week.

The park has well over 100 small **backcountry campsites,** which may be reserved. Backpackers should carry portable stoves, because wood fires are permitted at only a few sites with metal fire rings. In addition to the designated backcountry campsites, there are two dozen cross-country zones, in some of the least accessible sections of the park, which are recommended only for those with good map and compass skills.

The park's **Backcountry Office** should be the first stop for those planning backpacking trips. Rangers there know the trails and camping areas well and are happy to advise hikers on the best choices for their abilities and expectations. **Backcountry permits** are required for all overnight hikes. Technical climbers who expect to be out overnight usually set up a bivouac—a temporary open-air encampment that is normally at or near the base of a route or on the face of a climb. Designated bivouac zones have been established; **permits** are required.

Backcountry and bivouac permits are available at park headquarters and ranger stations. They cost $20 from May through October and are free from November through April. For information, call ✆ **970/586-1242.**

6 Other Sports & Activities

In addition to the businesses discussed below, **Estes Park Mountain Shop,** 2050 Big Thompson Ave., Estes Park (✆ **866/303-6548** or 970/586-6548; www.estesparkmountainshop.com), sells and rents equipment and has an indoor climbing gym. The company offers fly-fishing and climbing instruction and guided trips in and around the national park. It also offers a kids' outdoor adventure program in half- and full-day sessions.

BIKING As in most national parks, bikes are not permitted on the trails, only established roads. Bicyclists here will, in most cases, share space with motor vehicles along narrow roads with 5% to 7% grades. However, bikers still enjoy the challenge and scenery. A free park brochure provides information on safety, regulations, and suggested routes. One popular 16-mile ride, with plenty of beautiful mountain views, is the **Horseshoe Park/Estes Park Loop.** It goes from Estes Park west on U.S. 34 past Aspenglen Campground and the park's Fall River Entrance, and then back east at the Deer Ridge Junction, following U.S. 36 through the Beaver Meadows Entrance.

Tours, rentals, and repairs are available at **Colorado Bicycling Adventures,** 184 E. Elkhorn Ave., Estes Park (✆ **888/586-4129** or 970/586-4241; www.coloradobicycling.com). Bike rentals range from $18 to $55 for a half-day and $28 to $95 for a full day, depending on the type of bike, which ranges from very basic to absolutely fantastic. The company offers guided downhill trips in the park for about $75 per person (ages 10 and over only), and also leads a variety of free group bike rides in the Estes Park area from May through September (call or check the website for the current schedule).

CLIMBING & MOUNTAINEERING The **Colorado Mountain School,** 341 Moraine Ave., Estes Park, CO 80517 (✆ **800/836-4008,** ext. 3; www.totalclimbing.com), is an AMGA-accredited year-round guide service and the sole concessionaire for technical climbing and instruction in Rocky Mountain National Park. The school offers a wide range of programs. Among those we recommend are the 2-day mountaineering class for $425 and the guided group hike up Longs Peak for $220. The school also offers lodging in a hostel-type setting (see "Where to Stay," below).

CROSS-COUNTRY SKIING & SNOWSHOEING A growing number of people have discovered the joys of exploring the park on cross-country skis and snowshoes, which are conveniently available for rent at area stores (see below) outside the park.

If you're headed into the backcountry for cross-country skiing or snowshoeing, stop by park headquarters for maps, information on where the snow

Especially for Kids

The park offers a variety of special hikes and programs for children, including an especially popular trip to the park's beaver ponds. There are numerous ranger-led programs for kids from 6 to 12 years old covering the park's geology and wildlife through hands-on activities; see the park newspaper for a full schedule. The park's **Junior Ranger Program** lets kids earn badges by completing activities that teach them about the park's plants and animals and environmental concerns. Most of the activities are scheduled during the summer; check on schedules at any park visitor center.

is best, and a free backcountry permit if you plan to stay out overnight. Keep in mind that trails are not groomed. On winter weekends starting in February, rangers often lead guided snowshoe walks on the east side of the park and guided cross-country ski trips on the west side. Participants must supply their own equipment.

Popular winter recreation areas include Bear Lake, south of the Beaver Meadows Entrance. A lesser-known part of the park is Wild Basin, which is south of the park's east entrances, off Colo. 7 about a mile north of the community of Allenspark. A 2-mile road, closed to motor vehicles for the last mile in winter, winds through a subalpine forest to the Wild Basin trail head, which follows a creek to a waterfall, a rustic bridge, and eventually another waterfall. Total distance to the second falls is 2.7 miles. Along the trail, visitors have a good chance of spotting birds such as Clark's nutcrackers, Steller's jays, and the American dipper. On winter weekends, the Colorado Mountain Club often opens a warming hut at the Wild Basin Ranger Station.

Among shops that rent winter gear is **Estes Park Mountain Shop,** 2050 Big Thompson Ave. (© **866/303-6548** or 970/586-6548; www.estespark mountainshop.com), which charges $10 per day for a cross-country ski package and $5 per day for snowshoes.

EDUCATIONAL PROGRAMS The **Rocky Mountain Nature Association** (see "Information," earlier) offers a wide variety of seminars and workshops, lasting from a half-day to 1 full day, to several days. Subjects vary but might include songbirds, flower identification, edible and medicinal herbs, painting, wildlife photography, park animal tracking, and edible mushrooms. Rates are $75 to $100 for full-day programs and $160 and up for multiday programs. There are also kids' programs, including guided children's hikes and other special kids' programs starting at $15.

FISHING Four species of **trout** are fished in the park: brown, rainbow, brook, and cutthroat. Anglers must get a state fishing license and are permitted to use only artificial lures or flies. About a half-dozen lakes and streams, including Bear Lake, are closed to fishing; a free park brochure lists open and closed waters, and gives regulations and other information.

HORSEBACK RIDING Many of the national park's trails are open to horseback riders. Several outfitters provide guided rides inside and outside the park, including a 1-hour ride ($35) and the very popular 2-hour rides ($50). There are also all-day rides ($120, including lunch), plus breakfast and dinner rides and multiday pack trips. Recommended companies include **SK Horses** (www.cowpoke cornercorral.com), which operates **National Park Gateway Stables,** at the Fall River entrance of the national park on U.S. 34 (© **970/586-5269**), and the **Cowpoke Corner Corral,** at Glacier Lodge, 3 miles west of town, 2166 Colo. 66 (© **970/586-5890**). **Hi Country Stables** (www.colorado-horses.com) operates two stables inside the park: **Glacier Creek Stables** (© **970/586-3244**) and **Moraine Park Stables** (© **970/586-2327**).

SNOWMOBILING On the park's west side, a 2-mile section of the North Supply Access Trail is open to snowmobiles. It leads from the park into the adjacent **Arapaho National Forest.** This trail leaves U.S. 34 just north of the Kawuneeche Visitor Center and follows County Roads 491 and 492 west into the forest. Contact park visitor centers for current information.

WILDLIFE VIEWING & BIRD-WATCHING Rocky Mountain National Park is a premier wildlife-viewing area, especially in fall, winter, and spring. Look for large herds of elk in meadows and on mountainsides. During the fall rutting season, park volunteers called the **Rocky Mountain National Park Elk Bugle Corps** are stationed at elk-viewing areas in the evenings to help people get the best views while not disturbing the animals—elk are often just 30 or 40 feet away.

Park visitors also often see mule deer, beavers, coyotes, and river otters. Watch for moose among the willows on the west side of the park. The forests are home to an abundance of songbirds and small mammals; particularly plentiful are gray and Steller's jays, Clark's nutcrackers, chipmunks, and golden-mantled ground squirrels. You also have a chance of seeing bighorn sheep, marmots, pikas, and ptarmigan along Trail Ridge Road. For detailed and current wildlife-viewing information, stop by one of the park's visitor centers and check on the many interpretive programs, such as bird walks.

7 Camping

INSIDE THE PARK

The park has five campgrounds with a total of almost 600 sites, nearly half of them at Moraine Park. Moraine Park and Glacier Basin accept reservations from Memorial Day through early September, and they are strongly recommended, especially on holiday weekends (✆ **800/444-6777** or 518/885-3639; www.recreation.gov). In summer, arrive early if you hope to snare one of the first-come, first-served campsites. Campsites cost $20 per night during the summer or $14 in the off season, when water is turned off. No showers or RV hookups are available. Camping is limited to 3 days at Longs Peak and 7 days at other campgrounds.

NEAR THE PARK

THE EAST SIDE

Choices on the east side include the **Estes Park KOA,** 2051 Big Thompson Ave., Estes Park, CO 80517 (✆ **800/562-1887** for reservations, or 970/586-2888; www.estesparkkoa.com), 1 mile east of Estes Park on U.S. 34. Scenically located across the street from Lake Estes and within walking distance of the Big Thompson River, this KOA lacks a swimming pool but has cable-TV hookups, a basketball court, and a game room. In addition to the campsites, there are camping cabins ($55–$77 double) and cottages with kitchens and bathrooms ($105–$145 double). There are fire pits in the tent and cabin areas, but not at RV sites.

The most luxurious camping is at **Spruce Lake R.V. Park,** 1050 Mary's Lake Rd., Estes Park, CO 80517 (✆ **800/536-1050** or 970/586-2889; www.sprucelakerv.com), about a mile west of the intersection of U.S. 34 and Business U.S. 36. Here you'll be pampered with miniature golf, a heated swimming pool, a playground, a stocked private fishing lake (fee), large sites, cable TV hookups, and scheduled activities such as ice-cream socials. Fully equipped cabins that sleep up to eight are available ($130–$175). Ground tents are not permitted.

Two **Roosevelt National Forest** campgrounds lie within easy driving distance of the park's east entrances: **Olive Ridge,** 15 miles south of Estes Park along Colo. 7, has pleasant, shady, well-spaced sites and an amphitheater. A less developed campground, for those who carry their own drinking water, is **Meeker Park Overflow,** about 12 miles south of Estes Park on Colo. 7. Both campgrounds have vault toilets.

Campground	Elev.	Total Sites	RV Hookups	Dump Station	Toilets
Inside the Park					
Aspenglen	8,220	54	0	No	Yes
Glacier Basin	8,500	150	0	Yes	Yes
Longs Peak	9,405	26	0	No	Yes
Moraine Park	8,160	245	0	Yes	Yes
Timber Creek	8,900	98	0	Yes	Yes
Near the Park's East Side					
Estes Park KOA	7,500	62	62	Yes	Yes
Meeker Park	8,600	29	0	No	Yes
Olive Ridge	8,350	55	0	No	Yes
Spruce Lake RV Park	7,622	110	110	Yes	Yes
Near the Park's West Side					
Elk Creek	8,400	80	50	Yes	Yes
Green Ridge	8,500	78	0	Yes	Yes
Stillwater	8,350	129	20	Yes	Yes
Willow Creek	8,130	33	0	No	Yes
Winding River	8,672	150	98	Yes	Yes

In Estes Park, a **U.S. Forest Service Information Center** is at 161 Second St. (© **970/586-3440**); it's usually open daily in summer. For year-round information, contact the **Forest Service Information Center,** 2150 Centre Ave., Building E, Fort Collins, CO 80526-8119 (© **970/295-6700;** www.fs.fed.us/r2).

For reservations at Olive Ridge Campground only, contact the National Recreation Reservation Service (© **877/444-6777;** www.recreation.gov).

THE WEST SIDE

Covering more than 36,000 acres along the western edge of Rocky Mountain National Park in Arapaho National Forest, the **Arapaho National Recreation Area** (www.fs.fed.us/r2/arnf/recreation/anra/index.shtml) contains excellent fishing lakes (several with boat ramps) and opportunities for hiking, mountain biking, cross-country skiing, snowshoeing, snowmobiling, hunting, and camping. The recreation area has an entrance fee, in addition to camping fees, of $5 for 1 day, $10 for 3 days, and $15 for 1 week.

The recreation area's campgrounds offer shaded campsites plus picnic tables and fire pits. The most developed site, **Stillwater Campground,** is off U.S. 34 on the west bank of Lake Granby, about 7 miles south of Grand Lake. Stillwater has showers plus water and electric hookups, available only in summer; a limited number of sites are open in winter, when water is turned off.

Also in the Arapaho National Recreation Area, south of Grand Lake, are **Green Ridge Campground** (about 4 miles south on U.S. 34, then 1 mile south on C.R. 66), which lost most of its surrounding forest to pine beetles; and **Willow Creek** (about 10 miles south on U.S. 34, then about 4 miles west on C.R. 40). All three are on lakes with fishing and boat ramps. For information on both the forest and the recreation area, contact the **Sulphur Ranger District Office,** 9 Ten Mile Dr. (P.O. Box 10), Granby, CO 80446 (© **970/887-4100**). You can also obtain information from the **Forest Service Information Center,** 2150 Centre Ave., Building E, Fort Collins, CO 80526-8119 (© **970/295-6700;** www.fs.fed.us/r2). Campsite reservations (Stillwater and Green Ridge only) are available from the **National Recreation Reservation Service** (© **887/444-6777;** www.recreation.gov).

Several commercial campgrounds in the community of Grand Lake, just outside the park's west entrance, combine modern conveniences with a forest-camping atmosphere. **Elk Creek Campground,** Box 549, Grand Lake, CO 80447 (© **800/355-2733** or 970/627-8502; www.elkcreekcamp.com), is on Golf Course Road, off U.S. 34 on the north side of the village. It has tent and RV sites in a wooded setting, a pond with license-free trout fishing (there is a per-fish charge), a playground, a game room, and a convenience store. There are also 10 log cabins ($60 double). **Winding River Resort,** P.O. Box 629, Grand Lake, CO 80447 (© **800/282-5121,** 970/627-3215, 303/623-1121; www.windingriverresort.com), also offers forest camping, with hot showers, full RV hookups, and all the other

Drinking Water	Showers	Fire Pits/ Grills	Laundry	Reserve	Fees	Open
Yes	No	Yes	No	No	$20	Mid-May to mid-Sept
Yes	No	Yes	No	Yes	$20	Late May to mid-Sept
Yes	No	Yes	No	No	$14–$20	Year-round
Yes	No	Yes	No	Yes	$14–$20	Year-round
Yes	No	Yes	No	No	$14–$20	Year-round
Yes	Yes	No	Yes	Yes	$25–$51	May to mid-Oct
No	No	Yes	No	No	$9	Early June to Labor Day
Yes	No	Yes	No	Yes	$17–$20	Mid-May to late Sept
Yes	Yes	Yes	Yes	Yes	$40–$50	Apr–Sept
Yes	Yes	Yes	Yes	Yes	$26–$40	May –Oct
Yes	No	Yes	No	Yes	$17–$48	May–Oct
Yes	Yes	Yes	No	Yes	$20–$36	Year-round
Yes	No	Yes	No	No	$17	Memorial Day to mid-Oct
Yes	Yes	Yes	Yes	Yes	$29–$40	Mid-May to Sept

amenities of a commercial campground. In addition, Winding River has wireless Internet access, plus an abundance of activities, ranging from horseshoes to horseback riding, plus hayrides, ice-cream socials, and chuckwagon breakfasts. There's also a petting zoo. In addition to campsites, you can rent a camping cabin, which shares the campground's bathhouse ($50), plus there are full cabins, with their own bathrooms and all the amenities ($140–$220), and lodge units ($90–$115). From Grand Lake, head north on U.S. 34 about 1½ miles, turn left onto County Road 491 (across from the Kawuneeche Visitor Center), and continue 1½ miles to the resort.

8 Where to Stay

There is no lodging inside the park.

ESTES PARK AREA (EAST SIDE OF THE NATIONAL PARK)

For help in finding accommodations in and around Estes Park, contact the **Estes Park Convention and Visitors Bureau** (✆ **800/443-7837;** www.estesparkcvb.com). Among the independent motels, we especially like the **Saddle and Surrey Motel,** 1341 S. St. Vrain Ave., Estes Park, CO 80517 (✆ **970/586-3326;** www.saddleandsurrey.com), which has a pleasant indoor heated pool and rates of $90 to $150 double in summer and $55 to $85 at other times.

Chains in Estes Park include the **Best Western Silver Saddle,** 1260 Big Thompson Ave. (U.S. 34), Estes Park, CO 80517 (✆ **970/586-4476**), with rates of $99 to $259 double from June to mid-September, $79 to $199 double during of the rest of year; **Comfort Inn,** 1450 Big Thompson Ave., Estes Park, CO 80517 (✆ **970/586-2358**), charging $109 to $249 double in summer, $69 to $199 double during the rest of the year; and **Travelodge,** 1220 Big Thompson Ave., Estes Park, CO 80517 (✆ **970/586-4421**), charging $119 to $229 double in summer, $75 to $110 double during the rest of the year. Many campgrounds in Estes Park also offer cabin rentals (see "Camping," above).

Allenspark Lodge Bed & Breakfast We enjoy the historic ambience of this three-story lodge, built in 1933 of native stone and hand-hewn ponderosa pine logs. The lodge is 16 miles south of Estes Park at the southeast corner of the national park, not far from the Wild Basin Unit, and all rooms offer mountain views and original handmade 1930s pine furniture. Guests share the Great Room and its stone fireplace, games, puzzles, and videos in the recreation room, and books in the library. Rates include afternoon and evening coffee, tea, and cookies. Also available is The Apartment, with sleeping space for four at $150. The lodge has a hot tub, conference rooms, an espresso **coffee shop,** and a **wine and beer bar.** There are no in-room phones.

184 Main St., Colo. 7 Business Loop (P.O. Box 247), Allenspark, CO 80510. ✆ **303/747-2552.** www.allensparklodge.com. 13 units, 7 with bathroom. $95–$125 double. Rates include full breakfast. AE, DISC, MC, V. Children 13 and under not accepted.

Alpine Trail Ridge Inn This top-notch independent motel, next to the entrance to Rocky Mountain National Park, offers nicely maintained rooms, many with private balconies, with basic Western decor and plenty of functionality. There are rooms with kings and queens, two doubles, as well as a few two-room family units. Longtime managers Jay and Fran Grooters are also great sources for hiking advice—Fran's **Trail Tracks** (www.trailtracks.com) publishes excellent 3-D hiking maps of Rocky Mountain National Park and other hiking meccas. All units have refrigerators, coffeemakers, and hair dryers, and some have microwaves. The property also has free Wi-Fi; a restaurant, **The Sundeck** (American), serving three meals daily; and an outdoor heated pool. All units are nonsmoking.

927 Moraine Ave., Estes Park, CO 80517. ✆ **800/223-5023** or 970/586-4585. Fax 970/586-6249. www.alpinetrailridgeinn.com. 48 units. A/C, TV, TEL. Summer $70–$129 double; $130–$192 family unit. Closed mid-Oct through Apr. AE, DC, DISC, MC, V.

Baldpate Inn This is a good choice for those who seek an old-fashioned, historic lodge experience. Located 7 miles south of Estes Park, the Baldpate was built in 1917 and named for the novel *Seven Keys to Baldpate,* a murder mystery in which seven visitors believe each possesses the only key to the hotel. Guests can watch several movie versions of the story, read the book, and contribute to the hotel's collection of some 25,000 keys. Guests can also enjoy complimentary refreshments or use the free Wi-Fi network by the stone fireplace in the lobby, relax on the large sun deck, or view free videos on the library VCR or DVD player. But it might be difficult to stay inside once you experience the spectacular views from the inn's porch and see the nature trails beckoning. Each of the early-20th-century-style rooms is unique, with handmade quilts on the beds. Several of the rooms are a bit small, and although most of the lodge rooms share bathrooms (five bathrooms for nine units), each room does have its own sink. Among our favorites are the Mae West Room (yes, she was a guest here), with a red claw-foot tub and wonderful views of the valley; and the Pinetop Cabin, which has a whirlpool tub, canopy bed, and gas fireplace. In summer, an excellent **soup-and-salad buffet** is served for lunch and dinner daily (see "Where to Dine," below). Smoking is not permitted.

4900 S. Colo. 7 (P.O. Box 700), Estes Park, CO 80517. ✆ **866/577-5397** or 970/586-6151. www.baldpateinn.com. 14 units, 5 with bathroom; 4 cabins. $110 double with shared bathroom; $135 double with private bathroom; $200–$260 cabin. Rates include full breakfast. DISC, MC, V. Closed mid-Oct to Memorial Day weekend.

Boulder Brook on Fall River It would be hard to find a more beautiful setting for a lodging than this. Surrounded by tall pines, all suites face the Fall River, and all feature private riverfront decks and full or partial kitchens, Wi-Fi, hair dryers, and irons. The spa suites have two-person spas, fireplaces, sitting rooms with cathedral ceilings, and king-size beds. One-bedroom suites offer king-size beds, window seats, two TVs, and bathrooms with a whirlpool tub/showers. There's also a year-round outdoor hot tub. DVD/VCR combos and a large free video library are available, and special-occasion packages can be arranged year-round.

1900 Fall River Rd., Estes Park, CO 80517. ✆ **800/238-0910** or 970/586-0910. Fax 970/586-8067. www.boulderbrook.com. 19 units. TV, TEL. $119–$239 double. AE, DISC, MC, V.

Estes Park Center/YMCA of the Rockies This popular family resort is an ideal place to get away from it all. It makes a great home base while exploring the Estes Park area. Lodge units are simply decorated and perfectly adequate, but we prefer the spacious mountain cabins. They have two to four bedrooms (accommodating up to 10) and complete kitchens, and some have fireplaces. The center, which occupies 860 wooded acres, offers hiking, horseback riding, miniature golf, an indoor heated pool and children's pool, fishing, bicycle rentals, three tennis courts, and cross-country skiing. Other facilities include a self-serve laundry.

2515 Tunnel Rd., Estes Park, CO 80511-2550. ✆ **970/586-3341** or 303/448-1616 direct from Denver. Fax 970/586-6078. www.ymcarockies.org. 510 lodge rooms, 450 with bathroom; 205 cabins. Summer lodge rooms $99–$164, cabins $119–$364; winter lodge rooms $74–$109, cabins $99–$79. $10 nightly discount for YMCA membership. No credit cards. Pets are permitted in the cabins, but not the lodge rooms ($10 per night).

Lane Guest Ranch Lloyd Lane opened his guest ranch south of Estes Park in 1953 and built it into a great family resort with a focus on the great outdoors. For this, its location on 30 acres abutting Roosevelt National Forest and Rocky Mountain National Park is ideal. The calendar is pretty packed here, with activities ranging from guided hiking to silversmithing classes, and entertainment ranging from bingo to magic. The horseback rides run the gamut from standard trail rides to wine-and-cheese rides, overnight rides, and even a shopping-oriented ride! All meals are included, with nightly specials and a standard menu. The cabins here accommodate families up to six, complete with bunk beds, stocked fridges, and knotty pine furnishings. There is also the Doctor's House, a large house that accommodates up to 14.

South of Estes Park via Colo. 7 (P.O. Box 1766), Estes Park, CO 80517. ✆ **303/747-2493.** www.laneguestranch.com. 25 cabins. $182 per adult per night; $147 per child 7–11 per night; children 6 and under free without child care. Rates include all meals and activities. 3-night minimum. MC, V. Closed late Aug to mid-June. Pets accepted.

The Lodge at Colorado Mountain School This is lodging at its simplest: coed dormitory-style rooms furnished in light woods, clean and well maintained, with bunk beds, showers, and lockable private storage. Total Climbing also offers a year-round guide service and rock-climbing and mountaineering school (see "Climbing & Mountaineering," above).

341 Moraine Ave., Estes Park, CO 80517. ✆ **800/836-4008,** ext. 3. www.totalclimbing.com. 16 dormitory beds. Summer $35 per bed; winter $25 per bed. AE, DISC, MC, V. Closed Oct–mid-Dec. Office 8am–5pm (until 6pm on weekends).

McGregor Mountain Lodge A top midpriced choice on the east side of Rocky Mountain National Park, this smallish, spread-out property is a stone's throw from the park boundary at the foot of McGregor Mountain, a favorite hangout for bighorn sheep. With efficiencies, cottages, and one- and two-bedroom suites, the 19 rooms here are diverse and uniformly well maintained, and the place has a homey, faraway feel, despite its location off one of the area's main thoroughfares. There's an indoor hot tub and outdoor playground, and all units have kitchens and Wi-Fi. Many of the rooms have jetted tubs and balconies—all of them are great spots to unwind. The entire lodge is nonsmoking.

2815 Fall River Rd., Estes Park, CO 80517. ✆ **800/835-8439** or 970/586-3457. Fax 970/586-4040. www.mcgregormountainlodge.com. 19 units, including 15 cottages and suites. Early June to mid-Aug $142 double, $175–$340 cottage or suite; rest of year $95–$128 double, $109–$281 cottage or suite. DISC, MC, V.

Romantic RiverSong Inn Couples looking for some quiet romance while visiting Rocky Mountain National Park will enjoy this 1920 Craftsman mansion on the Big Thompson River. Owned and operated since 1986 by Gary and Sue Mansfield, the secluded and elegant bed-and-breakfast has 27 forested acres with hiking trails and a trout pond, as well as prolific wildlife and beautiful wildflowers. The comfortable rooms are decorated with a blend of antique and modern country furniture. All have tubs with separate showers and fireplaces, some have refrigerators, and many have jetted tubs for two. Gourmet candlelight dinners ($124 per couple) are available by advance arrangement, but you must supply your own alcoholic beverages. Breakfasts are often Southwestern, and the house specialty is Mountain Man Stuffed French Toast, stuffed with thin-sliced sausage and Muenster cheese. Although we can't imagine why you would want it, Wi-Fi is available. Smoking is not permitted.

1765 Lower Broadview Rd. (P.O. Box 1910), Estes Park, CO 80517. ✆ **970/586-4666.** Fax 970/577-1336. www.romanticriversong.com. 10 units. $165–$350 double. Rates include full breakfast. DISC, MC, V. Not suitable for small children.

Stanley Hotel Fans of the automotive, the historic, and the horrific should check out this hotel. F. O. Stanley, inventor of the Stanley Steam Car (the Stanley Steamer), built the elegant hotel in 1909, and it inspired Stephen King to write *The Shining* 6 decades later. The equal of European resorts the day it opened, the Stanley was constructed in solid rock at an elevation of 7,800 feet on the eastern slope of the Colorado Rockies. Today the hotel and its grounds are listed on the National Register of Historic Places as the Stanley Historic District. Each room differs in size and shape, offering a variety of views of Longs Peak and Lake Estes, and the most expensive rooms are allegedly haunted. All have free Wi-Fi access. There are several new lavish one- to three-bedroom condo units, but we prefer the deluxe rooms in the front of the building, with views of the park. There is a **spa,** a **restaurant,** an outdoor heated pool, a tennis court, and an exercise room.

333 Wonderview Ave. (P.O. Box 1767), Estes Park, CO 80517. ✆ **800/976-1377** or 970/586-3371. Fax 970/586-3673. www.stanleyhotel.com. 140 units. TV, TEL. $159–$479 double; $249–$369 suite; $400–$600 condominium; $1,500 presidential cottage. AE, DISC, MC, V.

GRAND LAKE AREA (WEST SIDE OF THE NATIONAL PARK)

For a complete listing of lodging and dining choices in the Grand Lake Area, contact the **Grand Lake Area Chamber of Commerce,** P.O. Box 429, Grand Lake, CO 80447 (✆ **800/531-1019** or 970/627-3402; www.grandlakechamber.com).

Black Bear Lodge Located 3 miles south of town across from Shadow Mountain Lake, this comfortable and well-maintained establishment is a great bet if you're looking for an attractive motel with Western ambience. Some units have two rooms, and some have kitchenettes. Of the 17 units, eight of the bathrooms have showers only; the rest have a tub/shower. The property has a small heated outdoor pool, a sauna, two whirlpools (indoors and outdoors), free Wi-Fi in the lobby, and a playground. All units are nonsmoking.

12255 U.S. 34 (P.O. Box 609), Grand Lake, CO 80447. ✆ **800/766-1123** or 970/627-3654. www.blackbeargrandlake.com. 17 units. TV, TEL. $88–$175 double. AE, MC, V.

Daven Haven Lodge Set among pine trees about 1 block from the lake, this group of cabins is a good choice for those seeking peace and quiet in a secluded mountain resort–type setting. There's a welcoming stone fireplace in the lobby plus old Coke machines, a friendly dog named Buddie, and several antique jukeboxes—they actually play 78 rpm records! The cabins vary in size, some sleeping as many as eight people; each has a kitchen and its own picnic table, and several have stone fireplaces. Decor and furnishings vary, but most have attractive light-wood walls and both solid-wood and upholstered furniture. You'll also find a lovely patio, volleyball court, horseshoes, and bonfire pit. The **Backstreet Steakhouse** (see "Where to Dine," below) serves dinner nightly in summer and 4 nights a week in winter. All cabins are nonsmoking; most have free Wi-Fi. Under the same ownership is **Wildwood Cabins** (www.wildwoodcabins.com).

604 Marina Dr. (P.O. Box 1528), Grand Lake, CO 80447. ✆ **970/627-8144.** Fax 970/627-5098. www.davenhavenlodge.com. 12 cabins. TV. Mid-June to Sept and Christmas holiday season $127–$226; other times $94–$182. DISC, MC, V. 3-night minimum required on reservations during holidays. Pets accepted in one cabin only ($15 per night).

The Inn at Grand Lake For modern lodging with an Old West feel, stay at this restored historic building, originally constructed in 1881 as Grand Lake's courthouse and jail. Rooms have a variety of bed combinations, and several sleep up to six. They're equipped with Western-style furniture, ceiling fans, white stucco walls, and Indian-motif draperies and bedspreads, and they have coffeemakers and hair dryers. Many of the units have refrigerators and microwaves; some have kitchenettes. The best views are on the street side of the building. The inn is located in the center of town, about a half-block from the lake. The **Sagebrush BBQ & Grill** (see "Where to Dine," below) serves three meals daily. All units are nonsmoking.

1103 Grand Ave. (P.O. Box 2087), Grand Lake, CO 80447. ✆ **800/722-2585** or 970/627-9234. Fax 970/627-2483. www.innatgrandlake.com. 10 units. TV, TEL. $85–$155 double; $125–$170 suite. AE, DISC, MC, V.

9 Where to Dine

There are no dining facilities inside the park.

ESTES PARK AREA (EAST SIDE OF THE NATIONAL PARK)

In addition to the restaurants described here, we like **Bob & Tony's Pizza,** 124 W. Elkhorn Ave. (✆ **970/586-2044**), a busy pizza joint with redbrick walls covered with chalk signatures.

Baldpate Inn AMERICAN Don't be misled by the simple cuisine—the buffet is delicious and plentiful. Everything is freshly prepared on the premises, with the cooks barely staying one muffin ahead of the guests. Soups—a choice of two is offered each day—include hearty stews, chili, chicken rice, garden vegetable, and classic French onion. The salad bar provides fresh greens and an array of toppings, chunks of cheese, and fruit and vegetable salads. Honey-wheat bread is a staple, plus rolls, muffins, and corn bread. Topping off the meal are fresh homemade pies and cappuccino.

4900 S. Colo. 7. ✆ **970/586-6151.** www.baldpateinn.com. Reservations recommended. Buffet $14 adults, $6 children 9 and under. DISC, MC, V. Memorial Day to Aug daily 11:30am–8pm. Shorter hours Sept to mid-Oct; closed the rest of the year.

The Dunraven Inn ITALIAN This is a great spot to celebrate a special occasion in an intimate setting, but not so fancy that you wouldn't want to take the (well-behaved) kids. The decor is eclectic, to say the least: Images of the *Mona Lisa* are scattered about, ranging from a mustachioed lady to opera posters, and autographed dollar bills are posted in the lounge area. House specialties include shrimp scampi, lasagna, and, our favorite, the Dunraven Italiano (a 10-oz. charbroiled sirloin steak in a sauce of peppers, onions, and tomatoes). There's a wide choice of pastas, fresh seafood, vegetarian plates, and desserts, plus a children's menu. The full bar is well stocked and the wine list reasonably priced.

2470 Colo. 66. ✆ **970/586-6409.** Reservations recommended. Main courses $8–$40. AE, DISC, MC, V. Daily 5–10pm; closes slightly earlier in winter.

The Egg & I AMERICAN A bright and cheery place to start your day, the Egg & I is decorated in warm earth tones, with magnificent views of the Rocky Mountains. Breakfast is available at any time, ranging from fried eggs to several variations of eggs Benedict, omelets, frittatas, crepes, skillet meals—and we do mean meals—plus pancakes and French toast. Those not opting for breakfast can choose among a variety of sandwiches, such as the Veggie Greek Wrap, with sun-dried tomatoes, artichoke hearts, spinach, and other veggies in a tomato tortilla. Soups and a number of salads are also available, and there is takeout.

393 E. Elkhorn at the corner of U.S. Hwys. 34 and 36. ✆ **970/586-1173.** Main courses $5–$9. AE, DISC, MC, V. Summer Mon–Sat 6am–2pm, Sun 7am–2pm; winter daily 7am–2pm.

Grumpy Gringo MEXICAN Dine in style at this classy Mexican restaurant without breaking the bank. The private booths, whitewashed plaster walls, green plants, bright poppies, and a few choice sculptures provide a posh atmosphere. And although the food is excellent and portions large, the prices are surprisingly low. Our choice here is a burrito, but which one to choose? Besides burritos, we recommend the huge Enchilada Olé. It's actually three enchiladas: one each of cheese, beef, and chicken. The fajitas (chicken or beef) are delicious. Diners choose from six homemade sauces, rated mild, semihot, or hot. Burgers and sandwiches are also available, as are several inexpensive lighter options. The house specialty drink is the Gringo Margarita, made with Sauza Gold tequila from an original (and secret) recipe.

1560 Big Thompson Ave. (U.S. 34). ✆ **970/586-7705.** www.grumpygringo.com. Main courses $5–$20. AE, DISC, MC, V. Summer daily 11am–10pm; shorter hours in winter. On U.S. 34, 1 mile east of the junction of U.S. Hwys. 34 and 36.

Poppy's ITALIAN/AMERICAN This bright, pleasant, and casual eatery right on the Big Thompson River serves up a menu of gourmet pizzas, sandwiches, and entree salads, and also has a good soup and salad bar. You can sit in its family-friendly room with hints of the West or on the great riverfront patio. We're partial to some of the Mexican-accented dishes, like the enchilada pizza or the green chile cheeseburger, not to mention the "Adult Italian Sodas," sweet and fizzy drinks that pack a mild punch.

342 E. Elkhorn Ave. (on the Riverwalk in Barlow Plaza). ✆ **970/586-8282.** www.poppyspizzaandgrill.com. Main courses $6–$11, pizzas $6–$27. AE, DISC, MC, V. Summer daily 11am–9pm; rest of year daily 11am–8pm.

The View STEAK/SEAFOOD While the restaurant is named for the picture-perfect panorama of the town and surrounding mountains, the food is also terrific. Chef Russell Stephens shows an inventive eye for detail with such dishes as the walnut-crusted rainbow trout, served with garlic mashers and a grapefruit beurre blanc sauce, and a pan-seared rib-eye with garlic–blue cheese crust and merlot sauce. The atmosphere is woodsy but refined, with hardwood floors and red-and-white checkered tablecloths, and there is often jazz or a Celtic guitarist.

At Historic Crags Lodge, 300 Riverside Dr. ✆ **970/586-6066.** Reservations recommended. Main courses $15–$23. AE, MC, V. Daily 5–9pm. Closed mid-Oct to mid-May.

GRAND LAKE AREA (WEST SIDE OF THE NATIONAL PARK)

Backstreet Steakhouse STEAKS This cozy, country inn–style restaurant in the Daven Haven Lodge (see above) offers fine dining in a down-home atmosphere. Steaks—from the 9-ounce filet mignon to the 12-ounce New York strip—are all USDA choice beef. The house specialty, Jack Daniel's pork chops (breaded, baked, and served with a creamy Jack Daniel's mushroom sauce), has been featured in *Bon Appétit* magazine. Also on the menu are pasta, chicken, and fish dishes, plus slow-roasted prime rib and children's items. Sandwiches and light entrees, such as smoked salmon and a wild game sausage platter, are served in the lounge. There is also a covered garden patio.

In the Daven Haven Lodge, 604 Marina Dr. ✆ **970/627-8144.** www.davenhavenlodge.com. Reservations recommended in summer and on winter weekends. Main courses in the dining room $16–$36, lounge menu $7–$16. DISC, MC, V. Summer and Christmas holidays daily 4:30–9:30pm; winter Thurs and Sun 4:30–8pm, Fri–Sat 4:30–9pm.

Sagebrush BBQ & Grill AMERICAN Come here to enjoy excellent barbecue, plus steaks, sandwiches, and seafood, in a historic building that also houses The Inn at Grand Lake. The atmosphere here is definitely Wild West, complete with Grand Lake's original jail doors, and so casual that you're encouraged to munch on peanuts and throw the shells on the floor. The specialty here is barbecue—try the super-tender fall-off-the-bone pork ribs—but we also suggest the New York strip steak, pan-fried rainbow trout, and elk medallions served with roasted raspberry chipotle sauce. Another good choice is the burrito—pork, chicken, or vegetarian—served with refried beans, green chiles, cheese, tomato, and lettuce.

1101 Grand Ave. ✆ **970/627-1404.** www.sagebrushbbq.com. Main courses lunch and dinner $6–$22. AE, DISC, MC, V. Sun–Thurs 7am–9pm; Fri–Sat 7am–10pm.

10 Picnic & Camping Supplies

The **Country Supermarket,** 900 Moraine Ave., Estes Park (✆ **970/586-2702**), is less than a mile from the Beaver Meadows entrance to the park in a small shopping center. Outside the Fall River Entrance Station, adjacent to the Fall River Visitor Center, **Rocky Mountain Gateway,** 3450 Fall River Rd. (✆ **970/577-0043;** www.rockymountaingateway.net), has a large gift shop and a convenience store with groceries, camping supplies, and clothing.

Those looking for top-quality camping and outdoor sports equipment should stop at **Outdoor World,** downtown at 156 E. Elkhorn Ave. (✆ **800/679-3600** or 970/586-2114; www.rmconnection.com), or **Estes Park Mountain Shop,** 2050 Big Thompson Ave. (✆ **866/303-6548** or 970/586-6548; www.estesparkmountainshop.com), which also has a rental department.

In Grand Lake, on the park's west side, the **Mountain Food Market,** 400 Grand Ave. (✆ **970/627-3470**), and the **Circle D,** 701 Grand Ave. (✆ **970/627-3210**), have good selections of groceries and picnic supplies. You can get fishing supplies and almost anything else you might need at **Lakeview General Store,** 14626 U.S. 34 (✆ **970/627-3479**).

31

Saguaro National Park, AZ

by Eric Peterson

The stately saguaro cactus, symbol of the American Southwest, is the king here, dominating the entire landscape. Although Saguaro National Park preserves a sizable chunk of the Sonoran Desert, it is one of America's few national parks dedicated to protecting one plant. Saguaros are plants with personalities. They often look human, standing tall and proud, their arms reaching toward the sky or pointing the way. Though some achieve heights of 50 feet and weigh up to 8 tons, saguaros grow slowly. It usually takes them 15 years to reach 1 foot in height, and they don't flower or produce fruit until they're about 30. They take about 100 years to reach a height of 25 feet. Their maximum life span is about 200 years.

One of the hottest and driest parts of North America, the Sonoran Desert has an amazing variety of life, more than any other desert on the continent. Although the saguaro forests dominate the horizon—and are consequently the first thing we notice here—this desert is home to dozens of other cacti, grasses, shrubs, flowers, and trees, as well as several hundred species of birds, mammals, and reptiles. Many of them are uniquely adapted to the demanding environment of this dry land. For instance, javelinas, those odd-looking piglike animals, have mouths so tough they can bite through prickly pear cactus pads in search of moisture, and kangaroo rats never need to drink—they extract all the water they need from seeds.

The park consists of two separate sections. The **Tucson Mountain District,** also called Saguaro West, covers 32 square miles of Sonoran Desert west of Tucson; the **Rincon Mountain District,** also called Saguaro East, covers 104 square miles of saguaro forest, desert, foothills, and mountain terrain on the east side of Tucson. The two sections are about 30 miles apart.

Both districts have scenic drives and trails, with good wildlife viewing and bird-watching. When the spring rain cooperates, there are also spectacular shows of wildflowers and cactus blooms.

AVOIDING THE CROWDS

Besides the two million commuters passing through the park every year, annual recreational visitation is about 750,000 people, with Saguaro West receiving the greater number. The park's busiest time is from Christmas through Easter. Those wanting to avoid crowds should visit at other times, although visitors who plan on hiking will want to avoid summer's extreme heat. Fall through mid-December can offer the best of both worlds: fewer crowds and lower temperatures.

Another way to avoid crowds, even at the busiest times, is to hike. Although the park gets a lot of visitors at busy times, many confine their activities to scenic drives and short walks. Within 15 minutes, you can easily leave the crowds behind.

1 Essentials

GETTING THERE & GATEWAYS

Saguaro National Park is in southern Arizona on the fringes of **Tucson,** about 116 miles southeast of Phoenix. There are two parts to the park: the **Rincon Mountain District (Saguaro East)** and the **Tucson Mountain District (Saguaro West),** each about 15 miles from downtown Tucson. To get to Saguaro East from Tucson, head east on Broadway Boulevard and turn right on **Old Spanish Trail,** which meanders southeast to the park. Watch for signs for the park as you go.

To get to Saguaro West from Tucson, go west on **Speedway Boulevard,** which first becomes Gates Pass Road and then ends at Kinney Road, where you turn right and continue to the park entrance.

From Phoenix, follow **I-10** toward Tucson and watch for signs directing you to the park.

THE NEAREST AIRPORT Tucson International Airport (© **520/573-8000;** www.tucsonairport.org) is served by most major airlines and all major car-rental agencies. See chapter 38 for website listings.

INFORMATION

Contact **Saguaro National Park,** 3693 S. Old Spanish Trail, Tucson, AZ 85730-5601 (© **520/733-5100;** www.nps.gov/sagu). Information is also

Tips from a Park Ranger

For those who have not experienced the Southwest's deserts, and particularly the Sonoran Desert of southern Arizona, Saguaro National Park can be an unusual experience, according to Tom Danton, the park's former chief of interpretation.

"Many visitors are petrified," he says. "It's essential they stop at the **visitor center** to learn about the park before going out into it." The park environment, with its extreme heat and forests of saguaro, is alien to most people's experiences. Visitors can be more frightened when they learn there are rattlesnakes, Gila monsters, and other poisonous creatures.

Among his suggestions for enjoying Saguaro West are hiking the 5.5-mile **Hugh Norris Trail.** "Within 30 minutes you feel like you're on the top of the world," he says. "You get a tremendous sense of accomplishment." For those with less ambition or time, he suggests the short Valley View Overlook Trail and the Desert Discovery Nature Trail, both also in the western district.

On the east side, he suggests the easy Freeman Homestead Trail, which passes by the site of a historic homestead, and the challenging Tanque Verde Ridge Trail, which, he says, is "steep and rugged, but gives you great views of Tucson and the mountains." To really be alone, he recommends trying some of the backcountry trails, where you'll be hiking from desert up into forests of Douglas fir and ponderosa pine.

The prettiest time at the park is spring, when the wildflowers and cacti are in bloom, but Danton says he would visit in midwinter, when the weather is best for hiking. In winter there are also many interpretive programs, such as moonlight walks, and you seldom see any poisonous reptiles.

Danton says that one problem for visitors going to Saguaro East is the lack of parking, even at the visitor center. He suggests that those with recreational vehicles use a smaller vehicle in the park, if they have one, or check with rangers about where to park their big rigs. At the pullouts just inside the Cactus Forest Drive, RVs can be parked when there's no room in the parking lot.

available at the website of the **Friends of Saguaro National Park,** 2700 N. Kinney Rd., Tucson, AZ 85743 (✆ **520/733-8610;** www.friendsofsaguaro.org). For information on other area attractions and services, contact the **Metropolitan Tucson Convention & Visitors Bureau,** 100 S. Church Ave., Tucson, AZ 85701 (✆ **800/638-8350** or 520/624-1817; www.visittucson.org).

Those particularly interested in the plants, animals, and geology of the park can get additional information from *Saguaro National Park* by Doris Evans and Sandra Scott, published in 2005 by the Southwest Parks and Monuments Association.

If you're spending more time in the Tucson area or looking to explore other parks in Arizona, we also recommend *Frommer's Arizona*, by Karl Samson, which includes chapters on Tucson, Phoenix, and all the major national and state parks, from the Four Corners area to the Grand Canyon.

VISITOR CENTERS

The park has two visitor centers, one in each district. Both visitor centers are open daily from 9am to 5pm (closed Dec 25). The park is open daily 7am until sunset.

On the west side of the park, in the Tucson Mountain District, the **Red Hills Visitor Center** (✆ **520/733-5158**) has a museum, an information desk, and a bookstore. The museum offers exhibits on desert life and a 15-minute program on the uniqueness and importance of deserts.

On the park's east side, in the Rincon Mountain District, the **visitor center** (✆ **520/733-5153**) has similar facilities on a smaller scale. There's an excellent 15-minute video on the flora and fauna of the park, and exhibits on saguaro and deserts.

FEES & PERMITS

Entry to the park (either side or both) costs $10 per private vehicle, or $5 per person on foot or bike. Permits for **backcountry camping** cost $6 per campsite per night and can be obtained in advance by writing the park, or at the Rincon Mountain District Visitor Center after arrival.

SPECIAL REGULATIONS & WARNINGS

Extreme heat, cactus spines, and poisonous reptiles are the main safety hazards here. Temperatures that soar to 115°F (46°C) in summer make hiking not only uncomfortable, but also often dangerous. Those who insist on hiking in the hot months can minimize the dangers by starting very early in the day, perhaps by 4am, and getting off the trails by noon. Hikers should carry plenty of water and drink it even if they do not feel thirsty.

Cactus spines can be very painful, as anyone who's backed into one while trying to line up a photo can tell you. The bites of rattlesnakes, Gila

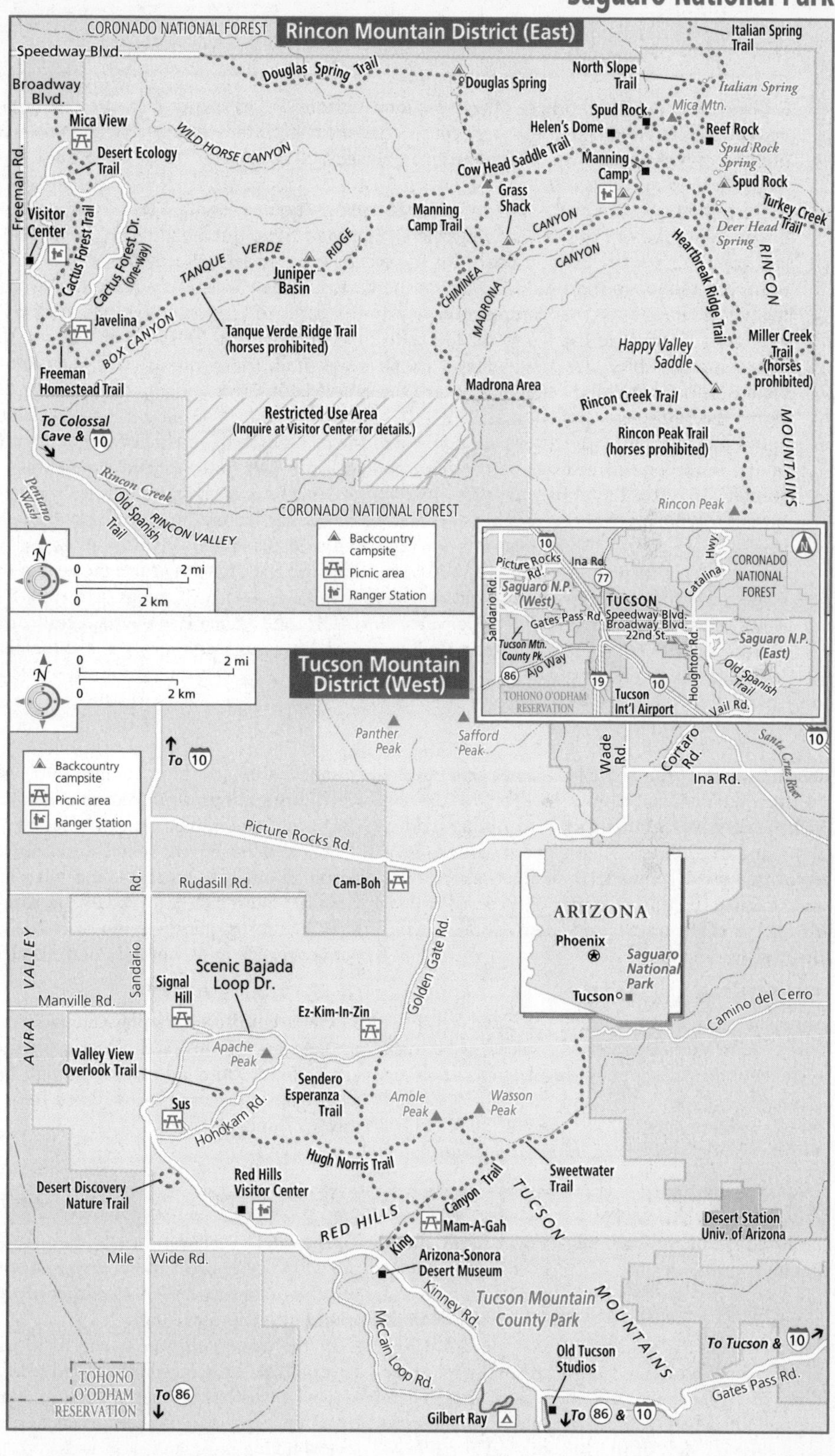
Rincon Mountain District (East)
CORONADO NATIONAL FOREST
Speedway Blvd.
Broadway Blvd.
Freeman Rd.
Mica View
Desert Ecology Trail
Visitor Center
Cactus Forest Trail
Cactus Forest Dr. (one-way)
Javelina
Freeman Homestead Trail
To Colossal Cave & 10
Douglas Spring Trail
Douglas Spring
WILD HORSE CANYON
TANQUE VERDE RIDGE
Juniper Basin
Tanque Verde Ridge Trail (horses prohibited)
BOX CANYON
Restricted Use Area
(Inquire at Visitor Center for details.)
Rincon Creek
Old Spanish Trail
RINCON VALLEY
Pantano Wash
CORONADO NATIONAL FOREST
Italian Spring Trail
North Slope Trail
Italian Spring
Spud Rock
Mica Mtn.
Helen's Dome
Reef Rock
Spud Rock Spring
Cow Head Saddle Trail
Manning Camp
Spud Rock
Grass Shack
Manning Camp Trail
CANYON
Turkey Creek Trail
Deer Head Spring
CHIMINEA
MADRONA
CANYON
Heartbreak Ridge Trail
RINCON
Happy Valley Saddle
Miller Creek Trail (horses prohibited)
Madrona Area
Rincon Creek Trail
Rincon Peak Trail (horses prohibited)
MOUNTAINS
Rincon Peak
Backcountry campsite
Picnic area
Ranger Station
N
0 2 mi
0 2 km
Picture Rocks Rd.
Ina Rd.
77
Saguaro N.P. (West)
TUCSON
Sandario Rd.
Gates Pass Rd.
Speedway Blvd.
Broadway Blvd.
22nd St.
Tucson Mtn. County Pk.
86
Ajo Way
19
10
TOHONO O'ODHAM RESERVATION
Tucson Int'l Airport
Houghton Rd.
Catalina Hwy.
CORONADO NATIONAL FOREST
Saguaro N.P. (East)
Old Spanish Trail
Vail Rd.
Tucson Mountain District (West)
N
0 2 mi
0 2 km
Backcountry campsite
Picnic area
Ranger Station
To 10
Panther Peak
Safford Peak
Wade Rd.
Cortaro Rd.
Santa Cruz River
Ina Rd.
10
Picture Rocks Rd.
Rudasill Rd.
Cam-Boh
Sandario Rd.
AVRA VALLEY
Manville Rd.
Golden Gate Rd.
ARIZONA
Phoenix
Saguaro National Park
Tucson
Camino del Cerro
Signal Hill
Scenic Bajada Loop Dr.
Ez-Kim-In-Zin
Apache Peak
Valley View Overlook Trail
Sus
Hohokam Rd.
Sendero Esperanza Trail
Amole Peak
Wasson Peak
Hugh Norris Trail
Sweetwater Trail
Desert Discovery Nature Trail
Red Hills Visitor Center
RED HILLS
King Canyon Trail
Mam-A-Gah
TUCSON MOUNTAINS
Desert Station Univ. of Arizona
Mile Wide Rd.
Arizona-Sonora Desert Museum
Kinney Rd.
Tucson Mountain County Park
McCain Loop Rd.
To Tucson & 10
Old Tucson Studios
Gates Pass Rd.
TOHONO O'ODHAM RESERVATION
To 86
Gilbert Ray
To 86 & 10

If You Have Only 1 Day

Saguaro National Park consists of two sections. Visitors should spend at least a day or two at each district, starting with the visitor centers, then the short interpretive walks, and finally a serious hike or two. Those with only a day can either see a bit of each district or explore one of them more thoroughly.

To see both sections of the park in 1 day, start in the **Tucson Mountain District** at the **Red Hills Visitor Center,** where you can examine the exhibits and try to get a handle on life in the Sonoran Desert. Check the bulletin board for the schedule of ranger-led activities; if your timing is right, you can join a short guided walk on the **Cactus Garden Trail,** just outside the visitor center, which serves as an excellent introduction to the park. You can also take this short walk on your own. Then drive the 9-mile **Bajada Loop Drive** through a thick stand of saguaro, taking time for a short hike along the **Valley View Overlook Trail.** Those interested in early American Indians will want to take a slight detour off the Bajada Loop Drive to ponder the rock art on the **Signal Hill Petroglyph Trail.**

By now it should be lunchtime. Stop in one of the picnic areas if you happened to bring food, or at a restaurant in Tucson as you drive through on your way to the **Rincon Mountain District.** Stop at the visitor center as you enter—by now you may have a few questions for the rangers, such as, "What were those two big eyes staring out at me from a hole in that old saguaro?" (Probably an elf owl.) Then head out onto the 8-mile **Cactus Forest Drive** for an easy close-up look at a forest of saguaro. About a third of the way into the drive, the road crosses the **Cactus Forest hiking trail,** where you can get out of your vehicle, stretch your legs, and walk a short way into the saguaro forest. If time remains, pull off at the Javelina Picnic Area access road and walk along the **Freeman Homestead Trail,** which offers good scenic views and a look at the remains of an old homestead.

monsters, and scorpions are poisonous. Park rangers recommend that you always look before putting your hands or feet under rocks or in other hidden spots, and that you use a flashlight at night to help avoid unwanted encounters. Weather-related dangers include lightning (stay off exposed ridges during thunderstorms) and flash floods (avoid drainages during rain).

SEASONS & CLIMATE

Summers are hot and winters comfortable, so the best time to visit, especially for hikers, is between October and April. Summer high temperatures are routinely between 100° and 115°F (38°C and 46°C), with lows generally in the 70s (20s Celsius). Visitors should also beware of occasional torrential thunderstorms in July, August, and September, which bring danger from lightning and flash floods.

During winter, high temperatures are usually in the 60s and low 70s (upper teens Celsius), with lows dropping into the upper 30s and 40s (single digits Celsius). Snow falls occasionally, is almost always light, and melts quickly. Winters are also known for periodic gentle rains, but most of the time it's sunny.

SEASONAL EVENTS

The best **wildflower displays** are from mid-March through mid-April. Cacti bloom a bit later—some kinds flower from mid-April through September, although the saguaro usually bloom from late April through June.

2 Exploring the Park by Car

Each section of the park has its own scenic drive. Before you set out on one, consider buying one of the inexpensive booklets about the park's terrain and vegetation at the visitor centers. The 9-mile **Bajada Loop Drive** in the western section begins at the Red Hills Visitor Center and proceeds through a dense forest of saguaro cacti, offering scenic views. There are pullouts where you can get out of your vehicle for a close-up view of the saguaro, and a trail head for the very worthwhile **Valley View Overlook Trail** (see "Day Hikes," below). Because 6 miles of the loop are gravel, those driving low-clearance vehicles or towing trailers should check on current conditions before starting.

In the eastern section of the park, the **Cactus Forest Drive** is a somewhat hilly and twisting 8-mile loop that wanders through a forest of saguaro. This paved one-way road provides access to picnic areas, several hiking trails, and short walks.

Organized Tours & Ranger Programs

Rangers guide hikes and give talks daily from mid-October through April. Activities vary, but they might include an easy cactus or bird identification walk, a 4-mile hike through the desert, a video program on desert life, or slide shows on wildflowers or bats. Check at the visitor centers for schedules.

3 Park Attractions

Both sections of the park contain impressive **rock art** believed to have been created by the Hohokam people, who lived here from about A.D. 700 to 1500. The best and easiest place to see rock art is on the **Signal Hill Petroglyph Trail** in the Tucson Mountain District. These petroglyphs (a type of rock carving) usually depict figures of humans and animals, plus many abstract designs, such as wavy lines and combinations of circles and spirals.

The park also contains reminders of the miners and settlers who arrived in the late 1800s. You can see the remains of the **Gould Mine,** active in the early 1900s, along the Sendero Esperanza Trail, in the Tucson Mountain District. In the Rincon Mountain District are what's left of an **adobe house** built in 1929 on the Freeman Homestead Trail, and several **limekilns,** built in about 1880, along the Cactus Forest Trail. See "Day Hikes," below.

4 Day Hikes

Desert hiking can be a killer, literally. Those planning to do any serious hiking at Saguaro National Park are strongly advised to talk with rangers about their plans before setting out, and then to carry at least a gallon of water per day per person. Rangers do not recommend hiking at all in the summer, when temperatures frequently reach a scorching 115°F (46°C). Because some of the longer trails are difficult to follow, hikers are advised to carry good topographical maps, available at the visitor centers.

TUCSON MOUNTAIN DISTRICT (SAGUARO WEST)

SHORTER TRAILS

Cactus Garden Trail A level nature walk just outside the visitor center, this wheelchair-accessible trail is a good introduction to the park and the Sonoran Desert environment. Interpretive signs identify a variety of desert plants. .15 mile RT. Easy. Access: Red Hills Visitor Center.

Desert Discovery Nature Trail This mostly level wheelchair-accessible trail has signs describing the plants, animals, and ecology of the Sonoran Desert. It also affords panoramic views of the Tucson Mountains. .5 mile RT. Easy. Access: Kinney Rd., 1 mile northwest of the Red Hills Visitor Center.

Signal Hill Petroglyphs Trail This trail zigzags up the side of a hill to an area containing examples of American Indian rock art, believed to have been left by the Hohokam people between 500 and 1,300 years ago (see "Park Attractions," above). .5 mile RT. Easy. Access: North of Signal Hill picnic area, off Golden Gate Rd., 5 miles northwest of the Red Hills Visitor Center.

Valley View Overlook Trail Built by the Civilian Conservation Corps in the 1930s, this trail passes through cactus forests and two washes before climbing to a ridge for splendid views of the surrounding desert and mountains. .75 mile RT. Easy. Access: Bajada Loop Dr., 3½ miles north of the Red Hills Visitor Center.

LONGER TRAILS

Hugh Norris Trail The longest and most difficult in the park's Tucson Mountain District, this trail begins with a series of switchbacks that lead to a ridge overlooking a huge forest of saguaro cactus. From there it offers panoramic views and passes old mines and intriguing rock formations. The trail climbs another series of switchbacks before finally making its way to the top of Wasson Peak, at 4,687 feet, from which you generally have spectacular views of Tucson and the surrounding mountains. The trail has a total elevation gain of 2,087 feet. 9.8 miles RT. Strenuous. Access: Bajada Loop Dr., 2½ miles north of the Red Hills Visitor Center.

King Canyon Trail This trail combines with the last .3 mile of the Hugh Norris Trail to take you from 2,800 feet in elevation to the top of 4,687-foot Wasson Peak, the highest point in the Tucson Mountains. Along the trail are petroglyphs believed to have been created by the Hohokam people, some open mine shafts that you'll want to avoid, and panoramic views once you get to the higher elevations. The trail is rocky in spots, so good hiking boots are recommended. 7 miles RT. Moderate to strenuous. Access: On Kinney Rd., directly across from the Arizona-Sonora Desert Museum, about 2 miles southwest of the Red Hills Visitor Center.

Sendero Esperanza Trail The trail leaves an old mining road and climbs through several steep switchbacks to a ridge, with spectacular views in all directions. It finally drops to the Mam-A-Gah Picnic

Area and a junction with the King Canyon Trail. Along the way, it passes the remains of the Gould Mine, which was enthusiastically but unproductively worked in the early 1900s. 6.4 miles RT. Moderate. Access: Golden Gate Rd., about 6 miles northeast of the Red Hills Visitor Center.

RINCON MOUNTAIN DISTRICT (SAGUARO EAST)

SHORTER TRAILS

Desert Ecology Trail Interpretive signs along this paved wheelchair-accessible walkway explain how plants and animals of the Sonoran Desert make the most of the limited amount of water available. .25 mile RT. Easy. Access: Cactus Forest Dr., east of the Mica View Picnic Area.

Freeman Homestead Trail This walk through gently rolling desert terrain offers good panoramic views, as well as close-up views of saguaro (including a 30-armed giant), ocotillo, and other desert plants. Along the way, you'll find several interpretive signs describing desert life, as well as the remains of the Freeman Homestead, a three-room adobe house built by Safford Freeman in 1929. All that's left is a mound of dirt from the adobe bricks. 1 mile RT. Easy. Access: Off Cactus Forest Dr., on the Javelina Picnic Area access road.

LONGER TRAILS

Cactus Forest Trail This sandy, level trail, which is also accessible from two points on the Cactus Forest Drive, is simply a very pleasant walk. It passes through though a forest of cactus, primarily saguaro; a variety of other desert plants, such as paloverde and mesquite; and large beehive-shaped limekilns dating from about 1880. Bicycles are permitted on a 2.5-mile section of the trail inside the loop made by Cactus Forest Drive. 5 miles one-way. Easy. Access: Near the east end of Broadway Blvd., just east of Freeman Rd.

Douglas Spring Trail This trail through the foothills of the Rincon Mountains starts off fairly level but gradually becomes steeper. It then alternates between steep and flat sections all the way to Douglas Spring Campground. Along the way, you'll find lots of cactus, especially prickly pear, and some interesting rock formations. Signs of damage from a devastating 1989 fire can still be seen here, as well as the results of revegetation. The trail continues beyond the campground, providing access to other backcountry trails. You need a backcountry permit to stay overnight at the campground (see "Camping," below). 6 miles one-way (to Douglas Spring Campground). Strenuous. Access: East end of Speedway Blvd.

Tanque Verde Ridge Trail This trail offers splendid panoramic views as it follows a ridgeline northeast into the wilderness area. You'll see saguaro, cholla, prickly pear, and other cactus for a while, and then pinyon, juniper, and some oak as you climb higher into the foothills. The Juniper Basin Campground, at 6,000 feet, is 2,900 feet higher than the trail head. Although the trail continues, this is a good spot for day hikers to turn around. See "Exploring the Backcountry," below, for information on forging ahead. 6.9 miles one-way (to Juniper Basin Campground). Strenuous. Access: Javelina Picnic Area off Cactus Forest Dr.

5 Exploring the Backcountry

All the park's backcountry hiking and camping opportunities are in the Rincon Mountain District (the eastern section), which includes the 59,930-acre **Rincon Mountain Wilderness.** Varying considerably in elevation, this area contains both hot desert sprinkled with saguaro and other cacti, and relatively cool forests of pine and mixed conifer. The main routes into the backcountry are the **Douglas Spring Trailhead** and **Tanque Verde Ridge trail head,** which are discussed above. From these two trails, you have access to more than 100 miles of trails, as well as the park's six backcountry campgrounds (see "Camping," below). Dirt roads lead to several other trail heads; check with park rangers for directions and current conditions. Rangers strongly suggest that those going into the backcountry carry topographical maps, which can be purchased at either visitor center. Backcountry camping requires a **permit** (see "Fees & Permits," above).

Campground	Elev.	Total Sites	RV Hookups	Dump Station	Toilets
Cactus Country RV Resort	3,300	263	258	Yes	Yes
Catalina State Park	2,650	120	95	Yes	Yes
Gilbert Ray	2,600	135	130	Yes	Yes
Molino Basin	4,370	37	0	No	Yes
Rose Canyon	7,000	74	0	No	Yes
Spencer Canyon	8,000	60	0	No	Yes

6 Other Sports & Activities

BIKING Bikes are permitted on the scenic drives in both districts; the Rincon loop was repaved in 2006 and features a bike-only lane, and bikes are allowed on a 2.5-mile stretch of the Cactus Forest Trail inside the loop. **Tucson Bicycles,** 4743 E. Sunrise Dr. (✆ **520/577-7374;** www.tucsonbicycles.com), rents road and mountain bikes for $25 to $35 per day.

HORSEBACK RIDING Horseback riding is permitted on most trails in both districts of the park, although horses are not allowed off-trail. Horses may be kept overnight in the backcountry campgrounds in the Rincon Mountain District. Manning Camp has a corral; at the other backcountry campgrounds, riders should secure horses with a picket rope slung between two trees. Get details from park rangers.

WILDLIFE VIEWING & BIRD-WATCHING Both sections of the park offer abundant opportunities for wildlife observation and bird-watching. Because Saguaro East has a greater range of elevations, and therefore climates, you'll see a larger variety of animals there.

In both sections of the park, look for holes punched in saguaro cacti by Gila woodpeckers and gilded flickers. These finicky birds sometimes make several cavities before settling on one as home for the year. They always punch out a new home when they return the following year. The extra holes are taken over by other desert inhabitants, including cactus wrens, Lucy's warblers, and little elf owls.

Among other birds you're likely to see in both sections of the park are black-throated sparrows, brown towhees, verdin, brown-crested flycatchers, Costa's hummingbirds, roadrunners, mourning doves, white-winged doves, Gambel's quail, American kestrels, and red-tailed hawks. In the eastern part of the park, you'll also see rufous-crowned sparrows, olive warblers, yellow-rumped warblers, solitary vireos, American robins, pygmy nuthatches, Steller's jays, mountain chickadees, violet-green swallows, broad-tailed hummingbirds, and Cooper's hawks.

Mammals commonly seen include desert cottontails, Harris ground squirrels, round-tailed ground squirrels, striped skunks, javelina, mule deer, and southern long-nose bats, which pollinate saguaro flowers while feeding on their nectar. You may also spot white-tailed deer in the higher elevations of Saguaro East. Reptiles commonly seen include zebra-tailed and western whiptail lizards, gopher snakes, and king snakes. In the desert and foothill areas, watch out for the many western diamondback rattlesnakes, which are poisonous.

7 Camping

INSIDE THE PARK

There are no drive-in campgrounds in the national park, but backpackers will find six backcountry campgrounds in the Rincon Mountain Wilderness. All the campgrounds have three sites, each except Manning Camp, which has six. Water is available at Manning year-round, but water availability at the other campgrounds is spotty—ask a ranger. To avoid illness, you must treat backcountry water before drinking. Backcountry camping is permitted only in designated campsites. Pick up the $6 **permit** at the Rincon Mountain District Visitor Center or by writing to the park.

NEAR THE PARK

Four miles south of the park's Tucson Mountain District is **Gilbert Ray Campground,** off Kinney Road on McCain Loop Road, operated by the Pima County Parks and Recreation Department (✆ **520/883-4200;** www.pima.gov/nrpr/camping). It offers an attractive desert mountain environment of saguaro, prickly pear, cholla, mesquite, and paloverde, with well-maintained gravel sites. The sites are first come, first served. No wood fires are permitted, and RV hookups offer electricity only.

Convenient for visitors to the national park's Tucson Mountain District, the campground at **Catalina State Park,** 9 miles north of Tucson on Ariz. 77 (✆ **520/628-5798;** www.pr.state.az.us),

Drinking Water	Showers	Fire Pits/ Grills	Laundry	Reserve	Fees	Open
Yes	Yes	Yes	Yes	Yes	$20–$38	Year-round
Yes	Yes	Yes	No	No	$10–$20	Year-round
Yes	No	No	No	No	$10–$20	Year-round
No	No	Yes	No	No	$10	Late Oct to late Apr
Yes	No	Yes	No	Yes	$18	Apr–Oct
Yes	No	Yes	No	No	$18	May–Oct

has nicely spaced and well-shaded sites, an abundance of rock squirrels, and splendid views of the Santa Catalina Mountains to the southeast.

There are also campgrounds in the Santa Catalina District of the **Coronado National Forest** (✆ **520/749-8700;** www.fs.fed.us/r3/coronado), north of the national park's Rincon Mountain District. Located along the Catalina Highway, they include **Molino Basin,** about 18 miles northeast of Tucson, which has limited facilities and can accommodate trailers up to 22 feet only; **Rose Canyon,** about 33 miles northeast of Tucson, which offers fishing at Rose Canyon Lake; and **Spencer Canyon,** near the top of Mount Lemmon about 39 miles northeast of Tucson, which can accommodate trailers up to 18 feet only. Of these, only a few sites at Rose Canyon can be reserved; call ✆ **877/444-6777.**

Among commercial campgrounds in the area are **Cactus Country RV Resort,** 10195 S. Houghton Rd. (✆ **800/777-8799** or 520/574-3000; www.abtucson.com), at I-10 exit 275, which has large spaces, some shade trees, and attractive desert landscaping. All RV sites have full hookups, including cable TV. There are only a few tent sites. Campers have access to free Wi-Fi and an outdoor heated pool, a hot tub, modem hookups, a game room, a playground, shuffleboard, and horseshoes.

8 Where to Stay

There are no accommodations inside the park.

NEAR THE PARK

In addition to the lodgings listed below, you'll find dozens of chain motels along I-10, including the **Motel 6–Tucson/Congress Street,** 960 S. Freeway, Tucson, AZ 85745 (exit 258; ✆ **520/628-1339**), and **Motel 6–Tucson/22nd Street,** 1222 S. Freeway, Tucson, AZ 85713 (exit 259; ✆ **520/624-2516**), which both charge $35 to $50 for a double. Among hotels near the airport are the **Best Western Las Brisas–Tucson Airport,** 7060 S. Tucson Blvd., Tucson, AZ 85706 (✆ **866/217-2140** or 520/746-0271), with rates of $89 to $119 double; and **La Quinta,** 750 W. Starr Pass Blvd., Tucson, AZ 85713 (exit 263A or B off I-10; ✆ **520/624-4455**), with rates of $69 to $89 double. See chapter 38 for the national chains' websites.

Casa Tierra If you've come to Tucson to really be a *part* of the desert, this is an excellent choice. A modern adobe home surrounded by 5 acres of cacti and paloverde, Casa Tierra is on the west side of Saguaro National Park's Tucson Mountain District, and it has fabulous views of a saguaro landscape and the surrounding mountains. Around a central courtyard with a desert garden and a fountain is a candlelit, covered portal—a seating area where guests congregate. The rooms have queen beds, brick floors, refrigerators, microwaves, hair dryers, and private patios; the family suite holds two bedrooms, a bathroom, a dining area, and a library. The gourmet breakfasts range from stuffed French toast with prickly-pear syrup to green-chile polenta. There's an exercise room, a Wi-Fi network, and a common area with TV, stereo, and games. Another perk: an outdoor whirlpool spa that makes a perfect stargazing spot at night (a telescope is provided)!

11155 W. Calle Pima, Tucson, AZ 85743. ✆ **866/254-0006** or 520/578-3058. Fax 520/578-8445. www.casatierratucson.com. 4 units. $135–$195 double; $165–$285 suite. 2-night minimum stay. Rates include full vegetarian breakfast. AE, DISC, MC, V.

Hacienda del Desierto On the east side of Tucson, within 5 minutes of the entrance to the Rincon Mountain District of Saguaro National Park, this stylish, sunny B&B is set amid 16 picturesque acres, with its own wildlife-filled nature trail and desert ponds. The inn, centered on an interior courtyard, features eclectic and colorful rooms (two of which have kitchenettes), and the standalone Casita (with a full kitchen). Full of personality, the inn can arrange massages and also offers guest use of an outdoor hydrotherapy spa to soothe muscles after a desert hike.

11770 E. Rambling Trail, Tucson, AZ 85747. ✆ **800/982-1795** or 520/298-1764. www.tucson-bed-breakfast.com. 4 units. A/C, TV. $129–$289 double, with a 2-night minimum stay in winter. Rates include continental breakfast. AE, DISC, MC, V.

Hotel Congress In the heart of Tucson's downtown arts district, the Hotel Congress once counted John Dillinger among its guests. Today it operates as a hipster hangout and economical historic hotel. Conveniently located near the Greyhound and Amtrak stations, the hotel is especially popular with students and European backpackers. The lobby has been restored to its original Southwestern elegance, and the guest rooms have been renovated. All have evaporative cooling instead of air-conditioning, some bathrooms have tubs only, and others have showers only. The property has free Wi-Fi, a **restaurant,** and a popular and noisy **bar** that's also hosts live music.

311 E. Congress St., Tucson, AZ 85701. ✆ **800/722-8848** or 520/622-8848. Fax 520/792-6366. www.hotelcongress.com. 40 units. TEL. $79–$119 double. AE, DISC, MC, V.

J.W. Marriott Starr Pass Opened in 2005, this dazzling, sprawling golf resort is one of the toniest places to hang your hat near the western district of Saguaro. It's nestled amid the cactus-speckled foothills, with commanding views of not only the scenery, but the surrounding golf course and picture-perfect outdoor pool. Little details—like a nightly tequila toast at sundown—evoke a desert vibe. In addition to the plush and comfortable rooms—equally good for business and leisure travelers—the hotel provides a lengthy list of amenities and facilities, including a lap pool (besides the one mentioned above), a spa, shops, three **restaurants,** a **lounge,** and valet parking.

6555 E. Speedway Blvd., Tucson, AZ 85710. ✆ **888/772-5809** or 520/792-3500. Fax 520/792-3351. www.jwmarriottstarrpass.com. 575 units, including 35 suites. A/C, TV, TEL. Mid-Sept to Jan $269–$299 double, $450–$600 suite; Jan to mid-May $349 double, $550–$700 suite; mid-May to mid-Sept $159–$109 double, $325–$500 suite. AE, DISC, MC, V.

Radisson Suites Tucson This all-suite hotel is a good choice for those who want plenty of space and aren't overly concerned about proximity to the park. The five-story brick building is arranged around two lushly landscaped garden courtyards, one of which has a large heated pool and a hydra-spa (a fixed-jet whirlpool). The two-room suites feature contemporary furnishings, and all have refrigerators, microwaves, coffeemakers, hair dryers, and irons and ironing boards. The hotel has a **restaurant** (American) serving three meals a day, limited room service, an exercise room, laundry service, and a coin-operated laundry.

6555 E. Speedway Blvd., Tucson, AZ 85710. ✆ **800/333-3333** or 520/721-7100. www.radisson.com. 299 suites. A/C, TV, TEL. Mid-Sept to mid-Jan $149–$179 double; mid-Jan to mid-May $189–$249 double; mid-May to mid-Sept $109–$159 double. AE, DISC, MC, V. Pets accepted; $25 refundable fee.

9 Where to Dine

There are no restaurants inside the park.

NEAR THE PARK

Anthony's in the Catalinas CONTINENTAL If you head north on Campbell Avenue up into the foothills of the Catalinas, you'll come to this fine-dining restaurant. In a modern hacienda-style building overlooking the city, Anthony's exudes Southwestern elegance. The waiters are smartly attired in tuxedos, and the guests are almost as well dressed. Quiet classical music plays in the background. In such a rarefied atmosphere, you'd expect only the finest meal, and that's what you get. The house-smoked salmon is a fitting beginning, followed by beef Wellington, baked in puff pastry with pâté and prosciutto. The wine list is quite likely the most extensive in the city. The pastry selection may tempt you, but if it's available, don't miss out on the day's soufflé.

6440 N. Campbell Ave. ✆ **520/299-1771.** www.anthonyscatalinas.com. Reservations highly recommended. Main courses $30–$43. AE, DC, DISC, MC, V. Daily 5:30–9pm.

Cafe Poca Cosa MEXICAN Mexican cuisine doesn't come much more refined or creative than chef-owner's Suzana Davila's unforgettable creations at Cafe Poca Cosa. The menu changes twice daily at this downtown eatery and is read by the waitstaff from handheld chalkboards, where it is listed in both Spanish and English. The flavors and presentations are remarkable, with seafood, poultry, beef, and vegetarian dishes concocted with contemporary twists on Mexican standbys. Rice, beans, and tortillas are served family style, and each plate comes with a heap of fresh fruit and salad.

110 E. Pennington Ave. ✆ **520/622-6400.** www.cafepocacosainc.com. Reservations recommended for dinner. Main courses $13–$15 lunch, $19–$25 dinner. AE, MC, V. Tues–Thurs 11am–9pm; Fri–Sat 11am–10pm. Closed mid-July to mid-Aug.

El Charro Café MEXICAN In an old stone building in El Presidio Historic District, El Charro claims to be the nation's oldest continuously open family-operated Mexican restaurant—it's been serving authentic Tucson-style Mexican food since 1922. A glassed-in porch makes for a greenhouse-like dining area overlooking the street, and there's also dining downstairs. Look at the roof of El Charro as you approach, and you might see a large metal cage containing beef drying in the sun. This is the main ingredient in *carne seca,* El Charro's well-known specialty, rarely found outside the Tucson area. The chimichangas, rellenos, and enchiladas are hard to beat, as is the volcanic El Topopo Salad—a conical heap of shredded lettuce, black olives, and your choice of meat or veggies on a tostada shell. And the salsa—green and red, served in syrup dispensers—is some of the best in the West. Besides the downtown original, there are four other El Charro locations in Tucson.

Picnic & Camping Supplies

Although there are no stores within the park's boundaries, you'll find plenty of places to stock up on supplies in Tucson, where there are numerous supermarkets, including **Basha's,** 100 S. Houghton Rd. (✆ **520/296-4700;** www.bashas.com). For camping, hiking, backpacking, and mountain-biking gear, as well as tips on outdoor recreation locations, stop at **Summit Hut,** 5045 E. Speedway Blvd. (✆ **520/325-1554;** www.summithut.com), which is open daily.

---

311 N. Court Ave. ✆ **520/622-1922.** www.elcharrocafe.com. Reservations recommended for dinner. Main courses $7–$18. AE, DC, DISC, MC, V. Daily 11am–9pm.

Little Anthony's Diner AMERICAN This is a great place for kids, although kids at heart will also enjoy the 1950s music and decor. The staff is good with children, and there's a video-game room and a rocket-ship ride outside. How about a Jailhouse Rock Burger or Hound Dog Hot Dog with a tower of onion rings? Or an old-fashioned banana split or a hand-dipped shake? Daily specials and bottomless soft drinks make feeding the family fairly inexpensive. Beer and wine are also served.

7010 E. Broadway Blvd. ✆ **520/296-0456.** www.littleanthonysdiner.com. Main courses $4–$9. MC, V. Mon–Thurs 11am–10pm; Fri 11am–11pm; Sat 7:30am–11pm; Sun 7:30–11am and noon–10pm.

Tucson McGraw's AMERICAN Owned by Lex McGraw since the early 1980s, this eatery is a southeast Tucson institution and a favorite of the Saguaro National Park staff. A friendly vibe complements the roadhouse atmosphere. The menu revolves around meat—ribs, burgers, steaks—and beer, although the menu also includes some good salads and what might be considered more healthy fare. The margaritas are some of Tucson's best.

4110 S. Houghton Rd. ✆ **520/885-3088.** www.tucsonmcgraws.com. Reservations accepted for large parties only. Main courses $5–$24. AE, DISC, MC, V. Mon–Sat 11am–10pm; Sun 11am–9pm.

32

Sequoia & Kings Canyon National Parks, CA

by Eric Peterson

In the heart of the Sierra Nevada, just south of Yosemite, are Sequoia and Kings Canyon national parks, home to the largest giant sequoia trees in the world, vast wilderness areas, and a deep, beautiful canyon. Sequoia and Kings Canyon are separate adjacent parks that are managed jointly; combined, they exceed Yosemite in size. Their peaks stretch across 1,350 square miles and include 14,505-foot Mount Whitney, the tallest point in the continental United States. The parks are also home to the Kaweah Range, a string of dark, beautiful mountains nestled amid the Sierra, and three powerful rivers: the Kings, Kern, and Kaweah. Despite their size and scenic beauty, these two parks attract less than half the number of Yosemite's annual visitors, making them a welcome alternative for those looking to avoid huge crowds.

The parks owe their existence to a small band of determined 19th-century conservationists. Alarmed by the wholesale destruction of the region's sequoia forests, these farsighted people pushed to make the area a protected park. Sequoia National Park was created in 1890, along with the tiny General Grant National Park, which was established to protect Grant Grove. In 1926, the park was expanded eastward to include the Kern Canyon and Mount Whitney, and in the 1960s Kings Canyon was finally protected. In 1978, Mineral King was added to Sequoia's half of the park.

AVOIDING THE CROWDS

Though Sequoia and Kings Canyon receive far fewer visitors than nearby Yosemite, they still get crowded, especially in summer. Luckily, there's a lot of space here, so it's relatively easy to find solitude. To get the most from the parks while avoiding traffic, try to visit before Memorial Day or after Labor Day, keeping in mind that snow can limit access in the high elevations. Fall provides some scenic color often missing from the California landscape. As always, a trip to the backcountry will help avoid the crowds.

You can also try taking a dead-end road into the parks. Mineral King, South Fork, and, to a lesser extent, Cedar Grove all lack the through traffic prevalent on the larger highways.

1 Essentials

GETTING THERE & GATEWAYS

There are two main entrances to the parks. **Calif. 198** through Visalia and the town of Three Rivers leads to the **Ash Mountain Entrance** in Sequoia National Park. **Calif. 180** from Fresno leads straight to the **Big Stump Entrance** near Grant Grove in Kings Canyon National Park. Three dead-end entrance roads are open only in the summer: the Kings Canyon Highway (a continuation of Calif. 180) to **Cedar Grove** in Kings Canyon National Park, and two smaller roads to **Mineral King** and to **South Fork,** both in the south part of Sequoia National Park.

The parks are roughly equidistant (5 hr. by car) from San Francisco and Los Angeles. The Ash Mountain Entrance is 36 miles, or about an hour, from Visalia. The Big Stump Entrance is 53 miles from Fresno, also about an hour's drive.

THE NEAREST AIRPORTS The closest major airport is **Fresno-Yosemite International Airport** (✆ **559/621-4500**), 53 miles from the Big Stump Entrance in Kings Canyon. Airlines include **Alaska, Allegiant, American/American Eagle, Delta, Horizon, Mexicana, United,** and **US Airways.** You'll find most major car-rental companies here. **Visalia Municipal Airport** (✆ **559/713-4201;** www.flyvisalia.com), 36 miles from the Ash Mountain Entrance, handles daily direct service to Los Angeles on **Great Lakes Airlines.**

See chapter 38 for website listings of airlines, car rental firms, and major motel/hotel chains.

INFORMATION

Contact **Sequoia & Kings Canyon National Parks,** 47050 Generals Hwy., Three Rivers, CA 93271-9700 (✆ **559/565-3341;** www.nps.gov/seki).

Sequoia & Kings Canyon National Parks

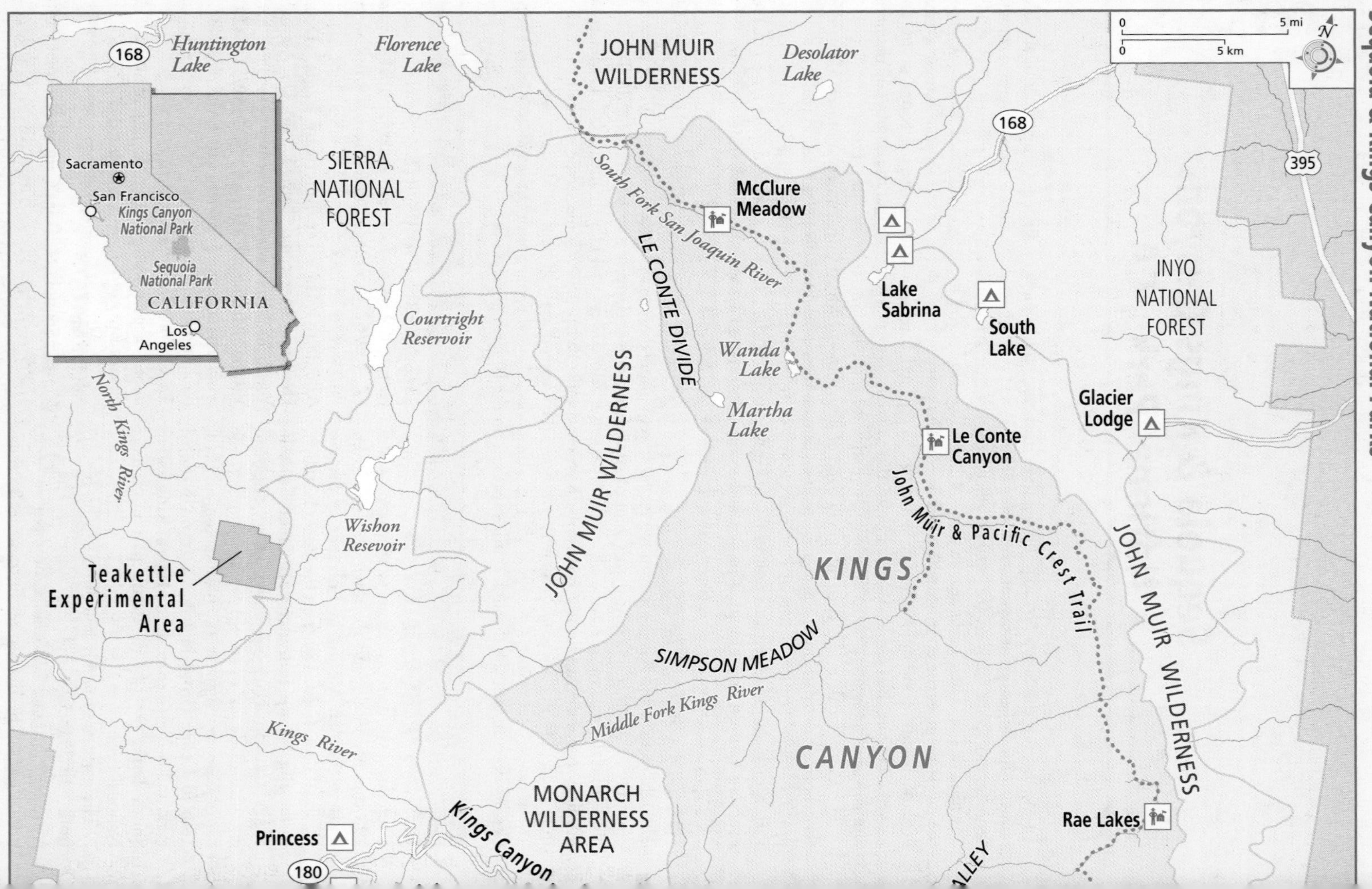

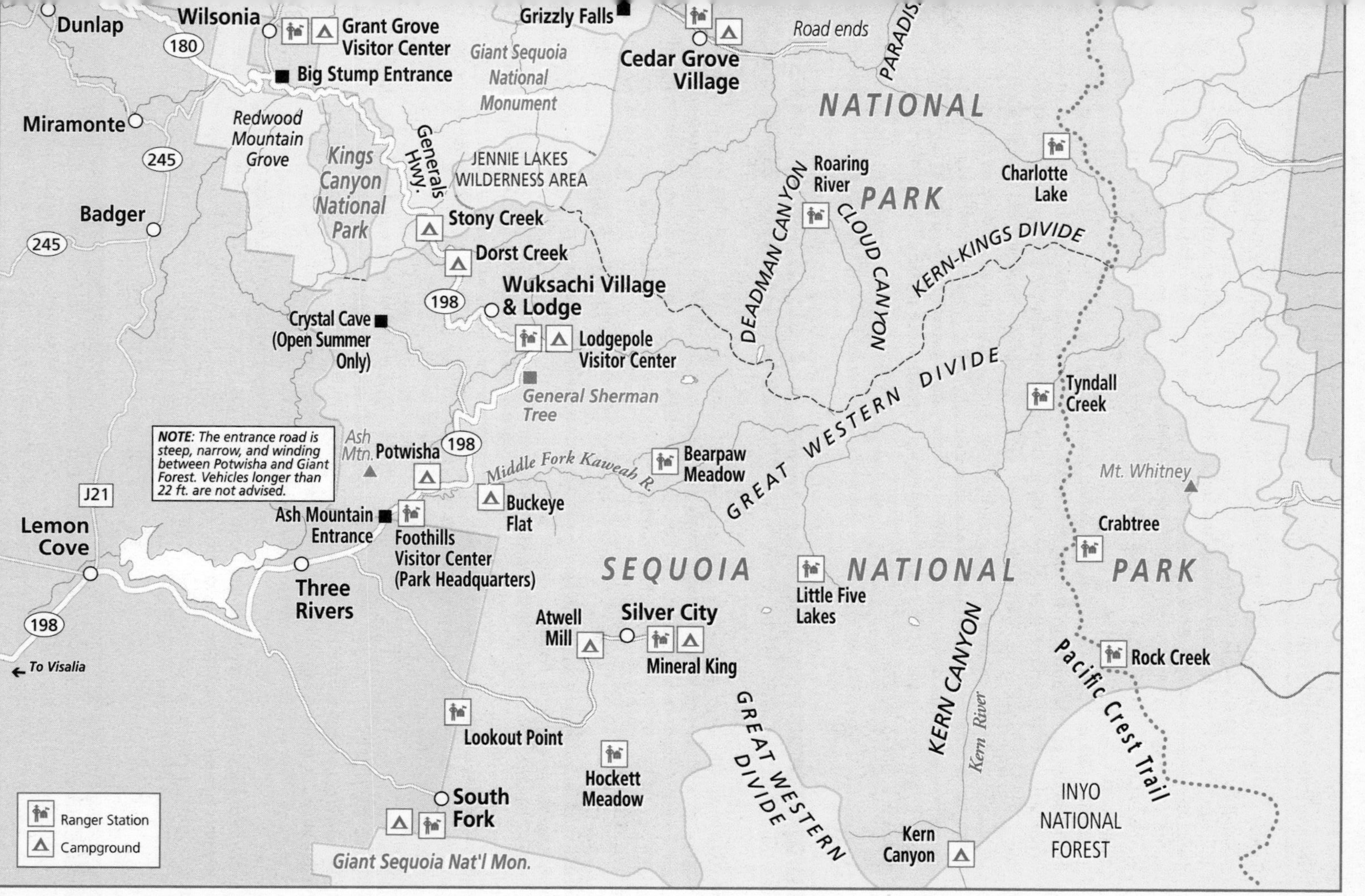

Dunlap
Wilsonia
180
Grant Grove Visitor Center
Big Stump Entrance
Grizzly Falls
Giant Sequoia National Monument
Cedar Grove Village
Road ends
PARADISE
NATIONAL PARK
Miramonte
245
Redwood Mountain Grove
Kings Canyon National Park
Generals Hwy.
JENNIE LAKES WILDERNESS AREA
Roaring River
Charlotte Lake
Badger
Stony Creek
Dorst Creek
DEADMAN CANYON
CLOUD CANYON
KERN-KINGS DIVIDE
198
Wuksachi Village & Lodge
Crystal Cave (Open Summer Only)
Lodgepole Visitor Center
General Sherman Tree
GREAT WESTERN DIVIDE
Tyndall Creek
NOTE: The entrance road is steep, narrow, and winding between Potwisha and Giant Forest. Vehicles longer than 22 ft. are not advised.
Ash Mtn.
Potwisha
Middle Fork Kaweah R.
Bearpaw Meadow
Mt. Whitney
J21
Buckeye Flat
Ash Mountain Entrance
Foothills Visitor Center (Park Headquarters)
Crabtree
Lemon Cove
Three Rivers
SEQUOIA NATIONAL PARK
Little Five Lakes
Atwell Mill
Silver City
Mineral King
KERN CANYON
Rock Creek
To Visalia
Pacific Crest Trail
Kern River
Lookout Point
Hockett Meadow
GREAT WESTERN DIVIDE
INYO NATIONAL FOREST
South Fork
Kern Canyon
Ranger Station
Campground
Giant Sequoia Nat'l Mon.

If You Have Only 1 Day

Eighty percent of park visitors come here on day trips—an amazing statistic, considering the geography of this place. Three to four days will do the park justice, but it is possible to drive through the park and take a short walk through a grove of big trees in one afternoon. Day-trippers should stick to **Grant Grove,** if possible—it's the most accessible area. Coming from the south, **Giant Forest** is a good alternative, although the trip on the steep and narrow Generals Highway takes some time. Cedar Grove and Mineral King are a bit farther afield and require an early start or an overnight stay.

Consider **driving from Giant Forest to Grant Grove,** or vice versa. It's about 2 hours through the park. Get your bearings by starting at a park visitor center—either the **Foothills Visitor Center** near the Ash Mountain Entrance or the **Kings Canyon Visitor Center.** You'll see the varied climate within the park as you pass through dense forest to exposed meadows and then through scrubby foothills covered in oaks and underbrush. In spring and summer, wildflowers dot much of the route. The southern portion of the drive runs along the Kaweah River. This route also passes near two large stands of giant sequoias, one at Grant Grove and the other at Giant Forest. Both have easy trails looping through the majestic stands. At Grant Grove, a footpath passes through a fallen sequoia.

VISITOR CENTERS

There are three year-round visitor centers in the parks, where you can talk with rangers, see exhibits, and buy books and maps. The biggest is in Sequoia National Park at **Lodgepole,** 4½ miles north of Giant Forest Village. It has exhibits on geology, wildlife, air quality, and park history. The **Foothills Visitor Center,** just inside the Ash Mountain Entrance to Sequoia National Park on Calif. 198, includes exhibits on the chaparral region's ecosystem. The visitor center in **Grant Grove** in Kings Canyon National Park shows exhibits on logging and the role of fire in the forests. Also, the **Giant Forest Museum** has exhibits on giant sequoias. The small visitor center at **Cedar Grove** and ranger station at **Mineral King** are open only during the summer.

FEES & PERMITS

It costs $20 per motor vehicle ($10 for individuals on foot, bike, or motorcycle) to enter the parks for up to a week. Park campgrounds charge $12 to $20 a night.

All overnight backpacking trips require a $15 **wilderness permit** per party (free in winter), available by mail, by fax, or in person at the ranger station closest to the hike you want to take.

SPECIAL REGULATIONS & WARNINGS

The roads in the parks are steep and winding, and those in RVs will find it easiest to travel on Calif. 180 from Fresno. All groundwater should be boiled, filtered, or otherwise purified before drinking. Rattlesnakes are common; look where you step and touch. In the foothills, check your clothes frequently for ticks. Beware also of black bears. When camping, store all food in lockers and put all garbage in bear-proof containers.

SEASONS & CLIMATE

Sequoia and Kings Canyon, for the most part, share a climate that varies considerably depending on the region of the park. A good rule of thumb is that the higher you go, the cooler it gets. During the summer, temperatures at lower elevations can climb into the 90s (30s Celsius) or higher, and drop into the 50s (10s Celsius) at night. Afternoon temperatures average in the 60s and 70s (upper teens and 20s Celsius) in spring and fall, and evenings are usually cool. Afternoon showers are fairly common year-round. Winter days average in the 40s and 50s (single digits and 10s Celsius) and seldom drop below zero, although much of the land is beneath several feet of snow. A particularly wet winter often leads to stunning wildflowers and spectacular waterfalls (and dangerous rivers and creeks) in spring and early summer.

2 Exploring the Park

SEQUOIA NATIONAL PARK

The best-known stand of sequoias in the world is in **Giant Forest,** part of Sequoia National Park. Named in 1875 by explorer and environmentalist John Muir, this park consists mostly of huge meadows and a large grove of giant trees. At the northern edge of the grove, you can't miss the **General Sherman Tree,** considered the largest living tree on the planet (although it is neither the tallest nor the widest). It is believed to be about 2,100 years old, and it's still growing. Every year it adds enough new wood to make another 60-foot-tall tree. The tree is part of the 2-mile **Congress Trail,** a foot trail that includes groups of trees with names such as the Senate and the House.

Another interesting stop in Giant Forest is **Tharp's Log,** a cabin named after the first non–American Indian settler in the area, Hale Tharp, who grazed cattle among the giant sequoias and built a summer cabin in the 1860s from a fallen sequoia hollowed by fire. It is the oldest cabin remaining in the park. You'll also encounter **Tunnel Log,** a toppled tree that you can drive under, and the Beetle Rock Education Center.

Nearby **Crescent Meadow** is a pristine clearing dotted with wildflowers and tall grasses. A trail wraps around the meadow. This is also the trail head for several backcountry hikes.

Also in the area is **Moro Rock,** a large granite dome that offers one of the most spectacular views in the Sierra. From atop the rock, the high-elevation, barren mountains in the Kaweah Range appear dark and ominous. Snow caps the ridgeline throughout the year. Although the cliffs appear towering and steep, they are smaller than the summit of the Sierra, which is obscured from view. The walk to the top takes visitors up hundreds of stairs and requires about a half-hour to complete. At the top is a narrow, fenced plateau with endless views. During a full moon, the mountain peaks shimmer like silver.

South of the Giant Forest is the turnoff for **Crystal Cave,** one of more than 200 caves in the park and one of just two in the area that offer guided tours. (Boyden Cavern in the neighboring Giant Sequoia National Monument is the other.) The cave consists of limestone that has turned to marble, and it contains a wonderful array of formations, many still growing, that range from sharply pointed stalactites and towering stalagmites to beautiful flowing draperies. To reach the entrance, drive 7 miles down the narrow, winding road (RVs, trailers, and buses are prohibited); the cave is an additional half-mile walk down a steep path (which you'll have to hike up after your cave tour). The Sequoia Natural History Association conducts 45-minute tours daily from 10:30am to 4:30pm from mid-May to Labor Day, and less often in late September. Tickets are sold at the Lodgepole and Foothills visitor centers, *not* at the cave. Cost is $11 for adults, $10 for seniors 62 and older, $6 for children 6 to 12, free for children under 6. A special summer-only **discovery tour** begins at 4:15pm weekdays. It is less structured and limited to 16 people, and has a minimum age of 13. The fee is $19 per person. Information is available at visitor centers and by telephone (✆ **559/565-3759**). It gets cold underground, so take a sweater or jacket.

Lodgepole, the most developed area in both parks, lies just northeast of the Giant Forest on the Generals Highway. Here you'll find the largest visitor center, a large market, several places to eat, a laundry, and a post office. Nearby is Wuksachi Village, with a restaurant, lodge, and gift shop.

About 16 miles south of Giant Forest is the region of the park known as the **Foothills.** Located near the Ash Mountain Entrance, the Foothills has a visitor center, several campgrounds, and **Hospital Rock,** a boulder with ancient pictographs believed to have been painted by the Monache Indians, who once lived here. Nearby are about 50 grinding spots once used to smash acorns into flour. A short trail leads down to a beautiful spot along the Kaweah River where the water gushes over rapids into deep pools. Hospital Rock also has a picnic area.

Mineral King is a relatively undeveloped region in the southern part of the park. This high-mountain valley was carved by glaciers and is bordered by the tall peaks of the Great Western Divide. To reach this area, patient drivers must follow the marked highway sign 3 miles outside Sequoia National Park's Ash Mountain Entrance. From the turnoff to Mineral King, it's a 28-mile trip that makes many tight turns and takes 1½ hours. Trailers, RVs, and buses are not allowed. The road is closed in winter.

The rocky landscape in Mineral King is as colorful as a rainbow—red and orange shales mix with white marble and black metamorphic shale and granite. In winter, this area is prone to avalanches. The most prominent point in the area is **Sawtooth Peak,** which reaches 12,343 feet. Sawtooth and other peaks in this region resemble the Rocky Mountains more than the rest of the Sierra Nevada because they are made of metamorphic rock. The trails in Mineral King begin at 7,500 feet and climb from there. Park rangers sometimes conduct hikes in this area.

KINGS CANYON NATIONAL PARK

With its rugged canyon, huge river, and desolate backcountry, Kings Canyon is a hiker's dream. It consists of Grant Grove and Cedar Grove, as well as portions of the Monarch Wilderness and Jennie Lakes Wilderness. ***Note:*** Between Grant Grove and Cedar Grove is a stretch of land that lies not in the park, but in Giant Sequoia National Monument (see the sidebar later in this chapter).

Grant Grove is the most crowded region in either park. Not only is it just a few miles from a main entrance, but the area is also a thoroughfare for travelers heading from Giant Forest to the south or

Cedar Grove to the east. The grove was designated General Grant National Park in 1890 and was incorporated into Kings Canyon National Park when it was created in 1940.

Here you'll find the towering **General Grant Tree** amid a grove of spectacular giant sequoias. The tree was discovered by Joseph Hardin Tomas in 1862 and named 5 years later to honor Ulysses S. Grant. It measures 267 feet tall and 108 feet around, is among the world's largest living trees, and is possibly 2,000 years old. This tree has been officially declared "The Nation's Christmas Tree" and is the cornerstone of the park's annual Christmas tree ceremony.

Two and a half miles southwest of the grove is the **Big Stump Trail,** an interpretive hike that winds among the remains of logged sequoias. Since sequoia wood decays slowly, you'll see century-old leftover piles of sawdust that remain from the logging days. Nearby, **Panoramic Point** visitors can stand atop a 7,520-foot ledge and see across a large stretch of the Sierra and across Kings Canyon. **Grant Grove Village** also has a restaurant, market, gift shop, post office, and visitor center.

The **Cedar Grove** section of the park is known for its lush landscape, tumbling waterfalls, and miles upon miles of solitude. Getting to it is half the fun. You drive through **Kings Canyon,** with sheer granite canyon walls towering above you and the wild South Fork of the Kings River racing by. One mile east of the Cedar Grove Village turnoff is **Canyon View,** where visitors can see the glacially carved U shape of Kings Canyon. Easily accessible nature trails in Cedar Grove include Zumwalt Meadow, Roaring River Falls, and Knapp's Cabin. **Zumwalt Meadow** is dotted with ponderosa pine and has good views of two rock formations, the **Grand Sentinel** and **North Dome.** The top of Grand Sentinel is 8,504 feet above sea level; North Dome, which some say resembles Half Dome in Yosemite, towers over the area at 8,717 feet. The mile-long trail around the meadow is one of the prettiest in the park. Begin this walk at a parking lot 4½ miles east of the turnoff for Cedar Grove Village.

Roaring River Falls is a 5-minute walk from a parking area 3 miles east of the turnoff to the village. Even during summer and dry years, water crashes through a narrow granite chute into a cold green pool below. During a wet spring, these falls are powerful enough to drench visitors who venture too close. The route to **Knapp's Cabin** is a short walk from a turnoff 2 miles east of the road to Cedar Grove Village. Here, during the 1920s, Santa Barbara businessman George Knapp commissioned lavish fishing expeditions. This tiny cabin was used to store tons of expensive gear.

Ten miles west of Cedar Grove, in the national monument and back toward Grant Grove, is the entrance to **Boyden Cavern,** the only other cave in the area where tours are available. Although it's not as impressive as Sequoia's Crystal Cave, Boyden is a scenic cave, known for a wide variety of formations including rare shields. Highlights include a flowstone formation known as **Mother Nature's Wedding Cake** and the aptly named **Baby Elephant** formation. The cave is open daily April through October. Hours are usually 10am to 5pm June but often are shorter at the beginning and end of the season. Visitors see the cave on guided 45-minute tours that follow a well-lighted, handrail-equipped trail. Tours leave approximately every hour on the hour. The cost is $13 for ages 14 and up, $8 for children 3 to 12; admission is free for children 2 and younger. Reservations are not required. For information, contact **Boyden Cavern Adventures** (✆ **559/338-0959;** www.caverntours.com).

In Cedar Grove is a small village with a store and gift shop, restaurant, laundry, showers, lodge, and campgrounds. This region of the park is often less crowded than others. It's closed from mid-November to mid-April.

The **Monarch Wilderness** is a 45,000-acre region protected under the 1984 California Wilderness Act. Part of it lies on the grounds of Sequoia National Forest, and it adjoins wilderness in Kings Canyon National Park. It's small, tough to reach, and so steep that it seems more appropriate for mountain goats than human hikers. You're near the wilderness area when you pass Kings Canyon Lodge and Boyden Cave.

The **Jennie Lakes Wilderness,** at 10,500 acres, is tiny enough to hike through in a day, but it exhibits a variety of wilderness features, including the 10,365-foot Mitchell Peak and wide lowland meadows. This region lies between the Generals Highway and Calif. 180, east of Grant Grove.

3 Organized Tours & Ranger Programs

Sequoia Field Institute, HCR 89, Box 10, Three Rivers, CA 93271 (✆ **559/565-4251;** www.sequoiahistory.org/sfi/sfi.htm), offers a number of field seminars in and around Sequoia and Kings Canyon National Parks. The programs typically run from 1 to 4 days, with fees ranging from around $50 for the 1-day seminars to $100 and up for the multiday programs. Topics vary but are likely to include subjects such as mountain wildflowers, black bears, photography, and, of course, giant sequoias. Some seminars have minimum age limits, and some are physically demanding. Daylong van tours of

Sequoia are available through **Sequoia Sightseeing Tours** (✆ **559/561-4189;** www.sequoiatours.com) for $88 adults, $52 kids under 13.

While it's not an organized tour, per se, the National Park Service and the City of Visalia have put together a transportation system that makes it possible to explore Sequoia National Park without a car. From Visalia (or Three Rivers), the **Sequoia Shuttle** (✆ **877/287-4453;** www.sequoiashuttle.com) will take you to the Giant Forest Museum for just $15 round-trip. From here, riders can connect with the **free park shuttle** to get to Wuksachi Lodge or one of the numerous trail heads en route. The former makes five runs between 7am and 6:30pm (reservations are accepted); the latter runs from 9am to 6pm. Both run in the summer only.

4 Day Hikes

NEAR GIANT FOREST

Big Trees Trail A scenic loop walk among the sequoias, Big Trees Trail skirts the edge of a pretty meadow and has trailside exhibits that explain why this area is such a good habitat for sequoias. There are usually abundant wildflowers in Round Meadow in early summer. The trail, which has a 60-foot elevation change, is mostly paved, with some wooden boardwalk sections, and is wheelchair accessible. 1.5 miles RT. Easy. Access: Giant Forest Museum.

Congress Trail This walk circles some of Sequoia National Park's best-known and best-loved giants. The trail is a paved loop with a 200-foot elevation gain. Here you'll find the General Sherman Tree, considered the largest living tree on Earth. Other giant sequoias along this loop include the President, Chief Sequoyah, General Lee, and McKinley trees. The Lincoln tree is nearby. Several groups of trees include the House and the Senate. Try standing in the middle of these small clusters of trees to gain the perspective of an ant at a picnic. 2 miles RT. Easy. Access: General Sherman Tree, just off the Generals Hwy., 2 miles northeast of Giant Forest Museum.

Crescent Meadow Loop The meadow is a large, picturesque clearing dotted with high grass and wildflowers, encircled by a forest of firs and sequoias. The park's oldest cabin (Tharp's Log) is along this paved route. This is a particularly nice hike in early morning and at dusk, when indirect sunlight allows photographers to take the best pictures. 1.8 miles RT. Easy. Access: Crescent Meadow parking area.

Hazelwood Nature Trail Follow the signs for a pleasant, informative walk with exhibits that explain the relationship of trees, fire, and humans while winding among several stands of sequoias. 1 mile RT. Easy. Access: South side of the Generals Hwy., across from the road to Round Meadow.

High Sierra Trail This is one gateway to the backcountry, but the first few miles also make a great day hike. Along the way are spectacular views of the Kaweah River's middle fork and the Great Western Divide. The trail runs along a south-facing slope and is warm in spring and fall. Get an early start in summer. From the trail head, cross two wooden bridges over Crescent Creek until you reach a junction. Tharp's Log is to the left, the High Sierra Trail to the right. Hike uphill and a bit farther on through the damage done by the Buckeye Fire of 1988, a blaze ignited by a discarded cigarette 3,000 feet below, near the Kaweah River. After .75 mile you'll reach Eagle View, which offers a picturesque vision of the Great Western Divide. To the south are the craggy Castle Rocks.

Continue to see Panther Rock, Alta Peak, and Alta Meadow. At 2.75 miles is a sign for the Wolverton Cutoff, a trail used as a stock route between the Wolverton trail head and the high country. A bit farther on are Panther Creek and a small waterfall. At 3.25 miles is another fork of Panther Creek, and above is pink and gray Panther Rock. Follow a few more creeks to reach the last fork of Panther Creek, down a steep, eroded ravine. 9 miles RT. Moderate. Access: Near Crescent Meadow parking area restrooms.

Huckleberry Trail This is a great hike with a lot of beauty and not a lot of people. It passes through forest and meadow, near a 100-year-old cabin and an old American Indian village. The first mile takes you along the Hazelwood Nature Trail. Head south at each junction until you see a big sign with blue lettering, which marks the start of the Huckleberry Trail. You pass a small creek and meadow before reaching a second sign for Huckleberry Meadow. The next mile is steep and runs beneath sequoias, dogwoods, and white firs. At the 1.5-mile point is a Squatter's Cabin, built in the 1880s. East of the cabin is a trail junction. Head north (left) up a short hill. At the next junction, veer left along the edges of Circle Meadow for about a quarter-mile before you reach another junction. The right is a short detour to Bear's Bathtub, a pair of sequoias hollowed by fire and filled with water. Legend has it that an old mountain guide named Chester Wright once surprised a bear taking a bath here. Continue on the trail heading northeast to the Washington Tree, almost as big as the General Sherman Tree, then on to Alta Trail. Turn west (left) to Little Deer Creek. On both sides of the creek are American Indian mortar holes. Some of the largest are 3 feet in diameter. At the next junction, head north (right) to return to the Generals Highway and the last leg of the Huckleberry Trail to the parking area. 4 miles RT. Moderate. Access: Hazelwood Nature Trail parking area, a little more than ¼ mile east of Giant Forest Museum on the Generals Hwy.

Moro Rock This walk climbs 300 feet up 400 steps that twist along the gigantic boulder perched perilously on a ridgetop. Take it slow. The view from the top is breathtaking. It stretches to the Great Western Divide, which looks barren and dark, like the end of the world; mountains are often snow-capped well into summer. During a full moon, the view is even stranger and more beautiful. .25 mile one-way. Moderate. Access: Moro Rock parking area.

Moro Rock and Soldiers Loop Trail This hike cuts cross-country from the Giant Forest to Moro Rock. An early section is parallel to a main road, but the trail quickly departs from the traffic and heads through a forest dotted with giant sequoias. A carpet of ferns occasionally hides the trail. It pops out at Moro Rock, and then it's just a quick heart-thumper to the top. 4.6 miles RT. Moderate. Access: 30 yd. west of cafeteria at Giant Forest Museum.

Trail of the Sequoias This trail offers a longer, more remote hike than other routes into Giant Forest, away from the crowds and along some of the more scenic points of this plateau. The first quarter-mile is along the Congress Trail before heading uphill at Alta Trail. (Look for signs that read TRAIL OF THE SEQUOIAS.) After 1.5 miles, including a .5-mile steep climb among giant sequoias, is the ridge of the Giant Forest. Here are a variety of specimens, young and old, fallen and sturdy. Notice the shallow root system of fallen trees, and the lightning-blasted tops of others still standing. The trail continues to Log Meadow, past Crescent Meadow and Chimney Tree, a sequoia hollowed by fire. At the junction with Huckleberry Trail, follow the blue and green signs north toward the General Sherman Tree and back to Congress Trail. 6 miles RT. Moderate. Access: Northeast end of General Sherman Tree parking area.

NEAR GRANT GROVE

Azalea Trail From the visitor center, walk past the amphitheater to Sunset Campground and cross Calif. 180. The first mile joins the South Boundary Trail as it meanders through Wilsonia and crisscrosses Sequoia Creek in a gentle climb. After 1.5 miles is the third crossing of Sequoia Creek. It may be dry in late summer, but the banks are lush with ferns and brightly colored azaleas. Return the way you came. 3 miles RT. Easy. Access: Kings Canyon Visitor Center.

Big Stump Trail This trail meanders through what was once a grove of giant sequoias. All that's left today are the old stumps and piles of 100-year-old sawdust. A brochure available at visitor centers (and at the trail head during the summer) describes the logging that occurred here in the 1880s. To continue, take the Hitchcock Meadow Trail (described below), which leads to Viola Fall. 1 mile RT. Easy. Access: Big Stump Picnic Area near entrance to Grant Grove from Kings Canyon.

Boole Tree Loop This trail loops through the once-proud forest in the ravaged Converse Basin to the 269-foot Boole Tree, one of the last reminders of the giants that were logged here. The world's eighth-largest sequoia (it was once thought to be the largest), the Boole Tree, is the highlight of the loop, and there are terrific views of Kings Canyon. 2.5 mile RT. Moderate. Access: The end of the Converse Basin rd. north of Grant Grove in Giant Sequoia National Monument.

Dead Giant Loop The Dead Giant Loop and the North Grove Loop (described below) share the first .75 mile. The trail descends a fire road and after a quarter-mile hits a junction. Take the lower trail. After another half-mile you'll break off from the North Grove Loop and head south around a lush meadow. It's another quarter-mile to a sign that reads DEAD GIANT. Turn west to see what's left of this tree. The trail climbs slightly as it circles a knoll and comes to Sequoia Lake Overlook. The lake was formed in 1899 when the Kings River Lumber Company built a dam on Mill Flat Creek. The water was diverted down a flume to the town of Sanger. During logging, millions of board feet (a unit of linear measurement of lumber) of giant sequoias were floated down that flume to be finished at a mill in Sanger. The lumber company went bankrupt and sold the operation to new owners, who moved it over to Converse Basin. The company then clear-cut Converse Basin, once the world's largest stand of sequoias. Continue around the loop back to the Dead Giant sign, then return to the parking area. 2.25 miles RT. Easy. Access: Lower end of General Grant Tree parking area, at a locked gate with a sign that reads NORTH GROVE LOOP.

General Grant Tree Trail The accessible trail leads to the huge General Grant Tree, which is also the nation's only living national shrine. Signs help visitors interpret forest features. .5 mile RT. Easy. Access: General Grant Tree parking area, 1 mile northwest of the visitor center.

Hitchcock Meadow Trail This trail takes you to pretty Viola Falls. The first half-mile mirrors the Big Stump Trail described above. From there, hike another quarter-mile to Hitchcock Meadow, a large clearing in Sequoia National Forest that is surrounded by sequoia stumps. Notice the small sequoias in this area—these are the descendants of the giant sequoias logged in the last century. From here the trail climbs slightly to a ridge, where it re-enters Kings Canyon National Park before descending a short series of steep switchbacks to Sequoia Creek. Cross the creek and look for a sign directing you to Viola Falls, a series of short steps that join into one fall when the water level is high. It is very dangerous to venture down the canyon, but above it are several flat places that make great picnic spots. 3.5 miles RT. Easy. Access: Big Stump Picnic Area near the entrance to Grant Grove from Kings Canyon.

North Grove Loop The trail follows an abandoned mill road from long ago. It cuts through stands of dogwood, sugar pine, sequoia, and white fir. A large dead sequoia shows evidence of a fire. 1.5 miles RT. Easy. Access: Lower end of General Grant Tree parking area.

Park Ridge Trail Begin this hike by walking south along the ridge, where views of the valley and peaks dominate. On a clear day, you can see Hume Lake in Sequoia National Forest, the San Joaquin Valley, and, occasionally, the coast range 100 miles away. Return the same way. 4.7 miles RT. Easy. Access: Panoramic Point parking area, a 2½-mile drive down a steep road from Grant Grove Village.

Sunset Trail The hike climbs 1,400 feet past two waterfalls and a lake. After crossing the highway, the trail heads left around a campground. After 1.25 miles, follow the South Boundary Trail toward Viola Falls. You'll reach a paved road where you can head to the right to see the park's original entrance. Return the way you came, or follow the road to the General Grant Tree parking area and walk to the visitor center. 6 miles RT. Moderate to strenuous. Access: Across the road from Kings Canyon Visitor Center.

NEAR CEDAR GROVE

Bubbs Creek Trail The trail begins by crossing and recrossing Copper Creek. This site was once an American Indian village, and shards of obsidian can still be found on the ground (please leave them in place). After the first mile, you'll enter a swampy area that offers a good place to watch for wildlife. The trail here closes in on the river, where deer and bear drink. At 2 miles, you'll come to a junction. The trail to Paradise Valley heads north (left); the hike to Bubbs Creek veers right and crosses Bailey Bridge, over the South Fork of the Kings River.

Continue hiking east over four small wooden bridges that cross Bubbs Creek. The creek was named after John Bubbs, a prospector and rancher who arrived here in 1864. The trail climbs on the creek's north side, following a few steep switchbacks, which provide alternating views of the canyon of Paradise Valley and Cedar Grove. At 3 miles is a large, emerald pool with waterfalls, and far above is a rock formation that John Muir named "the Sphinx." At 4 miles you reach Sphinx Creek, a good area to spend the day or night (with a wilderness permit). There are several campsites nearby. Hike back the way you came or along the Sentinel Trail (described below). 8 miles RT. Moderate to strenuous. Access: East end of parking area at Road's End.

Mist Falls This is one of the more popular trails leading to the backcountry, but it's also a nice day hike. The first 2 miles, before you reach Bubbs Creek Bridge, are dry. Take the fork to the left and head uphill. The first waterfall is not your destination, although it is a pretty spot to take a break. From here, the trail meanders along the river, through forest and swamp areas, before it comes out at the base of Mist Falls, a wide fall that flows generously in spring. There are dozens of great picnic spots along the way. Return along the same route, or cross over at Bubbs Creek Bridge and head back on the Sentinel Trail (described below). This will add a mile to the hike. From Mist Falls, you can also continue to Paradise Valley (described below). 8 miles RT. Moderate to strenuous. Access: Short-term parking area at Road's End; pass Cedar Grove Village and follow signs.

Muir's Rock This level, simple, short stroll takes you to one of the most historically significant spots in the park's modern-day history. From this wide, flat rock, John Muir delivered impassioned speeches about the Sierra. 100 yd. RT. Easy. Access: Parking area at Road's End, along the trail to Zumwalt Meadow.

Paradise Valley This is a great overnight hike because the valley is so pretty and there's much to explore. But it can also be an ambitious day hike. Follow the Mist Falls trail (described above), and then head up 3 miles of switchbacks to Paradise Valley. The beautiful valley is 3 miles long and relatively flat. Hike through the valley to connect with the John Muir Trail and the rest of the backcountry, or return the way you came. 12 miles RT. Moderate to strenuous. Access: Short-term parking area at Road's End; pass Cedar Grove Village and follow signs.

River Trail The trail hugs the river and can be shorter if you want to walk just to the waterfalls (.5 mile round-trip) or Zumwalt Meadows (3 miles round-trip; a shorter version is listed below). The waterfalls are .25 mile along the trail. The falls are short but powerful. Do *not* attempt to climb them. Just north of the falls, back toward the parking area, is a sign that reads ZUMWALT MEADOW—ROAD'S END. Take this trail, which hugs the highway before breaking off into a beautiful canyon.

At 1.5 miles is the Zumwalt Bridge. If you cross the bridge, you'll be a quarter-mile from the Zumwalt Meadow parking area. To stay on the River Trail, don't cross the bridge—continue up the canyon for another quarter of a mile to Zumwalt Meadow. From here there's a slight incline. In a half-mile you'll reach a fork; head uphill. The rest of the hike follows the riverbank, which has plenty of swimming and fishing holes. After 2.5 miles you'll come to another footbridge. Cross over, and it's a short (.5-mile) walk back to the Road's End parking area, where you can try to catch a ride. Otherwise, retrace your steps to your car. 5.5 miles RT. Easy. Access: From Cedar Grove Ranger Station, drive 3 miles to Roaring River Falls parking area.

Sentinel Trail Essentially, this hike encircles a small length of the South Fork of the Kings River. After following the river's north side for 2 miles, the trail splits and heads north to Mist Falls and Paradise Valley or east across Bailey Bridge toward Bubbs Creek. Follow the eastern trail, but instead of hiking to Bubbs Creek, follow a sign that reads ROAD'S END—2.6 MILES. This will take you through dense groves of pine and cedars, with occasional views of Grand Sentinel. You'll cross Avalanche Creek before emerging in a huge meadow and returning near the riverbank. At 2 miles, you can see Muir's Rock, the huge, flat boulder described above. At 2.25 miles, you'll find a footbridge that points back to the parking area. 4.6 miles RT. Easy. Access: Short-term parking area at Road's End; pass Cedar Grove Village and follow signs.

Zumwalt Meadow Cross the bridge and walk left for 100 yards to a fork. Take the trail that leads right for a bird's-eye view of the meadow before descending 50 feet to the ground below. The trail leads along the meadow's edge, where the fragrance of ponderosa pine, sugar pine, and incense cedar fills the air. The loop returns along the banks of the South Fork of the Kings River. Grand Sentinel and North Dome rise in the background. 1.5 miles RT. Easy. Access: Zumwalt Meadows parking area, 1 mile west of Road's End, on Calif. 180 past Cedar Grove Village.

OTHER HIKES

Cold Springs Nature Trail This easy loop illustrates the natural history and beauty of the region. It passes near private cabins that predate the area's addition to Sequoia National Park in 1978. The walk offers views of the Mineral King Valley and surrounding peaks. It can get hot and dry in summer, so carry additional water. 2 miles RT. Easy. Access: Mineral King's Cold Springs Campground, across from ranger station.

Deer Cove Trail This hike in the Monarch Wilderness, maintained by the U.S. Forest Service, starts at 4,400 feet and climbs to 5,600 feet. It follows short, steep switchbacks that climb through bear clover and manzanita. After the first .5 mile, it passes above a large spring. Deer Cove Creek is in a steep drainage area at the 2-mile mark. This area is heavily wooded with cedar, fir, and Jeffrey pine. To continue, see the description of the Wildman Meadow Trail (below). 4 miles RT. Strenuous. Access: In the Monarch Wilderness, on Calif. 180, about 2¾ miles west of Cedar Grove Village turnoff. Parking area is on north side of road.

Kings River National Recreation Trail It's a long drive to the trail head, but after hiking in upper Kings Canyon, this is a great place to see what it looks like from the bottom. The views here rival anything in the park, with peaks towering overhead and the river rushing nearby. The hike cuts through the Monarch Wilderness along the belly of Kings Canyon, although this trail, too, lies in the national forest, not the park. The trail starts along a dirt road and soon departs and follows the river, which is broad and powerful at this point. The first mile alternates between rapids and great fishing pools. At 1.5 miles is a view up Converse Creek and its rugged canyon.

At 3 miles you'll find Spring Creek, a short but pretty waterfall and a good place to rest. You can turn around here for a total hike of 6 miles, or proceed for the 10-mile option. The trail from here ascends the steep Garlic Spur, a ridge that ends suddenly at the ledge of the canyon. The trail above Spring Creek is flecked with obsidian. The nearest source of this rock is the Mono Craters, more than 100 miles north. For that reason, many believe the Monache Indians used this trail for trading. After the long, steep ascent, the trail heads down to Garlic Meadow Creek. A short way upstream are large pools and wide resting areas. Beyond the creek, the trail is not maintained. 6–10 miles RT. Easy to Spring Creek; strenuous to Garlic Meadow Creek. Access: On Calif. 180, 6 miles below Big Stump Entrance, turn north on F.S. 12S01 (a U.S. Forest Service rd.), a dirt road marked MCKENZIE HELIPORT, DELILAH LOOKOUT, camp 4½ miles. Drive 18 miles to the Kings River. Turn west and drive another 2½ miles to Rodgers Crossing. Cross the bridge and turn east, following signs to Kings River Trail. The trail head is at the east end of a parking lot another 7 miles ahead, at the road's end.

Marble Fork Trail This is one of the most scenic hikes in the Foothills area. The walk leads to a deep gorge where the roaring Marble Falls spill in a cascade over multicolored boulders. From the parking area, begin hiking north up the Southern California Edison flume. After crossing the flume on a wooden bridge, watch for a sign to the trail and head east (uphill). The trail crosses some steep switchbacks and near some large poison oak bushes with stems 3 inches wide. Watch out for these bare sticks in late fall and winter.

The trail will begin to flatten out and settle into a slight slope for the rest of the hike up to the waterfalls. Look for large yuccas and California bay along the way. After 2 miles, you can see the waterfalls as the hike cuts through white and gray marble, a belt of the rock that is responsible for seven caves in the park, including Crystal Cave near Giant Forest. Once you reach the falls, it's almost impossible to hike any farther; only very experienced hikers should attempt a walk downstream. The marble slabs break very easily, and the boulders in the area can get very slick. Be extra careful when water is high. This is a good hike year-round, but it can be very hot during summer afternoons. 6 miles RT. Strenuous. Access: Dirt road at upper end of Potwisha Campground, which is 3½ miles east of the Ash Mountain Entrance. A small parking area is past campsite no. 16.

Potwisha & River's Edge This was once the site of an American Indian village known as Potwisha, home to the Monache tribe. The main village was just about where the dump station is now, and on the bedrock are mortar holes where the women ground acorns into meal. From here the trail continues above the river to a sandy beach and a good swimming hole. The trail turns east upstream before the suspension bridge, then north up a short but steep hill. Near the top of the hill you'll run into Middle Fork Trail. Turn west (left) and hike the short distance back to the parking area. .5 mile RT. Easy. Access: From Ash Mountain Entrance, take highway to Potwisha Campground. At campground entrance (on the left), turn right down a paved road toward an RV dump station. Take paved road until it dead-ends at a parking area. Continue toward river on a footpath to open bedrock.

Wildman Meadow This hike through the Monarch Wilderness mirrors the first 2 miles of the hike to Deer Cove (described above). After reaching Deer Cove, it's a steep ascent to 7,500 feet—a 1,900-foot gain in 5 miles. From Deer Cove, hike 3.5 miles to a sandy knoll that has a good view into the rugged canyon drainage area of Grizzly Creek. At 6.5 miles, you'll top the ridge and cross over to the north-facing slope. A quick drop lands you in Wildman Meadow, where a large stock camp occupies the edge of the clearing. 14 miles RT. Strenuous. Access: Trail head for Deer Cove Trail, with which this trail connects, is in the Monarch Wilderness, on Calif. 180, about 2¾ miles west of the Cedar Grove Village turnoff. Parking area is on north side of road.

5 Exploring the Backcountry

Be aware of **bears** that frequent these regions, and in the summer take insect repellent for protection against mosquitoes. Stay off high peaks during thunderstorms, and don't attempt any climb if it looks as if a storm is rolling in; exposed peaks are often struck by lightning. In winter, snow buries many of these routes.

All overnight backpacking trips require a $15 **wilderness permit** per party (free in winter), available by mail, by fax, or in person at the ranger station closest to the hike you want to take. First-come, first-served permits can be issued the morning of your trip or after 1pm on the previous afternoon. **Reservations** can be made at least 14 days in advance, March 1 to September 10. To reserve a permit, you must provide a name, address, and telephone number; the number of people in your party; the method of travel (snowshoe, horse, foot); number of stock, if applicable; start and end dates; start and end trail heads; a principal destination; and a rough itinerary. Download the application from the park's website and mail it to **Wilderness Permit Reservations,** Sequoia and Kings Canyon National Parks, 47050 Generals Hwy. #60, Three Rivers, CA 93271, or fax it to ✆ **559/565-4239.** Reserved permits must be picked up by 9am. If you're delayed, call the ranger station or you risk forfeiting your permit. If your hike crosses agency boundaries, get the permit from the agency on whose land the hike begins. Only one permit is required.

Note: Eight ranger stations lie along the John Muir and Pacific Crest trails, and six are in the southern part of the park in the Sequoia backcountry. Most are not staffed from fall to spring. To find the ranger station closest to your trail head, consult the park map.

Alta Peak–Alta Meadow From Wolverton, hike on the Lakes Trail toward the Panther Gap Trail. Head right on the Panther Gap Trail, up through the 8,400-foot gap to Alta Trail. Turn left on Alta Trail and hike past the junction with Sevenmile Hill Trail and the junction with Alta Peak Trail. Left takes you up Alta Peak, a 2,000-foot ascent in 2 miles that offers spectacular vistas. If climbing isn't your idea of fun, plow straight ahead to Alta Meadow, which has a nice view and good places to camp. 13–16 miles RT. Strenuous. Access: From Giant Forest Museum, drive about 3 miles north on the Generals Hwy. and take the Wolverton Rd. turnoff (on the right). Look for the trail at the southeast end of the parking area at Wolverton Creek.

High Sierra Trail This trail is a popular route into the backcountry, and some utilize it as a one-way passage to Mount Whitney. It gets a lot of sun, so begin early. From the parking area, head out on a paved trail to the south, over several bridges to a junction. Turn right onto the High Sierra Trail. You will pass Eagle View, the Wolverton Cutoff, and Panther Creek. Hike at least 3 miles before setting up camp. For $175 to $250 for two people (meals included), a civilized overnight option is the 11-mile hike to the **Bearpaw High Sierra Camp** (✆ **559/565-4070;** www.visitsequoia.com) from Crescent Meadow. At least 10 miles RT. Moderate to strenuous. Access: Calif. 198 to Giant Forest; proceed to Crescent Meadow Rd. Bear right at the junction, passing the signed parking area for Moro Rock, and continue to the road's end and the Crescent Meadow parking area.

Jennie Lakes Trail This is a nice overnight hike that's not too demanding. You can extend it into the Jennie Lakes Wilderness Area. From the parking area, cross through the campground and continue across Big Meadow Creek. From here, the trail climbs. At Fox Meadow are a wooden trail sign and a register for hikers to sign. At the next junction, head right toward Jennie Lakes (left goes toward the Weaver Lake Trail) and up to Poop Out Pass. From here it's a drop down to the Boulder Creek drainage area and on to emerald-green Jennie Lakes. This hike can be combined with a second day hike to Weaver Lake. Just retrace your steps to the Weaver Lake turnoff. Weaver Lake is a relatively warm mountain lake surrounded by blueberry bushes that grow heavy with fresh fruit in July. At least 12 miles RT. Moderate to strenuous. Access: From Grant Grove, drive about 7 miles south on the Generals Hwy. to the turnoff for Big Meadows Campground. The trail head and parking area are on the south side of the road next to a ranger station.

Lakes Trail This trail traces a string of **tarns,** high-mountain lakes created by the scouring action of glaciers thousands of years ago. Heather Lake and Pear Lake are popular destinations along this route. From the trail head, go east, avoiding the Long Meadow Trail. Climb up a moraine ridge and soon you'll be hiking above Wolverton Creek, which darts through meadows strewn with wildflowers. At a junction with the Panther Gap Trail, head left toward Heather Lake. At a second junction, you have to choose. To the right is Hump Trail, a steep but always open trail. Left is the Watchtower Trail, which leads along a granite ledge blasted in the rock with dynamite. With the Tokopah Valley far below, this hike is not for those who suffer vertigo. Both trails wind up at Heather Lake. Camping is not allowed here but is permitted up the trail at Pear and Emerald lakes. At least 12.5 miles RT. Moderate to strenuous. Access: From Giant Forest, drive north on the Generals Hwy. to the Wolverton parking area. The trail head is on the left of the parking lot as you enter from the highway.

6 Other Sports & Activities

CROSS-COUNTRY SKIING There are 35 miles of marked backcountry trails in the parks. Call park concessionaires for information (✆ **559/335-5500** in Grant Grove and ✆ **559/565-4070** in the Wuksachi Lodge area). The **Pear Lake Ski Hut** is open to the public for backcountry accommodations in Sequoia from mid-December through April for $30 to $40 per person per night. Call ✆ **559/565-4222** for more information.

FISHING A section of the south fork of the **Kings River,** the **Kaweah** drainage, and the parks' lakes are open all year for trout fishing—rainbow, brook, German brown, and golden. Most other waters are open for trout fishing from late April through mid-November, and open for other species year-round. California **fishing licenses** (available at stores in the park) are required for anglers 16 and older, and you should also get a copy of the National Park Service's fishing regulations, available at visitor centers.

HORSEBACK RIDING Concessionaires in both parks and the adjacent national monument offer guided horseback and mule rides and overnight pack trips during the summer. In Kings Canyon, **Cedar Grove Pack Station** (✆ **559/565-3464** summer, 559/337-2314 winter) is about 1 mile east of Cedar Grove Village, and **Grant Grove Stables** (✆ **559/335-9292** summer, 559/337-2314 winter) is near Grant Grove Village. In Giant Sequoia National Monument, **Horse Corral Pack Station** is on Big Meadows Road, 10 miles east of Generals Highway (✆ **559/565-3404** summer, 559/564-6429 winter; www.horsecorralpackers.com). The pack stations offer hourly rides as well as overnight treks. The stables offer day rides only. Rates range from $30 to $40 for a 1-hour ride, to $100 to $200 for a full day in the saddle; call for rates for pack trips.

SNOWSHOEING On winter weekends, rangers lead introductory snowshoe hikes in **Grant Grove** (✆ **559/565-4307**) and **Giant Forest** (✆ **559/565-4436**). Snowshoes are provided, and a $1 donation is requested.

WHITE-WATER RAFTING The Kaweah and Upper Kings rivers in the parks are not open to boating, but several companies run trips just outside the parks. The thrilling roller-coaster ride through the rapids is a great way to not only see, but also to experience these scenic rivers. Offering trips on the Kaweah, Kings, Merced, and other rivers is **Whitewater Voyages** (✆ **800/400-7238;** www.whitewatervoyages.com), with rates that range from $109 to $219 for half- and full-day trips, and multiday trips are also available (call for rates). **Kings River Expeditions** (✆ **800/846-3674** or 559/233-4881; www.kingsriver.com) specializes in rafting trips on the Kings. For 1-day trips they charge $99 to $160 per person. Overnight trips are also available (call for rates).

A Nearby National Monument

Some of the most beautiful scenery in Sequoia and Kings Canyon national parks is not in either one, but in an adjacent section of the Sequoia National Forest now designated a national monument.

Covering 328,000 acres, **Giant Sequoia National Monument** was created by proclamation by President Bill Clinton in 2000. The monument contains 38 groves of sequoias, including some of the most magnificent giant trees anywhere. In addition, it has towering domes of granite, scenic Hume Lake (a popular destination for boaters and anglers), and the spectacular Kings Canyon—the deepest canyon in North America, with elevations ranging from 1,000 to 11,000 feet.

Among hiking trails in the monument is the **Boole Tree Trail,** a moderate 2.5-mile loop that leads to Boole Tree, the largest sequoia in the 1.1-million-acre Sequoia National Forest, and the eighth-largest tree in the world. This trail, located off Forest Road 13S55 off Kings Canyon Highway, includes forest and open country. You'll see sequoias, scenic vistas of the Kings River, and wildflowers in summer.

An easy walk on the quarter-mile (each way) **Chicago Stump Trail** leads to the stump of the General Noble Tree, which was cut down, cut into pieces, and then reassembled and displayed at the 1893 World's Fair in Chicago. Some fairgoers refused to believe that a tree could grow so big; they dubbed it "the California hoax."

Information about other attractions and facilities in the monument are discussed elsewhere in this chapter. For additional information, contact **Giant Sequoia National Monument,** Sequoia National Forest, Hume Lake Ranger District, 35860 E. Kings Canyon Rd. (Calif. 180), Dunlap, CA 93621 (✆ **559/338-2251;** www.fs.fed.us/r5/sequoia).

7 Camping

There are numerous camping opportunities both within and surrounding Sequoia and Kings Canyon national parks. It's important to remember that proper food storage is required for the sake of the black bears in the parks, as well as for your safety. See local bulletin boards for instructions.

INSIDE SEQUOIA NATIONAL PARK

The only national park campgrounds that accept reservations are Dorst and Lodgepole (✆ **877/444-6777;** www.recreation.gov); the other campgrounds are first come, first served. Reservations for Dorst and Lodgepole can be made up to 6 months in advance.

The two biggest campgrounds in the park are in the Lodgepole area. The **Lodgepole Campground,** which has flush toilets, is often crowded, but it's pretty and near big trees and enough backcountry trails to offer some solitude. In summer, you'll find a grocery store nearby, a restaurant, visitor center, children's nature center, evening ranger programs, and gift shop. From Giant Forest, drive 5 miles northeast on the Generals Highway. **Dorst Creek Campground,** 14 miles northwest of Giant Forest on the Generals Highway, is a high-elevation campground that offers easy access to Muir Grove and pleasant backcountry trails. It has flush toilets and evening ranger programs. Group campsites are available by reservation.

In the Foothills area, **Potwisha Campground** is small, with well-spaced sites tucked beneath oak trees along the Marble Fork of the Kaweah River. However, it does get hot in summer. The campground has flush toilets. From the Ash Mountain Entrance, drive 3 miles northeast on the Generals Highway to the campground entrance. The **Buckeye Flat Campground,** which is open to tents only, sits among oaks along the Middle Fork of the Kaweah River, and although it also gets hot in summer, its beauty makes it one of our favorites. It has flush toilets. From the Ash Mountain Entrance, drive about 6 miles northeast on the Generals Highway to the Hospital Rock Ranger Station. From there, follow signs to the campground, which is several miles down a narrow, winding road. **South Fork Campground,** just inside Sequoia's southwestern boundary, is the smallest and most remote campground in the park. It is along the South Fork of the Kaweah River and has pit toilets only. From the town of Three Rivers, go east on South Fork Road 23 miles to the campground.

The two campgrounds in the Mineral King area are open to tents only—no RVs or trailers. Pretty, small **Atwell Mill Campground** is near the East

Campground	Elev. (ft.)	Total Sites	RV Hookups	Dump Station	Toilets
Inside Sequoia National Park					
Atwell Mill	6,650	21	0	No	Yes
Buckeye Flat	2,800	28	0	No	Yes
Cold Springs	7,500	31	0	No	Yes
Dorst Creek	6,700	204	0	Yes	Yes
Lodgepole	6,700	204	0	Yes	Yes
Potwisha	2,100	42	0	Yes	Yes
South Fork	3,600	10	0	No	Yes
Inside Kings Canyon National Park					
Azalea	6,500	110	0	No	Yes
Crystal Springs	6,500	50	0	No	Yes
Moraine	4,600	120	0	No	Yes
Sentinel	4,600	82	0	No	Yes
Sheep Creek	4,600	111	0	No	Yes
Sunset	6,500	157	0	No	Yes
Outside the Parks					
Big Meadows	7,600	25	0	No	Yes
Horse Creek	300	80	0	Yes	Yes
Hume Lake	5,200	74	0	No	Yes
Landslide	5,800	9	0	No	Yes
Lemon Cove	500	55	40	Yes	Yes
Princess	5,900	90	0	Yes	Yes
Stony Creek	6,400	49	0	No	Yes
Ten Mile	5,800	13	0	No	Yes

Fork of the Kaweah River, at Atwell Creek. It has pit toilets. From Three Rivers, take Mineral King Road east for 20 miles to the campground. **Cold Springs Campground,** which also has pit toilets, is a beautiful place but not very accessible. Once you get there, you'll be rewarded with lovely scenery. It's near the Mineral King Ranger Station, making it a good starting point for many backcountry hikes. From Three Rivers, take Mineral King Road east for 25 miles to the campground.

For additional information, call the general Sequoia/Kings Canyon **information line** (✆ **559/565-3341**).

IN KINGS CANYON NATIONAL PARK

All of the campgrounds in Kings Canyon are first come, first served only; reservations are not available. All have flush toilets.

In the Grant Grove area are three attractive campgrounds near the big trees—**Azalea, Crystal Springs,** and **Sunset.** They have a pleasant, woodsy feeling, are close to park facilities, and offer evening ranger programs. From the Big Stump Entrance, take Calif. 180 east about 1¾ miles.

There are four attractive campgrounds in the Cedar Grove Village area, all accessible from Calif. 180 and close to the facilities in Cedar Grove Village. **Sentinel,** the first to open for the season, tends to fill quickly; **Moraine** is the farthest from the crowds. The others generally open on an as-needed basis. They are **Sheep Creek,** along picturesque Sheep Creek, and **Canyon View,** a group campground not listed in the accompanying table.

For additional information, call the general Sequoia/Kings Canyon **information line** (✆ **559/565-3341**).

OUTSIDE THE PARKS

The U.S. Forest Service operates a number of campgrounds in **Giant Sequoia National Monument,** a 327,769-acre section of Sequoia National Forest, which was given national monument status in April 2000. They provide a delightful forest camping experience and are usually less crowded than national park campgrounds. There is also primitive camping available—no fee, no facilities.

In the Hume Lake area, all the Forest Service campgrounds have pit toilets except the beautiful

Drinking Water	Showers	Fire Pits/ Grills	Laundry	Public Phones	Reservations	Fees	Open
Yes	No	Yes	No	No	No	$12	Late May–Oct
Yes	No	Yes	No	No	No	$18	Apr to early Sept
Yes	No	Yes	No	Yes	No	$12	Late May–Oct
Yes	No	Yes	No	Yes	Yes	$20	Late June to mid-Sept
Yes	Yes	Yes	Yes	Yes	Yes	$18–$20	Year-round
Yes	No	Yes	No	Yes	No	$18	Year-round
No	No	Yes	No	No	No	$12	Year-round
Yes	Yes	Yes	No	Yes	No	$10–$18	Year-round
Yes	Yes	Yes	No	Yes	No	$18	May–Sept
Yes	Yes	Yes	Yes	Yes	No	$18	May–Oct
Yes	Yes	Yes	Yes	Yes	No	$18	Late Apr–Oct
Yes	Yes	Yes	Yes	Yes	No	$14	May to mid-Nov (as needed)
Yes	Yes	Yes	Yes	No	No	$18	May to mid-Sept (as needed)
No	No	Yes	No	Yes	No	Free	May–Oct
Yes	Yes	Yes	No	Yes	Yes	$16	Year-round
Yes	No	Yes	No	Yes	Yes	$20	May–Oct
No	No	Yes	No	No	No	$16	May–Oct
Yes	Yes	Yes	Yes	Yes	Yes	$25–$35	Year-round
Yes	No	Yes	No	No	Yes	$18	May–Oct
Yes	Yes	Yes	No	Yes	Yes	$20	May–Oct
Yes	No	Yes	No	No	No	$16	May–Oct

Hume Lake Campground, which is on the banks of the lake and has flush toilets. It's about 3 miles south of Calif. 180 on Hume Lake Road. The largest campground in this area is **Princess,** on Calif. 180; two smaller campgrounds, both beyond Hume Lake on Ten Mile Road, are **Landslide** and **Upper Ten Mile.**

In the Stony Creek/Big Meadows area, you'll find vault toilets at all U.S. Forest Service campgrounds except **Stony Creek Campground,** off Generals Highway in Stony Creek Village, which has flush toilets. Among the larger campgrounds in this area is **Big Meadows,** which sits along Big Meadows Creek. Nearby trails lead to the Jennie Lakes Wilderness. From Grant Grove Village, drive 7 miles southeast on the Generals Highway, then turn east on Big Meadows Road and drive 5 miles to the campground.

For additional information on the above and other campgrounds in the national monument, contact **Giant Sequoia National Monument,** Sequoia National Forest, Hume Lake Ranger District, 35860 E. Kings Canyon Rd., Dunlap, CA 93621 (✆ **559/338-2251;** www.fs.fed.us/r5/sequoia).

Another great place to camp is **Horse Creek Campground,** operated by the U.S. Army Corps of Engineers. It's along the south shore of Lake Kaweah, in Lake Kaweah Recreation Area, about 6 miles east of the community of Lemon Cove off Calif. 198. The lake, which is about 5 miles long and a ½-mile wide, covers 1,900 acres when full. It is popular with boaters, who take to the water in kayaks, canoes, personal watercraft, fishing boats, and larger patio boats. There are several boat ramps, and boat rentals are available at the **Kaweah Marina** (✆ **559/597-2526;** www.kaweahmarina.com). Call for current rates and availability. This is also a popular fishing lake, where you're apt to catch large-mouth bass, crappie, bluegill, catfish, and rainbow trout. The number of campsites varies with the water level, with the fewest usually in spring, when the lake is at its highest; much of the campground is often flooded into July. There are some shady sites and some open, and most have good views across the lake. The campground has flush toilets. For information, contact **U.S. Army Corps of Engineers,** Lake Kaweah Recreation Area, P.O. Box 44270, Lemon Cove, CA 93244 (✆ **559/561-3155** or 559/597-2301). Campsite reservations are available (✆ **877/444-6777;** www.recreation.gov).

Those seeking a full-service commercial campground with RV hookups and all the usual amenities should head to **Lemon Cove/Sequoia Campground,** 32075 Sierra Dr., P.O. Box 44269, Lemon Cove, CA 93244 (✆ **559/597-2346;** www.lemoncovesequoiacamp.com). This attractive and convenient campground on the west side of Lemon Cove is 22 miles east of Visalia in the foothills of the Sierra Nevada. It can handle large rigs with slide-outs and offers cable-TV hookups, propane sales, a convenience store, grassy and shaded sites, a recreation room, a playground and volleyball court, and an outdoor swimming pool.

8 Where to Stay

INSIDE THE PARKS

Lodging in the parks ranges from rustic cabins to well-equipped motel-style accommodations, usually with a mountain-lodge atmosphere and great views. There are also several good choices in the nearby Giant Sequoia National Monument and in the gateway towns of Visalia, Three Rivers, and Lemon Cove (see "Outside the Parks," below).

Cedar Grove Lodge This motel offers comfortable rooms on the bank of the Kings River. Getting here is half the fun—it's a 36-mile drive down a winding highway that provides beautiful vistas along the way. The phone- and TV-free rooms are standard motel accommodations—comfortable, but nothing special—but what you're really paying for is the location, surrounded by tall trees with a pretty river. Most of the rooms are above the **Cedar Grove Café** (see "Where to Dine," below), with communal decks and river views. However, we prefer the three smaller, not quite as attractively appointed rooms on ground level, which have patios looking right out onto the river and their own refrigerators and microwaves.

Calif. 180, Cedar Grove, Kings Canyon National Park (mailing address: Sequoia Kings Canyon Park Services Company, 5755 E. Kings Canyon Rd., Ste. 101, Fresno, CA 93727). ✆ **866/522-6966** or 559/335-5500. www.sequoia-kingscanyon.com. 18 units. A/C. $119–$135 double. AE, DISC, MC, V. Closed Nov–Apr.

Grant Grove Cabins Although these are all cabins, they offer a wide range of amenities and prices, from handsomely restored cabins with private bathrooms that ooze historic charm, to rustic tent cabins that simply provide a comfortable bed out of the weather at a very low price. Those who want to rough it in style should reserve one of the nine cabins, built in the 1920s, that have electricity, indoor plumbing, and full private bathrooms. A bit less modern but still quite comfortable are the 43 rustic cabins that have kerosene lanterns for light and wood-burning stoves for heat; these share a bathhouse. Tent cabins, with wood floors and walls but canvas roofs, are available in summer only. All cabins have full linen service. It's a 10-minute walk to the Grant Grove Visitor Center from the cabins, which are also near the **Grant Grove Restaurant** (described under "Where to Dine," below). There is free Wi-Fi in the lobby area.

Calif. 180, Grant Grove Village, Kings Canyon National Park (mailing address: Sequoia Kings Canyon Park Services Company, 5755 E. Kings Canyon Rd., Ste. 101, Fresno, CA 93727). ✆ **866/522-6966** or 559/335-5500. www.sequoia-kingscanyon.com. 53 units, 9 with private bathroom. $63–$91 cabin with shared bath; $129–$140 cabin with private bath. Register at Grant Grove Village Registration Center, btw. the restaurant and gift shop. AE, DISC, MC, V.

John Muir Lodge This handsome log lodge, built in 1998, looks perfect in this beautiful national park setting. It is an excellent choice for visitors who want a mountain-lodge atmosphere and quiet, comfortable, modern rooms, with full bathrooms and the other comforts we've all come to appreciate. Standard rooms are simply but tastefully decorated, with two queen beds and wonderful views of the surrounding forest. Suites are pretty much two connecting lodge rooms, except that one of the rooms has a queen bed and a queen sofa sleeper instead of two queens. The lodge also has a gigantic, very attractive log-beam lobby.

Calif. 180, Grant Grove Village, Kings Canyon National Park (mailing address: Sequoia Kings Canyon Park Services Company, 5755 E. Kings Canyon Rd., Ste. 101, Fresno, CA 93727). ✆ **866/522-6966** or 559/335-5500. www.sequoia-kingscanyon.com. 30 units. $172–$188 double. Register at Grant Grove Village Registration Center, btw. the restaurant and gift shop. AE, DISC, MC, V.

Silver City Mountain Resort An excellent choice for those seeking a woodsy experience in a cabin surrounded by forest. There are three types of cabins, with a variety of bed combinations (some sleep up to eight) and woodstoves for heat. Blankets and pillows are provided, but guests need to bring their own sheets, pillowcases, towels, and trash bags. The top-of-the-line Swiss Chalets are finished in knotty pine with fully equipped kitchens, full bathrooms, and an outdoor barbecue. The midlevel units, dubbed Family Cabins, have two bedrooms and complete kitchens, propane wall lamps, small restrooms with toilets but no showers (there is a central bathhouse), and decks with barbecue grills. Historical Cabins, built in the 1930s, are the most basic units, with light from kerosene and propane lamps, and a camp kitchen. Some have refrigerators, and all share the bathhouse.

Mineral King, Sequoia National Park (mail: 3101 Cielo Grande, Atascadero, CA 93422). ✆ **559/561-3223** summer, or 805/461-3223 winter. Fax 805/461-3116. www.silvercityresort.com. 14 cabins, 7 with shared central bathhouse. $100–$395 cabin. 2- to 3-night minimum. Discounts approx. June 1–15 and after Sept 18. MC, V. Closed Nov–May. Take Calif. 198 through Three Rivers to the Mineral King turnoff. Silver City is 21 miles up Mineral King Rd.

Wuksachi Lodge The Wuksachi Lodge is by far the most upscale lodging in either park. The handsome main lodge has a **dining room** (see "Where to Dine," below), lounge, gift shop, conference rooms, Wi-Fi, and registration desk. Guest rooms are in three buildings separated from the lodge by parking lots. The rooms are attractively but simply decorated, with wood furnishings, light-colored plaster walls, and artwork depicting the area's attractions. Views of the forest and surrounding mountains dominate the scene. There are refrigerators, coffeemakers, hair dryers, ski storage racks, and phones with dataports. The standard rooms have one or two queen beds and a small desk; deluxe rooms are larger, with two queen beds or a king and a sofa bed, plus a table and two chairs. "Superior" rooms are minisuites, with two queen beds or one king, plus a sofa bed in an alcove sitting area with a sliding door (a good place for your teenager!).

Calif. 180 and 198 (P.O. Box 89), Sequoia National Park, CA 93262. ✆ **888/252-5757** or 559/253-2199. www.visitsequoia.com. 102 rooms. TV, TEL. May–Oct and holidays $194–$260; Nov–Apr $81–$115. AE, DISC, MC, V.

OUTSIDE THE PARKS

You'll pass many of these establishments as you travel to different sections of the parks. New in 2006, the luxury **Sequoia High Sierra Camp** (✆ **866/654-2877;** www.sequoiahighsierracamp.com) in Giant Sequoia National Monument looks to one-up its Yosemite counterparts in terms of upscale "roughing it." For $250 per person, you get 330-square-foot bungalows with plush furnishings and three "California-cuisine-style" meals a day. Guests can choose to drive to a trail head and hike 1 mile or take an 11-mile trail.

IN GIANT SEQUOIA NATIONAL MONUMENT

Montecito Lake Resort The Montecito is a well-stocked resort that caters to families with children and large groups, although guests of all ages will enjoy this well-run facility. It's open year-round and offers recreation of all types—from fishing to fencing, to cross-country skiing (85 miles of groomed trails begin here). The recently upgraded rooms, which all have private bathrooms, are in four separate buildings; 13 cabins share two bathhouses. Bed types and number vary, with units that sleep from two to eight. Meals are served buffet style. The resort has a small lake, with seasonal sailing and canoeing. Recreation is more limited in winter and includes snowshoeing and ice skating.

8000 Generals Hwy., Giant Sequoia National Monument (mailing address: Box 858, 8000 Generals Hwy., Kings Canyon National Park, CA 93633). ✆ **800/227-9900,** 800/843-8667, or 559/565-3388. Fax 559/565-3223. www.mslodge.com. 49 units, including 13 cabins. $99–$279 double. 6-night minimum in summer except Sat. Rates include all meals. AE, DISC, MC, V. Take Calif. 180 into Kings Canyon National Park, turn right at the fork, drive 8 miles south to the lodge access road, turn right, and follow the road about ½ mile to the parking lot.

Stony Creek Lodge This small lodge offers motel-style accommodations in a pretty setting in the Giant Sequoia National Monument, between the Grant Grove and Wuksachi sections of Kings Canyon National Park. Rooms are simply but attractively decorated and sleep two to four. The lodge's lobby is inviting, with a massive stone fireplace. The lodge has a **pizzeria** that serves lunch and dinner, a self-service laundry, a store, a gas station, and nature trails.

Generals Hwy., Giant Sequoia National Monument (mailing address: Sequoia Kings Canyon Park Services Company, 5755 E. Kings Canyon Rd., Ste. 101, Fresno, CA 93727). ✆ **866/522-6966** or 559/335-5500. www.sequoia-kingscanyon.com. 11 units. $149–$169 double. AE, DISC, MC, V. Closed Sept–May. Take the Stony Creek Village exit off the Generals Hwy., btw. Grant Grove Village and Wuksachi.

IN THE NEARBY GATEWAY TOWNS

In addition to the properties discussed below, chains in Visalia include the **Holiday Inn,** 9000 W. Airport Dr., Visalia, CA 93291 (✆ **559/651-5000**), which has rates of $89 to $149 double; and the **Super 8,** 4801 W. Noble Ave., Visalia, CA 93277 (✆ **559/627-2885**), charging $65 to $70 double. Lodging options in Three Rivers include the **Western Holiday Lodge,** 40105 Sierra Dr., Three Rivers, CA 93271 (✆ **559/561-4119**), which charges $89 to $199 double; and the **Comfort Inn and Suites,** 40820 Sierra Dr., Three Rivers, CA 93271 (✆ **800/331-2140** or 559/561-9000), charging $99 to $199 double. All have lower rates in the winter.

Ben Maddox House Our top choice for an enchanting place to stay in the Visalia area, the Ben Maddox House is named for one of Visalia's most prominent citizens during the late 1800s and early 1900s. Ben Maddox started the local newspaper and the area's first electric company. Located 4 blocks from downtown Visalia on a street with a number of other Victorian homes, the inn is replete with gardens, decks, and a citrus orchard that includes a 100-year-old lemon tree that is still producing. Palm trees grace the front yard. The house itself is impressive, with a large, triangular gable and a long covered porch, where you can relax and watch the world go slowly by. The house is furnished with antiques, including many Victorian pieces, and the comfortable and attractive guest rooms have 14-foot ceilings and white-oak floors. One room has a California king-size bed; the rest each have one queen bed. Breakfast is a treat, including terrific quiches with local veggies. There is free Wi-Fi.

601 N. Encina St., Visalia, CA 93291. ✆ **800/401-9800** or 559/739-0721. Fax 559/739-0729. www.benmaddoxhouse.com. 6 units. TV, TEL. $150–$185 double; $375 cottage. Rates include full breakfast. AE, DISC, MC, V. Children 12 or under not accepted.

Buckeye Tree Lodge Just a quarter-mile from the entrance to Sequoia National Park, this motel offers affordable and attractive rooms, not to mention rolling lawns that end at a picturesque river, and every room has a patio or balcony offering splendid views of the main fork of the Kaweah River. Rooms are clean, basic motel units, with a king bed or two queens (one has one queen). Eight rooms have showers only; the rest have a tub/shower.

46000 Sierra Dr., Three Rivers, CA 93271. ✆ **559/561-5900.** www.buckeyetree.com. 12 units. A/C, TV, TEL. $120–$136 double; lower rates in winter. Rates include continental breakfast. AE, DC, DISC, MC, V. Pets accepted by prior arrangement ($10 per night).

Lake Elowin Resort One of my favorite places to stay in the Sierra, this quirky resort is exactly what a national park lodging should be—a place to get away from it all. There are no phones and no televisions, just rustic but clean cabins nestled under huge trees, all looking out at Lake Elowin, a small body of water above the Kaweah River. Milton Melkonian purchased the 1920s-era resort in the 1970s with the idea of creating a place to coexist with nature, which now attracts all sorts of creative types, as well as anyone seeking an escape. Cabins can accommodate two to six people. I especially like cabin no. 1, sitting close to the lake with a delightful view, and the Master Cabin, boasting a fireplace, a deck, and a Jacuzzi. All cabins include linens and towels, cookware, barbecues, and canoes—just bring food, sunblock, and a good attitude.

43840 Dineley Dr., Three Rivers, CA 93271. ✆ **559/561-3460.** Fax 559/561-1300. $120–$145 double; $130–$195 cabin; $225 Master Cabin. AE, DISC, MC, V. From eastbound Sierra Dr. in Three Rivers, about 2½ miles before the park entrance, turn left on Dineley Dr. (the street sign says DINLEY) and drive across a bridge. Bear right and continue less than ½ mile to the resort's driveway.

Plantation Bed & Breakfast Step out of the Sierra Nevada and into the Old South at this fun bed-and-breakfast, where inspiration comes straight from *Gone With the Wind.* Honeymooners might enjoy the luxurious Scarlett O'Hara Room, with a king bed, velvet loveseat, fireplace, and marble bathroom with a Jacuzzi and separate shower. Our favorite, though, is the Belle Watling Room, done up in an elegant bordello style, with a king-size bed and an enormous mirror, a red crystal chandelier, and a claw-foot bathtub painted with a tasteful nude. Two rooms have showers only, while the others have showers and tubs. Secluded in an orange grove are a large swimming pool and a Jacuzzi, which are available at all hours. The wonderful breakfasts include fresh fruit, homemade granola, and a hot entree such as mushroom asparagus crepes.

33038 Calif. 198 (16 miles west of the park entrance), Lemon Cove, CA 93244. ✆ **800/240-1466** or 559/597-2555. Fax 559/597-2551. www.plantationbnb.com. 8 units. A/C. $149–$239 double. Rates include full breakfast. AE, DC, DISC, MC, V.

Sequoia Village Inn The sister property of the Buckeye Tree Lodge across the street, the Sequoia Village Inn offers charming cabin-style units that sleep 2 to 12 people. Stylishly decorated with lodgepole bed frames and hardwood floors, they're great for couples and families alike. Many feature full kitchens and decks with great views; the smaller units have microwaves and fridges only.

43175 Sierra Dr., Three Rivers, CA 93271. ✆ **559/561-3652.** www.sequoiavillageinn.com. 10 units. TV, TEL. $113–$319 double; lower rates in winter. AE, DC, DISC, MC, V.

Visalia Marriott The best hotel in Visalia—located a block off bustling Main Street—offers reliable Marriott service and style in its guest rooms and facilities. The property underwent a major renovation in 2007, and it shows. The rooms are chic and comfortable, with one king bed or two full-size beds. Units on the eighth floor feature private decks and great city views.

300 S. Court St., Visalia, CA 93291. ✆ **559/636-1111.** Fax 559/636-8224. www.visaliamarriotthotel.com. 195 rooms. A/C, TV, TEL. $109–$169 double; $169–$299 suite. Rates include full breakfast. AE, DISC, MC, V.

9 Where to Dine

INSIDE THE PARKS

Every Wednesday through Sunday from mid-June to early August, an all-you-can-eat barbecue takes place in the outdoor setting of Wolverton Meadow, just south of Lodgepole in Sequoia. Tickets can be purchased at the Wuksachi Lodge or Lodgepole Market. Call ✆ **866/807-3598** for information. There is also a seasonal pizzeria at Stony Creek Lodge on Generals Highway between Grant Grove and Wuksachi that serves lunch and dinner.

Cedar Grove Snack Bar AMERICAN The only dining option at Cedar Grove offers a simple but adequate menu at affordable prices, although those staying for several days will quickly tire of the limited choices. The cafe has a pleasant outdoor balcony seating area that overlooks the river.

Cedar Grove, Kings Canyon National Park. ✆ **559/565-0100.** Breakfast $4–$10; lunch and dinner $5–$20. AE, DISC, MC, V. Mid-June to mid-Aug daily 7am–2pm and 5–8pm; mid-May to mid-June and mid-Aug to mid-Oct Mon–Fri 8–10:30am, Sat–Sun 8am–2pm, daily 5–7pm. Closed mid-Oct to mid-May.

Grant Grove Restaurant AMERICAN This pleasant cafe-style restaurant, in the hub of activity in Kings Canyon National Park, is the primary option for a sit-down meal, with a simple but adequate menu and good service. Breakfast and lunch are typical American fare, including pizza—always a favorite with kids. Complete dinners include steaks, pastas, chicken, and trout dishes.

Grant Grove Village, Kings Canyon National Park. ✆ **559/335-5500**, ext. 305. Breakfast and lunch $5–$15; dinner $8–$30. AE, DISC, MC, V. Late May to early Sept daily 7am–2pm and 5–9pm; early Sept to late May daily 9am–2pm and 5–7pm (until 8pm Fri–Sat).

Lodgepole Market DELI/PIZZA The Watchtower Deli and the Harrison BBQ & Grill are two separate counter-service, fast-food restaurants in the Lodgepole Market Center. At the snack bar, you'll find burgers, hot dogs, and pizza. Healthier grown-up fare is available at the deli, which specializes in made-to-order deli-style sandwiches, wraps, and salads—and ice cream.

Lodgepole, Sequoia National Park. ✆ **559/565-3301.** Most items $4–$13. AE, MC, V. Daily 8am–8pm. Snack bar year-round with shorter hours fall to spring; deli closed Nov–Apr.

Wuksachi Dining Room AMERICAN A high, natural wood–beamed ceiling; huge stone fireplace; and large windows offering views of the surrounding forest make this upscale mountain lodge–style restaurant a delightful spot for a refined and relaxing meal. Standard American breakfast buffets are the morning fare, and a number of salads and sandwiches—such as a half-pound burger or citrus-marinated salmon with caramelized onion—are offered during lunch and dinner. The dinner entrees are creative and elegant, with a nice mix of meat and potatoes, seafood, and vegetarian fare.

Wuksachi Lodge, Sequoia National Park. ✆ **559/565-4070,** ext. 608. Dinner reservations required. Breakfast and lunch $5–$15; dinner entrees $16–$33. AE, DISC, MC, V. Daily 7–10am, 11:30am–2:30pm, and 5–10pm.

OUTSIDE THE PARKS

About 20 miles west of Kings Canyon on Generals Highway, **Clingan's Junction,** 35591 E. Kings Canyon Rd. (✆ **559/338-0160**), has been a foothills standby since 1938, with eggs Benedict, burgers, chicken sandwiches, and steaks. In Three Rivers, I also like **Serrano's,** 40869 Sierra Dr. (✆ **559/561-7283**), a good family-run Mexican restaurant with spicy salsa and tasty carne asada.

Anne Lang's Emporium DELI A great spot for a quick lunch or to pick up a picnic lunch before heading into the park. This busy, full-service deli has a half-dozen or so small tables inside, in a cafe-like atmosphere, plus a large deck out back (away from the hwy.) that overlooks the Kaweah River. You order at the counter, and the staff will prepare your sandwich to eat there or as a box lunch. In addition to the usual cold deli sandwiches, there are a few hot items, including burgers and chicken-breast sandwiches. There are also several luncheon salads, a soup of the day, fresh baked items, ice cream, and specialty drinks including espressos, smoothies, and Italian sodas.

41651 Sierra Dr. (Calif. 198), Three Rivers. ✆ **559/561-4937.** Most items $3–$7. AE, DISC, MC, V. Mon–Fri 10am–4pm; Sat–Sun 11am–4pm. Store/ice cream parlor Mon–Fri 9am–5pm; Sat–Sun 9am–5:30pm.

Brewbaker's Restaurant & Brewery MICROBREWERY At this terrific microbrewery in downtown Visalia, the brass bar is within arm's reach of their huge fermentation vats. Brick walls, a two-story ceiling, stained glass, and a social vibe round out the atmosphere. The beers are fantastic, and the food—including burgers, chili, fish and chips, and personal pizzas—is the best deal in town. Not only does the house brew beer, but it also makes its soda pop in-house in such flavors as orange and bubble gum. There are seating areas upstairs and down, as well as on the second-story cigar deck, with a great city view out back.

219 E. Main St., Visalia. ✆ **559/627-2739.** www.brewbakersbrewingco.com. Main courses $7–$22. AE, DISC, MC, V. Daily 11:30am–10pm. Bar open later.

Tommy's NEW AMERICAN With a contemporary design and a menu to match, Tommy's is the most creative restaurant in Visalia. Diverse influences show up from the Deep South (appetizers include fried green tomatoes), the Far East (Kobe burgers), and the Rocky Mountains (Colorado rack of lamb). I particularly enjoyed the root beer–glazed pork chop, served with a baked yam, as well as the side of bacon mac 'n' cheese and the make-your-own s'mores for dessert. The restaurant prides itself on its hand-cut Angus beef steaks, aged for at least 21 days, grilled, and finished with steak butter. There is a full bar and a good, California-centric wine list.

130 N. Encina St., Visalia. ✆ **559/627-6075.** www.tommysdowntown.com. Main courses items $19–$38. AE, MC, V. Tues–Thurs 5–9pm; Fri–Sat 5–10pm. Bar open later.

Vintage Press AMERICAN/CONTINENTAL A good pick for a romantic dinner, this stalwart restaurant's three dining rooms are elegant in the spirit of an upscale gin mill in Gold Rush–era San Francisco, featuring a handsome old bar imported from the city by the bay, and many antiques and leaded mirrors. There is also patio dining. The menu features several steaks alongside sautéed shrimp scampi, and crispy veal sweetbreads with a port–jalapeño–blue cheese sauce. There are also exotic appetizers like escargot, goat cheese rellenos, and ahi-halibut ceviche. Lunch brings smaller steaks, sandwiches, pastas, and salads. The restaurant's wine cellar offers more than 1,000 selections.

216 N. Willis St., Visalia. ✆ **559/733-3033.** Reservations recommended at dinner. Main courses $10–$17 lunch, $18–$37 dinner. AE, DC, MC, V. Mon–Sat 11:30am–2pm and 5:30–10pm; Sun 10am–2pm and 5–9pm.

10 Picnic & Camping Supplies

Stores throughout the parks stock basic camping supplies, such as flashlights, canteens, and tarps, and enough food that you won't starve, but you'll find better selections in nearby towns. In the parks, the **Lodgepole Market** has the widest selection available, including a good deli and grill. It's open from May through September only, as is the **Cedar Grove Market.** The **Grant Grove Market** is open year-round, and during the winter a small variety of goods is available at **Wuksachi,** in Sequoia.

For the best selection and prices on foodstuffs outside the parks, stop in Visalia at **Save Mart,** 1591 E. Noble St. at Calif. 198 and Ben Maddox Way (**© 559/636-0328**), on your way in. This is an excellent supermarket with a good bakery and a deli. Just east is a **Walmart** at 1819 E. Noble Ave. (**© 559/636-2302**), where you'll find a wide stock of camping supplies, along with clothing and practically everything else you might need.

Theodore Roosevelt National Park, ND

by Jack Olson

After he became president in 1901, Theodore Roosevelt pursued his love of nature and the outdoors by creating the U.S. Forest Service and signing the 1906 Antiquities Act, under which he proclaimed 18 national monuments.

He also obtained congressional approval to establish five national parks, as well as set aside millions of acres of land as national forests and 51 wildlife refuges. As a conservationist, Roosevelt is arguably without equal among American presidents. So it seems appropriate that he is the only president for whom a national park has been named, and that Theodore Roosevelt National Park is located in western North Dakota, where many of his early experiences formed his later environmental efforts.

Roosevelt first traveled to the North Dakota Badlands in 1883. Before returning home to New York, he became interested in the cattle business and joined two other men as partners in the Maltese Cross Ranch. The following year, Roosevelt returned to North Dakota and established a second open-range ranch, the Elkhorn, which became his principal residence in the area.

During his frequent visits, Roosevelt led what he called the "strenuous life" that he loved. When he wasn't studying botany or herding cattle, he hunted, fished, and enjoyed the camaraderie of fellow Dakotans, some of whom would later form the nucleus of his Rough Riders.

Roosevelt arrived in the Badlands soon after the last of the bison herds had been slaughtered, and he spent much time pondering what was being done to the animals and land around him. He carried those thoughts and convictions, born on the Dakota prairie, into his later political life. He wrote, "I would not have been President, had it not been for my experience in North Dakota."

BADLANDS & BUFFALO

The colorful, broken landscape of the North Dakota badlands provides the scenic backdrop for Theodore Roosevelt National Park. Carved over millions of years by the natural forces of wind and rain and the tireless waters of the Little Missouri River, this land is home to a variety of animals and plant life.

Tips from a Park Expert

After 18 years at Theodore Roosevelt National Park, a dozen years with the National Park Service in Alaska, and 6 years each in Death Valley and Crater Lake, recently retired Chief of Interpretation Bruce Kaye has some insights for prospective visitors.

Kaye encourages visitors to view Roosevelt's two ranch sites—the **Maltese Cross,** whose ranch house was relocated to the park in 1959 from the state capital in Bismarck, and the **Elkhorn Ranch** site, 35 miles north of Medora. Kaye said visitors should check with rangers before traveling to the Elkhorn site, to ensure that road conditions or high water will not impede their progress.

While visiting the park, Kaye says travelers should keep their eyes open for a wide variety of wildlife, including bison, elk, wild horses, mule deer, white-tailed deer, coyotes, antelope, a variety of birds, and the ever-abundant prairie dog.

"The best month to be without crowds at Theodore Roosevelt National Park, yet do the things you want to do in view of the weather, is September," Kaye says. "But even at the height of the summer season, most visitors will not be bothered by overcrowding." Kaye adds, "Summertime is not all that busy—you can still go out into the backcountry and not see people; you can even drive one of the park roads and not be inundated."

Kaye says that hiking, camping, and cross-country skiing are ideal experiences in the off season.

Theodore Roosevelt National Park

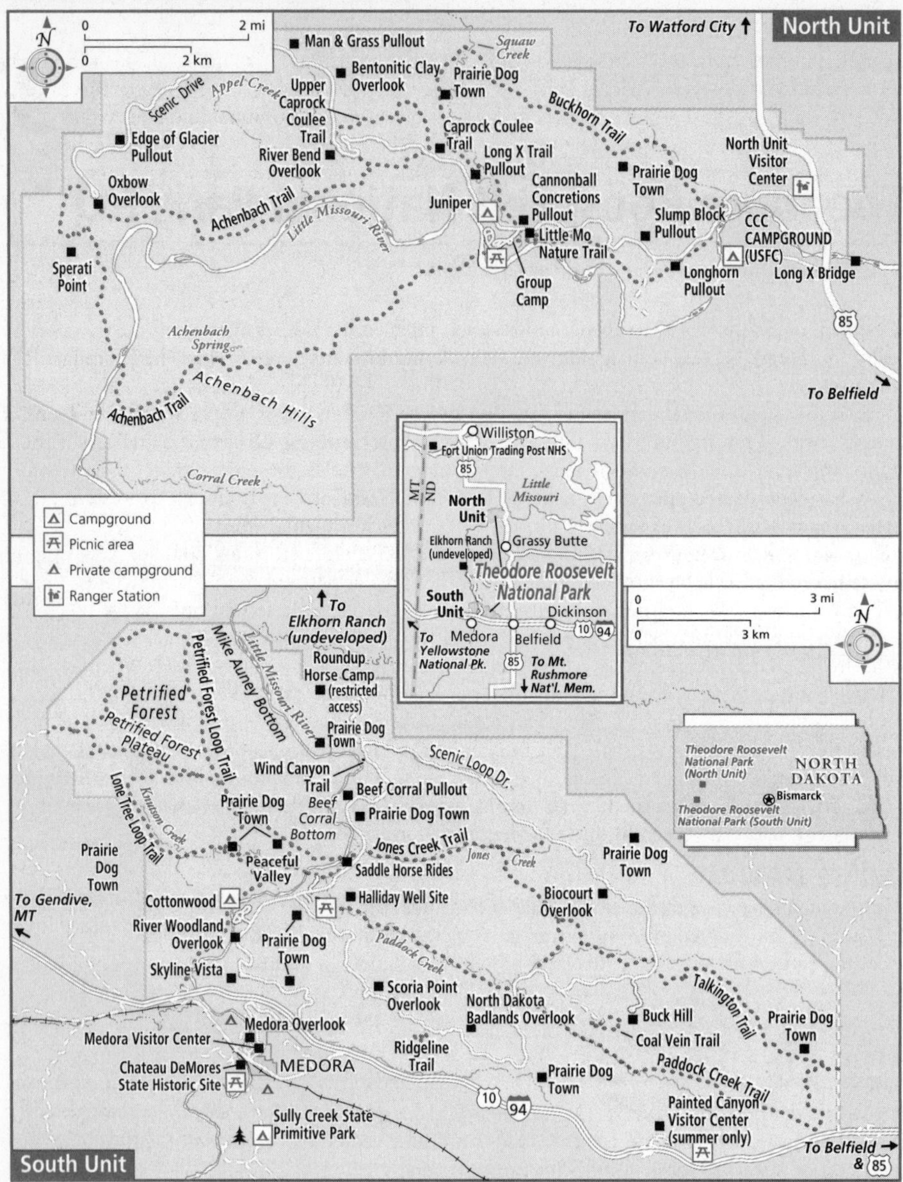

Some 60 million years ago, streams carried eroded materials eastward from the young Rocky Mountains, then deposited them on a vast lowland, today's Great Plains. During the warm, rainy periods that followed, dense vegetation grew, fell into swampy areas, and was later buried by new layers of sediment. Eventually, this plant material turned into lignite coal. Some plant life became petrified.

Even as layers of sediment were being deposited, streams began to carve through the soft strata, sculpting the infinite variety of buttes, tablelands, and valleys that comprise the Badlands today.

As inhospitable as this land looks, it is home to a large variety of creatures and plants. Rainfall supports an abundance of prairie grasses and wildflowers, and 186 species of birds have been observed.

Mule deer and white-tailed deer inhabit the park, and prairie dogs build their "towns" in the grasslands. Through careful management, some animals that nearly became extinct in the 19th and early 20th centuries are once again thriving. Bison and elk, for example, have been successfully reintroduced into the area.

The wealth of wildlife that first attracted Theodore Roosevelt and thousands of other avid sports enthusiasts to this area still exists. Bands of wild horses roam in the park's South Unit, just as they did when Roosevelt rode over this land and tended his cattle a century ago.

AVOIDING THE CROWDS

Since the park has 70,000 acres, three spread-out units, and fewer than a half-million visitors per year, avoiding crowds at Theodore Roosevelt National Park is not difficult. In general, you'll see fewer visitors in early morning and evening hours, particularly during the high-visitation months of June, July, and August. Early fall is especially appealing to those seeking a more contemplative experience. But even during the height of the summer, those enjoying backcountry treks and scenic drives are not likely to encounter throngs of vacationers: This national park is just too big, and visitation too low, to make that occur.

1 Essentials

GETTING THERE & GATEWAYS

The park's **South Unit** is 130 miles west of Bismarck and just north of Medora (exit 24 or 27 on **I-94**). The **North Unit** is 15 miles south of Watford City. From I-94, take exit 42 (Belfield); then you must continue north on **U.S. 85** another 50 miles to the North Unit Entrance. The park also includes **Theodore Roosevelt's Elkhorn Ranch,** which is located between the North and South Units, but visitors should ask rangers about road conditions before attempting to go there.

THE NEAREST AIRPORTS About 130 miles east of the park is **Bismarck Airport** (✆ **701/355-1808;** www.bismarckairport.com), served by **Allegiant Air, Delta,** and **United Express** airlines, with service to Chicago, Denver, Minneapolis, Phoenix, Salt Lake City, and Las Vegas, plus **Avis, Enterprise,** and **Hertz** car rentals. **Dickinson–Theodore Roosevelt Regional Airport** (✆ **701/483-1062;** www.dickinsonairport.com) is 35 miles from Medora and is served by **Great Lakes Airlines,** with service to Denver, and you can rent a car from **Budget.** The websites for the airlines and major car-rental agencies are in chapter 38.

INFORMATION

Contact the **Superintendent, Theodore Roosevelt National Park,** P.O. Box 7, Medora, ND 58645 (✆ **701/623-4466** for the South Unit, the main number, or 701/842-2333 for the North Unit; www.nps.gov/thro). The National Park Service has a variety of brochures that explore the park's cultural and natural resources, including a very useful road log guide, sold in the visitor center. Information and a variety of publications are available from the **Theodore Roosevelt Nature and History Association,** P.O. Box 167, Medora, ND 58645 (✆ **701/623-4730,** ext. 3419; www.trnha.org). The park produces *Frontier Fragments,* an excellent park newspaper. It's updated annually and filled with relevant stories on the park's history, wildlife, interpretive offerings, and visitor services.

For information about the area, contact the **Medora Chamber of Commerce,** P475 4th St., Medora, ND 58645 (✆ **701/623-4910;** www.medorandchamber.com).

VISITOR CENTERS

The park has three visitor centers. The **South Unit Visitor Center** (for the South Unit) is located just inside the park entrance at Medora and is open daily 8am to 4:30pm MT year-round. The **Painted Canyon Visitor Center,** located on **I-94,** is 7 miles east of Medora and open daily from April 1 to November 11. The **North Unit Visitor Center,** located just off U.S. 85, is open daily 9am to 5:30pm CT from early April through mid-November and Friday and Sunday the rest of the year.

FEES & PERMITS

Entry into the park for up to 7 days costs $10 per vehicle. Campsites cost $10 per night. Campsites are $5 per night with Senior or Access passes. Group campsites and the Roundup Horse Camp (South Unit) are by reservation only.

SPECIAL REGULATIONS & WARNINGS

The animals in the park are wild and should be viewed from a safe distance. (Even the prairie dogs can bite.) Watch out for ticks in late spring and early summer. Climbing on the steep, barren slopes of the badlands can be dangerous due to slippery clays and soft sediments that may yield underfoot, so stay on designated trails. Horses are prohibited in campgrounds, in picnic areas, and on self-guided nature trails.

SEASONS & CLIMATE

The climate in the badlands can be extreme, with bitter cold and snow in the winter and intense heat in the summer. Sudden, violent storms are possible.

2 Exploring the Park by Car

THE SOUTH UNIT

If you're traveling west on I-94, your first introduction to Theodore Roosevelt National Park is the **Painted Canyon Overlook and Visitor Center,** 7 miles east of Medora. Here, on the upper ridge of the badlands, is an unparalleled panorama of ragged ridges and colorful hues. Watch for wild horses, the descendants of former domestic ranching stock; you might even see bison grazing.

A highlight of the South Unit is a 36-mile **scenic loop road** with interpretive signs that explain some of the park's historical and natural phenomena. The scenic drive begins at the South Unit Visitor Center. If you've bought the road log, you'll want to travel counterclockwise around the loop. Descriptions of the shorter interpretive trails are incorporated into the driving tours for the North and South units; for more information on longer hiking opportunities, see "Exploring the Backcountry," below.

South Unit Scenic Drive In any season, the South Unit Scenic Drive can take you into some of the most remote areas of North Dakota. When Gen. Alfred Sully traveled through these badlands, he described them as "hell with the fires burned out." In reality, they are teeming with wildlife, wildflowers, and bird life. The South Unit comprises 46,158 acres, of which 10,510 acres are designated as wilderness.

Scoria Point is the first overlook you'll come to. Strictly speaking, scoria is volcanic in origin, but in the badlands, wherever a seam of coal has caught fire and baked the surrounding sand and clay, it's called scoria. You'll see it from this view point, where the topsoil has been stripped away by erosion and the harder material underneath is exposed.

About a mile farther, you'll come to the **Ridgeline Nature Trail.** If you choose to take this short (.6-mile loop) hike, you'll learn more about the Badlands and their ecology. This trail has some steep hills and may not be suitable for some people.

Next is the **North Dakota Badlands Overlook.** The view here is over Paddock Creek, and what you'll see is a surreal, striking landscape. This is because erosion has worn away the topsoil, leaving behind only the rocks and harder materials underneath the thin, top layer.

After crossing Paddock Creek, you'll come to the turnoff for the **Coal Vein Trail,** a short (.8-mile) loop that winds through an area where a fire burned in a coal seam from 1951 through 1977. The fire baked the clay and soil, changing the appearance of the terrain and altering the vegetation patterns. Here you'll be walking around the scoria (the same kind of formations you viewed from a distance at the Scoria Point Overlook earlier). You must drive down a short, unpaved road to reach the trail.

After returning to the main loop road, you'll next come to the turnoff for **Buck Hill.** It's only a short walk to the hill itself from the end of the road. The hill (at 2,855 ft.) has two very different slopes. On the south side, the slopes are hot and dry, and you'll see only shrubs and small plants. On the north side, which is wetter and cooler, you'll see trees.

Traveling several miles farther will bring you to the **Boicourt Overlook,** which affords one of the best views of the badlands in the South Unit.

The next stop is **Wind Canyon Trail.** This is a very short walk up to a ridge, where you'll have a great view of the Little Missouri River, which did much to create the landscape here. Beyond the river, to the west, is the virtually untouched wilderness of the South Unit. Pause here around sunrise to listen for the call of coyotes in the valley below.

After passing the **Beef Corral Pullout** and a prairie-dog town, which is just beyond the pullouts on either side of the road, you'll pass the parking lot for the **Jones Creek Trail.** This is one of two trail heads for the Jones Creek Trail on Scenic Loop Drive. (You passed the other one earlier; it was at the parking area btw. the Boicourt Overlook and the Wind Canyon Trail pullout.) The trail itself is 3.7 miles and leads into the heart of the badlands.

The final stop on the Scenic Loop Drive is in Peaceful Valley. The **Peaceful Valley Ranch,** which is on the National Historic Register, was established during the heyday of cattle ranching in the 1880s. The tall central section of the ranch house was constructed about 1885. The ranch offers trail rides from May through the end of September (see "Horseback Riding in the Backcountry," below).

THE NORTH UNIT

Fewer visitors take the time to travel to the park's North Unit, although paved roads provide easy

If You Have Only 1 Day

If you have only 1 day, you'll probably want to limit yourself to either the North or South Unit. Since it's more accessible from I-94, and more developed, it's likely you'll choose the **South Unit.**

If you're coming from the east, stop first at the **Painted Canyon Overlook and Visitor Center** to get a sweeping, panoramic view of the North Dakota badlands, then continue 7 miles west to Medora and the **South Unit Visitor Center.** Here you'll be able to view a film and listen to one or more ranger talks. There's also a museum with some of Theodore Roosevelt's personal effects. Be sure to stop in at the **Maltese Cross** cabin, behind the visitor center. Take the 36-mile **scenic driving loop** around the park, stopping at the overlooks (be sure to stop at one of the **prairie-dog towns**), and stop along the way to explore one of the scenic trails.

access. There are 24,070 acres in the North Unit, of which 19,410 acres are designated as wilderness. Stop at the visitor center at the entrance to the unit, and the rangers will help you plan your time.

North Unit Scenic Drive The 14-mile scenic drive (and State Scenic Byway) travels from the entrance station to the **Oxbow Overlook,** with plenty of turnouts and interpretive signs along the route. Keep your eyes open for longhorns between the entrance and Juniper Campground; these are the same type of cattle raised by ranchers during Roosevelt's time. At the Oxbow Overlook, you must double back along the same route.

Since less of the North Unit is developed, the thing to do here is to get out of the car at one of the scenic pullouts and take a hike. You'll be able to see dramatic scenery populated with many bison, but few people.

The **Little Mo Nature Trail,** which starts at Juniper Campground, offers a comfortable, leisurely walk through the Little Missouri River bottom. The trail cuts through woodlands near the river, as well as badlands formations, and gives you two options. The shorter portion of the loop is .7 mile, paved, and wheelchair accessible. But you can also extend your hike by .4 mile and take the unpaved portion. If you're more adventurous, you'll see additional formations and cross some wildlife trails that (mostly) bison use.

Just across the road from the Juniper Campground entrance road, stop at the **Cannonball Concretions Pullout.** A short walk reveals the well-named rock formations. Contrasting formations in the area make this stop a photographer's delight. Light doesn't hit the best "cannonball" until late morning.

The **Caprock Coulee Nature Trail,** 1.5 miles west of Juniper Campground, is another easy, self-guiding nature trail that winds through badlands and dry water gulches, then finds a welcome interruption in the grassy plains of the park. The total length round-trip is 1.6 miles.

If you want to do something more ambitious, combine the self-guided nature trail with the Upper Caprock Coulee Trail. Together they run a distance of 4.1 miles. (The latter portion is 3.3 miles.) You'll go farther into the wilderness this way; it also brings you back to the trail head so that you don't have to double back over the same route. Bighorn sheep were introduced into the North Unit in 1996. Be on the lookout for these majestic animals.

It's at this point that the North Unit Scenic Drive is often closed for the winter. If you continue, you'll end up at the **Oxbow Overlook,** another sweeping panoramic view of the badlands.

The **Sperati Point Trail** can be accessed from the Oxbow Overlook. This is the spur of the Achenbach Trail that leads to the Oxbow Bend Overlook and makes a less strenuous alternative if you want something shorter than the Achenbach's 16 miles. (The length of this trail is 1.5 miles round-trip.) The trail leads to the narrowest gateway in the badlands. The flow of the Little Missouri River once continued north to Hudson Bay. Blocked during the Ice Age, the river was forced to find a new course and finally broke through the gap between this point and the Achenbach Hills on the other side. The Little Missouri now drains into the Gulf of Mexico via the Missouri–Mississippi system. Take this trail for a taste of prairie country and long, sweeping views.

3 Exploring the Backcountry

If you wish to explore some of the wilderness the park has to offer, you'll need a free **backcountry permit** from the Medora or North Unit visitor center to do any overnight camping. You can also explore on horseback. If you bring a horse, you must camp either in the backcountry or at the Roundup Horse campsite (by reservation only) in the South Unit. You can also board your horse at the Peaceful Valley Ranch (see "Horseback Riding in the Backcountry," below). Your stay in the backcountry is limited to 14 consecutive days.

SPECIAL REGULATIONS

You cannot have a campfire in the backcountry, so you must bring a self-contained **camp stove.** You must **pack out** what you pack in (no burying of trash). The park requires that those with horses bring certified **weed-free hay.** Groups entering the backcountry are limited to 10 persons (or eight persons with eight horses). Finally, don't drink the water in the backcountry; there are no safe, approved water sources here.

The mother of all trails in the area is the **Maah Daah Hey Trail,** completed in summer 1999. The Maah Daah Hey is a 120-mile hiking, horseback, and mountain-biking trail that traverses the scenic and rugged North Dakota badlands. The trail passes through the **Little Missouri National Grasslands,** as well as state and private land, as it connects the North and South units of Theodore Roosevelt National Park. The north end of the trail begins at the U.S. Forest Service CCC Campground in McKenzie County, located 20 miles south of Watford City off Highway 85. The trail winds its way to its southern terminus at Sully Creek State Park in Billings County, south of Medora. Six fenced overnight campsites with hitching posts, vault toilets, and campfire rings have been constructed along the trail.

Organized Tours & Ranger Programs

From mid-June to early September, ranger programs, including nature walks and longer hikes, are offered at various locations. If snow conditions permit, rangers may conduct ski tours in winter.

For more information about this trail, contact the **U.S. Forest Service,** Medora Ranger District, 99 23rd Ave. W., Dickinson, ND 58601 (✆ **701/227-7800;** www.fs.fed.us/r1/dakotaprairie); or the **McKenzie Ranger District** office, at 1901 S. Main St., Watford City, ND 58854 (✆ **701/842-2393**).

4 Park Attractions

There are a variety of historic attractions, both in the national park and nearby.

A **museum** in the South Unit Visitor Center features personal items that belonged to Theodore Roosevelt, ranching artifacts, and natural history displays. Tours are conducted (free, about 20 min.) through the **Maltese Cross Cabin** from mid-June through Labor Day; you can take a self-guided tour during the rest of the year.

At the **Elkhorn Ranch site,** where Roosevelt started his second cattle ranch in the area, no buildings remain (save the foundation stones from the main ranch house). To get there, ask a ranger in the Visitor Center for detailed directions.

Chateau De Mores State Historic Site (✆ **701/623-4355;** www.state.nd.us/hist; click on "Historic Sites," then "Chateau De Mores"), near the town of Medora, is a 128-acre site that contains the Chateau de Mores, Chimney Park, and De Mores Memorial Park. The town of Medora was built by the Marquis de Mores, an entrepreneurial French nobleman, on the Northern Pacific Line and named for his American wife. The **Chateau de Mores,** a 26-room rustic summer home built in 1883, contains many of its original furnishings. The ruins of the Marquis's meat-packing plant, found in Chimney Park, recall his ambitious plans to revolutionize the meat-packing industry. A young Theodore Roosevelt was a business acquaintance of the Marquis. Admission costs $7 adults, $3 kids 6 to 15, under 6 free; group tour rates are available. Guided tours of the chateau are offered from May 16 to September 15, hours 8:30am to 6:15pm MDT, and winter hours 9am to 5pm.

Knife River Indian Villages National Historic Site, consisting of three villages along the Knife River in North Dakota, was inhabited by the Hidatsa, Mandan, and later the Arikara from the early 1500s to 1860. Located a half-mile north of Stanton, North Dakota (via C.R. 37), it offers insights into the life of the Northern Plains Indians. The site is open from 8am to 6pm (Mountain Daylight Time) daily from Memorial Day through Labor Day, 8am to 4:30pm daily the rest of the year. Admission is free. The exhibits and 15-minute orientation video depict life in the villages before and after Euro-American contact. Earthlodge tours are conducted daily Memorial Day through Labor Day. The annual **Northern Plains Indian Culture Fest** is held the last full weekend in July.

Special attention was focused on Knife River Indian Villages due to the Lewis & Clark Bicentennial. This area is believed to have been the home of Sacagawea, her new baby, and her husband before they joined the Corps of Discovery for the arduous trip west.

Various short trails lead to the three village sites. Other trails meander through prairie and woodland ecosystems. Check at the visitor center for trail hours. Some trails are wheelchair accessible. For information, contact the **Knife River Indian Villages NHS,** P.O. Box 9, Stanton, ND 58571 (✆ **701/745-3300;** www.nps.gov/knri).

Fort Union Trading Post National Historic Site preserves the restored Fort Union, which was, for nearly 4 decades in the 19th century, a bastion of John Jacob Astor's American Fur Company, which dominated the fur trade in the region of modern-day North Dakota, Montana, and Saskatchewan. The focal point of the site is Fort Union's Indian Trade House. Here goods were traded between the fur company representatives and Assiniboines, Crows, Crees, and Blackfeet. Also called the **Bourgeois House** (or Manager's House), this facility is now the visitor center and bookstore. The National Park Service and the Fort Union Association have meticulously restored and refurnished the Trade House to its appearance in 1851. It's about 2 hours north of Theodore Roosevelt National Park near Williston, North Dakota. The Bourgeois House Visitor Center is open from 8am to 8pm Memorial Day through Labor Day, from 9am to 5:30pm the remainder of the year. The Indian Trade House is open from 10am to 5:45pm daily during the summer only. Ranger tours are available daily during the summer, with self-guided tours the remainder of the year. Fort Union is in **two time zones;** you park in Montana (Mountain Time) and walk into North Dakota (Central Time).

Fort Union Trading Post was a focus of attention during the Lewis & Clark Bicentennial. Lewis and Clark stopped at the confluence of the Yellowstone and Missouri rivers in 1805, near the location where Fort Union was constructed 23 years later.

For scheduled dates of special programs, or for more information, contact the **Superintendent, Fort Union Trading Post NHS,** 15550 Hwy. 1804, Williston, ND 58801 (✆ **701/572-9083;** www.nps.gov/fous).

5 Day Hikes

SOUTH UNIT TRAIL

Petrified Forest Trail Pieces of petrified wood are scattered throughout this national park, but the greatest concentration can be reached only on foot or horseback along this trail, which leads up along Petrified Forest Plateau. Just don't take any souvenirs! 16 miles RT (from the east). Moderate. Access: You can get on the trail at the parking area at Peaceful Valley at the trail's eastern end; from the west, the trail head is at the end of a dirt road outside the park (ask park rangers for directions).

NORTH UNIT TRAILS

Achenbach Trail This route climbs from the river bottomlands up through the Achenbach Hills, drops down to the river again, climbs to the Oxbow Overlook on a spur trail, then returns along the river bottom to the campground. Before departing, ask a ranger about the condition of river crossings. The "spur" trail is the Sperati Point Trail described in "The North Unit," above. 16 miles RT. Moderate. Access: Juniper Campground.

Buckhorn Trail About a mile into this loop, hikers discover a large prairie-dog town. Of the five varieties of prairie dogs, only the black-tailed variety inhabits Theodore Roosevelt National Park. 11 miles RT. Moderate. Access: From the Caprock Coulee Nature Trail (see "The North Unit," above).

6 Camping

Cottonwood Campground in the South Unit and **Juniper Campground** in the North Unit are operated on a first-come, first-served basis. You'll find drinking water, flush toilets, public telephones (Cottonwood only), and fire grates in both campgrounds, but no showers or RV hookups. Juniper Campground has an RV dump station, but Cottonwood does not. Camping costs $10 per night; holders of Senior or Access passes pay $5. Campgrounds are open year-round, but the availability of water is limited during the winter.

Camping for organized groups is available at both campgrounds, and reservations are required.

Camping with horses is permitted only at the **Roundup Group Horse Campground** in the South Unit; reservations are required.

Other privately run and Forest Service campgrounds are located near both units of the park, and you can get a list from park offices.

7 Where to Stay & Dine

There are no accommodations or dining facilities in the park, but you will find hotels, motels, and bed-and-breakfasts, as well as a variety of modest restaurants in Medora, Belfield, and Beach near the South Unit, and in Watford City near the North Unit. Most are open year-round, but some may close in the winter. Rates are highest in summer.

IN MEDORA

The **AmericInn,** the most luxurious choice, is at 75 E. River Rd. S., 1 block south of the Medora Community Center (✆ **866/661-7615** or 800/396-5007; www.americinn.com). It has seasonal rates, ranging in the main tourist season from $85 to $220 double; American Express, Diners Club, Discover, MasterCard, and Visa are accepted.

The **Badlands Motel,** on Pacific Avenue, with 115 air-conditioned rooms, charges $69 (off season) up to $135 in high season for a double. It's open April to October and has a heated swimming pool and a miniature golf course. The **Rough Riders**

Horseback Riding in the Backcountry

Many backcountry trails are open to those on horseback; you can use your own horse or go on a guided ride with a park concessionaire. In the South Unit, contact **Peaceful Valley Ranch,** P.O. Box 308, Medora, ND 58645 (✆ **701/623-4568;** http://home.ctctel.com/peacefulvalley). They operate from Memorial Day to Labor Day and have regularly scheduled horseback rides lasting from 1½ to 5 hours. Trail rides run daily from 7:30am to evening, and all rides include a riding lesson.

Motel, at 301 3rd Ave., has been newly renovated and is opening 68 additional rooms in 2010, as well as a restaurant. Rates range from $179 to $199 double. Their season is June to September. Both take American Express, Discover, MasterCard, and Visa. For reservations at both motels, call ✆ **800/MEDORA-1** [633-6721] or 701/623-4444; www.medora.com.

Custer's Cottage, at 156 E. River Rd. S. in Medora, is a medium-size, air-conditioned house with two units, one main floor, and one lower level. Each unit has separate private entrances, full kitchens, large living rooms, cable TV, up to four bedrooms, and laundry facilities. It is open year-round by advance reservations (✆ **888/385-2574** or 701/623-4378; www.custerscottage.com); prices range from $50 to $105, depending on how many bedrooms are used and length of stay (one group or party per night per unit). Credit cards are not accepted for payment but may be used to reserve a room. The facility is 2 miles from Maah Daah Hey Trail. This is a smoke-free facility.

IN BELFIELD

The **Cowboy Inn** is west of U.S. 85 on U.S. 10 (✆ **866/901-4245** or 701/575-4245; www.cowboyinn-nd.com). A double costs $44 to $79, depending on the season; American Express, Discover, MasterCard, and Visa are accepted.

The **Trapper's Inn** is located at I-94 and U.S. 85 North, 15 minutes from Medora (✆ **800/284-1855** or 701/575-4261; www.trapperskettle.co). Rates range from $81 to $91 double in the peak season; American Express, Discover, MasterCard, and Visa are accepted.

IN BEACH

The **Buckboard Inn,** with 39 rooms, is located at I-94 and N. Dak. 16 South (✆ **888/449-3599;** 701/872-4794). A double costs $66 during the summer; American Express, Discover, MasterCard, and Visa are accepted. Pets are welcome.

IN WATFORD CITY

The **McKenzie Inn,** with 13 rooms, is on U.S. 85 West (✆ **800/842-3989** or 701/444-3980; www.mckenzieinn.com). The year-round rate is $59 for a double, $47 for a single; American Express, Discover, MasterCard, and Visa are accepted. Senior and AAA rates.

The **Roosevelt Inn & Suites,** on U.S. 85 West (✆ **800/887-9170** or 701/842-3686; www.rooseveltinn.com), with 50 rooms, has a swimming pool, spa, sauna, and game room. Rates year-round are $60 single, $73 double, suites $70 to $143; American Express, Discover, MasterCard, and Visa are accepted. Continental breakfast and handicapped facilities are available.

Yellowstone National Park, WY & Little Bighorn Battlefield National Monument, MT

by Eric Peterson

Yellowstone has shaped the American public's definition of nature for more than a century, and with good reason: There are more geysers, hot springs, and other thermal features here than on the rest of the planet combined. There's pristine snowmelt cascading into dazzling waterfalls, including one that's twice as high as Niagara Falls. Not to mention a canyon deep and colorful enough to fall into the "grand" category. Best of all, a significant chunk of the park's incredible terrain is reachable by a hiker of just average ability.

Then there's the wildlife: Ever focus your telephoto lens on a wild, untamed grizzly bear? Or a bald eagle? What about a wolf? Thousands of visitors have these experiences here every year.

By one biologist's estimate, Yellowstone has about 1,100 species of native plants; when wildflowers cover the meadows in spring, you won't just see them, you'll be overpowered by their fragrance. The mud pots and fumaroles have their own odors, though many are less pleasing than a wild lily. Your ears will fill with the sounds of geysers noisily expelling thousands of gallons of boiling water into the blue Wyoming sky. After sunset, coyotes break the silence of the night with their high-pitched yips.

It's possible to see the highlights of Yellowstone without ever leaving your car—park roads lead past most of the key attractions—but why would you want to? There's so much more to see if you actually get out of your vehicle. And there's even more to see by venturing into the backcountry, something only a small percentage of the park's visitors ever do. You can spend weeks hiking Yellowstone's backcountry or fishing its streams, and the crowds and traffic snarls become faint memories.

Aside from month-long closures in the fall and spring, Yellowstone's season is year-round. It's not nearly as crowded in the winter, and wildlife is more visible. Mammoth and Old Faithful serve as launching pads for thousands of skiers, snowmobilers, and wildlife watchers.

The beauty of Yellowstone's natural architecture comes from its geology. The area experienced three volcanic periods, beginning 2.1 million years ago, occurring every 600,000 to 800,000 years since. The last big bang happened 640,000 years ago, meaning that the area is ripe for another massive eruption—if Mother Nature's timetable holds to form.

During the biggest eruptions, thousands of square miles of landmass were blown skyward, leaving enormous *calderas* (volcanic depressions). This process has repeated itself several times—some areas hold geologic evidence of 27 layers of lava. Subsequently, glaciers covered the volcanic mountains during the ice ages. The powerful bulldozing caused by the movement of the gigantic blocks of ice shaped the valleys and canyons of the park.

Yellowstone National Park was officially created in 1872, when President Ulysses S. Grant signed legislation making it the first national park in the world. It then suffered from incompetent superintendents and shortages of cash until at last, in 1886, the U.S. Army took possession and helped rein in poaching and establish a sense of order. In 1916, the newly created National Park Service took control of the park. Yellowstone became one of the first parks to come under its stewardship.

AVOIDING THE CROWDS

If a few thousand people on the benches in front of Old Faithful is not your idea of a wilderness park experience, then skip Yellowstone's busy summer season, which is in full swing during July and August. Or if you can't avoid that time of year, head up the trails, away from the roads and car traffic. Fewer than 10% of the park's visitors venture into the backcountry.

Although the beautiful seasons between May and mid-June and after Labor Day are no longer the best-kept secret in the Rockies, they attract only a fraction of the midsummer traffic. Just be careful how far you

Yellowstone National Park

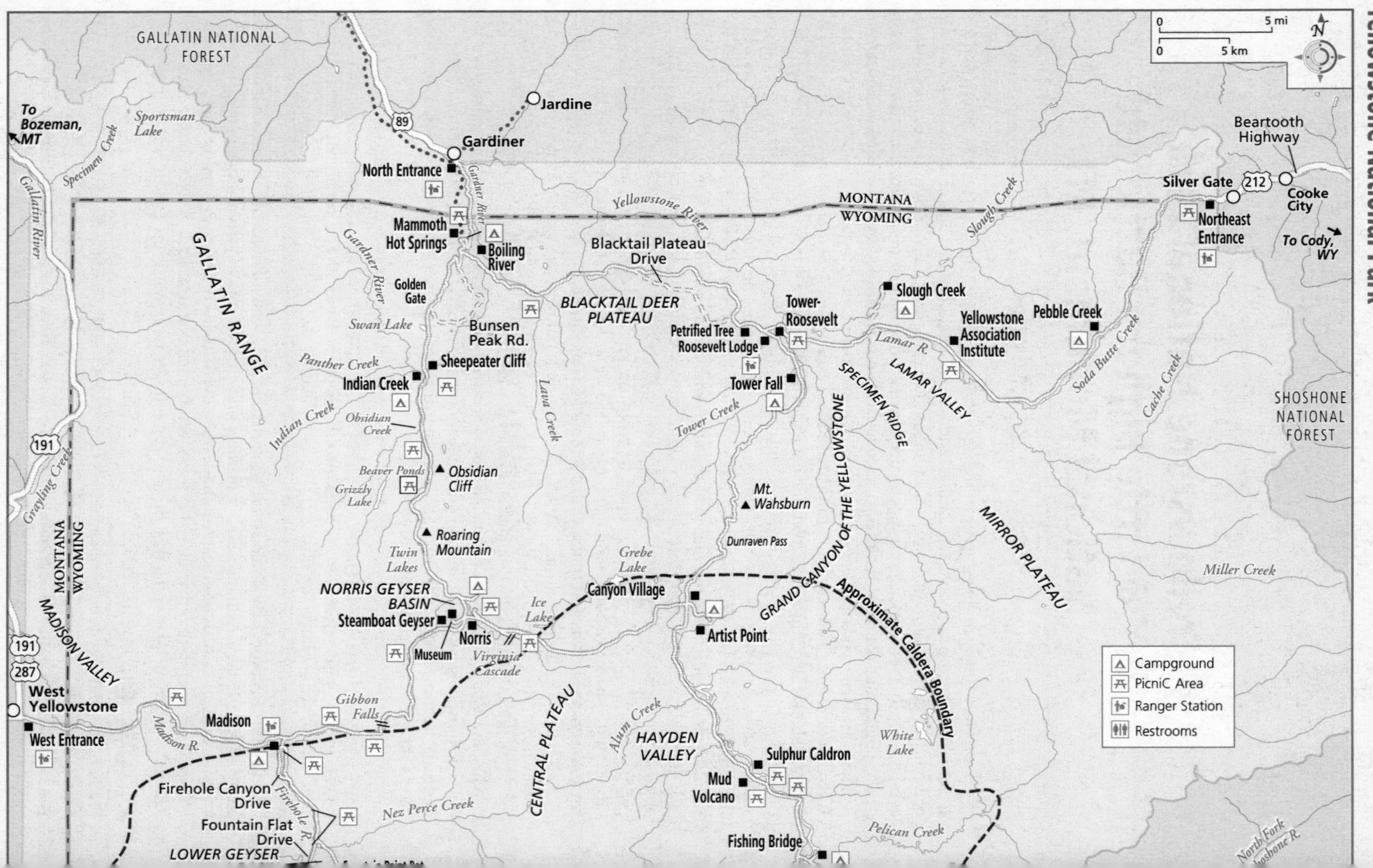

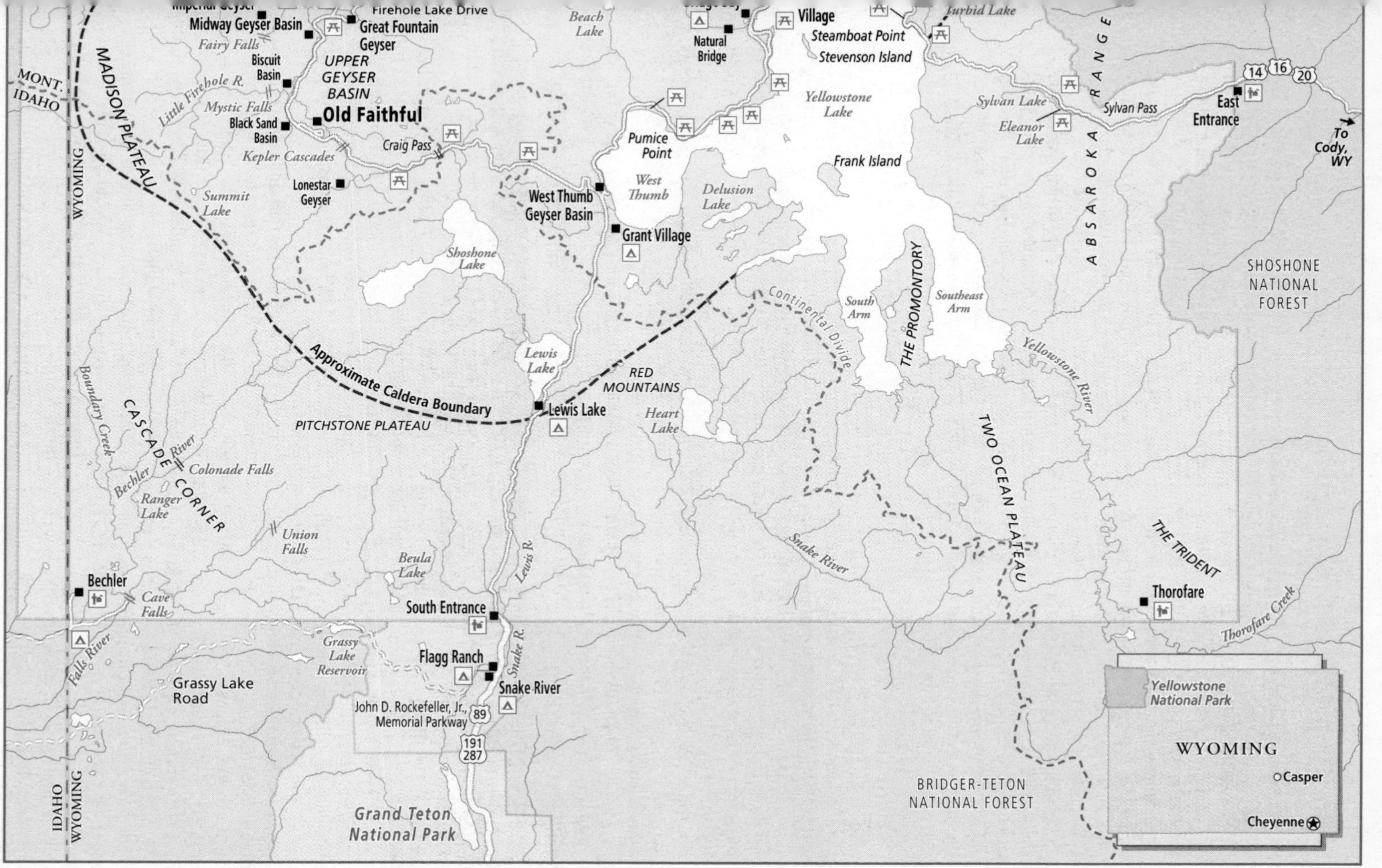

Firehole Lake Drive
Midway Geyser Basin
Great Fountain Geyser
Beach Lake
Village
Natural Bridge
Steamboat Point
Stevenson Island
Turbid Lake
MONT.
IDAHO
MADISON PLATEAU
Fairy Falls
Biscuit Basin
UPPER GEYSER BASIN
Little Firehole R.
Mystic Falls
Black Sand Basin
Old Faithful
Kepler Cascades
Craig Pass
Lonestar Geyser
Summit Lake
Yellowstone Lake
Pumice Point
West Thumb
West Thumb Geyser Basin
Delusion Lake
Frank Island
Grant Village
Sylvan Lake
Eleanor Lake
Sylvan Pass
ABSAROKA RANGE
14
16
20
East Entrance
To Cody, WY
SHOSHONE NATIONAL FOREST
WYOMING
Shoshone Lake
Lewis Lake
Approximate Caldera Boundary
RED MOUNTAINS
Lewis Lake
Heart Lake
PITCHSTONE PLATEAU
Continental Divide
South Arm
THE PROMONTORY
Southeast Arm
Yellowstone River
TWO OCEAN PLATEAU
Boundary Creek
CASCADE CORNER
Bechler River
Colonade Falls
Ranger Lake
Union Falls
Beula Lake
Lewis R.
Snake River
THE TRIDENT
Thorofare
Thorofare Creek
Bechler
Cave Falls
South Entrance
Falls River
Grassy Lake Reservoir
Flagg Ranch
Snake R.
Snake River
Grassy Lake Road
John D. Rockefeller, Jr., Memorial Parkway
89
191
287
Yellowstone National Park
WYOMING
Casper
Cheyenne
BRIDGER-TETON NATIONAL FOREST
Grand Teton National Park
IDAHO
WYOMING

The Great Fire of '88: Still a Burning Issue

Yellowstone's park managers faced the ultimate test of their noninterference philosophy of fire management in 1988, when nearly one-third of Yellowstone was burned by a series of uncontrollable **wildfires.** The violent conflagrations scorched more than 700,000 acres, leaving behind dead wildlife, damaged buildings, injured firefighters, and ghostly forests of stripped, blackened tree trunks.

The debate over park and public-land fire policies still rages, although things have quieted down some. After years of suppressing every fire in the park, Yellowstone, in 1988, was operating under a new "let it burn" policy, based on scientific evidence that fires were regular occurrences before the settlement of the West and part of the natural cycle of a forest.

What you will see as you travel Yellowstone today is a park that may be healthier than it was before: Saplings have sprouted from the long-dormant seeds of the lodgepole pine (fires stimulate the pine cones to release their seeds), and the old, tinder-dry forest undergrowth is being replaced with new, green shrubs, sometimes as thick as one million saplings per acre. Visitors who want to better understand the effects of the fires of 1988 should check out the exhibits at the Grant Village Visitor Center; the coverage there is the best in the park.

push it in this unpredictable climate. A beautiful Halloween weekend of rustling leaves and bright sun can become a winter wonderland overnight. Come too early in the spring—which is when the region gets most of its precipitation—and you'll be stuck at lower elevations while walls of snow melt on the higher trails. Try June and September or, if you like taking chances, the first 2 weeks in October. Any earlier or later, and you're on your own—truly on your own, because most of the inns in the park will have shut their doors.

Even if you schedule your visit during the park's busy months, you can still avoid the crowds: Take short hikes in popular spots at times of day when others are eating. Take a bag lunch—you can buy them at the Yellowstone General Stores—and avoid the lines at restaurants.

Better yet, take long walks into this grand wilderness. About 500 yards from a trail head, the crowd is a fading memory. Strap on a backpack, pick up a backcountry permit, and spend a night in the wilderness. You'll see some of the park's most beautiful landscapes, and there won't be a single tourist in the picture.

1 Essentials

GETTING THERE & GATEWAYS

To get to Yellowstone from I-90 and **Bozeman,** Montana (91 miles), take U.S. 191 south to its junction with U.S. 287 and head straight through the town of **West Yellowstone** to the park's west entrance. For visitor information on Bozeman, including lodging, dining, and getting to Yellowstone, visit the Convention and Visitor's bureau website at **www.bozemancvb.com**.

Billings, Montana, is 129 miles from Yellowstone's northeast entrance over Beartooth Pass (closed Oct 15 to Memorial Day). It's a 65-mile drive south from I-94 on U.S. 212 to Red Lodge, then 30 miles on the Beartooth Highway to the park. For visitor information on Billings, call the **Chamber of Commerce** at ✆ **406/245-4111** or visit www.billingschamber.com

Cody, Wyoming, is 52 miles from Yellowstone's east entrance (closed Nov–Apr) on U.S. 14/16/20. To Yellowstone's northeast entrance, it's 53 miles on Wyo. 120/296 to the Beartooth Highway (closed Oct 15–Memorial Day) intersection, and 14 miles beyond that to the entrance.

Jackson, Wyoming, is 57 miles south of Yellowstone's south entrance. Take U.S. 89/191 north through Grand Teton National Park. You can also approach this entrance from the east over Togwotee Pass on U.S. 26/287 from **Dubois,** Wyoming (83 miles).

From **Little Bighorn Battlefield National Monument,** an easy detour on the way to or from Yellowstone, take I-90 south from the monument into Wyoming about 50 miles to exit 9, and then follow U.S. 14 west about 190 miles to Yellowstone's east entrance (closed in winter).

For visitor information on any of the Wyoming gateway towns, contact **Wyoming Travel and Tourism** at ✆ **800/225-5996** or www.wyomingtourism.org.

THE NEAREST AIRPORTS You can fly into Bozeman, Montana's airport, **Gallatin Field** (✆ **406/388-8321;** www.gallatinfield.com), which handles daily service on **Delta, Northwest,** and **United,** as well as **Horizon** and **Frontier.** The West Yellowstone Airport, U.S. 191, 1 mile north of West Yellowstone (✆ **406/646-7631**), provides commercial air service seasonally, from June through September only, on Delta's commuter service, **SkyWest.** The airport in Billings, Montana, **Logan International** (✆ **406/238-8609;** www.flybillings.com), is the busiest in the state; it's on the rimrocks 2 miles north of downtown. Daily service within the region is provided by **Allegiant, Delta, Frontier, Horizon, Northwest,** and **United**. Cody, Wyoming's **Yellowstone Regional Airport** (✆ **307/587-5096;** www.flyyra.com) serves the east entrance of Yellowstone National Park with year-round commercial flights on **Delta** and **United.** Most of the major car-rental agencies operate in the gateway cities. For websites of major airlines, hotel chains, and car-rental agencies, see chapter 38.

INFORMATION

To receive maps and information before your arrival, contact **Yellowstone National Park,** WY 82190 (✆ **307/344-7381;** www.nps.gov/yell).

Information regarding lodging, some campgrounds, tours, boating, and horseback riding in Yellowstone is available from **Xanterra Parks & Resorts,** P.O. Box 165, Yellowstone National Park, WY 82190 (✆ **866/439-7375** or 307/344-7311; www.yellowstonenationalparklodges.com).

For information regarding educational programs in Yellowstone, contact the **Yellowstone Association,** P.O. Box 117, Yellowstone National Park, WY 82190 (✆ **406/848-2400;** www.yellowstoneassociation.org), which operates bookstores in park visitor centers, museums, and information stations, and oversees the excellent **Yellowstone Association Institute.** The institute conducts a varied curriculum at the old Lamar Buffalo Ranch in the park's northeast corner and at other locations. Its catalog of publications is available by mail and online at **http://yellowstoneassociation.org/institute**.

The following books are interesting and informative. If you cannot find them in your local bookstore, you can order many of them from the Yellowstone Association (see above). Look for *Yellowstone Trails,* Mark Marschall (Yellowstone National Park, WY: The Yellowstone Association) if you're a hiker. If you're traveling with kids, pick up *An Outdoor Family Guide to Yellowstone and Grand Teton National Parks,* Lisa Gollin Evans (The Mountaineers). For a more comprehensive guide, look for *Frommer's Yellowstone & Grand Teton National Parks* (Wiley), by the author of this chapter.

VISITOR CENTERS

There are five major visitor and information centers in the park, and each has something different to offer. The **Albright Visitor Center** (✆ **307/344-2263**), at Mammoth Hot Springs, is the largest and is open daily year-round. It provides visitor information and publications about the park, has exhibits depicting park history from prehistory through the creation of the National Park Service, and also houses displays on wildlife.

The **Canyon Visitor Center** (✆ **307/344-2550**), in Canyon Village, completed in 2007, is the place to go for books and an informative display about the park's geology, with a focus on the underlying volcanism. It's staffed with friendly rangers used to dealing with crowds.

A new, state-of-the-art **Old Faithful Visitor Center** (✆ **307/344-2750,** or 307/344-2751 for a recording of Old Faithful eruption predictions) is slated to open in 2010, showing a film on Yellowstone's thermal features throughout the day and featuring exhibits focusing on the park's thermal features and underlying volcanism. Rangers also post projected geyser-eruption times here.

The **Fishing Bridge Visitor Center** (✆ **307/344-2450**), near Fishing Bridge on the north shore of Yellowstone Lake, has an excellent display that focuses on the park's bird life. You can get information and publications here as well.

The **Grant Visitor Center** (✆ **307/242-2650**), in Grant Village, has information, publications, a video program, and a fascinating exhibit that examines the role of fire in Yellowstone.

Park literature and helpful staff are also found at several small information stations: the **Madison Information Station** (✆ **307/344-2821**), home of the **Junior Ranger Station;** the **Museum of the National Park Ranger** (no phone) and the **Norris Geyser Basin Museum and Information Station** (✆ **307/344-2812**), both at Norris; the **West Thumb Information Station** (no phone); and the **Visitor Information Center** at the West Yellowstone Visitors Information Center, 100 Yellowstone Ave. (✆ **307/344-2876**).

FEES & PERMITS

A pass to enter Yellowstone costs $25 per vehicle for a 7-day period (no matter the number of occupants) and covers both Yellowstone and Grand Teton national parks. Entering on a snowmobile or motorcycle costs $20 for 7 days, and someone who comes in on bicycle, skis, or foot pays $12. If you expect to visit the parks by car more than once in a year, buy an annual pass for $50.

You must have a **backcountry permit** for any overnight trip, whether on foot, on horseback, or by boat. See "Exploring the Backcountry," later in this chapter, for more information.

If You Have Only 1 Day

If you'll be coming into Yellowstone for 1 day and leaving the next, here's an itinerary that highlights the best of the best. If you'll be spending the night, try to reserve a room in one of the park hotels—either the Old Faithful Inn or the Lake Hotel—and you'll find yourself minutes from all of the major attractions. Expect to average about 30 mph during peak season.

The quickest route to the inner road loops of the park is on the west entrance road, so come in that way, perhaps stopping for a stroll along the banks of the **Madison River,** where you can see the forest recovering from the 1988 fires. You'll likely spot wildlife: ducks and trumpeter swans on the river, and grazing elk and bison near its banks. Turn north at Madison Junction to **Norris Geyser Basin,** where there are two boardwalk tours. Take the southern one if you don't have time for both, because there you can wait for the **Echinus Geyser** pool to fill and erupt.

You're now driving the **upper loop,** which goes north to **Mammoth Hot Springs,** east to **Tower-Roosevelt,** south to **Canyon Village,** and west again to Norris, finally returning to Madison Junction, a circuit of about 85 miles. But don't complete the loop—at Canyon, continue south on the Lower Loop, which will take you to **Fishing Bridge** and **Lake Village,** then by **West Thumb,** west over Craig Pass to **Old Faithful,** and back to Madison Junction from the south. If you do the entire loop, it covers 96 miles. Our recommendation: Do one loop the day you enter the park, spend the night, then do the second loop and leave the way you came. If this is part of a longer cross-country trip, you can enter one side of the park and leave the other.

THE UPPER LOOP The Norris Geyser basin is a major concentration of thermal attractions, including **Porcelain Basin** and legendary **Steamboat Geyser** (the park's largest, erupting only about once a decade historically but more often in recent years) and has a nice **museum.** Mammoth has one of the park's major attractions, the ever-growing terraces of **Mammoth Hot Springs.** In addition to the natural attraction, the Albright Visitor Center provides excellent historical background for everything you'll see in the park. There is a fine old hotel at Mammoth, and mom-and-pop and chain lodging just north of the park in Gardiner, but we recommend you continue farther around the loop on your first day. From Mammoth, the route winds through forested areas that lead to the edge of the **Lamar Valley,** a deep, rounded path for the Lamar River that is prime wildlife habitat. You could stop for the night at **Roosevelt Lodge** or continue south to Yellowstone's **Grand Canyon,** one of the most dramatic sights in the park, and on to Lake Yellowstone Hotel, at the north end of **Yellowstone Lake.**

THE LOWER LOOP This is a better way to go, in our opinion. You'll also see the two largest geyser areas in Yellowstone: **Norris** to the north and the park's signature attraction, **Old Faithful,** to the south. On the eastern side of this route, you'll find the **Grand Canyon of the Yellowstone** and **Hayden Valley,** where you'll often see herds of buffalo. Farther south, the **Yellowstone Lake** area is a haven for water lovers, with fishing, boating, and places for picnicking on the shore of the lake.

This circuit is called the **"Grand Loop,"** and it takes you through all the major areas of the park except the road between Norris and Canyon Village. If you have 2 days, then do both loops. You could do it in a day—it's about 150 miles long—but you'd scare a lot of other travelers as you sped by.

SPECIAL REGULATIONS & WARNINGS

It is unlawful to approach within 100 yards of a bear or within 25 yards of other wildlife. Feeding any wildlife is illegal. Wildlife calls such as elk bugles or other artificial attractants are forbidden. Because of wildlife and thermal activity, staying on the trails here is especially important.

SEASONS & CLIMATE

For general information on seasons and climate in the area, see "Seasons & Climate" in chapter 17, which covers nearby Grand Teton National Park. Keep in mind that Grand Teton is a bit lower in elevation than Yellowstone, so snows melt later in Yellowstone and temperatures are slightly lower.

ROAD OPENINGS

Scheduling a spring driving trip to Yellowstone can be a roll of the dice, because weather conditions can delay openings for weeks, especially at higher altitudes. A heavy snowstorm in October can compel early closure of the park gates. Depending upon weather, most other park roads remain open until the park season ends on the first Sunday in November (the Beartooth Hwy. btw. Cooke City and Red Lodge, Montana, closes mid-Oct). The only road open year-round is the **Mammoth Hot Springs–Cooke City Road.**

Plowing in Yellowstone begins in early March. The first roads open to motor vehicles usually include **Mammoth–Norris, Norris–Canyon, Madison–Old Faithful,** and **West Yellowstone–Madison.** The latter may open by the end of April. If the weather cooperates, the east and south entrances, as well as roads on the east and south sides of the park, will open early in May. Late-season snowfall on Dunraven Pass may delay opening of the **Tower–Roosevelt** to **Canyon Junction Road.**

The **Sunlight Basin Road** (also called the **Chief Joseph Hwy.**), connecting the entrance at Cooke City, Montana, with Cody, Wyoming, often opens by early May. The **Beartooth Highway** between Cooke City and Red Lodge, Montana, is generally open by Memorial Day weekend.

The road connecting **Gardiner** and **Cooke City,** Montana, remains open year-round, providing the only wintertime access to Cooke City. This presents late-season travelers with an opportunity to see the northeast area of the park and some of its abundant wildlife during the winter.

Call the park's main information number (© **307/344-7381**) for road conditions and closings.

2 Exploring the Park

Stretching your visit to several days will give you time to delve into some of the park's lesser-known but impressive offerings. Since the roads in Yellowstone are organized into a series of connecting loops that you can reach from any of the park's five entrances, it doesn't really matter where you begin your tour. To simplify things, we will discuss attractions and activities going clockwise along each section of the **Grand Loop Road,** beginning at **Madison Junction.** But you can enter the loop and pick up the tour at any point, as long as you are traveling clockwise. We haven't suggested an optimum amount of time to spend on each leg of the loop; that will depend on your particular interests. ***Note:*** Road maintenance is a continual process in the park, so expect delays.

WEST YELLOWSTONE TO NORRIS

Most of Yellowstone's visitors enter at the **West Yellowstone Entrance,** so we'll use that as a jumping-off point for an extended tour of the park. As you travel the 14 miles from the gate to **Madison Junction,** you will find the **Two Ribbons Trail,** which offers an opportunity to walk through and inspect the effects of the 1988 fire. Park maps don't identify all the observation points and side roads in the area, so now is the time to begin forming the habit of driving off the beaten path, even when you may not know where you're going. Keep a sharp eye peeled for the poorly marked **Riverside turnout** on the Madison River side of the road; it's a paved road on the north side of the highway about 6 miles from the entrance. This back road takes you along a river, removed from most traffic, with a number of turnouts perfectly situated to let you look for resident swans, enjoy a picnic, or test your fly-fishing ability.

As you continue toward **Madison Junction,** you'll see vivid evidence of the 1988 fire and, odds are, a herd of bison that frequents the area during summer months. As frightening as the fire was, it had its good points: When temperatures exceeded 500°F (260°C), pine seeds were released from fire-adapted pine cones, which has quickened the rebirth cycle. The thick carpet of tiny trees making their way through the soil is evidence that this forest is recovering very quickly.

The short **Harlequin Lake Trail** offers an excellent, easy opportunity to explore the area and see various types of waterfowl. An alternative hike, the **Purple Mountain Trail,** is more strenuous, but it is one of the best in the area. For descriptions of both, see "Day Hikes," later in this chapter.

Madison Junction marks the confluence of the Gibbon and Firehole rivers. The two famous trout streams meet to form the Madison River, one of three that join to form the Missouri. This is also where you'll enter the northern loop toward Norris Junction, along a winding 14-mile section of road that parallels the **Gibbon River.** At **Gibbon Falls,** which is 84 feet tall, you'll see water bursting out of the edge of a thermal vent in a rocky canyon, the walls of which were hidden from view for several hundred years until being exposed by the fire of 1988. There's a delightful **picnic area** just below the falls, on an open plateau overlooking the Gibbon River. Before arriving at Norris Junction, you'll discover the **Artist Paint Pot Trail** in Gibbon Meadows 4½ miles south of Norris Junction, an interesting yet easy half-mile stroll. Across the road from the trail head is **Elk Park,** where you are likely to see a large herd of elk.

NORRIS GEYSER BASIN

Perhaps more than any other area in Yellowstone, this basin is living testimony to the park's unique thermal activity. It changes from year to year as thermal activity and fierce weather create new and different ponds and landscapes. This is the location of one of the park's highest concentrations of thermal features, including the most active geysers, with underground water temperatures that reach 459°F (237°C).

There are two loop trails here, both mostly level with wheelchair access, to the Porcelain Basin and the Back Basin. If you take in both of them, you'll see most of the area's interesting thermal features. If you're pressed for time, opt for the shorter **Porcelain Basin Trail,** a boardwalk that takes 45 minutes. To us, this area is especially spectacular on summer days when thermal activity takes place on the ground with thunderstorms overhead.

The **Porcelain Basin Trail** is a .75-mile round-trip that can be completed in 45 minutes; on it are Black Growler Steam Vent, Ledge Geyser, and the descriptively named Whale's Mouth.

The 1.5-mile **Back Basin Loop** is easily negotiable in 1 hour and passes by **Steamboat Geyser,** which has been known to produce the world's highest and most memorable eruptions. However, these 400-foot waterspouts occur infrequently, so it will take some luck to see one—it erupted eight times between 2000 and late 2009, but blew its top only twice during the preceding 12 years and not at all between 1911 and 1961.

Among the many highlights of the area is the **Norris Geyser Basin Museum,** a single-story stone-and-log building with several excellent exhibits explaining the nature of the area. Also nearby is the **Museum of the National Park Ranger,** which is little more than a room full of artifacts in a small building near the campground (discussed later). Both museums open from mid- to late May, weather permitting, until September; hours vary by season, but you can expect the museums to be open from 9 or 10am to 5pm during the busiest times (roughly Memorial Day to Labor Day; again, weather is a factor).

NORRIS TO MAMMOTH HOT SPRINGS

From Norris Geyser Basin, it's a 21-mile drive north to Mammoth Hot Springs, past the **Twin Lakes,** beautiful, watery jewels surrounded by trees. During the early months of the park year, the water is milky green because of the runoff of ice and snow. This is an excellent place to call timeout and do some bird-watching.

This stretch of road, between Norris Junction and Mammoth Hot Springs, presents yet another excellent opportunity to see the effects of the 1988 fire. The large **meadow** on the west (left, if you are traveling north) side of the highway that begins 3 miles from Norris is popular with moose, thanks to water from bogs, marshes, and a creek. As you travel alongside **Obsidian Creek,** you'll notice the smell of sulfur in the air, evidence of thermal vents.

On the east (right, if you are traveling north) side of the road, 4 miles from Norris, is **Roaring Mountain,** a patch of ground totally devoid of brush and plant life, covered with trees and stumps from the fire. Its bareness is attributed to the fact that, as steam vents developed here, the ground became too hot and acidic, which bleached and crumbled the rock, taking the undergrowth with it. Historians say that the noise from the Roaring Mountain was once so loud that it could be heard as far as 4 miles away; these days it is nearly silent.

Just up the road 2 miles is the **Beaver Lake Picnic Area,** an excellent little spot for a snack right on Beaver Lake. It's also a good place to keep an eye out for moose.

As you wend your way a half-mile to **Obsidian Cliff,** across the road from the picnic area, the terrain changes quickly, and you'll find yourself driving through a narrow valley bisected by a beautiful green stream. Obsidian Cliff is where ancient peoples of North America gathered to collect obsidian, a hard, black rock that was used to make weapons and implements.

If you didn't stop at Beaver Lake, consider taking time for the 3-minute detour to **Sheepeater Cliffs** (unless you're driving an RV or pulling a trailer). This quiet, secluded spot on the banks of the Gardner River is home to yellow-bellied marmots that live in the rocks, safe from flying predators (such as eagles) and coyotes.

Exiting the valley, head north onto a high plateau, where you'll find **Swan Lake,** which is surrounded by Little Quadrant Mountain and Antler Peak to the west, and Bunsen Peak to the north.

At the northernmost edge of the Yellowstone Plateau, you'll begin a descent through **Golden Gate.** This steep, narrow stretch of road was once a stagecoach route constructed of wooden planks anchored to the mountain by a massive rock called the **Pillar of Hercules,** the largest rock in an unmarked pile that sits next to the road.

From the 45th parallel parking area on the north entrance road north of Mammoth Hot Springs, a short hike leads to the **Boiling River.** Here you can take a dip during daylight hours, where a hot spring empties into the Gardner River.

MAMMOTH HOT SPRINGS

The large **Albright Visitor Center,** near park headquarters, has more visitor information and publications than other centers. You'll probably want to stop in.

Though it's possible to see most of the wildlife and the major thermal areas from behind car windows, getting out of your vehicle will greatly enhance your experience of the park. Most people in average shape are capable of negotiating the trails, a significant percentage of which are level or only moderately inclined boardwalks. Even the more challenging trails frequently have rest areas where you can catch your breath and stop to absorb the magnificent views.

Two of Yellowstone's most fascinating areas are the **Upper** and **Lower terraces.** Strolling through them, you can observe Mother Nature going about the business of mixing and matching heat, water, limestone, and rock fractures to sculpt the area. With the exception of the Grand Canyon of the Yellowstone River, this is the most colorful area of the park; its tapestries of orange, pink, yellow, green, and brown, formed by masses of bacteria and algae, seem to change color before your eyes.

The mineral-rich hot waters that flow to the surface here do so at an unusually constant rate, roughly 750,000 gallons per day, which results in the deposit of almost 2 tons of limestone on these ever-changing terraces. Contours are constantly undergoing change in the hot springs, as formations are shaped by large quantities of flowing water, the slope of the ground, and trees and rocks that determine the direction of the flow.

On the flip side of the equation, nature has a way of playing tricks on some of her creatures: **Poison Spring** is a sinkhole on the trail, so named because carbon dioxide collects there, often killing creatures who stop for a drink. The **Lower Terrace Interpretive Trail** (see "Day Hikes," later in this chapter) is one of the best ways to see this area.

After passing **Palette Spring,** where bacteria create a collage of browns, greens, and oranges, you're on your way to **Cleopatra** and **Minerva terraces.** Minerva is a favorite of visitors because of its brightly colored travertine formations, the product of limestone deposits.

The hike up the last 150 feet to the Upper Terrace Loop Drive is slightly steeper, though there are benches at frequent intervals. From here you can see all the terraces and several springs—**Canary Spring** and **New Blue Spring** being the most distinctive—and the red-roofed buildings of **Fort Yellowstone,** which is now the park headquarters.

MAMMOTH HOT SPRINGS TO TOWER JUNCTION

Heading east from Mammoth on the Tower Road, a 6-mile drive will bring you to the **Forces of the Northern Range Self-Guiding Trail;** this flat, easy boardwalk stroll is an excellent opportunity to learn about the environmental effects of the fire.

Two miles later is **Blacktail Plateau Drive,** a 7-mile, one-way dirt road that offers wildlife-viewing opportunities and a bit more solitude. You'll emerge on the Mammoth–Tower Road, about a mile west of the turnoff to the Petrified Tree.

Turn right onto this half-mile-long road that dead-ends at the **Petrified Tree,** a redwood that, while standing, was burned by volcanic ash more than 50 million years ago.

TOWER-ROOSEVELT

Just beyond the Petrified Tree, you'll come to **Tower–Roosevelt,** the most relaxed of the park's villages and a great place to take a break from the more crowded attractions. Even if you aren't going to stay, you might want to take a look at the **Tower Soldier Station,** now the ranger residence at Tower Junction, one of three surviving outposts from the era of U.S. Cavalry management of the park. Also here is **Roosevelt Lodge,** a rustic building that commemorates President Teddy Roosevelt's camping excursion to this area of the park in 1903.

At **Specimen Ridge,** 2½ miles east of Tower Junction on the northeast entrance road, you'll find a ridge that entombs one of the world's most extensive fossil forests.

FROM TOWER JUNCTION TO THE GRAND CANYON OF THE YELLOWSTONE

A few minutes' drive from the Tower area is the **Calcite Springs Overlook.** A short loop along a boardwalk leads to the overlook at the rim of **The Narrows,** the narrowest part of the canyon. You can hear the river raging through the canyon some 500 feet below, and look across at the canyon walls made up of rock spires and bands of columnar basalt. Just downstream is the most prominent feature in the canyon, **Bumpus Butte.**

Continuing south, you travel through the **Washburn Range,** an area in which the 1988 fire ran especially hot and fast. The terrain changes dramatically as the road climbs, as well as along some major hills toward **Mount Washburn.** There are trail heads for the **Mount Washburn Trail,** one of our favorites, on each side of the summit.

As you approach **Dunraven Pass** (8,859 ft.), keep your eyes peeled for the shy mountain sheep—this is one of their prime habitats. One mile farther south is the **Washburn Hot Springs Overlook,** which offers sweeping views of the Grand Canyon. On a clear day, you can see 50 to 100 miles south, beyond Yellowstone Lake.

CANYON VILLAGE

You're in for yet another eyeful when you reach the **Grand Canyon of the Yellowstone River.** Compared to the Grand Canyon of Arizona, the Yellowstone canyon is relatively narrow; however, the sheer cliffs are equally impressive, descending hundreds of feet to the bottom of a gorge where the Yellowstone River flows. It's also equally colorful, with displays of oranges, reds, yellows, and golds. You won't find thermal vents in Arizona, but you will find them here, a constant reminder of ongoing underground activity.

You should plan on encountering crowds when you reach **Canyon Village.** Rebuilt in 2007, the **Canyon Visitor Center** (✆ **307/242-2550**) is the place to go for books and a geology exhibit.

An auto tour of the canyon follows **North Rim Drive,** a two-lane, one-way road that begins in Canyon Village, to your first stop, **Inspiration Point.** On the way, you'll pass a **glacial boulder** estimated to weigh 500 tons that was deposited by melting ice more than 10,000 years ago.

At Inspiration Point, a moderately strenuous descent down 57 steps takes you to an overlook with views of the Lower Falls and canyon. There are several other view points you can stop at along North Rim Drive before you reconnect with the main Canyon Village–Yellowstone Lake Road, which will take you down to South Rim Drive.

For the adventurous, an alternative to driving from one overlook to another is to negotiate the **North Rim Trail,** which is slightly more than 2.25 miles long, beginning at Inspiration Point. Unfortunately, the North Rim Trail is not a loop, so if you take the hike, you'll have to backtrack. The footpath brings you closer to what you want to see, and you won't be fighting for elbow room, as you will at the overlooks that are accessible only to cars.

Whether you drive or walk, you should go down to the **Upper Falls View,** where a .25-mile trail leads down from the parking lot to the brink of the **Upper Falls** and an overlook within splashing distance of the rushing river and the waterfall. At this point you won't just hear, but you'll feel the power of the river as it begins its course down the canyon.

The **South Rim Drive** leads to several overlooks and better views of the Lower Falls. The most impressive vantage point is from the bottom of **Uncle Tom's Trail,** a steep, 500-foot steel staircase that begins at the first South Rim parking lot.

South Rim Road continues to a second, lower parking lot and a trail that leads to **Artist Point.** The astounding view here, one of our favorites in the park, is best in the early morning.

CANYON VILLAGE TO FISHING BRIDGE

The road winds through the **Hayden Valley,** a vast expanse of green meadows accented by brown cuts where the soil is eroded along the banks of the Yellowstone River. The valley is a wide, sprawling area where bison and antelope play and where trumpeter swans, white pelicans, and Canada geese float along the river. This is also a prime grizzly habitat; during early spring, pay close attention to binocular-toting visitors grouped beside the road.

Nature is working at her acidic best at the **Sulphur Caldron** and **Mud Volcano** areas, 12 miles south of the Canyon Junction, which the frontier minister Edwin Stanley described as "unsightly, unsavory, and villainous." We think he was right on the money, so you'll not want to miss this area. After all, there's nothing quite like the sound of burping mud pots.

At **Dragon's Mouth Spring,** steam and sulfurous gases propel turbid water from an underground cavern to the surface, where it colors the earth shades of orange and green. The belching of steam and the attendant sound, which is due to the splash of 180°F (82°C) water against the wall in a subterranean cavern, creates a medieval quality, hence the name of the spring.

Nearby **Mud Volcano** is an unappetizing mud spring, the product of vigorous activity caused by escaping sulfurous gases and steam. The youngest feature in the area is **Black Dragon's Caldron,** which is often referred to as "the demon of the backwoods," and rightly so. The caldron emerged from its subterranean birthplace for the first time in 1948 when it announced its presence by blowing a hole in the landscape, scattering mature trees hundreds of feet in all directions. Since then, continual seismic activity and intermittent earthquakes in the area have caused it to relocate 200 feet south of its original position.

The road across the Yellowstone River at **Fishing Bridge** was once the only eastern exit in the park, the route leading over Sylvan Pass to Cody, Wyoming. The bridge, built in 1902, spans the Yellowstone River as it exits Yellowstone Lake, and is another prime spawning area for native trout. The **Fishing Bridge Visitor Center** (✆ **307/242-2450**) has a first-rate wildlife display. You'll find an excellent hiking trail, **Elephant Back Loop Trail,** leading off the short strip of highway between Fishing Bridge and the Lake Village area.

YELLOWSTONE LAKE AREA

As if the park didn't have enough record-setting attractions: At 7,773 feet, **Yellowstone Lake** is North America's largest high-altitude lake. The lake exhibits its multifaceted personalities daily, ranging from a placid, mirrorlike surface to a tantrum whipped by southerly winds that create 3- to 4-foot waves. Because the lake has the largest population of native cutthroat trout in North America, it makes an ideal fishing spot during the summer.

Lake Village, on the northwest shore of the lake, offers a wide range of amenities, the most prominent of which is the majestic century-old **Lake Yellowstone Hotel** (✆ **307/344-7311;** www.yellowstonenationalparklodges.com), perhaps the most beautiful structure in the park.

Just south of Lake Village is the **Bridge Bay Marina,** the center of the park's water activities. Here you can arrange for guided fishing trips or small boat rentals, or learn more about the lake during an informative and entertaining 1-hour narrated boat tour. The marina is usually open from mid-June to mid-September.

Though the **Natural Bridge,** near Bridge Bay, is well marked on park maps, it's one of the park's best-kept secrets, and you may end up enjoying it by yourself. The mile-long path down to the bridge, a geologic masterpiece consisting of a massive rock arch 51 feet overhead, spanning Bridge Creek, is an excellent bike route.

The **West Thumb** area along the western shoreline is the deepest part of Yellowstone Lake. Because of its craterlike contours, many scientists speculate that this 4-mile-wide, 6-mile-long, water-filled crater was created during volcanic eruptions approximately 125,000 years ago.

The **West Thumb Geyser Basin** is notable for a unique series of geysers. Some are right on the shores, some overlook the lake, and some can be seen beneath the lake surface. Three of the shoreline geysers, the most famous of which is **Fishing Cone,** are occasionally marooned offshore when the lake level rises. Fortunately, boardwalks surround the area, so it's easy to negotiate. Maps and details on the area are available in the **West Thumb Information Station** (no phone; daily in summer 9am–5pm).

As you depart the West Thumb area, you have two choices: head south toward Grand Teton National Park, or head west across the **Continental Divide** at Craig Pass, en route to Old Faithful.

GRANT VILLAGE TO THE SOUTH ENTRANCE

In contrast to the forgettable **Grant Village,** the 22-mile drive to **Grand Teton National Park** (see chapter 17), along high mountain passes and **Lewis Lake,** is beautiful. After the lake loses its winter coat of ice, it is a popular spot for early season anglers who are unable to fish streams clouded by the spring runoff.

Beyond the lake, the road follows the Lewis River through an alpine area and along the **Pitchstone Plateau,** a pile of lava more than 2,000 feet high and 20 miles wide that was created some 500,000 years ago. A high gorge overlooking the river provides views that are different from, but just as spectacular as, those in other sections of the park.

WEST THUMB TO OLD FAITHFUL

The most interesting phenomenon on the Old Faithful route is **Isa Lake** at Craig Pass. Unlike most lakes and streams in the park, it empties into both eastern and western drainages and ends up in the Pacific Ocean and the Gulf of Mexico. Amazingly, as a consequence of a gyroscopic maneuver, the outlet on the east curves west and eventually drains into the Pacific, and the outlet on the west curves east and drains into the Gulf.

Before you reach the Old Faithful geyser area, two additional detours are recommended. Southeast of Old Faithful 2½ miles is an overlook at the spectacular **Kepler Cascades,** a 150-foot stair-step waterfall on the Firehole River that is footsteps from the parking lot.

Near that parking lot is the trail head for the second detour, a 5-mile round-trip to the **Lonestar Geyser** (on the eponymous trail), which erupts every 3 hours, sending steaming water 30 to 50 feet from its 12-foot cone.

OLD FAITHFUL GEYSER AREA

Despite the overwhelming sight of the geysers and steam vents that populate the Old Faithful area, we suggest you resist the temptation to explore until you've stopped at the **Old Faithful Visitor Center** (✆ **307/545-2750**). Check the information board for estimated times of geyser eruptions, and plan accordingly.

The Old Faithful area is divided into four sections: **Upper Geyser Basin,** which includes **Geyser Hill, Black Sand Basin, Biscuit Basin,** and **Midway Geyser Basin.** All of these connect to the Old Faithful area by paved trails and roads. If time allows, hike the area; it's fairly level, and distances are relatively short. Between the Old Faithful area and Madison Junction, you'll also find the famous **Lower Geyser Basin,** including **Fountain Paint Pot** and the trails surrounding it. You can see some of these geysers on Firehole Lake Drive.

Though **Old Faithful** is not the largest or most regular geyser in the park, its image has been said to be the West's equivalent of the Statue of Liberty. Like clockwork, the average interval between eruptions is about 90 minutes, though it may vary 30 minutes in either direction. A typical eruption lasts 1½ to 5 minutes, during which 3,700 to 8,400 gallons of water are thrust upward to heights of 180 feet. For the best views and photo opportunities of the eruption in the boardwalk area, plan on arriving early to ensure a first-row view.

An alternative to a spot on the crowded boardwalk is a stroll from the Old Faithful Geyser up the **Observation Point Trail** to an observation area that provides better views of the entire geyser basin. The path up to the observation point is approximately .5 mile, and the elevation gain is only 200 feet, so it's an easy 15-minute hike. The view of the eruption of the geyser is more spectacular from here and the crowds less obtrusive.

Old Faithful Area

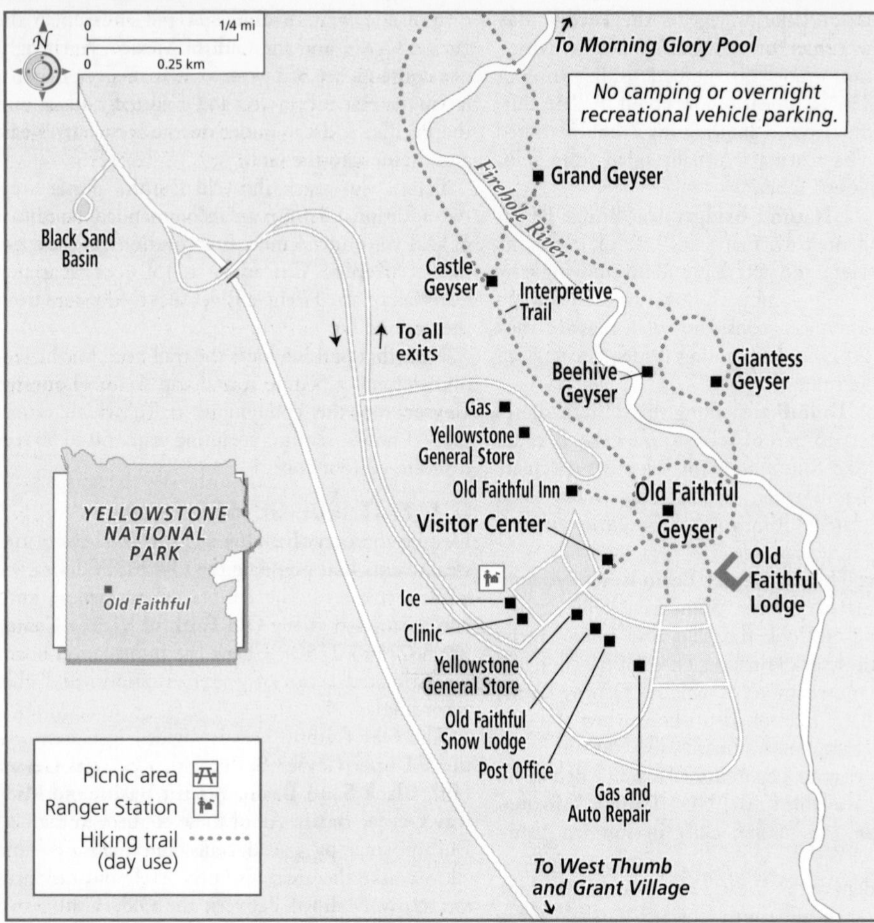

Accessible by walkways from Old Faithful Village, the **Upper Geyser Basin Loop** is designated as Geyser Hill on some maps. The 1.3-mile loop trail winds among several thermal attractions. **Anemone Geyser** may offer the best display of the various stages of a typical eruption as the pool fills and overflows, after which bubbles rising to the surface begin throwing water in 10-foot eruptions, a cycle that repeats every 7 to 10 minutes.

Two other stars of the show in the Upper Geyser Basin are **Castle Geyser** and **Grand Geyser.** Castle Geyser, with the largest cone of any geyser in the park, currently erupts for 20 minutes every 10 to 12 hours, after which a noisy steam phase may continue for half an hour. Grand Geyser, the tallest predictable geyser in the world, usually erupts every 7 to 15 hours with powerful bursts that produce streams of water that may reach 200 feet in height.

The **Riverside Geyser** is on the bank of the Firehole River, across from a large viewing area. One of the most picturesque geysers in the park, it generates a 75-foot column of water that creates an arch over the river. Just to the south, **Morning Glory Pool** was named for its likeness to its namesake flower in the 1880s, but it has since lost some of its beauty. Vandals have tossed so much debris into its core over the years that it now suffers from poor circulation and reduced temperatures, which are causing unsightly brown and green bacteria to grow on its surface.

The **Black Sand Basin** is a cluster of especially colorful hot springs and geysers located a mile north of Old Faithful. It is interesting primarily because of its black sand, a derivative of obsidian. **Biscuit Basin,** 2 miles farther up the road, was named for biscuitlike deposits that surrounded colorful **Sapphire Pool** until a 1959 earthquake caused the pool to erupt, sending them skyward. Both the Black Sand Basin and the Biscuit Basin can be viewed from flat, interpretive boardwalks.

The **Midway Geyser Basin** extends for about a mile along the Firehole River. The major attractions here are the **Excelsior Geyser,** the third-largest geyser in the world and once the park's most powerful geyser, and the well-known **Grand Prismatic**

Spring, the largest hot spring in Yellowstone and the second largest in the world.

OLD FAITHFUL TO MADISON JUNCTION

Believe it or not, there are more superb geysers and hot springs on **Firehole Lake Drive,** all visible without leaving your vehicle, along a 3-mile, one-way road. The turnoff for Firehole Lake Drive is about 8 miles north of the Old Faithful area. There are three geysers of interest on this road. The largest is **Great Fountain Geyser,** which erupts every 8 to 12 hours, typically spouting water some 100 feet high for periods of 45 to 60 minutes. However, the lucky visitor may see the occasional "superburst" that reaches heights of 200 feet or more.

Estimates are that **White Dome Geyser** has been erupting for hundreds of years. Unfortunately, the age and height of this massive cone are not matched by spectacular eruptions. The vent on top of the cone has been nearly sealed with deposits of "geyserite," so eruptions reach only 30 feet. However, a look at the cone itself is worth a trip.

Farther on, **Pink Cone Geyser** couldn't be closer to the road—crews cut into the geyser's mound during construction. The geyser still erupts occasionally, but the 30-foot spray goes mostly skyward and doesn't interfere with traffic.

About a half-mile north of where Firehole Lake Drive rejoins the Grand Loop Road is the **Fountain Paint Pots** area. See "Day Hikes," below.

3 Organized Tours & Ranger Programs

A number of tour companies offer bus and van tours of the park, originating in gateway communities: **Yellowstone Alpen Guides** (✆ **800/858-3502;** www.yellowstoneguides.com) takes travelers around the park from West Yellowstone; rates run about $50 per person for a 4-hour tour. Salt Lake City–based **AdventureBus** (✆ **888/737-5263;** www.adventurebus.com) takes groups to Yellowstone and Grand Teton between June and August; week-long tours run about $1,000 per person. I highly recommend **Escape Adventures** (✆ **800/596-2953;** www.escapeadventures.com), which offers supported 6-day road biking tours of Yellowstone and Grand Teton for about $1,500 if you camp or $2,300 if you stay in the park's accommodations. If you are looking for specialized guided trips—such as photo safaris—contact the chambers of commerce in the gateway community where you want to begin.

Within the park, the hotel concessionaire, **Xanterra Parks & Resorts** (✆ **307/344-7311;** www.yellowstonenationalparklodges.com), has a variety of general and specialized tours. Five different motorcoach tours are available from all of Yellowstone's villages. For about $70, you can explore the **Circle of Fire** (Old Faithful, Yellowstone Lake, the Hayden Valley) or you can do the **Yellowstone in a Day** tour. These are full-day tours, with stops at all the sights and talks by the guides. In 2007, eight restored **Old Yellow Buses** that roamed the Yellowstone roads here in the first half of the 20th century went back into service for Xanterra. Tours in the buses range from 1 to 4 hours ($15–$81). Other specialty trips include custom van tours, photo safaris, wildlife trips up the Lamar Valley, and Yellowstone Lake sunset tours in historic buses from the 1930s.

At Bridge Bay Marina, 1-hour **Scenicruiser tours** (✆ **307/344-7311**) depart throughout the day from June to the end of September for a trip around the northern end of giant Yellowstone Lake. You view the Lake Yellowstone Hotel from the water and visit Stevenson Island while a guide fills you in on the history, geology, and biology. Fares are $14 for adults and $9 for children ages 2 to 11. Guided fishing trips on 22-foot and 34-foot cabin cruisers are also available at Bridge Bay ($152 and $196 for 2 hr., respectively), and you can rent smaller outboards and rowboats.

Buses are replaced in the winter by **snowcoach tours.** These are closer in size to a van than a bus, mounted on tank treads with skis in front for steering. The snowcoach can pick you up at the south or west entrances or at Mammoth, and take you all over the park. You can spend a night at Old Faithful and then snowcoach up to Mammoth the next night, or do round-trip tours from the gates or wherever you're staying in the park. One-way and wildlife-watching trips range from roughly $30 to $60, while round-trips cost about $110 to $130. **Yellowstone Alpen Guides** (✆ **800/858-3502;** www.yellowstoneguides.com) offers snowcoach trips and tours from West Yellowstone for $110 per person and up.

Guided horseback trail rides lasting from 1 to 2 hours are available at Roosevelt Lodge and Canyon Village. Children must be at least 8 years old and 48 inches tall; adults cannot exceed 240 pounds. Tour prices are $35 for a 1-hour ride and $54 for a 2-hour ride (no discount for children). Check any activity desk for times and dates. Reservations are recommended and can be made at **Xanterra Parks & Resorts** activity centers in the hotels, although not before you leave home.

The **Yellowstone Association Institute** (✆ **406/848-2400;** www.yellowstoneassociation.org/institute) offers a slew of guided classes, from daylong hikes to multiday backcountry adventures, often with a historical or scientific bent. The Institute has teamed with

Xanterra Parks & Resorts to offer visitors days spent exploring trails with guides and nights at the comfortable lodgings throughout the park. These **Lodging and Learning** packages are excellent options for those who want to delve into the park without too much of the traditional "roughing it." Rates (starting at about $600 per person) include box lunches, breakfast, and in-park transportation. Contact **Xanterra Parks & Resorts** (✆ **866/439-7375;** www.yellowstonenationalparklodges.com).

In September, the Institute takes over **Roosevelt Lodge** with the **Roosevelt Rendezvous,** a series of 4-day educational experiences with a daily menu of different field trips led by park experts. There are also evening programs. Rates start at $679 per person, which includes tuition, a cabin, and three meals a day.

Ranger-led programs take place throughout the park during the summer, some at campground amphitheaters, some at visitor centers, some on hikes or at key landmarks. It's the best value in the park: free. **Evening campfire programs** run nightly in the summer at campgrounds at Mammoth Hot Springs, Norris, Madison, Grant, Bridge Bay, and Canyon. Many of these activities are accessible to travelers with disabilities. There are more tours and evening programs in the **Old Faithful** area than anywhere else in the park. The talks and walks, which can run as long as 1½ hours, usually focus on the geysers, their fragile plumbing, and their role in the Yellowstone ecosystem. Check the park newspaper when you enter the park for a current listing of ranger programs.

4 Day Hikes

WEST YELLOWSTONE TO MADISON

Artist Paint Pot Trail This interesting and worthwhile stroll along a relatively level path winds through a lodgepole pine forest in Gibbon Meadows, to a mud pot at the top of a hill. This thermal area contains some small geysers, hot pools, and steam vents. 1 mile RT. Easy. Access: Gibbon Meadow, 4½ miles south of Norris Junction.

Harlequin Lake Trail This is an excellent, easy opportunity to explore the area while winding through the burned forest to a small lake populated by various types of waterfowl. 1 mile RT. Easy. Access: West entrance road 1½ miles west of Madison Campground.

Purple Mountain Trail This hike requires some physical exertion. It winds through a burned forest to the top of what many consider only a tall hill, with an elevation gain of 1,400 feet. 6 miles RT. Easy. Access: Madison–Norris Rd., ¼ mile north of Madison Junction.

Two Ribbons Trail This trail offers an opportunity to inspect the effects of the 1988 fire. Along the boardwalk, you'll see evidence of not only the blaze that ravaged the area, but the beginning of a new cycle of life in the dense green shag of lodgepole saplings. 1.5 mile RT. Easy. Access: Turnout on north side of road 3 miles east of west entrance.

NORRIS GEYSER BASIN

Back Basin Loop This level boardwalk, easily negotiable in 1 hour, passes by Steamboat Geyser, which has been known to produce the world's highest and most memorable eruptions. However, these 400-foot waterspouts rarely occur more than once or twice a year (and sometimes only once or twice a decade), so it will take some luck to see one. 1.5 miles RT. Easy. Access: Norris Geyser Basin.

Porcelain Basin Trail This short trail, which can be completed in 45 minutes, is on a level boardwalk that, like the Back Basin Loop, is in a concentration of thermal attractions that may change every year. .5 mile RT. Easy. Access: Norris Geyser Basin.

MAMMOTH HOT SPRINGS AREA

Bunsen Peak Trail This trail leads to a short but steep 2.1-mile trip to the 8,564-foot summit, with a 1,300-foot gain in elevation. Park rangers say this is a favorite for watching the sunrise behind Electric Peak, off to the northwest, which glows with a golden hue. At the top of the peak, you will be 3,000 feet above the valley. 4.2 miles RT. Moderate. Access: Across road from Glen Creek Trailhead, 5 miles south of Mammoth on Mammoth–Norris Rd.

Forces of the Northern Range Self-Guiding Trail This level, easy stroll along a boardwalk presents an excellent opportunity to learn about the effects of fire on the environment. .8 mile RT. Easy. Access: Tower Rd., 8 miles east of Mammoth Hot Springs.

Lower Terrace Interpretive Trail This interpretive trail is one of the best ways to see the Mammoth area. The trail starts at 6,280 feet and climbs another 300 feet (an easy excursion) along marginally steep grades through a bare, rocky, thermal region to a flat alpine area and observation deck at the top. 1.5 miles RT. Easy. Access: South of the village on the road to Norris.

GRAND CANYON OF THE YELLOWSTONE RIVER AREA

Mount Washburn Trail The Mount Washburn Trail falls into the "If you can only do one hike, do this one" category. The 1,400-foot elevation gain is fairly gradual, and the rises are interspersed with long, fairly level stretches. At this elevation, the best method of attacking the mountain is to pace yourself, which has its own rewards: You have time to appreciate the views to the east of the Absaroka Mountains, south to Yellowstone Lake, and west to the Gallatin Mountains. You may see bighorn sheep—this is a popular summer grazing area—as well as yellow-bellied marmots and red foxes. The hike to the summit is an easy 90-minute walk at a steady pace, or 2 hours with breaks. At this elevation, where weather changes quickly, it's always a good idea to bring several layers of clothing. Fortunately, there's a warming hut in the base of the ranger lookout, as well as viewing telescopes and restrooms (but, alas, no hot-chocolate machine). 6 miles RT. Moderate. Access: End of Old Chittenden Rd. and at Dunraven Pass.

North Rim Trail This trail, which is described more fully in the Canyon Village section above, offers better views and less bustle than you'll find at the paved overlooks. 4 miles RT. Easy. Access: Inspiration Point.

South Rim Trail Like the North Rim Trail, this trail gives you more and better views of the canyon and river than you can see from a vehicle, and takes you away from the crowds. 6 miles RT. Easy. Access: Parking lot just beyond South Rim Dr. Bridge.

Uncle Tom's Trail The short trip is down 328 stairs and paved inclines that lead to an incredible perspective on Lower Falls. The staircase (shackled to the canyon's wall) is rather steep but can be negotiated in an hour, though it will be challenging for inexperienced hikers. 1 mile RT. Moderate. Access: South Rim parking lot.

YELLOWSTONE LAKE AREA

Elephant Back Loop Trail The hike is to an overlook that provides photographers with panoramic views of Yellowstone Lake and its islands, the Absaroka Range, and Pelican Valley. 3.6 miles RT. Easy. Access: Just before turnoff for Lake Yellowstone Hotel.

Storm Point Trail The Storm Point Trail follows a level path that terminates at a point jutting into the lake, with panoramic views. In the spring, this is a popular spot with grizzlies, so the trail may be closed; even when it's open, check with rangers regarding bear activity. 2.3 miles RT. Easy. Access: Directly across from Pelican Valley Trailhead (on lake side of road), 3½ miles east of Fishing Bridge.

OLD FAITHFUL AREA

Fairy Falls Trail Though considerably longer than the Mystic Falls Trail (see below), the Fairy Falls Trail is equally popular with the park staff because it leads to a taller waterfall. The hike begins at the Imperial Meadows Trailhead, 1 mile south of the Firehole River Bridge on Fountain Flat Drive. It winds through an area populated by elk along Fairy Creek, then past the Imperial Geyser. From here, it joins Fairy Creek Trail and travels east to the base of the falls. The total gain in elevation is only 100 feet. Up to 7 miles RT. Moderate. Access: Imperial Meadows in Biscuit Basin.

Fountain Paint Pot Trail This area is a very popular attraction, so you may have to wait for a parking place. All of the various types of thermal activity strut their stuff here. As you stroll along the easy half-mile boardwalk, you'll be in an area that may have six geysers popping their lids at the same time. .5 mile RT. Easy. Access: Fountain Paint Pot parking lot.

Geyser Hill Loop One of the most interesting, and easiest, loops in the area, this trail winds around several thermal attractions. Anemone Geyser may offer the best display of the various stages of a typical eruption as the pool fills and overflows. The Lion Group consists of four geysers connected beneath the surface, and Doublet Pool is popular with photographers, who are attracted by a complex series of ledges and deep-blue waters. Giantess Geyser is known for its violent eruptions. 1.4 miles RT. Easy. Access: Old Faithful boardwalk.

Lonestar Geyser Trail This trail falls into the "Gotta Do It" category, and its popularity is its only disadvantage. Despite the probability that you'll be sharing the territory with others, there are several compelling reasons to give it a go. From the trail head, you'll wend your way through a forested area along a trail that parallels the Firehole River. The payoff for your effort is the arrival at the geyser, sitting alone, a vanilla-chocolate ice-cream cone near the middle of a vast meadow partially covered by grass and trees, exposed rock, gravel, and volcanic debris. The geyser erupts about every 3 hours, and the eruption lasts about 30 minutes. Small, bubbling hot springs and steam vents surround it. The trail is popular with cross-country skiers in winter. 4.6 miles RT. Easy. Access: Parking lot opposite Kepler Cascades.

Mystic Falls Trail This is a favorite of park rangers. The trail leads to a waterfall on the Little Firehole River that drops more than 100 feet, one of the steepest in the park. The trail starts at Biscuit Basin, crosses the river, and then disappears into the forest. The total distance to the falls is only 1 mile; there's a trail to take you to the top.

To make your return more interesting, continue .2 mile to the Little Firehole Meadows Trail, which has an overlook that offers a view of Old Faithful in the distance. Best estimates are that the total time for the hike is an easy 2 hours, with an elevation gain of only 460 feet. 2.5 miles RT. Easy. Access: Imperial Meadows in Biscuit Basin.

Observation Point Trail—Solitary Geyser This trail leads to an observation area that provides better views of the entire geyser basin. The path up to the observation point is approximately .5 mile, and the elevation gain is only 200 feet, so it's an easy 15-minute hike. The view puts the entire Upper Geyser Basin into a different perspective; it is possible to see most of the major geysers, as well as steam vents located in the middle of wooded areas. From the top of the boardwalk, continue to the Solitary Geyser on a downhill slope that leads past the geyser, through the basin, and back to the inn, which completes the loop. 2 miles RT. Easy. Access: Old Faithful boardwalk.

5 Exploring the Backcountry

The backcountry season in Yellowstone is brief but glorious: For just 2 or 3 months, the snow melts off, the streams drop to fordable levels, and you can go deep into a domain of free-roaming wildlife and pristine natural beauty.

You must have a **backcountry permit** for any overnight trip on foot, on horseback, or by boat, and you can camp only in designated campsites, many of which are equipped with food-storage poles to keep wildlife out of your supplies. You can pick up a permit for hiking or boating the day before a trip, but if you'll be traveling during peak season, make a reservation in advance. It costs $20 to hold a site, and you can start making reservations for the upcoming year beginning April 1.

Contact the **Yellowstone Backcountry Office,** P.O. Box 168, Yellowstone National Park, WY 82190 (✆ **307/344-2160;** www.nps.gov/yell/planyourvisit/backcountryhiking.htm), and the staff will send you the useful *Backcountry Trip Planner,* with a detailed map showing where the campsites are, how to make reservations, and how to prepare. You can also download the trip planner and a reservation form at the URL above. Pick up your permit in the park within 48 hours of your departure at one of these ranger stations any day of the week during the summer: Bechler, Canyon, Mammoth, Old Faithful, Tower, West Entrance, Grant Village, Lake, South Entrance, and Bridge Bay.

BACKCOUNTRY GEYSERS If you just can't get your fill of geysers, or if you've had your fill of people, several trails lead to more isolated geysers. The **Shoshone Geyser Basin** and **Heart Lake Geyser Basin** contain active geysers, as do **Ponuntpa Springs** and the **Mudkettles** in the Pelican Valley Area, **Imperial Geyser** in the Firehole area, and the **Highland Hot Springs** on the Mary Mountain Trail. ***Safety warning:*** If you head in these directions, be careful about walking on unstable surfaces.

SHOSHONE LAKE Shoshone Lake is the park's largest backcountry lake and a popular spot for hikers. The shortest route is on the **Delacy Creek Trail,** which begins 8 miles east of Old Faithful on the Old Faithful–West Thumb Road. The trail winds 3 miles along Delacy Creek through moose country and the edge of the forest at the lake. From here you can head around the lake (a distance of 18 miles) in either direction. Assuming you take a clockwise track, you'll take the Delacy Creek Trail to its intersection with **Dogshead Trail,** then head west on the **Shoshone Lake Trail** until it intersects with the **North Shoshone Trail** and returns to your starting point.

A detour: At the western end of the lake, you'll arrive at the 1-mile-long **Shoshone Geyser Basin Trail,** which loops through a number of geysers, hot springs, and meadows that lie ankle deep in water and mud during the spring.

As you travel the lake's loop trail along the **Delacy Creek Trail,** you'll have views of the lake at the top of a 100-foot rise. Then, on the **Shoshone Lake Trail,** you'll cross the Lewis Channel, which may have thigh-high water as late as July. Beyond that, the trail is a series of rises that are easily negotiable by the average hiker, passing across shallow Moose Creek and through meadows where you may spot deer or moose early in the morning or evening.

The 8.4-mile **North Shoshone Trail** winds through a lodgepole-pine forest, over numerous ridges up to 200 feet high. The best views of the lake are from cliffs on this trail. The loop trail is especially popular with overnighters, since there are 26 campsites on the loop.

THE BECHLER REGION This area is often referred to as the Cascade Corner because it contains a majority of the park's waterfalls and it offers great opportunities to view thermal features. Many backpacking routes cut through this region, including one that leads to Old Faithful on the **Bechler River Trail.**

To begin your hike, drive into the park from Ashton, Idaho, and check in at the Bechler Ranger Station. To reach the ranger station, drive east 17 miles from Ashton on the Cave Falls Road; 3 miles before reaching Cave Falls, you'll find the ranger station turnoff. The ranger station is 1½ miles down the gravel road.

The **Bechler Meadows Trail** takes you into this rarely visited southwest corner, which is rich in waterfalls, cascades, and thermal areas. About 6 miles into the journey, the trail fords the river several times as it enters Bechler Canyon, where it passes Collonade and Iris Falls. This is a camping trip—you can cover a good 30 miles, depending on what turns you take—best made late in the summer to avoid high water during creek crossings. For a shorter trip, hike 3.5 miles along the **Bechler River Trail** to the **Boundary Creek Trail,** then return to the station on the **Bechler Meadows Trail,** a round-trip of 7 miles.

The most adventurous, and most scenic, route takes you 30 miles from the ranger station to the end of the trail at the **Lonestar Trailhead** near Old Faithful. Beyond Iris Falls, and then Ragged Falls, you'll reach a patrol cabin at Three Rivers Junction at the 13-mile mark, a popular camping area. If you continue toward Old Faithful, you'll intersect the **Shoshone Lake Trail** at the 23.5-mile mark and exit 6.5 miles later.

THOROFARE AREA When you enter this section, you're venturing into the most remote roadless area in the Lower 48. You can make a round-trip of around 70 miles deep into the wilderness, or shorter hikes, such as a trip from the park's east entrance road to the Yellowstone River inlet on Yellowstone Lake's southeast arm. The remoteness of this country discourages many hikers, so you'll have it mostly to yourself. The tepee rings and lean-tos that you may see are remnants of the presence of American Indians, who once used this area as the main highway between Jackson Hole and points north.

The trail follows the eastern shore of Yellowstone Lake and then the Yellowstone River into some of the most remote and beautiful backcountry in the Rockies. It's a lot of miles and climbing, but you'll be rewarded with views of the Upper Yellowstone Valley, Two Oceans Plateau, and abundant wildlife. You'll reach the Park Service's Thorofare Ranger Station at 32 miles, and a few miles farther along you'll come to Bridger Lake, outside the park, and a gorgeous alpine valley with a ranger station known as Hawk's Rest. Fishers love this area—as do grizzly bears, especially during the cutthroat trout spawning season in early summer. You'll be a good 35 miles from the trail head at the lake, and even the most capable hikers should consider riding with an outfitter. You can cut 9 miles off the journey by getting a boat shuttle to the mouth of the lake's southwest arm; call the **backcountry shuttle office** (© **307/242-3893**) for information. Only human-powered boats are allowed into the arm to the Yellowstone River outlet (you can canoe in, a wonderful trip in good weather). Or you can come into Thorofare through Bridger–Teton National Forest up the North Fork of the Buffalo Fork to the south; check with the forest's **Blackrock Ranger Station** (© **307/543-2386**).

Aside from grizzlies, the major obstacle to early season trips in the Thorofare is water; you'll encounter knee-deep water at **Beaverdam Creek** and at **Trapper Creek** as late as July.

THE SPORTSMAN LAKE TRAIL This moderate, 14-mile trail begins near Mammoth Hot Springs and extends west toward U.S. 191 to Sportsman Lake. From the Glen Creek trail head 5 miles south of Mammoth Hot Springs, you'll spend 2 miles on the Glen Creek Trail as you traverse a mostly level, wide-open plateau, covered with sagebrush, that is the home of herds of elk and a bear management area. At the **Sepulcher Mountain Trail** at the 3-mile mark, the terrain gets steeper as you continue northwest on the **Sportsman Lake Trail**—the elevation gain is approximately 2,300 feet to the Sepulcher summit (though you don't go to it on this route). The trail enters the forest and descends to a log that is used to cross Gardner River. Then it's uphill for another 4 miles to **Electric Divide,** another 2,000-foot gain in elevation. From there, the trail descends 2,100 feet in 3 miles to Sportsman Lake. The lake, which sits in a meadow populated by moose and elk, teems with cutthroat trout. There are two campsites.

6 Other Summer Sports & Activities

BIKING Yellowstone's narrow, twisty roads and lack of bike lanes make life difficult for bikers, and off-road opportunities are limited because of the small number of trails that permit bikes. The following trails are available to mountain bikers, but know that you will share the roads with hikers. The **Mount Washburn trail,** leaving from the Old Chittenden Road, is a strenuous trail that climbs 1,400 feet. The **Lonestar Geyser trail,** accessible at Kepler Cascade near Old Faithful, is an easy 1-hour ride on a user-friendly, partly paved road. Near Mammoth Hot Springs, **Bunsen Peak Road** and **Osprey Falls trails** present a combination ride and hike: The first 6 miles travel around Bunsen Peak; getting to the top requires a hike. A hike down to Osprey Falls adds 3 miles to the journey.

Bike rentals are available in the gateway towns of West Yellowstone, home to **Free Heel and Wheel** (© **406/646-7744;** www.freeheelandwheel.com), and Jackson, where you'll find **Hoback Sports** (© **307/733-5335;** http://hobacksports.com).

BOATING The best place to enjoy boating in Yellowstone is on **Yellowstone Lake,** which has easy access and beautiful, panoramic views. The lake is also one of the few areas where powerboats are allowed. Rowboats and outboard motorboats are for rent at **Bridge Bay Marina** (© **866/439-7375**). Motorboats, canoes, and kayaks can be used on

Lewis Lake as well. In West Yellowstone, kayak rentals and guided kayaking are available from **Lava Creek,** 433 Highway Ave. (✆ **406/646-5145;** www.lavacreekadventures.com).

FISHING Seven varieties of game fish live here: native cutthroat, rainbow, brown, brook, and lake trout; grayling; and mountain whitefish. Of the trout, only the cutthroat are native, and they are being pressured in the big lake by the larger lake trout, despite efforts to remove the exotic strains by gill-net fishing. As a result, you can't keep any pink-meat cutthroat caught anywhere in Yellowstone, and you *must* keep any lake trout.

The Yellowstone season typically opens on the Saturday of Memorial Day weekend and ends on the first Sunday in November. The exceptions are Yellowstone Lake's slightly shorter season, and the lake's tributaries, which are closed until July 15 to avoid conflicts between humans and grizzly bears, both of which are attracted to spawning trout.

In June, try the **Yellowstone River** downstream of Yellowstone Lake, where the cutthroat trout spawn. Fish the **Madison River** near the west entrance in July, and again in late fall for rainbow and some brown trout. In late summer, you can try to hook the cutthroats that thin out by September on the **Lamar River** in the park's northeast corner.

You can fish the **Yellowstone River** below the Grand Canyon by hiking down into **Seven Mile Hole,** a great place to cast (not much vegetation to snag on) for cutthroat trout from July to September. The best luck is around Sulphur Creek.

Other good fishing stretches include the **Gibbon** and **Firehole** rivers, which merge to form the Madison River on the park's west side, and the 3-mile **Lewis River Channel** between Shoshone and Lewis lakes during the fall spawning run of brown trout.

Fishing requires a special permit good only within the park. For anglers 16 and older, it's $15 for a 3-day permit or $20 for 7 days, and $35 for a season permit. Anglers 12 to 15 need a permit, too, but it's free. Children under 12 may fish without a permit when supervised by an adult. Permits are available at all ranger stations, visitor centers, and Yellowstone General Stores.

HORSEBACK RIDING People who want to pack their gear on a horse, llama, or mule must get permits to enter the Yellowstone backcountry, or hire an outfitter with a permit (see below). Other visitors who want to get in the saddle but not disappear in the wilderness can put themselves in the hands of the concessionaire, **Xanterra Parks & Resorts.** Stables are at Canyon Village, Roosevelt Lodge, and Mammoth Hot Springs. Roosevelt Lodge also offers **evening rides** from June into September. Choices are 1- and 2-hour guided trail rides daily aboard well-broken, tame animals for $37 and $56, respectively.

If you're looking for a longer, overnight horse-packing experience, contact the park and request a list of approved concessionaires that lead backcountry expeditions. Most offer customized, guided trips, with meals, horses, and camping and riding gear provided. Costs run from $250 to $500 per day per person, depending on the length of the trip and number of people. One good outfitter is **Rockin' HK Outfitters** (✆ **307/333-4505;** www.rockinhk.com), offering 3- to 10-day trips for about $450 per person per day. Out of Bozeman, **Greater Yellowstone Flyfishers** (✆ **406/585-4655;** www.gyflyfishers.com) offers fly-fishing pack trips in the park.

7 Winter Sports & Activities

The average snowfall in a Yellowstone winter is nearly 50 inches, creating a beautiful setting for sightseers and a wonderful resource for outdoor winter recreation. The steaming hot pools and geysers generate little islands of warmth and attract not just tourists, but wildlife as well. Frozen thermal vapors transform nearby trees into "snow ghosts." Bison become frosted, shaggy beasts, easily spotted as they take advantage of the more accessible vegetation on the thawed ground. Yellowstone Lake's surface freezes to an average thickness of 3 feet, creating a vast ice sheet that sings and moans as the huge plates of ice shift. But the ice is thinner where hot springs come up on the lake bottom, and you'll see otters surfacing at the breaks in the ice. Waterfalls become astounding pieces of frozen sculpture.

Only two of the park's hostelries, **Mammoth Hot Springs** and the **Old Faithful Snow Lodge,** provide accommodations from December through March, as does **Flagg Ranch,** just outside the park's south entrance. The only road that's open for cars is the **Mammoth Hot Springs–Cooke City Road.** Most visitors these days come into Yellowstone in winter from the west or south by snow coach or snowmobile.

For additional information on all of the following winter activities and accommodations, as well as snow-coach reservations, contact **Xanterra Parks & Resorts** (✆ **866/439-7375;** www.xanterra.com). For more information on snow-coach tours, see "Organized Tours & Ranger Programs," earlier in this chapter.

The **Yellowstone Association Institute** (✆ **406/848-2400;** http://yellowstoneassociation.org/institute) offers winter courses in various areas in the park. Past offerings have included 3-day classes devoted to wintertime photography, cross-country skiing, and wolf ecology.

CROSS-COUNTRY SKIING The Old Faithful area has 40 miles of cross-country trails, including the popular Lonestar Geyser Trail, an 8-mile trail in a remote setting that starts at the Old Faithful Snow Lodge; and the Fern Cascades trail, which winds for 3 miles through a rolling woodland landscape on a short loop close to the Old Faithful area. In the Mammoth area, try the Upper Geyser Basin and Biscuit Basin trail, which some say is the best in Yellowstone, though it may take an entire day to negotiate.

Equipment rentals (about $20 per day), ski instruction (about $30 per person for a group lesson), ski shuttles to various locations, and guided ski tours are available at the **Old Faithful Snow Lodge** and the **Mammoth Hot Springs Hotel.** A full-day guided excursion costs $75 to $125 per person (lunch may or may not be included).

ICE-SKATING The **Mammoth Hot Springs ice rink** is behind the Mammoth Hot Springs Recreation Center. On a crisp winter's night, you can rent skates (free) and glide across the ice while seasonal melodies play over the PA system. It's cold out there, but there's a warming fire at the rink's edge.

SNOWCOACH TOURS It is possible to enjoy the sights and sounds of Yellowstone without raising a finger—except to write a check or sign a credit card voucher—by taking one of the scenic snowcoach tours that originate at the south and west entrances, as well as at Mammoth and Old Faithful. One-way and wildlife-watching trips range from about $30 to $60, while round-trips cost about $110 to $140.

If you've never seen a snowcoach, you're in for a treat. Don't be fooled into thinking that this distinctively Yellowstone mode of transportation is merely a fancy name for a bus that provides tours during winter. Imagine instead an Econoline van with tank treads for tires and water skis extending from its front, and you won't be surprised when you see this unusual-looking vehicle. The interiors are toasty warm, with seating for a large group, and they usually allow each passenger two bags. They aren't the fastest, smoothest, or most comfortable form of transportation, but they do allow large groups to travel together, and they're cheaper and warmer than snowmobiles. They're also available for hire by groups at many snowmobile locations. Guides provide interesting and entertaining facts and stories of the areas as you cruise the park trails, and they give you opportunities to photograph scenery and wildlife.

For snowcoach information, contact **Xanterra Parks & Resorts** (✆ **866/439-7375;** www.xanterra.com). Out of West Yellowstone, **Yellowstone Vacations** (✆ **800/426-7669** or 406/646-9564; www.snowcoachyellowstone.com) and **Yellowstone Alpen Guides** (✆ **800/858-3502** or 406/646-9591; www.yellowstoneguides.com) provide service as well.

SNOWMOBILING This is an excellent way to sightsee at your own pace, but note that the courts are still debating long-term snowmobile policies for the parks. A driver's license and guide are required for rental at **Mammoth Hot Springs Hotel** or **Old Faithful Snow Lodge.** Day tours cost about $225 for a single rider or $250 double; custom tours are also available, but considerably more costly. A helmet is included with the snowmobile, as is a clothing package for protection against the bitter cold. **Warming huts** are located at Mammoth, Indian Creek, Canyon, Madison, West Thumb, and Fishing Bridge. They offer snacks, a hot cup of coffee or chocolate, and an excellent opportunity to recover from a chill.

Snowmobile rentals are also available in the **gateway communities** of Gardiner, Cooke City, and West Yellowstone. In West Yellowstone, try **Yellowstone Arctic/Yamaha,** 208 Electric St. (✆ **406/646-9636;** www.yellowstonearcticyamaha.com), or **Yellowstone Adventures,** 131 Dunraven St. (✆ **800/231-5991** or 406/646-7735; www.yellowstoneadventures.com). Most rental shops accept reservations weeks in advance, so reserving at least 2 weeks ahead of time is a good idea.

For snowmobile rentals in Jackson, contact **Leisure Sports,** 1075 S. Hwy. 89 (✆ **307/733-3040;** www.leisuresportsadventure.com), which charges $145 and up per day. For a guided trip, call **Wyoming Adventures,** 1050 S. Hwy. 89 (✆ **800/637-7147** or 307/733-2300; www.wyomingsnow.com), which offers three different loop trips through Yellowstone for $250 to $360.

8 Camping

There are 12 campgrounds in Yellowstone, five of them under the efficient management of **Xanterra Parks & Resorts,** the park concessionaire. The other seven are smaller, less expensive, and often less crowded. The seven campgrounds still run by the **National Park Service** are at Indian Creek, Lewis Lake, Mammoth, Norris, Pebble Creek, Slough Creek, and Tower Fall. They fill daily on a first-come, first-served basis. Our personal favorites are Slough Creek, in the Lamar Valley, and Norris, a shady riverside spot near the Norris Geyser Basin.

Xanterra runs the bigger campgrounds at Bridge Bay, Canyon, Grant Village, Madison, and Fishing Bridge. Reservations can be made by calling ✆ **866/439-7375** or 307/344-7311, or by writing Xanterra Parks & Resorts, P.O. Box 165, Yellowstone National Park, WY 82190. The only campground in the park equipped with RV hookups is at **Fishing Bridge RV**

Campground	Total Sites	RV Hookups	Dump Station	Toilets	Drinking Water
Inside the Park					
Bridge Bay*	425	No	Yes	Yes	Yes
Canyon*	250	No	No	Yes	Yes
Fishing Bridge*†	346	Yes	Yes	Yes	Yes
Grant Village*	400	No	Yes	Yes	Yes
Indian Creek	75	No	No	Yes	Yes
Lewis Lake	85	No	No	Yes	Yes
Madison*	277	No	Yes	Yes	Yes
Mammoth	85	No	No	Yes	Yes
Norris	100	No	No	Yes	Yes
Pebble Creek	30	No	No	Yes	Yes
Slough Creek	29	No	No	Yes	Yes
Tower Fall	32	No	No	Yes	Yes
Near the Park					
Bakers Hole†	73	Yes	No	Yes	Yes
Lonesomehurst	27	No	No	Yes	Yes
Rainbow Point†	86	No	No	Yes	Yes

* Reserve through Xanterra Parks & Resorts.
† Accepts hard-sided vehicles only.

Park. It accepts hard-sided vehicles only (no tents or tent trailers) and has electrical, water, and sewer hookups. Though there are no hookups at the other campgrounds, they all accommodate RVs.

Camping is allowed only in designated areas and is limited to 14 days between June 15 and September 15, and to 30 days the rest of the year. Checkout time for all campgrounds is 10am. Quiet hours are enforced between 8pm and 8am (10am to 7pm at Fishing Bridge), when no generators, radios, or other loud noises are allowed. See the chart above for amenities and prices at each campground.

INSIDE THE PARK

The **Tower Fall Campground,** which has forested sites, is near a convenience store, restaurant, and gas station at Roosevelt Lodge. The campground is 19 miles north of Canyon Village and 18 miles east of Mammoth.

Slough Creek Campground is in the Lamar Valley, near the northeast entrance, where there are fewer people, good fishing, and the possibility of a wolf howl to stimulate your dreams; however, restroom facilities are in pit toilets.

Canyon Campground is the busiest in the park, with sites in a heavily wooded area. It has a store, restaurants, a visitor center, and laundry nearby at Canyon Center.

Fishing Bridge RV Park is somewhat controversial because of its location in an area where bears feed in the spring; only hard-sided camping vehicles are allowed.

Bridge Bay Campground, near the shores of Yellowstone Lake, offers tremendous views, especially at sunrise and sunset. Unfortunately, though surrounded by the forest, much of the area has been clear-cut, so there's not a whole lot of privacy. It's close to boat-launching facilities and the boat-rental operation.

The **Madison Campground** is in a wooded area just south of the river. It has good access to fishing and hiking, and the location is a short drive from the amenities of West Yellowstone.

The attractive, wooded sites at **Norris Campground** are in the heart of the park's east side, close to wildlife activity, geothermal areas, and the Gibbon River.

NEAR THE PARK

There are three National Forest Service campgrounds in the **West Yellowstone** area, all in the Gallatin National Forest (**www.fs.fed.us/r1/gallatin**). They accommodate both RVs and tents, but during some periods in late summer they accept hard-sided vehicles only. All three are first come, first served, so it's best to stake out a spot early. The heavily forested **Bakers Hole,** just 3 miles north of West Yellowstone on U.S. 191, is popular because of its fishing access. Both tents and RVs are accepted, but there are no hookups. **Lonesomehurst,** 8 miles west of the park on U.S. 20, then 4 miles north on Hebgen Lake Road, is only one-third the size of Bakers Hole and fills up quickly in summer. It has tent and RV sites, some of them right on the shore of Hebgen Lake. To

Showers	Fire Pits/ Grills	Laundry	Public Phone	Reserve	Fees	Open
No	Yes	No	Yes	Yes	$19	Late May to mid-Sept
Yes	Yes	Yes	Yes	Yes	$19	June to mid-Sept
Yes	Yes	Yes	Yes	Yes	$35	Mid-May to mid-Sept
Yes	Yes	Yes	Yes	Yes	$19	Mid-June to Sept
No	Yes	No	No	Yes	$12	June–Sept
No	Yes	No	No	No	$12	Mid-June to Nov
No	Yes	No	Yes	Yes	$19	Early May to mid-Oct
No	Yes	No	Yes	No	$14	Year-round
No	Yes	No	Yes	No	$14	Mid-May to Sept
No	Yes	No	No	No	$12	Mid-June to Sept
No	Yes	No	No	No	$12	Late May to Oct
No	Yes	No	No	No	$12	Mid-May to late Sept
No	Yes	No	Yes	Yes	$14	Late May to mid-Sept
No	Yes	No	No	Yes	$14	Late May to mid-Sept
No	Yes	No	Yes	Yes	$14	Late May to mid-Sept

reach **Rainbow Point,** drive 5 miles north of West Yellowstone on U.S. 191, then 3 miles west on Forest Service Road 610, then north for 2 miles on Forest Service Road 6954. Tucked away in the forest near Hebgen Lake, it accommodates both tents and RVs (no hookups) and has boating and fishing access. For further information on these campgrounds, call the **Hebgen Lake Ranger District** (✆ **406/823-6961**).

9 Where to Stay

INSIDE THE PARK

If you're coming at the height of summer, book ahead! Contact **Xanterra Parks & Resorts,** P.O. Box 165, Yellowstone National Park, WY 82190 (✆ **866/439-7375** or 307/344-7311; www.yellowstonenationalparklodges.com), for lodging in the park. Accommodations are open from early summer to late October. Mammoth Hot Springs and Old Faithful Snow Lodge then reopen for the winter season, from mid-December through mid-March.

Another option is **Flagg Ranch Resort** (see chapter 17). Only 2 miles from Yellowstone's south entrance, it's a convenient jumping-off point for exploring the southern reaches of the park, as well as Grand Teton.

MAMMOTH HOT SPRINGS AREA

Mammoth's distance from attractions such as Old Faithful and the Grand Canyon of the Yellowstone makes it one of the last places to fill up. Despite that, it's a good base, home to the park's best visitor center, as well as colorful limestone terraces.

Mammoth Hot Springs Hotel and Cabins Below the steaming terraces of Mammoth Hot Springs, this is one of two Yellowstone hotels open during both summer and winter seasons. (The other is the Old Faithful Snow Lodge.) Established in 1911, the hotel itself is less distinguished than the Lake Yellowstone Hotel or the Old Faithful Inn, but it manages to blend a wide range of rooms into a satisfying whole. The only truly high-end accommodations are the suites. Standard rooms and cabins offer minimal amenities but make up for it with a fair amount of charm. Some have tubs only, some have showers only, and some share a bathroom down the hall. The cottage-style cabins are clustered in rings adjacent to the hotel and vary in quality. Make sure you drift into the **Map Room** (named for the massive inlaid map of the United States on one of the walls), a great place to spend an evening reading or listening to a pianist.

At Mammoth Hot Springs, P.O. Box 165, Yellowstone National Park, WY 82190. ✆ **866/439-7375** or 307/344-7311. Fax 307/344-7456. www.yellowstonenationalparklodges.com. 212 units, including 2 suites. $85–$121 double; $75–$107 cabin; $211 hot tub cabin; $449 suite. AE, DC, DISC, MC, V. Closed Oct to mid-Dec and early Mar to early May.

CANYON VILLAGE AREA

Standing at the center of Canyon Village, you may feel as though you're in a mall parking lot. With one of the park's biggest attractions close by, this is one of its busiest areas. It's certainly a plus, though, that the Grand Canyon of the Yellowstone is a short walk from the center of the village.

Canyon Lodge and Cabins This complex is one of the newer facilities in the park (both Cascade and Dunraven lodges were completed here in the 1990s), but it can't escape the bustle of Canyon Village. However, the lodges are located a mere half-mile from the Grand Canyon of the Yellowstone and Inspiration Point, one of the most photographed spots in the park. Cascade Lodge offers simple rooms appointed with tasteful log furnishings in the three-story building; the newer Dunraven is similar, although it is more modern (with an elevator); both are located adjacent to a woodland setting. The cabins are single-story duplex and fourplex structures with private bathrooms that are among the largest in the park. They're a bit weathered but generally acceptable, but, given the sheer number of units involved, this isn't the place to "get away from it all."

In Canyon Village, P.O. Box 165, Yellowstone National Park, WY 82190. ✆ **866/439-7375** or 307/344-7311. Fax 307/344-7456. www.yellowstonenationalparklodges.com. 605 units. $164 double; $70–$149 cabin. AE, DC, DISC, MC, V. Closed Oct to late May.

TOWER–ROOSEVELT AREA

This is a cheerful throwback to the early days of car camping in Yellowstone: no big complex of shops and services, not a lot of amenities. It's small, out of the way, and less crowded than other areas. Hiking trails and the corridor of the Lamar Valley and River that runs to the northeast entrance are nearby.

Roosevelt Lodge Cabins This is considered the park's family hideaway, a low-key operation with dinky, primitive cabins; stables; and a lodge restaurant that feels like a big ranch house. The bare-bones cabins are called Roughriders, and they're furnished with two simple beds, clean linens, a writing table, and a wood stove. A step up, the Frontier cabins have their own bathrooms and showers. The lodge is a rugged-but-charming stone edifice; its large, inviting porch is outfitted with rockers so guests can sit back and watch the world go by. Stagecoach rides, horseback trips, and Western trail cookouts give this place a cowboy flavor, and it's a less hectic scene than the other park villages.

At Tower Junction, P.O. Box 165, Yellowstone National Park, WY 82190. (At junction of Mammoth–Tower Rd. and Tower–Canyon Rd.) ✆ **866/439-7375** or 307/344-7311. Fax 307/344-7456. www.yellowstonenationalparklodges.com. 80 cabins, 14 with private bathroom. $64–$107 cabin. AE, DC, DISC, MC, V. Closed early Sept to June.

LAKE VILLAGE AREA

This resort along the lake is reminiscent of a less-hurried era. The location puts you near the lake's recreational opportunities and hiking trails, and you'll find accommodations in a historic hotel, as well as motel and cabin units and nearby lakeside camping sites. The food at the hotel is as good as any in the park, and lower-priced alternatives are in the neighborhood.

Lake Lodge Cabins These cabins surrounding Lake Lodge stand a little ways from the lake in a relatively quiet, traffic-free area. The old Western lodge's most attractive feature is a large porch with wicker rockers that invite visitors to sit and gaze out across the waters. The accommodations are in well-preserved, clean, freestanding cabins near a trout stream that threads through a wooded area. (Access is usually restricted when grizzlies emerge from hibernation.) The cabins come in two grades: Western cabins provide electric heat, paneled walls, two double beds (and, in some cases, an extra twin), and combination bathrooms, while Pioneer cabins are smaller and sparsely furnished, with one or two double beds each and small shower-only bathrooms. Because the dining room here is a tad short on atmosphere, you might want to make the short trek to the Lake Yellowstone Hotel for a more sumptuous meal in a more appetizing setting.

On Yellowstone Lake (P.O. Box 165), Yellowstone National Park, WY 82190. ✆ **866/439-7375** or 307/344-7311. Fax 307/344-7456. www.yellowstonenationalparklodges.com. 186 cabins. $66 Pioneer cabin; $138–$149 Western cabin. AE, DC, DISC, MC, V. Closed mid-Sept to early June.

Lake Yellowstone Hotel and Cabins The Ionic columns, dormer windows, and deep porticos on this classic yellow building faithfully recall the year it was built: 1891. It's an entirely different world from the rustic Western style of other park lodgings. The facility was restored in the early 1990s, and its better rooms are the most comfortable and roomy in the park, with soul-stirring views of the massive lake. The three- and four-story wings house the hotel rooms, and there's also a motel-style annex and an assortment of cabins. The upper-end rooms here are especially lavish for Yellowstone, with stenciled walls and traditional spreads on one queen-size or two double beds. Smaller rooms in the annex are fitted with two double beds and bring to mind a typical motel chain. The freestanding yellow-clad cabins here are passable, decorated with knotty pine paneling, and furnished with double beds and a writing table.

On the north side of the lake (P.O. Box 165), Yellowstone National Park, WY 82190. ✆ **866/439-7375** or 307/344-7311. Fax 307/344-7456. www.yellowstonenationalparklodges.com. 300 units. $143–$216 double; $128 cabin; $565 suite. AE, DC, DISC, MC, V. Closed early Oct to mid-May.

GRANT VILLAGE AREA

Though Grant Village is near the south end of beautiful Yellowstone Lake and has a good visitor center, this fairly recent addition to park accommodations lacks the character of the Lake and Old Faithful villages. It's also isolated from other park centers, so guests here are likely to frequent its tiny lounge and eat in one of its two decent restaurants overlooking the lake. Other guest services include a laundry facility, service station, and convenience store.

Grant Village The southernmost of the major overnight accommodations in the park, Grant Village was completed in 1984 and is one of the more contemporary choices in Yellowstone. It's not as architecturally distinctive as the Old Faithful options, consisting of six condo-style units (with motel-style rooms), but it's also less touristy and more isolated. Rooms are tastefully furnished, most outfitted with light wood furniture, track lighting, electric heat, and laminate counters. Nicer and more expensive rooms affording lake views have mullioned windows, one queen-size or one or two double beds, and full bathrooms.

On the West Thumb of Yellowstone Lake (P.O. Box 165), Yellowstone National Park, WY 82190. ✆ **866/439-7375** or 307/344-7311. www.yellowstonenationalparklodges.com. 300 units. $138–$143 double. AE, DC, DISC, MC, V.

OLD FAITHFUL AREA

At the Old Faithful area, you'll spend a night in the midst of the largest and most famous geyser basin in the world. Here you have more choices of rooms, restaurants, and services—including a visitor center, gas station, and Yellowstone General Store—than anywhere else in the park.

Old Faithful Inn This is undoubtedly the crown jewel of Yellowstone's man-made wonders. Seven stories tall, with dormers peaking from a shingled, steep-sloping roof, it's an architectural wonder designed by Robert Reamer to blend into the natural environment, first welcoming guests in 1904.

The cavernous, log-laden lobby is striking, with an ambience that is half elegant palace and half rugged wilderness lodge. You can climb the stairs to its internal balconies, but seismic activity eventually closed the crow's nest, where a chamber orchestra initially performed for the well-dressed guests below. Only 30 miles from the west entrance and 40 miles from the south entrance, this is the first place visitors head when they want a bed for the night, so make reservations well in advance.

Guest rooms are basic, appointed with conservative fabrics and park-theme art, but they don't all have private bathrooms; the wing rooms offer better facilities and more privacy.

At Old Faithful (P.O. Box 165), Yellowstone National Park, WY 82190. ✆ **866/439-7375** or 307/344-7311. Fax 307/344-7456. www.yellowstonenationalparklodges.com. 327 units. $119–$206 double with private bathroom; $93 double with shared bathroom; $397–$502 suite. AE, DC, DISC, MC, V. Closed mid-Oct to mid-May.

Old Faithful Lodge Cabins These are the leftovers from the days when crude cabins littered the landscape around the geyser. The ones closest to the geyser were hauled away years ago, but you still get a sense of what tourism was like in the park's early days, especially if you rent one of the budget cabins, which are only slightly less flimsy than tents and have basic beds and sinks, no more. Showers and restrooms are a short walk away. Frontier cabins are better, adding a private bathtub to other amenities. If amenities are irrelevant, these rustic, thin-walled cabins are an economical way to put a roof over your head in the park. The lodge is perhaps the busiest spot in the geyser area, featuring several snack shops and a huge cafeteria.

At Old Faithful (P.O. Box 165), Yellowstone National Park, WY 82190. ✆ **866/439-7375** or 307/344-7311. www.yellowstonenationalparklodges.com. 96 cabins, some without private bathroom. $69–$113 double. AE, DC, DISC, MC, V. Closed mid-Sept to mid-May.

Old Faithful Snow Lodge and Cabins If your childhood visit to Yellowstone included a stay at the Old Faithful Snow Lodge, put the memory out of your mind. The old dormitory-style lodge was torn down in 1998, and this new, award-winning structure could aptly be called the *New* Faithful Snow Lodge. Its contemporary big-beam construction and high ceiling in the lobby echo the Old Faithful Inn, and a copper-lined balcony curves above the common area, where guests can relax in wicker furniture. The folks behind the place paid attention to every last detail: The public areas have a contemporary (but appropriate) style, some of the lodge's wood was recycled from the same mill that provided the lumber for the Old Faithful Inn in 1904, and wrought-iron bears abound on everything from lamps to fireplace grates. The modern rooms are spacious and comfortable, second only to the upper-end accommodations at the Lake Yellowstone Hotel. There's also a small collection of surrounding cabins with motel-style furnishings (many of which were built after the 1988 fires) and—a rarity in the park—in-room coffeemakers.

At Old Faithful (P.O. Box 165), Yellowstone National Park, WY 82190. ✆ **866/439-7375** or 307/344-7311. Fax 307/344-7456. www.yellowstonenationalparklodges.com. 134 units. $191 double; $94–$140 cabin. AE, DC, DISC, MC, V.

NEAR THE PARK

WEST YELLOWSTONE

Make your reservations early if you want to visit in July or August, or if you're going to spend Christmas to New Year's here. If you're smart, you'll come in the fall, when there are plenty of empty rooms and better rates, and spend your days fishing the Henry's Fork or one of the other great streams in the vicinity. Rates for rooms often reflect the seasonal traffic, and prices fluctuate. Unless noted, all these establishments are open year-round.

You'll find chains like **Comfort Inn,** 638 Madison Ave. (✆ **406/646-4212;** www.comfortinn.com), with summertime doubles for $79 to $199; and **Days Inn** (✆ **800/548-9551** or 406/646-7656; www.daysinn.com), at 301 Madison Ave., with rates of $119 to $199 for a double. There are three **Best Western** affiliates, ranging from about $100 to $170 a night during the summer. Call ✆ **800/528-1234.** For major hotel/motel chain websites, see chapter 38.

The **One Horse Motel,** at 216 N. Dunraven St. (✆ **800/488-2750** or 406/646-7677; www.onehorsemotel.com), is a top-notch independent across from City Park, with doubles for $90 to $100 a night. Another inexpensive option (with more character than the chains), the 1912 **Madison Hotel,** 139 Yellowstone Ave. (✆ **800/838-7745** or 406/646-7745; www.madisonhotelmotel.com), has historic rooms for $59 to $89 for a double or $30 for a bunk in a dormitory, and newer motel doubles for $79 to $139. Another option with historic cachet—and a one-time favorite of broadcasting legend Charles Kuralt—is the **Parade Rest Guest Ranch,** 10 miles north of West Yellowstone at 1279 Grayling Rd. (✆ **800/753-5934** or 406/646-7217; www.paraderestranch.com), in a serene setting near Hebgen Lake. Rates are about $190 per day for adults and $110 to $150 for kids, all meals and horseback riding included.

Bar N Ranch One of the oldest brands in Montana, the Bar N is an excellent new lodging option in West Yellowstone, operating a spiffed-up lodge and cabin complex since 2004. Located on 200 acres of unsullied ranchland with 2 miles of the Madison River and a fishing pond, the lodge is an image of the New West, with a great river-rock fireplace and a knotty pine banister leading up to the rooms upstairs. The lodge rooms mix equal parts Ralph Lauren and Old West, exuding a simple but rich style with antler lamps, hardwood floors, and jetted tubs. The cabins are one- and two-bedroom units arranged in a half-circle around the lodge, with decor that echoes that of the lodge; all of them have fireplaces and private outdoor hot tubs. The staff can arrange for guides to take guests fishing, rafting, or horseback riding for an extra fee, and there's a good **restaurant** and Wi-Fi Internet access.

890 Buttermilk Creek Rd. (P.O. Box 250), West Yellowstone, MT 59758. ✆ **406/646-0300.** Fax 406/646-0301. www.bar-n-ranch.com. 15 units, including 8 cabins. Lodge rooms $223–$238 double; cabins $273–$345 double; 4-bedroom cabin $500–$600; lower rates Oct–June. AE, DC, DISC, MC, V.

Holiday Inn West Yellowstone This is the town's best modern hotel. The rooms are sizable and comfortable, well maintained, and regularly updated. At the tour desk, you can arrange fishing and rafting trips, bike and ATV rentals, and chuckwagon cookouts. The **Iron Horse Saloon** serves regional microbrews, and the **Oregon Short Line Restaurant** serves Western cuisine, including game and seafood. At the center of the restaurant sits a restored railroad club car that brought Victorian gents to Yellowstone a century ago.

315 Yellowstone Ave., West Yellowstone, MT 59758. ✆ **800/HOLIDAY** [465-4329] or 406/646-7365. www.doyellowstone.com. 123 units. A/C, TV, TEL. $99–$209 double; $119–$299 suite. AE, DISC, MC, V.

GARDINER

Chain motels include the **Comfort Inn,** 107 Hellroaring Dr. (✆ **800/424-6423** or 406/848-7536), and the **Super 8** on U.S. 89 South (✆ **800/800-8000** or 406/848-7401), with high-season rates ranging from $120 to $200 double; and the **Best Western by Mammoth Hot Springs,** on U.S. 89 (✆ **800/828-9080** or 406/848-7311), with doubles for $99 to $189 in the summer.

Absaroka Lodge Every room in this lodge has its own furnished balcony with jaw-dropping views of the Yellowstone River and the mountain scenery beyond it. The lodge's riverbank location—with a nice slope of lawn overlooking the river gorge—is just a few blocks from the village center, and the rooms are well appointed with queen-size beds. Suites with kitchenettes cost a little more; there is also a pair of cabins without balconies. Like most other properties in town, the lodge has staff ready and able to assist in arrangements with outfitters for fly-fishing, rafting, and, in the fall, hunting.

U.S. 89 at the Yellowstone River Bridge (P.O. Box 10), Gardiner, MT 59030. ✆ **800/755-7414** or 406/848-7414. Fax 406/848-7560. www.yellowstonemotel.com. 41 units. A/C, TV, TEL. Summer $110–$125 double; winter $45–$60 double. AE, DC, DISC, MC, V.

Yellowstone Suites Bed and Breakfast This quiet B&B on the south bank of the Yellowstone River is a good alternative to the motels that line U.S. Hwy. 89. Originally built in 1904, legend has it that the second story's quarried-stone exterior is actually a leftover from the Roosevelt Arch. The rooms are frilly and cozy, with a teddy bear motif in the Roosevelt Room and a Victorian theme in the Jackson Room; the Yellowstone Suite has satellite television and a kitchenette. The real perks here are the impeccably gardened backyard and the breakfasts, such as cinnamon rolls or cheese blintzes.

506 4th St. (P.O. Box 277), Gardiner, MT 59030. ✆ **800/948-7937** or 406/848-7937. www.yellowstonesuites.com. 4 units. Summer $112–$158 double; winter $80–$105 double. Rates include full breakfast. AE, MC, V.

COOKE CITY

If you choose to spend the night in little Cooke City, you have several options, none of which includes modern facilities or gourmet dining. Rooms at each of the properties listed below are clean and comfortable, but that's about all. A room for the night is less expensive than a stay in other gateway towns, anywhere from $60 to $120 a night. The **Soda Butte Lodge,** on Main Street (✆ **406/838-2251;** www.cookecity.com) is the biggest and poshest motel in town; on the premises are the good **Prospector Restaurant** and a small casino. The newest property in town is a woodsy **Super 8,** 303 Main St. (✆ **877/338-2070** or 406/838-2070; www.cookecitysuper8.com).

CODY

With some of the showmanship of its founder, William F. "Buffalo Bill" Cody, this town offers more than just a gateway to the east entrance. The night rodeo and the fine historical center are the big summer attractions.

Buffalo Bill Village Resort Consisting of three distinct lodging options at the same location, Buffalo Bill Village has something for everybody. The Holiday and Comfort inns are similar to their chain brethren elsewhere, while the village of historic cabins offers a rustic exterior and a more Western feel. The one- and two-bedroom cabins at Buffalo Bill Village are simply equipped—with a bed, phone, and TV—and surrounded by plenty of room for the kids to roam. The cabins themselves first housed the contractors who built the city circa 1920, and became the centerpiece of the resort in the 1950s. The Holiday Inn followed in the 1970s, the Comfort Inn in the '90s. Also on-site is an Old West–style **boardwalk** where you can shop or sign up for tours and river trips, an outdoor pool, and restaurants.

17th and Sheridan Ave., Cody, WY 82414. ✆ **800/527-5544.** Fax 307/587-2795. Comfort Inn: 75 units. A/C, TV, TEL. $79–$159 double. Rates include continental breakfast. Holiday Inn: 189 units. A/C, TV, TEL. $89–$169 double. Buffalo Bill Village Historic Cabins: 83 units. TV, TEL. $79–$159 double. AE, DC, DISC, MC, V. Buffalo Bill Village closed Oct–Apr.

The Chamberlin Inn A boardinghouse opened here in 1903, and the property evolved and devolved over the course of the next century until Ev and Susan Diehl took over the property in 2005 and completely restored it—and then some. Centered on a serene and green courtyard, the new-and-improved Chamberlin Inn is now Cody's best lodging option, just a block from the center of town and featuring charming historic rooms and apartment units. Of special note are the Hemingway Suite ("Papa" stayed here in 1932) with an angling motif and a small Hemingway library, and the lavish Courthouse unit, the original town courthouse reimagined as a luxury apartment.

1032 12th St., Cody, WY 82414. ✆ **888/587-0202** or 307/587-0202. www.chamberlininn.com. 24 units. A/C, TV, TEL. $145–$175 double; $235–$650 suite or apt. AE, DISC, MC, V.

The Cody The Cody became the top modern hotel in town when it opened in May 2008. On the west end of town near the rodeo grounds, the hotel has a colorful, thoroughly Western-chic design in both the common areas and the spacious guest rooms, which have one king bed or two queens, warm earth tones, and a Native American motif. Some have sleeper sofas; those on the west side have balconies with terrific views of Shoshone River Canyon. The facilities are also excellent, including the exercise room and indoor pool, and there are a number of special packages catering to anglers, rodeo-goers, and Yellowstone visitors.

232 W. Yellowstone Ave., Cody, WY 82414. ✆ **307/587-5915.** www.thecody.com. 75 units. A/C, TV, TEL. Summer $209–$249 double; off season $99–$169 double. Pets accepted. Additional person $14. Rates include hot breakfast buffet. AE, DISC, MC, V.

Cody Cowboy Village New in 2006, this property is a couples-oriented resort in a family-oriented town. The "village," consisting of a cluster of cabin units near the rodeo grounds, is a world away from the bustling boardwalks of downtown Cody. The log cabins meld contemporary and cowboy decor. All have a deck in front and free Wi-Fi; suites have microwaves and fridges. Most units have one king bed, but six have two queens.

203 W. Yellowstone Ave., Cody, WY 82414. ✆ **307/587-7555.** www.codycowboyvillage.com. 50 units. TV, TEL. $79–$159 double; $109–$199 suite. Rates include continental breakfast. AE, MC, V.

The Irma Hotel Buffalo Bill's entrepreneurial gusto ultimately left him penniless, but it also left us this century-old hotel (named for his daughter) in the heart of town. Cody hoped to corral visitors who got off the train on their way to Yellowstone, and one of his lures was an elaborate cherrywood bar, a gift from strait-laced Queen Victoria. You can still hoist a jar on Her Royal Highness's slab in the **Silver Saddle Saloon,** or spend the night in a renovated room that might have once housed a president or prince. Suites are named after local characters from the town's early days: The Irma Suite, on the corner of the building, has a queen-size bed, a writing table, a vanity in the bedroom area, a small sitting area, and an old-fashioned bathroom. While the Irma's aura will surely please history buffs, those acclimated to ultramodern convenience will probably want to look elsewhere. But the hotel's location in the middle of town and the regular schedule of reenacted gunfights out front help compensate.

1192 Sheridan Ave., Cody, WY 82414. ✆ **800/745-4762** or 307/587-4221. www.irmahotel.com. 73 units. A/C, TV, TEL. $105 double; $145 suite; lower rates in winter. AE, DC, DISC, MC, V.

The Mayor's Inn This two-story A-frame, built in 1905 for Mayor Frank Houx, found itself in the path of a wrecking ball in 1997. However, new owners moved it on a truck to its current location, a few blocks away. It's now one of Cody's best B&Bs, with rooms such as the Yellowstone, featuring a lodgepole-pine bed frame and black-and-white photos of the park's early years, and the Hart Mountain Suite, with romance and floral decor in spades. There's also a carriage house (breakfast not included) with a well-equipped kitchen. The breakfasts here are a hearty treat, featuring sourdough flapjacks and buffalo sausage, and innkeepers Bill and Dale Delph also run a gem of a dinner house here Thursday through Saturday nights in the summer.

1413 Rumsey Ave., Cody, WY 82414. ✆ **888/217-3001** or 307/587-0887. www.mayorsinn.com. 5 units. A/C, TV. $120–$160 double; $210 suite. Rates include full breakfast. AE, MC, V.

Pahaska Tepee Resort Buffalo Bill's hunting lodge, only a mile from the east entrance to Yellowstone, bore his Lakota name, "Pahaska" (long hair), when he opened the lodge in 1905. Near the top of the beautiful Wapiti Valley along U.S. 14/16/20, Pahaska is a popular stop for visitors to the Yellowstone area. The cabins are scattered on the hill behind the historic, colorfully decorated lodge. Accommodations have limited amenities and might best be described as "mini-motels" of two to five rooms, each with a private entrance. Some bathrooms have only showers, some tubs—it's best to ask in advance.

183 Yellowstone Hwy., Cody, WY 82414. ✆ **800/628-7791** or 307/527-7701. Fax 307/527-4019. 47 units. TEL. Mid-June to Aug $115–$175 double, $575 condo, $1,095 lodge; off season $70–$140 double, $450–$495 condo, $895–$995 lodge. DISC, MC, V. Closed mid-Oct to Apr.

10 Where to Dine

INSIDE THE PARK

Each dining room at the Mammoth Hot Springs Hotel, Old Faithful Inn, and Lake Yellowstone Hotel has a distinctive ambience, with solid, if none too adventurous, cuisine and servings aimed squarely at a hiker's appetite. For reservations, contact **Xanterra Parks & Resorts** (✆ **866/439-7375;** www.xanterra.com). The atmosphere is festive and just elegant enough that you might want to dress up a bit for dinner—put on socks, perhaps, and a shirt with a collar. The prices aren't bad, and the big halls absorb sound well enough that young children are rarely a bother. Reservations are recommended and sometimes required.

If you're not up for restaurant dining, there is counter-style fast-food service at the **Yellowstone General Stores,** and snack shops and cafeterias in the villages at Canyon, Mammoth, Grant Village, Yellowstone Lake Lodge, and Old Faithful.

MAMMOTH HOT SPRINGS

You'll find the **Terrace Grille** at the opposite end of the building that holds the Mammoth Hot Springs Hotel Dining Room. It serves typical restaurant fare in a less formal—and less pricey—dining room, but it doesn't take reservations.

Mammoth Hot Springs Hotel STEAK/SEAFOOD At Mammoth, there's a good balance between casual and formal because the dining room is reminiscent of an above-average neighborhood restaurant: comfortable and pleasant, without too much of the hotel's Victorian past. The view of the Old Fort Yellowstone buildings and surrounding slopes is also quite enjoyable. The breakfast buffet is essentially identical to what you'll find here at other locations, featuring eggs, pancakes, and the like. The lunch menu focuses on an array of sandwiches, including smoked turkey on Parmesan-crusted sourdough, a grilled vegetarian Reuben, and smoked salmon club. The dinner menu includes bison top sirloin and Montana whitefish, and the vegetarian entrees are surprisingly good.

Mammoth Hot Springs. ✆ **307/344-7311.** Reservations recommended in winter. Breakfast $4–$11; lunch $8–$12; dinner $13–$23. AE, DC, DISC, MC, V. Closed Oct to late Dec and early Mar to early May. May–Oct daily 6:30–10am, 11:30am–2:30pm, and 5–10pm; late Dec to early Mar daily 6:30–10am, 11:30am–2:30pm, and 5:30–8pm.

CANYON VILLAGE AREA

Arrayed around this busy village parking lot are a casual, soda fountain–style restaurant, a cafeteria, a takeout place, and a conventional dining room.

The **Canyon Glacier Pit Snack Bar,** operated by Yellowstone General Stores, shares a building with a convenience store and souvenir shop. Seating is on stools in the fashion of a 1950s soda fountain; you can expect to wait up to 30 minutes during peak hours. The **Canyon Lodge Cafeteria** is a fast-food alternative across the parking lot in the Canyon Lodge area. Next door is an inexpensive deli, **The Picnic Stop,** with sandwiches, salads, and other light fare.

Canyon Lodge Dining Room STEAK/SEAFOOD This is a spacious dining area, a tad sterile perhaps, and when it fills up, it's noisy. The salad bar is long and loaded, but otherwise the dinner fare is largely geared toward the carnivore, with a wide selection of steaks alongside some seafood and pasta selections. The breakfast buffet is a good way to start your day, with all the standard American fixings. The crowds can be large at Canyon Village, but there is a relaxed and unhurried feel to this place that you don't find at some of the park's other busy points.

Canyon Lodge. ✆ **307/344-7311.** Reservations not accepted. Breakfast $5–$12; lunch $8–$13; dinner $13–$23. AE, DC, DISC, MC, V. June to mid-Sept daily 7–10am, 11:30am–2:30pm, and 5–10pm.

TOWER–ROOSEVELT AREA

Roosevelt Lodge Dining Room STEAK/SEAFOOD This is supposed to be the cowboy alternative to the fancier cuisine served at the bigger Yellowstone hotels, but the unadventurous menu will win over only the most naive city slickers. For breakfast, it's eggs and flapjacks; lunch is burgers and sandwiches. Come suppertime, the menu is dominated by barbecue and steaks. A better idea: Join Roosevelt's Old West Dinner Cookout, and ride by horse or wagon through the Pleasant Valley to a chuckwagon dinner that includes cornbread, steak, watermelon, those famous beans, and apple crisp. It's a daily summer event (reservations required) that costs $66 to $80 for an adult, depending on the route of your horseback ride, or $55 if you go by wagon. Children pay $10 less.

Tower Junction. ✆ **307/344-7311.** Reservations not accepted, except for Old West cookouts. Breakfast $5–$9; lunch $7–$10; dinner $9–$24. AE, DC, DISC, MC, V. Summer daily 7–10am, 11:30am–3pm, and 4:30–9pm.

YELLOWSTONE LAKE

For the eat-on-the-run traveler, a **deli** in the Lake Yellowstone Hotel serves lighter fare in an area that is slightly larger than a broom closet. Just down the road, the **Yellowstone Park General Store** offers meals in a section of the store that is shared with tourist items; the best bet is breakfast or a burger. There is also a **cafeteria** serving three meals a day at Lake Lodge.

Lake Yellowstone Hotel CONTINENTAL This represents the finest dining Yellowstone has to offer, with a view of the lake stretching south from a vast dining room that doesn't feel crowded even when it's full. One of the best ways to start your day is with a breakfast buffet, but the stuffed French toast is also quite good. Lunch entrees are gourmet sandwiches and burgers. The dinner menu is the most adventurous in the park. Appetizers include chilled cucumber soup and lobster ravioli, while entrees include elk medallions and lobster tail, bison prime rib, and Idaho trout stuffed with mushrooms and tomatoes.

North side of the lake. ✆ **307/344-7311.** Dinner reservations required. Breakfast $5–$11; lunch $7–$12; dinner $17–$37. AE, DC, DISC, MC, V. Mid-May to early Oct daily 6:30–10:30am, 11:30am–2:30pm, and 5–10pm.

GRANT VILLAGE

The casual choice here is the **Lake House,** footsteps away from the Grant Village restaurant. It specializes in inexpensive fish entrees, as well as burgers and beer. No reservations are accepted. The **Village Grill** in the Yellowstone General Store here also serves three meals daily.

Grant Village Dining Room STEAK/SEAFOOD Breakfast and lunch at the Grant Village restaurant are much like those at the other restaurants in the park, although the chef often surprises diners with interesting dinner items that stray from the norm. Lunch might include pan-fried trout covered with toasted pecans and lemon butter, huge burgers, and ham and Brie on a pretzel roll. The dinner menu ranges from pistachio-crusted chicken to portabella mushroom cannelloni to prime rib, but the specialty is trout, pan-fried with pecans. Quality and ambience here are comparable to those of the better dining rooms at the major park hotels.

Grant Village. ✆ **866/439-7375.** Dinner reservations recommended. Breakfast $5–$11; lunch $7–$10; dinner $13–$24. AE, DC, DISC, MC, V. June–Sept daily 6:30–10am, 11:30am–2:30pm, and 5:30–10pm.

OLD FAITHFUL AREA

Choices abound here. For quick and inexpensive, the year-round **Geyser Grill** at the **Old Faithful Snow Lodge** and the cafeterias at the **Old Faithful Lodge Cafeteria and Bake Shop** serve lunch and dinner in a fast-food environment that fits the mood of a crowd on the move; the **Bear Paw Deli,** an ice-cream stand in the lobby of the **Old Faithful Inn,** is your best choice for dessert. The **Yellowstone General Store** also has a lunch counter.

Obsidian Dining Room STEAK/SEAFOOD In the snazzy new Snow Lodge, a spacious restaurant provides a comparatively contemporary alternative to the dining room at the Old Faithful Inn. It's a little quieter, a little less expensive, and a little less formal. It still has some flash on the menu—braised bison short ribs shank and linguine with Tuscan chicken, for instance—and there is a breakfast gem, the veggie breakfast burrito.

At the Old Faithful Snow Lodge. ✆ **307/344-7311.** Reservations not accepted in summer. Breakfast $5–$11; dinner $16–$33. AE, DC, DISC, MC, V. Early May to mid-Oct daily 6:30–10am and 5–10pm; mid-Dec to mid-Mar daily 6:30am–10am and 5–9:30pm.

Old Faithful Inn Dining Room STEAK/SEAFOOD The food notwithstanding, the true highlight is the gnarled log architecture of this distinguished historic inn. Breakfast is buffet or a la carte, and there's a lot to choose from. There's another buffet at lunchtime (headlined by barbecue beef and chicken), as well as a generous assortment of salads and sandwiches. Dinnertime brings yet another buffet, along with menu entrees like rib-eye steaks, fish, and a vegetarian dish. The fare has gotten more distinguished in recent years, with such creative options as wild game Bolognese and pan-seared elk medallions making regular appearances on the menu.

At the Old Faithful Inn. ✆ **307/344-7311.** Dinner reservations required. Breakfast and lunch $5–$14; dinner $16–$30. AE, DC, DISC, MC, V. Mid-May to mid-Oct daily 6:30–10:30am, 11:30am–2:30pm, and 5–10pm. Closed in winter.

NEAR THE PARK

WEST YELLOWSTONE

Beartooth Barbecue BARBECUE A bustling and funky space that plates up some mean Texas-style barbecue, this is my pick for a casual meal in West Yellowstone. At the bar or a table in the room laden with bric-a-brac (hanging from the walls are sleds, ristas [decorative pepper strings], a traffic light, and sports memorabilia), order a plate of St. Louis–cut spareribs or beef brisket for lunch or dinner (or a sandwich with brisket, sausage, or chicken), and plenty of tangy sauce. The bar has Montana micro beer on draft and serves wine by the glass, but no liquor is served.

111 Canyon St. ✆ **406/646-0227.** Lunch and dinner $10–$27. MC, V. Daily 11:30am–10pm.

The Canyon Street Grill AMERICAN It's hard not to like an establishment whose slogan is "We are not a fast-food restaurant. We are a cafe reminiscent of a bygone era when the quality of the food meant more than how fast it could be served." With checkerboard floors and shiny red booths, this delightful 1950s-style spot serves hearty food for breakfast, lunch, and dinner. Hamburgers and chicken sandwiches are popular, accompanied by milkshakes made with hard ice cream or a famous root beer float

22 Canyon St. ✆ **406/646-7548.** Main courses $4–$11. MC, V. May–Nov Mon–Sat 11am–10pm; shorter hours rest of year. Closed Apr.

Eino's Tavern AMERICAN Locals snowmobile out from West Yellowstone to Eino's (there's a trail that follows U.S. Hwy. 191) to become their own chefs at the grill here. It's a novel concept, and it keeps patrons coming back to this casual restaurant with a fine view of Hebgen Lake time and time again. There's usually a line out the door, but it's fun to check out the walls, plastered with dollar bills and other currency, as well as bras and funny photos, while you wait. After placing your order, keep a straight face when you're handed an uncooked piece of meat. Go to the grill, slap it on, and stand around, drink in hand, shooting the breeze with other patrons until your food is cooked the way you like it. Steaks and chicken come with your choice of a salad (or the place's trademark "hot potatoes" in winter); hamburgers come with chips.

8955 Gallatin Rd. (9 miles north of town on U.S. 191). ✆ **406/646-9344.** Reservations not accepted. Main courses $6–$26. No credit cards; ATM on premises. Winter daily 9am–9pm; spring to fall daily noon–9pm. Closed Thanksgiving to mid-Dec.

The Outpost Restaurant AMERICAN Tucked away in a downtown mall, this restaurant has a family-oriented, home-cooking style—exemplified in the beef stew. There's also salmon, steaks, trout, liver, and an excellent salad bar. For breakfast, if you're really hungry, you can't beat the Campfire Omelette, smothered in homemade chili, cheese, and onions. The menu isn't all that adventurous, and the restaurant offers none of the vices you'll find in the local taverns (no video poker, beer, wine, liquor, or smoking), but it serves solid fare in a quiet, family-friendly atmosphere.

In the Montana Outpost Mall, 115 Yellowstone Ave. ✆ **406/646-7303.** Breakfast $5–$16; lunch $6–$14; dinner $9–$25. AE, DISC, MC, V. Daily 6:30am–10:30pm. Closed mid-Oct to mid-Apr.

Sydney's Mountain Bistro CONTEMPORARY AMERICAN The most upscale option in a meat-and-potatoes town, Sydney's offers an intimate setting, an excellent wine list, and a menu that balances seafood and vegetarian fare with beef, poultry, and pork. With interesting preparations—such as flash-fried calamari for starters and entrees including sweet-chile salmon and a porterhouse pork chop with butternut squash—and a breezy patio complementing the upscale atmosphere inside, this is my pick for a special meal in West Yellowstone. At lunch, look for sandwiches, paninis, and burgers, as well as a quiche of the day and a savory pear-walnut salad.

38 Canyon St. ✆ **406/646-7660.** Brunch and lunch $5–$10; dinner $14–$26. MC, V. Daily 11am–3pm and 5–10pm.

GARDINER

The Chico Dining Room CONTINENTAL The Chico Hot Springs Resorts are 35 miles north of Gardiner, but if you're in the area, stop here for some of the best food in the Greater Yellowstone Ecosystem and a soak in this resort's hot springs. The carnivorous traveler will enjoy the selection of top-drawer beef, the pinenut–crusted Alaskan halibut is a seafood aficionado's dream, and wine lovers won't be disappointed one bit by the award-winning list. Many of the incredibly fresh veggies originate in the resort's garden and greenhouse, and the menu always includes a vegetarian selection. You'll want to linger over the food, so consider a night's stay.

Old Chico Rd., Pray, MT, 35 miles north of Gardiner. ✆ **406/333-4933.** Reservations recommended. Main courses $25–$30. AE, DISC, MC, V. Summer daily 5:30–10pm; winter Sun–Thurs 5:30–9pm, Fri–Sat 5:30–10pm; Sun brunch 8:30–11:30am.

Picnic & Camping Supplies

Pick up your food and camping supplies at the ubiquitous **Yellowstone General Stores,** which are in all the park villages, or at supermarkets in Cody, Gardiner, or West Yellowstone.

Helen's Corral Drive-In BURGERS Okay, so it's not much to look at, and the menu's most adventurous item is a basket of fried shrimp. But the half-pound beef, buffalo, and elk "hateful" hamburgers are the stuff of legend, topping out at 7 inches from top to bottom and featuring all of the fixings.

U.S. Hwy. 89 at Yellowstone St. ✆ **406/848-7627.** Reservations not accepted. Menu items $4–$14. No credit cards. May–Sept daily 11am–11pm. Closed Oct–Apr.

Pedalino's ITALIAN Gardiner's culinary standout, Pedalino's serves tasty Italian dishes in a woodsy room on the main drag, decked out with exposed rough-hewn logs and historic photos of the area. The menu features a number of pasta dishes—including the signature spicy penne *pazze*—"crazy"—as well as a selection of steaks, seafood, and ribs. There is a kids' menu and a full bar.

200 W. Park St. ✆ **406/848-9950.** Main courses $14–$26 dinner. AE, DISC, MC, V. Wed–Mon 5–9pm.

CODY

Cassie's Supper Club WESTERN Cassie's is the sort of classic roadhouse you might expect and look for in the West: big platters of beef; four bars serving drinks; and ornery roadhouse decor with taxidermy, antelope skulls, and assorted cowboy ephemera. Located along the highway west of town in what was once a "house of ill fame," Cassie's is now very respectable and quite good. Besides the requisite steaks—grilled to perfection—there's seafood (including a great walleye dinner), pasta, and chicken, plus a full menu of specialty drinks. In the **Buffalo Bar,** a 20-foot mural depicts horses, cowboys, and shootouts. The near-mythical dance floor bustles to the twang of live country music every night in summer.

214 Yellowstone Ave. ✆ **307/527-5500.** Reservations recommended. Lunch $7–$25; dinner $12–$40. AE, DISC, MC, V. Daily 11am–10pm.

Shiki SUSHI An anomalous standout in meat-and-potatoes Cody, Shiki is a superlative sushi bar. With spare Asian decor—consisting primarily of artfully hung cloth and an attractive water feature—and booth, tables, and bar seating, the setting matches the top-notch sushi rolls and tempura, teriyaki, and curry entree. The sushi includes traditional rolls like spicy tuna and eel, as well as a few regional variations—like the Heart Mountain, with crab, cucumber, avocado, and crunchy tempura flakes. Don't be alarmed by the lack of an ocean nearby: Fresh fish is flown in two to three times a week from both coasts.

1420 Sheridan Ave. ✆ **307/527-7116.** Reservations not accepted. Sushi rolls $5–$15; main courses $15–$26. AE, DISC, MC, V. Mon–Fri 11am–2pm and 4–9pm; Sat–Sun 4–8pm. Closed Sun in winter.

Wyoming's Rib & Chop House STEAKS One of an upscale regional chain with locations in Billings and Livingston, Montana, and Sheridan, Wyoming, this is the place to head for terrific ribs, chops, and steaks—from chicken-fried steaks to buffalo rib-eyes—but vegetarians will have difficulty finding a meatless main course. Chicken and seafood round out the menu, and desserts such as "Pecan Meltaway"—a chocolate crust filled with ice cream, pecans, and more chocolate—provide decadent finales.

1367 Sheridan Ave. ✆ **307/587-4917.** Lunch $6–$9; dinner $10–$33. AE, DISC, MC, V. Daily 11am–10pm.

11 A Side Trip: Little Bighorn Battlefield National Monument, MT

Little Bighorn Battlefield is a relatively easy detour on the way west or east if you are passing through this area, and worth a trip if you are anywhere close by. Most people who visit the battlefield include it in their trip to Grand Teton or Yellowstone National Park. For driving directions from the monument to Yellowstone, see "Getting There & Gateways," earlier in this chapter.

Like the Revolutionary War battlefield at Lexington, Massachusetts, and Civil War battlefields at Gettysburg, Pennsylvania, and Appomattox, Virginia, the Little Bighorn Battlefield National Monument in eastern Montana presents visitors with an opportunity to immerse themselves in American history. This is where Lt. Col. George Armstrong Custer and the 647 men of the 7th Cavalry were wiped out on June 25, 1876, after Custer and his troops attacked an American Indian village along the banks of the Little Bighorn River. Custer had divided his troops into three companies—he led one, while Maj. Marcus Reno and Capt. Frederick Benteen commanded the others. Custer expected little resistance, but he was surprised by what some have estimated at several thousand Lakota Sioux, Cheyenne, and Arapaho warriors, who surrounded and killed the soldiers.

Until 1991, the battlefield was known as the Custer Battlefield in honor of the soldiers who fought there. However, when activists protested that the battlefield recognized only one side of what occurred on its dusty soil, Congress changed the name. In late 2001, Congress approved $2.3 million for construction of a memorial at the national monument to the American Indian warriors who fought at Little Big Horn. The striking memorial, dedicated in 2003, includes bronze tracings of three warriors—a Sioux, a Cheyenne, and an Arapaho—and what is described as a "spirit gate."

Little Bighorn Battlefield National Monument

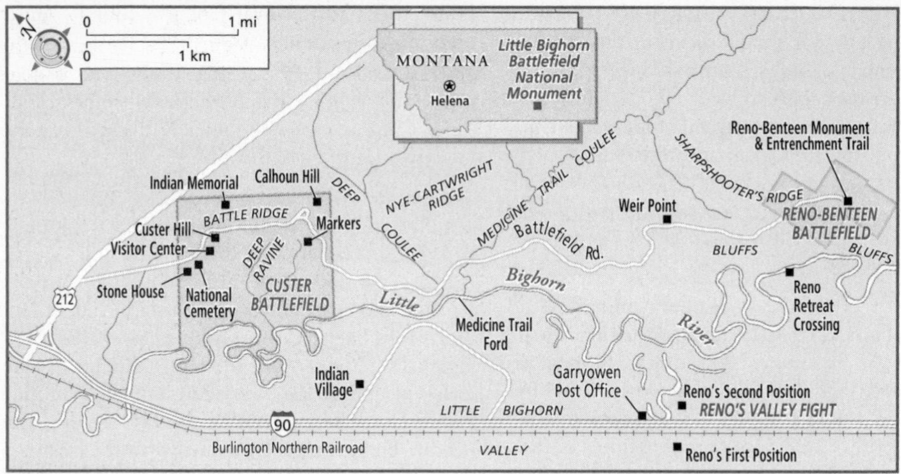

ESSENTIALS

WHEN TO GO

The national monument is popular, and visitation is highest between Memorial Day and Labor Day. The best advice if you wish to avoid crowds is to avoid these months, or to arrive early in the morning or late in the day. This is also good advice because summers in eastern Montana can get very hot, and there is no shade on the battlefield.

GETTING THERE

If you are coming from the west, from Billings, Montana, take **I-90** east 61 miles to the Little Bighorn Battlefield off-ramp at U.S. 212 (exit 510). If you are coming from the south, from Sheridan, Wyoming, take I-90 north (approximately 70 miles) to the same off-ramp at U.S. 212. If you are coming from the east, from the Black Hills of South Dakota, you will already be on **U.S. 212.** The battlefield is 42 miles west of Lame Deer, Montana.

INFORMATION & VISITOR CENTER

Contact the **Superintendent,** Little Bighorn Battlefield National Monument, P.O. Box 39, Crow Agency, MT 59022-0039 (✆ **406/638-2621;** www.nps.gov/libi).

At the **visitor center** just inside the park entrance, you'll see actual uniforms worn by Custer, read about his life, and view an eerie reenactment of the battles on a small-scale replica of the battlefield.

PARK HOURS & FEES

The park is open daily 8am to 9pm from Memorial Day through July, and 8am to 8pm August to Labor Day; spring and fall hours are 8am to 6pm; winter hours are 8am to 4:30pm. The visitor center is open the same hours. The park is closed on January 1, Thanksgiving, and December 25. The admission fee is $10 per vehicle, $5 per person on foot or bike.

RANGER PROGRAMS & A GUIDED TOUR

Hourly **interpretive talks** help visitors understand the battle and its participants. Subjects vary during the day and include discussion of the culture and life of the Northern Plains tribes that engaged in the battle, army life in the 1870s, weapons and tactics, and the significance of the battle.

For a unique perspective, take a guided tour with **Apsaalooke Tours** (✆ **406/638-3100**), a concessionaire at Little Bighorn Battlefield. American Indian guides lead 1-hour bus tours (summer only, five times daily) to the battle sites, starting at the visitor center. The cost is $8 for adults, $5 for seniors, and $2 for children.

EXPLORING THE MONUMENT

It's possible to view the site in less than a half-hour, but you should plan to spend enough time to explore the visitor center, listen to interpretive talks presented by rangers, and then tour the site. You'll leave with a greater appreciation for the monument and understanding of the history that led up to the battle.

After stopping at the **visitor center,** drive 4½ miles south to the **Reno–Benteen Monument Entrenchment Trail,** at the end of the monument road, and double back. Interpretive signs at the top of this bluff show the route followed by the companies under Custer, Benteen, and Reno as they approached the area from the south, and the positions from which they defended themselves from their American Indian attackers.

As you proceed north along the ridge, you'll pass **Custer's Lookout,** the spot from which the general first viewed the Indian village. This was the spot at which Custer sent for reinforcements, though he continued marching north.

Capt. Thomas Weir led his troops to **Weir Point** in hopes of assisting Custer, but was immediately discovered by the Indian warriors and forced to retreat to the spot held by Reno.

The **Medicine Trail Ford,** on the ridge, overlooks a spot well below the bluffs in the Medicine Trail Coulee on the Little Bighorn River, where hundreds of warriors who had been sent from the Reno battle pushed across the river in pursuit of Custer and his army.

Farther north, the Cheyenne warrior Lame White Man led an attack up **Calhoun Ridge** against a company of the 7th Cavalry that had charged downhill into the coulee. When the opponents' resistance overwhelmed the army, troops retreated back up the hill, where they were killed.

As you proceed to the north, you will find detailed descriptions of the events that occurred on the northernmost edges of the ridge, as well as white markers that indicate the places where army troops fell in battle. The bodies of Custer, his brothers Tom and Boston, and nephew Autie Reed all were found on Custer Hill.

Indian casualties during the rout are estimated at 60 to 100 warriors. Following the battle, which some say began early in the morning and ended within 2 hours, the Indians broke camp in haste and scattered to the north and south. Within a few short years, they were all confined to reservations.

The survivors of the Reno–Benteen armies buried the bodies of Custer and his slain army where they fell. In 1881, the graves that could be located were opened, and the bones reinterred at the base of a memorial shaft found overlooking the battlefield. Custer's remains were eventually reburied at the U.S. Military Academy at West Point.

There are three **walking trails** within the monument for visitors wishing to explore the battle in greater depth.

The adjacent **National Cemetery,** established in 1879, incorporates a self-guided tour to the graves of some of the more significant figures buried there. The **Indian Memorial** is also in this area.

35

Yosemite National Park, CA

by Eric Peterson

Yosemite's sky-scraping geologic formations, lush meadows, swollen rivers, and spectacular waterfalls make it a destination for travelers from around the world. It's home to three of the world's 10 highest waterfalls and the largest single piece of exposed granite anywhere, not to mention one of the world's largest trees and the most recognized rock formation.

The greatest thing about all this is that you don't have to be a mountaineer to enjoy the beauty. Yosemite's most popular attractions are accessible to everyone. No matter where you go, you'll see a view worth remembering. In the span of a mile, you can behold the quiet beauty of a forest, walk through a pristine meadow, observe a sunset from a towering granite cliff, hike to a half-mile-high waterfall, enjoy a moonlit night as bright as day, climb a rock, and eat a gourmet meal before falling asleep, be it under the stars or in a luxurious hotel.

Yosemite Valley, the destination of 95% of park visitors (more than three million people a year), is just a small sliver of the park—around 1% of its land area—but it holds the bulk of the region's jaw-dropping features. This is the place of record-setting statistics: the highest waterfall in North America and three of the tallest in the world (Upper Yosemite, Sentinel, and Ribbon falls), the biggest and tallest piece of exposed granite (El Capitan), and stands of giant sequoia.

This beautiful wilderness has experienced a disquieting sense of foreboding in recent years, with increasing traffic, litter, and noise. It seems that, in many ways, Yosemite is being loved to death. But the National Park Service has implemented a transportation plan aimed at getting visitors out of their cars, and we can already see improvements. Yosemite has also undergone changes due to Mother Nature. In recent years, floods and rock slides have altered the face of the park, destroying campgrounds and some trails.

AVOIDING THE CROWDS

Yosemite has its highest number of visitors during summer, especially during school vacations, so the best advice for avoiding crowds is to go when schools are in session. The campgrounds and lodgings are often full from June through August, and you can expect some crowds in late spring and early fall as well. Because of Yosemite's proximity to California's population centers, you'll also want to try to avoid weekends, especially holiday weekends. Winter is a great time to visit Yosemite—not only is the park almost empty, but it offers a number of activities, from skiing at Badger Pass to sledding, ice-skating, and snowshoeing. Keep in mind, however, that the high country along Tioga Pass Road is inaccessible to vehicles from mid-fall to early June, depending on snow levels.

Other ways to avoid humanity, at any time of the year, are to explore the less-visited sections of the park—which generally means anywhere outside Yosemite Valley—and to walk away from the crowds by getting out on the trails. The farther you go from the trail heads, the fewer people you'll encounter. Time of day is also important. Most people tour the park between 10am and 4pm, meaning that early morning, late afternoon, and early evening are the best times to see the park.

1 Essentials

GETTING THERE & GATEWAYS

Yosemite is a 3½-hour drive from San Francisco and a 6-hour drive from Los Angeles. Many roads lead to Yosemite's four entrances. From the west, the Big Oak Flat Entrance is 88 miles from Manteca on **Calif. 120** and passes through the towns of Groveland, Buck Meadows, and Big Oak Flat. The Arch Rock Entrance is 75 miles northeast of Merced on **Calif. 140** and passes through Mariposa and El Portal. The South Entrance is 64 miles north of Fresno and passes through Oakhurst, Bass Lake, and Fish Camp. From the east, the Tioga Pass Entrance is the only option. It is 10 miles west of Lee Vining on Calif. 120; the route is usually open only in the summer. To check on statewide road conditions, call ✆ **800/427-7623** in California (or 916/445-7623 elsewhere) or visit www.dot.ca.gov.

Daily bus transportation into the park from Merced, Mariposa, and nearby communities is provided by **YARTS,** the **Yosemite Area Regional Transportation System** (✆ **877/989-2787** or 209/388-9589; www.yarts.com). Buses are not subject to park entrance delays during peak season. From Merced, there are several departures daily from the airport, train station, and bus terminal. Round-trip fare is $25 adults, $14 for children under 13 and seniors 62 and older. There are stops in Mariposa at several lodgings and the visitor center, with round-trip rates of $12 adults, $8 for children under 13 and seniors 62 and older.

THE NEAREST AIRPORTS **Fresno–Yosemite International Airport** (✆ **559/621-4500;** www.fresno.gov), 90 miles from the South Entrance at Wawona, is the nearest major airport. It serves over 25 cities with more than 100 flights daily. Airlines include Alaska, Allegiant, American/American Eagle, Delta, Horizon, Mexicana, United, and US Airways. You can rent a car from Avis, Budget, Dollar, Enterprise, Hertz, or National/Alamo. **Mariposa County Airport** (✆ **209/966-2143**) has a tiny airstrip for private planes.

INFORMATION

Get general information from **Superintendent,** Yosemite National Park, P.O. Box 577, Yosemite, CA 95389 (✆ **209/372-0200;** www.nps.gov/yose). The park newspaper, the *Yosemite Guide,* is a vital source of information. The **Yosemite Association** (✆ **209/379-2646;** www.yosemite.org) publishes books and interpretive information.

VISITOR CENTERS

In the park, the best and biggest visitor center is the **Valley Visitor Center** in Yosemite Village (✆ **209/372-0200**). The year-round center offers tour information, daily ranger programs, lodging, and restaurants. The rangers here are helpful, insightful, and knowledgeable. Inside, information boards update road conditions and campsite availability, and serve as message boards. Maps, books, and videos are for sale. There are several exhibits on the park, its geologic history, and the history of the valley. Nearby is **Yosemite Valley Wilderness Center,** a small room with high-country maps, information on necessary equipment, and trail information. A ranger at the desk answers questions, issues permits, and offers advice about the high country. Elsewhere, the **Wawona Information Station** and **Big Oak Flat Information Center** dispense general park information. In the high country, stop at the **Tuolumne Meadows Visitor Center** for information and advice.

FEES & PERMITS

It costs $20 per vehicle per week to enter the park, or $10 per person per week if arriving on bike or on foot. Camping costs $5 to $20 a night.

Camping in the backcountry and fishing both require permits. See "Fishing" (under "Other Sports & Activities") and "Overnight Hikes," later in this chapter, for more information.

SPECIAL REGULATIONS & WARNINGS

In addition to the usual regulations about not damaging the natural resources, staying on established trails, and the like, special regulations at Yosemite are aimed at protecting the park's **bear** population, which has become much too familiar with the habits of humans. Under no circumstances should food be left in tents, cabins, or cars. There are storage lockers and bear-proof containers throughout the park—use them. Never feed a bear, or any animal, for that matter.

SEASONS & CLIMATE

For general information on the climate of Yosemite, see the "Seasons & Climate" section of chapter 32, which covers nearby Sequoia and Kings Canyon parks. The climate there is similar to Yosemite's. The high country in Yosemite receives up to 20 feet of snow annually, and visitors who plan a winter trip should be well experienced in winter travel.

SEASONAL EVENTS

January to February: Chefs' Holidays. Yosemite entertains nationally renowned chefs, who share their secrets with participants. Each session, which includes several talks and demonstrations throughout the day by noted chefs, concludes with a banquet in the Ahwahnee Dining Room. Packages that include overnight accommodations at the Ahwahnee are available. Call ✆ **801/559-5000** for reservations.

March: Heritage Holidays. Started in 2002 to celebrate the Ahwahnee's 75th birthday, this is a nostalgic treat for visitors, and many events—concerts, lectures, and movies—are free and open to the public. Lodging packages at the Ahwahnee and the Yosemite Lodge at the Falls are available. Call ✆ **801/559-5000** for more information.

November to December: Vintners' Holidays. California's finest winemakers hold tastings in the Ahwahnee Great Lounge. Each session concludes with a Vintners' Banquet. Two-, 3-, and 5-night packages are also available. Call ✆ **801/559-5000** for reservations.

December 15–26: The Bracebridge Dinner. This event transports diners to 17th-century England, with music, song, and course upon course of delectable dishes. This popular event requires reservations, which are secured by lottery. Applications are

Yosemite National Park

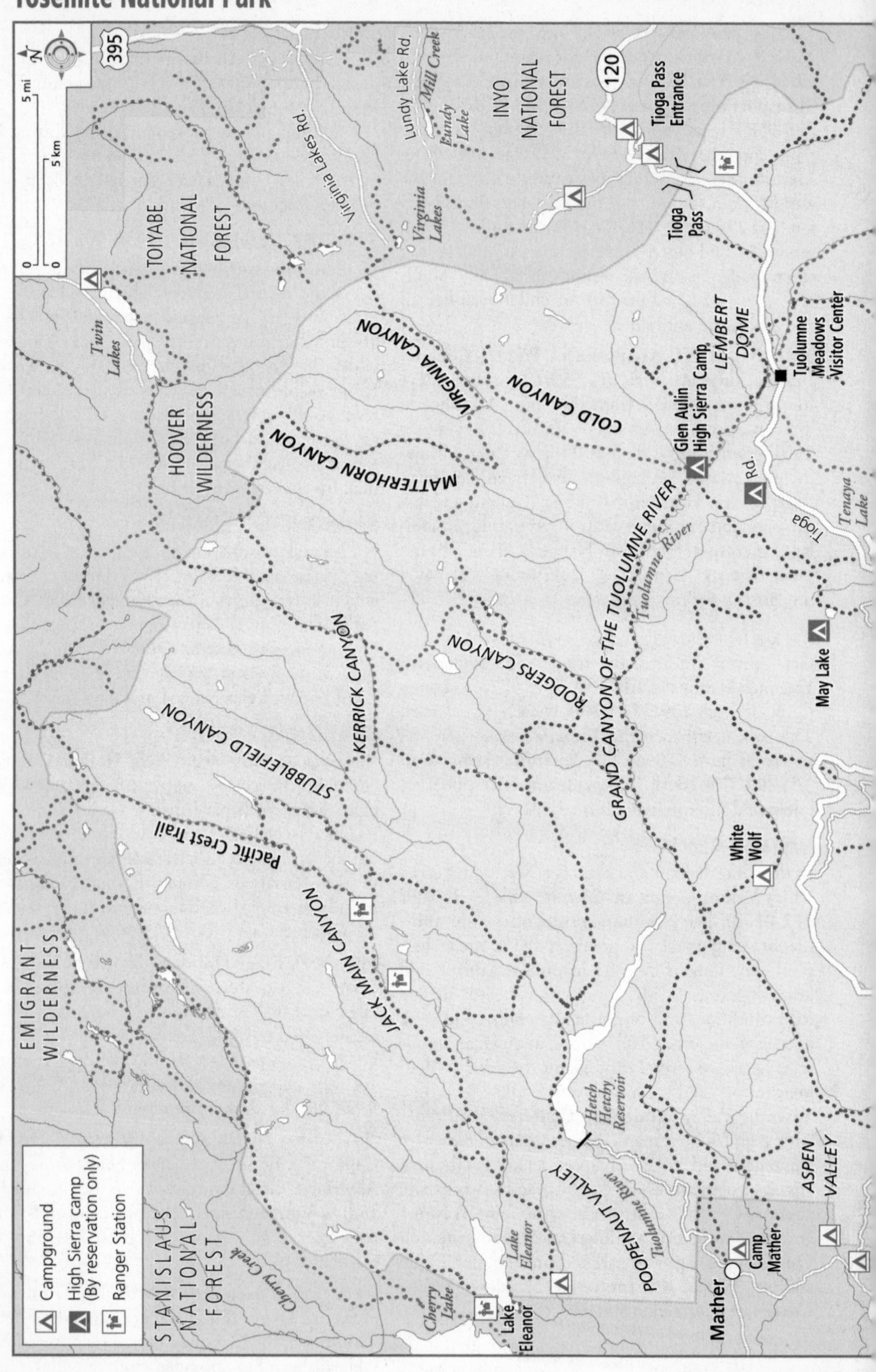

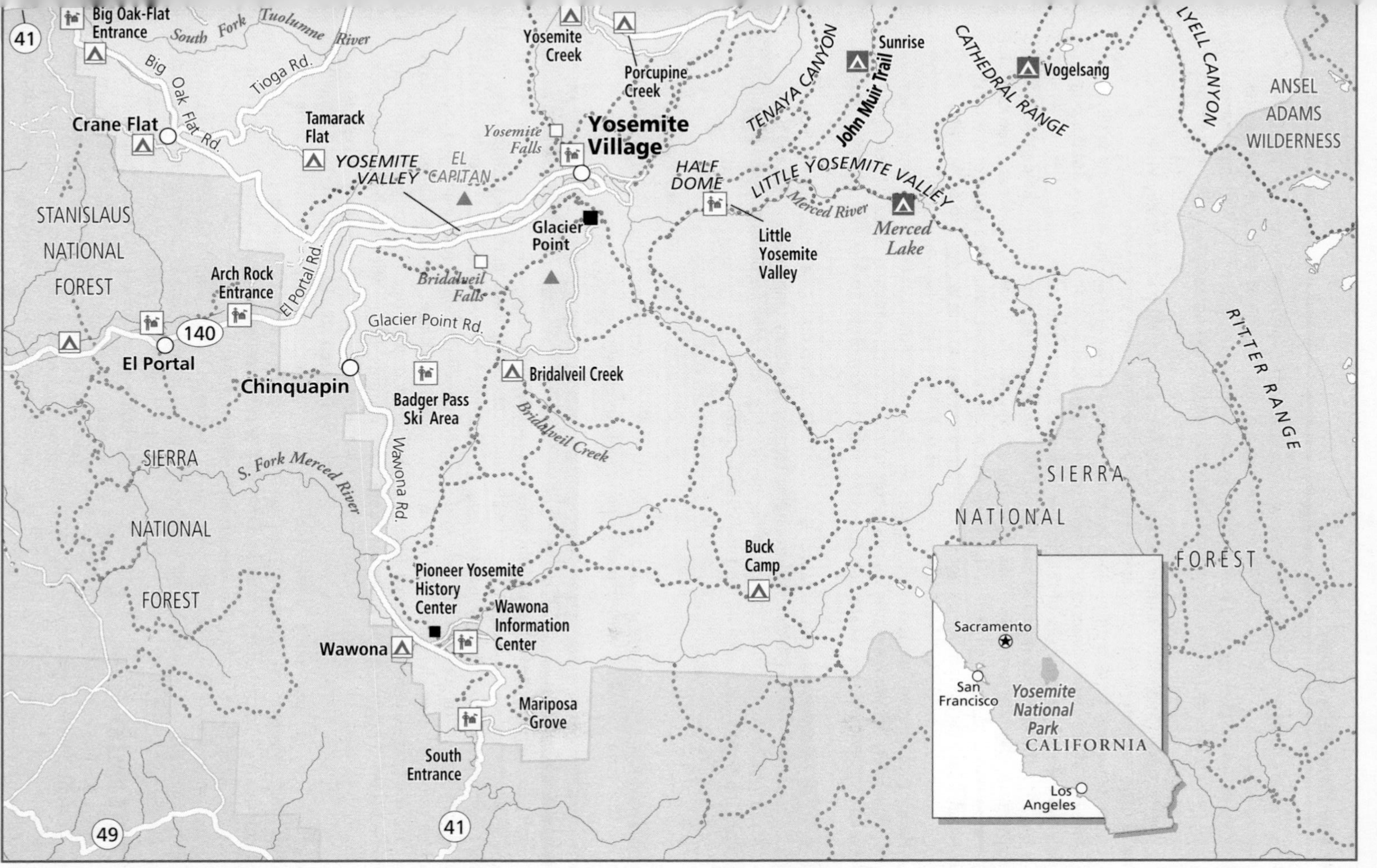

Big Oak-Flat Entrance
41
South Fork Tuolumne River
Yosemite Creek
Porcupine Creek
Sunrise
TENAYA CANYON
John Muir Trail
CATHEDRAL RANGE
Vogelsang
LYELL CANYON
ANSEL ADAMS WILDERNESS
Big Oak Flat Rd.
Tioga Rd.
Crane Flat
Tamarack Flat
Yosemite Falls
Yosemite Village
YOSEMITE VALLEY
EL CAPITAN
HALF DOME
LITTLE YOSEMITE VALLEY
Merced River
Merced Lake
Little Yosemite Valley
Glacier Point
STANISLAUS NATIONAL FOREST
Bridalveil Falls
Arch Rock Entrance
El Portal Rd.
Glacier Point Rd.
140
El Portal
Chinquapin
Badger Pass Ski Area
Bridalveil Creek
Bridalveil Creek
RITTER RANGE
SIERRA NATIONAL FOREST
S. Fork Merced River
Wawona Rd.
SIERRA NATIONAL FOREST
Buck Camp
Pioneer Yosemite History Center
Wawona Information Center
Wawona
Mariposa Grove
South Entrance
49
41
Sacramento
San Francisco
Yosemite National Park
CALIFORNIA
Los Angeles

If You Have Only 1 Day

This is a park that begs for an extended visit, but those with a limited amount of time will also have an enjoyable experience, especially if they use the park's free shuttle bus. The bus operates year-round, with fewer stops in winter. Bus stops are well marked and within walking distance of all parking lots. We've included shuttle bus stop numbers throughout the valley sections of this chapter.

You can get on and off the shuttles at any point, but be sure to stop at the **Valley Visitor Center** (shuttle bus stop no. 5 or 9) to see an exhibit on how the valley was created.

If you're not apt to take off on your own, one of the best ways to spend your time wisely is to take one of the **guided tours** (see "Organized Tours & Ranger Programs," below). But if group activities aren't really your cup of tea, try the following sites on your own.

The base of **Lower Yosemite Fall** (shuttle bus stop no. 6) is an easy walk from the parking lot across from Yosemite Lodge. The hike is described in greater detail below. From here, you can see a portion of the magnificent water show. During peak runoff, when the force of the falls sends spray in every direction, it's not uncommon to get wet. In late winter and early spring, a huge snow cone caused by freezing water rises up to 300 feet at the base of this fall.

Happy Isles (shuttle bus stop no. 16) is another major attraction. Located at the convergence of several inlets, it's the site of the valley's nature center. This is also the trail head for Vernal and Nevada falls, two staircase waterfalls accessible only on foot. Both are described later in this chapter.

Next, we recommend a visit to **Mirror Lake** (shuttle bus stop no. 17), a small lake named for the near-perfect way it reflects the surrounding scenery. It's slowly filling up with silt and is less dramatic and mirrorlike than it used to be, but its shore still offers a beautiful view of Half Dome. This short stroll is well marked and described below.

available December 1 to January 15 and are due February 15 for the following year. Expect to pay around $500 per person. Call ✆ **801/559-5000** for more information.

2 Exploring the Park

It's relatively easy to find your way around Yosemite. All road signs are clear and visible. You'll soon realize that everything leads to a one-way road that hugs the valley's perimeter. To get from one side to the other, you can either drive the entire loop or travel one of the few bridges over the Merced River. It's easy to find yourself heading in the wrong direction on the one-way road, so be alert whenever you merge.

In addition to the year-round shuttle bus in Yosemite Valley, Wawona and Tuolumne Meadows offer a similar service during summer months. Driving in any of these places during peak season—or even off season in the valley—is a surefire way to miss important sights and spend too much time stuck in traffic.

YOSEMITE VALLEY

Many people come to Yosemite National Park solely to see Yosemite Valley, which can be simply described as a giant study in shadow and light. In spring, after winter snow begins melting in the high country, waterfalls encircle the valley, shimmering like a diamond necklace. There are wide, beautiful meadows, towering trees, and the ever-present sound of rushing water in the background.

Yosemite Valley consists of three developed areas. Just about all the hotels, restaurants, and shops are in **Yosemite Village, Yosemite Lodge,** and **Curry Village.** Curry Village (also called Camp Curry) and Yosemite Lodge offer the bulk of the park's overnight accommodations. Curry Village is near shuttle bus stop nos. 13A, 13B, 14, 15, 20, and 21. Yosemite Lodge is at stop no. 8. Both locations have restaurants and a small grocery. The lodge has a large public pool, and Curry Village has an ice rink (open in winter).

Yosemite Village (shuttle bus stop nos. 1, 2, 4, 5, 9, or 10) is the largest-developed region in the valley. It is home to the park's largest visitor center and the headquarters for the National Park Service in Yosemite, as well as for DNC Parks & Resorts at Yosemite, the contractor that runs most of the park's accommodations and restaurants. The village has a host of stores and shops, including a grocery, restaurants, the valley's only medical clinic, a dentist, a post office, a beauty shop, and an ATM.

Also check out the **Yosemite Pioneer Cemetery,** a peaceful graveyard in the shade of tall sequoias with headstones dating from the 1800s. (Pick up the self-guiding booklet at the nearby visitor center.) There are about 36 marked graves, identifiable by horizontal slabs of rock, some etched with crude or faded writing. Buried here are some notables in Yosemite history, such as James Lamon, an early settler known for his apple trees—they still bear fruit—who died in 1875.

Next door, you'll find the **Yosemite Museum** and **Indian Cultural Exhibit.** Both are free and provide a historic picture of the park, before and after it was settled and secured as a national treasure. The museum entrance is marked by a crowd-pleaser—the cross-section of a 1,000-year-old sequoia with memorable dates identified on the tree's rings. Highlights include the signing of the Magna Carta in 1215, the landing of Columbus in the New World, and the Civil War. The ring was cut in 1919 from a tree that fell in the Mariposa Grove south of the valley in Wawona. The Indian Cultural Exhibit strives to explain the life of the American Indians who once lived here, and members of regional tribes regularly speak or give demonstrations of traditional arts. The Yosemite Museum Book Shop, next door, sells books as well as traditional American Indian arts and crafts.

The village of the **Ahwahneechee** is behind the museum and Indian Cultural Exhibit; a free self-guided walking tour is accessible from the back door of the visitor center. This exhibit guides visitors through the transformation of the Ahwahneechee, the tribe that inhabited Yosemite Valley until the mid-1850s. The village includes a ceremonial roundhouse that's still in use.

The **Ansel Adams Gallery** (✆ **209/372-4413;** www.anseladams.com) sells prints and cards of images made by the famed photographer. The shop also serves as a small gallery for current artisans, some with works for sale.

One mile east of Yosemite Village on a narrow, dead-end road is the majestic old **Ahwahnee** hotel (shuttle bus stop no. 3; see "Where to Stay," later in this chapter). It's definitely worth a visit for anyone interested in architecture and design.

The **Yosemite Valley Chapel** is on the south side of the Merced River (shuttle bus stop no. 11). From the bus stop, walk across the bridge and to the left for just under a quarter-mile. Schedules for worship services in the chapel are posted in the *Yosemite Guide* and available by phone (✆ **209/372-4831**).

The **LeConte Memorial Lodge** (shuttle bus stop no. 12) is an educational center and library. Built in 1903 in honor of University of California geologist Joseph LeConte, the Tudor-style granite building schedules a number of free educational programs. Talks are listed in the *Yosemite Guide.*

At the valley's far eastern end, beyond Curry Village, is the **Happy Isles Nature Center** (shuttle bus stop no. 16). Summer hours are 9am to 5pm daily; it's closed fall through spring. The nature center offers exhibits and books on the animal and plant life of Yosemite, and is a super place for children to explore. This is also where the park's Little Cub and Junior Ranger programs are held. Happy Isles is named for three nearby inlets labeled by Yosemite's guardian in 1880.

NORTH OF THE VALLEY

Hetch Hetchy and **Tuolumne Meadows** are remarkably different regions on opposite sides of the park. Hetch Hetchy is on the western border; take the turnoff just outside the park's Big Oak Flat Entrance. Tuolumne Meadows is on the eastern border, just inside Tioga Pass, and is inaccessible by motor vehicle during the winter.

Hetch Hetchy is home to the park's reviled reservoir, fought over for years by conservationist John Muir. In the end, Muir lost and the dam was built, ensuring water for the city of San Francisco. Many believe the loss exhausted Muir and hastened his death in 1914, a year after a bill was signed to fund the dam project. Construction began on the dam in 1919, and it was completed in 1923.

South of Hetch Hetchy, inside the park, are two large stands of giant sequoias. The Merced and Tuolumne groves offer a quiet alternative to the Mariposa Grove of Big Trees in Wawona. Both groves are accessible only on foot. The **Merced Grove** is a 4-mile round-trip walk that begins on Big Oak Flat Road about 4½ miles inside the Big Oak Flat Entrance. Although the trees don't mirror the majesty of the Mariposa Grove, the solitude makes this area a real treat for hikers. The **Tuolumne Grove** of about 25 trees is the destination of a 1-mile hike (2-hr. round-trip).

To get into Yosemite's **high country,** go about 1½ hours east along Tioga Road, which is closed in winter between Big Oak Flat and Tioga Pass. This subalpine region is low on amenities, which makes it a frequent haunt of those who enjoy roughing it, but even cushy-soft couch potatoes can enjoy the beauty up here. Glistening granite domes tower above lush green meadows, which are cut by silver swaths of streams and lakes. Many of Yosemite's longer hikes begin or pass through here.

Olmsted Point, midway between White Wolf and Tuolumne meadows, offers one of the most spectacular vistas anywhere in the park. Here the enormous walls of the Tenaya Canyon are exposed, and an endless view stretches all the way to Yosemite

Yosemite Valley

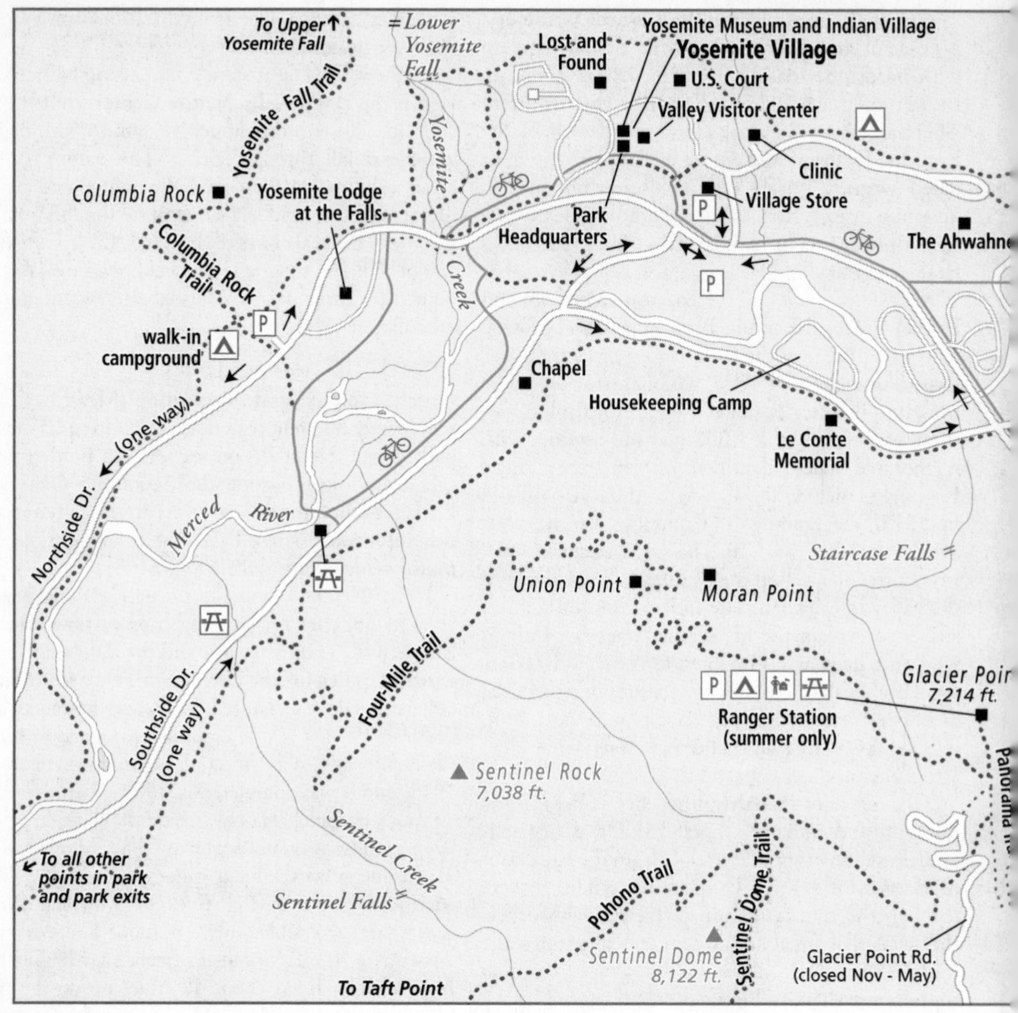

Valley. In the distance are Cloud's Rest and the rear of Half Dome. To the east, easily accessible Tenaya Lake, one of the park's larger lakes, glistens like a sapphire.

About 8 miles east of Tenaya Lake is **Tuolumne Meadows,** a huge subalpine area surrounded by domes and steep granite formations that offer exhilarating climbs. The meadow is a beautiful place to hike and fish, or just to admire the scenery while escaping the crowds of Yosemite Valley. North of the meadow is Lembert Dome at about 2 o'clock, and then, working clockwise, Johnson Peak at 7 o'clock, Unicorn Peak at 8 o'clock, Fairview Dome at about 10 o'clock, and Pothole Dome at 11 o'clock. Up the road is the central region of Tuolumne, where you'll find a visitor center, campground, canvas tent-cabins, and a store. Continue east to reach Tioga Lake and Tioga Pass.

SOUTH OF THE VALLEY

This region, which includes Wawona and the Mariposa Grove of Big Trees, is densely forested. It has a handful of granite rock formations, none as spectacular as those found elsewhere in the park. En route to Wawona you'll come across several wonderful views of Yosemite Valley. **Tunnel View,** a turnout just before the tunnel to Wawona, provides one of the park's most recognizable vistas, memorialized on film by photographer Ansel Adams. To the right is Bridalveil Fall, opposite El Capitan. Half Dome lies straight ahead.

Halfway between Yosemite Valley and Wawona is Glacier Point Road (closed in winter past the turnoff to Badger Pass Ski Area), which runs 16 miles to spectacular **Glacier Point.** From the parking area, it's a short hike to an amazing overlook that provides a view of the glacier-carved granite

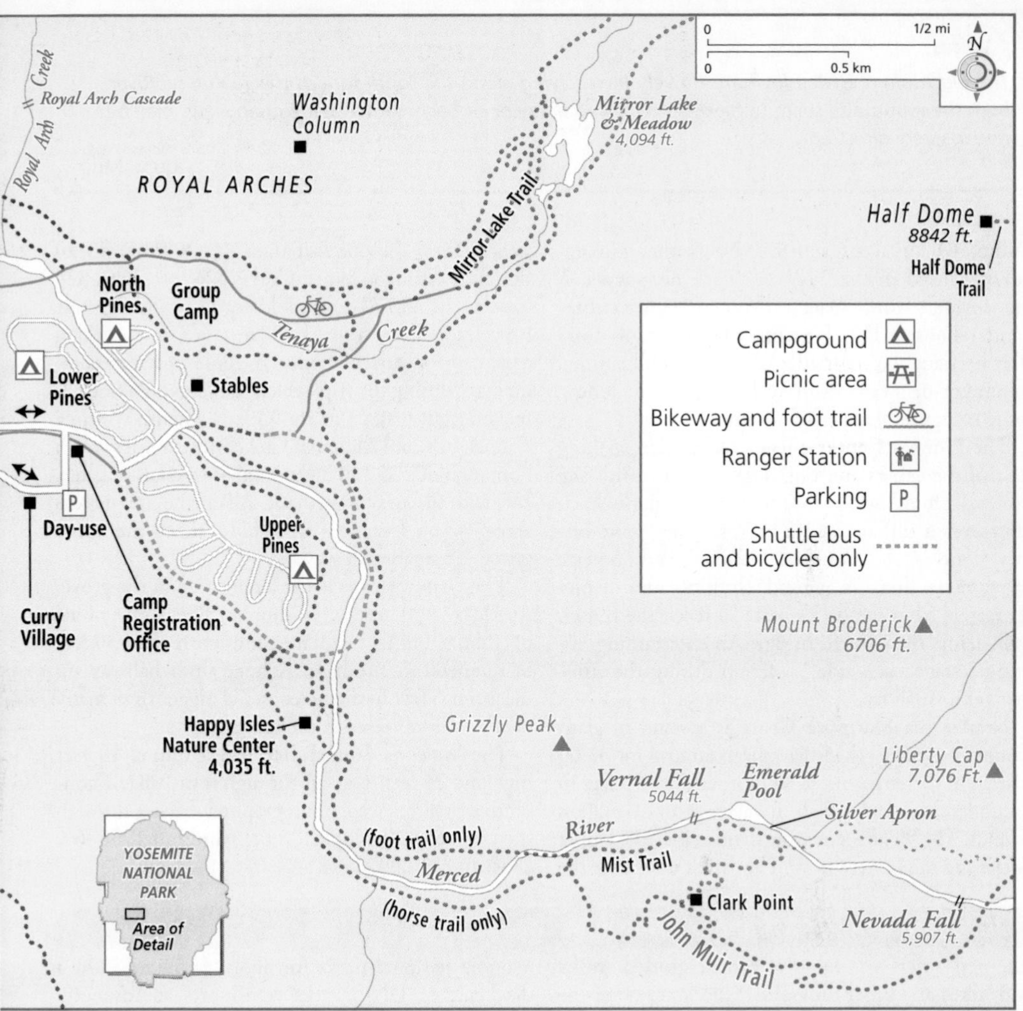

rock formations all along the valley and beyond. At this point you will be at eye level with **Half Dome,** which looks close enough to reach out and touch. Far below, Yosemite Valley resembles a green-carpeted ant farm. There are also some pretty sights of some waterfalls that are not visible from the valley floor. Glacier Point has a geology hut and a day lodge for wintertime cross-country skiers that is a gift store and snack shack during the rest of the year. It's accessible by both foot and bus (see "Organized Tours & Ranger Programs," below).

Continue south on Wawona Road to reach **Wawona,** a historic small town 30 miles from the valley. It was settled in 1856 by homesteader Galen Clark, who built a rustic waystation for travelers en route from Mariposa to Yosemite. The property's next owners, the Washburn brothers, built much of what is today the Wawona Hotel, including the large white building to the right of the main hotel, which was constructed in 1876. The two-story hotel annex went up 3 years later. When Congress established Yosemite National Park in 1890 and charged the U.S. Army with managing it, Wawona became its headquarters. Every summer, soldiers camped in what is today the Wawona Campground. For 16 summers, the cavalry out of San Francisco camped and mapped the park. When Yosemite Valley was added after the turn of the 20th century, the cavalry picked up and relocated to the valley.

As Yosemite grew in popularity, so did the Wawona Hotel and the town itself. When the Wawona was added to the park in 1932, Section 35 (the number assigned to the plot in its legal description) was allowed to remain under private ownership. The town is still there today, just east of the hotel off Wawona Road.

Near the Wawona Hotel are the Thomas Hill Studio and Pioneer Yosemite History Center. The

Voices

The big Tuolumne Meadows are flowery lawns, lying along the south fork of the Tuolumne River ... here the mountains seem to have been cleared away or sit back, so that wide-open views may be had in every direction.

—John Muir

studio, which keeps sporadic hours that are frequently listed in the *Yosemite Guide* newspaper, is the former work space of noted 19th-century painter Thomas Hill. He came to Wawona in 1885 after his daughter married a Washburn. Hill painted a number of award-winning landscapes, including some recognizable ones of Yosemite.

The **Pioneer Center** offers a self-guided walking tour of the cabins and buildings moved to this site in 1961 from various locations in the park. Each represents a different time in Yosemite's short history. During the summer, National Park Service interpreters dress in period clothing and depict characters from the park's past. To reach the center, walk across the covered bridge. An entertaining 10-minute stagecoach ride is offered during the summer for a small fee.

Nearby, the **Mariposa Grove** is a stand of giant sequoias, some of which have been around for 3,000 years. They stretch almost 300 feet tall, are 50 feet in circumference, and weigh an average of 2 million pounds. The 500 trees here are divided into the Upper Grove and the Lower Grove. The easiest way to see the trees is from the open-air tram (© **209/372-4386**) that runs during summer. Cost is $26 for adults, $24 for seniors, and $18 for children; kids under 5 ride free. Trams leave from the Mariposa Grove parking area; call for current hours. A guide provides commentary during the trip, which lasts about an hour. It makes regular stops at the Grizzly Giant, Wawona Tunnel Tree, and Mariposa Grove Museum. It's worth hopping out and walking around as often as possible. Just take the next tram back. All of the area is also accessible on foot. It is an uphill walk to the upper grove, 2.5 miles each way.

The Grizzly Giant is the largest tree in the grove. At "just" 200 feet, it is shorter than some of its neighbors, but its trunk measures more than 30 feet in diameter at the base. A huge limb halfway up measures 6 feet in diameter and is bigger than many of the "young" trees in the grove.

The Wawona Tunnel Tree had a tunnel 10 feet high and 26 feet long cut through it in 1881. Thousands of visitors were photographed driving through the tree before it toppled in the winter of 1968–69, a victim of heavy snow.

3 Organized Tours & Ranger Programs

The park offers a number of **ranger-guided walks and hikes** and other programs. Check at one of the visitor centers or in the *Yosemite Guide* for current topics, start times, and locations. Walks may vary from week to week, but you can always count on nature hikes, evening discussions on park anomalies (floods, fires, or critters), and the sunrise photography program aimed at replicating some of Ansel Adams's works. The sunrise photo walk always gets rave reviews from the early risers who venture out at dawn. All photo walks require advance registration. The living history evening program outside at Yosemite Lodge is great for young and old alike.

Several organizations also conduct guided trips. **Southern Yosemite Mountain Guides,** 621 Highland Ave., Santa Cruz, CA 95060 (© **800/231-4575;** www.symg.com), offers hiking, backpacking, fishing, and rock-climbing trips. Trips last from a day to over a week; prices run about $150 to $200 a day. **California Alpine Guides,** P.O. Box 84846, Mammoth Lakes, CA 93456 (© **877/686-2546;** www.californiaalpineguides.com), offers multiday climbing and backpacking trips in Yosemite and Sequoia national parks for about $150 to $200 a day. Part of DNC Parks & Resorts at Yosemite, **Yosemite Mountaineering** (© **209/372-8344;** www.yosemitemountaineering.com) offers a variety of guided climbing and backpacking trips. Both the **Evergreen Lodge** and the **Yosemite Bug** (see "Where to Stay," later in this chapter) also give tours of the park; the latter offers van tours, as well as backpacking and hiking excursions.

Yosemite Sightseeing Tours (© **559/658-8687;** www.yosemitetours.com) conducts scheduled tours as well as customized trips. Costs run about $75 for adults, $65 for teens 17 and under, and free for kids under 13. Tours are operated on small air-conditioned buses with huge picture windows. The sightseeing includes Mariposa Grove, Yosemite Valley, and Glacier Point. Geology, flora, and fauna are pointed out along the way. Stops are scheduled for lunch, shopping, and photo opportunities. Pickup can be arranged from various motels throughout Oakhurst and Bass Lake.

If you're staying in the valley, the **National Park Service** and **DNC Parks & Resorts at Yosemite** present evening programs on the park's history and culture. Inquire about current programs upon check-in at your hotel or at the information booth outside the visitor center. Most programs are held in Yosemite Valley, but a few campgrounds in other areas of the park offer programs in the summer.

Spring through fall, the **Yosemite Theater** offers inexpensive theatrical and musical programs designed to supplement Park Service programs. They tend to repeat from year to year; favorites include a conversation with John Muir, a film on Yosemite's future, and singalongs.

A variety of **guided bus tours** are also available. You can buy tickets at tour desks at Yosemite Lodge, at the Ahwahnee, at Curry Village, or beside the Village Store in Yosemite Village. Advance reservations are suggested for all tours; make them in person or by phone (✆ **209/372-4386**). Always double-check at tour desks for updated departure schedules and prices. Most tours depart from Yosemite Lodge, the Ahwahnee, or Curry Village, and prices range from $25 for adults for a 2-hour tour, to $92 for adults for full-day trips with lunch. Children's rates are usually half that, and discounts are offered for seniors.

The 2-hour **Valley Floor Tour** is a great way to get acclimated to the park. It provides a good selection of photo ops, such as El Capitan, Tunnel View, and Half Dome. This ride is also available on nights when the moon is full or near full. It's an eerie but beautiful scene when moonlight illuminates the valley's granite walls and gives visitors a rare picture of Yosemite. Blankets and hot cocoa are provided. Dress warmly, though, because it can get mighty chilly after the sun goes down.

The **Glacier Point Tour** is a 4-hour scenic bus ride through the valley to Glacier Point. Tours also depart from Yosemite Valley to **Mariposa Grove.** The trip takes 6 hours and includes the Big Trees tram tour that winds through the grove and stops for lunch at Wawona (lunch not provided). You can combine the trip to Glacier Point and Mariposa Grove in an 8-hour bus ride.

4 Day Hikes

A nature-lover's paradise, Yosemite has some of the most beautiful scenery anywhere, and the best way to experience the park is to get out onto the trails.

IN & NEAR THE VALLEY

Base of Bridalveil Fall Bridalveil Fall measures 620 feet from top to bottom. In the spring, expect to get wet. This walk is wheelchair accessible with strong assistance. .5 mile RT. Easy. Access: Bridalveil Fall parking area, about 3 miles west of Yosemite Village (accessible by car or on foot). Follow trail markers.

Columbia Rock This hike mirrors the initial ascent of the waterfall trail but stops at Columbia Rock, 1,000 feet above the valley. You won't have a valley view, but the sights here are still impressive. The trail is also less likely to get an accumulation of snow, because it's on the sunny side of the valley. 2 miles RT. Moderate. Access: Trail head for Upper Yosemite Fall.

Four-mile Trail to Glacier Point This trail climbs 3,200 feet, but your efforts will be rewarded with terrific views of Yosemite Valley's north rim. Check on current trail conditions before setting out; it's usually closed in winter. The trail ends at Glacier Point. If you'd like to extend the hike, you can connect there to the Panorama Trail (see below). The combined round-trip distance is 14 miles. 9.6 miles RT. Strenuous. Access: Trail head 1¼ miles from Yosemite Village, at Four Mile parking area, post V-18. Or shuttle bus to Yosemite Lodge stop (no. 8); walk behind lodge over Swinging Bridge to Southeast Dr., and trail head is .25 mile west.

Half Dome This long, steep trip, which about 1,000 hikers do each summer day, climbs 4,900 feet. From Happy Isles, take the Mist Trail or the John Muir Trail past Vernal and Nevada falls, and up into Little Yosemite Valley. Leave the John Muir Trail for the Half Dome Trail. Hiking the final 600 feet up the back of Half Dome requires the use of cables, and a strong heart is helpful, too. Half Dome has a small level spot on top, at an elevation of 8,800 feet. It's possible to cut the length of the trip by camping in Little Yosemite Valley (you'll need a wilderness permit). 17 miles RT. Very strenuous. Access: Happy Isles (shuttle bus stop no. 16).

Lower Yosemite Fall Lower Yosemite Fall reaches 320 feet, but it packs the accumulated punch of the entire 2,425-foot waterfall, and from early spring through midsummer, you're likely to get wet. You can also take this trip from Yosemite Village by following the path from the Valley Visitor Center to the trail head. Add another half-mile (40 min.) each way. This walk is wheelchair accessible with assistance. 1 mile RT. Easy. Access: From shuttle bus stop no. 6, follow paved path from Yosemite Fall parking area to base of waterfall.

Mirror Lake This paved trail climbs about 60 feet along the west side of Tenaya Creek to Mirror Lake, where you'll see overhanging rock formations reflected in the lake's still surface. This trail connects with a delightful 3-mile loop around the lake. 2 miles RT. Easy. Access: Shuttle bus stop no. 17.

Mist Trail to Vernal Fall This hike begins on the famous 211-mile John Muir Trail to Mount Whitney in Sequoia National Park. From the Happy Isles Bridge, the trail climbs 400 feet to the Vernal Fall Bridge, which offers a good view of what lies ahead, as well as water and restrooms. From this point, you can either take a series of switchbacks along the side of the mountain and come out above the fall, or you can ascend the Mist Trail (our preference), which is a steep climb with 500 steps—it's wet, picturesque, and refreshing. The Mist Trail is so named because the spray from the fall drenches anyone who tackles this route, especially in spring. ***Be warned:*** It's slick and requires careful placement of your feet. Once you reach the top, you can relax on a series of smooth granite benches and soak in the cool, refreshing water before hiking back down. You can continue up 1.4 miles to Nevada Fall and leave the crowds behind for a round-trip of 5.8 miles. 3 miles RT. Moderate to strenuous. Access: From Happy Isles (shuttle bus stop no. 16), walk to Happy Isles Bridge. Cross bridge and follow signs to the trail.

Panorama Trail From Glacier Point, this trail drops 3,200 feet. At one of its prettiest points, it crosses Illilouette Fall about 1.5 miles from Glacier Point. The path continues along the Panorama Cliff and eventually winds up at Nevada Fall, where it's a straight descent to Yosemite Valley on the Mist or John Muir trail. You can hike this trail in conjunction with the Four-mile Trail, and it's also possible to take a bus to Glacier Point and hike only one-way. 8.5 miles one-way. Moderate to strenuous. Access: Glacier Point, at east end of the parking area.

Upper Yosemite Fall Climb 2,700 feet on this trail and you'll be rewarded with spectacular views from the ledge above the fall. This hike is not for the faint of heart. Take it slow, rest often, and absorb the scenery as you ascend higher and higher above the valley. One mile up, you'll reach Columbia Rock, which offers a good view. The rest of the trail dips and climbs, and you'll get a bit of mist from the fall above. The last quarter-mile is rocky and steep, with a series of tortuous, seemingly endless switchbacks that ascend through underbrush before opening at a clearing near the top of the fall, but beware—the view here can induce vertigo. After completing the trail, it's a worthwhile walk upstream to see the creek before it takes its half-mile tumble to the valley floor below. Hikers with the proper permits and equipment can stay here overnight. 7.2 miles RT. Strenuous. Access: Shuttle bus stop no. 7; trail head next to Camp 4 Walk-in Campground, behind Yosemite Lodge.

SOUTH OF THE VALLEY

Chilnualna Falls from Wawona This trek offers a satisfying glimpse of a stunning waterfall. One of the tallest outside Yosemite Valley, the fall cascades down two chutes. The one at the bottom is narrower and packs a real punch after a wet winter. A series of switchbacks leads to the top fall. 8.2 miles RT. Moderate. Access: From Wawona, take Chilnualna Rd., just north of the Merced River's south fork, until it dead-ends at "The Redwoods," a little more than 1¼ miles. This is the trail head.

Grizzly Giant This is the walking alternative to the Mariposa Grove tram tour described above. It's a nice stroll to see an impressive tree, and the hike climbs only 400 feet. 1.6 miles RT. Easy. Access: Sign near map dispenser at east end of Mariposa Grove parking lot.

Mariposa Grove The hike sounds long, but a one-way option in the summer uses the Wawona shuttle bus service for the return trip, cutting the distance almost in half. The trail climbs through a forest, then ascends the Wawona Dome and Wawona Basin, both of which provide excellent views. 12 miles RT. Moderate to strenuous. Access: Park at Wawona Store parking area and walk east .25 mile to Forest Dr. Trail head is on the right.

Sentinel Dome This hike offers broad views of Yosemite Valley. At the starting point, you'll be able to see Sentinel Dome on your left. The trail descends slightly and, at the first fork, bears right. It winds through manzanita and pine before beginning its ascent. It's a steep scramble to the top of Sentinel Dome, and you have to leave the trail on the north side to scramble up. The view from the top offers a 180-degree panorama of Yosemite Valley that includes a host of impressive and recognizable geologic landmarks. 2.2 miles RT. Moderate. Access: Glacier Point Rd. to Sentinel Dome parking lot, about 3 miles from Glacier Point.

Taft Point The walk to Taft Point crosses a broad meadow dotted in early summer by wildflowers. Near Taft Point, note the deep chasms, known as "fissures," in the rock. Some of the cracks are 40 feet long and 20 feet wide at the top and 100 feet deep. The wall of Yosemite actually overhangs the narrow ravine below, and if you carefully peer over the cliff, you'll notice that your head seems to be on the opposite side of a stream running far beneath you. A small pipe railing farther on marks the 6-by-3-foot Taft Point overlook hanging over Yosemite Valley. 2.2 miles RT. Moderate. Access: Follow directions to Sentinel Dome (above). At fork, head left.

Wawona Meadow Loop This relaxing stroll encircles Wawona Meadow, curving around at its east end and heading back toward the road. It crosses the highway and winds through forest until it returns to the Wawona Hotel. Some cars still use this road, so watch out. This trail is also open to pets. 3.5 miles RT. Easy. Access: Dirt road through golf course, and 50-yd. walk to the trail.

NORTH OF THE VALLEY

Some of the hikes discussed below can be either long day hikes or overnight backpacking trips; see "Overnight Hikes," below.

Cathedral Lakes These lakes are set in granite bowls cut by glaciers, and the views of the peaks and domes around both Lower and Upper Cathedral lakes are worth the hike alone. Lower Cathedral Lake is next to Cathedral Peak and is a good place to stop for a snack before heading up the hill to enjoy the upper lake. 8 miles RT. Moderate. Access: Trail head off Tioga Rd., at west end of Tuolumne Meadows, west of Budd Creek.

Cloud's Rest This hike descends through a wooded area, heading toward Sunrise Lake. Ascend out of Tenaya Canyon and bear right at the junction (watch for the signposts); the vistas will appear almost at once. The sight line to your destination will be clear—a good thing, since the trail is sketchy at this point. The last stretch to the top is a little spooky, with sheer drops on each side, but your perseverance will be amply rewarded with spectacular views of the park's granite domes. Overnight stays (with a permit) offer the added incentive of beautiful sunrises. 14 miles RT. Strenuous. Access: Tioga Rd. to Tenaya Lake. Trail leaves from parking area on east side of road near southwest end of lake.

Dog Lake This easy climb through forests offers great views of Mount Dana. Dog Lake is warm, shallow, and great for swimming. 2.8 miles RT. Easy. Access: Tioga Rd. to access road for Tuolumne Lodge. Pass ranger station and leave your vehicle at a parking lot on the left. Walk north (back toward the hwy.), up an embankment, and recross Calif. 120 to find Dog Lake Trail.

Elizabeth Lake This popular day hike attracts a slew of people, which can be a bummer, but it's nonetheless magnificent for its beauty; Elizabeth Lake glistens like ice. Don't forget your camera and some extra film—the entire route is one long Kodak moment. 4.8 miles RT. Moderate. Access: Tioga Rd. to group camping area of Tuolumne Meadows Campground, where trail begins.

Gaylor Lakes This trail begins with a climb, then descends to the alpine lakes. It's a particularly pretty hike in summer, when wildflowers dot the mountainsides. 2 miles RT. Moderate. Access: Tioga Rd. to Tioga Pass. Trail head is on northwest side of the road.

Glen Aulin This hike takes you to an impressive waterfall with grand views along the way. Start by heading across a flat meadow toward Soda Springs and Glen Aulin. The trail is well marked, and signs along the way describe the area's history. This was once the old Tioga Road, built in 1883 to serve the Great Sierra Mine at Tioga Pass. The hike offers a view of the landmarks of Tuolumne Meadows. Behind you, Lembert Dome rises almost 900 feet above the meadow. About .4 mile from the trail head, the road forks; head right up a grassy slope. In less than 500 feet is a trail that leaves the road on the right and a steel sign that says GLEN AULIN IS 4.7 MILES AHEAD. Along the way you'll pass Fairview Dome, Cathedral Peak, and Unicorn Peak. The crashing noise you'll hear in early to midsummer is Tuolumne Falls, a cascade of water that drops first 12 feet, then 40 feet down a series of ledges. There's a hikers' camp nearby if you want to spend the night. 11 miles RT. Strenuous. Access: Tioga Rd. toward Tuolumne Meadows, about 1 mile east of Tuolumne Meadows Visitor Center and just a few yd. east of the bridge over Tuolumne River. Follow marked turnoff and take the paved road on your left. The trail head begins about .3 mile ahead, at a road that turns right and heads up a hill toward the stables.

Lembert Dome This hike offers a bird's-eye view of Tuolumne Meadows—and it's a great vista. A well-marked trail leads you to the top, and from there you'll see the peaks that encircle the valley and get good views of this lovely meadow. It's a great place to watch sunrises and sunsets. 2.8 miles RT. Moderate. Access: Trail head at parking lot north of Tioga Rd. in Tuolumne Meadows, at road marker T-32. Follow nature trail that starts here and take off at marker no. 2.

Lyell Canyon This section of the John Muir Trail follows the Lyell Fork of the Tuolumne River up an idyllic green canyon to the rocky Donohue Pass, nearly 12 miles from the trail head and over 2,000 feet above it. While this is a good starting point for a backcountry expedition, a shorter hike up Lyell Canyon—say, 3 miles each way—is perfect for a picnic-centered day hike for most any group of hikers. Backpackers can continue into the Ansel Adams Wilderness Area; day hikers can loop back through the Vogelsang area. Up to 11.9 miles one-way. Easy to strenuous. The trail head is at the Dog Lake parking lot near Tuolumne Meadows Lodge.

May Lake Winding through forests and granite, this picturesque hike offers ample opportunities to fish, but swimming is not allowed. May Lake is in the center of Yosemite National Park and is a good jumping-off point for other high-country hikes. The peaks surrounding the lake include 10,855-foot Mount Hoffman, which rises behind the lake. A hikers' camp lies on the south side of the lake. 2.5 miles RT. Easy. Access: Tioga Rd. east past White Wolf; turn off at road marker T-21 and drive 2 miles to May Lake parking area.

Mono Pass You'll pass some historical cabin sites, then hike down to Walker Lake, and return by the same route. The hike loops into the Inyo National Forest and the Ansel Adams Wilderness, and it climbs to an elevation of 10,600 feet. Hikers enjoy a stupendous view of Mono Lake from the top of the trail. 8 miles RT. Moderate to strenuous. Access: Trail head on south side of Tioga Rd. as you enter the park from Lee Vining. Drive about 1½ miles from park entrance to Dana Meadows, where trail begins on an abandoned road and up alongside Parker Creek Pass.

Mount Dana This climb is an in-your-face reminder that Mount Dana is Yosemite's second-highest peak. The mountain rises 13,053 feet, and the trail gains a whopping 3,100 feet in 3 miles. The views at the top are wonderful, and once you catch your breath, you can again stand upright. You can see Mono Lake from the summit. In summer, the wildflowers add to this hike's beauty. 5.8 miles RT. Very strenuous. Access: Trail head on southeast side of Tioga Rd./Calif. 120 at Tioga Pass.

North Dome This hike offers amazing views of Yosemite Valley. Walk south down the abandoned road toward the Porcupine Creek Campground. A mile past the campground, the trail hits a junction with the Tenaya Creek and Tuolumne Meadows Trail. Pass a junction toward Yosemite Falls and head uphill toward North Dome. The ascent is treacherous because of loose gravel, but from the top you can catch an all-encompassing view of Yosemite Valley, second only to the view from Half Dome. 8.8 miles RT. Moderate. Access: Tioga Rd. east to Porcupine Flat Campground, past White Wolf. About 1 mile past campground is a sign for Porcupine Creek, at a closed road. Park in designated area.

Polly Dome Lake This hike is easily the road least traveled. The trip to Polly Dome Lake is a breeze, and you'll find nary another traveler in sight. Several lakes beneath Polly Dome can accommodate camping. The trail fades in and out, so watch for markers. It crosses a rocky area en route, then skirts southeast at a pond just after the rocky section. Polly Dome Lake is at the base of—you guessed it—Polly Dome, a visual aid to help hikers stay the course. 12.5 miles RT. Easy to moderate. Access: Tioga Rd. past White Wolf to Tenaya Lake. Drive about ½ mile to picnic area midway along lake. Trail head is across road from picnic area.

Soda Springs This trail crosses Tuolumne Meadows and then the Tuolumne River on a wooden bridge. It's peaceful and beautiful, with the sound of the river gurgling along as it winds slowly through the wide expanse of Tuolumne Meadows. The trail leads to a carbonated spring where you can taste the water, although it gets mixed reviews. For years, the spring was administered and owned by the Sierra Club, which operates the nearby Parsons Lodge, now an activity center. Also nearby is the historical McCauley Cabin, which is used for employee housing in the summer. 1.5 miles RT. Easy. Access: Trail head at crosswalk just east of Tuolumne Meadows Visitor Center. Or from parking lot north of Tioga Rd. at road marker T-32; follow gravel road around a locked gate.

Sunrise Lakes This hike leads through quiet wooded glades while affording occasional glimpses of distant vistas. Look for a sign that says SUNRISE, then follow the level road to Tenaya Creek, cross the creek, and follow the trail to the right. The hike parallels Tenaya Creek for about .25 mile, then moves away through a wooded area and climbs gently up a rocky rise. After a while, the trail descends quickly to the outlet of Mildred Lake. There you'll be able to see Mount Hoffmann, Tuolumne Peak, and Tenaya Canyon. At the halfway mark, the trail passes through a hemlock grove, then comes to a junction. Head left. (The trail on the right goes toward Cloud's Rest.) About .25 mile from the junction, you'll reach Lower Sunrise Lake, tucked into the slope of Sunrise Mountain. The trail climbs past Middle Sunrise Lake and continues upward along a cascading creek coming from Upper Sunrise Lake. The trail follows the lake's shore and opens in less than .5 mile onto a wide, bare sandy pass. It's all downhill from here. Before you is the snowcapped Clark Range. The trail begins its descent, sharply switching back and forth in some places. A backpackers' camp lies a short distance above Upper Sunrise Lake. 7 miles RT. Moderate to strenuous. Access: Tioga Rd. to Tenaya Lake. Trail begins in parking area on east side of road near southwest end of lake.

Tioga Lake to Dana Lake This is a less crowded alternative to the above hike to Mount Dana; it doesn't top the mountain, although that option is available for experienced hikers on the Mount Dana Trail. The trail is not maintained, although it is fairly visible. This area is easily damaged, so be sure to tread lightly. Mount Dana looms large from the lake's shore. 4.6 miles RT. Moderate to strenuous. Access: Calif. 120 to Tioga Lake. Trail head is on west side of lake, about 1 mile east of the pass.

Vogelsang This hike climbs to a high meadow offering spectacular views. The trail goes south through the woods to a footbridge over the Dana Fork. Cross the bridge and follow the John Muir Trail upstream. Head right at the next fork. The trail crosses the Lyell Fork on a footbridge. Take the left fork a couple hundred feet ahead. Continue onward, and just before you cross the bridge at Rafferty Creek, you'll reach another junction. Veer right and prepare for switchbacks up a rocky slope. The trail climbs steeply for about .25 mile, then levels off as it darts toward and away from Rafferty Creek for the next 4 miles. The trail ascends to Tuolumne Pass, crossing many small creeks and tributaries en route. Two small tarns mark the pass. One drains south and the other north. Just south of the tarns, the trail splits. Veer left. (The right fork offers a 2-mile round-trip jaunt to Boothe Lake.) You'll climb to a meadow with great views, at 10,180 feet. 14 miles RT. Moderate to strenuous. Access: Tioga Rd. to Tuolumne Meadows; watch for signposted trail head for John Muir Trail and Lyell Fork.

5 Overnight Hikes

Of the more than four million people who visit Yosemite each year, 95% never leave the valley, but the brave 5% who do are well rewarded. A wild, lonelier Yosemite awaits just a few miles from the crowds. You'll find some of the most grandiose landscapes in the Sierra, as well as excellent opportunities for backpacking. Check with park rangers for tips on where to go and how to prepare for your backpacking trip.

All overnight backpacking stays require a **wilderness permit,** available by phone, by mail, by fax, or in the park. Permits can be reserved 2 days to 4 months in advance and cost $5 plus $5 each individual on the permit. Call ✆ **209/372-0740** or write to Wilderness Permits, P.O. Box 545, Yosemite National Park, CA 95389. You can download a reservation form at **www.nps.gov/yose/planyourvisit/wildpermits.htm**.

If planning isn't your style, first-come, first-served permits are available up to 24 hours before your trip. Permit stations are at the Yosemite Valley Visitor Center and Wawona Information Station year-round, and at Big Oak Flat Information Station in Tuolumne Meadows in summer. Permits for the popular trails, such as those leading to Half Dome, Little Yosemite Valley, and Cloud's Rest, go quickly. Call ✆ **209/372-0200** for permit station locations and hours.

6 Other Sports & Activities

About the only thing you can't do in Yosemite is surf. In addition to sightseeing, the park is a great place to bike, ski, rock-climb, fish, and even golf.

BICYCLING Twelve miles of designated bike trails cross the eastern end of Yosemite Valley, which is the best place to ride because roads and shuttle bus routes are usually crowded and dangerous for bicyclists. Children under 18 are required by law to wear helmets. Single-speed bikes are for rent by the hour ($10) or the day ($26) at Curry Village (✆ **209/372-8319**) in summer only, and at Yosemite Lodge (✆ **209/372-1208**) year-round. Bike rentals include helmets for all ages.

CROSS-COUNTRY SKIING The park has more than 350 miles of skiable trails and roads, including 25 miles of machine-groomed track and 90 miles of marked trails in the Badger Pass area. Equipment rentals, lessons, and day and overnight ski tours are available from **Badger Pass Cross-Country Center and Ski School** (✆ **209/372-8444;** www.yosemitepark.com).

FISHING Several species of trout can be found in Yosemite's streams. California fishing licenses are required for those 16 and older; information is available from the **California State Department of Fish and Game** (✆ **559/243-4005;** www.dfg.ca.gov). **Village Sport Shop** in Yosemite Valley has fishing gear and sells licenses. There are also special fishing regulations in Yosemite Valley; get information at the visitor centers.

GOLF The park has one golf course, and several others are nearby. **Wawona** (✆ **209/375-6572**) is a 9-hole, par-35 course that alternates between meadows and fairways. Greens fees are $36 to $42 for 18 holes, cart included.

HORSEBACK RIDING Several companies offer guided horseback rides in and just outside the national park, with rates starting at about $60 for 2 hours, $80 for a half-day, and $120 for a full day. **Yosemite Stables** (✆ **209/372-8348**) offers rides from Yosemite Valley, Tuolumne Meadows, and Wawona, and leads multiday pack trips into the backcountry (call for details). **Yosemite Trails Pack Station** (✆ **559/683-7611;** www.yosemitetrails.com) offers rides south of Wawona, and **Minarets Pack Station** (✆ **559/868-3405;** www.highsierrapackers.org) leads day trips to Yosemite and Ansel Adams Wilderness.

ICE SKATING The outdoor ice rink at Curry Village, with great views of Half Dome and Glacier Point, is open from early November to March, weather permitting. Admission is $8 for adults, $6 for children; skate rental costs $3. Call ✆ **209/372-8319** for current hours.

RAFTING A raft-rental shop is located at Curry Village (✆ **209/372-4386**). Daily fees are $26 for adults, $16 for children under 13. Fees include a raft, paddles, mandatory life preservers, and transportation from Sentinel Beach to Curry Village. Swift currents and cold water can be deadly. Talk with rangers and shop people before venturing out to be sure you're planning a trip that's within your abilities.

ROCK CLIMBING Yosemite is considered one of the world's premier playgrounds for experienced rock climbers and wannabes. The **Yosemite Mountaineering School** (✆ **209/372-8344;** www.yosemiteountaineering.com) provides instruction for beginning, intermediate, and advanced climbers in the valley and Tuolumne Meadows from April through October. Classes last anywhere from a day to a week, and private lessons are available. Rates vary according to the class or program. All equipment is provided.

Campground	Elev. (ft.)	Total Sites	RV Hookups	Dump Station	Toilets
Inside Yosemite National Park					
Bridalveil Creek	7,200	110	0	No	Yes
Camp 4	4,000	35	0	No	Yes
Crane Flat	6,191	166	0	No	Yes
Hodgdon Meadow	4,872	105	0	No	Yes
Lower Pines	4,000	60	0	Nearby	Yes
North Pines	4,000	81	0	Nearby	Yes
Porcupine Flat	8,100	52	0	No	Yes
Tamarack Flat	6,315	52	0	No	Yes
Tuolumne Meadows	8,600	304	0	Nearby	Yes
Upper Pines	4,000	238	0	Yes	Yes
Wawona	4,000	93	0	Nearby	Yes
White Wolf	8,000	74	0	No	Yes
Yosemite Creek	7,659	75	0	No	Yes
Outside the Park					
Big Bend	7,800	17	0	No	Yes
Ellery Lake	9,500	21	0	No	Yes
Jerseydale	4,000	8	0	No	Yes
Junction	9,600	13	0	No	Yes
Lost Claim	3,100	10	0	No	Yes
Lumsden	1,500	10	0	No	Yes
Lumsden Bridge	1,500	9	0	No	Yes
The Pines	3,200	11	0	No	Yes
Saddlebag Lake	10,000	20	0	No	Yes
South Fork	1,500	8	0	No	Yes
Summerdale	5,000	29	0	No	Yes
Summit	5,800	6	0	No	Yes
Sweetwater	3,000	12	0	No	Yes
Tioga Lake	9,700	13	0	No	Yes
Yosemite–Mariposa KOA	2,400	89	51	Yes	Yes

SKIING Yosemite's **Badger Pass Ski Area** (© **209/372-8430;** www.yosemitepark.com) is usually open from Thanksgiving through Easter, weather permitting. The small resort 22 miles from Yosemite Valley was established in 1935. There are 10 runs, rated 35% beginner, 50% intermediate, and 15% advanced, with a vertical drop of 800 feet from its highest point of 8,000 feet. There are five lifts—one triple chair, three double chairs, and a cable tow. Full-day adult lift tickets cost $35 to $42, and full-day lift tickets for kids 7 to 12 are $16 to $20; half-day tickets are $30 to $33 and $16, respectively.

The ski area has several casual restaurants, a ski shop, ski repairs, a day lodge, and lockers. There's also an excellent ski school, thanks to "Ski Ambassador" Nic Fiore, a Yosemite ski legend who arrived in the park in 1947 to ski for a season and never left. Fiore became director of the ski school in 1956, and park officials credit Fiore with making Badger Pass what it is today—a family-oriented ski area where generations have come to ski.

7 Camping

Important note: When camping in this area, proper food storage is *required* for the sake of the black bears in the parks, as well as for your safety. See local bulletin boards for instructions.

INSIDE THE PARK

First, the bad news: Yosemite Valley lost half of its roughly 800 campsites during a flood in early 1997. The lost campsites will eventually be replaced

Drinking Water	Showers	Fire Pits/ Grills	Laundry	Public Phone	Reservations	Fees	Open
Yes	No	Yes	No	Yes	No	$14	July to early Sept
Yes	Nearby	Yes	Nearby	Yes	No	$5	Year-round
Yes	No	Yes	No	Yes	Yes	$20	June–Sept
Yes	No	Yes	No	Yes	May–Sept	$20	Year-round
Yes	Nearby	Yes	Nearby	Yes	Yes	$20	Mar–Oct
Yes	Nearby	Yes	Nearby	Yes	Yes	$20	Apr–Sept
No	No	Yes	No	Yes	No	$10	June–Sept
No	No	Yes	No	Yes	No	$10	June to early Sept
Yes	Nearby	Yes	No	Yes	Yes	$20	July–Sept
Yes	Nearby	Yes	Nearby	Yes	Yes	$20	Year-round
Yes	No	Yes	No	Yes	May–Sept	$20	Year-round
Yes	No	Yes	No	Yes	No	$14	July to early Sept
No	No	Yes	No	Yes	No	$10	July–Sept (tent only)
Yes	No	Yes	No	No	No	$19	Late Apr to mid-Oct
Yes	No	Yes	No	No	No	$19	June to mid-Oct
Yes	No	Yes	No	No	No	Free	May–Nov
No	No	Yes	No	No	No	$14	June–Oct
Yes	No	Yes	No	No	No	$14–$28	May to Labor Day
No	No	Yes	No	No	No	Free	Year-round
No	No	Yes	No	No	No	Free	Mid-Apr to Oct
Yes	No	Yes	No	No	No	$14	Year-round
Yes	No	Yes	No	No	No	$17	June to mid-Oct
No	No	Yes	No	No	No	Free	Mid-Apr to Oct
Yes	No	Yes	No	No	Yes	$19	June–Nov
No	No	Yes	No	No	No	Free	June–Oct
Yes	No	Yes	No	No	No	$17	Apr–Oct
Yes	No	Yes	No	No	No	$19	June to mid-Oct
Yes	Yes	Yes	Yes	Yes	Recommended	$40–$50	Mar to mid-Oct

elsewhere in the park, but no one's predicting when. Campsite reservations are a really good idea. Reservations are accepted in 1-month blocks beginning on the 15th of each month and can be made up to 5 months in advance. Make your reservations (© **877/444-6777;** www.recreation.gov) as soon as you can, especially for sites in the valley. Unless noted otherwise, pets are accepted in the following campgrounds. Additional campground information is available by phone (© **209/372-0200**).

Wilderness permits are required for all overnight backpacking trips in the park (see "Overnight Hikes," above), and no wilderness camping is allowed in Yosemite Valley.

The busiest campgrounds in the park are in Yosemite Valley. All four of the following have flush toilets and access to the showers nearby at Curry Village ($2). Upper, Lower, and North Pines campgrounds require reservations. **Upper Pines** is pretty and shady, but you won't find peace and quiet here in the summer. Parking is available, or take the shuttle bus to stop no. 15 or 19. **Lower Pines Campground** is wide open, with lots of shade but limited privacy. Still, it's a nice place with clean bathrooms, and sits just south of a picturesque meadow. Parking is available, or take the shuttle bus to stop no. 19. **North Pines,** which we particularly like, is beautifully situated beneath a grove of pine trees that offer little privacy but a lot of shade. It's near the river, roughly a mile from Mirror Lake. Parking is available, or take the shuttle bus to stop no. 18. **Camp 4** (also called Sunnyside Walk-In) has tent sites only. It's a small campground that's become a magnet for hikers and climbers taking off or just returning from trips. It's behind Yosemite Lodge and the trail head for Yosemite Fall, and near rocks frequently used by novice rock climbers. Pets are not permitted. Parking is available about 50 yards away, or take the shuttle bus to stop no. 7.

Elsewhere in the park, **Bridalveil Creek Campground** at Glacier Point has flush toilets. Near beautiful Glacier Point, this campground is set off from the valley crowds but a moderate drive from the valley sights. It's along Bridalveil Creek, which flows to Bridalveil Fall, a beauty of a waterfall, especially after a snowy winter or wet spring. The campground can accommodate some pack animals; call park offices for information. Take Wawona Road (from either direction) to Glacier Point Road. The campground is about 8 miles down the road.

Several campgrounds are near Big Oak Flat Entrance, roughly 20 to 25 miles from Yosemite Valley. About 1 mile inside the entrance is **Hodgdon Meadow,** which has flush toilets and RV and tent sites, including some walk-in sites. It's open all year and requires reservations from May through September. This campground is along North Crane Creek, near the Tuolumne River's south fork. The Big Trees are 3 miles southeast. About 8 miles farther, not far from the Tioga Road turnoff, is **Crane Flat,** a large but pleasant campground with flush toilets. It's near the Big Trees and away from valley crowds. **Tamarack Flat Campground** is a bit off the beaten path and therefore more secluded and less busy than most. Equidistant from Yosemite Valley and Tuolumne Meadows, it has pit toilets and does not allow pets. Head east on Tioga Road about 3 miles, and turn right onto the access road; the campground is another 3 miles down the road.

Campgrounds in the White Wolf area include **Porcupine Flat,** which has shade, shrubs, and trees, although facilities are pretty much limited to pit toilets. It's near Yosemite Creek; you may find a spot here if you're in a pinch. Pets are not permitted. It's along Tioga Road, 16 miles west of Tuolumne Meadows and 38 miles east of Yosemite Valley. The **White Wolf Campground,** secluded in a forest, is a delightful campground where you might want to spend several days. It has flush toilets and offers easy access to nearby hiking, with trails that lead to several lakes, including Grant Lake and Lukens Lake. There's a dirt road to Harden Lake and, beyond that, a trail to Smith Peak, which overlooks the Hetch Hetchy Reservoir. On the down side, mosquitoes make their presence felt here in summer. From Big Oak Flat Road, head east on Tioga Road for 15 miles to White Wolf Road and turn left. The road dead-ends at the campground.

Among Yosemite's other campgrounds are **Tuolumne Meadows,** the biggest campground in the park and, amazingly, often the least crowded. Its location in the high country makes this a good spot from which to head off with a backpack. It's also near the Tuolumne River, making it a good choice for anglers. In addition to its standard RV and tent sites, the campground has 25 walk-in spaces for backpackers and 8 group sites that can accommodate up to 30 people each. There are flush toilets, and showers nearby at Tuolumne Lodge (for a fee). From Big Oak Flat Road, drive about 45 miles east on Tioga Road.

Wawona Campground, which requires reservations from May through September and is first come, first served the rest of the year, has flush toilets and can accommodate pack animals; call park offices for information. There's not much seclusion here, but the location, shaded beneath towering trees, is beautiful. The campground is near the Mariposa Grove of Big Trees and close to the Merced River, which offers some of the better fishing in the park. It's about 1 mile north of Wawona. The **Yosemite Creek Campground,** along Yosemite Creek, has pit toilets and little else, but it may have sites available when the park's other campgrounds are full. From Big Oak Flat Road, head east on Tioga Road about 30 miles, turn right on the access road, and go another 5 miles.

OUTSIDE THE PARK

Yosemite sits amid national forests that offer comparable public campgrounds to the ones in the park, although often less developed and less crowded. There are also private campgrounds, which usually provide level sites, complete RV hookups, hot showers, coin-operated laundries, convenience stores, and other amenities.

ALONG CALIF. 120

The following campgrounds, along Calif. 120 west of the park, are all in the Stanislaus National Forest's **Groveland Ranger District,** 24545 Calif. 120, Groveland, CA 95321 (✆ **209/962-7825;** www.fs.fed.us/r5/stanislaus/groveland). They all have vault toilets and can accommodate rigs up to 22 feet long.

Lumsden Campground is along the Tuolumne River, on a scenic stretch between the Hetch Hetchy and Don Pedro reservoirs. It offers fishing in a primitive setting, and it can get unbelievably hot in the summer. From Groveland, take Calif. 120 about 9 miles east to Ferretti Road, turn left and drive about 1 mile to Lumsden Road, where you turn right and travel about 5 miles on a steep, narrow dirt road to the campground. **Lumsden Bridge Campground** is about 1½ miles past Lumsden Campground (on Lumsden Rd.). Set in a pine and oak forest along the Tuolumne River, it is a favorite of rafters because it's close to some of the Tuolumne River's best (and most scenic) stretches of white water. The **South Fork Campground,** also along Lumsden Road, near Lumsden and Lumsden Bridge campgrounds, is a pretty spot near the Tuolumne River. Trailers and vehicles with low ground clearance are not recommended for any of the above three campgrounds.

The **Pines Campground** is about 9 miles east of Groveland on Calif. 120, and although it's in a mixed conifer forest, it can get hot in the summer. Drinking water is available only in the summer. **Lost Claim Campground,** about 12 miles east of Groveland by way of Calif. 120, is easily accessible by road. There are some trees, and the river is nearby. Drinking water is supplied by a hand pump. Trailers are not recommended. Pretty **Sweetwater Campground,** 15 miles east of Groveland on Calif. 120, is in a mixed conifer forest with shady sites, but it also gets hot in summer.

ALONG CALIF. 140

Jerseydale Campground, in the Sierra National Forest, 1600 Tollhouse Rd., Clovis, CA 93611-0532 (✆ **559/297-0706;** www.fs.fed.us/r5/sierra), is a great base for exploring the area. It also allows you to stay away from the crowds. There are vault toilets and hiking trails, and you can get to the Merced River from a nearby trail head. From Mariposa, drive 12 miles northwest on Calif. 49 to Jerseydale Road, which leads to the campground and adjacent Jerseydale Ranger Station.

A good choice for those who want all the amenities of a top-notch commercial campground is the **Yosemite–Mariposa KOA,** 7 miles northeast of Mariposa at 6323 Calif. 140 (P.O. Box 545), Midpines, CA 95345 (✆ **800/562-9391** for reservations or 209/966-2201; www.koa.com). Located 23 miles from the park entrance, this KOA has trees shading many of the sites, a catch-and-release fishing pond, pedal boats in the summer, a pool, and a playground. There's also a convenience store and propane sales. A favorite of kids is the train caboose containing video games. There are also a dozen camping cabins (you share the bathhouse with campers), with rates of $68 to $155.

ALONG CALIF. 41

Two Sierra National Forest campgrounds (see contact information under Jerseydale Campground, above) offer pleasant camping, with vault toilets, in a woodsy atmosphere along Calif. 41, southwest of Yosemite. **Summerdale Campground** is about a mile north of Fish Camp on Calif. 41, on the south fork of the Merced River; call ahead (✆ **877/444-6777;** www.recreation.gov), as it's often full for the weekend by noon Friday. **Summit Campground,** in the Chowchilla Mountains, about 5 miles west of Fish Camp on a Forest Service Road, is a little campground that's often overlooked.

ALONG CALIF. 120

The Inyo National Forest operates a number of small, attractive campgrounds along Calif. 120 east of the national park. These include **Big Bend Campground,** with flush toilets, 7 miles west of Lee Vining on Calif. 120. Located on the eastern Sierra along Lee Vining Creek, this campground is sparse but breathtaking. **Ellery Lake Campground,** which also has flush toilets, is at scenic Ellery Lake, about 9 miles west of Lee Vining on Calif. 120. **Junction Campground** is near Ellery and Tioga lakes, with easy access to the Tioga Tarns Nature Trail. It has vault toilets and is 10 miles west of Lee Vining along Calif. 120.

The highest (in elevation) drive-in campground in the state, at 10,000 feet, beautiful **Saddlebag Lake Campground** is along Saddlebag Lake and near Lee Vining Creek. It's a good place to stay a while, or you can head out from here into the wilderness with a backpack. It has flush toilets. From Lee Vining, drive 10 miles west on Calif. 120, then turn north on Saddlebag Lake Road and go about 2 miles to the campground. Another high-elevation campground, **Tioga Lake Campground,** is a pretty place to camp and has flush toilets. From Lee Vining, drive 10 miles west on Calif. 120.

Information on these U.S. Forest Service campgrounds is available from the **Mono Basin Scenic Area Visitor Center,** on the west shore of Mono Lake (P.O. Box 429), Lee Vining, CA 93541; ✆ **760/647-3044**), and the **Inyo National Forest,** 351 Pacu Lane, Ste. 200, Bishop, CA 93514 (✆ **760/873-2400;** www.fs.fed.us/r5/inyo).

8 Where to Stay

Choices abound in and near Yosemite National Park. Yosemite Valley is the hub for lodging, dining, and other services in the park. It is usually quite crowded in summer, but it offers the best location, close to Yosemite's main attractions and with easy access to the park's shuttle bus system. A narrower scope of choices is available outside the valley, but still in the park, during the summer at Wawona, Tuolumne Meadows, White Wolf, and other areas. In addition, there are some delightful (and generally less expensive) accommodations outside the park in the gateway communities of El Portal, Mariposa, Oakhurst, and Groveland.

INSIDE THE PARK

Most lodging in the park is under the management of **DNC Parks & Resorts at Yosemite** (✆ **801/559-5000;** TTY 559/252-2846; www.yosemitepark.com). Rooms can be reserved up to 366 days in advance by phone, online, and by mail (Yosemite

Reservations, 6771 N. Palm Ave. Fresno, CA 93704).

More than 130 private homes in the park can be rented through the **Redwoods in Yosemite,** P.O. Box 2085, Wawona Station, Yosemite National Park, CA 95389 (✆ **888/225-6666;** www.redwoodsinyosemite.com). Offerings range from cabins to vacation homes, and all are furnished and equipped with linens, cookware, and dishes. Rates range from $180 a night for a one-bedroom cabin to $500 a night or more for a five-bedroom spread; there are usually 3-night minimum stays in summer, and 2-night minimums the rest of the year.

The Ahwahnee This hotel's accommodations are fit for a king or queen, and it has hosted both. Queen Elizabeth II slept here, as have presidents, star athletes, actors, artists and other celebrities. It's tough to top the Ahwahnee, a six-story concrete and stone structure that offers beautiful views from nearly every window. The hotel has a number of common rooms on the ground floor. There are three fireplaces large enough to stand in, and the rooms are furnished with overstuffed sofas and chairs, perfect for reading or playing games after a day of hiking. The Sunroom Suite is a bright pair of rooms in lime and yellow, with comfy lounges and floor-to-ceiling French windows that open out onto the valley. The Library Room's rich decor includes a fireplace and walls of books. Regular rooms offer a choice of two doubles or one king-size bed, with a couch, plush towels, and snuggly comforters.

Yosemite Valley. ✆ **801/559-5000.** www.yosemitepark.com. 123 units. A/C, TEL. $408 guest rooms and cottages; $562–$1,053 2-room suites; from $1,127 3-room suites. AE, DC, DISC, MC, V. Parking available, or take the shuttle bus (stop no. 3).

Curry Village Curry Village is best known as a mass of more than 300 white canvas tents tightly packed together on the valley's south slope. It was founded in 1899 as a cheap lodging option for valley visitors at a mere $2 a day, but guests can kiss those $2 days goodbye. Still, it's an economical place to crash and gives you something of the feeling of a camping vacation without the hassle of bringing your own tent. Since these tents are basically canvas affairs, and this is bear country, you'll need to lock up all foodstuffs and anything that bears might think is food in bear-proof lockers which may be a healthy walk from your tent-cabin. Curry Village also has over 50 attractive wood cabins with private bathrooms; 14 wood cabins that, like the tent-cabins, share a large bathhouse; and 18 motel rooms. Canvas tents have wood floors, sleep two to four people, and are equipped with beds, bedding, dressers, and electrical outlets; some have propane heaters. The wood cabins are much more substantial and comfortable.

Yosemite Valley. ✆ **801/559-5000.** www.yosemitepark.com. 500 units. $94 double tent-cabin; $102 double cabin without bathroom; $140 double cabin with bathroom; $179 double motel room. AE, DC, DISC, MC, V. Parking is available, or take the shuttle bus (stop no. 13A, 13B, 14, or 20).

Housekeeping Camp A fun, funky place to spend the night, this is the closest thing to camping without pitching a tent. The sites are fence-enclosed, canvas-roofed cinder-block cabins built on concrete slabs, each with a table, cupboard, electrical outlets, shelves, a mirror, and lights. The sleeping areas have two single-size bunks and a double bed. There is a grocery store on premises.

Yosemite Valley. ✆ **801/559-5000.** www.yosemitepark.com. 266 units, all with shared bathrooms and shower house. $79 per site (up to 4 people; $5 per extra person). AE, DC, DISC, MC, V. Closed Nov–Mar.

Tuolumne Meadows Lodge This is a group of canvas tent cabins. Like those at White Wolf Lodge (see below), they have tables and wood-burning stoves; they sleep up to four. This is prime hiking territory, with numerous trail heads, and the lodge is home base for wilderness trekkers and backcountry campers. There's a restaurant (see "Where to Dine"), tour desk, general store, gas station, mountaineering store, post office, and stables.

Tioga Rd., Tuolumne Meadows, Yosemite National Park. ✆ **801/559-5000.** www.yosemitepark.com. 69 canvas tent cabins, all with shared bathroom and shower house. $93 double; additional $10 per adult or $6 per child. AE, DC, DISC, MC, V. Parking available in an adjacent lot. Closed winter. From Yosemite Valley, take Big Oak Flat and Tioga rds. north and east 60 miles (about 1½ hr.) toward Tioga Pass.

Wawona Hotel This is a classic Victorian-style hotel made up of six stately white buildings set near towering trees in a green clearing. Don't be surprised if a horse and buggy round the driveway by the fishpond—it's that kind of place, with wide porches, a nearby 9-hole golf course, and vines cascading from one veranda to the next. The entire place was designated a National Historic Landmark in 1987. The 1876 Clark Cottage is the oldest building, and the main hotel was built in 1879. Rooms are comfortable and quaint, with a choice of a double and a twin, a king, or one double bed (most of the one-double units share bathrooms). All rooms open onto wide porches and overlook green lawns. Clark Cottage is the most intimate. The main hotel has the widest porches and plenty of Adirondack chairs, and at night a pianist plays in the downstairs sunroom. Check out the whistling maintenance man who hits every high note in "The Star-Spangled Banner" while the American flag is hoisted each morning (leaving many bystanders speechless as more than a few Wawona employees chime in to complete the whistling orchestra).

An adjacent dining room serves great food and an awesome Sunday brunch (see "Where to Dine").

There is also a lounge, large outdoor pool, outdoor tennis court, golf course, grocery store, gas station, and stable.

Wawona Rd., Wawona, Yosemite National Park. ✆ **801/559-5000.** www.yosemitepark.com. 104 units, 54 with shared bathroom. $145 double with shared bathroom; $217 double with private bathroom. Additional charge for extra adults $13–$21. AE, DC, DISC, MC, V. From Yosemite Valley, take Wawona Rd. south 27 miles toward Fresno.

White Wolf Lodge Imagine a smaller, quieter, cleaner Curry Village with larger tents, each equipped with a wood-burning stove. White Wolf Lodge is not a lodge, but a cluster of canvas tent cabins, with a few wooden ones out front. This small outpost was bypassed when Tioga Road was rebuilt. It's halfway between the valley and the high country, and it generally isn't overrun with visitors. It's a popular spot for midweek hikers and weekend stopovers. Though it can get crowded, it retains a homey feeling. There's no electricity after 11pm, when the generator shuts off. Wood cabins all have a private bathroom and resemble a regular motel room, with neat little porches and chairs out front. Canvas cabins beat the Curry Village style by a mile. Each sleeps four in any combination of twin and double beds. The helpful staff will show guests how to work the wood-burning stove. Benches outside provide a place to rest weary feet and watch the stars. Bathrooms here are clean, and guests control access to the facilities except for a few midday hours when nearby campers can pay for showers. There's also a restaurant (see "Where to Dine") and a tiny general store.

Tioga Rd., White Wolf, Yosemite National Park. ✆ **801/559-5000.** www.yosemitepark.com. 24 canvas tent-cabins, 4 cabins. All canvas cabins share bathroom and shower house. $84–$96 double. Additional charge of $10 per adult and $6 per child. AE, DC, DISC, MC, V. Parking available across the road. Closed winter. From Yosemite Valley, take Big Oak Flat and Tioga rds. north and east 33 miles toward Tioga Pass.

Yosemite Lodge at the Falls The comfortable motel-type rooms here are popular because of the lodge's location; some units offer views of Yosemite Falls. Rooms have two double beds or one double with two twins, and most have balconies or patios. It's not uncommon to see deer and other wildlife scamper through this area. Spring mornings offer a wonderful orchestra of songbirds and some stunning views of Yosemite Falls at sunrise. The complex contains a food court (see "Where to Dine," below), lounge, large outdoor swimming pool, bicycle rentals, children's programs, ice-cream stand, general store, Wi-Fi in the lobby, and babysitting.

Yosemite Valley. ✆ **801/559-5000.** www.yosemitepark.com. 245 units. TV. $179–$207 double. Additional charge of $7–$10 per adult; additional children are free. Lower rates Nov–Mar. AE, DC, DISC, MC, V. Parking available, or take the shuttle bus (stop no. 8).

Yosemite West Lodging For the unforgettable experience of living in Yosemite National Park (if only for a few nights) rather than just visiting, what could be better than renting a private home, cottage, or condominium in the park? Yosemite West rents a variety of privately owned accommodations, ranging from fairly simple rooms with a kitchenette, suitable for one or two people, to luxurious vacation homes with full-size kitchens, two bathrooms, living rooms, and beds for up to eight people. Kitchens and kitchenettes are fully equipped, all bedding is provided, and lodgings have TVs, VCR/DVD players, and outdoor decks. All units also have automatic or wood-burning fireplaces and charcoal grills. The homes are in a forested section of the park, about 10 miles from Yosemite Valley and 8 miles from Badger Pass.

P.O. Box 36, Yosemite National Park, CA 95389. ✆ **559/642-2211.** www.yosemitewestreservations.com. Number of units varies. TV. $95–$295 double. Lower rates early Sept through mid-Dec and early Jan through early May. Take Wawona Rd. 12 miles north of Wawona.

OUTSIDE THE PARK

If you choose to stay outside the park, you'll find a plethora of choices, many of which are less expensive than the lodging in the park.

ALONG CALIF. 120 (WEST OF THE PARK)

Evergreen Lodge A rough-and-tumble Prohibition-era entertainment destination for the workers who built the dam that flooded nearby Hetch Hetchy Valley, Evergreen Lodge was reborn as one of the best cabin resorts in the Sierra Nevada. Located 7 miles from the roar of the highway, the lodge underwent a major renovation after new ownership took over in 2004 and built new cabins and renovated others. The end results are tremendous: rustic art made from peach boxes, rockers on the decks and porches, a fresh and comfortable feel, and space for two to six guests. (Also available: "Custom Camping" sites with tents furnished with cushy foam mattresses and the necessary gear.) The lodge's recreation program is excellent, including guided bike rides and hikes, live music, basket-weaving and dancing classes, and s'mores on the campfire. The **restaurant** is also top-notch, and the original woodsy bar a classic.

33160 Evergreen Rd., Groveland, CA 95321. ✆ **800/935-6343** or 209/379-2606. www.evergreenlodge.com. 86 units, plus 15 "Custom Camping" sites. $89–$269 double; $65 campsite. AE, DISC, MC, V.

Groveland Hotel Owner-operators Peggy and Grover Mosley have poured their hearts into this standout hotel. The building was vacant for years when the Mosleys decided to forgo a quiet retirement to renovate and reopen the hotel. They've done a great job, and the hotel is now a national historic landmark. The hotel consists of two buildings—one constructed in 1849 to house gold miners and the other built in 1914 for workers constructing the dam in Hetch Hetchy Valley. Standard rooms are spacious, with feather beds, antiques, thick down comforters, and plush robes. Suites have large spa bathtubs and fireplaces. Many rooms are named after women of the Sierra and local characters, although Lyle's Room is named for the hotel's resident ghost. Then there's Charlie's Room, named for a hard-driving, tobacco-spitting stagecoach driver and farmer. When he died, the townspeople learned that he was a she.

18767 Calif. 120, Groveland, CA 95321. ✆ **800/273-3314** or 209/962-4000. Fax 209/962-6674. www.groveland.com. 17 units. A/C, TV, TEL. $145–$185 double; $235–$285 suite. Extra person $25. Rates include buffet breakfast. AE, DC, DISC, MC, V. Pets accepted with approval ($15 per night).

Hotel Charlotte Walking into the Charlotte is like stepping back in time. Built in 1918 by an Italian immigrant of the same name, it's warm, comfortable, and a good choice for those who enjoy the ambience of a small historic hotel. Cheerily wallpapered and wainscoted, the hotel's rooms—which are primarily upstairs—are small, quaint, and nicely maintained. Several rooms adjoin each other and have connecting bathrooms (perfect for families) with claw-foot-tub/shower combos. There's an excellent restaurant, **Café Charlotte** (see "Where to Dine"). The pancake buffet breakfast is great—with coffee, cereals, fruit, juices, flapjacks, and scrambled eggs.

18736 Calif. 120, Groveland, CA 95321. ✆ **800/961-7799** or 209/962-6455. Fax 209/962-6254. www.hotelcharlotte.com. 10 units. A/C, TV, TEL. $98–$149 double. Rates include full breakfast. AE, MC, V.

Sunset Inn Just 2 miles from Yosemite's entrance gates, the Sunset Inn is the perfect antidote to the hubbub you encounter in the valley. Surrounded by old-growth forest, the inn's 2 acres were once a logging camp, then became a tourist camp, and are now a world apart, complete with a frog pond, chicken coop, and hiking trails in every direction. The three cabins here have been lovingly restored by Bill Nickell, the carpenter-innkeeper who owns and operates the place with his wife, Lauren. (They've called the property home since the 1970s.) Each cabin has attractive woodwork, quilts, a wood-burning or gas stove, and a full kitchen. The comfy indoors are matched outdoors with picnic tables, barbecue grills, and porches that are ideal to watch the phenomenon from which the inn took its name. The Nickells also manage a pair of homes a few miles west.

33569 Harden Flat Rd., Groveland, CA 95321. ✆ **888/962-4360** or 209/962-4360. www.sunsetinnusa.com. 3 cabins, 2 houses. $140–$230 cabin; $250–$400 vacation home. AE, MC, V.

Yosemite Rose Located on 210 acres of working ranchland, this beautiful Victorian B&B was actually built in 2000, modeled after the Mountain View, California, home of Henry Rengstorff, the 19th-century owner of the spot now known as Silicon Valley. From the public rooms (featuring a pool table, murals, and a player piano) to the grounds (with a stocked fishing pond, stables, and an olive orchard) to the rooms (with top-end soft goods and compelling antiques), innkeeper Katherine Davalle has left little to chance here. A good many of the furnishings here have amazing stories behind them: The Scelestia Room's antique Danish headboard has the face of a demon in the grain, and the bedstead in the cottage was brought in on a settler's wagon.

22830 Ferretti Rd., Groveland, CA 95321. ✆ **866/962-6548.** Fax 209/962-7750. www.yosemiterose.com. 7 units, 1 cottage. A/C. $161 double; $185 suite; $220 cottage. Rates include full breakfast. AE, DISC, MC, V.

ALONG CALIF. 140

Highland House Bed & Breakfast Secluded on 10 forested acres, with easy access to hiking and horseback trails that lead into the nearby Sierra National Forest, this inn is a wonderful place to relax. A mix of Cape Cod and Colonial styles of architecture, Highland House is comfortably and tastefully decorated. Common areas include the living room, with a large stone fireplace with woodstove insert, and a great den, with books and a pool table. All three rooms here have forest views; we like the Forest Retreat, with a four-poster king, a fireplace, and a soaking tub and separate shower. The big deal, though, is breakfast, with fresh baked goods and a hot entree such as blueberry pancakes or orange French toast.

3125 Wild Dove Lane, Mariposa, CA 95338-9037. ✆ **209/966-3737.** www.highlandhouseinn.com. 3 units. TV. $125–$165 double. Rates include full breakfast. AE, MC, V. From Mariposa, head east (toward Yosemite National Park) on Calif. 140 for about 4 miles, turn south (right) onto Triangle Rd. for about 6 miles, and shortly after a 1-lane bridge, turn left onto Jerseydale Rd. Go 1½ miles and turn right onto Wild Dove Lane, then watch for marked driveway on the right.

Mariposa Lodge Three generations of the Gloor family have run this reliable and well-maintained motel on Mariposa's main drag for over 30 years, and their standards are surprisingly high. The place has grown over the years from one building to three, with smaller rooms in the original structure, and larger rooms in the newer two. The largest rooms have Mission decor and impressive vanities, and many have private balconies. Landscaping is also superlative for a roadside motel, especially the garden courtyard around the pool. Free Wi-Fi access is a modern touch.

5052 Calif. 140 (P.O. Box 733), Mariposa, CA 95338. ✆ **800/966-8819** or 209/966-3607. Fax 209/742-7038. 45 units. A/C, TV, TEL. $59–$129 double. AE, DISC, MC, V.

Poppy Hill Bed & Breakfast This restored country farmhouse, surrounded by large oak and pine trees, provides a delightful escape from the hustle and bustle of the developed areas of the park and gateway communities. The inn is decorated with a variety of antiques, most from the 1800s, but also including "new" furnishings such as the 1925 Wurlitzer baby grand piano in the parlor. Each of the attractive rooms declares its name in its individual decor—Mariposa Lily, Iris, Willow, and, of course, Poppy. Rooms have queen-size beds (Mariposa Lily also has a twin), down comforters, antique furnishings, and bathrobes. Outside, a rolling lawn is punctuated by flower gardens—one hillside bursts into color when the poppies bloom in spring. The second-floor balcony overlooks an ancient oak tree, which entices the birds to entertain you while you relax in quietude. Breakfast is a big event, with such entrees as eggs picante, puffed apple pancake, or croissant French toast.

5218 Crystal Aire Dr., Mariposa, CA 95338. ✆ **800/587-6779** or 209/742-6273. www.poppyhill.com. 4 units. A/C. $125–$150 double. AE, DC, DISC, MC, V. Take Calif. 140 east out of Mariposa (toward Yosemite National Park) 3 miles, turn left on East Whitlock Rd., go 1¼ miles, turn right onto Crystal Aire Dr., and continue ¼ mile to the B&B.

Yosemite View Lodge Just outside the National Park's Arch Rock entrance, this lodge offers guests nice accommodations on the Merced River. A number of the rooms are brand new or recently refurbished, and many feature fireplaces, private decks or patios, kitchenettes, and spa tubs and showers for two. The Yosemite View's sister property, the Yosemite Cedar Lodge, is 15 miles down the road, with similar accommodations and rates. Just beyond the Cedar Lodge is **Yosemite Resort Homes** at historic Savage's Trading Post, featuring newly renovated, fully equipped vacation abodes that sleep up to 12, with rates of $300 to $600 a night.

11136 Calif. 140 (P.O. Box D), El Portal, CA 95318. ✆ **800/321-5261** or 209/379-2681. Fax 209/379-2704. www.yosemiteresorts.us. 335 units. A/C, TV, TEL. $95–$194 double; $155–$450 suite. AE, MC, V.

River Rock Inn Mariposa's oldest motel (1941) recently received a much-needed update that transformed it from a roadside has-been to a bright and cheery boutique motel. Each of the small rooms has been uniquely decorated and is comfortably chic. There is a coffeehouse, the **Deli Garden Café,** where guests enjoy their breakfast of pastries, fresh fruit, and strong coffee.

4993 7th St., Mariposa, CA 95338. ✆ **209/966-5793.** www.riverrockncafe.com. 7 units. A/C, TV. $79–$95 double. Rates include continental breakfast. AE, MC, V.

Yosemite Bug Rustic Mountain Resort & Spa The Yosemite Bug started as a hostel in 1996, but it grew and grew, and is now much, much more. The place has something for everybody, with accommodations that range from dorm rooms and tent-cabins to delightful private rooms, a good restaurant, a spa, and loads of personality. Situated in the forest, most of the units have woodsy, national park–like views. The dorm rooms are basic, with bunk beds, heat, air-conditioning, individual lockable storage boxes, and conveniently located communal bathrooms and kitchen. The tent-cabins have wooden floors and framing, no heat, and different bed combinations, including family units with a double and two single beds. Private rooms are themed (Western to hippie), with a variety of bed combinations. The Yosemite Bug is along the route for the YARTS bus into Yosemite National Park and also offers transportation and tours on the **Bug Bus** (www.yosemitebugbus.com). Maybe the best feature of all is the idyllic swimming hole right down the slope from the main lodge, especially on those dog days of summer.

6979 Calif. 140 (P.O. Box 81), Midpines, CA 95345. ✆ **866/826-7108** or 209/966-6666. Fax 209/966-9667. www.yosemitebug.com. 67 hostel beds, 14 private rooms with private bathrooms, 8 private rooms with shared bathrooms, 16 tent-cabins, 1 studio, 1 private house. Hostel beds $22–$25 per person; private room with bathroom (2–5 people) $75–$125; private room with shared bathroom (2–5 people) $50–$90; tent-cabin $30–$55; studio/private house $125–$300. AE, DISC, MC, V.

ALONG CALIF. 41

Château du Sureau and Spa One of the standout B&Bs in California (or anywhere), the lavish Château du Sureau is as close as you get to Europe on the west side of the Atlantic. A world away from the rest of Oakhurst, the 9,000-square-foot inn has an elegant, near-magical ambience to it (that you pay for in spades), which radiates from the château that houses the stylish, uniquely decorated guest rooms—such as the extraordinary Saffron Room with a king-size ebony and ivory bedroom set from 1834, and the Sweet Geranium Room, with a private balcony overlooking sumptuous gardens. There are details both time-tested (fresh fruit and fireplaces) and modern (CD players), and scads of impressive objects of art around every corner. The grounds here are similarly phenomenal—featuring a spa and a lawn-size chessboard with 3-foot-high pawns—and the restaurant, **Erna's Elderberry House,** is sublime (see "Where to Dine").

48688 Victoria Lane (P.O. Box 577), Oakhurst, CA 93644. ✆ **559/683-6860.** Fax 559/683-0800. www.chateausureau.com. 11 units. A/C. $385–$585 double; $2,950 guesthouse. Rates include full breakfast. AE, MC, V.

The Homestead Secluded on 160 acres of woodland with plenty of trails, this off-the-beaten-path establishment is a gem. The delightful cottages here are rustic yet modern, with four-poster log beds, Saltillo tile floors, stone fireplaces, and separate sitting and dining areas, plus the conveniences of TVs, satellite radio, and air-conditioning. Each unit has its own unique bent, from the romantic Garden

Cottage to the cozy Star Gazing Loft, to the two-bedroom Ranch House (the most family-friendly option here). There are kitchens in all the rooms; smoking is not allowed.

41110 Rd. 600, Ahwahnee, CA 93601. ✆ **559/683-0495.** Fax 559/683-8165. www.homesteadcottages.com. 5 cottages, 1 house. A/C, TV. $145–$219 double; $349–$374 house. AE, DISC, MC, V. Go 4½ miles north of Oakhurst on Calif. 49, then south on Rd. 600 for 2½ miles.

Hounds Tooth Inn With a Victorian look and a 1997 birth date, the Hound's Tooth is a good choice for those who want easy access to Yosemite from the south but more intimacy than a motel or sprawling resort can offer. Set a few hundred feet from the highway, the guest rooms offer the convenience of kitchenette and hot tub, plus the flair of antique reproductions. There's also a private summer house (850 sq. ft.) with a king bed and a kitchenette, plus a Jacuzzi and private patio. The garden area out back is something of a work of art, perfect for whiling away an evening in peace and quiet. The inn is smoke-free.

42971 Calif. 41, Oakhurst, CA 93644. ✆ **888/642-6610** or 559/642-6600. Fax 559/658-2946. www.houndstoothinn.com. 13 units. A/C, TV, TEL. $95–$199 double; $225 cottage. AE, DC, DISC, MC, V.

Tenaya Lodge at Yosemite The top-rated Tenaya Lodge seems to have one foot in the Adirondack Mountains and another in the Southwest. This three- and four-story resort is on 35 acres surrounded by Sierra National Forest and features a full slate of organized recreational activities. The comfortable rooms are modern, and the grand lobby has an impressive fireplace built of river rock that towers three stories. In 2008, the lodge acquired the adjacent **Apple Tree Inn** and renovated its 53 cottages. Tenaya Lodge is an especially cozy choice for winter visitors.

1122 Calif. 41, Fish Camp, CA 93623. ✆ **800/635-5807** or 559/683-6555. Fax 559/683-0249. www.tenayalodge.com. 297 units. A/C, TV, TEL. $155–$379 double; $375–$719 suite; $250–$450 cottage. Children stay free in parent's room. Buffet breakfast $30 per couple. AE, DC, DISC, MC, V.

ALONG U.S. 395 (LEE VINING)

El Mono Motel Built in the 1920s, this artfully renovated European-style lodging is our pick on the east side of the park in Lee Vining. Fronted by attractive porches and a barbecue area, the rooms feature vibrant color schemes and down comforters; the drawback is their small size and the fact that some of them share bathrooms. El Mono also has a coffeehouse and organic garden. All in all, this eclectic lodging is a perfect place to bunk after an expedition in Tuolumne Meadows.

51 U.S. 395, Lee Vining, CA 93541. ✆ **760/647-6310.** www.elmonomotel.com. 11 units, 6 with shared bathroom. A/C, TV. $60–$92 double. MC, V. Closed Nov–late Apr.

Lake View Lodge Spread across several green lawns populated by birds and butterflies, this former chain property is now a first-rate independent. With king beds or a pair of queens, the rooms are reliably clean and well-maintained rooms and a few cottages set off from the main highway.

51285 U.S. 395, Lee Vining, CA 93541. ✆ **800/990-6614.** www.lakeviewlodgeyosemite.com. 53 units. A/C, TV, TEL. $89–$134 double; $89–$209 cottage. AE, DISC, MC, V.

9 Where to Dine

There are plenty of dining possibilities in and near the park, so you certainly won't go hungry. However, you won't find many bargains!

IN THE VALLEY

Ahwahnee Dining Room AMERICAN/INTERNATIONAL The Ahwahnee Dining Room is where the great outdoors meets four-star cuisine, and it's a wonderful place to celebrate a special occasion. The cavernous room, its candelabra chandeliers hanging from the 34-foot-high beamed ceiling, seems intimate once you're seated at a table. Don't be fooled—it actually seats 350. The menu changes frequently and offers a good variety of creative yet recognizable dishes, such as pan-roasted Alaskan halibut, bone-in rib-eye, and rack of lamb. An extensive wine list featuring wines from California and abroad is offered at lunch and dinner. Breakfast includes a variety of egg dishes, hotcakes, and the like, plus specialties such as a thick apple crepe filled with spiced apples and raspberry purée. Lunch choices include sautéed trout, a grilled portobello sandwich, and a variety of plates and salads. Sunday brunch is a big event. ***Note:*** The dinner dress code requires men to wear a collared shirt and long pants, and women to wear a dress, skirt, or pants with a blouse; no shorts anytime.

The Ahwahnee, Yosemite Valley. ✆ **209/372-1489.** Dinner reservations required. Breakfast $7–$21; lunch $15–$23; dinner $30–$49; Sun brunch $49 adults, $24 children. AE, DC, DISC, MC, V. Mon–Sat 7–10:30am, 11:30am–3pm, and 5:30–9pm; Sun 7am–3pm and 5:30–9pm. Shuttle bus stop 3.

Curry Village Coffee Corner COFFEE SHOP Specialty coffees and fresh-baked pastries are the fare here, and ice cream after 11am.

Curry Village. Most items $1–$4. AE, DC, DISC, MC, V. Summer daily 6am–10pm; winter daily 7am–10pm. Shuttle bus stops 13A, 13B, 14, and 20.

Curry Village Pavilion AMERICAN A good spot for the hungry. All-you-can-eat breakfast and dinner buffets offer a wide variety of well-prepared basic American selections at reasonable prices.

Curry Village, Yosemite Valley. Breakfast $9 adults, $7 children; dinner $12 adults, $10 children. DC, DISC, MC, V. Daily 7–10am and 5:30–8pm. Shuttle bus stops 13A, 13B, 14, and 20.

Curry Village Pizza Patio PIZZA Need to watch ESPN? This is the place, but you may have to wait in line. One of the park's few public TVs is inside, and if you're a sports buff, this is the place to be. The scenic outdoor patio offers large umbrellas, table service, and a great view of Mother Nature, plus or minus a hundred kids. The lounge also taps a few brews—nothing special, but a mix aimed to please. This is a great place to chill after a long day.

Curry Village, Yosemite Valley. Pizza $8–$20. AE, DC, DISC, MC, V. Summer daily noon–10pm; winter daily noon–9pm. Shuttle bus stops 13A, 13B, 14, and 20.

Curry Village Taqueria MEXICAN A good place for a quick bite, this taco stand offers daily specials like carne asada and chili verde, along with spicy tacos, burritos, taco salads, beans, and rice.

Curry Village, Yosemite Valley. Most items $3–$10. AE, DC, DISC, MC, V. Mon–Thurs 11am–5pm; Fri–Sun 8am–5pm. Closed in winter. Shuttle bus stops 13A, 13B, 14, and 20.

Degnan's Café AMERICAN Adjacent to Degnan's Deli, this cafe offers specialty coffee drinks, fresh pastries, and ice cream. It's a good place for a quick bite when you're in a hurry, and one of the few spots in the park with Internet-access kiosks (25¢ per minute).

Yosemite Village. Most items $1–$7. DC, DISC, MC, V. Daily 7am–7pm. Shuttle bus stops 4 and 10.

Degnan's Deli SANDWICHES A solid delicatessen with a large selection of sandwiches made to order (plus incidentals), this is our top choice for a quick, healthy lunch or supper. Sometimes the line to order gets long, but it moves quickly. This place is half market and half deli; in addition to sandwiches there is a selection of prepared items—soups, salads, sandwiches, desserts, and snacks—to carry off for a day on the trail. There's also a good selection of beer and wine.

Yosemite Village. Most items $3–$8. DC, DISC, MC, V. Daily 7am–7pm. Shuttle bus stops 4 and 10.

Degnan's Loft ITALIAN This cheery restaurant, with a central fireplace and high-beamed ceilings, is adjacent to Degnan's Deli and Degnan's Cafe. This is a good choice for families due to the restaurant's kid-friendly atmosphere. The menu features pizza, pasta, salads, and desserts.

Yosemite Village. Entrees $4–$21. DC, DISC, MC, V. Daily noon–9pm. Closed in winter. Shuttle bus stops 4 and 10.

Mountain Room Restaurant AMERICAN The best thing about this restaurant is the view. The food's excellent, too, with an emphasis on local organic ingredients, but the floor-to-ceiling windows overlooking Yosemite Falls are spectacular. There's not a bad seat in the house. We suggest the half chicken, which is flavorful and moist, as are the rainbow trout and the Pacific salmon. Meals come with vegetables and bread. Soup or salad is extra. There are entrees for vegetarians and an amazing dessert tray. The Mountain Room also has a good wine list, and the **Mountain Room Lounge** has an open-air fireplace and an a la carte menu.

Yosemite Lodge. Entrees $17–$34. AE, DC, DISC, MC, V. Daily 5:30–9pm. Shuttle bus stop 8.

Village Grill AMERICAN The Village Grill is a fast-food joint that's a decent place to pick up a quick bite. It offers burgers, chicken sandwiches, and the like, and has outdoor seating.

Yosemite Village. Most items $5–$10. AE, DC, DISC, MC, V. Daily 11am–5pm. Closed in winter. Shuttle bus stop 2.

Yosemite Lodge Food Court AMERICAN You'll find breakfast, lunch, and dinner at this busy restaurant (serving about 2,000 meals each day), which is a vast improvement over the traditional cafeteria. It's set up with a series of food stations, where you pick up your choices before heading to the centralized cashier and then to a table either inside or at the outside seating area, which features tables with umbrellas and good views of Yosemite Falls. Food stations specialize in pasta (with a choice of sauces), pizza, deli sandwiches and salads, a grill (offering burgers, hot dogs, and hot sandwiches), meat-based and vegetarian entrees, desserts and baked goods, and beverages. There's also a hot breakfast food station offering traditional American breakfast items and coffee.

Yosemite Lodge. Entrees $5–$15. AE, DC, DISC, MC, V. Daily 6:30–10am, 11:30am–2pm, and 5–8:30pm (until 7:30pm in winter). Shuttle bus stop 8.

ELSEWHERE IN THE PARK

Tuolumne Meadows Lodge AMERICAN One of the two restaurants in Yosemite's high country, the lodge offers something for everyone. The breakfast menu features the basics, including eggs, pancakes, fruit, oatmeal, and granola. Dinners always include a beef, chicken, fish, pasta, and vegetarian specialty, all of which change frequently. The mountain trout, citrus salmon pasta, prime rib, and New York steak are consistently good.

Tuolumne Meadows, Calif. 120. ✆ **209/372-8413.** Reservations required for dinner. Breakfast $7–$11; dinner $6–$28. AE, DC, DISC, MC, V. Daily 7–9am and 6–8pm.

Wawona Hotel Dining Room AMERICAN The Wawona Hotel's dining room mirrors the hotel's ambience—wide open, lots of windows, and sunlight. Dinners are delectable. In addition to some exceptional entrees, such as grilled plum-glazed pork tenderloin skewers with barley, wehani rice pilaf, and plum compote; rib-eye steak; and several seafood and veggie dishes, there are amazing appetizers like split pea fritters and crab Louie. Lunch features a variety of sandwiches and salads.

Wawona Hotel, Wawona Rd. ✆ **209/375-1425.** Lunch $7–$12; dinner $17–$33. AE, DC, DISC, MC, V. Mon–Sat 11:30am–1:30pm and 5:30–9pm; Sun 10:30am–1:30pm and 5:30–9pm.

White Wolf Lodge AMERICAN A changing menu in this casual restaurant, with a mountain lodge atmosphere, offers a variety of American standards with generous portions. Breakfast choices include eggs, pancakes, omelets, or biscuits and gravy; dinner always includes a choice of beef, chicken, fish, pasta, and vegetarian dishes. Takeout lunches are also available from noon to 2pm.

White Wolf, Tioga Rd. ✆ **209/372-8416.** Reservations required for dinner. Breakfast $5–$11; dinner $8–$24. AE, DC, DISC, MC, V. Daily 7:30–9:30am and 5–8:30pm.

NEAR THE PARK

To sip a cup of coffee, buy a book, shop for gear, check your e-mail, and relax in a hammock, visit **Mountain Sage,** 18653 Main St., Groveland (✆ **209/962-4686;** www.mtnsage.com).

Cafe at the Bug AMERICAN Ask the Mariposa locals for their favorite place to get a great meal at a reasonable price, and if they'll tell you, it will likely be this bustling eatery. It's a noisy, busy, somewhat self-service restaurant at the Yosemite Bug Rustic Mountain Resort & Spa. This casual space contains several rooms with knotty-pine walls, oak floors, wooden chairs and tables, and an open-beamed ceiling. You order at a counter and your food is delivered to your table. Emphasizing organic ingredients, many from a garden on-site, the food—innovative American dishes with Mediterranean and Californian influences—is great, with different offerings every night. You might have top sirloin, or a trout filet with lime butter, or stuffed portobello mushrooms. There is at least one vegetarian and one vegan option at every meal. Breakfasts here range from bacon and eggs to buckwheat pancakes or granola; and lunches include sandwiches and sack lunches to go.

At the Yosemite Bug Rustic Mountain Resort & Spa, 6979 Calif. 140, Midpines. ✆ **209/966-6666.** Breakfast and lunch items $5–$10; dinner entrees $8–$16. AE, DISC, MC, V. Daily 7am–9pm.

Café Charlotte MEDITERRANEAN You'll find generous portions of beef, seafood, and pastas in a fine-dining atmosphere in the small dining room at this historic hotel. A variety of seasonal specials are offered, and staples include filet mignon, New York steaks, and daily seafood specials. You'll also find artichoke chicken on the menu, as well as several vegetarian and vegan choices. All meals include veggies, potato or rice, and bread, and the wine list is quite good. There are daily wine tastings in the evening, where six tastes of local wines will set you back only $5.

At Hotel Charlotte, 18736 Calif. 120, Groveland. ✆ **209/962-7872.** Reservations recommended. Entrees $10–$23. AE, MC, V. Summer daily 11:30am–4:30pm and 5:30–10pm; fall to spring Thurs–Sun 5:30–9pm.

Castillo's Mexican Food MEXICAN Established in 1955, this cheerful, cozy cantina serves generous portions of well-prepared Mexican favorites. Entrees come with salad, rice, and beans, and can also be ordered a la carte. A house specialty, the *tostada compuesta,* fills a hungry belly with your choice of meat, plus beans, lettuce, and cheese, stuffed into a bowl-shaped crisp flour tortilla and topped with avocado dip and sour cream. A variety of Mexican combo plates are served, and you can also choose steak specialties or seafood dishes such as jumbo shrimp fajitas. For those who like their hot food with extra fire, there's *camarones a la diabla*—shrimp sautéed in butter, garlic, and crushed red chile peppers. The outdoor seating in a garden area is our favorite spot here.

4995 5th St., Mariposa. ✆ **209/742-4413.** Reservations recommended in summer. Lunch entrees $6–$13; dinner entrees $8–$17. AE, DISC, MC, V. Mon–Thurs 11am–9pm; Fri 11am–9:30pm; Sat 11:30am–9:30pm; Sun 11:30am–2:30pm and 5–8:30pm. Closes 1 hr. earlier in winter.

Cellar Door NEW AMERICAN Top-notch food in a rich and refined atmosphere is what you'll experience at this fine restaurant in the landmark Groveland Hotel. Chef Greg Luckes's menu has something for everyone and is constantly changing to reflect what's fresh and in season. There's a sumptuous local rack of lamb, grilled ahi tuna with wasabi mashers, duck and mushroom risotto, and more. The *Wine Spectator*–lauded wine list—owner Peggy Mosley's passion—is fantastic, and in summer there is also courtyard dining, as well as regularly scheduled concerts under the stars.

At the Groveland Hotel, 18767 Calif. 120, Groveland. ✆ **800/273-3314** or 209/962-4000. Reservations suggested in summer. Lunch entrees $8–$16; dinner entrees $14–$30. AE, DC, DISC, MC, V. Summer Fri–Sun 11am–2pm and daily 6–9pm winter Tues–Sun 6–8pm.

Charles Street Dinner House AMERICAN Famous for its steaks, the Charles Street Dinner House has been the locals' choice for fresh seafood and a variety of other specialties for more than 25 years. We recommend the New Zealand rack of lamb, broiled, with mint glaze; and the breast of duck with pomegranate glaze. Or try the scallone—abalone and scallops sautéed with lemon butter and toasted almonds. The restaurant is in a historic building from the 1800s, and decor is straight out of the Old West, with a huge wagon wheel in the front window and touches that include family photos and fresh flowers. Service is excellent.

5043 Charles St., Mariposa. ✆ **209/966-2366.** Reservations recommended. Entrees $13–$46. AE, DISC, MC, V. Tues–Sat 5–9pm.

Erna's Elderberry House CONTEMPORARY One of the most renowned eateries in California, this elegant restaurant at Château du Sureau is a feast for the eyes, with a contemporary seating area with purple walls and modern prints adjoining a more traditionally elegant room. Likewise, it is a feast for the taste buds, with a nightly changing menu that might include any number of European culinary traditions sculpted into a meal that is definitively Californian. Offerings might range from marinated mussels and chilled carrot-coconut soup to pan-seared Tasmanian sea trout with oatmeal crust to red pepper and prosciutto-wrapped beef tenderloin, spinach gnocchi, and blueberry-yogurt terrine. Each menu comes with a list of recommended wines. Proprietor Erna Kubin-Clanin and company also offer regular gourmet cooking classes here.

48688 Victoria Lane (at Château du Sureau), Oakhurst. ✆ **559/683-6800.** www.elderberryhouse.com. Reservations recommended. Prix-fixe dinners $95; prix-fixe brunch $44. AE, DISC, MC, V. Daily 5:30–8:30pm; Sun also 11am–1pm.

Happy Burger Diner AMERICAN One of the best fast-food joints we've seen anywhere, the Happy Burger offers practically any type of fast food you can think of—it has the region's largest menu—with everything cooked to order. It takes a few minutes longer than at your usual chain fast-food restaurants, but it's worth it. Breakfasts (served until 11:30am) include numerous egg dishes, French toast, pancakes, oatmeal, and the like. The lunch and dinner menu, served all day, features a multitude of charbroiled burgers, sandwiches, stuffed potatoes, Mexican dishes, salads, and dinner plates such as top sirloin and fried shrimp.

In typical fast-food style, you order your food at the counter, then sit at booths among the record album covers from the '60s and '70s and a vintage pinball game, where your piping-hot food is delivered an instant later.

5120 Calif. 140 (at 12th St.), Mariposa. ✆ **209/966-2719.** www.happyburgerdiner.com. Menu items $3–$15. AE, DISC, MC, V. Daily 6am–9pm.

Iron Door Saloon and Grill AMERICAN In 1852, this family-friendly establishment started serving whiskey from an "obligatory plank over two flour barrels," making it California's oldest bar. Now it's the colorful anchor to a city block of businesses (including a soda fountain and a general store), with scads of dollar bills hanging from the ceiling alongside rusted mining equipment, a menagerie of taxidermy, and odd little displays on such topics as the origin of Groveland's name and the career of Black Bart. The menu is fairly basic, with steaks, burgers, poultry, fresh fish, and pasta. You can eat in the 150-year-old bar or the dining room, which is more upscale, with tiled floors, rock walls, and historic photographs. Lunch features wraps and salads (and floats and shakes from the soda fountain). The food and service don't quite live up to the colorful atmosphere, but the Iron Door is a can't-miss nonetheless.

18761 Calif. 120, Groveland. ✆ **209/962-6244.** www.iron-doorsaloon.com. Lunch entrees $7–$11; dinner entrees $10–$23. MC, V. Mon–Thurs 11am–9pm; Fri–Sat 11am–10pm. Bar open later.

Savoury's NEW AMERICAN Opening in 2003 and moving to bigger and better quarters in 2009, this is my favorite restaurant in Mariposa. Proprietor-chef Mirriam Wackerman had catered in the area for years, and customers urged her to follow her dreams and open a restaurant. Now that she has, the results are extraordinary, with a menu of simple, fresh dishes that meld culinary traditions near and far: jambalaya linguini, chipotle pesto chicken, spicy shrimp diabla, and hand-cut steaks. For dessert, bite into a decadent dish of pannacotta, on a bed of strawberry sauce. The dining room is sleek and stylish, decorated with dried plants and nature photos and art.

5034 Calif. 140, Mariposa. ✆ **209/966-7677.** Entrees $13–$30. AE, DISC, MC, V. Summer daily 5–9:30pm; Thurs–Tues 5–9:30pm.

Whoa Nellie Deli DELI/NEW AMERICAN What looks to be an ordinary gas station is home to a truly extraordinary eatery that serves thousands of people on a summer day. Inside the Tioga Gas Mart—aka. "The Mobil"—Chef Matt "Tioga" Toomey offers some of the most tantalizing plates in the Sierra Nevada, as well as some plump to-go sandwiches and pizzas. Sit down in a booth or on the popular patio and enjoy the mind-blowing cuisine. The menu includes fish tacos with mango salsa and ginger slaw, pork tenderloin with apricot-berry glaze, and wild buffalo meatloaf with garlic mashers, but we especially liked the lobster taquitos with tomatillo salsa—and the transcendent chocolate cake. All of the plates overflow with excellent salads and heaps of fresh fruit, making the deli the best post-backpacking eatery in the area.

Calif. 120 just west of U.S. 395, Lee Vining. ✆ **760/647-1088.** Breakfast and lunch $6–$12; entrees $10–$20. MC, V. Daily 7am–9pm. Closed Nov–Apr.

Yosemite Forks Mountain House AMERICAN A reliable stop between Oakhurst and the South Entrance, this woodsy family restaurant does a good job with American staples three meals a day. For breakfast, there are egg dishes, pancakes, and the like; lunch, burgers and sandwiches; and pasta, steak, and seafood for dinner. With exposed beams and log chairs, the woodsy atmosphere matches the hearty portions.

Calif. 41 at the Bass Lake turnoff, Oakhurst. ✆ **559/683-5191.** Breakfast and lunch entrees $5–$11; dinner entrees $10–$25. DISC, MC, V. Mon–Thurs 7am–9pm; Fri–Sun 6am–9pm.

10 Picnic & Camping Supplies

The best place to get supplies and camping equipment in the valley is the **Yosemite Village Store,** which stocks groceries, film, and maps, and has an ATM. Nearby, the **Village Sport Shop** has fishing, camping, and other outdoor gear and sells fishing licenses. The **Yosemite Lodge Gift Shop** and **Curry Village General Store** stock some supplies. The **Curry Village Mountain Shop** sells clothing and equipment for day hikes and for backcountry excursions. The **Tuolumne Meadows Gift & Mountain Shop** also carries backpacking supplies, including maps and dehydrated food. The **Badger Pass Sport Shop** (open only during the snow season) stocks ski clothing and other winter supplies. There are also several small convenience stores throughout the park.

In **Mariposa,** you'll find a good selection of groceries, plus a deli, at **Pioneer Market,** 5034 Coakley Circle, behind the town rest area (© 209/742-6100). Our choice for a grocery store in **Oakhurst** is **Raley's** at 40041 Calif. 41 (© 559/683-8300). Just outside the park's El Portal Entrance, on Calif. 140, is the well-stocked **El Portal Food Market** (© 209/379-2632). For natural and organic foods, the upscale **Mono Market** (© 760/647-1010) in Lee Vining can't be beat. For better prices, you can stop at the **major supermarket and discount chains** in **Merced** or **Fresno,** the largest cities in the park vicinity.

Zion National Park & Cedar Breaks National Monument, UT

by Don & Barbara Laine

It's fairly easy to conjure up a single defining image of most national parks, but Zion, a collage of images and secrets, is impossible to pin down. Zion National Park is not simply the towering Great White Throne, the deep Narrows Canyon, or the cascading waterfalls and emerald green pools. You'll discover an entire smorgasbord of experiences, sights, sounds, and even smells here, as you explore everything from the massive stone sculptures and monuments to the lush forests and rushing rivers.

Today, 150 years after the Mormon settler Isaac Behunin named his homestead here "Little Zion," the park still casts a spell as you gaze upon its sheer multicolored walls of sandstone, explore its narrow canyons, hunt for hanging gardens of wildflowers, and listen to the roar of the churning, tumbling Virgin River. The park means different things to different people: a day hike down a narrow canyon, a rough climb up the face of a massive stone monument, the red glow of sunset over majestic peaks. To some degree, each of these experiences is possible only because of the rocks and the processes that have changed them—uplifting, shifting, breaking, and eroding. The most important of Zion's nine rock layers that create its colorful formations is Navajo sandstone, the thickest rock layer in the park, at up to 2,200 feet.

Millions of years ago, a shallow sea covered the sand dunes here. It caused minerals, including lime from the shells of sea creatures, to glue sand particles together, forming sandstone. Later, movements in the earth's crust lifted the land, draining away the sea but leaving rivers that gradually carved the soft sandstone into the spectacular shapes we see today.

But where do the marvelous colors of the rocks come from? Essentially, from rust. Most of the rocks at Zion are colored by iron or hematite (iron oxide), either contained in the original stone or carried into the rocks by groundwater. Although iron often creates red and pink hues, seen in many of Zion's sandstone faces, it can also result in blacks, browns, yellows, and even greens. Sometimes the iron seeps into the rock, coloring it through, but often it just stains the surface in vertical streaks. Rocks are also colored by bacteria that live on their surfaces. The bacteria ingest dust and expel iron, manganese, and other minerals, which stick to the rock and produce a shiny black, brown, or reddish surface called "desert varnish."

Because of its extremes in elevation (3,666–8,726 ft.) and climate, Zion harbors a vast array of flora and fauna. Wildlife here includes pocket gophers, mountain lions, hundreds of birds (including golden eagles), and dozens of snakes. As for plants, about 800 native species have been found, including cactus, yucca, and mesquite in the hot, dry desert areas; ponderosa pine trees on the high plateaus; and cottonwoods and box elders along the rivers and streams. Watch for the red claret cup cactus, which has spectacular blooms in the spring; for wildflowers such as manzanita, which has tiny pink blossoms; and for the bright red hummingbird trumpet, sometimes called the "Zion Lily." And don't miss the hanging gardens of plant life clinging to the sides of the sandstone cliffs.

AVOIDING THE CROWDS

Try to avoid the peak summer months of June through August, when temperatures are hot and Zion receives almost half its annual visitors. The quietest months are December, January, and February, but you may have to contend with some snow and ice. Good times to visit, if your schedule permits, are April, May, September, and October, when the weather is pleasant and the park is less crowded than in the summer.

Once in the park, the best way to avoid crowds is to walk away from them, either on the longer and more strenuous hiking trails or on treks into the backcountry. It's sad but true: Most visitors to Zion never bother to venture far from the main view points. Their loss can be your gain. You can also avoid the hordes by spending time in Kolob Canyons, in the far northwest section of the park; it's spectacular and receives surprisingly little use, at least in comparison to Zion Canyon.

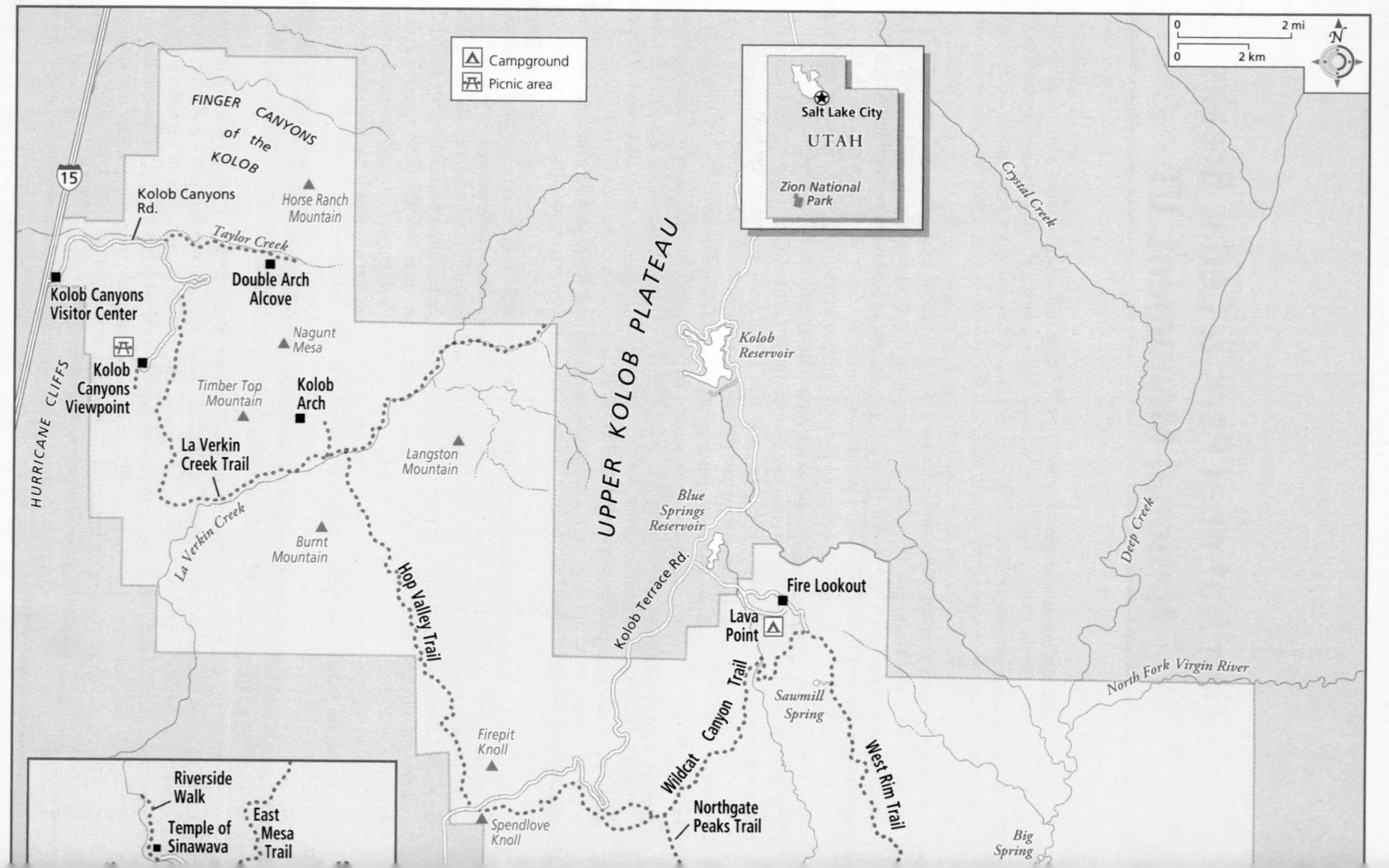

0
2 mi
0
2 km
N
Campground
Picnic area
Salt Lake City
UTAH
Zion National Park
FINGER CANYONS of the KOLOB
15
Kolob Canyons Rd.
Horse Ranch Mountain
Taylor Creek
Double Arch Alcove
Kolob Canyons Visitor Center
Nagunt Mesa
Kolob Canyons Viewpoint
HURRICANE CLIFFS
Timber Top Mountain
Kolob Arch
La Verkin Creek Trail
Langston Mountain
La Verkin Creek
Burnt Mountain
Hop Valley Trail
UPPER KOLOB PLATEAU
Kolob Reservoir
Crystal Creek
Deep Creek
Blue Springs Reservoir
Kolob Terrace Rd.
Fire Lookout
Lava Point
North Fork Virgin River
Wildcat Canyon Trail
Sawmill Spring
West Rim Trail
Firepit Knoll
Spendlove Knoll
Northgate Peaks Trail
Big Spring
Riverside Walk
Temple of Sinawava
East Mesa Trail

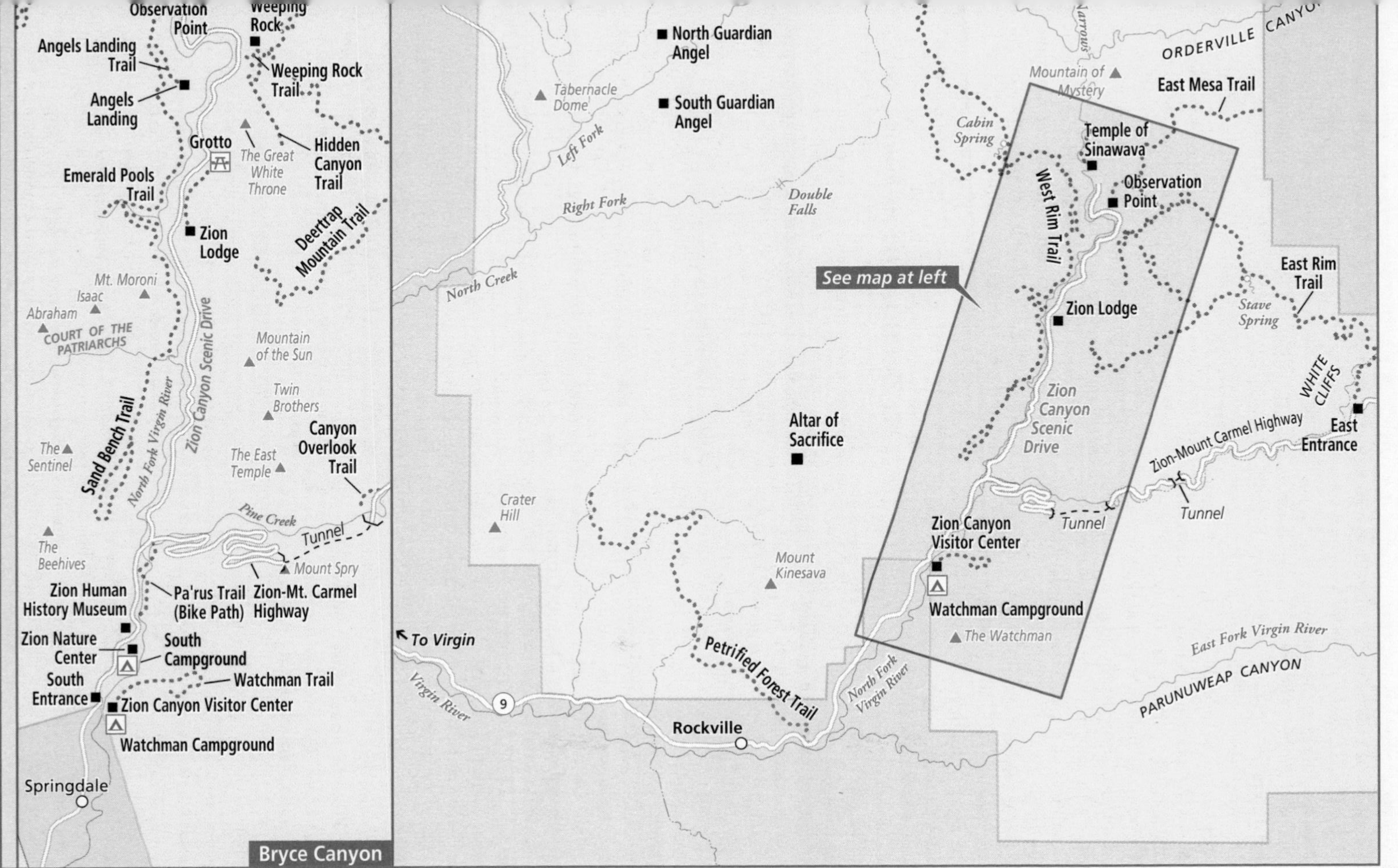

Observation Point
Weeping Rock
Angels Landing Trail
Weeping Rock Trail
Angels Landing
Grotto
The Great White Throne
Hidden Canyon Trail
Emerald Pools Trail
Zion Lodge
Deertrap Mountain Trail
Mt. Moroni
Isaac
Abraham
COURT OF THE PATRIARCHS
Zion Canyon Scenic Drive
Mountain of the Sun
Twin Brothers
Sand Bench Trail
North Fork Virgin River
The Sentinel
The East Temple
Canyon Overlook Trail
Pine Creek
Tunnel
The Beehives
Mount Spry
Zion Human History Museum
Pa'rus Trail (Bike Path)
Zion-Mt. Carmel Highway
Zion Nature Center
South Campground
South Entrance
Watchman Trail
Zion Canyon Visitor Center
Watchman Campground
Springdale
Bryce Canyon
North Guardian Angel
Tabernacle Dome
South Guardian Angel
Left Fork
Right Fork
Double Falls
North Creek
Narrows
Mountain of Mystery
ORDERVILLE CANYON
East Mesa Trail
Cabin Spring
Temple of Sinawava
West Rim Trail
Observation Point
See map at left
Zion Lodge
East Rim Trail
Stave Spring
WHITE CLIFFS
East Entrance
Zion Canyon Scenic Drive
Altar of Sacrifice
Zion-Mount Carmel Highway
Crater Hill
Tunnel
Tunnel
Zion Canyon Visitor Center
Mount Kinesava
Watchman Campground
The Watchman
To Virgin
East Fork Virgin River
Petrified Forest Trail
PARUNUWEAP CANYON
North Fork Virgin River
Virgin River
9
Rockville

1 Essentials

GETTING THERE & GATEWAYS

Zion National Park is in the southwestern corner of Utah, 83 miles southwest of Bryce Canyon National Park and 120 miles northwest of the North Rim of Grand Canyon National Park in northern Arizona. It's 309 miles south of Salt Lake City, 42 miles northwest of Kanab, and 158 miles northeast of Las Vegas, Nevada. The park consists of two main parts: Zion Canyon, the main section, and the less visited Kolob Canyons, in the northwest corner. The closest towns with airport service are St. George (46 miles southwest of the park) and Cedar City (60 miles north).

The easiest way to get to the park is to approach from the west on **I-15,** which runs north to Salt Lake City and southwest through Arizona to Nevada. This route is more direct than the eastern approach, avoids possible delays at the Zion–Mount Carmel Tunnel, and delivers you to Springdale, just outside the park's south entrance, where most of the area's lodging and restaurants are located. From I-15, go east on Utah 9 if approaching from the south, or go south on Utah 17 and then east on Utah 9 if approaching from the north; Utah 9 continues east to the park's south entrance.

The eastern approach to the park is less direct but far more beautiful. From the south or the north, take **U.S. 89** to Utah 9 at Mount Carmel, then go west on Utah 9, a spectacularly scenic 24-mile drive. However, be aware that this route into the park drops more than 2,500 feet in elevation, passes through the mile-long Zion–Mount Carmel Tunnel, and winds down six steep switchbacks. Oversize vehicles pay $15 to use the tunnel (see "Special Regulations & Warnings," below).

The Kolob Canyons section, in the park's northwest corner, is accessible on the short Kolob Canyons Road off I-15, exit 40.

INFORMATION

Contact **Zion National Park,** Springdale, UT 84767 (© **435/772-3256;** www.nps.gov/zion). The nonprofit **Zion Natural History Association,** Zion National Park, Springdale, UT 84767 (© **800/635-3959** or 435/772-3265; www.zionpark.org), sells books, maps, and videos related to the park, some available in foreign languages. Those wanting to help the association can join ($45 single or $60 family annually) and get a 20% discount on purchases, a 20% discount on most Zion Canyon Field Institute classes, and discounts at most other nonprofit bookstores at national parks, monuments, historic sites, and recreation areas. Those planning to spend a lot of time on the trails and in the backcountry should purchase the association's *Zion Topographic Map.* The association also publishes a handy pocket-size *Zion Canyon Shuttle Guide.* The free *Zion Map & Guide,* a small newspaper-format guide, is packed with extremely helpful information.

VISITOR CENTERS

The park has two visitor centers. The **Zion Canyon Visitor Center,** near the south entrance to the park, has a wide variety of outdoor exhibits. Rangers answer questions and provide backcountry permits; free brochures are available; and books, maps, videos, postcards, and posters are sold. In summer it is open from 8am to 8pm, with shorter hours the rest of the year. The **Kolob Canyons Visitor Center,** in the northwest corner of the park, right off I-15, provides information, permits, books, and maps. It is open from 8am to 5pm in summer, with shorter hours the rest of the year.

The **Zion Human History Museum,** about 1 mile inside the south entrance, offers museum exhibits, park information, and an orientation program, plus a bookstore. It's open daily in summer from 9am to 7pm, with shorter hours at other times.

Both visitor centers and the museum are closed on Christmas Day.

FEES & PERMITS

Entry into the park (for up to 7 days), which includes unlimited use of the shuttle bus, costs $25 per private car, pickup truck, van, or RV, or $12 per individual 16 or older on bicycle, foot, or motorcycle; those under 16 admitted free. Oversize vehicles are charged $15 for use of the Zion–Mount Carmel Tunnel on the east side of the park (see "Special Regulations & Warnings," below).

Backcountry permits, available at either visitor center, are required for all overnight hikes in the park, as well as for any slot canyon hikes. Permits cost $10 for 1 or 2 persons, $15 for 3 to 7 people, and $20 for 8 to 12 people. Camping costs $16 per night for basic campsites and $18 to $20 per night for sites with electric hookups (located in Watchman Campground).

SPECIAL REGULATIONS & WARNINGS

The mile-long Zion–Mount Carmel Tunnel was **not built for big vehicles.** It is too narrow for two-way traffic involving anything larger than passenger cars and pickup trucks. Therefore, any vehicle more than 7 feet, 10 inches wide (including mirrors) or 11 feet, 4 inches tall (including luggage racks) can pass only by driving down the center of the tunnel after all other traffic has been stopped. The charge is $15, good for two trips through the tunnel during a 7-day period. Drivers pay the fee at the entrance stations. Call the park headquarters if you have questions about your vehicle's accessibility.

Tips from a Park Ranger

"One of the most spectacular places on Earth," is how Ron Terry, Zion National Park's chief of interpretation and visitor services, describes the park. "Its beauty and grandeur are overpowering. You cannot visit Zion without being inspired and awestruck by the immensity of the towering sandstone cliffs and deep, narrow canyons."

Even though Zion is the most visited national park in Utah, Terry says it is still possible to find solitude in its numerous out-of-the-way places.

"One of Zion's lesser-known but stunningly beautiful areas is **Kolob Canyons,**" Terry says. "The Kolob Canyons Scenic Drive includes numerous pullouts providing a chance to get out of the car and drink in the beauty of the red sandstone cliffs and hanging valleys of the Finger Canyons of the Kolob.

"The hike up the Middle Fork of Taylor Creek to Double Arch Alcove is well worth the trip, as is the more strenuous hike to Kolob Arch," he says.

Choosing the right time to visit Zion National Park can also enhance your experience. "If you visit Zion in March, April, October, or November, you will be sharing the park with fewer people and still have access to most of the park's trails," Terry says.

"October and November are particularly beautiful," he adds. "The yellow and gold leaves of the trees along the Virgin River and in its side canyons contrast wonderfully with the reddish-colored sandstone of the canyon walls."

Your first stop in the park should be at a **visitor center,** Terry advises, to get current weather and flash-flooding-potential information, purchase any needed backcountry permits, and get advice from rangers on which trails and attractions are best for you.

Attending one of the park's **ranger naturalist programs** will also enhance your park experience, according to Terry. During warmer months, programs run nightly in the campgrounds and at Zion Lodge, and there are daily talks and ranger-guided shuttle tours.

Terry also suggests a visit to the **Zion Human History Museum,** which opened in 2002 and features exhibits on how humans have interacted with the geology, water, plants, and animals of the park. An informative orientation film shows in the museum auditorium.

Although the vast majority of Zion's visitors have a thoroughly enjoyable experience with no serious problems, the park does have some serious potential dangers.

The Narrows hike, in which hikers spend most of their time in the water, is one of the most popular but also one of the most potentially dangerous. Before attempting this or any hike in a narrow canyon, visitors need to check at the visitor center.

"Cold and swift water, slippery and uneven walking surfaces, potential flash flooding, and potential hypothermia are all factors to be considered when planning for this hike," Terry says. "Good footwear with ankle support is a must. A walking stick to provide greater stability and better balance will make the experience much more enjoyable."

Also popular at Zion are canyoneering and rock climbing. "Canyoneering is a strenuous activity involving traversing narrow slot canyons usually requiring rappelling equipment and skills," Terry says, adding that climbing the towering vertical cliffs in the park is a high-risk activity that should be attempted only by expert climbers.

The soft sandstone of Zion's cliffs and the prohibition against drilling into the rock make climbing in the park doubly dangerous, according to Terry, and climbers who are not experts should obtain their experience in less extreme conditions elsewhere.

"Zion is in a desert environment, and the summer sun can be very hot," Terry says. "Whatever activity you are participating in should include carrying and drinking plenty of water. Hats and sunscreen are a must. Know your limits, and don't be afraid to end an activity and return another day."

All vehicles more than 13 feet, 1 inch tall, and certain other particularly large vehicles, are prohibited from driving anywhere on the park road between the east entrance and Zion Canyon.

Bicycles are prohibited in the Zion–Mount Carmel Tunnel, in the backcountry, and on all trails except the Pa'rus Trail.

If You Have Only 1 Day

Those with just a day in the park should stop first at the **Zion Canyon Visitor Center** to see the exhibits and look through the free *Zion Map & Guide,* which describes the various options for exploring the park. Then hop on the shuttle bus, which hits the major Zion Canyon roadside view points. When you get to the **Temple of Sinawava,** instead of just taking a quick look and jumping on the next shuttle, hike the easy 2-mile round-trip **Riverside Walk,** which follows the Virgin River through a narrow canyon past hanging gardens. Then take the shuttle bus back to the lodge (total time: 2–4 hr.), where you might stop at the gift shop and possibly have lunch in the lodge restaurant.

Near the lodge you'll find the trail head for the **Emerald Pools.** Especially pleasant on hot days, this easy walk through a forest of oak, maple, fir, and cottonwood trees leads to a waterfall, a hanging garden, and the shimmering lower pool. This walk should take about an hour round-trip. Those with a bit more ambition may want to add another hour and another mile to the loop by taking the moderately strenuous hike on a rocky, steeper trail to the upper pool.

If time and energy remain, head back toward the south park entrance and stop at **Watchman trail head.** Here a moderately strenuous 2-mile, 2-hour round-trip hike takes you to a plateau with beautiful views of several rock formations and the town of Springdale. That evening, take in the campground amphitheater program.

Backcountry hikers should practice minimum-impact techniques and are prohibited from building fires. A limit on the number of people allowed in various parts of the backcountry may be in force during your visit; prospective backcountry hikers should check with rangers before setting out. You can purchase a backcountry permit at the visitor center the day before or the day of your trip. Permits can also be reserved in advance through the park's website (**www.nps.gov/zion**) but must be picked up in person at the visitor center. A free booklet, *Backcountry Travel,* lists all regulations and has descriptions of close to 20 backcountry trails.

SEASONS & CLIMATE

Zion experiences all four seasons, although the winters are mild and rarely bring snow. The best times to visit the park are spring and fall, when the temperatures range from lows in the 40s (single digits Celsius) to pleasant highs in the 80s (upper 20s Celsius). Remember that summer daytime highs often soar above 100°F (38°C), with lows in the 70s (lower 20s Celsius). During the summer, do your hiking in the early morning to avoid both the heat and the frequent afternoon thunderstorms (in July and Aug), which can change a babbling brook into a raging torrent in minutes.

2 Exploring the Park

If you enter the park from the east, along the steep **Zion–Mount Carmel Highway,** you'll travel 13 miles to the **Zion Canyon Visitor Center,** passing between the White Cliffs and Checkerboard Mesa, a massive sandstone rock formation covered with horizontal and vertical lines that make it look like a huge fishing net. Continuing, you'll pass through a fairyland of fantastically shaped rocks of red, orange, tan, and white, and you'll encounter the **Great Arch of Zion,** carved high in a stone cliff by the forces of erosion. At the east end of the Zion–Mount Carmel Tunnel is the trail head parking for the **Canyon Overlook Trail,** a relatively easy 1-mile walk to a great view point. After driving through the tunnel, you'll traverse a number of long switchbacks as you descend to the canyon floor.

A shuttle bus system has been implemented in the main section of the park to reduce traffic congestion and the resultant problems of pollution, noise, and damage to the park. The shuttle system consists of **two loops:** one in the town of Springdale and the other along Zion Canyon Scenic Drive. The loops connect at the visitor center just inside the south park entrance. From April through October, access to Zion Canyon Scenic Drive (above Utah 9) is limited to shuttle buses, hikers, and bikers. The only exceptions are overnight Zion Lodge guests and tour buses connected with the lodge—both have access as far as the lodge. Shuttle stops are at all the major-use areas in the park, and shuttles run frequently (about every 6 min. at peak times). In winter, when visitation is lowest, visitors are permitted to drive the full length of Zion Canyon Scenic Drive in their own vehicles.

ZION CANYON SCENIC DRIVE The ride through Zion Canyon is impressive by any standards, with massive stone reaching straight up to the heavens and the North Fork of the Virgin River threading its way through the maze of rocks. The views in every direction are awe inspiring. Stops along the road provide access to view points and hiking trails.

The first stop is across from the **Court of the Patriarchs,** where a short trail leads to an impressive view point. The next stop is **Zion Lodge.** Across the road from the lodge is the trail head for the **Emerald Pools Trail system.** The Grotto Picnic Area is about a half-mile beyond the lodge, accessible on a trail that parallels Zion Canyon Scenic Drive. Across from the Grotto Picnic Area parking lot is a footbridge that leads to the Emerald Pools, Angels Landing, and West Rim trails.

Continuing north into Zion Canyon, the road passes the **Great White Throne** on the right and then **Angels Landing** on the left before coming to the turnoff to the **Weeping Rock trail head** parking area. From here, the road closely traces the curves of the river, with a couple of stops to allow different views of **the Organ,** which to some resembles a huge pipe organ. The road ends at the **Temple of Sinawava,** where the paved **Riverside Walk** follows the Virgin River toward **The Narrows,** one of the most incredible sights in Zion.

KOLOB CANYONS ROAD To escape the crowds of Zion Canyon, head to the northwest corner of the park. The Kolob Canyons Road runs 5 miles among spectacular red and orange rocks, ending at a high vista. Allow about 45 minutes round-trip, which includes time for stopping at the numbered view points. Be sure to get a copy of the "Kolob Canyons Road Guide" at the Kolob Visitor Center. Here's what you'll pass along the way:

Leaving **Kolob Canyons Visitor Center,** you'll drive along the Hurricane Fault to **Hurricane Cliffs,** a series of tall, gray limestone cliffs, and onward to **Taylor Creek,** where a pinyon-juniper forest clings to life on the rocky hillside, providing a home to bright-blue scrub jays.

Your next stop is **Horse Ranch Mountain,** which, at 8,726 feet, is the national park's highest point. Passing a series of colorful rock layers, where you might be lucky enough to spot a golden eagle, your next stop is **Box Canyon,** along the South Fork of Taylor Creek, with sheer rock walls soaring more than 1,500 feet high. Along this stretch you'll see multicolored layers of rock, pushed upward by tremendous forces from within the earth, followed by a side canyon with large, arched alcoves boasting delicate curved ceilings.

Head on to a view of **Timber Top Mountain,** which has a sagebrush-blanketed desert at its base and a stately fir and ponderosa pine forest at its peak. Watch for mule deer on the brushy hillsides, especially between October and March, when they might be spotted just after sunrise or just before sunset. From here, continue to **Rockfall Overlook;** a large scar on the mountainside marks the spot where a 1,000-foot chunk of stone crashed to the earth in July 1983, the victim of erosion. Finally, stop to see the canyon walls themselves, colored orange-red by iron oxide and striped black by mineral-laden water running down the cliff faces.

3 Ranger & Educational Programs

Zion National Park has some of the best **ranger programs** we have encountered, and they're all free. **Evening programs,** which last about 45 minutes, take place at the Watchman Campground Amphitheater and Zion Lodge Auditorium. They usually include a slide show, take place most evenings from April through September, and include topics such as the animals or plants of the park, geology, the night sky, mankind's role in the park, or some unique aspect of Zion, like slot canyons. Rangers also give **short talks** on similar subjects during the day at various locations, including the Zion Lodge auditorium and Zion Human History Museum. Ranger-guided **hikes and walks,** which may require reservations, might take you to little-visited areas of the park, on a trek to see wildflowers, or for a night hike under a full moon. These range from easy to very difficult. Rangers also lead shuttle tours during summer. The 2-hour **Ride with a Ranger** trip offers an opportunity to see the scenic drive and learn about Zion Canyon from a park ranger's perspective.

Schedules of the various ranger programs and activities are posted on bulletin boards at the visitor centers, campgrounds, and other locations.

The **Zion Canyon Field Institute,** operated by the nonprofit Zion Natural History Association, Zion National Park, Springdale, UT 84767 (© **800/635-3959;** 435/772-3265; or 435/772-3264 for the field institute; www.zionpark.org), offers a variety of single- and multiday outdoor workshops and classes, covering subjects in the sciences, arts, and humanities. Programs take place year-round in Zion National Park and nearby Cedar Breaks National Monument (discussed later). Recent programs have included Bird Watching, Hanging Gardens of Zion, Zion Geology, Wasps & Ants, Bat Biology & Conservation, Zion by Moonlight, Fall Foliage Photo Workshop, Zion Narrows, Watercolor Journaling, and Winter Photography.

Although all the Field Institute's programs are rewarding, we especially recommend the **photo workshops,** led by institute director Michael Plyler, an excellent photographer and teacher. Fees for most of the programs range from $25 to $100 per day, with a minimum age of 15 or 16, depending on the program. Members of the **Zion Natural History Association** receive a 20% discount on most Zion Canyon Field Institute programs.

4 Park Attractions

There are no major historic sites in Zion National Park, but there is some evidence of the early peoples who inhabited the area. Just outside the Zion Canyon Visitor Center, the short but steep **Archeology Trail** (.4 mile round-trip, with an 80-ft. elevation gain) leads to the outlines of small prehistoric storage buildings. There are also some trailside exhibits and interpretive signs.

Hikers with sharp eyes may see potsherds, pieces of ancient stone tools, rock art, and other archaeological objects throughout the park. Rangers ask that you do not touch these artifacts (skin oils can damage them), but report their location to them.

The park's **Zion Human History Museum,** 1 mile from the park's south entrance, features exhibits on how humans have interacted with the geology, water, plants, and animals of the park. An informative orientation film shows in the museum auditorium. The museum is open daily in summer from 9am to 7pm, with shorter hours at other times.

5 Day Hikes

Zion offers a wide variety of hiking options, ranging from easy half-hour walks on paved paths to grueling overnight hikes over rocky terrain. Hikers with a fear of heights should be careful when choosing trails, because many include steep, dizzying, and potentially fatal drop-offs. Water in streams in the park is not safe to drink. Smoking is prohibited on all trails. Several local companies offer guided hiking, rock climbing, and biking trips in the park and surrounding area, including **Zion Adventure Company,** 36 Lion Blvd., at the corner of Lion Boulevard and Zion Park Boulevard (P.O. Box 523), Springdale, UT 84767 (© **435/772-1001;** www.zionadventures.com); and **Zion Rock & Mountain Guides,** 1458 Zion Park Blvd. (P.O. Box 623), Springdale, UT 84767 (© **435/772-3303;** www.zionrockguides.com). Shuttle service for backcountry hikers and bikers is available on the park's shuttle service, and each shuttle bus has racks for two bikes.

SHORTER TRAILS

Canyon Overlook This self-guided trail takes you to an overlook with a magnificent view of lower Zion Canyon and Pine Creek Canyon. Be aware that there are some long drop-offs and that the sandy trail can be slippery. Trail guide booklets are available at the visitor center and at the trail head. 1 mile RT. Moderate. Access: East side of Zion–Mount Carmel Tunnel.

Emerald Pools Trails This is a wonderful trail, especially on a hot day, when you'll especially enjoy the spray of water from the falls. It can be either an easy 1-hour walk or a moderately strenuous 2-hour hike with steep drop-offs, depending on how much you choose to do. A .6-mile paved path leads from the Emerald Pools parking area, through a forest of oak, maple, fir, and cottonwood, to several waterfalls, a hanging garden, and the picturesque Lower Emerald Pool.

From here, a steeper, rocky trail continues .25 mile to the Middle Emerald Pool, and then climbs another .33 mile past cactus, yucca, and juniper to Upper Emerald Pool, which has another waterfall. Total elevation gain is 69 feet to Lower Emerald Pool, 150 feet to the Middle Emerald Pool, and 400 feet from the trail head to Upper Emerald Pool. 1.2–2.5 miles RT. Easy to moderate. Access: Across from Zion Lodge.

Hidden Canyon Trail A particularly scenic hike, this trail climbs 850 feet through a narrow, water-carved canyon, ending at the canyon's mouth. Those wanting to extend the hike can go another .6 mile to a small natural arch. Hidden Canyon Trail includes long drop-offs and is not recommended for anyone with a fear of heights. 2 miles RT. Moderate to strenuous. Access: Weeping Rock parking lot.

Pa'rus Trail This paved trail (fully accessible to wheelchairs) follows the Virgin River, providing views of the rock formations in lower Zion Canyon. Unlike other park trails, this one is open to bicycles and leashed pets. The elevation gain is only 50 feet. 3.5 miles RT. Easy. Access: Either the entrance to Watchman Campground, near amphitheater parking area, or near the Nature Center at South Campground.

Riverside Walk and the Gateway to The Narrows This paved trail follows the Virgin River upstream to the Zion Canyon Narrows, past trailside exhibits and, in spring and summer, hanging wildflowers. Accessible to those in wheelchairs with some assistance, the trail has an elevation change of only 57 feet. At The Narrows, the pavement ends and you have to decide whether to turn around or continue upstream into The Narrows itself (yes, you will get wet), where the canyon walls are about 20 feet apart in some areas and more than 1,000 feet high. ***Warning:*** The bottom of a very narrow slot canyon is definitely not a place you want to be in a rainstorm (common in July–Aug), when flash floods are a serious threat. Before entering The Narrows, check the weather forecast and discuss your plans with park rangers. Permits are required for longer treks in The Narrows but not for short day hikes (see The Narrows, below). 2 miles RT. Easy. Access: Temple of Sinawava parking lot.

Watchman Trail This moderately strenuous but relatively short trail gets surprisingly light use, possibly because it can be very hot in the middle of the day. Climbing to a plateau near the base of the Watchman formation, it offers splendid views of lower Zion Canyon, Oak Creek Canyon, the Towers of the Virgin, the West Temple formations, and the town of Springdale. The trail takes about 2 hours and has an elevation gain of 368 feet. 2.7 miles RT. Moderate. Access: Zion Canyon Visitor Center.

Weeping Rock Trail This is among the park's shortest and easiest rambles, although it is steep in spots. A self-guiding nature trail, the route leads to a rock alcove with a spring and hanging gardens of ferns and wildflowers. Although paved, the trail is relatively steep (gaining 98 ft.) and slippery, and not suitable for wheelchairs. .5 mile RT. Easy to moderate. Access: Weeping Rock parking lot.

LONGER TRAILS

Angels Landing Trail This strenuous 4-hour hike is most certainly not for anyone with even a mild fear of heights. The trail climbs 1,488 feet to a summit that offers spectacular views into Zion Canyon. ***But be prepared:*** The final half-mile follows a narrow, knife-edge trail along a steep ridge, where footing can be slippery even under the best of circumstances. Support chains have been set along parts of the trail. 5 miles RT. Strenuous. Access: Grotto picnic area.

Hop Valley Trail This backcountry trail loses about 1,000 feet as it meanders through sunny fields and past Gambel oak, partly following an old jeep road and then a stream, before taking you to La Verkin Creek. Some hikers connect with the La Verkin Creek/Kolob Arch Trail to see Kolob Arch. Hikers should allot a full day for this trail. 13.4 miles RT. Moderate to strenuous. Access: Trail head on Kolob Terrace Rd.

La Verkin Creek/Kolob Arch Trail Although there are no drop-offs, this backcountry trail is quite strenuous. Descending almost 700 feet, it follows Timber and La Verkin creeks, ending at Kolob Arch, which, at 310 feet long, may be the world's largest freestanding arch. Some people choose to camp on this hike. You can camp at La Verkin Creek if you have a permit and have been assigned a campsite at the visitor center. 14 miles RT. Strenuous. Access: Kolob Canyons Rd. at Lee Pass.

The Narrows Hiking The Narrows doesn't really involve hiking a trail at all; it consists of walking or wading along the bottom of the Virgin River, through a spectacular 1,000-foot-deep chasm that, at a mere 20 feet wide, definitely lives up to its name. Passing sculptured sandstone arches, hanging gardens, and waterfalls, this moderately strenuous hike is recommended for those in good physical condition who are up to fighting currents, which can sometimes be strong. Those who want just a taste of The Narrows can walk and wade in from the end of the Riverside Walk (see above), but more than a short trip will involve a long full- or 2-day trek, which includes arranging a shuttle to the starting point at Chamberlain's Ranch and then transportation from the Temple of Sinawava, where you'll leave the canyon.

The Narrows is subject to flash flooding and can be very treacherous. Park Service officials remind hikers that they are responsible for their own safety, and they should check on current water conditions and weather forecasts. This hike is *not* recommended when rain is forecast or threatening. Permits ($5) are required for full-day and overnight hikes, and must be purchased at the visitor center the day before your hike. 16 miles one-way. Moderate to difficult. Access: Chamberlain's Ranch (outside the park). By permit only.

Taylor Creek Trail This is a 4-hour hike along the middle fork of Taylor Creek. You might get your feet wet fording the creek. The trail leads past two historic cabins to Double Arch Alcove, with an elevation gain of 450 feet. 5 miles RT. Moderately strenuous. Access: Kolob Canyons Rd., about 2 miles from Kolob Canyons Visitor Center.

6 Exploring the Backcountry

The park offers many backpacking opportunities, and a number of the day hikes discussed above are actually more comfortably done in 2 or more days. In addition to the park's established trails and the famous Narrows, there are a number of off-trail routes for those experienced in using topographical maps—get information at the Backcountry Desk at the Zion Canyon Visitor Center.

Backcountry permits are required for all overnight hikes in the park as well as for slot canyon hikes. You can get permits at either visitor center. They cost $10 for 1 or 2 people, $15 for 3 to 7, and

$20 for 8 to 12. You can purchase a permit the day before or the day of your trip. You can also make reservations for permits in advance through the park's website (**www.nps.gov/zion**), but you must pick them up in person.

The difficult **West Rim Trail** climbs more than 3,500 feet into the high country to a view point overlooking the Right Fork of North Creek Canyon (at 14 miles), then continues to Lava Point. The round-trip distance is 28 miles. Access is at the Grotto Picnic Area. There are striking views from most points on the trail.

7 Other Sports & Activities

BIKING & MOUNTAIN BIKING Although bikes are prohibited on almost all trails and are forbidden to travel cross-country within the national park boundaries, Zion is among the West's most bike-friendly parks. The bike-friendly **Pa'rus Trail** runs a little under 2 miles along the Virgin River, from the south park entrance and South Campground to Zion Canyon Scenic Drive. The trail crosses the river and several creeks, and it provides good views of the Watchman, West Temple, the Sentinel, and other lower-canyon formations. The trail is paved and open to bicyclists, pedestrians, pets on leashes, strollers, and wheelchairs, but is closed to cars.

From early April through late October, the **Zion Canyon Scenic Drive,** beyond its intersection with the Zion–Mount Carmel Highway, is closed to private motor vehicles, except to motorists with reservations at Zion Lodge. However, during that time, the road is open to hikers and bicyclists as well as shuttle buses. Cyclists should stay to the right to allow shuttle buses to pass.

Bicycles can also be ridden on other park roads, though not through the Zion–Mount Carmel Tunnel.

Although mountain bikes are prohibited on the trails of Zion National Park (except the Pa'rus Trail), just outside the park—mostly on Bureau of Land Management and state property—are numerous rugged jeep trails that are great for mountain biking, plus more than 100 miles of slickrock cross-country trails and single-track trails. Talk with the knowledgeable staff at **Zion Cycles,** 868 Zion Park Blvd., behind Zion Pizza & Noodle (P.O. Box 624), Springdale, UT 84767 (© **435/772-0400;** www.zioncycles.com), about the best trails for your interests and abilities. This full-service bike shop offers maps, a full range of bikes and accessories, repairs, and rentals ($38–$50 for a full day, $28–$40 for a half-day).

For guided mountain or road bike trips, contact **Zion Adventure Company** (see "Day Hikes," above). A guided hike and road-bike trip into the park costs $139 for a half-day and $179 for a full day, per person for two people, with lower per-person rates for larger groups. Guided mountain-biking trips outside the park start at $10 per person higher. **Zion Rock & Mountain Guides** (see "Day Hikes," above) also offers guided mountain-bike excursions outside the national park at similar rates.

FISHING Though not the most popular pastime in the park, fishing in the Virgin River is permitted with a Utah fishing license, available at sporting goods stores and other businesses throughout Utah; contact the **Utah Division of Wildlife Resources,** 1594 W. North Temple (P.O. Box 146301), Salt Lake City, UT 84114-6301 (© **801/538-4700;** www.wildlife.utah.gov), for more details. Anglers occasionally catch a few trout, but the stream is not stocked.

HORSEBACK RIDING Guided rides in the park are available March through October from **Canyon Trail Rides,** P.O. Box 128, Tropic, UT 84776 (© **435/679-8665;** www.canyonrides.com), with ticket sales and information near Zion Lodge. A 1-hour ride along the Virgin River costs $40, and a half-day ride on the Sand Beach Trail costs $75. Riders must weigh no more than 220 pounds, and children must be at least 7 years old for the 1-hour ride and 10 years old for the half-day ride. Reservations are advised.

ROCK CLIMBING Expert technical rock climbers like the tall sandstone cliffs in Zion Canyon, although rangers warn that much of the rock is loose, or "rotten," and climbing equipment and techniques

Campground	Elev.	Total Sites	RV Hookups	Dump Station	Toilets
East Zion Riverside	5,191	12	12	Yes	Yes
Lava Point	7,980	6	0	No	Yes
South	4,000	127	0	Yes	Yes
Watchman	4,000	164	95	Yes	Yes
Zion Canyon	3,800	200	125	Yes	Yes

that are suitable for granite are often less effective (and therefore less safe) on sandstone. Backcountry permits, available at visitor centers, are required for overnight climbs and cost $10 for 1 or 2 people, $15 for 3 to 7, and $20 for 8 to 12. Because some routes may be closed at times, such as during peregrine falcon nesting from early spring through July, climbers should check at the Zion Canyon Visitor Center before setting out. **Zion Adventure Company** and **Zion Rock & Mountain Guides** (see "Day Hikes," above) offer a variety of guided rock climbing and hiking trips, as well as instruction. Typical per-person rates are $125 for a half-day and $160 for a full day for two people, with lower per-person rates for larger groups. The company also offers equipment rentals and sales.

WILDLIFE VIEWING & BIRD-WATCHING

It's a rare visitor to Zion who doesn't spot a critter of some sort, from **mule deer**—often seen along roadways and in campgrounds year-round—to the many varieties of **lizards** that you're likely to see from spring through fall. The park's largest lizard, the chuckwalla, can grow to 20 inches. The **ringtail cat,** a relative of the raccoon, prowls Zion Canyon at night and is not above helping itself to your camping supplies. Along the Virgin River you'll see **bank beaver,** so named because they live in burrows instead of dams. The park is also home to coyotes, black-tailed jackrabbits, cottontails, chipmunks, several types of squirrels, voles, skunks, porcupines, gophers, and a variety of bats.

The **peregrine falcon,** among the world's fastest birds, sometimes nests in the Weeping Rock area, where you could also see birds like the American dipper, the canyon wren, and the white-throated swift. Bald eagles sometimes winter in the park, and you might also see golden eagles. Snakes include the **Great Basin rattlesnake,** usually found only below 8,000 feet, as well as nonpoisonous king snakes and gopher snakes. **Tarantulas** are often seen in the late summer and fall.

8 Camping

INSIDE THE PARK

The best places to camp are the **national park campgrounds,** just inside the park's south entrance. Reservations for **Watchman Campground** can be made from early April through October (✆ **877/444-6777;** www.recreation.gov). Reservations are not accepted for **South Campground,** and it often fills by noon in the summer, so get there early in the day to claim a site.

Both of Zion's main campgrounds have paved roads, well-spaced sites, lots of trees, flush toilets, and that national park atmosphere you came here to enjoy. **Lava Point,** on the Kolob Terrace, is more primitive (vault toilets) but has a delightful wooded setting. There are no showers in the national park, but the commercial campgrounds listed below will let you use their showers for a fee. There are no RV hookups at South Campground, but electric hookups are available in two loops in Watchman.

NEAR THE PARK

Outside the park entrances, on both the east and south sides, are commercial campgrounds with all the usual amenities. Keep in mind that the park's visitor center, campgrounds, and most of its developed attractions are closer to the south entrance than the east.

Zion Canyon Campground is at 479 Zion Park Blvd., Springdale, UT 84767 (✆ **435/772-3237;** www.zioncamp.com), a half-mile south of the park's south entrance. Although quite crowded in summer, the campground is clean and well maintained, with tree-shaded sites (including big rig sites) and grassy tent areas. Some sites are along the Virgin River, and the campground has free cable TV hookups, a pool, a game room, a playground, and a store. Dogs are permitted at RV sites but not tent sites. There is a **Quality Inn** (42 units) on the grounds (✆ **435/772-3237;** fax 435/772-3844), with rates starting at $110 double.

East Zion Riverside RV Park is located in the Best Western East Zion Thunderbird Lodge complex in Mt. Carmel Junction, about 13 miles east of the east entrance to the national park (P.O. Box 5536, Mt. Carmel Junction, UT 84755; ✆ **435/648-2203;** www.zionnational-park.com). Especially good for self-contained RVs, the park sits along the

Drinking Water	Showers	Fire Pits/ Grills	Laundry	Reserve	Fees	Open
Yes	No	No	Yes	Yes	$15	Year-round
No	No	Yes	No	No	Free	June to mid-Oct
Yes	No	Yes	No	No	$16	Mid-Mar to Oct
Yes	No	Yes	No	Yes	$16–$20	Year-round
Yes	Yes	Yes	Yes	Yes	$30–$35	Year-round

banks of the East Fork of the Virgin River in the shade of cottonwood trees and offers campers use of the pool, hot tub, and other amenities at the adjacent Thunderbird Lodge. All sites are back-in.

In addition to the campgrounds discussed here, there is also camping at Cedar Breaks National Monument (see p. 490).

9 Where to Stay

INSIDE THE PARK

Zion Lodge This handsome facility, the only lodging in the park, is a wonderful place to stay, but its main appeal is the splendid location. Built in 1925 by the Union Pacific Railroad, the original Zion Lodge was destroyed by fire in 1966 but has been rebuilt and restored. Set in a valley with spectacular views of the park's rock cliffs, the charming and historic cabins are our first choice because they fit the national park ambience. Each cabin has a private porch, stone (gas-burning) fireplace, two double beds, and pine board walls. The comfortable motel units are good for those who prefer more modern accommodations, with two queen-size beds, a private porch or balcony, and all the usual amenities except televisions. The motel suites, plush and spacious, have one king-size bed, a sitting room with a queen-size hide-a-bed, and a refrigerator. Ranger programs take place in the lodge auditorium during the summer. The lodge has two restaurants, the **Castle Dome Café** and **Red Rock Grill** (see "Where to Dine," below). All units are nonsmoking.

In Zion National Park. Information and reservations: Xanterra Parks & Resorts, Central Reservations, 6312 S. Fiddlers Green Circle, Ste. 600N, Greenwood Village, CO 80111. ✆ **888/297-2757** or 303/297-2757. Fax 303/297-3175. www.zionlodge.com. ✆ **435/772-7700** (direct line to lodge). 121 units. A/C, TEL. Mid-Mar to Nov motel rooms $159 double; $173 cabin double; $183 suite double. Discounts (sometimes up to 50% off) and packages available rest of the year. AE, DISC, MC, V.

NEAR THE PARK

The lodgings listed below are in Springdale, a village of some 450 people at the park's south entrance, or in Mount Carmel Junction, an even smaller community about 13 miles east of the park's east entrance.

Best Western East Zion Thunderbird Lodge A well-maintained two-story motel with Southwest decor, the Thunderbird offers quiet, spacious, comfortable rooms with king- or queen-size beds, wood furnishings, photos or artwork depicting area scenery, and a private balcony or patio. All units have Wi-Fi, and some have refrigerators and microwaves. There is a large outdoor heated pool (Apr–Oct), a whirlpool, a 9-hole golf course, a gas station, a convenience store, and a restaurant, **The Thunderbird** (see "Where to Dine," below), on the premises. Also under the same management is a nearby house with two budget rooms (one queen bed, bathroom with shower only, and TV) for $62 and several restored cabins (one queen bed, full bathroom, and TV) for $65. All units are nonsmoking.

At the junction of Utah 9 and U.S. 89 (P.O. Box 5536), Mt. Carmel Junction, UT 84755. ✆ **888/848-6358** or 435/648-2203. Fax 435/648-2239. www.zionnational-park.com. 61 units. A/C, TV, TEL. May–Oct $104–$119 double; Nov–Mar $81–$90 double. AE, DC, DISC, MC, V.

Best Western Zion Park Inn This is a good choice for those who are seeking an upscale, reliable chain motel with no surprises. Rooms in the handsome two-story complex, 1½ miles from the park, are tastefully appointed in Southwest style, with two queen-size beds or one king-size bed, dataports, coffeemakers, hair dryers, and irons. The grounds are nicely landscaped, with phenomenal views of the area's red rock formations. Facilities include a heated outdoor swimming pool (Apr–Oct), a whirlpool (year-round), a **restaurant,** a gift shop, a convenience store, guest laundry, a liquor store, and conference and meeting rooms.

1215 Zion Park Blvd., Springdale, UT 84767. ✆ **800/934-7275** or 435/772-3200. Fax 435/772-2449. www.zionparkinn.com. 120 units. A/C, TV, TEL. Apr–Oct $105–$135 double, $140–$160 suite or family unit; Nov–Mar $65–$75 double, $90–$125 suite or family unit. No charge for children 17 and younger. AE, DC, DISC, MC, V. One pet accepted ($25 fee).

Canyon Ranch Motel Consisting of a series of two- and four-unit cottages set back from the highway, this motel's buildings ooze charm, with the look of 1930s-style cabins on the outside, while providing modern motel rooms inside. Rooms have Wi-Fi and most have refrigerators. Options include one queen- or king-size bed, two queen-size beds, or one queen-size and one double. Some rooms have showers only, while others have a tub/shower. Room no. 13, with two queen-size beds, offers spectacular views of the Zion National Park rock formations; views from most other rooms are almost as good. The units surround a lawn with trees and picnic tables, and the property has an outdoor pool and whirlpool. All units are smoke-free.

668 Zion Park Blvd. (P.O. Box 175), Springdale, UT 84767. ✆ **866/946-6276** or 435/772-3357. www.canyonranchmotel.com. 22 units. A/C, TV, TEL. Apr–Oct $84–$99 double; Nov–Mar $59–$89 double; kitchenettes $10 more year-round. AE, DISC, MC, V. Pets accepted ($10 per pet).

Cliffrose Lodge & Gardens With river frontage and 5 acres of lawns that boast shade trees and flower gardens, the Cliffrose offers a beautiful setting just outside the entrance to Zion National Park. The modern, well-kept rooms have all the standard motel appointments, plus unusually large bathrooms with a tub/shower, refrigerators, and Wi-Fi. We especially like the four very luxurious Canyon View Suites, which sleep up to six guests each. On the lawns, you'll find comfortable seating, including a swing, plus a playground, a whirlpool, and a large outdoor heated pool. Guests have use of a coin-op laundry.

281 Zion Park Blvd., Springdale, UT 84767. ✆ **800/243-8824** or 435/772-3234. Fax 435/772-3900. www.cliffroselodge.com. 40 units. A/C, TV, TEL. Apr–Oct and holidays $149–$199 per unit; rates lower at other times. AE, DISC, MC, V.

Desert Pearl Inn This imposing property offers luxurious, comfortable accommodations with beautiful views from private terraces or balconies. Spacious rooms are decorated in modern Southwest style, with either two queens or one king-size bed. Units have Wi-Fi, dataports, refrigerators, microwaves, wet bars, coffeemakers, hair dryers, and safes. The grounds are nicely landscaped, and facilities include a huge outdoor heated pool and a whirlpool. All units are nonsmoking.

707 Zion Park Blvd., Springdale, UT 84767. ✆ **888/828-0898** or 435/772-8888. Fax 435/772-8889. www.desertpearl.com. 61 units. A/C, TV, TEL. Summer $148–$183 double, $348 suite; winter $98–$118 double, $198 suite. AE, DISC, MC, V.

Driftwood Lodge Beautiful lawns and gardens enhance this attractive, well-kept motel—a quiet, lush complex perfect for sitting back and admiring the spectacular rock formations that practically surround the town. The spacious rooms have light walls and wood-grain furnishings; all have patios or balconies. Most standard rooms have two queen-size beds; others have one king-size. Two family suites each have one king-size and two queen-size beds, and the handsome king suites have a separate sitting room, king-size bed, and microwave. The restaurant has a delightful outdoor patio with views into the national park. There is Wi-Fi in the lobby and restaurant only. There's an outdoor heated pool with a sun deck, a whirlpool, a coin-op laundry, and a **restaurant** that serves basic American cuisine.

1515 Zion Park Blvd. (P.O. Box 447), Springdale, UT 84767. ✆ **888/801-8811** or 435/772-3262. Fax 435/772-3702. www.driftwoodlodge.net. 42 units. A/C, TV, TEL. Apr–Nov $129–$149 double, $169–$209 family unit and suite; Dec–Mar $59–$79 double, $89–$129 family unit and suite. AE, DC, DISC, MC, V. Pets accepted at management's discretion ($10 fee).

Flanigan's Inn A mountain-lodge atmosphere suffuses this very attractive complex of natural wood and rock set among trees, lawns, and flowers, just outside the entrance to Zion National Park. This is a place where you will actually want to spend time relaxing. The rooms are artfully decorated in what we might describe as a spa-like atmosphere, with top-line amenities, and most units have decks or patios and large windows overlooking a natural courtyard including a koi pond, heated pool, and hot tub. Suites have microwaves in addition to small refrigerators, and the two villas are completely furnished and beautifully decorated upscale homes separate from the main inn. A nature trail leads to a hilltop labyrinth and spectacular vistas. There is a heated outdoor pool, outdoor hot tub, and full-service spa, including a salon and yoga exercise room, and bicycles are available for guests' use. The restaurant, the **Spotted Dog Café,** serves breakfast and dinner (see "Where to Dine," below). The inn is 50% wind powered and entirely nonsmoking.

428 Zion Park Blvd., Springdale, UT 84767. ✆ **800/765-7787** or 435/772-3244. Fax 435/772-3396. www.flanigans.com. 36 units. A/C, TV, TEL. Mid-Mar through Nov and holidays $119–$159 double, $249–$349 suites and villas; lower rates at other times. AE, DISC, MC, V.

Harvest House Bed & Breakfast at Zion Personal touches and yummy breakfasts make this B&B a fine alternative to a standard motel. Built in 1989, the house is Utah territorial style (a style similar to Victorian) and has a cactus garden out front and a garden sitting area in back, with a koi pond and spectacular views of the national park's rock formations. Rooms are charming, comfortable, and quiet, with king- or queen-size beds and Wi-Fi. The units are furnished with an eclectic mix of contemporary items, and original art dots the walls. One upstairs room faces west and has grand sunset views, while the other two have private decks facing the impressive formations of Zion. There's a big-screen TV in the living room, and the gourmet breakfasts are sumptuous, with fresh-baked breads, fresh-squeezed orange juice, granola, fruit, yogurt, and a hot main course. Facilities include an outdoor whirlpool tub.

29 Canyon View Dr., Springdale, UT 84767. ✆ **800/719-7501** or 435/772-3880. www.harvesthouse.net. 4 units. A/C. $100–$135 double. Rates include full breakfast. DISC, MC, V. Children 7 and older welcome.

Historic Pioneer Lodge and Restaurant Old West ambience and style coupled with modern amenities and comfortable beds are what you'll find at the Historic Pioneer Lodge. Standard rooms have a homey feel with one king or two queen beds and some of the quietest heating/air-conditioning units around (and heating and cooling is all remote control). There are 40 rooms and three suites/apartments, and all units have rustic log furnishings, good lighting, full carpeting, granite counters, Wi-Fi, refrigerators, microwaves, coffeemakers, and hair dryers. There's a seasonal outdoor heated pool, whirlpool tub, and coin-op laundry, as well as a gift shop selling the work of local artists, an Internet cafe with espresso bar, and a reasonably priced **restaurant** where lodge guests receive a 10% discount during their stay. All units are nonsmoking.

828 Zion Park Blvd., Springdale, UT 84767. ✆ **888/772-3233** or 435/772-3233. Fax 435/772-3165. www.pioneerlodge.com. 45 units.

A/C, TV, TEL. Summer $119–$139 double; $179–$299 suite/apt. Lower rates the rest of the year. AE, DISC, MC, V.

Under the Eaves Bed & Breakfast English owners Steve and Deb Masefield have furnished this lovely 1931 home with many family antiques, creating an inn that is both attractive and comfortable. We especially enjoy the historic ambience, but the wireless Internet access is nice, too. On the first floor there are two cheerful rooms, decorated in a mix of antique and country furnishings, each with one double bed. Upstairs is a 1,200-square-foot suite with a vaulted ceiling, a wood-burning stove, a kitchenette, and a claw-foot tub plus separate shower in the bathroom. You'll find a queen-size bed and two single beds, and windows provide views of the gardens and the national park. The cute Garden Cottage, which was moved here from inside the national park, contains two small but comfortable rooms on the main floor, each with one queen-size bed; and a lower level hikers' room, more rustic, with two single beds. In the backyard is an attractive garden area with seating. All units are nonsmoking.

980 Zion Park Blvd. (P.O. Box 29), Springdale, UT 84767. ✆ **866/261-2655** or 435/772-3457. www.undertheeaves.com. 6 units. A/C. $75–$185 double. Rates include full breakfast. AE, DISC, MC, V. Children accepted at management's discretion.

Zion Mountain Ranch The upscale log cabins and family lodges here, just outside the east entrance to the national park, provide a luxurious way to "rough it" while visiting Zion. The spacious log cabins have lodgepole king-size beds, refrigerators, microwaves, and coffeemakers. The basic cabins range from 325 to 450 square feet and have one or two king-sized beds and gas fireplaces. There are larger and more upscale cabin suites, which add two-person jetted tubs and other amenities, and "family lodges"—1,000 to 1,500 square feet—that sleep from 7 to 10 people and include fully equipped kitchens. The property covers 1,000 partly wooded acres, where you're very likely to see the resort's bison herd. There is hiking, horseback riding ($35 for a 1-hr. ride), fishing, and a restaurant that serves three meals daily. Custom massages are available at $90. All units are nonsmoking.

9065 W. Utah 9, Mt. Carmel, UT 84755 (3 miles east of the Zion National Park east entrance). ✆ **866/648-2555** or 435/648-2555. www.zionmountainresort.com. 50 units. A/C, TV. Apr–Oct $120–$160 double in cabin, $150–$495 cabin suite and family lodge; Nov–Mar $80–$116 double in cabin, $110–$440 cabin suite and family lodge. AE, DISC, MC, V.

Zion Park Motel This economical modern motel offers comfortable, attractively furnished rooms. Bathrooms have showers or tub/shower combos. All rooms have refrigerators and microwaves, and two suites have full kitchens. The family unit sleeps six. Facilities include a seasonal outdoor heated pool, a picnic area, and a playground. A self-service laundry, a small but well-stocked grocery store with camping supplies and an ATM, and a restaurant are adjacent.

865 Zion Park Blvd. (P.O. Box 365), Springdale, UT 84767. ✆ **435/772-3251**. www.zionparkmotel.com. 21 units. A/C, TV, TEL. $79 double; $99–$139 family unit and suite. AE, DISC, MC, V.

10 Where to Dine

INSIDE THE PARK

Castle Dome Café SNACK BAR At the north end of the lodge, this fast-food restaurant offers an outdoor dining patio serving burgers, sandwiches, hot dogs, pizza, ice cream, frozen yogurt, and similar fare. No alcoholic beverages are served.

Zion National Park. ✆ **435/772-3213.** $4–$10. No credit cards. Summer daily 7am–9pm; shorter hours the rest of the year.

Red Rock Grill AMERICAN Try to have at least one meal here during your national park vacation. The restaurant's mountain lodge decor competes for your attention with the spectacular rock formations visible through the dining room's large windows. For an even better view, dine on the outside patio. Breakfasts offer all the usuals, including a good buffet. At lunch, you'll find grilled salmon burgers, beef burgers, sandwiches, and salads. House specialties at dinner usually include the excellent Santa Fe flatiron steak (grilled and topped with bleu cheese crumbles, pico de gallo, and seasoned onion straws), roasted loin of pork with apple-cranberry chutney, chipotle tilapia fillets, and trout amandine. Vegetarian items include Pasta Zion—pasta topped with garlic, mushrooms, carrots, broccoli, zucchini, and oven-roasted tomatoes. We heartily recommend the lodge's specialty desserts, such as the white chocolate raspberry cheesecake. There is full liquor service.

Zion Lodge, Zion National Park. ✆ **435/772-7760.** www.zionlodge.com. Dinner reservations required in summer. Breakfast $6–$10; lunch $7–$11; main dinner courses $14–$24. AE, DC, DISC, MC, V. Daily 6:30–10am, 11:30am–3pm, and 5:30–9pm.

NEAR THE PARK

All of the following restaurants, except the Thunderbird Restaurant in Mount Carmel, are in Springdale, just outside the park's south entrance.

Bit & Spur Restaurant & Saloon MEXICAN/SOUTHWESTERN Rough wood-and-stone walls and an exposed-beam ceiling give this restaurant the look of an Old West saloon, but it's actually much more than that, with a family dining room, patio dining, and original art decorating the walls. The food here is also a lot better than you'll find in the average saloon, closer to what we expect in an upscale Santa Fe restaurant. The menu changes seasonally but usually includes Mexican standards such as burritos, flautas, chiles rellenos, and a traditional green chile stew with pork and rice. You'll also often find seafood, such as grilled salmon steak, and our personal favorites, barbecued pork baby back ribs with red chile ketchup barbecue glaze, and steak or chicken fajitas. The Bit & Spur has full liquor service—try the fresh fruit margaritas—an extensive wine list, and an excellent variety of microbrewed beers.

1212 Zion Park Blvd., Springdale. ✆ **435/772-3498.** www.bitandspur.com. Reservations recommended. Main courses $12–$30. AE, DISC, MC, V. Feb–Nov (Dec–Jan Thurs–Mon) daily 5–10pm. Closed Christmas Eve and Christmas.

Spotted Dog Café AMERICAN/REGIONAL This restaurant's art-filled interior makes the most of the scenery with large windows for inside diners plus a Euro-style outdoor patio with spectacular views of Zion Canyon. Selections vary by season and may include Rocky Mountain trout, lamb, free-range poultry, hormone-free beef, environmentally farmed fish, hearty pastas, fresh summer salads, plus local specialties. There is also a surprisingly healthy children's menu. It offers an Express Breakfast Buffet daily at 7am featuring country potatoes, bacon, link sausage, plus selections of eggs, cereal, pastries, yogurt, fresh fruit, French toast, waffles, and freshly baked specialties. The Spotted Dog has an excellent wine cellar, microbrewed draft beers, and complete liquor service.

Flanigan's Inn, 428 Zion Park Blvd., Springdale. ✆ **435/772-0700.** Reservations recommended. Main courses $12–$26. AE, DISC, MC, V. Daily 7–11:30am and 5–10pm; reduced hours in winter.

Thunderbird Restaurant AMERICAN You won't go wrong stopping here for basic American food at reasonable prices. The spacious dining room offers both booths and tables in a comfortable Southwest setting. The breakfast menu includes pancakes, French toast, cereal, fruit, breads, numerous egg dishes, and even a hearty steak and eggs platter. Lunch consists of a wide variety of burgers plus hot and cold sandwiches. Dinner entrees include steak, seafood, and chicken, plus the popular country-fried steak. The restaurant has great homemade pies, breads, and soups, and a soup and salad bar is open at dinner during the summer. Beer and wine are served.

At the junction of Utah 9 and U.S. 89 in the Best Western East Zion Thunderbird Lodge. ✆ **435/648-2262.** Reservations not accepted. Lunch $7–$14; dinner entrees $9–$17. AE, DC, DISC, MC, V. Summer daily 7am–10pm; winter daily 7am–8pm. Closed Christmas.

Zion Park Gift & Deli SANDWICHES This is our choice for a top-quality, deli-style sandwich at a good price. You can eat at one of the cafe-style tables inside or on the patio outside, or you can carry your sandwich off on a hike or to a national park picnic ground. All baked goods, including the excellent sandwich breads and sub rolls, are made in-house. Order at the counter and wait as your sandwich is prepared with your choice of bread, meats, cheeses, and condiments. This is also a good breakfast stop for those who enjoy fresh-baked cinnamon rolls, muffins, banana nut bread, and similar goodies, with a cup of espresso. Locally made candy, including 14 flavors of excellent fudge, and 24 flavors of ice cream and frozen yogurt are offered. No alcohol is served.

866 Zion Park Blvd., Springdale. ✆ **435/772-3843.** $5–$10. AE, DISC, MC, V. Summer Mon–Sat 8am–9pm; reduced hours in winter.

Zion Pizza & Noodle PIZZA/PASTA A favorite of locals and visitors—including us—this busy cafe offers good pizza and pasta in a funky atmosphere—a former Mormon church with a turquoise steeple. The dining room has small, closely spaced tables and black-and-white photos on the walls. The pizzas, with lots of chewy crust, are baked in a slate stone oven. You can choose one of the house favorites, such as the Southwest burrito pizza or barbecue chicken pizza, but also get a basic cheese pizza or create your own by adding any of the roughly 17 extra toppings, from pepperoni to green chiles to pineapple. The menu also offers pastas, such as chicken parmesan, or penne pasta with grilled chicken, broccoli, carrots, fresh cream, and cheese; plus calzones and stromboli. Takeout and delivery service are provided. Beer is served inside and in the delightful year-round beer garden.

868 Zion Park Blvd., Springdale. ✆ **435/772-3815.** www.zionpizzanoodle.com. Reservations not accepted. Entrees $9–$15. No credit cards. Summer daily from 4pm; call for winter hours.

11 Picnic & Camping Supplies

You'll find most of the groceries and camping supplies you want just outside the park's south entrance at **Sol Foods Supermarket & Deli,** 95 Zion Park Blvd. (✆ **435/772-0277;** www.solfoods.com). This well-stocked store has a good selection of groceries, including fresh produce, meats, and dairy products, plus a very good deli. It also stocks camping supplies, souvenirs, and digital memory cards; rents DVDs; and has a restaurant. It is open daily year-round, 7am to 10pm in summer, with shorter hours at other times.

In downtown Springdale is **Lawrence's "Mini" Mini Mart,** with milk, bread, and other basics, at the Zion Park Motel complex, 865 Zion Park Blvd. (✆ **435/772-3251;** www.zionparkmotel.com). Call for current hours. On the south end of Springdale (the opposite side of town from the national park) is the **Springdale Fruit Company,** 2491 Zion Park Blvd. (✆ **435/772-3222;** www.springdalefruit.com), which is open only from mid-March through mid-November (daily 9am–7pm) and sells fresh organic fruits, vegetables, and juices (try the fruit smoothies), plus trail mix and baked goods. It also has a picnic area and free wireless Internet.

Those in need of outdoor equipment, hiking boots, clothing, sleeping bags, stoves, and the like will find what they need at **Zion Rock & Mountain Guides,** 1458 Zion Park Blvd. (✆ **435/772-3303;** www.zionrockguides.com), which offers both rentals and sales.

12 Nearby Entertainment

Just outside the south entrance to Zion National Park, in Springdale, are two worthwhile attractions.

The **Tanner Twilight Concert Series** presents a varied performing arts program from May through August each year in the stunning 2,000-seat outdoor **Tanner Amphitheater,** just off Zion Park Boulevard. Performances range from orchestra concerts and dance performances to rock, jazz, and gospel shows. Shows begin at 8pm and cost $10 for adults and $5 for youths (18 and younger). Contact **Dixie State College,** in St. George (✆ **435/652-7994;** www.dixie.edu/tanner/index.html).

The **Zion Canyon Theatre,** 145 Zion Park Blvd. (✆ **888/256-3456** or 435/772-2466; www.zioncanyontheatre.com), boasts a huge screen—some 60 feet high by 82 feet across. Here you can see the dramatic film *Zion Canyon: Treasure of the Gods,* with scenes of events around the Zion National Park area, including a hair-raising flash flood through Zion Canyon's Narrows and some dizzying bird's-eye views. The theater also shows a variety of other Hollywood and large-format films. Admission is $10 adults, $8 children 3 to 11, and free for children under 3. The theater is open daily from 11am in summer; call for winter hours. The theater complex also contains a tourist information center, an ATM, a picnic area, gift and souvenir shops, restaurants, and a grocery store.

13 Cedar Breaks National Monument

A delightful little park, Cedar Breaks is a wonderful place to spend anywhere from a few hours to several days, gazing down from the rim into the spectacular natural amphitheater, hiking the trails, and camping among the spruce and fir trees and the summer wildflowers.

The park forms a natural coliseum more than 2,000 feet deep and over 3 miles across, filled with stone spires, arches, and columns shaped by the forces of erosion and painted in ever-changing reds, purples, oranges, and ochers. Why the name Cedar Breaks? The pioneers who came here called such badlands "breaks," and they mistook the juniper trees along the cliff bases for cedars.

ESSENTIALS

WHEN TO GO

At more than 10,000 feet elevation, Cedar Breaks is always pleasantly cool. At night it actually gets cold, so take a jacket or sweater, even if the temperature is scorching down the road in St. George. The monument opens for its short summer season only after the snow melts, usually in late May, and closes in mid-October. If you happen to have a snowmobile or a pair of cross-country skis or snowshoes, you can visit anytime.

GETTING THERE

Cedar Breaks National Monument is 85 miles north of the main section of Zion National Park. From Zion's south entrance, head west on Utah 9, then north on Utah 17 to I-15. Follow **I-15** north to exit 57 (Cedar City), turn and head east on Utah 14, then turn north on Utah 148, which goes straight into the monument. From the Kolob Canyons section of Zion, which is off exit 40 of I-15, it is only 40 miles to Cedar Breaks.

The national monument is 23 miles east of Cedar City, 56 miles west of Bryce Canyon National Park, and 247 miles south of Salt Lake City. If you're coming from Bryce Canyon or other points east, the park is accessible from the town of Panguitch on Utah 143. If you're coming from the north, take the Parowan exit off I-15 and head south on Utah 143. It's a steep climb from whichever direction you choose, so take care, especially if your vehicle is prone to vapor lock or (like many motor homes) to loss of power on hills.

INFORMATION & VISITOR CENTER

One mile from the south entrance gate, you'll find the **visitor center,** which is usually open daily from late May through mid-October, 8am to 6pm (closed the rest of the year). The visitor center has exhibits on the geology, flora, and fauna of Cedar Breaks. You can purchase books and maps here, and rangers can help you plan your visit. For advance information, contact the Superintendent, **Cedar Breaks National Monument,** 2390 West Utah 56, Ste. 11,

Cedar City, UT 84720 (© **435/586-9451;** www.nps.gov/cebr).

FEES

Admission for up to 1 week, charged from late May through mid-October, is $4 per person for all those 16 and older, free for under 16. Admission is free the rest of the year. Camping costs $14 per night.

HEALTH & SAFETY CONCERNS

The high elevation—10,350 feet at the visitor center—is likely to cause shortness of breath and tiredness. Those with heart or respiratory conditions should consult their doctors before making the trip to Cedar Breaks. During thunderstorms, avoid overlooks and other high, exposed areas—they're often targets for lightning.

RANGER PROGRAMS

During the monument's short summer season, rangers offer nightly campfire talks at the campground, including periodic star parties, with telescopes provided, to take advantage of Cedar Breaks clear night skies. There are also talks on the area's geology at Point Supreme, a view point near the visitor center (daily on the hr. from 10am–5pm), and guided hikes on Saturday and Sunday mornings. A complete schedule is posted at the visitor center and the campground.

EXPLORING CEDAR BREAKS BY CAR

The 5-mile road through Cedar Breaks National Monument offers easy access to the monument's scenic overlooks and trail heads. Allow 30 to 45 minutes to make the drive. Start at the visitor center and nearby **Point Supreme** for a panoramic view of the amphitheater. Then drive north, past the campground and picnic ground turnoff, to **Sunset View,** for a closer look at the amphitheater and its colorful canyons. From each of these overlooks you'll be able to see out across Cedar Valley, over the Antelope and Black mountains, and into the Escalante Desert.

Continue north to **Chessman Ridge Overlook,** so named because the stone hoodoos below the overlook seem like massive chess pieces. Watch for swallows and swifts soaring among the rock formations. Back in your car, head north to **Alpine Pond,** to walk among the wildflowers on the self-guided nature trail (see "Hiking," below). Finally, proceed to **North View,** which offers perhaps the best views of the amphitheater and its rock statues.

SUMMER SPORTS & ACTIVITIES

HIKING The fairly easy 2-mile round-trip **Alpine Pond Nature Trail** loop leads through woodlands of bristlecone pines to a forest glade and a pond surrounded by wildflowers, offering panoramic views of the amphitheater along the way. A trail guide pamphlet is available at the trail head.

A somewhat more challenging hike, the 4-mile round-trip **Spectra Point/Ramparts Overlook Trail** follows the rim more closely than the Alpine Pond Trail, offering changing views of the colorful rock formations. It also takes you through fields of wildflowers and by bristlecone pines that are more than 1,600 years old. You'll need to be especially careful of your footing along the exposed cliff edges and allow yourself some time to rest—there are lots of ups and downs along the way.

The 1-mile round-trip **Campground Trail** connects the campground with the visitor center, providing views of the amphitheater along the way. It is the only trail where pets are permitted.

There are no trails from the rim to the bottom of the amphitheater completely within the monument, but there are trails just outside the monument that go into the amphitheater. Check with the visitor center for details and directions.

WILDLIFE WATCHING Because of its relative remoteness, Cedar Breaks is a good place for spotting wildlife. You're likely to see mule deer grazing in the meadows along the road early and late in the day. Marmots make their dens near the rim and are often seen along the Spectra Point Trail. You'll spot ground squirrels, red squirrels, and chipmunks everywhere. Pikas, related to rabbits, are here too, but it's unlikely you'll see one. They're small, with short ears and stubby tails, and prefer the high, rocky slopes.

Birders should have no trouble spotting the Clark's nutcracker, with its gray torso and black-and-white wings and tail, in the campground. The monument is also home to swallows, swifts, blue grouse, and golden eagles.

WINTER SPORTS & ACTIVITIES

The monument's facilities shut down from mid-October to late May or even later. The thick blanket of snow keeps cars out but makes Cedar Breaks perfect for snowmobilers, snowshoers, and cross-country skiers, who usually come over from nearby Brian Head ski area. Snowshoers and cross-country skiers have numerous options, but snowmobilers are restricted to the main 5-mile road through the monument, which is groomed and marked.

CAMPING

A 28-site campground in a beautiful high-mountain setting, **Point Supreme,** just north of the visitor center, is open from mid-June to late September, with tent, car, and RV sites available on a first-come, first-served basis. The campground has restrooms, drinking water, picnic tables, grills, and an

The Summer Wildflowers of Cedar Breaks

During its brief summer season, Cedar Breaks makes the most of the warmth and moisture in the air with a spectacular wildflower show. The rim comes alive in a blaze of color—a sight to behold! The dazzling display begins practically as soon as the snow melts and reaches its peak during late July and August. Watch for mountain bluebells, spring beauty, beard tongue, and fleabane early in the season; then comes the columbine, larkspur, Indian paintbrush, wild roses, and other flowers.

amphitheater for the ranger's evening campfire programs. There are no showers or RV hookups. The camping fee is $14 per night. Keep in mind that, even in midsummer, temperatures can drop into the 30s (single digits Celsius) at night at this elevation, so bring cool-weather gear.

37

Field Guide to Western Wildlife

by Kurt Repanshek

1 Canyon Country

MAMMALS & OTHER DESERT CRITTERS

Besides the plants and animals pictured here, you might see North American elk (p. 495), mountain lion (p. 495), and bobcat (p. 496).

Coyote

COYOTE

These wild dogs are midway in size between wolves and foxes. Their natural habitat is in the deserts and grasslands of the West, but when hunting killed all the wolves in the Lower 48 states, coyotes spread out and changed their behavior. They now act more like wolves, hunting in packs and going for bigger game, like deer. In the Southwest, they're more solitary, eating reptiles, rodents, insects, and fruit.

JACK RABBIT

Jack Rabbit

You can tell a jack rabbit by its long ears and strong back legs. This rabbit is tan and white and about 2 feet tall. Jack rabbits are active at night, and you often see them in your headlights when driving. If you're camping, keep an eye out for their eyes reflecting the light of your fire or lantern from the woods.

MULE DEER

You might see elk, which are larger, but mule deer are much more common in this region. They are 4 to 6 feet long, have big ears like a mule, and have brown coats in the summer. Generally, mule deer in groups are females with offspring, while bucks travel alone.

Mule Deer

RATTLESNAKE

Watch out for these guys, and if you find one, just back off. Most people who get bitten step on one accidentally or are messing with the snake; it attacks an animal as large as a person only in self-defense. Rattlesnakes are dormant in the winter and come out only at night in the hot summer months. There are many kinds, including one that lives only in the Grand Canyon, but I wouldn't recommend getting close enough to check which one you're seeing.

SIDE-BLOTCHED LIZARD

There are 3,000 kinds of lizards in the world, many of which look alike, and you often don't see them for long—be happy just to say it was a lizard. This one is 4 to 6 inches long and is brown with spots. Like snakes and other reptiles, lizards are coldblooded. They use the environment around them to set their body temperature, hiding in the shade or basking on warm rocks to get it right.

Rattlesnake

SQUIRRELS

You might see many kinds of squirrels, but the rare Abert's squirrel is noticeable because it has tall tufts of hair that stick up behind its ears. The back is gray, with white running on the underside from the belly to the tip of the tail. It's found only in pine and juniper forests, especially on the South Rim of the Grand Canyon.

Abert's Squirrel

The rare Kaibab squirrel, on the North Rim, evolved separately after the canyon formed and has an all-black body and a white tail.

Kaibab Squirrel

BIRDS

In addition to the birds below, you might also spot a golden eagle (p. 496) or a hairy woodpecker (p. 496).

CALIFORNIA CONDORS

These birds with wingspans that can reach 9 feet are making a comeback in canyon country, thanks to efforts by federal agencies and nonprofit groups. When not soaring on air currents, they like to perch on canyon walls.

RAVEN

You can see the raven, a black bird like a larger version of a crow, and hear its throaty caw all over the West into Alaska. The raven is common in the stories of many Native American cultures as a wily trickster and powerful creator. Ravens are extremely intelligent birds, able to solve problems. They eat many kinds of food, but a favorite seems to be garbage.

Raven

WESTERN BLUEBIRD

This is a striking bird, with a bright blue back and a red breast. Males compete for nest holes, using a red breast like the robin's to show other males that they're willing to fight for their place. Look for them in open areas where there are trees for nesting.

2 The Rockies

MAMMALS

In addition to the creatures here, you might want to check out the black bear (p. 496), bobcat (p. 485), white-tailed deer, mule deer (p. 493), and rattlesnake (p. 493).

BIGHORN SHEEP

Bighorn Sheep

The strong bodies and huge curling horns of bighorns are unmistakable. In the fall, the males fight for the right to mate by bashing their horns together. You can hear it a mile away. At Rocky Mountain, you can often see bighorn in the late spring and early summer on Hwy. 34 at Sheep Lakes in Horseshoe Park, where they come to eat minerals they don't get enough of in their winter diet. They come to the area so predictably that the Park Service posts crossing guards on the highway. Later in the year, you can see them in alpine areas, sometimes along Trail Ridge Road or on the Crater Trail.

BISON (OR BUFFALO)

Bison (Buffalo)

When settlers first came to the West, 60 million bison roamed in huge herds across the plains. By 1890, excessive hunting had left fewer than 1,000 alive. Now there are more than 200,000 in North America, mostly on farms. The wild herds at Yellowstone and Grand Teton national parks are unique and number a few thousand animals. Bison eat grass, often near roads where you can see them. In Yellowstone, the Hayden Valley and Lamar Valley are good spots to see them; in Grand Teton, look in the Antelope Flat area and along the Snake River. Amazingly, I saw people walking right up to bison. These animals are the size of a small truck, can run fast, and have horns that can inflict great damage. People get hurt every year.

GRIZZLY BEAR

Grizzly bears once lived in much of the United States, but they need large areas of undisturbed land. Now some biologists fear they don't have enough room left even in their last Lower 48 habitat, in the northern Rockies. Only about 500 to 600 live in the greater Yellowstone ecosystem, which includes Yellowstone and

Grand Teton national parks, and more live in Glacier National Park. About 30,000 live in Alaska. The best way to tell a grizzly from the smaller and more common black bear is by the hump on the grizzly's back and the black bear's straighter face profile. A grizzly's brown or blond color isn't a good guide, because blacks can be brown and grizzlies can be black. Grizzlies mostly eat roots, berries, and the like, but they are predators. Adult males weigh more than 500 pounds in this area.

Grizzly Bear

MOOSE

Moose are the largest member of the deer family, with males growing up to 1,600 pounds. They like brushy areas, willows, and swamps or shallow ponds, where they stand deep in the water and eat weeds from the bottom. They're excellent swimmers. Look for moose along the Snake River and near Jackson Lake Lodge at Grand Teton, and in the Kawuneechee Valley at Rocky Mountain. Only the males have antlers.

Moose

MOUNTAIN LION

Your chances of seeing a mountain lion are extremely slim because they're rare and appear only when they want to—and if a mountain lion wants you to see it, then you could be in danger. They are big cats and feed on large mammals like deer. Attacks on humans are rare but have happened, and are another good reason to keep your children near when you are hiking, especially in brush.

Mountain Lion

NORTH AMERICAN ELK (OR WAPITI)

These large, noble-looking deer show up all over the Rockies, spending the summer in alpine meadows and moving down for the winter. They show up at many places in all four parks; at Yellowstone you commonly see them along the road. In the winter, elk are fed at a refuge between Grand Teton National Park and the town of Jackson. At Glacier, a good place to find elk is in the roadside meadows near Saint Mary Lake. Only the males have antlers.

North American Elk (Wapiti)

PIKA

The pika is a cute little animal that lives in rocky areas high in the mountains. Pikas grow to 8 inches long and are related to rabbits but don't have long ears. Their coat blends in with the rocks, so look around carefully to see them.

WOLVES

Wolves once roamed throughout the United States, but as settlers colonized parts of the country, they drove out these predators. With wolves no longer part of the ecosystem, populations of their prey, such as elk and deer, ballooned unusually high and overgrazed the landscape. In 1995, in an effort to make Yellowstone's animal kingdom complete, federal agencies began a wolf recovery program. Today about 400 wolves lope through the greater Yellowstone ecosystem, preying predominantly on elk. The result is a smaller, but healthier, elk herd and a healthier landscape. The best place to spot Yellowstone's wolves is in the Lamar Valley in late spring and early summer. Some wolves can be found in Grand Teton National Park, although they're not as visible to park visitors. Glacier National Park also has a wolf population.

Pika

BIRDS

Besides the birds listed here, you may see some that are described in other sections, such as the raven (p. 494), western bluebird (p. 494), and Steller's jay (p. 497).

Golden Eagle

BALD & GOLDEN EAGLES

These majestic birds can have wingspans of over 7 feet; they glide in the air before swooping down and grabbing their prey. While golden eagles will grab a rabbit or other rodent in its ferocious talons, bald eagles might also pluck a fat trout from a river or lake. While the bald eagle is known for its white head and tail feathers, the golden eagle is all brown, with a lighter brown neck.

HAIRY WOODPECKER

Mountain Chickadee

The hairy woodpecker is roughly the size of a robin, with black and white feathers; the male has a red spot on his head. It lives in deciduous forests (where trees have leaves). Male woodpeckers have long, hard beaks that they hammer against tree trunks to make holes. Females have shorter beaks that are better for prying. Together they dig insects out of the wood.

MOUNTAIN CHICKADEE

Trumpeter Swan

This little bird looks a lot like the common black-capped chickadee but has an extra white stripe on its head, and gray sides. It is easy to find high in the mountains, hunting insects and flitting around the alpine forests.

TRUMPETER SWAN

These huge, graceful white swans are among the largest birds in North America. They are somewhat easy to find on the lakes of Yellowstone and Grand Teton national parks, but are found nowhere else except Canada and Alaska. They nearly disappeared, but conservation brought them back.

3 The Sierra Nevada

MAMMALS & REPTILES

Besides the creatures listed here, see the jack rabbit (p. 493), pika (p. 495), bighorn sheep (p. 494), mule deer (p. 493), coyote (p. 493), and rattlesnake (p. 493).

BLACK BEAR

Black Bear

Growing to 5 or 6 feet tall, black bears are common in the Sierra. Major problems have resulted from humans living in black bear country. Careless campers and picnickers have allowed bears to get their food and garbage, and now many bears are so used to thinking of humans as sources of food that they walk right through busy campgrounds and rip open cars. Blackies normally eat berries, nuts, and plants, with an occasional squirrel thrown in. You might be able to tell a black bear from the larger brown or grizzly bear (no longer found in California) by size or color. The sure signs are that the grizzly has a raised hump over the shoulders and its nose sticks out from its face, while a black bear's back and neck slope fairly evenly, and its nose and face form a smooth profile.

BOBCAT

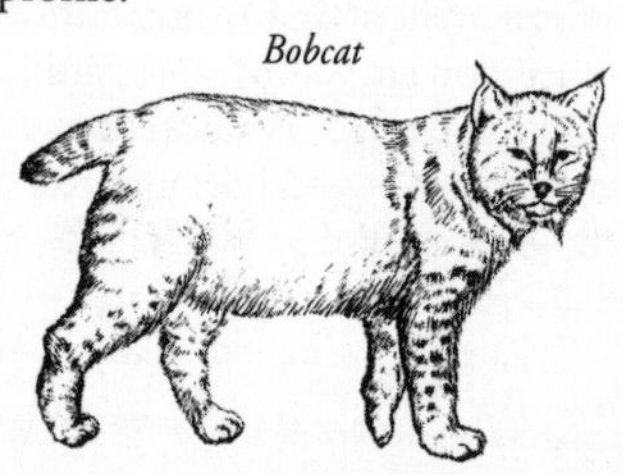
Bobcat

Bobcats are common in the foothills and lower Sierra, but you're very lucky if you see one. They hunt rabbits, squirrels, and other animals, often at night, hiding under logs in rocky areas to sleep. If you hear a bloodcurdling howl at night, it could be a bobcat. They're about as large as a middle-size dog, growing to 2½ feet long.

SIERRA NEVADA GOLDEN-MANTLED GROUND SQUIRREL

These brave little guys will come right into campsites to raid picnic baskets. They have small tails and black-and-white stripes on the sides of their bodies. They look like chipmunks but are larger (the body is about 6 in. long) and don't have stripes on their heads as chipmunks do.

BIRDS

In addition to the birds listed here, you might see some described in other sections, such as the raven (p. 494), western bluebird (p. 494), mountain chickadee (p. 496), golden eagle (p. 496), and hairy woodpecker (p. 496).

STELLER'S JAY

Steller's Jay

This striking blue-and-black bird has a large black crest—it's the only Western jay with a crest. Steller's jays live in Sierra pine forests and often visit campgrounds to pick up crumbs. They also live in the Rockies, the Pacific Northwest, and coastal Alaska. They bear the name of the naturalist Georg Steller, who helped discover Alaska in 1741.

WHITE-HEADED WOODPECKER

Common in the Yosemite Valley, these 9-inch-long birds are black except for white heads and wing patches; they're the only woodpeckers in the Sierra with white heads. They can blend in and be hard to spot until they take flight. They feed by peeling scales of bark off trees, not by hammering them like other woodpeckers.

4 Olympic & Sequoia National Parks

MAMMALS & MARINE LIFE

Besides those discussed below, the following can also show up in this region: bobcat, coyote (p. 493), harbor seal, hermit crab, humpback whale, jack rabbit (p. 493), mountain lion (p. 495), mule deer (p. 493), sea star or starfish, and white-tailed deer.

GRAY WHALE

Gray Whale

In the spring, these animals, which weigh up to 80,000 pounds, pass close to shore on their migration from winter calving grounds off western Mexico to summer feeding grounds off western Alaska. They return in late fall and winter. They don't have fins on their backs. To feed, they dive down and sift food out of the gunk from the bottom through the comb-shaped baleen in their mouths. Watching from shore is popular at the Olympic Peninsula.

KILLER WHALE (OR ORCA)

Killer Whale (Orca)

These whales either travel in organized family groups called pods, feeding mostly on salmon and other fish, or are loners, prowling for prey that could include sea lions or even humpback or gray whales. On the water you'll usually see only the whales' shiny black backs and long dorsal fins. When the whale sounds (dives), the flukes of the tail appear. Like people swimming, orcas turn head down when they want to go deeper. Orcas grow up to 30 feet long.

LIMPET

Limpets are common in West Coast tide pools. Their shells are shaped like small, shallow cones. There are many varieties, some large enough to be used as food or decorations for Native American costumes. Most limpets eat algae, but they also can consume tiny mussels and barnacles that have just attached to rocks.

SEA ANEMONE

These are among the most fun and bizarre animals to find in a tide pool. They look like huge flowers with thick stalks, but the flower petals really are sticky tentacles that grab and poison fish or other small animals that come too close. Any gentle contact will make an anemone quickly close up, leaving it looking like a rock. Sea anemones come in many varieties, in different sizes and colors.

Sea Anemone

SEA LION

Groups of sea lions have certain rocks called haul-outs, where they rest together, and rookeries, where they mate and give birth. Like whales, otters, and seals, they're mammals and have to hold their breath to dive deep for the fish they catch. They are larger than seals and feed on salmon and other fish that people also eat, so commercial fishing can reduce their food supply and lower the number that can live in an area.

Sea Lion

SEA OTTER

Shiny otters float on their backs in groups called rafts, tying kelp around their legs to stay in place. Otters use their tummies as tables for food or to carry their babies. Unlike other marine mammals, they don't have a layer of fat to keep them warm. Instead, otters rely on their fur, which is the finest and most thickly spaced fur of any animal, and on their bodies' ability to produce heat from the huge amounts of food they eat. Otters like clams, crabs, and sea urchins, which they pick off the bottom of the ocean during long dives when they hold their breath.

Sea Otter

SEA URCHIN

These animals have spines that stick out like pins from a pincushion. The spines protect the urchin and allow it to move, like a centipede's legs. They fall off when the urchin dies, leaving a delicate, beautifully etched shell. Kelp is a favorite food, although they eat almost anything, and sea otters are an important predator. Many kinds of urchins are common and interesting to find in tide pools; some have eggs that are eaten as sushi.

Sea Urchin

TULE ELK & ROOSEVELT ELK

Tule elk like the open, grassy lands on Point Reyes National Seashore north of San Francisco. Commercial hunts killed them off during the gold rush in the 1850s, but they were brought back in the 1970s and now are easy to find in a reserve on Tomales Point, at the north end of Point Reyes. Roosevelt elk, also rare, are the largest elk. They prefer the forests of Olympic National Park, where I've seen them in the Hoh and Quinault rainforests. Both kinds of elk make a big difference in their ecosystems. Tule elk helped keep Point Reyes's grasslands from turning into bushes and forest. Roosevelt elk, which like to eat hemlock sprouts but not Sitka spruce, may help keep hemlocks from taking over the rainforest.

BIRDS

Besides the birds listed here, you may see some osprey, herring gull, sanderling, great blue heron, raven (p. 494), hairy woodpecker (p. 496), and Steller's jay (p. 497).

COMMON LOON

These large, striking birds with sharply contrasting black-and-white coloring have an unforgettable, mournful cry that is symbolic of America's outdoors. In the summer, they nest on northern lakes. They spend the winter fishing in coastal waters all over the United States.

COMMON MURRE

The size and shape of a football, these birds don't look as if they'd be able to fly, but they do. Their little wings flap like crazy as they skim over the waves. Murres live in huge colonies on rocky islands, making them very vulnerable to oil spills and climate changes. Each female has only one egg a year. They depend on having a lot of birds together on the rocks for protection, so recovery from die-offs is slow.

GREAT HORNED OWL

This big owl, found all over North America south of the Arctic, is a fierce hunter at the top of the food chain. It preys on rabbits, ducks, and even other owls, including the endangered spotted owl of the old-growth forest in the Pacific Northwest. The owl's powerful flight, hypnotic eyes, and "hoo-hoo-hoo hooooo" call even give shivers to some people.

Great Horned Owl

38

Airline, Hotel & Car Rental Websites

1 Airlines

AirTran Airways
www.airtran.com

Alaska Airlines/Horizon Air
www.alaskaair.com

Allegiant Air
www.allegiantair.com

American Airlines
www.aa.com

Continental Airlines
www.continental.com

Delta Air Lines
www.delta.com

Frontier Airlines
www.frontierairlines.com

Great Lakes Airlines
www.greatlakesav.com

JetBlue Airways
www.jetblue.com

Midwest Airlines
www.midwestairlines.com

Northwest Airlines
www.nwa.com

Olympic Airlines
www.olympicairlines.com

Southwest Airlines
www.southwest.com

Spirit Airlines
www.spiritair.com

United Airlines
www.united.com

US Airways
www.usairways.com

2 Major Hotel & Motel Chains

Best Western International
www.bestwestern.com

Clarion Hotels
www.choicehotels.com

Comfort Inns
www.ComfortInn.com

Courtyard by Marriott
www.marriott.com/courtyard

Crowne Plaza Hotels
www.ichotelsgroup.com/crowneplaza

Days Inn
www.daysinn.com

Doubletree Hotels
www.doubletree.com

Econo Lodges
www.choicehotels.com

Embassy Suites
www.embassysuites.com

Fairfield Inn by Marriott
www.fairfieldinn.com

Four Seasons
www.fourseasons.com

Hampton Inn
http://hamptoninn1.hilton.com

Hilton Hotels
www.hilton.com

Holiday Inn
www.holidayinn.com

Howard Johnson
www.hojo.com

Hyatt
www.hyatt.com

InterContinental Hotels & Resorts
www.ichotelsgroup.com

La Quinta Inns and Suites
www.lq.com

Loews Hotels
www.loewshotels.com

Marriott
www.marriott.com

Motel 6
www.motel6.com

Omni Hotels
www.omnihotels.com

Quality
www.QualityInn.ChoiceHotels.com

Radisson Hotels & Resorts
www.radisson.com

Ramada Worldwide
www.ramada.com

Red Carpet Inns
www.bookroomsnow.com

Red Lion Hotels
www.redlion.rdln.com

Red Roof Inns
www.redroof.com

Renaissance
www.renaissancehotels.com

Residence Inn by Marriott
www.marriott.com/residenceinn

Rodeway Inns
www.RodewayInn.com

Sheraton Hotels & Resorts
www.starwoodhotels.com/sheraton

Super 8 Motels
www.super8.com

Travelodge
www.travelodge.com

Vagabond Inns
www.vagabondinn.com

Westin Hotels & Resorts
www.starwoodhotels.com/westin

Wyndham Hotels & Resorts
www.wyndham.com

3 Major Car-Rental Agencies

Advantage
www.advantage.com

Alamo
www.alamo.com

Avis
www.avis.com

Budget
www.budget.com

Dollar
www.dollar.com

Enterprise
www.enterprise.com

Hertz
www.hertz.com

National
www.nationalcar.com

Payless
www.paylesscarrental.com

Rent-A-Wreck
www.rentawreck.com

Thrifty
www.thrifty.com

Index

D

E